BOLLINGEN SERIES LXXI · 2

THE
COMPLETE WORKS OF
ARISTOTLE

THE REVISED OXFORD TRANSLATION

Edited by

JONATHAN BARNES

VOLUME TWO

BOLLINGEN SERIES LXXI · 2

PRINCETON UNIVERSITY PRESS

THIS IS PART TWO OF THE SEVENTY-FIRST
IN A SERIES OF WORKS SPONSORED
BY BOLLINGEN FOUNDATION

Library of Congress Cataloging in Publication Data
ARISTOTLE.
The complete works of Aristotle.
(Bollingen series ; 71:2)
Includes index.
1. Philosophy—Collected works. I. Barnes, Jonathan. II. Title. III. Series.
B407.s6 1984   185   82-5317
ISBN 0-691-01651-8

Princeton University Press books are printed on acid-free paper and meet the
guidelines for permanence and durability of the Committee on Production Guidelines
for Book Longevity of the Council on Library Resources

Printed in the United States of America

Second Printing, 1985

Fourth Printing, 1991

Sixth Printing, with Corrections, 1995

14 13 12 11 10

CONTENTS

vi   C O N T E N T S

* and **: See the Note to the Reader

ACKNOWLEDGMENTS

THE TRANSLATIONS of the *Categories* and the *de Interpretatione* are reprinted here by permission of Professor J. L. Ackrill and Oxford University Press (© Oxford University Press, 1963); the translation of the *Posterior Analytics* is reprinted by permission of Oxford University Press (© Oxford University Press, 1975); the translation of the third book of the *Economics* is reprinted by permission of The Loeb Classical Library (William Heinemann and Harvard University Press); the translation of the fragments of the *Protrepticus* is based, with the author's generous permission, on the version by Professor Ingemar Düring.

NOTE TO THE READER

THE TRADITIONAL *corpus aristotelicum* contains several works which were certainly or probably not written by Aristotle. A single asterisk against the title of a work indicates that its authenticity has been seriously doubted; a pair of asterisks indicates that its spuriousness has never been seriously contested. These asterisks appear both in the Table of Contents and on the title pages of the individual works concerned.

The title page of each work contains a reference to the edition of the Greek text against which the translation has been checked. References are by editor's name, series or publisher (OCT stands for Oxford Classical Texts), and place and date of publication. In those places where the translation deviates from the chosen text and prefers a different reading in the Greek, a footnote marks the fact and indicates which reading is preferred; such places are rare.

The numerals printed in the outer margins key the translation to Immanuel Bekker's standard edition of the Greek text of Aristotle of 1831. References consist of a page number, a column letter, and a line number. Thus "1343ᵃ" marks column one of page 1343 of Bekker's edition; and the following "5," "10," "15," etc. stand against lines 5, 10, 15, etc. of that column of text. Bekker references of this type are found in most editions of Aristotle's works, and they are used by all scholars who write about Aristotle.

NOTE (1994): This is an unrevised reprint of the first edition; but a small number of typographical errors have been corrected. Many of these errors were generously communicated to the editor by Mr. M. W. Dunn, who recorded the translation for the blind.

THE COMPLETE WORKS
OF ARISTOTLE

ON PLANTS **

E. S. Forster

BOOK I

1 · Life is found in animals and plants; but while in animals it is clearly   815ᵃ10
manifest, in plants it is hidden and not evident. For before we can assert the
presence of life in plants, a long inquiry must be held[1] as to whether plants possess a
soul and a distinguishing capacity for desire and pleasure and pain. Now Anaxagoras and Empedocles say that they are influenced by desire; they also assert that they   15
have sensation and sadness and pleasure. Anaxagoras declared that plants are
animals and feel joy and sadness, deducing this from the fall of their leaves; while
Empedocles held the opinion that sex has a place in their composition. Plato indeed   20
declares[2] that they feel desire only on account of their compelling need of
nutriment. If this be granted, it will follow that they also feel joy and sadness and
have sensation. I should also like to reach some conclusion as to whether they are
refreshed by sleep and wake up again, and also whether they breathe, and whether   25
they have sex and the mingling of the sexes or not. But the great diversity of opinion
on these subjects involves too long an inquiry, and the best course is to pass over
these topics and not to waste time on the unprofitable investigation of details. Some   30
have asserted that plants have souls, because they have seen that they are generated
and receive nutriment and grow, and have the bloom of youth and the dissolution of
old age—characteristics which nothing inanimate shares with plants; if plants
possess these characteristics, they believed them also to be affected by desire.   815ᵇ10

Let us first examine their obvious characteristics, and afterwards those which
are less evident. I say that whatsoever takes food desires food, and feels pleasure in
satiety and pain when it is hungry, and that these dispositions do not occur without
the accompaniment of sensation. The view of Plato, then, who held that plants have
sensation and desire was remarkable, but not unsound; but Anaxagoras and   15
Democritus and Empedocles declared that they possessed intellect and intelligence.
These views we must repudiate as unsound and pursue a sane statement of the case.
I assert, then, that plants have neither sensation nor desire; for desire can only   20

TEXT: J. Bussemaker, *Aristotelis Opera Omnia,* Vol. IV, Firmin-Didot, Paris, 1878
[1]Omitting *constaret enim.*
[2]See *Timaeus* 77AC.

proceed from sensation, and the end proposed by our volition changes in accordance with sensation. In plants we do not find sensation nor any organ of sensation, nor any semblance of it, nor any definite form or capacity to pursue objects, nor
25 movement or means of approach to any object perceived, nor any sign whereby we may judge that they possess sense-perception corresponding to the signs by which we know that they receive nutriment and grow. Of this we can only be certain because nutrition and growth are parts of the soul, and when we find a plant to be
30 possessed of such a nature, we perceive of necessity that some part of a soul is present in it which lacks sensation; but we ought not to allow that a plant is a thing possessed of sense, because while sensation is the cause of the glorification of life, nutrition is the cause of growth in the living thing.

35 These differences of opinion come into consideration in their own proper place. It is certainly difficult to find a state intermediate between life and the absence of
816ᵃ1 life. Some, too, will urge that a plant, if it be alive, is therefore an animal; for it is difficult to assign any principle to the life of plants except that of the life of nutrition. But, when men deny that plants have life, they do so because plants do not
5 possess sensation—for there are certain animals which lack foresight and intelligence. For nature, which destroys the life of the animal in death, preserves it in the continuation of its kind by generation, and it is wrong for us to suppose any
10 intermediate state between the animate and the inanimate. We know that sea-shells are animals which lack foresight and intelligence and are at once plants and animals. The only reason, therefore, for their being called animals is that they have sensation; for genera give names and definitions to the species which fall under them, while the species give names to the individuals, and the genus ought to rest on
15 a common cause present in the several individuals and not on several causes; but the nature of the cause, on which the genus is based, is not familiar to every one. Now there are animals which have no female sex, and some which do not procreate their kind, and some which lack the power of movement, and some in which the colour
20 varies, and some which produce an offspring unlike themselves, and some which grow from the earth or from trees.

What, therefore, is the principle of life in animals? What is it that raises the noble animal, i.e. that which surrounds the heavens, the sun and the planets, from
25 the sphere of perplexity and doubt? For the heavenly bodies feel no outside influence, and sensation is an effect produced on a sentient being. Now a plant has no movement of itself, for it is fixed in the earth, which is itself immovable. Whence, then, shall we infer any similarity which may enable us to attribute life to the plant?
30 For there is no one thing which includes all of them. We therefore assert that sensation is common to all animal life, because sensation marks the distinction between life and death; but the heavens, which pursue a nobler and more sublime path than we do, are far removed from life and death. But it is fitting that animals should have[3] some common characteristic perfect in itself but less sublime, and this
35 is the acquisition and deprivation of life. And one ought not to shrink from the use of these terms on the ground that there is no mean between the animate and the

[3]Reading *habeat*.

inanimate, between life and the deprivation of life; indeed, there is a mean between life and the inanimate, because the inanimate is that which has no soul nor any portion of it. But a plant is not one of those things which entirely lack a soul, because there is some portion of a soul in it; and it is not an animal, because there is no sensation in it, and things pass one by one gradually from life into non-life. We can put the matter in a different way and say that a plant is animate. I cannot, however, assert that it is inanimate as long as it possesses soul and some form of sensation; for that which receives food is not entirely without soul. And every animal has soul, but a plant is imperfect, and, whereas an animal has definite limbs, a plant is indefinite in form, and a plant derives its own particular nature from the motion which it possesses in itself. Someone might say that a plant has soul, because the soul is that which causes locomotion and desire to arise, and locomotion can only arise when sensation is present. But the absorption of food is in accordance with a natural principle, and is common both to animals and plants, and no sensation at all will accompany the absorption of food; for everything that absorbs food employs two qualities in feeding, namely, heat and cold, and an animal properly requires moist food and dry food, for coldness is always found in dry food; for neither of these two natures is ever unaccompanied by the other. And so food is continuously being supplied to that which feeds on it till the time when it begins to decay, and animals and plants have to be provided with food similar in kind to themselves.

2 · Let us now investigate what we have already mentioned, namely, desire in plants, their movement, and their soul and its function. A plant has not respiration, although Anaxagoras declared that it has; and we even find many animals which have not respiration. We can see by ocular demonstration that plants do not sleep and wake, for waking is due to an effect of sensation, and sleeping is an enfeebled condition of sensation, and nothing of this kind is found in that which vegetates at all times in the same condition, and is itself naturally without sensation. When an animal takes food, a vapour rises from the food into its head and it falls asleep, and, when the vapour which rises to its head is consumed, it wakes up. In some animals this vapour is plentiful and yet they sleep but little. Sleep is the suppression of motion and this involves the quiescence of the thing moved.

The most important and appropriate subject of inquiry which arises in this science is that proposed by Empedocles, namely, whether female and male sex is found in plants, or whether there is a combination of the two sexes. Now we assert[4] that when the male generates it generates *in* another, and when the female generates it generates *from* another, and both are mutually separate. This is not found to be the case in plants; for in a particular species the produce of the male plant will be rougher, harder, and stiffer, while the female will be weaker but more productive. We ought also to inquire whether the two kinds are found in combination in plants as Empedocles states that they are. But my opinion is that this is not the case, for things which mingle together ought first to be simple and separate, and so the male will be separate and the female separate; they afterwards mingle, and

---

[4]Omitting *sicut diximus.*

15   the mingling will only take place when it is produced by generation. A plant, therefore, would have been discovered before the mingling had taken place, and it ought therefore to be at the same time an active and a passive agent. The two sexes cannot be found combined in any plant; if this were so, a plant would be more
20   perfect than an animal, because it would not require anything outside itself in order to generate; whereas the plant *does* require the right season of the year and sunshine and its natural temperature more than anything. Thus it requires them at the time when the tree sprouts, and while the nutritive principle in plants is derived from the
25   earth, the principle which generates seeds is derived from the sun. Hence Anaxagoras said that the seeds of plants derive from the air, and others call[5] the earth the mother and the sun the father of plants. But we must suppose that the mingling of the male and the female in plants takes place in some other way, because the seed of a plant resembles the embryo in animals, being a mixture of the male and female
30   elements. And just as in a single egg there exists the force to generate the chicken and the material of its nutriment up to the time when it reaches perfection and emerges from the egg, and the female lays the egg in a short space of time; so too
35   with the plant. And Empedocles is right when he said the tall trees do not bear their young; for that which is born can only be born from a portion of the seed, and the rest of the seed becomes at first the nutriment of the root; and the plant begins to move as soon as it is born. This, then, is the opinion which we ought to hold about
817ᵇ1   the mingling of the male and female in plants, similar to that which we hold about animals. This process is the cause of plants under a certain disposition of circumstances; for in the case of an animal when the sexes mingle the powers of the
5   sexes mingle after they have separated, and a single offspring is produced from them both. But this is not the case with plants. And if nature has mingled the male and the female together, she has followed the right course; and in plants the only
10   operation which we find is the generation of fruits; and an animal is only separated at the times when it is not having sexual intercourse, and this separation is due to its multifarious activities and intellectual pursuits.
       But there are some who hold that the plant is complete and perfect because of
15   its possession of these two powers, and because of the food which is adapted to feeding it, and the length of its existence and duration. When it bears leaves and fruit its life will continue and its youth return to it. No excrement will be produced
20   from plants. A plant does not require sleep for many reasons, for it is placed and planted in the earth and attached to it and has no movement of itself; nor has it any definite bounds to its parts, nor does it possess sensation or voluntary motion, or a
25   perfect soul; indeed it has only part of a soul. Plants are only created for the sake of animals, and animals are not created for the sake of plants. Some one will urge that a plant requires food which is easily obtained and poor, yet it needs it very regularly and continuously, and without interruption. If it were agreed that a plant has an
30   advantage over an animal, it would follow that things which are inanimate were better and nobler than those which are animate; yet we see that the function of the animal is nobler and better than all those of the plant, and we find in the animal all

[5]Reading *dicunt alii* for *dicit lechineon.*

the virtues which are present in the plant and many others. Empedocles said that   35
plants had their birth when the world was yet small and its perfection not attained,
while animals were born after it was completed. But this account does not suit the
facts, for the world is a whole, perpetual and eternal, and has never ceased to
produce animals and plants and all their species. In every kind of plant there is   818ª1
natural heat and moisture, and, when these are consumed, the plant will become
weak and grow old and decay and dry up. Some people call this corruption, others
do not.

3 · Some trees contain a gummy substance, such as resin and almond-gum   5
and myrrh, and frankincense, and gumarabic. Some trees have knots and veins and
core and wood and bark and marrow within them; some trees consist almost wholly
of bark. In some the fruit is underneath the bark, that is, between the bark and the
wood. Some parts of the tree are simple, such as the moisture found in it and the   10
knots and veins; other parts are compounded from these, such as the branches and
twigs and the like. These are not all found in all plants; for some have composite and
some simple parts, while others do not have them. Plants possess various other parts
as well—roots, twigs, leaves, branches, flowers, catkins, tendrils, and bark   15
surrounding the fruit.

Just as in the animal, so also in the plant there are homogeneous parts, and all
the composite parts of a plant are like the members of an animal: the bark of a plant
resembles the skin of an animal, while the root of a plant is like the mouth of an   20
animal, and its fibres are like an animal's sinews, and so with its other parts. Any of
these parts can be divided on one principle into similar parts, or a division can be
made by dissimilar parts (just as mud can be divided in one way into earth only and
in another into water; similarly the lungs and flesh can be divided up on one
principle so that they are pieces of flesh, while on the other principle they can be   25
divided into their elements or radical parts). But a hand cannot be divided up into
another hand, nor a root into another root, nor leaves into other leaves; but these
roots and leaves are themselves the result of composition. Some fruits are composed   30
of few parts, some of many—olives, for example, which are made up of bark and
flesh and a shell and a seed. Some fruits[6] have as many as three coverings. All seeds
have two barks. We have now mentioned the parts of which individual plants   35
consist. The aim of our discussion is to determine the parts of the plant and its
coverings and its variations—this is very difficult—and in particular, to define its
essential nature and its colour, and the period of its duration, and the effects which
are produced upon it. Plants have not fixed habits of mind and the power of action   818ᵇ1
like that possessed by animals; and if we compare the parts of an animal with those
of a plant, our discussion will be a long one, and we shall hardly avoid considerable
differences of opinion in naming the parts of plants. For a part of a thing is of its   5
own kind and of its own particular substance, and, when it is once produced, each
kind will remain in its original condition, unless it departs from it owing to some
long continued infirmity. Flowers, fruits, and leaves will, in some cases, be produced   10

---

[6]Reading *semen. et fructus quidam.*

annually, in others they are not, nor do they remain as the bark does . . .[7] This does
not happen in plants; for various undetermined parts of plants are often shed (like
15   hair in the case of man and claws in the case of animals), and in their stead other
parts grow either where the lost parts were, or elsewhere in some other place. It is
clear from this that it is not determined whether the parts of a plant are really parts
or not. It is wrong for us to say that those things with which an animal grows and by
20   which it reaches completion are not parts of it; but the leaves and everything that is
found in a plant[8] are parts of that plant, although they are not determined and are
25   gradually shed; for the antlers of a stag and the hair of certain animals, and the fur
of certain of those which hibernate in hollows underground, fall off, and this process
resembles the shedding of leaves.

We ought, therefore, to treat of the subjects which we mentioned first, and
30   begin to name the parts which are peculiar to certain plants and those which are
common to all, and their differences. Let us say, therefore, that there is a great
diversity in the parts of plants in respect of number and fewness, largeness and
smallness, and in respect of strength and weakness. The reason of this is that the
35   moisture which is found in large trees, is in some trees, the fig, for example, like
milk, in others it is like pitch, as in the pine, in others it is watery, like the liquid
found in the vine, in others it is acrid, like that found in marjoram and in the herb
called opigaidum. There are also plants which have their parts dry. Some plants
have their parts well defined, and neither alike nor equal in size; others have parts
which are similar to one another but not equal, in others they are equal but not
819ª1   similar, and their position is not fixed. The differences of plants are recognized in
their parts—differences in form and colour and sparseness and density and
roughness and smoothness, and all their incidental differences in equality of size,
5   numerical increase and decrease, largeness and smallness. Some plants, too, will not
be uniform, but will show great variation, as we have already said.

4 · Some plants produce their fruit above their leaves, others beneath; in
10   some plants the fruit is suspended from the stock of the tree, in others it grows from
the root, as in the Egyptian trees which are called vargariaton; in some cases it
grows in the middle of the plant. In some plants the leaves and knots are not
separated; in others the leaves are equal in size and similar to one another, and some
15   of those which have branches have branches equal in size. The following parts,
which we will name, are found in all plants, and admit of growth and addition—
namely, the root, the shoots, the stem, and the branches; these resemble the limbs of
animals which include all the other limbs. The root acts as an intermediary between
20   the plants and its food, and for that reason the Greeks call it the root and cause of
life in plants, for it supplies the plant with the cause of life. The stem is the only part
which grows out of the ground and forms and is like the stature of a tree. The
25   suckers are the parts which sprout from the root of a tree, while the branches are

[7]The next sentence is unintelligible: *et corpus cadens aere abiciente ipsum propter causam.*
[8]Reading *illa.*

above the suckers. They are not found in all plants; and in some plants which have branches these are not permanent, but only last from year to year. There are plants which do not have branches or leaves, fungi, for example, and mushrooms. 30 Branches are only found on trees. Bark and wood and the pith of a tree are produced from moisture; some call this pith the womb of the tree, others the viscera, others the heart. The knots and veins and flesh of the whole plant are made up from the 35 four elements. Parts are often found which are adapted to reproduction, leaves, for example, and flowers and small twigs (which are flowers outside the plant); similarly with the fruit and leaves of a plant, and what is produced from the seed 40 and the shell which surrounds it.

Of plants some are trees, some are midway between trees and herbs and are called bushes, some are herbs, and some are vegetables. Almost every plant falls 819^b1 under one of these names. A tree is a plant which has a stem growing from its root, from which stem numerous branches grow, olive-trees, for example, and fig-trees. A 5 plant which is something between a tree and a small herb, and is called a bush, has many branches growing out of its roots, like the thorntree and bramble. Vegetables are plants which have a number of stems growing out of one root and a number of 10 branches, rue, for example, and cabbage. Herbs are plants which have no stem, but their leaves grow out of their roots. Some plants are produced and dry up every year, wheat, for example, and vegetables. We can only indicate these various classes of plants by general inferences, and by giving examples and descriptions. Some plants 15 verge towards two extremes, mallow, for example (since it is both a herb and a vegetable), and likewise beet. Some plants grow at first in the form of low bushes and afterwards become trees, as, for instance, the nut-tree, the chaste-tree, and the 20 plant called 'goatberry'. Perhaps myrtles, apple-trees, and pear-trees fall also under this class, for all of them have a number of superfluous stems growing from their roots. It is worth while to specify these that they may serve for purposes of example 25 and inference, but we must not investigate the definitions of every kind of plant.

Some plants are indoor plants, others garden plants, and others wild, in the same way as animals. I think, too, that all species of plants which are not cultivated become wild. Some plants produce fruit, others do not; some produce oil, others do 30 not; some have leaves and not others; some plants shed their leaves, others do not; some have branches, others do not. Plants differ greatly in their large or small size, 35 in beauty and ugliness, and in the excellence, or the contrary, of their fruits. Trees in a wild state bear more fruit than garden trees, but the fruit of the garden tree is better than that of the wild. Some plants grow in dry places, some in the sea, others 40 in rivers. Plants which grow in the Red Sea will there reach a great size, whereas they are only small in other places. Some plants grow on the banks of rivers, others in standing water. Of plants which grow in dry places, some grow on mountains, 820^a1 others in the plain; some plants grow and flourish in the most arid districts, as, for example, in the land of the Ethiopians which is called Zara, and increase there better than anywhere else. Some plants live at high altitudes, some on moist ground, 5 others in dry, others equally well in either, as, for instance, willow and tamarisk. A plant changes very much with a difference of locality, and such variations must be taken into consideration. 10

5 · A plant which is fixed in the ground does not like to be separated from it. Some places are better for certain plants than others; similarly some fruits are better in one place than in another. In some plants the leaves are rough, in others smooth; in some they are small, in others they are cleft as in the vine. Some trees have a single bark, as the fig, others have several layers of bark, as in the case of the pine; some are bark throughout, as, for example, the mediannus. Some plants have joints, reeds, for example; some have thorns, like the bramble. Some have no branches, others have a great number, like the sycamore. Other plants show various differences; for instance, suckers grow from some and not from others; this can only be due to a difference in the root. Some plants have a single root only, the squill for example; for it grows in a single shoot and spreads by expansion underground, and will increase as it grows more and more and approaches the sunlight, because the sun draws out its shoots.

Of the juices which are found in fruits, some are drinkable, as, for instance, the juice of grapes, pomegranates, mulberries, and myrtles. Some juices are oily, as in the olive and pine-nut; others are sweet like honey, as in the date and fig; others are hot and pungent, as in marjoram and mustard; others bitter, as in wormwood and centaury. Some fruits are made up of a fleshy and a bony substance and a seed, plums for example; others, cucumbers for instance, are made up of a fleshy substance and seeds, others of moisture and seeds like the pomegranate. Some have rind outside and flesh inside, others flesh outside and seed inside; in others one comes immediately upon the seed with the envelope which encloses it, as in dates and almonds; in others this is not so. Fruits are edible or inedible accidentally, and some people can eat certain fruits while others cannot, and certain animals can eat certain fruits while others cannot. Some fruits, again, are in pods, like seeds; others in sheaths, like[9] weapons, wheat for example; others are enclosed in a fleshy substance, dates for instance; others in husks, acorns for example, and some in several husks, a cuticle and a shell, nuts for example. Some fruits mature quickly, like mulberries and cherries, others slowly, as do all or most wild fruits. Some plants produce their leaves and fruits quickly, others slowly—and of these some wait for the winter before coming to maturity. The colours of fruits and flowers vary very much. One plant is green throughout, another has a tendency to blackness, another to whiteness, another to redness. Also the conformation of the fruit, if it be wild, varies considerably; for all fruits are not angular, nor do they take the form of straight lines.

6 · In aromatic trees it is sometimes the root which is aromatic, sometimes the bark, sometimes the flower, and sometimes the wood; in other cases every part is aromatic, in the balsam for example.

Some trees come into existence by being planted, some from seeds, others spontaneously. Those which are planted are separated either from the root, the stem, the branches, or the seed, or else the whole is transplanted; some are slightly bruised before being planted. Some are planted in the earth again, others are

---

[9]Reading *ut tela*.

planted, that is, grafted, on other trees. It is better to graft on trees which are   35
similar and have the same proportions; the best results are obtained in the grafting,
for instance, of apple on pear, fig on fig, or vine on vine. Sometimes grafting of
different species is resorted to, bay, for example, on wild plane, olive-trees on
terebinth, mulberries on a number of different trees, and wild trees on garden trees.   821ᵃ1
Every plant does not produce a seed similar to that from which it is sprung; some
produce a better seed, others a worse, and good trees sometimes grow from bad   5
seeds, as in the case of bitter almonds and pomegranates. In some trees too, when
they are weak, the seed fails, in the pine for example, and the palm. But a good plant
is not likely to be produced from a bad seed, nor a bad tree from a good seed. This   10
often occurs, however, among animals.

A tree which has hard bark and has become barren, if its root be split and a
stone inserted in the cleft will become fruitful again. In palms too, if the leaves or
pollen or bark of the male palm be applied to the leaves of the female palm so as to   15
cohere,[10] its fruits will come to maturity quickly, and it will prevent their falling off.
The male can be distinguished from the female palm, because it sprouts first and its
leaves are small, and also because of its odour; sometimes all these conditions are
present, sometimes only some of them. It will perhaps happen that the wind will   20
bear the odour of the male to the female palm, and then the dates will come to
maturity; the foliage of the male will also cohere to that of the female palm when
they catch in one another. Wild fig-trees, too, spread along the ground and
contribute to garden fig-trees; similarly wild olives contribute to olives, when they   25
are planted together.

7 · Again, some plants change into other species, the nut-tree, for example,
when it becomes old. It is also said that catmint changes into mint, and basil, if   30
plucked up and planted by the Persian Gulf, will perhaps turn into thyme. Also
wheat and flax change into tares. The poisonous nightshade which grows in Persia
changes its nature if transplanted into Egypt and Jerusalem and becomes edible.   35
Almond-trees and pomegranates change their condition for the better under
cultivation. Pomegranates are improved by being manured with pigs' dung and
watered with fresh cold water. Almond-trees with pegs driven into them exude gum
for a long while. Many wild plants are thus artificially changed into garden plants.   821ᵇ1
Position and care, and, above all, the season of planting, contribute to this process.
Some plants require some one to plant them, others do not. Most plants are planted
in the spring, a few in the winter and autumn, very few in the summer after the   5
rising of the dogstar; planting at this season takes place in few places—nowhere
except in the Crimea. In Egypt planting only takes place once in the year.

Some trees produce leaves from their roots, some from their buds, some from   10
the wood, others from every part. In some they are near the ground, in others far
from it, in others they are neither high nor low; others produce a few leaves at
various times. Some trees bear fruit once a year, others several times, and their fruit
does not mature, but remains unripe. Certain trees are very fruitful over a long

---

[10]Reading *cohaereant*.

15 period, as, for instance, fig-trees. Some bear fruit one year and then recuperate for a year, as do olive-trees, although they produce a number of boughs which cover them. Some trees are more productive when they are young than when they are old; others, on the contrary, are more fertile when they are old, almond-trees, for
20 example, and pear-trees and holm-oaks. Wild and garden plants can be distinguished by virtue of the male and female, each being recognizable by its peculiar characteristics; for the male is thicker and harder and has more branches and less
25 moisture and a smaller fruit, and does not reach such maturity; the leaves, too, and likewise the suckers are different.

In considering this we should form some conjectures whereby we may know trees and their seeds apart, and similarly in the case of small herbs. We must
30 consider what the ancients have said on these points, and examine the works written upon them. We shall only be able to take a brief survey and extract the essence of them. This means that we shall consider those plants which contain oil, those which
35 produce seeds, and those which produce wine, and plants which have medicinal properties, and those which destroy life. All these particulars about trees and plants are well known. But in order to know their causes, we ought to inquire into their production, and discover why certain plants grow in certain places and not in others, and at certain seasons and not at others; we must examine their methods of planting, their roots, their differences of sap and odour and juice and gum, and the
822ᵃ1 excellence and defects of particular plants, and the fact that the fruits of some trees last but not those of others, and why some fruits putrefy quickly, others more slowly. We must inquire into the properties of all plants, and particularly those of
5 their roots; and why some fruits grow soft while others do not; and why some arouse lust, others cause sleep, and others are fatal to life; and many other differences; and why the fruits of some produce milk, of others not.

BOOK II

10   1 · A plant has three powers, the first derived from the element of earth, the second from that of water, the third from that of fire. From the earth the plant
15 derives its fixity, from water its solidity, and from fire the unity of its fixity. We see much the same thing in vessels of pottery, which contain three elements—clay, which is, as it were, the material of pottery; secondly, water, which binds the pottery
20 together; and, thirdly, fire, which draws its parts together, until it completes the process of manufacture. The appearance, then, of complete unity is due to the fire; because rarity is present in pottery according to the composition of its parts, and, when the fire heats them, the moist matter is completed, and the parts of the clay
25 will cohere together. Dryness will thus take the place of moisture, owing to the predominance of the fire and the process of concoction which takes place in all animals, plants, and metals. For concoction takes place where moisture and heat are present, when the struggle between them is allowed to run its course; and this is
30 what will take place in the concoction of stone and metals. It is not so in animals and

plants; for their parts are not closely compacted, and so there is an escape of moisture from them. But in metals there is no such escape of moisture or sweating, because their parts have no rarity, and therefore they can give up nothing except parts of themselves to correspond to certain residues which are given off by animals and plants. This escape of moisture can only take place where rarity is present; and so where there is no rarity, nothing at all can be given off. Therefore that which   35
cannot be increased is solid, because that which can increase requires space in which to dilate and grow; and therefore stones, salt, and earth are always the same, neither increasing nor growing. There is motion in plants in a secondary sense, and   822^{b}1
this is a form of attraction, namely, the force of the earthly element which attracts moisture; in this attraction there will be motion, and the moisture makes for a certain position, and the process of concoction is thus in a certain way completed. And so small plants usually come into being in the short space of a single day, unlike   5
animals; for the nature of animals is in itself different; for no concoction will take place except by the use of material in the animal itself. But the material of which the plant is formed is near at hand, and therefore its generation is quick, and it   10
grows and increases, because it is rare, more quickly than if it were dense. For that which is dense requires many powers on account of the diversity of its form and the extension of its parts in relation to one another. Consequently the generation of a plant is quicker on account of the similarity of its parts to one another, and the   15
completion of its growth is speedier. Now the parts of plants are usually rare, because the heat draws the moisture into the extremities of the plant, and the material is distributed through all its parts, and that which is superfluous will flow away; just as in a bath the heat attracts the moisture and turns it into vapour which   20
rises, and, when it is present in superfluity, it will turn into drops of water. Similarly in animals and plants, the superfluities ascend from the lower into the upper parts and then descend in their action from the upper to the lower parts.

We find the same phenomenon in streams which are generated underground   25
and come forth from mountains, and whose material is rain. When the waters increase and are confined within the earth, an excess of vapour will be produced from them on account of their compression underground, and the vapour will break its way through the earth and fountains and streams will appear, which were   30
formerly hidden.

2 · We have set forth the causes which produce springs and rivers in the book on *Meteorology*. An earthquake frequently discloses springs and rivers which had   35
not before been visible, when the earth is rent by vapour. We also often find that springs and rivers are submerged when an earthquake takes place. But this does not happen in the case of plants, because air is present in the rarity of their parts. This is   823^{a}1
indicated by the fact that an earthquake never takes place in sandy localities, but only where the ground is hard, that is in districts of water and mountains. Earthquakes occur similarly in these districts, because water and stone are solid,   5
and it is the nature of warm, dry air to ascend. When, therefore, the particles of air become massed together, they gain force and thrust up the ground and the vapour

10 makes its way out; whereas, if the ground were rare, the vapour would make its way
out gradually from the first. But the ground being solid, it does not make its way out
15 gradually, but its parts collect, and it is then strong enough to rend the earth. This,
then, is the cause of earthquakes in solid bodies; there will, therefore, be nothing to
20 correspond to an earthquake in the parts of plants and animals, though it will occur
in other things—often, for example, in pottery and glass, and in some cases in
minerals. Any body which has considerable rarity tends to rise upwards, for the air
supports it. This we often see when we throw a gold coin or some other heavy
substance into the water and it immediately sinks; whereas if we throw in a piece of
wood, which has rarity in it, it does not sink. A gold coin sinks not because of its
25 leaf-like form nor on account of its weight, but because it is solid. That which has
rarity can never altogether sink. Ebony and similar substances sink because there is
very little rarity in them, and therefore there will not be air present to support them;
30 and so they sink, because their parts are practically solid. Oil and leaves always
float on the surface of water. We will now prove this. We know that heat and
moisture are present in these substances; and it is characteristic of moisture to
35 cohere with particles of water, while it is characteristic of heat that it causes things
to rise and makes its way towards the particles of air; and it is the habit of water to
raise objects to its surface, and of air to rise upwards; and water does not rise above
40 its surface, because the whole surface of the water is one and the same, and
consequently the air rises with the oil above the water. Some stones too float on
823ᵇ1 water, because rarity is present in them and is greater in quantity than the matter of
which they are formed, and consequently[11] the space occupied by air will be greater
than that occupied by the earthly element. It is the nature of water to take up a
position above the earth, and of air to rise above water; the material, therefore,
which composes the stone, which is of the element of earth, sinks in the water, while
5 the element of air enclosed in the stone rises above the water. Each element
therefore attracts its like in a contrary direction to the element with which it is
combined. If, then, one element is equal to the other, half the stone will be
submerged and half will project above the surface; but if the air is present in greater
10 quantity, the stone will float above the water. The weight of trees is made up in the
same way. (These stones are due to a violent collision of waves, and are originally
foam which forms an oily milk; when the wave is dashed against the sand, the sand
will collect the oily foam, and the dryness of the sea will dry it up together with the
15 superfluous salt, and the particles of sand will collect, and thus in the long process of
time stones will be formed.)
       The presence of sand under the sea is explained by the fact that earth always
20 has a fresh flavour, and when water stands it will be prevented from undergoing any
change, and will form an enclosed mass of water in the place where it is, and the air
will not draw it up; the particles of earth, therefore, gain the upper hand and
25 become salty, and gradually acquire heat. (Now soil is found in its natural state in
fresh running water, because there the water is sweet and light.) And because the
30 dryness of the earth gains the upper hand in the water, it changes it into an earthy

---

[11]Reading *ideo* for *idem.*

nature, or something like it, and makes both the earth and water crisp; and this process of drying goes on as long as the earth remains in its place and there is water still left, and it splits up the soil into small particles; and for this reason the earth near the sea is always sandy. The same thing happens on plains which have nothing   35 to protect them from the sun, and which are far from fresh water; the sun has dried up the particles of fresh moisture and that which is of the nature of earth has remained; and because the sun shines continually upon an exposed place of this   40 kind, the parts of the soil become separated and sand is thus formed. A further sign of this is that if we dig deep down in a desert, we shall find natural soil. Natural soil, therefore, will be the basis of sand, and will only become sand accidentally and   824^{a}1 under certain circumstances, namely, when the sun's rays dwell on it for a long time and it is far removed from fresh water. The saltness of the sea is to be accounted for in a similar way; for the basis of all water is fresh water, and saltness is accidental,   5 occurring only under the circumstances which we have mentioned. The fact that the earth is below the sea and the sea naturally and necessarily above the earth is a self-evident proof of this. Some, however, have held that the common element is   10 that which is present in the greatest quantity, and that there is a greater quantity of water in the sea than elsewhere, and that, therefore, sea-water is the element present in all water. But water naturally has its position above the earth and is lighter than it; for we have already shown that water is at a higher elevation than   15 the earth according to the altitude at which the mass of water stands. Let us take two vessels of the same size and place fresh water in one and salt water in the other; then let us take an egg and place it in the fresh water; it will sink, whereas, if we   20 place it in the salt water, it will float. It therefore rises above the particles of salt water because these particles do not let it sink,[12] as do those of fresh water, but they can uphold the weight, which therefore does not sink. So in the Dead Sea no animal   25 can sink, nor is any animal life produced in it, because dryness predominates in it and it is like the form of earth. It is clear, therefore, that dense water finds a lower level than water which is not dense; for the dense is of the nature of earth, the rare of   30 the nature of air; therefore, fresh water stands at a higher elevation than any other water, and is therefore further removed from earth. Now we already know that the water which is furthest removed from earth is the natural water, and we have shown that fresh water is higher in position than all other kinds of water; as this sign shows,   35 then, it certainly and necessarily is the natural water. Salt water is also produced in pools, because fresh water becomes salt. The saltness, therefore, of the earth prevails over that saltiness, and the air will remain enclosed, and the mass of water will not therefore be fresh. Saltness may also be produced from water by being given   824^{b}1 off from it like sweat.

3 · So too in the case of plants: their species will be formed, not from a simple element, but by a process of composition, just as saltness and the substance of sand   5 are formed from the water of the sea. For vapours which rise, when they become solidified, will be able to conceive these plants, and the air will descend and bedew   10

---

[12]Reading *mergunt*.

the ground, and from it will come forth the form of their seeds through the powerful influence of the stars. But plants must necessarily have some material, and this material is water. There are, however, different kinds of water, and water only rises if it is fresh, and salt water is heavier than fresh; and so that which rises above water is rarer than water. When, therefore, the air draws it up, it will become rarefied and rise still higher; and this is why fountains and streams are formed in mountains. Similarly phlegm and blood rise to the brain, and all foods also rise; so too all water rises. Even salt water rises in that part of it which heat dries out into the element of air, and, because air is always higher than water, that which rises above salt water is fresh. We often find the same thing taking place in baths. When heat takes hold of salt water, its parts will be rarefied, and vapour will rise in a contrary direction to the depth of the bath, and the particles of salt and the natural moisture become separated, for the latter is of the nature of air and follows the vapour; and cloud after cloud of vapour rises upwards, and when they reach the roof they press upon it. The vapour will thus collect and become condensed, and will turn into drops of fresh water dripping down, and so in salt baths the vapour will always be fresh.

Plants ought not to grow in salt water, on account of its low temperature and dryness. This is because a plant needs two things—its proper material and a position suitable to its nature; when these two conditions are present a plant will grow. Now we find that snow is the substance furthest removed from an equable temperature, and its most striking characteristic is the impossibility of its existing in a temperate region. We do not, therefore, find plants growing in snow; yet we often find plants appearing in the snow, and animals of all kinds, especially worms (for they are bred in the snow), and mullein and all bitter herbs. But it is not the snow which causes this to be so; but a certain characteristic of snow is active. The reason is that snow falls like smoke, and the wind congeals it and the air binds it together. There is therefore rarity amongst its parts, and air will be retained in it and will grow hot, and foul water flows from it, which had before enclosed the air; and when the air is present in considerable quantities and the sun shines upon it, the air which is enclosed in the snow will burst its way out, and a foul moisture will appear and will be solidified by the heat of the sun. But if the place is covered up, plants will grow in it, but without leaves, because it is cut off from the equable temperature of the earth which is congenial to it. This is the reason why there are numerous flowers and leaves on small plants in places where the air and water are temperate, and few flowers and leaves on a plant which occurs in the snow. So too in very salty and dry places plants do not usually appear, because these places are far from being temperate; and the ground is impoverished, because heat and moisture, which are the characteristics of fresh water, are absent. So the soil that is fresh is the mountain soil, and there plants grow quickly.

But in warm places, because there the water is fresh and the heat plentiful, the process of concoction proceeds for two reasons, partly as a result of the position and the air which is found there, and partly because there is a concoction of the air owing to the heat of the sun there. On mountains, because they attract moisture and the clearness of the air assists the process, concoction proceeds apace; and therefore plants are generally found on mountains. In deserts the saltness gains the upper

hand, as we have already shown, and rarities resembling one another are left 35
between the particles of sand; the sun has therefore no power to produce or
perpetuate any continuous plant life; and so in deserts separate species of plants will
not occur, but species similar to one another.

4 . Plants which grow on the surface of the water will only do so when there
is density in the water; the reason of this is that, when heat touches water which has 825[b]1
no current to move it, something of the nature of a cloud comes over it and retains a
little of the air, and the moisture putrefies and the heat draws it up, and it spreads
over the face of the water. Such a plant has no root, because roots will only attach 5
themselves to the hard particles of the earth, and the particles of water are loose and
scattered. The heat then comes forth with the putrefaction which takes place on the
surface of the water. Such a plant has no leaves because it is produced under 10
conditions which are far from temperate, and its parts are not compact, because the
parts of water are not compact. It is for this reason too that such plants grow like
threads.[13] It is because the parts of earth are compact that the plants too which grow
in the earth are compact. Sometimes putrefactions are set up in damp, smoky
ground, and hold the air—the sun causing them to appear when rain and winds are 15
frequent—and the dryness of the earth will make their roots dry up and solidify,
and thus fungi and mushrooms and the like will be produced. In places that are
exceedingly warm, because the heat concocts the water in the interior of the earth 20
and the sun holds the heat, a vapour is formed and a plant is thus produced. This
process takes place in all warm places, and the formation of the plant is thus
completed. A cold locality causes a similar but contrary process; the cold air forces 25
the heat downwards and its particles collect together, and the ground undergoes
concoction with the moisture present in it; the ground is then cleft open and a plant
emerges from it. Where the ground is fresh, water is generally not far away. When, 30
therefore, the air which is enclosed in the earth is stirred into motion, the moisture
of the water will remain behind, and the air will solidify inside the water and a plant
is produced, such as the water-lily and various kinds of small plants; these plants
grow straight up and do not expand, because their roots are above the earth. In 35
places too where there is warm water running, plants often grow, because the heat
of the water attracts the vapours which are retained in the earth, and draws the cold
moisture upwards, and air is solidified from the moisture, which it concocts owing to
the heat of the water, and a plant appears, but only after a long lapse of time. Small 826[a]1
plants too appear in sulphurous places: and when the wind blows violently upon the
brimstone, it will recoil back again, and the air which is in it will be stirred up, and
the place will become hot, and fire will be produced from it, and will continue to be 5
produced from it, because it exists deep down in the brimstone, which is due to
impurities deposited by the air; the fire attracts the air when the sulphur putrefies,
and a plant will be produced from it. Such a plant, as we have shown before, will not
generally have many leaves, because it is produced under conditions which are far 10
from equable.

[13]Reading *fila*.

Edible products will grow from plants in positions which are warm even, and elevated, especially in the third and fourth zones; and products almost edible grow
15 in cold and high districts. Many species are produced in cold, high positions owing to the attraction of the moisture and the temperate conditions which prevail in the warmth of the sun on spring days. Similarly natural soil readily produces plants which are full of oil; such soil, as we have already seen, is found where there is fresh water.

20   5 · A plant which grows upon solid rock takes a long time to grow; for the air which is enclosed in the stone strives to rise, and when it cannot find a way, owing to the resistance of the stone, it retreats back again and becomes heated, and attracts the residuum of the moisture in the stone upwards, and with this moisture a vapour
25 comes forth accompanied by a resolution of small particles of the stone; and because the sun often acts upon the stone, it assists the moisture in the process of concoction, and as a result a plant is produced. Such plants do not generally grow to any height,
30 unless they are near some soil or moisture. The rest of the plant requires soil, water, and air. If you look at the matter, you will see that if a plant faces the east, it will grow quickly, and slowly if it faces the west. A plant, when water is the predominant element in it, will retain the air and will not allow it to rise, and thus the plant is not
35 nourished. Similarly, when dryness predominates, the natural heat will be diverted into the extremities of the plant and will block up the ducts through which the flow of water passed, and the plant does not receive nourishment.

        6 · Every plant needs four things (just as an animal needs four things), namely, a definite seed, a suitable position, and a suitable supply of water and air.
826ᵇ1 When these four conditions are fulfilled, a plant will grow and increase; but if they are lacking, the plant will be correspondingly weakened. A plant which is used for medicinal purposes will be more serviceable and suitable for such purposes if it grows on high mountains; its fruit, however, will be harder to concoct and will
5 contain less nourishment. Places which are secluded from the sun's rays will not produce much plant life (just as they will not produce much animal life), because the sun makes the day long according to the duration of its absence, and it is the sun which draws out the moisture; and so plants which grow in sunless places will not
10 have the strength to produce leaves and fruit. As for plants which grow in watery places, when the water is still, a foulness is formed, and there will be no power in the air to rarefy the particles of water, and the air will be imprisoned inside the earth,
15 and this will prevent the thick matter in the water from rising; then the wind will invade[14] the spot and the earth will be cleft open, and the air which is enclosed will retreat into the earth, and the wind will solidify the moisture, and from this condition of moisture marsh plants will spring. Usually such plants do not differ from one another in form on account of the constant presence of water and its thick
20 consistency and the heat of the sun overhead. The plants which grow in damp places will appear like patches of verdure on the surface of the earth. In such a place there

_____
[14]Reading *inundabit*.

is, in my opinion, little rarity, and when the sun falls upon it, it will stir up the moisture and the spot will grow warm through the resulting motion and the heat   25
which is enclosed within the earth; and so there is nothing to cause the upward growth of the plant, while the moisture helps its expansion; and so it spreads over the earth in a sheet of verdure and produces no leaves. A kind of plant also grows which appears above the surface of the water and is smaller in quantity than that   30
just mentioned, because it is like the nature of earth, and it neither grows upwards nor expands. Often, too, one plant grows out of another plant of a different form from itself, without any root, and spreads all over the plant. For when a plant which   35
has numerous thorns and contains an oily juice moves, its parts will open and the sun will cause its putrefactions to turn into vapour, and the putrefied place of its own accord will produce a plant, and the wind and a moderate heat assist, and the plant grows in the form of threads and extends over the original plant. This is a peculiarity of very thorny plants, dodder and the like.   827ᵃ1

There is also a class of plant which has neither root nor leaves, and another which has a stalk, but no fruit or leaves, the tamarisk, for example.[15]

All herbs and all things that grow above or in earth have their origin in one of five ways, namely, either from seed, or from putrefaction, or from the moisture of   5
water, or from being planted, or from growing as parasites on other plants. These are the five causes of plants.

7 · Trees have three different methods of production; they produce their fruit either before their leaves, or at the same time as their leaves, or else after their leaves have grown. We have already described these three methods. A plant which   10
produces its fruit before its leaves contains a considerable amount of oily juice, and when the heat which is natural to the plant has concocted the juice, its maturity will quickly follow, and the juice will acquire force and boil up within the branches of   15
the plant and will prevent the moisture from rising; the result is that the fruit appears before the leaves. But in plants which produce their leaves more quickly than their fruits, the effects of the moisture are various. When the heat of the sun   20
begins to disperse the particles of water, the sun attracts the particles of this moisture upwards, and the process of ripening will be delayed, because the concoction of the fruit will only take place through coagulation, and so the leaves come before the fruit. A plant which produces its leaves and fruit simultaneously has much moisture, and frequently also contains an oily juice. When the heat has concocted the moisture, it will, as a result, rise upward, carrying the juice with it,   25
and the air and sun will draw it out, and the oily juice which forms the fruit will come out, while the moisture will produce the leaves, leaves and fruit coming forth together. The wise men of old used to assert that all leaves were really fruits, but so much moisture was present, because the fruit did not mature or solidify owing to the   30
presence of heat above and the sudden attraction exerted by the sun, and consequently the moisture on which the process of concoction had had no effect changed into leaves; the leaves, they said, are simply intended to attract the   35

---

[15]This sentence occurs in the MSS after 'have grown', in line 10.

moisture and serve as a protection to the fruit from the violence of the sun. The leaves ought therefore, they said, to be equally regarded as fruit. But the truth is that the moisture rises above them and the leaves are converted into real fruits, as we have already said. The same theory applies to olives, which often fail to produce 827ᵇ1 fruit; for when nature brings about concoction of moisture, some of the thin moisture, which has not matured, will rise first, and this will produce leaves and its concoction will produce flowers, and when in the second year the process of concoction is completed, the fruit will grow and will eventually use up all the 5 available material according to the space which it has in it.

Thorns are not characteristic of plants or natural to them. My opinion is that there is rarity present in a plant, and concoction will take place at the beginning of its existence, and moisture and cold rise upwards, and they are accompanied by a 10 slight concoction; this circulates where there is rarity, and the sun causes it to solidify, and thus the thorns will be produced. Their form is pyramidal; for they begin by being thin at the point and gradually grow thicker, because when the air is withdrawn from the plant its parts increase, and the material expands. The same is 15 true of any plant or tree which is pyramidal at the top.

8 · Greenness must be the most common characteristic of plant life; for we see that trees are white internally and green externally. The reason is that the 20 material which supplies their nutriment is more readily accessible: it follows therefore that there is greenness in all plants, because their material is absorbed and rarefies the wood of the tree, and the heat causes a slight concoction, and the moisture remains in the tree and appears externally: consequently there will be greenness. This is also the case with the leaves, unless the concoction in them is 25 unusually powerful; and leaves are in respect of strength midway between bark and wood. But greenness does not persist, nor indeed come into existence without the presence of moisture, and is of the element of earth, and is the intermediate colour between that of earth and water. This is indicated by the fact that when the bark of 30 trees dries up it turns black, and the wood inside the tree becomes white, and the green, which comes between these two colours, is the colour presented by the outward appearance of the plant.

The shapes of plants fall under three classes. Some spread upwards, others downwards, while others are intermediate. The upward extension is due to the fact 35 that the nutritive material makes its appearance in the marrow of the plant, and the heat draws it up, and the air, which is present in the rarities of the plant, compresses it, and it assumes a pyramidal form, just as fire assumes a pyramidal form in bodies in which it is present and rises upwards. Downward extension is due to the blocking of ducts in the plant, and, when the material is concocted, the water, which contains 828ᵃ1 the marrow of the plant, will thicken, and the rarefied portion proceeds on its upward course, while the water returns to its former position in the lower portion of the plant, and by its weight presses the plant downwards. In the plants which are intermediate between the two classes already mentioned, the moisture is rarefied and the natural state of the plant is very nearly a temperate condition during the

process of concoction, and the ducts are open through the middle of the plant, and 5
the nutritive material spreads upwards and downwards. There is a double process of
concoction; the first takes place below the plant, while the second takes place in the
marrow which comes out of the earth and is in the middle of the plant; afterwards
the nutritive materials make their appearance fully matured and are distributed 10
through the plant, and do not undergo a third concoction. In animals there is a third
process of concoction; this is due simply to the diversity of their limbs and to the
distinctness of their parts from one another. Plants, on the other hand, are more 15
homogeneous and repeat the same members over and over again, and the nutritive
material generally has a downward tendency. The shapes of plants will depend on
the quantity of the seed, while the flower and fruit is dependent on the water and
nutritive material. In all animals the first process of maturation and concoction 20
takes place within the animal; there is no exception to this rule. But in plants the
first concoction and maturation takes place in the nutritive material. Every tree
continues to grow up, until its growth is completed and it dies. The reason is that,
while in any animal its height is much the same as its width, in a plant it is far from 25
being so, because water and fire, the elements which compose it, rise quickly, and
therefore the plant grows. Variety in the branches of a plant is due to excessive
rarity, and, when the moisture is intercepted there, the process of nature will cause
it to grow hot and will hasten the concoction, and thus boughs will form and leaves 30
will appear, as we have already said.

9 . The shedding of leaves from trees will be due to the tendency to fall,
induced by quickly formed rarity. When the moisture is concocted with the
nutritive material, it will assume a pyramidal form, and therefore the ducts within 35
will be wide and will afterwards become narrow and pyramidal; when the nutritive
material makes its appearance already concocted and formed, it will close up the
extremities of the ducts above, and the leaves will have no nutritive material, and
therefore dry up. When the contrary process to the one we have described takes
place, the leaves do not fall from the trees. When coldness dominates in the plant, it 40
will affect its colour owing to the secretion of heat in the middle of the plant and the
presence of cold outside in its extremities; the result is that the leaves are blue-grey 828^{b}1
and do not fall, as in the olive, and myrtle, and similar trees. When trees or plants
exercise a violent force of attraction, fruit will be produced once a year; when they 5
do not exercise such a force, nature will employ the process of concoction on
successive occasions and at each concoction they produce fruit, and so some plants
bear fruit several times in the year. Plants which are of the nature of water bear
fruit with difficulty on account of the predominance of moisture in them, and the 10
wideness of their ducts and the tendency of their roots to fall off; when the heat is
intense, the concoction will be quick and will be rarefied owing to the water and will
not solidify; this we find to be the case in all small herbs and in some vegetables. 15

A grey colour will occur where the ground is exceedingly hot; here there will be
little moisture and the ducts will become narrow, and when nature wishes to bring
about concoction it will not have sufficient moisture to supply the nutritive material

20 and the ducts will become narrow. The process of concoction therefore will be
reversed and the heat will cause it to continue, and the plant will be seen to have a
colour intermediate between white and black. When this happens it will have black
wood or anything like it between white and ebony, that is, any of the whole range of
25 colours from that of ebony to that of elm;[16] and so such wood sinks in water because
its parts are compact and the ducts in it are narrow, and no air enters into them.
When white wood sinks the reason will be the narrowness of the ducts and the
30 presence of superfluous moisture, which blocks up the ducts so that the air does not
enter; consequently it sinks. Every flower is composed only of rarefied material
when concoction first begins; and so the flower generally precedes the fruit in
plants. We have already shown why it is that plants produce their leaves before their
fruits. In the case of plants which have slender parts the colour of the flower will
35 resemble a bright blue; when the parts are not closely compressed, it will tend to
whiteness; under medium conditions it will be a blue-grey. The absence of flowers in
certain plants is usually due to the solidity of their parts or their rarity or their
roughness or thickness. The palm and similar trees therefore have no flowers.

829ª1   A plant which has thick bark expands owing to the pressure of moisture and
the impelling force of heat; we see this in the pine and palm. A plant which gives
5 forth a milky juice will have such juice within it; there will be powerful heat within
and an oily substance will be present there. When the heat begins to cause
concoction, the oily substance will be turned into moisture, and the heat will solidify
it to a slight extent, and local warmth will be caused, and an oily liquid will be
produced similar to milk, and vapour will rise from the moisture which attracts the
10 milky substance into the extremities of the plant, and the moisture will retain the
heat which appears. The milky substance will not be solidified, because it is the
function of heat to solidify it and any milk requires a great deal of solidification. If
there is cold present in the tree, the milky substance will solidify when it has left its
15 original position in the tree, and the result will be the formation of gum. Gum comes
out warm from the tree by distillation, and, when it comes into contact with the air,
it will solidify. Some gums flow in temperate places, and these will be of the
consistency of water; others flow out and solidify as hard as stone or shell. Gum
20 which flows drop by drop keeps its form, as in the tree which is known as *aletafur*.
The gum which changes into a stony substance will be very cold on its first
appearance, and its appearance will be caused by heat, and when it has flowed out it
will turn to stone; it will occur where the soil is very hot. Some trees undergo a
25 change in the winter and will become sometimes green and sometimes blue-grey,
and neither their leaves nor their fruits decay; for trees in which this occurs have a
great quantity of heat and rarefied water in their lower reservoirs. Thus as the year
30 goes on this water will retain its heat on account of the coldness of the air; and
because the heat goes out to the cold, it carries the moisture out with it, and the
moisture tinctures it with the colour of heat, and therefore the colour is seen in the
appearance of the tree. Consequently cold and heat are converted into activity, and
35 the moisture retains heat, and therefore another colour makes its appearance.

[16]Reading *ulmum*.

10 · Fruit will be bitter because the heat and moisture have not completed the process of concoction (cold and dryness hindering the completion of this process), and so fruit turns bitter. This is indicated by the fact that what is bitter, when put into fire, becomes sweet. Trees which grow in sour water produce sweet 829ᵇ1 fruit, because the sourness assisted by the heat of the sun attracts that which is of its own quality, namely, cold and dryness. Sweet liquids therefore make their appearance inside the tree, and the innermost part of the tree becomes hot when the sun shines continuously above it, and the flavour of the fruit will be successively 5 sour, and then, when the process of concoction has taken place, the sourness will be gradually dissolved until it disappears, and sweetness will make its appearance. Consequently the fruit will be sweet, while the leaves and extremities of the tree will be acid. When the maturation is complete, the fruit will be bitter: this is due to a superfluity of heat with very little moisture. The moisture is used up and the fruit 10 makes the heat rise, and so the fruit will be bitter, and the stones in the fruit will be pyramidal in form on account of the upward attraction of the heat and the downward attraction of the cold and moisture which are of the same nature as sour 15 water; and the moisture remains in the trunk of the tree, which consequently thickens, while its extremities are thin. If trees are planted in temperate soil, they reach maturity quickly before the days of spring, because, when the heat is almost temperate and the moisture has made its appearance and the air is clear, the fruit 20 will not require much heat during the process of concoction. Consequently maturity comes quickly and takes place before the days of spring. Bitterness or harshness of flavour is prevalent in all trees when they are first planted. The reason is that when 25 the moisture is in their extremities and has concocted the parts that are in the middle of the tree, from which the material of the fruit comes, the dryness comes forth and follows the moisture, and the first concoction will be sour or bitter or harsh. The reason is that the concoction takes place in the heat and moisture, and 30 when moisture or dryness prevails over the heat, the fruit so produced will not at first have undergone proper concoction, and consequently the production of fruit is at first without sweetness.

The fruit of the bennut-tree when it first appears is sweet, but subsequently becomes harsh in flavour and finally bitter. The reason for this is that the tree has 35 excessive rarity in it, and at the time of concoction, when the ducts are wide, the heat will follow the moisture and will cause the fruit to mature; consequently the fruit will be sweet at first. Subsequently the heat attracts the dryness which resembles its own nature, and will cause the ducts to contract, and cold and dryness 40 will prevail over heat and moisture; the fruit, therefore, will change to a harsh flavour. Next, the sun with its heat will prevail through the attraction of 830ᵃ1 superfluous[17] moisture in the seed, which is present at the first appearance of the tree, and the cold will prevail over the dryness; the fruit will therefore become exceedingly harsh in flavour. Next, the natural heat will rise upwards, and the heat 830ᵇ1 of the sun outside will assist it; therefore the heat and dryness will prevail, and the fruit will become bitter.

---

[17]Reading *superfluae.*

ON MARVELLOUS THINGS
HEARD**

L. D. Dowdall

830ᵃ5   1 · Men say that in Paeonia, on the mountain called Hesaenus, which forms the boundary between the Paeonian and Maedian districts, there is found a wild beast, which is called Bolinthos, but by the Paeonians is named Monaepos. They state that this in its general nature is similar to the ox, but surpasses it in size and

10   strength, and moreover is distinguished from it by its mane; for like the horse it has a mane hanging down very thick from the neck, and from the crown of the head as far as the eyes. It has horns, not such as oxen have, but bent downwards, the tip

15   being low down near the ears; and these severally contain more than three pints, and are very black, and shine as though they were peeled; and when the hide is stripped off it occupies a space capable of containing eight couches. When the animal is struck with a weapon it flees, and only stops when it is quite exhausted. Its flesh has an agreeable taste. It defends itself by kicking, and voiding excrement over

20   a distance of about twenty-four feet. It easily and frequently employs this kind of defence, and the excretion burns so severely that the hair of the dogs is scraped off. They say, however, that the excrement produces this effect only when the animal is disturbed, but when it is undisturbed it does not burn. When they bring forth young, assembling in larger numbers and being all gathered closely together, the full-grown ones bring forth, and void excrement as a defence round their young; for the animal discharges a large quantity of this excretion.

830ᵇ5   2 · The camels in Arabia, they say, do not copulate with their mothers, but that even if someone tries to force them they are unwilling. For it is said that once, when there was no stallion present, a keeper disguised the mother and set her foal on

10   her. And the foal, it seems, finished its task then, but a little later bit the keeper and killed him.

3 · Men say that the cuckoos in Helice, when about to breed, do not build a nest, but lay their eggs in the nests of ring-doves or turtle-doves, and neither sit on their eggs, nor hatch them, nor rear their young; but when the chick is born and

TEXT: O. Apelt, Teubner, Leipzig, 1888

reared, it expels its companions from the nest. Moreover, it appears, it grows large   15
and beautiful, so that it easily overcomes the rest. They say that the ring-doves also
take such a delight in it that they even assist it to drive out their own young.

4 · The she-goats in Crete, when they are shot with arrows, seek, it would   20
appear, for the dittany, which grows there; for as soon as they have eaten it, they
straightway expel the arrows from their bodies.

5 · Men say that some of the stags in Achaea, when they have shed their
horns, proceed to places of such a kind that they cannot be easily found; and that
they act in this way because they have no means of defence, and also because the   831ᵃ1
parts from which they have shed their horns give them pain; and it is stated that, in
the case of many of these animals, ivy is seen growing in the place of the horns.

6 · Men say that in Armenia a certain poison grows, which is called leopard's
bane. So, when a leopard is seen, they anoint a victim with this, and let it go. When   5
the leopard touches it, she goes, it would appear, in quest of human excrement.
Therefore the hunters put excrement in a vessel, and suspend it from a tree, so that
the leopard, by leaping up towards it and becoming exhausted, may be paralysed by
it, and fall into their power.   10

7 · Men say that in Egypt the sandpipers fly into the mouths of the
crocodiles, and clean their teeth, pulling out the pieces of flesh, which stick in their
snouts, while the crocodiles are pleased, and do them no harm.

8 · Men say that the hedgehogs in Byzantium perceive when north or south   15
winds are blowing, and immediately change their holes; and, when the winds are
southerly, make their holes opening out of the ground, but, when they are northerly,
out of the walls.

9 · The she-goats in Cephallenia do not drink, as it appears, like other
quadrupeds; but daily turning their faces towards the sea, open their mouths, and   20
take in the breezes.

10 · They say that in Syria one of the wild donkeys leads the herd, and that
when one of the younger foals mounts a female the leader gets angry and chases him
until he catches him; and then, ducking down to his back legs, he tears off his   25
genitals with his teeth.

11 · Men say that tortoises, when they have eaten part of a viper, eat
marjoram as an antidote, and, if the creature fails to find it at once, it dies; that
many of the countryfolk, wishing to prove whether this is true, whenever they see it
acting in this manner, pluck up the marjoram, and when they have done so, the   30
tortoise is presently seen dying.

831^b1   12 · They say that the penis of the marten is not like that of the other animals, but is always stiff like a bone, whatever state the marten may be in. They say that it is one of the best drugs for strangury and is given in powdered form.

5   13 · Men say that the bird called the woodpecker climbs upon the trees like lizards, both hanging from and standing on the branches. It is further stated that it feeds upon the grubs out of the trees, and digs so deeply into the trees, in its search for the grubs, that it even brings the trees down.

10   14 · Men say that the pelicans dig up the mussels that are found in the rivers, and swallow them; then, when they have devoured a large quantity of these, they vomit them up again, and thereupon eat the meat of the mussels, but do not touch the shells.

     15 · Men say that in Cyllene in Arcadia the blackbirds are born white, 15 which happens nowhere else, and that they give utterance to various sounds, and go forth by the light of the moon; but that, if any one should attempt to capture them by day, they are caught with great difficulty.

     16 · It is stated by certain persons that what is called flower-honey is 20 produced in Melos and Knidos, and that, while fragrant in smell, it lasts for only a short time; and that in it bee-bread is produced.

     17 · In some parts of Cappadocia they say that the honey is made without a honey-comb, and that in consistency it resembles olive-oil.

     18 · At Trapezus in Pontus the honey gathered from the box-tree is 25 produced, having an oppressive smell, and they say that this drives out of their senses those who are sound in mind, while it completely cures those who suffer from epilepsy.

     19 · Men say that in Lydia also the honey is gathered from the trees in abundance, and that the inhabitants form out of it balls without wax, and cutting 30 off portions by very violent rubbing make use of it. It is produced indeed in Thrace likewise, not so solid, but as it were of a sandy nature. They say that all honey when 832^a1 congealed preserves an equal volume, not like water and all other liquids.

     20 · The grass of Chalcis and almonds are most useful for making honey; for they say that a very large quantity is produced by them.

     21 · People say that bees are stupefied by unguents, and are unable to 5 endure the smell of them; while some say that they especially sting those who have been anointed.

22 · They say that among the Illyrians those who are called Taulantians make wine out of honey. When they have squeezed out the honey-combs, they pour water on the honey, and boil it in a caldron until half is consumed; then they pour it out into earthen jars, fill them half full, and lay them on boards; and on these they 10 say it ferments for a long time, and becomes like wine, while for the rest it is sweet and strong. But now they state that this mode of preparation was adopted also among some of the inhabitants of Greece, so that the drink did not differ from old wine, and that in later times, when they inquired into the method of mixing it, they were unable to discover it.

23 · They relate that in Thessaly once upon a time so large a number of serpents was bred alive that, if they had not been exterminated by the storks, the 15 inhabitants would have left the country. That is why they also honour the storks, and it is unlawful to kill them, and, if any one kills them, he becomes liable to the same penalties as a homicide.

24 · Likewise also it is related that there was once in Lacedaemon so great a multitude of serpents that the Lacedaemonians, owing to a scarcity of corn, used 20 them as food; whence also they say that the Pythian priestess called them 'serpent-necked'.

25 · It is said that in the island of Gyaros the mice eat iron.

26 · Men say that among the Chalybians, in an islet situated beyond them, gold is collected by mice in large numbers: that is why also, as it appears, they cut up those that are found in the mines. 25

27 · It is said that travellers going from Susa to Media meet with an immense multitude of scorpions at the second stage. So the King of the Persians, whenever he was passing through the place, remained there for three days, ordering all his men to hunt them down; and he gave a prize to him who caught the greatest number. 30

28 · Men say that in Cyrene there is not merely one sort of mouse, but several kinds differing both in forms and in colours; for some are broad-faced, like 832ᵇ1 weasels, and some like hedgehogs, which they call 'hedgehogs'.

29 · In Cilicia they say that there is a whirlpool, in which birds, and animals besides, that have been suffocated, when immersed come to life again. 5

30 · Among the Scythians who are called Geloni, they say that there is a certain wild animal, excessively rare indeed, which is named Tarandos. Now this is said to change the colour of its hair, according to the place in which it may be; and 10 for this reason it is hard to catch; for it becomes in colour like to trees and places,

and its surroundings generally. But the most wonderful thing is its changing its hair;
15 for other animals change the colour of the skin, such as the chameleon and octopus.
In size it resembles an ox, while the form of its face is like that of a stag.

31 · It is said that a certain man in Abydos being deranged in mind, and
going to the theatre on many days looked on (as though actors were performing a
20 play), and applauded; and, when he was restored to his senses, he declared that that
was the happiest time he had ever spent.

32 · Moreover they say that at Tarentum a certain wine-merchant was mad
at night, but sold his wines during the day: he also kept the key of the cellar attached
to his belt, and though many tried to steal it from him and get possession of it, he
25 never lost it.

33 · In the island of Tenos they say there is a small bowl containing a
mixture, from which people kindle fire very readily. Moreover in the Thracian
Bithynia there is found in the mines the stone which is called 'the chaffinch' from
30 which they say that fire is kindled.

34 · People say that in the island of Lipara there is a certain place where the
air is sucked down into the earth, and that if they bury a pot there they can put in it
whatever they please and boil it.

833ᵃ1   35 · Both in Media and in Psittacene, a district of Persia, there are fires
burning, that in Media small, but that in Psittacene large and with a bright flame;
for which reason also the King of the Persians constructed kitchens near it. Both
5 these are in level, not in elevated places. These fires are conspicuous both by night
and by day, while those in Pamphylia are seen only at night.

36 · They say also that at Atitania, near the borders of the district of
Apollonia, there is a certain rock, and fire rising from it is not visible, but whenever
10 oil is poured on it it blazes up.

37 · It is said that the places outside the Pillars of Hercules burn, some
constantly, others at night only, as Hanno's *Circumnavigation* relates. The fire also
in Lipara is visible and flaming, yet not by day, but only at night. They say also that
15 in Pithecusae the ground is fiery, and extraordinarily hot, yet not burning.

38 · Xenophanes states that the fire in Lipara once failed for sixteen years,
but returned in the seventeenth year. They say that the lava-stream in Etna is
neither flaming nor continuous, but returns only after an interval of many years.

20 39 · It is said that in Lydia a vast amount of fire blazed up, and continued
burning for seven days.

40 · The lava-stream in Sicily is an extraordinary phenomenon. The breadth of the fire that blazes up amounts to forty stadia, while the height to which it is carried amounts to three.

41 · They say that the stone in Thrace which is called 'the chaffinch' burns when split in two, and that it also, like charcoal-embers, when put together again, and sprinkled with water, burns; and that the stone called 'marieus' does the same.

42 · At Philippi in Macedonia they state that there are mines, the refuse from which, they say, increases and produces gold, and that this is an observable fact.

43 · They say that in Cyprus, at the place called Tyrrhias, copper is produced in like manner; for men having cut it up, as it appears, into small pieces, sow it, and then, when the rains have come on, it grows and springs up, and so is collected.

44 · They say that in the island of Melos, in those parts of the ground that are dug up, the earth fills itself up again.

45 · In Paeonia they state that when continuous showers have fallen, and the ground is thoroughly soaked, there is found what is called gold without fire. They state, too, that in Paeonia the ground is so rich in gold that many persons have found gold even exceeding a pound in weight. And they say that certain persons, who had found them, brought two nuggets to the king, one weighing three pounds, the other five; and they say that these are set beside him on the table, and, if he eats anything, he first offers a libation upon them.

46 · They say that among the Bactrians also the river Oxus carries down numerous small nuggets of gold, and moreover that in Iberia the river called Theodorus both throws out much gold on its banks, and likewise also carries it down the stream.

47 · They state also that in Pieria, a district of Macedonia, some uncoined gold was buried by the ancient kings, and, while there were four cavities, from one of them gold grew up a span in length.

48 · It is said that the production of the Chalybian and Amisenian iron is very peculiar; for it grows together, as at least they assert, from the sand that is carried down by the rivers. Some say that they simply wash this, and smelt it in a furnace; but others that, after frequently washing the deposit left by the first washing, they burn it, and insert what is called the fire-proof stone which is abundant in the country. This iron is far more beautiful than the other kinds. But if it were not burnt in the furnace it would not at all differ, as it appears, from silver. Now they say that it alone is not liable to rust, but that it is not very plentiful.

834ª1   **49** · They say also that among the Indians the copper is so bright, pure, and free from rust that it cannot be distinguished in colour from gold; moreover that among the cups of Darius there are certain goblets, and these not inconsiderable in 5   number, as to which, except by their smell, one could not otherwise decide whether they are of copper or gold.

50 · They say that Celtic tin melts much more quickly than lead. A proof of its fusibility is that it is believed to melt even in water: at any rate, it seems, it stains 10   quickly. Now it melts in the cold also, when the weather is frosty, because, as they say, the hot substance inherent in it is by reason of its weakness shut up and compressed within.

51 · In the Pantheon there is an olive-tree, which is called that 'of the beautiful crowns'. But all its leaves are contrary in appearance to those of other 15   olive-trees; for it has the pale-green outside, instead of inside, and it sends forth branches, like those of the myrtle, suitable for crowns. From this Heracles took a shoot, and planted it at Olympia, and from it are taken the crowns which are given to the competitors. This tree is near the river Ilissus, sixty stadia distant from the 20   river. It is surrounded by a wall, and a severe penalty is imposed on any one who touches it. From this the Eleians took the shoot, and planted it in Olympia, and from it they took the crowns which they bestowed.

52 · In the Lydian mines near Pergamos, which also Croesus had worked, 25   the following incident occurred. When a certain war arose the workmen fled to them; but, as the mouth was built up, they were suffocated; and a long time afterwards, when the mines were cleared out, vessels, which they used to employ for 30   daily uses, such as jars and the like, were found petrified. These, being filled with whatever liquid it might be, had been turned to stone, as well as the bones of the men.

53 · In the Ascanian lake the water is so impregnated with soda that garments have need of no other detergent; if one leaves them too long in the water they fall to pieces.

54 · Near the Ascanian lake is Pythopolis, a village about one hundred and twenty stadia distant from Cius, in which all the wells are dried up in the winter, so 834ᵇ1   that one cannot dip a pitcher into them; but in the summer they are filled up to the brim.

55 · The strait between Sicily and Italy increases and diminishes along with the changes of the moon.

5   **56** · On the road to Syracuse there is in a meadow a spring, neither large nor containing much water; but, when once a great crowd met at the place, it supplied water in abundance.

57 · There is also a certain spring in Palici in Sicily, about as large as the space ten couches would occupy. This throws up water to the height of six cubits, so that it is thought by those who see it that the plain will be inundated; and again it returns to its original state. There is also a form of oath, which is considered to be sacred there; whatever oaths a man swears he writes on a little tablet, and throws into the water. If therefore he swears truly, the tablet floats on the top; but if he swears falsely, they say that the tablet grows heavy and disappears, while the man is burnt. That is why the priest takes security from him that some one shall purify the temple.

58 · Demonesus, the island of the Chalcedonians, received its name from Demonesus, who first cultivated it. The place contains the mine of cyanos and gold-solder. Of this latter the finest sort is worth its weight in gold, for it is also a remedy for the eyes. In the same place there is also copper, obtained by divers, two fathoms below the surface of the sea, from which was made the statue in Sicyon in the ancient temple of Apollo, and in Pheneus the so-called statues of mountain-copper. On these is the inscription—'Heracles, son of Amphitryon, having captured Elis, dedicated them'. Now he captured Elis guided, in accordance with an oracle, by a woman, whose father, Augeas, he had slain. Those who dig the copper become very sharp-sighted, and those who have no eyelashes grow them: that is why also physicians use the flower of copper and Phrygian ashes for the eyes.

59 · Now in the same place there is a cave which is called the pretty cave. In this pillars have been formed by congelation from certain drippings of water: and this is evident at the point where they join the ground, for the narrowest part is there.

60 · Of the offspring of a pair of eagles, so long as they pair together, every second one is a sea-eagle. Now from the sea-eagles springs an osprey, and from these black eagles and vultures: yet these on the other hand do not bring the breed of vultures to a close, but produce the great vultures, and these are barren. And a proof is this, that no one has ever seen a nest of a great vulture.

61 · A wonderful thing they say happens among the Indians with regard to the lead there; for when it has been melted and poured into cold water it jumps out of the water.

62 · Men say that the copper of the Mossynoeci is very brilliant and white, no tin being mixed with it; but there is a kind of earth there, which is smelted with it. They state that the man who discovered the mixture did not inform any one; so the copper vessels formerly produced in these parts were excellent, but those subsequently made were no longer so.

63 · Men state that in Pontus some birds during the winter are found lurking in holes, and not discharging excrement, and when people pluck out their feathers

they do not feel it, nor yet when they are pierced on a spit, but only when they have been burnt through with fire. They say that many fishes also, when trimmed and cut round, have no perception of it, but only when they have been warmed through by fire.

20

64 · The bee is thought to announce the solstices by going to its labours, which the bee-keepers also use as a sign, for then they have rest. The grasshoppers also appear to chirp only after the solstices.

25

65 · They say also that the hedgehog continues without food for a year.

66 · It is said that the spotted lizard, when it has stripped off its slough, like snakes, turns round and swallows it, because physicians look out for it, from its being serviceable to those who suffer from epilepsy.

30

67 · Men state also that the fat of the bear, when it has been congealed owing to the winter, increases as long as the bear lies hidden in its den, and overflows the vessels in which it is kept.

68 · They say that the frogs in Cyrene are altogether dumb, and that in Macedonia, in the country of the Emathiotae, the swine have solid hoofs.

835ᵇ1

69 · They say that in Cappadocia there are fertile mules, and in Crete black poplars which yield fruit.

70 · They say also that in Seriphos the frogs do not croak; but if they are transferred to another place they croak.

5

71 · Among the Indians, in what is called the Horn, it is stated that there are little fishes, which wander about on the dry land, and run away again into the river.

72 · Some say also that in the neighbourhood of Babylon certain fishes remain in the holes, which contain moisture, while the river is drying up; that they go out to the threshing-floors and feed, and walk upon their fins, and move the tail to and fro, and when they are pursued they flee, enter into their holes, and stand facing their pursuer; for people often approach and tease them. Their head is like that of the sea-frog, while the rest of the body resembles that of the gudgeon, and they have gills like other fishes.

10

15

73 · At Heraclea in Pontus, and in Rhegium, they say there are fish obtained by digging, especially in places near rivers, and such as are well watered; and that it sometimes happens that when these places dry up at certain seasons, the fish shrink under the earth, and then when this dries up still more, they, in search of

humidity, enter into the mud; then when this becomes dry, they remain in the   20
moisture, like animals which continue in their holes; but, when they are dug up
before the waters come on, they then move.

74 . They say also that in Paphlagonia the fish obtained by digging are met
with deep in the ground, and that these are of an excellent quality, though neither is   25
water to be seen close at hand, nor do rivers flow into the place; the earth engenders
them of itself.

75 . Men say that the stags in Epirus bury their right horn, when they have
shed it, and that this is useful for many purposes.

76 . They say that the lynx too covers up its urine, because of its being useful   30
for signet-rings as well as for other things.

77 . They also state that the seal, when taken, vomits out rennet, and that
this is medicinal and serviceable to those who suffer from epilepsy.

78 . It is said that on the Circaean mountain in Italy there grows a deadly
poison, which is so potent that, if it be sprinkled on any one, it straightway causes   836ᵇ1
him to fall, and the hairs of his body to drop off, and generally the limbs of his body
to waste away, so that the surface of the body of those who are dying is a pitiable
sight. They say too that Aulus the Peucestian and Gaius were detected when about
to administer this poison to Cleonymus the Spartan, and that having been examined   5
they were put to death by the Tarentines.

79 . In the island of Diomedeia, which lies in the Adriatic, they say there is a
temple of Diomedes, wonderful and holy, and round the temple there sit in a circle
birds of a large size, having great hard beaks. These birds, they state, if Greeks land   10
at the place, keep quiet; but if any of the barbarians who live around them
approach, they fly up, and soaring in the air swoop down upon their heads, and,
wounding them with their beaks, kill them. The story goes that the companions of   15
Diomedes were metamorphosed into these, when they had been shipwrecked off the
island and Diomedes was treacherously slain by Aeneas, who was then king of those
regions.

80 . Among the Umbrians they say that the cattle bring forth young three   20
times in a year, and that the earth yields many times more fruit than the seed that is
sown: that the women also are prolific, and rarely bring forth only one child at a
time, but most of them have two or three.

81 . In the Amber islands, which are situated in the corner of the Adriatic,   25
they say that there are two statues erected, the one of tin, the other of bronze,
wrought after the ancient fashion. It is stated that these are works of Daedalus, a

memorial of old times, when he, fleeing before Minos from Sicily and Crete, put in
30   to these places. But they say that the river Eridanus formed these islands by alluvial
deposit. Moreover, as it appears, there is near the river a lake, containing hot water,
and a smell exhales from it heavy and unpleasant, and neither does any animal
836ᵇ1   drink from it, nor does a bird fly over it, but falls and dies. It has a circumference of
two hundred stadia, a width of about ten. Now the inhabitants tell the story that
Phaethon, when struck by the thunderbolt, fell into this lake; and that therein are
many black poplars, from which falls what is called amber. This, they say,
5   resembles gum, and hardens like a stone, and, when collected by the inhabitants, is
carried over to the Greeks. To these islands, therefore, they state that Daedalus
came, and, having obtained possession of them, dedicated in one of them his own
10   statue, and in the other that of his son Icarus; but that afterwards, when the
Pelasgians, who had been expelled from Argos, sailed against them, Daedalus fled,
and arrived at the island of Icarus.

15   82 · In Sicily, in the neighbourhood of the place called Enna, there is said to
be a cave, round about which they assert that there not only grows a quantity of
other kinds of flowers at every season of the year, but that especially an immense
space is covered with violets, which fill the adjoining country with fragrance, so that
the huntsmen are unable to track the hares, as their dogs are overcome by the smell.
20   Through this chasm there is an invisible subterranean passage, by which they say
Pluto carried off Proserpine. In this place it is said that wheat is found, resembling
neither the native sorts, which people use, nor other kinds that are imported, but
possessed of a great peculiarity. And this they use as an argument to prove that the
25   wheat-fruit appeared first among themselves; whence also they lay claim to
Demeter, affirming that the goddess was born among them.

83 · In Crete men say that there are no wolves, bears, and vipers, and
similarly no wild beasts like them, because Zeus was born there.

30   84 · In the sea outside the Pillars of Hercules they say that an island was
discovered by the Carthaginians, desolate, having wood of every kind, and
navigable rivers, and admirable for its fruits besides, but distant several days'
837ª1   voyage from them. But, when the Carthaginians often came to this island because
of its fertility, and some even dwelt there, the magistrates of the Carthaginians gave
notice that they would punish with death those who should sail to it, and destroyed
all the inhabitants, lest they should spread a report about it, or a large number
5   might gather together to the island in their time,[1] get possession of the authority,
and destroy the prosperity of the Carthaginians.

85 · From Italy as far as the country of the Celts, Celtoligurians, and
Iberians, they say there is a certain road, called the 'road of Heracles', by which
10   whether a Greek or a native travels, he is watched by the neighbouring tribes, so

[1]Retaining ἐπ᾽ αὐτῶν.

that he may receive no injury; for those among whom the injury has been done must pay the penalty.

86 · They say that among the Celts there is a poison called by them 'arrow-poison', which they assert produces corruption so quickly that the Celtic huntsmen, when they have shot a stag, or any other animal, run up to it in haste, and cut out the wounded part of the flesh, before the poison spreads, as well for the sake of the food as to prevent the animal from putrefying. They say, however, that the bark of the oak was found to be an antidote for this; but others maintain that the antidote is something different, a leaf, which they call ravenswort, because a raven, which had tasted the poison, and become sick, was observed by them to hasten for this leaf, and, after devouring it, to be delivered from its pain.

87 · In Iberia they say that, when the coppices were set on fire by certain shepherds, and the earth was heated by the wood, the country visibly flowed with silver; and when, after some time, earthquakes succeeded, and the ground in different places burst asunder, a large quantity of silver was collected, which brought in no ordinary revenue to the Massilians.

88 · In the islands called Gymnesiae, that lie off the coast of Iberia, which they assert to be the largest, after the so-called seven islands, they say that oil is not produced from olives, but from the turpentine-tree in very large quantities, and adapted for every purpose. Moreover they affirm that the Iberians, who inhabit those islands, are so fond of women that they give to the merchants four or five males in exchange for one female. When they receive their pay, while serving with the Carthaginians, they purchase, it seems, nothing else but women; for no man among them is allowed to have gold or silver. But as a reason for their forbidding the introduction of money, some such statement as this is added, that Heracles made his expedition against Iberia for the sake of the riches of the inhabitants.

89 · In the country of the Massilians, on the borders of Liguria, they say there is a certain lake, and that this boils up and overflows, and casts out so great a quantity of fish as to surpass belief. But whenever the Etesian winds blow the soil is heaped up upon it (such dust arises there), and its surface becomes solid like the ground, and the natives, piercing it with tridents, easily take out of it as many fish as they please.

90 · It is said that some of the Ligurians sling so skilfully that, when they see several birds, they contend with one another about which bird each is preparing to strike, presuming that all will easily hit their mark.

91 · They say that there is also this peculiarity among them: the women give birth while engaged in work, and after washing the child with water, they immediately dig and hoe, and attend to their other household duties, which they were obliged to perform before the time of their delivery.

92 · This is also a marvel among the Ligurians: they say that there is a river in their country whose stream is lifted up on high and flows along so that those on the other side cannot be seen.

93 · In Etruria there is said to be a certain island named Aethaleia, in which out of a certain mine in former days copper was dug, from which they say that all the copper vessels among them have been wrought; that afterwards it could no longer be found: but, when a long interval of time had elapsed, from the same mine iron was produced, which the Etrurians, who inhabit the town called Populonium, use to the present day.

94 · Now in Etruria there is a certain city called Oenarea, which they say is exceedingly strong; for in the midst of it there is a lofty hill, rising upwards to the height of thirty stadia, and having at its foot wood of all sorts, and waters. They say, therefore, that the inhabitants, fearing lest some one should become despot, set over themselves those of their slaves who had been manumitted, and these have dominion over them; but every year they appoint others of the same class in their stead.

95 · At Cumae in Italy there is shown, it appears, a subterranean bed-chamber of the prophetic Sibyl, who, they say, was of a very great age, and had always remained a virgin, being a native of Erythrae, but by some of the inhabitants of Italy called a native of Cumae, and by some named Melancraera. It is said that this place is under the sway of the Lucanians. They state moreover that in those parts about Cumae there is a certain river called Cetus, and they say that whatever is thrown into this is after a considerable time first coated over, and finally turns into stone.

96 · Men say that for Alcimenes, the Sybarite, a mantle was prepared of such magnificence, that it was exhibited at Lacinium during the festival of Hera, to which all the Italians assemble, and that it was admired more than all the things that were shown there. Of this they say that Dionysius the Elder obtained possession, and sold it to the Carthaginians for one hundred and twenty talents. It was of purple, fifteen cubits in width, and was adorned on either side with little figures inwoven, above with Susa, below with Persians; in the middle were Zeus, Hera, Themis, Athene, Apollo, and Aphrodite. Near each extremity was Alcimenes, and on both sides Sybaris.

97 · In the neighbourhood of the Iapygian promontory, from a certain place in which, as the legends relate, the fight of Heracles with the giants took place, they say that ichor flows in great abundance, and of such a nature that, owing to the oppressiveness of the smell, the sea off that place is not navigable. They state besides that in many parts of Italy many memorials of Heracles still exist on the roads by which he travelled. Near Pandosia in Iapygia footprints of the god are shown, on which no one must tread.

98 · There is also in the neighbourhood of the Iapygian promontory a stone   838[b]1
big enough to load a waggon, which they say was lifted up by him and transferred to
this spot, and it was actually moved with one finger.

99 · In the city of the Orchomenians in Boeotia they say that a fox was seen,
which, being pursued by a dog, entered into a certain subterranean passage, and   5
that the dog entered along with her and, barking, produced a great noise, as though
he found a wide space about him; but the huntsmen, thinking there was something
marvellous there, broke open the entrance, and forced their way in as well: and that,
seeing the light coming in by certain holes, they had a clear view of all that was in   10
the cave, and went and reported it to the magistrates.

100 · In the island of Sardinia they say there are many beautiful buildings
constructed in the ancient Greek style, and, among others, domes carved in
remarkable proportions. It is said that these were built by Iolaus, son of Iphicles,   15
when he, having taken with him the Thespiadae, the sons of Heracles, sailed to
those parts with the intention of settling there, considering that they belonged to
him through his relationship with Heracles, because Heracles was lord of all the   20
western land. This island, as it appears, was formerly called Ichnussa, because it
was shaped in its outline very similarly to a human footstep. It is stated to have been
previously fertile and productive; for the legend states that Aristaeus, whom they
assert to have been most skilful in agriculture among the ancients, ruled over these
parts, which were formerly occupied by many large birds. At the present day,   25
however, it is no longer fertile, because when ruled by the Carthaginians it had all
its fruits that were useful for food destroyed, and death was fixed as the penalty for
the inhabitants if any one should plant again anything of the kind.

101 · In one of the seven so-called islands of Aeolus, which bears the name   30
Lipara, the legend goes that there is a tomb, about which they tell many other
portentous stories, and agree in asserting that it is unsafe to approach that place at
night; for from it are distinctly heard the sound of drums and cymbals, and   839[a]1
laughter, along with uproar and the rattle of castanets. But they state that a still
more prodigious event occurred with regard to the cave; for a certain man, under
the influence of wine, fell asleep in it before daylight, and continued to be sought for
by his servants for three days; but on the fourth, being found apparently dead, he   5
was conveyed by his servants to his own tomb, and after obtaining all the usual rites,
he suddenly rose up, and related all that had befallen him. This story seems to me
somewhat fabulous, yet it was necessary for me not to leave it unmentioned, while   10
giving a record of circumstances connected with that place.

102 · Near Cumae in Italy there is a lake called Avernus, containing in
itself, as it seems, nothing wonderful; for they say that hills lie round about it not   15
less than three stadia in height; that it is itself circular in form and of unsurpassable

depth. But this is what seems marvellous: while trees stand thickly above it, and
20   some lean over it, one cannot see a single leaf floating upon the water, while the
water is so very pure that those who behold it wonder. On the mainland not far
distant from it hot water springs forth from many parts, and all the place is called
25   Pyriphlegethon. But to say that no bird flies over it is a lie; for those who have been
there maintain that there is a large number of swans in it.

103 · They say that the Siren islands are situated in Italy at the point of the
headland in the strait, which lies before the promontory separating the two bays,[2]
30   i.e. the one surrounding Cumae and the one which cuts off from it the city called
Posidonia; on this promontory also a temple of the Sirens has been built, and they
are honoured exceedingly by the neighbouring peoples with diligent sacrifices, and
they, making mention of their names, call one Parthenope, another Leucosia, and
the third Ligeia.

104 · It is stated that between the Mentoric district and that of Istria there
839b1   is a mountain named Delphium with a high crest. When the Mentores, who dwell
near the Adriatic, ascend this crest they can discern, as it appears, the ships sailing
5   into the Pontus: there is also a spot, half-way between, at which when a common
market is held, Lesbian, Chian, and Thasian wares are sold by the merchants
coming up from the Pontus, and Corcyraean jars by the merchants from the
Adriatic.

105 · Men say that the Ister, flowing from what are called the Hercynian
10   woods, divides, and in one direction flows into the Pontus, and in the other
discharges its waters into the Adriatic. And we have seen a proof not only in the
present times, but also more fully in antiquity, that the waters there are not[3]
innavigable; for they say that Jason sailed into the Pontus by the 'Dark Rocks',
15   while he sailed out of it by the Ister; and for this, besides alleging not a few other
evidences, they point out altars set up by Jason in the country, and in one of the
islands in the Adriatic a costly temple of Artemis erected by Medea. Moreover they
20   affirm that Jason could not have sailed past the 'Wandering Islands', if he were not
sailing away from that quarter. And moreover in the island of Aethaleia, which lies
in the Tyrrhenian Sea, they point to other memorials of the chiefs of the Argonautic
Expedition, and also to what is said respecting the pebbles; for they say that along
the shore there are pebbles of various colours; and the Greeks who inhabit the island
25   say that they received their colour from the oil and dirt which the heroes scraped
off, while anointing themselves; for, according to the legend, neither before these
times were such pebbles seen nor afterwards had any such been found. Moreover
they mention still clearer proofs of this, that they did not sail out through the
30   Symplegades, citing the poet himself as a witness in the case of those regions; for

---

[2]Reading τοὺς κόλπους.
[3]Reading μὴ εἶναι.

(say they) he, pointing out the gravity of the danger, states that it is impossible to
sail past the place—

Planks of ships and bodies of men together are carried
By the waves of the sea and storms of fire destructive.[4]

As regards the 'Dark Rocks' indeed it is not said that they send forth fire; but it   840ᵃ1
happens near the strait which divides Sicily from Italy, as the eruptions of fire are
found on both sides; while not only is the island continually burning, but also the
stream of lava round Etna often spreads over the country.   5

106 · In Tarentum they say that at certain times people offer sacrifices to
the shades of the Atridae, Tydidae, Aeacidae, and Laertiadae, and besides that they
celebrate a sacrifice separately to the Agamemnonidae on another special day, on
which it is unlawful for the women to taste the victims offered to those heroes.   10
There is also amongst them a temple of Achilles. Now it is said that after the
Tarentines had taken it, the place which they at present inhabit was called
Heraclea; but in the early times, when the Ionians were in possession, it was named
Pleum and at a still earlier date it was called Sigeum by the Trojans, who had   15
gained possession of it.

107 · Among the Sybarites Philoctetes is said to be honoured; for on his
return from Troy he founded in the Crotonian territory the town called Macalla,
which they say is one hundred and twenty stadia distant; and they relate that he
dedicated the bow and arrows of Heracles in the temple of Apollo the sea-god: but   20
from there they say that the Crotonians, during their dominion, took them, and
dedicated them in the temple of Apollo in their own city. Now it is said that having
died there he lies by the river Sybaris, after he had given help to the Rhodians, who
along with Tlepolemus had been carried out of their course to those parts, and had   25
engaged in battle with the barbarians who inhabited that country.

108 · In that part of Italy which is called Gargaria, close to Metapontum,
they say there is a temple of Athene Heilenia, where they state that the tools of
Epeus were dedicated, which he had prepared for the construction of the wooden
horse; he gave the goddess this name—for Athene appeared to him in a dream and   30
desired him to dedicate the tools; and he being therefore delayed in putting out to
sea was cooped up in the place, unable to sail out: hence the temple was called that
of Athene Heilenia.

109 · In the district which bears the name of Daunia, there is said to be a   840ᵇ1
temple called that of the Achaean Athene, in which bronze axes and the arms of
Diomedes and his companions are dedicated. In this place they state that there are
dogs which do no harm to such of the Greeks as come there, but fawn upon them, as   5
though they were most familiar to them. Now all the Daunians and the neighbouring tribes, both men and women, wear black garments, apparently for the

---

[4]*Odyssey* XII 67.

following reason—because it is said that the Trojan women, who had been taken
10 captives, and had come to those parts, fearing that they might experience hard
slavery at the hands of the women who already belonged to the Achaeans in their
native land, set fire to their ships, in order that they might escape from the expected
slavery, and at the same time, that they, being united in wedlock with those men,
15 now compelled to stay, might have them for their husbands. The poet has also very
admirably described them; for one may see those women likewise, it seems,
'robe-trailing' and 'deep-bosomed'.

110 · In the country of the Peucetians they say there is a temple of Artemis,
20 in which, they state, is dedicated the bronze necklace celebrated in those parts, with
the inscription—'Diomede to Artemis'. Now the legend relates that he put it round
the neck of a stag, and that it adhered there; and in this way having been afterwards
found by Agathocles, king of the Sicilians, it was, they affirm, dedicated in the
temple of Zeus.

25 111 · On the promontory of Sicily, called the promontory of Pelorus, it is
stated that so much saffron grows that, while by some of the Greeks dwelling in
those parts it is not known what sort of flower it is, on the promontory of Pelorus all
30 who wish bring home large waggon loads of it, and in the spring-time strew their
beds and stages with saffron.

112 · Polycritus, who has written the history of Sicily in verse, states that in
a certain part of the interior there is a little lake, with a circumference about that of
a shield, and this contains water transparent indeed, but somewhat turbid. Now if
841ª1 any one enters this, intending to wash himself, it increases in breadth; and if a
second person enters, it grows wider still; and finally, having grown larger, it
becomes wide enough for the reception of even fifty men. But whenever it has
5 received this number, swelling up again from the bottom it casts the bodies of the
bathers high in the air and out on the ground; and as soon as this has occurred, it
returns once more to the original form of its circumference. And not only in the case
of men does this occur with regard to it, but also, if a quadruped enters, it
experiences the same result.

10 113 · In the dominion of the Carthaginians they say there is a mountain
which is called Uranion, full of all kinds of wood and variegated with many flowers,
so that the contiguous places over a wide extent partaking of its fragrance waft to
15 the travellers a most agreeable odour. Near this spot they say that there is a spring
of oil, and that it has a smell like that of cedar sawdust. But they say that the person
who approaches it must be chaste, and, if this is the case, it spouts up the oil in
greater abundance, so that it can be safely drawn.

20 114 · Men say that near this spring also there is a natural rock of great size.
Now they say that when summer is come it sends up a flame of fire, but when winter

arrives, from the same place it sends gushing up a stream of water so cold that, when compared with snow, it does not differ from it. And this, they declare, is not a secret occurrence, nor does it appear for only a short time; but it sends forth the fire   25 throughout the whole summer, and the water throughout the whole winter.

115 · It is reported that in that part of Thrace which is called the country of the Sinti and Maedi, there is a certain river named Pontus, in which are carried down certain stones which burn, and are of a nature opposed to that of charcoal   30 from wood; for while fanned they are quickly extinguished, but when sprinkled with water they blaze up and kindle better. Now, when they are burning, they have a smell similar to that of bitumen, so bad and pungent that no creeping thing remains   841ᵇ1 in the place while they are burning.

116 · They say, moreover, that in their country there is a certain place, not very small, about twenty stadia in extent, that bears barley, which the men indeed use; but the horses and oxen, or any other animal, will not eat it: indeed, not even   5 does any pig or dog venture to taste the excrement of men who after eating a cake or bread made from this barley have voided it, as death results from it.

117 · At Scotussae in Thessaly they say there is a little fountain from which flows water of such a kind that in a moment it heals wounds and bruises both of men   10 and of beasts of burden; and if any one throws wood into it, without having quite broken it, but having merely split it, this unites, and is restored again to its original state.

118 · In Thrace above Amphipolis they say that a thing happens, which is   15 wonderful and incredible to those who have not seen it; for the boys, going forth from the villages and neighbouring districts to catch little birds, take the hawks to help in catching them, and they do so in this manner:—When they have advanced to a suitable spot they call the hawks by name with a loud cry; and, when they hear the   20 boys' voice, they come and frighten away the birds; these in terror of them take refuge in the bushes, where the boys strike them down with sticks and capture them. But what one would be most of all surprised at is this—whenever the hawks   25 themselves have seized any of the birds, they throw them down to the bird-catchers, while the boys return home, after giving some portion of all their booty to the hawks.

119 · Another marvel also they say occurs among the Heneti: that countless myriads of jackdaws are frequently borne to their country, and eat up the corn when   30 the people have sown it. To them the Heneti offer gifts, before the birds are about to fly to the borders of the land, throwing before them seeds of all kinds of fruits. Now   842ᵃ1 if the jackdaws taste these they do not come over into their country, and the Heneti know that they will be in peace; but, if they do not taste them, the people thereupon expect an attack to be made upon them by their enemies.

120 · In the Thracian Chalcidice, near Olynthus, they say there is a place called Cantharolethros, a little larger in size than a threshing-floor; and that when any other living creature reaches the spot it departs again; but none of the beetles that come there do so; but they going round and round the place die from hunger.

121 · Among the Thracian Cyclopes there is a little spring containing water, which in appearance indeed is pure, transparent, and like all others; but when an animal drinks of it, straightway it perishes.

122 · Men say that in Crastonia, near the country of the Bisaltae, the hares that are captured have two livers; and that there is a certain place, about a rood in extent, into which whatever animal enters dies. There is in the same place, besides, a temple of Dionysus, large and beautiful, in which, when the festival and sacrifice take place, it is said that a great blaze of fire is seen when the god is going to produce a good season, and that all those who are assembled round the sacred enclosure see it; when, however, he intends to cause unfruitfulness, this light is not seen, but darkness extends over the place, as during the other nights.

123 · In Elis they relate that there is a certain building about eight furlongs distant from the city, in which, at the festival of Dionysus, they place three empty copper cauldrons. Having done this, they request any of the Greeks staying in the city, who wishes, to examine the vessels, and to seal the doors of the house: then, when they are about to open them, they point out the seals to the citizens and strangers first of all, before they do so. They on entering find the cauldrons full of wine, but the floor and the walls uninjured, so that it is impossible to entertain a suspicion that they accomplish this by some trick. Moreover, they say that among the same people there are kites, which snatch the meat from those who carry it through the marketplace, but do not touch the flesh of the sacred victims.

124 · It is said that at Coronea in Boeotia moles cannot live, or dig up the ground, while the rest of Boeotia possesses a large number of them.

125 · At Lusi in Arcadia men say there is a certain spring in which field-mice are found and dive, passing their lives in it. The same thing is said to occur likewise at Lampsacus.

126 · At Crannon in Thessaly they say there are only two crows in the city. When these have hatched their young, they depart from the place, as it appears, but leave behind as many others of their offspring.

127 · In Apollonia, which lies near to the country of the Taulantii, they say there is bitumen obtained by digging, and pitch springing up from the earth, in the same manner as springs of water, in no respect differing from that of Macedonia, except that it is naturally blacker and thicker than that. And not far from this place there is a fire burning at all times, as those who dwell in the neighbourhood assert.

The burning place, it appears, is not large, but about the size of the space occupied by five couches. This spot smells of sulphur and alum, and thick grass grows around, at which one would be most surprised, and also large trees, not four cubits distant 25 from the fire. Moreover, a fire burns constantly in Lycia and near Megalopolis in the Peloponnese.

128 · It is said also that among the Illyrians the cattle bring forth young twice in the year, and that most of them have twins, and that many goats bring forth three or four kids at a time, and some even five or more; and, besides, that they readily yield nine pints of milk. They say too that the hens do not lay merely once, as 30 among other nations, but twice or thrice in the day.

129 · It is said that the wild oxen in Paeonia are far larger than those that are found in other nations, and that their horns contain twenty-four pints, and those of some of them even more.

130 · Concerning the Sicilian Strait, apart from what many other writers 843ᵃ1 have written, this author states that a portentous occurrence takes place: the billows, he says, being carried with a loud whistling sound from the Tyrrhenian Sea, dash against both the promontories, that of Sicily and that of Italy, which is called 5 Rhegium, and being borne from a great sea are shut up in a narrow space; and when this occurs they raise the waves with a loud roar in mid-air to a very great height, as they dash upwards, so that the rising of the waters is visible to those who are far 10 away, not resembling the rising of the sea, but white and foaming, and similar to the sweeping movements which take place in excessively violent storms: and that sometimes the waves meet each other on both the promontories and produce a collision incredible in description, and unendurable for the eyes to behold; but at 15 other times parting, after dashing against each other, they show an abyss, so deep and horrible to those who are compelled to look on, that many are unable to restrain themselves, and fall, blinded with terror. But when the waves, after dashing on 20 either of the two places and being carried to the tops of the promontories, have descended again into the sea flowing beneath, then again with loud bellowing and great and swift eddies the sea boils up, and is lifted on high from the depths in confusion, and assumes alternately all kinds of hues, for it appears at one time dark, 25 at another blue, and often of a purplish colour: but no creeping thing can endure either to hear or to see the quick rush and length of this sea, and besides these its ebb, but all flee to the low-lying skirts of the mountains; but, when the heaving of the billows ceases, the eddies are borne on high, making such various twistings that 30 they seem to produce movements resembling the coils of presteres, or some other large snakes.

131 · Men say that, while the Athenians were building the temple of 843ᵇ1 Demeter at Eleusis, a brazen pillar was found surrounded with rocks, on which had been inscribed—'This is the tomb of Deïope', whom some state to have been the wife of Musaeus, others the mother of Triptolemus. 5

132 · In one of the islands, called the islands of Aeolus, they say that a large number of palm-trees grow, whence it is also called 'Palm-island'; therefore that could not be true which is asserted by Callisthenes, that the tree received its name from the Phoenicians, who inhabited the sea-coast of Syria. But some state that the Phoenicians themselves received this name from the Greeks, because they, first of all sailing over the sea, slew and murdered all, wherever they landed. And moreover in the dialect of the Perrhaebians the verb 'phoenixai' means 'to stain with blood'.

133 · In what is called the Aeniac district, in the neighbourhood of the city named Hypate, an old pillar is said to have been discovered; and the Aenianians, wishing to know to whom it belonged, as it had an inscription in ancient characters, sent certain persons to take it to Athens. But as they were proceeding through Boeotia, and were communicating to some of their guest friends the object of their journey, it is said that they were conducted into the so-called Ismenium at Thebes; for there the meaning of the inscription could be most easily discovered, they said, adding that there were in that place some ancient dedicatory offerings having the forms of the letters similar to those of the one in question: whence they say that, having found an explanation of the objects of their inquiry, from what was already known to them, they copied down the following lines:—

I Heracles offered the grove to the beaming goddess Cythera,
When I had Geryon's herds, and Erytheia for spoil;
For with desire for her the goddess had vanquished my heart.
But here my wife Erythe brings forth Erython as her offspring,
Nymph-born maid Erythe, to whom I yielded the plain,
Sacred memorial of love under the shade of the beech.

With this inscription both that place corresponded, being called Erythus, and also the fact that it was from there, and not from Erytheia, that he drove away the cows; for they say that nowhere either in the parts of Libya or Iberia is the name of Erytheia to be found.

134 · In the city called Utica in Libya, which is situated, as they say, on the gulf between the promontory of Hermes and that of Hippos, and about two hundred furlongs beyond Carthage (now Utica also is said to have been founded by Phoenicians two hundred and eighty-seven years before Carthage itself, as is recorded in the Phoenician histories), men state that salt is obtained by digging at a depth of eighteen feet, in appearance white and not solid, but resembling the most sticky gum; and that when brought into the sun it hardens, and becomes like Parian marble; and they say that from it are carved figures of animals, and utensils besides.

135 · It is said that those of the Phoenicians who first sailed to Tartessus, after importing to that place oil, and other small wares of maritime commerce,

obtained for their return cargo so great a quantity of silver, that they were no longer able to keep or receive it, but were forced, when sailing away from those parts, to   20 make of silver not only all the other articles which they used, but also all their anchors.

136 · They say that the Phoenicians who inhabit the city called Gades, when they sail outside the Pillars of Heracles under an easterly wind for four days,   25 arrive at certain desolate places, full of rushes and seaweed, and that these places are not covered with water, whenever there is an ebb, but, whenever there is a flood, they are overflowed, and in these there is found an exceeding great number of tunnies, of a size and thickness surpassing belief, when they are stranded. These   30 they salt, pack up in vessels, and convey to Carthage. They are the only fish which the Carthaginians do not export; on account of their excellence for food, they consume them themselves.

137 · In the district of Pedasa in Caria a sacrifice is celebrated in honour of Zeus, at which they send in the procession a she-goat, with regard to which they say   844^{b}1 that a marvellous thing occurs; for while it proceeds from Pedasa a distance of seventy furlongs, through a dense crowd of people looking on, it is neither disturbed in its progress, nor is turned out of the way, but, being tied with a rope, advances   5 before the man who holds the priesthood.

What is wonderful is that two crows stay continually about the temple of Zeus, while no other approaches the spot, and that one of them has the front part of its neck white.

138 · In the country of those Illyrians who are called Ardiaei, near the   10 boundaries separating them from the Antariates, they say there is a great mountain, and near this is a valley, from which water springs up, not at every season, but during the spring, in great abundance, which the people take, and keep during the day in a cellar, but during the night they set it in the open air. And, after they have done this for five or six days, the water congeals, and becomes the most   15 excellent salt, which they preserve especially for the sake of the cattle: for salt is not imported to them, because they live at a distance from the sea, and have no intercourse with others. They have therefore most need of it for their cattle; for they   20 supply them with salt twice in the year; but if they fail to do this, the result is that most of their cattle perish.

139 · In Argos they say there is a species of locust which is called the scorpion-fighter; for, as soon as it sees a scorpion, it attacks him, and likewise the   25 scorpion attacks it. It chirps as it goes round him in a circle. The other, they say, raises his sting, and turns it round against his adversary in the same spot; then he gradually lets his sting drop, and at last stretches himself out altogether on the ground, while the locust runs round him. At last the locust approaches and devours him. They say that it is good to eat the locust as an antidote against the scorpion's   30 sting.

140 · They say that the wasps in Naxos, when they have tasted the flesh of the viper (and its flesh, as it appears, is agreeable to them), and when they have afterwards stung any one, inflict so much pain, that their sting seems more dangerous than that of the vipers.

141 · They say that the Scythian poison, in which that people dips its arrows, is procured from the viper. The Scythians, it would appear, watch those that are just bringing forth young, and take them, and allow them to putrefy for some days. But when the whole mass appears to them to have become sufficiently rotten, they pour human blood into a little pot, and, after covering it with a lid, bury it in a dung-hill. And when this likewise has putrefied, they mix the sediment, which is of a watery nature, with the corrupted blood of the viper, and thus make it a deadly poison.

142 · At Curium in Cyprus they say there is a species of snake, which has similar power to that of the asp in Egypt, except that, if it bites in the winter, it produces no effect, whether from some other reason, or because when congealed with cold the reptile loses its power of movement, and becomes completely powerless, unless it be warmed.

143 · In Ceos they say there is a species of wild pear of such a kind that, if any one be wounded by its thorn, he dies.

144 · In Mysia they say there is a white species of bears, which, when they are hunted, emit a breath of such a kind as to rot the flesh of the dogs, and likewise of other wild beasts, and render them unfit for food. But, if any one approaches them with violence, they discharge, it appears, from the mouth a very great quantity of phlegm, which the animal blows upon the faces of the dogs, and of the men as well, so as to choke and blind them.

145 · In Arabia they say there is a certain kind of hyaena, which, when it sees some wild beast, before being itself seen, or steps on the shadow of a man, produces speechlessness, and fixes them to the spot in such a way that they cannot move their body; and it is said that they do this in the case of dogs also.

146 · In Syria they say there is an animal, which is called the lion-killer; for the lion, it seems, dies, whenever he eats any of it. He does not indeed do this willingly, but rather flees from the animal; but when the hunters, having caught and roasted it, sprinkle it, like white meal, over some other animal, they say that the lion, after tasting it, dies on the spot. This animal injures the lion even by making water upon it.

147 · It is said also that vultures die from the smell of unguents, if any one anoints them, or gives them something smeared with an unguent to eat: likewise they say that beetles also die from the smell of roses.

148 · They say that both in Sicily and Italy the star-lizards have a deadly 5
bite, and not like those among ourselves a weak and soft bite: moreover that there is
a sort of mouse, which flies at people, and, when it bites, causes them to die.

149 · In Mesopotamia, a region of Syria, and at Istrus, they say that there
are certain little snakes, which do not bite the people of the country, but do great 10
injury to strangers.

150 · At the Euphrates they say that this especially happens; for that many
are seen about the edges of the river, swimming also towards either bank; so that
while seen in the evening on this side, at daybreak they appear on the other side; and
that they refrain from biting such of the Syrians as are taking their repose, but do
not spare the Greeks. 15

151 · In Thessaly they say that the snake which is called sacred destroys all
persons, not merely if it bites, but even if it touches them; and so when it appears
(but it appears rarely), and they hear its voice, both serpents and vipers, and all the 20
other wild beasts flee. It is not large, but of a moderate size. In the city of Tenos in
Thessaly they say it was once destroyed by a woman, and that its death happened in
the following manner:—The woman, having described a circle and put the charms
in it, entered into the circle, herself and her son, and then imitated the hissing of the 25
beast; it answered the sound of her voice and approached; but, while it was hissing,
the woman fell asleep, and the more profoundly, the closer it approached, so that
she could not overcome the power of sleep: but her son, sitting beside her, aroused
her by striking her, as she had bidden him to do, saying that, if she fell asleep, both 30
she and he would perish, whereas if she used force, and drew the animal towards
her, they would be saved. But the snake, when it came up to the circle, immediately
withered away.

152 · It is said that near Tyana there is water sacred to Zeus Horcios—they
call it Asbamaeon—whose spring rises very cold, but boils up like caldrons. This 846ª1
water is sweet and propitious to those who observe their oaths; but punishment
follows on the heels of the perjured; for it falls upon their eyes, hands, and feet, and
they are seized with dropsies and consumptions; and it is not even possible to get
away beforehand, but they are held on the spot, and lament beside the water, 5
confessing the perjuries they have committed.

153 · At Athens they say that the sacred branch of the olive tree in one day
buds and increases, but quickly shrinks together again.

154 · When the craters in Etna once burst forth, and the lava was carried
hither and thither over the land like a torrent, the deity honoured the race of the 10
pious; for when they were hemmed in on all sides by the stream, because they were
bearing their aged parents on their shoulders, and were trying to save them, the
stream of fire, having come near to them, was cleft asunder, and turned aside one

15   part of the flame in this direction, another in that, and preserved the young men unharmed, along with their parents.

155 · It is said that the sculptor Phidias, while constructing the Athene in the Acropolis, carved his own face in the centre of her shield, and connected it by an

20   imperceptible artifice with the statue, so that, if any one wished to remove it, he must necessarily break up and destroy the whole statue.

156 · They say that the statue of Bitys in Argos killed the man who had caused the death of Bitys, by falling upon him while he was looking at it. It appears therefore that such events do not happen at random.

25   157 · Men say that dogs pursue wild beasts only to the summits of the so-called Black Mountains, but turn back when they have pursued them as far as these.

30   158 · In the river Phasis it is related that a rod called the 'White-leaved' grows, which jealous husbands pluck, and throw round the bridal-bed, and thus preserve their marriage from adultery.

159 · In the Tigris they say there is a stone found, called in the barbarian language Modon, with a very white colour, and that, if any one possesses this, he is not harmed by wild beasts.

160 · In the Scamander they say a plant grows, called the Rattle, resem-

35   bling a chick-pea, and that it has seeds that shake, from which fact it has obtained its name: those who possess it (so it is said) fear neither demon nor apparition of any kind.

161 · In Libya there is a vine, which some people call mad, that ripens some

846ᵇ1   of its fruit, others it has like unripe grapes, and others in blossom, and this during a short time.

162 · On Mount Sipylus they say there is a stone like a cylinder, which, when pious sons have found it, they place in the sacred precincts of the Mother of

5   the Gods, and never err through impiety, but are always affectionate to their parents.

163 · On Mount Taÿgetus (it is said) there is a plant called the love-plant, which women in the beginning of spring fasten round their necks, and are loved more passionately by their husbands.

10   164 · Othrys is a mountain of Thessaly, which produces serpents that are called Rotters, which have not a single colour, but always resemble the place in which they live. Some of them have a colour like that of land snails, while the scales

of others are of a bright green; but all of them that dwell in the sands become like these in colour. When they bite they produce thirst. Now their bite is not rough and 15 fiery, but malicious.

165 · When the dark-coloured adder copulates with the female, the female during the copulation bites off the head of the male; therefore also her young ones, as though avenging their father's death, burst through their mother's belly. 20

166 · In the river Nile they say that a stone like a bean is produced, and that, if dogs see it, they do not bark. It is beneficial also to those who are possessed by some demon; for, as soon as it is applied to the nostrils, the demon departs. 25

167 · In the Maeander, a river of Asia, they say that a stone is found, called by contradiction 'sound-minded'; for if one throws it into any one's bosom he becomes mad, and kills some one of his relations.

168 · The rivers Rhine and Danube flow towards the north, one passing the Germans, the other the Paeonians. In the summer they have a navigable stream, but 30 in the winter they are congealed from the cold, and form a plain over which men ride.

169 · Near the city of Thurium they say there are two rivers, the Sybaris and the Crathis. Now the Sybaris causes those that drink of it to be timorous, while the Crathis makes men yellow-haired when they bathe in it. 35

170 · In Euboea there are said to be two rivers; the sheep that drink from one of them become white—it is called Cerbes; the other is the Neleus, which makes them black.

171 · Near the river Lycormas it is said that a plant grows, which is like a 847ᵃ1 lance, and is most beneficial in the case of dim sight.

172 · They say that the fountain of Arethusa at Syracuse in Sicily is set in motion every five years.

173 · On Mount Berecynthius it is said that a stone is produced called 'the 5 Sword', and if any one finds it, while the mysteries of Hecate are being celebrated, he becomes mad, as Eudoxus affirms.

174 · On Mount Tmolus it is said that a stone is produced like pumice-stone, which changes its colour four times in the day; and that it is only seen by maidens who have not yet attained to years of discretion.

175 · On the altar of the Orthosian Artemis it is said that a golden bull 847ᵇ1 stands, which bellows when hunters enter the temple.

176 · Among the Aetolians it is said that moles see, but only dimly, and do not feed on the earth, but on locusts.

177 · They say that elephants are pregnant during the space of two years, while others say during eighteen months; and that in giving birth they suffer hard labour.

178 · They say that Demaratus, the pupil of the Locrian Timaeus, having fallen sick, was dumb for ten days; but on the eleventh, having slowly come to his senses after his delirium, he declared that during that time he had lived most agreeably.

MECHANICS**

Our wonder is excited, firstly, by phenomena which occur in accordance with 847ᵃ10
nature but of which we do not know the cause, and secondly by those which are
produced by art despite nature for the benefit of mankind. Nature often operates
contrary to human interest; for she always follows the same course without 15
deviation, whereas human interest is always changing. When, therefore, we have to
do something contrary to nature, the difficulty of it causes us perplexity and art has
to be called to our aid. The kind of art which helps us in such perplexities we call
Mechanical Skill. The words of the poet Antiphon are quite true: 20

> Mastered by Nature, we o'ercome by Art.

Instances of this are those cases in which the less prevails over the greater, and
where forces of small motive power move great weights—in fact, practically all
those problems which we call Mechanical Problems. They are not quite identical 25
nor yet entirely unconnected with Natural Problems. They have something in
common both with Mathematical and with Natural Speculations; for while
Mathematics demonstrates *how* phenomena come to pass, Natural Science demonstrates *in what medium* they occur.

Among questions of a mechanical kind are included those which are connected 847ᵇ10
with the lever. It seems strange that a great weight can be moved with but little
force, and that when the addition of more weight is involved; for the very same
weight, which one cannot move at all without a lever, one can move quite easily with
it, in spite of the additional weight of the lever. 15

The original cause of all such phenomena is the circle. It is quite natural that
this should be so; for there is nothing strange in a lesser marvel being caused by a
greater marvel, and it is a very great marvel that contraries should be present
together, and the circle is made up of contraries. For to begin with, it is formed by 20
motion and rest, things which are by nature opposed to one another. Hence in
examining the circle we need not be much astonished at the contradictions which
occur in connexion with it. Firstly, in the line which encloses the circle, being
without breadth, two contraries somehow appear, namely, the concave and the 25
convex. These are as much opposed to one another as the great is to the small; the
mean being in the latter case the equal, in the former the straight. Therefore just as,

TEXT: O. Apelt, Teubner, Leipzig, 1888

848ᵃ1 if they are to change into one another, the greater and smaller must become equal before they can pass into the other extreme; so a line must become straight in passing from convex into concave, or on the other hand from concave into convex and curved. This, then, is one peculiarity of the circle.

Another peculiarity of the circle is that it moves in two contrary directions at the same time; for it moves simultaneously to a forward and a backward position. Such, too, is the nature of the radius which describes a circle. For its extremity comes back again to the same position from which it starts; for, when it moves continuously, its last position is a return to its original position, in such a way that it has clearly undergone a change from that position.

Therefore, as has already been remarked, there is nothing strange in the circle being the origin of any and every marvel. The phenomena observed in the balance can be referred to the circle, and those observed in the lever to the balance; while practically all the other phenomena of mechanical motion are connected with the lever. Furthermore, since no two points on one and the same radius travel with the same rapidity, but of two points that which is further from the fixed centre travels more quickly, many marvellous phenomena occur in the motions of circles, which will be demonstrated in the following problems.

Because a circle moves in two contrary forms of motion at the same time, and because one extremity of the diameter, A, moves forwards and the other, B, moves backwards, some people contrive so that as the result of a single movement a number of circles move simultaneously in contrary directions, like the wheels of brass and iron which they make and dedicate in the temples. Let AB be a circle and CD another circle in contact with it; then if the diameter of the circle AB moves forward, the diameter CD will move in a backward direction as compared with the circle AB, as long as the diameter moves round the same point. The circle CD therefore will move in the opposite direction to the circle AB. Again, the circle CD will itself make the adjoining circle EF move in an opposite direction to itself for the same reason. The same thing will happen in the case of a larger number of circles, only one of them being set in motion. Mechanicians seizing on this inherent peculiarity of the circle, and hiding the principle, construct an instrument so as to exhibit the marvellous character of the device, while they obscure the cause of it.

848ᵇ1   1 · First, then, a question arises as to what takes place in the case of the balance. Why are larger balances more accurate than smaller? And the fundamental principle of this is, why is it that the radius which extends further from the centre is displaced quicker than the smaller radius, when the near radius is moved by the same force? Now we use the word 'quicker' in two senses; if an object traverses an equal distance in less time, we call it quicker, and also if it traverses a greater distance in equal time. Now the greater radius describes a greater circle in equal time; for the outer circumference is greater than the inner.

The reason of this is that the radius undergoes two displacements. Now if the two displacements of a body are in any fixed proportion, the resulting displacement must necessarily be a straight line, and this line is the diagonal of the figure, made by the lines drawn in this proportion.

Let the proportion of the two displacements be as AB to AC, and let A[1] be brought to B, and the line AB brought down to GC. Again, let A be brought to D 15 and the line AB to E; then if the proportion of the two displacements be maintained, AD must necessarily have the same proportion to AE as AB to AC. Therefore the small parallelogram is similar to the greater, and their diagonal is the same, so that 20 A will be at F. In the same way it can be shown, at whatever points the displacement be arrested, that the point A will in all cases be on the diagonal.

Thus it is plain that, if a point be moved along the diagonal by two displacements, it is necessarily moved according to the proportion of the sides of the parallelogram; for otherwise it will not be moved along the diagonal. If it be moved 25 in two displacements in no fixed ratio for any time, its displacement cannot be in a straight line. For let it be a straight line. This then being drawn as a diagonal, and the sides of the parallelogram filled in, the point must necessarily be moved according to the proportion of the sides; for this has already been proved. Therefore, 30 if the same proportion be not maintained during any interval of time, the point will not describe a straight line; for, if the proportion were maintained during any interval, the point must necessarily describe a straight line, by the reasoning above. So that, if the two displacements do not maintain any proportion during any interval, a curve is produced.

Now that the radius of a circle has two simultaneous displacements is plain from these considerations, and because the point from being vertically above the 849ª1 centre comes back to the perpendicular,[2] so as to be again perpendicularly above the centre.

Let ABC be a circle, and let the point B at the summit be displaced to D, and come eventually to C. If then it were moved in the proportion of BD to DC, it would 5 move along the diagonal BC. But in the present case, as it is moved in no such proportion, it moves along the curve BEC. And, if one of two displacements caused by the same forces is more interfered with and the other less, it is reasonable to suppose that the motion more interfered with will be slower than the motion less interfered with; which seems to happen in the case of the greater and less of the radii 10 of circles. For on account of the extremity of the lesser radius being nearer the stationary centre than that of the greater, being as it were pulled in a contrary direction, towards the middle,[3] the extremity of the lesser moves more slowly. This is the case with every radius, and it moves in a curve, naturally along the tangent, 15 and unnaturally towards the centre. And the lesser radius is always moved more in respect of its unnatural motion; for being nearer to the retarding centre it is more constrained. And that the less of two radii having the same centre is moved more 20 than the greater in respect of the unnatural motion is plain from what follows.

Let BCED be a circle, and XNMO another smaller circle within it, both having the same centre A, and let the diameters be drawn, CD and BE in the large 25 circle, and MX and NO in the small; and let the rectangle DYRC be completed. If the radius AB comes back to the same position from which it started, i.e. to AB, it is

[1]Reading τὸ μὲν A.
[2]Omitting κατ' εὐθεῖαν.
[3]Placing a comma after, not before, ἐπὶ τὸ μέσον.

plain that it moved towards itself; and likewise AX will come to AX. But AX moves
more slowly than AB, as has been stated, because the interference is greater and
AX is more retarded.

Now let AHG be drawn, and from H a perpendicular upon AB within the
circle, HF; and, further, from H let HZ be drawn parallel to AB, and ZU and GK
perpendiculars on AB; then ZU and HF are equal. Therefore BU is less than XF;
for in unequal circles equal straight lines drawn perpendicular to the diameter cut
off smaller portions of the diameter in the greater circles; ZU and HF being equal.

Now the radius AH describes the arc XH in the same time as the extremity of
the radius BA has described an arc greater than BZ in the greater circle; for the
natural displacement is equal and the unnatural less, BU being less than XF.
Whereas they ought to be in proportion, the two natural motions in the same ratio to
each other as the two unnatural motions.

Now the radius AB has described an arc GB greater than ZB. It must
necessarily have described GB in this time; for that will be its position when in the
two circles the proportion between the unnatural and natural movements holds
good. If, then, the natural movement is greater in the greater circle, the unnatural
movement, too, would agree in being proportionally greater in that case only, where
B is moved along GB while X is moved along XH. For in that case the point B comes
by its natural movement to G, and by its unnatural movement to K, GK being
perpendicular from G. And as GK to BK, so is HF to XF. Which will be plain, if B
and X be joined to G and H. But, if the arc described by B be less or greater than
GB, the result will not be the same, nor will the natural movement be proportional
to the unnatural in the two circles.

So that the reason why the point further from the centre is moved quicker by
the same force, and the greater radius describes the greater circle, is plain from
what has been said; and hence the reason is also clear why larger balances are more
accurate than smaller. For the cord by which a balance is suspended acts as the
centre, for it is at rest, and the parts of the balance on either side form the radii.
Therefore by the same weight the end of the balance must necessarily be moved
quicker in proportion as it is more distant from the cord, and some weight must be
imperceptible to the senses in small balances, but perceptible in large balances; for
there is nothing to prevent the movement being so small as to be invisible to the eye.
Whereas in the large balance the same load makes the movement visible. In some
cases the effect is clearly seen in both balances, but much more in the larger on
account of the amplitude of the displacement caused by the same load being much
greater in the larger balance. And thus dealers in purple, in weighing it, use
contrivances with intent to deceive, putting the cord out of centre and pouring lead
into one arm of the balance, or using the wood towards the root of a tree for the end
towards which they want it to incline, or a knot, if there be one in the wood; for the
part of the wood where the root is is heavier, and a knot is a kind of root.

2 · How is it that if the cord is attached to the upper surface of the beam of a
balance, if one takes away the weight when the balance is depressed on one side, the
beam rises again; whereas, if the cord is attached to the lower surface of the beam, it

does not rise but remains in the same position? Is it because, when the cord is 5
attached above, there is more of the beam on one side of the perpendicular than on
the other, the cord being the perpendicular? In that case the side on which the
greater part of the beam is must necessarily sink until the line which divides the
beam into two equal parts reaches the actual perpendicular, since the weight now 10
presses on the side of the beam which is elevated.

Let BC be a straight beam, and AD a cord. If AD be produced it will form the
perpendicular ADM. If the portion of the beam towards B be depressed, B will be
displaced to E and C to F; and so the line dividing the beam into two halves, which
was originally DM, part of the perpendicular, will become DH when the beam is 15
depressed; so that the part of the beam EF which is outside the perpendicular AM
will be greater by HP than half the beam. If therefore the weight at E be taken
away, F must sink, because the side towards E is shorter. It has been proved then
that when the cord is attached above, if the weight be removed the beam rises 20
again.

But if the support be from below, the contrary takes place. For then the part
which is depressed is more than half of the beam, or in other words, more than the
part marked off by the original perpendicular; it does not therefore rise, when the
weight is removed, for the part that is elevated is lighter. Let NO be the beam when
horizontal, and KLM the perpendicular dividing NO into two halves. When the 25
weight is placed at N, N will be displaced to S and O to R, and KL to LH, so that
KS is greater than LR by HLK. If the weight, therefore, is removed the beam must
necessarily remain in the same position; for the excess of the part in which SK is
over half the beam acts as a weight and remains depressed.

3 · Why is it that, as has been remarked at the beginning of this treatise, the 30
exercise of little force raises great weights with the help of a lever, in spite of the
added weight of the lever; whereas the less heavy a weight is, the easier it is to move,
and the weight is less without the lever? Does the reason lie in the fact that the lever
acts like the beam of a balance with the cord attached below and divided into two 35
unequal parts? The fulcrum, then, takes the place of the cord, for both remain at
rest and act as the centre. Now since a longer radius moves more quickly than a
shorter one under pressure of an equal weight; and since the lever requires three
elements, viz. the fulcrum—corresponding to the cord of a balance and forming the
centre—and two weights, that exerted by the person using the lever and the weight
which is to be moved; this being so, as the weight moved is to the weight moving it, 850^{b}1
so, inversely, is the length of the arm bearing the weight to the length of the arm
nearer to the power. The further one is from the fulcrum, the more easily will one
raise the weight; the reason being that which has already been stated, namely, that
a longer radius describes a larger circle. So with the exertion of the same force the 5
motive weight will change its position more than the weight which it moves, because
it is further from the fulcrum.

Let AB be a lever, C the weight to be lifted, D the motive weight, and E the
fulcrum; the position of D after it has raised the weight will be G, and that of C, the
weight raised, will be K.

4 · Why is it that those rowers who are amidships move the ship most? Is it because the oar acts as a lever? The fulcrum then is the thole-pin (for it remains in the same place); and the weight is the sea which the oar displaces; and the power that moves the lever is the rower. The further he who moves a weight is from the fulcrum, the greater is the weight which he moves; for then the radius becomes greater, and the thole-pin acting as the fulcrum is the centre. Now amidships there is more of the oar inside the ship than elsewhere; for there the ship is widest, so that on both sides a longer portion of the oar can be inside the two walls of the vessel. The ship then moves because, as the blade presses against the sea, the handle of the oar, which is inside the ship, advances forward, and the ship, being firmly attached to the thole-pin, advances with it in the same direction as the handle of the oar. For where the blade displaces most water, there necessarily must the ship be propelled most; and it displaces most water where the handle is furthest from the thole-pin. This is why the rowers who are amidships move the ship most; for it is in the middle of the ship that the length of the oar from the thole-pin inside the ship is greatest.

5 · Why is it that the rudder, being small and at the extreme end of the ship, has such power that vessels of great burden can be moved by a small tiller and the strength of one man only gently exerted? Is it because the rudder, too, is a lever and the steersman works it? The fulcrum then is the point at which the rudder is attached to the ship, and the whole rudder is the lever, and the sea is the weight, and the steersman the moving force. The rudder does not take the sea squarely, as the oar does; for it does not move the ship forward, but diverts it as it moves, taking the sea obliquely. For since, as we saw, the sea is the weight, the rudder pressing in a contrary direction diverts the ship. For the fulcrum turns in a contrary direction to the sea; when the sea turns inwards, the fulcrum turns outwards; and the ship follows it because it is attached to it. The oar pushing the weight squarely, and being itself thrust in turn by it, impels the ship straight forward; but the rudder, as it has an oblique position, causes an oblique motion one way or the other. It is placed at the stern and not amidships, because it is easiest to move a mass which has to be moved, if it is moved from one extremity. For the fore part travels quickest, because, just as in objects that are travelling along, the movement ceases at the end; so too, in any object which is continuous the movement is weakest towards the end, and if it is weakest in that part it is easy to check it. For this reason, then, the rudder is placed at the stern, and also because, as there is little motion there, the displacement is much greater at the extremity, since the equal angle stands on a longer base in proportion as the enclosing lines are longer. From this it is also plain why the ship advances in the opposite direction more than does the oar-blade; for the same bulk moved by the same force progresses more in air than in water. For let AB be the oar and C the thole-pin, and A the end of the oar inside the ship, and B, that in the sea. Then if A be moved to D, B will not be at E: for BE is equal to AD, and so B, if it were at E, would have changed its position as much as A, whereas it has really, as we saw, traversed a shorter distance. B will therefore be at F. H then cuts AB not at C but below it. For BF is less than AD, so that HF is less than DH, for the triangles

are similar. The centre C will also have been displaced; for it moves in a contrary   25
direction to B, the end of the oar in the sea, and in the same direction as A, the end
in the ship, and A changes its position to D. So the ship will also change its position,
and it advances in the same direction as the handle of the oar. The rudder also acts
in the same way, except that, as we saw above, it contributes nothing to the forward   30
motion of the ship, but merely thrusts the stern sideways one way or the other; for
then the bow inclines in the contrary direction. The point where the rudder is
attached must be considered, as it were, the centre of the mass which is moved,
corresponding to the thole-pin in the case of the oar; but the middle of the ship
moves in the direction to which the tiller is put over. If the steersman puts it   35
inwards, the stern alters its position in that direction, but the bow inclines in the
contrary direction; for while the bow remains in the same place, the position of the
ship as a whole is altered.

6 · Why is it that the higher the yard-arm is raised, the quicker does a vessel
travel with the same sail and in the same breeze? Is it because the mast is a lever,
and the socket in which it is fixed, the fulcrum, and the weight which it has to move $851^{b}1$
is the boat, and the motive power is the wind in the sail? If the same power moves
the same weight more easily and quickly the further away the fulcrum is, then the
yard-arm, being raised higher, brings the sail also further away from the mast-
socket, which is the fulcrum.   5

7 · Why is it that, when sailors wish to keep their course in an unfavourable
wind, they draw in the part of the sail which is nearer to the steersman, and,
working the sheet, let out the part towards the bows? Is it because the rudder cannot
counteract the wind when it is strong, but can do so when there is only a little wind,   10
and so[4] they draw in sail? The wind then bears the ship along, while the rudder turns
the wind into a favouring breeze, counteracting it and serving as a lever against the
sea. The sailors also at the same time contend with the wind by leaning their weight
in the opposite direction.

8 · Why is it that spherical and circular forms are easier to move? A circle   15
can revolve in three different ways: either along its circumference, the centre
correspondingly changing its position, as a carriage wheel revolves; or round the
centre only, as pulleys move, the centre being at rest; or it can turn, as does the   20
potter's wheel, parallel to the ground, the centre being at rest. Do not circular forms
move quickest, firstly because they have a very slight contact with the ground (like
a circle in contact at a single point), and secondly, because there is no friction, for
the angle is well away from the ground? Further, if they come into collision with   25
another body, they only are in contact with it again to a very small extent. (If it were
a question of a rectilinear body, owing to its sides being straight, it would have a
considerable contact with the ground.) Further, he who moves circular objects
moves them in a direction to which they have an inclination as regards weight. For

[4]Reading διό for ὅ.

when the diameter of the circle is perpendicular to the ground, the circle being in
30   contact with the ground only at one point, the diameter divides the weight equally
on either side of it; but as soon as it is set in motion, there is more weight on the side
to which it is moved, as though it had an inclination in that direction. Hence, it is
easier for one who pushes it forward to move it; for it is easier to move any body in a
direction to which it inclines, just as it is difficult to move it contrary to its
35   inclination. Some people further assert that the circumference of a circle keeps up a
continual motion, just as bodies which are at rest remain so owing to their
resistance. This can be illustrated by a comparison of larger with smaller circles;
larger circles can be moved more readily with an exertion of the same amount of
force and move other weights with them, because the angle of the larger circle as
compared with that of the smaller has an inclination which is in the same proportion
852ªl   as the diameter of the one is to the diameter of the other. Now if any circle be taken,
there is always a lesser circle than which it is greater; for the lesser circles which can
be described are infinite in number.

Now if it is the case that one circle has a greater inclination as compared with
another circle, and is correspondingly easy to move, then it is also the case that if a
5   circle does not touch the ground with its circumference, but moves either parallel to
the ground or with the motion of a pulley, the circle and the bodies moved by the
circle will have a further cause of inclination; for circular objects of this kind move
most easily and move weights with them. Can it be that this is due to a reason other
than that they have only a very slight contact with the ground, and consequently
encounter little friction? This reason is that which we have already mentioned,
namely, that the circle is made up of two forms of motion—and so one of them
10   always has an inclination—and those who move a circle move it when it has, as it
were, a motion of its own, when they move it at any point on its circumference. They
are moving the circumference when it is already in motion; for the motive force
pushes it in a tangential direction, while the circle itself moves in the motion which
takes place along the diameter.

15   9 . How is it that we can move objects more easily and quickly when they are
lifted or drawn along by circles of large circumference? Why, for example, are large
pulleys more effective than small, and similarly large rollers? Is it because the
longer the radius is the further the object is moved in the same time, and so it will do
20   the same also with an equal weight upon it? Just as we said that large balances are
more accurate than small; for the cord is the centre and the parts of the beam on
either side of the cord are the radii.

10 . Why is it that a balance moves more easily without a weight upon it
25   than with one? So too with a wheel or anything of that nature, the smaller and
lighter is easier to move than the heavier and larger. Is it because that which is
heavy is difficult to move not only vertically, but also horizontally? For one can
move a weight with difficulty contrary to its inclination, but easily in the direction
of its inclination; and it does not incline in a horizontal direction.

11 · Why is it that it is easier to convey heavy weights on rollers than on   30
carts, though the latter have large wheels and the former a small circumference? Is
it because a weight placed upon rollers encounters no friction, whereas when placed
upon a cart it has the axle at which it encounters friction? For it presses on the axle
from above in addition to the horizontal pressure. But an object on rollers is moved   35
at two points on them, where the ground supports them below and where the weight
is imposed above; the circle revolves at both these points and is thrust along as it
moves.

12 · Why is it that a missile travels further from a sling than from the hand,
although he who casts it has more control over the missile in his hand than when he   852ᵇ1
holds the weight suspended? Further, in the latter case he moves two weights, that
of the sling and the missile, while in the former case he moves only the missile. Is it
because he who casts the missile does so when it is already in motion in the sling (for
he swings it round many times before he lets it go), whereas when cast from the   5
hand it starts from a state of rest? Now any object is easier to move when it is
already in motion than when it is at rest. Or, while this is one reason, is there a
further reason, namely, that in using a sling the hand becomes the centre and the
sling the radius, and the longer the radius is the more quickly it moves, and so a cast
from the hand is short as compared with a cast from a sling?   10

13 · Why is it that longer bars are moved more easily than shorter ones
round the same capstan, and similarly lighter windlasses are moved more easily by
the same force than stouter windlasses? Is it because the windlass and the capstan
form a centre and the outer masses the radii? For the radii of greater circles are
moved more readily and further by the same force than those of lesser circles; for   15
the extremity further from the centre is moved more readily by the same force.
Therefore in the case of the capstan they use the bars as a means whereby they turn
it more easily; and in the case of the lighter windlasses the part outside the central
cylinder is more extended, and this portion forms the radius of the circle.   20

14 · Why is it that a piece of wood of the same size is more easily broken
against the knee, if one breaks it holding the ends at equal distance from the knee,
than if it is held close to the knee? And if one leans a piece of wood upon the ground
and places one's foot on it, why does one break it more easily if one grasps it at a   25
distance from the foot rather than near it? Is it because in the former case the knee,
and in the latter the foot is the centre, and the further an object is from the centre
the more easily is it always moved, and that which is to be broken must be moved?

15 · Why is it that the so-called pebbles found on beaches are round, though
they are originally formed from stones and shells which are elongated in shape? Is it   30
because objects whose outer surfaces are far removed from their middle point are
borne along more quickly by the movements to which they are subjected? The

middle of such objects acts as the centre and the distance from there to the exterior becomes the radius, and a longer radius always describes a greater circle than a shorter radius when the force which moves them is equal. An object which traverses
35 a greater space in the same time travels more quickly, and objects which travel more quickly from an equal distance strike harder against other objects, and the more they strike the more they are themselves struck. It follows, therefore, that objects in which the distance from the middle to the exterior is greater always become broken, and in this process they must necessarily become round. So in the case of pebbles,
853ᵃ1 because the sea moves and they move with it, the result is that they are always in motion, and, as they roll about, they come into collision with other objects; and it is their extremities which are necessarily most affected.

5   16 · Why is it that the longer a plank of wood is, the weaker it is, and the more it bends when lifted up? Why, for example, does a short thin plank about two cubits long bend less than a thick plank a hundred cubits long? Is it because the
10 length of the plank when it is lifted forms a lever, a weight, and a fulcrum? The first part of it, then, which the hand raises becomes, as it were, a fulcrum, and the part towards the end becomes the weight; and so the longer the space is from the fulcrum to the end, the more the plank must bend; for it must necessarily bend more the
15 further away it is from the fulcrum. Therefore the ends of the lever must be subject to pressure. If, then, the lever is bent, it must bend more when it is lifted up. This is exactly what happens in the case of long planks of wood; whereas in the case of shorter planks, the extremity is near the fulcrum which is at rest.

20   17 · How is it that great weights and masses can be split and violent pressure be exerted with a wedge, which is a small thing? Is it because the wedge forms two levers working in opposite directions, and each has a weight and fulcrum which presses upwards or downwards? Further, the impetus of the blow causes the weight which strikes the wedge and moves it to be very considerable; and it has all the more
25 force because by reason of its speed it is moving what is already moving. Although the lever is short, great force accompanies it, and so it causes a much more violent movement than we should expect from an estimate of its size. Let ABC be the wedge, and DEGF the object which is acted upon by it; then AB is a lever and the weight is below at B, and the fulcrum is FD. On the opposite side is the lever BC.
30 When AC is struck it brings both of these into use as levers; for it presses upwards at the point B.

      18 · Why is it that if one puts two pulleys on two blocks which are in
35 opposite positions, and places round them a cord with one end attached to one of the blocks and the other supported by or passed over the pulleys, if one pulls at the end of the cord, one can move great weights, even if the force which draws them is small? Is it because the same weight is raised by less force, if a lever is employed,
853ᵇ1 than by the hand, and the pulley acts in the same way as a lever, so that a single

pulley will draw more easily and draw a far heavier weight with a slight pull than the hand alone can? Two pulleys raise this weight with more than double the velocity; for the second pulley draws a still less weight than if it drew alone by itself, when the rope is passed on to it from the other pulley; for the other pulley makes the weight still less. Thus if the cord is passed through a greater number, the difference is great, even when there are only a few pulleys, so that, if the load under the first weighs four *minae,* much less is drawn by the last. In building operations they easily move great weights; for they transfer them from one pulley to another and thence again to windlasses and levers, and this is equivalent to constructing a number of pulleys.

19 . How is it that, if you place a heavy axe on a piece of wood and put a heavy weight on the top of it, it does not cleave the wood to any considerable extent, whereas, if you lift the axe and strike the wood with it, it does split it, although the axe when it strikes the blow has much less weight upon it than when it is placed on the wood and pressing on it? Is it because the effect is produced entirely by movement, and that which is heavy gets more movement from its weight when it is in motion than when it is at rest? So when it is merely placed on the wood, it does not move with the movement derived from its weight; but when it is put into motion, it moves with the movement derived from its weight and also with that imparted by the striker. Furthermore, the axe works like a wedge; and a wedge, though small, can split large masses because it is made up of two levers working in opposite directions.

20 . Why is it that steelyards weigh great weights of meat with a small counterpoise, the whole forming only a half balance? For a pan is fixed only at the end where the object weighed is placed, and at the other end there is nothing but the steelyard. Is it because the steelyard is at once a beam and a lever? For it is a beam, inasmuch as each position of the cord becomes the centre of the steelyard. Now at one end it has a pan, and at the other instead of a pan the counterpoise which is fixed in the beam, just as if one were to place the other pan with the counterpoise in it at the end of the steelyard; for it is clear that it draws the same weight when it lies in this second pan. But in order that the single beam may act as many beams, many such positions for the cord are situated along a beam of this kind, in each of which the part on the side of the counterpoise forms half the steelyard and acts as the weight,[5] the positions of the cord being moved through equal intervals, so that one can calculate how much weight is drawn by what lies in the pan, and thus know, when the steelyard is horizontal, how much weight the pan holds for each of the several positions of the cord, as has been explained. In short, this may be regarded as a balance, having one pan in which the object weighed is placed, and the other in which is the weight of the steelyard, and so the steelyard at the other end is the counterpoise. Hence it acts as an adjustable balance beam, with as many forms as

5

10

15

20

25

30

35

854ᵃ1

5

---

[5]Placing a comma after, not before, καὶ ὁ σταθμός.

there are positions of the cord. And in all cases, when the cord is nearer the pan and the weight upon it, it draws a greater weight, on account of the whole steelyard
10 being an inverted lever (for the cord in each position is a fulcrum, although it is above, and the weight is what is in the pan), and the greater the length of the lever from the fulcrum, the more easily it produces motion in the case of the lever, and in the case of the balance causes equilibrium and counterbalances the weight of the
15 steelyard near the counterpoise.

21 · How is it that doctors extract teeth more easily by applying the additional weight of a tooth-extractor than with the bare hand only? Is it because
20 the tooth is more inclined to slip in the fingers than from the tooth-extractor? or does not the iron slip more than the hand and fail to grasp the tooth all round, since the flesh of the fingers being soft both adheres to and fits round the tooth better? The truth is that the tooth-extractor consists of two levers opposed to one another, with the same fulcrum at the point where the pincers join; so they use the
25 instrument to draw teeth, in order to move them more easily.

Let A be one extremity of the tooth-extractor and B the other extremity which draws the tooth, and ADF one lever and BCE the other, and CHD the fulcrum, and let the tooth, which is the weight to be lifted, be at the point I, where the two levers
30 meet. The doctor holds and moves the tooth at the same time with B and F; and when he has moved it, he can take it out more easily with his fingers than with the instrument.

22 · Why is it that men easily crack nuts, without striking a blow upon them, in the instruments made for this purpose? For with nut-crackers much power is lost, namely, that of motion and violent impetus. Further, if one crushes them with a
35 hard and heavy instrument, one can crack them much more quickly than with a light wooden instrument. Is it because the nut is crushed on two of its sides by two levers, and weights can easily be divided with a lever? For the nut-cracker consists
854^{b}1 of two levers, with the same fulcrum, namely, A, their point of connexion. As, therefore, E and F would have been easily pushed apart, so they are easily brought together by a small force,[6] the levers being moved at the points D and C. So EC and
5 FD being levers exert the same or even greater force than that which the weight exerted when the nut was cracked by a blow; for when weight is put upon the levers they move in opposite directions and compress and break the object at K. For this very reason, too, the nearer K is to A, the sooner it is subjected to pressure; for the further the lever extends from the fulcrum, the more easily and more powerfully does it move an object with the exercise of the same force. A, then, is the fulcrum,
10 and DAF and CAE are the levers. The nearer, therefore, K is to the angle at A, the nearer it is to the point where the levers are connected, and this is the fulcrum. So with the same force bringing them together, F and E must be subjected to more weight; and so, when weight is exerted from two contrary directions, more

[6]Omitting ὑφ' ὧν.

compression must take place, and the more an object is compressed, the sooner it 15
breaks.

23 · Why is it that in a rhombus, when the points at the extremities are
moved in two movements, they do not describe equal straight lines,but one of them a
much longer line than the other? Further (and this is the same question), why does
the point moving along the side describe a resultant line less than the side? For the
point describes the diagonal, the shorter distance, and the line moves along the side, 20
the longer distance; and yet the line has but one movement, and the point two
movements.

For let A move along AB to B, and B to A with the same velocity; and let the
line AB move along AC parallel to CD with the same velocity. Then the point A
must move along the diagonal AD, and B along BC; and both must describe these 25
diagonals simultaneously, while AB moves along the side AC.

For let A be moved the distance AE, and the line AB the distance AF, and let
FG be drawn parallel to AB, and a line drawn from E to complete the parallelogram. The small parallelogram then thus formed is similar to the whole parallelogram. Thus AF equals AE, so that A has been moved along the side AE, while the 30
line AB would be moved the distance AF. Thus A will be on the diagonal at H, and
so must always move along the diagonal; and the side AB will describe the side AC,
and the point A the diagonal AD simultaneously. In the same way it may be proved 35
that B moves along the diagonal BC, BE being equal to BG. For, if the
parallelogram be completed by drawing a line from G, the interior parallelogram
will be similar to the whole parallelogram; and B will be on the diagonal at the point
where the sides meet; and the side will describe the side; and the point B describes 855ᵃ1
the diagonal BC.

At the same time then B will describe a line which is much longer than AB, and
the side will pass along the side which is shorter, though the velocity is the same, in
the same time (and the side has moved further than A, though it is moved by only 5
one movement). For as the rhombus becomes more acute, AD becomes the lesser
diagonal and BC greater, and the side less than BC. For it is strange, as has been
remarked, that in some cases a point moved by two movements travels more slowly
than a point moved by one, and that, while both the given points have equal velocity,
either one of them describes a greater line. 10

The reason is that, when a point moves from an obtuse angle, the sides are in
almost opposite directions, namely, that in which the point itself is moved and that
in which it is moved down by the side; but when it moves from an acute angle, it
moves, as it were, in actual fact towards the same position. For the angle of the sides
contributes to increase the speed of the diagonal; and in proportion as one makes the
one angle more acute and the other more obtuse, the movement is slower or quicker. 15
For the sides are brought into more opposite direction by the angle becoming more
obtuse; but they are brought into the same direction by the sides being brought
nearer together. For B moves in practically the same direction in virtue of both its
movements; thus one contributes to assist the other, and more so, the more acute the 20

angle becomes. And the reverse is the case with A; for it itself moves towards B, while the movement of the side brings it down to D; and the more obtuse the angle is, the more opposite will the movements be; for the two sides become more like a
25   straight line. If they became actually a straight line, the components would be absolutely in opposite directions. But the side, being moved in one direction only, is interfered with by nothing. In that case it naturally moves through a longer distance.

24 · There is a question why a large circle traces out a path equal to that of a
30   smaller circle, when they are placed about the same centre, but when they are rolled separately, their paths are to one another in the proportion of their dimensions. And, further, the centre of both being one and the same, at one time the path which they trace is of the same length as the smaller traces out alone, and at another time
35   of the length which the larger circle traces. Now it is manifest that the larger circle traces out the longer path. For by mere observation it is plain that the angle which the circumference of each makes with its own diameter is greater in the case of the larger circle than in the smaller; so that, by observation, the paths along which they
855^{b}1   roll will have this same proportion to one another. But, in fact, it is manifest that, when they are situated about the same centre, this is not so, but they trace out an equal path; so that it comes to this, that in the one case the path is equal to that
5   traced by the larger circle, in the other to that traced by the smaller.
       Let DFC be the greater circle, EGB the lesser, A the common centre, FI the path along which the greater circle moves by its own motion, and GK the path of the smaller circle by its own motion, equal to FL.
10   When, then, I move the smaller circle, I move the same centre A; and now let the large circle be fixed to it. Whenever, therefore, AB becomes perpendicular to GK, AC at the same time becomes perpendicular to FL; so that they will always have traversed an equal distance, GK representing the arc GB, and FL representing
15   the arc FC. And if one quadrant traces an equal path, it is plain that the whole circle will trace out a path equal to that of the other whole circle; so that whenever the line GB comes to K, the arc FC will move along FL; and the same is the case with the whole circle after one revolution.
       In like manner if I roll the large circle, fastening the smaller circle to it, about
20   the same centre, AB will be perpendicular and vertical at the same time as AC, the latter to FI, the former to GH. So that, whenever the one shall have traversed a distance equal to GH and the other a distance equal to FI, and FA again becomes perpendicular to FL and AG to GK, they will be in their original position at the points H and I. And, since there is no halting of the greater for the lesser, so as to be
25   at rest during an interval at the same point (for in both cases both are moved continuously), nor does the lesser skip any point, it is strange that in one case the greater should traverse a distance equal to that traversed by the lesser, and in the other case the lesser a distance equal to that traversed by the greater. And, further,
30   it is wonderful that, though there is always only one movement, the centre that is moved should be rolled forward in one case a great and in another a less distance.

For the same thing moved at the same velocity naturally traverses an equal distance; and to move a thing at the same velocity is to move it an equal distance in both cases.

As to the reason, this may be taken as a principle, that the same, or an equal force, moves one mass more slowly and the other more quickly.

Suppose that there is a body which is not naturally in motion of itself; if another body which is naturally in motion move it and itself as well, it will be moved more slowly than if it were being moved by its own motion alone; and if it be naturally in motion and nothing is moved with it, the same is the case. So it is quite impossible for any body to be moved more than that which moves it; for it is not moved according to any rate of motion of its own, but at the rate of that which moves it.

Let there be two circles, a greater A and a lesser B. If the lesser were to push along the greater, when the greater is not rolling alone, it is plain that the greater will traverse so much distance as it has been pushed by the lesser. And it has been pushed the same distance as the small circle has moved; so that they have both traversed an equal straight line. Necessarily, therefore, if the lesser be rolling while it pushes the greater, the latter will be rolled, as well as pushed, just so far as the lesser has been rolled, if the greater have no motion of its own; for in the same way and so far as the moving body moves it, so far must the body which is moved be moved thereby. So, indeed, the lesser circle has moved the greater so far and in the same way, viz., in a circle and for the distance of one foot (for let that be the extent of the movement); and consequently the larger circle has moved that distance.

So too, if the large circle move the lesser, the lesser circle will have been moved just as far as the large circle, in whatever way[7] the latter be moved, whether quickly or slowly, by its own motion; and the lesser circle will trace out a line at the same velocity and of the same length as the greater traced out by its natural movement. And this is just what causes the difficulty, that they do not act any longer when they are joined together in the same way as they acted when they were not connected; that is to say, when one is moved by the other not according to its natural motion, nor according to its own motion. For it makes no difference whether one is fixed round the other or fitted inside it, or placed in contact with it; for in all these cases, when one moves and the other is moved by it, the one will be moved just so far as the other moves it.

Now when one moves a circle by means of another circle in contact with it, or suspended from it, one does not revolve it continuously; but if one places them about the same centre, the one must be continuously revolved by the other. But nevertheless, the former is not moved in accordance with its own motion, but just as if it had no proper motion; and if it has a proper motion, but does not make use of it, it comes to the same thing.

Whenever, therefore, the large circle moves the small circle affixed to it, the small circle moves the same distance as the large, and vice versa. But when they are separate each has its own motion.

[7] Placing a comma after καὶ ὁ μείζων, and reading ὁποτερωσοῦν.

If any one raises the difficulty that, when the centre is the same and is moving the two circles with equal velocity, they trace out unequal paths, he is reasoning falsely and sophistically. For the centre is, indeed, the same for both, but only
35   accidentally, just as the same thing may chance to be musical and white; for to be the centre of each of the circles is not the same for it in the two cases.

In conclusion, when it is the smaller circle that moves the greater, the centre and source of motion is to be regarded as belonging to the smaller circle; but when the greater circle moves the lesser, it is to be regarded as belonging to the greater circle. Thus the source of motion is not the same absolutely, though it is in a sense the same.

25 · Why do they construct beds so that one dimension is double the other,
856ᵇ1   one side being six feet long or a little more, the other three feet? And why do they not stretch bed-ropes diagonally? Do they make them of this size so as to fit the
5   body? Thus they have one side twice the length of the other, being four cubits long and two cubits wide.

The ropes are not stretched diagonally but from side to side, so that the wooden frame may be less likely to break; for wood can be cleft most easily if split thus in the natural way, and when there is a pull upon it, it is subject to a considerable strain. Further, since the ropes have to be able to bear a weight, there will be less of
10   a strain when the weight is put upon them if they are strung crosswise rather than diagonally. Again, less rope is used up by this method.

Let AFGI be a bed, and let FG be divided into two equal parts at B. There is an equal number of holes in FB and FA; for the sides are equal, each to each, for the
15   whole side FG is double the side FA. They stretch the rope on the method already mentioned from A to B, then to C, D, H, and E, and so on until they turn back and reach another angle; for the two ends of the rope come at two different angles.

Now the parts of the rope which form the bends are equal, e.g. AB, BC are
20   equal to CD, DH—and so with other similar pairs of sides, for the same demonstration holds good in all cases. For AB is equal to EH; for the opposite sides of the parallelogram BGKA are equal, and the holes are an equal distance apart from one another. And BG is equal to KA; for the angle at B is equal to the angle at G (for the exterior angle of a parallelogram is equal to the interior opposite angle);
25   and the angle at B is half a right angle, for FB is equal to FA, and the angle at F is a right angle. And the angle at B is equal to the angle at G; for the angle at F is a right angle, since the bed is a rectangular figure, one side of which is double the other, and divided into two equal parts; so that BC is equal to EG, as also is KH; for it is
30   parallel. So that BC is equal to KH, and CE to DH. In like manner it can be demonstrated that all the other pairs of sides which form the bends of the rope are equal to one another. So that clearly there are four such lengths of rope as AB in the bed; and there is half the number of holes in the half FB that there is in the whole
35   FG. So that in the half of the bed there are lengths of rope, such as AB, and they are of the same number as there are holes in BG, or, what comes to the same thing, in AF, FB together. But if the rope be strung diagonally, as in the bed ABCD, the
857ᵃ1   halves are not of the same length as the sides of both, AF and FG; but they are of the

same number as the holes in FB, FA. But AF, FB, being two, are greater than AB, so that the rope is longer by the amount by which the two sides taken together are greater than the diagonal.

26 · Why is it more difficult to carry a long plank of wood on the shoulder if 5 one holds it at the end than if it is held in the middle, though the weight is the same? Is it because, as the plank vibrates, the end prevents one from carrying it, because it tends to interrupt one's progress by its vibration? No, for if it does not bend at all 10 and is not very long, it is nevertheless more difficult to carry if it is held at the end. It is easier to carry if one holds it in the middle rather than at the end, for the same reason for which it is easier to lift in that way. The reason is that, if one lifts it in the middle, the two ends always lighten one another, and one side lifts the other side up. For the middle, where the lifter or carrier holds it, forms, as it were, the centre, and 15 each of the two ends inclining downwards raises up and lightens the other end; whereas if it is lifted or carried from one end, this effect is not produced, but all the weight inclines in one direction. Let A be the middle of a plank which is raised or carried, and let B and C be the extremities. When the plank is lifted or carried at the point A, B inclines downwards and raises C up, and C inclines downwards and 20 raises B up; the effect is produced by their being raised up at the same moment.

27 · Why is a very long object more difficult to carry on the shoulder, even if one carries it in the middle, than a shorter object of the same weight? In the last case we said that the vibration was not the reason; in this case it is the reason. For 25 the longer an object is, the more its extremities vibrate, and so it would be more difficult for the man to carry it. The reason of the increased vibration is that, though the movement is the same, the extremities change their position more the longer the piece of wood is. Let the shoulder, which is the centre (for it is at rest), be at A, and 30 let AB and AC be the radii; then the longer the radius AB or AC is, the greater is the amplitude of movement. This point has already been demonstrated.

28 · Why do they construct swing-beams by the side of wells by attaching the lead as a weight at the end of the bar, the bucket being itself a weight, whether it 35 is empty or full? Is the reason that, the drawing of water being divided into two operations distinct in time (for the bucket has to be dipped and then drawn up), it is an easy task to let it down when it is empty, but difficult to raise it when it is full? It 857ᵇ1 is therefore of advantage to lower it rather more slowly with a view to lightening the weight considerably when it is drawn up again. This effect is produced by the lead or stone attached to the end of the swing-beam. In letting it down there is a heavier 5 weight to lift than if one has merely to lower the empty bucket; but when it is full, the lead, or whatever the weight attached is, helps to draw it up; and so the two operations taken together are easier than on the other method.

29 · Why is it that when two men are carrying an equal weight on a piece of wood or something of the kind, the pressure on them is not equal unless the weight is 10 in the middle, but it presses more on the person carrying it to whom it is nearest? Is

it because the wood, when they hold it in this way, becomes a lever, and the load
15   forms the fulcrum, and the carrier nearer to the load becomes the weight which is to
be moved, while the other carrier becomes the mover of the weight? The further the
latter is from the weight, the more easily he moves it, and the more he presses down
the other man, since the load placed on the wood and acting as a fulcrum, as it were,
offers resistance. But if the load is placed in the middle, one carrier does not act as a
weight on the other any more than the other on him, or exercise any motive force
20   upon him, but each is equally a weight upon the other.

30 · Why is it that when people rise from a sitting position, they always do so
by making an acute angle between the thigh and the lower leg and between the
chest and the thigh, otherwise they cannot rise? Is it because equality is always a
cause of rest, and a right angle causes an equality and so causes equilibrium? So in
25   rising a man moves towards a position at equal angles to the earth's circumference;
for it is not the case that he will actually be at right angles to the ground. Or is it
because when a man rises he tends to become upright, and a man who is standing
must be perpendicular to the ground? If, then, he is to be at right angles to the
30   ground, that means that he must have his head in the same line as his feet, and this
occurs when he is rising. As long, then, as he is sitting, he keeps his feet and head
parallel to one another and not in the same straight line. Let A be the head, AB the
line of the chest, BC the thigh, and CD the lower leg. Then AB, the line of the chest,
35   is at right angles to the thigh, and the thigh at right angles to the lower leg, when a
man is seated in this way. In this position, then, a man cannot rise; but to do so he
must bend the leg and place the feet at a point under the head. This will be the case
if CD be moved to CF, and the result will be that he can rise immediately, and he
858ᵃ1   will have his head and his feet in the same straight line;[8] and CF will form an acute
angle with BC.

31 · Why is it that a body which is already in motion is easier to move than
one which is at rest? For example, a wagon which is in motion can be propelled more
5   quickly than one which has to be started. Is it because, in the first place, it is very
difficult to move in one direction a weight which is already moving in the opposite
direction? For though the motive force may be much quicker, yet some of it is lost;
for the propulsion exerted by that which is being pushed in the opposite direction
must necessarily become slower. And so, secondly, the propulsion must be slower if
the body is at rest; for even that which is at rest offers resistance. When a body is
10   moving in the same direction as that which pushes it, the effect is just as if one
increased the force and speed of the motive power; for by moving forward it
produces of itself exactly the effect which that power would have upon it.

32 · Why is it that an object which is thrown eventually comes to a
15   standstill? Does it stop when the force which started it fails, or because the object is
drawn in a contrary direction, or is it due to its downward tendency, which is

---

[8]Reading εὐθείας.

stronger than the force which threw it? Or is it absurd to discuss such questions, while the principle escapes us?

33 · How is it that a body is carried along by a motion not its own, if that which started it does not keep following and pushing it along? Is it not clear that in the beginning the impelling force so acted as to push one thing along, and this in its turn pushes along something else? The moving body comes to a standstill when the force which pushes it along can no longer so act as to push it, and when the weight of the moving object has a stronger inclination downwards than the forward force of that which pushes it. 20

34 · Why is it that neither small nor large bodies travel far when thrown, but they must have due relation to the person who throws them? Is it because that which is thrown or pushed must offer resistance to that from which it is pushed, and whatever does not yield owing to its mass, or does not resist owing to its weakness, does not admit of being thrown or pushed? A body, then, which is far beyond the force which tries to push it, does not yield at all; while that which is far weaker offers no resistance. Or is it because that which travels along does so only as far as it 30 moves the air to its depths, and that which is not moved cannot itself move anything either? Both these things are the case here; that which is very large and that which 858ᵇ1 is very small must be looked upon as not moving at all; for the latter does not move anything, while the former is not itself at all moved. 25

35 · Why is it that an object which is carried round in whirling water is 5 always eventually carried into the middle? Is it because the object has magnitude, so that it has position in two circles, one of its extremities revolving in a greater and the other in a lesser circle? The greater circle, then, on account of its greater velocity, draws it round and thrusts it sideways into the lesser circle; but since the object has breadth, the lesser circle in its turn does the same thing and thrusts it into 10 the next interior circle, until it reaches the centre. Here the object remains because it stands in the same relation to all the circles, being in the middle; for the middle is equidistant from the circumference in the case of each of the circles. Or is it because an object which, owing to its magnitude, the motion of the whirling water cannot 15 overcome, but which by its weight prevails over the velocity of the revolving circle, must necessarily be left behind and travel along more slowly? Now the lesser circle travels more slowly—for the greater and the lesser circle do not[9] revolve over the same space in an equal time when they move round the same centre—and so the object must be left revolving in a lesser and lesser circle until it reaches the middle. 20 If the force of the whirling water prevails at first, it will go on doing so to the end; for one circle must prevail and then the next over the weight of the object owing to their velocity, so that the whole object is continually being left behind in the next circle towards the centre. For an object over which the water does not prevail must be carried either inwards or outwards. Such an object cannot then be carried along in 25

---

[9]Reading οὐ τὸ αὐτό.

its original position; still less can it be carried along in the outer circle, for the velocity of the outer circle is greater. The only alternative is that the object over which the water does not prevail is transferred to the inner circle. Now every object

30 has a tendency to resist force; but since the arrival at the middle puts an end to motion, and the centre alone is at rest, all objects must necessarily collect there.

PROBLEMS*

E. S. Forster

BOOK I
PROBLEMS CONNECTED
WITH MEDICINE

1 · Why is it that great excesses cause disease? Is it because they engender   859ª1
excess or defect, and it is in these after all that disease consists?

2 · But why is it that diseases can often be cured if the patient indulges in
excess of some kind? And this is the treatment used by some doctors; for they cure   5
by the excessive use of wine or water or salt, or by over-feeding or starving the
patient. Is it because the causes of the disease are opposites of one another, so that
each reduces the other to the mean?

3 · Why is it that the changes of the seasons and the winds intensify or stop   10
diseases and bring them to a crisis and engender them? Is it because the seasons are
hot and cold and moist and dry, while diseases are due to excess of these qualities
and health to their equality? In that case, if the disease is due to moisture or cold, a
season which has the opposite characteristics stops it; but if a season of the opposite
kind follows, the same admixture of qualities being caused as before intensifies the
disease and kills the patient. For this reason the seasons even cause disease in   15
healthy persons, because by their changes they destroy the proper admixture of
qualities; for it is at the same time improved by suitable seasons, times of life, and
localities. The health therefore requires careful management at times of change.
And what has been said generally as to the effect of the seasons applies also in
detail; for changes of winds and of age and of locality are to some extent changes of   20
season. These also therefore intensify and stop diseases and bring them to a crisis
and engender them, as do the seasons and the risings of certain constellations, such
as Orion and Arcturus and the Pleiads and the Dogstar, since they cause[1] wind and
rain and fine weather and storms and sunshine.

TEXT: C. A. Ruelle, Teubner, Leipzig, 1922
[1]Reading αἰτίαι οὖσαι for ὥσπερ.

25   **4** · Why ought emetics to be avoided at the changes of the seasons? Is it in order that there may be no disturbance when the excretions are being altered by such changes?

859ᵇ1   **5** · Why is it that the feet swell both of those who are bilious and of those who are suffering from starvation? Is it in both cases the effect of wasting? For those who are starving waste because they do not receive any nourishment at all, while the bilious waste because they do not derive any benefit from the nourishment which they take.

5   **6** · Why is it that, though the diseases due to bile occur in the summer (the season when fevers are at their height), acute diseases due to bile occur rather in the winter? Is it because, being accompanied by fever, they are acute because they are violent, and violence is unnatural? For fervent inflammation is set up when certain parts of the body are moist, and inflammation, being due to an excess of heat,
10   engenders fevers. In the summer, therefore, diseases are dry and hot, but in the winter they are moist and hot and consequently acute (for they soon kill the patient), for concoction will not take place because of the abundance of the excretion.

15   **7** · Why is it that the plague alone among diseases infects particularly persons who come into contact with those who are under treatment for it? Is it because it is the only disease to which all men alike are liable, and so the plague affects any one who is already in a low state of health? For they quickly become infected by the inflammatory matter caused by the disease which is communicated
20   by the patient.

        8 · Why is it that, when north winds have been prevalent in the winter, if the spring is rainy and characterized by south winds the summer is unhealthy with fever and ophthalmia? Is it because the summer finds the body full of alien humours, and
25   the earth, and any place in which men dwell, becomes moist and resembles localities which are regarded as permanently unhealthy? The result is that, first, ophthalmia occurs when the excretion in the region of the head liquefies, and, secondly, fever
860ª1   ensues. For it is noticeable that anything which admits of extreme cold also admits of extreme heat,—water, for example, and a stone, of which the former boils quicker than other things, the latter burns more.[2] As, therefore, in the air a stifling heat occurs when it grows warm owing to its density, so likewise in the body stifling
5   and heat are engendered, and heat in the body is fever and in the eyes ophthalmia. Generally speaking the change which occurs when a warm, dry summer follows immediately on a wet spring, being violent has a deleterious effect upon the body. The effect is still worse if the summer is rainy; for then the sun finds material, which
10   it will cause to boil in the body as in the earth and air; the result is fever and ophthalmia.

$$^2\text{Reading } \tau\grave{o} \ \mu\grave{\epsilon}\nu \ \zeta\tilde{\alpha}, \ \grave{o} \ \delta\grave{\epsilon} \ \kappa\acute{\alpha}\epsilon\iota.$$

9 · Why is it that, if the winter is characterized by south winds and rainy and if the spring is dry with the wind in the north, both the spring and the summer are unhealthy? Is it because in the winter owing to the heat and moisture the body assimilates its condition to that of the season, since it must necessarily be moist and   15
relaxed? When the body is in this state, the spring being cool congeals and hardens it owing to its dryness. The result is that women who are pregnant run a risk of abortion in the spring because of the inflammation and mortification caused by the dry cold, since the necessary moisture is not secreted, and the foetus in the womb   20
becomes weakly and defective owing to the excess of cold; for children who are born at this season in fine weather become strong and receive nourishment in the womb. In the case of other persons—because in the spring the phlegm is not purged away owing to its excess (as happens when the weather is warm), but congeals owing to   25
the cold—when the summer and warmth succeeds, setting up violent liquefaction, humours form in those who are bilious and dry because their bodies lack moisture and are naturally parched; but these humours are slight and so such people suffer from dry ophthalmia. Those on the other hand who are phlegmatic are afflicted   30
with sore throats and catarrh of the lungs. Women suffer from dysentery owing to their natural moisture and cold; while elderly persons are afflicted with apoplexy, when moisture being all set free at once overcomes them and solidifies owing to the weakness of their natural heat.

10 · Why is it that, when the summer is dry and northerly winds prevail and   35
the autumn on the contrary is wet and characterized by south winds, headaches and sore throats and coughs occur in the ensuing winter and then terminate in phthisis? Is it because the winter finds a considerable amount of matter in the body and so it   860ᵇ1
is a difficult task for it to solidify the moisture and form phlegm? Consequently, when moisture is engendered in the head, it causes a feeling of heaviness, and if it is plenteous and cold, it causes mortification; but if, owing to its abundance, it does   5
not solidify, it flows into the nearest region of the body, and thus coughs are caused and sore throats and wasting.

11 · But why is it that if the summer and autumn are dry and northerly winds prevail, this weather suits those who are phlegmatic, and women? Is it because in both cases nature tends to an excess in one direction, and so the season   10
exerting its influence in the opposite direction establishes an equable temperament, and they are healthy at the time, unless they themselves do anything which harms them, and, when the winter comes on, they are not in a moist condition, having heat in them with which to resist the cold?

12 · Why is it that a dry summer and autumn in which northerly winds   15
prevail is unhealthy for those who are bilious? Is it because their bodily condition and the season have the same tendency and it is like adding fire to fire? For the body becoming dry (the freshest element in it becoming evaporated) and being

20   overheated, dry ophthalmia must necessarily ensue owing to solidification;[3] but because the remaining humours are full of bile[4] and these become overheated, acute fevers must ensue caused by the bile, which is undiluted, and in some cases madness, where black bile is naturally present; for the black bile comes to the 25 surface as the contrary humours are dried up.

13 · Why do they say that a change of drinking-water is unhealthy, but not a change of air? Is it because water becomes nutriment, with the result that it gets into one's system and has an effect upon one, which is not the case with air? Further there are many kinds of water differing intrinsically from one another, but not of 30 air; this then may also be a reason. For even when we change our place of dwelling we continue to breathe practically the same air, but we drink different waters. It is, therefore, probably a right opinion that change of drinking-water is unhealthy.

35   14 · Why is it that a change of drinking-water is more unhealthy than a change of food? Is it because we consume more water than anything else? For water is found in farinaceous and other foods and whatever we drink consists mainly of water.

861ª1   15 · But why is a change unhealthy? Is it because every change both of season and of age is liable to disturbance? For extremities, such as beginnings and ends, are particularly liable to disturbance. So too foods, when they are different, corrupt one another; for some have only just entered the system, while others have 5 not yet done so. Further, just as a varied diet is unhealthy (for the concoction is then disturbed and not uniform), so those who change their drinking-water are using a varied diet in what they drink; and liquid nourishment has more effect than dry food because it is greater in bulk and because the moisture from the foods themselves forms nourishment.

10   16 · Why does a change of drinking-water cause an increase of lice in those who suffer from lice? Is it because, owing to the disturbance set up by the different water in those who frequently change their drinking-water, the unconcocted state of the liquid causes a moist condition, especially in that part where the conditions are suitable? Now the brain is moist, and therefore the head is always the moistest part 15 of the body (as is shown by the fact that hair grows there more than elsewhere), and it is the moisture of this part which generates lice. This is clear in the case of children; for their heads are moist and they frequently have either runny noses or discharge of blood, and persons of this age suffer particularly from lice.

20   17 · Why is it that from the rising of the Pleiads until the west wind blows those who suffer from chronic diseases are most likely to die, and the old rather than the young? Is it because two things are fatal to life, excess and cold? For life is heat,

---

[3]Reading συμπήξεις.
[4]Reading χολώδεις.

whereas this season has both the above characteristics, for it is cold, and winter is
then at its height, the subsequent season being spring. Or is it because those who   25
suffer from chronic diseases are in a similar condition to the old? For the occurrence
of a long illness is like premature old age, since in both the body is dry and cold,—in
the one case owing to the time of life, in the other from disease. Now winter and
frosts constitute an excess of coldness and dryness; therefore to those who are in a   30
condition where a very little will turn the scale, winter is like fire added to fire and
so causes death.

18 · Why is it that in marshy districts sores on the head are quickly cured,
but those on the legs only with difficulty? Is it because the moisture, owing to the
fact that it contains an earthy element, is heavy, and heavy things are carried   35
downwards? Thus the upper parts of the body are cleared out because the
impurities are carried to the lower parts, and these become full of excretions which
easily putrefy.

19 · Why is it that, when a very dry summer follows after northerly winds   861ᵇ1
have prevailed in the winter and the spring has been damp and rainy, the autumn is
universally fatal, especially to children, while in other people dysentery and
prolonged quartan fevers occur then? Is it because, when there is a moderate   5
amount of rain in the summer, the moisture boiling within us, which collected in the
damp spring, is cooled and becomes quiescent? If on the other hand this does not
happen, children, because they are moist and hot, are in a state of excessive boiling,
because they are not cooled; and anything which does not as it were[5] boil out in the
summer, does so in the autumn. If the excretions do not cause death immediately,   10
but settle round the lungs and windpipe—for they collect first in the upper part of
the body, because we are warmed by the air, for it is owing to this that ophthalmia
occurs before fever in an unhealthy summer—if then, as I have said, the excretions
in the upper parts of the body do not immediately kill the patient, they descend in an   15
unconcocted condition into the stomach; and thus dysentery is caused, because the
moisture owing to its abundance is not discharged. If the dysentery ceases, quartan
fevers arise in those patients who survive; for the sediment of the unconcocted
moisture remains very persistently in the body and becomes active, just like black
bile.   20

20 · Why is it that, if the summer and the autumn have been rainy and
damp, the ensuing winter is unhealthy? Is it because the winter finds the body in a
very moist state, and also the change from great heat is violent and not gradual,
because the autumn as well as the summer has been hot, and so acute diseases are   25
caused in some persons, if they have no rarity in their bodies (for in such persons the
moist excretions tend to collect in the upper part of the body, because these parts
provide room for them, whereas the lower parts differ in this respect)? Those then
whose flesh is solid do not allow of much excretion. When therefore the excretion in   30

⁵Reading οἷον.

the upper parts of the body cools (as happens in drunken persons when they grow cold), the above-mentioned diseases are engendered. On the other hand when fevers are set up in persons in whose bodies there is more rarity, the fevers caused by a large quantity of unconcocted moisture become burning fevers, because in such
35 people the humours are distributed more through the whole body than in solid-fleshed people, and, when the flesh is contracted by the winter-cold, the humours being heated cause fever. For excessive heat in the whole body is fever, and, when it
862ª1 is intensified by the abundance of moisture already present there, it turns into a burning fever.

21 · Why is it that when a large amount of vapour is drawn out of the earth
5 by the sun, the year is pestilential? Is it because it is necessarily a sign that the year is damp and rainy and the ground is necessarily damp? The conditions of life will then resemble those under which people live in a marshy district, and these are unhealthy. The body must then have in it an abundance of excretion and so contain unhealthy matter in the summer.

10 22 · Why is it that those years are unhealthy in which small toad-like frogs are produced in abundance? Is it because everything flourishes in its natural environment, and these frogs are naturally moist and so signify that the year is moist and damp? Now such years are unhealthy; for then the body being moist
15 contains abundant excretion, which is a cause of diseases.

23 · Why is it that south winds which are dry and do not bring rain cause fever? Is it because they cause alien moisture and heat (for they are naturally moist
20 and hot), and this is what causes fever, for it is due to the combined excess of moisture and heat? When therefore south winds blow without bringing rain, they engender this condition in us, whereas, when they bring rain with them, the rain cools us. Now south winds from the sea are also beneficial to plants, for they are
25 cooled by the sea before they reach them; whereas blight is due to alien moisture and heat.

24 · Why is it that men feel heavier and weaker when the wind is in the south? Is it because moisture becomes abundant instead of scanty, being melted by
30 the heat, and moisture, which is heavy, takes the place of breath, which is light? Further, our strength is in our joints, and they are relaxed by south winds (as is shown by the fact that things which have been glued together creak); for the viscous matter in the joints, if it hardens, prevents us from moving, whereas, if it is too moist, it prevents us from exerting ourselves.

35 25 · Why are people more liable to fall ill in the summer while those who are ill are more liable to die in the winter? Is it because in the winter, owing to the fact that the hot matter from its density becomes collected within the body and we suffer more through the excretions which solidify in us, if we cannot concoct them, the
862ᵇ1 commencement of the disease must necessarily be violent, and being of this

character it is likely to prove fatal? In the summer on the other hand, because the whole body is in a state of rarity and cool and too much relaxed for great exertion, there must necessarily be many commencements of disease owing to fatigue and to the fact that we do not concoct all that we swallow (for summer is the season of 5 fresh fruit); but such diseases are not so violent, and therefore yield easily to treatment.

26 · Why is it that deaths are particularly likely to occur during the hundred days following each solstice? Is it because in each case the excess of heat or cold extends over this period, and excess causes disease and death in the weakly? 10

27 · Why is it that the spring and the autumn are unhealthy? Is it because changes are unhealthy? The autumn is more unhealthy than the spring, because we are more apt to contract disease when heat turns to cold than when cold turns to heat, and it is in spring that cold turns to heat and in autumn that heat turns to 15 cold.

28 · Why is it that illnesses are rarer in the winter than in the summer, but more often fatal? Is it because illnesses arise from slight causes in the summer but not in the winter? For in winter we are in a better condition for concoction and at the very height of our health, so that naturally illnesses which arise from more 20 serious causes are themselves more serious and more likely to prove fatal. We see the same thing in athletes and generally among those who are in a healthy condition; for they either are not afflicted with disease, or, if they are, they rapidly succumb, for they only become ill from some serious cause.

29 · Why is it that in the autumn and winter burning fevers are more likely 25 to occur when the weather is cold, while in the summer chills are most troublesome when it is hot? Is it due to the fact that of the humours in man the bile is hot and the phlegm cold? As a result, in summer the cold matter is set free, and being diffused in the body gives rise to chill and shivering; in the winter, on the other hand, the hot 30 matter is overpowered by the weather and cooled. Burning fevers are more troublesome in the winter and autumn, because, owing to the cold, the hot matter collects within, and the fever is within and not on the surface; it is natural therefore that burning fevers should occur during this part of the year. This can be well illustrated by contrasting those who bathe in cold water and those who use warm 35 water in the winter; those who wash in cold water, though they feel chilled for a short time while they are actually washing, suffer no ill effects from the cold during the rest of the day, while those who use hot water continue to be less able to resist 863ᵃ1 the cold. For the flesh of those who wash in cold water becomes solid, and the hot matter collects within; but the flesh of those who use warm water becomes rare, and the hot matter is diverted to the outside of the body. 5

30 · In what does the virtue of a poultice consist? Would it, owing to its dissolvent action, set up perspiration and evaporation?

31 · How can the presence of an abscess be diagnosed? Is it true that, if, when hot water is poured over it, a change takes place, there is an abscess, but none if there is no change?

32 · In what cases ought cauterization to be employed, and in what cases the surgeon's knife? Is it true that wounds which have large openings and do not close up quickly ought to be cauterized, so that a scab may form? If this is done, there will be no festering.

33 · In what does the virtue of a remedy for stanching blood consist? Is it because it has a drying effect and stops the discharge of excretions without making a scab or causing decay of the flesh? If so, the wound must be free from inflammation and likely to heal up. For if there is no discharge, it will be free from inflammation, and being dry it will close up; whereas it will not close up as long as it is discharging moisture. Most remedies, therefore, for stanching blood are pungent, so as to cause contraction.

34 · When ought drugs to be employed and not the knife or cauterization? Ought drugs to be used for the armpits and groin? For sores in these parts are sometimes painful and sometimes dangerous after they are cut open. Flat growths and those which project considerably and are situated in parts which are venous and not fleshy, should be cauterized; but those which collect at an acute point and are not situated in solid parts of the body should be treated with the knife.

35 · Why is it that, if one is cut with a bronze instrument, the wound heals more quickly than if the cut is made with iron? Is it because bronze is smoother and so tears the flesh and bruises the body less? Or must we reject this explanation, since, if iron takes a better edge, the cleavage is easier and less painful? Yet even so bronze has a medicinal power of its own, and it is the beginning that is important, and so the drug, by its immediate action as soon as the cut is made, causes the wound to close up.

36 · Why is it that burns inflicted by bronze heal more quickly than others? Is it because bronze contains more rarity and is less substantial, and the more solid a thing is the more heat it contains?

37 · Is barley-gruel lighter and better for use in sickness than that made from wheat? For the latter commends itself to some people who argue from the fact that among bakers those who handle wheaten flour have a much better colour than those who employ barley meal, and furthermore that barley is moister and that which is moister requires more concoction. But is there any reason why barley should not have some qualities which make it more difficult of concoction and others which make it more serviceable because of its lightness? For barley is not only moister than wheat, but it is also colder, and porridge and any other food which is served to one who is in a fever ought to be such that it will provide him with a little

nourishment and also cool him. Now barley-gruel has these qualities; for, because it is moist rather than substantial, it gives nourishment which is small in bulk and at the same time has a cooling effect.   10

38 · Why do purslane and salt stop inflammation of the gums? Is it because purslane contains some moisture? This is seen if one chews it or if it is crushed together for some time; for the moisture is then drawn out of it. This glutinous matter sinks into the gum and drives out the acidity. For that there is an affinity between the disease and the remedy is shown by the acidity; for the juice of purslane   15 has a certain acidity. Salt on the other hand dissolves and draws out the acidity. Why then do lye and soda not have this effect? Is it because they have an astringent instead of a dissolvent action?

39 · Why is it that fatigue must be cured in summer by baths, in winter by anointing? Is anointing employed in the latter case because of the cold and the   20 changes which it causes in the body? For the fatigue must be got rid of by heat which will warm the body, and olive-oil contains heat. In summer, on the other hand, the body requires moisture, because the season is then dry and chills are not to be feared, because the natural inclination is towards heat. A sparing diet of solid food and a liberal indulgence in liquid nourishment are appropriate to the summer,   25 the latter being peculiar to summer, while the former is commoner then than at other seasons; for indulgence in drinking is peculiar to the summer because of the dryness of the season, but a sparing diet is found at all seasons but is more general in the summer; for then, owing to the weather, heat is engendered by food.

40 · Why do some drugs relax the stomach and not the bladder, others the   30 bladder and not the stomach? Is it true that anything which is naturally moist and full of water, if it has medicinal properties, relaxes the bladder? For it is there that the unconcocted moisture settles; for the bladder is a receptacle for any moisture which is not concocted in the stomach; and such moisture does not remain there, but passes away without undergoing or causing any change. But anything which partakes of the nature of earth, if it has medicinal properties, relaxes the stomach;   864^{a}1 for it is to the stomach that anything of an earthy nature is carried, so that, if it has any motive power, it causes a disturbance in the stomach.

41 · Why is it that some things affect the upper part of the stomach, hellebore for example, others the lower part, for instance scammony, while others like elaterium and the juice of thapsia affect both parts? Is it because some of the   5 drugs which affect the stomach are hot and others cold, so that some of them, owing to their heat, as soon as they reach the upper part of the stomach are carried thence to the upper region of the body, melting in particular anything there which is most alien to them and least substantial; and if the drug be powerful or has been administered in a dose stronger than nature can withstand, it carries these   10 liquefactions and any excretions that there may be down into the upper part of the stomach, and by its heat stirring up the breath, which it engenders in great quantity,

checks their progress and causes vomiting? Drugs of a cold nature, on the other hand, owing to their weight are carried downwards before undergoing or causing any change and, borne thence, have the same action as those which affect the upper part of the body; for passing thence upwards through the ducts and setting in motion any excretions or liquefactions over which they prevail, they carry them with them in the same direction. Drugs which partake of both these kinds and are a mixture of hot and cold, possessing both qualities, have both these effects, and are the composite drugs which doctors now make up.

42 · Why is it that drugs have a purgative effect, while other things, though they surpass them in bitterness and astringency and other such qualities, do not have this effect? Is it because the purgative effect is not due to these qualities but to the fact that they are unconcocted? For anything which, though small in bulk, owing to its excessive heat or cold is unconcocted and of such a nature as to overcome, and not be overcome by, animal heat, if it is easily dissolved in the two stomachs, is a drug. For when such drugs enter the stomach and become dissolved, they are carried into the vein by the ducts through which the food passes, and, not being concocted but themselves prevailing, they make their way out, carrying with them anything which gets in their way; and this is called purging. Bronze and silver and the like, although they are not concocted by animal heat, are not easily dissolved in the stomach. Oil and honey and milk and other such foods have a purgative effect; but this depends, not on any quality which they possess, but on quantity; for, if they act as a purge, they only do so when they are unconcocted owing to their quantity. For things can be unconcocted for two reasons, either because of their quality or because of their quantity. So none of the above-mentioned foods are drugs, because they do not purge owing to their quality. Astringency and bitterness and unpleasant odour are characteristic of drugs, because a drug is the opposite of a food; for that which is concocted by a natural process amalgamates with the body and is called a food; but that whose nature it is to refuse to be overcome and which enters into the veins and causes disturbance there owing to its excess of heat or cold, this is of the nature of a drug.

43 · Why is it that pepper if taken in large quantities relaxes the bladder, but if taken in small quantities affects the stomach, whereas scammony if taken in large quantities relaxes the stomach, but if taken in small quantities and when it is old affects the bladder? Is it because each has more effect on one part of the body? For pepper promotes urine, while scammony is purgative. Pepper therefore if taken in large quantities is carried into the bladder and does not dissolve in the stomach, but if taken in small quantities it is overcome and relaxes the stomach and acts upon it as a drug. Scammony, on the other hand, if it is taken in large quantities, is overcome to such an extent that it is dissolved, and being dissolved it becomes a drug for the reason mentioned above; but, if it is taken in small quantities, it is swallowed with what is drunk and passes into the ducts and is quickly carried into the bladder before it can cause any disturbance, and there by its own force it carries off all the excretions and liquefactions which are on the surface. When it is taken in large

quantities, as has already been remarked, owing to its strength it remains a long time in the stomach and effects an extensive purgation of the earthy element.

44 · Why do some cure by cooling the same inflammations which others bring to a head by heating them? Surely it is because the latter collect the inflammation by applying external heat, the former by cooling the heat already present in the body.   30

45 · Why is it necessary to change poultices? Is it in order that[6] they may be more felt? For as, in things which we eat, that to which we have grown accustomed no longer acts as a drug but becomes a food, so poultices lose their effect.   35

46 · Why does it promote health to reduce one's diet and increase one's exercise? Is it because an excess of excretion causes disease, and this occurs when we take too much nourishment or too little exercise?   865ª1

47 · Why is it that drugs, and bitter and evil-smelling substances generally, have a purgative effect? Is it because anything which is evil-smelling and bitter does not admit of concoction? Drugs therefore are bitter and evil-smelling; for they are   5
drugs because, in addition to being bitter, they do not admit of concoction and can cause motion; and if they are administered in too large doses, they are destructive of life. But substances which are destructive of life even if given in small quantities are not drugs but deadly poisons. Nor again do we give the name of drugs to those substances which are not purgative through their natural qualities; for indeed many   10
foods have the effect of drugs, if taken in sufficient quantity—milk, for example, and olive oil and unfermented wine; all these things, because they are not easily concocted, have a purgative effect on those by whom they are not easily concocted. For different things are easy or difficult of concoction to different people; and so the same things do not act upon every one as drugs, but particular things act upon certain people. For, generally speaking, a drug ought not only to be difficult of   15
concoction, but also ought to have the power to produce movement; just as also exercises, whether external or internal, expel alien matter.

48 · Why is it that sweet-smelling seeds or plants promote the flow of urine? Is it because they contain heat and are easily concocted, and such things have this   20
effect? For the heat in them causes quick digestion, and their odour has no corporeal existence; for even strong-smelling plants, such as garlic, promote the flow of urine owing to their heat, though their wasting effect is a still more marked characteristic; but sweet-smelling seeds contain heat.

49 · Why is it that unclean and foul sores require to be treated with dry,   25
pungent, and astringent drugs, while clean, healthy sores require moist, porous[7] remedies? Is it because something must be drawn out from unclean sores, and it is

---

[6]Reading ὅπως.
[7]Reading μανοῖς.

foreign moisture which must be extracted? Now biting, pungent, and astringent
30   substances have this effect, and the dry rather than the moist. Clean sores, on the
other hand, only require to skin over.

50 · Why is it that sexual excess is beneficial to diseases caused by phlegm?
Is it because the semen is the secretion of an excrement and in its nature resembles
phlegm, and so sexual intercourse is beneficial because it draws off a quantity of
phlegm-like matter?
35   Is it better to give the patient nourishment at first or later? Ought nourishment
to be given at the beginning, so that the inflammation, when it sets in, may not find
the patient already weak? Or ought the patient to be reduced at once? Or ought the
following to be the treatment, namely, that the patient should first take nourish-
865ᵇ1 ment in the form of draughts, since food of this kind is milder and more readily
swallowed and dissolved, and it is easier for a sick person to receive nourishment
from this sort of food? For where⁸ the food has first to be acted upon in the
stomach,—namely, both dissolved and heated—these processes cause pain to the
5   body.

51 · Why is it that, in order to examine urine to see if it is concocted, one
must stop the flow of urine rather than continue to pass it? Is it because it is a sign of
concoction if it is reddish in colour, and this is better detected if the flow is stopped?
10   Or is it because anything that is liquid forms as it were a better mirror of its colour
in a small than in a large quantity? For form is better discerned in a large quantity,
but colour in a small quantity, in dew, for example, and drops of rain and tears on
the eyelids. If urine, therefore, is allowed to flow it becomes greater in quantity, but,
15   if it is checked, it takes on colour more readily; and so if it has already taken on this
character by concoction, this can be better observed if the flow of urine is stopped
and light thus refracted and a mirror formed.

52 · Why should the flesh be made rare rather than dense in order to
promote health?⁹ For just as a city or locality is healthy which is open to the breezes
20   (and this is why the sea too is healthy), so a body is healthier in which the air can
circulate. For either there ought to be no excrement present in the body or else the
body ought to get rid of it as soon as possible and ought always to be in such a
condition that it can reject the excrement as soon as it receives it, and be in a state of
motion and never at rest. For that which remains stationary putrefies (standing
25   water, for example), and that which putrefies causes disease; but that which is
rejected passes away before it becomes corrupt. This then does not occur if the flesh
is dense, the ducts being as it were blocked up, but it does happen if the flesh is rare.
One ought not therefore to walk naked in the sun; for the flesh thereby solidifies and
30   acquires an absolutely fleshy consistency, and the body becomes moister; for the
internal moisture remains, but the surface moisture is expelled, a process which also
takes place in meat when it is roasted rather than boiled. Nor ought one to walk

---

⁸Reading οὐ.
⁹Reading διὰ τί.

about with the chest bare; for then the sun draws the moisture out of the best constructed parts of the body, which least of all require to be deprived of it. It is rather the inner parts of the body which should be submitted to this process; 35 because they are remote, it is impossible to produce perspiration from them except by violent effort, but it is easy to produce it from the chest because it is near the surface.

53 · Why is it that both cold and hot water are beneficial to chilblains? Is it 866ᵃ1 because chilblains are caused by an excess of moisture? If so, the cold water thickens and hardens the moisture, while the hot water causes it to evaporate and enables the vapour to escape by rarefying the flesh.

54 · Why is it that cold both causes and stops chilblains, and heat both 5 causes and stops burns? Is the cause the same in both cases, namely, that they cause them by setting up liquefaction and stop them by drying them up?

55 · In fevers liquid nourishment ought to be administered often and in small quantities. For a large quantity flows away and is wasted, but a small quantity taken frequently sinks in and penetrates into the flesh. For as the rain, if it comes 10 down upon the earth in torrents, runs to waste, but, if it comes down in small quantities, merely moistens the ground; so the same thing occurs in fever patients. In irrigation, if the water is allowed to flow gradually, the channel sucks it up; whereas, if the same amount of water is allowed to flow all at once, it makes its way wherever it is directed.

Next the patient ought to lie as still as possible, because fire also obviously dies 15 down if one does not stir it. And he ought not to lie in a draught, because the wind stirs up the fire, and, being fanned, it becomes great instead of small. For this reason the patient ought to be well wrapped up, because fire is extinguished if it is not 20 allowed to draw in air; and the garments ought not to be removed until damp heat is present, for the fire if exposed to the air dries up the moisture—just as happens also in nature.

In the case of intermittent fevers one must make preparations beforehand by washing[10] the patient and applying fomentations to his feet, and he must rest well 25 wrapped up, in order that there may be as much heat as possible in him before the attack begins. For a flame will not be able to burn where there is a great fire; for the great fire will absorb the little fire. Consequently a great fire must be prepared beforehand in the body; for fever has but little fire in it, and so the great fire will absorb the little fire. 30

56 · In quartan fevers the patient must not be allowed to get thin, and heat must be introduced and engendered in his body. Exercises must also be employed. On the day on which the attack is expected he must bathe himself and avoid sleep. A heating diet is beneficial, because a quartan fever is weak; for if it were not so, it 35

---

[10]Reading ἐκλούοντα.

would not occur only every fourth day. For, mark you, where there is a great fire, a flame cannot burn; for the great fire attracts and absorbs the little fire. For this reason it is necessary to engender great heat in the body, because fever has but little fire in it. The daily treatment consists in introducing at one time heat and at another time moisture into the body. Some diseases are caused by heat, others by moisture; those which are caused by heat are cured by moisture, and those which are due to moisture are cured by heat, for heat dries up moisture.

BOOK II
PROBLEMS CONNECTED
WITH PERSPIRATION

1 · Why is it that perspiration is caused neither when the breath is expanded nor when it is held in, but rather when it is relaxed? Is it because, when it is held in, the breath fills out the veins and so does not allow the perspiration to escape, just as the water in a water clock cannot escape if you turn it off when the clock is full? But when the perspiration does come out, it does so in great abundance, because it has gradually collected during the actual period that it has been checked.

2 · Why is it that the parts of the body that are immersed in hot water do not perspire, even though they are themselves hot? Is it because the water prevents liquefaction, while perspiration is formed when matter which is not properly attached to the flesh[1] is expelled by heat?

3 · Why is perspiration salty? It is because it is caused by movement and heat which rejects any foreign matter in the process by which nourishment passes into blood and flesh? For such matter quickly separates, because it has no affinity with the body, and evaporates externally. It is salty because the sweetest and lightest part of the food is taken up by the body, while the unsuitable and unconcocted part is discharged. This when it is excreted below is called urine, in the flesh it is sweat; both of these are salty for the same reason.

4 · Why is it that the upper parts of the body perspire more freely than the lower? It is because heat rises upwards and remains there, and this carries the moisture upwards? Or is it because breath causes sweat, and the breath is in the upper parts of the body? Or is it because sweat is unconcocted moisture, and such moisture resides in the upper parts because the process of its composition takes place there?

[1]Omitting ὃ κωλύει τήκεσθαι.

5 · Why is it that sweat is produced most copiously if we exercise the arms while we keep the other parts of the body in the same position? Is it because we have most strength in this region of the body? For it is in this region, which is nearest to 35 the strongest part of us, that we hold our breath; and we gain strength by violent exertion, and, having gained strength, we can hold the breath more easily. Furthermore, we feel the effect of friction more in the arm than when any other part 867ª1 of the body is rubbed; for it is by holding the breath that we get exercise, both when we are rubbed and when we rub.

6 · Why is it that sweat given off from the head either has no odour or less than that from the body? Is it because air circulates freely in the region of the head? 5 That the head possesses rarity is shown by the fact that it produces hair. And it is those regions of the body and the substances of which they are composed through which the air does not circulate that are malodorous.

7 · Why is it that those who take athletic exercise, if they wrestle after a period of rest, perspire more freely than if they wrestle continuously? Is it because the sweat collects while they are resting, and then the wrestling afterwards brings 10 out this sweat? Continuous exercise, on the other hand, dries up the sweat, just as does the heat of the sun.

8 · Why is it that one sweats more freely if one has not for a long time employed means to induce perspiration? Is it because sweat is not caused by moisture alone, but is also due to the fact that the pores are opened wider and the 15 body becomes porous? In those, therefore, who take no measures to induce perspiration the pores become closed up, whereas if they do take such measures the pores are kept open.

9 · Why is it that, although the sun warms those who are naked more than those who are clothed, the latter perspire more freely? Is it because the sun by burning causes the pores to close up? Or is it because it dries up the moisture? 20 These processes are less likely to happen in those who are clothed.

10 · Why is it that the face gives off the most perspiration? Is it because the sweat can find a way out through parts which are particularly porous and moist? Now the head seems to be the source of moisture, and it is owing to the presence of 25 copious moisture that the hair grows; and the region of the head is rare and porous, and so the sweat naturally finds a way out.

11 · Why is it that one perspires most freely, not when the heat is applied all at once or when it is gradually diminished, but when it is gradually increased? For those who are in vapour baths perspire under these conditions more freely than if all 30 the heat be applied at once. Is it because it is the presence of anything in proper proportions which produces each required effect, and so, if it produces this effect, its presence in greater quantity will not produce a greater effect, or will rather produce

the contrary effect, for it is because a thing is proportionate that it produces a certain effect? For this reason then increased perspiration is not induced as the result of greater heat; but because to each increment of heat there answers a 35 different proportion, and that which has already produced its effect produces no greater effect, increased perspiration is rather the result of successive additions of heat. For it is not the same cause which prepares the way and creates a favourable condition for a series of effects and then begins to produce the effect, but a different cause. So a small quantity of heat prepares the way and predisposes the body to 867^{b}1 perspire better than a large quantity; but another and a greater proportion is required actually to produce the perspiration, but this does not continue to produce the effect which it originally produced, but must be followed by another application of heat different again in its proportions.

12 · Why does the sweat flow more freely if a scraper be used than if it be 5 allowed to remain on the body? Is it because the presence of external sweat induces cooling? Or is it because the external sweat forms as it were a lid over the pores and so prevents the movement of the internal sweat?

13 · Why is it that rue and certain unguents give the perspiration an evil 10 odour? Is it because things which have a heavy scent, mixing with the excretory fluids, make the odour of these still more unpleasant?

14 · Why do we perspire more on the back than on the front of the body? Is it because in the front of the body there is an interior region into which the moisture is drained, but this is not the case with the back, but there the excretion of moisture 15 must be external? (It is for the same reason that we perspire less on the stomach than on the chest.) A further reason is the fact that the back and hinder parts hold the perspiration more than the front, because the latter become more cooled than the former. (This is the reason too why the armpits perspire most readily and freely; 20 for they are least subject to cooling.) Further, the regions about the back are fleshier than those in front and therefore moister; and there is more moisture in the hinder parts, because the marrow in the spine causes considerable humidity.

25 15 · Why is it that we do not perspire in those parts of the body on which we are lying? Is it because the area with which we come into contact with anything is hot and therefore prevents the perspiration from passing forth, for it dries it up? Furthermore it is compressed, and pressure causes the blood to disperse, and, when this happens, the part tends to become cool. This can be illustrated from numbness, 30 which is a condition due to cooling and is caused by pressure or by a blow.

16 · Why do those who are asleep perspire more freely? Is it due to the heat being driven inwards? For the heat collects inside and expels the moisture.

17 · Why is it that one perspires most freely on the face, though it is far from 35 being fleshy? Is it because parts which are rather moist and rare perspire freely, and

the head has these characteristics? For it possesses an abundance of natural moisture; this is shown by the veins which extend from it and the discharges which it produces and the brain-fluid and the numerous pores. That there are numerous pores extending outwards is shown by the presence of the hair. The perspiration then comes not from the lower parts of the body but from the head; and so one 868ª1 perspires most readily and freely on the forehead, for it is the first thing below the top of the head, and moisture flows down and not up.

18 · Why is it that those who are perspiring are apt to vomit if they are 5 cooled either by water or by air? Is it because the moisture when cooled ceases to move and collects together, whereas before it was not at rest because it was in a state of flux? Or is it because the breath which turns into perspiration by being cooled as it passes out, being cooled internally before passing out turns into moisture and, attacking the body, causes vomiting?

19 · Why is it that sweat is given off from the head and feet of those who are 10 heated more freely than from any other part of the body? Is it because the part which is heated attracts the moisture to itself, and the moisture has nowhere where it can expend itself in these regions of the body, because they are bony, and therefore it finds its way out?

20 · Why do those who exert themselves perspire when they cease to exert 15 themselves? For since the exertion is the cause, they ought to perspire while they are exerting themselves. Is it because during their exertion the veins, being inflated with breath, cause the pores to close up, whereas, when they stop, the veins contract, and so the pores become wider and the moisture finds an easier outlet? Or is it because during the exertion the motion expels air from the solidified moisture and, 20 owing to the heat caused by the motion, the moisture becomes breath on the surface of the body; while on the other hand, when the exertion ceases, the heat also stops at the same time, and then the moisture, which we call perspiration, is generated from the condensation of the breath? 25

21 · Is it more necessary to induce perspiration in the summer or in the winter? Is it not more necessary to do so at a time when, unless care be taken, the body would become too moist and in a dangerous condition? If so, it would be more necessary to perspire in the summer,[2] when a violent change takes place in the body and the excretions are not thoroughly concocted. Again in the winter, since the body 30 is cool, it is also unnatural to perspire. It is clearly, therefore, more necessary to induce perspiration in the summer; for moisture of all kinds is then more apt to putrefy and should therefore be drawn off. This was the opinion of all the ancients and for the above reason.

22 · Why is it that, although the body is in a state of continual flux, and 35 effluvia are given off from the excrements, the body is only lightened if it perspires?

---

[2]Reading θέρους for χειμῶνος.

Is it because the excretion in the form of effluvia is too little? For when liquid is transformed into air, much air is formed out of little liquid; for what is excreted in 868ᵇ1 liquid form is more abundant. The process of excretion, therefore, takes longer to begin, both for the above reason and because the excretion takes place through smaller pores. Further, the viscous and adhesive matter is expelled with the moisture, because it mingles with it, but it cannot be expelled with the breath; and it 5 is this thick matter in particular that causes pain. Therefore also vomiting lightens the body more than sweating, because that which is vomited, being thicker and more substantial, carries away this viscous matter with it. Or is there a further reason, namely, that the region in which the viscous and the adhesive matter is, is situated at a distance in relation to the flesh (and so it is difficult to make it change 10 its position), but near the stomach? For it is engendered either in or close to it; and therefore it is difficult to get rid of it in any other way.

23 · Why is it that one perspires less during actual exertion than when one ceases? Is it because while one is exerting oneself one is engendering perspiration, but the process of engendering it is only complete when the exertion is ended? This then is naturally the time when it is expelled from the body in greater quantities; for during exertion it is coming into being, but, when the exertion is finished, it actually 15 exists. Or is it because during exertion the pores of the flesh are closed, because the breath is held, but when the pressure of the breath is relaxed the pores open again? Consequently one perspires less when one is holding the breath.

24 · Why is it that perspiration is more copious not when one is running and the body is in motion, but when one stops? Is it because the same thing happens as 20 when flowing water is checked by the hand or by some other means and collects from every direction, and, when it is released, flows in greater volume than before; so perspiration can be stopped by the breath—like water in a water clock—and also 25 in the bladder, which keeps the moisture within. So too, while there is considerable movement, the breath is cut off inside the body, and so the veins are distended, the moisture being unable to find its way out. The moisture then, being cut off, collects, and when the breath is relaxed comes all out at once.

25 · Why is it that, when one is drinking, one perspires less if one eats 30 something as well? Is it because the food sucks up the moisture, as though a sponge were applied, and, just as a stream can be stopped by blocking up its channels, so by stopping³ the pores through administering food it is possible to a large extent to prevent the flowing of moisture?

26 · Why is that the feet of those who are nervous perspire and not the face? 35 For it would be more natural that the feet should perspire only when the whole body perspires; for the feet are the coldest region of the body and therefore least liable to

³Reading τῷ ἐπιλαβεῖν.

perspire. Also in sickness physicians order the feet in particular to be wrapped up, because they are especially susceptible to cold and so readily give rise to cold in the rest of the body also. Is it because nervousness does not cause a displacement of 869ᵃ1 heat—such as takes place from the upper to the lower parts of the body under the influence of fear (hence the relaxation of the bowels in those who are alarmed)—but an increase of heat such as is caused by anger? For anger causes the heat round the heart to boil up; and one who is nervous is affected not by fear or cold, but by an 5 increase of heat.[4]

27 · How is it that one can become red in the face without perspiring? Is it due to excessive warmth which results in the heat on the surface drying up the 10 moisture in the face, while it liquefies the moisture in the feet because, though less than the heat on the surface, it is more powerful than the natural heat already existent in the feet?

28 · Why is it that we perspire more when asleep than when awake? Is it because perspiration originates internally, and the interior parts of the body are hotter, and so the internal heat melts and expels the internal moisture? Or[5] is it 15 because in all probability there is always something given off from the body, but it is not apparent because there is nothing with which it can come into contact and by which its escape can be arrested? That this is so is shown by the fact that the hollow parts of the body perspire continually.

29 · Why is it that persons in vapour baths perspire more freely when it is cold? Is it because the heat does not find a way out, because it is surrounded by the 20 cold, which prevents its exit, but collects internally, and, remaining there, dissolves the moisture in our body and engenders perspiration from it?

30 · Why is it that perspiration, even though it be less profuse, is more beneficial if it be induced by running naked rather than clothed? Is it because 25 exertion in general is better than non-exertion, and perspiration which is induced by exertion is better than that which is produced without exertion, and that which is due in a greater degree to exertion is better than that which is due in a less degree? Now perspiration involves more exertion if induced by running about naked: for a naked man cannot perspire at all unless he runs with considerable energy; whereas, 30 if he be clothed, owing to the heat produced by his garments, he soon perspires although he runs only moderately fast. Those too who run naked in the summer have a healthier colour than those who wear garments; for just as those who live in regions open to the air have a better colour than those who live in a stifling 35 atmosphere, so too a man, when he is as it were in a well-aired condition, acquires a better colour than when he is stifled and surrounded by considerable heat, as he is more likely to be when he runs clothed. For this reason too those who sleep much 869ᵇ1

[4]Reading διὰ τὸ μᾶλλον ἐκθερμαίνεσθαι.
[5]Reading ἢ ὅτι.

have a less healthy colour than those who sleep a moderate amount; for a man who is asleep is in a stifled condition.

31 · Why is it that our feet perspire, but not our faces, when we are in a state of nervousness, whereas under ordinary conditions our faces perspire most and our feet least? Is it because nervousness is a kind of fear connected with the beginning of an action, and fear causes a cooling in the upper part of the body; this is also why those who are nervous are pale-faced. On the other hand they move and dance their feet about, thus resembling those who are taking exercise; therefore they naturally perspire in those parts which they are exercising. Also they rub their hands together and bend and stretch themselves and keep jumping up and can never remain still; for they are eager for action, because the heat within them is collected in the region of the chest, which is one of the more substantial parts of the body, and this heat and the blood rushing thence through their whole body results in frequent and varied movement. But they perspire most in the feet, because these are being continually exerted, whereas the other parts of the body obtain rest in the changes of position and movement.

32 · Why is it that in a vapour bath one perspires most freely not when the heat is applied all at once nor when it is gradually diminished, but when it is gradually increased? For if the heat is gradually introduced into the vapour bath, one perspires more freely than if the full amount were admitted at first. Is it because heat which is great from the beginning, finding the flesh on the surface dry, burns the skin and bakes it hard, and the flesh when it is in this condition holds the perspiration within?[6] Less heat on the other hand tends to relax and rarefy the flesh and as it were stimulates the internal moisture to separate itself and come forth. This condition being established, when more heat is gradually introduced and penetrates deep into the flesh owing to its rarity, it vaporizes the already softened humours and separating those which are light expels them with the breath.

33 · Is it more necessary to induce perspiration in the summer or in the winter? In winter does not the heat collecting within the body concoct and vaporize our internal humours, and so, because all or most of them are expended, there is no need to supply an appropriate method of expelling them? In the summer, on the other hand, because the flesh is in a state of rarity, the heat escapes and our internal humours become less concocted and therefore need to be drawn off. For if they are allowed to remain, they putrefy owing to the season and cause disease; for anything that putrefies does so owing to heat that is not its own, whereas its own natural heat causes concoction. Consequently in the summer the external heat prevails, and so everything within the body tends to putrefy; but in the winter the natural heat predominates, and so the winter does not cause putrefaction.

34 · Why is it that, whereas perspiration is due to internal heat or else to

[6]Reading στέγει.

heat attacking the body from without, yet we sometimes shiver while we perspire? Is it because, when owing to the internal heat the perspiration is expelled from a large area into a small space, it collects[7] on the surface of the body and entirely blocks up the channels through which the heat circulates, and so shivering ensues?   10 Another reason is that the flesh becomes saturated and the heat escapes. On the other hand the external heat attacking the flesh at first rarefies it, and then the internal natural heat as it is given off causes the shivering.

35 · Why are hot sweats considered to be better than cold? Is it because all   15 perspiration is the rejection of some excretion, and it is natural that a small excretion should become heated, whereas a more abundant excretion is less likely to do so, and so a cold sweat would be an indication of a copious excretion; consequently the disease, the presence of which it indicates, is likely to last longer?   20

36 · Why is it that, although perspiration is caused by heat, we perspire less in front of a large fire? Is it because, when the body is subjected to considerable heat, the humours are dissolved into vapour; or else we do not feel the moisture, because it makes its way out and quickly dries on the surface?   25

37 · Why is it that, though the sun heats us more if we wear no clothing, yet we perspire[8] more freely when we are clothed? To this we shall give the same answer as to the last problem.

38 · Why is it that, though brisk movements are generally regarded as more heating than slow movements, walking up a steep hill, which is a slower movement,   30 induces more perspiration and obstructs the breathing, as though it were more heating than walking down hill? Is it because it is natural for heavy things to be carried downwards and unnatural for them to be carried upwards? Consequently the nature of the heat which carries us along does not undergo any strain when we   35 are going down hill, but has to bear a continual burden when we are walking up hill; and so it grows exceedingly hot by movement of this kind and causes more profuse perspiration and obstructs the breath. The bending, too, of the body involved in walking up hill contributes to prevent the free passage of the breath by obstructing   870^b1 it.

39 · Why is it that, although more perspiration is induced by additional clothing, it is not those who wear most clothing that perspire most? To this question we shall give the same answer as we gave above.   5

40 · Why is it that, although our bodies are drier in the summer than in the winter, we are more disposed to perspire in the summer? Is it because, our bodies

---

[7]Reading συστελλομένοι.
[8]Reading ἱδρῶτες μᾶλλον.

being in a condition of rarity in the summer, not much natural heat is contained in them? This, therefore, dissolves the humours into vapour. In the winter on the
10 contrary, our bodies being externally in a dense condition, the considerable amount of natural heat enclosed within does not dissolve the humours into vapour. Moreover, in the summer we swallow liquid in large quantities, but in small quantities in the winter.

41 · Why is it that in healthy persons spontaneous perspiration is not
15 considered to be as good as that produced by exertion? Is it because exertion continually drains off the superfluous moisture and makes the flesh drier, so that the hollows of the pores are healthy and there is no obstruction to the straining off of
20 the heat? On the other hand the so-called spontaneous perspiration (which really occurs of necessity when the natural pores are disturbed by excessive moisture, and the heat is not completely retained, but can still resist and expel the moisture) is rightly regarded as a sign of disease. For then, owing to the presence of a more than
25 proportionate amount of moisture, a natural process of cooling takes place, and the flesh becoming saturated assumes a most unhealthy condition.

42 · Why is it that in the winter perspiration is given off less freely and we do not feel the same desire to induce it, although our bodies are moister in the winter?
30 Do we perspire less, because in winter our humours are congealed and solidified to a considerable extent, and are consequently less easily dissolved? The reason why we do not think it necessary to induce perspiration in the winter is because the condition in which we are is a healthy one, and any one who induces perspiration dissolves and upsets that condition; moreover, by creating in the body a condition of
35 greater rarity than it ought to have, he expels and reduces the natural heat, so that it cannot so effectively resist the surrounding cold; also external moisture will more easily burst its way into the body when the pores are rarefied by process of perspiration.

BOOK III

PROBLEMS CONNECTED WITH THE DRINKING
OF WINE AND DRUNKENNESS

871ª1   1 · Why is it that, though wine is hot, the drunken are unable to endure cold and are very readily attacked by pleurisy and similar diseases? Is it because a large quantity of moisture, if it be cooled, forms a mass of cold and so overpowers the
5 natural heat? For this is similar to what happens when, if a garment is soaked in cold water, the flesh beneath it also becomes cold.

2 · Why is it that it is not those who are very drunk that are most troublesome in their cups, but those who are only half blotto? Is it because they

have neither drunk so little that they still resemble the sober nor so much that they
are in the incapacitated state of those who have drunk deep? Further, those who are   10
sober have more power of judgement, while those who are very drunk make no
attempt to exercise their judgement; but those who are only half blotto can still
exercise their judgement because they are not very drunk, but they exercise it badly
because they are not sober, and they are ready to despise some of their neighbours
and imagine that they are being slighted by others.   15

3 · Why is it that those who drink slightly diluted wine have worse hangovers
than those who drink wine absolutely unmixed? Is it because owing to its lightness
diluted wine penetrates better into more numerous and narrower parts of the body
than unmixed wine, and so is less easy to get rid of? Or is it because those who drink   20
unmixed wine drink a less quantity, because it is impossible to drink more, and
vomit more readily? Furthermore unmixed wine, being hotter, causes concoction in
other things and in itself; whereas watery wine has the opposite effect.

4 · Why is the semen of drunkards generally infertile? Is it because the
composition of their body has become full of moisture, and the semen is fertile not   25
when it is liquid but when it has body and consistency?

5 · Why do drunkards tremble, and more so the more they drink unmixed
wine? Now wine is heating; but trembling is chiefly due to cold, and so those who
are chilled tremble very much. Yet many people before now, who have taken   30
unmixed wine as their only form of nourishment, have been seized with such violent
trembling as to throw off those who were trying to hold them down; and when they
wash in hot water, they have no perception of it. Is it because trembling is due to
cooling, and cooling takes place either when the heat is driven within by external
cold, as happens in winter, or when the natural heat is extinguished either by its   35
opposite or by lapse of time, as in old age, or by the excess of extraneous heat which
is caused in that which is exposed to the sun or to a blazing fire? This occurs also in
those who take unmixed wine. The wine, being hot, when on mingling with the
proper heat of the body it exceeds it in power,[1] quenches the bodily heat; and the   871[b]1
heat being thus extinguished and the body cooled, trembling ensues. But there is
also another process of cooling differing from all those described above; namely,
when the matter whereby the heat in anything is fed is removed, and, as a result,   5
the heat dies down. This can be illustrated in the inanimate world from the lamp; for
when the oil is expended, the light goes out; and in living beings old age and long,
wasting diseases have a similar effect. For when that which feeds the heat is   10
removed or diminished, the result is that the heat fails;[2] for heat is fed by moisture,
not, however, by any kind of moisture but by that which is smooth and fat.[3] In those,
therefore, who are suffering from the diseases mentioned above and in those who
are growing old, when moisture of this kind becomes corrupted and changed

[1] Reading ὑπερτείνῃ τῇ δυνάμει.
[2] Reading ἐκλείπειν.
[3] Reading πίονι.

15 (becoming harsh and dry instead of smooth and oily), as a result the heat fails. A proof of the above is afforded by the treatment applied to those who are wasting to death; for, whenever they have any nourishing liquid administered to them, the result is that their vitality[4] is revived, which implies that their bodily dissolution is
20 due to the lack of such a substance. The same cause seems to operate in those who drink unmixed wine. For the wine, being warm, co-operating with the heat already naturally present in the body, tends to use up the supply already present in the body
25 for the natural heat; consequently some drunkards become dropsical, others rheumatic, while in others the stomach is affected. For the other humours in them are harsh, and what they imbibe, being soft, does not acquire consistency owing to the weakness of the natural heat. Their heat is weak because the matter in which it
30 is still contained is itself weak; like a fire fed by reeds, which, because its material is weak, is weaker than a wood-fire.

6 · Why is it that, though wine is hot, the drunken are unable to endure cold and are very readily attacked by pleurisy and similar diseases? Is it because a large
35 quantity of moisture, if it be cooled, forms a mass of cold, and so overpowers the natural heat? Now the moister anything is the hotter it is by nature, as is shown by the fact that external agencies cause heat but do not cause liquefaction; but where there is less heat, it is clear that either the heat or the moisture is failing too quickly,
872ᵃ1 and so, cold humours only being left, it is natural that the drunken should be colder and show the proper symptoms of chill.

7 · Why is it that children, who have a hot temperament, are not fond of wine, although the Scythians and all who are courageous are fond of wine because
5 they have a hot temperament? Is it because the latter, though they are hot, are also dry (for this is the natural condition of a man), whereas children are hot and moist? Now fondness for drink is due to a desire for moisture; and so their moist condition prevents children from being thirsty, for desire is a lack of something.

10 8 · Why is it that men are more sensitive to salty and bad water when they are drunk than when they are sober? Is it because that which is like and similarly constituted is unaffected by its like, but opposites are very sensitive to opposites? A drunken man then has sweet liquids in him (for such seems to be the nature of
15 wine), and so is more sensitive to bad liquids; but the sober man has harsh and salty liquids in him, and so, when his food becomes concocted, the excretory humours come to the surface and these are unaffected by their like and cause the man in whose body they are to be similarly unaffected.

9 · Why is it that to those who are very drunk everything seems to revolve in
20 a circle, and as soon as the wine takes hold of them they cannot see objects at a distance, and so this is used by some as a test of drunkenness? Is it because the vision is continually disturbed by the heat of the wine? It makes no difference then

----

[4]Reading συμβαίνει τὸ ζωτικόν.

whether it is the vision that is disturbed or the object seen; for the result is the same in producing the above-mentioned phenomenon. And since the vision of drunken persons is often mistaken about objects near at hand, it is only natural that it should   25 be even more so in looking at distant objects. So the latter are not visible to them at all, while objects near at hand are not seen in their proper places, but appear to revolve in a circle and not to be near or far,because the circular motion makes it less possible for the sight to be directed towards distant objects; for it is difficult to do   30 two contrary things at the same time. Now distant vision is movement in a straight line,[5] but circular vision is restricted to the area implied by its name. For the above-mentioned reasons then the vision does not travel to a distance. Secondly, if it could travel to both near and distant objects, it would not see them, for that which was seen in the same place would fail at the next moment, and, if it did so,[6] the eye   35 could not see it. The circular movement is due to the present constitution of his sight; for it is a cone, the base of which is a circle, and, moving in this circle, the sight always sees the same thing,[7] because it never fails, but it is deceived as to its   872[b]1 position, because it never directs the same glance upon it; for just the same thing would happen whether the object moved in relation to the eye or the eye in relation to the object.

10 · Why is it that to those who are drunk one thing at which they are looking sometimes appears to be many? Is it because, as has already been   5 remarked, the vision is disturbed, with the result that the same glance does not rest on the same object for any length of time? Now that which is seen differently at the same time appears to exist later in time; for that which is seen is seen by contact with the vision, and it is impossible for several objects to be in contact with the same thing at the same time. But because the intervening time, during which the vision   10 comes into contact with and passes away from the object seen, is imperceptible, the moment during which it has been in contact and passed away seems to be one; and so when several glances come into contact with the same object at the same time, the objects seen appear to be several, because it is impossible for the glances to be in contact with the same[8] thing at the same time.[9]

11 · Why is it that those who are drunk are incapable of having sexual   15 intercourse? Is it because to do so a certain part of the body must be in a state of greater heat than the rest, and this is impossible in the drunken owing to the large quantity of heat present in the whole body; for the heat set up by the movement is extinguished by the greater surrounding heat, because they have in them a considerable quantity of unconcocted moisture? Furthermore the semen is derived   20 from food and all food is concocted, and those who are satiated with food are more inclined for sexual intercourse. This is why some people say that with a view to the

[5]Reading ἐπ' εὐθείας φορά.
[6]Reading ἀπολεῖπον.   [7]Reading ταὐτό.
[8]Reading ταὐτοῦ for ταῦτα.
[9]Reading χρόνον for τρόπον.

sexual act one ought to take a plenteous midday meal but a light supper, so that
25   there may be less unconcocted than concocted matter in the body.

12 · Why is it that sweet wine and unmixed wine and mead if drunk from
time to time during a drinking bout make men sober? And why do those who drink
from large vessels become less drunk? Is the reason in all cases the same, namely
30   the repression of heat on the surface of the body? For drunkenness takes place when
the heat is in the region of the head.

13 · Why is it that, though that which is sweet tends to rise to the surface, if
any one who is already drunk takes a sweet draught the wine which he has drunk
before is concocted and causes less discomfort? Is it because that which is sweet is
35   both soothing and adhesive (which is the reason why it blocks up the pores), while
that which is bitter has a roughening effect? The latter makes it easy for the heat to
rise, but the sweet draught keeps it in by blocking up the pores; and it has already
873ᵃ1   been remarked that drunkenness is due to the upper parts of the body becoming
heated. Furthermore sweet wine is odourless, but bitter wine is not, and any odour
oppresses the head.

14 · Why is it that wine which is mixed but tends towards the unmixed
5   causes a worse headache the next morning than entirely unmixed wine? Is it
because unmixed wine is composed of heavy particles and so does not find its way
into the pores of the head, which are narrow, but only its power, namely its odour
and heat, reaches the head? Diluted wine on the other hand, being mixed with
water, which is light, itself penetrates to the head and having body, as well as much
10   of the power of unmixed wine, is much less easily concocted; for moist things are
most difficult of all to concoct, and actual substances are more difficult of
concoction than their powers.

15 · Why is it that those who do not take physical exercise are better able to
drink themselves into a condition of drunkenness, and throw it off more easily, than
15   those who take such exercise? Is it because those who have excretions and moisture
in their bodies are more inclined to pass urine? This enables them to drink and
afterwards to be relieved of the effects, because much vinous moisture does not
remain in them. Those who take no exercise are moist and full of excretions; but
those who do take exercise are dry, and so the vinous moisture penetrates into their
20   body, and its impetus immediately checks the flow of urine, and the moisture
remaining afterwards behind forms a weight in the body.

16 · Why has wine the effect both of stupefying and of driving to frenzy
those who drink it? For these are contrary states, the frenzied being in a state of
excessive movement and the stupefied in a condition of too little movement. Is it
25   true, as Chaeremon says, that

Wine mingles with the temper of the drinker?

It therefore has the opposite effect not on the same but upon the unlike, just as fire dries up some things but liquefies others, but does not have both these effects on the same things—for instance it melts ice, but hardens salt. So wine, being in its nature moist, excites the slow and makes them quicker, while it ener- 30 vates the quick. Therefore some of those who are naturally of a melancholic temperament become entirely enervated as the result of a drunken debauch. For just as a bath makes supple those who have a well-knit and hard frame, while it relaxes those who are supple and moist, so wine has this effect, acting 35 as an internal bath.

17 · Why is it that cabbage stops hangovers? Is it because its juice is sweet and has a cleansing effect (and so doctors use it to purge the bowels), while in itself 873ᵇ1 it is cold? This is shown by the fact that doctors use it in cases of acute diarrhoea, boiling it thoroughly and draining off the juice[10] and letting it cool. In those with hangovers the effect of the juice of cabbage is to draw off the internal humours, 5 which are vinous and unconcocted, into the stomach, while the cabbage itself remains in the upper part of the stomach and cools the body. As the body cools, the light humours are carried into the bladder. Thus since the humours throughout the body are expelled by these two methods and it becomes cool, hangovers naturally 10 vanish; for wine is moist and hot. A further result of the humours being drawn downwards and expelled is that breath is thereby carried down into the body, and it is only from there that breath can be carried from the wine into the head and cause stupor and hangovers. But if the breath is carried downwards and the body cooled in 15 the manner mentioned above, the pain of the hangover is relieved. For the hangover is due to a seething and to inflammation as it dies down; but it is more painful than drunkenness, because the latter drives men out of their senses, but the hangover causes them pain when they are in full possession of their wits. Just as those who are 20 in a fever are delirious rather than in pain, but feel pain when they are relieved of the fever and recover their senses; for just the same thing happens with hangovers and drunkenness.

18 · Why is it that watery wine is more apt to cause vomiting than water and than unmixed wine? Is it because anything that tends to rise to the surface and is 25 unpleasant to the taste is most likely to cause vomiting? Now wine has the effect of repression; while water is light and not unpleasant, and, therefore, being light[11] it quickly penetrates downwards, but, not being unpleasant, it does not cause heartburn. Now excessively diluted wine is not light enough to percolate through 30 quickly, and because it has a little wine in it, it is unpleasant; for it disturbs the sense of taste by setting up two kinds of movement, one produced by the wine and the other by the water, both of which make themselves felt. But the proper mixing of wine does away with the taste of water and gives the wine a soft taste, which makes

[10]Reading ἀποχυλίζοντες.
[11]Omitting καὶ οὐκ ἀηδές.

35   it pleasant to drink. But watery wine, being unpleasant to the taste, has a tendency to rise, and anything which does this is apt to cause vomiting.

874ᵃ1   **19** · Why is it that men are more sensitive to salty and bad water when they are drunk than when they are sober? Is it because anything which has an unpleasant taste is more perceptible to those who feel no desire, but is not noticed by those who feel desire? A man therefore who is in a state of lacking something[12] resembles one who feels a desire, and the sober man is in this condition; whereas the drunken man is satiated.

5   **20** · Why is it that to those who are very drunk everything seems to revolve in a circle, and as soon as the wine takes hold of them they cannot count objects at a distance, and so this is used by some as a test of drunkenness? Is it because the vision is continually disturbed by the heat of the wine? The same thing then
10   happens to those who are drunk as when an object appears double if one puts it close to the eye. For it makes no difference if you move the eye instead of[13] putting the object close to it, and whether the movement is within the eye or outside it; for the effect on the vision is the same in both cases. The result will be that the object seen appears not to be at rest, and more so if it is at a distance (for it has less hold upon
15   the vision when the latter is extended to a distance); and this near movement causes a still greater variation at the farthest point to which the eye reaches; and if the vision is moved violently and regularly up and down, it has still less hold upon the distant object. Now anything which is extended to a distance moves in a circle, arrows, for example, and objects suspended; and so the same thing happens to the vision owing to its weakness, as though it were actually projected to a distance. It
20   makes no difference whether it is the vision which moves or the object seen; for the effect on the appearance of the object is the same.

21 · Why is it that, when a quantity of wine is drunk at once, the stomach becomes drier, whereas it ought to be rendered moister by the additional liquid? Is it because the stomach has no action upon a large amount of liquid swallowed at
25   once, but it goes unaltered to its proper place (and the proper place for unconcocted liquid is the bladder), whereas the stomach acts upon a small quantity and concocts it, so that it remains in the stomach and makes it moist?

22 · Why is it that those who drink wine properly diluted suffer more from hangovers than those who drink unmixed wine? Is it because diluted wine, being
30   light, finds its way into more parts of the body (just as it penetrates into clothing), and is more difficult to expel (water by itself being of a thinner consistency but easier to expel)? Or is it because the amount of unmixed wine which is drunk is less because of the impossibility of drinking a large quantity, and there is more liability

---

[12]Reading ἐνδεῶς.
[13]Reading μή for μέν.

to vomiting? Moreover unmixed wine concocts everything else as well as itself. This is the same problem.

23 · Why is it that death ensues from the drinking of unmixed wine in large   35
quantities by one who is already in a lean condition? On the other hand, those who
are addicted to drinking, if they are not in a lean condition, often become dry from
drinking a large quantity at a time; for both wine and life seem to be of the nature of
hot things, whereas death is a process of cooling. Is it because death by drinking   874ᵇ1
resembles death by hemlock, the natural heat being gradually extinguished? But
the process is different in the two cases; for hemlock by its coldness congeals the
moisture and heat, whereas wine by its own heat parches up the natural heat. So
just as a small fire is extinguished by a large blaze and by the heat of the sun, so too   5
the heat in the body is extinguished by that in the wine, if the latter surpasses it in
strength.

24 · Why are the drunken more easily moved to tears? Is it because they
become hot and moist, and so they have no command over themselves and are
affected by trifling causes?   10

25ᵃ · Why do those who drink from large vessels become less drunk? Is the
reason in all cases the same, namely the repression of heat; that is to say, on the
surface of the body? For drunkenness takes place in the region of the head.

25ᵇ · Why do those who are drunk not go to sleep? Is it because to induce
sleep warm moisture must be present, for it is easily concocted? But if no moisture is
present, or[14] only a little, or moisture which is difficult of concoction, sleep does not   15
come on. Therefore men become sleepiest when they are fatigued and after meat
and drink, owing to the heat. But sleeplessness afflicts the melancholic and those
who are in a high fever,[15] the former because the moisture in them is cooled, the
latter because there is little or no moisture in them; these facts must clearly be   20
looked to as the causes of sleeplessness in these two[16] cases.

26 · Why do drunkards tremble, and the more so the more they drink
unmixed wine? Now wine is heating, and trembling is chiefly due to cold; and so it is
principally those who are chilled that tremble. Yet many people before now who   25
have taken unmixed wine as their only form of nourishment, have been seized with
such violent trembling as to throw off those who were trying to hold them down, and
when they wash with hot water they have no perception of it. Others who live in this
way, but also undergo massage and take meat as part of their diet, have been
stricken with apoplectic seizures; these are less subject to trembling, because they   30

---

[14]Reading ἢ ὀλίγη.
[15]Reading τοῖς μεγάλως πυριῶσιν.
[16]Reading ἑκάτερον.

are unable to move, but they suffer from violent pain and an inability to rest. Trembling is due to cooling; for, as has been remarked, it is those who are chilled who suffer from it and the very old, the cause being in the former their cold condition, in the latter their age. Wine, on the other hand, is very heating; so that it ought to have the opposite effect. Is there any reason why the same effect should not be produced by contraries working in a different manner? For example, burning is caused both by frost and by heat, when the frost collects the heat in one place. Thus there is a sense in which the same condition is produced both by contrary causes and by the same cause. Now trembling is due to lack of heat,—not, however, of any kind of heat, but of natural heat. Heat perishes either by dying down or by being extinguished; it is extinguished by its contraries, cold and moisture, and it dies down either through lack of material, as lamps do when they have no more fuel or oil, or under the influence of external heat, as the fire goes out in the sunlight and lamps when they are exposed to the fire. Those then who are chilled tremble because the heat in them is extinguished by the cold. This is why the pouring of hot water over a person makes his hair bristle; for the cold being enclosed within and being compressed causes the hair to stand on end. The coldness of one who is beginning to suffer from fever is due to a like cause. In old age the heat dies down because the material which feeds it fails; for moisture is the food of heat, and old age is dry. Now it is because their own heat dies down that drunkards tremble and any others in whom this effect is produced by wine; but they do not do so in the same way as those who tremble from old age, but there is, as we saw, a third way in which the heat is destroyed. For when too much wine is taken, the heat being considerable in the body extinguishes or weakens our own heat, in which our strength consists; for trembling arises when the motive power loses control over that which it moves, just as the extremity of a long and large piece of wood trembles if one has not a good hold[17] upon it, and this happens because either that which is being held is too large or that which is moving it is too weak. So, when the heat is extinguished (for heat appears to be the cause of motion in animals), the natural control of the body is lost. That this condition is induced in drunkards and the aged by a process of cooling is proved by the fact that the trembling is unaccompanied by chill.

27 · Why is it that one who is tipsy is more troublesome in his cups than one who is more drunk and than the sober man? Is it because the sober man exercises his judgment properly, whereas one who is quite drunk, because his senses are blocked up, being unable to resist the heaviness which oppresses him, cannot exercise his judgement at all, and, this being so, is not troublesome in his cups? But he who is tipsy uses his judgement, but, owing to the wine which he has drunk, he uses it amiss, and so is troublesome in his cups. He is like Satyrus of Clazomenae, who was given to abuse, and so when he was defendant in a lawsuit, in order that he might speak to the point and not abuse his adversary, they stopped up his ears, so that he might not hear anything and become abusive; but as his adversary was finishing his speech, they uncovered his ears, and he, hearing a few words at the end

[17]Reading ἐγκρατῶς.

of the speech, could not restrain himself and began to revile him, because he could use his senses but could not use his judgement aright.

28 · Why is it that men do not become drunkards by being addicted to sweet 875ᵇ1 wine, which is pleasanter to the taste? Is it because sweet wine possesses a flavour other than that of wine? He then who is addicted to sweet wine will be a lover of what is sweet rather than of wine.

29 · Why is it that drunkards take a particular delight in the warmth of the 5 sun? Is it because they need concoction? Another reason is the fact that they are cooled by the wine; which is also a reason why apoplectic seizures and torpidity very readily occur after drinking.

30 · Why is it that drunkards when looking at a single object sometimes see several objects? Is it because the sources of vision (like the whole head) are 10 disturbed internally by the wine, and, this being so, the vision of the two eyes cannot meet at the same point, but as it were moves to different parts of the object seen; consequently the object appears to be two? The same thing happens if one presses one eye from below; for this disturbs the source of its vision, so that it no longer falls 15 upon the same point as the other eye. This then is an external disturbance, while that caused by wine is internal; but there is no real difference, the effect being the same whatever the cause of the disturbance.

31 · Why is it that the tongue of those who are drunk stumbles? Is it because, just as the whole body staggers in drunkenness, so also the tongue staggers 20 and stumbles and cannot articulate clearly? Or is it because the flesh of the tongue is spongy? It therefore becomes saturated and swells up, and when this happens it is more difficult to move, owing to the thickness caused by its increased bulk, and it cannot articulate distinctly. Or is it because, just as we cannot speak under water 25 through lack of air, so we cannot speak when we take liquid into the mouth? So in a state of drunkenness we cannot articulate because the tongue is surrounded by a large quantity of moisture; for a stumbling speech is due to inability to articulate. Or is it because in drunkenness the soul is affected and stumbles? If the soul is in this condition, it is only natural that the tongue should suffer likewise; for the soul is 30 the source of speech. This is why, apart from drunkenness, if the soul is affected, the tongue is affected also, as for example in those who are frightened.

32 · Why is it that drunkards and those who have to do with the sea delight in the sun? Is it because drunkards require concoction and at the same time certain 35 parts of their bodies have become cooled? This is why apoplectic seizures and torpor follow after drinking. Those who have to do with the sea like the sun because they live always amid moisture.

33 · Why is it that those who are drunk are incapable of having sexual intercourse? Is it because to do so a certain part of the body ought to be in a state of

876ᵇ1 greater heat than the rest, and this is impossible in the drunken owing to the large quantity of heat in them; the heat therefore caused by the movement is extinguished, being heated by the surrounding heat? Or is it because for sexual intercourse the lower parts of the body must be heated, whereas wine naturally rises upwards and so creates heat in the upper parts and withdraws it from the lower
5   parts? Also people are least inclined for sexual intercourse after food and are recommended to take a heavy midday meal and a light supper with a view to it, for the heat and moisture move upwards when the food is unconcocted and downwards when it is concocted; and the semen is formed from concocted food. Those who are fatigued emit semen during sleep, because fatigue is a moist and hot condition; if
10 therefore the excretion takes place in this part of the body, the result is that semen is emitted during sleep. This also occurs for the same reason in certain forms of illness, and likewise in those who are frightened and in the dying.

15   34 · Why is it that the young wet their beds more, when they are drunk, than the old? Is it because they are hot and moist, and so the excretion which collects is abundant, because the body does not expend the moisture, and so it overflows; but as they become older, the body owing to its dryness absorbs the excess of moisture?
20 Or is it because the young are more inclined to sleep than the old? Consequently, without their being aware of it, the flow of urine finds its way out while they are asleep, before they can wake up, whereas the old are aware of it, just as they are more alive to any external movement than the young. This is confirmed by the fact
25 that the young themselves wet their beds most when they are most sound asleep.

      35 · Why is it that oil is beneficial against drunkenness and sipping it enables one to continue drinking? Is it because it promotes the flow of urine and so prepares a way for the liquor?

BOOK IV
PROBLEMS CONNECTED WITH
SEXUAL INTERCOURSE

30   1 · Why is it that one who is having sexual intercourse, and also a dying person, casts his eyes upwards, while a sleeper casts them downwards? It is because the heat going out in an upward direction makes the eyes turn in the direction in which it is itself travelling, whereas during sleep the heat collects in the lower part of the body and so inclines the eyes downwards? The eyes close because there is no
35 moisture left in them.

      2 · Why do the eyes and buttocks of those who indulge too frequently in sexual intercourse sink very noticeably, though the latter are near and the former

far from the sexual organs? Is it because these parts co-operate very noticeably in the effort made in the act of coition, contracting at the time of the emission of the 876^b1 semen? It is from these parts then in particular that any easily liquefied nourishment which is present there is squeezed out by the pressure. Or is it because these parts become overheated and waste away most, and sexual intercourse operates through heat, and those parts are most heated which are moved in the act of 5 coition? Now the eyes and the parts about the buttocks noticeably co-operate in the sexual act; for it is impossible to emit the semen without drawing the buttocks together and closing the eyes, for the buttocks by their contraction press out the semen (just as the liquid can be expelled from the bladder by the pressure of the hand), while the bringing together of the eyelids presses out the moisture in the 10 brain. That the eyes and the region near them have considerable influence in procreation is shown by the fact that childless and fruitful women alike try the experiment of anointing them, thinking that strength must pass by this way into the semen. These two parts, the fundament and the eyes, are always in all persons full of fatness; and, because they co-operate in the act of coition, they share in the heat 15 which it engenders and are made lean thereby, and much of their substance is excreted into the semen. For unless a part of the body is fat, the heat will not melt it properly, nor will it do so if the part is fat but does not co-operate in the sexual act, as is the case with the stomach. (The kidneys, however, have more sensation in sexual intercourse than other parts of the body because of their nearness to the organs employed.) Moreover, the mere passage of the semen through these parts, 20 which is quite perceptible by these parts, is sufficient to make them lean; for its proximity takes away something without adding anything to them.

3 · Why is it that both those who indulge in sexual excess and eunuchs, who never do so, alike lose their sharpness of vision? Is it because in the former owing to 25 their desire, and in the latter owing to their mutilation, the upper parts of the body become drier than they ought to be, and this is most noticeable in those organs which have delicate work to do, such as the eye? So when the moisture is drawn away downwards, the upper parts become dry. It is quite obvious that sexual 30 intercourse has this effect. In eunuchs the legs swell and the bowels are easily relaxed, which shows that the moisture has moved downwards.

4 · Why is it that man alone grows hair when he begins to be capable of sexual intercourse, whereas this does not happen in the other animals which have hair? Is it because on coming to maturity the characteristics of animals change to 35 their opposites? For the voice becomes deep instead of shrill, and they become hairy instead of bare; it is clear therefore that animals which are hirsute from birth ought to become bare and not continue to be hirsute when they begin to secrete semen. But this is not so, because animals which emit semen become drier and rarer, conditions which are favourable to the growth of hair. This is shown by the fact that hair does 877^a1 not grow on scars, for scars are of a close texture and not rare; nor does hair grow upon women and children, both of whom are moist and not dry.

5   5 · Why is it that having the feet bare is prejudicial to sexual intercourse? Is
it because the body, when it is about to have sexual intercourse, ought to be warm
and moist internally? This condition is attained during sleep rather than when one
is awake; and so emission of semen takes place readily and without effort during
10   sleep, but requires exertion in those who are awake. When the body is moist and
warm, the feet are even more so; as is shown by the fact that the feet of those who
are asleep are warm, being in this condition simultaneously with the interior of the
body. But bareness of the feet has the opposite effect of causing dryness and cold. So
since it is either difficult or impossible to have sexual intercourse when the feet are
15   not warm, bareness of the feet must necessarily be prejudicial to the performance of
the sexual act.

        6 · Why is it that man is more languid after sexual intercourse than any
other animal? Is it because in proportion to his bulk he emits more semen than any
other animal? But why does he do so? Is it because man digests his food with less
effort and is naturally moister and hotter than all the other animals? His moistness
20   then creates an abundance of semen, while his heat creates a natural condition
favourable to it; for the semen must be moist and hot as long as it is kept in the
body.

        7 · Why is it that, whereas sexual intercourse takes place by means of heat,
25   and fear and death have a cooling effect, yet semen is sometimes emitted by those
who are frightened and by the dying? Is it because, though some parts are cooled,
others become somewhat warmed, since they already have their own heat and
receive additional heat from the parts which are cooling? So that, though such
persons are growing cold, the emission of semen is due not to cooling but to the
30   simultaneous heating. Observation proves this to be so in those who are frightened;
for the blood leaves the upper parts of the body, and the lower parts become moist,
and the bowels and bladder are relaxed. Thus under the influence of fright the heat
makes its way downwards, and at death it travels upwards from below, and, because
it creates a state of moisture by its warmth, it causes the emission of semen.

35   8 · Why is it that one ought not to have sexual intercourse or vomit or sneeze
or emit a deep breath, unless one is aroused? Is it because if we are not aroused, we
are in the condition of plants torn up from the earth with which something which
does not belong to them is torn up also, or of which some part is torn off and left in
877^{b}1   the ground? Now anything which ought to be removed, but of which a part is
detached and remains behind, will cause trouble for a long while. And if one
disturbs something external to oneself, this will cause trouble, because it is not in its
proper place; and this is what will happen if we do any of the above-mentioned
things when we are not aroused.

5   9 · Why is it that one can have sexual intercourse more readily when
fasting? Is it because the ducts of the body are emptier in those who are fasting and

full in those who are full? In the latter case they prevent the moisture from passing through into the semen. This is seen to be the case with the bla'dder; for when it is full it is impossible to have sexual intercourse readily.

10 · Why is it that the young, when they first begin to have sexual   10
intercourse, feel loathing after the act for those with whom they have had intercourse? Is it due to the fact that the change caused in them is great? For they are only conscious of the ensuing feeling of discomfort, and so avoid those with whom they have had intercourse as being the cause of this feeling.

11 · Why is it that those who are continually on horseback are more inclined   15
for sexual intercourse? Is it because owing to the heat and movement they are in the same condition as during sexual intercourse? So as growth takes place with increasing age in the region of the genital organs, these parts become enlarged. Since then they are always in this state of movement, their bodies become open-pored and in a condition which disposes them for sexual intercourse.   20

12 · Why is it that when sexual powers begin to be present the flesh has an unpleasant odour which is not present in men or women before puberty? Is it because unconcocted matter always has a worse taste—being more acid or salty or bitter—and a more unpleasant odour, while concocted matter has a pleasant, or less unpleasant, taste and a more agreeable, or less disagreeable, odour? This is clear   25
from an observation of the whole vegetable and animal world. If the properly concocted matter is removed, that which is left is unconcocted,—for instance in ashes, the sweet portion having been consumed, the dust which remains is bitter, and similarly perspiration is salty. Now the natural heat concocts the semen, which   30
though small in amount is very strong, being a large quantity in a concentrated form. When, therefore, it leaves the body, the latter usually becomes languid and cold; and so the juices in it are subject to less concoction, since the pores are opened owing to the excretion of the semen. Consequently the perspiration of adults is saltier and has a more unpleasant odour than that of children, because it is   35
unconcocted; and if their natural condition is such that the residue of their perspiration has an unpleasant odour, it is still more evident in such persons, and particularly in those parts, such as the armpit, in which it is especially evident in other people also.

13 · Why is it that we regard the creature which is born from our own semen   878ᵃ1
as our offspring, while that which is produced from any other part of us or from any other excretion is not looked upon as our own? For many things are produced by putrefaction, even from semen. Why then is that which resembles us claimed as our own, while that which is alien to us is not so considered? For either all or none ought   5
to belong to us. Is the reason that, in the first place, what is produced from the semen is born from what is our own, but that which is produced otherwise originates from something which is not ours, namely, from what is purged or excreted from

us? In a word, nothing in a creature procreates another creature except the semen;
10 and that which is harmful and evil, and also that which is alien, is not claimed by
anything as its own; for it is not the same thing to be part of a thing and to be alien to
it and other than it and evil. Now our excretions and putrefactions are not our own
but are other than us and alien to our nature. For all things that grow in the body
must not be considered as belonging to the body, for even boils grow on it and these
15 are removed and got rid of. In a word, all things that are contrary to nature are alien
to the body, and many of the things that grow there are contrary to nature. If
therefore the semen is the only thing in us from which a creature can be born, we
should be right in regarding as our own offspring that only which is produced from
the semen. Moreover anything else which is produced from the semen, as for
instance, when it putrefies, a worm, or the so-called monstrosities, when there is
20 corruption in the womb, are not to be reckoned as offspring. In a word, anything
which is produced from corruption is no longer produced from that which is our own
but from that which is alien to us, like that which is generated from excretions such
as ordure. That all such things are produced from corruption is proved by the fact
25 that what is generated from uncorrupted semen is of such a nature as to resemble
that from which the semen came, a horse being born from a horse and a man from a
man. And we do not value the semen in itself or everything that is being completed
in the process of coming into being (for it is sometimes moisture and a mere mass
30 and flesh which is coming into being),[1] because it has not yet its true nature but only
so much of its nature as is implied in the fact that it is so disposed as to produce
something resembling ourselves; and nothing even of this kind can be produced
from corrupted semen. For these reasons we do not regard as our offspring that
which is produced either from anything else in us except the semen, or from the
semen when it is corrupted or fails to achieve perfection.

35   14 · Why are people less able to have sexual intercourse in the water? Is it
because in water none of those things liquefy which liquefy with heat—lead, for
example, or wax? Now the semen obviously liquefies with heat, for it does not
liquefy until it is warmed by the friction. Fishes, however, have sexual intercourse
without friction.

878^b1   15 · Why is it that sexual intercourse is the most pleasant of all things to
animals, and is it so of necessity or with some purpose in view? Is it pleasant because
the semen comes either from the whole body, as some declare, or not from the whole
5 body but only from the area over which all the ducts of the veins extend? The
pleasure then of the friction being similar in both cases, the sensation extends as it
were over the whole body. Now the friction is pleasant, since it involves the emission
of vaporous moisture enclosed unnaturally in the body; but the act of generation is
10 an emission of similar matter for its natural purpose. It is pleasant both of necessity
and for the sake of something,—of necessity, because the way to a natural result is

_____
[1]Reading γίνεται ποτέ, διά.

pleasant, if it is realized by the senses; and for the sake of something, namely, the procreation of animal life. For it is the pleasure more than anything else which incites animals to sexual intercourse.

16 · Why is it that sexual excess is beneficial in some diseases caused by phlegm? Is it because it involves the emission of an excretion, and so a considerable 15 amount of excreted matter is rejected with it, and phlegm is an excretion?

17 · Why does sexual intercourse cool and dry the stomach? Does it cool it because the heat is expelled in coition? Coition causes dryness, because, as the heat goes out, the moisture is vaporized and finds its way out as the body cools, while at 20 the same time the heat caused by the act of copulation has a drying effect.

18 · Why are those whose eyelashes fall off accounted lustful? Is it for the same reason as that for which the bald also are so accounted? For the eyelashes and the hair of the head really belong together. The reason is that all the congenital hair 25 which does not increase as a man gets older, falls off owing to lustfulness. For the hair of the head and the eyebrows and eyelashes are congenital hair; and of these the eyebrows alone sometimes grow thicker with advancing years (the reason for this has been stated elsewhere), while the hair of the head and the eyelashes both fail from the same cause, viz., that lustfulness cools the upper parts of the body 30 which are deficient in blood, and so this portion of the body does not concoct any of the nourishment, and the hair not receiving any nourishment drops off.

19 · Why is it that those who wish to pass urine cannot have sexual intercourse? Is it because the ducts become full? Now that which is full of moisture cannot admit any more moisture. 35

20 · Why is it that varicose veins prevent both man and any other animals which suffer from them from procreating? Is it because varicose veins are due to a displacement of breath, and this is why they are beneficial to melancholic diseases? Now sexual intercourse also is accompanied by an emission of breath. If therefore a 879ª1 rush of breath makes its way along when sexual intercourse is taking place, it fails to impart movement to the semen and the latter becomes cold; consequently it enfeebles the erection of the penis.

21 · Why do those who have sexual intercourse usually become languid and weaker? Is it because the semen is an excretion from the whole body, and so the 5 composition of the body, like the harmony of a building, is disturbed by the loss of any portion of it—if, for example, all the blood or any other component part of it is removed? So important is that which the body loses in sexual intercourse, being indeed formed from a large amount of nourishment though itself small in quantity, just as a cake is made from wheaten flour. 10

22 · Why is it that the penis is greatly distended in those who have sexual intercourse at a time when they desire to pass urine? Is it because, owing to the ducts being full of moisture, the semen, passing out through a narrower space, swells the bulk of the penis and lifts it up, for it is situated close to the ducts.

15   23 · What is the cause of the erection and swelling of the penis? Are there two reasons, first, that it is raised by a weight applied behind the testicles, the latter acting as the fulcrum, and, secondly, that the pores become full of breath? Or does its bulk become greater from the increase of the moisture and its change of position, 20   or from the formation of moisture? Now very large objects are less easily moved, because the weight is farther away from the fulcrum.

24 · Why is it that those who have sexual intercourse or are capable of it have an evil odour and what is called a goat smell, whereas children do not? Is it because, as has already been said, in children the breath concocts the moisture and 25   perspiration, whereas the perspiration of grown men remains unconcocted?

25 · Why is it that in summer men are less capable of sexual intercourse and women more so? As the poet says,

Men, when the artichoke blooms, are weaker and women more wanton.[2]

30   Is it because the testicles hang down lower then than in the winter, and they must be drawn up if sexual intercourse is to take place? Or is it because hot natures collapse in summer when the heat is excessive, but cold natures are invigorated by it? Now a man is dry and hot, but a woman is cold and moist; consequently a man's strength is impaired, but a woman's is invigorated, its deficiency being compensated by its 35   opposite.

26 · Why is it that some persons find pleasure in submitting to sexual intercourse, and some take pleasure in performing the active part, and others do 879ᵇ1   not? Is it because each form of excretion has a region in which it is naturally secreted and, when an effort is made, the breath in finding its way out causes the excretion to swell and expels it; for example, urine collects in the bladder, food from which the moisture has been extracted in the bowels, tears in the eyes, mucous 5   matter in the nostrils, and blood in the veins? Similarly the semen collects in the testicles and penis. In those whose ducts are not in a natural condition, owing either to the blocking up of the ducts leading to the sexual organs (as in the case of eunuchs or other victims of sexual disablement) or to some other cause, all such moisture collects in the region of the fundament; for it is by this way that it passes 10   out of the body. That this is so is proved by the contraction of that part in sexual intercourse and the wasting of that region of the body. If therefore through wantonness a man has a superfluity of semen, it all collects there; and so, when desire comes upon him, the part in which it is collected desires friction. This desire may be due to diet or to thought. When desire is stirred from any cause, the breath

²Hesiod, *Works and Days* 582.

collects and secretion of this kind flows to its natural place. If the secretion be thin 15
and full of air, when the breath finds its way out the desire ceases (just as the
erection in boys and older persons sometimes ceases without the discharge of any
moisture); but when the moisture dries up . . .[3] And if neither of these things occurs,
the desire continues till the one or the other of them takes place. But those who are 20
effeminate by nature are so constituted that little or no semen is secreted where it is
secreted by those who are in a natural state, but it collects in this part of the body.
The reason for this is that they are unnaturally constituted; for, though male, they
are in a condition in which this part of them is necessarily incapacitated. Now
incapacity may involve either complete destruction or else perversion; the former, 25
however, is impossible, for it would involve a man becoming a woman. They must
therefore become perverted and aim at something other than the discharge of
semen. The result is that they suffer from unsatisfied desires, like women; for the
moisture is scanty and has not enough force to find its way out and quickly cools. 30
When it finds its way to the fundament only, there is a desire to submit to sexual
intercourse; but if it settles both there and in the sexual organs, there is a desire both
for performing and submitting to the sexual act, and the desire for one or other is
greater as more semen is present in either part. This condition is sometimes the
result of habit; for men take a pleasure in whatever they are accustomed to do and
emit the semen accordingly. They therefore desire to do the acts by which pleasure 35
and the emission of semen are produced, and habit becomes more and more a
second nature. For this reason those who have been accustomed to submit to sexual
intercourse about the age of puberty and not before, because recollection of the past 880ᵃ1
presents itself to them during the act of copulation and with the recollection the idea
of pleasure, desire to take a passive part owing to habit, as though it were natural to
them to do so; frequent repetition, however, and habit become a second nature. All
this is more likely to occur in the case of one who is both lustful and effeminate. 5

27 · Why is it that those who desire to submit to sexual intercourse feel a
great shame about confessing it, which they do not feel in confessing a desire for
meat or drink or anything of that kind? Is it because the desire for most things is
necessary and its non-satisfaction is sometimes fatal to life, but sexual desires
proceed from something beyond mere necessity? 10

28 · Why is it that men are more inclined for sexual intercourse in the winter
and women in the summer? Is it because men are hotter and drier in their nature,
and women moister and cooler? In men therefore during the winter the moisture
and heat are sufficient to cause the impulse (and it is moisture and heat which give 15
rise to the production of the semen), whereas in women the heat is less and the
moisture is congealed owing to the lack of fire. But in summer in women[4] the heat is
well proportioned, whereas in men it is more than sufficient; for the excess dissolves
much of their strength. For this reason also children are thinner during the summer; 20
for it is a case of 'fire added to fire'.

---

[3]Ruelle marks a lacuna.
[4]Reading θέρους ταῖς μέν ἐστι.

29 · Why is it that those who are hot by nature, when they are strong and well nourished, if they do not have sexual intercourse are often oppressed by bile, which makes its way down in a very bitter condition, and a salty phlegm is
25 engendered, and their complexion changes? Is it because some excretion always comes away with the semen? (That is why also the semen of some men who emit a large quantity of excretion[5] is said to smell of the water in which fish have been washed.) So when they have sexual intercourse, this excretion comes away with the semen and so causes no inconvenience; but if they abstain from copulation, the excretion becomes bitter or salty.

30   30 · Why are the melancholic particularly inclined for sexual intercourse? Is it because they are full of breath, and the semen is a discharge of breath? If so, those whose semen is full of breath must necessarily often desire to purge themselves of it; for thus they are relieved of it.

31 · Why are birds, and men with thick hair, lustful? Is it because they have
35 a large amount of moisture? Or is this not true (for the female sex is moist and not hairy), but is the real reason that the natures both of birds and of thickhaired men are able owing to their heat to concoct a large quantity of moisture? This is indicated by the presence of hair and feathers. Or is it because the moisture is plentiful and is overpowered by the heat? For if the moisture were not plentiful or
880ᵇ1 were not overpowered, hair would not grow on human beings nor feathers on birds. Now the semen is formed most plentifully under conditions of locality and at seasons that have these characteristics, in spring for example, which is naturally moist and hot. Birds and lame men are lustful for the same reason, namely, that in
5 both, owing to the deficiencies of their legs, the nourishment is carried downwards in small quantities only, while the rest travels into the upper region of the body and is converted into semen.

32 · Why is it that when a man has sexual intercourse his eyes grow very weak? Is it not clear that this happens because the moisture leaves them? This is
10 proved by the fact that the semen is cold; for it does not become moist unless the heat warms it thoroughly. Nor does it require melting, for it is dispersed about the body like blood.

BOOK V
PROBLEMS CONNECTED WITH FATIGUE

15   1 · Why is it that long walks are more fatiguing and short walks less fatiguing over level ground than over uneven country? Is it because much movement and violent movement causes fatigue, and spasmodic movement is violent, and continuous and monotonous movement is much movement? In walking

---

[5]Reading περιττωματικῶν.

therefore on hilly ground, if the distance be long, the change provides a rest, and the   20
same movement is not continued for long, even in the case of horses, owing to the
change. On even ground, on the other hand, the similarity of position continues
uninterruptedly and gives the limbs no rest, but helps to make the movement
continuous. Now if the distance is short, no fatigue is caused on flat ground by
long-continued motion; whereas over hilly ground the violent change to an opposite   25
kind of movement, sometimes uphill and sometimes down, gives rise to fatigue.
Such, in our opinion, is movement over hill country, and that over level ground is the
contrary.

2 · Why is it that those who faint and those who collapse after physical   30
exertion are generally held to become smaller in bulk and their voices shriller? Is it
because their voices, appearing to be less, seem shriller (this can be illustrated by
the fact that those who imitate distant voices make shrill sounds), while their bulk
appears less?

3 · Why is it that only the stomach becomes thinner in those who take
physical exercise? Is it because the greatest quantity of fat is found round the
stomach?   35

4 · Why is it that the fat is consumed in those who exert themselves? Is it
because fat melts when heated, and the movement causes heat, whereas flesh does
not melt?

5 · Why is it that the parts round the belly are fattest? Is it because they are
near to the nourishment? While then the other parts of the body receive something   881ᵃ1
from the belly, the belly itself often receives something. Or is it because the belly is
exerted less than the other parts, because it has no joints?

6 · Why is it that fatigue ceases more readily if one mixes water with the oil
with which one rubs oneself? Is it because the oil sinks in farther when mixed with   5
water, whereas by itself it does not penetrate so well, because it has a tendency to
remain on the surface? If, therefore, it sinks in, the body is more softened; for oil is
naturally hot, and hot things have a drying and hardening effect, and dryness and
hardness are inexpedient in fatigue; but when applied with water the oil has a less   10
drying effect.

7 · Why is it that vomiting is prescribed for those who are suffering from
fatigue, although vomiting is itself fatiguing? Is it because fatigue is caused by the
crushing and pressure and weariness of the bones, and this can be caused either by
some external or by some internal agency, and in the latter case from one of two   15
causes, either because the flesh overreaches its own strength, or because one bodily
constituent mingles in a large quantity with the rest of the body and does not keep to
its proper place, as happens with the excretions? For any burdens which are put

upon us externally cause more fatigue than our own members, even though they are
20   lighter than these in weight. This can be illustrated by the fact that those who have
eaten or drunk somewhat freely, though they have exerted themselves less than
when they were fasting, yet feel more fatigue, because the food, being unconcocted,
is not in its proper place. And since fatigue causes liquefaction, and liquefaction is
25   an excretion, it is the latter which produces fatigue in us, wandering about at
random and attacking the bones and sinews and the interior parts of the flesh, which
are rare and open. Consequently vomiting, by dislodging the excretion which is the
cause of fatigue, naturally makes us less fatigued; for it leaves the body in the state
30   in which it was when the exertion began. Vomiting is fatiguing, not because of the
excess of movement caused while it is taking place, but when it does not happen to
be thoroughly carried out; for fatigue caused by vomiting occurs when a considerable amount of food is left behind and this contains excretions, which, as we have
already said, happens in those who have eaten largely. If, therefore, in the latter it is
35   not exertion which causes fatigue, but they feel fatigue because of the condition in
which they are, so vomiting could not be the cause of fatigue in those who do not get
rid of all the food which is in them; for in that case every one who vomited would feel
fatigue, whereas many through vomiting become less fatigued.

8 · Why is it more fatiguing to the arm if one casts with the hand empty than
881ᵇ1   with a stone in it? Is it because the movement is more spasmodic if the hand be
empty, for the hand has nothing to rest upon, such as the thrower finds in the missile
which he holds in his hand? Similarly the competitor in the pentathlon finds
resistance in the weights which he holds, and the runner in his arms which he
5   swings; so the former jumps farther if he holds weights than if he does not, and the
latter runs more quickly if he swings his arms than if he does not do so.

9 · Why is it that quick running causes a tendency to disease in the head both
in man and in the other animals? Yet generally speaking running appears to draw
10   the excretions downwards, as does walking; for which reason also those who walk
much grow fat in the legs, because both the nourishment and the excretions settle
down from the upper into the lower parts. Is it true that while motion has the same
effect, yet quick motion, owing to the strain and the holding of the breath which it
involves, causes heat in the head and inflates the veins in it and renders them liable
15   to be affected by external influences, such as cold and heat, and by the contents of
the trunk; and that if these can enter the head, disease is necessarily engendered in
that region?

10 · Why is it more fatiguing to walk on level than on uneven ground,
whereas one can walk more quickly on an even than on an uneven road? Is it
20   because it is less fatiguing if one does not move continually in the same position, and
this is the case rather in traversing uneven ground? On the other hand one
progresses more quickly the less one's movement is contrary to nature. On even
ground, therefore, the raising and planting of the foot is a slight but frequent

movement, while the opposite occurs on uneven ground. Now to raise the foot is unnatural (for raising anything requires an effort); and the slight movement of 25 raising the foot at each step becomes considerable when repeated many times.

11 · Why is it more fatiguing to lie down on a flat than on a concave surface? Is it for the same reason that it is more fatiguing to lie on a convex than on a flat surface? For the weight being concentrated in one place in the sitting or 30 reclining position causes pain owing to the pressure. This is more the case on a convex than on a straight surface, and more on a straight than on a concave; for our body assumes curved rather than straight lines, and in such circumstances concave surfaces give more points of contact than flat surfaces. For this reason also couches and seats which yield to pressure are less fatiguing than those which do not do so. 35

12 · Why are short walks fatiguing? Is it because they involve abrupt change, for they necessitate coming often to a standstill? Now frequent change from one extreme to another is fatiguing, for it does not allow one to become accustomed to either extreme, and this is tiring; and one cannot become accustomed 882ª1 to both things at once.

13 · Why is it that those who ride on horseback water more freely at the eyes the quicker the horse goes? Is it because the stream of air which meets them is colder according as it is for a shorter time in contact with the body (as happens in 5 the case of naked runners), and it is the cold which makes the eyes water? Or is the reason the contrary of this, namely, that heat makes the eyes water (the sun, for instance), and movement engenders heat? Or is it due to the impact of the air? For as blasts of wind coming from an opposite direction trouble the eyes, so the air all 10 the more deals a gentle blow the quicker the horse is driven.

14 · Why is it that the other parts of the body become more fleshy when subjected to friction, but the stomach becomes leaner? Or is it true that the stomach does not become gradually leaner but solider? The flesh, however, is not similarly 15 affected, and this is the point of the problem; for, speaking generally, the stomach does become leaner as the result of exercise and exertion. The reason is that the fat parts, and those which naturally admit of more expansion, liquefy when heated. Now the skin naturally admits of expansion; but, because it very quickly fattens, it 20 always contains some fat, unless any disease is present. The reason for this is that it is near the nourishment. Since, therefore, generally speaking, fat is not natural but adventitious, and is not one of the necessary constituents of the body, as is the flesh, the movements set up by exercise and friction warm and melt it and distribute the 25 superfluous nourishment in the other portions of the body. It is for this reason that sitting still makes the stomach fat and the rest of the body thin; whereas movement and friction make the stomach thin and fill out the rest of the body.

15 · Why is it that after long and violent walking or running, if one stands on

30 tiptoe, the heels quiver and are hastily drawn[1] down again? Is it because, owing to the continuity and violence of the movement, the quivering of the muscles in the man does not cease? For the mind often controls the body as a whole, but does not control certain parts of it, when they have been set in motion in a certain way, the 35 heart, for example, and the sexual organ. The reason is that a considerable quantity of breath is consumed by heat round the muscles, which does not cool off immediately a man comes to a standstill. This breath, therefore, is drawn down, making him quiver, as it were dragging him down by its movement, and leaves him little control over the most distant part of his body—in this case over his heels. A similar phenomenon occurs in the trembling of the lower lip in those who are angry.

882ᵇ1 16 · Why is it that those who are not running very hard respire rhythmically? Is it because every rhythm is measured by a definite movement, and the movement at regular intervals which occurs in running is of this nature? As soon, therefore, as they begin to run they respire; and so the respiration taking place at 5 equal intervals, because it is measured out by a uniform movement, creates a rhythm. Or is it because all respiration without exception takes place at intervals in those who respire naturally and do not hold their breath? The rhythm then is not obvious in those who are sitting or walking, because the movement of the body is 10 slight; and in those who are running vigorously we cannot get a complete view of the rhythm of the respiration, because our senses cannot follow the movement. But in those who are running moderately fast the movement allows the measure observed by the breathing to be perceptible, and so shows the rhythm.

17 · Why is it that, when we are running, the air seems to turn into breath? 15 Is it because, while we are moving in the act of running, we set in motion a stream of air continuous with our bodies, and this is breath? That is why the air not only seems to turn into breath, but actually does so. Or is it because in running we come into collision with the air, and, when this happens, we have a more acute perception of the air owing to the movement? It is only natural, therefore, that it should seem 20 to us to turn into breath; for the phenomenon occurs through the rush of our movement.

18 · Why is it that one is more liable to fall when running than when walking? Is it because in the former case one raises oneself higher before moving? For this is the difference between running and walking.

25 19 · Why is it that in ascending a slope our knees feel the strain, and in descending our thighs? Is it because when we ascend we throw the body upwards and the jerk of the body[2] from the knees is considerable, and so we feel the strain in the knees? But in going downhill, because the weight is carried by the legs, we are

---

[1]Reading σπῶνται.
[2]Omitting καί.

supported by our thighs, and so they feel the strain. Furthermore, whatever is   30
unnatural causes strain and pain. Now it is natural for the knees to bend forwards
and the thighs to bend backwards. In going uphill then the knees are bent
backwards owing to one's desire to support oneself, but in going downhill the thighs   35
are bent forwards because the body has a tendency to fall forwards.

20 · Why is it that on journeys the middle of the thigh is the part which feels
the strain most? Is it because in anything that is prolonged and continuous and fixed
the strain falls most upon the centre, and so it is most likely to break at that point?
Now the thigh is of this nature, and so it is in the middle of it that we feel the strain   883ᵃ1
most.

21 · Why is it that persons of a moist temperament easily choke as a result of
exertion and through heat? Is it because their moisture when heated becomes air
and the excess of it burns more fiercely? When, therefore, it cannot find its way out   5
owing to its abundance, the process of cooling does not take place; and so it quickly
catches fire owing to the natural and adventitious heat. It is for this reason that
perspiration induced by taking physical exercise, and by exerting oneself generally,
and the emission of breath are beneficial; for breath is formed by the separation and
rarefaction of moisture.   10

22 · Why is it that bodies of an equable temperament often feel weariness
but throw it off more easily? Is the cause the same in both cases? For that which is
equable is uniform, and that which is uniform is the more subject to similar
influences; so if any part suffers, the whole straightaway suffers in sympathy. But
that which is not equable, being more disunited, is not sympathetically affected by   15
its parts. A body of equable temperament therefore often feels weariness, but
throws it off more easily, because the whole body shares it; for the suffering, being
distributed over a larger area, is weaker and therefore more easily got rid of. But a
body which is not of an equable temperament, inasmuch as it has no communion
with its members, is less often afflicted with weariness, but has greater difficulty in   20
shaking it off; for its suffering is acute.

23 · Why is it more fatiguing to walk on level than on uneven ground,
whereas one can walk more quickly on an even than on an uneven road? Is it
because it is least fatiguing if one does not move continually in the same position,
and this is the case rather in traversing uneven ground?³ But one travels more   25
quickly when the foot has to be lifted less in any equal period of time. On level
ground the raising of the foot is a slight but frequent movement, on uneven ground
the reverse; but the slight⁴ movement of raising the foot at each step becomes
considerable when repeated many times.

---

³Reading ἐν τῷ αὐτῷ σχήματι ποιεῖσθαι τὴν κίνησιν, ὃ συμβαίνει ἐν τῇ ἀνωμάλῳ κτλ.
⁴Reading γινόμενον μικρόν.

24 · Why is it that in descending a slope we feel the strain most in the thighs, and in ascending in the legs? Is it because in ascending the strain is due to the raising of the body? For the whole body becomes a burden; and so the part upon which it all rests and with which we raise it (that is, the legs) feels the strain most. For the leg is an extremity, having length but not having width, as the foot has; consequently it is shaken. So we may cite in illustration the fact that we move weights with the shoulder and rest them upon it, and therefore feel the strain most in the shoulder. But when we are descending, the strain is caused by the body falling downwards and thrusting us forward unnaturally, so that we feel the strain most in the part on which it falls most and which it shakes. Now the leg remains unaffected, and the trunk forms the weight; but it is the thigh which receives the weight and is shaken, because it has extension and is forced from above into a bent position where the trunk presses on it.

25 · Why is it that a journey seems longer when we traverse it without knowing its length than when we do know it, all other conditions equal? Is it because to know its length is to be able to connect a number with it, and the indeterminate is always more than the determinate? Just as, therefore, if one knows that a journey is a certain length, it must necessarily be finite, so, if one does not know, as though the proposition was convertible, the mind draws a false conclusion, and the distance appears infinite. Furthermore, a quantity is determinate, and that which is determinate is a quantity; therefore when a thing appears not to be determinate, it appears to be as it were infinite, because that which is of a nature to be determined, if it is not so, is infinite; so that what appears not to be determined necessarily appears in a sense unlimited.

26 · Why is it that the thighs feel fatigue more than the legs? Is it because they are nearer to the part of the body which contains the excrement, so that, when that part overflows with heat owing to the movement, the thighs contract more readily and to a greater extent? Or is it because the thighs are more closely connected by growth with one another, for they suffer considerably owing to the separation of what is really continuous? For indeed, if one feels fatigue when there is no excrement in the body, even so it is the thighs and loins which suffer more than the other parts. Or is it because, just as swellings in the groin are caused, if one receives a blow, owing to the close connexion of the veins and sinews, so the thigh is similarly affected? For the thigh is nearer than the leg to the source of the veins. Or is it because the thigh remains more in the same position than the legs, and this is more fatiguing? Or is it because the thigh is fleshy, and therefore the natural heat[5] there is considerable?

27 · Why is it that in some people sores are formed as the result of exertion? Is it because, when the body contains impurities, movement heats it and causes other excretions to exude with the perspiration? These excretions, being thick and

[5]Reading τὸ κατὰ φύσιν θερμὸν ἔχειν.

containing harmful humours of an acid, bitter, and salty nature, cannot be expelled   30
owing to their thickness, but swell up through the flesh and cause sores owing to the
bitterness of the humour which they contain.

28 · Why is it that food is not given immediately after exercise and after
medicine has been administered? It is because the body is still being purged and has
not yet rested from its toil, and the excretions have not yet been expelled?   35

29 · Why is it more difficult to run than to walk? Is it because the runner
has a heavier burden, since, when he is raised in the air, he has his whole weight to
support? But a man who is walking continues to put his weight on the part of him
which is at rest, like a man leaning against a wall.

30 · Why is it that one does not feel hungry immediately after exercise? Is it   884ᵃ1
because liquefaction still remains until the concoction of anything is complete? Or
is it owing to the breath which the exertion engenders from the moisture? Or is it
owing to the thirst which is due to the heat caused by the exertion? All these
possible causes are present.   5

31 · Why is it that those who are fatigued and those who are suffering from
phthisis are apt to emit semen during sleep? Is it because generally speaking those
who are warm and moist are inclined to do so, since the semen naturally has these
characteristics? Now such a thing is most likely to happen in persons in these
conditions, when the heat engendered by sleep is added; for the body requires a   10
slight impulse only, which must be internal and not external. This condition is
fulfilled in those who are suffering from phthisis and in those who are fatigued; the
latter being full of hot liquid owing to their fatigue and movement, and the former
owing to their state of flux and the heat engendered by their inflamed condition.   15

32 · Why is it more difficult to apply prolonged friction oneself to the left leg
than to the right? Is it because, though our right is the side which is capable of
exertion, yet the rubbing of the left leg, since it involves a distorted attitude, is
unnatural, and anything which is unnatural is difficult? The difficulty of rubbing
the right side with the left hand is not obvious, because the left hand has no strength   20
whichever side it is applied to.

33 · Why is it healthy to reduce the amount of nourishment and to increase
the amount of exercise? Is it because abundance of excretion is the cause of disease?
Now this is due either to excess of nourishment or to lack of exercise.   25

34 · Why should the flesh be made rare rather than dense in order to
promote health? For just as a city or locality is healthy which is open to the breezes
(and that is why the sea too is healthy), so a body is healthier in which the air can
circulate. For either there ought to be no excrement present in the body, or else the

30   body ought to get rid of it as soon as possible and ought to be in such a condition that
      it can reject the excrement as soon as it receives it and be always in a state of motion
      and never at rest. For that which remains stationary putrefies (water, for example),
      and that which putrefies and does not move causes disease; but that which is
35   rejected passes away before it becomes corrupt. This then does not occur if the flesh
      is dense, the ducts being as it were blocked up, but it does happen if the flesh is rare.
      One ought not, therefore, to walk naked in the sun; for the flesh thereby solidifies
      and acquires an absolutely fleshy consistency, and the body becomes moister, for
      the internal moisture remains, but the surface moisture is expelled, a process which
884ᵇ1 also takes place in meat when it is roasted rather than boiled.[6] Nor ought one to
      walk about with the chest bare; for then the sun draws the moisture out of the best
      constructed parts of the body, which least of all require to be deprived of it. It is
      rather the inner parts of the body which should be submitted to this process; for,
      because they are remote, it is impossible to produce perspiration from them except
5   by violent effort, but it is easy to produce it from the chest because it is near the
      surface.

      35 · Why is it that short walks are fatiguing? Is it because one often comes
      to a standstill and there is no uniform movement in the joints, and this is
10   fatiguing?

      36 · Why do those who stand still in the sun become warmer than those who
      move, and this although movement is productive of heat? Is it true that every kind
      of movement does not produce heat, but some kinds have a cooling effect, as
      happens, for example, when one blows upon or keeps in motion kitchen-pots which
15   have boiled up? If then the heat remains when one stands still and, doing so, heats
      us more than if it were in motion (for our own body always gives off a warm steam,
      which heats the neighbouring air, as though there were a burning brand there),
      then, if we remain motionless, the air surrounding us becomes warm for the reasons
20   already stated; whereas, if we move, a wind is set up which cools us, for wind always
      has a cooling effect.

      37 · Why is it that those who ride on horseback water more freely at the eyes
      the quicker the horse goes, and those on foot the quicker they run? Is it due to the
25   fact that the air which meets them is cold? For cold causes the eyes to water; for by
      contracting and solidifying the flesh it purges out the moisture. Or is the reason the
      contrary of this, namely, that the heat causes perspiration, and watering at the eyes
      is a form of perspiration? Therefore both perspiration and watering at the eyes are
30   due to heat and are alike salty; and it is movement which causes heat. Or is it due to
      the impact of the air? For as blasts of wind coming from an opposite direction
      trouble the eyes, so too the quicker a man drives or runs the more does the air deal a
      gentle blow, and this causes the eyes to water, because the ducts of the eye are
35   rarefied by the blow; for every blow has the effect either of cleaving or crushing.

      ⁶Reading τὰ ὀπτὰ τῶν ἐφθῶν.

38 · Why is it that fatigue must be cured in the summer by baths, in the winter by anointing? Is it because the latter, owing to the cold and the changes which it causes in the body, must be got rid of by heat, which will cause warmth, and olive-oil contains heat? In summer, on the other hand, the body requires moisture; for the season is dry and chills are not engendered, because it is warm. A 885ᵃ1 sparing diet of solid food and a liberal indulgence in liquid nourishment are characteristic of the summer, the latter being peculiar to the summer, while the former is commoner than at other seasons; for indulgence in drinking is peculiar to the summer because of the dryness of the season, but a sparing diet is found at all seasons, but is more general in the summer; for then owing to the season more heat is engendered by food. 5

39 · Why is it that those who are running vigorously experience the greatest shock, if any one impedes them in their course? Is it because a thing is being drawn apart most vigorously when it is being dragged or moved violently in a contrary direction? If therefore any one impedes one who is running and whose limbs are being vigorously thrust forward, the result is that he wrenches him back at the same 10 time as his limbs are still moving forward, and so the more vigorously he is running the more violent is the shock which he receives.

40 · Why is it that walking along roads over uneven ground is less fatiguing than along a flat, straight surface? Is it because an upright carriage is natural to 15 everybody, but walking over even surfaces is more fatiguing than over uneven ground, since walking over even ground causes a continuous strain on the same members, whereas walking over uneven ground distributes the strain over the whole body? Now walking in warm weather tends more to make the body thin than in cold weather; for it causes more strain upon the outer parts, and so causes thinness by 20 engendering perspiration. Walking in cold weather makes the flesh more solid and causes a great desire for food; for it engenders an increase of heat in the inner parts and, since they become less liable to be affected by the cold, it cleans the inner 25 region by increasing the heat there, while it makes the flesh firm, since it cannot prevail over the whole of it. In like manner walking uphill is a greater exertion and tends more to cause thinness than walking downhill. For walking uphill causes most strain to the loins (whereas walking downhill is most trying to the thighs, for the whole weight falls upon them and so usually causes fatigue in them); for as they are 30 forcibly carried⁷ upwards in an unnatural manner, heat is engendered. Walking uphill therefore induces perspiration and causes thinness by heightening the respiration and engenders pain in the loins; for the legs, being lifted with difficulty, cause the loins to bend and draw them up, which naturally causes a very great 35 strain. Walking on hard, resisting ground causes fatigue to the muscles and tendons of the legs; for it causes tension in the sinews and muscles, because the pressure upon them is violent. Walking on soft ground is fatiguing to the joints; for it causes 885ᵇ1

⁷Omitting ὑπὸ τοῦ θερμοῦ and reading φερομένους.

frequent bending of the joints, because the surface trodden gives way. This is the same problem.

41 · Why do we walk with difficulty up a steep slope? Is it because all progression is made up of raising the feet and putting them down again? Now raising the foot is unnatural and putting it down is natural, while putting the foot forward is a mean between the two. Now in walking up a steep slope the unnatural motion preponderates.

42 · Why are riders on horseback less likely to fall? Is it because owing to their fear they are more careful?

BOOK VI

PROBLEMS CONNECTED WITH THE POSITIONS ASSUMED IN LYING DOWN AND IN OTHER POSTURES

1 · Why is it that sitting down makes some persons fat and others lean? Is it because bodily conditions differ, some men being hot, others cold? Those therefore who are hot grow fat (for the body owing to its heat prevails over the nourishment); but those who are cold, owing to the fact that their body requires heat introduced from without and derives it chiefly from movement, cannot concoct their food while they are at rest. Or is it because the hot are full of superfluities and require movement to expend them, while the cold are not so?

2 · Why is it necessary that the parts of the body should be distended, as happens when a man takes athletic exercise? Is it because the ducts must be purged by their own breath?

3 · Why is it better to lie in a curved position and why do many physicians prescribe this? Is it because the stomach concocts food more quickly when it is kept warm, and it keeps warmer in this position? Furthermore it is necessary to give the vapours a place where they can settle; for then there is less likely to be pain from flatulence. (It is on this account that swollen veins and abscesses of all kinds help to restore a healthy condition, because they form hollows in which they receive the vapours.) When the body then is extended no hollow is formed (for the internal organs occupy all the space); but a hollow is formed when the body is curved.

4 · Why is dizziness more likely to occur in those who are standing than in those who are sitting? Is it because, when one is still, the moisture all inclines to one part of the body? This is why raw eggs cannot be spun round and round but fall over. The same thing occurs when the moisture in the body is put in motion. So one stands up after having been at rest, when one is in this condition; but one sits down

after having been in motion, when the moisture is evenly and uniformly distributed.

5 · Why is it that sleep comes more readily if one lies on the right side? Is it
because the conditions when we are awake and when we are asleep are the contrary
of one another? Since, therefore, when we are awake we recline on the left side, the   5
contrary will occur when another principle, namely, the contrary, is at work. Or is it
because sleep is the absence of movement? The parts then of the body which are
most active must be at rest; and the parts of the body on the right are most active.
So, if one is lying on this side, a waking principle is as it were enchained.

6 · Why does one feel numbness? And why more in the hands and feet than   10
elsewhere? Is it because numbness is a process of cooling, being due to deprivation
of blood and its transference elsewhere? Now these parts, especially the feet, are
least fleshy and most muscular, and so they are naturally disposed to cool quickly.

7 · Why do we find it comfortable to recline on the left side, but sleep better   15
on the right side? Is it because by turning away we avoid looking towards the light,
since in the dark sleep comes on more readily? Or is it because we keep awake when
reclining on the left side, and in this position we can easily employ ourselves in any
particular function; and so for the contrary purpose the contrary position[1] is
advantageous; for each position invites to a particular function.   20

BOOK VII

PROBLEMS CONNECTED WITH SYMPATHETIC
ACTION

1 · Why do men generally themselves yawn when they see others yawn? Is it   25
because, if they are reminded of it when they feel a desire to perform any function,
they then put it into execution, particularly where the desire is easily stirred, for
example, that of passing urine? Now a yawn is a breath and a movement of
moisture; it is therefore easy of performance, if only one sees some one else yawning;
for the yawn is always ready to come.

2 · Why is it that, although we do not imitate the action if we see a man
stretching out his hand or foot or doing anything else of the kind, yet we ourselves   30
yawn if we see some one else doing so? Or does this not always occur, but only when
the body happens to feel a desire and is in such a condition that its moisture becomes
heated? For then it is recollection which gives the impulse, as also in sexual desire
and hunger; for it is that which causes recollection to exist that provides the
stimulus towards the condition observed in another person.   35

---

[1]Reading πρὸς τὸ ἐναντίον τὸ ἐναντίον σχῆμα.

3 · Why is it that if we stand by a fire we desire to pass urine, and if men stand near water (for example, near a river) they actually pass urine? Is it because 886ᵇ1 water in general reminds us of the water in our own bodies, and the neighbourhood of water incites our internal moisture to come out? Fire of itself dissolves anything which is solidified in the body, just as the sun melts the snow.

4 · Why is it that those who come into contact with certain diseases become 5 affected by them, but no one ever becomes healthy through contact with health? Is it because disease is a state of movement, while health is a state of rest? If so, disease can set up movement, but health cannot. Or is it because disease comes to us against our will, while health comes by our own wish? Things then which occur against our will are different from those which occur by our wish and deliberate choice.

5 · Why is it that not only do some unpleasant sounds make us shudder—for 10 example, when a saw is being sharpened, or pumice-stone cut, or a stone ground—but the signs of effects produced in others conveyed by the sight cause those very effects in ourselves? For our teeth are set on edge when we see others eating anything bitter, and some people faint when they see any one being 15 strangled. Is it because every sound or noise is a breath, and this penetrating into us naturally causes disturbance? Now it will cause greater disturbance if it comes either in great quantity or with an unusually violent impact, setting up a new condition or causing some alteration within us. Therefore breaths which, though large in bulk, are yet soft, stir the actual seat of sensation, and such have a pleasant 20 effect; but those which are rough, causing a violent impact, shake the seat of sensation and affect a wide area owing to the force of their impact. Now things which are cold also affect a wide area, for coldness is a kind of force; therefore, as has been already said, it causes shuddering. But things which are rough, because they cause a series of frequent impacts, striking on the base of the hair thrust it in 25 the opposite direction; for when the hair is thrust out, its ends must necessarily assume a contrary position, with the result that it stands upright; for hair always naturally lies flat. The direction taken by the breath which is conveyed to the body by the hearing is downwards from above. The sounds, therefore, which we have mentioned being harsh, the hair bristles for the reasons stated. The bristling occurs 30 more on the rest of the body than on the head, because the hair there is weaker and the effect produced is weaker. The sensation produced by hearing being blunter than that produced by sight, the effects produced by it are confined to the surface of the body; the bristling of the hair is an effect of this kind, so it occurs from many dissimilar causes. The sensation produced by sight being very distinct, its results too are correspondingly more distinct; therefore the same effects are produced by it as 887ᵃ1 occur in reality, but more mildly than in reality. But as a result of hearing our hair stands on end for fear, not of the actual sounds, but of the anticipation which they arouse; for it is an anticipation of grievous ill.

6 · Why is yawning caused by the sight of others yawning, and so also the

passing of urine, particularly in beasts of burden? Is it due to recollection? For 5
when recollection occurs the part of the body concerned is stimulated. In men then,
because their sensations are finer, when they see something stimulation and
recollection occur simultaneously. But in the beasts the sight is not sufficient by
itself, but they require another sense to be called into activity; so the sense of smell
must also be employed, this being a more easily stimulated sense in unreasoning 10
animals. So the other animals always pass urine in the same spot as the first one; for
the stimulus is most acute when the sense of smell is employed; and the sense of
smell is called into play when they are near the spot.

7 · Why is it that when we see any one cut or burned or tortured or 15
undergoing any other painful suffering, we share mentally in his pain? Is it because
nature is common to us all, and it is this which shares in the sufferer's pain, when we
see any of these things happening to him, through kinship with him? Or is it
because, just as the nose and hearing according to their particular faculties receive
certain emanations, so also the sight does the same as the result of things pleasant 20
and painful?

8 · Why is it that those who come into contact with phthisis or ophthalmia or
scurvy become affected by them, but there is no contagion from dropsy or fevers or
apoplexy and the rest? In ophthalmia is contagion due to the fact that the eye is very
easily affected and more than the other senses assimilates itself to that which it 25
sees—for example, it moves when it sees something else moved—and so it very
readily becomes disordered when it sees another eye in that condition? In phthisis is
the contagion due to the fact that phthisis makes the breath weak and laboured, and
those diseases are most quickly contracted which are due to the corruption of the
breath, as is seen in plagues? He therefore who comes into contact with the sufferer 30
inhales this corrupted breath, and so himself becomes ill, because the breath is
unhealthy; and he catches the disease from one person only, because that person
exhales this particular breath, which is different from that which others exhale; and
he catches the same disease, because, in inhaling the breath by which he becomes
infected, he is inhaling just such breath as he would if he were already suffering
from the disease. Scurvy is more catching than the other diseases, such as leprosy
and the like, because it affects the surface of the body and causes a glutinous
discharge (for this is the nature of itching diseases), and so this disease, being on the 35
surface of the body and glutinous, can be conveyed by contact. Other similar
diseases are not so conveyed, because either they are not on the surface, or else,
being on the surface, they do not remain there, because they are dry.

9 · Why do purslane and salt stop inflammation of the gums? Is it because 887ᵇ1
purslane contains some moisture? This is seen to be so if one chews it or if it be
crushed together[1] for some time; for the moisture is then drawn out of it. The
glutinous matter sinks into the gum and draws out the acidity. For that there is an

---

[1]Reading συνθλασθῇ.

affinity between the disease and the remedy is shown by the acidity; for the juice of
5 the purslane has a certain acidity. Salt, on the other hand, dissolves and draws out
the acidity. Why then do lye and soda not have this effect? Is it because they have
an astringent instead of a dissolvent effect?

BOOK VIII
PROBLEMS CONNECTED WITH CHILL AND SHIVERING

10   1 · Why is it that those who are chilled become livid? Is it because the blood
is congealed by the cold and, as it congeals, becomes black through the absence of
heat? (A white colour, on the other hand, is to be attributed to fire.) For this reason
also the flesh of the aged is particularly livid, because it contains very little heat.

15   2 · Why is it that those who are chilled cannot sleep? Is it because any one
who is chilled tends to hold his breath, but a sleeper exhales rather than inhales, so
that it is difficult for one who is cold to sleep, since it is impossible to do contrary
things simultaneously?

20   3 · Why is it that those who are ill or in pain or angry become more active
under the influence of cold? Is it because a cold condition makes a man stronger?

   4 · Why is it that athletes in good training do not bear the cold well? Is it
because their condition is clean and airy and free from fat? Such a condition is
easily accessible to the air, since it is permeable and does not contain any heat; fat,
25 on the other hand, is hot, unless it is saturated with moisture.

   5 · Why are the extremities most affected by cold? Is it due to their narrow
shape? Also the ducts in them, being narrow, hold little blood, and therefore little
heat; for the blood is hot.

   6 · Why are the feet more liable to become chilled when they are suspended
30 in mid air? Is it because the wind blows more underneath then? Or is it because the
blood is contracted into a narrower space below, and so the rest of the foot is more
easily chilled, because the heat leaves it?

   7 · Why is it that stout persons are especially liable to chill, although fat is
warm? Is it because, owing to the greatness of their bulk, their extreme parts are far
from the internal heat, while their near parts are far from the external cold?

35   8 · Why do people shiver after sneezing and after passing urine? Is it
because in both processes the veins are emptied, and when they are empty the cold
air enters, and this causes shivering?

9 . Why is it that ravenous hunger is felt in cold weather and in winter rather than in summer? Is it because ravenous hunger is brought on through lack of dry   888ᵃ1
nourishment, and in the cold and winter the internal heat contracts into a narrower space and its internal nourishment soon fails, and when this happens ravenous hunger is more likely to occur? The faintness and weakness due to ravenous hunger occur when liquefaction takes place in the body owing to the collection of heat in   5
one place. This liquefied matter flows into the region usually occupied by the nourishment and itself becomes nourishment for the body; if it attacks the seat of respiration, loss of voice and weakness ensue, the loss of voice being due to the obstruction of the passage of the breath, while the weakness is caused by the lack of nourishment in the body and internal liquefaction. Treatment in such cases can be   10
quickly and simply applied, because the cause of the trouble is external; for it is the external[1] cold making our heat contract which causes the ravenous hunger. So just as one trembles and turns pale from fear, but, when freed from the danger, one recovers immediately; so too those who are suffering from ravenous hunger, after   15
taking a little bread, quickly recover, having undergone a violent and unnatural disturbance, but not having been permanently injured thereby; for the same thing which resists the tendency of nature also restores us to our natural course. Once relax the force which is straining against nature, and the body slips back into its natural state as suddenly as children who are playing at tug-of-war with a rope, if   20
the rope is let go, fall on their backs.

10 · Why is it that those who have undergone athletic training do not bear the cold so well as those who have not done so? Is it because the fat is got rid of by   25
their exercises, and it is the fat which gives warmth, since that which is oily is hot? Or is it because the body is in a more airy and rare condition, because the fat and the excretions have been got rid of, so that there is nothing to keep out the cold? Or is it because through the opening of the pores by perspiration a number of doors are as it were removed? It is clear that the same condition does not conduce both to health and to strength; for obviously a condition of health is one of fatness, while a   30
condition of strength is a state of rarity.

11 · Why do we shiver both when hot and when cold water is poured over us? For it is strange that contraries should produce the same result. Is it because, when cold water is poured over us, the extinguishing of the internal heat causes shivering, whereas, as the effect of warm water, the superficial cold is enclosed in   35
one place and massed together by its inward rush? So both effects are due to the same cause, but in one case it operates from within and in the other from without.

12 · Why do the hairs bristle upon the skin? Is it because they naturally stand erect when the skin is contracted, and this contraction occurs owing to cold and certain other conditions?

¹Reading ἐκτός for ἐντός.

888[b]1   13 · Why is it that one shivers at the last emission of urine? Is it because, whilst the warm liquid is still within, the bladder and the passages round it are full, but when it has passed out they fill up again with cold air, for nothing can be empty,
5   but must be full either of something corporeal or of air? Inasmuch then as cold air enters, shivering is a natural result.

14 · Why is it that the tongue of those who are chilled, like that of the drunken, stumbles? Is it because, as it stiffens and hardens with the cold, it becomes
10   difficult to move, and, when this happens, it cannot speak plainly? Or is it because, the outer parts of the body being solidified by the cold, the moisture flows together within and saturates the tongue, and so it cannot perform its function, as has been already described in the case of the drunken? Or is it because owing to the trembling produced by chill, the movement of the tongue is irregular and it cannot
15   articulate the words which it utters, and consequently it stumbles?

15 · Why do the hairs stand erect on the bodies of those who are chilled? Is it because as a result of cooling the heat collects in the inner region of the body, and the flesh, as the heat leaves it, contracts more and more, and, as it is drawn together,
20   the hairs become more upright? Or is it because . . .

16 · Why in the winter are we more likely to become chilled through running than through standing still? Is it because the air surrounding the body, when we stand still, no longer causes discomfort when once the body is thoroughly warm, but on the other hand, when we are running, we are continually encountering more and more cold air, and so are more liable to become chilled? Moreover also air
25   is cold when it is in motion, and it is for the most part such air that meets us in running.

17 · Why is it that it is colder at dawn, although the sun is nearer to us? Is it because the period of the sun's absence is then at its longest, so that the earth has become more cooled? Or is it because towards daybreak the dew falls, as does the
30   hoar-frost, and both of these are cold? Or do they too fall because the heat which rises from the earth is overpowered, the reason that it is overpowered being the absence of the sun? So that they do not fall when the sun is farther away, but when it is nearer they fall and become congealed, because the longer the sun is absent the
35   cooler the ground becomes. Or is it because the nocturnal breezes tend to cause cold towards daybreak? Or do we only imagine that it is colder because then the food within us is concocted and, the stomach being emptier, we are more liable to feel the cold? This can be illustrated by the fact that we feel very cold after vomiting.

18 · Why is it that those who are chilled feel pain if they are taken straight to the fire, whereas they do not do so if they are warmed gradually? Is it because one
889[a]1   contrary immediately succeeding another contrary always sets up a violent change? We may compare the fact that if one bends a tree by degrees, it does not suffer, but if one bends it with greater violence and not gradually, it breaks off. If therefore like

is unaffected by like, and the heat of a man who is chilled collects and concentrates   5
within him and the moisture and cold are left behind, and a contrary is destructive
of its contrary, it follows that, if one is warmed by degrees, the heat comes out
gradually and less pain is caused, but, if the warming is not gradual, the heat is
rather drawn out.

19 . Why is it that when we are chilled the same heat causes more burning   10
and pain? Is it because owing to its density the flesh holds the heat which comes into
contact with it? This is the reason why lead becomes hotter than wool. Or is the
passage of the heat violent because the pores are congealed by the cold?

20 . Why is it that those who are angry do not become cold? Is it because   15
anger and wrath are the opposite of cowardice? Now anger is the result of fiery
heat, for by retaining a large quantity of fiery heat within us we become warm. This
is particularly noticeable in children. For grown-up men when angry become
distracted, but children first of all take in breath in large quantities and then blush;   20
for the amount of heat in them being very great and causing liquefaction makes
them blush, since, if one were to pour a quantity of cold water on them, they would
cease from their wrath, for their heat would be quenched. The opposite occurs in
cowards and those who are afraid; for they are chilled and become cold and pale; for
the heat leaves the superficial region of their bodies.   25

21 . Why is it that when we shiver, the hairs stand erect? Do they lie down[2]
because they grow in moisture? For the weight[3] of the hair prevails over the
moisture. Now shivering is caused by the cold, for the cold naturally congeals the
moisture. When therefore the moisture, out of which the hair grows, undergoes a   30
change and congeals, it is natural that the hair should undergo a change also. If
therefore it changes into a contrary condition, it either remains permanently in that
condition, or else the hair will again prevail over the moisture. It is not, however,
likely that the hair can by its weight overpower the moisture when it is congealed
and condensed; and if it is impossible for the hair to lie down anywhere because the   35
moisture is congealed, the only thing left for it to do is to stand erect. Or is it
because, as a result of cooling, the heat collects in the interior region of the body,
and the flesh, as the heat leaves it, contracts more and more, and, as it draws
together, the hair grows more upright, just as when one fixes a twig or some other
object in the ground and fills the space round it and collects the soil on every side, it   889[b]1
is more likely to remain erect than if one leaves the soil loose round it?

22 . Why is it that those who are chilled find it particularly difficult to go to
sleep? Is it because one who is chilled holds his breath rather than exhales, and a   5
sleeper exhales rather than inhales? Chill therefore induces a condition which is
directly opposed to sleep.

---

[2]Reading κατακέκλιυται.
[3]Reading βάρος.

BOOK IX

PROBLEMS CONNECTED WITH BRUISES,
SCARS, AND WEALS

1 · Why is it that weals can be prevented by the application of newly flayed hides, particularly those of rams, and by breaking eggs over the part affected? Is it because both these things prevent the collection of moisture and the consequent swelling? For the wounded place swells owing to the heat. Now eggs owing to their glutinous consistency cause adhesion and prevent swelling (their effect resembling that of cautery), acting as a kind of glue. The hide owing to its glutinous condition adheres and at the same time by its heat sets up concoction and stops the inflammation, for they do not remove it for several days. Rubbing with salt and vinegar is also employed with the object of drawing out the inflammation.

2 · Why is it that scars are black on the rest of the body but white on the eye? Is it because a scar, like everything else which is diseased, takes on the contrary of its original colour, and it is in the black part of the eye that wounds are inflicted? However, scars on the body do not become black immediately, but are white at first; nor are scars in the eye always white,[1] but it is only after a while that they become absolutely or comparatively so.

3 · Why does a fennel-stalk make the parts round the place which is struck red and the centre of it white? Is it because it presses the blood away from the middle, at the point where, being round, it strikes deepest? Or would one not expect the blood for this reason to return there again, the redness being due to the rush of blood and such a rush taking place towards the part which is struck?

4 · Why is it that, when a violent blow is struck with a fennel-stalk, the middle of the flesh which is struck turns white and the surrounding parts red, whereas, if an ordinary stick is used, the middle is the reddest part? Is it because the fennel-stalk owing to its lightness, if it strikes a hard blow, disperses the blood on the surface, and so the part from which the blood has retired has a white appearance, but the parts to which it flows in greater quantities become redder? When the part struck swells up, the dispersed blood does not readily return to its place, because it is scanty and the course which it must follow is upwards; for it needs the force imparted by mass to make it follow an unnatural course. But blows dealt with hard objects owing to their weight and strength cause compression and crushing. The compression, therefore, produces a hollow, while the crushing causes rarity; for crushing is a mild form of cutting and cleaving. The middle of the part struck becoming hollow and rare, the blood flows into it from the surrounding surface; for it naturally flows downwards and into the rare parts, because they give way before it. The blood collecting there naturally makes this part red, while the surrounding regions, from which the blood retires, turn white.

---

[1] Reading λευκαί.

5 · Why do those who are splenetic have black scars? Is it because their 10
blood is corrupted by the admixture of vitiated and watery blood from the spleen?
Now the scar occupies only a small depth of the skin on the surface, but the blood,
which is black because it is watery and hot, shows through the skin and gives the
scar also a black appearance. Moreover, very often the scar meanwhile becomes 15
blacker and blacker; this is due to the same cause, for owing to the weakness of the
skin the blood cools, and as the heat evaporates, turns blacker. Similarly in the aged
the flesh becomes blacker, and their congenital scars are blacker than those of the
young; for their whole body assumes as it were the condition of a bruise owing not to 20
the thinness of their skin but to the fact that their heat fails.

6 · Do things which cause the same effect possess the same power for the
production of that effect, or not? For example, seeing that bronze and radishes and
mashed beans and sea-lungs and clay and various other things take away bruises, do 25
they do so in virtue of the same power? Or does bronze produce this effect because
of its rust, which has a medicinal value, and beans and sea-lungs and clay because
they have an attractive force owing to their rarity, and other things for various other
reasons? Or is the ultimate effect the same in all these cases (for many of them 30
possess contrary qualities, for example heat and cold), while the earlier effects may
nevertheless be different?

7 · Why do all other scars turn black, while those in the eye are white? Is it
because they cause a change in respect of colour in the parts in which they occur,
and so scars which occur in the eye, which is black, must necessarily be white? 35

8 · Why is the blow of a fennel-stalk more painful than that of some much
harder instruments, if in dealing the blow one considers their comparative effects?
For it would be much more natural to suppose that the stroke of a harder instrument
would be more painful, for it deals a heavier blow. Is it because the flesh is pained 890^{b}1
not only by receiving a blow but also by dealing one? When it is struck by hard
substances, it only receives a blow (for it yields to them because they are hard); but
when it is struck by a fennel-stalk, two effects are produced—it receives a blow and
it also deals one, because it does not yield owing to the lightness of the weight 5
imposed upon it; and so the blow is of a double nature.

9 · Why are thapsia and metal ladles used to stop bruises (the former being
applied immediately, the latter at a later stage), containing as they do opposite
qualities? For a ladle is cold, as the poet says,

Between his teeth the chilly bronze he bit;[2] 10

whilst thapsia is hot and burning. Does the ladle have the same effect that water has
upon the fainting? For its coldness encounters the heat and prevents it from
escaping out of the blood, which collects on the surface owing to the blow and

---

[2]Homer, *Iliad* V 75.

congeals when the heat passes out. For just as would happen if it congealed outside,
15 so the blood congeals near the outer surface while it is still under the skin; but[3] if the
heat is prevented from escaping by the coldness of the bronze, the blood does not
congeal, but disperses again and returns to the area from which it was collected.
Thapsia being hot has the same effect; for by its heat it prevents congelation.

20　　　10 · Why are bruises dispersed by the application of copper objects such as
ladles and the like? Is it because copper is cold? It therefore prevents the escape of
the heat from the blood which collects as the result of the blow, and it is the loss of
heat from the surface which causes the bruise. The ladle must therefore be applied
quickly before congelation takes place. Thapsia, too, mixed with honey is a good
25 remedy for the same reason; for being hot it prevents the blood from becoming
cold.

　　　11 · Why is it that if a wound occurs several times in the same place, the scar
turns black? Is it because, whenever a wound is dealt, the part affected is always
30 weak and becomes weaker the more often it is wounded? Now that which is weak is
chilled and full of moisture; therefore it has a black appearance. Again[4] large and
inveterate wounds form black scars, and to receive frequent wounds is equivalent to
having one wound for a long time.

　　　12 · Why do we apply metal ladles to bruises? Is it because, when we are
35 struck, the part affected is cooled and the heat leaves it? So the application of the
ladle, the material of which, being copper, is cold, prevents the heat from
escaping.

　　　13 · Why is it that hairs do not grow on scars? Is it because the pores, from
which the hairs grow, become blocked up and displaced?

891ᵃ1　　　14 · Why do blows cause swelling and discoloration? Is it because the
moisture in the part affected is dispersed and, after breaking its way into the
adjoining regions, recoils again and collects owing to the conglutination of the
moisture? Also if any small veins are burst, a collection of bloodshot matter is
5 formed.

BOOK X

A SUMMARY OF PHYSICAL PROBLEMS

　　　1 · Why is it that some animals cough, while others do not, for example a
man coughs, but an ox does not? Is it because in most animals the excretion is
10 directed to some other part, but in man to this part? Or is it because in man the
brain is very copious and liquid, and coughing occurs when phlegm flows down?

---

[3]Reading δὲ ἐξιέναι.
[4]Reading φαίνεται. εἶτα τά.

2 · Why is it that in man alone of the animals blood flows from the nostrils? Is it because his brain is very copious and liquid, whence the veins, becoming full of excretion, send forth a stream through the ducts? For unhealthy blood (that is, blood which is mixed with excretions from the brain) is thinner than pure blood and resembles lymph.

3 · Why is it that some animals are fat under the flesh, others in the flesh, and others in both these places? Is it because in those whose flesh is dense the moisture collects between the skin and the flesh, because the skin there is naturally loose,[1] and this moisture being concocted turns into fat? Those, on the other hand, who have rare flesh and a tightly fitting[2] skin, become fat in the flesh; while those who have both these characteristics are fat both in and under the flesh.

4 · Why are boys and women less liable to white leprosy than men, and old women more than young? Is it because white leprosy is due to the escape of breath, and the bodies of boys are dense and do not allow the passage of breath, and those of women do so less than those of men, for the breath is diverted into the menstrual fluids? The density of their flesh is shown by its smoothness. But the bodies of middle-aged and old women allow the passage of breath; for they alone, like old buildings, have a loose structure of their component parts.

5 · Why is it that man alone has white leprosy? Is it because he is the thinnest-skinned and at the same time the fullest of breath amongst the animals? An indication of this is the fact that leprosy appears most abundantly and soonest on the parts of the body where the skin is thinnest. Or, while this is true, is there a further reason, namely, that in man alone of the animals the hair turns grey? For in leprosy the hair becomes grey, and so it is impossible for leprosy to occur in those in whom the hair does not turn grey.

6 · Why is it that goats and sheep yield the most milk, although their bodies are not the largest, whereas women and cows produce proportionately less? Is it because in the latter two cases the available material is used up to form bulk, while in the other animals it goes into excretions, and in sheep and goats the residue of the excretion all becomes milk? Or is it because sheep and goats are more prolific than the large animals, and so draw off more excretion, because they have more offspring to nourish? Or is it because owing to the weakness of their bodies more excretion is formed during the period of gestation, and the milk comes from the excretion?

7 · Why is it that in some animals (goats, for example) a change of water causes a change in their colour, which assimilates to that of other animals in the new locality, whereas with other animals (man, for example) this is not so? Or, to put the question generally, why do some animals change and others not (the crow, for

[1] Reading τὸ ταυτῇ εἶναι τὸ δέρμα ἀφεστός.
[2] Reading προσεστός.

example)? Do those animals not change in whom the element of moisture does not predominate, birds, for example, which consequently have no bladder? Why is it that while such creatures do not themselves change, yet their offspring do so? Is it
20 because the offspring is weaker than its parents?

8 · Why are males usually larger than females? Is it because they are hotter, and heat is productive of growth? Or is it because the male is complete in all its parts, whereas the female is defective? Or is it because the male takes a long time to attain perfection, the female a short time?

25 9 · Why is it that some animals bear their young quickly, but in others the period of gestation is a long one? Is it because the longer-lived animals come to perfection more slowly? It is the longer-lived animals that take a long time to bear their young. This is not, however, true of the longest-lived of all animals; for example, the horse is slower in bearing its young but shorter-lived than man. The
30 reason for this is the hardness of the uterus; for the uterus of a mare may be compared to a dry soil which does not readily bring the crops to maturity.

10 · Why is it that the young of all other animals resemble their parents in nature more closely than do those of man? Is it because man's mental condition is more varied at the moment of sexual intercourse, and so the offspring varies
35 according to the condition of the male and female parents? The other animals, or most of them, are wholly absorbed in the sexual act; further, owing to this avidity, impregnation does not usually take place.

892ᵃ1 11 · Why is it that fair men and white horses usually have grey eyes? Is it because there are three colors in eyes, black, greenish, and grey, and the colour of
5 the eyes follows that of the body, resulting in this case in greyness?

12 · For what reason are there dwarfs? Or to put the question more generally, why are some creatures quite large, others small? Let us examine the latter question. The causes of smallness are two, either space or nourishment— space, if it be narrow, and nourishment, if it be scanty; as happens when attempts
10 are made to make animals small after their birth, for example by keeping puppies in quail-cages. Those who suffer from lack of space become pygmies; for they have width and depth corresponding to the dimensions of their parents, but they are quite
15 small in stature. The reason for this is that owing to the narrowness of the space in which they are confined the straight lines become crushed and bent. So pygmies are like figures painted on shops which are short in stature but are seen to be of ordinary width and depth. Those who fail to come to perfection from lack of nourishment
20 clearly have the limbs of children, and one sometimes sees persons who are very small and yet perfectly proportioned, like Maltese lap-dogs. The reason is that the process of growth has a different effect from that of space.

13 · Why is it that some animals come into being from the sexual intercourse of animals with one another, others from the compounding of certain elements—a process resembling the original production of their species? Just as the 25 writers on natural phenomena explain the first origin of animals as being due to powerful changes and movements in the world and universe; so now, if it is to happen again, some similar movements must take place. For the beginning of anything is the most important part, being indeed half of the whole; and in this case 30 the seed is the beginning. The reason then why small animals which are not produced by sexual intercourse resemble the species as it originally came into being, is the smallness of the seed; for the smaller a thing is, the smaller is its first beginning. So the changes even of this are sufficient to produce a seed for it. And this is what actually happens; for it is under conditions of change that such 35 creatures usually come into being. In the larger animals a greater change is necessary for their production.

14 · Why is it that some animals are prolific, such as the pig, the dog, and the hare, whilst others are not so, for instance man and the lion? Is it because the 892^{b}1 former class has a number of wombs which they desire to fill and moulds into which the semen is distributed, while with the latter the opposite is the case?

15 · Why has man a smaller distance between his eyes in proportion to his size than any other animal? Is it because man is the most natural of creatures and 5 perception is naturally of that which is in front, since it is necessary to see beforehand that to which the movement is directed? Now the greater the distance between the eyes, the more will the sight incline sideways. So if the sight is to accord with nature, the distance between the eyes ought to be as small as possible, for then 10 it will travel most directly forward. Further, the other animals must necessarily turn their gaze sideways, since they do not possess hands; their eyes therefore are farther apart, especially those of sheep, because they generally advance bending their heads downwards.

16 · Why is it that the other animals seldom or never emit semen during 15 sleep? Is it because no animal except man sleeps on its back and no emission of semen takes place except in that position? Or is it because the other animals dream less than man, and the emission of semen only takes place when the imagination is stirred?

17 · Why is it that some animals move their heads and others not? Is it 20 because some have no necks and so cannot move their heads?

18 · Why does man sneeze more than the other animals? Is it because in him the ducts are wide through which the breath and smells pass in? For it is with these, when they fill with breath, that he sneezes. That these ducts are wide is shown by the fact that man has a weaker sense of smell than any other animal; and the 25

narrower the ducts, the keener is the sense of smell. Since, therefore, the moisture, the evaporation of which causes sneezing, enters in larger quantities and more often into wide ducts, and man more than any other animal has such ducts, he might
30   naturally be expected to sneeze most often. Or is it because his nostrils are particularly short and so the heated moisture can quickly turn into breath, whereas in the other animals, owing to the length of their nostrils, it cools before it can evaporate?

19 · Why is it that in no animal is the tongue of a fatty consistency? Is it because that which is fat is dense, whereas the tongue is naturally rare in order that
35   it may recognize different flavours?

20 · Why is it that females pass urine with an effort, but males without an effort? Is it because in the female the bladder is farther away both in depth of position and in distance, since the womb is situated between the fundament and the
893ᵃ1   bladder? It therefore requires a greater effort to drive the urine owing to the distance of the womb; and the requisite force is exercised by an effort of the breath.

21 · Why is it that all such animals as do not fly shed their winter coats,
5   except the pig? The dog, for example, does so, and the ox. Is it because the pig is very hot and its hairs grow out of a hot substance (for that which is fat is hot)? In the other animals the hair is shed because either the moisture cools or else the natural heat cannot concoct the nourishment. But the pig[3] does not shed its hair,
10   either because the moisture in it undergoes no change or because its nourishment is properly concocted; for whenever any cause is present to make it shed its hair, the fat is sufficient to prevent it. Sheep and men are unaffected owing to the quantity
15   and density of their hair; for the cold cannot penetrate deep enough to congeal the moisture or to prevent the heat from concocting it.

22 · Why is it that in sheep the hair grows again softer when it is plucked out, but in man it is harder? Is it because the hair of sheep grows out of the surface,
20   and so can be plucked out without causing pain, the source of its nourishment, which is in the flesh, remaining unimpaired? So the pores being opened, the excretions evaporate more readily, and the wool receives the natural nourishment of the flesh, the latter being fed by soft, sweet nourishment. The hair of man, on the other hand, since it grows from a great depth, can only be plucked out by force and
25   painfully. This is shown by the fact that it draws blood with it. The place therefore from which it is plucked is wounded and scarred. So at last the hair ceases to grow on those who pluck it out, and as long as it does grow again, it grows hard, because all the nourishing food in the flesh fails, and it is from the excretions of this food
30   that the hair grows. This can be illustrated by the fact that in all those who inhabit a southerly clime the hair is hard, because the exterior heat penetrates deeply and

---

[3]Reading ἢ δὲ ὗς ἢ διά.

vaporizes the well-concocted nourishment; but the hair of those who dwell in northern climes is soft, because in them the blood and sweet humours are nearer the surface, for which reason also they have a healthy complexion.   35

23 . Why is it that in sheep the longer the hair grows the harder it is, whereas in man it is softer? Is it because the hair of sheep, obtaining the nourishment described above, receives less food because it is far removed from the source of it, and the nourishment already present in it easily evaporates out of it owing to the heat as a result of concoction? And as the hair dries it becomes harder;[4]   893ᵇ1 for it is the moisture which makes it soft. Human hair, on the other hand, receives less nourishment but is situated nearer to the source of it; and the nourishment is more thoroughly concocted because it is less abundant, and, being concocted, it makes the hair softer, because anything that is concocted is softer than that which is   5 unconcocted; for human hair is derived more from excretion than that of sheep. This is shown by the fact that the wool of young sheep is softer than that of old.

24 . Why is it that thick-haired men and birds with thick feathers are   10 lustful? Is it because they are naturally hot and moist? Now both these characteristics are necessary for sexual intercourse; for the heat causes excretion, and the moisture is the form which the excretion takes. Lame men are lustful for the same reason; for, owing to the deficiencies of their legs, the nourishment is carried downwards in small quantities only, but travels into the upper region of the body in   15 large quantities, and is there converted into semen.

25 . Why has man no mane? Is it because he has a beard, and so the nourishment consisting of the necessary excretion, which in animals goes into the mane, in man goes to the jaws?

26 . Why is it that all animals have an even number of feet? Is it because it   20 is impossible to move (except by jumping), unless some part is at rest? Since, then, progression involves two things, namely, movement and rest, we immediately get here a pair and an even number. Quadrupeds have two more legs;[5] for they move two, while the other two are at rest. Six-footed animals have an additional pair,[6] of   25 which one moves while the other is at rest.

27 . Why is it that in horses and asses hair grows out of scars, but not in man? Is it because in the other animals the skin is part of the flesh, but in man it is only as it were a condition of the flesh? For in man the surface of the flesh seems to   30 become harder through cooling and resembles what we call the crust of boiled meal; just, then, as this crust is really only boiled meal, so what is called man's skin would really be only flesh. Now when a man receives a wound or is chafed, the result is

---

[4]Reading σκληρότεραι.
[5]Reading δύο ἔτι for διότι.
[6]The text is uncertain at this point.

35   that his flesh becomes denser; and so, the surface of the flesh having undergone a change, the wounded parts do not assume the same nature as the original skin; and, as the flesh has undergone a change, it is not to be wondered at that what grew from it no longer does so—a phenomenon also occurring in what is called baldness, which is also due to a corruption and change in the surface of the flesh. When, however,

894ᵃ1   beasts of burden have been chafed and recover again, the parts of the body affected fill out again with the same substance, but it is weaker than it was before; and since their skin too is a part of them, the hair (which grows out of the skin) must come

5   forth and grow, but it is white, because the skin which was formed is weaker than the original skin, and white hair is the weakest kind of hair.

28 · Why is it that among the other animals twins though differing in sex are just as likely to survive, but this is not so with the young of man? Is it because human twins are particularly weak, for man naturally produces only one offspring

10   at a time? Now in twins it is unnatural to find a diversity of sex; and so what is most contrary to nature is also weakest.

29 · Why is it that in horses and asses hair grows out of scars, but not in man? Is it because the scar impedes the growth of the hair, either owing to the condensation of the flesh or because its nutrition is impaired? In man, therefore, it

15   absolutely prevents the growth owing to the weakness of the hair; but in horses it does not prevent, but merely impairs, the growth.

30 · Why have animals an even number of feet? Is it because in anything that moves something must necessarily be at rest, and this could not happen if there were an odd number of feet (for[7] it was the arrangement of the feet in pairs which

20   originally made movement possible)?

31 · Why is it that animals are asleep for a shorter time than they are awake, and their sleep is not continuous? Is it because all the excretion is not concocted at the same time, but, when some is concocted, the animal is relieved and wakes up? Again, they more often wake up when the region in which the excretion

25   is concocted becomes cold; for it quickly and frequently ceases to do its work, and this cessation causes awakening. Sleep not unnaturally[8] seems to be pleasant, because it gives us rest; but the rest which we take in sleep does not last longer than the time taken by our natural activities, nor do we eat for a longer period than that during which we abstain from food, in spite of the fact that eating is pleasanter than fasting.

30   32 · Why is it that some animals imitate their parents immediately after birth, while others, like man, do so late, or hardly at all, or never? Is it because some quickly attain a state of physical perfection,[9] while others are late in doing so, and

---

[7]Reading ἅπερ.
[8]Reading ὡς εἰκός.
[9]Reading τὴν ἐπιτέλεσιν τοῦ σώματος for τὸ γνωρίζειν.

some are without a perception of what is for their good, while others possess such a perception? Those therefore which possess both these qualities, namely, perception of what is for their good and physical perfection, imitate their parents, 35 but those who have not both these qualities do not do so; for physical and perceptive powers are both requisite.

33 . Why is it that white leprosy does not occur in animals other than man? Is it because, while it is a disease which afflicts other animals, only in man does the hair and skin turn partially white? (But, if so, one might raise the question why $894^{b}1$ diversity of colour in animals occurs at birth and not afterwards.) Or is it because the skin of other animals is hard, whereas man has naturally very thin skin? Now white leprosy is an excretion of breath, which in the other animals is prevented from 5 escaping by the thickness of their skin.

34 . Why is it that in white leprosy the hair turns grey, but it does not necessarily follow that leprosy is always present where there is grey hair? Is it because the hair grows from the skin, and greyness is as it were a corruption of the hair? When therefore the skin is in a morbid condition, the hair that grows from it is 10 necessarily affected; but when the hair is unhealthy the skin is not necessarily so.

35 . Why is it that some animals are ill-tempered after bearing young, dogs, for example, and pigs, but others are not noticeably so, for instance women and sheep? Is it because those animals which are full of excretions are mild-tempered, for that which causes them pain passes out at the time of birth? Those,[10] on the 15 other hand, who in bearing young lose healthy material, are made irritable by the reduced condition in which they are; just as hens are bad-tempered, not just when they have laid, but when they are sitting, from want of food.

36 . Why is it that eunuchs, when they are emasculated, in other respects change into the likeness of the female,—for they have the voice, the shrillness, and 20 the lack of articulation which characterize women, and so undergo a violent change, as do other animals when castrated (in bulls and rams, however, we find the horns assuming contrary forms, the reason being that their females have contrary kinds of horns, and so bulls when they are castrated grow larger horns and rams smaller horns)—in respect of size, however, alone eunuchs change into the likeness of the 25 male, for they become larger? Now size is characteristic of the male, for the female is smaller than the male. Or is it not after all a change into the likeness of the female rather than the male? For it is not a change in every dimension, but only in height, whereas the male is characterized by width and depth as well; for this is what his 30 full growth involves. Furthermore, as is the female to the male, so within the female sex is the maiden to the woman; for the latter has reached the full nobility of form, while the former has not yet done so. It is into the likeness of *their* nature then that

[10]Omitting ὥστε.

the eunuch changes; for their growth is in height. So Homer well says,

> Stature chaste Artemis gave them,

35   as being able to give what, being a maiden, she herself possessed. When, therefore, a
eunuch changes in size, he does not change into the likeness of the male; for the
change is not in the direction of physical perfection, but eunuchs increase in size
only in respect of height.

37 · Why is it that eunuchs either never suffer from varicose veins, or do so
895ᵃ1   less than others? Is it because, by their being castrated, their nature changes into
that of persons lacking generative power? Now boys and women lack this power,
and neither has varicose veins except women very occasionally.

38 · Why is man better able to utter many voices, while other animals of one
5   and the same species utter only one voice? Has man too really only one voice, but
many forms of speech?

39 · And why has man different forms of speech, while the other animals
have not? Is it because men in their speech make use of a number of letters, but the
other animals employ either none or only two or three consonants? (Now it is
10   consonants combined with vowels that form speech.) Now speaking is signifying
something not merely by the voice but by certain conditions of the voice, and not
merely to signify pain or pleasure; and it is the letters which regulate these
conditions. But children express what they want to say in just the same way as wild
beasts; for young children cannot yet make use of the letters in speech.

15   40 · Why is it that of all animals man alone is apt to hesitate in his speech?
Is it because he is also liable to be dumb, and hesitancy of speech is a form of
dumbness, or at any rate the organ of speech is not perfect? Or is it because man
partakes more of rational speech, while the other animals only possess voice, and
hesitancy of speech, as its name implies, is simply[11] being unable to explain one's
meaning continuously?

20   41 · Why is it that man more than the other animals is apt to be lame from
birth? Is it because the legs of animals are strong (for quadrupeds and birds have
bony and sinewy legs), but human legs are fleshy, and so owing to their softness they
more easily become damaged through movement? Or is it because in man alone of
25   animals the period of gestation varies? For he may be born after the seventh or the
eighth or the tenth month. For the other animals there is one fixed time for coming
to perfection without any further delay; but in man the period of delay is long, and
so, when the foetus moves, its extremities being soft are more liable to become
30   broken in the longer period.

[11]Reading κατὰ τὸ ὄνομα οὐδὲν ἢ οὐ.

42 · Why have eunuchs sore and ulcerated legs? Is it because this is also characteristic of women, and eunuchs are effeminate? Or, while this is true, is the cause in women as well this, that the heat has a downward tendency? (Menstruation shows that this is so.) So neither eunuchs nor women grow thick hair, owing to 35 the presence of copious moisture in them.

43 · Why is it that no animal except man suffers from gall-stones? Is it because in beasts of burden and cloven-hoofed animals the ducts of the bladder are wide? Those animals which produce their young alive not immediately but after an interval, like certain of the fishes, never have bladders, but the sediment which 895^{b}1 might form gall-stones is forced into the bowels (as happens also in birds), and so easily passes out with the excrement. But man has a bladder and a stalk to the bladder, which is narrow in proportion to his size; so, because he has this part, the 5 earthy matter is forced into the bladder (and so chamber-pots become discoloured by it) and, owing to the heat in that region, it becomes concocted and thickens still more and remains there and increases owing to the narrowness of the urethra; for the earthy sediment, being unable to make its way out easily, coheres together and 10 forms a gall-stone.

44 · Why is it that beasts of burden and cattle and horned animals and birds do not belch? Is it owing to the dryness of their stomachs? For the moisture is quickly used up and percolates through; whereas belching results when the 15 moisture remains and evaporates. In animals with long manes and tails, owing to the length of their necks, the breath tends to travel downwards, and therefore they generally break wind backwards. Birds and horned animals neither belch nor break wind; and ruminating animals do not belch, because they have several stomachs and the so-called 'reticulum'; and so the breath finds a passage up and down through 20 many channels, and the moisture is taken up before it can become vaporized and cause either belching or breaking of wind.

45 · Why is it that tame animals are invariably found also in a wild state, but wild animals are not always found also in a tame condition? For even men certainly exist in a wild state in some places, and wild dogs are found in India and 25 horses elsewhere; but lions and leopards and vipers and many other animals are never found in a tame state. Is it because the inferior condition is more easily acquired at first and it is easier to degenerate into it, since it is not the original but the ultimate nature which is difficult to attain to at once? For this reason all tame animals are at first wild rather than tame (for example the child is greedier and 30 more quick-tempered than the man), but physically weaker. So we find the same state of affairs in the products of nature as in those of the arts. For among the latter there are always badly-made objects, and the bad are more numerous than the good, beds for instance and garments and the like; and, where a good object is 35 produced, it is always possible to find also a bad one, but, where a bad object is produced, it is not also possible always to find a good one. This can be seen from an

examination of the works of the primitive painters and sculptors; for in their day
there was not yet any good painting or sculpture anywhere, but only inferior work.
896ª1 So likewise nature always produces inferior specimens and in a greater number, and
superior specimens in a smaller number and in some cases not at all. Now the tame
is superior and the wild inferior. It is, I suppose, easier for nature—not the primitive
nature but that towards which animals develop—to make the good kinds also tame;
but the opposite kinds never, or scarcely ever, become tame, and it is only under
5   certain conditions of locality and time that sooner[12] or later owing to a general
admixture of circumstances all animals can become tame. The same thing happens
in plants of all kinds; those which are garden plants are also found in a wild state,
but it is impossible for all to be cultivated, but some are so peculiarly conditioned in
many respects in their natural soil that, though neglected and left wild, they grow
10   better and more like cultivated plants than those which are carefully tilled in other
soil.

46 · Why is it that men have large navels, whereas in the other animals they
are inconspicuous? Is it because in the latter, owing to the long period of gestation,
15   they wither off and project outwards and swell all up into sores, and so the
navel sometimes even becomes mis-shapen? Now man comes forth from the womb
in an imperfect condition, and so his navel comes away still full of moisture and
blood. That some animals are perfect and others imperfect at birth is shown by the
fact that some animals can fend for themselves at once, but children require looking
after.

20   47 · Why is it that some animals copulate only once, others frequently, and
some only at certain seasons of the year and others at no fixed time? For example,
man does so at all times but wild animals only occasionally, and the wild boar only
does so once but the domesticated pig frequently. Is it the effect of nourishment and
warmth and exercise, since 'Cypris depends on fullness'? Again, the same species
25   bears young once in some localities but several times in others; for instance, the
sheep in Magnesia and Libya have young twice a year. The reason is the prolonged
period of gestation; for animals, when their desire is satisfied, feel desire no longer,
just as, when they have fed, they no longer desire food. Also animals when pregnant
feel less desire for sexual intercourse, because the menstrual purgation does not take
place.

30   48 · Why is it that men who have widely-spaced teeth are generally
short-lived? Is it a sign that the skull is thick? For the brain is weak if it is not well
ventilated, and so, being moist, it quickly decays, just as all other things decay if
they are not in motion and cannot evaporate. For this reason too man has very thick
35   hair upon the head, and the male is longer-lived than the female because of the
sutures in his skull. But we must next consider length of life in relation to other
conditions.

[12]Reading ἄρτι.

49 · Why then are men long-lived who have a line right across their palms?
Is it because animals whose limbs are badly articulated are shortest-lived, aquatic
animals for example? And if those which are badly articulated are short-lived,   896ᵇ1
clearly those that are well articulated must be the opposite. Now the latter are those
in which even those parts are best articulated which are by nature badly articulated;
and the inside of the hand is the least well articulated part of the body.

50 · Why is it that man alone squints, or at any rate does so more than any   5
other animal? Is it because he alone, or more than other animals, is liable to seizure
in infancy, when distortion of the vision also always begins?

51 · Why is man more affected by smoke than other animals? Is it because
he is most prone to shed tears, and shedding tears is one of the effects of smoke?

52 · Why does horse take pleasure in and desire horse, and man take   10
pleasure in man, and generally why do animals delight in animals which are akin to
and like them? For every[13] animal is not equally beautiful, and desire is of the
beautiful. The beautiful then ought to be pleasanter; but in actual fact it is truer
that not every kind of beauty is pleasant,[14] nor are pleasure and the beautiful
equally pleasing to all men; for example, one creature takes greater pleasure in
eating or drinking and another in sexual intercourse. The question why each   15
creature prefers and takes greatest pleasure in sexual intercourse with a creature
that is akin to it is dealt with elsewhere; but to add that what is akin is also most
beautiful is not true. But we regard as beautiful that which is pleasing with a view to
sexual intercourse, because, when we feel desire, we delight in looking upon the   20
object of our desire. And indeed the same thing happens in other forms of desire; for
example, when we are thirsty we take greater pleasure in the sight of something to
drink. So that which is beautiful in view of a certain use of it seems to be most
pleasant because we particularly desire it. (But this is not true of that which is
beautiful in itself, as is proved by the fact that even grown men appear to us   25
beautiful, when we look at them without[15] any idea of sexual intercourse. Do they
then appear beautiful in such a way as to give our eyes more pleasure than those
who are of an age for sexual intercourse? There is no reason why they should not,
provided we do not happen to feel a desire for sexual intercourse.) Thus something
to drink appears to us as particularly good; for, if we happen to be thirsty, we shall
see it with considerable pleasure.

53 · Why is it that in man the front of the body is more thickly covered with
hair than the posterior portion, but in quadrupeds the posterior part is hairiest? Is it   30
because all two-footed animals have the front part of the body more thickly
covered? For the birds resemble man in this respect. Or is nature always

---

[13]Reading ὁτιοῦν for ὅτι πᾶν.
[14]Omitting τὸ καλὸν καὶ τὸ ἡδύ.
[15]Reading οὐ πρός.

accustomed to protect the weaker parts and is every creature weak in some respect?
35 Now in all quadrupeds the posterior portions are weaker than the front parts owing
to their position; for they are more liable to suffer from cold and heat; but in man
the front portions of the body are weaker and suffer likewise under these
conditions.

897ᵃ1   54 · Why is it that man sneezes more than any other animal? Is it because
he also suffers most from running at the nose? The reason for this is that, the heat
being situated in the region of the heart and being naturally disposed to rise
upwards, in the other animals its natural direction is towards the shoulders and
5 thence, splitting up owing to refraction, it travels partly into the neck and head and
partly into the backbone and flanks, because these parts are all in the same straight
line and parallel to the ground on which the animal stands. Now the heat,[16] as it
travels along, distributes the moisture uniformly to these parts alike; for the
10 moisture follows the heat. Four-footed animals therefore do not suffer either much
from running at the nose or sneeze; for sneezing is due to the rush either of a mass of
breath, when moisture evaporates more quickly than the body, or of unconcocted
moisture (hence it precedes a cold in the head);[17] and these forms of moisture are
15 not found in the other animals, because the rush of heat is equally distributed
between the fore and hind parts of an animal. Man being naturally, like the plants,
at a right angle to the ground on which he stands, the result is that a very copious
and violent rush of heat takes place in the direction of the head, and the heat in its
course thither rarefies and heats the ducts in the region of the head. Now these
20 ducts being in this condition are better able to receive the moisture than those
leading downwards from the heart. When, therefore, a man happens to have
become in too moist a condition and to have been cooled off externally,[18] the result is
that the heat obtaining nourishment and collecting within increases, and as it does
25 so it is carried to the head and the ducts there. Into these the moisture, which is thin
and unconcocted, follows the heat and fills them up and causes cold in the head and
likewise sneezing. For at the beginning of a cold the heat, being carried along in
advance of the moisture and inflating the ducts, causes sneezing by the expulsion of
30 the breath and by the drawing off[19] of those humours which are light and pungent.
Hence it happens that after sneezing from a cold in the head one wipes away watery
matter. These all having been set in motion, the continuous and solid[20] humours
follow closely upon them and block up the ducts in the region of the head and
35 nostrils. If they become swollen and distended, they cause pain in the region of the
head. That the ducts are blocked is shown by the fact that no breath can pass out
through them;[21] so those who suffer from running at the nose neither sneeze nor can
they use their sense of smell. Sneezing unaccompanied by running at the nose is due
to the same causes, but has some slight and insignificant origin; and so the humours,

---

[16]Omitting τὸ σῶμα.
[17]Putting a comma after ἀπέπτων, and placing διό . . . γίνεται in parentheses.
[18]Putting a comma after instead of before ἔξωθεν.
[19]Omitting πρό.   [20]Reading πάχος ἔχοντα.
[21]Reading τὸ μηδὲν ἐκτὸς δι' αὐτῶν.

being collected by the heat and vaporized by it owing to their small mass, are   897ᵇ1
precipitated down the nostrils. The noise made by the breath is due quite as much to
the violence of its rush as to its quantity. For the heat, being carried along in a direct
line to the brain and rushing into it, is refracted into the nostrils, because the ducts   5
there lead out from the brain. The rush made by the breath in breaking out into the
nostrils, being unnatural, is consequently violent, and therefore makes loud noises.
Amongst the other animals birds are most liable to running at the nose, because   10
they most resemble man in form; but they are less liable to it than man, because
they usually hold their heads down, since they derive their food from the ground.

55 · Why are marine animals larger and better nourished than land
animals? Is it because the sun consumes the outer surface of the earth and takes the   15
nourishment out of it? (For this reason too those animals which are enclosed in the
earth are better nourished.) Marine animals then are free from all these disadvantages.

56 · Why is it that the other animals provide themselves more often with dry
than with moist food, but man takes more moist than dry nourishment? Is it   20
because man is naturally very hot and therefore requires most cooling?

57 · Why is it that eunuchs do not become bald? Is it because they have a
large amount of brain-matter? Now this is the result of their not having sexual
intercourse with women; for the semen passes from the brain through the spine. For   25
this reason too bulls which have been castrated appear to have large horns after
castration. For the same reason also, apparently, women and children are not bald.

58 · Why is it that some animals are able to feed themselves directly after   30
birth, while others cannot? Are those who can do so the shorter-lived among those
animals which are capable of memory? It is for this reason that they always die
sooner.

59 · Why does man produce more moist than dry excrement, but horses and
asses more dry than moist? Is it because the latter animals take more dry food,   35
whereas man takes more moist than dry nourishment? For all excrement comes
from food, and a greater amount of food produces a greater quantity of excrement.
Some animals then take more moist food, others more dry food, because some are
naturally dry and others moist. Animals then which are naturally dry feel more   898ᵃ1
desire for moist food, since they require it more; but those which are naturally moist
desire dry food, for they stand more in need of it.

60 · Why is it that birds and men and the courageous animals have hard
frames? Is it because high spirit is accompanied by bodily heat, since fear is a   5
process of cooling? Those then whose blood is hot are also courageous and
high-spirited; for the blood gives them sustenance. Plants too which are watered
with warm water become harder.

61 · Why is it that quadrupeds of a small size most often give birth to
10 monstrosities, whereas man and the larger quadrupeds, such as horses and asses, do
so less often? Is it because the small quadrupeds, such as dogs, pigs, goats, and
sheep, have much more abundant progeny than the larger animals, which either
always or usually produce only one offspring at a time? Monstrosities come into
15 being when the semen becomes confused and disturbed either in the emission of the
seminal fluid or in the mingling which takes place in the uterus of the female. So
birds too produce monstrosities; for they lay twin eggs, and their monstrosities are
born from such eggs in which the yolk is not separated by the membrane.

20 62 · Why is the head in man more hairy than the rest of the body—in fact
quite disproportionately so—while in the other animals the opposite is the case? Is it
because some of the other animals send an excessive amount of their nutritive
material into teeth, others into horns, others into hair? Those who expend their
25 nourishment on horns have less thick hair on the head; for the available material is
used up in the horns. Those whose nourishment goes into teeth have thicker hair on
the head than horned animals (for they have manes), but less thick than such
creatures as birds. For birds have the same sort of covering as man; but, whereas in
birds the covering is distributed all over the body owing to its abundance, in man it
breaks out only on the head; for man is neither on the one hand devoid of hair, nor
30 on the other hand has he sufficient to cover the whole body.

63 · Why is it that in man alone of the animals the hair turns white? Is it
because most of the animals shed their coats every year, for instance the horse and
the ox, while others, though they do not do so, are short-lived, such as sheep and
others (in which case the hair does not turn white, because it does not as it were
35 grow old)? But man does not change his hair and is long-lived, and so he grows
white owing to age.

64 · Why is it that those in whom the distance from the navel downwards is
898ᵇ1 longer than that from the navel to the chest are short-lived and weak? Is it because
their stomach is cold owing to its small size, and therefore it tends to cause excretion
rather than concoction? Now such persons are unhealthy.

65 · Why is it that some animals come into being not only from the sexual
5 intercourse of animals with one another but also spontaneously, while others, such
as man and the horse, can only be born as the result of sexual intercourse? Is it due,
if to no other cause, at any rate to the fact that the former have a short period of
coming to birth, so that the moment of birth is not protracted and can take place at
the change of the seasons; but of the latter class the coming to birth is much
10 protracted, since they are born after a year or ten months, so that they must
necessarily be born from the intercourse of animals with each other or not at all?[22]

---

[22]Reading ἢ μὴ γίνεσθαι.

66 · Why is it that the teeth of Ethiopians are white—indeed whiter than those of other nations, but their nails are not correspondingly white? Are their nails dark because their skin also is black and blacker than that of others, and the nails grow out of the skin? But why are their teeth white? Is it because those things turn 15 white out of which the sun extracts the moisture without adding any colour to them, as happens in the case of wax? Now the sun colours the skin, but it does not colour the teeth, but the moisture is evaporated out of them by the heat.

67 · Why is it that, when the head is removed, some animals die immedi- 20 ately or very soon, while others do not? Does death occur less quickly in the bloodless animals, which require little nourishment, since they do not need food immediately and the heat in them is not diffused in moisture, whereas full-blooded animals cannot live without food and heat? The former can live after their heads are cut off, for they can live longer without breathing. The reason for this has been 25 stated elsewhere.

BOOK XI
PROBLEMS CONNECTED WITH
THE VOICE

1 · Why is it that of all the senses the hearing is most liable to be defective from birth? Is it because the sense of hearing and the voice may be held to arise from the same source? Now language, which is a kind of voice, seems to be very 30 easily destroyed and to be very difficult to perfect; this is indicated by the fact that we are dumb for a long time after our birth, for at first we simply do not talk at all and then at length begin only to lisp. And because language is easily destroyed, and language (being a kind of voice) and hearing both have the same source, hearing is, 35 as it were, *per accidens,* though not *per se,* the most easily destroyed of the senses.[1] Further evidence of the fact that the source of language is eminently easy to destroy may be taken from the other animals; for no animal other than man talks, and even 899ᵃ1 he begins to do so late, as has already been remarked.

2 · Why is it that the deaf always speak through their nostrils? Is it because they are near to being dumb? Now the dumb make sounds through their nostrils; 5 for the breath escapes by that way because their mouth is closed, and it is closed because they make no use of their tongue for vocal purposes.

3 · Why have all hot-natured men big voices? Is it because they necessarily have a large amount of cold air in them? For their breath, which is hot, attracts the 10 air to itself, and the more of it there is the more it attracts. Now a big voice arises

----

[1]Reading (φωνὴ γάρ τις) καὶ τῆς ἀκοῆς, ὥσπερ καὶ ἐκ.

from setting in motion a large quantity of air, and when the motion is swift, the voice is shrill, and when it is slow, it is deep.

15   **4** · Why do the deaf always speak through their nostrils? Is it because the deaf breathe more violently? For they are near to being dumb; the passage therefore of the nostrils is distended by the breath, and those who are in this condition speak through the nostrils.

5 · Why are sounds more audible at night? Is it because there is more quiet 20 then owing to the absence of great heat? For this reason too there is usually less disturbance; for it is the sun which is the source of movement.

6 · Why do voices sound shriller at a distance? For example, those who try to imitate persons shouting from a very great distance utter shrill noises, like those of 25 an echo; and the sound of an echo is distinctly shriller, and it is a distant sound, being the result of refraction. Since then in sound the swift is shrill and the slow is deep, one would have expected voices to seem deeper from a distance, for all moving bodies move more slowly the farther they progress from their starting-point, and at 30 last fall. May not the explanation be that these mimics use a feeble and thin voice[2] when they imitate a distant sound? Now a thin voice is not deep, and it is impossible to emit a small and feeble sound that is deep, but such a sound is necessarily shrill. Or is it true that not only do the mimics imitate for this reason, but also the sounds themselves become shriller? The reason is that the air which travels makes the 35 sound; and just as that which first sets the air in motion causes the sound, so the air in its turn must do likewise and be partly a motive power and partly itself set in motion. That is why sound is continuous, motive power continually succeeding to 899^{b}1 motive power, until the force is spent, which results in falling in the case of bodies when the air can no longer impel the missile, while in the case of sound the air can no longer impel other air. Continuous sound is produced when air is impelled by air, while the missile continues its progress as long as there is air to keep a body in 5 motion. In the latter it is always the same body that is carried along until it drops, in the former it is always different air. Smaller objects travel more quickly at first, but do not go far. Therefore voices are shriller and thinner at a distance; for that which moves more quickly is shrill—a question which we have already raised. It is for the 10 same reason that children and invalids have shrill voices, whereas grown men and healthy persons have deep voices. That from near at hand one cannot clearly distinguish degrees of deepness and shrillness and that altogether the conditions are not the same as those of heavy bodies thrown, is due to the fact that the body thrown is one and preserves its identity throughout; whereas sound is air impelled by air. 15 Consequently a body falls in one particular spot, while the voice scatters in every direction, just as though a body thrown were, in the course of its flight, to be broken into infinitely many pieces, some particles even returning on their track.

---

[2]Reading μιμοῦνται καὶ λεπτῇ.

7 . Why are newly plastered houses more resonant? Is it because their smoothness gives greater facility for refraction? They are smoother because they are free from cracks and their surface is continuous. One must, however, take a house which is already dry and not one which is still quite wet; for damp clay gives no refraction of sound. It is for this reason that stucco has a higher degree of resonance. Perhaps the absence of disturbance in the air also contributes something; for when the air is massed together it beats back the air that strikes against it.

8 . Why is it that if a large jar or empty earthenware vessels are buried in the ground and lids placed on them, the buildings in which they are have more resonance, and the same is true if there is a well or cistern in the house? Is it because, since an echo is due to refraction, the air when enclosed is necessarily massed together, and so the sound has something dense and smooth upon which it can strike[3] and from which it can be refracted, these being the most favourable conditions for an echo? A well, then, or a cistern causes the contraction and massing together of air, and jars and earthenware vessels also have dense surrounding walls, and so the phenomenon in question results in both cases. For anything which is hollow is particularly resonant; for which reason bronze vessels are particularly so. That resonance still continues when the vessels are buried need not surprise us; for the voice is carried downwards as much as in any other direction—indeed one conceives of it as being carried in a circle in every direction.

9 . But why is it that there is more resonance where vessels are buried than where they are not? Is it because covered vessels receive the air and retain it better? The result is that the impact of sound upon them is more violent.

10 . Why does cold water poured out of a jug make a shriller sound than hot water poured from the same vessel? Is it because the cold water falls at a greater speed, being heavier, and the greater speed causes the sound to be shriller? Heat, on the other hand, makes water lighter by rarefying it and causing it to rise. We may compare the phenomenon that torches deal softer blows when they are alight.

11 . Why is it that the voice is rougher when one has passed a sleepless night? Is it because the body, owing to absence of concoction, is moister than usual, especially in its upper part (which is also the cause of heaviness in the head), and moisture in the region of the windpipe necessarily makes the voice rougher? For roughness is due to unevenness, whilst depth is due to congestion; for the passage of sound is then slower.

12 . Why does the voice become broken very readily after meals? Is it because the region in which it is produced is thoroughly heated by constant impacts, and, becoming heated, attracts the moisture? The moisture too is itself more copious and readier to hand when food is being taken.

[3]Reading $\pi\rho\sigma\pi\iota\pi\tau\omega\nu$.

20   13 · Why is the sound of weeping shrill, whereas that of laughing is deep? Is it because those who weep either set only a little breath in motion, because they are weak, or else exhale violently, which makes their breath travel quickly? Now speed makes for shrillness; for that which is hurled from a body which is tense travels quickly. (On the other hand, a man who is laughing is in a relaxed condition.) Those

25   who are weak make shrill sounds, for they set only a little air in motion, in some cases merely on the surface. Further, the air emitted by those who are laughing is warm, while the breath of those who are weeping is colder, just as pain is a chilling of the region round the breast. Now heat sets a great mass of air in motion, so that its progress is slow, whereas cold imparts movement to a little air only. The same

30   thing happens with flutes; when the player's breath is hot, the sound produced is much deeper.

          14 · Why do children and the young of other animals have shriller voices than the full-grown of their species, and that though shrillness involves a quality of violence? Is it because[4] the voice is a movement of the air, and the swifter the

35   movement the shriller is the sound? Now a little air can be moved more easily and quickly than a large quantity, and it is set in motion owing either to its concretion or to its dissolution by heat. Now since we draw in cold air when we inhale, the air within us can become concreted by the act of inhalation; but exhalation, when heat sets air in motion, can become voice, for it is when we are exhaling that we speak,

900ᵇ1   not when we are inhaling. And since the young are hotter than their elders, and their interior passages are narrower, they may well have less air in them. So, as there is less in them of that which is moved and more motive power, namely heat, for

5   both reasons the movement of the air may be quicker; and, for the reasons already stated, the quicker the movement the shriller the voice.

          15 · Why is the sound of weeping shrill and of laughter deep? Is it because those who weep, in uttering their cries, strain and contract the mouth? Owing to the

10   tension the air that is in them is impelled into swift motion, and the contraction of the mouth, through which it passes, makes its speed still greater. For both these reasons the voice becomes shrill. On the other hand, those who laugh relax the tension in doing so and open the mouth. Since then for this reason they emit the air from the mouth through a wide aperture and slowly, their voice is naturally deep.

15   16 · Why is it that persons without generative power, such as boys, women, men grown old, and eunuchs, have shrill voices, while adult men have deep voices? Is it because[5] the thin voice has only one dimension, just as the line and other thin things have one dimension, while thick things have more than one? Now it is easier to create and set in motion one thing than several things. Now the breathing of the

20   persons mentioned above is feeble and sets little air in motion; and the air which has only one dimension is very small in quantity, for it will be thin for the reasons

---

[4]Reading ἢ ὅτι.
[5]Reading ἢ ὅτι.

already stated. And the voice produced from it will be of the same quality, and a thin voice is shrill. This then is the reason why persons without generative power have shrill voices; whereas men who are vigorous set a large quantity of air in motion with their breath, and the air, being large in quantity, is likely to move slowly and causes the voice to be deep. For shrillness of voice is, as we have seen, produced by a movement at once swift and thin, neither of which conditions is fulfilled in an adult man.

17 · Why are our voices deeper in the winter? Is it because then the air both inside and outside us is thicker, and, being such, its movement is slower and the voice therefore deeper? Further, we are drowsier in the winter than in the summer and sleep longer, and we are heavier after sleeping. In the period then during which we sleep for a longer time than we are awake (namely, the winter), we may expect to have deeper voices than in the season when the contrary happens. For during the short interval of wakefulness the condition set up during sleep persists and causes a tendency to drowsiness.

18 · Why is the voice deeper as a result of drinking and vomiting and cold weather? Is it due to the congestion of the larynx caused by phlegm, which makes fluid matter collect in it? In some people vomiting and drinking, in others the season and the constriction resulting therefrom, make the larynx narrower, so that the passage of breath is slower; and its slow passage makes the voice deep.

19 · Why is it that a deeper voice is more audible close at hand, but less so at a distance? Is it because a deeper voice sets a greater amount of air in motion, but not at a distance? So we hear it less well at a distance, because it travels less far, but better from near at hand, because a greater mass of air strikes upon our sensory organ. A shrill sound is audible at a distance, because it is thinner; and that which is thin has greater longitudinal extension. It might also be said that the motion which causes it is quicker; this would be so, if the breath which sets the air in motion were at the same time dense and narrow. For, in the first place, air which is small in bulk moves more readily (for the air which is set in motion by that which is narrow is small in bulk); and, secondly, that which is dense deals more impacts, and it is these which cause the sound. This can be illustrated from musical instruments; for, all other conditions being the same, it is the thinner strings that give shriller sounds.

20 · Why does the voice seem shriller to those standing at a distance, whereas shrillness depends on the rapidity with which the voice travels, and that which travels moves more slowly the farther it goes? Is it because the shrillness of the voice depends not only on the rapidity with which it travels but also on the attenuation of sound? The farther one is away the more attenuated is the voice when it reaches one, because very little air is set in motion. For the motion gradually diminishes; and just as number in diminishing terminates in the unit, so a body terminates in a single dimension, and this in a body is tenuity. So it is also with the voice.

30   21 · Why is it that both those who have taken violent exercise and those who are weak speak shrilly? Is it because those who are weak set only a little air in motion, and a little air travels more quickly than a larger quantity? Those who have taken violent exercise, on the other hand, set the air in vigorous motion, and air which is in vigorous motion travels more quickly, and in the voice quickness of motion causes shrillness.

901^b1   22 · Why do those who shout after meals spoil their voices? Indeed, we can see how those who are training their voices, such as actors and chorus-men and all such persons, practise early in the morning and on an empty stomach. Is it because the spoiling of the voice is simply the spoiling of the region through which the voice
5   passes out? So too those who have sore throats have their voices spoilt, not because the breath which causes the voice is any worse, but because the windpipe is roughened. This region by its nature is especially liable to be roughened by violent
10   heat, and so neither can those who are in a fever sing, nor can those who have been suffering from a violent fever sing immediately after it leaves them; for their larynx is roughened by the heat. The consumption of food naturally increases and heats the breath, and it is reasonable to suppose that the breath being in this state makes the
15   windpipe sore and rough as it passes through; and when this happens the voice is naturally spoilt.

      23 · Why is it that the voice, which is air that has taken a certain form and is carried along, often loses its form by dissolution, but an echo, which is caused by such air striking on something hard, does not become dissolved, but we hear it distinctly? Is it because in an echo refraction takes place and not dispersion? This
20   being so, the whole continues to exist and there are two parts of it of similar form; for refraction takes place at the same angle. So the voice of the echo is similar to the original voice.

      24 · Why is it that, although the young of all other animals and infants have
25   shriller voices than the full-grown of their species, calves have deeper voices than full-grown oxen? Is it because in each species the young resembles the female of the same kind? Now among cattle cows have deeper voices than bulls, and the calves resemble the former rather than the latter; but in all other species the males have deeper voices.

30   25 · Why is it that when the orchestra of a theatre is spread with straw, the chorus makes less sound? Is it because, owing to the unevenness of the surface, the voice does not find the ground smooth when it strikes upon it and is therefore less uniform, and so is less in bulk, because it is not continuous? Similarly light too shines more on smooth surfaces, because it is not cut off by anything which intercepts it.

902^a1   26 · Why does salt make a noise when it is thrown on fire? Is it because salt has a little moisture in it which is evaporated by the heat and violently bursting forth rends the salt? Now anything which is rent makes a noise.

27 · Why is it that some children, before they reach the age at which it is time for them to express themselves clearly, find voice and say something distinctly, and then go on as before until the usual age for speaking arrives? Some regard such incidents as portents; and before now cases have been reported of children who spoke immediately after birth. Is it because generally the majority of children at birth[6] follow the usual course of nature (and so the phenomenon in question occurs only in a few), and their faculties keep pace with one another; and so they hear and find voice and understand what they hear and speak and express themselves clearly all at the same time? Sometimes, however, these things do not go together, but some children understand before the faculty by which they converse is set free for use, while in others the opposite happens. The latter, then, would not converse intelligently (for they merely repeat what they hear); but when the time comes at which they can both speak and understand, they make a natural use of both functions. But in those in whose souls perception through hearing has been perfected before the organ[7] by which the voice is first set in motion and speech is formed, the full power and freeing of the organ of speech sometimes comes to pass when they already understand a great deal. This is especially likely to happen after sleep—the reason being that sleep makes the body and the faculties more sluggish by giving them a rest—or, if not after sleep, after some other similar change has taken place. We can do many things of this sort which require some short-lived opportunity—after which the conditions are no longer suitable—when the organ of speech is in this state of freedom; and when there has been obviously present to their sensation something by which thought was stirred, in virtue of having heard it the child returns to it and utters it. Now tunes and phrases often occur to us without our choosing, but if we originally utter them by choice, we afterwards speak or sing them without choosing and cannot get rid of them from our lips. So too when this happens in children, the part relapses again into its natural condition, until the time comes for it to become strong and to be separately constituted.

28 · Why do some objects, chests for example, suddenly make a noise and move, when nothing perceptible sets them in motion? Yet that which causes motion is stronger than that which is moved. The same question arises in connexion with corruption and old age; for everything which is said to be 'destroyed by time' is destroyed by something imperceptible. Is it similar to dripping water and stones lifted by the growth of plants, namely, that it is not the final effort but its continuity which raises or moves the object? This continuity of effort is imperceptible, but it results in a movement which is perceptible. So too that which is contained within perceptible spaces of time moves and can be divided into imperceptible portions, but these cause motion and corruption by their sum and their continuity? Now

The markers in the margin read: 5, 10, 15, 20, 25, 30, 35 (for section 27), and 902[b]1, 5 (for section 28).

---

[6]Retaining γινομένων.
[7]Reading ἢ ᾧ.

continuity is not in the present time but in the period of time terminated by the present.

29 · Why does one hear less well when one is yawning? Is it because a quantity of breath emitted in the yawn finds its way also into the ears from inside, so that the motion which it sets up in the neighbourhood of the ears makes a distinct impression on the perception, especially after sleep? Now sound is air or a certain condition of it. The sound then from outside enters the ear, and that from within comes into collision with it, and the movement thus caused checks the progress of the sound from without.

30 · Why do children hesitate more in their speech than grown men? Is it because, just as when we are children, we always have less control over our hands and feet and at a still earlier age cannot walk at all, so the young cannot control their tongue? Now when they are quite small, they cannot speak at all but can only make sounds like the animals, because they lack control. This is the cause not only of hesitancy in speech but also of lisping and stammering. Lisping is due to the inability to master a letter—not any letter but some particular one; stammering is due to the dropping out of some particular letter or syllable; hesitancy is due to the inability to join one syllable to another sufficiently quickly. All three are due to want of power; for the tongue is not an efficient servant of the intelligence. The same thing occurs in those who are drunken and in the old; but always to a less extent than in children.

31 · Why is it that the voice trembles in those who are nervous or afraid? Is it because the heart is shaken by the passing out of the heat? For this happens in both conditions, being an effect both of nervousness and of fear. When the heart is shaken, the impact is not one but many, like that from strings which are not properly stretched.

32 · Why is it that those who are nervous have deep voices, but those who are afraid speak shrilly? Is it because in those who are afraid the region about the heart is chilled, because the heat passes downwards, and so they set only a little air in motion? For the force which sets the air in motion is derived from heat. In those who are nervous the heat travels upwards, as happens in those who are ashamed; for it is through shame that nervousness is felt. In those who are ashamed the heat travels upwards to the face, as is shown by the fact that they tend to blush. The heat therefore dissolves and thickens the air with which they speak, and such air can only be propelled slowly; and in the voice that which is slow is deep.

33 · Why are sounds more audible in the night than in the day? Is it for the reason that Anaxagoras gives, namely, that in the day-time the air, heated by the sun, hisses and roars, but at night it is still because the heat has ceased, and that when there is no noise hearing is easier? Or is it because one hears more easily

through a comparative void than through a *plenum*? Now in the day the air is dense, being full of light and of the sun's rays; but at night it is rarer, for then the fire and the rays, which are bodies, have gone out of it. Or is it because in the day-time the various bodies around us distract our intelligence, and so it is less able to distinguish[8] what it hears? Also because we do all that we have to do preferably in the day rather than at night, our intelligence[9] too is busy then; and the perception apart from intelligence does, if one may say so, only an imperceptible amount of work—as the saying is, 'It is the mind which sees, the mind which hears'. But at night when our sight has no work to do and our intelligence is more at liberty, the channel of hearing, being wider open, is just as receptive of sounds and better able to report them to the intelligence, because the latter is neither busy nor distracted by the sight, as it is in the day-time.

34 · Why is it that persons without generative power, such as boys, women, men grown old, and eunuchs, have shrill voices, while adult men have deeper voices? Is it because of the weakness of the organ which sets the air in motion? For that which is weak sets only a little in motion; and a little air travels quickly, and that which travels quickly is shrill. Or is it because the first passage through which the air passes is narrow in those who are without generative power, so that that which expels the air from it has little force, and the air, being small in volume, travels quickly through the larynx above, which is wide? But in the adult and fully developed men this passage is wide (just as also is that leading to the testicles), and so the quantity of the air expelled is also greater; and so passing through more slowly it makes a deeper sound.

35 · Why is it that those who hesitate in their speech cannot speak softly? Is it because they are hindered from using their voice by some impediment? Since, then, there is not equal force exerted and similar movement set up when there is some impediment to the movement and when there is none, a violent effort is required. Now the voice is a movement, and those who use more force speak louder; and so, since they have to force the hindrance out of the way, those who hesitate in their speech must necessarily speak louder.

36 · Why do those who hesitate in their speech become worse when they are nervous, but better under the influence of drunkenness? Is it because their condition is a state resembling apoplexy of some interior part of the body which they cannot move and which by its coldness hinders their speech? Wine then, being naturally hot, tends to get rid of the coldness, but nervousness creates coldness; for it is a form of fear, and fear is a chilling condition.

37 · Why is it easier to hear sounds from outside in a house than those from inside a house outside it? Is it because the sound from inside becomes dispersed

---

[8]Reading εὐκρινής.
[9]Reading αὐτή.

because it travels over an immense space, so that each component part of the sound
15 is not sufficiently strong to make itself heard, or at any rate is less audible? On the
other hand, a voice from without entering within into a smaller space and into
stagnant air arrives in a close mass, and so being greater in bulk is more audible.

38 · Why are those who hesitate in their speech melancholic? Is it because
20 melancholy is due to their responding too quickly to appearances? Now this is
characteristic of those who hesitate in their speech; for the impulse to speak
outstrips their power to do so, the mind responding too quickly to that which has
appeared to it. The same thing occurs in those who lisp; for in them the organs
employed in speech are too slow.[10] This is shown by the fact that men under the
25 influence of wine become lispers, since then they respond most to the appearances
and not so much to the mind.

39 · Why do leeks contribute to loudness of the voice (for we find that this is
so even with partridges)? Is it because, whereas boiled garlic makes the throat
smooth, leeks contain a certain amount of adhesive matter, and this cleanses the
larynx?

30 40 · Why is it that in all other creatures the sounds made are shriller when
more violence is used, but man speaks more shrilly when he is weak? Is it because
then he sets less air in motion, and this passes along quickly and its speed makes the
sound shrill?

41 · Why can one hear better when one holds one's breath than when one
35 exhales? This is why people when hunting tell one another not to breathe. Is it
because the power of perception rises into the upper parts of the body when the veins
are distended? For it sinks when one is asleep; and so those who are sleeping exhale
904ª1 rather than inhale, and lose the sense of hearing. Or does the blood rise upwards
when one exhales, so that the lower parts of the body become void, and one can hear
better in a void? Or is it because breathing is a noise, and when it takes place in the
act of exhaling it impedes the hearing?

42 · Why do small quantities of salt make a noise and explode more quickly,
5 but large quantities more violently? Is it because in the former case the particles
burst quickly because they are small (for the fire does not have far to penetrate), but
in the latter case slowly, since a large mass is more difficult to burst than a small? A
small quantity makes a small noise because the impact is small, whereas a large
10 quantity makes a loud noise because the impact is greater; and sound is an impact.
The stronger an object is, the greater is the explosion if it is struck; for it is less
yielding.

[10]Reading βραδύτερα.

43 · Why is it that if the same quantity of salt is thrown on to a large fire, it makes less noise than if thrown on a small fire, or else makes no noise at all? Is it because it is burnt up before it can burst? For it burns because the moisture is used up, and it makes a noise because it bursts.   15

44 · Why does one hear less well when one is yawning? Is it because the action of yawning cuts off the breath internally and the breath so cut off accumulates in the region of the ears? This is shown by the fact that there is a noise in the ears when one yawns. Now the breath thus cut off hinders the hearing. Further one also makes a noise when one yawns, and this tends to impede the hearing. Also the organs of hearing must necessarily become compressed by the   20 distension of the mouth in yawning.

45 · Why is it that though the voice, since it is a kind of stream, is naturally inclined to travel upwards, yet it is more audible below from above than above from below? Is it because the voice is a kind of air mingled with moisture, and this air   25 being weighed down by the moisture is carried downwards instead of upwards, since it is the natural characteristic of moisture to be carried downwards? For this reason one hears better when one is below. Or is such a result characteristic only of the voice of a living creature (for it contains moisture), while the phenomenon which we are discussing is found also in other sounds? Just as the sight then, if it be allowed to   30 fall from a higher to a lower object, makes an upwards reflexion and vice versa, so the voice, which has a natural tendency to rise, coming into collision with the air which bars its progress, cannot overpower the air, which is greater in mass and   35 heavier, but the air which is set in motion by the voice, being refracted, is carried in a contrary direction and downwards, and so, being scattered in a downward direction, it is more audible below. Somewhat similar is that which happens in an echo, which is due to the refraction of the voice in a contrary direction.

46 · Why are the voices of drunken persons more broken than those of the   904ᵇ1 sober? Is it because their voice breaks easily owing to their state of repletion? This can be illustrated by the fact that chorus-men and actors practise not after a meal but on an empty stomach. Now since a person in a state of drunkenness is in a   5 condition of greater repletion, his voice is naturally more broken.

47 · Why can one hear shriller voices at a greater distance? Is it because shrillness in the voice is rapidity, and what is carried forcibly along moves more rapidly, and what is carried violently along is carried farther?   10

48 · Why can we hear better if we hold the breath? Is it because breathing makes a noise? It is only natural therefore that we should hear better when the noise is less; for the noise is less when we hold the breath.

49 · Why is it that light cannot penetrate through dense objects, whereas   15

sound can do so, although light is rarer and travels[11] farther and quicker than
sound? Is it because light travels in a straight line, and so, if anything blocks its
direct course, it is completely cut off, but sound, because it is a breath, can also
20 travel in a line that is not direct? So we can hear those who make sounds from any
direction and not only those who are in a straight line with our ears.

50 · Why is the sound of laughing deep, whereas that of weeping is shrill? Is
it because a voice which comes from those who are in a state of tension is shrill, and
that which is shrill is weak? Now both these characteristics are found rather in
25 those who are weeping; for they are in a state of greater tension and they are
weaker.

51 · Why is it that the voice, being air which has assumed a certain form and
is carried along,[12] often loses its form by dissolution, but an echo, which is formed by
such air striking on something hard, does not become dissolved, but we hear it
30 distinctly? Is it because in an echo refraction takes place, not dispersion? It starts
then as a complete whole and continues to be so. Also, the effect produced upon it is
due to a similar agency; for it is refracted from the air in the hollow, not from the
hollow itself.

52 · Why is it that when one person makes a sound and a number of persons
35 make the same sound simultaneously, the sound produced is not equal nor does it
reach correspondingly farther?[13] Is it because each of them thrusts forward his own
portion of air and they do not all impel the same air, except to a very small extent?
The result is much the same as when a number of persons throw stones but each
throws a different stone, or at any rate most of them do so. Neither in the latter case
905ª1 will any missile travel far (or at any rate not correspondingly farther), nor in the
former case will the voice reach farther. For this great voice is that of many, not of
one; so at a short distance it appears correspondingly greater (just as a number of
missiles reaches the same spot), but at a great distance this is no longer so.

5   53 · Why do those who are nervous have deep voices, but those who are
afraid speak shrilly, though a feeling of shame is a kind of fear? Or are the two
conditions really very different? For those who feel shame blush (and nervousness is
a kind of shame), whereas those who are afraid turn pale. It is clear then that in
those who are afraid the heat fails in the upper part of the body, so that the breath,
10 being weak, sets only a little air in motion; and that which is small in bulk travels
quickly, and in the voice quickness is shrillness. But in those who feel shame the
heat in the region of the breast travels upwards, as is shown by the fact that they
blush. Now a strong force sets a great mass of air in motion, and a great mass travels
15 slowly, and in the voice slowness is deepness.

---

[11]Reading πόρρω ἰόν.
[12]Reading φερόμενος, διαλύεται.
[13]Reading γεγώνασιν.

54 · What is the cause of hesitation of speech? Is it due to the chilling of the region in which the sound is produced, and to a condition resembling apoplexy in that part of the body? This is why those who hesitate, if warmed with wine and deriving thence a continuity of speech, are better able to connect their words together.

55 · Why is it that of all animals man alone is apt to become hesitating in   20
speech? Is it because he alone possesses the power of uttering words, while the other animals only have voices? Now those who hesitate in their speech use their voice, but they cannot connect their words together.

56 · Why is the voice shriller in winter and in those who are sober, and   25
deeper in summer and in those who are drunken? Is it because the quicker a voice is the shriller it is, and it is quicker when it proceeds from one who is in a state of tension? The bodies of those who are sober are in a more solid condition than those of the drunken, and bodies are in a more solid condition in winter than in summer; for heat and warmth have a dissolvent effect upon the body.

57 · Why does the voice come to perfection later in man than in any other   30
creature capable of sound? Is it because there are many variations and kinds of sounds in the human voice? For the other animals can express few or no letters; and that which is most elaborate and contains a large number of variations takes a long time to perfect.

58 · Why is it that the sight cannot pass through hard objects, but the voice   35
can do so? Is it because the course of the sight can only take one direction, namely, a straight line (as is shown by the rays of the sun and the fact that we can only see what is directly opposite us), whereas the voice can take many directions, since we can hear from everywhere? When therefore the sight is prevented from making its way through in a straight line, because there is no continuous passage between the eye and the object, it is impossible to see through the impeding matter. But the air   905^{b}1
and the voice, since they travel everywhere, find their way everywhere and make themselves audible. On the other hand, the sight can penetrate through liquids, but voices cannot be heard through them or hardly at all, although the liquid is rarer than the earth, because the passages are small and close together and continuous,   5
and so the sight is not prevented from travelling in a straight line. For the same reason it is possible to see through glass, although it is dense, but not through a fennel-stalk, although it contains rarities, because in the former the pores are continuous, in the latter they are irregular, and their size is no advantage if they are not straight.[14] The voice is not audible through water, because the empty air-spaces   10
in it are too small and so cannot admit the voice or let it pass through, or only with difficulty; for the voice is a kind of air. For that which is rarer is not necessarily more penetrable, unless at the same time the passages are adapted to that which is

[14]Reading διορᾶται, ὅτι.

passing through. So also that which is rarer is not necessarily more compressible,
15   unless its passages are of such a kind as to admit the passage of other bodies. But, it
may be urged, that which is rare is soft and compressible. True, but in some things
compression is impossible owing to the smallness of the passages—in glass, for
example; for its passages cannot be contracted, although it may be rarer than a
20   fennel-stalk, for the reason already mentioned. So too with water and the like. This
then is clear, that, although the rare and the soft are either identical or else of a very
similar nature, yet it does not follow that the rarer a thing is the more it admits of
contraction. The reason in all these cases is the same.

59 · Why is it that the sound produced becomes less if some of those who
25   produce it are withdrawn, but its character is unchanged? Is it because their voice
had formed part of a general mingling of sound, and that which is mingled is not
mingled in one part and not in another, but is mingled throughout? So when some of
those who make the sound are withdrawn, the volume of sound comes forth in the
same way as before from the various voices, and must therefore, though smaller,
necessarily retain the same characteristics.

60 · What is the cause of hesitancy in speech? Are those who hesitate in too
30   great a hurry because of the heat that is in them, and so they stumble and stop? If
so, they resemble those who are angry, for they too become full of panting, with the
result that a large quantity of breath comes together. Or do they pant owing to the
boiling of the heat, because it is abundant and cannot come forth before the proper
moment of exhalation? Or is the right explanation the exact contrary, namely, that
35   it is the chilling rather than the heating of the region in which the sound is
produced—a state resembling apoplexy in that part of the body? That is why those
who hesitate, when warmed with wine and deriving thence a continuity of speech,
are better able to connect their words together.

61 · Why are voices deeper in the winter? Is it because then the air is thicker
and as a consequence its movement is slower, and therefore the voice is deeper? Or
906ª1   is it because the air passes more slowly through narrow passages, and the region
round the larynx is closed by the cold and by the phlegm which flows into it?

62 · Why is it that boys, women, eunuchs, and old men have shrill voices? Is
5   it because the movement of air which creates a shriller sound is quicker? Now it is
more difficult to move a greater amount of the same thing, and so those who are in
the prime of life draw in the air in greater quantities, and therefore this air, since it
travels more slowly, makes the voice deeper. In boys and eunuchs the contrary
occurs, because they contain less air. Old men's voices tremble because they cannot
10   control them, just as, when invalids and children take hold of a long stick by one
end, the other end shakes, because they have no control over it; this too is the cause
of trembling in old men, namely lack of control. We must suppose also that
trembling of the voice in those who are nervous or afraid or chilled is due to the

same cause. For in one whose voice is in this state, since most of the heat collects   15
within as a result of the above conditions, the rest, which is small in quantity, cannot
control the voice; consequently it shakes and trembles. This is the reason why artists
who belong to the class of those who are conscious of nervousness speak in a low
voice at first, until they settle down to their work; for by keeping the voice low they   20
can control it.

BOOK XII
PROBLEMS CONNECTED WITH THINGS
OF PLEASANT ODOUR

1 · Why is it that perfumes produced by burning affect the senses less at a
short distance? Is it because the effluvium is pleasanter when mingled with the air
in a weak form, as happens in medicinal myrrh? Or can the contrary of this be the   25
explanation, namely, that the fire destroys the odour in the immediate neighbourhood of the flames? For the odour is produced when the perfume evaporates; that is
why near the embers the effluvium has no odour, but it appears purer and thinner
the farther away it is.

2 · Why is it that the odours of burning perfumes and of flowers are less   30
sweet-scented at a close distance? Is it because particles of earth are given off with
the odour, and these, owing to their weight, fall more quickly to the ground, and
therefore the odour is pure at a greater distance? Or is the effluvium not at its
strongest either quite near to its source or very far from it? For close at hand it has
not yet gained strength, while at a distance it has become dissipated.   35

3 · It is said that trees become sweet-scented upon which the rainbow has
fallen. Is this true or false? And if it is true, what can be the cause of the
phenomenon? That it does not happen always and as a universal rule is obvious; for   906ᵇ1
rainbows often occur without any visible effect on the trees. When it does happen
(for it does occur sometimes and this has given rise to the saying), the effect is not
produced on every kind of wood. The cause can only be attributed to the rainbow   5
per accidens, especially if the rainbow does not really occur in nature but is an effect
produced on the eye by refraction. Now the phenomenon, as we said, does not occur
whatever the condition of the wood; for shepherds say that sweet odour is noticeable
after the rains which accompany the rainbow not in green or in dry trees but in   10
burnt wood, and in particular where briars and brambles grow and trees which have
sweet-scented flowers. The reason for the sweet scent is the same as in the soil; for
where the soil is hot and burnt through and through, anything which grows from it
is at first sweet-scented. For things which contain but little moisture, if they are
burnt at all, become sweet-scented; for the heat concocts this moisture. (So, of the   15
whole world, those parts towards the sun have a sweeter odour than those towards

the north; and of the former those towards the east have a sweeter odour than those
towards the south, for the districts of Syria and Arabia have more soil, but Libya is
20 sandy and free from moisture.) For there must not be a large amount of
moisture—for much moisture is difficult to concoct—nor must there be a complete
absence of it, or else there will be no evaporation. These conditions are fulfilled in
newly burnt wood and wood which naturally has a sweet odour in itself. This is
proved to be true by the flowers, for it is through them that the wood emits its scent.
25 The theory that sweet odour is engendered in any trees upon which the rainbow
rests is due to the fact that this cannot happen without the presence of water; for it is
when the wood has been wetted and has then concocted the moisture by the heat
which is in it, that it gives out the vapour which is being engendered in it. But there
must not be a large amount of water; for too much water drenches the tree and
30 extinguishes the heat previously caused by the burning. Now the rains which follow
the rainbow, so far from being heavy, may almost be called slight. Also if there is a
number of rainbows, the rain is not heavy, but it falls little and often. It is therefore
natural under these circumstances that men notice nothing unusual except the
rainbow and attribute to it the cause of the sweet odour.

35   4 · Why is it that flowers and burnt perfumes smell sweeter at a distance,
whereas close at hand they have rather the smell either of vegetation or of smoke? Is
it because scent is a form of heat and sweet-scented things are hot? Now heat is
907ª1 light, and so, the further the perfumes penetrate, the more does their scent become
purified from other concomitant odours produced by their leaves and by smoke,
which is a watery steam; at a short distance, on the other hand, the mingled odours
are simultaneously perceptible in the plants in which they are present.

5   5 · Why do things always emit a stronger odour when they are in motion? Is
it because they fill a larger space of air than when they are at rest? The result is that
the odour is thus transmitted more quickly to our perception.

6 · Why is it that we perceive odours less in the winter, especially in frosty
weather? Is it because the air is more free from motion when it is cold? The motion
10 therefore set up by the body which produces the odour cannot have such a
far-reaching effect owing to the difficulty of imparting motion to the effluvium and
to the air in which it is present.

7 · Why do perfumes have a more pungent odour when they are burnt on
ashes than on the fire? And why is their odour stronger and more persistent when
15 they are burnt on ashes? Is it because their odour is less thoroughly concocted on
ashes, and therefore greater in bulk? Now fire by quickly concocting their natural
force alters their odour; for concoction involves alteration in that which is
concocted.

20   8 · Why do those roses in which the centres are rough smell sweeter than
those in which they are smooth? Is it because those roses smell sweetest which

partake most of the natural characteristics of the rose? Now the rose is naturally thorny, and so it smells sweeter when its characteristics are more natural.

9 · Why are the odours both of burnt perfumes and of flowers less pleasant at a short distance? Is it because at a short distance the earthy element is transmitted with the scent, and so mixing with it lessens its strength, whereas the odour travels to a distance? It is for this reason too that flowers when rubbed lose their scent.

10 · Are scents smoke [or air]¹ or vapour? For it makes a difference, in that the former is produced by fire, the latter without it. And is something transmitted from the sense to the objects producing the scent or vice versa, causing a continuous motion in the adjoining air? Also, if any effluvium is given off by these objects, one would expect them to become less; yet we see that those things which have the strongest scent last the longest.

11 · Why have perfumes a more pungent odour when they are burnt on ashes than on fire? Is it because their odour is less thoroughly concocted on ashes and is therefore greater in bulk? Consequently a large quantity of the earthy element is vaporized in the process and becomes smoke; but the fire burns up the earthy element before it can escape, and so the odour is purer and reaches the senses untainted by the smoke. This is also the reason why flowers when rubbed smell less sweet; for the rubbing imparts motion to the earthy element and the slow heat does not destroy it.

12 · Why is it that sweet-smelling seeds and plants promote the flow of urine? Is it because they contain heat and are easily concocted,² and such things have this effect? For the heat which is in them causes quick digestion and their odour has no corporeal existence; for evil-smelling plants, such as garlic, by reason of their heat promote the flow of urine, but their wasting effect is a still more marked characteristic. But sweet-smelling seeds contain heat, because odour is in general engendered by heat; while evil-smelling things are unconcocted. Now anything which is to promote the flow of urine must be not only hot but also easily concocted, in order that it may accompany the liquids in their downward course and effect their digestion.

13 · Why is it that wines mixed with water have a less strong odour³ than when they are unmixed? Is it because wine mixed with water is weaker than unmixed wine? Now the weaker is more easily changed by any force acting upon it than the stronger. So wine mixed in the water is more easily affected than unmixed wine. Now it is characteristic of that which is easily affected⁴ to yield⁵ to something

---

¹Excised by Forster.
²Reading εὔπεπτα for λεπτά.
³Reading ἧττον for θᾶττον.   ⁴Reading εὐπετεστέρου.
⁵Reading ὑπᾶξαι.

else or to receive something which does not belong to it; unmixed wine, therefore, has a strong odour, but wine mixed with water is odourless.

BOOK XIII

PROBLEMS CONNECTED WITH THINGS
OF UNPLEASANT ODOUR

20   1 · Why is it that urine acquires a more unpleasant odour the longer it remains in the body, whereas ordure becomes less unpleasant to the smell? Is it because the latter becomes drier the longer it remains in the body (and what is dry is
25   less liable to putrefaction), but urine thickens, and the fresher it is the more like it is to the original liquid drunk?

2 · Why is it that things of unpleasant odour do not seem to have an odour to those who have eaten them? Is it because, owing to the fact that the scent penetrates to the mouth through the palate, the sense of smell soon becomes satiated and so it
30   no longer perceives the odour inside the mouth to the same extent—for at first every one perceives the odour, but, when they are in actual contact with it, they no longer do so, as though it had become part of themselves—and the similar odour from without is overpowered by the odour within?

3 · Why have flowers an unpleasant odour when they are rubbed? Is it because the earthy element, which is in the flower, mingles with the odour?

35   4 · Why is it that no living creature is pleasant to the smell except the leopard—which is pleasing even to animals, for they are said to find pleasure in its odour—and when they decay they are unpleasant to the smell, but many plants when they decay and wither become still more pleasant to the smell? Is it because
908ª1   the cause of evil odour is an unconcocted condition of excretion? For this reason the perspiration of some people is sometimes unpleasant, particularly in those whose perspiration is not usually unpleasant, as the result of disease. Also farts and belches of those who are in an unconcocted state are unpleasant. The same cause
5   must be ascribed for evil odour in the flesh and in that which is analogous to it (by which I mean that which in other animals corresponds to flesh); for here too there is sometimes unconcocted excretion. This then when it putrefies is a cause of evil odour in living creatures and in decaying bodies. For this reason too the fat and the bony parts and the hair have no evil odour, because the fat and bones are already
10   concocted, while the hair contains no moisture. Now plants contain no excretion. Or is there excretion in them also, but, because plants are naturally dry and hot, is the moisture in them more easily concocted and not of a muddy consistency? This can be illustrated from the soil, which is pleasant to the smell in hot regions, such as Syria
15   and Arabia, and from the fact that the plants which come from there are

sweet-smelling, because they are dry and hot; and such plants are not liable to decay. But animals are not dry and hot, and so their excretions are unconcocted and malodorous, and likewise their exhalations, and when they decay the moisture putrefies. This does not happen in plants, because they contain no excretions.

5 · Why are things of unpleasant odour more unpleasant when they are hot   20
than when they are cool? Is it because odour is a vapour and an effluvium? A vapour, then, and an effluvium is caused by heat; for a movement takes place, and heat is the source of the movement. Cold, on the contrary, is a source of stagnation and contraction and downward movement; but heat and all odours have an upward   25
tendency, because they are in the air, and the organ which perceives them is above and not below; for odour penetrates to the brain and so causes perception.

6 · Why, if one eats garlic, does the urine smell of it, whereas this does not happen when other things are eaten which have a strong odour? Is it because, as some of the followers of Heraclitus say, vaporization takes place in the body just as   30
in the universe, and then, when the process of cooling succeeds, moisture is formed in the universe and urine in the body, so the vaporization from the food, when it is formed by intermixture, causes the odour(for it is odour after it has undergone change)? If so, should not all the foods too which have a strong odour produce this   35
effect, which we know they do not? Furthermore, concretions from vapour do not resume their original form—which would result in wine, for example, being produced from the vapour of wine instead of water, as actually happens—and so this part of their theory is also untrue. The truth is that garlic, alone of foods which   908^{b}1
have an odour which is strong and also promotes the flow of urine, has the quality of inflating the lower part of the belly; all other such foods (radishes, for example) engender breath higher up or else do not promote the flow of urine. But garlic[1] has these three qualities: it promotes the flow of urine, it engenders breath, and it does so in the lower part of the body. The region round the privy parts and the bladder   5
feels the effect of such foods owing to its nearness and because it is liable to admit breath; that this is so is shown by the distension of the privy parts. It is clear therefore that the excretion of garlic is more liable than that of any other such food to reach the bladder with the breath, and this excretion mingling with the urine imparts its odour to it.   10

7 · Why is it that the mouths of those who have eaten nothing, but are fasting, have a stronger odour, 'the smell of fasting', as it is called, but when they eat the odour ceases, when one would expect it to increase? Is it because, as the stomach becomes empty, the air becomes hotter from the absence of motion and causes the breath and the excretions of phlegm to putrefy? That the air becomes hotter is   15
proved by the fact that fasting also induces an increase of thirst. When food is

[1]Reading τούτῳ for κάτω.

taken, the odour ceases because it is less than that of the food; for the heat in the food overcomes the internal heat, so that it cannot undergo any process of change.

20　　8 · Why has the armpit a more unpleasant odour than any other part of the body? Is it because it is least exposed to the air? Such parts have a particularly unpleasant odour because putrefaction takes place in them owing to the stagnation of fat. Or is it because the armpit is not moved and exercised?

9 · Why is it that those who have a goaty odour are still more unpleasant
25　　when they anoint themselves with unguents? Is it because this kind of thing happens in many instances; for example, if something acid and something sweet are mixed, the resulting whole is sweeter? Now any one who perspires has an unpleasant odour, and unguents are productive of heat and therefore induce perspiration.

10 · Why is it that the odour of the breath of those who are bent and
30　　deformed is more unpleasant and oppressive? Is it because the region round the lungs is contracted and bent out of an upright position, so that it does not give a free passage to the air, but the moisture and the breath, which tends to be enclosed within, putrefies?

11 · Why is it that most unguents are unpleasant when they mingle with
35　　perspiration, but others have a sweeter or at any rate not a more unpleasant odour? Do those which change as a result of movement or friction deteriorate in odour, whereas those which do not are improved? There are some such perfumes, just as
909ᵃ1　　there are some flowers from which scents are made, which deteriorate when rubbed or heated or dried, white violets, for example; but others remain the same, for instance roses. The unguents too made from flowers of the former class change, while those made from the latter do not; and so rose-perfume is least liable to
5　　change. Also unguents have a more unpleasant odour on those whose perspiration is malodorous, through mingling with their opposite, just as honey when mixed with salt becomes not sweeter but less sweet.

12 · Why do objects always produce a stronger odour when they are in motion? Is it because they fill up the air? The result is that the odour is thus
10　　transmitted more quickly to our perception.

BOOK XIV

PROBLEMS CONNECTED WITH THE EFFECT OF LOCALITY ON TEMPERAMENT

1 · Why are those who live under conditions of excessive cold or heat brutish in character and aspect? Is the cause the same in both cases? For the best mixture
15　　of conditions benefits the mind as well as the body, but excesses of all kinds cause

disturbance, and, as they distort the body, so do they pervert the mental temperament.

2 · Why is it that in Pontus corn, if exposed to the cold, keeps intact for many years? Is it because the extraneous moisture is evaporated together with the heat, as happens in grapes? For some things are evaporated by the cold and others with the   20 heat.

3 · Why do burning fevers occur more frequently in the coldest season? Is it because the cold imprisons the heat within? In the summer the contrary occurs, the interior of the body being cooler than the exterior. Burning fever is the inflammation in which,[1] the exterior of the body being cold, the interior is in a condition of   25 excessive heat.

4 · Why are the Ethiopians and the Egyptians bandy-legged? Is it because the bodies of living creatures become distorted by heat, like logs of wood when they become dry? The condition of their hair too supports this theory; for it is curlier than that of other nations, and curliness is as it were crookedness of the hair.   30

5 · Why is it that in damp regions copulation is more likely to lead to the birth of female offspring? Is it because a large amount of moisture thickens more slowly, and in damp regions the semen is moister owing to the presence of more moisture in the temperament?

6 · Why is it that in marshy districts sores on the head are quickly cured, but   35 those on the legs only with difficulty? Is it because the moisture, since it contains an earthy element, is heavy, and heavy things are carried downwards? Thus the upper parts of the body are easily concocted, because the impurities are carried downwards; but the lower parts become full of abundant excretion which easily putrefies.

7 · Why is it that those who live in airy regions grow old slowly, but those   909ᵇ1 who inhabit hollow and marshy districts age quickly? Is it because old age is a process of putrefaction, and that which is at rest putrefies, but that which is in motion is either quite free from, or at any rate less liable to, putrefaction, as we see in water? In lofty regions, therefore, owing to the free access of the breezes, the air   5 is in motion, but in hollow districts it stagnates. Furthermore, in the former, owing to its movement, the air is always pure and constantly renewed, but in marshy districts it is stagnant.

8 · Why are the inhabitants of warm regions cowardly, and those who dwell in cold districts courageous? Is it because there is a natural tendency which   10 counteracts the effects of locality and season, since if both had the same effect

---

[1]Reading πυρετὸς ἐν ᾧ τῶν.

mankind would inevitably be soon destroyed by heat or cold? Now those who are hot by nature are courageous, and those who are cold are cowardly. But the effect of hot regions upon those who dwell in them is that they are cooled, while cold regions engender a natural state of heat in their inhabitants. Both races are large of stature—those who live in cold regions because of the innate heat in them, and those who inhabit hot districts owing to the heat in which they live; for increase of stature occurs both in those who are hot and as a result of heat, whereas cold has a contracting effect. Since then those who live in cold districts have a powerful principle of growth in themselves, and those who live in hot regions encounter no external cold which prevents their growth, both naturally admit of considerable increase in stature. But this is less true of those who live in our latitudes, because the principle of growth in them is less strong, and those who live in cold regions feel the contracting effect of cold.

9 · Why are those who live in hot regions longer-lived? Is it because their natural condition is drier, and that which is drier is less liable to putrefaction and more lasting, and death is as it were a kind of putrefaction? Or is it because death is due to the chilling of the interior heat, and everything is chilled by a surrounding medium which is colder than itself? Now in warm regions the surrounding air is hot, but in cold regions it is cold and so more quickly and effectively destroys the interior heat of the body.

10 · Why are those who live in hot regions longer-lived? Is it because they preserve their heat and moisture better? For death is the corruption of these.

11 · Why is it that we become drowsier in marshy districts? Is it because there we are more cooled, and cooling, being a kind of rest, induces sleep, and sleep occurs during rest?

12 · Why is it that those who live on board ship, though they spend their time on the water, have a healthier colour than those who live in marshes? Is the weather and the free access of the breezes the cause? Now water makes men pale when it putrefies, a process which is due to the absence of movement; that is why those who live in marshy regions are rather pale.

13 · Why is suffocating heat very frequently experienced in wintry regions, much more so than in warm districts? Is it because of the moisture in the air? For as a result of the same heat applied to it water becomes hotter than air, and therefore damper air[2] becomes hotter than dry air.[3] Or perhaps the air is not really hotter[4] in these regions, but only seems so by contrast with the general coolness, as the sun emerging from a cloud seems hotter in contrast with its effect when it is behind a cloud.

[2]Reading ὁ ἀὴρ ὁ ὑγρότερος.
[3]Reading ξηροῦ for θερμοῦ.
[4]Reading θερμότερος for ξηρότερος.

14 · Why do those who live in southerly climes tend to have black eyes? Is blueness of the eyes due to excess of internal heat, whereas blackness is due to its absence, as Empedocles affirms? Just, therefore, as those who dwell in the north 15 have blue eyes, because the internal heat is prevented from escaping owing to the external cold; so in those who dwell in southerly climes the moisture cannot escape owing to the surrounding heat, but the heat escapes because there is nothing to bar its exit, and the moisture left behind causes blackness; for when light departs that 20 which is left behind is dark. Or does the pigmentation of the eye assimilate itself to the colour of the rest of the body? If so, the eyes of those who live towards the north are blue, because they are themselves white (for blue is akin to white); and those who dwell in the south being black, their eyes also are black. 25

15 · Why are those who live in warm regions wiser than those who dwell in cold districts? Is it for the same reason as that for which the old are wiser than the young? For those who live in cold regions are much hotter, because their nature recoils owing to the coldness of the region in which they live, so that they are very like the drunken and are not of an inquisitive turn of mind, but are courageous and 30 sanguine; but those who live in hot regions are sober because they are cool. Now everywhere those who feel fear make more attempt to inquire into things than do the self-confident, and therefore they discover more. Or is it because the race of those who live in warm regions is more ancient, the inhabitants of the cold regions having perished in the Flood, so that the latter stand in the same relation to the 35 former as do the young to the old?

16 · Why are the inhabitants of warm regions cowardly, and those who dwell in cold regions courageous? Is it because human beings have a natural tendency which counteracts the effect of locality and season (for, if both had the 910ᵇ1 same tendency, they would soon be destroyed)? Now those who are hot by nature are courageous and those who are cold are cowardly. The effect of hot regions upon their inhabitants is to cool them (for, their bodies having rarities, the heat escapes out of them), but those who live in a cold climate become heated in their nature, 5 because their flesh is condensed by the external cold, and when it is in this condition the heat collects internally.

BOOK XV
PROBLEMS CONNECTED WITH
MATHEMATICAL THEORY

1 · Why is it that of all the lines which divide a rectilinear figure into two 10 parts that drawn from angle to angle alone bears the name of diameter? Is it because the diameter, as its name implies, divides the figure of which it is the diameter into two parts without destroying it? The line therefore which divides it at

15   its joints (by which I mean the angles) will be the diameter; for it does not destroy the figure but divides it, like those who divide up implements of war for distribution. But a division which cuts through a composite figure in the lines which form it destroys the figure; for a rectilinear figure is constructed on angles.

2 · Why is the diameter so called? Is it because it is the only line which divides a rectilinear figure into two parts, as though one should call it the
20   'dichameter'?[1] And why[2] is it the only one that bears this name of all the lines which divide a rectilinear figure into two parts? Is it because it is the only line which divides the figure at the points where its limbs bend, whereas all other lines divide it in its sides?

3 · Why do all men, barbarians and Greeks alike, count up to 10 and not up to any other number, saying for example, 2, 3, 4, 5 and then repeating them,
25   one-five, two-five, just as they say eleven, twelve?[3] Or why do they not stop at some point beyond ten and repeat from there? For every number is made up of one, two, &c., combined with a preceding number, and thus a different number is formed; but the counting always proceeds in fixed sets of ten. For it is clearly not the result
30   of chance that all men invariably count in tens; and that which is invariable and universal is not the result of chance, but is in the nature of things. Is it because ten is a perfect number? For it combines every kind of number, odd and even, square and cube, length and surface, prime and composite. Or is it because ten is the original
35   number, since one, two, three, and four together make ten? Or is it because the bodies which move in the heavens are nine in number? Or is it because in ten proportions four cubic numbers result, from which numbers the Pythagoreans declare that the whole universe is constituted? Or is it because all men have ten fingers and so, as though possessing counters that indicate the numbers proper to
911ᵃ1   man, they count all other things by this quantity? One race among the Thracians alone of all men count in fours, because their memory, like that of children, cannot extend farther and they do not use a large number of anything.

5   4 · ... because the earth is a centre? For the shapes which appear to us are always similar. This does not seem[4] to be so unless one views them from the centre, but they would sometimes appear triangular, sometimes irregular foursided figures, and sometimes take other forms. Now the earth would appear to us to be the centre of the universe, if we could view it from the heavenly bodies.[5] For the earth being spherical, the centre of the universe and of the earth will be the same. But we dwell
10   on the surface of the earth, so that it is not from the centre but at the distance of half the diameter that the heavenly bodies appear to have the shapes that they do appear to have. What reason then is there why the appearance of their shapes should not remain the same when the distance is increased?

---

[1]διχάμετρος as from δίχα ('into two parts').
[2]Reading διὰ τί for διότι.
[3]A literal translation of the Greek for 'eleven' is 'one-ten'.
[4]Reading οὐ δοκεῖ.
[5]The text of this sentence is quite uncertain.

5 · Why is it that, although the sun moves with uniform motion, yet the increase and decrease of the shadows is not the same in any equal period of time? Is 15 it because the angles to the objects seen, that is the angles made by the rays of the sun and subtending equal arcs, are equal? Now if these are equal, so also are the angles which the rays when produced⁶ make in the triangle formed by the first ray and the object seen and the shadow. If the angles are equal, the line which is farther from the object seen must be greater than that which is less far; for we know that 20 this is so. Let the circumference, therefore, be divided into any number of equal parts, and let the object seen be H. When therefore the sun at A falling on H makes the shadow HL⁷, the ray must fall on L. But when the sun comes to B, the ray from B will fall within HL, and similarly again when the sun comes to C; otherwise one 25 straight line will touch another straight line at two points. Since therefore AB is equal to BC, the angles which subtend them at D will also be equal, for they are situated about the centre. But if the angles on this side of D are equal, so also are the corresponding angles in the triangle; for they are at the apexes of the first pair of angles. So while the angle is divided into two equal parts, the line LE will be greater 30 than the line EF within LH.⁸ So too with the other angles formed by the rays from the circumference. At the same time it is clear that the shadow must be shortest at midday and that then its increases are least. For the sun is most over our head at midday, and stifling heat occurs both for the reason just mentioned and because 35 there is no wind; for wind is caused when the sun dissipates the air near the earth. If therefore it does so simultaneously in both hemispheres, midnight and midday 911ᵇ1 would naturally be windless.

6 · Why does the sun penetrating through quadrilaterals form not rectilinear shapes but circles, as for instance when it passes through wicker-work? Is it because the projection of the vision is in the form of a cone, and the base of a cone is a circle, 5 so that the rays of the sun always appear circular on whatever object they fall? For the figure also formed by the sun must be contained by straight lines, if the rays are straight; for when they fall in a straight line on to a straight line, they form a figure contained by straight lines. And this is what happens with the rays; for they fall on 10 the straight line of the wicker-work, at the point where they shine through, and are themselves straight, so that their projection is a straight line. But because the parts of the vision which are cut off towards the extremities of the straight lines are weak, the parts of the figure about the angles are not seen; but what there is of straight line 15 in the cone describes a straight line, while the rest does not, but the sight falls on part of the figure without perceiving it. For there are many things to which the sight penetrates without our seeing them, objects, for instance, which are in darkness. A similar phenomenon is the fact that a quadrilateral figure appears polygonal, and at a greater distance circular. Now since the projection of sight is in the form of a cone, 20 when the figure is removed to a distance the parts of the vision which are cut off towards the angles, because they are weak and few, do not see anything when the

⁶Reading καὶ ἃς ἐκβαλλόμεναι ποιοῦσιν αἱ ἀκτῖνες.
⁷Reading (here and below) Λ for A.
⁸Reading ἐν τῇ ΛΘ.

distance is increased; but the parts of the vision which fall upon the centre of the
25 figure, being numerous and strong, are more persistent. When, therefore, the figure
is near at hand, they can[9] see the parts in the angles; but, when the distance is
greater,[10] they cannot do so. For this reason too a curved line removed to a distance
appears straight, and the moon on the eighth day seems to be contained by straight
30 lines, if the vision falls upon the line which encloses it and not on its breadth. For
when the circumference is near, the sight can discern how much nearer one part of
the circumference is than another; but when it is distant, the sight does not perceive
it clearly, and it seems to be equally distant; and so it appears to be straight.

35   7 · Why, though the moon is spherical, do we see it straight when it is
half-full? Is it because our vision and the circumference of the circles which the sun
912ᵃ1 makes when it falls upon the moon are in the same plane? Whenever this happens,
the sun appears as a straight line; for since that which casts its vision on a sphere
must see a circle, and the moon is spherical, and the sun looks down upon it, there
5 must be a circle which is caused by the sun. When therefore this is opposite to us,
the whole is visible and the moon appears to be full; but when it changes owing to
the altered position of the sun, its circumference becomes on a plane with our sight
and so it appears straight, and the rest appears circular, because a hemisphere is
10 opposite our vision, and this has the appearance of a semicircle; for the moon is
always facing our vision, but when the sun sheds its rays we do not see it. And after
the eighth day it begins to fill out from the middle, because the sun as it passes on
makes the circle incline more towards us; and the circle being thus presented to view
15 resembles the section of a cone. It assumes a crescent-like appearance when the sun
changes its position; for when the circle of the sun reaches the extreme points, which
make the moon seem half-full, the circumference of the circle appears; for it is no
longer in a straight line with the vision, but passes beyond it. When this happens and
the circle passes through the same points, it must necessarily appear to have a
20 crescent shape; for a part of the circle is directly on a plane with the eye (a part of
the circle, that is, which was formerly opposite to us), so that part of the brightness
is cut off. Then the extremities too remain in the same position, so that the moon
must have a crescent shape to a greater or less extent according to the sun's
movement; for when the sun changes its position, the circle upon which it looks also
25 turns, remaining on the same points; for it might assume an infinite number of
inclinations, since an infinite number of the largest circles can be described through
the same points.

    8 · Why is it that the sun and moon, which are spherical, have the
appearance of being flat? Is it because all things of which the distance is uncertain
30 seem to be equidistant, when they are more or less distant? And so in a single body
composed of parts, provided that it is uniform in colour, the parts must necessarily
appear equidistant, and the equidistant must appear to be uniform and flat.

[9]Reading δύνανται.
[10]Reading πλείονος δ' αὐτοῦ.

9 · Why does the sun make long shadows as it rises and sets, and shorter when it is high in the heavens, and shortest of all at midday? Is it because, as it rises, 35 it will at first make a shadow parallel to the earth and cast it to an infinite distance,[11] and then make a long shadow, which grows ever less because the straight line from the higher point falls within that from the lower point. Let *AB* be the gnomon, and *C* and *D* two positions of the sun. The ray from *C*, the line *CF*, will fall outside the line *DE*;[12] and the shadow *BE* is formed when the sun is higher in the 912[b]1 heavens, and *BF* when it is lower, and it will be shortest when[13] the sun is at its highest and over our head.

10 · Why are the shadows thrown by the moon longer than those thrown by the sun, though both are thrown by the same perpendicular object? Is it because the 5 sun is higher than the moon, and so the ray from the higher point must fall within that from the lower point? Let *AD* be the gnomon, *B* the moon, and *C* the sun. The ray from the moon is *BF*, so that the shadow will be *DF*; but the ray from the sun is *CE*, and its shadow therefore will necessarily be less, viz. *DE*. 10

11 · Why is it that during eclipses of the sun, if one views them through a sieve or a leaf—for example, that of a plane-tree or any other broad-leaved tree—or through the two hands with the fingers interlaced, the rays are crescent-shaped in the direction of the earth? Is it because, just as, when the light shines through an aperture with regular angles, the result is a round figure, namely a cone (the reason 15 being that two cones are formed, one between the sun and the aperture and the other between the aperture and the ground, and their apexes meet), so, when under these conditions part is cut off from the orb in the sky,[14] there will be a crescent on the other side of the aperture from the illuminant, that is, in the direction of the earth (for the rays proceed from that part of the circumference which is a 20 crescent)? Now as it were small[15] apertures are formed between the fingers and in a sieve, and so the phenomenon can be more clearly demonstrated than when the rays pass through wide apertures. Such crescents are not formed by the moon, whether in eclipse or waxing or waning, because the rays from its extremities are not clearcut, but it sheds its light from the middle, and the middle portion of the 25 crescent is but small.

12 · Why does the parhelion not occur either when the sun is in mid-heaven or above the sun or below it, but only at the side of it? Is it because the parhelion is produced when our visual ray to the sun is refracted, and this stationary condition of 30 the air, on the occasion of which the vision is refracted, cannot occur either near the sun or far away from it? For, if it is near, the sun will dissolve it, whereas, if it is far away, the sight will not be refracted; for, if it is strained to a distance, it is weak

---

[11]Omitting ὡς ἄνισον.
[12]Reading Δ for Γ.
[13]Reading ὅταν for ὅσω. [14]Reading τοῦ ἄνωθεν κύκλου.
[15]Reading μικραὶ δέ.

when refracted from a small refractor. (So too a halo does not form.) If then a
35   refractor forms opposite the sun and near to it, the sun will dissolve it, whereas if it
be far away, the incidence of the sight upon it will be too weak. If, however, it forms
at the side of the sun, it is possible for the refractor to be at such a distance that
neither does the sun dissolve it nor does the sight ascend weakened[16] by passing
under the earth. It does not form below the sun because, being near the earth, it
913ᵃ1   would be dissolved by the sun; whereas, if it were above the sun when the sun is in
mid-heaven, the sight would be distracted. And it cannot form at all even at the side
of the sun when it is in mid-heaven, because, if the sight is directed too far under the
earth, very little of it will reach the refractor, so that, when it is refracted, it will be
very weak.

5   13 · Why does the extremity of the shadow caused by the sun seem to
tremble? For it is not due to the fact that the sun is travelling along; for it is
impossible for it to move in contrary directions, and it is of such motion that
trembling consists. (Moreover it is uncertain why a shadow changes its position, as
also why the sun itself moves.) Is it due to the movement of the so-called motes in
10   the air? These can be seen in the rays which enter through a window; for they move
even when there is no wind. These then being constantly carried from the shadow
into the light and from the light into the shadow, the common boundary between the
light and the shadow is seen to move similarly. For changing[17] from side to side of it,
these motes cause as it were shadow in one place and light in another; so that the
15   shadow appears to move, though it is not really it but the motes which move in this
way.[18]

BOOK XVI

PROBLEMS CONNECTED WITH
INANIMATE THINGS

1 · Why is it that the bases of bubbles in water are white, and if they are
20   placed in the sun they do not make any shadow, but, while the rest of the bubble
casts a shadow, the base does not do so but is surrounded on all sides by sunlight?
And, what is still more wonderful, even if a piece of wood is placed on the water in
the sunlight, the shadow is cut off by the water at that point.[1] Is no shadow really
formed? Is the shadow dissolved by the sun? If then a shadow is to be defined as
25   anything which is not visible to the sun, the whole mass of the object all round must
be visible to the sun; but the impossibility of this has been demonstrated in the

---

[16]Reading ἀσθενῆ.
[17]Reading μεταβάλλοντα.
[18]Reading ἐκεῖνα.
[1]Reading ταύτῃ.

treatises on optics, for even the largest optical system cannot see the whole circumference of the smallest visible object.

2 · Why are bubbles hemispherical? Is it because the radii between the centre and the outer air extend in every direction upwards to the same distance and thus necessarily produce a hemispherical form? The corresponding hemisphere   30 below is cut off by the watery surface in which the central point is situated.

3 · Why is it that in magnitudes of uneven weight,[2] if you set the lighter part of them in motion, the object thrown revolves in a circle, as happens, for example, with loaded dice if you throw them with the unweighted side turned towards you? Is   35 it because the heavier part cannot travel at the same speed as the lighter when hurled with the same force? Now the object must travel as a single whole, but cannot move alike in all its parts; therefore if the parts were moved with equal speed   913ᵇ1 they would move in the same line, while since one part travels more quickly than the other, the object necessarily revolves as it moves; for it is only in this manner that the parts which are always opposite one another can follow unequal paths in the same time.   5

4 · Why is it that objects which fall to the earth and rebound describe similar angles to the earth's surface on either side of the point at which they touch the surface? Is it because all things naturally tend to travel at right angles to the earth? Objects, therefore, which fall upon the ground at right angles, striking the surface perpendicularly and diametrically, when they rebound, form angles of that size,   10 because the diameter divides the angle at the surface into equal parts. But objects which fall obliquely, since they do not strike the ground perpendicularly but at a point above the perpendicular, when they are thrust back by that against which they strike, travel in the opposite direction. This in the case of round objects is due to the   15 fact that, striking against it in their course, they revolve in an opposite direction to that in which they are thrust back, whether their central point is at rest or changes its position. In the case of rectilinear objects it is due to the fact that their perpendicular is thrown backwards after being brought forward;[3] just as happens to those whose legs are sheared away from under them or whose scrotum is pulled   20 downwards, for such persons always fall in a contrary direction and backwards, because their perpendicular is raised above the ground[4] and then thrust forward. For clearly the opposite of perpendicularity will be to fall backwards and downwards, and objects carried downwards would be heavier. That, therefore, which in these persons involves a fall, becomes movement in rebounding objects.   25 Neither round nor rectilinear objects therefore rebound at right angles, because the perpendicular divides the objects in motion into two parts depthways,[5] and there

[2]Reading βάρος.
[3]Reading προσενεχθεῖσαν.
[4]Omitting ἰσάζειν αὐτά.
[5]Reading βάθει.

30 cannot be several perpendiculars to the same plane surface cutting one another, which will happen if a perpendicular is formed at the moment of their impact at the point where the object in motion strikes the plane surface;[6] so that the original perpendicular along[7] which it travelled must necessarily be cut by the new perpendicular. Now since the object will be borne back, but will not be borne back 35 at a right angle, it remains that the angle on either side of the point of impact with the plane surface must be an acute angle; for the right angle forms the division between the opposite angles.

5 · Why is it that a cylinder, when it is set in motion, travels straight and describes straight lines with the circles in which it terminates, whereas a cone revolves in a circle, its apex remaining still, and describes a circle with the circle in 914ᵃ1 which it terminates? Both move with a circular motion, but the cylinder describes straight lines on the plane surface, while the cone describes circles because the circles which compose the cone are unequal and the greater circle always moves more quickly than the less about the same centre. Now since all the circles 5 composing the cone move at different rates, it results that the outermost circles travel over most space and describe the longest line in the same time (hence they must move in a circle); for all the circles are described by the same straight line, and when the straight line revolves the various points on it do not describe an equal line 10 in the same time, but can travel along an equal line only if they proceed in a straight direction. But in the cylinders, since all the circles are equal and about the same centre, the result is that, since they touch the plane surface at all the points on them at the same time, as they roll they travel at a uniform speed (because cylinders are 15 uniform throughout), and reach the plane surface again simultaneously when each has completed its own circuit; thus the straight lines described on the plane surface are also equal, for the circles describe them by contact, since they both are equal and travel at the same speed. Now the lines described by the same line travelling in a straight direction are straight, and so the cylinder would travel straight along 20 them; for it makes no difference whether you drag the cylinder over the plane surface at the line where it first[8] touched the plane surface, or whether you roll it over it; for the result will always be that an equal and similar line made up of points on the cylinder will touch the plane surface, both when the cylinder is dragged and when it is rolled along.

25 6 · Why is it that if a scroll is cut level and straight, then if you cut it parallel to the base, the edge becomes straight when unrolled, but if it is cut obliquely, the edge becomes crooked? Is it due to the fact that, since the circles in the first section are in the same plane, the result is that the oblique section is not parallel but is 30 partly more and partly less distant from the first section, so that, when the roll is unfolded, the circles, which are in the same plane and have their origin in the same plane, assume, when unrolled, the line which they themselves form? For the

---

[6]Omitting δισχοτομεῖσθαι . . . συμβήσεται.
[7]Reading ἐφ' ἧς.
[8]Reading ᾗ πρώτῃ.

resulting line is formed from the circles which are in the same plane, so that the line, being on a plane, is also straight. But the line of the oblique section when it is 35 unrolled, not being parallel to the first section, but partly more and partly less distant from it (this being the position of the section relative to it), will not be on a plane and therefore not straight either; for part of a straight line cannot be in one plane and part in another.

7 · Why is it that magnitudes always appear less when divided up than when 914ᵇ1 taken as a whole? Is it because, though things which are divided always possess number, in size they are smaller than that which is single and undivided? For that which is great is said to be great owing to its continuity and because it is of a certain size, but the number of its parts is always greater than the number of any undivided 5 magnitude. So it is only natural that the whole should appear greater than the parts into which it is divided; for, though the whole and its parts are identical, the whole, being continuous, possesses more of the quality of magnitude, while the parts have more of the quality of number.

8 · Of the phenomena which occur in the water-clock the cause seems to be in general that ascribed by Anaxagoras; for the air which is cut off within it is the 10 cause of the water not entering when the tube has been closed. The air, however, by itself is not the cause; for if one plunges the water-clock obliquely into the water, having first blocked up the tube, the water will enter. So Anaxagoras does not adequately explain how the air is the cause; though, as has been said, it certainly is 15 the cause. Now air, whether impelled along or travelling of itself without any compelling force, naturally travels in a straight line like the other elements. When therefore the water-clock is plunged obliquely into the water, the air preserving its straight course is driven out by the water through the holes opposite to those which 20 are in the water, and, as it goes out, the water flows in. But if the water-clock is plunged upright into the water, the air not being able to pass straight up, because the upper parts are closed, remains round the first holes; for it cannot contract into itself.[9] The fact that the air can keep out the water by its immobility can be 25 illustrated by what happens with the water-clock itself. For if you fill the bulb itself of the water-clock with water, having stopped up the tube, and invert it with the tube downwards, the water does not flow along the tube to the outlet. And when the outlet is opened, it does not immediately flow out along the tube but only after a moment's interval, since it is not already at the outlet of the tube but passes along it 30 afterwards, when it is opened. But when the water-clock is full and in an upright position, the water passes through the strainer as soon as ever the tube is opened, because it is in contact with the strainer, whereas it is not in contact with the extremities of the tube. The water does not, therefore, flow into the water-clock, for 35 the reason already mentioned, but flows out when the tube is opened because the air in it being set in motion up and down causes considerable movement[10] in the water inside the water-clock. The water then, being thrust downwards and having itself

---

[9]Reading σάττεσθαι γὰρ εἰς αὐτόν.
[10]Reading κίνησιν.

also a tendency in that direction, naturally flows out, forcing its way through the air
915ᵃ1 outside the water-clock, which is set in motion and is equal in force to the air which
impels it but weaker than it in its power of resistance, because the interior air, since
it passes through the tube, which is narrow, flows more quickly and violently and
forces the water on. The reason why the water does not flow when the tube is closed
5 is that the water on entering into the water-clock drives the air forcibly out of it.
(That this is so is shown by the breath and noise engendered in it.) As the water
enters, driving the air forcibly along, it rushes into the tube itself, and[11] like wedges
of wood or bronze driven in by cleavage, remains in position without anything else to
10 hold it together, until it is expelled from the opposite direction, as pegs which are
broken in wood are knocked out. This occurs when the tube is opened for the reasons
already mentioned. If this is the reason, it is only natural that it should not flow out
or make its way forth, since the air forcibly prevents it and becomes inflated.[12] (The
15 noise which is made shows that the water is drawn up by the air, and this is a
common phenomenon.) All the water then, being drawn up and being in itself
continuous, remains in the same position under the pressure of the air, until it is
thrust away again by it; and, since the first part of the water remains in the same
position, the rest of the water is dependent from it in one continuous mass. It is only
20 natural that this should be so; for it is the property of the same thing to move
something from its own place and to hold it when it has moved it,[13] and to do so for a
longer time, if that which holds and that which is held are of equal force, or if that
which holds is stronger, as occurs in the present case; for air has greater force than
water.

25   9 · Why is it that the parts of plants and of animals which are not
instrumental are all round—in plants, for instance, the stem and the shoots, and in
animals the calves, thighs, arms, and chest—and no whole or part is triangular or
polygonal? Is it due, as Archytas used to say, to the fact that in natural movement
30 the proportion of equality is always present (for he holds that all things move in a
proportion), and that this is the only proportion which can return to itself, and so it
forms circles and rotundities wherever it occurs?

     10 · Why do extremities always take rounded forms? Is it because nature
makes everything as excellent and as beautiful as the available material permits,
35 and a rounded form is the most beautiful, being as uniform as possible?

     11 · Why does a circular object when it is thrown at first describe a straight
line, but, as it ceases to move, describe a spiral, until it falls? Does it describe a
straight line at first, because the air on either side of it alike keeps it upright? The
915ᵇ1 inclination then to either side being equal, the line also which it describes must be of
such a nature that it divides the space on either side of it equally, and such a line is a
straight line. But when it inclines to one side, because the air on either side of it is

----

[11]Reading αὐτὸν καί for αὐτοῦ.
[12]The text of this sentence is quite uncertain.
[13]Reading ὡς ἐκίνησεν.

not even, it no longer describes an equal line with its inner and with its outer edge, but is forced to describe a circular line.   5

12 · Why is it that in magnitudes of uneven weight,[14] if you set the lighter part of them in motion, the object thrown revolves in a circle, as happens for example with loaded dice if you throw them with the unweighted side towards you? Is it because the heavier part cannot travel at the same speed as the lighter when   10 hurled with the same force? Now since it must necessarily move, but cannot do so in the same manner, that is in a straight line, it must take an inward direction and revolve; just as, if part of the object had as a whole remained motionless owing to a weight in the centre, the part next to the person setting the object in motion would have moved so as to occupy the position of the part away from him, while the farther side would have moved towards him. But when the whole object moves and, as it   15 travels, has a weight in the middle, it must necessarily behave in the same manner.

13 · Why is it that objects which are travelling along, when they come into collision with anything, rebound in a direction opposite to that in which they are naturally travelling, and at similar angles? Is it because they move not only with the impetus which accords with their own nature but also with that which is due to the   20 agent which throws them? Their own impetus then ceases when they reach their own proper position (for everything comes to rest when it reaches the position to which it is naturally carried), but, owing to the extraneous impetus, it is forced to continue to move, not, however, in a forward direction, because it is prevented from doing so, but either sideways or in a direct line. Now every object rebounds at   25 similar angles, because it is travelling to the point to which it is carried by the impetus which was imparted by the person who threw it; and at that point it must be travelling at an acute angle or at a right angle. Since then the repelling object stops the movement in a straight line, it stops alike the moving object and its impetus. As   30 then in a mirror the image appears at the end of the line along which the sight travels, so the opposite occurs in moving objects, for they are repelled at an angle of the same magnitude as the angel at the apex (for it must be observed that both the angle and the impetus are changed), and in these circumstances it is clear that moving objects must rebound at similar angles.   35

BOOK XVII
PROBLEMS CONNECTED WITH
ANIMATE THINGS

1 · Why do those who are unsymmetrical appear larger when set side by side with other men than by themselves? Is it because that which is symmetrical is one, and symmetry more than anything else gives unity to a thing, and that which is one   916ᵃ1

---

[14]Reading βάρος.

tends to be indivisible, and the indivisible is smaller, whereas asymmetry by causing diversity creates a multiplicity? When things therefore are seen by themselves, their dimensions are less likely to be noticed; but this is not so when they are seen side by 5 side with one another. That then which is indivisible appears to be one, and the impression which it makes on the beholder is one because of its symmetry. But that which is unsymmetrical makes a greater impression, as though it were many, and appears greater because, though in reality only one, it seems to be many; for it partakes of the nature of magnitude, because it is continuous, and of number, 10 because of the inequality of its parts; and so being increased in both these respects, it naturally appears great by the side of that which is simple and one.

2 · Why do animals and plants grow more in length than otherwise? Is it because length increases three times over, width twice, and depth once? For length 15 is the first and original dimension, and so it increases both of itself, and secondly in combination with width, and thirdly in combination with depth. But width implies an increase in two dimensions only, in itself and at the same time in depth.[1]

In what sense must we understand the terms 'prior' and 'posterior'? As those who lived in the time of Troy are prior to us, so are those who lived before them prior 20 to them and so on *ad infinitum?* Or since there is a beginning and a middle and an end of the universe, and when a man, as he becomes old, reaches the limit and turns again towards the beginning, that which is nearer to the beginning is earlier, what prevents our being nearer to the beginning than to the end, in which case we should 25 be prior? Just as the course[2] of the firmament and of each of the stars is a circle, why should not also the coming into being and the decay of perishable things be of such a kind that these things again come into being and decay? This agrees with the saying that 'human life is a circle'. To demand that those who are coming into being 30 should always be numerically identical is foolish, but one would more readily accept that they were identical in kind. And so we should ourselves be prior, and one might suppose the arrangement of the series to be such that it returns back in a circle to the point from which it began and thus secures continuity and identity of composition. For Alcmaeon declares that men perish because they cannot link 35 together the beginning to the end—a clever saying, if one supposes that he uses it metaphorically and the literal meaning is not insisted upon. If then human life is a circle, and a circle has neither beginning nor end, we should not be prior to those who lived in the time of Troy nor they prior to us by being nearer to the beginning.

---

[1]Reading βάθει.
[2]Reading ἡ φορά.

BOOK XVIII
PROBLEMS CONNECTED WITH
LITERARY STUDY

1 · Why is it that some people, if they begin to read, are overcome by sleep even against their will, whereas others wishing to be overcome by sleep are kept awake by taking up a book? Is it because in those in whom movements of breath take place owing to the coldness of their nature or of melancholic humours, which 5 by their coldness engender an unconcocted excretion of breath—in such people, the intelligence, when it is set in motion and does not think of anything with concentrated attention, is checked by the second movement, which has a cooling effect, and this causes a tendency to sleep? But when they fix the intelligence firmly upon something, as happens in reading, they are impelled by the heating movement, 10 which is unchecked by anything, and so they cannot go to sleep. In those who are in a natural condition, however, when the intelligence, which is very powerful, stands at a single point and does not keep changing from one subject to another, every function in that region (whose inactivity involves sleep) is at a standstill;[1] and when the intelligence stands still and is as it were weary, being situated in the head, it 15 weighs it down and produces sleep. But as long as the mind moves naturally, it does not go to sleep; for it is then that it is most alive, and wakefulness rather than sleeping is the cause of life.

2 · Why are contentious disputations useful as a mental exercise? Is it because they involve frequent victories and defeats? They therefore quickly instil a 20 spirit of rivalry; for, when men are victorious, they are induced by their joy to contend yet more, and, when they are defeated, they continue the struggle in hopes of turning defeat into victory. Those engaged in struggles of other kinds act in the same way, and so when fighting and getting the worst of it often refuse to come to terms.

3 · Why is it that in rhetorical displays men prefer examples and stories 25 rather than enthymemes? Is it because they like to learn and to learn quickly, and this end is achieved more easily by examples and stories, since these are familiar to them and are of the nature of particulars, whereas enthymemes are proofs based on generalities, with which we are less familiar than with the particular? Further, we 30 attach more credence to any evidence which is supported by several witnesses, and examples and stories resemble evidence, and proofs supported by witnesses are easily obtained. Further, men like to hear of similarities, and examples and stories display similarities.

4 · Why do we talk of an orator, or a general, or a business man as being 35 clever, but not use the term of a musician or of an actor? Is it because the powers of

---

[1]Reading ἵσταται.

the two last are exercised apart from any desire of gaining an advantage (for their aim is pleasure), whereas the three first aim at some advantage? For a good orator or general or business man is one who can gain some advantage, and cleverness consists mainly in getting the better of some one else.

5 · Why is the philosopher generally regarded as superior to the orator? Is it because the philosopher treats of the nature of injustice, while the orator says that such and such a person is unjust, and the orator states that such and such a person is a tyrant, while the philosopher discusses the nature of tyranny?

6 · Why is it that some men spend their time in pursuits which they have chosen, though these are sometimes mean, rather than in more honourable professions? Why, for example, should a man who chooses to be a conjurer or an actor or a piper prefer these callings to that of an astronomer or an orator? Is it because some men would prefer to undertake the more honourable professions but do not do so because they do not feel confident that they would succeed in them? Or is it because each man chooses the calling in which he thinks he can excel and devotes himself to that which he chooses, giving up the greater part of each day to it, in order that he may improve his own proficiency in it? Now when men have chosen a calling from the first and have become accustomed to it, they lose the power of discriminating between the higher and the lower; for their mind is warped by their bad choice.

7 · Why is it that some persons, if they begin to read, are overcome by sleep even against their will, whereas those who wish to go to sleep are made unable to do so if they take up a book?[2] Is it because in those in whom movements of breath take place owing to the coldness of their nature or of melancholic humours, which by their coldness engender an unconcocted excretion of breath—in these when the intelligence is set in motion and does not think of anything with concentrated attention, the intelligence is checked by the second movement,[3] and so they undergo a great mental change and go to sleep (for the movement of breath is overcome)? But when they fix their intelligence on something, as happens in reading, they are impelled by the movement of breath unchecked by anything, and so cannot sleep. But in those who are in a natural condition, when the intelligence is fixed on one thing and does not keep changing from one subject to another, every function in that region (the inactivity of which involves sleep) is at a standstill. (Similarly during a rout, if the leader halts, all the forces under his command halt also.) For naturally that which is light rises, while the heavy sinks. As long, therefore, as the mind moves naturally, it does not go to sleep; for it is then that it is most alive.[4] When the mind stands still and is as it were weary, the intellect undergoes a change, and the corporeal elements rise to the head and produce sleep. Reading might be expected to prevent sleep; but wakefulness is not due to the fact that we are thinking (for then

---

[2]Reading οὐ ποιεῖ.
[3]Reading τῇ ἑτέρᾳ κινήσει.   [4]Reading μάλιστα ζῇ for ἔχει.

our mind is most concentrated) but to the constant change; for the intellectual activities which cause wakefulness are those in which the mind searches and finds   917ᵇ1 difficulties rather than those in which it pursues continual contemplation; for the former cause lack of concentration, while the latter do not.

8 · Why is it that in contentious disputes no verbosity can ever occur? Is it because such reasoning is apparent deduction, and deduction involves only a brief   5 discussion; and, if it be prolonged, after a time the false reasoning is detected and the disputant can withdraw the premises which he has granted?

9 · Why do we feel more pleasure in listening to narratives in which the attention is concentrated on a single point than in hearing those which are concerned with many subjects? Is it because we pay more attention to and feel more   10 pleasure in listening to things which are more easily comprehended, and that which is definite is more easily comprehended than that which is indefinite? Now a single thing is definite, but a plurality partakes of the nature of the infinite.

10 · Why do we like to hear of events which are neither very old nor quite new? Is it because we discredit events which occurred long before our time and take no pleasure in events which we discredit, while we can still as it were perceive very   15 recent events and so take no pleasure in hearing about them?

BOOK XIX
PROBLEMS CONNECTED WITH MUSIC

1 · Why do those who are grieving and those who are enjoying themselves alike have the flute played to them? Is it in order that the distress of the former may be lessened and the pleasure of the latter increased?   20

2 · Why is it that, when the same person uses the same vocal power, the sound travels farther when he is singing or shouting with others than when he does so by himself? Is it because the doing of anything with a number of other people—compressing, for instance, or pushing something—does not produce an effect in simple proportion to the number of persons; but, just as a line two feet long describes a circle which is not double but quadruple that described by a line a foot long, so collective actions have greater force in proportion to their number than   25 when they are carried out separately? When, therefore, a number of persons sing together, the force of their voice unites, and impels the air simultaneously, so that it travels many times as far; for the voice produced by all is the multiple of each single voice.

30   3 · Why does the voice waver most when singing *parhypate* and to no less a degree than when singing *nete* and the higher notes, although the interval is greater? Is it because the interval is more difficult to sing and is in primary element? Now the difficulty is due to the straining and pressure of the voice; and these require an effort, and things which require an effort are more likely to fail.

35   4 · But why is *parhypate* difficult to sing, but *hypate* easy, although there is only a quarter-tone between them? Is it because *hypate* is accompanied by relaxation of the voice and also because after tension it is easy to slacken?[1] It is probably for the same reason that what a man says with violence,[2] he says with this note or *paranete*. For one must . . . with a consciousness of the character which one
918ᵃ1   is representing and under conditions most akin to it according to one's purpose. But what is the cause of concordant music?[3]

        5 · Why do men take greater pleasure in listening to those who are singing such music as they already know than music which they do not know? Is it because,
5   when they recognize what is being sung, it is more obvious that the singer is as it were achieving his aims, and this is pleasant to contemplate? Or is it because it is less[4] pleasant to learn? And the reason for this is that in the one case there is acquisition of knowledge, in the other the use and recognition of it. Further, that which is familiar is always pleasanter than the unfamiliar.

10   6 · Why does recitation with a musical accompaniment have a tragic effect when introduced into singing? Is it owing to the resulting contrast? For the contrast gives an expression of feeling and implies extremity of calamity or grief, whereas uniformity is less mournful.

        7 · Why did the ancients, when they gave the scale seven notes, leave in
15   *hypate* and not *nete*? Is this a false statement, since they left in both and omitted *trite,* or is the truer answer that the lower note contains the sound of the higher note,[5] so that *hypate* gives the impression of the octave above better than *nete* for the high note is a sign of more force, while the low note is easier to utter?

        8 · Why does the low note contain[6] the sound of the high note? Is it because
20   the low note is greater and resembles an obtuse angle, while the high note resembles an acute angle?

        9 · Why do we listen with greater pleasure to a solo when a man sings it to the accompaniment of a flute or lyre? Yet the same tune is sung note for note with or without accompaniment. For if there is more of the same thing, it ought to be still

---

[1]Reading ἀναχαλᾶν for ἄνω βάλλειν.
[2]Reading βίαν for μίαν.
[3]The text of the last two sentences is uncertain.
[4]Reading ἧττον ἡδύ.   [5]Reading ἴσχει.
[6]Reading ἴσχει.

more pleasant when accompanied by a large number of flute-players. Is it because 25
the singer is more obviously achieving his aim when he is accompanied by a flute or
lyre? And the accompaniment of a number of flute-players or lyres does not add to
the pleasure, because it drowns the singing.

10 · Why, if the human voice is more pleasant than an instrument, is the
voice of a man singing without words—as, for example, when singing nonny- 30
noes—not so pleasant as a flute or lyre? Or is it true that even in the case of an
instrument we get less pleasure if it is not expressive of meaning? The instrument,
however, has an advantage even in its actual effect; for while the human voice is
pleasanter, instruments strike the note better than the human mouth, which is why
they are pleasanter to hear than nonny-noes.

11 · Why is the voice higher when it echoes back? Is it because it is smaller, 35
having become weaker?

12 · Why does the lower of two strings sounded together always give the
tune? For if one omits *paranete,* when one should sound it with *mese,* the tune is
given none the less; but if one omits *mese,* when one should sound both, the tune is
lost.⁷ Is it because the low note is large and therefore strong, and the less is
contained in the greater? So too if *hypate* is stopped down in the centre, two *netes* 918ᵇ1
are produced.

13 · Why is it that the low note in the octave gives the effect of unison with
the high, but not vice versa? Is it because, if possible, the sound of both notes is in
both notes, but, failing that, in the low note, since it is greater? 5

14 · Why does the accord in the octave escape notice, and why does there
appear to be a simple unison, as for example in the Phoenician lyre and in the
human voice? For the upper and lower notes do not give the same sound but are
analogous to one another at the octave. Is it because their sound appears to be 10
practically the same because analogy is equality in sounds, and equality is of the
one? The same deception occurs also in the pipes.

15 · Why were 'nomes' not composed in antistrophes like all other songs,
that is, choric songs? Is it because the 'nomes' were assigned to virtuosi, and as these
were already able to imitate different characters and sustain their parts, the songs 15
composed for them became long and elaborate? Like the words, therefore, the
music conformed to the imitation, becoming constantly different; for it was more
essential for the music to be imitative than the words. (For this reason too
dithyrambs, since they have become imitative, no longer have antistrophes, as they
had formerly.) The reason is that in old days free citizens themselves formed the 20

⁷Following Monro's text.

choruses; it was difficult, therefore, for a large number to sing together like virtuosi, so they sang enharmonic songs. For it is easier for a single person to make many changes than for a large chorus, and for a professional than for those who are preserving the character of the music. And so they made the music more simple for 25 them. Now the antistrophic song is simple; for there is one rhythm[8] and one unit of metre. For the same reason songs executed from the stage are not antistrophic, but those sung by the chorus are so; for the actor is a virtuoso and an imitator, but the chorus is less imitative.

30   16 · Why is antiphonal accompaniment more pleasing than symphonic accompaniment? Is it because in the former the consonance is more obvious than when the accompaniment of the singing is symphonic? For of the two notes played by the instrument one must be in unison with the note sung, and so two notes contending against one drown the other note.

17 · Why is it that singing in fifths does not give the effect of antiphony? Is 35 it because the symphonic notes are not the same as are the notes which are an octave apart? For in the octave the deep note in the lower part of the scale is analogous to the high note in the upper part; it is, therefore, as it were at once the same and different. But this does not occur in fifths and fourths so that the sound of the antiphonal note does not appear, for it is not identical.

18 · Why is it that the accord in the octave alone is used in singing? For in 919ª1 'magadizing', this and no other accord is used. Is it because it alone is made up of antiphonal notes, and with antiphonal notes, if but one be sung, the same effect is produced as if both were sung? For the one note in a way contains the sounds of both, so that, when one is sung, the concordant note at this interval is also sung; and 5 when they sing both, or when one note is sung and the other played on the flute, they both as it were sing one note. Therefore the accord in the octave alone is sung, because the antiphonal notes have the sound of one note.

19 · But why does the power of producing the effect of a single note belong 10 only to antiphonal notes? Is it because they alone are equidistant from *mese?* The presence then of this mean creates a certain similarity in their sounds, and the ear seems to tell us that it is the same note and that they are both extremes.

20 · Why is it that, if after tuning the other strings, one alters *mese* and uses the instrument, the ear is offended and an unmusical effect is produced not only 15 when *mese* is used, but in the rest of the piece as well, whereas, if *lichanos* or any other string is altered, it only seems to make a difference when that particular string is used? Surely this is only natural; for in all good music *mese* occurs frequently,

----

[8]Reading εἰς ῥυθμός.

and all good composers have frequent recourse to *mese*, and, if they leave it, they 20
soon return to it, as they do to no other note. Similarly in language, if certain
connecting particles are removed, such as τε and καί, the language is no longer
Greek; whereas the omission of some particles does not offend the ear, because
certain particles must be frequently used, if there is to be language, but others not. 25
So *mese* is as it were a connective among sounds, and particularly in good music,
because its sound occurs more often.

21 · Why is it that of singers those who are singing low notes are more
conspicuous if they sing out of tune than those who are singing high? So too those 30
who make mistakes in time in the lower notes[9] are more conspicuous. Is it because
the period of time occupied by the low note is longer, and this longer period is more
perceptible (for,[10] lasting for a greater time, it creates a ·deeper sense-impression),
whereas a quick,[11] high note escapes notice owing to its swiftness? 35

22 · Why does a large choir keep better time than a small one? Is it because
they look more to one man, their leader, and begin more slowly and so more easily
achieve unity? For mistakes occur more frequently in quick singing.

23 · Why is *nete* double *hypate*? Is it because in the first place, when half 919[b]1
the string is struck and when the whole string is struck an accord in the octave is
produced? So too with wind instruments, the sound produced through the middle
hole and that produced through the whole flute give an accord in the octave. Again, 5
in the flutes an accord in the octave is obtained by doubling the length, and this is
how flute-makers produce it. Similarly they obtain a fifth by means of a length in
the ratio of 3 to 2.[12] Again, those who construct Pan-pipes stuff wax into the
extreme end of the *hypate*-reed, but fill up the *nete*-reed to the middle. Similarly 10
they obtain a fifth by means of a length in the ratio of 3 to 2, and a fourth by means
of a length in the ratio of 4 to 3. Further, *hypate* and *nete* on triangular stringed
instruments, when they are equally stretched, give an accord in the octave when one
is double the other in length.

24 · Why, if one strikes *nete* and then stops it down, does *hypate* alone seem 15
to resound? Is it because the vibration produced from *hypate* is very much of the
same nature as the sound of *nete*, because it is in accord with it? When it is
increased by the addition of its like, it alone is audible, the other sounds being
imperceptible owing to their smallness.

25 · Why is *mese* so called in the scale, though there is no middle of eight 20
notes? Is it because in the old days scales had seven notes, and seven has a middle?

---

[9]Retaining βαρυτέρῳ.   [10]Reading αἰσθητός, ὅτι.
[11]Retaining ταχύ.
[12]Ruelle excises this sentence.

26 · Why do most men sing high when they sing out of tune? Is it because it is easier to sing high than low? Or is it because singing high is worse than singing low, and a mistake is doing what is worse?

27 · Why is it that of all things which are perceived by the senses that which is heard alone possesses character? For music, even if it is unaccompanied by words, yet has character; whereas a colour and an odour and a savour have not. Is it because that which is heard alone has movement, not, however,[13] the movement in us to which the sound gives rise (for such movement exists also in the other things which affect our senses, for colour also moves our sight), but we perceive the movement which follows such and such a sound? This movement resembles character both in the rhythms and in the melodic disposition of the high and low notes, but not in their commingling; for symphony does possess character. This does not occur in the other objects of sense-perception. Now these movements are connected with action, and actions are indicative of character.

28 · Why are the 'nomes' which are sung so called? Is it because before men knew the art of writing they used to sing their laws in order not to forget them, as they are still accustomed to do among the Agathyrsi? They, therefore, called the earliest of their subsequent songs by the name as their earliest songs.

29 · Why do rhythms and tunes, which after all are only voice, resemble characters, whereas savours do not, nor yet colours and odours? Is it because they are movements, as actions also are? Now activity possesses and instils character, but savours and colours have no similar effect.

30 · Why is neither the Hypodorian nor the Hypophrygian mode suitable for use by the chorus in tragedy? Is it because they do not admit of antistrophic melody? They are used, however, from the stage, because they are imitative.[14]

31 · Why were Phrynichus and his contemporaries primarily musicians? Is it because in those days the lyrical portions of tragedies were many times longer than the purely metrical?

32 · Why is the diapason so called and not named after the number of notes an octave, like the fourth and the fifth? Is it because the notes were originally seven in number, and then Terpander took away *trite* and added *nete,* and in his time it was called diapason and not octave, since there were seven?

33 · Why is it more satisfactory to pass from a high to a low note than from a low to a high note? Is it because the former amounts to beginning at the beginning,

---

[13]Reading μόνον, οὐχί.
[14]Reading μιμητικά.

for the *mese,* or leader,[15] is the highest note in the tetrachord? But in passing from a low to a high note one begins not at the beginning but at the end. Or is it because a low note is nobler and more euphonious after a high note?

34 · Why are a double fifth and a double fourth not concordant, whereas a double octave is? Is it because neither a double fifth nor a double fourth is . . .[16] though a fourth and a fifth are so?

35 · Why is the accord in the octave the most beautiful of all? Is it because its ratios are contained within integral terms, while those of the others are not so contained? For since *nete* is double *hypate,* as *nete* is two, so *hypate* is one; and as *hypate* is two, *nete* is four; and so on. But *nete* is to *mese* in ratio of 3 to 2 (for a fifth is in this ratio), and that which is in the ratio of 3 to 2[17] is not contained within integral terms; for as the lesser number is one, so the greater number is one with the addition of a half, so that it is no longer a comparison of whole numbers, but parts are left over. The like happens also with the fourth; for the ratio of 4 to 3 gives the lesser[18] plus a third of it. Or is it because the accord which is made up of both the other two is the most perfect, and because it is the measure of the melody?

. . .[19] in any body which is displaced the movement is most violent in the middle and gentler at the beginning and end, and when the movement is most violent the sound of that which is displaced is shriller? For this reason also strings which are tightly stretched give a shriller note, for their movement is quicker. Now if a sound is the displacement of air or of something else, a sound which is in the middle of its course must be shrillest. If this were not so, there would be no displacement of anything.

36 · Why is it that if *mese* is altered, the sound of the other strings also is spoilt,[20] but if on the other hand *mese* is left alone and one of the other strings altered, the note which is altered alone is spoilt?[21] Is it because for all strings being in tune means standing in a certain relation to *mese,*[22] and the arrangement of each is already determined by *mese*? If, therefore, that which is the cause of their being in tune and which holds them together is taken away, their proper relationship appears to be no longer maintained. But if one string is out of tune but *mese* is not altered, naturally the defect lies in that string only;[23] for all the others are in tune.

37 · Why is it that, though height in a voice is in accordance with smallness and lowness in accordance with largeness (for a low note is slow owing to its

[15]Omitting καί after ἡγεμών.   [16]Ruelle marks a lacuna here.
[17]Reading διὰ πέντε ἡμιόλιον, τὸ δ' ἡμιόλιον.   [18]Reading τ' ἐκεῖνο for τεμεῖν ὅ.
[19]There is a lacuna in the text here.   [20]Reading φθειρομέναι.
[21]Reading ἡ κινηθεῖσα μόνη φθείρεται.
[22]Omitting δέ before ἔχειν and ἁπάσαις after μέσην.
[23]Reading ἐκλείπει μόνον.

largeness, and a high note quick owing to its smallness), yet more effort is required to sing a high than a low note, and few can sing the top notes, and the 'Orthian
20   songs' and high music are hard to sing owing to the strain which they involve? Yet it requires less effort to set in motion that which is small than that which is large, and this ought to be true also of the air. Is it because the possession of a naturally high voice and the singing of high notes are not the same thing, but naturally high voices are always due to weakness because of the inability to set more than a little air in
25   motion, and the little air thus set in motion is carried quickly along? But height of note in singing is a sign of strength; for that which is carried violently along is carried swiftly—so that height of note in singing is a sign of strength. Hence persons in robust health[24] can sing high. And it requires an effort to sing the high notes, but the low notes are easier.[25]

30   **38** · Why do all men delight in rhythm and melody and concords in general? Is it because we naturally rejoice in natural movements? This is shown by the fact that children rejoice in them as soon as they are born. Now we delight in the various types of melody because of habit; and we delight in rhythm because it contains a familiar and ordered number and moves us in a regular manner; for ordered
35   movement is naturally more akin to us than disordered, and is therefore more in accordance with nature. This is shown by the fact that by working and eating and drinking in an ordered manner we preserve and improve our nature and strength, whereas if we do these things irregularly we destroy and derange our nature; for
921ª1   diseases are disturbances of the natural order[26] of the body. And we delight in concord because it is the mingling of contraries which stand in proportion to one another. Proportion, then, is order, which, as we have said, is naturally pleasant. Now that which is mingled is always more pleasant than that which is unmingled,
5   especially if, being perceived by the senses, it contains equally the force of both extremes; and in a concord the proportion has this characteristic.[27]

39 · Why is 'antiphony'[28] more pleasant than 'homophony'? Is it because 'antiphony' is concord in the octave? For 'antiphony' is produced by young boys and
10   men whose voices are separated in pitch as *nete* is from *hypate*. Now any concord is more pleasing than a simple note for the reasons already stated, and of concords that in the octave is the most pleasing; whereas 'homophony' produces only a simple sound. 'Magadizing' is in the concord of the octave, because, just as in verses the
15   feet stand to one another in the proportion of equal to equal, or two to one, or some other proportion, so too the sounds in a concord stand in a proportion of movement to one another. In the other concords the termination of one of the two notes is incomplete since it coincides with the end of only a half of the other; and so they are

[24]Reading εὐεκτικοί.
[25]Reading ῥᾷον for κάτω.
[26]Omitting οὐ.
[27]Reading δύναμιν ἔχῃ · τοῦτο δ' ἔχει.
[28]Reading ἀντίφωνον for σύμφωνον.

not equal in force, and being unequal they make a different impression on the
sense-perception, as happens in a chorus when at the conclusion they are singing   20
louder than others. Furthermore, *hypate* happens to have the same conclusions to
the periods in its sounds; for the second stroke which *nete* makes upon the air is
hypate. As, then, these notes, though they do not do the same thing, terminate
together, the result is that they carry out one common task, like those who are
playing a stringed accompaniment to a song; for these, though they do not play the   25
same other notes as the singer, yet, if they finish on the same note, give more
pleasure by their conclusion than they give pain by the differences which occur
earlier in the piece, because after diversity the unity due to the accord in the octave
is very pleasing.[29] Now 'magadizing' is made up of contrary notes, and for this   30
reason it is carried out in the octave.

40 · Why do men take greater pleasure in listening to those who are singing
tunes which they already know than if they do not know them? Is it because it is
more obvious that the singer is as it were achieving his aim when they recognize
what is being sung, and when they recognize it the contemplation of it is pleasant?   35
Or is it because the listener is in sympathy with one who sings what he himself
knows? For he sings with him; and every one enjoys singing when he is under no
compulsion to sing.

41 · Why are a double fifth and a double fourth not concordant, whereas a   921[b]1
double octave is? Is it because a fifth is in the ratio of 3 to 2, and a fourth in that of 4
to 3? Now in a series of three numbers[30] in a ratio of 3 to 2 or 4 to 3, the two extreme
numbers will have no ratio to one another; for neither will they be in a superparticu-
lar ratio nor will one be a multiple of the other. But, since the octave is in a ratio of 2   5
to 1, if it be doubled the extreme numbers would be in a fourfold ratio. So, since a
concord is a compound of sounds which are in a ratio[31] to one another, and sounds
which are at an interval of two octaves from one another are in a ratio to one another   10
(while double fourths and double fifths are not), the sounds constituting the double
octave would give a concord (while the others would not) for the reasons given
above.

42 · Why is it that, if one strikes *nete* and then stops it down, *hypate* seems
to respond? Is it because *nete*, as it ceases and dies down, becomes *hypate*? (This is   15
indicated by the fact that it is possible to sing *nete* from *hypate*; for the similarity
can be taken from *hypate* as being a response to *nete*.[32]) And since an echo is a
response to a note,[33] and when *nete* ceases a sound is set in motion[34] which is the
same as the note of *hypate*, it is only natural owing to the similarity that *nete* should   20

[29]Omitting τό before ἐκ διαφόρων.
[30]Retaining τριῶν.   [31]Reading λόγον for εὔλογον.
[32]Reading οὔσης ἀντωδῆς τῆς νεάτης.
[33]Reading ἠχὼ ἀντωδὴ τίς ἐστι φωνῆς, καὶ τῆς.
[34]Reading κινεῖται.

seem to set *hypate* in motion. For we know that *nete* is not[35] in motion, because it is stopped down, and seeing that *hypate* itself is not stopped down and hearing its note we think that it is *hypate* which is giving forth a sound. (This kind of thing is quite
25 common, where we cannot grasp the exact truth either by reasoning or by the senses.) Again, it would be nothing extraordinary if, after *nete* is struck when it is very tightly stretched, the bridge were set in motion; and it would not be strange if, when the bridge moved, all the strings were set in motion with it and made a sound.
30 Now the sound of *nete* is alien to the other notes both in its end and in its beginning, but is the same as *hypate* in its end. This having been added to the movement of *hypate* itself, it would not be strange that the sound should seem to be entirely that of *hypate*; and it will be louder than the combined sound of the other notes, because the latter, being as it were impelled by *nete,* give only a soft sound, whereas *nete,*
35 being the most violent of notes, sounds with its full force; and so naturally its second sound would be louder than that of the others, especially if only a slight movement has taken place in them.[36]

922ª1 **43** · Why do we listen[37] with greater pleasure to a solo sung to a flute than to one sung to a lyre?[38] Is it because anything becomes still more pleasant when mingled with what is more pleasant?[39] Now the flute is more pleasant than the lyre, so that singing would be more pleasant when it mingles with the flute than with the lyre. Further,[40] that which is mingled is more pleasant than that which is
5 unmingled, if there is a simultaneous perception of both the elements. For wine is pleasanter than honey-wine, because natural mixtures are more thoroughly mingled than those which we make ourselves. For there is also wine which is mingled of bitter and sweet savours, as is shown by the so-called vinous pomegranates. Singing,
10 then, and the flute mingle with one another owing to their similarity, for they are both produced by breath. But the sound of the lyre, since it is not produced by breath or is less perceptible than the sound of the flute, mingles less well with the voice and, causing a contrast in the perception, has a less pleasing effect, as has been said of savours. Furthermore, the flute by its own sound and by its likeness to the
15 voice covers up many of the mistakes of the singer; but the sounds of the lyre, which are isolated and mingle less well with the voice, since they are observed show up the mistakes of the singing separately, actually[41] providing as it were a standard for criticizing it. And when there are many mistakes in the singing, the combined effect
20 of the singing and the accompaniment must necessarily be worse.

44 · Why is *mese*[42] so called, though there is no middle of eight notes? Is it because in the old days the scales had seven notes, and seven has a middle? Again, since of the points which fall between two extremes the middle alone forms a kind of

---

[35]Reading ὅτι οὐ for οὖ.
[36]Reading ἄλλως τε καὶ βραχείας κινήσεως αὐταῖς γεγενημένης.
[37]Reading ἀκούομεν for ἐστίν.   [38]Reading ἢ ἐὰν πρὸς λύραν.
[39]Reading πᾶν τῷ ἡδίονι μιχθὲν ἥδιον ἔτι ἐστίν.
[40]Reading ἔτι for ἐπεί.   [41]Omitting ὄντες αὐτοῖς.
[42]Omitting τῶν μὲν ὀκτώ.

starting-point, that which lies between the points which verge towards either end in   25
an extended space, being also a starting-point—*that* will be the middle.[43] And since
nete and *hypate* are the extremes of the scale[44] and the other sounds lie between
them, of which the one which is called *mese* alone is the starting-point of the second
tetrachord, the name *mese* is amply justified; for of the points lying between certain
extremities, as has been shown, the middle alone forms a starting-point.

45 · Why does a large chorus keep the rhythm better than a small one? Is it   30
because they look more to one man, their leader, and begin more slowly, and so
more easily achieve unity? For mistakes occur more frequently in quick singing.
Now a large chorus attends to its leader, and no one by differing from the rest would   35
render himself conspicuous by making himself heard above the rest: in a small
chorus, on the other hand, individuals make themselves more conspicuous; they,
therefore, vie with one another instead of looking to their leader.

46 · Why do most men sing high when they sing out of tune? Is it because it
is easier to sing a high note than a low note? They have at all events a tendency to   922[b]1
sing high and make mistakes in what they sing.

47 · Why did the ancients, when they made the scales consist of seven
strings, leave in *hypate* but not *nete*? Or should we say that they omitted not *nete*
but what is now called *paramese* and the interval of a tone? They treated *mese*,   5
then, as the lower note of the upper 'pycnon'; whence came the name *mese*. Or is it
because it was the end of the upper tetrachord and the beginning of the lower, and
was in pitch in an intermediate relation between the extreme notes?

48 · Why do the choruses in tragedy not sing either in the Hypodorian or in   10
the Hypophrygian mode? Is it because these modes have very little of the kind of
tune which is specially necessary to a chorus? Now the Hypophrygian mode has a
character of action (hence in the *Geryone* the sortie and arming are composed in
this mode); and the Hypodorian is magnificent and steadfast, and so is the most
suitable of all the modes to accompaniment by the lyre. Now both these are   15
unsuited to the chorus and more proper for the characters on the stage; for the latter
imitate heroes, and among the ancients the leaders alone were heroes, and the
people, of whom the chorus consists, were mere men. So a mournful and quiet
character and type of music are suited to the chorus, for they are human. These   20
characteristics belong to the other modes, but least to the Phrygian among
them—for it is exciting and orgiastic. In accordance with this mode, then, we are
affected in a certain way, and the weak are more readily affected than the strong;
and so this mode is appropriate to choruses. When we use the Hypodorian and
Hypophrygian modes, on the other hand, we are active, and action is not fitting for   25

---

[43]The text of this sentence is quite uncertain.
[44]Reading μέν for μέσον.

choruses; for the chorus is in attendance and takes no active part, for it simply shows goodwill towards those with whom it is present.

49 · Why is it that of the sounds which form a consonance the softer is the lower note? Is it because melody is in its own nature soft and tranquil, but becomes harsh and full of movement by the admixture of rhythm? Now since the low note is soft and tranquil, and the high note full of movement, of the notes which maintain the same melody the lower would rather be softer in the same melody; for melody in itself,[45] as has been shown, is soft.

50 · Why is it that the sounds produced from two jars of the same size and quality, one empty and the other half-full, give an accord in the octave? Is it because the sound produced from the half-full jar is double that produced from the empty jar? This surely is just what happens in the pipes. For the quicker the movement, the higher seems the note, and in larger spaces the air collects more slowly, and in double the space in double the time, and proportionately in the other spaces. A wine-skin too which is double the size of another, gives an accord in the octave with one which is half its size.

BOOK XX
PROBLEMS CONCERNING SHRUBS
AND VEGETABLES

1 · Why is it that celery can endure salt water, but the leek cannot? Is it because the roots of the latter are weak, but those of the former are strong, and that which is stronger is less liable to be affected?

2 · What is the reason for the saying:

Mint should neither be eaten nor planted in season of warfare?

Is it because mint has a cooling effect upon the body, as is shown by the corruption which it causes in the semen? This is opposed to courage and spirit, being the same in kind.

3 · Why is it that some plants, though they have blossom, have no fruit, such as the cucumber and the pumpkin and the pomegranate? Or have they fruit, the blossom being the fruit? For example the part which blossoms is a fruit-case, and the cucumber is a fruit-case.

4 · Why is it that some plants are edible only after they have been boiled,

---

[45]Reading αὐτό.

while others can be eaten raw? Do the juices of such plants as are not at first edible
become sweeter when the plants have been warmed by heat, whilst in others the
juices are originally sweet, and these can be eaten raw?   20

5 · Why is it that some plants are boiled, others roasted? Is it because the
moister plants are not dry enough, while the drier plants must not be further dried?
Now anything which is boiled becomes moister and softer, and that which is less
moist becomes dry if exposed to the fire.

6 · Why are some plants edible and others inedible? Is it owing to their   25
juices? For plants which in their raw state have unconcocted juices and, when
heated, do not undergo change, are inedible. Now those of which the juice is edible
but somewhat strong are used as condiments; for plants which have a strong savour
in a small compass serve to flavour those of which the savour is distributed over a
large bulk.

7 · Why is it that some plants live only until they have produced seeds and   30
having borne seeds dry up—grass, for instance, and the so-called herbs—while
others do not, but bear seeds time after time? And of those which live only until they
have produced seed why are the majority annuals, while horse-parsley produces its
fruit in the second year and having done so dries up? Is it because all things flourish   35
until they are at their prime as far as their seed is concerned (for man too continues
to grow until the age of thirty, sometimes in mass and sometimes in bulk), but when
they can no longer produce seed, as in the case of man, they begin to dry up and
grow old—in some cases slowly and in proportion? The reason why some forms of   923^{b}1
life are long-lived and others short-lived is to be the subject of another treatise. But
since the perfection of the seed is the limit in all cases, it necessarily follows that the
short-lived bear fruit only once or only a few times, and the long-lived many times;   5
so that the weakest bear only once and so necessarily dry up; and those of them
which can bear seed in a year are annuals, whilst others, like horse-parsley, do so in
the second year, both plants and trees alike.

8 · Why is it that if one digs down to the roots of celery and surrounds them   10
with barley-husks, and puts earth over these and then waters the plants, the roots
become very large? Is it because the barley-husks, being hot and spongy, hold the
nourishment in a mass so that it does not rise upwards, but, being hot, causes
concoction, and so considerable growth takes place?   15

9 · Why is it that if one buries gourds or pumpkins in the ground when they
are still small, they become large? Is it because the wind and the sun dry everything
up and prevent growth, and make everything smaller in bulk but closer in texture?
(As can be seen in the difference between trees growing in windy and sunny[1]   20

¹Reading εἰλώδεσι.

localities and those in hollow and moist places, the latter being large and spongy in texture, the former small and dense.) Now the burying of things in the earth is the contrary of this and produces a contrary result. (A similar difference occurs in fruits placed in vessels; if cucumbers are placed in hollow fennel-stalks or boxes, and pomegranates or apples in earthenware jars, the apples become large and spongy, but the cucumbers become small and hard because they grow against a resisting surface.)² The reason then is that the nutriment is increased, because it is not dispersed by the wind or dried up; for the covering of earth prevents it from being thus affected.

10 · Why are the seeds of pungent plants more pungent than the roots and the leaves? Is it because everything is derived from the seed and distributed to the other parts from it, as it were pre-existing in it, as some contend, including the juices and odours, since the odours always become distinctive as soon as the seeds are formed? If, therefore, the pungency in the rest of the plant is derived from the seed, it is only natural that it should be present in the greatest degree in the seed.³

11 · Why are thin radishes more pungent? Is it because the larger radishes are more concocted owing to the lapse of time?

12 · Why is it that the caper-plant will not grow easily in tilled ground—for the experiment has often been made of transplanting the roots or sowing the seed (for in some places it is more profitable than roses)—but grows best among the tombs because the ground is most untrodden? As regards this and similar questions the principle must be accepted that all things do not come into being and grow from the same matter, but some things originally come into being and grow from the corruption of other things—for instance lice and the hair on the body when its nutriment is corrupted and when the body is in a state of continual deterioration. As therefore in the body certain products are engendered from the excrement of nutriment (which means that concoction is incomplete), and since, when nature cannot prevail over the excrement, the commonest excretions are absorbed into the bladder and bowels, while from others living organisms are engendered (and so these attain the greatest growth in old age and disease), so in the earth some products are engendered and grow from the concoction of nutriment, others from excretions and matter that is in a condition which is the opposite of concoction. Now tillage concocts the nutriment and makes it productive, and from this the cultivated fruits are formed. The products, therefore, of this cultivation are called cultivated because they are benefited by art, undergoing as it were a kind of training. Plants, on the other hand, which cannot be so benefited or are formed from an opposite condition, are 'wild' and will not grow in a highly tilled soil. For tillage spoils them by trying to train them; for they are engendered from corruption. It is to this class that the caper-plant belongs.

²Omitting μή.
³Reading αὐτῷ.

3 · Why is it that, when radishes are in their prime in the winter, if one cuts   25
off the leaves and heaps earth round them and treads it in so as to keep out the
water, they grow to an extraordinary size in the summer? Is it because the heaping
up of the earth round them secures them from becoming corrupted by preventing
the water from rotting them, and the nutriment, which the plant used to send into
the shoot, enters into the radish, so that it must either itself increase in size or send   30
out lateral shoots and grow other roots, as do onions? For onions, if they are not
pulled up each year but are left in the ground during the winter, become multiplied.
Now onions are among the plants which send out shoots laterally; but the radish
does not do so, and must therefore increase in bulk, because it absorbs all the   35
nutriment.

14 · Why is it that if one plants pumpkins or cucumbers near a well and,
when they are ripe, lets them down into the well and covers them over, they remain
green for a whole year? Is it because the vapour from the water cools them and
prevents them from drying up and keeps them in good condition, and the covering of   924^{b}1
them up fosters the breath which has formed in them? Their conservation is due to
the fact that they still receive nutriment, because their roots are left undisturbed;
for even if one removes the shoots, when they have borne fruit, and after cutting
them away heaps earth round the roots and treads it down, the plant will produce
early cucumbers, because the roots can survive; for the cucumber is not a biennial.   5
The plants themselves will bear fruit more quickly than seedlings, because the root,
the most important part of their organism, is already present in their growth,
whereas in seedlings the roots must grow first. Furthermore,[4] the heaping of earth
round the root engenders warmth, so that it is preserved and sends up a shoot more   10
quickly. So too if one sows cucumber seeds during the winter in small wicker baskets
and waters them with hot water and carries them out into the sun and places them
by the fire, very early cucumbers will be produced if one plants them out in the
ground, as they are, in the baskets, when the proper season arrives.

15 · Why are plants watered at dawn or at night or in the evening? Is it in   15
order that the sun may not consume the water? Or is it because, when the water is
warm it corrupts the plants which are watered with it?

16 · Why is it that sweet-smelling seeds and plants promote the flow of
urine? Is it because they contain heat and are easily concocted, and such things
have this effect? For the heat which is in them causes quick digestion, and their
odour has no corporeal existence; for evil-smelling plants, such as garlic, owing to   20
their heat, promote the flow of urine, but their wasting effect is a more marked
characteristic. But sweet-smelling seeds contain heat, because odour is entirely
engendered by the presence of some heat; but evil-smelling things are unconcocted.
Now anything which is to promote the flow of urine must be not only hot but also   25

---

[4]Reading ἔτι δὲ ἡ περίσαξις.

easily concocted, so that it may accompany the liquids in their downward course and effect their digestion.

17 · Why is it that vegetables which are produced from older seed (for example two or three years old) produce more stalk than those grown from fresh seeds? Is it because, just as in animals that which is at its prime produces semen most readily, so too very old seeds lose their vigour by evaporation, and those which are produced from fresh seeds are too weak because they still contain excrement which is alien to them, but those which are of moderate age are strongest, because the moisture has left them, and so they produce seed more readily? And the production of seed is the same process as the production of stalk, since the seed comes from the stalk.

18 · Why does rue grow best and most abundantly if it is grafted on to a fig-tree? Now it is grafted inside the bark and plastered with clay. Is it because the roots of the rue require heat and warmth (and this is why they are benefited by being surrounded with ashes), and the fig-tree contains heat? That this is so is shown by the fact that its sap is the most pungent of all and by the amount of smoke which it produces when burnt. It therefore possesses the same kind of heat and moisture as ashes, so that if ashes benefit rue, it must necessarily flourish greatly when grafted on the fig-tree, since, whereas ashes give off no fluid, the flow of liquid from the fig-tree is continuous, its moisture being never exhausted.

19 · Why do some plants always produce empty stalks? Are they among those plants which have to produce something other than stalk?

20 · Why is it that in Attica, while all other fruits are very sweet, thyme is very bitter, yet thyme is a kind of fruit? . . .[5] so that the plants which grow there do not contain much moisture? In plants, then, which are naturally sweet, owing to the moderate quantity of moisture which they contain, when the sun has absorbed the greater part of it the remainder is easily concocted; for it is difficult for a large amount, but easy for a moderate amount, to be ripened. Fruits, therefore, which are naturally sweet become more so; but in those which are naturally dry and not sweet, the natural moisture fails, because it is scanty, and is very far from being sweet. For the sun absorbs the sweetest and lightest part of it; and these fruits have no superfluous moisture, as have other fruits.

21 · Why do pennyroyal and narcissi and onions bloom if hung up at the time of the summer solstice? Is it because there is unconcocted nutriment in them, which[6] in winter does not become concocted owing to the cold, but at the summer solstice owing to the season becomes concocted, and so the growth takes place? This growth, however, because there is no influx of moisture, quickly dies down; for if

---

[5]There is a lacuna at this point in the MSS.
[6]Reading ἥ for ἤ.

they have not some source of nutriment or influx of moisture, they dry up. A similar phenomenon occurs in Scythia, where, owing to the presence of abundant snow, the corn remains a long time in the earth and then suddenly shoots up. 25

22 · Why does the onion alone make the eyes smart to such an excessive degree (hence it is said to derive its name because it makes one cover up the pupil), whereas marjoram and other pungent plants do not have this effect? For the nasturtium, though it is more stinging, does not cause tears to the same extent if 30 placed near the eyes, whereas the onion has this effect both when so placed and when eaten. Is it because many differences attach to each of the pungent plants, which give each its peculiar property? The nasturtium then, because it is hotter, is so dry that it prevails over the liquefaction which it causes; for it causes tears when 35 it is eaten, but it does not cause tears when placed near the eyes, because it does not give off any thin vapour, being too dry and hot to do so. But marjoram and such warm plants are dry, though only slightly so; and that which is to cause tears must 925^b1 be stinging and moist and viscous. This is why olive oil causes tears, though its sting is weak; for it penetrates owing to its viscosity and tenuity and causes pain, and the pain causes melting. Now the onion has such properties that its moisture and the 5 vapour which it gives off are hot and tenuous and viscous; and so, when it is placed near the eye, it causes tears, because the vapour which it gives off is of such a character and carries with it a thin moisture; and, when it is eaten, the exhalation penetrates . . .[7] Garlic, on the other hand, is hot and pungent and contains moisture, 10 but is not viscous; and so does not cause tears.

23 · Why is it that myrtle-berries which have been compressed in the hand seem to us sweeter than those which have not been so compressed? Is it for the same reason as makes dried grapes sweeter than fresh clusters and undried grapes? For 15 dried grapes are, it appears, flavoured by the must, which is naturally sweet (for they are even externally saturated by it), but the grapes which are still in the cluster are not so flavoured. So too myrtle-berries, which are naturally sweet and have their sweetness within, like grapes when they are compressed, become saturated by the 20 sweetness which is within them and are clearly sweeter externally.

24 · Why is it that, the smaller myrtle-berries are, the more they tend to have no stones, and the same is also true of dates and clusters of grapes, in which[8] the small grapes have no stones at all or only smaller stones? Is it because, being less 25 perfect, they have less distinctly formed stones? For the purpose of the stone is to contain the seed. Now the berries are smaller, because they are mere offshoots and imperfect, and they are less sweet than those which have proper stones; for they are less concocted, and concoction is a process which produces perfection.

25 · Why is it that in some fruits the parts which are near the root are more 30

---

[7]There is a lacuna in the MSS here.
[8]Omitting δέ.

bitter (for example in the cucumber), but in others the parts towards the upper extremity (for example in acorns)? Is it because in the former the nutriment in that part is unconcocted, because there is a continual influx along the root; while the latter are naturally dry, and so, when the sweetness is drawn off from the extremity and has become concocted, they are henceforward dry and the bitterness is left
35 behind like salt? Now as anything becomes dry, it becomes more bitter, just as olives and acorns become bitter as they grow old.

926ᵃ1   26 · Why do some plants sprout when they are not in the earth, but either cut off or placed in store, lily-stalks, for example, and garlic and onions? Is it because they all have nutriment within themselves and not in some separate place?⁹
5 [It is therefore their superabundance of nutriment which makes them sprout, as is clear from the fact that squills and purse-tassels do the same.]¹⁰ Now each of them grows not merely because it contains nutriment, but only when that nutriment is concocted and distributed; it therefore contains nutriment before, but it only grows when the season comes at which this process takes place owing to the concoction caused by the season, as happens also to crocodiles' eggs. The growth, however, is
10 not continuous, because there is no influx of more nutriment.

27 · Why is it that garlic and onions grow better according as they are drier when planted, whilst other plants grow worse under such conditions? Is it because all plants of this kind are exceedingly full of moisture? If, then, they are planted in
15 this condition, they enjoy equable conditions. A further reason is that they are less likely to rot if they are dried before being planted.

28 · Why is it that garlic and onions alone among plants sprout when they are stored away? Is it because they are full of moisture and nutriment? It is abundance of nutriment, then, which makes them sprout, as is clear from the fact
20 that squills and purse-tassels do the same. But they grow only when the proper season for each of them comes.

29 · Why is it that plants which are watered with cold water are sweeter than those watered with warm water? Is it because the warm water when it becomes enclosed in the plant is saltier (just as that which is saltier is hotter, and that which is sweet is the opposite, that is, in a sense, cold)? Now the nutriment of vegetables is
25 liquid, and it is this which gives them their juices.

30 · Why is it that garlic has a stronger odour when it has run to stalk than when it is young? Is it because, when it is young, there is still a large quantity of alien moisture in it which deprives it of its strength? When, however, the plant has ripened, the alien moisture having been already excreted, it then has its own proper

⁹Omitting οὐθὲν φυτόν.
¹⁰This sentence is excised by Ruelle.

odour; and this is naturally pungent. Similarly, all other fruits when they are young   30
are more watery. This is the reason why young onions are less pungent.

31 · Why is it that, if myrtle-branches are not preserved, the berries rather
than the leaves drop off, whereas, if they are preserved with seaweed, the leaves
drop off but the berries do not? Is it what naturally happens if the branches are not   35
preserved, for the berries naturally drop off when they become ripe? This does not
occur when the branches are stored away, but the moisture in the seaweed only
prevents the moisture in the berries from undergoing change. The leaves, on the
other hand, drop off as the branches become dry, and the seaweed, which is salty,   926ᵇ1
has a drying effect upon them. The leaves thus undergo different processes when
they remain on the tree and when they are stored away.

32 · Why do melons grow best in marshy plains which are humid, for   5
example, round Orchomenus and in Egypt, which appears to be a well-watered
country? Now marshy districts are full of water and melons themselves are
somewhat moist; and this is why those grown in gardens are poor. Is it because they
have to be planted deep owing to the hardness of the ground? For clayey, flat
ground becomes very hard, and plants grow best which are deeply planted. Or is it   10
because the ground must be dry, because the plant itself is naturally moist? For
thus being pulled in opposite directions it will attain the mean. Now ground which
is somewhat marshy but deep contains nutriment owing to the depth of the soil and
the locality, but not in an excessive quantity, because the ground dries up again.   15

33 · Why is it that rue and certain unguents give the perspiration an evil
odour? Is it because things which have a heavy and pungent odour, mixing with the
excretory fluids, make the odour of these still more unpleasant?

34 · Why is rue said to be a remedy against the evil eye? Is it because men   20
think they are victims of the evil eye when they eat greedily or when they expect
some enmity and are suspicious of the food set before them? For instance, when
they take anything for themselves from the same course, they offer some one else a
portion, adding the words, 'so that you may not cast the evil eye upon me'. All
therefore will take with alarm of what is offered them, whether liquid or solid, of   25
those foods, the constriction or vomiting forth of which causes the solids to be
carried upwards and ejected or the flatulence from the liquid to give rise to pain and
writhing. Rue, therefore, being eaten beforehand, since it is naturally warming,
rarefies the organ which receives the food and the whole body, with the result that   30
passes out the flatulence enclosed within it.

35 · Why is it that marjoram, being thrown into the must, makes the wine
sweet, and two cupfuls are thrown into a jar of wine? Is it because it takes away the
elements which cause harshness by absorbing into itself by its dryness the watery   35
and sedimentary parts? That it is these which cause harshness is shown by the fact

that wines are less soft if water is added or if they have been allowed to stand a long time on the lees. Also when they make sweet wine, they expose the grapes for a long time to the sun, which draws out the watery element and concocts the remainder.
927ª1 Now marjoram produces the same result, for it is dry and hot, and so naturally has a lasting effect.

36 · Why do black myrtle-trees have thicker foliage than white? Is it because they are a wilder species? That they are so is proved by the fact that they
5 grow in the fields and undergo very little modification as a result of cultivation. Now wild plants invariably have denser foliage; for, because their fruit is less concocted, the nutriment is diverted into the foliage.

BOOK XXI
PROBLEMS CONCERNING BARLEY-MEAL, BARLEY-CAKE, AND THE LIKE

10   1 · Why is it that barley-gruel and wheaten-flour become whiter if oil is poured on to them, though oil is reddish in colour? Is it because oil naturally foams when it is mixed with liquid, and foaming causes whiteness? Now mixing is carried out by pounding and motion, and is most complete in the case of corporeal
15 substances. This process occurs in foods which are boiled, and so makes them whiter.

2 · Why is it that foods made from wheat suit our bodies best and are more nourishing than those made from barley? Is it because wheat contains a moderate
20 amount of stickiness, and food ought to have this quality, since it ought to cling and adhere to the body, and its stickiness causes it to do so? But barley[1] is less cohesive, and so cakes in which the barley is well kneaded are more nourishing than those in which it is not kneaded.

3 · Why is it that of wheaten-flour that which is ground first is whiter, but of barley-meal that which is ground last? Is it because barley, being dry, breaks into
25 pieces, whereas wheat is soft and crushes? Now in both it is the inner part which is whitest.

4 · Why do loaves appear whiter when they are cold than when they are hot? Is it somehow for the same reason that stale oil is whiter than fresh? For the cause
30 of the blackness is the water which in both cases is present in larger quantities when they are fresh; but after a time, owing to evaporation, the water remaining near the surface becomes less. Now it is either the passage of time or the heat of the sun

[1] Reading ἀλλ' ἡ κριθὴ ψαθυρώτερον.

which causes evaporation from the oil; and from loaves the heat goes forth as they cool and has entirely departed when they are cold, whereas it is still present when they are warm.

5 . Why do loaves which contain no salt weigh heavier than those which are 35 salted, the other ingredients being exactly the same? The contrary would be expected, since salt is added, and salt is heavier than water. Is it because the salt causes drying to take place? This is why things which are preserved with salt remain uncorrupted; for the moisture in them is taken up and dried up by the salt, and it is the moisture in things that is corrupted by heat. So too in bread the moisture is 927ᵇ1 taken up by the salt and evaporates outside. Stale bread therefore is lighter than hot bread, since it is cooler. Now in loaves which do not contain salt this moisture is present in greater quantities and makes them heavier. 5

6 . Why is it that loaves which have become cold, if they are moistened and placed in contact with one another, do not cohere, whereas hot loaves do so? Is it because the cold loaves give off with the vapour the sticky moisture which is in them, and, because this has gone forth, do not cohere (for the water with which they were wetted is too uncohesive); but the hot loaves contain a certain amount of 10 stickiness, and so, when they are moistened and the vapour comes forth, the heat, owing to its rarity, is given off, but the sticky matter, which comes out with it and mingles with the moisture, causes the loaves to adhere together?[2]

7 . Why is it that of wheaten-flour that which is ground first[3] is whiter, but 15 of barley-meal that which is ground last? Is it because barley, being dry, breaks into pieces, and this happens most when it is ground for a very long time, but the flour which is inside the wheat is soft and fine and is crushed out at first? Now in both cases it is the inner part which is whitest. 20

8 . Why is it that barley-cake becomes more indigestible the more it is kneaded, whereas wheaten-bread becomes easier to digest? Is it because dough becomes less by being much kneaded (and this is the nature of that which is sticky), but the moisture has been expelled from every part of the loaf by the fire, so that, when the moisture has been entirely expelled, the loaf becomes more uncohesive the 25 more it is kneaded, because in the kneading it is divided up into smaller particles? Now that which is uncohesive is more easily concocted. Barley-cake, on the other hand, the more it is kneaded becomes more sticky, as the liquid mingles in it; and that which is sticky is not easily divided up, and such foods are not easily concocted; 30 for that which is to be concocted must be split up into small parts.

9 . Why does barley-cake become less when it is kneaded, whereas dough becomes more? Is it because barley-meal when moistened and kneaded unites

²Reading προσέχεσθαι ποιεῖ ἑαυτοῖς.
³Reading πρῶτα for ἄλφιτα.

35   owing to the binding quality of the moisture, because it is of even texture and
granulated, but wheaten-flour rises, because it is very dense? For that which is
dense grows hot when kneaded and, when it is hot and inflated, it rises, as does the
flesh.

928ª1   10 · But why does dough increase more when it is heated than barley-cake
does? Is it because dough contains moisture which is not separated in such a way
that it can escape when warmed, owing to the kneading? When therefore it is
warmed, breath is engendered, and more breath is necessarily engendered from a
greater amount of moisture.

5   11 · Why is it that although honey is more adhesive than water, wheaten-
flour is more uncohesive, when it is boiled or baked, if it is mixed with honey-water
than with water? Is it because water becomes stiff and solid under the influence of
the heat, whereas the honey becomes solid but also has a drying effect, and so makes
10   the food more uncohesive (for this quality is produced by dryness)?

12 · Why do twice-baked loaves, when they are cool, not become hard? Is it
because wheat has in it a certain sweet and sticky juice, which is as it were its 'soul'?
This can be illustrated by the fact that when it is dried it becomes quite empty, but,
15   when it is wetted, it expands. This juice, therefore, being present also in wheaten-
flour, especially in that of the purest quality, when the flour is made into dough and
the dough is kneaded the same thing[4] happens, as is proved by the fact that when it
is boiled it becomes more digestible. When, therefore, the bread is baked for the
first time, the thin and light part of the moisture[5] is evaporated from the bread, and
20   the part of the flour which most resembles chaff is burnt out. But when the dough is
taken out and kneaded again, the smoothest part of the flour and the stickiest part
of the moisture being left mingle more with one another, owing to the fact that they
have become smoother and stickier, and owing to the effect of the heat; for their
25   mixing resembles the process of dyeing, so that the dough, when subsequently
kneaded, is like boiled flour. For when the dough is kneaded and the lightest flour
and the stickiest moisture are left, the bread, when it has been exposed to the fire,
becomes glutinous and does not dry up; for that which is sticky cannot be separated,
30   and that which is dense does not of itself give up any moisture. Twice-baked bread
then undergoes this same process[6] for the reasons mentioned above, and, always
containing moisture, does not become hard.

13 · Why is it that we can go on partaking of some kinds both of solid and of
35   liquid food for a long period—for instance, food made from barley-meal and
wheaten-flour and dry wines, and water—whereas we cannot partake continually of
others, though they are pleasanter to the taste? Is it because some of the foods

---

[4]Reading ταὐτό.
[5]Omitting δέ.
[6]Reading προίεται ὑγρόν. ταὐτὸ οὖν τοῦτο καὶ δίπυρος.

which we take tend to float on the stomach and are highly nutritious, so that when one has discharged them, though their first nutriment has been consumed, a considerable force still remains in the body, concocted for the first bodily process but unconcocted for its final purpose and for the succeeding process? Now most of the pleasing foods belong to this class; for the fatty and sweet and rich foods seem pleasantest to our taste, and these, however they differ from one another, are all foods which are nutritious, and not difficult of concoction, and apt to float on the stomach; their force is therefore lasting, if one takes one's fill of them, and the perception of them does not quickly pass away;[7] for the feeling of satiety does not only continue while they are in the stomach but also when their nutriment has been distributed to other parts of the body. Or is this not the only reason, and is there a further reason, namely, that some foods are naturally suited and akin to us? For our bodies accept all such foods more readily because they are natural, while they accept less readily those which are unnatural. And different foods suit different temperaments; for example, honey is the natural food of bees, so that they take no other, though they are physically weak; so that what they consume must be small in amount, but must be to their strength as what men eat is to theirs. And so any pleasing foods which are of this kind seem pleasing because they are present in small quantities in our nature, but they only appear so for a short time, and then soon cause a feeling of satiety. But we always need the natural foods, so that we feel less satiety from foods continually taken other than those which are most pleasing in themselves.

14 · Why is it that the same things seem pleasant when we are becoming accustomed to them and not pleasant if we partake of them too continuously, though being accustomed to anything is doing it often and continuously? Is it because custom engenders a receptive habit but does not bring satiety, whereas taking anything continuously fills up the desire, just as a vessel[8] is filled; for desire is a kind of void?[9] Now habits, when exercised, increase and grow, but vessels when they are filled full do not become any bigger. Hence custom, being an exercise, increases the receptive habit; but that which is continuously taken fills up and satisfies the desire, and, when this is satisfied, we no longer receive any more, and nothing can increase the desire for the reasons already stated regarding the filling of vessels. Furthermore, custom is not pleasant through constantly giving pleasure (for such things too cause pain through continual practice), but because we enter upon the beginning of the process with pleasure and can continue doing the same thing longer than if we were unaccustomed to it. In the same way then as custom, which is pleasant, causes pain, so too do all other pleasant things; for things which happen and foods which are taken continuously, both alike cause pain. The reason is that the powers of acceptance and action which we possess in ourselves are not unlimited but limited, and when they have reached their full capacity (and this is continually

928ᵇ1 appears in margin at line 3
5 margin
10 margin
15 margin
20 margin
25 margin
30 margin
35 margin
929ᵃ1 margin

---

[7] Reading ἐκλιπεῖν.
[8] Reading ἀγγεῖον for αἴτιον.
[9] Reading κενόν for καί.

visible to an increasing extent) the receptive powers are satisfied, and the powers for
5   action can no longer function.

15 · Why does dough become white when it is kneaded, while barley-cake
becomes blacker? Is it because the surface of the barley-meal becomes drier, and it
is the[10] heat in the moisture which causes the whiteness? Or is it because, through
exposure to the heat, the surface of barley-meal attracts the moisture, since it
10 consists of larger particles?

16 · Why does barley-meal adhere better together when mixed with water
than with oil, though oil is more viscous? Yet that which is viscous is more binding,
and oil is more viscous than water. Is it because water is thinner and so penetrates
15 into everything and makes the barley-meal soft, and the grains adhere together
better and are compressed into one another, even though pressed together without
any kneading?

17 · Why does bread which is either not kneaded or very much kneaded
break up? Does the unkneaded bread do so because it is not sufficiently bound
together? Now it is the kneading that binds the bread; so that unkneaded bread is
20 already on the way to breaking up. Further, it contains much moisture not properly
mixed in. Bread which is very much kneaded is dry, because it has very little
moisture; for when it is heated, the moisture all escapes. So that in both cases the
bread breaks up because much moisture goes forth; for much moisture is actually
present in the unkneaded bread, and in the over-kneaded bread much escapes[11]
compared to what remains behind.

25 18 · Why is the admixture of barley-meal and liquid lighter than the two
things together when unmixed? Is it because, when they are mixed, air is enclosed in
them? Or is it because part of the water is evaporated by the heat in the
barley-meal, and so the mixture becomes smaller in bulk? The air, however, if it
were also mixed in, would not make the mixture any lighter; for air enclosed in air
30 possesses weight.

19 · Why do milk and sweet wine appear sweeter if drunk with barley-meal?
Do they appear sweeter in contrast with anything which is not sweet (for
barley-meal is not sweet)? Or is it because the barley-meal continues to hold
35 sweetness, and so the perception of it is prolonged?

20 · Why does the same potion seem less strong if it is drunk with
barley-meal? Is it because the barley unites what has one quality with what has
another, or because the barley-meal interferes with the potion and destroys it,
absorbing it into itself?

[10]Reading τὸ δὲ ἐν ὑγρῷ θερμὸν ποιεῖ.
[11]Adding ἔξεισι after ὑπόλοιπον.

21 · Why does gruel take up more water than the wheat from which such ⁹²⁹ᵇ1 gruel is made? Is it because the gruel is a kind of flour, and flour takes up more water (for its bulk is greater than that of the wheat, for even the particles of the wheat are packed closely together)? Now that which is more holds more both for this reason[12] and also because both flour and gruel contain heat, and heat both 5 attracts the moisture more and expends it by evaporation.

22 · Why does wheaten-flour increase much more in proportion than barley-meal when it is kneaded? Is it because flour admits a large quantity of water, but barley-meal only a little? (But why does it admit more, for barley-meal would 10 naturally be expected to do so, because it has been exposed to heat, whereas the flour has not, and that which has been exposed to heat is drier?) Or is it because flour admits of more kneading, the reason being that it is composed of smaller particles? As therefore it is potentially as it were more manifold by reason of the smallness of its parts, so much the more water does it take up. For it uses the water 15 as a glue—a metaphor employed by Empedocles in the *Physics,* when he says 'gluing barley with water'—and it consumes much water for this reason.

23 · Why does dough increase more when it has been heated than barley-cake does? Is it because it contains moisture which is not separated in such a way that it can escape when it is warmed, and this[13] moisture, becoming breath and not 20 being able to escape (as it can in the barley-cake) owing to the density of the dough (for that which is made up of smaller particles is dense), makes the dough, therefore, rise and causes the mass to be greater? Furthermore, the moisture which it contains is more considerable, and it is from this, when it is heated, that the breath is engendered; and from the greater amount of moisture more breath must necessarily be engendered. 25

24 · Why is it that, of persons engaged in the preparation of cereals, those who handle barley become pale and are subject to catarrh, while those who handle wheat are healthy? Is it because wheat is more easily concocted than barley, and therefore its emanations are also more easily concocted?

25 · Why is it that bread, if one toasts it, becomes harder, whereas, if one 30 warms it, it becomes moister up to a certain point? Is it because, when it is toasted, the moisture goes out of it, and so it becomes harder, whereas, when it is warmed, the moisture having acquired consistency is liquefied again by the fire, and so the bread becomes moister?

26 · Why does flour, as it cools, become less closely packed, but barley-meal 35 more so? Is it because things which are made up of small particles contain no vacant spaces, and heavy things, by the pressure which they exert, take up the same space

---

[12]Reading πλέον καὶ διὰ τοῦτο καί.
[13]Reading ὅ for οὐ.

whether they are more or less[14] numerically? Barley-meal then is soft; when it cools, therefore, it becomes less, so that the less is more compressed.[15] But wheaten-flour already consists of small particles, and so it does not cool because of this, but in such a way as to become lighter and not so as to become more closely packed by compression; for wheaten-flour is naturally heavier than barley-meal.

930ᵃ1

BOOK XXII

PROBLEMS CONNECTED WITH FRUIT

5   1 · Why is it that the volume of food necessary for repletion is not proportionate in the same persons if they eat fruit at the beginning and at the end of a meal? Is it because fruit is much heavier than solid food? This can be illustrated by the fact that figs, though eaten last, are vomited out last. If, therefore, they are eaten first, owing to their weight they sink downwards and leave ample space above, so that one can easily contain the volume of solid food. If, however, the converse takes place, the solid food when it enters in, because it does not sink downwards, quickly occupies the vacant upper space.

10

2 · Why is it that, although sweet foods are more akin to us than pungent, we are more quickly sated by the former? For the contrary might have been expected, since we might naturally be supposed to be less sated by foods which are akin to us. Is it because the organ whereby we receive replenishment and the body, which is nourished, are not sated equally quickly, but sometimes the stomach is full, in those, for instance, who are thirsty, but the thirst is not less? For we do not cease being thirsty because the stomach is full, but when each part of the body has drawn in its own particular moisture; and we cease being thirsty only when they have received this in sufficiency. The same thing also occurs when we are hungry.

15

20

3 · Why are we more quickly sated by sweet than by pungent foods? Is it because we cease desiring sweet things sooner? Or, while it is not generally admitted[1] that we become satiated as the stomach is filled by sweet foods, yet might it not be said that our desire is more quickly sated by them? Or is it because desire is simply a lack, which occurs when we no longer have any nutriment in us or very little? Pungent foods then are not nourishing, but contain little nutriment and a considerable amount of excrement. We therefore naturally seek to eat them in large quantities, and yet do not satiate our desire with them, because we still lack nutriment and they do not contain it. But all sweet foods are nutriment, and the body derives a large amount of nutriment from a small quantity of them. When,

25

30

35

[14]Reading πλείω ἢ ἐλάττω.
[15]Reading συμπιέζεται for συμπιέζει τό.
[1]Placing a comma before οὐχ ὁμολογεῖται.

therefore, it derives a large amount of nutriment, it can no longer eat, because it cannot tolerate more. We are therefore naturally more quickly satisfied by sweet foods.

4 · Why is it that fruits and meat and the like remain uncorrupted if placed in skins, when these are tightly inflated, as also do substances placed in closely covered vessels? Is it because all things become corrupt through being in motion, and things which are full are without motion (for it is impossible for anything to be moved without there being a void), and these vessels are full? 930^{b}1

5 · Why does wine seem bitter when drunk after the eating of rotten fruits? Is it because such rottenness contains bitterness? That, then, which remains on the tongue, mingling with the draught and becoming diffused in it, makes the draught bitter. The fruit by itself, when eaten, seems less bitter, because juice of this kind takes effect at many different points and is divided up into small particles. 5

10

6 · Why should dried fruits be eaten? Is it in order that we may drink sufficiently? For we ought not only to drink to satisfy the thirst which is engendered by solid food, but also when the solid food is finished.

7 · Why do roasted nuts deteriorate when they become cool, and also bread and acorns and many such things, but improve when they are heated again? Is it because, when they become cold, the juice congeals, but when they are warmed up it becomes liquid again, and it is the juice which is pleasing? 15

8 · Why is it that, for the proper enjoyment of fruits such as figs and the like, one ought to drink with them either unmixed wine or water, which are the opposites of one another? Is it because fruit is both hot and moist owing to the manner of its growth? For it contains much both of fire and of moisture; and so, owing to the fire, the juice causes as it were a boiling within, such as must makes on the surface (though the others, the hard-shelled fruit, also have this force, but in a less degree), while the large quantity of moisture causes an unconcocted condition. Water then, owing to its coldness, extinguishes the boiling, as wine also usually does by its heat; for it takes away its power, just as one fire sometimes diminishes the force of another if the latter be less. And wine by its heat is better able to concoct the moisture, and by its weight it prevails over the scum formed on the surface by the boiling. 20

25

30

9 · Why is it that those dried figs are sweetest which are cut in half and not those which are cut either many times or not at all? Is it because, if they are cut many times, most of the sweetness escapes and evaporates with the moisture, whereas in those which are entirely closed the watery element is considerable, because it has not been turned into vapour? Those, however, which have been cut but not many times, do not suffer from either of these disadvantages. 35

10 · Why is it that figs when they are cooled in an oven are harder if they are 931ᵃ1 left to cool in the oven than if they are taken out to cool? Is it because in the oven all the moisture is evaporated by the heat, whereas outside the surrounding air cools the moisture and prevents it from escaping and the moisture retains its consistency 5 rather than evaporates?[2] Now what is dry is hard, and what is moist is soft.

11 · Why is it that wine and water seem sweeter when taken with something sour, if, for instance, one munches acorns or myrtle-berries or something of the kind? Is not this natural and does it not happen in other things too? For everything seems to assert its identity more forcibly when compared with its contrary and here 10 the tastes of the contraries are in a way opposed. Or is it because, as in objects which are being dyed, the tongue has already been permeated by the sour matter and opens its pores, and so the sweetness can penetrate better? For objects which are being dyed are for this reason first of all moistened in sour liquid—because what is 15 permeated takes the dye better.

12 · Why do sweet things seem to be less sweet when they are hot than when they are cold? Is it because two sensations of the two qualities are present together, and so that of heat dispels the other? Or is it because that which is sweet[3] is also hot, and it is therefore a case of 'fire upon fire', and thus the heat prevents the perception 20 of the sweetness? Or is it because fire takes away the power of everything, since it causes motion? Things, then, which are hot are nearer to change, but when they cool they become stable again.

13 · Why is it that chaff concocts hard fruits and does not corrupt those which are already concocted? Is it because chaff is both hot and absorbent? It, 25 therefore, by its heat causes concoction, while owing to its absorbent property it attracts the corrupted sap, which therefore does not cause corruption.

14 · Why do figs, which are soft and sweet, destroy the teeth? Do they, owing to their stickiness, penetrate into the gums, and, because they are soft, 30 insinuate themselves into the spaces between the teeth, and, being hot, quickly cause decay? Perhaps also, owing to the hardness of the seeds, the teeth are quickly caused to ache in the process of chewing them up.

---

[2]Reading συνίσταται μᾶλλον ἢ ἐξατμίζει.
[3]Reading γλυκύ.

BOOK XXIII
PROBLEMS CONNECTED WITH SALT WATER
AND THE SEA

1 · Why is it that the waves do not ripple in the deep open sea, but only where 35 it is confined and shallow? Is it because a small amount of liquid, as it is carried along, is more divided up by the wind than a large amount?

2 · Why do the waves sometimes begin to move before the winds reach them? Is it because the portion of the sea near the source of the wind being impelled along first has continually the same effect upon the adjoining part, and so, since the 931ᵇ1 sea is continuous, the same effect is caused in every part of it, as though from one continuous impetus? Now this occurs simultaneously, with the result that the first and the last parts of the sea are set in motion at the same time. This effect is not produced in the air, because it is not a single body (since many hindrances affect it 5 from all sides, which often cut short the first and most vigorous movement); the sea, however, suffers from no such impediments, because it is heavier and less easily disturbed than the air.

3 · Why do ships seem to be more heavily loaded in harbour than out at sea, and why do they travel more quickly from the open sea towards the land than from 10 the land towards the open sea? Is it because the greater quantity of water offers more resistance than[1] the less, and the vessel sinks deeper into the latter, because it prevails more over it, for it pushes up the water from below? Now in a harbour the sea is shallow, but deep out at sea; so that a vessel will seem to carry a heavier load 15 in harbour and will move with greater difficulty, because it is sunk deeper into the water, which offers less resistance. But in the open sea the contrary happens.

4 · Why is it that if anything (for example an anchor) is thrown into the sea when it is rough, a calm ensues? Is it because the sea is stopped by the descending 20 object, with which a certain amount of air is carried down, and this air, carried in a direct course downwards and drawn thither, draws with it also the lateral force which is disturbing the sea? Now a wave does not move downwards from above but along the surface, and, when it ceases, a calm ensues. Furthermore, the sea, as it 25 closes in upon the space opened by the descending object, makes an eddy, and eddies move in a circle. Now since a straight line touches a circle at a point (and waves travel obliquely in a straight line), the result would be that the waves touch the circumference of the eddy only at a point, both for the reasons stated and because the eddy pushes the wave off as soon as it comes into contact with it. The place, 30 then, where the eddy is, being without waves, the result is that there is a calm where the surface is broken, because the air, which descended with the object thrown in, subsequently ascending and thrusting the sea upwards, causes it as it were to

---

[1]Omitting ἐκ.

35   bubble; for a bubble consists of moisture thrust up by air from below. Now every
bubble is smooth and still. An indication that the above process takes place is given
by the fact that the sea at the point where the object is thrown in rises a moment
later to a higher level than the surrounding sea.

5 · Why is it that sometimes vessels which are journeying over the sea in fine
932ᵃ1   weather are swallowed up and disappear so completely that no wreckage even is
washed up? Is it because, when a cavernous space breaks open in the earth beneath
the sea, the ship at the same time follows the rush of air into the sea and into the
cavern? And in like manner the sea, being carried everywhere round in a circle, is
5   borne downwards; and this constitutes a whirlpool. And ships in the Straits of
Messina suffer the same fate owing to the flow of water, which causes eddies, and
are swallowed up into the abyss, for the reasons stated above and also because the
sea is deep and the land cavernous to a great distance. The eddies, therefore,
overpower the ships and carry them thither, and so no wreckage is washed up. The
10   flow occurs when, the former wind having stopped, a contrary wind blows over the
sea when it is running under the impulse of the former wind, and especially when
the contrary wind is the south wind. For the currents flowing against one another
try to thrust one another aside, as happens in rivers, and eddies are formed. And the
15   original movement, which is strong, is borne whirling round and round from above.
Since then the currents cannot travel laterally (for they are mutually repelled), they
must be thrust down into the depths, and so whatever is caught by the eddy must
necessarily be carried down too. Hence they build ships with slanting ends; for cases
20   have been recorded before now in which a ship with straight ends has been
swallowed up.

6 · Why is the water whiter in the Black Sea than in the Aegean? Is it owing
to the refraction of the vision from the sea into the air? For in the region of the
25   Black Sea the air is thick and white, so that the surface of the sea appears to be
similar, whereas in the Aegean it is blue, because it is clear to a great distance, and
so the sea too reflecting the air appears to be similar. Or is it because all lakes are
whiter than the sea, and the Black Sea has the character of a lake because many
30   rivers flow into it? Now lakes are whiter than the sea, and than rivers; at any rate,
painters picture rivers as pale yellow and the sea as blue. Or is it because the sight
cannot penetrate quickly through fresh water and is refracted into the air,[2] but is
not refracted upwards from the sea, because the water is not smooth, but the sight
35   tires of trying to penetrate into the depths, and so the sea appears black? But in seas
of a lake-like character, since the fresh water is on the surface and the salt water
below, the sight does not penetrate, but is refracted towards the daylight; and so the
surface of the sea appears white.

7 · Why is the sea less cold than fresh water, and salt water in general than
932ᵇ1   sweet? Is it because the sea is denser and has more body? Now such things are less

---

[2]Omitting οὐκ before ἀνακλᾶται and inserting οὐ before διέρχεται.

susceptible to cold, just as they are more easily heated; for owing to their density they are better able to retain heat. Or is it because the sea is of a more fatty composition and so does not extinguish fire? (And similarly in other cases.) And the 5 more fatty anything is the hotter it is. Or is it because it contains much earth and is therefore drier, and the drier a thing is the hotter it is?

8 · Why is the sea more transparent than fresh water, although it is thicker? For fresh water is rarer than salt. Or is the cause not its rarity but the fact that in it there are direct interstices which are very numerous and wide? Fresh water, 10 therefore, has density owing to the small particles of which it is composed, whereas salt water contains great voids. Or is it because the sea is purer? For there is no earth in it, but the sand, which is heavy, is precipitated; but fresh water is earthy, and the earth floating in its midst is easily stirred into mud. 15

9 · Why is the sea more transparent when the wind is in the north than when it is in the south? Is it because the sea has colour when it is calm? For there is something fatty in the juice of salt water, as is shown by the fact that in hot weather an oily substance is excreted from the sea. When, therefore, the sea is calm and 20 warmer, juice of this kind forms on the surface of the sea owing to its lightness. This is less likely to happen when the wind is in the north, owing to the cold. Now water is more transparent than oil; for oil has colour, but water, presenting itself without colour to the vision, gives a clearer image.

10 · Why does one dry more quickly after washing in the sea, although sea 25 water is heavier than fresh? Is it because the sea is thicker and earthy? Since, therefore, it has little moisture in it, it dries more quickly.

11 · Why are the waves windy? Is it because they are a sign of wind in the future? For wind is a massing together of air, which[3] occurs because the air is 30 continually thrust forward. But the wind begins to thrust the air forward when it is not yet blowing continuously but only just beginning. The first breath of wind then as it were dies down before having any effect, but it thrusts forward another breath and drives on another mass of air and then dies away. It is clear therefore, when the wave which is thrust forward is already present, that that which sets it in motion 35 will also come; for it causes this effect when it first begins to blow.

12 · Why do the waves break forth before the wind? Is it because the wind does not cease to blow[4] and the sea to be rough at the same time, but the sea ceases later? For[5] it is possible that the wind which set the wave in motion perishes before 933ᵃ1 it becomes perceptible; and so the wave is not prior to the wind, but the former is noticeable, while the latter is not. Or do the winds not blow everywhere at the same

---

[3]Reading ἤ for ἥ.
[4]Omitting τό before πνέον.
[5]Reading θάλαττα; ἐνδέχεται γάρ.

time, but at first only in the quarter from which they arise? Now as soon as they begin to blow, they set in motion the sea which is near them, and this sets in motion
5   the adjoining sea; and thus it would be possible for the wave to break forth before the wind reaches it. For the movement is due to the sea and not to wind, being a movement of the sea which travels more quickly than that of the air.[6]

13 · Why is it easier to swim in the sea than in a river? Is it because the
10 swimmer always leans on the water as he swims, and we receive more support from that which is of a more corporeal nature, and sea water is more corporeal than river water, for it is thicker and able to offer more resistance to pressure?

14 · Why can one remain longer in the sea than in a river? Is it because river
15 water is rare and therefore penetrates more into the body and chokes one?

15 · Why is the sea combustible, while water is not? Or does water also burn, while the reason why the sea has less power to extinguish fire is because it is of a more fatty composition? (And that it is so indicated by the fact that an oil is given
20 off from sea water.) Or are the interstices less able to adapt themselves to fire because they are too wide, and all the more so owing to the presence also of salt? As, therefore, that which is dry has less power to quench than that which is moist, so that which is drier is proportionately more capable of being burnt, one thing being
25 more so than another, since the drier a thing is the more closely allied is it to heat;[7] and the sea possesses both these qualities to a greater extent.

16 · Why is it that the wind blows cold in early morning from rivers, but not from the sea? Is it because the sea extends over open spaces, but rivers are in narrow
30 places? The breeze, therefore, from the sea is dispersed over a wide area and is consequently weak; whereas the breeze from a river is carried along in a mass and is stronger and therefore naturally seems colder. Or is the reason other than this,
35 namely, that the rivers are cold, but the sea is neither hot nor cold? Now a breeze or an exhalation is due to the heating or cooling of liquids; for whichever of these two processes they undergo, evaporation takes place, and, when water evaporates, the resultant air is set in motion, and this is a breeze. That which is produced from cold liquids naturally blows cold, while that which blows from very hot liquids cools and becomes cold. One would, therefore, find that all the rivers are cold, but that the sea
933ᵇ1 is neither very hot nor very cold. That which blows from it, therefore, is not cold, because it is not itself cold, nor does it cool quickly, because it is not very hot.

5   17 · Why do waves calm down more slowly in the wider open sea than in shallow waters? Is it because everything calms down more slowly after much motion than after little? Now in the wide open sea the ebb and flow is greater than

in shallow waters; there is, therefore, nothing strange if that which is greater is more slow in calming down. 10

18 · Why is it that salt water when it is cold is not fresh, but becomes more fresh when it is heated, and when it is heated and then cooled? Is it because a thing naturally changes from one opposite into the other? Now fresh water is the opposite of salt water; and, when salt water is heated, the salt is boiled out, and, when it 15 cools, is precipitated.

19 · Why is it that waters near the sea are usually sweet and not salty? Is it because water which is strained becomes more fresh, and the nearer water is to the sea the more it is strained? 20

20 · Why does salt water not flow readily? Is it because that which is heavy is stationary, and salt water is heavy? Hence only warm salt waters flow readily, for they have lightness in them which prevails over the heaviness which is in their saltness; for that which is hot is lighter. Furthermore, water which flows readily is 25 strained through the earth; and if water is strained, the thickest and heaviest part of it is always carried to the bottom, while the light and clean element becomes separated. For salt water is heavy and sweet water is light. And so flowing water is sweet. It is for the same reason that salt water, when it is set in motion and 30 undergoes change, becomes sweeter; for it becomes lighter and weaker owing to the motion.

21 · Why is it that in Libya, if one digs a hole near the sea, the water that first comes is fresh, but afterwards quickly becomes salty, but this happens less elsewhere? Is it because the water which comes first is the water which was already 35 there and has been concocted by the earth, but after a time the sea also is strained through and, because it is new, makes the water more salty? Elsewhere, however, there is either no water or abundant water, because the ground is not dried up.

22 · Why does salt water melt salt more quickly than fresh water? Is it 934ª1 because the process of melting anything is its dissolution by moisture or heat penetrating into it so that it becomes liquid? Now those things do not cause melting which either cannot penetrate at all or penetrate in such a way as not to touch the substance. Those things which pass through easily scarcely cause any melting, but 5 those which enter in with violence dissolve substances very quickly. Now those liquids which are composed of very large particles do not penetrate, for they are too large for the pores; while those which are composed of small particles pass through without touching. Now fresh water is rare, while salt water is thicker; and so the former, passing through easily owing to its rarity, scarcely causes any melting, 10 whereas the latter penetrates, but percolates through[8] to a less extent, because it is composed of larger particles, and forces its way in more quickly.

[8]Reading διαρρεῖ.

23 · Why does water appear less white when it is in motion, for instance when there is a ripple? Whence Homer says that, when the wind begins to blow,

15   the sea grows blacker beneath it.[9]

Are there two reasons? Firstly, because, when the sight is near to it, it can penetrate farther through the water when it is still, but when it is in motion the sight cannot pass directly through it. (And that which is transparent appears white, for that through which the sight cannot pass is what Homer calls black; therefore the air appears black from a distance but white near at hand, and the part of the sea which
20 is near is white, while that which is distant is blue or black.) And, secondly, because, when the sight is at a distance and is subject in any way to disturbance, it is refracted back in a mass towards the light, if the water is still, but cannot be refracted when it is in motion.

25   24 · Why is it that the waves do not ripple in the deep, open sea, but only on small expanses? Is it because a small amount of water, as it is carried along, is more divided by the air than a large amount? Hence it beats more and is broken up. Now in deep water the quantity which is set in motion is great, but in shallow water it is small.

30   25 · Why are the waters saltier in regions facing the south wind? Do they become mixed because the sea is driven under the earth by the south wind?

26 · Why does the salty element in water come to the surface more in sweet than in dry wine? Is it because sweet wine, like raisin wine, has more earth in it? Or
35 is it because sweet wine is heavier and stickier and so mixes less, and, as it does not mix,[10] the salty element comes to the surface?

27 · Why does the salty element, being earthy, float on the surface at all (for
934ᵇ1 its natural tendency is to sink)? Is it[11] owing to its heat, as happens with salt (for it resembles an efflorescence)? Or is there some other reason? For if it is for no other reason,[12] it is not unreasonable that it should be for this reason that it floats specially on the surface of sweet wine; for that is the hottest of wines.

28 · Why do the waves sometimes begin to move before the winds reach them? Is it because they also cease to move later? For the first breath of wind as it
5   were dies down before the wave which has been impelled by it into motion; and it is not the wave which is first set in motion that arrives, but there is a successive impetus given to the adjoining water.

---

[9]*Iliad* VII 64.
[10]Reading μιγνυμένου.
[11]Omitting ὅτι μᾶλλον ἔχει γῆν ὁ γλυκύς; ἤ.
[12]Placing a comma after οὐ instead of after μᾶλλον.

29 · Why is it that the ground where the waves break more violently becomes solid, often to such an extent as to appear to have been artificially levelled, and why is the ground where the waves break solid, whereas further from the sea it is loose? Is it because the fine sand is not cast up from a long way off by the waves, but rather the coarser sand, just as it is not possible to throw a very small object far with the hand? Then, many objects being mingled in confusion, the smallest particles fall together and form into a mass, and the motion of the wave, as it recedes, levels them and no longer disturbs them. Since, then, the smallest particles cannot leap far, a mass is formed of very small objects; and since it is in frequent motion, it becomes continuous, the sand falling in amongst it until it unites it together; it is then levelled by the last waves, and the slight moisture causes it to adhere together. But the ground farther from the sea, being dry, becomes disintegrated, and is formed of larger pebbles and is unlevelled.

30 · Why is it that the upper parts of the sea are saltier and hotter than the depths? So, too, in wells of fresh water the upper water is saltier than that at the bottom; yet salty water, being heavier, ought to stand at a lower level. Is it because the sun and the air always attract the lightest part of liquid? Now the fresher is always lighter, and the sun can more easily attract things from the nearest parts. And so that which is left on the surface both of the sea and of fresh water is saltier (since the sweet element has been extracted) than that from which little or nothing has been withdrawn. For this reason the upper part is also hotter; for salt water is hotter than fresh. Therefore some of the followers of Heraclitus declare that stones and earth are formed from the drying and solidifying of fresh water and that the sun draws up vapours from the sea.

31 · Why are the waters of the sea sweeter which are nearer the land? Is it because they are more continuously in motion? Now salt water becomes sweeter through motion. Or is it because the water is saltier in its depths, and the part of the sea near the land is less deep? Hence also water which shelves quickly is salty and less sweet. The reason for this is that the salty element being heavy is carried down more into deep water.

32 · Why is sea water the only kind of water that is combustible, whereas fresh water and river water are not? Is it because it has much earth in it, as is proved by the presence of the salt in it? Or is it because it is of a fatty composition, as is proved by the oil which forms on the surface[13] of salt water?

33 · Why does sand not form in lakes, or at any rate less than in the sea and in rivers? Is it because rocks form in the sea and the earth has been to a great extent burnt out of them? Now sand is rock which has been broken up into small and minute particles, and it is broken up by the impetus of the waves. But in lakes pure

[13]Reading ἐφιστάμενον.

rocks are not formed to the same extent, nor are they broken to the same extent,
15 because there are not waves to the same extent. But sand is formed more in rivers, because they carry down the earth and break up the rocks with their impetus.

34 · Why is it that, when a lake either falls or dries up, the corn in the adjoining plain is more likely to be frosted? Is it because the moisture in the lake
20 evaporates and warms the air with its vapour, and so makes the frosts slighter and weaker than in hollow and marshy districts? Or is it from the earth, as men say, that the cold begins and penetrates unnoticed? If then the lake becomes dry, owing to
25 the larger space of earth greater cold attacks the crops and freezes them and frosts them to a greater extent; and on such ground the cold comes from below, as indeed seems to be the case. And yet the earth is warm in winter; but the surface heat which is in the earth, owing to the fact that it is moist, becomes cooled, for the
30 moisture is neither so far in as not to be affected by cold, owing to the heat which is present in liquids, nor so slight as to have no force, since the earth is permeated with water. For instance, owing to its becoming cold, one walks and lives upon ice.

35 · Why is the sea salty and bitter? Is it because the juices in the sea are
35 numerous? For saltness and bitterness appear at the same time.

36 · Why do shells and stones which are in the sea become round? Is it because the breaking off of their extremities equally on every side causes them to
935ᵇ1 assume a round form? For the outer surface of this shape is the same on all sides, and the sea by moving objects in every direction breaks off their extremities equally.

37 · Why is it that sometimes, if one digs a hole near the sea, the first water which enters is fresh but afterwards it becomes salty? Is it because the water comes
5 from the sea itself which is strained under the earth? The water which first comes is, therefore, naturally sweet; for sweet water is lighter than salt water, and the sea has some sweetness in it, which mingling with the earth tends to come to the surface. But the salt water, owing to its weight and to the fact that it has power to penetrate, is carried downwards. Whether this is so or whether the sweet water flows from the
10 mainland into the sea through the earth's veins, it would naturally float on the surface of the sea which mingles with it; but, the passages being opened, the salt water, owing to its greater volume, subsequently prevails and makes the whole sea salty. For if the passages are blocked the result is that the inflowing salt water finds
15 another way higher up;[14] but when they are opened, it is all carried there, just as happens in the veins in the body.

38 · Why is it that the sea, which is heavier than fresh water, is more transparent? Is it because of its fattier composition? Now oil poured on the surface
20 of water makes it more transparent, and the sea, having fat in it, is naturally more

[14]Reading τῶν πόρων ἄνω.

transparent. Or is that which is lighter not always more transparent also? For oil itself is lighter than water but not more transparent. Or is the sea not really more transparent, but only apparently so? For fresh water comes from the earth or from streams, and its source sends forth earth also with the water, so that the streams, not being pure, bring down with them the earth and sediment. This then is the reason why fresh water is less transparent. 25

39 · Why do the bowels of those who swim in the sea open readily? For if it is because they take violent exercise, those who run also take very violent exercise, yet their bowels do not open. Or does not every form of exertion cause the bowels to open, but only such exercise as does not cause liquefaction? Now staying in the sea seems to make men, generally speaking, hungrier and opens the bowels; for the vapour given off by it is both hot and dry. 30

40 · Why does the Lake of Paesus,[15] of which the water is fresh, wash and also remove the stains from garments? For water which is sweet washes, but that which is bitter removes stains, and water cannot have both these qualities at the same time. Are stains removed not because the water is bitter, but by the quality of stickiness which has this power? Hence animals' hoofs have this effect, and anything which contains mucous matter; and so also any bitter substances which partake of this character do the same. Now in this lake it so happens that the bitter element of the quality of soda has been burnt out, but the fatty and sticky element remains. It is by virtue of this that it removes stains, and it washes because it is fresh. 35

936ᵃ1

41 · Why does the part of the sea which is calm appear white, while that which is agitated appears black? Is it because that which is less visible appears blacker, and water which is in motion is less seen than that which is still? Or is it because that which is transparent is white, while that which is not so is black, and that which is in motion is less transparent? 5

10

BOOK XXIV

PROBLEMS CONCERNING HOT WATER

1 · Why is it that, if one is anointed with oil, hot water poured over one seems less hot, in spite of the fact that oil contains heat? Is it because owing to the smoothness caused by the oil the water glides off and sinks in less? 15

2 · Why is it that in the summer the water in wells becomes warm after midday? Is it because by that hour the heat has mastered the air, whereas before

---

[15]Reading Παῖσα λίμνη.

midday the heat is dissolving and putting an end to the cold; but the one does not
20 prevail as soon as the other has ceased, but only after time has elapsed?

3 · Why is it that water, which sometimes becomes hotter than a flame, does
not burn wood, whereas the flame does so? Is it because the flame, and the breath
which comes from it, consist of small particles, whereas water is made up of large
particles and so does not penetrate? Now flame and the heat from coals owing to
25 their rarity can penetrate and destroy.

4 · Why is it that boiling water has not the power to melt, while the stomach
possesses this power? Is it because the heat which is in the stomach penetrates
owing to its rarity, whereas water cannot penetrate because of its density? Or is it
because liquid prevents other things also from melting (for nothing melts in liquid)?
30. In the stomach, however, the liquid flows down into the bladder and so permits the
process of melting.

5 · Why is it that the bottom of a vessel containing boiling water does not
burn, but one can carry it holding it by the bottom, whereas if the water be removed
it burns? Is it because the heat as it is engendered in the bottom of the vessel is
35 extinguished by the water? That is also why substances which can be melted do not
melt if any liquid is added to them.[1]

6 · Why is it that water does not boil over so much in winter as in summer,
although heated not only up to the same temperature but even higher, and although
936ᵇ1 equally hot or even hotter? Is it because boiling over is due to the rising of bubbles?
The water then itself becomes just as hot in winter as in summer,[2] but the bubbles
cannot rise to the same extent, because the surrounding air is cold, but they rise
5 smaller in size, being compressed by the cold, and soon burst, being broken by the
air. They are, therefore, smaller in bulk and fewer in number in the winter, and the
contrary in summer. Now boiling over is due to the number and size of the bubbles
forming the froth.

10 7 · Why does hot water cause wrinkles, but fire, though it is hot, not do so?
Is it because fire produces breath and so causes swelling (for it distends the skin),
whereas it is the curving of the skin which makes wrinkles?

8 · Why is it that the bottoms of vessels in which water is being heated are
hotter while the water is still cold? Is it because, while the water is still cool, the heat
15 is enclosed and driven inwards, being prevented from making its way out, but, when
the water in the vessel becomes thoroughly heated, since the fire no longer holds the
heat but expends itself and becomes less, the bottom of the vessel becomes cooler,

---

[1]Reading ὑγρόν τι for μὴ ψόφος.
[2]Reading θέρους for ψύχους.

just as a bath does? For a bath is hotter in winter than in summer, because the heat   20
is more enclosed in winter than in summer by the surrounding air which is cold.

9 . Why is it that water when it boils does not form a scum, as do pea-soup
and lentil-soup? And yet water is lighter than these, and light substances ought to
be able to project themselves more easily to a distance. The same thing happens in
the case of silver when it is being purified; for those who clean out the mint make   25
gains by appropriating the remnants, sweeping up the silver which is scattered
about. Is it because the heat causes the scum by vaporizing and subjecting to force
anything which opposes its own natural impetus? Water, therefore, owing to its   30
lightness and rarity is not subjected to force, and so no great heat is collected in it,
but the heat which continually passes into it cuts its way through before it can
become massed together. But substances which have body in them, like thick soups
and silver, since, owing to their weight, they contain much corporeal matter and
offer resistance,[3] because they are subjected to violent force as the heat tries to   35
make its way out, form bubbles wherever the heat prevails; for, owing to their
density, the heat cannot pass through them, but the density prevails until it is
thrown off by the heat which flows into it. The result is a sudden impact, and not a
continuous pressure, owing to the heat passing up quickly from below.

10 . Why, if substances are moistened in hot water for a short time, do they   937ᵃ1
swell, but, if for a long time, collapse and become wrinkled? Is it because the heat
makes a thing liquid instead of solid and produces breath from liquid and rarefies
what is dense? At first, therefore, it heats things which are solid and makes them
moister, and producing breath from the moisture distends and swells them; but   5
when it heats them still more, it rarefies their outer part,[4] so that the vapour is given
off, and the drying up of moisture causes their bulk to collapse. Now, as anything
collapses, its outer skin shrivels up, and where it shrivels up unevenly, wrinkles are
formed.   10

11 . Why are stones formed by hot water rather than by cold? Is it because a
stone is produced from the failure of moisture, and moisture fails more through the
operation of heat than of cold, in other words petrifaction is the result of heat—as
Empedocles says that both rocks and stones come into being through the action of[5]   15
hot waters? Or, while it is true that heat petrifies, can petrifaction also take place
through cold, because an extremely hard frost consumes the moisture and causes
hardening? That cold, pure and simple, produces this effect is clear from the fact
that its excess does so.

12 . Why is it that if one has one's foot in hot water, if the foot is kept still   20
the water appears to be less hot, but hotter if it is moved? Does the same thing

---

[3]Placing a comma before instead of after βία.   [4]Placing a comma before instead of after τὸ πέριξ.
[5]Reading διά for καί.

happen as in the body, viz. that, when one runs in the wind, the opposing air becomes increasingly colder, and the farther one goes the more one notices it?

25   13 · Why do hot things cool off more in the sun than in the shade? Is it because the lesser heat is destroyed by the greater? Or is it because in the shade the surrounding cold represses the interior heat and does not allow it to make its way out, producing the same effect as the pouring of cold water produces upon those who 30   are fainting[6] (for it encloses the heat and prevents it from escaping); and speaking generally the interior parts of anything are warmer in the winter? But in the sun, since there is nothing which intercepts it, the heat is free to move and vanishes more quickly.

      14 · Why is it that water heated by the sun is not more wholesome for 35   washing purposes? Is it because, owing to the fact that it is cooling, it causes shivering while it is still upon the body?[7] Or, while it has this effect, is it unhealthy if used often for washing? For hot water, generally speaking, produces concoction and has a drying effect, whereas cold water has an astringent effect, and so both do 937^{b}1   good. Therefore cold water and water heated over a fire are both beneficial to those who wash in them; but water heated by the sun owing to the weakness of its heat produces the effect of neither of these, but merely has the effect of moistening—like the light of the moon.

5   15 · Why is water which has been heated in the sun not wholesome? Is it because that which is cooling causes shivering?

      16 · Why are the hot waters at Magnesia and at Atarneus fresh? Is it because more water pours into the hot water as it flows out, and so its saltness 10   disappears, but its heat remains?

      17 · Why is it that in Magnesia the hot waters ceased to be hot but the water remained salty? Is it because more cold water from elsewhere was poured at the same time into the springs and extinguished the heat? Now the earth was salty, but 15   not hot owing to the abundance of water flowing into it. (A similar process occurs in water which is strained through hot ashes; for the water being strained through the hot ashes cools the ashes and itself becomes cold, but is salty and bitter owing to the ashes.) But when the water which was added had become transformed, the heat in 20   the earth for a different reason prevailed over the coldness of the water owing to its small volume, and hot waters flowed again.

      18 · Why are waters from hot springs all salty? Is it because they usually percolate through earth which contains alum (as is shown by the smell of the water) and has been burnt? Now the ashes of anything are salty and smell of sulphur. The

---

[6]Reading ἐκθνῄσκουσι.
[7]Reading ψύχεσθαι καὶ ἔτι ἐπὶ τῷ σώματι ὄν.

earth therefore burns the water like a thunderbolt. Many hot springs therefore are   25
due to strokes of thunderbolts.

19 · Why are hot bathing-places sacred? Is it because they are due to two
very sacred things, sulphur and the thunderbolt?

BOOK XXV

PROBLEMS CONNECTED WITH THE AIR

1 · Why is it that pain is caused if the limbs are enclosed in inflated skins? Is   30
it due to the pressure of the air? For just as the air does not yield to pressure applied
to the skin from outside but repels it, so the air also presses upon the limbs enclosed
within. Or is it because the air is held within by force and is compressed, and so,   35
having naturally an outward impetus in every direction, it presses against the body
enclosed within?

2 · Why is it that in marshes near rivers the so-called 'bellowings' take place,
which according to the fable are uttered[1] by the sacred bulls of the god? That which
is produced is certainly a noise which resembles the roaring of a bull, so much so   938ª1
that it has the same effect on cows when they hear it as the bellowing of a bull. Is it
due to the fact that this phenomenon always occurs wherever rivers stagnate into
marshes,[2] or are driven back by the sea, or give forth wind in unusually large
quantities? The reason is that hollows in the earth form, and the water making its   5
way in (for there is always a flow of water in marshy ground of this kind) thrusts the
air also through a narrow entrance into a wider hollow, just as a noise like roaring is
produced if one makes a sound through the aperture into an empty jar; for it is by a
similarly shaped organ that a bull's roaring is produced. Now, if the hollows have   10
irregular forms, a variety of strange noises is produced; for if one takes off the lid of
a vessel and rubs it against the bottom, drawing it in and out,[3] it makes enough noise
to frighten away wild animals when orchard-watchers employ this device.   15

3 · Why does the air not become moist when it comes into contact with
water? For all other things become moist when they touch water. Is it because the
extremities of the air and water meet, but the surface of each remains distinct?[4] All
other things then are heavier, but the air does not sink below the outer extremity of   20
the water. It therefore touches it, because there is nothing between them; but it does
not become wet, because it always remains above the water.

---

[1]Reading ἰέναι for εἶναι.
[2]Omitting ἢ ὅσα ἕλη λιμνάζονται.
[3]Omitting εἰ τρίψει διὰ τοῦ καταδήματος.
[4]Omitting οὐχ.

4 · Why does calm weather occur most often at midnight and at midday? Is it because calm is immobility of the air, and the air is most at rest when it either has the mastery or is overmastered, and it is in movement when it is struggling? Now it has the mastery most at midnight and is overmastered at midday; for at the former time the sun is farthest away and at the latter nearest at hand. Again, the winds begin to blow either about dawn or about sunset; and the wind which blows at dawn dies down when it is overpowered, and that which blows at sunset dies down when it ceases to have the mastery. Consequently the former dies down at midday, the latter at midnight.

5 · Why is it colder when dawn is breaking and it is already early morning than at night, although the sun is nearer to us? Is it because towards daybreak dew and hoar-frost fall, and both of these are cold? The whole ground then being as it were sprinkled with cold moisture, a process of cooling takes place.

6 · Why is it that in Pontus both intense cold and stifling heat occur? Is it because of the thickness of the air? For in the winter it cannot be thoroughly warmed, and in the summer, when it is heated, it burns because it is thick. It is for the same reason also that marshy regions are cold in winter and hot in summer. Or is it because of the course of the sun? For in the winter it is far away, and in the summer near at hand.

7 · Why is the sky finer at night than by day? Is the sun the cause of wind and disturbance? For these occur when some movement takes place; the cause therefore is the heat. So, when the heat is not present, everything is at rest, and there is more rest when the sun is rising than when it is sinking. And the saying,

> Having no fear of a cloud from the land,

means that, where there is most movement, there must be least permanence and consistency, that which is trying to hold together being irregular and unable to gain the mastery. And this is what happens on the sea in winter and on land in summer.

8 · Why is it that when liquid which fills a jar is poured into skins the jar not only holds the liquid and the skins as well but also has room for more liquid? Is it because there is air present in the liquid? This then, when it is in the jar, cannot be given off owing to the size of the jar; for the larger anything is the more difficult it is to press any moisture or air out of it, as can be seen in sponges. But when it is divided up into small portions, it is pressed out of the skin together with the air already there, so that the space occupied by the air becomes empty; and so the jar can hold the skins and additional liquid as well. This is more especially the case with wine, because there is more air in wine than in water. Similarly the same vessel can hold the same quantities of ashes and water together as it can hold of each poured in separately. For there are apparently many empty spaces in ashes, and so the water, being thinner, sinks in more and saturates the ashes, so that they become dense, because the saturation takes place in one part after another (for a thing always

becomes more thoroughly saturated if the process takes place little by little than all   30
at once), and, as this takes place, the ashes gradually sink, at the same time
absorbing the liquid because they contain hollows. (But ashes thrown into water
while still hot cleave the water and cause it to evaporate.) And the same thing
happens if the water is poured in first and the ashes put in afterwards, so that the   35
water also would seem to contain hollows and empty spaces. Or do the ashes take up
the water, and not the water the ashes? For it is only natural that that which is
composed of smaller particles should be that which finds its way into something
else. (Further, this can be illustrated by an experiment; for when ashes are sprinkled
water is attracted to any spot where they are sprinkled; whereas the contrary would   939ª1
have taken place if it were the water which takes up the ashes.) Or does this process
not occur if the water be poured in first and fill the vessel to the brim, but, if
anything then be added, does it overflow? But if the water once overflows and the
ashes settle down, then it does occur; for it was the ashes which took up the water.   5
There is a parallel to this in the fact that trenches do not hold all the earth which has
been dug out of them; for apparently some air occupies the space excavated, and for
this reason it does not hold all the earth.

9 . Why is it that, though air is denser than light, it can pass through solids?   10
Is it because light travels in a straight line only, and so the sight cannot see through
porous substances like pumice-stone, in which the pores are irregular, whereas they
are not so in glass? The air, on the other hand, is not obstructed, because it does not
travel in a straight line through anything through which it passes.   15

10 . Why is it that the air becomes cold by touching water but not moist,
even though one blows so hard upon water as to cause waves? That it becomes cold
is clear from the change which it undergoes; for the air from water causes cold. Is it
because it is the nature of air to be cold or hot, and it changes by touching anything   20
with which it comes into contact; but it does not also become moist, because it is too
light and so never penetrates below the level of the water, but always remains in
contact only with the surface, even though it be forced downwards, and the water
then recedes still lower, so that the air can never penetrate into its depth?

11 . Why is the air from bubbles and the air which comes up from beneath   25
the water never wet? Is it because the moisture is not retained, but the water drops
off? The water on the surface of a bubble is also too little to moisten anything.

12 . Why is it that air cannot saturate anything, but water can? For water
even when it is transformed into air is moist. Is it for the same reason as that for   30
which stone cannot do so? For everything has not this faculty of saturating other
things, but only that which is viscous or liquid.

13 . . . . Is it because the air in it is carried upwards? For when the skin is
empty it sinks; but when it is inflated, it remains on the surface, because the air
supports it. But if the air makes it lighter and prevents it from sinking, why does a   35

skin become heavier when it is inflated? And how is it that when it is heavier it floats, and when it is lighter it sinks?

14 · Why is it that the air does not rise upwards? For if the winds are the result of air being moved by heat and it is the nature of fire to rise upwards, the wind ought to travel upwards, since that which sets it in motion rushes upwards and that which is set in motion has a natural tendency to travel in the same direction. As a matter of fact, however, the air obviously travels in an oblique direction.

15 · Why is the hour of dawn colder than the evening? Is it because the former is nearer to midnight and the latter to midday? Now midday is the hottest time, because it is nearest to the sun, and midnight is colder for the opposite reason.

16 · Why is it that in hot weather the nights are more stifling than the days? Is it owing to the absence of wind? For the periodical winds and the 'forerunners' blow less at night.

17 · Why is it that substances enclosed in inflated skins and closely covered vessels remain uncorrupted? Is it because things which are in motion become corrupt, and all things that are full are without motion, and such skins and vessels are full?

18 · Why is it that it is colder when the sky is clear than when it is overcast, though the stars and the heaven are warm? Is it because in clear weather there is nothing to hold the vapour, but it is diffused everywhere, whereas in cloudy weather it is contained? For the same reason it is colder when the wind is in the North than when it is in the South; for the South wind attracts cloud, whereas the North wind dispels it, and more evaporation appears to take place when the wind is in the North than when it is in the South, and in winter than in summer. Or is it because of dissimilarity? Or because vapour is formed when that which is hot cools?

19 · Why is it that a smaller amount of air is warmer than a larger quantity (for confined spaces are always warmer)? Is it because a larger quantity is subjected to more motion, and motion makes a thing cold? This can be seen from the fact that hot things become cold if set in motion.

20 · Why is it that water and earth become corrupt, but air and fire do not? Is it because anything which is corrupted must become very hot, but there is nothing hotter than fire? Or is it because a thing must be chilled before it can be corrupted, but fire is always hot and the air is full of fire? So nothing becomes corrupted when it is hot, but only when it is chilled. Now earth and water[5] can become hot and cold.

---

[5]Omitting καὶ ἀήρ.

21 · Why is cloudy weather hotter than clear weather? Is it because, as the men of old said, the stars are cold? Or is this too absurd a doctrine, and is the real reason that in clear weather vaporization takes place? That this is so can be inferred 35 from the fact that, when there is no wind, dew and hoar-frost are formed. When, therefore, the weather is clear, the hot substance, by which the moisture is taken up, is blown about, and so the air becomes cold; for which reason also the moisture which the hot substance lets fall forms dew. But when the weather is cloudy the moisture is contained; and therefore there is no dew or hoar-frost in cloudy weather. 940ª1 The heat, therefore, remaining in the neighbourhood of the earth makes the weather warm.

22 · Why is it that in lofty rooms the air constantly ebbs and flows, especially in calm weather? Is it because the air contains much void in its composition? When, therefore, it begins to flow in, the air inside the room gives way 5 and contracts; and when in course of time this air becomes massed together, the air outside becomes more full of voids and contains much vacant space. Into this space then the air from the room rushes, since it is near at hand, and passes into it, because it is suspended and the nature of the void cannot resist. So when this happens in 10 many parts of it, the adjoining air follows it owing to the forward impetus;[6] and then, since a large quantity of air rushes out,[7] the space within becomes full of voids, while the air outside is denser and so rushes in again from outside. Thus these two currents continually interchange. 15

BOOK XXVI
PROBLEMS CONNECTED
WITH THE WINDS

1 · Why does the North-East wind (Caecias) alone of the winds attract the clouds to itself? Is it because it blows from higher regions? For the parts towards the East are higher than those towards the West, as is shown by the extent and 20 depth of the sea towards the West. Now Caecias, blowing from above to a contrary direction, describes in its course a line which follows an upward curve in relation to the earth;[1] and falling, as has been said, upon the western regions of the earth and massing the clouds together as a result of the form of line which it follows, on its 25 return it thrusts the clouds before it towards itself. It is the only one of all the winds which does this, because for some the opposing regions are higher,[2] towards which their course, either starting from a lower level or proceeding in a straight line, as a

[6]Reading πρόωσιν.
[7]Reading ἔξω.
[1]Reading κυρτά.
[2]Reading τοῖς μὲν ὑψηλοτέρους τοὺς ἐναντίους.

result travels in a downward curve[3] towards the earth, so that there can be no return
30   of the wind to its source because it ends its course round the earth, where, besides,
there are no clouds.[4] The East wind (Apeliotes) and the other winds which follow a
less curving course do not form clouds because they have no moisture. Since, then, it
forms no clouds, the effect produced by the East wind (Apeliotes) is less obvious
than that produced by Caecias.

35   2 · Why do the North winds occur at a fixed period of the year, whereas the
South winds do not? Or do South winds occur annually but are they not continuous,
because the source of the South wind is far away from us, and we live close to the
North wind? Further, the annual North winds blow when the air is still (for they
940ᵇ1   blow in summer); whereas the South winds occur in the spring, when the region of
the air is less stable. Again, the South wind is moist, and the upper region of the
atmosphere is unfavourable to moisture; so any moisture which is formed in it is
quickly dissolved. Also moisture is erratic; and so the South wind, because it does
5   not remain in the same place, helps to set up changes in the movement of the air.
And since the air does not remain in the same place when it moves, other winds are
consequently set up; for a wind is a movement of air.

      3 · Why does the South wind blow after a hoar-frost? Is it because hoar-frost
occurs when concoction takes place, and after concoction and cleansing a change to
10   the opposite condition takes place? Now the South wind is the opposite of the North
wind. For the same reason also the South wind blows after snow. In a word, both
snow and hail and rain and all such processes of cleansing are a sign of concoction;
15   therefore after rain and similar storms the winds fall.

      4 · Why do the alternating winds blow? Is it for the same reason as causes
the change of current in straits? For both sea and air are carried along until they
flow; then, when the land-winds encounter opposition and can no longer advance,
because the source of their motion and impetus is not strong, they retire in a
20   contrary direction.

      5 · Why do the alternating winds come from the sea? Is it because the sea is
close at hand? Or is it because the alternating wind is the opposite of the land-wind
and as it were the reverse of it? Now the land-wind is the breeze which blows from
25   the land towards the sea, and the alternating wind is the reflux of the land-wind, so
that it must necessarily come from the sea. Or is it because the air which has been
set in motion collects out at sea? The reason of its not collecting on land and of its
being thrown back is the fact that the sea is in a hollow, and air, like water, flows
always into the deepest hollow it can find.

30   6 · Why do cloud-winds stop sooner when rain falls? Is it because, when it
rains, the hollows of the cloud, in which the source of the wind is formed, collapse?

[3]Reading κοῖλα.
[4]Reading τῷ περὶ τὴν γῆν ἔχειν τὴν τελευτὴν τῆς φορᾶς.

7 · Why are not the same winds everywhere rainy? Is it because the same winds do not everywhere blow against mountains, but different winds are opposed to different mountains? For example, when the winds blow laboriously against steep mountains, the clouds are more likely to form there, since the wind cannot push them farther forward; and when the clouds form and are compressed, they burst.

8 · Why are sunsets, if they are clear, a sign of fine weather; if they are disturbed, a sign of stormy weather? Is it because a storm occurs when the air is dense and thick? When, therefore, the sun prevails, it breaks up and clears the air; but, if it is itself overpowered, an overcast sky results. If, therefore, the density is excessive, a storm occurs as soon as the day dawns; whereas if it is weaker but not completely overpowered, the denseness which forms is driven towards the setting sun and remains there, because the air round the earth is thicker than the storm. And the rest of the air quickly densifies, because a beginning of the process has already been made and there is a rallying point to receive and collect anything which comes to it,[5] the same thing occurring in the air as happens in a rout, where, if one man makes a stand, the rest also remain firm. Hence the sky sometimes becomes quickly and suddenly overcast. When, therefore, there is a disturbed sunset, it is a strong indication that the sun has not got the mastery over the density, though it has struggled long against it, so that probably further condensation has taken place. This is a less alarming symptom when it occurs after a storm than in calm weather; for in the former circumstances it is probably the remnant of a storm, but in the latter the beginning of condensation.

9 · What is the origin of the saying,

Boreas blows not at night when once the third sun has arisen?

Is it because the breezes which come from the north are weak when they blow at night? A proof that the amount of air which is set in motion is not great is the fact that they blow at a time when there was a small amount of heat; and a small amount of heat was moving a small amount of air. Now all things terminate in multiples of three, and things which are very small terminate at the end of the first triad; and that is what this wind does.

10 · Why does the North wind blow more frequently than the South wind? Is it because the North wind, being near the inhabited portion of the world, attracts our notice in spite of its short duration (for it is with us as soon as it begins to blow), whereas the South wind does not reach us, because it blows from a distance?

11 · Why does the South wind blow as much[6] on winter nights as on winter days? Is it because during the night the sun is near the southern region, and the

---

[5] Omitting καθάπερ ὄρθρος.   [6] Reading οὐχ ἧττον.

nights there are warmer than are the days in the north? Much air, therefore, is set in
35 motion and not less than by day; but the warmer days prevent the wind from
blowing more strongly by drying up the moisture.

12 · Why does the South wind blow at the time of the dog-star, and why does
this happen regularly like any other natural phenomenon? Is it because the
southern regions are warm, since the sun is not far[7] away, and so the evaporation is
considerable? The South winds would blow frequently if it were not for the annual
941ᵇ1 winds; as it is, these prevent their blowing. Or is it because a sign occurs at the
setting and rising of any star, and especially of the dog-star? It is clear that winds
blow most of the time of and after its rising, and since it causes stifling heat, it is
5 only natural that the hottest winds should be set in motion when it rises; and the
South wind is hot. And since things are most accustomed to pass from contraries
into contraries, and the 'forerunners', which are northern winds, blow before the
rising of the dog-star, the South wind naturally blows after the dog-star appears,
10 since a sign then occurs, and the occurrence of a sign[8] at the time when stars rise
means a change in the air. Now all winds change either into their contraries or into
those on their right; but since the North wind cannot[9] change into the winds on its
right, the only thing left for it to do would be to change into a South wind. Now on
the fifteenth day after the winter solstice the wind is in the south, because the
15 solstice marks as it were a fresh start and the sun sets in motion air which is nearest
to it[10] and at this solstice it is near the south. Just as, therefore, when it sets the
region of the east in motion it stirs up the East winds, so when it sets in motion the
southern region it stirs up the South winds. It does not do this immediately after the
20 solstice, because the changes which it sets up extend at first over a very small area,
but only on the fifteenth day, because this date corresponds to the first sensible
impression made by the change; for the said date is simply the most significant part
of a whole.

13 · Why are the days most changeable during the period of Orion, and why
25 is there then such variability in the wind? Is it because during a period of change all
things are always most indeterminate, and Orion rises at the beginning of autumn
and sets in the winter, so that, since there is not yet one settled season, but one is
coming on and the other coming to an end, the winds must therefore necessarily be
30 unsettled, because those of each season are passing into one another? And Orion is
said to be dangerous both in his setting and in his rising owing to the uncertainty of
the season; for it must be full of confusion and inconsistency.

14 · Why does the North wind which blows at night cease on the third day?
35 Is it because it comes from a small and weak source and the third day marks the

---

[7]Reading οὐ πόρρω.
[8]Reading ἄστροις τὸ ἐπισημαίνειν.
[9]Reading ἐπιδεξίους οὐ μεταβάλλει.
[10]Reading καθ' αὐτὸν.

crisis? or is it because it expends itself all at once like the cloud-winds, and therefore quickly dies down again?

15 · Why do the North winds blow more than the other winds? Is it owing to the fact that the inhabited portion of the earth is near the region of the north, which is high and outside the tropics and full of snow, which never leaves some of the mountains? As, therefore, frozen matter is usually melting there, a wind often arises, and this wind is the North wind which comes from the region of the pole.

942ᵃ1

16 · Why do the South winds blow during winter and at the beginning of spring and the end of the autumn, and why are they boisterous and whirling in their course and why are they cold to the inhabitants of Libya in like manner as the North winds are to us? Is it because, the sun being near, the winds must necessarily be set in motion? Now during the winter the sun travels towards the south, and at the beginning of the spring and at the end of autumn it is giving forth heat; whereas during the summer the sun travels towards the north and leaves those other regions. The South wind is hot, because it mingles its breath with the air in the region of Libya, which is hot; and so it is boisterous and makes the summer rainy, sweeping down on the sea.

5

10

15

17 · Why does the South wind cause evil odours? Is it because it makes bodies moist and hot, and they are then most liable to corruption? South winds, however, which come from the sea are good for plants—for it falls on them from the sea, as it does on the Thriasian Plain in Attica—and the reason is that it is cooled before it arrives.[11] Now mildew is caused by moisture which is hot and comes from without.

20

18 · Why does wind usually occur before eclipses, at nightfall before midnight eclipses and at midnight before those which occur at dawn? Is it because the heat which comes from the moon becomes faint, because its course is already getting near the earth, and when it is quite near the eclipse will take place? Now when the heat, by which the air is held back and kept still, is set free, the air begins to move again and a wind springs up later in time according as the eclipse is later.

25

19 · Why is the South wind rainy not when it is beginning but when it is ending? Is it because it collects the air from a distance? For the rain comes when the South wind masses the air together, and it masses the air together only after it begins to blow. Or is it because, when the South wind begins to blow, the air is still hot, because it comes from a hot region, but in course of time it becomes cool, and then tends to become massed into rain?

30

20 · Why is it that the South wind, when it is less strong, brings clear weather, but, when it is strong, brings clouds and lasts longer? Is it, as some say

35

---

[11]Placing a comma after προσπίπτει and a full stop after πεδίῳ.

owing to the source from which it comes? For if it comes from a weaker source it brings clear weather, but if it starts from a stronger source it brings clouds. Or is it because it is weaker when it begins, so that it does not propel much air, but in the end it usually becomes strong? Hence comes the proverb,

When the South wind begins and when Boreas ceases his blowing.

21 · Why is it that in the winter the winds come forth from the east, but in the summer also from the west? Is it because, when the sun no longer prevails, the air flows freely? When, therefore, the sun sinks, it leaves clouds behind it, which cause the West winds, and anything which it carries with it to the inhabitants of the southern hemisphere becomes an East wind. And, contrariwise, when it sinks in the southern region of the earth, it will cause West winds for the inhabitants of that region and East winds in our part of the world from the air which accompanies it. For this reason too, if it finds another wind blowing, that wind becomes stronger when the sun rises, because it adds something to it.

22 · Why are hounds least able to find the scent when a West wind is blowing? Is it because it disperses the scent most owing to the fact that of all the winds it blows most continuously and down on to the earth?

23 · Why, when there are shooting stars, is it a sign of wind? Is it because they are carried along by the wind, and the wind occurs where they are, before it reaches us? For this reason also the wind rises in that quarter from which the stars are set in motion.

24 · Why is it that of all the winds the West wind drives the largest clouds? Is it because it blows from the open sea and over the deep, so that it collects clouds from a large area?

25 · Why are the winds strongest which are at their ending? Is it because when they expend themselves all at once, what remains is very little?[12]

26 · Why is it that, if the South-West wind (Lips) blows about the time of the equinox, rain results? Is it because the sun sets the winds in motion from any part of the universe in which it is? Hence the succession of the winds corresponds to the course of the sun. Now since the equinox is the boundary between winter and summer, when it happens that the sun, according to the equinox as it appears to us, has passed the exact boundary or falls short of it and is rather in the wintry region, the result is that the winds from that region blow, of which the first is the South-West wind, which is naturally moist. Now when the sun is rather in the

---

[12]Reading λοιπόν for θερμόν.

wintry region of the universe and stirs up the winds there, the result is that the typical conditions of winter result; one of which is wet weather. Again, since the equinox is as it were winter and summer equally balanced, if anything is added to either one of them it causes a distinct inclination in one direction, just as happens in the case of equally balanced scales. But, since the South-West wind is of the wintry order and naturally moist, its addition at the equinox causes an inclination towards winter and rainy weather; for rain is the wintry weather most akin to the wind that has begun to blow.

35

943ᵃ1

27 · Why are the South wind and the South-East wind (Eurus), which are warmer than their respective contraries, the North wind and the West wind, more rainy, although water is engendered from the air by cold? For it is not true that the clouds form because the North wind thrusts them away from our part of the world; for the West and South-East winds both alike—for they are similarly at the sides of the world—drive away clouds from the quarter from which they blow, as also do all the other winds. Is it because the more the heat exists outside, the more the cold is driven within? Or is it due in some degree to the quarter from which they blow that certain winds bring clear weather? For the South-East wind rises from the dawn (and the region is warm), while the West wind is situated towards the evening.[13] But is there not a further reason, namely, that air, like water, cools most quickly and thoroughly when it is previously heated? The air then brought by the South-East wind arrives warm from the rising sun, as does that brought by the South wind from the midday sun; when, therefore, they reach the colder region, they quickly condense and become massed into rain. And the South-East wind has a greater tendency to form rain, because it brings the air more directly from the sun and equally hot; but the South wind is rainy as it ceases to blow, because the first air that is brought comes cold from the sea, whereas the last air, which is very warm, is brought[14] from the land. Or is there not a further reason, namely, that the South wind is stronger as it ceases to blow (hence the proverb applied to it, 'When the South wind begins . . .'), and stronger winds are colder, and so the South wind masses the clouds together at the end of its duration? Is not this why it is more rainy then than when it first begins to blow?

5

10

15

20

25

28 · Why do the winds, though they are cold, cause dryness? Is it because the colder winds cause evaporation? But why should they do so more than the sun? Is it because they carry off the vapour, whereas the sun leaves it where it is and consequently causes more moisture and less dryness?

30

29 · Why does the North-East wind (Caecias) alone of all the winds attract the clouds towards itself, as the proverb has it, 'Drawing it to himself, as Caecias draws clouds'? For the other winds simply drive forward the clouds from the quarter from which they blow. Is this phenomenon to be attributed to the fact that

35

---

[13]Reading χώρα θερμή· πρὸς δέ.
[14]Reading κομίζεται.

the contrary wind blows at the same time? But would not this have been obvious, and is it not more likely that the North-East wind naturally follows a circular course? The other winds therefore blow round the earth, but the North-East wind

943ᵇ1 has the concave side of its course towards the heavens and not towards the earth, and so, blowing towards its source, it attracts the clouds to itself.

30 · Why is it that the wind blows cold in the early morning from rivers but

5 not from the sea? Is it because the sea extends over open spaces, but rivers are in narrow places? The breeze, therefore, from the sea is dispersed over a wide area and is consequently weak; whereas the breeze from a river is carried along in a mass and

10 is stronger and therefore naturally appears colder. Or is the reason other than this, namely, that the rivers are cold, but the sea is neither hot nor cold? Now a breeze or exhalation is due to the heating or cooling of liquids; for whichever of these two processes they undergo, evaporation takes place, and, when water evaporates, the resultant air is set in motion, and this is a breeze. That which is produced from cold

15 liquids naturally blows cold, while that which blows from very hot liquids cools and becomes cold. One would therefore find that all the rivers are cold, but the sea is neither very hot nor very cold. That which blows from it therefore is not cold, because the sea is not itself very cold, nor does it cool quickly because the sea is not

20 very hot.

31 · Why is the West wind always considered to bring fair weather and to be the pleasantest of the winds? So, for instance, Homer says that in the Elysian Plains.

Ever the breezes blow of the Zephyr.[15]

Is it because in the first place it contains a mixture of air? For it is neither hot like

25 the winds from the south and east, nor cold like that from the north, but is[16] on the boundary between the cold and the hot winds; and, being near to them both, it partakes of their qualities, and is consequently temperate and breathes most of spring. Furthermore, the winds change either into their contraries or into those on

30 their right; blowing therefore after the North wind (for the west is on the right of the north), it enjoys a good reputation, as being mild as compared with an inclement wind. Also as soon as wintry weather ceases, fine weather usually follows; and the North wind is a wintry wind. [The East wind, though it lies between the warm and the cold winds, partakes less of them; for, when it blows, it sets in motion the winds

35 towards the south (for when it changes it does so in that direction), but though it sets them in motion it does not mingle with them. The West wind is set in motion by the South winds, and when it blows it sets the North winds in motion; for there the

944ᵃ1 succession of the winds ceases. Hence the West wind, constituting as it does the end of some winds and the starting-point of others, justly is and is considered to be a pleasant wind.][17]

---

[15]*Odyssey* IV 567.
[16]Reading ἐστι for ἐπί.
[17]Excised by Ruelle.

32 · Why does the South wind blow at the time of the dog-star? Is it because a sign occurs at the setting or rising of any star, and especially of the dog-star? It is clear then that the wind blows most at the time of and after its rising. And since it causes stifling heat, it is only natural that the hottest winds should be set in motion when it rises; and the South wind is hot.

33 · Why does the West wind blow towards evening and not in the early morning? Is the sun at its rising and setting usually the cause of breezes? For when it concocts and dissolves the air, which is moist, by thoroughly heating it, it dissolves it into breath; and if the air is full of breath, it becomes still more evaporated by the sun. When, therefore, the sun is in the east, it is far away from the West wind, for the latter blows from the setting sun; but when the sun is already near its setting, the breath is then thoroughly dissolved, and from midday onwards and towards evening the sun is most suitably situated for heating and dissolving the air. It is for this reason also that the East wind begins to blow in the early morning; for since the air above the earth becomes charged with moisture during the night and owing to its weight approaches the earth, the sun from dawn onwards dissolves it and sets in motion first the air which is nearest to itself. Now the East wind gets its name Apeliotes because it is the wind which blows from the rising sun.

34 · Why is it that when the sun rises the winds both rise and fall? Is it because a wind is the movement either of the air or of moisture carried up? Now this movement, when it is only slight, is quickly absorbed by the sun, so that no wind occurs; but when it is greater, the movement is increased when the sun rises, for the sun is a source of movement.

35 · Why does the West wind blow in the evening? Is it because all the winds blow when the sun disperses the moisture? For the moisture being already in a mass, the power of heat, when it approaches it, concocts it.[18] Now the West wind blows from the setting sun; it is only natural then that it should rise in the evening, for then the sun reaches the quarter proper to that wind.

The North and the South winds are the most frequent of winds, because, when one contrary is overcome by its direct contrary, it is least able to continue, whereas it is better able to resist a wind blowing against it from an angle. Now the South and the North winds blow from regions on either side of the sun's course, while the other winds blow rather in a straight line with it.

36 · Does the wind come from a source, as water does, and is it unable to rise to a higher level than that source, or is this not so? And does it come from a single point or from a wider area? There are indeed in the wind certain similarities to that which seems to occur in water; for water flows faster when it travels downhill, whereas it stagnates on flat and level ground, and the winds act similarly, for on

[18]Reading ἐκπέττει.

10 promontories and high ground the air is always in motion, whereas in hollows it is often at rest and there is a calm. Moreover on exceedingly high mountains there is no wind at all—on Mount Athos, for example, amongst others, as is proved by the fact that offerings which persons sacrificing leave there one year are, so it is said,
15 found there still in the following year. It is clear then that the course of the wind starts as it were from a source of some kind. It cannot, therefore, rise any higher. Hence the above phenomenon occurs on high mountains, to which what happens to water would be a close parallel; for apparently neither a strong flow of water nor a
20 violent wind is found in high mountains.

37 · Why is it that when the South wind blows the sea becomes blue, but when the North wind blows it becomes dark? Is it because the North wind disturbs the sea less, and that which is less disturbed appears to be all black?

25 38 · Why do the South winds when they blow gently cause no overclouding, but when they become strong overcloud the sky? Is it because, when they blow gently, they cannot produce many clouds? They therefore cover only a small area with cloud; but, when they blow strongly, they thrust along many clouds, and therefore seem to cause more overclouding.

30 39 · Why is the North wind strong when it begins to blow, but weak as it ceases, whereas the South wind is weak when it begins, but strong as it ceases? Is it because the North wind is near to us and the South wind distant? The former then, when it begins, blows immediately in our part of the world, whereas the beginning of the latter becomes dispersed owing to the long time it takes to travel, and little of
35 its first breath reaches us; and we feel the end of the North wind, but that of the South wind not at all. It is, therefore, only natural that the North wind should be weak as it ceases (for the end of all things is weak), while the South wind is not weak at its close, since we do not feel its ending at all.

945ª1 40 · Why do alternating winds blow where there are bays, but not where there is a wide expanse of open sea? Is it because the wind, when it pours into the bays, is less broken up and travels for the most part in a collected mass, whereas
5 over open expanses of sea the land-winds tend to be broken up as they begin to flow, and when they move the same thing happens to them, because they are free to travel in many directions? For an alternating wind is the reflux of a land-wind.[19]

41 · What is the origin of the saying,

When the South wind begins and when Boreas ceases his blowing?

Is it because the North wind, owing to the fact that we live near it and our
10 habitation is towards the pole, immediately blows strongly, for it is with us as soon

[19]Reading ἀπογέας.

as it begins? Hence, as it ceases, it blows pleasantly; for it then blows weakly. The South wind, on the other hand, because it is far away, reaches us later in greater strength.

42 · Why is it that men feel heavier and weaker when the wind is in the south? Is it because moisture becomes abundant instead of scanty, being melted by the heat, and moisture, which is heavy, takes the place of breath, which is light, and under these conditions men's strength becomes languid?

43 · Why are men hungrier when the wind is in the north than when it is in the south? It is because the North winds are colder?

44 · Why does the South wind not blow in Egypt itself in the regions towards the sea nor for the distance of a day and a night's journey inland, while in the regions beyond Memphis and for the distance of a day and a night's journey it blows freshly; and does not blow to the west for the distance of two days' and two nights' journey, while to the east the South-West wind (Lips) blows? Is it because Egypt in its lower regions is hollow, so the South wind passes over above it, but to the south and farther away the regions are loftier?

45 · Why is it that the South wind is weak when it begins to blow, but becomes stronger as it ceases, while with the North wind the contrary is the case, hence the proverb,

Sail when the South wind begins and when Boreas ceases his blowing?

Is it because we dwell rather towards the pole than towards the midday sun, and the North wind blows from the pole, while the South wind blows from the midday sun? It is only natural, therefore, that the North wind, when it begins, immediately attacks with violence the regions nearer to it, and afterwards transfers its violence to the dwellers farther south. The South wind, on the contrary, when it begins, presses upon those who dwell towards the midday sun, and, when it has passed them by, blows freshly upon those who dwell towards the pole.

46 · What is the origin of the saying,

Straightway the winter comes, if the South wind call to the North wind?

Is it because it is the nature of the South wind to collect clouds and much rain? When therefore the North wind blows under these conditions, since there is abundant material, the North wind freezes it and brings on the winter. Hence the saying,

When Boreas findeth the mire, soon cometh the season of winter.

Now mud and rain in general are usually, if not invariably, due to the South wind.

5   47 · Why does the North wind follow quickly upon the South wind, but not the South wind upon the North wind? Is it because the North wind arrives from near at hand, but the South wind from a distance, since our habitation is towards the north?

48 · Why is it that the winds are cold, although they are due to movement caused by heat? Is movement caused by heat not invariably hot, but only when it
10   occurs in a certain manner? If it comes forth in a mass, it burns with its heat the very thing which emits it; but if it passes out gradually through a narrow space, it is itself hot, but the air which is set in motion by this process completes the movement in accordance with whatever was its original nature. This can be seen in the human
15   body; for there is a saying that from the same organ we breathe both hot and cold, but this is untrue, since all that proceeds from the mouth is hot, as is shown by the fact that it appears hot if the hand is placed close to the mouth. It is the manner in which it comes forth which makes the difference. For if in yawning we emit breath from a wide opening, it appears hot because we can feel it; but if it be emitted
20   through a narrow opening, being more violent, it impels the air in its immediate neighbourhood, which in its turn impels the adjoining air. If the air is cold, its movement is also cold. May not the same thing happen also in the winds, and their first movement be through a narrow channel and then set in motion the adjoining air, and then other air begin to rush onwards? So in the summer the winds are hot,
25   in winter they are cold, because in each case this is the temperature of the air which is already there; for that the air does not follow this course because it is either set in motion by itself or overpowered by the heat, is clear not only from the fact that it heats the winds when there is more heat in it, but also because it was originally
30   being carried upwards. For fire is of this nature; whereas cold naturally travels downwards. The winds move horizontally and for good reason; for since the heat presses upwards and the cold downwards and neither prevails, and the air cannot remain still, it is only natural that its motion should be sideways.

35   49 · Why are the South winds cold in Libya as the North winds are with us? Is it primarily because the sources of these winds are respectively nearer to us and to them? For if, as we have already said, the winds pass through a narrow channel, they will be colder to those who are nearer to them owing to the violence of their
946ᵃ1   movement; for when their movement proceeds farther, they become dispersed. Hence the North winds are cold in our part of the world, because we are nearer to them and dwell quite near the pole.

50 · Why is it that those South winds which are dry and do not bring rain
5   cause fever? Is it because they engender unnatural moist heat in the body? For they are by nature moist and hot, and this causes fever, which is due to a combined excess of these two things. When, therefore, the South winds blow under the influence of the sun without bringing rain, they engender this condition in us;[20] whereas, when they bring rain with them, the rain cools us.

[20]Reading διάθεσιν for τάξιν.

51 · Why do the periodical winds always blow at the season at which they do   10
blow and with the force with which they blow? And why do they cease at close of
day and not blow during the night? Is this due to the fact that the melting of snow
by the sun ceases towards evening and at night? Now these winds blow in general
when the sun begins to prevail and melt the northern ice. When the ice begins to
melt, the 'forerunners' blow; when it is already melting, the periodic winds blow.   15

52 · Why is the West wind at once the gentlest of winds and also cold, and
why does it blow mainly at two seasons, namely, spring and autumn, and towards
evening, and usually in the direction of the land? Is it cold because it blows from the   20
sea and from extended areas? It is less cold indeed than the North wind, because it
blows from evaporated water and not from snow; but it *is* cold, because it blows
either after the winter, when the sun is only just beginning to prevail, or in the
autumn, when the sun no longer has power. For it does not have to wait for its
proper matter,[21] as it would if it were a land-wind, but wanders freely, because it has   25
travelled over water. For the same reason it blows evenly; for it does not blow from
mountains or from forcibly melted matter, but flowing gently as through a channel.
For the regions towards the north and south are mountainous; but towards the west
there is neither mountain nor land but the Atlantic Ocean, so that it travels in the
direction of the land. Further, it blows towards evening owing to the quarter from   30
which it comes; for the sun then approaches that quarter. It ceases at night because
the movement set up by the sun dies down.

53 · Why do all things appear larger when the South-East wind (Eurus)
blows? Is it because it makes the air very gloomy?

54 · Why is it that during the winter the winds blow early and from the east,   35
but in summer in the evening and from the setting sun? Is it because what happens
in our part of the world during the summer occurs during the winter among those
who inhabit the opposite hemisphere of the earth, and with us in the winter the
winds blow early and from the east, because the air, which during the night is full of
moisture, is dissolved and set in motion by the sun in the early morning, the air   946^{b}1
nearest the sun being the first to be affected? The sun begins to produce this effect
even before it rises; therefore the breezes blow just as much before sunrise. Since
then the sun attracts the moisture to itself and in the winter before its rising sets in   5
motion in our part of the earth the air which is moist, it is clear that it would also
attract the moisture when it is in the southern hemisphere, and it would be evening
there when it is early morning with us. The result would be that the air, which the
sun attracts to itself before its rising in our part of the world would become a West   10
wind to the dwellers in the south and would blow in the evening. Now what happens
during our winter happens to them at dawn, and what happens in the summer to
them happens to us in the evening; for when it is summer here, it is winter there, and
our evening is their early morning, at which time they have breezes from the east,

15   while we have West winds for the same reasons as are mentioned above. In the
summer breezes do not blow from the east, because the sun, when it rises, finds the
air in our part of the earth still too dry, owing to the short period of its absence; and
West winds do not blow in the evening during the winter, because East winds do not
blow in the southern hemisphere either at that time for the aforesaid reasons, in
20   virtue of which the sun attracts the moisture to itself and produces the West wind in
our part of the earth.

55 · Why is the West wind always considered to bring fair weather and to be
the pleasantest of the winds? Is it because it is on the boundary between the hot and
the cold winds, and being near to them both it partakes of their qualities, and is
therefore temperate? The East wind, though it also lies between the hot and the cold
25   winds, partakes less of them; for when it blows it sets in motion the winds towards
the south (for, when it changes, it does so in that direction), but, though it sets them
in motion, it does not mingle with them. The West wind is set in motion by the
South winds and, when it blows, it sets the North winds in motion; for there the
succession of the winds ceases. Hence the West wind, constituting as it does the end
30   of some winds and the starting-point of others, justly is and is considered to be a
pleasant wind.

56 · Why are different winds rainy in different places; for example, Hellespontias (the East wind) in Attica and the islands, the North wind on the Hellespont
and in Cyrene, and the South wind round Lesbos? Is it because rain occurs
35   wherever there is a collection of clouds, since density collects wherever it can
settle? It is for this reason that there is more rain among the mountains than where
the mass of clouds can find a free passage, for that which is confined becomes dense
as a necessary consequence; also it rains more in calm weather. In the Hellespont
947ᵃl   the North wind, blowing from its upper end, masses together many clouds, which
Hellespontias (the East wind) drives towards Attica and the islands, being thus
provided with material; for most clouds come round from the north.
Round Lesbos the South-East (Eurus) and South winds bring much cloud
5   from the open sea and drive it against the land. Similar instances might be quoted
for the other winds.

57 · What is the origin of the saying,

Have no fear of a cloud from the land in the season of winter,
But if it come from over the deep have a care; and in summer
Ever distrust the cloud that sweeps from the gloom of the mainland?

Is it because in the winter the sea is warmer, so that, if any cloud has formed, it must
10   have done so from some powerful cause, otherwise it would have been dissolved,
because the region in which it forms is warm? Now in the summer the sea is cold, as
also are the sea breezes, but the land is hot, so that if any cloud comes from the land,
it must have been formed from some considerable cause; for it would have been
dissolved if it had been weak.

58 · Why is it that in Arcadia, which is high, the winds are no colder than   15
elsewhere, but when there is no wind and it is cloudy, it is cold, just as it is in flat,
marshy districts? Is it because Arcadia resembles a marshy district, since it has no
outlet for its waters to the sea, for which reason also there are many chasms there?
When, therefore, there is a wind, it winnows away the exhalations from the earth,   20
which are cold, but the winds themselves are not cold, because they arrive from the
sea; but when there is no wind the vapour which rises from the stagnant water
causes the cold.

59 · Why is it that the wind lasts a long time when it begins to blow at dawn?   25
Is it because, when the sun rises, the impetus given to the wind is very violent and
can therefore maintain its character? That this is so is shown by the fact that it
forms a strong mass.

60 · Why is it that the North wind is keen during the day but falls at night?
Is it because it is generated from frozen rain when this is evaporated by the sun? It   30
falls at night, because the process does not go on as before, but is reversed; for at
night the North wind expends itself, but it is less apt to do so during the day.

61 · Why is it that when many spiders' webs are borne through the air, they
are a sign of wind? Is it because the spider works in fine weather, but the webs are   35
set in motion because the air, as it cools, collects on the ground, and this cooling
process is the beginning of winter, so that the movement of the webs is a sign? Or is
it because after rain and storms the spiders[22] are borne through the air in large
numbers, since they work in fine weather (for they do not appear at all in the winter,
the spider being unable to support the cold), and as they are borne along by the wind   947[b]1
they unwind a quantity of web? Now after rain winds usually blow.

62 · Why is it that the strong North winds in winter cause clouds in the cold
regions, but outside them bring a clear sky? Is it because they are at the same time   5
cold and strong, and in the regions near the north they are colder and so congeal the
clouds before they can drive them along, and the clouds, when they are congealed,
remain where they are owing to their weight? Elsewhere, however, it is their
strength rather than their coldness which takes effect.

[22]Reading ἀραχνῶν.

BOOK XXVII
PROBLEMS CONNECTED WITH FEAR
AND COURAGE

10   1 · Why do those who are afraid tremble? Is it due to the process of chilling? For the heat fails and contracts; that is also why the bowels usually are loosened.

15   2 · Why do men become thirsty under certain conditions, those, for example, who are about to be punished? For this ought not to be so, since they are chilled. Is it because the chilling and heating do not occur in the same region, but the former takes place on the surface of the body, from which the heat departs, but the heating takes place in the interior, so that it warms it, as is proved by the fact that the bowels become loosened? For thirst occurs when the sovereign region of the body becomes
20   dry. The same thing seems to happen as occurs in those suffering from ague, who are thirsty and cold at the same time; for in their case too the same part of the body is not hot and cold.

3 · Why is it that under the influence of anger men become heated and bold (the heat collecting in the interior of the body), whereas in a state of fear they are in
25   a contrary condition? Is it because they are not affected in the same region, but in those who are angry the heat collects in the region of the heart—hence they become courageous and red in the face and full of breath—the course of the heat being upwards, whereas in those who are afraid the blood and heat both retreat in a downward direction—hence the bowels become loosened. For the beating of the
30   heart is different, since in those who are frightened it is frequent and strongly punctuated, as would naturally occur from the failure of heat, while in those who are angry it has the character which one would expect when a greater quantity of heat collects. Hence the expressions about anger 'boiling up' and 'rising' and 'being stirred up' and the like are apt and fitting. Is the thirst also due to this cause, since
35   dry-spitting and the parching of the tongue and the like are due to the simultaneous upward rush of breath and heat? Thirst, moreover, is clearly due to the body becoming heated. How then can the same region, namely, that in which we feel thirst, become dried up both in one who is afraid and in one who is angry? That fear
948ª1   tends to produce thirst is clearly shown in the case of routed soldiers; for under no other condition is such thirst experienced. The same is true of those suffering from great anxiety; therefore they wash out their mouths and swallow liquid, as did Parmenon the actor. Or is it in such cases not thirst but dryness due to the flight of
5   blood (whence also they become pale)? This is indicated by the fact that they do not drink much but simply take a gulp; routed soldiers on the other hand are undergoing violent exertion. So those who are about to be punished feel thirst, and in this there is nothing strange. In war some brave men even, when they are drawn up in battle array, actually tremble when they are not distraught but confident; and they often
10   beat their bodies with a flat cane or, failing that, with the hand, in order that they

may be warmed.[1] It seems probable that owing to the violence and impetus of the heat a disturbing inequality of the temperature is set up in the body.

4 · Why are brave men generally fond of wine? Is it because the brave are full of heat, and the heat is in the region of the chest? (For it is there also that fear shows itself, acting as a process of cooling; with the result that less[2] heat remains in the region of the heart, and in some men the heart beats violently as it is cooled.) Those then who have an abundance of blood in their lungs have hot lungs, as though they were drunk, and so the presentiment of danger does not chill them. Such men are fond of drinking; for the desire for drink is due to the heat of this region, as has been stated elsewhere, and the desire is for that which has power to stop the heat. Now wine is naturally hot and satisfies the thirst better than water, particularly in those whom we are now considering;[3] the reason for this has been stated elsewhere. Hence those who are suffering from inflammation of the lungs and those who are mad both desire wine, though the lungs of the former are hot owing to the fever, and those of the latter owing to their state of disturbance. Since, then, the same people are usually of a thirsty and of a brave kind, and those who are thirsty desire wine and are therefore fond of drinking, it necessarily follows that the two characteristics of bravery and fondness for wine usually go together. Hence those who are drunk are braver than those who are not.

5 · Why do states honour courage more than anything else, though it is not the highest of the excellences? Is it because they are continually either making war or having war made against them, and courage is most useful in both these circumstances? They, therefore, honour not that which is best, but that which is best for themselves.

6 · Why do those who are afraid tremble most in the voice, the hands, and the lower lip? Is it because this affection is due to the departure of heat from the upper parts of the body? If so, their pallor is due to the same cause. The voice, then, trembles owing to the departure of heat from the chest, the region in which the voice is set in motion thus becoming cooled. So too with the hands; for they are attached to the chest. The lower lip trembles, and not the upper, because the upper lip hangs downwards[4] in the direction of its natural tendency; but the upward direction of the lower lip is contrary to nature and it is held steady in that position by the heat. When, therefore, the heat is withdrawn as the process of cooling takes place, it trembles. For the same reason the lip hangs down when a man is angry, as can be seen clearly in children; for the heat rushes together into the heart.

7 · Why do those who are afraid tremble, especially in the voice, the hands, and the lower lip? Is it because the heat fails in the region of the body in which the

---

[1] Reading ἵν' ἀναθερμανθῇ.
[2] Omitting τοῖς μέν.
[3] Reading τῶν τοιούτων.
[4] Reading ἄνωθεν τρέμει, διότι τὸ ἄνωθεν κάτω.

voice is situated, while the trembling of the lip and hands is due to the fact that they are very easily set in motion and contain very little blood? Those who are afraid also emit bile and their sexual organs contract, the emission of bile being due to the heat which descends and causes liquefaction, while the contraction of the sexual organs is due to the fact that fear comes from outside, and therefore the rush of heat is in the contrary direction.

8 · Why do those who are afraid feel both thirst and cold, these being contrary affections? Do they feel cold because they are chilled, and thirst because they are heated, since under the influence of fear the heat and the moisture leave the upper parts of the body? That this happens is shown by the change of colour and by the effect on the bowels; for the face becomes pale and the bowels are sometimes loosened. The cold, therefore, is caused by the departure of the heat, and the thirst by the departure of the moisture, from the upper parts of the body.

9 · Why is it that, although both fear and pain are a kind of grief, those who are in pain cry out, but those who are afraid keep silence? Is it because those who are in pain hold their breath (and so it is emitted all at once and comes forth with a loud cry), whereas the body of those who are afraid is chilled and the heat is carried downwards and creates breath? It creates breath in the particular region to which it is carried; hence those who are frightened fart. Now the voice is a rush of breath upwards in a particular manner and through certain channels; and the reason why those who are in pain hold the breath is that when we suffer anything (just as the other animals use their horns or teeth or claws in self-defence) we invariably make use straightway and without thought of the resources which we have in ourselves by nature, and against all or most forms of pain heat is helpful. This is what occurs when a man holds his breath; for he applies heat and concoction to the pain by collecting heat within him by means of the breath.

10 · Why is it that in those who are afraid the bowels are loosened and they desire to pass urine? Is it because the heat in us is as it were alive? It therefore flees whenever it is afraid of anything. Since, then, the fears due to nervousness and the like come from without and pass from the upper to the lower parts of the body and from the surface to the interior, the regions round the bowels and bladder becoming heated are loosened and make these organs ready to function. For anise and wormwood and all substances which promote the flow of urine have heating properties. Similarly the drugs which affect the bowels are those which cause heat in the lower parts of the body, and some of those which are applied merely[5] have a loosening effect, while others set up a further process of liquefaction, like garlic, which passes into the urine. Now heat coming from the surfaces of the body and meeting in these regions has the same effect as such drugs.

[5]Reading μόνον.

11 · Why do the sexual organs contract in those who are afraid? For one would expect the contrary to happen, namely, that they should become relaxed,   10 since the heat collects in this region in those who are afraid. Is it because those who are afraid are almost always as it were chilled? Their sexual organs therefore contract, because the heat has left the surface of the body; hence also those who are greatly frightened have internal rumblings. The surface of the body and the skin of those who are cold seems to contract, because the heat is driven out; and it is for this reason too that they shiver. Now the scrotum too contracts upwards and the testicles   15 also are lifted up with it as it is drawn in. This is more readily seen in the effect on the sexual organs; for fear causes excretion, and an emission of semen often occurs[6] in those who are nervous or greatly alarmed.   20

BOOK XXVIII

PROBLEMS CONNECTED WITH TEMPERANCE AND INTEMPERANCE, CONTINENCE AND INCONTINENCE

1 · Why is it that some men become ill when, after having been accustomed to live intemperately, they adopt a temperate mode of life? For example, Dionysius   25 the tyrant, when during the siege he ceased drinking for a short time, immediately became consumptive, until he changed his manner of life and began to drink again. Is it because in every one habit is a matter of importance, since it soon becomes nature? Just, then, as a fish would fare ill if it continued long in the air or a man if he continued long in the water, so those who alter their manner of life suffer from   30 the change, and a resumption of their accustomed mode of life is just as much their salvation as if they were returning to a natural condition. Furthermore, men waste away if they have been accustomed to large quantities of a particular diet; for if they do not receive their usual food, they are reduced to the condition in which they would be if they had no nourishment at all. Moreover, the excretions, when mixed   35 with a large quantity of food, disappear, but by themselves they rise to the surface and are carried to the eyes or lungs; whereas, if one takes nourishment, they mix with it and become diluted and harmless. But in those who live an intemperate life   949[b]1 the excretions become superabundant up to a certain point, when they cease from their accustomed mode of life, owing to the fact that much undigested matter is still present in them from their former manner of living; and, when this is melted, like a mass of snow, by the natural heat, the result is that violent fluxes take place.   5

2 · Why is it that we speak of men as incontinent in connexion with two only of the senses, namely, touch and taste? Is it because of the pleasures that result from these in us and in the other animals? Being then shared by the animals, they are

[6]Reading συμβαίνει.

held in least honour and so are regarded as the only pleasures deserving of reproach,
or at any rate more so than any others. So we blame a man who is a slave to them
and call him incontinent and intemperate, because he is a slave to the worst
pleasures.

3 · Why are men called incontinent in respect only of their desires, although
incontinence is possible also in anger? Is it because an incontinent man is one who
acts in some way contrary to reason, and incontinence is a mode of life which is
contrary to reason, and the desires are, generally speaking, contrary to reason?
Feelings of anger, on the other hand, are in consonance with reason, not in the sense
that reason prompts them, but in the sense that reason informs us of the insult or of
the charge made against us.

4 · Why is it that we approve most of continence and temperance in the
young and wealthy, and of justice in the poor? Is it because we feel most admiration
if a man abstains from what he most needs, rather than from the contrary? Now a
poor man needs resources, while a rich young man needs enjoyment.

5 · Why can men tolerate thirst less easily than hunger? Is it because thirst is
more painful? A proof that it is so is the fact that there is more pleasure in drinking
when one is thirsty than in eating when one is hungry. Now the contrary of what is
pleasant is more painful. Or is it because the heat whereby we live requires moisture
more?[1] Or is it because thirst is a desire for two things, namely, drink and food, but
hunger is a desire for only one, namely, food?

6 · Why can we endure thirst less than hunger? Is it because the former
causes us more pain? A proof of the pain it causes is the fact that the pleasure it
gives is more intense. Further, he who is thirsty needs two things, nourishment and
cooling, and drink provides both of these; but he who is hungry needs one of them
only.

7 · Why are men called incontinent if they indulge to excess in the pleasures
connected with touch and taste? (For those who are intemperate in sexual
intercourse and the enjoyments of eating and drinking are called incontinent; and in
the joys of eating and drinking the pleasure is partly in the tongue and partly in the
throat; hence Philoxenus longed for the throat of a crane.) And why is the term
incontinent never extended to the pleasures of sight and hearing? Is it because the
pleasures of touch and taste are common to us and the other animals? Being, then,
shared by the animals they are held in least honour and so are regarded as the only
pleasures deserving of reproach, or at any rate more so than any others. So we
blame a man who is a slave to them and call him incontinent and intemperate,
because he is a slave to the worst pleasures. Now the senses being five in number,
the other animals find pleasure only in the two already mentioned; in the others they

find no pleasure, or, if they do, it is only incidentally. For the lion[2] rejoices when he sees or scents his prey, because he is going to enjoy it;[3] and when he has satisfied his hunger, such things do not please him, just as the smell of dried fish gives us no   15 pleasure when we have eaten our fill of it, though, when we wanted to partake of it, it was pleasant.[4] The scent of the rose, on the other hand, is always pleasant.

8 · Why are men less able to restrain their laughter in the presence of friends? Is it because, when anything is especially elated, it is easily set in motion? Now benevolence causes elation,[5] so that laughter more readily moves us.   20

BOOK XXIX
PROBLEMS CONNECTED WITH JUSTICE
AND INJUSTICE

1 · Why is it that, although injustice is greater according as the good which is injured is greater, and honour is a greater good, yet injustice in the matter of money seems to be more serious and those who are unjust as regards money are considered more unjust? Is it because men prefer money to honour, and money is   25 common to all, whereas honour comes only to a few and its enjoyment is a rare occurrence?

2 · Why is it a more terrible thing to rob a man of a deposit than of a loan? Is it because it is disgraceful to wrong a friend? Now he who robs another of a deposit does wrong to a friend; for no one places a deposit with another unless he trusts him.   30 A creditor, on the other hand, is not a friend; for, if a man is a friend, he gives and does not lend. Or is it because the injustice is greater, since, in addition to the loss inflicted, he also violates his good faith, for the sake of which, if for no other reason, he ought to abstain from doing the wrong? Further, it is base not to requite like with like; for the one party in making the deposit regarded the other as his friend, but the   35 latter in robbing him treated him as an enemy; but a lender does not lend in the spirit of friendship. Again, a deposit is handed over to be guarded and returned, whereas the lender lends for his own advantage as well. Now we are less angry at losing if we are in pursuit of gain, like fishermen when they lose their bait; for the   950ᵇ1 risk is obvious. Again, those who make deposits are generally the victims of plots or misfortune, but it is the rich who lend money; and it is more terrible to wrong the unfortunate than the fortunate.

3 · Why is it that in some law courts the jury give their verdict in accordance   5 with the birth of the litigants rather than the provisions of the will? Is it because

---

[2]Reading ὁ λέων for ὁ ὁρῶν.
[3]Reading ἀπολαύσει.
[4]Reading ἡδέα.
[5]Reading ἡ δ' εὔνοια ἐξαίρει, ὥστε κινεῖ μᾶλλον τὸ γελοῖον.

about birth it is impossible to lie, but the truth must be declared, whereas before now many wills have been proved to be forged?

4 · Why is it that poverty is more commonly found amongst the good than
10 amongst the bad? Is it because, being universally hated and despised, she takes refuge with the good, thinking that with them she is most likely to find safety and a place of habitation; whereas she thinks that if she goes to the wicked, they would never remain content with the same condition but would steal or plunder, in which
15 case she could no longer remain with them? Or is it because she thinks that the good will treat her better than any one else and that she is least likely to be insulted by them? So, just as we place deposits of money with good men, so she of her own accord ranges herself with them. Or is it because, being of the female sex, she is
20 more helpless, so that she needs the assistance of the good? Or is it because, being herself an evil, she will not betake herself to that which is evil, since if she were to choose the evil, her position would be quite irremediable?

5 · Why is it that wrongs in other matters are not so liable to be committed on a large scale as those in respect of money?[1] For example, a man who has spoken a light word would not therefore necessarily divulge a secret, nor[2] would one who has
25 betrayed an individual also betray a city, as a man who has stolen an obol would steal a talent also. Is it because, though there are forms of unjust disposition which are worse, the acts resulting from them are less serious owing to lack of power?

6 · Why is it more disgraceful[3] to rob a man of a small deposit than of a large loan? Is it because he who robs another of a deposit is deceiving a man who thought
30 him to be honest? Or is it because he who commits the one crime would commit the other also?

7 · Why is it that man, who of all animals has the advantage of most education, is yet the most unjust of all? Is it because he possesses the power of reasoning to the greatest degree, and has therefore most carefully estimated the
35 pleasures and happiness, and these are impossible of attainment without injustice?

8 · Why is it that wealth is more often found in the hands of the wicked than in those of the good? Is it because, being blind, it cannot read men's hearts and choose the best?

951ᵃ1 **9** · Why is it considered more just to defend the dead than the living? Is it because those who are alive can look after themselves, but a dead man can no longer do so?

---

[1]Reading χρήματα.
[2]Reading οὐδέ for ἀλλά.
[3]Reading αἴσχιον.

10 · Why is it that a man who associates with one who is healthy does not himself become any healthier, nor does association with the strong or beautiful improve a man's condition, whereas association with the just and temperate and good does have this effect? Is it because some qualities can, and others cannot, be imitated by the soul, goodness being a quality of the soul and health of the body? A man can, therefore, accustom himself to feel pleasure and pain under the proper circumstances; but his association with the healthy does not produce this result, for health does not consist in taking pleasure or not in certain things, since none of these things can produce health.

11 · Why is it more terrible to kill a woman than a man, although the male is naturally superior to the female? Is it because she is weaker and so he commits a greater[4] injustice? Or is it because it is not a manly act to use one's strength against that which is greatly inferior?

12 · Why is the defendant given the position on the right hand in a law court? Is it from a desire to equalize matters? Since, then, the plaintiff possesses other advantages, the defendant is given the advantage of position. Further, as a rule defendants are under guard; and, if the defendant has the right-hand position, the guard is on his right.

13 · Why is it that, when the votes for the plaintiff and for the defendant are shown to be equal, the defendant wins the case? Is it because the defendant has heard only during the course of the trial itself[5] the charges against which he has to make his defence and produce the witnesses to refute the accusations,[6] if any advantage is to be obtained from them? Now it is not easy for a man to foresee of what he ought to provide witnesses or some other kind of evidence to prove his innocence. The plaintiff, on the other hand, can act as he pleases, and can begin to take action before having the summons issued; and even after he has summoned his opponent he can invent and bring against him any plausible accusation he likes. The lawgiver, then, recognizing that the defendant has the disadvantage in all these respects, has given him any advantage which may accrue from the disagreement of the jury. And, indeed, that defendants are at a disadvantage is shown by the fact that when men are in a state of alarm they omit much of what they ought to have said or done, and defendants are, generally speaking, always in greater danger; and so, if they omit necessary parts of their defence, when they are put on a level with their opponents in respect of their claims, they would clearly have been victorious if they had not omitted anything.

Further, any one of us would prefer to pass a sentence acquitting a wrong-doer rather than condemn as guilty one who is innocent, in the case, for example, of a

---

[4]Reading μείζω for ἐλάττω.
[5]Reading αυτῷ.
[6]Omitting τό and ἔχεσθαι.

man being accused of enslavement or murder. For we should prefer to acquit either of such persons, though the charges brought against them by their accuser were
5   true, rather than condemn them if they were untrue; for, when any doubt is entertained, the less grave error ought to be preferred; it is a serious matter to decide that a slave is free; yet it is much more serious to convict a freeman of being a slave.

Further, if one man brings a charge and another disputes his claim to any piece
10 of property, we do not consider that we ought to award the disputed property immediately to the plaintiff, but that the man in possession ought to enjoy it until the matter is decided. Similarly, when a number of persons are involved in a case and the numbers of those who declare that a wrong has been committed and of those who deny it are equal—just as in the case cited above when one man brought an accusation, while another denied the truth of it—we consider that the lawgiver is
15 right in not handing over the disputed property to the accuser but allowing the defendant to remain in possession until the plaintiff[7] has established some superiority. Similarly, when the votes of the jury are equal and so neither side has the superiority, the lawgiver has allowed matters to be left as they are.

Again, in serious crimes the punishments are also heavy, so that, if the jury
20 pass an unjust sentence and then change their mind,[8] it is impossible to take the opportunity of remedying the mistake; if, on the other hand, they acquit the accused when they ought not to do so, if he lives so circumspectly as never to commit any crime again, how can the jury have made a serious mistake in failing to condemn such a man to death? If, however, he subsequently commits a crime, the law would
25 consider that he ought to be punished for both crimes.

Or is it because it is the mark of a more unjust man to commit acts of injustice for which one is less likely to be unjustly accused.[9] For wrong-doing may be due to anger or fear or desire and to many other causes, and not only to intent, but an
30 unjust accusation is generally due to intent. So when the votes have proved equal, indicating both[10] that the accuser has brought an unjust charge and that the defendant is in the wrong, the unjust accuser being judged the offender, the lawgiver has awarded the legal victory to the defendant.

Again, we ourselves adopt the attitude towards our servants that, when we
35 suspect that they have committed a crime and have no certain knowledge, but nevertheless think that they have done the deed, we do not immediately proceed to punish them; and when we cannot pursue our inquiries any further, we acquit them
952ª1 of blame.

Further, he who from intent commits a crime does a greater wrong than he who does not act from intent. Now the man who brings a vexatious charge against another always does wrong from intent, whereas he who commits any other crime may happen to do so either under compulsion or through ignorance or by some other
5   chance. But when the votes are equal, the prosecutor has been judged by half the

---

[7]Reading διώκων for ἀδικῶν.
[8]Reading μεταγνοῦσιν.
[9]The text of this sentence is uncertain.
[10]Reading τό τ'.

jury to be committing a wrong from intent, while the defendant is considered by the remainder to be in the wrong, but not from intent; and so, since the prosecutor is judged guilty of a more serious wrong than the defendant, the lawgiver has rightly decided that he who has committed the less serious wrong wins the case.

Further, a man is always more unjust who does not expect to escape the   10
observation of the man whom he wrongs and nevertheless commits the wrong, than he who expects to remain undiscovered. Now he who brings a vexatious charge against another does not expect to escape the observation of the man whom he falsely accuses, whereas those who commit any other crime usually try to commit an injustice with the expectation of doing so without the knowledge of their victims, so that plaintiffs ought to be regarded as more unjust than defendants.   15

14 · Why is it that, if a man steals from the baths or the wrestling-school or the market or any similar place, he is punished with death, whereas if he steals from a house he merely pays back double the value of what he has stolen? Is it because in houses it is possible in some way or other to safeguard one's property? For the wall   20
is strong and there is a key, and it is the business of all the slaves in the house to see that the contents of the house are kept safe. At the baths, however, and in places which are similarly public, it is easy for any one who wishes to commit a crime; for those who place their property there have no sure means of guarding it except their   25
own eyes, so that, if one takes one's eye off it for a moment, it is immediately placed at the mercy of the thief. Hence the lawgiver, considering that bathers are not able to guard their property, has set the law to guard against thieves by threatening that they shall lose their lives if they appropriate the possessions of others.

Further, the owner of a house is responsible for admitting into it whom he   30
wishes and for introducing into it any one whom he does not trust; but the man who deposits any property in a bath cannot prevent any one from coming in, nor can he prevent him, when he has entered, from placing his garments next to his own when he has stripped himself; but, contrary to his wishes, the clothing of the thief and of   35
the man who is about to be robbed lie together in a confused heap. Therefore the lawgiver has prescribed not very heavy penalties to help the man who of his own free will and by his own mistake has admitted the thief to his house, but has clearly fixed   952ᵇ1
heavy penalties for theft to aid those who are obliged to share with others the right of entrance and the promiscuity of the baths.

Further, it is obvious that all those who commit theft in places the entrance to which is open to any one who wishes to come are bad men,[11] and so, if they are   5
allowed to live, do not desire to have the semblance of honest men even for the future advantage which they can gain from it, regarding it as useless to pretend to be honest in the eyes of those who know their real character; they therefore continue henceforward to be openly wicked. Those, on the other hand, whose wickedness is known to one person only, try to persuade that person by bribery not to make known   10
their real character to the rest of the world; they are not likely therefore to be

---

[11] Reading πονηροί.

completely wicked for ever, and so the penalty which the lawgiver has fixed for them is less severe.

Further, of all crimes those which are committed in the most crowded
15 meetings and assemblies bring most disgrace upon the city, just as public orderliness brings the greatest credit; for it is at public gatherings that the citizens are most conspicuous to each other and the rest of the world. The result, therefore, of such thefts is that not only is the man who loses his property personally injured, but also abuse is heaped upon the city. This is why the lawgiver has fixed heavier
20 penalties for such thieves than for those who abstract property from a private house.

Again, the man who loses anything from a private house is in a place where it is easy for him to bear his misfortune, since he is in his own home and neither suffers anything nor is jeered at by others. But the man who is robbed at the baths finds it
25 difficult to leave without his clothing, and, in addition, is usually jeered at by others; and this is harder to bear than the actual loss. Therefore the lawgiver has prescribed heavier penalties to assist such persons.

Again, many legislative parallels can be found for these penalties. For example, if any one speaks evil of a magistrate the punishment is severe, but there is no penalty for speaking evil of an ordinary individual; and rightly so, for the
30 legislator considers that the slanderer not only commits an offence against the magistrate but also insults the city. Similarly, a man who commits a theft at the harbour is considered not only to harm the individual whom he robs, but also to bring disgrace upon the city. And the same is true of any crime committed in a place
35 of public meeting.

15 · Why is it that in law courts, if equal votes are given for the two adversaries, the defendant wins the case? Is it because the defendant has remained
953ᵃ1 unaffected by the action of the plaintiff, and in a position of equality with him he would probably have won?

16 · Why is it that for theft the punishment is death, whereas for assault, which is a more serious crime, the penalty or fine is assessable in court? Is it because
5 to commit an assault is an act of human weakness, of which all more or less partake, whereas there is no force which compels us to theft? A further reason is the fact that a man who tries to commit theft would think nothing of committing assault also.

BOOK XXX

PROBLEMS CONNECTED WITH PRACTICAL WISDOM, INTELLIGENCE, AND WISDOM

10   1 · Why is it that all those who have become eminent in philosophy or politics or poetry or the arts are clearly of an atrabilious temperament, and some of them to such an extent as to be affected by diseases caused by black bile, as is said to

have happened to Heracles among the heroes? For he appears to have been of this nature, and that is why epileptic afflictions were called by the ancients 'the sacred disease' after him. That his temperament was atrabilious is shown by the fury which he displayed towards his children and the eruption of sores which took place before his disappearance on Mount Oeta; for this often occurs as the result of black bile. Lysander the Lacedaemonian also suffered from similar sores before his death. There are also the stories of Ajax and Bellerophon, of whom the former became insane, while the latter sought out habitations in desert places; that is why Homer writes,

> And since of all the gods he was hated,
> Verily o'er the Aleïan plain alone he would wander,
> Eating his own heart out, avoiding the pathway of mortals.[1]

And many others of the heroes seem to have been similarly afflicted, and among men of recent times Empedocles, Plato, and Socrates, and numerous other well-known men, and also most of the poets. For many such persons have bodily afflictions as the result of this kind of temperament, while some of them obviously possess a natural inclination to affections of this kind; in a word, they all, as has been said, are naturally atrabilious. The cause of this may be understood if we first take an example from the effect of wine, which if taken in large quantities appears to produce such qualities as we attribute to the atrabilious, inducing, as it is drunk, many different characteristics, making men for instance irritable, benevolent, compassionate, or reckless; whereas no such results are produced by honey or milk or water or anything similar. One can easily see that wine has a variety of effects by observing how it gradually changes those who drink it; for, finding them chilled and taciturn as the result of abstinence, a small quantity makes them more talkative, while a larger quantity makes them eloquent and bold, and, when they proceed to action, reckless, and a still larger quantity makes them insolent and afterwards frenzied, while outrageous excess enfeebles them and makes them stupid like those who have been epileptic from childhood, and very similar to those who are exceedingly atrabilious. As, therefore, an individual as he drinks and takes wine in different quantities changes his character, so there are men who embody each character. For the temporary condition of one man when he is drunk is the permanent character of another, and one man is loquacious, another emotional, another easily moved to tears; for wine has this effect also on some people and therefore Homer writes,

> He says that I swim in tears, like a man that is heavy with drinking.[2]

Others become compassionate or savage or taciturn; for some maintain a complete silence, especially those atrabilious subjects who are out of their minds. Wine also makes men amorous; as is shown by the fact that a man who is drinking is induced to kiss those whom, owing to their appearance or age, no sober person would kiss. Wine then gives a man extraordinary characteristics, but for a short time only,

[1] *Iliad* VI 200.
[2] *Odyssey* XIX 122.

while nature gives them permanently for the period of a lifetime; for some men are
20   bold, others taciturn, others compassionate, and others cowardly by nature. It is
therefore clear that each characteristic is produced by wine and by nature by the
same means; for the whole body functions under the control of heat. Now both the
juice and the atrabilious temperament are full of wind; and that is why the
25   physicians say that flatulence and disorders of the stomach are due to black bile.
Now wine has the quality of containing air; so wine and the atrabilious temperament are similar in nature. The froth which forms on wine shows that it contains air;
for oil does not produce froth, although it is hot, but wine produces it in large
30   quantities and red wine more than white because it contains more heat and
substance. It is for this reason that wine excites sexual desire, and Dionysus and
Aphrodite are rightly coupled together, and atrabilious persons are generally
lustful. For sexual desire is due to the presence of breath, as is shown by the fact
35   that the penis quickly increases from a small to a large size by inflation; also boys
before they are capable of emitting semen find a certain pleasure in rubbing their
sexual organs through lust when they are approaching the age of puberty, and the
swelling of the organ becomes manifest because breath passes through the passages
through which the semen subsequently passes; also the effusion and impetus of the
954ª1   semen in sexual intercourse is clearly due to propulsion by the breath. So those
foods and liquids which fill the region of the sexual organs with breath are rightly
regarded as aphrodisiac. Thus red wine more than anything else produces the
5   condition found in atrabilious persons.[3] This condition is obvious in some individuals; for most atrabilious persons are thin and their veins stand out, the reason being
the abundance not of blood but of breath. The reason why all atrabilious persons are
10   not thin[4] or dark, but only those who contain particularly unhealthy humours, is
stated elsewhere.
     But to return to our previous subject of discussion, this humour, namely, the
atrabilious, is originally mingled in the bodily nature, for it is a mixture of heat and
cold, of which two things the bodily nature consists. Black bile, therefore, becomes
15   both very hot and very cold, for the same thing naturally admits both heat and cold,
like water, which, though cold, yet when it is sufficiently heated (for example, when
it boils) is hotter than the actual flame which heats it, and similarly a stone or a
piece of iron when thoroughly heated becomes hotter than charcoal, though they
20   are naturally cold. (This subject has been dealt with more clearly in the treatise on
fire.) Now black bile, which is naturally cold and not on the surface, being in the
condition mentioned above, if it abounds in the body, produces apoplexy or torpor or
despondency or fear; but when it is overheated, it produces cheerfulness accompa-
25   nied by song, and frenzy, and the breaking forth of sores, and the like. In most
people then black bile engendered from their daily nutriment does not change their
character, but merely produces an atrabilious disease. But those who naturally
possess an atrabilious temperament immediately develop diverse characters in
30   accordance with their various temperaments; for example, those who are originally

---

[3]Omitting πνευματώδεις.
[4]Reading σκληροί.

full of cold black bile become dull and stupid, whereas those who possess a large quantity of hot black bile become frenzied or clever or erotic or easily moved to anger and desire, while some become more loquacious. Many too, if this heat approaches the region of the intellect, are affected by diseases of frenzy and possession; and this is the origin of Sibyls and soothsayers and all inspired persons, when they are affected not by disease but by natural temperament. Maracus, the Syracusan, was actually a better poet when he was out of his mind. Those in whom the excessive heat dies down[5] to a mean temperature are atrabilious, but they have more practical wisdom and are less eccentric and in many respects superior to others either in education or in the arts or in public life. In respect too of facing dangers an atrabilious state causes great variation, in that many of those who are in this condition are inconsistent under the influence of[6] fears; for they vary from time to time according to the state in which their bodies happen to be in respect of their atrabilious temperament. Now this temperament is itself also inconsistent, just as it produces inconsistency in those suffering from the diseases which it causes; for, like water, it is sometimes cold and sometimes hot. And so the announcement of something alarming, if it occurs at a time when the temperament is rather cold, makes a man cowardly; for it has already prepared a way for the entrance of fear, and fear has a chilling effect (as is shown by the fact that those who are greatly alarmed tremble). If, however, the temperament is inclined to be hot, fear reduces it to a moderate temperature and causes a man to be in his senses and unexcited. So too with the despondency which occurs in everyday life (for we are often in the condition of feeling grief without being able to ascribe any cause for it, while at other times we feel cheerful without knowing why), such feelings and those usually called superficial[7] feelings occur to a slight degree in every one, for something of the force which produces them is mingled in everyone; but those who are thoroughly penetrated by them acquire them as a permanent part of their nature. For as men differ in appearance not because they possess faces but because they possess certain kinds of faces, some handsome, others ugly, others with nothing remarkable about them (those, that is, who are naturally ordinary); so those who possess an atrabilious temperament in a slight degree are ordinary, but those who have much of it are quite unlike the majority of people. For, if their condition is quite complete, they are very atrabilious; but, if they possess a mixed temperament, they are men of genius. If they neglect their health, they have a tendency towards the atrabilious diseases, the part of the body affected varying in different people; in some persons epileptic symptoms declare themselves, in others apoplectic, in others violent despondency or terrors, in others over-confidence, as happened to Archelaus, King of Macedonia. The force which gives rise to such a condition is the temperament according as it contains heat or cold. If it is cold beyond due measure, it produces groundless despondency; hence suicide by hanging occurs most frequently among the young, but sometimes also among older men. Many men too put an end to

---

[5]Reading ἐπανεθῇ ἡ ἄγαν θερμότης.
[6]Reading ἐν for μέν.
[7]Reading ἐπιπόλαια for παλαιά.

themselves after drunkenness, and some atrabilious persons continue in a state of despondency after drinking; for the heat of the wine quenches their natural heat. Heat in the region in which we think and form hopes makes us cheerful; and for this reason all men are eager to drink until they become intoxicated, for abundance of wine makes all men hopeful, just as their youth makes children sanguine; for old age is despairing but youth is full of hope. There are a few who are seized with despondency while they are drinking, for the same reason as makes others despondent after drinking. Those then who become despondent as the heat in them dies down tend to hang themselves. Hence the young are more likely than the old to hang themselves; for old age makes the heat die down, and so, in the young, does their condition, which is itself natural.[8] When the heat is extinguished suddenly, most men make away with themselves to the general astonishment of all, since they have given no previous sign of any such intention. When the temperament caused by the admixture of black bile is colder, it gives rise, as has been already remarked, to despondency of various kinds, but when it is hotter to cheerfulness. Hence the young are more cheerful, the old more despondent, the former being hot and the latter cold; for old age is a process of cooling. Extinction takes place suddenly from external causes, just as objects which have been heated in the fire are cooled by unnatural processes, as for example when water is poured over hot coals. Hence men sometimes commit suicide after drunkenness; for the heat of the wine is introduced from outside, and when it is extinguished the condition which leads to suicide is set up. Also after sexual intercourse most people tend to be despondent; those, however, who emit a considerable amount of excrement with the semen become more cheerful, for they are relieved of an excess of excrement and breath and heat. But those who indulge in sexual intercourse are often more despondent, for by so doing they become cooled, because they lose something which is valuable, as is shown by the fact that the amount of semen which is emitted is not great.

To sum the matter up, owing to the fact that the effect of black bile is variable, atrabilious persons also show variation; for the black bile becomes very hot and very cold. And because it has an effect upon the character (for heat and cold have such an effect to a greater extent than anything else in us), like wine mingling in a stronger or weaker form in the body, it gives us our own special characters. Now both wine and black bile are full of breath. And since it is possible for a variable state to be well tempered and in a sense a favourable condition, and since it is possible for the condition to be hotter and then again cold, when it should be so, or to change to the contrary owing to excess, the result is that all atrabilious persons have remarkable gifts, not owing to disease but from natural causes.

2 · Why do we say that we acquire a disposition as the result of pursuing some sciences but not others? Are we said to acquire a disposition only by such sciences as enable us to make discoveries, since discovery is the result of a habit?

---

[8]Omitting τὸ μαραινόμενον θερμόν.

3 · Why is it that of all the animals man has most practical wisdom? Is it
because he has the smallest head in proportion to his body? Or is it because he is   5
abnormally small in certain parts? For that is why his head is small, and among
men those who have smaller heads have more practical wisdom than those who have
larger heads.

4 · Why is it that a journey seems longer when we traverse it without
knowing its length than when we know it, all other conditions being equal? Is it   10
because to know its length is to be able to connect a number with it? For that which
cannot be numbered is the same as the infinite, and the infinite is always more than
the determinate. Just as, therefore, if one knows that a journey is a certain length it
must necessarily be finite, so if one does not know its length one as it were converts   15
the proposition and the mind draws a false conclusion, and this journey appears
infinite. Furthermore,[9] a quantity is determinate, and that which is determinate is a
quantity; therefore when a thing does not appear determinate it will appear to be as
it were infinite, because that which is of a nature to be determined, if it is not so, is
infinite, and that which appears not to be determined necessarily appears in a sense   20
unlimited.

5 · Why is it that, whereas we become more intelligent as we grow older, yet
the younger we are the more easily we can learn? Is it because God has given us two
instruments within ourselves, which enable us to use external instruments, providing the body with the hand and the soul with intelligence? For intelligence is among   25
the things implanted in us by nature, being as it were an instrument; and, whereas
the sciences and arts are among the things created by us, intelligence is one of the
gifts of nature. So just as we cannot use the hand to the best advantage immediately
after birth, but only when nature has perfected it (for the hand can perform its   30
particular function best as age progresses), in like manner of our natural endowments reason is of most assistance to us not in early life but as we get old, and is then
at its highest perfection, unless it becomes incapacitated by anything, as may
happen also to the other natural endowments. Intelligence comes to us later than
the faculty of using the hands, because the instruments used by the intelligence are   35
posterior to those used by the hands. For science is an instrument of the intelligence
(for it is useful to the intelligence just as flutes are useful to the flute-player), and
many things in nature are instruments of the hands, but nature itself and its
creations are prior to science. Now it is natural that where the instruments are
prior, the faculties should also come into being in us first (for it is by using the
instruments that we acquire a disposition); and the instrument of each faculty is   956ᵃ1
related similarly to that faculty, and conversely, as the instruments are to one
another, so are the faculties of which[10] they are the instruments to one another.
Intelligence then for this reason comes to us when we are older; but we learn more
quickly when we are young because we do not yet know anything, and when we   5

---

⁹Reading ἔτι.   ¹⁰Reading οὕτως ὦν.

know more we are no longer so well able to acquire knowledge,[11] just as we remember best what we come upon early in the day, and then, as the day goes on, are less able to remember what happens, because we have come into contact with a
10   number of incidents.

6 · Why should man be obeyed more than any other animal? Is it because, as Plato answered Neocles, he alone of all the animals can count? Or is it because he is the only animal that believes in gods? Or is it because he is the most imitative (for it is for this reason that he can learn)?

15   7 · Why is it that we feel no pleasure in the contemplation or anticipation of the fact that the interior angles of a triangle are equal to two right angles, and similar geometrical truths—except in so far as we enjoy the speculation, and the pleasure of this is always the same and would be equally great if these angles were equal to three or more right angles—but we rejoice at the recollection of an
20   Olympic victory or the sea-battle at Salamis, and at the anticipation of such events, but not in their opposites? Is it because[12] we rejoice in such events as having taken place or taking place, but as regards what happens in the course of nature the contemplation of the real state of affairs alone causes us pleasure, whereas actions
25   give rise to the pleasure caused by their results? Since, then, actions are various, their results too are sometimes painful and sometimes pleasant; and we avoid and pursue anything in accordance with pleasure and pain.

8 · Why do doctors continue their treatment only until health is restored? For the doctor reduces the patient, and next dries his body, then creates a healthy
30   condition and at that point stops. Is it because it is impossible for any other condition to be produced from health? Or, if it is possible, is it the task of another science, and will what is produced from health be something different? Now, if health is produced from conditions which are its opposite or are intermediate between health and sickness, it is obvious that the patient is sick because he is too moist or too dry or something else. The doctor, then, from a state of cold creates a
35   less extreme condition and, finally, a condition of a certain heat or dryness or moisture by change from the opposite or intermediate condition, until he achieves a state which is such as to constitute a condition of health; and from this no condition can be produced except one which is intermediate between health and sickness. The possessor of the art can, then, create some new condition; for, when he has reached a certain point, he can retrace his steps and undo his work; but the doctor's *art* has nothing to do with such a course, for its aim is always to create a better condition. So neither the doctor's art nor any other art will create anything else out of health; for
956ᵇ1   either nothing would be being produced, or else the opposite of health, if the same science were being employed (so too out of a house nothing could make its contrary): nor is there any other art[13] which can make anything out of health,

---

[11]Reading δυνάμεθα δέχεσθαι for δυνάμεθα. δυνάμεθα δὲ ἔχεσθαι.
[12]Reading τοιούτοις; ἢ ὅτι.
[13]Reading ἄλλη for ἐν ἄλλῃ.

except as making a whole out of a part, as, for example, when the cobbler's art makes a shoe out of the front part of a shoe; for these two things can be produced out of one another by two processes, one of composition and the other of destruction.   5

9 · Why is it generally considered that the philosopher is superior to the orator? Is it because the philosopher spends his time in studying the actual forms of things, while the orator deals with what participates in them—the former considering what injustice and tyranny are, the latter urging that a certain individual is unjust or dealing with the character of a tyrant?   10

10 · Why are theatrical artists generally persons of bad character? Is it because they partake but little of reason and wisdom,[14] because most of their life is spent in the pursuit of the arts which provide their daily needs, and because the greater part of their life is passed in incontinence and often in want, and both these things prepare the way to villainy?   15

11 · Why did the men of old institute prizes for physical contests but none for wisdom? Is it because in all fairness the judges should in the intellectual sphere be either the superiors or at any rate not the inferiors of the competitors? Now if those who were pre-eminent in wisdom had to compete and a prize had been offered,   20 they would have no one to act as judges. In athletic contests, however, anyone can judge by merely using his eyes. Further, the original institutor of the games did not wish to propose to the Greeks such a contest[15] as would be likely to produce violent disputes and enmity; for when one is rejected or accepted in a contest of bodily   25 strength, men do not altogether harbour any grievance nor feel sentiments of enmity towards the judges, but they feel great wrath and indignation against those who decide their relative wisdom or worthlessness; and this is a quarrelsome and bad state of affairs. Furthermore, the prize ought to be better than the contest; for   30 in athletic games the prize is more desirable than, and superior to, the contest. But what prize could be found superior to wisdom?

12 · Why is it that man in particular thinks one thing and does another? Is it because the same science deals with contraries? Or is it because the intelligence has many objects, desire one? Now man usually lives by the intelligence, the animals by   35 appetite, passion, and desire.

13 · Why is it that some prudent men spend their time acquiring rather than using? Is it because they are following the habit of doing so? Or is it due to the pleasure of anticipation?

14 · Why do those who sleep deeply and most pleasantly see no visions? Is it because sensation and thought function because the mind is at rest? And this seems

---

[14]Reading λόγου καὶ σοφίας.
[15]Reading ἐξ ἧς for ἐξ ὧν.

957ᵃ1 to be knowledge because knowledge brings the soul to rest; for when it is in motion and being carried along it can neither have sensation nor think. Hence it is that children and those who are drunk and the insane are senseless; for, owing to the abundance of heat present in them, they are in a state of considerable and very
5 violent movement, but when this ceases they become more sensible; for, when the thought is undisturbed, they can control it better. Those who have visions during their sleep dream because thought is checked, and in proportion as it is at rest. For the mind is greatly moved during sleep, since, when heat collects in the interior from
10 the rest of the body, there is very considerable and violent movement; and it is not true, as most people suppose, that it is most at rest and by itself, and especially so when no vision is seen. The contrary is really true; for because it is in considerable movement and never rests for a moment, it cannot think. And it is naturally in most
15 movement when it sleeps most pleasantly, because it is then in particular that the greatest amount of heat collects in the interior of the body. That, when it is in motion, the mind cannot think, not only in its waking hours but also in sleep, is proved by the fact that one is least likely to see visions during the sleep which
20 follows the taking of food; now this is the time when the mind is most disturbed owing to the nourishment which has been introduced into the body. A vision occurs when sleep comes over us while we are thinking or letting things pass before our eyes. Hence we usually see things which we are doing or intend or wish to do; for it is
25 on these things that our thoughts and fancies most often dwell. And the better men are, the better are their dreams, because they think of better things in their waking hours, while those who are less well disposed in mind or body have worse dreams. For there is a close correspondence between the disposition of the body and the
30 images of our dreams; for, when a man is ill, the ideas proposed by his thoughts are bad, and furthermore, owing to the disturbance which reigns in his body, his mind cannot rest. It is for this reason that atrabilious persons start in their sleep, because, owing to the excess of heat, the mind is in a state of too much movement, and, when
35 the movement is too violent, they cannot sleep.

BOOK XXXI

PROBLEMS CONNECTED
WITH THE EYES

1 · Why does rubbing the eye stop sneezing? Is it because by this means evaporation is given to the moisture? For the eye sheds tears after friction, and
957ᵇ1 sneezing is due to an abundance of moisture. Or is it because the lesser heat is destroyed by the greater? Now the eye when it is rubbed acquires more heat than is contained in the nose; and for this reason even if we rub the nose itself the sneezing stops.

2 . Why can one see more accurately with one eye than with both eyes? Is it 5
because more movements are set up by the two eyes, as certainly happens in those
who squint? The movement of the two eyes, therefore, is not one, but that of a single
eye is one; therefore one sees less accurately with both eyes.

3 . Why do the eyes tend to become very red in those who are angry, and the
ears in those who are ashamed? Is it because the eyes are chilled in those who are 10
ashamed (for 'shame dwells in the eyes'), so that[1] they cannot look straight in front
of them? (Cowardice also involves a cooling in the same region.) Now the heat[2]
travels in a direction away from the forepart of the head, and the ears are situated in
the opposite part of the head, and therefore they redden most under the emotion of
shame. But under the influence of provocation assistance is sent to the more 15
sensitive and easily affected part, as though it were suffering violence; for in those
who are frightened it fails altogether there.

4 . Why is it that, if one eye is held down, the other has a more intent gaze?
Is it because the origins of sight in the two eyes are connected at one source? So
when one eye moves, the common source of sight is also set in motion; and when this 20
moves, the other eye moves also. When one eye therefore is held down, all the
movement will be concentrated on the other eye, which consequently will be able to
gaze more intently.

5 . Why is it that those who are blind from birth do not become bald? Is it
because the eye is injured by the presence of a large quantity of moisture in the
region of the head? This is why they cauterize the veins round the temples of those 25
who suffer from running at the eyes (thus closing the ducts through which the
humours flow), and scrape the head, cutting into the skin upon it. Since, therefore,
it is the excretion gathering in the head which injures the eyes, this same excretion
by collecting in too great quantities in the head might prevent the eyes from
originally coming into being at all. And since the hair grows from excretions, and 30
the excretion in the head of those who are blind from birth is abundant, it is only
natural that they are not bald.

6 . Why are those whose eyes protrude affected more than others by smoke?
Is it because smoke reaches the projecting parts most quickly?

7 . Why is it that we can turn the gaze of both eyes simultaneously towards 35
the right and the left and in the direction of the nose, and that of one eye to the left
or to the right, but cannot direct them simultaneously one to the right and the other
to the left? Similarly, we can direct them downwards and upwards; for we can turn
them simultaneously in the same direction, but not separately. Is it because the

[1]Reading ὥστ' ἀντιβλέπειν.
[2]Reading τὸ θερμόν.

eyes, though two, are connected at one point, and under such conditions, when one
958ᵃ1 extremity moves, the other must follow in the same direction, for one extremity
becomes the source of movement to the other extremity? Since, therefore, it is
impossible for one thing to move simultaneously in contrary directions, it is
impossible also for the eyes to do so; for the extremities would move in opposite
5 directions if one moved up and the other down, and the source of the movement of
both of them would have to make corresponding movements, which is impossible.
The squinting of the eyes is due to the fact that the eyeballs possess a moving
principle and turn, to a certain extent,[3] upwards and downwards and sideways.
When, therefore, being so placed that they are in a similar position to one another
10 and midway between an upward and a downward and an oblique movement, the
two eyeballs catch the visual ray on corresponding points of themselves, they do not
have a squint and their gaze is perfectly steady (though when they catch the visual
rays on corresponding points of themselves, although the vision does not squint they
15 differ.) Yet, if you turn up the whites of the eyes, part of the pupil is obscured, as for
example in those who are about to sneeze; others have oblique vision, madmen for
example; in others the gaze is turned towards the nose, as in tragic masks and in
those who are nervous, for their glance denotes concentrated thought. But those
who keep their gaze fixed on one point without having their eyeballs similarly
situated, or who have them similarly situated but do not keep them fixed on the
20 same point, both these have squints; they therefore scowl and screw up the eyes, for
they try to fix one eyeball in the same position as the other; so they leave one eye
alone and try to bring the other into position. If the vision of both eyes does not rest
on the same point,[4] they must squint; for the same thing happens as in those to
25 whom, when they press under the eye, a single object appears double, for in these
too the source of vision is disturbed. If, therefore, the eye is moved upwards, the
terminus of the vision is lowered; if downwards, it is raised. And if the position of
30 one eye is changed, the object of the vision therefore seems to move up or down,
because the vision also does so, but it does not appear double unless the vision of
both eyes is in use. A similar squint[5] occurs also in one whose eyes do not
correspond, causing him to see double; but this is due to the position of the vision,
because it is not in the middle of the eye.

35   8 · Why do those who are short-sighted write in small characters? For it is
strange that those who have not acute vision should do what requires such vision. Is
it because small things appear large when they are near at hand, and the
short-sighted hold what they are writing close to their eyes? Or is it because they
screw up their eyes when they write? For owing to the feebleness of their sight, if
958ᵇ1 they write with their eyes wide open, the vision, being dispersed, can only see dimly;
but when the eyes are screwed up, it all falls on one point, and, since it forms a small
angle, it necessarily causes the writing of small characters.

³Reading μέχρι του.
⁴Reading κατὰ ταὐτό.
⁵Reading ὦσιν. καὶ διαστροφή.

9 . Why can some people see more clearly after suffering from ophthalmia? Is it because their eyes are thus purged? For often the external thickening blocks the vision, but is dissolved when the eye discharges. Hence also it is beneficial that the eyes should be made to smart, with onion for example; but a substance of the opposite kind, such as marjoram, has an adverse effect.

10 . Why are those who see with only one eye less liable to disturbance of the vision? Is it because their mind is less affected, and so the disturbance of the vision is less felt?

11 . Why do objects appear double to those whose eyes are distorted? Is it because the movement does not reach the same point on each of the eyes? So the mind thinks that it sees two objects when it really sees one twice. A similar phenomenon occurs if one crosses the fingers; for a single object appears to be two to a single person touching it twice.

12 . Why is it that the senses on the right side of the body are not superior to those on the left side, but in all other respects the right side of the body is superior? Is it a question of habit, namely, that we accustom ourselves immediately to perceive equally well with the senses on both sides of the body? And it seems that the superiority of the right-hand parts of the body is due to habit, for we can accustom ourselves to be ambidextrous. Or is it because to feel sensation is to be passive, and the right parts of the body are superior in that they are more active and less passive than the left?

13 . Why is it that in all other respects the right side of the body is superior, but in sensation the two sides are alike? Is it because we habitually practise the equal use of sensation on both sides? Moreover, to feel sensation is to be passive, and the superiority of the right side of the body is shown in activity, not in passivity.

14 . Why is physical exercise detrimental to acuteness of vision? Is it because it makes the eye dry, as it does the rest of the body? Now dryness hardens every kind of skin; so it has that effect also on the skin covering the pupil. This is also the reason why the aged have not acute vision; for their eyes have a hard and wrinkled surface, and so the vision is obscured.

15 . Why do the short-sighted, though they have not acute vision, write in small characters? Yet it is characteristic of acute vision to see what is small. Is it because, having weak sight, they screw up their eyes? For when the sight proceeds forth in a concentrated glance it sees better, but when the eye is wide open its vision is dispersed. So owing to the feebleness of their sight they bring their eyelids close together, and, because their vision proceeds from a small area, they see magnitude

959ᵃ1   on a small scale, and the characters which they write are on the same scale as their vision.

16 · Why do the short-sighted bring their eyelids close together when they look at anything? Is it due to the weakness of their sight, so that, just as a man in
5   looking at a distant object puts his hand up to his eyes, they close the eyelids to look at objects near at hand? They do so in order that the vision may proceed forth in a more concentrated form, since it passes through a narrower opening, and that it may not be immediately dispersed by passing out through a wide aperture. A wider vision, however, covers a larger field.

17 · Why is it that if the eye be moved sideways a single object does not
10   appear double? Is it because the source of sight is still in the same line? It can only appear double when the line is altered upwards or downwards; and it makes no difference if it is altered sideways, unless it is also at the same time altered upwards. Why, then, is it possible in sight for a single object to appear double if the eyes are in a certain position in relation to one another, but impossible in the other senses? Is it
15   not the case also in touch that one thing becomes two if the fingers are crossed? But with the other senses this does not happen, because they do not perceive objects which extend to a distance away from them, nor are they duplicated like the eyes. It takes place for the same reason as it does with the fingers; for then the touch is imitating the sight.

20   18 · Why is it that, though in the rest of the body the left side is weaker than the right, this is not true of the eyes, but the sight of both eyes is equally acute? Is it because the parts of the body on the right side are superior in activity but not in passivity, and the sight is passive?

19 · Why is it that when we keep our gaze fixed on objects of other colours
25   our vision deteriorates, whereas it improves if we gaze intently on yellow and green objects, such as herbs and the like? Is it because we are least able to gaze intently on white and black (for they both mar the vision), and the above-mentioned colours come midway between these, so that, the conditions of vision being of the nature of a
30   mean, our sight is not weakened thereby but improved? Perhaps, just as we take harm from over-violent physical exertion but moderate exercise is beneficial, so too is it with the sight; for we over-exert the sight if we gaze intently on solid objects, but we do not strain it in looking at objects which contain moisture, since there is nothing in them to resist the vision. Now green things are only moderately solid and
35   contain a considerable amount of moisture; they therefore do not harm the sight at all, but compel it to rest upon them, because the admixture of their colouring is suited to the vision.

20 · Why is it that we see other things better with both eyes, but we can judge of the straightness of lines of writing better with one eye, putting it close to

the letters? Do both eyes falling on the same point cause confusion, as the writers on   959ᵇ1
optics say, whereas, when we look with one eye, straightness is more apparent to the
straight vision, just as it is when a measuring rod is used?

21 · Why does smoke make the eyes smart more than any other part of the   5
body? Is it because they alone are very weak, since the inner parts of the body are
always the weakest? (This is shown by the fact that vinegar and anything pungent
causes not the outer but the inner flesh to smart, because the latter is the rarest flesh
in the body and contains most pores.) For the vision finds its exit through certain
pores, and so what causes most stinging within is drawn away from the outer flesh.   10
The onion too has a similar effect and anything else which causes the eye to smart,
and of liquids olive-oil more than any other, because it is composed of very small
particles and so sinks in through the pores. Vinegar is used as a medicament for the
rest of the flesh.

22 · Why is it that the eye, although it is very weak, is the only part of the   15
body which does not feel the cold? Is it because the eye is of a fatty consistency and
does not partake of the nature of flesh, and such substances are unaffected by the
cold? For if the eye is really a fire, this is not the reason why it does not feel cold, for
its fire is not at any rate of such a character as to engender heat.

23 · Why are tears warm when we let them fall in weeping, but cold when   20
we shed them owing to an affection of the eyes? Is it because that which is
unconcocted is cold, while that which is concocted is hot? Now every malady
certainly proceeds from lack of concoction, and the tears of those whose eyes are
affected are unconcocted and therefore cold. It is for this reason that physicians   25
regard cold sweating as a sign of serious illness, while on the contrary they consider
that hot sweating tends to get rid of disease. For if the excretion is abundant, the
internal heat cannot concoct it, so that it must necessarily be cold; but when it is
scanty, the internal heat prevails over it. Now all diseases are caused by
excretions.   30

24 · Why is it that, though the parts of the body on the right side are more
easily moved, the left eye can be closed more easily than the right? Is it because the
parts of the body on the left always contain more moisture, and things that are moist   35
naturally close up more easily?[6]

25 · Why is it that though both a short-sighted and an old man are affected
by weakness of the eyes, the former places an object, if he wishes to see it, near the
eye, while the latter holds it at a distance? Is it because they are afflicted with
different forms of weakness? For the old man cannot see the object; he therefore   960ª1
removes the object at which he is looking to the point at which the vision of his two

[6]Omitting the final sentence.

eyes meets, expecting them to be able to see it best in this position; and this point is at a distance. The short-sighted man, on the other hand, can see the object but cannot proceed to distinguish which parts of the thing at which he is looking are
5 concave and which convex, but he is deceived on these points. Now concavity and convexity are distinguished by means of the light which they reflect; so at a distance the short-sighted man cannot discern how the light[7] falls on the object seen; but near at hand the incidence of light can be more easily perceived.

26 · Why is man alone, or at any rate more than the other animals, liable to
10 squinting? Is it because he alone, or more than the other animals, suffers from epilepsy in his youth, at which time squinting always begins?

27 · Why are men alone among the animals liable to squinting? Is it because they have the smallest distance between their eyes and their eyes are in a straight
15 line, so that any distortion is very obvious? Or is it because the eyes of the other animals tend to be of one colour only, and if the eyes were of uniform colour there could be no squinting? Or is it because man alone in the animal world is liable to epilepsy, and epilepsy, whenever it occurs, causes squinting as in the other parts of the body? Squinting, however, sometimes occurs quite late in life, namely, in those
20 to whom the illness comes late.

28 · Why is it that we can see better against the light of a lamp or the sun, if we place the hand in front of the light? Is it because the light of the sun or of the lamp falling on our vision makes it weaker by its excess of brightness, since by this
25 excess it destroys those very things which are akin to it? But if the light is shaded by the hand, it does not hurt the sight, and the object seen is equally in the light; so the sight sees[8] better and the object seen is just as visible.

29 · Why is there a difference between the left and the right hand and foot,
30 while this is not so with the eyes and ears? Is it because the elements, when they are pure, show no variation, but variations occur where the elements are compounded? Now these senses consist of pure elements—the sight of fire and the hearing of air.

BOOK XXXII
PROBLEMS CONNECTED
WITH THE EARS

35 1 · Why is it that, though the ears are the most bloodless part of the face, they are most affected by blushing in those who feel shame? Is it because extraneous moisture naturally makes its way most easily into a void, and so, when

---

[7] Reading τὴν αὐγήν.
[8] Reading ὁρᾷ for ὁρᾷ.

the moisture is dissolved by the heat engendered in those who feel shame, it collects   960ᵇ1
in the ears? Or is it because the ears are near the temples, where the moisture most
collects? Now under the emotion of shame the moisture flows into the face and
causes blushing. But the ears have less depth than any other part of the face and are
naturally very warm and fresh coloured, unless they have been long numbed by the
cold; they are then the most fresh coloured of all the parts of the face, and so the   5
heat, when it is dispersed, being nearest the surface in the ears, makes them red.

2 · Why is it that the ear-drums of divers burst in the sea? Is it because the
ear, as it fills with water, is subject to violent pressure, because it retains the breath?
Surely, if this is the reason, the same thing ought to happen in the air. Or is it   10
because a thing breaks more easily if it does not yield, and more readily under
pressure from what is hard than from what is soft? Now that which is inflated is less
yielding, and the ears, as has been said, are inflated because the breath is retained in
them; and so the water, which is harder than the air, when it presses upon them
bursts them.

3 · Why do divers tie sponges round their ears? Is it in order that the sea may   15
not rush violently in and burst the ear-drums? For thus the ears do not become full,
as they do when the sponges are removed.

4 · Why is the wax in the ears bitter? Is it because sweat is corrupt? It is,
therefore, a salty, corrupt substance; and that which is corrupt and salty is bitter.   20

5 · Why do sponge-divers slit their ears and nostrils? Is it in order that the
breath may pass more freely? For it is by this way that the breath seems to pass
out;[1] for it is said that they suffer more from difficulty of breathing by being unable
to expel the breath, and they are relieved when they can as it were vomit the breath   25
forth. It is strange, then, that they cannot achieve respiration for the sake of its
cooling effect; this appears to be a greater necessity. Is it not quite natural that the
strain should be greater when the breath is held, since then they are swollen and
distended? But there appears to be a spontaneous passage of the breath outwards;
and we must next consider whether breathing inwards is so also. Apparently it is;   30
for they enable the divers to respire equally well by letting down a cauldron; for this
does not fill with water, but retains the air, for it is forced down straight into the
water; since, if it inclines at all from an upright position, the water flows in.

6 · Why do some people cough when they scrape their ears? Is it because the   35
hearing is connected with the same duct as the lungs and the wind-pipe? This is
shown by the fact that, if these parts are filled up, a man becomes deaf. When,
therefore, heat is set up by friction, moisture is caused by melting and flows
downwards from the duct[2] into the wind-pipe and causes coughing.

---

[1] Omitting ἀνατέμνουσι δὲ . . . εὔπνοιαν.
[2] Reading πόρου.

7 · Why is it that, if a hole is pierced in the left ear, it generally closes up
961ᵃ1   more quickly than in the right ear? It is for this reason that women call the right ear
the 'male' and the left the 'female'. Is it because the left parts of the body are
moister and hotter, and such things close up very quickly? This is why green plants
5   grow together again; and why wounds close up more readily in the young than in the
old. This is a sign that the parts on the left side of the body are moister and,
generally speaking, partake rather of feminine characteristics.

8 · Why is it that in those who feel shame the extremities of the ears turn red,
but in those who are angry it is the eyes that do so? Is it because shame is a cooling
10   in the eyes accompanied by fear, so that the heat naturally leaves the eyes? So,
when it withdraws thence, it travels to the region best adapted to receive it, and this
is the extremity of the ears; for the region of the face is otherwise bony. In those who
are angry the heat travels in the other direction and makes itself most manifest in
15   the eyes owing to their white colour.

9 · Why is it that buzzing in the ears ceases if one makes a sound? Is it
because the greater sound drives out the less?

10 · Why is it that, if water has flowed into the ear, one pours olive oil in,
though the moisture in the ear cannot pass out through another liquid? Is it because
20   the oil floats on the surface of the water and, owing to the adhesive nature of the oil,
the water clings to it when it comes out, the object being to make the water come out
with the oil? Or is it in order that the ear may be lubricated and the water therefore
come out? For oil being smooth acts as a lubricant.

11 · Why is it that the ear-drums of divers are less liable to burst if they pour
25   olive-oil beforehand into them? Does the reason for their bursting already
mentioned still hold good, but the oil poured into the ears cause the sea-water,
which subsequently enters the ear, to glide smoothly over its surface, just as
happens on the exterior parts of the bodies of those who anoint themselves? The
sea-water gliding smoothly along does not make a violent impact upon the inside of
30   the ear, and so does not break the drum.

12 · Why is it that, although the ears are the most bloodless part of the face,
they turn red in those who feel shame? Is everything carried to that part which is
most devoid of it? Now in a man who feels shame the blood seems to be carried
upwards in a heated condition; it therefore passes into the part which is most devoid
of it and causes it to become red. The same thing happens also in the cheeks. A
35   further reason is that the skin of the ears, which is tightly stretched, is very thin and
therefore very transparent.

13 · Why is it that no one scrapes out his ears while yawning? Is it because,
when one yawns, the drum of the ear, by means of which he hears, is inflated? That

this is so is shown by the fact that one hears least well while yawning; for the breath, as happens also in the mouth, finds its way into the interior of the ears and thrusts the membrane outwards and prevents the sound from entering. If, therefore, one 961ᵇ1 touches the seat of hearing when in this condition in such a way as to scrape it, one might cause considerable damage to it; for the impact would be against a resisting and unyielding surface inflated by the breath, and it is obvious that the skin and the membrane are far from being solid; and so great pain is caused and a wound might 5 result.

BOOK XXXIII
PROBLEMS CONCERNING THE NOSE

1 · Why is it that sneezing stops hiccuping but does not stop belching? Is it because they are not affections of the same region, but belching is a cooling and lack 10 of concoction in the stomach, while hiccuping is a similar affection of breath and moisture in the region of the lungs? Now the regions about the head (the ears,[1] for example) are closely connected with the lungs. This is proved by the facts that deafness and dumbness are found together, and that the diseases of the ears become diverted into affections of the lungs; also in some persons coughing results when the 15 ears are scratched. That there is a connection between the region of the nose, in which the sneeze takes place, and the lungs is shown by the fact that both share in respiration; and so, while the nose sneezes when that region becomes hot, the lower region, where hiccuping takes place, also sneezes in sympathy. Now heat causes concoction; hence vinegar stops hiccups, as also does holding the breath if the 20 hiccup is only slight, for it heats the breath which is constricted. So too in sneezing the counter-constriction of the breath has this effect and exhalation takes place properly and from the upper region; for it is impossible to sneeze without exhaling. The impetus then dispels the enclosed breath which is the cause of the hiccup. 25

2 · Why is it that if, when one is about to sneeze, one rubs the eye, one sneezes less? Is it because what causes the sneeze is a kind of heat, and friction produces heat, which, owing to the close proximity to the eyes of the region in which 30 the sneeze occurs, destroys the other heat, just as the lesser fire fades away before the greater?

3 · Why is it that one generally sneezes twice, and not once or many times? Is it because there are two nostrils? The channel, therefore, through which the breath passes is divided between the two. 35

4 · Why is it that one sneezes more after one has looked at the sun? Is it

[1]Reading τὰ ὦτα.

because the sun engenders heat and so causes movement, just as does tickling the nose with a feather? For both have the same effect; by setting up movement they cause heat and create breath more quickly from the moisture; and it is the escape of this breath which causes sneezing.

962ᵃ1   5 · Why do sneezing and holding the breath and vinegar stop hiccups? Does sneezing, since it is a displacement of the lower breath, act in the same sort of way as medicines which, though applied in the upper part of the body, affect the lower part of the stomach? Holding the breath stops weak hiccups, because the slight
5   impetus of the breath which comes forth represses and stifles and completely dispels the hiccup, just as happens in coughing, which[2] ceases if you hold it back. Vinegar stops hiccuping because by its heat it vaporizes the surrounding moisture, which prevents belching; for belching takes place when the moisture in the upper part of
10   the stomach is vaporized and concocted, whereas hiccuping occurs when by the action of moisture breath is retained in an excessive quantity in the region of the lungs; for this, gaining impetus and being unable to break through, causes a spasm, and this spasm is called a hiccup. Hence hiccuping seizes those who are cold, because the cold causes the moisture to acquire consistency[3] from the breath, and
15   the rest of the breath, being still enclosed, gives a leap, and its movement is hiccuping.

      6 · Why do we sometimes pour cold water over a person's face when his nose is bleeding? Is it because the heat is thus driven inwards? If, therefore, the blood is
20   near the surface, it tends to liquefy it.

      7 · Why do we regard sneezing as divine, but not coughing or running at the nose? Is it because it comes from the most divine part of us, namely, the head, which is the seat of reasoning? Or is it because the other affections are the results of disease, but sneezing is not?

25   8 · Why does rubbing the eye stop sneezing? Is it because by this means evaporation is given to the moisture? For the eye sheds tears after friction, and sneezing is due to an abundance of moisture. Or is it because the lesser heat is destroyed by the greater? Now the eye when rubbed acquires more heat than is
30   contained in the nose; and for this reason, even if we rub the nose itself, the sneezing stops.

      9 · Why is it that the emission of other kinds of breath, e.g. farting and belching, are not regarded as sacred, but that of a sneeze is so regarded? Is it because of the three regions of the body—the head, the thorax, and the lower
35   stomach—the head is the most divine? Now farting is breath from the lower stomach and belching is from the upper stomach, but sneezing is from the head;

---

[2]Reading βῆχα ἤ, ἐάν.
[3]Reading συνεστάναι.

because, therefore, this region is most sacred, the breath also from it is revered as sacred. Or is it because all discharges of breath show that the above-mentioned parts are in a better state generally (for without any discharge of excrement the breath in its passage out lightens the body), and so too sneezing shows that the region of the head is in a healthy condition and capable of concoction? For when the heat in the head overcomes the moisture, the breath turns into a sneeze. This is why men test the dying by applying something which will cause sneezing, with the idea that, if this does not affect them, their case is indeed desperate. Thus sneezing is revered as sacred as being a sign of health in the best and most sacred region of the body, and is regarded as a good omen.

962ᵇ1

5

10 · Why does man sneeze most of all animals? Is it because in him the ducts are wide through which the breath and scent[4] pass in? For it is with these when they are full of breath that he sneezes. That these ducts are wide is shown by the fact that man has a weaker sense of smell than any other animal, and those who have narrow ducts have a keener sense of smell. If, therefore, the moisture, the evaporation of which causes sneezing, enters in larger quantities and more often into wide ducts, and man more than any other animal has such ducts, he might naturally be expected to sneeze more often. Or is it because[5] his nostrils are particularly short, and so the heated moisture can quickly become breath and be expelled, whereas in other animals owing to the length of their nostrils it cools before it can evaporate?

10

15

11 · Why is sneezing between midnight and midday regarded as a bad thing, but between midday and midnight as a good thing? Is it because sneezing seems rather to check those who are commencing anything and are at the beginning? And so, if it occurs when we are intending or beginning something, we are deterred from action.[6] Now early morning and the period after midnight are as it were a new beginning; therefore we carefully avoid sneezing so as not to hinder the action which has been begun. But towards evening and up to midnight there is as it were an ending and the contrary of the earlier period, so that the same thing that was undesirable becomes, under contrary conditions, desirable.

20

25

12 · Why do the old sneeze with difficulty? Is it because the ducts through which the breath passes have become partially closed? Or is it because they are no longer able to raise the breath up with ease, and, when they have done so, they expel it downwards with a violent effort?

30

13 · Why is it that, if one holds the breath, hiccuping ceases? Is it because hiccuping is the result of cooling (hence those who are frightened and those who are chilled hiccup), whereas the breath when it is held back warms the interior region?

⁴Reading ὀσμή for ῥύμη.
⁵Reading ἢ ὅτι for ὅσοις.
⁶Reading ὅταν μέλλουσιν ἢ ἀρχομένοις συμβῇ.

35   **14** · Why do the deaf usually talk through their noses? Is it because they suffer from lung trouble, since deafness is simply a congestion in the region of the lungs? The voice therefore does not easily find a passage; but, just as the breath of those who are panting or gasping accumulates owing to their inability to exhale it, so it is with the voice of the deaf. It therefore forces its way even through the

963ª1   nostrils, and, as it does so, owing to the friction, causes the echoing sound. For talking through the nose takes place when the upper part of the nose, where the openings to the roof of the mouth are situated, becomes hollow in form; it then resounds like a bell, its lower part being narrow.

5   **15** · Why is sneezing the only phenomenon which does not occur when we are asleep, but takes place practically always while we are awake? Is it because sneezing is the result of heat of some kind causing motion in the region from which the sneeze proceeds (and this is why we look up at the sun when we want to sneeze)?

10   Or is it because when we are asleep the heat is driven inwards? This is why the lower parts become warm in those who are asleep, and the large quantity of breath which collects there is the cause of the emission of semen during sleep. It is only natural, therefore, that we do not sneeze; for when the heat (which naturally sets in motion the moisture in the head, the evaporation[7] of which causes the sneeze) is withdrawn

15   from the head, it is only natural that the phenomenon which it causes does not take place. Men fart and belch rather than sneeze when they are asleep rather than awake, because, as the region about the stomach becomes hot during sleep, the moisture there becomes vaporized and, as it does so, is carried into the nearest parts;

20   for it is thrust together there by the breath engendered during sleep. For a man who is asleep is better able to hold than to expel the breath; therefore he collects the heat within him. Now when a man holds his breath he forces it downwards; for a downward course is unnatural to the breath, and that is why it is difficult to hold the

25   breath. The same thing is the cause of sleep also; for since waking is movement and this movement occurs to a great extent in the organs of sensation while we are awake, it is plain that we should go to sleep when our organs of sense are at rest.[8] And since it is fire which creates movement in our parts, and this during sleep is

30   driven inwards and leaves the region of the head, where the seat of sensation is situated, our organs of sense would then be most at rest, and this must be the cause of sleep.

        16 · Why do people shiver after sneezing and passing urine? Is it because by both actions the veins are emptied of the warm air which was previously in them,

35   and, when they are empty, other air enters from without, colder than that which was previously in the veins; and such air entering in causes shivering?

        17 · Why does sneezing stop hiccuping? Is it because hiccuping (unlike belching, which comes from the stomach when it receives food) comes from the

---

[7]Reading ἐξαερουμένου.
[8]Omitting ἡμῶν.

lungs⁹ and generally results from cooling as an effect of chill or pain or medicine 963ᵇ1
entering from above? For the region of the lungs, being naturally hot, when it is
cooled does not emit all the breath but forms as it were bubbles. This is why
hiccuping stops if the breath is held (for the region then becomes warm); and the
application of vinegar, which is heating, has the same effect. Heat then collecting 5
from the heat of the brain also (for the upper regions are connected by passages
with the lungs) and the lungs being warm, the holding of the breath which precedes
the sneeze, and the downward impetus from above, dissolve the hiccuping.

18 · Why is it that those who have crisp hair and whose hair curls are 10
usually rather snub-nosed? Is it because crispness resides in fatness, and fatness is
accompanied by hardness, and the blood being hard is hot, and heat does not
produce excrement, and boniness is formed from excrement, and the cartilage of the
nose is bony—therefore a scantiness of this part is a natural result? This theory is
supported by the fact that young children are always snub-nosed. 15

BOOK XXXIV
PROBLEMS CONCERNING THE MOUTH
AND THE PARTS THEREIN

1 · Why is it that those who have widely-spaced teeth are not long-lived? Is it
because the long-lived have more teeth, for instance males have more than females,
men than women, and rams than ewes? Those men who have widely-spaced teeth 20
apparently resemble those who have fewer teeth.

2 · Why is it that, though the teeth are stronger than the flesh, yet they are
more sensitive to cold? Is it because they are closely connected with the pores, in
which the heat, because it is small, is quickly overcome by the cold and causes 25
pain?

3 · Why are the teeth more sensitive to cold than to heat, while the contrary
is true of the flesh? Is it because the flesh partakes of the mean and is well
tempered, but the teeth are cold and therefore more sensitive to cold?¹ Or is it
because the teeth consist of narrow pores in which the heat is scanty, so that they
are quickly affected by the opposite of heat? Now the flesh is warm, so that it is 30
unaffected by the cold, but is quickly sensitive to heat; for it is a case of 'fire added
to fire'.

⁹Reading πνεύμονος for πνεύματος.
¹Reading ψυχροῦ for ἐναντίου.

4 . Why is it that the tongue is indicative of many things? For in acute
diseases it indicates fever by the presence of blisters upon it; also the tongues of
35 sheep are particoloured if the sheep are so. Is it because the tongue is capable of
taking up moisture and is situated near the lungs, which are the seat of fevers? Now
all things which are particoloured are so because their humours are particoloured,
and that part first takes on colour through which the humour first passes; and this is
what happens to the tongue. Now blisters collect on the tongue because it is spongy;
for a blister is as it were an eruption which has not been concocted within.

964ᵃ1   5 . Why is it that the tongue becomes bitter and salty and acid but never
sweet? Is it because these qualities are corruptions and so the tongue cannot
perceive its own real nature?

6 . Why is it that the coloration of the tongue corresponds with that of the
5   skin? Is it because it is really an external part of the body, though it is enclosed in
the mouth, and is it because the skin on it is thin that even a slight variegation of
colour makes itself visible? Or is it because it is liquid that causes change of colour,
and the tongue is most affected by what is drunk?

10   7 . Why is it that one can emit both hot and cold breath from the mouth? For
one can puff out cold breath and huff out warm breath. That the breath is warm can
be demonstrated by placing the hand near the mouth. Or is the air which is set in
motion warm[2] in both cases, but does he who puffs out breath not set the air in
motion all at once but blow through a partly closed mouth, so that, though he emits
15   but little breath, he sets up motion over a large area of the outer air, in which the
warmth from his mouth is not apparent owing to its scantiness? But one who huffs
emits it all at once, and therefore it is warm. For it is characteristic of puffing out
breath to[3] pack the air into a particularly small place; whereas huffing is emitting it
all at once.

8 . Why is it that, if one exhales violently and with all the breath at once, it is
20   impossible to exhale again? So too with violent inhalation, which cannot be
repeated again immediately. Is it because exhalation is a local dilatation, and
inhalation a local contraction, both of which can be carried out within certain
limits? Clearly, therefore, the two processes must be carried out one after another,
but neither can be performed twice consecutively.

25   9 . Why is it that, though there is one passage through which meat and drink
pass and another through which we breathe, if we swallow too large a morsel we
choke? In this there is nothing strange; for not only do we choke if something
penetrates into this passage, but we choke still more if it be blocked. Now the
30   passages through which we take food and through which we breathe are parallel to

---

[2]Reading θερμός for ψυχρός.
[3]Reading τό for τῷ.

one another; when, therefore, too large a morsel is swallowed, the respiration is also blocked, so that there is no way out for the breath.

10 · Why is it that men are very long-lived who have a line right across the palm? Is it because those animals which are badly articulated are short-lived and weak? As an instance of weakness we may take young animals, and of shortness of   35 life the aquatic creatures. Clearly then those who are well articulated must be the opposite, namely, those in whom even those parts are best articulated which are by nature badly articulated. Now the inside of the hand is the least well articulated part of the body.

11 · Why is it that, in deep breathing, when we draw in the breath the stomach contracts, but when we exhale it fills out? Now the contrary of this might   964^{b}1 be expected to occur. Is it because in breathing the stomach is compressed downwards by the flanks and then appears to expand again, like bellows?

12 · Why do we respire? Does the breath dissolve into fire, just as the   5 moisture dissolves into breath? The heat, then, of nature, when the greater part of the breath produces fire, causes pain and pressure upon the ducts; and that is why we emit the fire with the breath. Now when the breath and fire go forth,[4] the ducts contract and are cooled, and pain results; we therefore draw the breath in again.   10 Then when we have opened the ducts of the body and given them relief, fire is again engendered and we again feel discomfort, and therefore expel it and continue to do so indefinitely; just as we continually blink as the part round the eye cools and becomes dry. Also we walk without[5] giving attention to the manner of our walking,   15 the intellect by itself[6] guiding us. In like manner, therefore, we carry out the process of breathing; for we do so by contriving to draw in air, and then continue to draw it in.

BOOK XXXV
PROBLEMS CONNECTED WITH THE
EFFECTS OF TOUCH

1 · Why do we shudder more when some one else touches us than when we   20 touch ourselves? Is it because the touch of a part of some one else has more power to produce sensation than that of a part of oneself, since that which is connected by growth with the sense-organ is imperceptible? Also anything which occurs unawares and suddenly is more frightening, and fright is a process of cooling; and both these qualities are possessed by the touch of another as contrasted with one's   25

[4]Ruelle accidentally omits this clause.
[5]Reading οὐ for οὖν.
[6]Reading αὐτῆς for αὐτοῖς, without a lacuna.

own touch. And, speaking generally, passive sensation is produced either solely by some one else or at any rate in a greater degree than by oneself; as happens for example in tickling.

30   2 · Why do we feel tickling in the armpits and on the soles of the feet? Is it owing to the thinness of the skin? And do we feel it most where we are unaccustomed to being touched, as in these parts and the ears?

    3 · Why is it that every one does not shudder at the same things? Is it because, just as we do not all feel pleasure or pain at the same things, so we do not shudder at the same things? For the same sort of cooling process takes place. So
35 some people shudder when a garment is torn, others when a saw is being sharpened or drawn through wood, others when pumice-stone is being cut, others when the millstone is grinding on stone.

    4 · Why is it that, though the summer is warm and the winter cold, bodies
965ᵃ1 are colder to the touch in summer than in winter? Is it because perspiration and the act of perspiring cool the body, and this takes place in summer but not in winter? Or
5 is it because cold and heat are driven inwards inversely to the seasons, and in the summer the cold takes refuge within and therefore causes perspiration to be given off, whereas in winter the cold keeps the perspiration in and the body vaporizes it, as does the earth?

    5 · Why do the hairs bristle upon the skin? Is it because they naturally stand erect when the skin is contracted, and this contraction occurs owing to cold and
10 certain other conditions?

    6 · Why is it that no one can tickle himself? Is it because one also feels tickling by another person less if one knows beforehand that it is going to take place, and more if one does not foresee it? A man will therefore feel tickling least when he is causing it and knows that he is doing so. Now laughter is a kind of derangement
15 and deception (and so men laugh when they are struck in the midriff; for it is not just any part of the body with which one laughs). Now that which comes unawares tends to deceive, and it is this also which causes the laughter, whereas one does not make oneself laugh.

    7 · Why is it that we feel tickling in particular on the lips? Is it because the part which feels tickling must be situated not far from the seat of sensation? Now
20 the lips are essentially in this position, and so of all parts of the head the most sensitive to tickling are the lips, which are fleshy, and therefore very easily set in motion.

    8 · Why is it that a man bursts out laughing if one scratches the region of his armpits, though he does not do so when any other part is tickled? And why does a
25 man sneeze if he tickles his nostrils with a feather? Is it because these parts are

regions where the small veins are situated, and when these are cooled or undergo the opposite process they become moist or dissolve into breath as the result of the moisture? (Similarly, if one compresses the veins in the neck of one who is asleep, an extraordinarily pleasant sensation is caused.[1]) And when the breath is engendered in greater abundance, we emit it in a single mass. Similarly also in sneezing, when 30 we warm the moisture in the nostrils and scratch them with a feather, we dissolve it into breath; and when the breath becomes superabundant we expel it.

9 . Why is it that we often shudder after taking solid food? Is it because when food which is cold enters the body it prevails at first over the natural heat rather than vice versa? 35

10 . Why is it that an object which is held between two crossed fingers appears to be two? Is it because we touch it with two sense-organs? For when we hold the hand in its natural position we cannot touch[2] an object with the outer[3] sides of the two fingers.

BOOK XXXVI
PROBLEMS CONNECTED WITH
THE FACE

1 . Why is the face chosen for representation in portraits? Is it because the 965ᵇ1 face shows best what the character of a person is? Or is it because it is most easily recognized?

2 . Why is it that one perspires most freely on the face, though it is far from being fleshy? Is it because parts which are rather moist and rare perspire freely, and 5 the head has these characteristics? For it contains an abundance of natural moisture; this is shown by the veins which extend from it and the discharges which it produces, and the fluidity of the brain and the numerous pores. That there are numerous pores extending outwards is shown by the presence of the hair. The perspiration then comes not from the lower parts of the body but from the head; and 10 so one perspires most readily and freely on the forehead, for it is highest in position and moisture flows down and not up.

3 . Why do eruptions occur more frequently on the face than elsewhere? Is it because this part contains rarities and moisture? That this is so is shown by the 15 growth of hair on it and by its power of sensation; and an eruption is as it were an efflorescence of unconcocted moisture.

---

[1] Reading καθεύδουσιν ἡμῖν, ἡδονὴ θαυμασία.
[2] Reading θιγεῖν for εἰπεῖν.
[3] Reading ἐκτός for ἐντός.

BOOK XXXVII
PROBLEMS CONNECTED WITH
THE WHOLE BODY

20   1 · Why is it that, though the body is in a state of continual flux, and effluvia are given off from the excrements, the body is only lightened if it perspires? Is it because the excretion in the form of effluvia is too little (for when liquid is transformed into air, much air is formed out of little liquid)? For what is excreted is
25   more, which accounts for excretion taking longer to begin.

2 · And what is the reason for this? Is it because its exit takes place through smaller pores? For the viscous and the adhesive matter is expelled with the moisture because it mingles with it, but it cannot be expelled with the breath; and it is this
30   thick matter in particular which causes pain. Therefore also vomiting lightens the body more than sweating, because that which is vomited, being thicker and more substantial, carries away this viscous matter with it. Or is there a further reason, namely, that the region in which the viscous and the adhesive matter is, is situated at a distance in relation to the flesh (and so it is difficult to make it change its position), but near to the stomach? For it is engendered either in or close to it; and
35   therefore it is difficult to get rid of it in any other way.

3 · Why is it that friction produces flesh? Is it because heat has great power to increase what is in the body? For the bulk of what already exists in it becomes greater if the body is in continual motion and if our internal humours are carried
966ᵃ1   upwards and vaporized, and this occurs as a result of friction; whereas in the absence of this, the body wastes away and decreases. Or is it because the flesh increases in bulk by nutriment[1] as the result of heat (for anything which is hot has the power to attract moisture, and the nutriment distributed in the flesh is moist and
5   the flesh takes up nutriment better by being rare, for the rarer a thing is the more it can absorb, like a sponge), whereas friction makes the flesh well ventilated and rare and prevents congestion in the body? Now if there is no congestion, there can be no
10   wasting either; for atrophy and wasting are the result of conglomeration. But the better ventilated and the rarer and the more homogeneous the parts of the body are, the more likely they are to acquire bulk, for they are better able to take up nutriment and to get rid of excrements, since the flesh must be rarefied and not condensed in order to promote health. For just as a city or locality is healthy which
15   is open to the breezes (and that is why the sea too is healthy), so the body is healthier if the air can circulate in it than when it is in the contrary condition. For either there ought to be no excrement in the body, or else the body ought to be able to get rid of it as soon as possible and be in such a condition that it can reject the excrement as soon as it receives it and be always in a state of motion and never at
20   rest. For that which remains stationary putrefies (standing water, for example), and that which putrefies creates disease; but that which is rejected passes away before it

---

[1]Reading τῇ τροφῇ.

becomes corrupt. This then does not occur if the flesh is dense (the ducts being as it were blocked up), but it does happen if the flesh is rare. One ought not therefore to walk naked in the sun; for the flesh thereby solidifies and acquires an absolutely 25 fleshy consistency; for the internal moisture remains, but the surface moisture is expelled in the form of a vapour, just as in roast meat in the inner portions are moister than in boiled meat. Nor ought one to walk in the sun with the chest bare, 30 for then the sun draws out the moisture from the best constructed parts of the body, which[2] least require to be deprived of it; but it is rather the inner parts which need to be dried, for, because they are remote, it is impossible to produce perspiration except by a violent effort; but it is easy to exhaust the moisture in the chest, because it is near the surface.

4 · Why is it that, when we are chilled, the same heat causes more burning 35 and pain? Is it because owing to its density the flesh holds the heat which comes into contact with it? This is the reason why lead becomes hotter than wool. Or is the passage of the heat violent because the body is congealed by cold?

5 · Why does dry friction render the flesh solid? Is it because heat is 966ᵇ1 engendered by the friction and the moisture is used up? Furthermore, the flesh when rubbed becomes dense, and everything becomes denser and solider the more it is rubbed. This can be seen in many examples; dough, for instance, and clay and 5 similar substances, if you pour water into them and spread them out, remain moist and fluid, but, if you apply more friction, they quickly become dense, solid and viscous.

6 · Why does friction produce more flesh than running? Is it because 10 running cools the flesh and makes it less absorbent of nutriment, but part of the nutriment is shaken downwards, while the part on the surface,[3] owing to the exhaustion of the natural heat, becomes quite thin and is expelled in the form of breath? But the hand by friction makes the flesh rare and able to take up nutriment. 15 Moreover, the external contact, opposing by its pressure the natural impetus of the flesh, makes it compact and drives it back upon itself.

BOOK XXXVIII
PROBLEMS CONCERNING THE COLORATION
OF THE FLESH

1 · Why is it that the sun bleaches wax and olive oil, but darkens the flesh? Is 20 it because it bleaches the former by extracting the water from them (for that which is moist is naturally black owing to the admixture of the earthy element), whereas it scorches the flesh?

²Reading ἅ
³Reading ἐπιπολῆς.

25　　2 · Why have fishermen reddish hair, and divers for murex, and in short all who work on the sea? Is it because the sea is hot and full of dryness because it is salty? Now that which is of this nature, like lye and orpiment, makes the hair reddish. Or is it because they are warmer in their outer parts, but their inner parts
30　are chilled, because, owing to their getting wet, the surrounding parts are always being dried by the sun? And as they undergo this process, the hair being dried becomes fine and reddish. Furthermore all those who live towards the north have fine, reddish hair.

35　　3 · Why is it that running in clothing and anointing the body under the clothing with oil makes men pale skinned, whereas running naked makes them ruddy? Is it because ventilation produces a ruddy colour, while suffocation has the opposite effect and causes pallor, because the moisture on the surface is heated up and does not cool? Now perspiring in clothes and anointing the body under the
967ᵃ1　clothing both have the same effect, namely, that the heat is enclosed. But running naked makes the flesh ruddy for the opposite reason, because the air cools the excrements which form and ventilates the body. Further, the oil, which is moist and thin, being smeared over the body under the clothing and blocking up the pores,
5　　does not allow either the moisture and breath from the body to escape or the external air to penetrate inwards. Therefore the moist excrements being choked in the body decay and produce pallor.

　　4 · Why is it that the ventilation of the flesh makes it ruddy? Is it because pallor is as it were a corruption of the flesh? When, therefore, the surface is moist
10　and hot, it becomes yellow unless it is cooled and gives off the heat in the form of breath.

　　5 · Why is it that those who perspire are ruddy as a result of their exercises, whereas athletes are pale? Is it because as the result of moderate exertion the heat is
15　burnt up and comes to the surface, whereas by constant exertion it is drained off with the perspiration and breath, the body being rarefied by exertion? When, therefore, the heat comes to the surface, a man becomes ruddy, just as he does when he is hot or ashamed; but when the heat fails, he is pallid. Now ordinary persons indulge in moderate exercise, whereas athletes are constantly training.

20　　6 · Why are men more sunburnt who sit still in the sun than those who take exercise? Is it because those who are in motion are as it were fanned by the breath owing to the movement of the air which they set up, whereas those who are sitting still do not undergo this process?

　　7 · Why does the sun scorch, while fire does not? Is it because the heat of the
25　sun is finer and can penetrate farther into the flesh? Fire, on the other hand, if it does scorch, only raises the surface of the flesh by creating what we call blisters, and does not penetrate within.

8 · Why is it that fire does not make men black, whereas the sun does so, and   967^b1
why does fire blacken earthenware, while the sun does not? Or do they produce
their effects by dissimilar means, the sun blackening the flesh by scorching it and
the fire permeating the earthenware with the soot which it sends up? (Now soot
consists of fine coal-dust, formed by the simultaneous breaking-up and burning of   5
the charcoal.) The sun, then, makes men black, while the fire does not do so,
because the heat of the sun is gentle and owing to the smallness of its parts it can
scorch the flesh itself; and so, because it does not set the flesh on fire, it does not
cause pain, but it blackens it because it scorches it. Fire, on the other hand, either
does not kindle at all or else penetrates within; for what is burnt by fire also becomes   10
black, but it does not burn merely that part of the body in which the colour is
situated.

9 · Why do men become darker complexioned as they become older? Is it
because anything which decays becomes blacker, except mildew? And old age and
decay are the same thing. Further, since the blood when it dries up becomes blacker,   15
it is only likely that older men are darker; for it is the blood which naturally gives
colour to our bodies.

10 · Why is it that, of persons engaged in the preparation of cereals, those
who handle barley become pale and are subject to catarrh, while those who handle   20
wheat are healthy? Is it because wheat is more easily concocted than barley, and
therefore its emanations are also more easily concocted?

11 · Why is it that sun bleaches olive oil but darkens the flesh? Is it because
it extracts the earthy element from the olive oil, and this, like the earthy element in
wine, is the black part of it? Now it darkens the flesh because it burns it; for that   25
which is earthy always becomes black when burnt.

ON INDIVISIBLE LINES**

H. H. Joachim

^{968ª1} Are there indivisible lines? And, generally, is there something partless in every class of quanta, as some say?

For if, where 'many' and 'large' apply, so do their opposites, 'few' and 'small'; and if that which admits practically an infinite number of divisions is many not few, then what is few and what is small will clearly admit only a finite number of divisions. But if the divisions are finite in number, there must be a partless magnitude. Hence in all classes of quanta there will be found something partless, since in all of them 'few' and 'small' apply.

Again, if there is an Idea of line, and if the Idea is first of the things called by its name, then, since the parts are by nature prior to their whole, the Ideal Line must be indivisible. And, on the same principle, the Ideal Square, the Ideal Triangle, and all the other Ideal Figures—and, generalizing, the Ideal Plane and the Ideal Solid—must be without parts; for otherwise it will result that there are things prior to each of them.

Again, if body consists of elements, and if there is nothing prior to the elements, and if parts are prior to their whole, then fire and, generally, each of the elements which are the constituents of body must be indivisible. Hence there must be something partless in the objects of sense as well as in the objects of thought.

Again, Zeno's argument proves that there must be partless magnitudes. For it is impossible to touch an infinite number of things in a finite time, touching them one by one; and the moving body must reach the half-way point before it reaches the end; and there always is a half-way point in any non-partless thing.

But even if the body, which is moving along the line, does touch the infinity of points in a finite time; and if the quicker the movement of the moving body, the greater the stretch which it traverses in an equal time; and if the movement of thought is quickest of all movements:—it follows that thought too will come successively into contact with an infinity of objects in a finite time. And since thought's coming into contact with objects one-by-one is counting, it is possible to count infinitely many objects in a finite time. But since this is impossible, there must be such a thing as an indivisible line.

Again, the being of indivisible lines (it is maintained) follows from the mathematicians' own statements. For if commensurate lines are those which are

TEXT: M. Timpanaro Cardini, Milan, 1970

measured by the same unit of measurement, and if all commensurate lines are being measured,[1] there will be some length by which all of them will be measured. And this length must be indivisible. For if it is divisible, its parts—since they are commensurate with the whole—will involve some unit of measurement. Thus half 10 of a certain part will be double it. But since this is impossible, there must be an indivisible unit of measurement. And just as all the lines which are compounded of the unit are composed of partless elements, so also are the lines which the unit measures once.

And the same can be shown to follow in the plane figures too. For all which are 15 drawn on the rational lines are commensurate with one another; and therefore their unit of measurement will be partless.

But if any such plane be cut along any prescribed and determinate line, that line will be neither rational nor irrational, nor will any of the other kinds of lines which produce rational squares, such as the 'apotome' or the 'line ex duobus nominibus'. Such lines will have no nature of their own at all; though, relatively to 20 one another, they will be rational or irrational.

Now in the first place, it does not follow that that which admits an infinite number of divisions is not small or few. For we apply the predicate 'small' to place and magnitude, and generally to the continuous (and we apply 'few' where that is 25 applicable); and nevertheless we affirm that these quanta admit an infinite number of divisions.

Moreover, if in the composite magnitude there are contained indivisible lines,[2] the predicate 'small' is applied to these indivisible lines, and each of them contains an infinite number of points. But each of them, *quâ* line, admits of division at a 969ᵃ1 point, and equally at any and every point: hence each of these non-indivisible lines would admit an infinite number of divisions. Moreover, some amongst the non-indivisible lines are small. The ratios are infinite in number; and every non-indivisible line admits of division in accordance with any prescribed ratio. 5

Again, since the great is compounded of certain small things, the great will either be nothing, or it will be identical with that which admits a finite number of divisions. For the whole admits the divisions admitted by its parts. It is unreasonable that, whilst the small admits a finite number of divisions only, the great should admit an infinite number; and yet this is what the advocates of the theory postulate. 10

It is clear, therefore, that it is not *quâ* admitting a finite and an infinite number of divisions that quanta are called small and great respectively. And to argue that, because *in numbers* what is few admits a finite number of divisions, therefore *in lines* the small line must admit only a finite number of divisions, is childish. For in numbers the development is from partless objects, and there is a determinate something from which the whole series of the numbers starts, and every number 15 which is not infinite admits a finite number of divisions; but in magnitudes the case is not parallel.

<hr/>

[1]Reading ὅσαι δ' εἰσὶ σύμμετροι, πᾶσαί εἰσι μετρούμεναι.
[2]Reading ἐν τῷ συνθέτῳ ἄτομοί εἰσι γραμμαί.

As to those who try to establish indivisible lines by arguments drawn from the Ideal Lines, we may perhaps say that, in positing Ideas of these quanta, they are assuming a premiss too narrow to carry their conclusion; and, by arguing thus, they in a sense destroy the premisses which they use to prove their conclusion. For their arguments destroy the Ideas.

Again, as to the corporeal elements, it is childish to postulate them as partless. For even though some do as a matter of fact make this statement about them, yet to assume this for the present inquiry is to assume the point at issue. Or rather, the more obviously the argument would appear to assume the point at issue, the more the opinion is confirmed that solids and lengths are divisible in bulk and distance.

The argument of Zeno does not establish that the moving body comes into contact with the infinite number of points in a finite time in the same way. For the time and the length are called infinite and finite and admit of the same divisions.

Nor is thought's coming into contact with the members of an infinite series one-by-one *counting,* even if it were supposed that thought does come into contact in this way with the members of an infinite series. Such a supposition perhaps assumes what is impossible: for the movement of thought does not, like the movement of moving bodies, essentially involve *continua* and *substrata.*

If, however, the possibility of thought moving in this fashion be admitted, still this moving is not counting; for counting is movement combined with pausing.

It is surely absurd that, because you are unable to solve Zeno's argument, you should make yourselves slaves of your inability, and should commit yourselves to still greater errors, in the endeavour to support your incompetence.

As to what they say about commensurate lines—that all lines are measured by one and the same unit of measurement—this is sheer sophistry; nor is it in the least in accordance with the mathematical assumption as to commensurability. For the mathematicians do not make the assumption in this form, nor is it of any use to them.

Moreover, it is actually inconsistent to postulate both that every line becomes commensurate, and that there is a common measure of all commensurate lines.

Hence their procedure is ridiculous, since, whilst professing that they are going to demonstrate their thesis in accordance with[3] the opinions of the mathematicians, and by premisses drawn from the mathematicians' own statements, they lapse into an argument which is a mere piece of contentious and sophistical dialectic—and such a feeble piece of sophistry too! For it *is* feeble in many respects, and totally unable to escape paradox and refutation.

Moreover, it would be absurd for people to be led astray by Zeno's arguments, and to be persuaded—because they cannot refute it—to invent indivisible lines; and yet because of the movement of a straight line to make a semicircle, which must touch infinitely many arcs and distances in between, and because of its movement to form a circle, which readily shows that it must move at every point if it moves to make a semicircle, and because of other similar considerations about lines—to

---

[3]Reading κατὰ τὰς ἐκείνων δόξας . . . φάσκοντας.

refuse to accept that a movement can be generated such that in it the moving thing does *not* fall successfully on each of the intervening points before reaching the end-point. For the theorems in question are more generally admitted, than the arguments of Zeno. 25

It is clear, then, that the being of indivisible lines is neither demonstrated nor rendered plausible—at any rate by the arguments which we have quoted. And this conclusion will grow clearer in the light of the following considerations.

In the first place, our result will be confirmed by reflection on the conclusions proved in mathematics, and on the assumptions there laid down—conclusions and assumptions which must either stand or be overthrown by more convincing arguments. 30

For neither the definition of line, nor that of straight line, will apply to the indivisible line, since the latter is not between any terminal points, and does not possess a middle.

Secondly, all lines will be commensurate. For all lines—both those which are commensurate in length, and those which produce commensurate squares—will be measured by the indivisible lines. 970ª1

And the indivisible lines are all of them commensurate in length (for they are all equal to one another), and therefore also they all produce commensurate squares. But if so, then the square on any line will always be rational. 5

Again, since the line applied to the longer side determines the breadth of the figure, the rectangle, which is equal in area to the square on the indivisible line (e.g. on the line one foot long), will, if applied to a line double the indivisible line, have a breadth determined by a line shorter than the indivisible line: for its breadth will be less than the breadth of the square on the indivisible line.

Again, since any three given straight lines can be combined to form a triangle, a triangle can also be formed by combining three given indivisible lines. But in every equilateral triangle the perpendicular dropped from the apex bisects the base. Hence, it will bisect the indivisible base too. 10

Again, if the square can be constructed of partless lines, then let its diagonal be drawn, and a perpendicular be dropped. The square on the side will be equal to the square on the perpendicular together with the square on half the diagonal. Hence it will not be the smallest line. 15

Nor will the area which is the square on the diagonal be double the square on the indivisible line. For if from the diagonal a length equal to the side of the original square be subtracted, the remaining portion of the diagonal will be less than the partless line. For if it were equal the square on the diagonal would have been four times the original square.

And one might collect other similar absurdities to which the doctrine leads; for indeed it conflicts with practically everything in mathematics. 20

Again, what is partless admits of only one mode of conjunction, but a line admits of two: for one line may be conjoined to another either along the whole length of both lines, or by contact at either of its opposite terminal points.

Further, the addition of a line will not make the whole line any longer; for partless items will not, by being added together, produce an increased total magnitude.

25 Further, every continuous quantum admits more divisions than one, and therefore no continuous quantum can be formed out of two partless items. And since every line (other than the indivisible line) is continuous, there can be no indivisible line.

Further, if every line (other than the indivisible line) can be divided both into equal and into unequal parts—every line, even if it consist of three or any odd number of indivisible lines—it will follow that the indivisible line is divisible.

And the same will result if every line admits of bisection; for then every line
30 consisting of an odd number of indivisible lines will admit of bisection.

And if not *every* line, but only lines consisting of an even number of units admit of bisection, and if it is possible to cut the line being bisected any number of times, still, even so, the 'indivisible' line will be divided, when the line consisting of an even number of units is divided into unequal parts.

970ᵇ1 Again, if a body has been set in motion and takes a certain time to traverse a certain stretch, and half that time to traverse half that stretch, it will traverse less than half the stretch in less than half the time. Hence if the stretch be a length consisting of an odd number of indivisible unit-lines, we shall here again find[4] the
5 bisection of the indivisible lines, since the body will traverse half the stretch in half the time: for the time and the line will be correspondingly divided.

So that none of the composite lines will admit of division both into equal and into unequal parts; and if they are divided in a way corresponding to the division of the times, there will not be indivisible lines. And yet (as we said) the truth is, that
10 the same argument implies that all these things consist of partless items.

Further, every line which is not infinite has two terminal points; for line is defined by these. Now, the indivisible line is not infinite, and will therefore have a terminal point. Hence it is divisible: for the terminal point and that which it terminates are different from one another. Otherwise there will be a third kind of line, which is neither finite nor infinite.

15 Further, there will not be a point contained in every line. For there will be no point contained in the indivisible line; since, if it contains one point only, a line will be a point, whilst if it contains more than one point it will be divisible. And if there is no point in the indivisible line, neither will there be a point in any line at all: for all the other lines are made up of the indivisible lines.

Moreover, there will either be nothing between the points, or a line. But if
20 there is a line between them, and if all lines contain more points than one, the line will not be indivisible.

Again, it will not be possible to construct a square on every line. For a square will always possess length and breadth, and will therefore be divisible, since each of its dimensions is a determinate something. But if the square is divisible, then so will be the line on which it is constructed.

Again, the limit of the line will be a line and not a point. For it is the ultimate

⁴Reading ἀνευρεθήσεται.

thing which is a limit, and it is the indivisible line which is ultimate. For if the 25
ultimate thing be a point, then the limit to the indivisible line will be a point, and one
line will be longer than another by a point. But if the point is contained *within* the
indivisible line, because two lines united so as to form a continuous line have one and
the same limit at their juncture, then the partless line will after all have a limit
belonging to it.

And, indeed, how will a point differ at all from a line on their theory? For the
indivisible line will posses nothing characteristic to distinguish it from the point, 30
except the name.

Again, there must, by parity of reasoning, be indivisible planes and solids too.
For if one is indivisible, the others will follow suit; for each divides at one of the
others. But there is no indivisible solid; for a solid contains depth and breadth. 971ᵃ1
Hence neither can there be an indivisible line. For a solid is divisible at a plane, and
a plane is divisible at a line.

But since the arguments by which they endeavour to convince us are weak and
false, and since their opinions conflict with all the most convincing arguments, it is 5
clear that there can be no indivisible line.

And it is further clear from the above considerations that a line cannot be
composed of points. For the same arguments, or most of them, will apply.

For it will necessarily follow that the point is divided, when the line composed
of an odd number of points is divided into equal parts, or when the line composed of
an even number of points is divided into unequal parts. 10

And it will follow that the part of a line is not a line, nor the part of a plane a
plane.

Further it will follow that one line is longer than another by a point; for it is by
its constituent elements that one line will exceed another. But that this is impossible
is clear both from what is proved in mathematics and from the following argument.
For it would result that a moving body would take a time to traverse a point. For, as 15
it traverses an equal line in an equal time, it will traverse a longer line in a greater
time: and that by which the greater time exceeds the equal time is itself a time.

Perhaps, however, time consists of 'nows', and both theses belong to the same
way of thinking.

Since, then, the now is a beginning and end of a time, and the point a beginning
and end of a line; and since the beginning of anything is not continuous with its end,
but they have an interval between them; it follows that neither nows nor points can 20
be continuous with one another.

Again, a line is a magnitude; but the putting together of points constitutes no
magnitude, because several points put together occupy no more space than one. For
when one line is superimposed on another and coincides with it, the breadth is in no
way increased. And if points too are contained in the line, neither would points 25
occupy more space. Hence points would not constitute a magnitude.

Again, whenever one thing is contiguous with another, the contact is either
whole-with-whole, or part-with-part, or whole-with-part. But the point is without
parts. Hence the contact of point with point must be a contact whole-with-whole.

But if one thing is in contact with another whole-with-whole, the two things must be one. For if either of them is anything in any respect in which the other[5] is
30 not, they would not be in contact whole-with-whole.

But if the partless items are together, then a plurality occupies the same place
971ᵇ1 which was formerly occupied by one; for if two things are together and neither admits of being extended, just so far[6] the place occupied by both is the same. And since the partless has no dimension, it follows that a continuous magnitude cannot be composed of partless items. Hence neither can a line consist of points nor a time of nows.

5 Further, if a line consists of points, point will be in contact with point. If, then, from K there be drawn the lines AB and CD, the point in the line AK and the point in the line KD will both be in contact with K. So that they will also be in contact with one another; for what is partless when in contact with what is partless is in contact whole-with-whole. So that the points will occupy the same place as K, and, being in
10 contact, will be in the same place with one another. But if they are in the same place with one another, they must also be in contact with one another; for things which are in the same primary[7] place must be in contact. But, if this is so, one straight line will touch another straight line at two points. For the point in the line AK touches both the point KC[8] and another. Hence the line AK touches the line CD at more points than one.

15 And the same argument would apply not only where two lines were in contact but also if there had been any number of lines touching one another.

Further, the circumference of a circle will touch the tangent at more points than one. For both the point on the circumference and the point in the tangent touch the point of junction and also touch one another. But since this is not possible, neither is it possible for point to touch point. And if point cannot touch point,
20 neither can a line consist of points; for if it did,[9] they would necessarily be in contact.

Moreover, how will there any longer be straight *and* curved lines? For the conjunction of the points in the straight line will not differ in any way from their conjunction in the curved line. For the contact of what is partless with what is partless is contact whole-with-whole, and no other mode of contact is possible. Since, then, the lines are different, but the conjunction of points is the same, clearly
25 a line will not depend on the conjunction: hence neither will a line consist of points.

Further, the points must either touch or not touch one another. Now if the next in a series must touch the preceding term, the same arguments will apply; but if there can be a next without its being in contact yet by the continuous we mean
30 nothing but a composite whose constituents are in contact. So that even so the points must be in contact, in so far as the line must be continuous.[10]

---

⁵Reading ἢ θάτερον.
⁶Retaining ἐπέκτασιν, κατὰ ταῦτα.   ⁷Reading πρώτῳ.
⁸Reading καὶ τῆς ΚΓ.   ⁹Reading οὕτω γὰρ.
¹⁰Reading ἢ εἶναι γραμμὴν συνεχῆ.

Again, if it is absurd for a point to be by a point, or a line by a point, or a plane   972ᵃ1
by a line, what they say is impossible.[11] For if the points form a series, the line will
be divided not at either of the points, but between them; whilst if they are in contact,
a line will be the place of the single point. And this is impossible.   5
    Further, all things would be divided, i.e. be dissolved, into points; and the point
would be a part of a solid, since a solid consists of planes, a plane of lines, and lines
of points. And since those constituents, of which (as primary immanent factors) the
various groups of things are composed, are elements, points would be elements of   10
bodies. Hence elements would be synonymous, and not specifically different.
    It is clear, then, from the above arguments that a line does not consist of
points.
    But neither is it possible to subtract a point from a line. For, if a point can be
subtracted, it can also be added. But if anything is added, that to which it was added   15
will be bigger than it was at first, if that which is added be such as to form one whole
with it. Hence a line will be bigger than another line by a point. And this is
impossible.
    But though it is not possible to subtract a point *as such* from a line, one may
subtract it *incidentally,* viz. in so far as a point is contained in the line which one is
subtracting from another line. For since, if the whole be subtracted, its beginning   20
and its end are subtracted too; and since the beginning and the end of a line are
points: then, if it be possible to subtract a line from a line, it will be possible also
thereby to subtract a point. But such a subtraction of a point is accidental.
    But if the limit *touches* that of which it is the limit (touches either *it* or some   25
one of its parts), and if the point *quâ* limit of the line, touches the line, then the line
will be greater than another line by a point, and the point will consist of points. For
there is nothing between two things in contact.
    The same argument applies in the case of division, since the division is a point
and, *quâ* dividing-point,[12] is in contact with something. It applies also in the case of
a solid and a plane. And the solid must consist of planes, the plane of lines.   30
    Neither is it true to say of a point that it is the smallest constituent of a line.
    For if it be called the smallest of the things contained in the line, what is
smallest is also *smaller* than those things of which it is the smallest. But in a line   972ᵇ1
there is contained nothing but points and lines: and a line is not bigger than a point,
for neither is a plane bigger than a line. Hence a point will not be the smallest of the
constituents in a line.
    And if a point is commensurate with a line, yet, since the smallest involves   5
three degrees of comparison, the point will not be the *smallest* of the constituents of
the line; and there are other things in the length besides points and lines; for it will
not consist of points. But, since that which is in place is either a point or a length or a
plane or a solid, or some compound of these; and since the constituents of a line are   10

---

[11]Reading ἔτι εἰ ἄτοπον στιγμὴν ἐπὶ στιγμῆς εἶναι ἢ γραμμὴν ἐπὶ στιγμῆς ἢ ἐπὶ γραμμῆς ἐπίπεδον. But the text
is quite uncertain, even by the standards of the rest of the treatise.
[12]Reading ἢ τομή.

in place (for the line is in place); and since neither a solid nor a plane, nor anything compounded of these, is contained in the line:—there can be absolutely nothing in the length except points and lines.

Further, since that which is called greater than that which is in place is a length or a surface or a solid; then, since the point is in place, and since that which is contained in the length besides points and lines is none of the aforementioned:—the point cannot be the smallest of the constituents of a length.

Further, since the smallest of the things contained in a house is so called, without in the least comparing the house with it,[13] and so in all other cases:—neither will the smallest of the constituents in the line be determined by comparison with the line. Hence the term 'smallest' applied to the point will not be suitable.

Further, that which is not in the house is not the smallest of the constituents of the house, and so in all other cases. Hence, since[14] a point can exist by itself, it will not be true to say of it that it is the smallest thing in the line.

Again, a point is not an indivisible joint.

For a joint is always a limit of two things, but a point is a limit of *one* line. Moreover a point is a limit, but a joint is more of the nature of a division.

Again, a line and a plane will be joints; for they are analogous to the point. Again a joint *is* in a sense on account of movement (which explains the verse of Empedocles 'a joint binds two'[15]); but a point is found also in immovable things.[16]

Again, nobody has an infinity of joints in his body or his hand, but he has an infinity of points. Moreover, there is no joint of a stone, nor has it any; but it has points.

---

[13]Omitting Apelt's πρὸς τὴν οἰκίαν συμβάλλεται μήτε, and reading μή τι τῆς for μήτε τῆς.
[14]Reading ἐνδέχεται δέ.
[15]Reading δύω δέει ἄρθρον: frag. 32 Diels-Kranz.
[16]Omitting τό.

THE SITUATIONS AND
NAMES OF WINDS**

E. S. Forster

Boreas. At Mallus this wind is called Pagreus; for it blows from the high cliffs   973ᵃ1
and two parallel ranges known as the Pagrean Mountains. At Caunus it is called
Meses; in Rhodes it is known as Caunias, for it blows from Caunus, causing storms   5
in the harbour of that place. At Olbia, near Magydum in Pamphylia, it is called
Idyreus; for it blows from an island called Idyris. Some people identify Boreas and
Meses, amongst them the Lyrnatians near Phaselis.

Caecias. In Lesbos this wind is called Thebanas; for it blows from the plain of   10
Thebe, north of the Elaitic Gulf in Mysia. It causes storms in the harbour of
Mitylene and very violent storms in the harbour of Mallus. In some places it is
called Caunias, which others identify with Boreas.

Apeliotes. This wind is called Potameus at Tripolis in Phoenicia; it blows from
a plain resembling a great threshing-floor, which lies between the mountains of
Libanus and Bapyrus; hence it is called Potameus. It causes storms at Posidonium.   15
In the Gulf of Issus and the neighbourhood of Rosus it is known as Syriandus; it
blows from 'the Syrian Gates', the pass between the Taurus and the Rosian
Mountains. In the Gulf of Tripolis it is called Marseus, from the village of Marsus.   20
In Proconnesus, Teos, Crete, Euboea, and Cyrene it is known as Hellespontias. It
causes storms in particular at Caphereus in Euboea, and in the harbour of Cyrene,
which is called Apollonia. It blows from the Hellespont. At Sinope it is called
Berecyntias, because it blows from the direction of Phrygia. In Sicily it is known as   973ᵇ1
Cataporthmias, because it blows from the Straits. Some people identify it with
Gaecias, and also call it Thebanas.

Eurus. This wind is called Scopeleus at Aegae, on the borders of Syria, after
the cliff at Rosus. In Cyrene it is known as Carbas after the Carbanians in   5
Phoenicia; hence some people call this same wind Phoenicias. Some people identify
it with Apeliotes.

Orthonotus. Some call this wind Eurus, others Amneus.

Notus bears the same name everywhere. It is derived from the fact that this
wind is unwholesome, while out of doors it brings showers; thus there are two
reasons for its name.   10

TEXT: O. Apelt, Teubner, Leipzig, 1888

Leuconotus likewise derives its name from its effect; for it clears the sky.

Lips. This wind gets its name from Libya, whence it blows.

Zephyrus. This wind is so named because it blows from the west, and the west. . . .

Iapyx. At Tarentum it is called Scylletinus from the place Scylletium. At Dorylaeum in Phrygia. . . . Some people call it Pharangites, because it blows from a certain ravine in Mount Pangaeus. Many call it Argestes.

Thracias is called Strymonias in Thrace, for it blows from the river Strymon; in the Megarid it is known as Sciron, after the Scironian cliffs; in Italy and Sicily it is called Circias, because it blows from Circaeum. In Euboea and Lesbos it goes by the name of Olympias, which is derived from Pierian Olympus; it causes storms at Pyrrha.

I have drawn for you the circle of the earth and indicated the positions of the winds, and the directions in which they blow, so that they may be presented to your vision.

ON MELISSUS,
XENOPHANES, AND
GORGIAS**

T. Loveday and E. S. Forster

1 · Melissus says that, if anything is, it is eternal, since it is impossible that 974ᵃ1 anything can come into being from nothing. For suppose that either all things or some things have come into being, in either case they must be eternal; for otherwise, in coming into being, they would do so out of nothing. For if all things come into being, then nothing can pre-exist; whilst if some things were ever and others are added, that which is must have become more and greater, and that by which it is more and greater must have arisen out of nothing; for the more is not originally existent in the less, nor the greater in the smaller.

Since it is eternal, it is unlimited; for it has no beginning from which it has come into being, and no end at which it ever ceased coming into being.

Being all and unlimited it is one; for if it were two or more, these would be limits for one another.

Being one it must be similar throughout; for if it were dissimilar, it would be several and therefore no longer one but many.

Being eternal and unlimited and alike throughout, the One is without motion; for it could not move without passing somewhere else, and it can only pass either into that which is full or into that which is empty; but of these the former could not admit it, while the latter is nothing at all.

Such being the nature of the One, it is unaffected by grief and pain, and is healthy and free from disease, and cannot change either by transposition or by change of form or by mixture with anything else; for under all these circumstances the One becomes many, and what is not is necessarily generated and what is is destroyed; but these are impossibilities. For, indeed, if it were maintained that any One is the result of a mixture of several constituents—suppose, that is, that things

5
10
15
20
25

TEXT: H. Diels, Abh. Ak. Berlin, phil.-hist. Kl. 1, Berlin, 1900

were many and moved into one another, and that their mixture were either by way of the composition of the many in one, or, being due to the constituents fitting in with one another, resulted in their covering one another from view—then in the former case the constituents mixed would be easily discernible, if you separated them; whilst, if they covered one another, rubbing would reveal each constituent, the successive layers being uncovered as the upper layers were removed. Now neither of these things happens. But according to Melissus it is only in these ways that many things could both be and also appear to us; and since these ways are impossible, that which is cannot be many, and the belief that it is is erroneous, like many other fancies which are due to the senses; but argument does not prove either that things come into being or that what is, is many, but that it is one and eternal and unlimited and similar throughout.

Now surely one ought firstly to begin by taking not any and every opinion, but those which are most firm. If, then, all our opinions are incorrectly conceived, it is perhaps quite wrong to adopt this doctrine too, that nothing can ever come into being out of nothing; for this is but a single opinion and an incorrect one too, which we somehow all of us[1] have often been led to believe from our sense-perceptions. But if not all that appears to us is false, and some beliefs even of objects of sense are correct, either one ought to demonstrate the nature of such a correct belief and then adopt it, or else demonstrate and adopt those which appear most likely to be correct; and these must always be more firm than the conclusions which are apt to follow from the arguments of Melissus. For supposing that we really had to do with two contrary opinions, as Melissus thinks (for if there are many things, he says they must arise from what is not; and if this is impossible, what is, is not many; for, being ungenerated, anything which is, is unlimited, and therefore one), supposing this so, still, if we admit both propositions equally, unity is no more proved than multiplicity, and it is only if one proposition is more firm than the other, that the conclusions following from it are better proved. Now, as a matter of fact, we do entertain both these beliefs, namely, that nothing can come to be out of nothing, and also that existents are many and are in motion; and of the two the latter is more generally credited, and every one would more readily give up the former opinion than this. Now if it were the case that the two propositions are contrary to one another, and it were impossible that at the same time things should come to be of what is not, and there should fail to be a multiplicity of things, each of these views would refute the other. But why should his premises be correct? Some one else might assert the exact opposite. For he has not argued his case either by showing that it is a correct opinion from which he starts, or by taking a more firm opinion than that with which his proof is concerned. For it is usually considered more likely that things come to be from what is not than that there is not a multiplicity of things; it is confidently asserted about existents that things which do not exist come into being, indeed often have come into being, out of non-existents, and those who have asserted this are no ordinary men, but some of those who are looked upon as sages. To being with,

---

[1]Retaining πάντες.

Hesiod says:

> First of all in the world was Chaos born, and thereafter
> Broad-bosomed earth arose, firm seat of all things forever
> And Love that shineth bright amid the host of Immortals.[2]

All other things, he says, came into being from these, but these came into being out of nothing. Secondly, there are many who say that nothing is but all things become, declaring that whatever becomes does not arise from existents; for then their statement that all things become would be false. So much, therefore, is clear, that there are some people of the opinion that becoming even out of non-existents is possible.

2 · But had we not better leave aside the possibility or impossibility of his conclusions, and confine ourselves to what may very well be a distinct problem— namely, whether these conclusions follow from the premises which he takes, or whether nothing prevents things from being otherwise. And first of all, granted his first assumption, that nothing can come to be from what is not, does it necessarily follow that all things are ungenerated? Or is there no reason why one thing should not have come to be out of another, and so on in an endless series? Or may it not go on in a circular process, in such a way that one thing has come to be out of another, there thus being always something in existence, and all things having come to be out of one another an endless number of times? In that case, although it be agreed that nothing can come to be out of what is not, everything may very well have come to be. (And none of the attributes which are attached to the One prevents our calling existents unlimited in Melissus's sense of the word. For he himself attributes to the unlimited that it actually is, and is said to be, everything. And even if existents are not unlimited, there is no reason why they should not come to be by the circular process.) Further, if all things come to be and nothing is, as some declare, how can they be eternal? Yet he certainly argues as though the existence of something were real and agreed. For, he says, if a thing has not come to be but is, it must be eternal, as though being were necessarily inherent in things. Moreover, however impossible it may be for what is not to come to be, or for what is to be destroyed, yet what prevents some existing things from having come to be and others from being eternal, as Empedocles also affirms? For after admitting all this, namely, that

> Out of that which is not can nothing come into being;
> And whatsoever exists, no art nor device can destroy it;
> For it will always abide, where'er 'tis implanted, for ever,[3]

he yet declares that of existents some are eternal, namely, fire, water, earth, and air, but that the rest of things come to be and have come to be out of these. For in his

---

[2]*Theogony* 116–120.
[3]Frag. 12 Diels-Kranz.

opinion there is no other process whereby existents can come to be,

> Save the mingling of things and exchanging of things that are mingled;
> This in the speech of men is called the work of Begetting.[4]

10 But he denies that the being of the eternal things and of what really is, is the result of a process of coming to be; for this he considers impossible. For he says:

> How could aught bring increase to the All and whence have arisen?[5]

But the Many come to be by the mixture and composition of fire and the other elements, and perish again when those elements are exchanged and separated; that

15 is, by mixture and separation many things are at any time, but by nature there are only four apart from the causes, or else only one. Or again if these elements out of the composition of which things come to be, and by the dissolution of which they are destroyed were from the first unlimited—which is what some affirm that Anaxagoras means when he says that things which come to be do so out of things that are always existent and unlimited—even so not all things would be eternal, but there

20 would be some things coming to be and having come to be from things that are, and passing by destruction into other modes of being. Furthermore, there is no reason why one form should not constitute the universe (as Anaximander and Anaximenes say, the former declaring that the universe is water, while Anaximenes says that it is

25 air, and as others say who have contended along these lines that the universe is one), and why this, but assuming various shapes and greater or less bulk—that is, by coming to be in a rare or dense state—should not make up the many unlimited objects which exist and come to be and compose the whole. Again, Democritus declares that water and air and each of the many things that exist are essentially the

30 same, but differ in their 'rhythm'. Why should not the many come to be and be destroyed in *this* way, the One changing continually from being to being by the above-mentioned differences, and the whole becoming not a whit either greater or less? Furthermore, why should not bodies from time to time come to be from other bodies and be dispersed into bodies, and thus by dissolution the processes of generation and decay always balance one another?

35 But if one were to make these concessions and allow that what is both exists and is ungenerated, how is its unlimitedness thereby more clearly demonstrated? For Melissus declares it to be unlimited, if it exists but has not come to be; for the beginning and end of the process of coming to be are, he says, limits. Yet what in his argument prevents a thing which is ungenerated from having a limit? For if a thing

976ᵃ1 has come to be, he contends that it has as a beginning that from which it began coming to be. Now why should it not have a beginning, even if it has not come to be—not, however, one from which it has come to be, but some other—and why should not existents, though eternal, be limited in relation to one another? Again,

5 why should not the whole, being ungenerated, be unlimited, but the things which come to be within it be limited by having a beginning and end of coming to be?

---

[4]Frag. 8, lines 3–4, Diels-Kranz.
[5]Frag. 14, Diels-Kranz.

Again, as Parmenides says, what prevents the universe, though it be one and ungenerated, from being nevertheless limited and

> Like to the mass of a sphere on all sides carefully rounded,
> Everywhere equally far from the midst; for Fate hath appointed
> That neither here nor there should it either be greater or smaller?[6]   10

Now, if it has a centre and extremities, it has a limit though it is ungenerated; since if it be one and a body, as Melissus himself asserts, it has parts of its own as well, and these all alike. For when he says that the universe is similar, he does not use the term of similarity to something else (this is just the point that Anaxagoras[7] raises in disproving that the unlimited is similar, i.e. that what is similar is similar to   15 something else, so that being two or more it would no longer be one, nor yet unlimited), but perhaps he means similar in relation to itself—in other words, that it is homogeneous, being all water or earth or something else of the kind. For he clearly holds that in this case it would be one; but each of the parts being a body is not unlimited (for it is the whole which is unlimited), and therefore they are limited   20 in relation to one another, although they are ungenerated.

     Further, if it is both eternal and unlimited, how could it be one, being a body? For if it were heterogeneous,[8] it would be many. Melissus himself contends that it would then be many. But if it is all water or all earth, or whatever this being is, it would have many parts (as Zeno, too, attempts to prove of that which is one in this   25 sense); its parts would then be many, being some of them smaller and less than others; so that in this way it would vary throughout, without any body being added to it or taken away from it. But if it has no body or width or length, how could the One be unlimited? Or why should there not be many, indeed innumerable, existents   30 of this kind? Further, if there are more existents than one, why should they not be unlimited in size, just as Xenophanes asserts that the depth both of the earth and of the air is unlimited? Empedocles shows this; for, as though certain people urged such views, he makes the criticism that, if this is the nature of earth and air, it is impossible for them ever to meet,   35

> If the depths of the earth are unbounded and ample the ether,
> As the words that come forth from the lips of mortals unnumbered,
> Empty and meaningless, say; they have seen of the whole but a little.[9]

Further, if it is one, there is nothing absurd in supposing that it is not similar everywhere. For if the universe is water or fire or something of that kind, there is no   976ᵇ1 reason why we should not suppose several kinds of this one being, each kind individually similar to itself. For there is no reason why one kind should not be rare and another dense, as long as the rarity does not involve a void. For in the rare there is not a void isolated in particular parts in such a way that of the whole part is dense   5

---

⁶Frag. 28, lines 43–5, Diels-Kranz.
⁷Reading ὅπερ Ἀναξαγόρας ἐλέγχει.
⁸Reading ἀνομοιομερές.
⁹Frag. 39 Diels-Kranz.

and part not dense (rarity then meaning that the whole is like this); but rarity is produced when the whole is uniformly full, but uniformly less full than in the dense.

But suppose it exists and is ungenerated, and suppose it were granted that for this reason it is unlimited, and that more than one thing cannot be unlimited, and it must therefore be said to be one, and it is impossible. . . .[10] For how, if what is unlimited is a whole, can the void, not being a whole, exist?

Now Melissus declares that it is without motion, if a void does not exist; for everything moves by changing its place. In the first place, then, this does not agree with the opinion of many, which is that a void does exist, yet it is not a body, but is of the nature of the Chaos, as Hesiod describes it first coming into being in the birth of things, considering space to be a prime necessity for things which exist; and the void is, as it were, a vessel in which we expect to find an interior space. But even if there is no void, why should it be less likely to move? For Anaxagoras, who devoted his attention to this subject, and for whom it was not enough merely to declare that a void does not exist, declares that things which are, are in motion, although there is no void. Similarly Empedocles says that they are ever in motion continually all through the period of aggregation, but that there is no void; for he says that

Nought of the whole can be void; whence then could any be added?[11]

while when all has been aggregated into a single form, so as to be one,

Emptiness there is none, nor aught that is overflowing.[12]

For why should not things assume one another's position and go through a circle of simultaneous movements, one thing taking the place of another, and that the place of something else, and something else the first position? And what is there in what he has said that precludes a movement taking place in things, consisting in a change of form in an object which remains in the same position (what he, like every one else, terms alteration), as, for example, when white turns into black, or bitter into sweet? For the non-existence of a void and the inability of that which is full to receive any addition does not at all preclude the possibility of alteration.

Thus neither are all things necessarily eternal nor is it necessarily unlimited (but many things are unlimited), nor is it one, nor similar, nor unmoved, whether it be one or whether it be many. If this is admitted, if there would be nothing in what he has said to prevent existents from being either transposed or altered; if there is one thing, the movement is of the whole, which differs in quantity, and alters without the addition or abstraction of any body; while, if there is a multiplicity of existents, their movement is due to their mutual mixture and segregation. For it is not likely that the process of mixture is either a placing of elements one above another, or a putting of them together, such as he supposes, by which either they are

---

[10]Diels marks a lacuna. The text here and in the next two lines is far from certain.
[11]Frag. 14 Diels-Kranz.
[12]Frag. 13 Diels-Kranz.

immediately distinct, or else they appear each distinct from one another, if the layers above one another are successively rubbed away; but they are so arranged that any part of that which is mixed comes into such a relation to any part of that with which it is mixed, that even the smallest particles would be found not merely placed together but mixed. For since there is no smallest body, every part is mixed   10
with every other part, just as the whole is mixed.

3 · Xenophanes declares that if anything is, it cannot possibly have come into being, and he argues this with reference to God, for that which has come into   15
being must necessarily have done so either from that which is similar or from that which is dissimilar; and neither alternative is possible. For it is no more possible for like to have been begotten by like than for like to have begotten like (for since they are *equal*, all the same qualities inhere in each and in a similar way in their relations to one another), nor could unlike have come into being from unlike. For if the stronger could come into being from the weaker, or the greater from the less, or the   20
better from the worse, or conversely worse things from better, then what is not could come to be from what is, or what is from what is not; which is impossible. Accordingly for these reasons God is eternal.

Now if God is supreme over all, he says that he must be one. For if there were two or more gods, he would no longer be supreme and the best of all; for then   25
each of the many , being a god, would likewise be supreme. For what God and God's power means is that he is supreme and never inferior, and that he possesses supremacy over all. So far then as he is not superior, he is not God. Now if there were several gods, supposing they were superior to one another in some respects and   30
inferior in others, they would not be gods; for it is the nature of the divine not to be inferior. But supposing they were equal, they would not possess God's nature, for God must be supreme; whereas that which is equal is neither better nor worse than that to which it is equal. So that if God be, and be of this nature, God is one only. For otherwise he could not even do whatsoever he wished; for if there were more   35
gods than one, he could not do so; therefore he is One only.

Being one he is similar in every part, seeing and hearing and possessing the other senses in every part of him. For otherwise the parts of God would be superior and inferior to one another; which is impossible.

Being similar in every part, he is spherical; for he is not of a certain nature in $977^{b}1$
one part and not in another, but in every part.

Being eternal and one and similar and spherical, he is neither unlimited nor limited. For what is not is unlimited; for it has neither middle nor beginning and end, nor any other parts, and such is the nature of the unlimited. But what is could   5
not be of the same nature as what is not. On the other hand, if things were several, mutual limitation would occur. But the One has no likeness either to what is not or to the many; for that which is one has nothing in which it can find a limit.

A One, then, of the kind which Xenophanes declares God to be can, he says, be neither moved nor unmoved; for immobility belongs to what is not (for nothing else   10

can go into it, nor can it go into anything else); while movement belongs to a plurality, for one body must move into another's place. Now nothing can ever move into what is not, for what is not is nowhere. On the other hand, if it moved in the way
15 of things changing into one another, than the One would be more than one. For these reasons motion belongs to a pair of things, or any number more than one, while rest and immobility belong to that which is nothing. But the One is neither still nor is it moved; for it is similar neither to what is not nor to the many; but being
20 in every respect of this nature—eternal and one and similar and spherical—God is neither unlimited nor limited, neither at rest nor in motion.

4 · In the first place, then, Xenophanes also, like Melissus, assumes that what comes into being does so from that which already is. Yet why should not that which comes into being do so not from something either similar or dissimilar, but from what is not? Further, God is no more ungenerated than anything else, even if
25 we suppose that all things have come into being from something similar or dissimilar, which is impossible; so that either there is nothing except God or everything else is also eternal. Further, he assumes that God is supreme, meaning by this that he is most powerful and best. This does not seem to agree with the customary opinion, which holds that some gods are in many respects superior to
30 others. It was not, therefore, from accepted opinion that he took this admission about God. It is said that he understands the supremacy of God in the sense that his nature is superior, not in relation to anything else, but in his own disposition; since surely in relation to something else there would be nothing to prevent his excelling,
35 not by his own goodness and strength, but owing to the weakness of all others. But no one would wish to say that God is supreme in this latter sense, but rather that he is in himself as excellent as possible, and there is nothing lacking in him of what is good and noble; if this is so, his supremacy would perhaps follow. But even if there were more gods than one, nothing would prevent their being of this nature, all
978ᵃ1 possessing the greatest possible excellence and being superior to all else, but not to one another. Now there are, it seems, other things besides God; for he says that God is supreme, and he must necessarily be supreme over something.
But supposing that he is one, it does not follow that he sees and hears in every
5 part; for if he does not see in one part, he does not see worse in that part, but does not see at all. But perhaps perceiving in every part means that he would possess the highest excellence if he were similar in every part.
Further, if this were his nature, why should he be spherical, and why should he have that shape rather than any other, just because he hears in every part and is
10 supreme in every part? For just as when we say of white lead that it is white in all its parts, we merely mean that the colour whiteness is present in every portion of it, why should we not say similarly of God that sight and hearing and supremacy are present in every part, in the sense that whatsoever portion of him one takes will be
15 found to be possessed of these characteristics? But God is not necessarily spherical for this reason any more than white lead is.
Further, how is it possible that, being a body and having magnitude, God can

be neither unlimited nor limited? For that is unlimited which, being capable of limitation, has no limit, and limit occurs in magnitude and multitude and any kind of quantity; and therefore any magnitude which has no limit is unlimited. Again, if God is spherical, he must have a limit; for he has extremities, if he has a centre within himself from which they are at the greatest distance. But anything which is spherical has a centre; for that is spherical in which the extremities are equidistant from the centre. Now it is the same thing to say that a body has extremities, and that it has limits. . . .[13] For if what is not is unlimited, why should not what is also be unlimited? For why should not some identical attributes be assigned to what is and to what is not? For no one can perceive at this moment what does not exist, while something may exist at this moment without any one's perceiving it;[14] yet both can be the subject of speech and thought. . . .[15] And what is not is not white; either, then, for this reason everything that is is white (this is in order that we may not assign an identical quality to that which exists and to the non-existent), or else, I think, there is nothing to prevent anything which exists from being not white. And so what is would still more easily admit a negative predicate, namely, the unlimited, if, as was said just now, a thing is unlimited owing to its not having a limit; and so what is too either is unlimited or has a limit. But perhaps to attribute unlimitedness to what is not is also absurd; for we do not call everything which has not a limit unlimited, just as we should not say that what is not equal is unequal. Again, why should not God, although he be one, yet be limited, though not by anything which is God. But if God is one only, then his parts also must be one only. Further, it is also absurd that if in fact the many are limited in relation to one another, for this reason the One should not have a limit. For many of the same predicates belong to the many and to the One; being, for instance, is common to them both. It would therefore, perhaps, be absurd if we were to declare that God does not exist for the reason that the Many exist, so that he may not be like[16] them in this respect. Again, though God be One, why should he not be limited and have limits? Even as Parmenides says that, being One, he is

20

25

30

35

978ᵇ1

5

> Like to the mass of a sphere on all sides carefully rounded   10
> Everywhere equally far from the midst.[17]

For the limit must be a limit of something, but not necessarily in relation to something else: that which has a limit does not necessarily have it in relation to something else (as when it is limited in relation to the unlimited which comes next to it), but being limited means the possession of extremities, and when a thing has extremities it need not necessarily have them in relation to something else. Some things, therefore, may happen both to be limited and to adjoin something else, while   15 others may be limited, but not in relation to something else.

Again, as regards what is and what is not being unmoved, we must say that to

---

[13]Diels marks a lacuna here.
[14]Reading τό τε γὰρ οὐκ ὄν . . . αἰσθάνοιτο νῦν.
[15]Diels marks a lacuna here.
[16]Reading ὅμοιος.
[17]Frag. 8, lines 43–4, Diels-Kranz.

suppose that what is not is unmoved because what is is moved, is perhaps just as absurd as the cases given above. And further, surely one cannot suppose that not-moving and unmoved are the same thing, but the former is the negation of

20 moving (like not-equal, which can be correctly used even of the non-existent), while 'unmoved' is used of an actual state (as 'unequal' is used), and to express the contrary of moving (that is, being at rest), just as words with the negative prefix are generally used to express contraries. Not-moving is therefore true of the non-

25 existent, but being at rest cannot belong to the non-existent; similarly 'unmoved', which means the same thing,[18] cannot belong to it. Yet Xenophanes uses 'not moving' in the sense of 'being at rest', and says that what is not is at rest because it undergoes no change of position. As we said above, it is perhaps absurd, if we attach some predicate to what is not, to assert that it does not apply to what is, especially if

30 the predicate used is a negation, such as 'not moving' and 'not changing its position'. For, as has been said, it would preclude a number of predicates from being used of existing things: for it would not be true to say that many is not one, since the non-existent also is not one. Furthermore, in some cases the contrary predicates

35 seem to follow from the mere[19] negations; for example, a thing must be either equal or unequal if it is a multitude or magnitude, and odd or even, if it is a number; similarly, perhaps, what is, if it be a body, must be either at rest or in motion.

979ᵃ1 Further, if God and the One do not move, just because the many move by passing into one another, why should not God also move into something else? For he nowhere states that God is one only, but what he says is that there is only one God. But even supposing God were one only, why should not the parts of God move into

5 one another and God himself thus revolve? For he will not, like Zeno, declare that such a One is many. For he himself asserts that God is a body, whether he calls it the universe or by some other name; for if he were incorporeal, how could he be spherical? Again, it would only be possible for him neither to move nor to be at rest if he were nowhere; but since he is a body, what would prevent this body from

10 moving, as has been said?

5 · Gorgias declares that nothing exists; and if anything exists it is unknowable; and if it exists and is knowable, yet it cannot be indicated to others. To prove that nothing exists he collects the statements of others, who in speaking about what

15 is seem to assert contrary opinions (some trying to prove that what is is one and not many, others that it is many and not one; and some that existents are ungenerated, others that they have come to be), and he argues against both sides. For he says that if anything exists, it must be either one or many, and either be ungenerated or have come to be. If therefore, it cannot be either one or many, ungenerated or having

20 come to be, it would be nothing at all. For if anything were, it would be one of these alternatives. That what is, then, is neither one nor many, neither ungenerated nor having come to be, he attempts to prove by following partly Melissus and partly Zeno, after first stating his own special proof that it is not possible either to be or not

---

[18] Reading ὃ σημαίνει.
[19] Reading αὐτὰς τὰς ἀποφάσεις.

to be. For, he says, if not being is not being, then what is not would *be* no less than   25
what is. For what is not *is* what is not and what is *is* what is, so that things no more
are than are not. But if not being *is,* then, he argues, being, its opposite, is not; for if
not being is, it follows that being is not. So that on this showing, he says, nothing   30
could be, unless being and not being are the same thing. And if they are the same
thing, even so nothing would be; for what is not is not, nor yet what is since it is the
same as what is not. Such, then, is his first argument.

6 · Now it does not at all follow from what he has said that nothing is. For
the proof which he and others attempt is thus refuted: if what is not is, it either is   35
simply, or else it is in a similar sense something that is not. But this is not
self-evident, nor a necessary deduction; but if there are, as it were, two things of
which one is and the other is not, you can truly say of the former that it is, but not of
the latter, because that which is, is existent, but that which is not is non-existent.   979^b1
Why, then, is it not possible either to be or not to be? And why should not both or
either be possible? For, he says, not being, if not being were, as he thinks,
something, would *be* just as much as being, while no-one allows that not being has
any kind of existence. But even if what is not is not, yet it does not follow that what   5
is not is in a similar way to what is; for the former is something that is not, while the
latter actually is as well. But even if he could say of it that it is simply (yet how
strange it would be to say that what is not is), still granted that it were so, does it any
more follow that everything is not rather than is? For the exact opposite seems then
to become the consequent; since, if what is not is something that is and what is is
something that is, all things are; for both the things which are, and the things which   10
are not, are. For it does not necessarily follow that if what is not is, what is is not.
Even if one were to concede the point and allow that what is not is and what is is not,
nevertheless, something would be; for the things which are not would be, according
to his argument. But if being and not being are the same thing, even so it would not   15
follow that nothing is, rather than that something is. For just as he argues that if
what is not and what is are the same thing, what is and what is not alike are not,
therefore nothing is; so, reversing the position, it is equally possible to argue that
everything is; for what is not is and what is is, therefore everything is.

After this argument Gorgias declares that if anything is, it must either be   20
ungenerated or else have come to be. If it is ungenerated, he assumes by the axioms
of Melissus that it is unlimited, and declares that the unlimited cannot exist
anywhere. It cannot, he argues, exist in itself, or in anything else (for, on the latter
supposition, there would be two unlimiteds, that which is in something else and the
something else in which it is); and, being nowhere, it is nothing, according to the
argument of Zeno about space. It is not, therefore, ungenerated. Nor, again, has it   25
come to be; for, surely, he argues, nothing could come to be out of either what is or
what is not. For if what is were to change, it would no longer be anything that is, just
as also, if what is not were to come to be, it would no longer be a thing that is not.
Nor, again, could it come to be, save from what is; for if what is not is not, nothing   30
could come to be out of nothing; while on the other hand, if what is not is, it could
not come to be out of what is not for that reason. So if anything that is, necessarily

either is ungenerated or else has come to be, and these are impossibilities, it is
35 impossible for anything to be.

Further, if anything is, either one or more things must be; if neither one nor
more, nothing is. And there cannot be one thing because what is truly one, insofar as
it has no magnitude, is incorporeal. (This he adopts from Zeno's argument.) But if
there is not one thing, there will be nothing at all; for if there is not one thing, there
cannot be many things. But if there is neither one thing nor many things, he says,
there is nothing.[20]

980ª1 Nor, he says, can anything move. For if it were to move it would no longer be in
the same condition, but what is would not be and what is not would have come to be.
And further, if it moves and is transferred to a different position, what is, being no
5 longer continuous, is divided, and, where it is divided, it no longer exists; and so, if it
moves in all its parts, it is divided in all its parts, and if this is so, it ceases to exist in
all its parts. For where it is divided, he argues, there it lacks being; he uses 'divided'
to mean a void, as is written in the so-called 'Arguments of Leucippus'.

These are the proofs which he employs to show that nothing exists. . . .[21] For all
10 objects of cognition must exist, and what is not, if it really does not exist, could not
be cognized either. But were this so, nothing could be false, not even (he says)
though one should say that chariots are racing on the sea. For all things would be
just the same. For the objects of sight and hearing are for the reason[22] that they are
15 in each case cognized. But if this is not the reason—if just as what we see is not the
more because we see it, so also what we think is not the more for that[23] (and, were it
otherwise, just as in the one case our objects of vision would often be just the same,
so in the other our objects of thought would often be just the same) . . . ; but of
which kind the true things are is uncertain. So that even if things are, they would be
unknowable by us.

20 But even if they are knowable by us, how, he asks, could any one indicate them
to another? For how, he says, could any one communicate by word of mouth that
980ᵇ1 which he has seen? And how could that which has been seen be indicated to a
listener if he has not seen it? For just as the sight does not recognize sounds, so the
hearing does not hear colours but sounds; and he who speaks, speaks, but does not
speak a colour or a thing. When, therefore, one has not a thing in the mind, how will
5 he get it there from another person by word or any other token of the thing except by
seeing it, if it is a colour, or hearing it, if it is a noise? For he who speaks does not
speak a noise at all, or a colour, but a word; and so it is not possible to think a colour,
but only to see it, nor a noise, but only to hear it. But even if it is possible to know
things, and to express whatever one knows in words, yet how can the hearer have in
10 his mind the same thing as the speaker? For the same thing cannot be present

---

[20]This paragraph is very corrupt in the MSS. The translation is based on the following tentative restoration:
καὶ ἓν μὲν οὐκ ἂν εἶναι ὅτι ἀσώματον ἂν εἴη τὸ ὡς ἀληθῶς ἕν, καθὸ οὐδὲν ἔχον μέγεθος (ὃ λαμβάνει τῷ τοῦ
Ζήνωνος λόγῳ) · ἑνὸς δὲ μὴ ὄντος οὐδ' ἂν ὅλως εἶναι οὐδέν · μὴ γὰρ ὄντος ἑνὸς μηδὲ πολλὰ εἶναι. εἰ δὲ μήτε ἕν,
φησίν, μήτε πολλὰ ἔστιν, οὐδὲν ἔστιν.
[21]Reading ὅτι μὲν οὖν οὐδὲν ἔστι, ταύτας τὰς ἀποδείξεις λέγει (followed by a lacuna).
[22]Omitting Diels' addition.
[23]Placing a comma after διανοούμεθα.

simultaneously in several separate people; for in that case the one would be two. But if, he argues, the same thing *could* be present in several persons, there is no reason why it should not appear dissimilar to them, if they are not themselves entirely similar and are not in the same place; for if they were[24] in the same place they would be one and not two. But it appears that the objects which even one and the same man perceives at the same moment are not all similar, but he perceives different things by hearing and by sight, and differently now and on some former occasion; and so a man can scarcely perceive the same thing as someone else.

Thus nothing exists; and even if anything were to exist, nothing is knowable; and even if anything were knowable, no one could indicate it to another, firstly because things are not words, and secondly because no one can have in his mind the same thing as someone else. This and all his other arguments are concerned with difficulties raised by earlier philosophers, so that in examining their views these questions have to be discussed.

[24]Reading εἴησαν.

METAPHYSICS

W. D. Ross

BOOK I (A)

1 · All men by nature desire to know. An indication of this is the delight we take in our senses; for even apart from their usefulness they are loved for themselves; and above all others the sense of sight. For not only with a view to action, but even when we are not going to do anything, we prefer sight to almost everything else. The reason is that this, most of all the senses, makes us know and brings to light many differences between things.

980ᵃ25

By nature animals are born with the faculty of sensation, and from sensation memory is produced in some of them, though not in others. And therefore the former are more intelligent and apt at learning than those which cannot remember; those which are incapable of hearing sounds are intelligent though they cannot be taught, e.g. the bee, and any other race of animals that may be like it; and those which besides memory have this sense of hearing, can be taught.

980ᵇ25

The animals other than man live by appearances and memories, and have but little of connected experience; but the human race lives also by art and reasonings. And from memory experience is produced in men; for many memories of the same thing produce finally the capacity for a single experience. Experience seems to be very similar to science and art, but really science and art come to men *through* experience; for 'experience made art', as Polus says, 'but inexperience luck'. And art arises, when from many notions gained by experience one universal judgement about similar objects is produced. For to have a judgement that when Callias was ill of this disease this did him good, and similarly in the case of Socrates and in many individual cases, is a matter of experience; but to judge that it has done good to all persons of a certain constitution, marked off in one class, when they were ill of this disease, e.g. to phlegmatic or bilious people when burning with fever,—this is a matter of art.

981ᵃ1

5

10

With a view to action experience seems in no respect inferior to art, and we even see men of experience succeeding more than those who have theory without experience. The reason is that experience is knowledge of individuals, art of universals, and actions and productions are all concerned with the individual; for

15

TEXT: W. D. Ross, *Aristotle's Metaphysics*, Clarendon Press, Oxford, 1924

the physician does not cure a man, except in an incidental way, but Callias or Socrates or some other called by some such individual name, who happens to be a   20
man. If, then, a man has theory without experience, and knows the universal but does not know the individual included in this, he will often fail to cure; for it is the individual that is to be cured. But yet we think that *knowledge* and *understanding* belong to art rather than to experience, and we suppose artists to be wiser than men   25
of experience (which implies that wisdom depends in all cases rather on knowledge); and this because the former know the cause, but the latter do not. For men of experience know that the thing is so, but do not know why, while the others know the 'why' and the cause. Hence we think that the master-workers in each craft are more   30
honourable and know in a truer sense and are wiser than the manual workers, because they know the causes of the things that are done (we think the manual   981ᵇ1
workers are like certain lifeless things which act indeed, but act without knowing what they do, as fire burns,—but while the lifeless things perform each of their functions by a natural tendency, the labourers perform them through habit); thus we view them as being wiser not in virtue of being able to act, but of having the   5
theory for themselves and knowing the causes. And in general it is a sign of the man who knows, that he can teach, and therefore we think art more truly knowledge than experience is; for artists can teach, and men of mere experience cannot.

Again, we do not regard any of the senses as wisdom; yet surely these give the   10
most authoritative knowledge of particulars. But they do not tell us the 'why' of anything—e.g. why fire is hot; they only say that it is hot.

At first he who invented any art that went beyond the common perceptions of man was naturally admired by men, not only because there was something useful in   15
the inventions, but because he was thought wise and superior to the rest. But as more arts were invented, and some were directed to the necessities of life, others to its recreation, the inventors of the latter were always regarded as wiser than the inventors of the former, because their branches of knowledge did not aim at utility.   20
Hence when all such inventions were already established, the sciences which do not aim at giving pleasure or at the necessities of life were discovered, and first in the places where men first began to have leisure. This is why the mathematical arts were founded in Egypt; for there the priestly caste was allowed to be at leisure.

We have said in the *Ethics* what the difference is between art and science and   25
the other kindred faculties; but the point of our present discussion is this, that all men suppose what is called wisdom to deal with the first causes and the principles of things. This is why, as has been said before, the man of experience is thought to be   30
wiser than the possessors of any perception whatever, the artist wiser than the men of experience, the master-worker than the mechanic, and the theoretical kinds of knowledge to be more of the nature of wisdom than the productive. Clearly then   982ᵃ1
wisdom is knowledge about certain causes and principles.

2 · Since we are seeking this knowledge, we must inquire of what kind are the causes and the principles, the knowledge of which is wisdom. If we were to take   5
the notions we have about the wise man, this might perhaps make the answer more

evident. We suppose first, then, that the wise man knows all things, as far as possible, although he has not knowledge of each of them individually; secondly, that

10   he who can learn things that are difficult, and not easy for man to know, is wise (sense-perception is common to all, and therefore easy and no mark of wisdom); again, he who is more exact and more capable of teaching the causes is wiser, in every branch of knowledge; and of the sciences, also, that which is desirable on its

15   own account and for the sake of knowing it is more of the nature of wisdom than that which is desirable on account of its results, and the superior science is more of the nature of wisdom than the ancillary; for the wise man must not be ordered but must order, and he must not obey another, but the less wise must obey *him*.

20   Such and so many are the notions, then, which we have about wisdom and the wise. Now of these characteristics that of knowing all things must belong to him who has in the highest degree universal knowledge; for he knows in a sense all the subordinate objects. And these things, the most universal, are on the whole the

25   hardest for men to know; for they are furthest from the senses. And the most exact of the sciences are those which deal most with first principles; for those which involve fewer principles are more exact than those which involve additional principles, e.g. arithmetic than geometry. But the science which investigates causes is also more capable of teaching, for the people who teach are those who tell the

30   causes of each thing. And understanding and knowledge pursued for their own sake are found most in the knowledge of that which is most knowable; for he who chooses to know for the sake of knowing will choose most readily that which is most truly

982ᵇ1   knowledge, and such is the knowledge of that which is most knowable; and the first principles and the causes are most knowable; for by reason of these, and from these, all other things are known, but these are not known by means of the things

5   subordinate to them. And the science which knows to what end each thing must be done is the most authoritative of the sciences, and more authoritative than any ancillary science; and this end is the good in each class, and in general the supreme good in the whole of nature. Judged by all the tests we have mentioned, then, the name in question falls to the same science; this must be a science that investigates the first principles and causes; for the good, i.e. that for the sake of which, is one of

10   the causes.

      That it is not a science of production is clear even from the history of the earliest philosophers. For it is owing to their wonder that men both now begin and at first began to philosophize; they wondered originally at the obvious difficulties, then

15   advanced little by little and stated difficulties about the greater matters, e.g. about the phenomena of the moon and those of the sun and the stars, and about the genesis of the universe. And a man who is puzzled and wonders thinks himself ignorant (whence even the lover of myth is in a sense a lover of wisdom, for myth is composed

20   of wonders); therefore since they philosophized in order to escape from ignorance, evidently they were pursuing science in order to know, and not for any utilitarian end. And this is confirmed by the facts; for it was when almost all the necessities of life and the things that make for comfort and recreation were present, that such

25   knowledge began to be sought. Evidently then we do not seek it for the sake of any

other advantage; but as the man is free, we say, who exists for himself and not for another, so we pursue this as the only free science, for it alone exists for itself.

Hence the possession of it might be justly regarded as beyond human power; for in many ways human nature is in bondage, so that according to Simonides 'God alone can have this privilege', and it is unfitting that man should not be content to seek the knowledge that is suited to him. If, then, there is something in what the poets say, and jealousy is natural to the divine power, it would probably occur in this case above all, and all who excelled in this knowledge would be unfortunate. But the divine power cannot be jealous (indeed, according to the proverb, 'bards tell many a lie'), nor should any science be thought more honourable than one of this sort. For the most divine science is also most honourable; and this science alone is, in two ways, most divine. For the science which it would be most meet for God to have is a divine science, and so is any science that deals with divine objects; and this science alone has both these qualities; for God is thought to be among the causes of all things and to be a first principle, and such a science either God alone can have, or God above all others. All the sciences, indeed, are more necessary than this, but none is better.

Yet the acquisition of it must in a sense end in something which is the opposite of our original inquiries. For all men begin, as we said, by wondering that the matter is so (as in the case of automatic marionettes or the solstices or the incommensurability of the diagonal of a square with the side; for it seems wonderful to all men who have not yet perceived the explanation that there is a thing which cannot be measured even by the smallest unit). But we must end in the contrary and, according to the proverb, the better state, as is the case in these instances when men learn the cause; for there is nothing which would surprise a geometer so much as if the diagonal turned out to be commensurable.

We have stated, then, what is the nature of the science we are searching for, and what is the mark which our search and our whole investigation must reach.

3 · Evidently we have to acquire knowledge of the original causes (for we say we know each thing only when we think we recognize its first cause), and causes are spoken of in four senses. In one of these we mean the substance, i.e. the essence (for the 'why' is referred finally to the formula,[1] and the ultimate 'why' is a cause and principle); in another the matter or substratum, in a third the source of the change, and in a fourth the cause opposed to this, that for the sake of which and the good (for this is the end of all generation and change). We have studied these causes sufficiently in our work on nature, but yet let us call to our aid those who have attacked the investigation of being and philosophized about reality before us. For obviously they too speak of certain principles and causes; to go over their views, then, will be of profit to the present inquiry, for we shall either find another kind of cause, or be more convinced of the correctness of those which we now maintain.

Of the first philosophers, most thought the principles which were of the nature

30

983ᵃ1

5

10

15

20

25

30

983ᵇ1

5

---

[1]In the translation of the *Metaphysics* 'formula' (or 'definitory formula') renders 'λόγος'.

of matter were the only principles of all things; that of which all things that are consist, and from which they first come to be, and into which they are finally
10 resolved (the substance remaining, but changing in its modifications), this they say is the element and the principle of things, and therefore they think nothing is either generated or destroyed, since this sort of entity is always conserved, as we say Socrates neither comes to be absolutely when he comes to be beautiful or musical,
15 nor ceases to be when he loses these characteristics, because the substratum, Socrates himself, remains. So they say nothing else comes to be or ceases to be; for there must be some entity—either one or more than one—from which all other things come to be, it being conserved.

Yet they do not all agree as to the number and the nature of these principles.
20 Thales, the founder of this school of philosophy, says the principle is water (for which reason he declared that the earth rests on water), getting the notion perhaps from seeing that the nutriment of all things is moist, and that heat itself is generated from the moist and kept alive by it (and that from which they come to be is a
25 principle of all things). He got his notion from this fact, and from the fact that the seeds of all things have a moist nature, and that water is the origin of the nature of moist things.

Some think that the ancients who lived long before the present generation, and
30 first framed accounts of the gods, had a similar view of nature; for they made Ocean and Tethys the parents of creation, and described the oath of the gods as being by water, which they themselves call Styx; for what is oldest is most honourable, and the most honourable thing is that by which one swears. It may perhaps be uncertain
984ª1 whether this opinion about nature is primitive and ancient, but Thales at any rate is said to have declared himself thus about the first cause. Hippo no one would think fit to include among these thinkers, because of the paltriness of his thought.
5 Anaximenes and Diogenes make air prior to water, and the most primary of the simple bodies, while Hippasus of Metapontium and Heraclitus of Ephesus say this of fire, and Empedocles says it of the four elements, adding a fourth— earth—to those which have been named; for these, he says, always remain and do
10 not come to be, except that they come to be more or fewer, being aggregated into one and segregated out of one.

Anaxagoras of Clazomenae, who, though older than Empedocles, was later in his philosophical activity, says the principles are infinite in number; for he says almost all the things that are homogeneous are generated and destroyed (as water
15 or fire is) only by aggregation and segregation, and are not in any other sense generated or destroyed, but remain eternally.

From these facts one might think that the only cause is the so-called material cause; but as men thus advanced, the very facts showed them the way and joined in forcing them to investigate the subject. However true it may be that all generation
20 and destruction proceed from some one or more elements, why does this happen and what is the cause? For at least the substratum itself does not make itself change; e.g. neither the wood nor the bronze causes the change of either of them, nor does the
25 wood manufacture a bed and the bronze a statue, but something else is the cause of

the change. And to seek this is to seek the second cause, as *we* should say,—that from which comes the beginning of movement. Now those who at the very beginning set themselves to this kind of inquiry, and said the substratum was one, were not at all dissatisfied with themselves; but some at least of those who maintain it to be one—as though defeated by this search for the second cause—say the one   30 and nature as a whole is unchangeable not only in respect of generation and destruction (for this is an ancient belief, and all agreed in it), but also of all other change; and this view is peculiar to them. Of those who said the universe was one,   984ᵇ1 none succeeded in discovering a cause of this sort, except perhaps Parmenides, and he only insomuch that he supposes that there is not only one but in some sense two causes. But for those who make more elements it is more possible to state the second   5 cause, e.g. for those who make hot and cold, or fire and earth, the elements; for they treat fire as having a nature which fits it to move things, and water and earth and such things they treat in the contrary way.

When these men and the principles of this kind had had their day, as the latter were found inadequate to generate the nature of things, men were again forced by the truth itself, as we said, to inquire into the next kind of cause. For surely it is not   10 likely either that fire or earth or any such element should be the reason why things manifest goodness and beauty both in their being and in their coming to be, or that those thinkers should have supposed it was; nor again could it be right to ascribe so great a matter to spontaneity and luck. When one man said, then, that reason was   15 present—as in animals, so throughout nature—as the cause of the world and of all its order, he seemed like a sober man in contrast with the random talk of his predecessors. We know that Anaxagoras certainly adopted these views, but Hermotimus of Clazomenae is credited with expressing them earlier. Those who   20 thought thus stated that there is a principle of things which is at the same time the cause of beauty, and that sort of cause from which things acquire movement.

4 · One might suspect that Hesiod was the first to look for such a thing—or some one else who put love or desire among existing things as a principle, as Parmenides does; for he, in constructing the genesis of the universe, says:—   25

> Love first of all the Gods she planned.

And Hesiod says:—

> First of all things was chaos made, and then
> Broad-breasted earth, and love that foremost is
> Among all the immortals,

which implies that among existing things there must be a cause which will move   30 things and bring them together. How these thinkers should be arranged with regard to priority of discovery let us be allowed to decide later; but since the contraries of the various forms of good were also perceived to be present in nature—not only order and the beautiful, but also disorder and the ugly, and bad things in greater   985ᵃ1 number than good, and ignoble things than beautiful, therefore another thinker

introduced friendship and strife, each of the two the cause of one of these two sets of qualities. For if we were to follow out the view of Empedocles, and interpret it according to its meaning and not to its lisping expression, we should find that
5   friendship is the cause of good things, and strife of bad. Therefore, if we said that Empedocles in a sense both mentions, and is the first to mention, the bad and the good as principles, we should perhaps be right, since the cause of all goods is the
10   good itself.

These thinkers, as we say, evidently got hold up to a certain point of two of the causes which we distinguished in our work on nature—the matter and the source of the movement,—vaguely, however, and with no clearness, but as untrained men
15   behave in fights; for they go round their opponents and often strike fine blows, but they do not fight on scientific principles, and so these thinkers do not seem to know what they say; for it is evident that, as a rule, they make no use of their causes except to a small extent. For Anaxagoras uses reason as a *deus ex machina* for the making of the world, and when he is at a loss to tell for what cause something
20   necessarily is, then he drags reason in, but in all other cases ascribes events to anything rather than to reason. And Empedocles, though he uses the causes to a greater extent than this, neither does so sufficiently nor attains consistency in their use. At least, in many cases he makes friendship segregate things, and strife
25   aggregate them. For when the universe is dissolved into its elements by strife, fire is aggregated into one, and so is each of the other elements; but when again under the influence of friendship they come together into one, the parts must again be segregated out of each element.

Empedocles, then, in contrast with his predecessors, was the first to introduce
30   this cause in a divided form, not positing one source of movement, but different and contrary sources. Again, he was the first to speak of four material elements; yet he
985ᵇ1   does not *use* four, but treats them as two only; he treats fire by itself, and its opposites—earth, air, and water—as one kind of thing. We may learn this by study of his verses.

This philosopher then, as we say, spoke of the principles in this way, and made
5   them of this number. Leucippus and his associate Democritus say that the full and the empty are the elements, calling the one being and the other non-being—the full and solid being, the empty non-being (that is why they say that what is is no more than what is not, because body no more is than the void); and they make these the
10   material causes of things. And as those who make the underlying substance one generate all other things by its modifications, supposing the rare and the dense to be the sources of the modifications, in the same way these philosophers say the differences in the elements are the causes of all other qualities. These differences,
15   they say, are three—shape and order and position. For they say that what is is differentiated only by 'rhythm' and 'inter-contact' and 'turning'; and of these rhythm is shape, inter-contact is order, and turning is position; for A differs from N in shape, AN from NA in order, Ⅱ from H in position. The question of movement—whence or how it belongs to things—these thinkers, like the others,
20   lazily neglected.

Regarding the two causes, then, as we say, the inquiry seems to have been pushed thus far by the early philosophers.

5 · Contemporaneously with these philosophers and before them, the Pythagoreans, as they are called, devoted themselves to mathematics; they were the first to advance this study, and having been brought up in it they thought its principles were the principles of all things. Since of these principles numbers are by nature the first, and in numbers they seemed to see many resemblances to the things that exist and come into being—more than in fire and earth and water (such and such a modification of numbers being justice, another being soul and reason, another being opportunity—and similarly almost all other things being numerically expressible); since, again, they saw that the attributes and the ratios of the musical scales were expressible in numbers; since, then, all other things seemed in their whole nature to be modelled after numbers, and numbers seemed to be the first things in the whole of nature, they supposed the elements of numbers to be the elements of all things, and the whole heaven to be a musical scale and a number. And all the properties of numbers and scales which they could show to agree with the attributes and parts and the whole arrangement of the heavens, they collected and fitted into their scheme; and if there was a gap anywhere, they readily made additions so as to make their whole theory coherent. E.g. as the number 10 is thought to be perfect and to comprise the whole nature of numbers, they say that the bodies which move through the heavens are ten, but as the visible bodies are only nine, to meet this they invent a tenth—the 'counter-earth'. We have discussed these matters more exactly elsewhere.

But the object of our discussion is that we may learn from these philosophers also what they suppose to be the principles and how these fall under the causes we have named. Evidently, then, these thinkers also consider that number is the principle both as matter for things and as forming their modifications and states, and hold that the elements of number are the even and the odd, and of these the former is unlimited, and the latter limited; and the 1 proceeds from both of these (for it is both even and odd), and number from the 1; and the whole heaven, as has been said, is numbers.

Other members of this same school say there are ten principles, which they arrange in two columns of cognates—limit and unlimited, odd and even, one and plurality, right and left, male and female, resting and moving, straight and curved, light and darkness, good and bad, square and oblong. In this way Alcmaeon of Croton seems also to have conceived the matter,[2] and either he got this view from them or they got it from him; for he expressed himself similarly to them. For he says most human affairs go in pairs, meaning not definite contrarieties such as the Pythagoreans speak of, but any chance contrarieties, e.g. white and black, sweet and bitter, good and bad, great and small. He threw out indefinite suggestions about

[2]Some authorities read: 'For Alcmaeon lived during the old age of Pythagoras, and he expressed himself. . .'.

986ᵇ1 the other contrarieties, but the Pythagoreans declared both how many and which
their contrarieties are.

From both these schools, then, we can learn this much, that the contraries are
the principles of things; and how many these principles are and which they are, we
can learn from one of the two schools. But how these principles can be brought
5 together under the causes we have named has not been clearly and articulately
stated by them; they seem, however, to range the elements under the head of matter;
for out of these as immanent parts they say substance is composed and moulded.

From these facts we may sufficiently perceive the meaning of the ancients who
10 said the elements of nature were more than one; but there are some who spoke of the
universe as if it were one entity, though they were not all alike either in the
excellence of their statement or in regard to the nature of the entity. The discussion
of them is in no way appropriate to our present investigation of causes, for they do
not, like some of the natural philosophers, assume what exists to be one and yet
15 generate it out of the one as out of matter, but they speak in another way; those
others add change, since they generate the universe, but these thinkers say the
universe is unchangeable. Yet this much is appropriate to the present inquiry:
Parmenides seems to fasten on that which is one in formula, Melissus on that which
20 is one in matter, for which reason the former says that it is limited, the latter that it
is unlimited; while Xenophanes, the first of this school of monists (for Parmenides is
said to have been his pupil), gave no clear statement, nor does he seem to have
grasped either of these two kinds of unity, but he contemplates the whole heaven
25 and says the One is God. Now these thinkers, as we said, must be neglected for the
purposes of the present inquiry—two of them entirely, as being a little too naïve, viz.
Xenophanes and Melissus; but Parmenides seems to speak with somewhat more
insight. For, claiming that, besides the existent, nothing non-existent exists, he
thinks that the existent is of necessity one and that nothing else exists (on this we
30 have spoken more clearly in our work on nature), but being forced to follow the
phenomena, and supposing that what is³ is one in formula but many according to
perception, he now posits two causes and two principles, calling them hot and cold,
987ᵃ1 i.e. fire and earth; and of these he ranges the hot with the existent, and the other
with the non-existent.

From what has been said, then, and from the wise men who have now sat in
council with us, we have got this much—both from the earliest philosophers, who
regard the first principle as corporeal (for water and fire and such things are
5 bodies), and of whom some suppose that there is one corporeal principle, others that
there are more than one, but both put these under the head of matter; and from
some others who posit both this cause and besides this the source of movement,
which is stated by some as one and by others as two.

10 Down to the Italian school, then, and apart from it, philosophers have treated
these subjects rather obscurely, except that, as we said, they have used two kinds of
cause, and one of these—the source of movement—some treat as one and others as

---

³Reading τὸ ὄν ἓν μέν.

two. But the Pythagoreans have said in the same way that there are two principles, but added this much, which is peculiar to them, that they thought finitude and infinity were not attributes of certain other things, e.g. of fire or earth or anything else of this kind, but that infinity itself and unity itself were the substance of the things of which they are predicated. This is why number was the substance of all things. On this subject, then, they expressed themselves thus; and regarding the question of essence they began to make statements and definitions, but treated the matter too simply. For they both defined superficially and thought that the first subject of which a given term would be predicable, was the substance of the thing, as if one supposed that double and 2 were the same, because 2 is the first thing of which double is predicable. But surely to be double and to be 2 are not the same; if they are, one thing will be many—a consequence which they actually drew. From the earlier philosophers, then, and from their successors we can learn this much.

6 · After the systems we have named came the philosophy of Plato, which in most respects followed these thinkers, but had peculiarities that distinguished it from the philosophy of the Italians. For, having in his youth first become familiar with Cratylus and with the Heraclitean doctrines (that all sensible things are ever in a state of flux and there is no knowledge about them), these views he held even in later years. Socrates, however, was busying himself about ethical matters and neglecting the world of nature as a whole but seeking the universal in these ethical matters, and fixed thought for the first time on definitions; Plato accepted his teaching, but held that the problem applied not to any sensible thing but to entities of another kind—for this reason, that the common definition could not be a definition of any sensible thing, as they were always changing. Things of this other sort, then, he called Ideas, and sensible things, he said, were apart from these, and were all called after these; for the multitude of things which have the same name as the Form exist by participation in it. Only the name 'participation' was new; for the Pythagoreans say that things exist by imitation of numbers, and Plato says they exist by participation, changing the name. But what the participation or the imitation of the Forms could be they left an open question.

Further, besides sensible things and Forms he says there are the objects of mathematics, which occupy an intermediate position, differing from sensible things in being eternal and unchangeable, from Forms in that there are many alike, while the Form itself is in each case unique.

Since the Forms are the causes of all other things, he thought their elements were the elements of all things. As matter, the great and the small were principles; as substance, the One; for from the great and the small, by participation in the One, come the numbers.[4]

But he agreed with the Pythagoreans in saying that the One is substance and not a predicate of something else; and in saying that the numbers are the causes of the substance of other things, he also agreed with them; but positing a dyad and constructing the infinite out of great and small, instead of treating the infinite as

[4]The MSS read τὰ εἴδη εἶναι τοὺς ἀριθμούς, 'come the Forms, i.e. the numbers'.

one, is peculiar to him; and so is his view that the numbers exist apart from sensible things, while *they* say that the things themselves are numbers, and do not place the objects of mathematics between Forms and sensible things. His divergence from the

30 Pythagoreans in making the One and the numbers separate from things, and his introduction of the Forms, were due to his inquiries in the region of definitory formulae (for the earlier thinkers had no tincture of dialectic), and his making the other entity besides the One a dyad was due to the belief that the numbers, except those which were prime, could be neatly produced out of the dyad as out of a plastic material.

988ª1 Yet what happens is the contrary; the theory is not a reasonable one. For they make many things out of the matter, and the form generates only once, but what we observe is that one table is made from one matter, while the man who applies the

5 form, though he is one, makes many tables. And the relation of the male to the female is similar; for the latter is impregnated by one copulation, but the male impregnates many females; yet these are imitations of those first principles.

Plato, then, declared himself thus on the points in question; it is evident from what has been said that he has used only two causes, that of the essence and the

10 material cause (for the Forms are the cause of the essence of all other things, and the One is the cause of the essence of the Forms); and it is evident what the underlying matter is, of which the Forms are predicated in the case of sensible things, and the One in the case of Forms, viz. that this is a dyad, the great and the small. Further, he has assigned the cause of good and that of evil to the elements,

15 one to each of the two, as we say some of his predecessors sought to do, e.g. Empedocles and Anaxagoras.

7 · Our account of those who have spoken about first principles and reality and of the way in which they have spoken, has been concise and summary; but yet

20 we have learnt this much from them, that of those who speak about principle and cause no one has mentioned any principle except those which have been distinguished in our work on nature, but all evidently have some inkling of *them*, though only vaguely. For some speak of the first principle as matter, whether they

25 suppose one or more first principles, and whether they suppose this to be a body or to be incorporeal; e.g. Plato spoke of the great and the small, the Italians of the infinite, Empedocles of fire, earth, water, and air, Anaxagoras of the infinity of homogeneous things. These, then, have all had a notion of this kind of cause, and so

30 have all who speak of air or fire or water, or something denser than fire and rarer than air; for some have said the prime element is of this kind. These thinkers grasped this cause only; but certain others have mentioned the source of movement, e.g. those who make friendship and strife, or reason, or love, a principle.

The essence, i.e. the substance of things, no one has expressed distinctly. It is

988ᵇ1 mentioned chiefly by those who believe in the Forms; for they do not suppose either that the Forms are the matter of sensible things, and the One the matter of the Forms, or that they are the source of movement (for they say these are causes rather of immobility and of being at rest), but they furnish the Forms as the essence of

5 every other thing, and the One as the essence of the Forms.

That for the sake of which actions and changes and movements take place, they assert to be a cause in a way, but not in this way, i.e. not in the way in which it is its *nature* to be a cause. For those who speak of reason or friendship class these causes as goods; they do not speak, however, as if anything that exists either existed or came into being for the sake of these, but as if movements started from these. In the same way those who say the One or the existent is the good, say that it is the cause of substance, but not that substance either is or comes to be for the sake of this. Therefore it turns out that in a sense they both say and do not say the good is a cause; for they do not call it a cause *qua* good but only incidentally.

All these thinkers, then, as they cannot pitch on another cause, seem to testify that we have determined rightly both how many and of what sort the causes are. Besides this it is plain that when the causes are being looked for, either all four must be sought thus or they must be sought in one of these four ways. Let us next discuss the possible difficulties with regard to the way in which each of these thinkers has spoken, and with regard to his views about the first principles.

8 · Those, then, who say the universe is one and posit one kind of thing as matter, and as corporeal matter which has spatial magnitude, evidently go astray in many ways. For they posit the elements of bodies only, not of incorporeal things, though there are incorporeal things. And in trying to state the causes of generation and destruction, and in giving an account of the nature of all things, they do away with the cause of movement. Further, they err in not positing the substance, i.e. the essence, as the cause of anything, and besides this in lightly calling any of the simple bodies except earth the first principle, without inquiring how they are produced out of one another,—I mean fire, water, earth, and air. For some things are produced out of others by combination, others by separation, and this makes the greatest difference to their priority and posteriority. For in a way the property of being most elementary of all would seem to belong to the first thing from which they are produced by combination, and *this* property would belong to the most fine-grained and subtle of bodies. Therefore those who make fire the principle would be most in agreement with this argument. But each of the other thinkers agrees that the element of corporeal things is of this sort. At least none of the later philosophers who said the world was one claimed that earth was the element, evidently because of the coarseness of its grain. (Of the other three elements each has found some judge on its side; for some maintain that fire, others that water, others that air is the element. Yet why, after all, do they not name earth also, as most men do—for people say all things are earth. And Hesiod says earth was produced first of corporeal things; so ancient and popular has the opinion been.) According to this argument, then, no one would be right who either says the first principle is any of the elements other than fire, or supposes it to be denser than air but rarer than water. But if that which is later in generation is prior in nature, and that which is concocted and compounded is later in generation, the contrary of what we have been saying must be true,—water must be prior to air, and earth to water.

Let this suffice, then, as our statement about those who posit one cause such as we mentioned; but the same is true if we suppose more of these, as Empedocles says the matter of things is four bodies. For he too is confronted by consequences some of which are the same as have been mentioned, while others are peculiar to him. For we see these bodies produced from one another, which implies that the same body does not always remain fire or earth (we have spoken about this in our works on nature); and regarding the moving cause and the question whether we must suppose one or two, he must be thought to have spoken neither correctly nor altogether plausibly. And in general those who speak in this way must do away with change of quality, for on their view cold will not come from hot nor hot from cold. For if it did there would be something that accepted those very contraries, and there would be some one entity that became fire and water, which Empedocles denies.

As regards Anaxagoras, if one were to suppose that he said there were two elements, the supposition would accord thoroughly with a view which Anaxagoras himself did not state articulately, but which he must have accepted if any one had developed his view. True, to say that in the beginning all things were mixed is absurd both on other grounds and because it follows that they must have existed before in an unmixed form, and because nature does not allow any chance thing to be mixed with any chance thing, and also because on this view modifications and accidents could be separated from substances (for the same things which are mixed can be separated); yet if one were to follow him up, piecing together what he means, he would perhaps be seen to be somewhat modern in his views. For when nothing was separated out, evidently nothing could be truly asserted of the substance that then existed. I mean, e.g. that it was neither white nor black, nor grey nor any other colour, but of necessity colourless; for if it had been coloured, it would have had one of these colours. And similarly, by this same argument, it was flavourless, nor had it any similar attribute; for it could not be either of any quality or of any size, nor could it be any definite kind of thing. For if it were, one of the particular forms would have belonged to it, and this is impossible, since all were mixed together; for the particular form would necessarily have been already separated out, but he says all were mixed except reason, and this alone was unmixed and pure. From this it follows, then, that he must say the principles are the One (for this is simple and unmixed) and the Other, which is of such a nature as we suppose the indefinite to be before it is defined and partakes of some form. Therefore, while expressing himself neither rightly nor clearly, he means something like what the later thinkers say and what is now more clearly seen to be the case.

But these thinkers are, after all, at home only in arguments about generation and destruction and movement; for it is practically only of this sort of substance that they seek the principles and the causes. But those who extend their vision to all things that exist, and of existing things suppose some to be perceptible and others not perceptible, evidently study both classes, which is all the more reason why one should devote some time to seeing what is good in their views and what bad from the stand-point of the inquiry we have now before us.

The 'Pythagoreans' use stranger principles and elements than the natural philosophers (the reason is that they got the principles from non-sensible things, for the objects of mathematics, except those of astronomy, are of the class of things without movement); yet their discussions and investigations are all about nature; for they generate the heavens, and with regard to their parts and attributes and functions they observe the phenomena, and use up the principles and the causes in explaining these, which implies that they agree with the others, the natural philosophers, that what exists is just all that which is perceptible and contained by the so-called heavens. But the causes and the principles which they mention are, as we said, sufficient to act as steps even up to the higher realms of reality, and are more suited to these than to theories about nature. They do not tell us at all, however, how there can be movement if limit and unlimited and odd and even are the only things assumed, or how without process and change there can be generation and destruction, or how the bodies that move through the heavens can do what they do. Further, if we either granted them that spatial magnitude consists of these elements, or this were proved still how would some bodies be light and others have weight? To judge from what they assume and maintain, they speak no more of mathematical bodies than of perceptible; hence they have said nothing whatever about fire or earth or the other bodies of this sort, I suppose because they have nothing to say which applies *peculiarly* to perceptible things.

Further, how are we to combine the beliefs that the modifications of number, and number itself, are causes of what exists and happens in the heavens both from the beginning and now, and that there is no other number than this number out of which the world is composed? When in one particular region they place opinion and opportunity, and, a little above or below, injustice and sifting or mixture, and allege as proof of this that each one of these is a number, but when there happens to be already in each place a plurality of the extended bodies composed of numbers, because these modifications of number attach to the various groups of places,—this being so, is this number, which we must suppose each of these abstractions to be, the same number which is exhibited in the material universe, or is it another than this? Plato says it is different; yet even he thinks that both these bodies and their causes are numbers, but that the *intelligible* numbers are causes, while the others are *sensible*.

9 · Let us leave the Pythagoreans for the present; for it is enough to have touched on them as much as we have done. But as for those who posit the Ideas as causes, firstly, in seeking to grasp the causes of the things around us, they introduced others equal in number to these, as if a man who wanted to count things thought he could not do it while they were few, but tried to count them when he had added to their number. For the Forms are practically equal to or not fewer than the things, in trying to explain which these thinkers proceeded from them to the Forms. For to each set of substances there answers a Form which has the same name and exists apart from the substances, and so also in the case of all other groups in which there is one character common to many things, whether the things are in this changeable world or are eternal.

Further, of the ways in which we prove that the Forms exist, none is convincing; for from some no inference necessarily follows, and from some it follows that there are Forms of things of which we think there are no Forms.

For according to the arguments from the existence of the sciences there will be

Forms of all things of which there are sciences, and according to the argument that there is one attribute common to many things there will be Forms even of negations, and according to the argument that there is an object for thought even when the thing has perished, there will be Forms of perishable things; for we can have an image of these.

15 Further, of the more accurate arguments, some lead to Ideas of relations, of which we say there is no independent class, and others involve the difficulty of the 'third man'.

And in general the arguments for the Forms destroy the things for whose existence we are more anxious than for the existence of the Ideas; for it follows that 20 not the dyad but number is first, i.e. that the relative is prior to the absolute— besides all the other points on which certain people by following out the opinions held about the Ideas have come into conflict with the principles of the theory.

Further, according to the assumption on which our belief in the Ideas rests, there will be Forms not only of substances but also of many other things (for the 25 concept is single not only in the case of substances but also in the other cases, and there are sciences not only of substance but also of other things, and a thousand other such conclusions also follow). But according to the necessities of the case and the opinions held about the Forms, if they can be shared there must be Ideas of 30 substances only. For they are not shared incidentally, but a thing must share in its Form as in something not predicated of a subject (e.g. if a thing shares in double itself, it shares also in eternal, but incidentally; for eternal happens to be predicable of the double). Therefore the Forms will be substance; and the same terms indicate 991ᵃ1 substance in this and in the ideal world (or what will be the meaning of saying that there is something apart from the particulars—the one over many?). And if the Ideas and the particulars that share them have the same Form, there will be something common to these; for why should 2 be one and the same in the perishable 5 2's or in those which are many but eternal, and not the same in the 2 itself as in the particular 2? But if they have not the same Form, they must have only the name in common, and it is as if one were to call both Callias and a wooden image a man, without observing any community between them.

Above all one might discuss the question what on earth the Forms contribute to 10 sensible things, either to those that are eternal or to those that come into being and cease to be. For they cause neither movement nor any change in them. But again they help in no way towards the *knowledge* of the other things (for they are not even the substance of these, else they would have been in them), nor towards their being, if they are not *in* the particulars which share in them; though if they were, they 15 might be thought to be causes, as white causes whiteness in that with which it is mixed. But this argument, which first Anaxagoras and later Eudoxus and certain others used, is too easily upset; for it is not difficult to collect many insuperable objections to such a view.

20 But further all other things cannot come from the Forms in any of the usual senses of 'from'. And to say that they are patterns and the other things share them is to use empty words and poetical metaphors. For what is it that works, looking to the Ideas? Anything can either be, or become, like another without being copied from

it, so that whether Socrates exists or not a man might come to be like Socrates; and   25
evidently this might be so even if Socrates were eternal. And there will be several
patterns of the same thing, and therefore several Forms, e.g. animal and two-footed
and also man himself will be Forms of man. Again, the Forms are patterns not only
of sensible things, but of themselves too, e.g. the Form of genus will be a genus of   30
Forms; therefore the same thing will be pattern and copy.

Again it must be held to be impossible that the substance and that of which it is   991ᵇ1
the substance should exist apart; how, therefore, can the Ideas, being the substances
of things, exist apart?

In the *Phaedo* the case is stated in this way—that the Forms are causes both of
being and of becoming; yet when the Forms exist, still the things that share in them
do not come into being, unless there is some efficient cause; and many other things   5
come into being (e.g. a house or a ring), of which we say there are no Forms.
Clearly, therefore, even the other things can both be and come into being owing to
such causes as produce the things just mentioned.

Again, if the forms are numbers, how can they be causes? Is it because existing
things are other numbers, e.g. one number is man, another is Socrates, another   10
Callias? Why then are the one set of numbers causes of the other set? It will not
make any difference even if the former are eternal and the latter are not. But if it is
because things in this sensible world (e.g. harmony) are ratios of numbers, evidently
there is some one class of things of which they are ratios. If, then, this—the
matter—is some definite thing, evidently the numbers themselves too will be ratios   15
of something to something else. E.g. if Callias is a numerical ratio between fire and
earth and water and air, his Idea also will be a number of certain other underlying
things; and the Idea of man, whether it is a number in a sense or not, will still be a
numerical ratio of certain things and not a number proper, nor will it be a number
merely because it is a numerical ratio.   20

Again, from many numbers one number is produced, but how can one Form
come from many Forms? And if the number comes not from the many numbers
themselves but from the units in them, e.g. in 10,000, how is it with the units? If
they are specifically alike, numerous absurdities will follow, and also if they are not
alike (neither the units in the same number being like one another nor those in   25
different numbers being all like to all); for in what will they differ, as they are
without quality? This is not a plausible view, nor can it be consistently thought out.
Further, they must set up a second kind of number (with which arithmetic deals),
and all the objects which are called intermediate by some thinkers; and how do
these exist or from what principles do they proceed? Or why must they be
intermediate between the things in this sensible world and the things-in-   30
themselves? Further, the units in 2 must each come from a prior 2; but this is
impossible. Further, why is a number, when taken all together, one? Again, besides   992ᵃ1
what has been said, if the units are *diverse* they should have spoken like those who
say there are four, or two, elements; for each of these thinkers gives the name of
element not to that which is common, e.g. to body, but to fire and earth, whether   5
there is something common to them, viz. body, or not. But in fact they speak as if the
One were *homogeneous* like fire or water; and if this is so, the numbers will not be

substances. Evidently, if there is a One-in-itself and this is a first principle, 'one' is being used in more than one sense; for otherwise the theory is impossible.

10 When we wish to refer substances to their principles, we state that lines come from the short and long (i.e. from a kind of small and great), and the plane from the broad and narrow, and the solid from the deep and shallow. Yet how then can the plane contain a line, or the solid a line or a plane? For the broad and narrow is a 15 different class of things from the deep and shallow. Therefore, just as number is not present in these, because the many and few are different from these, evidently no other of the higher classes will be present in the lower. But again the broad is not a genus which includes the deep, for then the solid would have been a species of plane. Further, from what principle will the presence of the points in the line be derived? 20 Plato even used to object to this class of things as being a geometrical fiction. He called the indivisible lines the principle of lines—and he used to lay this down often. Yet these must have a limit; therefore the argument from which the existence of the line follows proves also the existence of the point.

In general, though philosophy seeks the cause of perceptible things, we have 25 given this up (for we say nothing of the cause from which change takes its start), but while we fancy we are stating the substance of perceptible things, we assert the existence of a second class of substances, while our account of the way in which they are the substances of perceptible things is empty talk; for sharing, as we said before, means nothing. Nor have the Forms any connexion with that which we see to be the 30 cause in the case of the sciences, and for whose sake mind and nature produce all that they *do* produce,—with this cause we assert to be one of the first principles; but mathematics has come to be the whole of philosophy for modern thinkers, though they say that it should be studied for the sake of other things. Further, one might 992ᵇ1 suppose that the substance which according to them underlies as matter is too mathematical, and is a predicate and differentia of the substance, i.e. of the matter, rather than the matter itself; i.e. the great and the small are like the rare and the 5 dense which the natural philosophers speak of, calling these the primary differentiae of the substratum; for these are a kind of excess and defect. And regarding movement, if the great and the small are to *be* movement, evidently the Forms will be moved; but if they are not, whence did movement come? If we cannot answer this the whole study of nature has been annihilated.

10 And what is thought to be easy—to show that all things are one—is not done; for by 'exposition' all things do not come to be one but there comes to be a One-in-itself, if we grant all the assumptions. And not even this follows, if we do not grant that the universal is a class; and this in some cases it cannot be.

Nor can it be explained either how the lines and planes and solids that come 15 after the numbers exist or can exist, or what meaning they have; for these can neither be Forms (for they are not numbers), nor the intermediates (for those are the objects of mathematics), nor the perishable things. This is evidently a distinct fourth class.

In general, if we search for the elements of existing things without distinguishing the many senses in which things are said to exist, we cannot succeed, especially 20 if the search for the elements of which things are made is conducted in this manner.

For it is surely impossible to discover what acting or being acted on, or the straight, is made of, but if elements can be discovered at all, it is only the elements of substances; therefore to seek the elements of all existing things or to think one has them is incorrect. And how could we *learn* the elements of all things? Evidently we cannot start by knowing something before. For as he who is learning geometry, 25 though he may know other things before, knows none of the things with which the science deals and about which he is to learn, so is it in all other cases. Therefore if there is a science of all things, as some maintain, he who is learning this will know 30 nothing before. Yet all learning is by means of premises which are (either all or some of them) known before,—whether the learning be by demonstration or by definitions; for the elements of the definition must be known before and be familiar; and learning by induction proceeds similarly. But again, if the science is innate, it is 993ª1 wonderful that we are unaware of our possession of the greatest of sciences. Again, how is one to *know* what all things are made of, and how is this to be made *evident?* This also affords a difficulty; for there might be a conflict of opinion, as there is about certain syllables; some say *za* is made out of *s* and *d* and *a*, while others say it 5 is a distinct sound and none of those that are familiar. Further, how could we know the objects of sense without having the sense in question? Yet we should, if the elements of which all things consist, as complex sounds consist of their proper elements, are the same. 10

10 · It is evident, then, even from what we have said before, that all men seem to seek the causes named in the *Physics,* and that we cannot name any beyond these; but they seek these vaguely; and though in a sense they have all been described before, in a sense they have not been described at all. For the earliest 15 philosophy is, on all subjects, like one who lisps, since in its beginnings it is but a child. For even Empedocles says bone exists by virtue of the ratio in it. Now this is the essence and the substance of the thing. But it is similarly necessary that the ratio should be the substance of flesh and of everything else, or of none; there it is on 20 account of this that flesh and bone and everything else will exist, and not on account of the matter, which *he* names,—fire and earth and water and air. But while he would necessarily have agreed if another had said this, he has not said it clearly.

On such questions our views have been expressed before; but let us return to enumerate the difficulties that might be raised on these same points; for perhaps we 25 may get some help towards our later difficulties.

BOOK II (*a*)

1 · The investigation of the truth is in one way hard, in another easy. An indication of this is found in the fact that no one is able to attain the truth adequately, while, on the other hand, no one fails entirely, but every one says 993ᵇ1 something true about the nature of things, and while individually they contribute little or nothing to the truth, by the union of all a considerable amount is amassed.

5   Therefore, since the truth seems to be like the proverbial door, which no one can fail
to hit, in this way it is easy, but the fact that we can have a whole truth and not the
particular part we aim at shows the difficulty of it.

Perhaps, as difficulties are of two kinds, the cause of the present difficulty is
10 not in the facts but in us. For as the eyes of bats are to the blaze of day, so is the
reason in our soul to the things which are by nature most evident of all.

It is just that we should be grateful, not only to those whose opinions we may
share, but also to those who have expressed more superficial views; for these also
contributed something, by developing before us the powers of thought. It is true that
15 if there had been no Timotheus we should have been without much of our lyric
poetry; but if there had been no Phrynis there would have been no Timotheus. The
same holds good of those who have expressed views about the truth; for from the
better thinkers we have inherited certain opinions, while the others have been
responsible for the appearance of the better thinkers.

20   It is right also that philosophy should be called knowledge of the truth. For the
end of theoretical knowledge is truth, while that of practical knowledge is action
(for even if they consider how things are, practical men do not study what is eternal
but what stands in some relation at some time). Now we do not know a truth
without its cause; and a thing has a quality in a higher degree than other things if in
25 virtue of it the similar quality belongs to the other things (e.g. fire is the hottest of
things; for it is the cause of the heat of all other things); so that that which causes
derivative truths to be true is most true. Therefore the principles of eternal things
must be always most true; for they are not merely sometimes true, nor is there any
cause of their being, but they themselves are the cause of the being of other things,
30 so that as each thing is in respect of being, so is it in respect of truth.

994ª1   2 · Evidently there is a first principle, and the causes of things are neither an
infinite series nor infinitely various in kind. For, on the one hand, one thing cannot
proceed from another, as from matter, *ad infinitum*, e.g. flesh from earth, earth
from air, air from fire, and so on without stopping; nor on the other hand can the
5   efficient causes form an endless series, man for instance being acted on by air, air by
the sun, the sun by Strife, and so on without limit. Similarly the final causes cannot
go on *ad infinitum*,—walking for the sake of health, this for the sake of happiness,
10 happiness for the sake of something else, and so one thing always for the sake of
another. And the case of the formal cause is similar. For in the case of an
intermediate, which has a last term and a prior term outside it, the prior must be the
cause of the later terms. For if we had to say which of the three is the cause, we
should say the first; surely not the last, for the final term is the cause of none; nor
15 even the intermediate, for it is the cause only of one. It makes no difference whether
there is one intermediate or more, nor whether they are infinite or finite in number.
But of series which are infinite in this way, and of the infinite in general, all the
parts down to that now present are alike intermediates; so that if there is no first
there is no cause at all.

20   Nor can there be an infinite process downwards, with a beginning in the upper

direction, so that water should proceed from fire, earth from water, and so always some other kind should be produced. For one thing comes *from* another in two ways (if we exclude the sense in which 'from' means 'after', as we say 'from the Isthmian games come the Olympian'), (*a*) as the man comes from the boy, by the boy's 25 changing, or (*b*) as air comes from water. By 'as the man comes from the boy' we mean 'as that which has come to be from that which is coming to be, or as that which is finished from that which is being achieved' (for as becoming is between being and not being, so that which is becoming is always between that which is and that which is not; and the learner is a man of science in the making, and this is what is meant when we say that *from* a learner a man of science is being made); on the 30 other hand, coming from another thing as water comes from air implies the destruction of the other thing. This is why changes of the former kind are not reversible,—the boy does not come from the man (for what comes to be *from* the process of coming to be is not what *is* coming to be but what exists *after* the process 994ᵇ1 of coming to be; for it is thus that the day comes from the morning—in the sense that it comes after the morning; and therefore the morning cannot come from the day); but changes of the other kind are reversible. But in both cases it is impossible that the number of terms should be infinite. For terms of the former kind being intermediates must have an end, and terms of the latter kind change into *one* 5 another; for the destruction of either is the generation of the other.

At the same time it is impossible that the first cause, being eternal, should be destroyed; for while the process of becoming is not infinite in the upward direction, a first cause by whose destruction something came to be could not be eternal.

Further, the *final cause* is an end, and that sort of end which is not for the sake of something else, but for whose sake everything else is; so that if there is to be a last 10 term of this sort, the process will not be infinite; but if there is no such term there will be no final cause. But those who maintain the infinite series destroy the good without knowing it. Yet no one would try to do anything if he were not going to come to a limit. Nor would there be reason in the world; the reasonable man, at least, always acts for a purpose; and this is a limit, for the end is a limit. 15

But the *formal cause,* also, cannot be referred always to another definition which is fuller in expression. For the original definition is always more of a definition, and not the later one; and in a series in which the first term is not correct, the next is not so either.—Further, those who speak thus destroy knowledge; for it is 20 not possible to have this till one comes to what is indivisible. And knowledge becomes impossible; for how can one think things that are infinite in this way? For this is not like the case of the line, to whose divisibility there is no stop, but which we cannot think of if we do not make a stop; so that one who is tracing the infinitely divisible line cannot be counting the possibilities of section. 25

But further, the *matter* in a changeable thing must be cognized.[1]

Again, nothing infinite can exist; and if it could, at least being infinite is not infinite.

---

[1]Retaining τὴν ὕλην ἐν κινουμένῳ.

But if the *kinds* of causes had been infinite in number, then also knowledge would have been impossible; for we think we know, only when we have ascertained
30   the causes, but that which is infinite by addition cannot be gone through in a finite time.

3 · The effect which lectures produce on a hearer depends on his habits; for
995ª1   we demand the language we are accustomed to, and that which is different from this seems not in keeping but somewhat unintelligible and foreign because it is not customary. For the customary is more intelligible. The force of custom is shown by the laws, in whose case, with regard to the legendary and childish elements in them,
5   habit has more influence than our knowledge about them. Some people do not listen to a speaker unless he speaks mathematically, others unless he gives instances, while others expect him to cite a poet as witness. And some want to have everything done accurately, while others are annoyed by accuracy, either because they cannot
10   follow the connexion of thought or because they regard it as pettifoggery. For accuracy has something of this character, so that as in trade so in argument some people think it mean. Therefore one must be already trained to know how to take each sort of argument, since it is absurd to seek at the same time knowledge and the way of attaining knowledge; and neither is easy to get.
15   The minute accuracy of mathematics is not to be demanded in all cases, but only in the case of things which have no matter. Therefore its method is not that of natural science; for presumably all nature has matter. Hence we must inquire first what nature is: for thus we shall also see what natural science treats of [and whether it belongs to one science or to more to investigate the causes and the principles of
20   things].[2]

BOOK III (B)

1 · We must, with a view to the science which we are seeking, first recount
25   the subjects that should be first discussed. These include both the other opinions that some have held on certain points, and any points besides these that happen to have been overlooked. For those who wish to get clear of difficulties it is advantageous to state the difficulties well; for the subsequent free play of thought implies the solution of the previous difficulties, and it is not possible to untie a knot
30   which one does not know. But the difficulty of our thinking points to a knot in the object; for in so far as our thought is in difficulties, it is in like case with those who are tied up; for in either case it is impossible to go forward. Therefore one should have surveyed all the difficulties beforehand, both for the reasons we have stated
35   and because people who inquire without first stating the difficulties are like those

_____

[2]Excised by Ross (see 995ᵇ6).

who do not know where they have to go; besides, a man does not otherwise know even whether he has found what he is looking for or not; for the end is not clear to such a man, while to him who has first discussed the difficulties it is clear. Further, he who has heard all the contending arguments, as if they were the parties to a case, must be in a better position for judging. 995ᵇ1

The first problem concerns the subject which we discussed in our prefatory remarks. It is this—whether the investigation of the causes belongs to one or to more sciences, and, if to one, whether this should survey only the first principles of substance, or also the principles on which all men base their proofs, e.g. whether it is possible at the same time to assert and deny one and the same thing or not, and all other such questions. And if the science in question deals with substance, whether does *one* science deal with all substances, or more than one, and if more, whether are all akin, or must some of them be called forms of wisdom and the others something else? And this itself is also one of the things that must be discussed—whether sensible substances alone should be said to exist or others also besides them, and whether these others are of one kind or there are several classes of substances, as is supposed by those who believe both in Forms and in mathematical objects intermediate between these and sensible things. We must inquire, then, as we say, into these questions, and also whether our investigation is concerned only with substances or also with the essential attributes of substances. Further, with regard to the same and other and like and unlike and contrariety, and with regard to prior and posterior and all other such terms, about which the dialecticians try to inquire, starting their investigation from reputable premises only,—whose business is it to inquire into all these? Further, we must discuss the essential attributes of these themselves; and we must ask not only what each of these is, but also whether one thing always has one contrary. Again, whether the principles and elements of things are the *classes,* or the *parts* present in each thing into which it is divided; and if they are the classes, whether they are the classes that are predicated proximately of the individuals, or the highest classes, e.g. whether animal or man is the first principle and the more independent of the individual instance? And we must inquire and discuss especially whether there is, besides the matter, any thing that is a cause in itself or not, and whether this can exist apart or not, and whether it is one or more in number. Once more, is there something apart from the concrete thing (by the concrete thing I mean the matter with something predicated of it), or is there nothing apart, or is there something in some cases though not in others, and what sort of cases are these? Again we ask whether the principles are limited in number or in kind, both those in the formulae and those in the substratum; and whether the principles of perishable and of imperishable things are the same or different; and whether they are all imperishable or those of perishable things are perishable. Further, there is the question which is hardest of all and most perplexing, whether unity and being, as the Pythagoreans and Plato said, are not attributes of something else but are the substance of existing things, or this is not the case, but the substratum is something else,—as Empedocles says, love; as someone else says, fire; while one says water and one air. Again we ask whether the 5

10

15

20

25

30

35

996ᵃ1

5

10 principles are universal or like individual things, and whether they exist potentially
or actually; further, whether they are potential or actual in any other sense than in
reference to movement; for these questions also would present much difficulty.
Further, whether numbers and lines and figures and points are a kind of substance
15 or not, and if they are substances whether they are separate from sensible things or
present in them? With regard to all these matters not only is it hard to get possession
of the truth, but it is not easy even to think out the difficulties well.

2 · First then with regard to what we mentioned first, does it belong to one or
to more sciences to investigate all the kinds of causes? How could it belong to one
20 science to know the principles if these are not contrary?
Further, there are many things to which not all the principles pertain. For how
can a principle of change or the nature of the good be present in unchangeable
things, since everything that in itself and by its own nature is good is an end, and a
25 cause in the sense that for its sake the other things both come to be and are, and
since an end or purpose is the end of some action, and all actions imply change; so
that in unchangeable things this principle could not exist nor could there be a
good-in-itself. This is why in mathematics nothing is proved by means of this kind of
30 cause, nor is there any demonstration of this kind—'because it is better, or worse';
indeed no one even mentions anything of the kind. And so for this reason some of the
Sophists, e.g. Aristippus, ridiculed mathematics; for in the arts, even in handicrafts,
e.g. in carpentry and cobbling, the reason always given is 'because it is better, or
worse', but the mathematical sciences take no account of goods and evils.
996ᵇ1 But if there are several sciences of the causes, and a different science for each
different principle, which of these sciences should be said to be that which we seek,
or which of the people who possess them has the most scientific knowledge of the
5 object in question? The same thing may have all the kinds of causes, e.g. the moving
cause of a house is the art or the builder, the final cause is the function it fulfils, the
matter is earth and stones, and the form is the definitory formula. To judge from
our previous discussion of the question which of the sciences should be called
wisdom, there is reason for applying the name to each of them. For inasmuch as it is
10 most architectonic and authoritative and the other sciences, like slave-women, may
not even contradict it, the science of the *end* and of the *good* is of the nature of
wisdom (for the other things are for the sake of the end). But inasmuch as it was
described as dealing with the first causes and that which is in the highest sense
knowable, the science of *substance* must be of the nature of wisdom. For as men
15 may know the same thing in many ways, we say that he who knows what a thing is
by the characteristics it has knows more fully than he who knows it by the
characteristics it has not, and in the former class itself one knows more fully than
another, and he knows most fully who knows what a thing is, not he who knows its
quantity or quality or what it can by nature do or have done to it; and further in all
other cases also (i.e. where demonstration is possible) we think that the knowledge
20 of each thing is present when we know what it is, e.g. what squaring a rectangle is,
viz. that it is the finding of a mean; and similarly in all other cases. And we know
about becomings and actions and about every change when we know the *source of*

the movement; and this is other than and opposed to the end. Therefore it would seem to belong to different sciences to investigate these causes severally. 25

But, regarding the starting-points of demonstration also, it is a disputable question whether they are the object of one science or of more. By the starting-points of demonstration I mean the common beliefs, on which all men base their proofs, e.g. that everything must be either affirmed or denied, and that a thing cannot at the same time be and not be, and all other such propositions; the question 30 is whether the same science deals with them as with substance, or a different science, and if it is not one science, which of the two must be identified with that which we now seek.—It is not reasonable that these topics should be the object of one science; for why should it be peculiarly appropriate to geometry or to any other science to understand these matters? If then it belongs to every science alike, and cannot belong to all, it is not peculiar to the science which investigates substances, 997ª1 any more than to any other science, to know about these topics.—And, at the same time, in what way can there be a *science* of the first principles? For we are aware even now what each of them is; at least even other sciences use them as familiar. And if there is a demonstrative science which deals with them, there will have to be 5 an underlying kind, and some of them must be attributes and others must be axioms (for it is impossible that there should be demonstration about all things); for the demonstration must start from certain premises and be about a certain subject and prove certain attributes. Therefore it follows that all attributes that are proved must belong to one class; for all demonstrative sciences use the axioms.—But if the 10 science of substance and the science which deals with the axioms are different, which of them is more authoritative and prior? The *axioms* are most universal and are principles of all things. And if it is not the business of the philosopher, to whom else will it belong to inquire what is true and what is untrue about them?

In general, do all substances fall under one science or under more than one? If 15 the latter, to what sort of substance is the present science to be assigned? On the other hand, it is not reasonable that one science should deal with all. For then there would be one demonstrative science dealing with all attributes. For every demonstrative science investigates with regard to some subject its essential attributes, 20 starting from the common beliefs. Therefore to investigate the essential attributes of one subject, starting from one set of beliefs, is the business of one science. For the subject belongs to one science, and the premises belong to one, whether to the same or to another; so that the attributes also are investigated either by these sciences or by one derived from them. 25

Further, does our investigation deal with substances alone or also with their attributes? I mean for instance, if the solid is a substance and so are lines and planes, is it the business of the same science to know these and to know the attributes of each of these classes (the attributes which the mathematical sciences prove), or of a different science? If of the *same,* the science of substance also must 30 be a demonstrative science; but it is thought that there is *no* demonstration of the essence of things. And if of *another,* what will be the science that investigates the attributes of substance? This is a very difficult question.

Further, must we say that sensible substances alone exist, or that there are others besides these? And are substances of one kind or are there several kinds of substances, as those say who assert the existence both of the Forms and of the intermediates with which they say the mathematical sciences deal?—In what sense we say the Forms are causes and substances in themselves has been explained in our first remarks about them; while this presents difficulties in many ways, the most paradoxical thing of all is the statement that there are certain things besides those in the material universe, and that these are the same as sensible things except that they are eternal while the latter are perishable. For they say there is a man-in-himself and a horse-in-itself and health-in-itself, with no further qualification,—a procedure like that of the people who said there are gods, but in human form. For they were positing nothing but eternal men, nor are they making the Forms anything other than eternal sensible things.—Further, if we are to posit besides the Forms and the sensibles the intermediates between them, we shall have many difficulties. For clearly on the same principle there will be lines besides the lines-in-themselves and the sensible lines, and so with each of the other classes of things; so that since astronomy is one of these mathematical sciences there will also be a heaven besides the sensible heaven, and a sun and a moon (and so with the other heavenly bodies) besides the sensible ones. Yet how are we to believe these things? It is not reasonable even to suppose these bodies immovable, but to suppose their *moving* is quite impossible. And similarly with the things of which optics and mathematical harmonics treat. For these also cannot exist apart from the sensible things, for the same reasons. For if there are sensible things and sensations intermediate between Form and individual, evidently there will also be animals intermediate between animals-in-themselves and the perishable animals.—We might also raise the question, with reference to *which kind* of existing things we must look for these additional sciences. If geometry is to differ from mensuration only in this, that the latter of these deals with things that we perceive, and the former with things that are not perceptible, evidently there will be a science other than medicine, intermediate between medical-science-in-itself and this individual medical science, and so with each of the other sciences. Yet how is this possible? There would have to be also healthy things besides the perceptible healthy things and the healthy-in-itself. And at the same time not even this is true, that mensuration deals with perceptible and perishable magnitudes; for then it would have perished, when they perished. And astronomy also cannot be dealing with perceptible magnitudes nor with this heaven above us. For neither are perceptible lines such lines as the geometer speaks of (for no perceptible thing is straight or curved in this way; for a hoop touches a straight edge not at a point, but as Protagoras said it did, in his refutation of the geometers), nor are the movements and complex orbits in the heavens like those of which astronomy treats, nor have geometrical points the same nature as the actual stars.—Now there are some who say that these so-called intermediates between the Forms and the perceptible things exist, not apart from the perceptible things, however, but in these; the impossible results of this view would take too long to enumerate, but it is enough to consider such points as the following:—It is not reasonable that this should be so only in the case of these *intermediates,* but clearly the *Forms* also might be in the perceptible things; for the same account applies to both. Further, it follows from this theory that there are two solids in the same place, and that the intermediates are not immovable, since they are in the moving perceptible things. And in general to what 15 purpose would one suppose them to *exist,* but to exist *in* perceptible things? For the same paradoxical results will follow which we have already mentioned; there will be a heaven besides *the* heaven, only it will be not apart but in the same place; which is still more impossible.

3 · Apart from the difficulty of stating the case truly with regard to these 20 matters, it is hard to say, with regard to the first principles, whether it is the genera that should be taken as elements and principles, or rather the primary constituents of a thing; e.g. it is the primary parts of which all articulate sounds consist that are thought to be elements and principles of articulate sound, not the common genus—articulate sound; and we give the name of 'elements' to those geometrical 25 propositions, the proofs of which are implied in the proofs of the others, either of all or of most. Further, both those who say there are several elements of corporeal things and those who say there is one, say the parts of which bodies consist and are compounded are principles, e.g. Empedocles says fire and water and the rest are the 30 constituent elements of things, but does not describe these as genera of existing things. Besides this, if we want to examine the nature of anything else, we examine 998ᵇ1 the parts of which, e.g., a bed consists and how they are put together, and then we know its nature. To judge from these arguments, then, the principles of things would not be the genera; but in so far as we know each thing by its definition, and the genera are the principles of definitions, the genera must also be the principles of 5 definable things. And if to get the knowledge of things is to get the knowledge of the species according to which they are named, the genera are at least starting-points of the *species.* And some also of those who say unity and being, or the great and the small, are elements of things, seem to treat them as genera.—But, again, it is not 10 possible to describe the principles in *both* ways. For the formula of the substance is one; but definition by genera will be different from that which states the constituent parts of a thing.

Besides this, even if the genera are in the highest degree principles, should one regard the first of the genera as principles, or those which are predicated directly of 15 the individuals? This also admits of dispute. For if the universal is always more of a principle, evidently the uppermost of the genera are the principles; for these are predicated of all things. There will, then, be as many principles of things as there are primary genera, so that both being and unity will be principles and substances; 20 for these are most of all predicated of all things. But it is not possible that either unity or being should be a genus of things; for the differentiae of any genus must each of them both have being and be one, but it is not possible for the genus to be predicated of the differentiae taken apart from the species (any more than for the 25 species of the genus to be predicated of the proper differentiae of the genus); so that if unity or being is a genus, no differentia will either be one or have being. But if

unity and being are not genera, neither will they be principles, if the genera are the
principles.—Again, the intermediate classes, whose concepts include the differentiae, will on this theory be genera, down to the individuals; but as it is, some are
thought to be genera and others are not thought to be so. Besides this, the
differentiae are principles even more than the genera; and if these also are
principles, there comes to be practically an infinite number of principles, especially
if we suppose the highest genus to be a principle.—But again, if unity *is* more of the
nature of a principle, and the indivisible is one, and everything indivisible is so either
in quantity or in species, and that which is so in species is prior to the divisible, and
genera are divisible into species (for man is not the *genus* of individual men), that
which is predicated directly of the individuals will have more unity.—Further, in
the case of things in which the distinction of prior and posterior is present, that
which is predicable of these things cannot be something apart from them; e.g. if two
is the first of numbers, there will not be a number apart from the kinds of numbers;
and similarly there will not be a figure apart from the kinds of figures; and if the
genera of these things do not exist apart from the species, the genera of other things
will scarcely do so; for genera of these things are thought to exist if any do. But in
the indivisible species one member is not prior and another posterior. Further,
where one is better and another worse, the better is always prior; so that of these
also no genus can exist. From these considerations, then, the species predicated of
individuals seem to be principles rather than the genera.—But again, it is not easy
to say in what sense these are to be taken as principles. For the principle or cause
must exist alongside of the things of which it is the principle, and must be capable of
existing in separation from them; and for what reason should we suppose any such
thing to exist alongside of the individual, except that it is predicated universally and
of all? But if this is the reason, the more universal must be supposed to be more of a
principle; so that the highest genera would be the principles.

4 · There is a difficulty connected with these, the hardest of all and the most
necessary to examine, and to this our argument has now brought us. If, on the one
hand, there is nothing apart from individual things, and the individuals are infinite
in number, how is it possible to get knowledge of the infinite individuals? For all
things that we know, we know in so far as they have some unity and identity, and in
so far as some attribute belongs to them universally.—But if this is necessary, and
there must be something apart from the individuals, it will be necessary that the
genera exist apart from the individuals,—either the lowest or the highest genera;
but we found by discussion just now that this is impossible.—Further, if we admit in
the fullest sense that something exists apart from the concrete thing, whenever
something is predicated of the matter, must there, if there is something apart, be
something corresponding to each set of individuals, or to some and not to others, or
to none? If there is nothing apart from individuals, there will be no object of
thought, but all things will be objects of sense, and there will not be knowledge of
anything, unless we say that sensation is knowledge. Further, nothing will be eternal
or unmovable; for all perceptible things perish and are in movement. But if there is

nothing eternal, neither can there be a process of coming to be; for that which comes to be, and that from which it comes to be, must be something, and the ultimate term in this series cannot have come to be, since the series has a limit and nothing can come to be out of that which is not.—Further, if generation and movement exist there must also be a limit; for no movement is infinite, but every movement has an end, and that which is incapable of completing its coming to be cannot be in process of coming to be; and that which has completed its coming to be must *be* as soon as it has come to be.—Further, since the matter exists, because it is ungenerated, it is *a fortiori* reasonable that the substance, that which the matter is at any time coming to be, should exist; for if neither substance nor matter is, nothing will be at all. And since this is impossible there must be something besides the concrete thing, viz. the shape or form.—But again if we are to suppose this, it is hard to say in which cases we are to suppose it and in which not. For evidently it is not possible to suppose it in all cases; we could not suppose that there is a house besides the particular houses.—Besides this, will the substance of all the individuals, e.g. of all men, be one? This is paradoxical, for all the things whose substance is on this view one would be one. But are they many and different? This also is unreasonable.—At the same time, how does the matter become each of the individuals, and how *is* the concrete thing these two elements?

Again, one might ask the following question also about the first principles. If they are one *in kind* only, nothing will be numerically one, not even unity-itself and being-itself. And how will it be possible to know, if there is not to be something common to a whole set of individuals? But if there is a common element which is *numerically* one, and each of the principles is one, and the principles are not as in the case of perceptible things different for different things (e.g. since this particular syllable is the same in kind whenever it occurs, the elements of it are also the same in kind; only in kind, for these also, like the syllable, are numerically different in different contexts),—if the principles of things are not one in this sense, but are numerically one, there will be nothing else besides the elements; for there is no difference of meaning between 'numerically one' and 'individual'. For this is just what we mean by the individual—the numerically one, and by the universal we mean that which is predicable of the individuals. Therefore it is just as, if the elements of articulate sound were limited in number, all the literature in the world would be confined to the ABC, since there could not be two or more letters of the same kind.

One difficulty which is as great as any has been omitted both by modern philosophers and by their predecessors—whether the principles of perishable and those of imperishable things are the same or different. If they are the same, how are some things imperishable and others perishable, and for what reason? The school of Hesiod and all the mythologists thought only of what was plausible to themselves, and had no regard to us. For asserting the first principles to be gods and born of gods, they say that the beings which did not taste of nectar and ambrosia became mortal; and clearly they are using words which are familiar to themselves, yet what they have said, even about the very application of these causes is above our comprehension. For if the gods taste nectar and ambrosia for their pleasure, these are in no wise the causes of their existence; and if they taste them to maintain their existence, how can gods who need food be eternal?—But into the subtleties of the mythologists it is not worth our while to inquire seriously; those, however, who use

20 the language of proof we must cross-examine and ask why, after all, things which consist of the same elements are, some of them, eternal in nature, while others perish. Since these philosophers mention no cause, and it is unreasonable that things should be as they say, evidently the principles or causes of things cannot be the

25 same. Even the man whom one might suppose to speak most consistently— Empedocles,—even he has made the same mistake; for he maintains that strife is a principle that causes *destruction,* but strife would seem none the less to *produce* everything, except the One; for all things excepting God proceed from strife. At least he says:—

From which grew all that was and is and will be hereafter—
30   Trees, and men and women, and beasts and birds
And water-nourished fish, and long-aged gods.

The implication is evident even apart from these words; for if strife had not been
1000^{b}1 present in things, all things would have been one, as he says—'when they have come together, strife stands outermost'. Hence it also follows on his theory that God most blessed is less wise than all others; for he does not know all the elements; for he has

5 in him no strife, and knowledge is of the like by the like. 'For by earth,' he says,

we see earth, by water water,
By ether godlike ether, by fire wasting fire,
Love by love, and strife by gloomy strife.

But—and this is the point we started from—this at least is evident, that on his
10 theory it follows that strife is as much the cause of existence as of destruction. And similarly friendship is not specially the cause of existence; for in collecting things into the One it destroys all other things.—And at the same time Empedocles mentions no cause of the change itself, except that things are so by nature.

But when strife waxed great in the limbs.
15   And sprang to honour as the time was fulfilled
Which is fixed for them in turn by a mighty oath.

This implies that change was necessary; but he shows no cause of the necessity. But yet so far at least he alone speaks consistently; for he does not make some things perishable and others imperishable, but makes all perishable except the elements.
20 The difficulty we are speaking of now is, why some things are perishable and others are not, if they consist of the same principles.

Let this suffice as proof of the fact that the principles cannot be the same. But if there are different principles, one difficulty is whether these themselves will be imperishable or perishable. For if they are *perishable,* evidently these also must

consist of certain elements; for all things that perish, perish by being resolved into 25
the elements of which they consist; so that it follows that prior to the principles there
are other principles. And this is impossible, whether the process has a limit or
proceeds to infinity. Further, how will perishable things exist, if their principles are
to be destroyed? But if the principles are *imperishable,* why will things composed of
some imperishable principles be perishable, while those composed of the others are 30
imperishable? This is not probable, but is either impossible or needs much proof.
Further, no one has even tried to maintain different principles; they maintain the
same principles for all things. But they swallow the difficulty we stated first as if 1001ª1
they took it to be something trifling.

The hardest inquiry of all, and the one most necessary for knowledge of the
truth, is whether being and unity are the substances of things, and whether each of 5
them, without being anything else, is being or unity respectively, *or* whether we
must inquire what being and unity are, with the implication that they have some
other underlying nature. For some people think they are of the former, others think
they are of the latter character. Plato and the Pythagoreans thought being and 10
unity were nothing else, but this was their nature, their substance being just unity
and being. But the natural philosophers take a different line; e.g. Empedocles—as
though referring it to something more intelligible—says what unity is; for he would
seem to say it is love: at least, this is for all things the cause of their being one. 15
Others say this unity and being, of which things consist and have been made, is fire,
and others say it is air. A similar view is expressed by those who make the elements
more than one; for these also must say that being and unity are precisely all the
things which they say are principles. If we do not suppose unity and being to be 20
substances, it follows that none of the other universals is a substance; for these are
most universal of all. If there is no unity-itself or being-itself, there will scarcely be
in any other case anything apart from what are called the individuals. Further, if
unity is not a substance, evidently number also will not exist as an entity separate 25
from the individual things; for number is units, and the unit is something whose
essence it is to be one.—But if there is a unity-itself and a being-itself, their
substance must be unity and being; for it is not something else that is predicated
universally of them, but just unity and being. But if there is to be a being-itself and a
unity-itself, there is much difficulty in seeing how there will be anything else besides 30
these—I mean, how things will be more than one in number. For what is different
from being does not exist, so that it necessarily follows, according to the argument
of Parmenides, that all things that are are one and this is being.—There are 1001ᵇ1
objections to both views. For whether unity is not a substance or there *is* a
unity-itself, number cannot be a substance. We have already said why this result
follows if unity is not a substance: and if it is, the same difficulty arises as arose with
regard to being. For whence is there to be another one besides the unity-itself? It 5
must be not-one; but all things are either one or many, and of the many each is
one.—Further, if the unity-itself is indivisible, according to Zeno's doctrine it will
be nothing. For that which neither when added makes a thing greater nor when
subtracted makes it less, he asserts to have no being, evidently assuming that

10 whatever has being is a spatial magnitude. And if it is a magnitude, it is corporeal; for the corporeal has being in every dimension, while the other objects of mathematics, e.g. a plane or a line, added in one way will increase what they are added to, but in another way will not do so, and a point or a unit does so in no way. But since he argues crudely, an indivisible thing *can* exist, so that the position may

15 be defended even against him; for the indivisible when added will make the number, though not the size, greater. But how can a *magnitude* proceed from one such indivisible or from many? It is like saying that the line is made out of points. But

20 even if one supposes the case to be such that, as some say, number proceeds from the unity-itself and something else which is not one, none the less we must inquire why and how the product will be sometimes a number and sometimes a magnitude, if the not-one was inequality and was the same principle in either case. For it is not evident how magnitudes could proceed either from the one and this principle, or

25 from some number and this principle.

5 · A question connected with these is whether numbers and bodies and planes and points are substances or not. If they are not, it baffles us to say what being is and what the substances of things are. For modifications and movements

30 and relations and dispositions and ratios do not seem to indicate the substance of anything; for all are predicated of a subject, and none is a 'this'. And as to the things which might seem most of all to indicate substance, water and earth and fire and

1002ᵃ1 air, of which composite bodies consist, heat and cold and the like are modifications of these, not substances, and the body which is thus modified alone persists as something real and as a substance. But, on the other hand, a body is surely less of a

5 substance than a surface, and a surface less than a line, and a line less than a unit and a point. For a body is bounded by these; and they are thought to be capable of existing without body, but a body cannot exist without these. This is why, while most of the philosophers and the earlier among them thought that substance and being were identical with body, and that all other things were attributes of this, so

10 that the first principles of bodies were the first principles of being, the more recent and those who were held to be wiser thought *numbers* were the first principles. As we said, then, if these are not substance, there is no substance and no being at all; for surely it is not proper to call the accidents of these, beings. But if this is admitted,

15 that lines and points are substance more than bodies, but we do not see to what sort of bodies these could belong (for they cannot be in perceptible bodies), there can be no substance.—Further, these are all evidently divisions of body,—one a division in

20 breadth, another in depth, another in length.—Besides this, no sort of shape is present in the solid more than any other; so that if the Hermes is not in the stone, neither is the half of the cube in the cube as something determinate; therefore the surface is not in it either; for if any sort of surface were in it, the surface which marks off the half of the cube would be in it too. And the same account applies to

25 the line and to the point and the unit. Therefore, if on the one hand body is in the highest degree substance, and on the other hand these things are so more than body, but these are not even instances of substance, it baffles us to say what being is and

what the substance of things is.—For besides what has been said, the questions of generation and destruction confront us with further paradoxes. For if substance, not having existed before, now exists, or having existed before, afterwards does not exist, this change is thought to be accompanied by a process of becoming or perishing; but points and lines and surfaces cannot be in process of becoming nor of perishing, though they at one time exist and at another do not. For when bodies come into contact or are separated, their boundaries instantaneously become one at one time—when they touch, and two at another time—when they are separated; so that when they have been put together one boundary does not exist but has perished, and when they have been separated the boundaries exist which before did not exist. For it cannot be said that the point (which is indivisible) was divided into two. And if the boundaries come into being and cease to be, from what do they come into being? A similar account may also be given of the 'now' in time; for this also cannot be in process of coming into being or of ceasing to be, but yet seems to be always different, which shows that it is not a substance. And evidently the same is true of points and lines and planes; for the same argument applies, as they are all alike either limits or divisions.

6 · In general one might raise the question why, besides perceptible things and the intermediates, we have to look for another class of things, such as the Forms which we posit. If it is for this reason, because the objects of mathematics, while they differ from the things in this world in some other respect, differ not at all in that there are many of the same kind, so that their first principles cannot be limited in number (just as the elements of all the language in this sensible world are not limited in number, but in kind, unless one takes the elements of this individual syllable or of this individual articulate sound—whose elements will be limited even in number—, so is it also in the case of the intermediates; for there also the members of the same kind are infinite in number), so that if there are not—besides perceptible and mathematical objects—others such as some maintain the Forms to be, there will be no substance which is one in number as well as in kind, nor will the first principles of things be determinate in number, but only in kind—if then this must be so, the Forms also must therefore be held to exist. Even if those who support this view do not express it distinctly, still this is what they mean, and they must be maintaining the Forms just because each of the Forms is a substance and none is by accident. But if we are to suppose that the Forms exist and the principles are one in number, not in kind, the impossible results that we have mentioned necessarily follow.

Closely connected with this is the question whether the elements exist potentially or in some other way. If in some other way, there will be something else prior to the first principles; for the potency is prior to the actual cause, and it is not necessary for everything potential to be actual.—But if the elements exist potentially, it is possible that everything that is should not be. For even that which is not yet is capable of being; for that which is not comes to be, but nothing that is incapable of being comes to be.

We must not only raise these questions about the first principles, but also ask whether they are universal or what we call individuals. If they are universal, they will not be substances; for everything that is common indicates not a 'this' but a
10 'such', but substance is a 'this'.—And if we can actually posit the common predicate as a single 'this', Socrates will be several animals—himself and man and animal, if each of these indicates a 'this' and a single thing.—If, then, the principles are universals, these results follow; if they are not universals but of the nature of individuals, they will not be knowable; for the knowledge of anything is universal.
15 Therefore if there is to be knowledge of the principles there must be other principles prior to them, which are universally predicated of them.

BOOK IV (Γ)

1 · There is a science which investigates being as being and the attributes which belong to this in virtue of its own nature. Now this is not the same as any of the so-called special sciences; for none of these others deals generally with being as
25 being. They cut off a part of being and investigate the attributes of this part—this is what the mathematical sciences for instance do. Now since we are seeking the first principles and the highest causes, clearly there must be some thing to which these belong in virtue of its own nature. If then our predecessors who sought the elements of existing things were seeking these same principles, it is necessary that the
30 elements must be elements of being not by accident but just because it *is* being. Therefore it is of being as being that we also must grasp the first causes.

2 · There are many senses in which a thing may be said to 'be', but they are related to one central point, one definite kind of thing, and are not homonymous.
35 Everything which is healthy is related to health, one thing in the sense that it preserves health, another in the sense that it produces it, another in the sense that it is a symptom of health, another because it is capable of it. And that which is
1003ᵇ1 medical is relative to the medical art, one thing in the sense that it possesses it, another in the sense that it is naturally adapted to it, another in the sense that it is a function of the medical art. And we shall find other words used similarly to these.
5 So, too, there are many senses in which a thing is said to be, but all refer to one starting-point; some things are said to be because they are substances, others because they are affections of substance, others because they are a process towards substance, or destructions or privations or qualities of substance, or productive or generative of substance, or of things which are relative to substance, or negations of
10 some of these things or of substance itself. It is for this reason that we say even of non-being that it *is* non-being. As, then, there is one science which deals with all healthy things, the same applies in the other cases also. For not only in the case of things which have one common notion does the investigation belong to one science, but also in the case of things which are related to one common nature; for even these

in a sense have one common notion. It is clear then that it is the work of one science   15
also to study all things that are, *qua* being.—But everywhere science deals chiefly
with that which is primary, and on which the other things depend, and in virtue of
which they get their names. If, then, this is substance, it is of substances that the
philosopher must grasp the principles and the causes.

Now for every single class of things, as there is one perception, so there is one
science, as for instance grammar, being one science, investigates all articulate   20
sounds. Therefore to investigate all the species of being *qua* being, is the work of a
science which is generically one, and to investigate the several species is the work of
the specific parts of the science.

If, now, being and unity are the same and are one thing in the sense that they
are implied in one another as principle and cause are, not in the sense that they are
explained by the same formula (though it makes no difference even if we interpret   25
them similarly—in fact this would strengthen our case); for one man and a man are
the same thing and existent man and a man are the same thing, and the doubling of
the words in 'one man' and 'one existent man' does not give any new meaning (it is
clear that they are not separated either in coming to be or in ceasing to be); and
similarly with 'one', so that it is obvious that the addition in these cases means the   30
same thing, and unity is nothing apart from being; and if, further, the essence of
each thing is one in no merely accidental way, and similarly is from its very nature
something that *is*:—all this being so, there must be exactly as many species of being
as of unity. And to investigate the essence of these is the work of a science which is
generically one—I mean, for instance, the discussion of the same and the similar   35
and the other concepts of this sort; and nearly all contraries are referred to this
source; but let us take them as having been investigated in the 'Selection of   1004ᵃ1
Contraries'.—And there are as many parts of philosophy as there are kinds of
substance, so that there must necessarily be among them a first philosophy and one
which follows this. For being falls immediately into genera; and therefore the   5
sciences too will correspond to these genera. For 'philosopher' is like 'mathematician'; for mathematics also has parts, and there is a first and a second science and
other successive ones within the sphere of mathematics.

Now since it is the work of one science to investigate opposites, and plurality is   10
opposite to unity, and it belongs to one science to investigate the negation and the
privation because in both cases we are really investigating unity, to which the
negation or the privation refers (for we either say simply that unity is not present, or
that it is not present in some particular class; in the latter case the characteristic
difference of the class modifies the meaning of 'unity', as compared with the
meaning conveyed in the bare negation; for the negation means just the absence of   15
unity, while in privation there is also implied an underlying nature of which the
privation is predicated),—in view of all these facts, the contraries of the concepts we
named above, the other and the dissimilar and the unequal, and everything else
which is derived either from these or from plurality and unity, must fall within the
province of the science above-named.—And contrariety is one of these concepts, for   20
contrariety is a kind of difference, and difference is a kind of otherness. Therefore,

since there are many senses in which a thing is said to be one, these terms also will have many senses, but yet it belongs to one science to consider them all; for a term belongs to different sciences not if it has different senses, but if its definitions
25   neither are identical nor can be referred to one central meaning. And since all things are referred to that which is primary, as for instance all things which are one are referred to the primary one, we must say that this holds good also of the same and the other and of contraries in general; so that after distinguishing the various senses of each, we must then explain by reference to what is primary in each term,
30   saying how they are related to it; some in the sense that they possess it, others in the sense that they produce it, and others in other such ways.

It is evident then that it belongs to one science to be able to give an account of these concepts as well as of substance. This was one of the questions in our book of problems.

And it is the function of the philosopher to be able to investigate all things. For
1004ᵇ1   if it is not the function of the philosopher, who is it who will inquire whether Socrates and Socrates seated are the same thing, or whether one thing has one contrary, or what contrariety is, or how many meanings it has? And similarly with
5   all other such questions. Since, then, these are essential modifications of unity *qua* unity and of being *qua* being, not *qua* numbers or lines or fire, it is clear that it belongs to this science to investigate both the essence of these concepts and their properties. And those who study these properties err not by leaving the sphere of philosophy, but by forgetting that substance, of which they have no correct idea, is
10   prior to these other things. For number *qua* number has peculiar attributes, such as oddness and evenness, commensurability and equality, excess and defect, and these belong to numbers either in themselves or in relation to one another. And similarly the solid and the motionless and that which is in motion and the weightless and that
15   which has weight have other peculiar properties. So too certain properties are peculiar to being as such, and it is about these that the philosopher has to investigate the truth.—An indication of this may be mentioned:—dialecticians and sophists assume the same guise as the philosopher, for sophistic is philosophy which exists
20   only in semblance, and dialecticians embrace all things in their dialectic, and being is common to all things; but evidently their dialectic embraces these subjects because these are proper to philosophy.—For sophistic and dialectic turn on the same class of things as philosophy, but this differs from dialectic in the nature of the faculty required and from sophistic in respect of the purpose of the philosophic life.
25   Dialectic is merely critical where philosophy claims to know, and sophistic is what appears to be philosophy but is not.

Again, in the list of contraries one of the two columns is privative, and all contraries are referred to being and nonbeing, and to unity and plurality, as for instance rest belongs to unity and movement to plurality. And nearly all thinkers
30   agree that being and substance are composed of contraries; at least all name contraries as their first principles—some name odd and even, some hot and cold, some limit and the unlimited, some love and strife. And everything else is evidently referred to unity and plurality (this reference we must take for granted), and the

principles stated by other thinkers fall entirely under these as their genera. It is 1005ª1
obvious then from these considerations too that it belongs to one science to examine
being *qua* being. For all things are either contraries or composed of contraries, and
unity and plurality are the starting-points of all contraries. And these belong to one 5
science, whether they have or have not one common notion. Probably they have not;
yet even if 'one' has several meanings, the other meanings will be related to the
primary meaning—and similarly in the case of the contraries.—And if being or
unity is not a universal and the same in every instance, or is not separable from the
particular instances (as in fact it probably is not; the unity is in some cases that of 10
common reference, in some cases that of serial succession),—just for this reason it
does not belong to the geometer to inquire what is contrariety or completeness or
being or unity or the same or the other, but only to presuppose these concepts.—
Obviously then it is the work of one science to examine being *qua* being, and the
attributes which belong to it *qua* being, and the same science will examine not only 15
substances but also their attributes, both those above named and what is prior and
posterior, genus and species, whole and part, and the others of this sort.

3 · We must state whether it belongs to one or to different sciences to inquire
into the truths which are in mathematics called axioms, and into substance. 20
Evidently the inquiry into these also belongs to one science, and that the science of
the philosopher; for these truths hold good for everything that is, and not for some
special genus apart from others. And all men use them, for they are true of being
qua being, and each genus has being. But men use them just so far as to satisfy their 25
purposes; that is, as far as the genus, whose attributes they are proving, extends.
Therefore since these truths clearly hold good for all things *qua* being (for this is
what is common to them), he who studies being *qua* being will inquire into them
too.—And for this reason no one who is conducting a special inquiry tries to say 30
anything about their truth or falsehood,—neither the geometer nor the arithmetician. Some natural philosophers indeed have done so, and their procedure was
intelligible enough; for they thought that they alone were inquiring about the whole
of nature and of being. But since there is one kind of thinker who is even above the
natural philosopher (for nature is only one particular genus of being), the discussion
of these truths also will belong to him whose inquiry is universal and deals with
primary substance. Natural science also is a kind of wisdom, but it is not the first 1005ᵇ1
kind.—And the attempts of some who discuss the terms on which truth should be
accepted, are due to a want of training in logic; for they should know these things
already when they come to a special study, and not be inquiring into them while 5
they are pursuing it.—Evidently then the philosopher, who is studying the nature of
all substance, must inquire also into the principles of deduction.

But he who knows best about each genus must be able to state the most certain
principles of his subject, so that he whose subject is being *qua* being must be able to 10
state the most certain principles of all things. This is the philosopher, and the most
certain principle of all is that regarding which it is impossible to be mistaken; for
such a principle must be both the best known (for all men may be mistaken about

things which they do not know), and non-hypothetical. For a principle which every
15 one must have who knows anything about being, is not a hypothesis; and that which
every one must know who knows anything, he must already have when he comes to a
special study. Evidently then such a principle is the most certain of all; which
principle this is, we proceed to say. It is, that the same attribute cannot at the same
20 time belong and not belong to the same subject in the same respect; we must
presuppose, in face of dialectical objections, any further qualifications which might
be added. This, then, is the most certain of all principles, since it answers to the
definition given above. For it is impossible for any one to believe the same thing to
25 be and not to be, as some think Heraclitus says; for what a man says he does not
necessarily believe. If it is impossible that contrary attributes should belong at the
same time to the same subject (the usual qualifications must be presupposed in this
proposition too), and if an opinion which contradicts another is contrary to it,
obviously it is impossible for the same man at the same time to believe the same
30 thing to be and not to be; for if a man were mistaken in this point he would have
contrary opinions at the same time. It is for this reason that all who are carrying out
a demonstration refer it to this as an ultimate belief; for this is naturally the
starting-point even for all the other axioms.

4 · There are some who, as we have said, both themselves assert that it is
1006ª1 possible for the same thing to be and not to be, and say that people can judge this to
be the case. And among others many writers about nature use this language. But we
have now posited that it is impossible for anything at the same time to be and not to
be, and by this means have shown that this is the most indisputable of all
5 principles.—Some indeed demand that even this shall be demonstrated, but this
they do through want of education, for not to know of what things one may demand
demonstration, and of what one may not, argues simply want of education. For it is
impossible that there should be demonstration of absolutely everything; there would
be an infinite regress, so that there would still be no demonstration. But if there are
10 things of which one should not demand demonstration, these persons cannot say
what principle they regard as more indemonstrable than the present one.
We can, however, demonstrate negatively even that this view is impossible, if
our opponent will only say something; and if he says nothing, it is absurd to attempt
to reason with one who will not reason about anything, in so far as he refuses to
15 reason. For such a man, as such, is seen already to be no better than a mere plant.
Now negative demonstration I distinguish from demonstration proper, because in a
demonstration one might be thought to be assuming what is at issue, but if another
person is responsible for the assumption we shall have negative proof, not
demonstration. The starting-point for all such arguments is not the demand that our
20 opponent shall say that something either is or is not (for this one might perhaps take
to be assuming what is at issue), but that he shall say something which is significant
both for himself and for another; for this is necessary, if he really is to say anything.
For, if he means nothing, such a man will not be capable of reasoning, either with
himself or with another. But if any one grants this, demonstration will be possible;

for we shall already have something definite. The person responsible for the proof,   25
however, is not he who demonstrates but he who listens; for while disowning reason
he listens to reason. And again he who admits this has admitted that something is
true apart from demonstration [so that not everything will be 'so and not so'.]¹

First then this at least is obviously true, that the word 'be' or 'not be' has a
definite meaning, so that not everything will be so and not so.—Again, if 'man' has   30
one meaning, let this be 'two-footed animal'; by having one meaning I understand
this: if such and such is a man, then if anything is a man, that will be what being a
man is. And it makes no difference even if one were to say a word has several
meanings, if only they are limited in number; for to each formula there might be   1006ᵇ1
assigned a different word. For instance, we might say that 'man' has not one
meaning but several, one of which would be defined as 'two-footed animal', while
there might be also several other formulae if only they were limited in number; for a
special name might be assigned to each of the formulae. If, however, they were not   5
limited but one were to say that the word has an infinite number of meanings,
obviously reasoning would be impossible; for not to have one meaning is to have no
meaning, and if words have no meaning reasoning with other people, and indeed
with oneself has been annihilated; for it is impossible to think of anything if we do
not think of one thing; but if this *is* possible, one name might be assigned to this   10
thing. Let it be assumed then, as was said at the beginning, that the name has a
meaning and has one meaning; it is impossible, then, that being a man should mean
precisely not being a man, if 'man' is not only predicable of one subject but also has
one meaning (for we do not identify 'having one meaning' with 'being predicable of   15
one subject', since on that assumption even 'musical' and 'white' and 'man' would
have had one meaning, so that all things would have been one; for they would all
have been synonymous).

And it will not be possible for the same thing to be and not to be, except in
virtue of an ambiguity, just as one whom we call 'man,' others might call 'not-man';   20
but the point in question is not this, whether the same thing can at the same time be
and not be a man in name, but whether it can in fact. Now if 'man' and 'not-man'
mean nothing different, obviously 'not being a man' will mean nothing different
from 'being a man'; so that being a man will be not being a man; for they will be one. 25
For being one means this—what we find in the case of 'raiment' and 'dress'—viz.
that the definitory formula is one. And if 'being a man' and 'not being a man' are to
be one, they must mean one thing. But it was shown earlier that they mean different
things. Therefore, if it is true to say of anything that it is a man, it must be a
two-footed animal; for this was what 'man' meant; and if this is necessary, it is   30
impossible that the same thing should not be a two-footed animal; for this is what
'being necessary' means—that it is impossible for the thing not to be. It is, then,
impossible that it should be at the same time true to say the same thing is a man and
is not a man.

The same account holds good with regard to not being man, for 'being man'   1007ª1

¹Excised by Ross.

and 'being not-man' mean different things, since even 'being white' and 'being man' are different; for the former terms are much more opposed, so that they must mean 5 different things. And if any one says that 'white' means one and the same thing as 'man', again we shall say the same as what was said before, that it would follow that *all* things are one, and not only opposites. But if this is impossible, then what has been said will follow, if our opponent answers our question.

And if, when one asks the question simply, he adds the contradictories, he is 10 not answering the question. For there is nothing to prevent the same thing from being both man and white and countless other things: but still if one asks whether it is true to call this a man or not our opponent must give an answer which means one thing, and not add that it is also white and large. For, besides other reasons, it is 15 impossible to enumerate the accidents, which are infinite in number; let him, then, enumerate either all or none. Similarly, therefore, even if the same thing is a thousand times man and not-man, we must not add, in answering the question whether this is a man, that it is also at the same time not a man, unless we are bound to add also all the other accidents, all that the subject is or is not; and if we do this, 20 we are not observing the rules of argument.

And in general those who use this argument do away with substance and essence. For they must say that all attributes are accidents, and that there is no such thing as being essentially man or animal. For if there is to be any such thing as being essentially man this will not be being not-man or not being man (yet these are 25 negations of it); for there was some one thing which it meant, and this was the substance of something. And denoting the substance of a thing means that the essence of the thing is nothing else. But if its being essentially man is to be the same as either being essentially not-man or essentially not being man, then its essence *will* be something else. Therefore our opponents must say that there cannot be such 30 a definition of anything, but that all attributes are accidental; for this is the distinction between substance and accident—white is accidental to man, because though he is white, whiteness is not his essence. But if *all* statements are accidental, there will be nothing primary about which they are made, if the accidental always 1007ᵇ1 implies predication about a subject. The predication, then, must go on *ad infinitum*. But this is impossible; for not even more than two terms can be combined. For an accident is not an accident of an accident, unless it be because both are accidents of the same subject. I mean, for instance, the white is musical and the latter is white, 5 only because both are accidental to man. But Socrates is musical, not in this sense, that both terms are accidental to something else. Since then some predicates are accidental in this and some in that sense, those which are accidental in the latter sense, in which white is accidental to Socrates, cannot form an infinite series in the upward direction,—e.g. Socrates the white has not yet another accident; for no 10 unity can be got out of such a sum. Nor again will white have another term accidental to it, e.g. musical. For this is no more accidental to that than that is to this; and at the same time we have drawn the distinction, that while some predicates are accidental in this sense, others are so in the sense in which musical is accidental 15 to Socrates; and the accident is an accident of an accident not in cases of the latter kind, but only in cases of the other kind, so that not *all* terms will be accidental. There must, then, even in this case be something which denotes substance. And it has been shown that, if this is so, contradictories cannot be predicated at the same time.

Again, if all contradictories are true of the same subject at the same time, evidently all things will be one. For the same thing will be a trireme, a wall, and a man, if it is equally possible to affirm and to deny anything of anything,—and this premise must be accepted by those who share the views of Protagoras. For if any one thinks that the man is not a trireme, evidently he is not a trireme; so that he also is a trireme, if, as they say, the contradictory is true. And we thus get the doctrine of Anaxagoras, that all things are mixed together; so that nothing really exists. They seem, then, to be speaking of the indeterminate, and, while fancying themselves to be speaking of being, they are speaking about non-being; for that which exists potentially and not actually is the indeterminate. But they must predicate of every subject every attribute and the negation of it indifferently. For it is absurd if of every subject its own negation is to be predicable, while the negation of something else which cannot be predicated of it is not predicable of it; for instance, if it is true to say of a man that he is not a man, evidently it is also true to say that he is either a trireme or not a trireme. If, then, the affirmative can be predicated, the negative must be predicable too; and if the affirmative is not predicable, the negative, at least, will be more predicable than the negative of the subject itself. If, then, even the latter negative is predicable, the negative of 'trireme' will be also predicable; and, if this is predicable, the affirmative will be so too.—Those, then, who maintain this view are driven to this conclusion, and to the further conclusion that it is not necessary either to assert or to deny. For if it is true that a thing is man and not-man, evidently also it will be neither man nor not-man. For to the two assertions there answer two negations. And if the former is treated as a single proposition compounded out of two, the latter also is a single proposition opposite to the former.

Again, either the theory is true in all cases, and a thing is both white and not-white, and being and not-being, and all other contradictories are similarly compatible, or the theory is true of some statements and not of others. And if not of all, the exceptions will be agreed upon; but if of all, again either the negation will be true wherever the assertion is, and the assertion true wherever the negation is, or the negation will be true where the assertion is, but the assertion not always true where the negation is. And in the latter case there will be something which fixedly *is not,* and this will be an indisputable belief; and if non-being is indisputable and knowable, the opposite assertion will be more knowable. But if what it is necessary to deny it is equally necessary to assert, it is either true or not true to separate the predicates and say, for instance, that a thing is white, and again that it is not-white. And if it is not true to apply the predicates separately, our opponent is not really applying them, and nothing at all exists; but how could non-existent things speak or walk, as he does? Also all things will on this view be one, as has been already said, and man and God and trireme and their contradictories will be the same. For if

20

25

30

35

1008ᵃ1

5

10

15

20

25

contradictories can be predicated alike of each subject, one thing will in no wise differ from another; for if it differ, this difference will be something true and peculiar to it. And if one may with truth apply the predicates separately, the above-mentioned result follows none the less.

Further, it follows that all would then be right and all would be in error, and our opponent himself confesses himself to be in error.—And at the same time our discussion with him is evidently about nothing at all; for he says nothing. For he says neither 'yes' nor 'no', but both 'yes' and 'no'; and again he denies both of these and says 'neither yes nor no'; for otherwise there would already be something definite.—Again, if when the assertion is true, the negation is false, and when this is true, the affirmation is false, it will not be possible to assert and deny the same thing truly at the same time. But perhaps they might say we had assumed the very thing at issue.

Again, is he in error who judges either that the thing is so or that it is not so, and is he right who judges both? If he is not right, what can they mean by saying that the nature of existing things is of this kind? And if he is not right, but more right than he who judges in the other way, being will already be of a definite nature, and this will be true, and not at the same time also not true. But if all are alike both right and wrong, one who believes this can neither speak nor say anything intelligible; for he says at the same time both 'yes' and 'no'. And if he makes no judgement but thinks and does not think, indifferently, what difference will there be between him and the plants?—Thus, then, it is in the highest degree evident that neither any one of those who maintain this view nor any one else is really in this position. For why does a man walk to Megara and not stay at home thinking he ought to walk? Why does he not walk early some morning into a well or over a precipice, if one happens to be in his way? Why do we observe him guarding against this, evidently not thinking that falling in is alike good and not good? Evidently he judges one thing to be better and another worse. And if this is so, he must judge one thing to be man and another to be not-man, one thing to be sweet and another to be not-sweet. For he does not aim at and judge all things alike, when, thinking it desirable to drink water or to see a man, he proceeds to aim at these things; yet he ought, if the same thing were alike man and not-man. But, as was said, there is no one who does not obviously avoid some things and not others. Therefore, as it seems, all men make unqualified judgements, if not about all things, still about what is better and worse. And if this is not knowledge but opinion, they should be all the more anxious about the truth, as a sick man should be more anxious about his health than one who is healthy; for he who has opinions is, in comparison with the man who knows, not in a healthy state as far as the truth is concerned.

Again, however much all things may be so and not so, still there is a more and a less in the nature of things; for we should not say that two and three are equally even, nor is he who thinks four things are five equally wrong with him who thinks they are a thousand. If then they are not equally wrong, obviously one is less wrong and therefore more right. If then that which has more of any quality is nearer to it, there must be some truth to which the more true is nearer. And even if there is not, still there is already something more certain and true, and we shall have got rid of the unqualified doctrine which would prevent us from determining anything in our thought. 5

5 · Again, from the same opinion proceeds the doctrine of Protagoras, and both doctrines must be alike true or alike untrue. For on the one hand, if all opinions and appearances are true, all statements must be at the same time true and false. For many men hold beliefs in which they conflict with one another, and all think 10 those mistaken who have not the same opinions as themselves; so that the same thing must be and not be. And on the other hand, if this is so, all opinions must be true; for those who are mistaken and those who are right are opposed to one another in their opinions; if, then, reality is such as the view in question supposes, all will be right in their beliefs. Evidently, then, both doctrines proceed from the same way of 15 thinking.

But the same method of discussion must not be used with all opponents; for some need persuasion, and others compulsion. Those who have been driven to this position by difficulties in their thinking can easily be cured of their ignorance; for it is not their expressed argument but their thought that one has to meet. But those 20 who argue for the sake of argument can be convinced only by emending the argument as expressed in words.

Those who really feel the difficulties have been led to this opinion by observation of the sensible world. They think that contradictions or contraries are true at the same time, because they see contraries coming into existence out of the same thing. If, then, that which is not cannot come to be, the thing must have 25 existed before as both contraries alike, as Anaxagoras says all is mixed in all, and Democritus too; for *he* says the void and the full exist alike in every part, and yet one of these is being, and the other non-being. To those, then, whose belief rests on these 30 grounds, we shall say that in a sense they speak rightly and in a sense they err. For 'that which is' has two meanings, so that in some sense a thing can come to be out of that which is not, while in some sense it cannot, and the same thing can at the same time be and not be—but not in the same respect. For the same thing can be potentially at the same time two contraries, but it cannot actually. And again we 35 shall ask them to believe that among existing things there is another kind of substance to which neither movement nor destruction nor generation at all belongs.

And similarly some have inferred from the sensible world the truth of 1009^{b}1 appearances. For they think that the truth should not be determined by the large or small number of those who hold a belief, and that the same thing is thought sweet by some who taste it, and bitter by others, so that if all were ill or all were mad, and only two or three were well or sane, these would be thought ill and mad, and not the 5 others. And again, many of the other animals receive impressions contrary to ours; and even to the senses of each individual, things do not always seem the same. Which, then, of these impressions are true and which are false is not obvious; for the one set is no more true than the other, but both are alike. And this is why 10

Democritus, at any rate, says that either there is no truth or to us at least it is not evident. And in general it is because these thinkers suppose knowledge to be sensation, and this to be a physical alteration, that they say that what appears to our senses must be true; for it is for these reasons that Empedocles and Democritus and, one may almost say, all the others have fallen victims to opinions of this sort. For Empedocles says that when men change their condition they change their knowledge;

> For wisdom increases in men according to their present
> state

And elsewhere he says:

> So far as their nature changes, so far to them always
> Come changed thoughts into mind.

And Parmenides also expresses himself in the same way:

> For as in each case the much-bent limbs are composed,
> So is the mind of men; for in each and all men
> 'Tis one thing thinks—the substance of their limbs:
> For that of which there is more is thought.

A saying of Anaxagoras to some of his friends is also related,—that things would be for them such as they supposed them to be. And they say that Homer also evidently had this opinion, because he made Hector, when he was unconscious from the blow, lie 'thinking other thoughts',—which implies that even those who are bereft of thought have thoughts, though not the same. Evidently, then, if both are forms of thought, the real things also are at the same time so and not so. And it is in this direction that the consequences are most difficult. For if those who have seen most of what truth is possible for us (and these are those who seek and love it most)—if these have such opinions and express these views about the truth, is it not natural that beginners in philosophy should lose heart? For to seek the truth would be to pursue flying game.

But the reason for this opinion is that while these thinkers were inquiring into the truth of that which is, they thought that which is was identical with the sensible world; in this, however, there is largely present the nature of the indeterminate—of that which exists in the peculiar sense which we have explained; and, therefore, while they speak plausibly, they do not say what is true. For it befits us to put the matter so rather than as Epicharmus put it against Xenophanes. And again, they held these views because they saw that all this world of nature is in movement, and that about that which changes no true statement can be made; at least, regarding that which everywhere in every respect is changing nothing could truly be affirmed. It was this belief that blossomed into the most extreme of the views above mentioned, that of the professed Heracliteans, such as was held by Cratylus, who finally did not think it right to say anything but only moved his finger, and criticized

Heraclitus for saying that it is impossible to step twice into the same river; for *he* thought one could not do it even once.

But we shall say in answer to this argument also, that there is some real sense 15 in their thinking that the changing, when it is changing, does not exist. Yet it is after all disputable; for that which is losing a quality has something of that which is being lost, and of that which is coming to be, something must already be. And in general if a thing is perishing, there will be present something that exists; and if a thing is 20 coming to be, there must be something from which it comes to be and something by which it is generated, and this process cannot be *ad infinitum*. But leaving these arguments, let us insist on this, that it is not the same thing to change in quantity and in quality. Grant that in quantity a thing is not constant; still it is in respect of its form that we know each thing.—And again, it would be fair to criticize those 25 who hold this view for asserting about the whole material universe what they saw only in a minority even of sensible things. For only that region of the sensible world which immediately surrounds us is always in process of destruction and generation; but this is—so to speak—not even a fraction of the whole, so that it would have been 30 juster to acquit this part of the world because of the other part, than to condemn the other because of this. And again, obviously we shall make to them also the same reply that we made before; we must show them and persuade them that there is something whose nature is changeless. Indeed, from the assertion that things at the 35 same time are and are not, there follows the assertion that all things are at rest rather than that they are in movement; for there is nothing into which they can change, since all attributes belong already to all subjects.

Regarding the nature of truth, we must maintain that not everything which 1010^{b}1 appears is true. Firstly, even if sensation—at least of the object special to the sense in question—is not false; still appearance is not the same as sensation.—Again, it is fair to express surprise at our opponents for raising the question whether magnitudes are as great, and colours are of such a nature, as they appear to people at a 5 distance, or as they appear to those close at hand, and whether they are such as they appear to the sick or to the healthy, and whether those things are heavy which appear so to the weak or those which appear so to the strong, and whether truth is what appears to the sleeping or to the waking. For obviously they do not think these 10 to be open questions; no one, at least, if when he is in Libya he fancies one night that he is in Athens, straightway starts for the Odeum. And again with regard to the future, as Plato says, surely the opinion of the physician and that of the ignorant man are not equally weighty, for instance, on the question whether a man will get well or not.—And again, among sensations themselves the sensation of a foreign 15 object and that of the special object, or that of a kindred object and that of the object of the sense in question, are not equally authoritative, but in the case of colour, sight, not taste, has the authority, and in the case of flavour, taste, not sight; each of which senses never says at the same moment of the same object that it at the same time is so and not so.—But not even at different moments does one sense 20 disagree about the quality, but only about that to which the quality belongs. I mean, for instance, the same wine might seem, if either it or one's body changed, at one

time sweet and at another time not sweet; but at least the sweet, such as it is when it exists, has never yet changed, but one is always right about it, and that which is to
25 be sweet must of necessity be of such and such a nature. Yet all these views destroy this distinction, so that as there is no substance of anything, so nothing is of necessity; for the necessary cannot be in this way and also in that, so that if anything is of necessity, it will not be both so and not so.

30 And, in general, if only the sensible exists, there would be nothing if animate things were not; for there would be no faculty of sense. The view that neither the objects of sensation nor the sensations would exist is doubtless true (for they are affections of the perceiver), but that the substrata which cause the sensation should
35 not exist even apart from sensation is impossible. For sensation is surely not the sensation of itself, but there is something beyond the sensation, which must be prior
1011ᵃl to the sensation; for that which moves is prior in nature to that which is moved, and if they are correlative terms, this is no less the case.

6 · There are, both among those who have these convictions and among those who merely profess these views, some who raise a difficulty by asking, who is the
5 judge of the healthy man, and in general who is likely to judge rightly on each class of questions. But such inquiries are like puzzling over the question whether we are now asleep or awake. And all such questions have the same meaning. These people demand that a reason shall be given for everything; for they seek a starting-point,
10 and they wish to get this by demonstration, while it is obvious from their actions that they have no conviction. But their mistake is what we have stated it to be; they seek a reason for that for which no reason can be given; for the starting-point of demonstration is not demonstration.

These, then, might be easily persuaded of this truth, for it is not difficult to
15 grasp; but those who seek merely compulsion in argument seek what is impossible; for they demand to be made to contradict themselves, while they are contradicting themselves from the very first.—But if not all things are relative, but some exist in their own right, not everything that appears will be true; for that which appears
20 appears to some one; so that he who says all things that appear are true, makes all things relative. And, therefore, those who ask for an irresistible argument, and at the same time demand to be called to account for their views, must guard themselves by saying that the truth is not that what appears exists, but that what appears exists *for him to whom* it appears, and *when,* and *in the sense in which,* and *in the way in which* it appears. And if they give an account of their view, but do not
25 give it in this way, they will soon find themselves contradicting themselves. For it is possible that a thing may for the same man appear as honey to the sight, but not to the taste, and that, as we have two eyes, things may not appear the same to each, if the eyes are unlike. For to those who for the reasons named above say that what
30 appears is true, and therefore that all things are alike false and true, for things do not appear either the same to all men or always the same to the same man, but often have contrary appearances at the same time (for touch says there are two objects when we cross our fingers, while sight says there is one),—to these we shall say 'yes,

but not to the same sense and in the same part of it and in the same way and at the same time', so that what appears *is* under these qualifications true. But perhaps for this reason those who argue thus not because they feel a difficulty but for the sake of argument, should say that this is not true, but true for this man. And as has been already said, they must make everything relative—relative to thought and perception, so that nothing either has come to be or will be without some one's first thinking so. But if things *have* come to be or will be, evidently not all things will be relative to opinion.—Again, if a thing is one, it is in relation to one thing or to a definite number of things; and if the same thing is both half and equal, still the equal is not correlative to the double. In relation to that which thinks, then, if the same thing is a man, and is that which is thought, that which *thinks* will not be a man, but only that which *is thought*. Again, if each thing is to be relative to that which thinks, that which thinks will be relative to an infinity of specifically different things.

Let this, then, suffice to show that the most indisputable of all beliefs is that contradictory statements are not at the same time true, and what consequences follow from the denial of this belief, and why people do deny it. Now since it is impossible that contradictories should be at the same time true of the same thing, obviously contraries also cannot belong at the same time to the same thing. For of the contraries, no less than of the contradictories, one is a privation—and a privation of substance; and privation is the denial of a predicate to a determinate genus. If, then, it is impossible to affirm and deny truly at the same time, it is also impossible that contraries should belong to a subject at the same time, unless both belong to it in particular relations, or one in a particular relation and one without qualification.

7 . But on the other hand there cannot be an intermediate between contradictories, but of one subject we must either affirm or deny any one predicate. This is clear, in the first place, if we define what the true and the false are. To say of what is that it is not, or of what is not that it is, is false, while to say of what is that it is, and of what is not that it is not, is true; so that he who says of anything that it is, or that it is not, will say either what is true or what is false; but neither what is nor what is not is said to be or not to be.—Again, either the intermediate between the contradictories will be so in the way in which grey is between black and white, or as that which is neither man nor horse is between man and horse. If it were of the latter kind, it could not change, for change is from not-good to good, or from good to not-good; but as a matter of fact it evidently always does, for there is no change except to opposites and to their intermediate. But if it is really intermediate, in this way too there is a difficulty—there would have to be a change to white, which was not from not-white; but as it is, this is never seen.—Again, the understanding either affirms or denies every object of understanding or reason—this is obvious from the definition—whenever it is true or false. When it connects in one way by assertion or negation, it is true, and when it does so in the other way, it is false.—Again, there must be an intermediate between *all* contradictories, if one is not arguing merely for

1011ᵇ1

5

10

15

20

25

30

1012ᵃ1

5

the sake of argument; so that it will be possible for a man to say what is neither true nor untrue. And there will be a middle between that which is and that which is not, so that there will also be a kind of change intermediate between generation and destruction.—Again, in all classes in which the negation of an attribute means the

10   assertion of its contrary, even in these there will be an intermediate; for instance, in the sphere of numbers there will be number which is neither odd nor not-odd. But this is impossible, as is obvious from the definition.—Again, the process will go on *ad infinitum,* and the number of realities will be not only made half as great again, but even greater. For again it will be possible to deny this intermediate with reference both to its assertion and to its negation, and this new term will be some

15   definite thing; for its substance is something different.—Again, when a man, on being asked whether a thing is white, says 'no', he has denied nothing except that it is; and its not being is a negation.

Some people have acquired this opinion as other paradoxical opinions have been acquired; when men cannot refute eristical arguments, they give in to the

20   argument and agree that the conclusion is true. This, then, is why some argue in such fashion; others do so because they demand a reason for everything. And the starting-point in dealing with all such people is definition. Now the definition rests on the necessity of their meaning something; for the formula, of which the word is a

25   sign, becomes its definition.—The doctrine of Heraclitus, that all things are and are not, seems to make everything true, while that of Anaxagoras, that there is an intermediate between the terms of a contradiction, seems to make everything false; for when things are mixed, the mixture is neither good nor not-good, so that one cannot say anything that is true.

8 · In view of these distinctions it is obvious that the one-sided theories which

30   some people express about all things cannot be valid—on the one hand the theory that nothing is true (for, they say, there is nothing to prevent every statement from being like the statement 'the diagonal of a square is commensurate with the side'),—on the other hand the theory that everything is true.—These views are practically the same as that of Heraclitus; for that which says that all things are true and all are false also makes each of these statements separately, so that since

1012ᵇ1   they are impossible, the double statement must be impossible too.—Again, there are obviously contradictories which cannot be at the same time true. Nor on the other hand can all statements be false; yet this would *seem* more possible in view of

5   what has been said.—But against all such arguments we must postulate, as we said above, not that something is or is not, but that people mean something, so that we must argue from a definition, having got what falsity or truth means. If that which it is true to affirm is nothing other than that which it is false to deny, it is impossible

10   that all statements should be false; for one side of the contradiction must be true.—Again, if it is necessary with regard to everything either to assert or to deny it, it is impossible that both should be false; for it is *one* side of the contradiction that is false.—Further, all such arguments are exposed to the often-expressed objection,

15   that they destroy themselves. For he who says that everything is true makes the

statement contrary to his own also true, so that his own is not true (for the contrary statement denies that it is true), while he who says everything is false makes himself also false.—And if the former person excepts the contrary statement, saying it alone is not true, while the latter excepts his own as being alone not false, none the less they are driven to postulate the truth or falsehood of an infinite number of statements; for that which says the true statement is true, is true, and this process will go on to infinity.   20

Evidently again those who say all things are at rest are not right, nor are those who say all things are in movement. For if all things are at rest, the same statements will always be true and the same always false,—but they obviously are not; for he 25 who makes a statement himself at one time was not and again will not be. And if all things are in motion, nothing will be true; everything therefore will be false. But it has been shown that this is impossible. Again, it must be that which is that changes; for change is from something to something. But again it is not the case that all things are at rest or in motion *sometimes,* and nothing *for ever;* for there is 30 something which always moves the things that are in motion, and the first mover must itself be unmoved.

BOOK V (Δ)

1 · We call an origin[1] (1) that part of a thing from which one would start first, e.g. a line or a road has an origin in either of the contrary directions. (2) That from which each thing would best be originated, e.g. we must sometimes begin to 1013ª1 learn not from the first point and the origin of the thing, but from the point from which we should learn most easily. (3) That from which (as an immanent part) a thing first arises, e.g. as the keel of a ship and the foundation of a house, while in 5 animals some suppose the heart, others the brain, others some other part, to be of this nature. (4) That from which (*not* as an immanent part) a thing first arises, and from which the movement or the change naturally first proceeds, as a child comes from the father and the mother, and a fight from abusive language. (5) That by whose choice that which is moved is moved and that which changes changes, e.g. the 10 magistracies in cities, and oligarchies and monarchies and tyrannies, are called origins, and so are the arts, and of these especially the architectonic arts. (6) That from which a thing can first be known; for this also is called the origin of the thing, 15 e.g. the hypotheses are the origins of demonstrations. (Causes are spoken of in an equal number of senses; for all causes are origins.) It is common, then, to all to be the first point from which a thing either is or comes to be or is known; but of these some are immanent in the thing and others are outside. Therefore the nature of a thing is an origin, and so are the elements of a thing, and thought and choice, and 20

---

[1]'Origin' translates 'ἀρχή', elsewhere often 'source' or '(first) principle'. In Greek 'ἀρχή' also means 'rule' or 'office', whence the illustration under (5).

substance, and that for the sake of which—for the good and the beautiful are the origin both of the knowledge and of the movement of many things.

2 · We call a cause (1) that from which (as immanent material) a thing comes into being, e.g. the bronze of the statue and the silver of the saucer, and the classes which include these. (2) The form or pattern, i.e. the formula of the essence, and the classes which include this (e.g. the ratio 2:1 and number in general are causes of the octave) and the parts of the formula. (3) That from which the change or the freedom from change first begins, e.g. the man who has deliberated is a cause, and the father a cause of the child, and in general the maker a cause of the thing made and the change-producing of the changing. (4) The end, i.e. that for the sake of which a thing is, e.g. health is the cause of walking. For why does one walk? We say 'in order that one may be healthy', and in speaking thus we think we have given the cause. The same is true of all the means that intervene before the end, when something else has put the process in motion (as e.g. thinning or purging or drugs or instruments intervene before health is reached); for all these are for the sake of the end, though they differ from one another in that some are instruments and others are actions.

These, then, are practically all the senses in which causes are spoken of, and as they are spoken of in several senses it follows that there are several causes of the same thing, and in no accidental sense, e.g. both the art of sculpture and the bronze are causes of the statue not in virtue of anything else but *qua* statue; not, however, in the same way, but the one as matter and the other as source of the movement. And things can be causes of one another, e.g. exercise of good condition, and the latter of exercise; not, however, in the same way, but the one as end and the other as source of movement.—Again, the same thing is sometimes cause of contraries; for that which when present causes a particular thing, we sometimes charge, when absent, with the contrary, e.g. we impute the shipwreck to the absence of the steersman, whose presence was the cause of safety; and both—the presence and the privation—are causes as sources of movement.

All the causes now mentioned fall under four senses which are the most obvious. For the letters are the causes of syllables, and the material is the cause of manufactured things, and fire and earth and all such things are the causes of bodies, and the parts are causes of the whole, and the hypotheses are causes of the conclusion, in the sense that they are that out of which these respectively are made; but of these some are cause as *substratum* (e.g. the parts), others as *essence* (the whole, the synthesis, and the form). The semen, the physician, the man who has deliberated, and in general the agent, are all *sources of change* or of rest. The remainder are causes as the *end* and the good of the other things; for that, for the sake of which other things are, is naturally the best and the end of the other things; let us take it as making no difference whether we call it good or apparent good.

These, then, are the causes, and this is the number of their kinds, but the *varieties* of causes are many in number, though when summarized these also are comparatively few. Causes are spoken of in many senses, and even of those which are of the same kind some are causes in a prior and others in a posterior sense, e.g. both the physician and the professional man are causes of health, and the ratio 2:1 and number are causes of the octave, and the classes that include any particular cause are always causes of the particular effect. Again, there are accidental causes and the classes which include these, e.g. while in one sense the sculptor causes the 35 statue, in another sense Polyclitus causes it, because the sculptor happens to be Polyclitus; and the classes that include the accidental cause are also causes, e.g. a 1014ª1 man—or in general an animal—is the cause of the statue, because Polyclitus is a man, and a man is an animal. Of accidental causes also some are more remote or nearer than others, as, for instance, if the white and the musical were called causes 5 of the statue, and not only Polyclitus or a man. But besides all these varieties of causes, whether proper or accidental, some are called causes as being able to act, others as acting, e.g. the cause of the house's being built is the builder, or the builder when building.—The same variety of language will be found with regard to the 10 effects of causes, e.g. a thing may be called the cause of this statue or of a statue or in general of an image, and of this bronze or of bronze or of matter in general; and similarly in the case of accidental effects. Again, both accidental and proper causes may be spoken of in combination, e.g. we may say not 'Polyclitus' nor 'the sculptor', 15 but 'Polyclitus the sculptor'.

Yet all these are but six in number, while each is spoken of in two ways; for (1) they are causes either as the individual, or as the class that includes the individual, or as the accidental, or as the class that includes the accidental, and these either as combined, or as taken simply; and (2) all may be taken as acting or as having a capacity. But they differ inasmuch as the acting causes and the individuals exist, or 20 do not exist, simultaneously with the things of which they are causes, e.g. this particular man who is curing, with this particular man who is recovering health, and this particular builder with this particular thing that is being built; but this is not always so with potential causes; for the house does not perish at the same time as the builder. 25

3 · We call an element that which is the primary component immanent in a thing, and indivisible in kind into other kinds, e.g. the elements of speech are the parts of which speech consists and into which it is ultimately divided, while *they* are no longer divided into other forms of speech different in kind from them. If they *are* divided, their parts are of the same kind, as a part of water is water (while a part of 30 the syllable is not a syllable). Similarly those who speak of the elements of bodies mean the things into which bodies are ultimately divided, while *they* are no longer divided into other things differing in kind; and whether the things of this sort are one or more, they call these elements. The elements of geometrical proofs, and in 35 general the elements of demonstrations, have a similar character; for the primary demonstrations, each of which is implied in many demonstrations, are called 1014ᵇ1 elements of demonstrations; and the primary deductions, which have three terms and proceed by means of one middle, are of this nature.

People also transfer the word 'element' from this meaning and apply it to that which, being one and small, is useful for many purposes; for which reason the small

5 and simple and indivisible is called an element. Hence come the facts that the most universal things are elements (because each of them being one and simple is present in a plurality of things, either in all or in as many as possible), and that unity and the point are thought by some to be first principles. Now, since the so-called genera are

10 universal and indivisible (for there is no formula of them), some say the genera are elements, and more so than the differentia, because the genus is more universal; for where the differentia is present, the genus accompanies it, but where the genus is, the differentia is not always. It is common to all the meanings that the element of

15 each thing is the first component immanent in each.

4 · We call nature (1) the genesis of growing things—the meaning which would be suggested if one were to pronounce the υ in φύσις long. (2) The primary immanent element in a thing, from which its growth proceeds. (3) The source from which the primary movement in each natural object is present in it in virtue of its

20 own essence. Those things said to grow which derive increase from something else by contact and organic unity, or organic adhesion as in the case of embryos. Organic unity differs from contact; for in the latter case there need not be anything besides the contact, but in organic unities there is something identical in both parts, which

25 makes them grow together instead of merely touching, and be one in respect of continuity and quantity, though not of quality.—(4) Nature is the primary matter of which any non-natural object consists or out of which it is made, which cannot be modified or changed from its own potency, as e.g. bronze is said to be the nature of a

30 statue and of bronze utensils, and wood the nature of wooden things; and so in all other cases; for when a product is made out of these materials, the first matter is preserved throughout. In this way people call the elements of *natural* objects also their nature, some naming fire, others earth, others air, others water, others

35 something else of the sort, and some naming more than one of these, and others all of them.—(5) Nature is the substance of natural objects, as with those who say the

1015ᵃ1 nature is the primary mode of composition, or as Empedocles says:—

> Nothing that is has a nature,
> But only mixing and parting of the mixed,
> And nature is but a name applied to them by men.[2]

Hence as regards the things that are or come to be by nature, though that *from which* they naturally come to be or are is already present, we say they have not their

5 nature yet, unless they have their form or shape. That which comprises both of these exists *by* nature, e.g. the animals and their parts; and nature is both the first matter (and this in two senses, either first, counting from the thing, or first in general, e.g. in the case of works in bronze, bronze is first with reference to them, but in general

10 perhaps water is first, if all things that can be melted are water), and the form or substance, which is the end of the process of becoming. And from this sense of 'nature' every substance in general is in fact, by an extension of meaning, called a 'nature', because the nature of a thing is one kind of substance.

<hr>

²Frag. 8 Diels-Kranz.

From what has been said, then, it is plain that nature in the primary and strict sense is the substance of things which have in themselves, as such, a source of movement; for the matter is called the nature because it is qualified to receive this,   15 and processes of becoming and growing are called nature because they are movements proceeding from this. And nature in this sense is the source of the movement of natural objects, being present in them somehow, either potentially or actually.

5 · We call the necessary (1) that without which, as a condition, a thing   20 cannot live, e.g. breathing and food are necessary for an animal; for it is incapable of existing without these.—(2) The conditions without which good cannot be or come to be, or without which we cannot get rid or be freed of evil, e.g. drinking the medicine is necessary in order that we may be cured of disease, and sailing to Aegina is necessary in order that we may get our money.—(3) The compulsory and   25 compulsion, i.e. that which impedes and hinders contrary to impulse and choice. For the compulsory is called necessary; that is why the necessary is painful, as Evenus says: 'For every necessary thing is ever irksome'. And compulsion is a form of   30 necessity, as Sophocles says: 'Force makes this action a necessity'.[3] And necessity is held to be something that cannot be persuaded—and rightly, for it is contrary to the movement which accords with choice and with reasoning.—(4) We say that that which cannot be otherwise is necessarily so. And from this sense of necessary all the   35 others are somehow derived; for as regards the compulsory we say that it is necessary to act or to be acted on, only when we cannot act according to impulse 1015^b1 because of the compelling force,—which implies that necessity is that because of which the thing cannot be otherwise; and similarly as regards the conditions of life and of good, when in the one case good, in the other life and being, are not possible   5 without certain conditions, these are necessary, and this cause is a kind of necessity.—Again, (5) demonstration is a necessary thing, because the conclusion cannot be otherwise, if there has been demonstration in the full sense; and the causes of this necessity are the first premises, i.e. the fact that the propositions from which the deduction proceeds cannot be otherwise.

Now some things owe their necessity to something other than themselves;   10 others do not, while they are the source of necessity in other things. Therefore the necessary in the primary and strict sense is the simple; for this does not admit of more states than one, so that it does not admit even of one state and another; for it would thereby admit of more than one. If, then, there are certain eternal and unmovable things, nothing compulsory or against their nature attaches to them.   15

6 · We call one (1) that which is one by accident, (2) that which is one by its own nature. (1) Instances of the accidentally one are Coriscus and musical, and musical Coriscus (for it is the same thing to say 'Coriscus' and 'musical', and 'musical Coriscus'), and musical and just, and musical Coriscus and just Coriscus.   20 For all these are called one by accident, just and musical because they are accidents

---

[3] *Electra* 256.

of one substance, musical and Coriscus because the one is an accident of the other;
and similarly in a sense musical Coriscus is one with Coriscus, because one of the
25   parts in the formula is an accident of the other, i.e. musical is an accident of
Coriscus; and musical Coriscus is one with just Coriscus, because both have parts
which are accidents of one and the same subject. The case is similar if the accident
is predicated of a class or of any universal term, e.g. if one says that man is the same
30   as musical man; for this is either because musical is an accident of man, which is one
substance, or because both are accidents of some individual, e.g. Coriscus. Both,
however, do not belong to him in the same way, but one doubtless as genus and in
the substance, the other as a state or affection of the substance.
35   The things, then, that are called one by accident, are called so in this way. (2)
Of things that are called one in virtue of their own nature some (*a*) are so called
1016ª1 because they are continuous, e.g. a bundle is made one by a band, and pieces of
wood are made one by glue; and a line, even if it is bent, is called one if it is
continuous, as each part of the body is, e.g. the leg or the arm. Of these themselves,
the continuous by nature are more one than the continuous by art. A thing is called
5   continuous which has by its own nature one movement and cannot have any other;
and the movement is one when it is indivisible, and indivisible in time. Those things
are continuous by their own nature which are one not merely by contact; for if you
put pieces of wood touching one another, you will not say these are one piece of
wood or one body or one *continuum* of any other sort. Things, then, that are
10   continuous in any way are called one, even if they admit of being bent, and still more
those which cannot be bent, e.g. the shin or the thigh is more one than the leg,
because the movement of the leg need not be one. And the straight line is more one
than the bent; but that which is bent and has an angle we call both one and not one,
15   because its movement may be either simultaneous or not simultaneous; but that of
the straight line is always simultaneous, and no part of it which has magnitude rests
while another moves, as in the bent line.
         (*b*) Things are called one in another sense because the substratum does not
differ in kind; it does not differ in the case of things whose kind is indivisible to the
20   sense. The substratum meant is either the nearest to, or the furthest from, the final
state. For, on the one hand, wine is said to be one and water is said to be one, *qua*
indivisible in kind; and, on the other hand, *all* juices, e.g. oil and wine, are said to be
one, and so are all things that can be melted, because the ultimate substratum of all
is the same; for all of these are water or air.
         (*c*) Those things are called one whose genus is one though distinguished by
25   opposite differentiae; and these are all called one because the genus which underlies
the differentiae is one (e.g. horse, man, and dog are one, because all are animals),
and in a way similar to that in which the matter is one. These are sometimes called
one in this way, but sometimes it is the higher genus that is said to be the same (if
30   they are *infimae species* of their genus)—the genus above the proximate genera,
e.g. the isosceles and the equilateral are one and the same *figure* because both are
triangles, but they are not the same triangles.
         (*d*) Two things are called one, when the formula which states the essence of

one is indivisible from another formula which shows the essence of the other (though *in itself* every formula is divisible). Thus even that which has increased or is diminishing is one, because its formula is one, as, in the case of planes, is the formula of their form. In general those things, the thought of whose essence is indivisible and cannot separate them either in time or in place or in formula, are most of all one, and of these especially those which are substances. For in general those things that do not admit of division are one in so far as they do not admit of it, e.g. if something *qua* man does not admit of division, it is one man; if *qua* animal, it is one animal; if *qua* magnitude, it is one magnitude.—Now most things are called one because they do or have or suffer or are related to something else that is one, but the things that are primarily called one are those whose substance is one,—and one either in continuity or in form or in formula; for we count as more than one either things that are not continuous, or those whose form is not one, or those whose formula is not one.

(*e*) While in a sense we call anything one if it is a quantity and continuous, in a sense we do not unless it is a whole, i.e. unless it has one form; e.g. if we saw the parts of a shoe put together anyhow we should not call them one all the same (unless because of their continuity); we do this only if they are put together so as to be a shoe and have thereby some one form. This is why the circle is of all lines most truly one, because it is whole and complete.

What it is to be one is to be a beginning of number; for the first measure is the beginning, for that by which we first know each class is the first measure of the class; the one, then, is the beginning of the knowable regarding each class. But the one is not the same in all classes. For here it is a quartertone, and there it is the vowel or the consonant; and there is another unit of weight and another of movement. But everywhere the one is indivisible either in quantity or in kind. That which is indivisible in quantity and *qua* quantity is called a unit if it is not divisible in any dimension and is without position, a point if it is not divisible in any dimension and has position, a line if it is divisible in one dimension, a plane if in two, a body if divisible in quantity in all—i.e. in three—dimensions. And, reversing the order, that which is divisible in two dimensions is a plane, that which is divisible in one a line, that which is in no way divisible in quantity is a point or a unit,—that which has not position a unit, that which has position a point.

Again, some things are one in number, others in species, others in genus, others by analogy; in number those whose matter is one, in species those whose formula is one, in genus those to which the same figure of predication applies, by analogy those which are related as a third thing is to a fourth. The latter kinds of unity are always found when the former are, e.g. things that are one in number are one in species, while things that are one in species are not all one in number; but things that are one in species are all one in genus, while things that are so in genus are not all one in species but are all one by analogy; while things that are one by analogy are not all one in genus.

Evidently 'many' will have uses corresponding to those of 'one'; some things are many because they are not continuous, others because their matter—either the

5 proximate matter or the ultimate—is divisible in kind, others because the formulae which state their essence are more than one.

7 · Things are said to be (1) in an accidental sense, (2) by their own nature.
(1) In an accidental sense, e.g., we say the just is musical, and the man is
10 musical and the musical is a man, just as we say the musical builds, because the builder happens to be musical or the musical happens to be a builder; for here 'one thing is another' means 'one is an accident of another'. So in the cases we have mentioned; for when we say the man is musical and the musical is a man, or the
15 white is musical or the musical is white, the last two mean that both attributes are accidents of the same thing; the first that the attribute is an accident of that which is; while the musical is a man means that musical is an accident of man. In this sense, too, the not-white is said to be, because that of which it is an accident is. Thus
20 when one thing is said in an accidental sense to be another, this is either because both belong to the same thing, and this is, or because that to which the attribute belongs is, or because the subject which has as an attribute that of which it is itself predicated, itself is.

(2) Those things are said in their own right to be that are indicated by the figures of predication; for the senses of 'being' are just as many as these figures.
25 Since some predicates indicate what the subject is, others its quality, others quantity, others relation, others activity or passivity, others its place, others its time, 'being' has a meaning answering to each of these. For there is no difference between 'the man is recovering' and 'the man recovers', nor between 'the man is walking' or
30 'cutting' and 'the man walks' or 'cuts'; and similarly in all other cases.

(3) 'Being' and 'is' mean that a statement is true, 'not being' that it is not true but false,—and this alike in affirmation and negation; e.g. 'Socrates is musical' means that this is true, or 'Socrates is not-white' means that this is true; but 'the diagonal of the square is not commensurate with the side' means that it is false to say it is.

(4) Again, 'being' and 'that which is', in these cases we have mentioned, some-
1017ᵇ1 times mean being potentially, and sometimes being actually. For we say both of that which sees potentially and of that which sees actually, that it is seeing, and both of that which can use knowledge and of that which is using it, that it knows, and both
5 of that to which rest is already present and of that which can rest, that it rests. And similarly in the case of substances we say the Hermes is in the stone, and the half of the line is in the line, and we say of that which is not yet ripe that it is corn. When a thing is potential and when it is not yet potential must be explained elsewhere.

10 8 · We call substances (1) the simple bodies, i.e. earth and fire and water and everything of the sort, and in general bodies and the things composed of them, both animals and divine beings, and the parts of these. All these are called substance because they are not predicated of a subject but everything else is
15 predicated of them.—(2) That which, being present in such things as are not predicated of a subject, is the cause of their being, as the soul is of the being of

animals.—(3) The parts which are present in such things, limiting them and marking them as individuals, and by whose destruction the whole is destroyed, as the body is by the destruction of the plane, as some say, and the plane by the destruction of the line; and in general number is thought by some to be of this 20 nature; for if it is destroyed, they say, nothing exists, and it limits all things.—(4) The essence, the formula of which is a definition, is also called the substance of each thing.

It follows, then, that substance has two senses, (a) the ultimate substratum, which is no longer predicated of anything else, and (b) that which is a 'this' and separable—and of this nature is the shape or form of each thing. 25

9 · We call the same (1) that which is the same in an accidental sense, e.g. white and musical are the same because they are accidents of the same thing, and man and musical because the one is an accident of the other; and the musical is man because it is an accident of man. And the complex notion is the same as either of the 30 simple ones and each of these is the same as it; for man and musical are said to be the same as musical man, and this is the same as they. This is why all of these statements are made not universally; for it is not true to say that *every* man is the same as musical; for universal attributes belong to things in virtue of their own nature, but accidents do not belong to them in virtue of their own nature, but are 1018ª1 predicated without qualification only of the individuals. For Socrates and musical Socrates are thought to be the same; but 'Socrates' is not predicable of more than one subject, and therefore we do not say 'every Socrates' as we say 'every man'.

Some things are said to be the same in this sense; (2) things are said to be the 5 same by their own nature in as many ways as they are said to be one; for both the things whose matter is one either in kind or in number, and those whose substance is one, are said to be the same. Clearly, therefore, sameness is a unity of the being either of more than one thing or of one thing when it is treated as more than one, i.e. when we say a thing is the same as itself; for we treat it as two.

Things are called other if either their kinds or their matters or the formulae of 10 their substance are more than one; and in general 'other' has uses corresponding to those of 'the same'.

We call different (1) those things which though other are the same in some respect, only not in number but either in species or in genus or by analogy; (2) those whose genus is other, and contraries, and all things that have their otherness in their substance.

Those things are called like which have the same attributes in every respect, 15 and those which have more attributes the same than different, and those whose quality is one; and that which shares with another thing the greater number or the more important of the attributes (each of them one of two contraries) in respect of which things are capable of altering, is like that other thing. The uses of 'unlike' correspond to those of 'like'.

10 · We call opposites contradictories, and contraries, and relative terms, 20

and privation and possession, and the extremes from which and into which generation and dissolution take place; and the attributes that cannot be present at the same time in that which is receptive of both, are said to be opposed,—either themselves or their constituents. Grey and white do not belong at the same time to the same thing; therefore their constituents are opposed.

25 We call contraries (1) those attributes that differ in genus, which cannot belong at the same time to the same subject, (2) the most different of the things in the same genus, (3) the most different of the attributes in the same receptive material, (4) the most different of the things that fall under the same capacity, (5) 30 the things whose difference is greatest either absolutely or in genus or in species. The other things that are called contrary are so called, some because they possess contraries of the above kind, some because they are receptive of such, some because they are productive of or susceptible to such, or are producing or suffering them, or 35 are losses or acquisitions, or possessions or privations, of such. Since 'one' and 'being' have many senses, the other terms which are used with reference to these, and therefore 'same', 'other', and 'contrary', must correspond, so that they must be 'other' for each category.

1018ᵇ1 Things are said to be other in species if they are of the same genus but are not subordinate the one to the other, or if, while being in the same genus they have a difference, or if they have a contrariety in their substance; and contraries are other than one another in species (either all contraries or those which are so called in the 5 primary sense), and so are those things whose formulae differ in the *infima species* of the genus (e.g. man and horse are indivisible in genus, but their formulae are different), or which being in the same substance have a difference. 'The same in species' is used correspondingly.

11 · We call things prior and posterior (1) in some cases (on the assumption 10 that there is a first, i.e. a beginning, in each class) because they are nearer some beginning determined either absolutely and by nature, or by reference to something or in some place or by certain people, e.g. things are prior in place because they are nearer either to some place determined by nature, e.g. the middle or the last place, or to some chance object; and that which is further is posterior.—Other things are 15 prior in time; some by being further from the present, i.e. in the case of past events (for the Trojan war is prior to the Persian, because it is further from the present), others by being nearer the present, i.e. in the case of future events (for the Nemean games are prior to the Pythian, if we treat the present as beginning and first point, because they are nearer the present).—Other things are prior in movement; for the 20 things that are nearer the first mover are prior (e.g. the boy is prior to the man); and the prime mover also is a beginning absolutely.—Others are prior in power; for that which exceeds in power, i.e. the more powerful, is prior; and such is that according to whose choice the other—i.e. the posterior—must follow, so that if the prior does 25 not set it in motion the other does not move, and if it sets it in motion it does move; and here choice is a beginning.—Others are prior in arrangement; these are the things that are placed at certain intervals in reference to some one definite thing according to some rule, e.g. the second member of the chorus is prior to the third,

and the second-lowest string is prior to the lowest; for in the one case the leader and in the other the middle string is the beginning.

These, then, are called prior in this sense, but (2) in another sense that which is 30 prior for knowledge is treated as absolutely prior; of these, the things that are prior in formula are different from those that are prior in perception. For in formula universals are prior in perception. For in formula universals are prior, in perception individuals. And in formula also the accident is prior to the whole, e.g. musical to musical man, for the formula cannot exist as a whole without the part; yet 35 musicalness cannot exist unless there is someone who is musical.

(3) The attributes of prior things are called prior, e.g. straightness is prior to smoothness; for one is an attribute of a line as such, and the other of a surface.   1019ª1

Some things then are called prior and posterior in this sense, others (4) in respect of nature and substance, i.e. those which can be without other things, while the others cannot be without *them*,—a distinction which Plato used. If we consider the various senses of 'being', firstly the subject is prior (so that substance is prior); 5 secondly, according as capacity or actuality is taken into account, different things are prior, for some things are prior in respect of capacity, others in respect of actuality, e.g. in capacity the half line is prior to the whole line and the part to the whole and the matter to the substance, but in actuality these are posterior; for it is only when the whole is dissolved that they will exist in actuality. In a sense, 10 therefore, all things that are called prior and posterior are so called according to this fourth sense; for some things can exist without others in respect of generation, e.g. the whole without the parts, and others in respect of dissolution, e.g. the part without the whole. And the same is true in all other cases.

12 · We call a capacity (1) a source of movement or change, which is in 15 another thing or in the same thing *qua* other, e.g. the art of building is a capacity which is not in the thing built, while the art of healing, which is a capacity, might be in the man healed, but not in him *qua* healed. Capacity then is the source, in general, of change or movement in another thing or in the same thing *qua* other, and also the source of a thing's being moved by another thing or by itself *qua* other. For 20 in virtue of that principle, in virtue of which the patient suffers anything, we call it capable of suffering; and this we do sometimes if it suffers anything at all, sometimes not in respect of everything it suffers, but only if it suffers a change for the better.—(2) The capacity of performing this well or according to choice; for sometimes we say of those who merely can walk or speak but not well or not as they choose, that they *cannot* speak or walk. The case of passivity is similar.—(3) The 25 states in virtue of which things are absolutely impassive or unchangeable, or not easily changed for the worse, are called capacities; for things are broken and crushed and bent and in general destroyed not by having a capacity but by not having one and by lacking something, and things are impassive with respect to such 30 processes if they are scarcely and slightly affected by them, because of a capacity and because they can do something and are in some positive state.

As capacity is used in so many ways, the capable in one sense will mean that which can begin a movement (or a change in general, for even that which can bring

things to rest is a capable thing) in another thing or in itself *qua* other; and in one
sense that over which something else has such a capacity; and in one sense that
which has a capacity of changing into something, whether for the worse or for the
better (for even that which perishes is thought to be capable of perishing, for it
would not have perished if it has not been capable of it; but, as a matter of fact, it
has a certain disposition and cause and principle which fits it to suffer this;—
sometimes it is thought to be of this sort because it has something, sometimes
because it is deprived of something; but if privation is in a sense having, everything
will be capable by having something, so that things are capable both by having
something, i.e. a principle, and by having the privation of the positive principle, if it
is possible to *have* a privation; and if privation is *not* in a sense having, things are
called capable homonymously); and a thing is capable in another sense because
neither any other thing, nor itself *qua* other, has a capacity or principle which can
destroy it. Again, all these are capable either merely because the thing might
chance to happen or not to happen, or because it might do so *well*. This sort of
capacity is found also in lifeless things, e.g. in instruments; for we say one lyre can
be made to sound, and another cannot be made to sound at all, if it has not a good
tone.

Incapacity is privation of capacity—i.e. of such a principle as has been
described—either in general or in the case of something that would naturally have
the capacity, or even at the time when it would naturally already have it; for the
senses in which we should call a boy and a man and a eunuch incapable of begetting
are distinct.—Again, to either kind of capacity there is a corresponding incapacity—both to that which only *can* produce movement and to that which can produce it
well.

Some things, then, are called incapable in virtue of this kind of incapacity,
while others are so in another sense, i.e. possible and impossible. The impossible is
that of which the contrary is of necessity true, e.g. that the diagonal of a square is
commensurate with the side is impossible, because such a statement is a falsity such
that not only is the contrary true but it is *necessary;* that it is commensurate, then, is
not only false but of necessity false. The contrary of this, the possible, is found when
it is not necessary that the contrary is false, e.g. that a man should be seated is
possible; for that he is not seated is not of necessity false.—The possible, then, in one
sense, as has been said, means that which is not of necessity false; in another, that
which is true; in another, that which is capable of being true.—A 'capacity'[4] in
geometry is so called by extension of meaning.—These senses of 'possible' involve
no reference to capacity. But the senses which involve a reference to capacity all
refer to the primary kind of capacity; and this is a source of change in another thing
or in the same thing *qua* other. For other things are called 'capable', some because
something else has such a capacity over them, some because it has not, some
because it has it in a particular way. The same is true of the things that are
incapable. Therefore the proper definition of the primary kind of capacity will be a
source of change in another thing or in the same thing *qua* other.

---

[4] I.e. a power.

13 · We call a quantity that which is divisible into two or more constituent parts of which each is by nature a one and a 'this'. A quantity is a plurality if it is numerable, a magnitude if it is measurable. We call a plurality that which is divisible potentially into non-continuous parts, a magnitude that which is divisible into continuous parts; in magnitude, that which is continuous in one dimension is length, in two breadth, in three depth. Of these, limited plurality is number, limited length is a line, breadth a surface, depth a solid.

Again, some things are called quantities in virtue of their own nature, others accidentally, e.g. the line is a quantity by its own nature, the musical is one accidentally. Of the things that are quantities by their own nature some are so as substances, e.g. the line is a quantity (for a certain kind of quantity is present in the formula which states what it is), and others are modifications and states of this kind of substance, e.g. much and little, long and short, broad and narrow, deep and shallow, heavy and light, and the other terms of this sort. And also great and small, and greater and smaller, both in themselves and when taken relatively to each other, are by their own nature attributes of quantity; but these names are transferred to other things also. Of things that are quantities accidentally, some are so called in the sense in which it was said that musical and white were quantities, viz. because that to which they belong is a quantity, and some are quantities in the way in which movement and time are so; for these are called quantities and continuous because the things of which these are attributes are divisible. I mean not that which is moved, but the space through which it is moved; for because that is a quantity movement also is a quantity, and because this is a quantity time is so.

14 · We call a quality (1) the differentia of the substance, e.g. man is an animal of a certain quality because he is two-footed, and the horse is so because it is four-footed; and a circle is a figure of particular quality because it is without angles,—which shows that the differentia with reference to substance is a quality.—This, then, is one meaning of quality—differentia of substance, but (2) there is another sense in which it applies to the unmovable objects of mathematics; i.e. the numbers have a certain quality, e.g. the composite numbers which are not in one dimension only, but of which the plane and the solid are copies (these are those which have two or three factors); and in general that which exists in the substance of numbers besides quantity is quality; for the substance of each is what it is once, e.g. that of 6 is not what it is twice or thrice, but what it is once; for 6 is once 6.

(3) All the attributes of substances in motion (e.g. heat and cold, whiteness and blackness, heaviness and lightness, and others of this sort), in virtue of which, when they change, bodies are said to alter. (4) Quality in respect of excellence and badness and, in general, of good and bad.

Quality, then, seems to have practically two meanings, and one of these is the more proper. The primary quality is the differentia of substance, and of this the quality in numbers is a part; for it is a differentia of substances, but either not of things in motion or not of them *qua* in motion. Secondly, there are the modifications of things in motion *qua* in motion, and the differentiae of movements. Excellence and badness fall among these modifications; for they indicate differentiae of the

20   movement or activity, according to which the things in motion act or are acted on
well or badly; for that which can be moved or act in one way is good, and that which
can do so in another—the contrary—way is vicious. Good and bad indicate quality
25   especially in living things, and among these especially in those which have choice.

15 · Things are relative (1) as double to half and treble to a third, and in
general that which contains something else many times to that which is contained
many times in something else, and that which exceeds to that which is exceeded; (2)
as that which can heat to that which can be heated, and that which can cut to that
30   which can be cut, and in general the active to the passive; (3) as the measurable to
the measure and the knowable to knowledge and the perceptible to perception.

(1) Relative terms of the first kind are numerically related either indefinitely
or definitely, either to various numbers or to 1, e.g. the double is in a definite
numerical relation to 1, and that which is many times as great is in a numerical, but
not in a definite, relation to 1, i.e. not in this or in that relation to it; the relation of
1021ᵃ1   that which is 3/2 of something else to its reciprocal is a definite numerical relation to
a number; that which is 1 and a bit times something else is in an indefinite relation
to its reciprocal, as that which is many times as great is in an indefinite relation to 1;
the relation of that which exceeds to that which is exceeded is numerically quite
5   indefinite; for number is always commensurable, and number is not said of the
non-commensurable; but that which exceeds is, in relation to that which is
exceeded, so much and something more; and this something is indefinite; for it can,
indifferently, be either equal or not equal to that which is exceeded.—All these
relations are numerically expressed and are determinations of number, and so in
10   another way are the equal and the like and the same, for all refer to unity. Those
things are the same whose substance is one; those are like whose quality is one; those
are equal whose quantity is one; and 1 is the beginning and measure of number, so
that all these relations imply number, though not in the same way.
15   (2) The active and the passive imply an active and a passive capacity and the
actualization of the capacities, e.g. that which is capable of heating is related to that
which is capable of being heated, because it *can* heat it, and, again, that which is
heating is related to that which is being heated and that which is cutting to that
which is being cut, because they are actually doing these things. But *numerical*
relations are not actualized except in the sense which has been elsewhere stated;
20   actualizations in the sense of movement they have not. Of relations which imply
capacity some further imply particular periods of time, e.g. that which has made is
relative to that which has been made and that which will make to that which will be
made. For it is in this way that a father is called father *of his son;* for the one has
acted, and the other has been acted on in a certain way. Further, some relative
25   terms imply *privation* of capacity, i.e. 'incapable' and terms of this sort, e.g.
'invisible'.

Relative terms which imply number or capacity, therefore, are all relative
because their very essence includes in its nature a reference to something else, not
because something else is related to *it;* but (3) that which is measurable or knowable

or thinkable is called relative because something else is related to it. For the 30
thinkable implies that there is thought of it, but the thought is not relative to that of
which it is the thought; for we should then have said the same thing twice. Similarly
sight is the sight of something, not of that of which it is the sight (though of course it 1021ᵇ1
is true to say this); in fact it is relative to colour or to something else of the sort. But
according to the other way of speaking the same thing would be said twice,—'it is
the sight of that which is the object of sight'.

Things that are by their own nature called relative are called so sometimes in
these senses, sometimes because the classes that include them are of this sort, e.g.
medicine is thought to be relative because its genus, knowledge, is thought to be 5
relative. Further, there are the properties in virtue of which the things that have
them are called relative, e.g. equality is relative because the equal is, and likeness
because the like is. Other things are relative by accident, e.g. a man is relative
because he happens to be double of something and double is a relative term; or the 10
white is relative, if the same thing happens to be double and white.

16 · We call complete (1) that outside which it is not possible to find even
one of the parts proper to it, e.g. the complete time of each thing is that outside
which it is not possible to find any time which is a part proper to it.—(2) That which
in respect of excellence and goodness cannot be excelled in its kind, e.g. a doctor is 15
complete and a flute-player is complete, when they lack nothing in respect of their
proper kind of excellence. And thus we transfer the word to bad things, and speak of
a complete scandal-monger and a complete thief; indeed we even call them good, i.e.
a good thief and a good scandal-monger. And excellence is a completion; for each 20
thing is complete and every substance is complete, when in respect of its proper kind
of excellence it lacks no part of its natural magnitude.—(3) The things which have
attained a good end are called complete; for things are complete in virtue of having
attained their end. Therefore, since the end is something ultimate, we transfer the 25
word to bad things and say a thing has been completely spoilt, and completely
destroyed, when it in no way falls short of destruction and badness, but is at its last
point. This is why death is by a figure of speech called the end, because both are last
things. The ultimate thing for the sake of which is also an end.—Things, then, that 30
are called complete in virtue of their own nature are so called in all these senses,
some because they lack nothing in respect of goodness and cannot be excelled and
no part proper to them can be found outside, others in general because they cannot
be exceeded in their several classes and no part proper to them is outside; the others
are so called in virtue of these first two kinds, because they either make or have 1022ᵃ1
something of the sort or are adapted to it or in some way or other are referred to the
things that are called complete in the primary sense.

17 · We call a limit the last point of each thing, i.e. the first point beyond
which it is not possible to find any part, and the first point within which every part 5
is; it is applied to the form, whatever it may be, of a spatial magnitude or of a thing
that has magnitude, and to the end of each thing (and of this nature is that towards

which the movement and the action are—not that from which they are, though sometimes it is both, that from which and that to which the movement is—and that for the sake of which), and to the substance of each thing, and the essence of each; for this is the limit of knowledge; and if of knowledge, of the thing also. Evidently, therefore, 'limit' has as many senses as 'beginning', and yet more; for the beginning is a limit, but not every limit is a beginning.

18 · 'That in virtue of which' has several meanings, (1) the form or substance of each thing, e.g. that in virtue of which a man is good is the good itself, (2) the proximate subject in which an attribute is naturally found, e.g. colour in a surface. 'That in virtue of which', then, in the primary sense is the form, and in a secondary sense the matter of each thing and the proximate substratum of each.—In general 'that in virtue of which' will be found in the same number of senses as 'cause'; for we say 'in virtue of what has he come'? or 'for what end has he come'? and 'in virtue of what has he inferred wrongly, or inferred at all'? or 'what is the cause of the inference, or of the wrong inference'?—Further (3) 'that in virtue of which' is used in reference to position, e.g. 'in which he stands' or 'in which he walks'; for all such phrases indicate place and position.

Therefore 'in virtue of itself' must have several meanings. It applies to (1) the essence of each thing, e.g. Callias is in virtue of himself Callias and the essence of Callias; (2) whatever is present in the 'what', e.g. Callias is in virtue of himself an animal. For 'animal' is present in the formula that defines him; Callias is a particular animal.—(3) Whatever attribute a thing receives in itself directly or in one of its parts, e.g. a surface is white in virtue of itself, and a man is alive in virtue of himself; for the soul, in which life directly resides, is a part of the man.—(4) That which has no cause other than itself; man has more than one cause—animal, two-footed—but man is man in virtue of himself.—(5) Whatever attributes belong to a thing alone and *qua* alone; hence also that which exists separately is 'in virtue of itself'.

19 · We call a disposition the arrangement of that which has parts, in respect either of place or of capacity or of kind; for there must be a certain position, as the word 'disposition' shows.

20 · We call a having (1) a kind of activity of the haver and the had—something like an action or movement. When one thing makes and one is made, between them there is a making; so too between him who has a garment and the garment which he has there is a having. This sort of having, then, evidently we cannot *have;* for the process will go on to infinity, if we can have the having of what we have.—(2) 'Having' means a disposition according to which that which is disposed is either well or ill disposed, either in itself or with reference to something else, e.g. health is a having; for it is such a disposition.—(3) We speak of a having if there is a portion of such a disposition; therefore the excellence of the parts is a having.

21 · We call an affection (1) a quality in respect of which a thing can be   15
altered, e.g. white and black, sweet and bitter, heaviness and lightness, and all
others of the kind.—(2) The already actualized alterations.—(3) Especially,
injurious alterations and movements, and, above all, painful injuries.—(4) Experi-   20
ences pleasant or painful when on a large scale are called affections.

22 · We speak of privation (1) if something has not one of the attributes
which a thing might naturally have, even if this thing itself would not naturally have
it, e.g. a plant is said to be deprived of eyes.—(2) If, though either the thing itself or
its genus would naturally have an attribute, it has it not, e.g. a blind man and a mole   25
are in different senses deprived of sight; the latter in contrast with its genus, the
former in contrast with his own normal nature.—(3) If, though it would naturally
have the attribute, and when it would naturally have it, it has it not; for blindness is
a privation, but one is not blind at any and every age, but only if one has not sight at
the age at which one would naturally have it. Similarly a thing suffers privation
when it has not an attribute in those circumstances, or in that respect and in that   30
relation and in that sense, in which it would naturally have it.—(4) The violent
taking away of anything is called privation.
　There are just as many kinds of privations as there are of words with negative
prefixes; for a thing is called unequal because it has not equality though it would
naturally have it, and invisible either because it has no colour at all or because it has   35
a poor colour, and footless either because it has no feet at all or because it has
imperfect feet. Again, a privative term may be used because the thing has little of
the attribute (and this means having it in a sense imperfectly), e.g. kernelless; or   1023ᵃ1
because it has it not easily or not well (e.g. we call a thing indivisible not only if it
cannot be divided but also if it cannot be easily or well divided); or because it has not
the attribute at all; for it is not the one-eyed man but he who is sightless in both eyes   5
that is called blind. This is why not every man is good or bad, just or unjust, but
there is also an intermediate state.

23 · 'To have' means many things. (1) To treat a thing according to one's
own nature or according to one's own impulse, so that fever is said to have a man,   10
and tyrants to have their cities, and people to have the clothes they wear.—(2) That
in which a thing is present as in something receptive is said to have the thing, e.g.
the bronze has the form of the statue, and the body has the disease.—(3) As that
which contains has that which is contained; for a thing is said to be had by that in
which it is contained, e.g. we say that the vessel has the liquid and the city has men   15
and the ship sailors; and so too that the whole has the parts.—(4) That which
hinders a thing from moving or acting according to its own impulse is said to have it,
as pillars have the incumbent weights, and as the poets make Atlas have the
heavens, implying that otherwise they would collapse on the earth, as some of the   20
natural philosophers also say. In this way that which holds things together is said to
have the things it holds together, since they would otherwise separate, each
according to its own impulse.
　'Being in something' has similar and corresponding meanings to 'having'.   25

24 · To come from something means (1) to come from something as from matter, and this in two senses, either in respect of the highest genus or in respect of the lowest species, e.g. in a sense all things that can be melted come from water, but in a sense the statue comes from bronze.—(2) As from the first moving principle, e.g. what does the fight stem from?—from abusive language, because this is the source of the fight.—(3) From the compound of matter and shape, as the parts come from the whole and the verse from the *Iliad* and the stones from the house; for the form is an end, and only that which attains an end is complete.—(4) As the form from its part, e.g. man from two-footed and syllable from letter; for this is a different sense to that in which the statue comes from bronze; for the composite substance comes from the sensible matter, but the form also comes from the matter of the form.—These, then, are some of the meanings of 'from', but sometimes (5) one of these senses is applicable only to part of a whole, e.g. the child comes from its father and mother and plants come from the earth, because they come from a part of those things.—(6) It means coming after a thing in time, e.g. night comes from day and storm from fine weather, because the one comes after the other. Of these things some are so described because they admit of change into one another, as in the cases now mentioned; some merely because they are successive in time, e.g. the voyage took place 'from' the equinox, because it took place after the equinox, and the Thargelia come 'from' the Dionysia, because after the Dionysia.

25 · We call a part (1) that into which a quantity can in any way be divided; for that which is taken from a quantity *qua* quantity is always called a part of it, e.g. two is called in a sense a part of three.—(2) It means, of the parts in the first sense, only those which measure the whole; this is why two, though in one sense it is, in another is not, a part of three.—(3) The elements into which the kind might be divided apart from the quantity, are also called parts of it; for which reason we say the species are parts of the genus.—(4) The elements into which the whole is divided, or of which it consists—'the whole' meaning either the form or that which has the form; e.g. of the bronze sphere or of the bronze cube both the bronze—i.e. the matter in which the form is—and the characteristic angle are parts.—(5) The elements in the formula which explains a thing are parts of the whole; this is why the genus is called a part of the species, though in another sense the species is part of the genus.

26 · We call a whole (1) that from which is absent none of the parts of which it is said to be naturally a whole, and (2) that which so contains the things it contains that they form a unity; and this in two senses—either as each and all one, or as making up the unity between them. For (*a*) that which is true of a whole class and is said to hold good as a whole (which implies that it is a kind of whole) is true of a whole in the sense that it contains many things by being predicated of each, and that each and all of them, e.g. man, horse, god, are one, because all are living things. But (*b*) the continuous and limited is a whole, when there is a unity consisting of several parts present in it, especially if they are present only potentially, but, failing

this, even if they are present actually. Of these things themselves, those which are so by nature are wholes in a higher degree than those which are so by art, as we said in the case of unity also, wholeness being in fact a sort of oneness. 35

Again, as quantities have a beginning and a middle and an end, those to which 1024ᵃ1 the position does not make a difference are called totals, and those to which it does, wholes, and those which admit of both descriptions are both wholes and totals. These are the things whose nature remains the same after transposition, but whose form does not, e.g. wax or a coat; they are called both wholes and totals; for they 5 have both characteristics. Water and all liquids and number are called totals, but 'the whole number' or 'the whole water' one does not speak of, except by an extension of meaning. To things, to which *qua* one the term 'total' is applied, the term 'all' is applied when they are treated as separate; 'this total number', 'all these units'. 10

27 · It is not any chance quantitative thing that can be said to be mutilated; it must be both divisible and a whole. For two is not mutilated if one of the two ones is taken away (for the part removed by mutilation is never equal to the remainder), nor in general is any number thus mutilated; for it is also necessary that the substance remain; if a cup is mutilated, it must still be a cup; but the number is no 15 longer the same. Further, even if things consist of unlike parts, not even these things can all be said to be mutilated, for in a sense a number has unlike parts, e.g. two and three. But in general of the things to which their position makes no difference, e.g. water or fire, none can be mutilated; to be mutilated, things must be such as in virtue of their substance have a certain position. Again, they must be continuous; 20 for a musical scale consists of unlike parts and has position, but cannot become mutilated. Besides, not even the things that are wholes are mutilated by the privation of *any* part. For the parts removed must be neither those which determine the substance nor any chance parts, irrespective of their position; e.g. a cup is not mutilated if it is bored through; but only if the handle or a projecting part is 25 removed. And a man is mutilated not if the flesh or the spleen is removed, but if an extremity is, and that not every extremity but one which when completely removed cannot grow again. Therefore baldness is not a mutilation.

28 · We call something a kind (1) if there is continuous generation of things which have the same form, e.g. 'while mankind lasts' means 'while the generation of 30 them goes on continuously'.—(2) A kind is that which first brought things into existence; for so some are called Hellenes in kind and others Ionians, because the former proceed from Hellen and the latter from Ion as their first begetter. And the word is used in reference to the begetter more than to the matter, though people also 35 get a kind-name from the female, e.g. the descendants of Pyrrha.—(3) There are kinds in the sense in which plane is the kind of plane figures and solid of solids; for 1024ᵇ1 each of the figures is in the one case a plane of such and such a kind, and in the other a solid of such and such a kind; and this is what underlies the differentiae. Again, in formulae their first constituent element, which is included in the essence, is the 5

kind, whose differentiae the qualities are said to be.—Kind then is used in all these ways, (1) in reference to continuous generation of the same sort, (2) in reference to the first mover which is of the same sort as the things it moves, (3) as matter; for that to which the differentia or quality belongs is the substratum, which we call matter.

10 Those things are said to be other in kind whose ultimate substratum is different, and which are not analysed the one into the other nor both into the same thing (e.g. form and matter are different in kind); and things which belong to different categories of being; for some of the things that are said to be signify essence, others a quality, others the other categories we have before distinguished;

15 these also are not analysed either into one another or into some one thing.

29 · We call false (1) that which is false as a *thing,* and that (*a*) because it is not put together or cannot be put together, e.g. 'that the diagonal of a square is

20 commensurate with the side' or 'that you are sitting'; for one of these is false always, and the other sometimes; it is in these two senses that they are non-existent. (*b*) There are things which exist, but whose nature it is to appear either not to be such as they are or to be things that do not exist, e.g. a sketch or a dream; for these are something, but are not the things the appearance of which they produce in us. We

25 call things false in this way, then,—either because they themselves do not exist, or because the appearance which results from them is that of something that does not exist.

(2) A false formula is the formula of non-existent objects, in so far as it is false. Hence every formula is false when applied to something other than that of which it is true, e.g. the formula of a circle is false when applied to a triangle. In a sense there is one formula of each thing, i.e. the formula of its essence, but in a sense there are

30 many, since the thing itself and the thing itself modified in a certain way are somehow the same, e.g. Socrates and musical Socrates. The false formula is not the formula of anything, except in a qualified sense. Hence Antisthenes foolishly claimed that nothing could be described except by its own formula,—one formula to one thing; from which it followed that there could be no contradiction, and almost

35 that there could be no error. But it is possible to describe each thing not only by its own formula, but also by that of something else. This may be done altogether falsely indeed, but in some ways it may be done truly, e.g. eight may be described as a

1025ª1 double number by the use of the formula of two.

These things, then, are called false in these senses, but (3) a false *man* is one who is ready at and fond of such formulae, not for any other reason but for their own sake, and one who is good at impressing such formulae on other people, just as we

5 say *things* are false, which produce a false appearance. This is why the proof in the *Hippias* that the same man is false and true is misleading. For it assumes that he is false who can deceive (i.e. the man who knows and is wise); and further that he who

10 is *willingly* bad is better. This is a false result of induction; for a man who limps willingly is better than one who does so unwillingly; by 'limping' Plato means 'mimicking a limp', for if the man were actually lame willingly, he would perhaps be worse in this case as in the corresponding case of character.

30 · We call an accident that which attaches to something and can be truly asserted, but neither of necessity nor usually, e.g. if one in digging a hole for a plant found treasure. This—the finding of treasure—happens by accident to the man who digs the hole; for neither does the one come of necessity from the other or after the other, nor, if a man plants, does he usually find treasure. And a musical man might be white; but since this does not happen of necessity nor usually, we call it an accident. Therefore since there are attributes and they attach to a subject, and some of them attach in a particular place and at a particular time, whatever attaches to a subject, but not because it is this subject, at this time or in this place, will be an accident. Therefore there is no definite cause for an accident, but a chance cause, i.e. an indefinite one. Going to Aegina was an accident, if the man went not in order to get there, but because he was carried out of his way by a storm or captured by pirates. The accident has happened or exists,—not in virtue of itself, however, but of something else; for the *storm* was the cause of his coming to a place for which he was not sailing, and this was Aegina.

'Accident' has also another meaning, i.e. what attaches to each thing in virtue of itself but is not in its substance, as having its angles equal to two right angles attaches to the triangle. And accidents of this sort may be eternal, but no accident of the other sort is. This is explained elsewhere.

BOOK VI (E)

1 · We are seeking the principles and the causes of the things that are, and obviously of things *qua* being. For there is a cause of health and of good condition, and the objects of mathematics have principles and elements and causes, and in general every science which is ratiocinative or at all involves reasoning deals with causes and principles, exact or indeterminate; but all these sciences mark off some particular being—some genus, and inquire into this, but not into being simply nor *qua* being, nor do they offer any discussion of the essence of the things of which they treat; but starting from the essence—some making it plain to the senses, others assuming it as a hypothesis—they then demonstrate, more or less cogently, the essential attributes of the genus with which they deal. It is obvious, therefore, from such a review of the sciences, that there is no demonstration of substance or of the essence, but some other way of revealing it. And similarly the sciences omit the question whether the genus with which they deal exists or does not exist, because it belongs to the same line of thought to show what it is and that it is.

And since natural science, like other sciences, confines itself to one class of beings, i.e. to that sort of substance which has the principle of its movement and rest present in itself, evidently it is neither practical nor productive. For the principle of production is in the producer—it is either reason or art or some capacity, while the principle of action is in the doer—viz. choice, for that which is done and that which is chosen are the same. Therefore, if all thought is either practical or productive or theoretical, natural science must be theoretical, but it will theorize about such being

as admits of being moved, and only about that kind of substance which in respect of
its formula is for the most part not separable from matter. Now, we must not fail to
notice the nature of the essence and of its formula, for, without this, inquiry is but
30   idle. Of things defined, i.e. of essences, some are like snub, and some like concave.
And these differ because snub is bound up with matter (for what is snub is a
concave *nose*), while concavity is independent of perceptible matter. If then all
1026ª1   natural things are analogous to the snub in their nature—e.g. nose, eye, face, flesh,
bone, and, in general, animal; leaf, root, bark, and, in general, plant (for none of
these can be defined without reference to movement—they always have matter), it
is clear how we must seek and define the essence in the case of natural objects, and
5   also why it belongs to the student of nature to study soul to some extent, i.e. so much
of it as is not independent of matter.—That natural science, then, is theoretical, is
plain from these considerations. Mathematics also is theoretical; but whether its
objects are immovable and separable from matter, is not at present clear; it is clear,
however, that it considers some mathematical objects *qua* immovable and *qua*
10   separable from matter. But if there is something which is eternal and immovable
and separable, clearly the knowledge of it belongs to a theoretical science,—not,
however, to natural science (for natural science deals with certain movable things)
nor to mathematics, but to a science prior to both. For natural science deals with
things which are inseparable from matter but not immovable, and some parts of
15   mathematics deal with things which are immovable, but probably not separable,
but embodied in matter; while the first science deals with things which are both
separable and immovable. Now all causes must be eternal, but especially these; for
they are the causes of so much of the divine as appears to us. There must, then, be
three theoretical philosophies, mathematics, natural science, and theology, since it
20   is obvious that if the divine is present anywhere, it is present in things of this sort.
And the highest science must deal with the highest genus, so that the theoretical
sciences are superior to the other sciences, and this to the other theoretical sciences.
One might indeed raise the question whether first philosophy is universal, or deals
25   with one genus, i.e. some one kind of being; for not even the mathematical sciences
are all alike in this respect,—geometry and astronomy deal with a certain particular
kind of thing, while universal mathematics applies alike to all. We answer that if
there is no substance other than those which are formed by nature, natural science
will be the first science; but if there is an immovable substance, the science of this
30   must be prior and must be first philosophy, and universal in this way, because it is
first. And it will belong to this to consider being *qua* being—both what it is and the
attributes which belong to it *qua* being.

2 · But since the unqualified term 'being' has several meanings, of which one
35   was seen to be the accidental, and another the true (non-being being the false),
while besides these there are the figures of predication, e.g. the 'what', quality,
1026ᵇ1   quantity, place, time, and any similar meanings which 'being' may have; and again
besides all these there is that which is potentially or actually:—since 'being' has
many meanings, we must first say regarding the *accidental*, that there can be no

scientific treatment of it. This is confirmed by the fact that no science—practical, productive, or theoretical—troubles itself about it. For on the one hand he who 5 produces a house does not produce all the attributes that come into being along with the house; for these are innumerable; the house that is made may be pleasant for some people, hurtful to some, and useful to others, and different—to put it shortly—from all things that are; and the science of building does not aim at producing any of these attributes. And in the same way the geometer does not 10 consider the attributes which attach thus to figures, nor whether a triangle is different from a triangle whose angles are equal to two right angles.—And this happens naturally enough; for the accidental is practically a mere name. And therefore Plato was in a sense not wrong in saying that sophistic deals with that which is not. For the arguments of the sophists deal, we may say, above all with the 15 accidental; e.g. the question whether musical and lettered are different or the same, and whether musical Coriscus and Coriscus are the same, and whether everything which is, but is not eternal, has come to be, with the paradoxical conclusion that if one who was musical has come to be lettered, he must also have been lettered and have come to be musical,—and all the other arguments of this sort; the accidental is 20 obviously akin to non-being. And this is clear also from arguments such as the following; of things which are in another sense there is generation and decay, but of things which are accidentally there is not. But still we must, as far as we can, say, regarding the accidental, what is its nature and from what cause it proceeds; for it 25 will perhaps at the same time become clear why there is no science of it.

Since, among things which are, some are always in the same state and are of necessity (nor necessity in the sense of compulsion but that which means the impossibility of being otherwise), and some are not of necessity nor always, but for 30 the most part, this is the principle and this the cause of the existence of the accidental; for that which is neither always nor for the most part, we call accidental. For instance, if in the dog-days there is wintry and cold weather, we say this is an accident, but not if there is sultry heat, because the latter is always or for the most part so, but not the former. And it is an accident that a man is white (for this is 35 neither always nor for the most part so), but it is not by accident that he is an animal. And that the builder produces health is an accident, because it is the nature not of the builder but of the doctor to do this,—but the builder happened to be a 1027ᵃ1 doctor. Again, a confectioner, aiming at giving pleasure, may make something wholesome, but not in virtue of the confectioner's art; and therefore we say it was an accident, and while there is a sense in which he makes it, in the full sense he does not make it.—For some accidental results sometimes tend to be produced by alien 5 capacities, but to others there corresponds no determinate art nor capacity; for of things which are or come to be by accident, the cause also is accidental. Therefore, since not all things are or come to be of necessity and always, but the majority of things are for the most part, the accidental must exist; for instance a white man is not always nor for the most part musical, but since this sometimes happens, it must 10 be accidental. If not, everything will be of necessity. The matter, therefore, which is capable of being otherwise than as it for the most part is, is the cause of the

15   accidental. And we must take as our starting-point the question whether everything
      is either always or for the most part. Surely this is impossible. There is, then, besides
      these something which is fortuitous and accidental. But while what is for the most
      part exists, can nothing be said to be always, or are there eternal things? This must
20   be considered later, but that there is no science of the accidental is obvious; for all
      science is either of that which is always or of that which is for the most part. For
      how else is one to learn or to teach another? The thing must be determined as
      occurring either always or for the most part, e.g. that honey-water is useful for a
      patient in a fever is true for the most part. But one will not be able to state when that
25   which is contrary to this happens, e.g. 'on the day of new moon'; for then it will be so
      on the day of new moon either always or for the most part; but the accidental is
      contrary to this. We have stated, then, what the accidental is and from what cause it
      arises, and that there is no science which deals with it.

          3 · That there are principles and causes which are generable and destruct-
30   ible without ever being in course of being generated or destroyed, is obvious. For
      otherwise all things will be of necessity, since that which is being generated or
      destroyed must have a cause which is not accidentally its cause. Will this be or
      not?—Yes if *this* happens; and if not, not. And this will happen if something else
      does. And thus if time is constantly subtracted from a limited extent of time, one
1027ᵇ1 will obviously come to the present. This man, then, will die by violence, *if* he goes
      out; and he will do this if he is thirsty; and he will be thirsty if something else
      happens; and thus we shall come to that which is now present, or to some past event.
      For instance, he will go out if he is thirsty; and he will be thirsty if he is eating
5   something pungent; and this is either the case or not; so that he will of necessity die,
      or not die. And similarly if one jumps over to the past, the same account will hold
      good; for this—I mean the past condition—is already present in something.
      Everything, therefore, that is to be, will be of necessity, e.g. it is necessary that he
      who lives shall one day die; for already something has happened—e.g. the presence
10   of contraries in the same body. But whether he dies by disease or by violence, is not
      yet determined, but depends on the happening of something else. Clearly then the
      process goes back to a certain starting-point, but this no longer points to something
      further. This then will be the starting-point for the fortuitous, and will have nothing
      else as cause of its coming to be. But to what sort of starting-point and what sort of
15   cause we thus refer the fortuitous—whether to matter or to that for the sake of
      which or to the motive power, must be carefully considered.

          4 · Let us dismiss the accidental; for we have sufficiently determined its
      nature. But since that which *is* in the sense of being true, or *is not* in the sense of
      being false, depends on combination and separation, and truth and falsehood
20   together are concerned with the apportionment of a contradiction (for truth has the
      affirmation in the case of what is compounded and the negation in the case of what
      is divided, while falsity has the contradictory of this apportionment—it is another
      question, how it happens that we think things together or apart; by 'together' and

'apart' I mean thinking them so that there is no succession in the thoughts but they become a unity—; for falsity and truth are not in things—it is not as if the good   25 were true, and the bad were in itself false—but in thought; while with regard to simple things and essences falsity and truth do not exist even in thought):—we must consider later what has to be discussed with regard to that which is or is not in this sense; but since the combination and the separation are in thought and not in the   30 things, and that which is in this sense is a different sort of being from the things that are in the full sense (for the thought attaches or removes either the 'what' or quality or quantity or one of the other categories), that which *is* accidentally and that which *is* in the sense of being true must be dismissed. For the cause of the former is indeterminate, and that of the latter is some affection of the thought, and both are   1028ª1 related to the remaining genus of being, and do not indicate any separate class of being. Therefore let these be dismissed, and let us consider the causes and the principles of being itself, *qua* being. [It was clear in our discussion of the various meanings of terms, that 'being' has several meanings.]¹   5

BOOK VII (Z)

1 · There are several senses in which a thing may be said to be, as we pointed   10 out previously in our book on the various senses of words; for in one sense it means what a thing is or a 'this', and in another sense it means that a thing is of a certain quality or quantity or has some such predicate asserted of it. While 'being' has all these senses, obviously that which is primarily is the 'what', which indicates the substance of the thing. For when we say of what quality a thing is, we say that it is   15 good or beautiful, but not that it is three cubits long or that it is a man; but when we say *what* it is, we do not say 'white' or 'hot' or 'three cubits long', but 'man' or 'God'. And all other things are said to be because they are, some of them, quantities of that which *is* in this primary sense, others qualities of it, others affections of it, and others some other determination of it. And so one might raise the question whether   20 'to walk' and 'to be healthy' and 'to sit' signify in each case something that is, and similarly in any other case of this sort; for none of them is either self-subsistent or capable of being separated from substance, but rather, if anything, it is that which walks or is seated or is healthy that is an existent thing. Now these are seen to be   25 more real because there is something definite which underlies them; and this is the substance or individual, which is implied in such a predicate; for 'good' or 'sitting' are not used without this. Clearly then it is in virtue of this category that each of the others *is*. Therefore that which is primarily and *is* simply (not is something) must be   30 substance.

Now there are several senses in which a thing is said to be primary; but substance is primary in every sense—in formula, in order of knowledge, in time. For

¹Excised by Ross.

35   of the other categories none can exist independently, but only substance. And in
     formula also this is primary; for in the formula of each term the formula of its
1028ᵇ1 substance must be present. And we think we know each thing most fully, when we
     know what it is, e.g. what man is or what fire is, rather than when we know its
     quality, its quantity, or where it is; since we know each of these things also, only
     when we know *what* the quantity or the quality *is*.

     And indeed the question which, both now and of old, has always been raised,
     and always been the subject of doubt, viz. what being is, is just the question, what is
5   substance? For it is this that some assert to be one, others more than one, and that
     some assert to be limited in number, others unlimited. And so we also must consider
     chiefly and primarily and almost exclusively what that is which *is* in this sense.

     2 · Substance is thought to belong most obviously to bodies; and so we say
10   that both animals and plants and their parts are substances, and so are natural
     bodies such as fire and water and earth and everything of the sort, and all things
     that are parts of these or composed of these (either of parts or of the whole bodies),
     e.g. the heaven and its parts, stars and moon and sun. But whether these alone are
     substances, or there are also others, or only some of these, or some of these and some
15   other things are substances, or none of these but only some other things, must be
     considered. Some think the limits of body, i.e. surface, line, point, and unit, are
     substances, and more so than body or the solid. Further, some do not think there is
     anything substantial besides sensible things, but others think there are eternal
     substances which are more in number and more real, e.g. Plato posited two kinds of
20   substance—the Forms and the objects of mathematics—as well as a third kind, viz.
     the substance of sensible bodies. And Speusippus made still more kinds of
     substance, beginning with the One, and making principles for each kind of
     substance, one for numbers, another for spatial magnitudes, and then another for
     the soul; and in this way he multiplies the kinds of substance. And some say Forms
25   and numbers have the same nature, and other things come after them, e.g. lines and
     planes, until we come to the substance of the heavens and to sensible bodies.

     Regarding these matters, then, we must inquire which of the common
     statements are right and which are not right, and what things are substances, and
     whether there are or are not any besides sensible substances, and how sensible
30   substances exist, and whether there is a separable substance (and if so why and
     how) or there is no substance separable from sensible substances; and we must first
     sketch the nature of substance.

     3 · The word 'substance' is applied, if not in more senses, still at least to four
     main objects; for both the essence and the universal and the genus are thought to be
35   the substance of each thing, and fourthly the substratum. Now the substratum is
     that of which other things are predicated, while it is itself not predicated of anything
     else. And so we must first determine the nature of this; for that which underlies a
1029ª1 thing primarily is thought to be in the truest sense its substance. And in one sense
     matter is said to be of the nature of substratum, in another, shape, and in a third
     sense, the compound of these. By the matter I mean, for instance, the bronze, by the

shape the plan of its form, and by the compound of these (the concrete thing) the   5
statue. Therefore if the form is prior to the matter and more real, it will be prior to
the compound also for the same reason.

We have now outlined the nature of substance, showing that it is that which is
not predicated of a subject, but of which all else is predicated. But we must not
merely state the matter thus; for this is not enough. The statement itself is obscure,
and further, on this view, *matter* becomes substance. For if this is not substance, it is   10
beyond us to say what else is. When all else is taken away evidently nothing but
matter remains. For of the other elements some are affections, products, and
capacities of bodies, while length, breadth, and depth are quantities and not
substances. For a quantity is not a substance; but the substance is rather that to   15
which these belong primarily. But when length and breadth and depth are taken
away we see nothing left except that which is bounded by these, whatever it be; so
that to those who consider the question thus matter alone must seem to be
substance. By matter I mean that which in itself is neither a particular thing nor of a   20
certain quantity nor assigned to any other of the categories by which being is
determined. For there is something of which each of these is predicated, so that its
being is different from that of each of the predicates; for the predicates other than
substance are predicated of substance, while substance is predicated of matter.
Therefore the ultimate substratum is of itself neither a particular thing nor of a
particular quantity nor otherwise positively characterized; nor yet negatively, for   25
negations also will belong to it only by accident.

For those who adopt this point of view, then, it follows that matter is substance.
But this is impossible; for both separability and individuality are thought to belong
chiefly to substance. And so form and the compound of form and matter would be
thought to be substance, rather than matter. The substance compounded of both,   30
i.e. of matter and shape, may be dismissed; for it is posterior and its nature is
obvious. And matter also is in a sense manifest. But we must inquire into the third
kind of substance; for this is the most difficult.

It is agreed that there are some substances among sensible things, so that we
must look first among these. For it is in an advantage to advance to that which is   1029^{b}1
more intelligible. For learning proceeds for all in this way—through that which is
less intelligible by nature to that which is more intelligible; and just as in conduct   5
our work is to start from what is good for each and make what is good in itself good
for each, so it is our work to start from what is more intelligible to oneself and make
what is intelligible by nature intelligible to oneself. Now what is intelligible and
primary for particular sets of people is often intelligible to a very small extent, and
has little or nothing of reality. But yet one must start from that which is barely   10
intelligible but intelligible to oneself, and try to understand what is intelligible in
itself, passing, as has been said, by way of those very things which one
understands.

4 . Since at the start we distinguished the various marks by which we
determine substance, and one of these was thought to be the essence, we must
investigate this. And first let us say something about it in the abstract. The essence

of each thing is what it is said to be in virtue of itself. For being you is not being
15 musical; for you are not musical in virtue of yourself. What, then, you are in virtue
of yourself is your essence.

But not the whole of this is the essence of a thing; not that which something is
in virtue of itself in the way in which a surface is white, because being a surface is
not being white. But again the combination of both—being a white surface—is not
the essence of surface. Why? Because 'surface' itself is repeated. The formula,
therefore, in which the term itself is not present but its meaning is expressed, this is
20 the formula of the essence of each thing. Therefore if to be a white surface is to be a
smooth surface, to be white and to be smooth are one and the same.

But since there are compounds of substance with the other categories (for
there is a substrate for each category, e.g. for quality, quantity, time, place, and
25 motion), we must inquire whether there is a formula of the essence of each of them,
i.e. whether to these compounds also there belongs an essence, e.g. to white man.
Let the compound be denoted by 'cloak'. What is being a cloak? But, it may be said,
this also is not said of something in its own right. We reply that there are two ways
in which a predicate may fail to be true of a subject in its own right, and one of these
30 results from addition, and the other not. *One* kind of predicate is not said of a thing
in its own right because the term that is being defined is added to something else,
e.g. if in defining the essence of white one were to state the formula of white *man*;
another because something else is added to it, e.g. if 'cloak' meant white man, and
1030ª1 one were to define cloak as white; white man is white indeed, but its essence is not to
be white. But is being a cloak an essence at all? Probably not. For the essence is
what something is; but when one thing is said of another, that is not what a 'this' is,
5 e.g. white man is not what a 'this' is since being a 'this' belongs only to substances.
Therefore there is an essence only of those things whose formula is a definition. But
we have a definition not where we have a word and a formula identical in meaning
(for in that case all formulae would be definitions; for there will be some name for
formula whatever, so that even the *Iliad* would be a definition), but where there is a
10 formula of something primary; and primary things are those which do not involve
one thing's being said of another. Nothing, then, which is not a species of a genus
will have an *essence*—only species will have it, for in these the subject is not thought
to participate in the attribute and to have it as an affection, nor to have it by
15 accident; but for everything else as well, if it has a name, there will be a formula of
its meaning—viz. that this attribute belongs to this subject; or instead of a simple
formula we shall be able to give a more accurate one; but there will be no definition
nor essence.

But after all, 'definition', like 'what a thing is', has several meanings; 'what a
thing is' in one sense means substance and a 'this', in another one or other of the
20 predicates, quantity, quality, and the like. For as 'is' is predicable of all things, not
however in the same sense, but of one sort of thing primarily and of others in a
secondary way, so too the 'what' belongs simply to substance, but in a limited sense
to the other categories. For even of a quality we might ask what it is, so that a
25 quality also is a 'what',—not simply, however, but just as, in the case of that which

is not, some say, in the abstract, that that which is not *is*—not *is* simply, but *is* non-existent. So too with a quality.

Now we must inquire how we should express ourselves on each point, but still more how the facts actually stand. And so now also since it is evident what language we use, essence will belong, just as the 'what' does, primarily and in the simple sense to substance, and in a secondary way to the other categories also,—not essence simply, but the essence of a quality or of a quantity. For it must be either homonymously that we say these *are*, or by making qualifications and abstractions (in the way in which that which is not known may be said to be known),—the truth being that we use the word neither homonymously nor in the same sense, but just as we apply the word 'medical' when there is a *reference* to one and the same thing, not *meaning* one and the same thing, nor yet speaking homonymously; for a patient and an operation and an instrument are called medical neither homonymously nor in virtue of one thing, but with reference to one thing. But it does not matter in which of the two ways one likes to describe the facts; this is evident, that definition and essence in the primary and simple sense belong to substances. Still they belong to other things as well in a similar way, but not primarily. For if we suppose this it does not follow that there is a definition of every word which means the same as any formula; it must mean the same as a particular kind of formula; and this condition is satisfied if it is a formula of something which is one, not by continuity like the *Iliad* or the things that are one by being bound together, but in one of the main senses of 'one', which answer to the senses of 'is'; now 'that which is' in one sense denotes an individual, in another a quantity, in another a quality. And so there can be a formula or definition of white man, but not in the sense in which there is a definition either of white or of a substance.

5 · It is a difficult question, if one denies that a formula with an addition is a definition, whether any of the things that are not simple but coupled will be definable. For we *must* explain them by an addition. E.g. there is the nose, and concavity, and snubness, which is compounded out of the two by the presence of the one in the other, and it is not by accident that the nose has the attribute either of concavity or of snubness, but in virtue of its nature; nor do they attach to it as whiteness does to Callias, or to man (because Callias, who happens to be a man, is white), but rather as 'male' attaches to animal and 'equal' to quantity, and as everything else which is said of something in its own right. And such attributes are those in which is involved either the *formula* or the *name* of the subject of the particular attribute, and which cannot be explained without this; e.g. white can be explained apart from man, but not female apart from animal. Therefore there is either no essence and definition of any of these things, or if there is, it is in another sense, as we have said.

But there is also a second difficulty about them. For if snub nose and concave nose are the same thing, snub and concave will be the same thing; but if snub and concave are not the same (because it is impossible to speak of snubness apart from the thing of which, in its own right, it is an attribute, for snubness is concavity *in the nose*), either it is impossible properly to say 'snub nose' or the same thing will have been said twice, concave nose nose; for snub nose will be concave nose nose. And so it is absurd that such things should have an essence; if they have, there will be an infinite regress; for in snub nose yet another nose will be involved.

1031ª1   Clearly then only substance is definable. For if the other categories also are definable, it must be by addition, e.g. [the qualitative is defined thus, and so is][1] the odd, for it cannot be defined apart from number; nor can female be defined apart from animal. (When I say 'by addition' I mean the expressions in which we have to

5   say the same thing twice, as in these instances.) And if this is true, coupled terms also, like 'odd number', will not be definable (but this escapes our notice because our formulae are not accurate). But if these also are definable, either it is in some other way or, as we said, definition and essence must be said to have more than one

10   sense. Therefore in one sense nothing will have a definition and nothing will have an essence, except substances, but in another sense other things will have them. Clearly, then, definition is the formula of the essence, and essence must belong to substances either alone or chiefly and primarily and in the unqualified sense.

15   6 · We must inquire whether each thing and its essence are the same or different. This is of some use for the inquiry concerning substance; for each thing is thought to be not different from its substance, and the essence is said to be the substance of each thing.

    Now in the case of things with accidental attributes the two would be generally
20   thought to be different, e.g. white man would be thought to be different from the essence of white man. For if they are the same, the essence of man and that of white man are also the same; for a man and a white man are the same, as people say, so
25   that the essence of white man and that of man would be also the same. But probably it is not necessary that things with accidental attributes should be the same. For the extreme terms are not in the same way the same.—Perhaps *this* might be thought to follow, that the extreme terms, the accidents, should turn out to be the same, e.g. the essence of white and that of musical; but this is not actually thought to be the case.

    But in the case of so-called self-subsistent things, is a thing necessarily the same as its essence? E.g. if there are some substances which have no other
30   substances nor entities prior to them—substances such as some assert the Ideas to be? If the essence of good is to be different from the Idea of good, and the essence of animal from the Idea of animal, and the essence of being from the Idea of being,
1031ᵇ1   there will, firstly, be other substances and entities and Ideas besides those which are asserted, and, secondly, these others will be prior substances if the essence is substance. And if the posterior substances are severed from one another, there will be no knowledge of the ones and the others will have no being. (By 'severed' I mean,
5   if the Idea of good has not the essence of good, and the latter has not the property of being good.) For there is knowledge of each thing only when we know its essence.

[1]Excised by Jaeger.

And the case is the same for other things as for the good; so that if the essence of good is not good, neither will the essence of being be, nor the essence of unity be one. And all essences alike exist or none of them does; so that if the essence of being is 10 not, neither will any of the others be. Again, that which has not the property of being good is not good. The good, then, must be one with the essence of good, and the beautiful with the essence of beauty, and so with all things which do not depend on something else but are self-subsistent and primary. For it is enough if they are this, even if there are no Forms; and perhaps all the more if there are Forms.—At 15 the same time it is clear that if there are Ideas such as some people say there are, the substratum of them will not be substance; for these must be substances, and not predicable of a substratum; for if they were they would exist only by being participated in.—Each thing then and its essence are one and the same in no merely accidental way, as is evident both from the preceding arguments and because to *know* each thing, at least, is to know its essence, so that even by the exhibition of 20 instances it becomes clear that both must be one.

(But of an accidental term, e.g. 'the musical' or 'the white', since it has two meanings, it is not true to say that it itself is identical with its essence; for both that to which the accidental quality belongs, and the accidental quality, are white, so 25 that in a sense the accident and its essence are the same, and in a sense they are not; for the essence of white is not the same as the man or the white man, but it is the same as the attribute white.)

The absurdity of the separation would appear also if one were to assign a name to each of the essences; for there would be another essence besides the original one, e.g. to the essence of horse there will belong a second essence. Yet why should not 30 some things be their essences from the start, since essence is substance? But not only are a thing and its essence one, but the formula of them is also the same, as is 1032ª1 clear even from what has been said; for it is not by accident that the essence of one, and the one, are one. Further, if they were different, the process would go on to infinity; for we should have the essence of one, and the one, so that in their case also the same infinite regress would be found. Clearly, then, each primary and self-subsistent thing is one and the same as its essence. 5

Now the sophistical objections to this position, and the question whether Socrates and to be Socrates are the same thing, are obviously answered in the same way; for there is no difference either in the standpoint from which the question would be asked, or in that from which one could answer it successfully. We have explained, then, in what sense each thing is the same as its essence and in what sense 10 it is not.

7 · Of things that come to be some come to be by nature, some by art, some spontaneously. Now everything that comes to be comes to be by the agency of something and from something and comes to be something. And the something which I say it comes to be may be found in any category; it may come to be either a 'this' or of some quantity or of some quality or somewhere. 15

Now natural comings to be are the comings to be of those things which come to be by nature; and that out of which they come to be is what we call matter; and that by which they come to be is something which exists naturally; and the something which they come to be is a man or a plant or one of the things of this kind, which we

20 say are substances if anything is. All things that come to be either by nature or by art have matter; for each of them is capable both of being and of not being, and this capacity is the matter in each. And, in general, both that from which they are produced is nature, and the type according to which they are produced is nature (for that which is produced, e.g. a plant or an animal, has a nature), and so is that by which they are produced—the so-called 'formal' nature, which is specifically the same as the nature of the thing produced (though it is in another individual); for

25 man begets man.

Thus, then, are natural products produced; all other productions are called 'makings'. And all makings proceed either from art or from a capacity or from

30 thought. Some of them happen also spontaneously or by chance just as natural products sometimes do; for there also the same things sometimes are produced without seed as well as from seed. Concerning these cases, then, we must inquire

1032ᵇ1 later, but from art proceed the things of which the form is in the soul. (By form I mean the essence of each thing and its primary substance.) For even contraries have in a sense the same form; for the substance of a privation is the opposite substance, e.g. health is the substance of disease; for it is by its absence that disease exists; and

5 health is the formula and the knowledge in the soul. The healthy subject, then, is produced as the result of the following train of thought; since *this* is health, if the subject is to be healthy *this* must first be present, e.g. a uniform state of body, and if this is to be present, there must be heat; and the physician goes on thinking thus until he brings the matter to a final step which he himself can take. Then the process

10 from this point onward, i.e. the process towards health, is called a 'making'. Therefore it follows that in a sense health comes from health and house from house, that with matter from that without matter; for the medical art and the building art are the form of health and of the house; and I call the essence substance without

15 matter. Of productions and movements one part is called thinking and the other making,—that which proceeds from the starting-point and the form is thinking, and that which proceeds from the final step of the thinking is making. And each of the intermediate steps is taken in the same way. I mean, for instance, if the subject is to be healthy his bodily state must be made uniform. What then does being made

20 uniform imply? This or that. And this depends on his being made warm. What does this imply? Something else. And this something is present potentially; and what is present potentially is already in the physician's power.

The active principle then and the starting-point for the process of becoming healthy is, if it happens by art, the form in the soul, and if spontaneously, it is that, whatever it is, which is the starting-point of his making for the man who makes by

25 art, as in healing the starting-point is perhaps the production of warmth, and this the physician produces by rubbing. Warmth in the body, then, is either a part of health or is followed (either directly or through several intermediate steps) by something which is a part of health; and this, viz. that which produces the part, is

the last step, and so are, e.g., the stones a part of the house, and so in all other cases.

Therefore, as we say, it is impossible that anything should be produced if there 30 were nothing before. Obviously then some part of the result will pre-exist of necessity; for the matter is a part; for this is present in the process and it is this that becomes something. But do some also of the elements in the *formula* pre-exist? 1033ª1 Well, we describe in both ways what bronze circles are; we describe both the matter by saying it is bronze, and the form by saying that it is such and such a figure; and figure is the proximate genus in which it is placed. The bronze circle, then, has its matter *in its formula.* 5

And as for that out of which as matter they are produced, some things are said, when they have been produced, to be not it but of it, e.g. the statue is not stone but of stone. But though what becomes healthy is a man, a man is not what the healthy product is said to come from. The reason is that though a thing comes both from its privation and from its substratum, which we call its matter (e.g. what becomes healthy is both a man and an invalid), it is said to come rather from its privation 10 (e.g. it is from an invalid rather than from a man that a healthy subject is produced). And so the healthy subject is not said to *be* an invalid, but to be a man, and a healthy man. But as for the things whose privation is obscure and nameless, e.g. in bronze the privation of a particular shape or in bricks and timber the 15 privation of arrangement as a house, the thing is thought to be produced *from* these materials, as in the former case the healthy man is produced *from* an invalid. And so, as there also a thing is not said to be that from which it comes, here the statue is not said to be wood but is said by a verbal change to be not wood but wooden, not bronze but of bronze, not stone but of stone, and the house is said to be not bricks but of bricks (since we should not say without qualification, if we looked at things carefully, even that a statue is produced from wood or a house from bricks, because 20 its coming to be implies change in that from which it comes, and not permanence). For this reason, then, we use this way of speaking.

8 · Since anything which is produced is produced by something (and this I call the starting-point of the production), and from something (and let this be taken 25 to be not the privation but the matter; for the meanings we attach to these have already been distinguished), and since something is produced (and this is either a sphere or a circle or whatever else it may chance to be), just as we do not make the substratum—the bronze, so we do not make the sphere, except incidentally, because the bronze sphere is a sphere and we make the former. For to make a 'this' is to 30 make a 'this' out of the general substratum. I mean that to make the bronze round is not to make the round or the sphere, but something else, i.e. to produce this form in something else. For if we make the form, we must make it out of something else; for 1033ᵇ1 this was assumed. E.g. we make a bronze sphere; and that in the sense that out of this, which is bronze, we make this other, which is a sphere. If, then, we make the sphere itself, clearly we must make it in the same way, and the processes of making will regress to infinity. Obviously then the form also, or whatever we ought to call 5

the shape of the sensible thing, is not produced, nor does production relate to it,—i.e. the essence is not produced; for this is that which is made to be in something else by art or by nature or by some capacity. But that there is a *bronze sphere,* this we make. For we make it out of bronze and the sphere; we bring the form into this

10 particular matter, and the result is a bronze sphere. But if the essence of sphere in general is produced, something must be produced out of something. For the product will always have to be divisible, and one part must be this and another that, I mean the one must be matter and the other form. If then a sphere is the figure whose circumference is at all points equidistant from the centre, part of this will be the

15 medium in which the thing made will be, and part will be in that medium, and the whole will be the thing produced, which corresponds to the bronze sphere. It is obvious then from what has been said that the thing, in the sense of form or substance, is not produced, but the concrete thing which gets its name from this is produced, and that in everything which comes to be matter is present, and one part of the thing is matter and the other form.

20 Is there then a sphere apart from the individual spheres or a house apart from the bricks? Rather we may say that no 'this' would ever have been coming to be, if this had been so. The 'form' however means the 'such', and is not a 'this'—a definite thing; but the artist makes, or the father generates, a 'such' out of a 'this'; and when it has been generated, it is a 'this such'. And the whole 'this', Callias or Socrates, is

25 analogous to this bronze sphere, but man and animal to bronze sphere in general. Obviously then the cause which consists of the Forms (taken in the sense in which some maintain the existence of the Forms, i.e. if they are something apart from the individuals) is useless with regard both to comings-to-be and to substances; and the Forms need not, for this reason at least, be self-subsistent substances. In some cases

30 it is even obvious that the producer is of the same kind as the produced (not, however, the same nor one in number, but in form), e.g. in the case of natural products (for man produces man), unless something happens contrary to nature, e.g. the production of a mule by a horse. And even these cases are similar; for that which would be found to be common to horse and ass, the genus next above them,

1034ª1 has not received a name, but it would doubtless be both, as the mule is both. Obviously, therefore, it is quite unnecessary to set up a Form as a pattern (for we should have looked for Forms in these cases if any; for these are substances if anything is so); the begetter is adequate to the making of the product and to the

5 causing of the form in the matter. And when we have the whole, such and such a form in this flesh and in these bones, this is Callias or Socrates; and they are different in virtue of their matter (for that is different), but the same in form; for their form is indivisible.

9 · The question might be raised, why some things are produced sponta-
10 neously as well as by art, e.g. health, while others are not, e.g. a house. The reason is that in some cases the matter which determines the production in the making and producing of any work of art, and in which a part of the product is present, is such as to be set in motion by itself and in some cases is not of this nature, and of the former kind some can move itself in the particular way required, while other matter is

incapable of this; for many things can be set in motion by themselves but not in 15
some particular way, e.g. that of dancing. The things then whose matter is of this
sort, e.g. stones, cannot be moved in the particular way required, except by
something else, but in another way they can move themselves; and so it is with fire.
Therefore some things cannot exist apart from some one who has the art of making
them, while others can exist without such a person; for motion can be started by
these things which have not the art but can move of themselves, i.e. either by *other* 20
things which have not the art or by a part of the product itself.

And it is clear also from what has been said that in a sense everything is
produced from another individual which shares its name (natural products are so
produced), or a part of itself which shares its name (e.g. the house produced by
reason is produced from a house; for the art of building is the form of the house), or
something which contains a part of it,—if we exclude things produced by accident. 25
For what directly and of itself causes the production is a part of the product. The
heat in the movement causes heat in the body, and this is either health, or a part of
health, or is followed by a part of health or by health itself. And so it is said to cause
health, because it produces that on which health follows. 30

Therefore substance is the starting-point of all production, as of deduction. It
is from the 'what' that deductions start; and from it also we now find processes of
production to start. And things which are formed by nature are in the same case as
these products of art. For the seed produces them as the artist produces the works of
art; for it has the form potentially, and that from which the seed comes has *in a* 1034^{b}1
sense the same name as the offspring; only in a sense, for we must not expect *all*
cases to have exactly the same name, as in the production of human being from
human being (for a woman also can be produced by a man—unless there is a
deformity: that is why it is not from a mule that a mule is produced). The natural
things which (like some artificial objects) can be produced spontaneously are those
whose matter can be moved even by itself in the way in which the seed 5
usually moves it; but those things which have not such matter cannot be produced
except by parents.

But not only regarding substance does our argument prove that its form does
not come to be, but the argument applies to all the primary classes alike, i.e.
quantity, quality, and the other categories. For as the bronze sphere comes to be, 10
but not the sphere nor the bronze, and so too in the case of bronze itself, if it comes
to be, (for the matter and the form must always exist before), so is it as regards both
'what' and quality and quantity and the other categories likewise; for the quality
does not come to be, but the wood of that quality, and the quantity does not come to 15
be, but the wood or the animal of that size. But we may learn from these instances a
peculiarity of substance, that there must exist beforehand another actual substance
which produces it, e.g. an animal if an animal is produced; but it is not necessary
that a quality or quantity should pre-exist otherwise than potentially.

10 · Since a definition is a formula, and every formula has parts, and as the 20
formula is to the thing, so is the part of the formula to the part of the thing, we are
already faced by the question whether the formula of the parts must be present in

the formula of the whole or not. For in some cases the formulae of the parts are seen
25 to be present, and in some not. The formula of the circle does not include that of the
segments, but that of the syllable includes that of the letters; yet the circle is divided
into segments as the syllable is into letters.—And further if the parts are prior to the
whole, and the acute angle is a part of the right angle and the finger a part of the
30 animal, the acute angle will be prior to the right angle and the finger to the man.
But the latter are thought to be prior; for in formula the parts are explained by
reference to them, and in virtue also of their power of existing apart from the parts
the wholes are prior.

Perhaps we should rather say that 'part' is used in several senses. One of these
is 'that which measures another thing in respect of quantity'. But let this sense be
set aside; let us inquire about the parts of which *substance* consists. If then matter is
1035ᵃ1 one thing, form another, the compound of these a third, and both the matter and the
form and the compound are substance, even the matter is in a sense called part of a
thing, while in a sense *it* is not, but only the elements of which the formula of the
5 form consists. E.g. flesh (for this is the matter in which it is produced) is not a part
of concavity, but of snubness it is a part; and the bronze is a part of the particular
statue, but not of the statue as form. (For each thing must be referred to by naming
its form, and as having form, but never by naming its material aspect as such.) And
so the formula of the circle does not include that of the segments, but the formula of
10 the syllable includes that of the letters; for the letters are parts of the formula of the
form, and not matter, but the segments are parts, in the sense of matter, on which
the form supervenes; yet they are nearer the form than the bronze is when
roundness is produced in bronze. But in a sense not even every kind of letter will be
15 present in the formula of the syllable, e.g. particular waxen letters or the letters as
sounds in the air; for these also are part of the syllable only in the sense that they are
its perceptible matter. For even if the line when divided passes away into its halves,
or the man into bones and muscles and flesh, it does not follow that they are
20 composed of these as parts of their substance, but rather as matter; and these are
parts of the concrete thing, but not of the form, i.e. of that to which the formula
refers; and therefore they will not be in the formulae either. Therefore of some
things the formula of such parts will be present, but in others it must not be present,
where the formula does not refer to the concrete object. For it is for this reason that
25 some things have as their constituent principles parts into which they pass away,
while some have not. Those things in which the form and the matter are taken
together, e.g. the snub, or the bronze circle, pass away into these material parts, and
the matter is a part of them; but those things which do not involve matter but are
without matter, and whose formulae are formulae of the form only, do not pass
30 away,—either not at all or at any rate not in this way. Therefore these materials are
principles and parts of the concrete things, while of the form they are neither parts
nor principles. And therefore the clay statue is resolved into clay and the ball into
bronze and Callias into flesh and bones, and again the circle into its segments; for
there is a sense of 'circle' in which it involves matter. For 'circle' is used
1035ᵇ1 homonymously, meaning both the circle in general and the individual circle,
because there is no name proper to the individuals.

The truth has really now been stated, but still let us state it yet more clearly, taking up the question again. The parts of the formula, into which the formula is 5 divided, are prior to it, either all or some of them. The formula of the right angle, however, does not include the formula of the acute, but the formula of the acute includes that of the right angle; for he who defines the acute uses the right angle; for the acute is less than a right angle. The circle and the semicircle also are in a like relation; for the semicircle is defined by the circle; and so is the finger by the whole 10 body, for a finger is such and such a part of a man. Therefore the parts which are of the nature of matter and into which as its matter a thing is divided, are posterior; but those which are parts of the formula, and of the substance according to its formula, are prior, either all or some of them. And since the soul of animals (for this is the substance of living beings) is their substance according to the formula, i.e. the 15 form and the essence of a body of a certain kind (at least we shall define each part, if we define it well, not without reference to its function, and this cannot belong to it without perception), therefore the parts of soul are prior, either all or some of them, to the concrete animal, and similarly in each case of a concrete whole; and the body and its parts are posterior to this its substance, and it is not the substance but the 20 concrete thing that is divided into these parts as its matter. To the concrete thing these are in a sense prior, but in a sense they are not. For they cannot even exist if severed from the whole; for it is not a finger in *any* state that is the finger of a living thing, but the dead finger is a finger only homonymously. Some parts are neither 25 prior nor posterior to the whole, i.e. those which are most important and in which the formula, i.e. the substance, is immediately present, e.g. perhaps the heart or the brain; for it does not matter which of the two has this quality. But man and horse and terms which are thus applied to individuals, but universally, are not substance but something composed of this particular formula and this particular matter treated as universal; but when we come to the individual, Socrates is composed of 30 ultimate individual matter; and similarly in all other cases.

   A part may be a part either of the form (i.e. the essence), or of the compound of the form and the matter, or of the matter itself. But only the parts of the form are parts of the formula, and the formula is of the universal; for being a circle is the same as the circle, and being a soul is the same as the soul. But when we come to the 1036ᵃ1 concrete thing, e.g. *this* circle, i.e. one of the individual circles, whether sensible or intelligible (I mean by intelligible circles the mathematical, and by sensible circles those of bronze and of wood), of these there is no definition, but they are known by 5 the aid of thought or perception; and when they go out of our actual consciousness it is not clear whether they exist or not; but they are always stated and cognized by means of the universal formula. But matter is unknowable in itself. And some matter is sensible and some intelligible, sensible matter being for instance bronze and wood and all matter that is changeable, and intelligible matter being that which 10 is present in sensible things not *qua* sensible, i.e. in the objects of mathematics. We have stated, then, how whole and part, and prior and posterior, are related.

   When any one asks whether the right angle and the circle and the animal are prior to that into which they are divided and of which they consist, i.e. the parts, we 15 must meet the inquiry by saying that the question cannot be answered simply. For if

the soul is the animal or the living thing, or the soul of each individual is the individual itself, and being a circle is the circle, and being a right angle and the essence of the right angle is the right angle, then the whole in one sense must be called posterior to the part in one sense, i.e. to the parts included in the formula and
20   to the parts of the individual right angle (for both the material right angle which is made of bronze, and that which is formed by individual lines, are posterior to their parts); while the immaterial right angle is posterior to the parts included in the formula, but prior to those included in the particular instance. But the question must not be answered simply. If, however, the soul is something different and is not identical with the animal, even so some parts must be called prior and others must
25   not, as has been said.

11 · The question is naturally raised, what sort of parts belong to the form and what sort not to the form, but to the concrete thing. Yet if this is not plain it is not possible to define anything; for definition is of the universal and of the form. If then it is not evident which of the parts are of the nature of matter and which are
30   not, neither will the formula of the thing be evident. In the case of things which are found to occur in specifically different materials, as a circle may exist in bronze or stone or wood, it seems plain that these, the bronze or the stone, are no part of the essence of the circle, since it is found apart from them. Of things which are *not* seen to exist apart, there is no reason why the same may not be true, e.g. even if all circles
1036ᵇ1   that had ever been seen were of bronze (for none the less the bronze would be no part of the form); but it is hard to effect this severance in thought. E.g. the form of man is always found in flesh and bones and parts of this kind; are these then also
5   parts of the form and the formula? No, they are matter; but because man is not found also in other matters we are unable to effect the severance.

Since this is thought to be possible, but it is not clear *when* it is the case, some are in doubt even in the case of the circle and the triangle, thinking that it is not
10   right to define these by lines and by continuous space, but that all these are to the circle or the triangle as flesh or bones are to man, and bronze or stone to the statue; and they bring all things to numbers, and they say the formula of line is that of two. And of those who assert the Ideas some make two the line itself, and others make it
15   the form of the line; for in some cases they say the Form and that of which it is the Form are the same, e.g. two and the Form of two; but in the case of line they say this is no longer so.

It follows then that there is one Form for many things whose Form is evidently different (a conclusion which confronted the Pythagoreans also); and that it is possible to make one thing the very Form of all, and to hold that the others are not
20   Forms; but thus all things will be one.

Now we have stated that the question of definitions contains some difficulty, and why this is so. Therefore to bring all things thus to Forms and to eliminate the matter is useless labour; for some things surely are a particular form in a particular matter, or particular things in a particular state. And the comparison which
25   Socrates the younger used to make in the case of animal is not good; for it leads

away from the truth, and makes one suppose that man can possibly exist without his parts, as the circle can without the bronze. But the case is not similar; for an animal is something perceptible, and it is not possible to define it without reference to movement—nor, therefore, without reference to the parts and to their being in a certain state. For it is not a hand in *any* state that is a part of man, but the hand which can fulfil its work, which therefore must be alive; if it is not alive it is not a part.

Regarding the objects of mathematics, why are the formulae of the parts not parts of the formulae of the wholes, e.g. why are not the formulae of the semicircles parts of the formula of the circle? It cannot be said, 'because these parts are perceptible things'; for they are not. But perhaps this makes no difference; for even some things which are not perceptible must have matter; for there is some matter in everything which is not an essence and a bare form but a 'this'. The semicircles, then, will be parts, not of the universal circle, but of the individual circles, as has been said before; for while one kind of matter is perceptible, there is another which is intelligible.

It is clear also that the soul is the primary substance and the body is matter, and man or animal is the compound of both taken universally; and Socrates or Coriscus, if even the soul of Socrates is Socrates, is taken in two ways (for some mean by such a term the soul, and others mean the concrete thing), but if he is simply this particular soul and this particular body, the individual is analogous to the universal.

Whether there is, apart from the matter of such substances, any other substance, and one should look for some substance other than these, e.g. numbers or something of the sort, must be considered later. For it is for the sake of this that we are trying to determine the nature of perceptible substances, since in a sense the inquiry about perceptible substances is the work of natural science, i.e of second philosophy; for the natural scientist must not only know about the matter, but also about the substance in the sense of the formula, and even more than about the other. And in the case of definitions, how the elements in the formula are parts of the definition, and why the definition is one formula (for clearly the thing is one, but in virtue of *what* is the thing one, although it has parts?)—this must be considered later.

What the essence is and in what sense it is independent, has been stated universally in a way which is true of every case, and also why the formula of the essence of some things contains the parts of the thing defined, while that of others does not; and we have stated that in the formula of the substance the material parts will not be present (for they are not even parts of the substance in that sense, but of the concrete substance; but of this there is in a sense a formula, and in a sense there is not; for there is no formula of it with its matter, for this is indefinite, but there is a formula of it with reference to its primary substance—e.g. in the case of man the formula of the soul—, for the substance is the indwelling form, from which along with the matter the so-called concrete substance is derived; e.g. concavity is a form of this sort, for from this and the nose arise snub nose and snubness; ['nose' will be found to be involved twice in these terms]);[2] but in the concrete substance, e.g. a snub nose or Callias, the matter also will be present. And we have stated that the essence and the individual thing are in some cases the same; i.e. in the case of primary substances, e.g. curvature and the essence of curvature, if this is primary. (By a primary substance I mean one which does not imply the presence of something in something else, i.e. in a substrate which acts as matter.) But things which are of the nature of matter or of wholes which include matter, are not the same as their essences, nor are accidental unities like that of Socrates and musical; for these are the same only by accident.

12 · Now let us treat first of definition, in so far as we have not treated of it in the *Analytics*; for the problem stated in them is useful for our inquiries concerning substance. I mean this problem:—wherein consists the unity of that, the formula of which we call a definition, as for instance in the case of man, two-footed animal; for let this be the formula of man. Why, then, is this one, and not many, viz. animal *and* two-footed? For in the case of 'man' and 'white' there is a plurality when one term does not belong to the other, but a unity when it does belong and the subject, man, has a certain attribute; for then a unity is produced and we have the white man. In the present case, on the other hand, one does not share in the other; the genus is not thought to share in its differentiae; for then the same thing would share in contraries; for the differentiae by which the genus is divided are contrary. And even if the genus does share in them, the same argument applies, since the differentiae present in man are many, e.g. endowed with feet, two-footed, featherless. Why are these one and not many? Not because they are present in one thing; for on this principle a unity can be made out of any set of attributes. But surely all the attributes in the definition *must* be one; for the definition is a single formula and a formula of substance, so that it must be a formula of some one thing; for substance means a 'one' and a 'this', as we maintain.

We must first inquire about definitions arising out of divisions. There is nothing in the definition except the first-named genus and the differentiae. The other genera are the first genus and along with this the differentiae that are taken with it, e.g. the first may be animal, the next animal which is two-footed, and again animal which is two-footed and featherless, and similarly if the definition includes more terms. And in general it makes no difference whether it includes many or few terms,—nor, therefore, whether it includes few or simply two; and of the two the one is differentia and the other genus, e.g. in 'two-footed animal' 'animal' is genus, and the other is differentia. If then the genus absolutely does not exist apart from the species which it as genus includes, or if it exists but exists as matter (for the voice is genus and matter, but its differentiae make the species, i.e. the letters, out of it), clearly the definition is the formula which comprises the differentiae.

But it is also necessary in division to take the differentia of the differentia; e.g. endowed with feet is a differentia of animal; again we must know the differentia of

---

[2] Excised by Ross.

animal endowed with feet *qua* endowed with feet. Therefore we must not say, if we are to speak rightly, that of that which is endowed with feet one part has feathers and one is featherless; if we say this we say it through incapacity; we must divide it into cloven-footed or not-cloven; for these are differentiae in the foot; cloven- 15 footedness is a form of footedness. And we always want to go on so till we come to the species that contain no differences. And then there will be as many kinds of foot as there are differentiae, and the kinds of animals endowed with feet will be equal in number to the differentiae. If then this is so, clearly the *last* differentia will be the substance of the thing and its definition, since it is not right to state the same things 20 more than once in our definitions; for it is superfluous. And this does happen; for when we say 'animal which is endowed with feet, and two-footed' we have said nothing other than 'animal having feet, having two feet'; and if we divide this by the proper division, we shall be saying the same thing many times—as many times as there are differentiae.

If then a differentia of a differentia be taken at each step, one differentia—the 25 last—will be the form and the substance; but if we divide according to accidental qualities, e.g. if we were to divide that which is endowed with feet into the white and the black, there will be as many differentiae as there are processes of division. Therefore it is plain that the definition is the formula which contains the differentiae, or, according to the right method, the last of these. This would be 30 evident, if we were to change the order of such definitions, e.g. that of man, saying 'animal which is two-footed and endowed with feet'; for 'endowed with feet' is superfluous when 'two-footed' has been said. But order is no part of the substance; for how are we to think the one element posterior and the other prior? Regarding the definitions, then, which arise out of divisions, let this much be taken as stated in 35 the first place as to their nature.

13 · Let us again return to the subject of our inquiry, which is substance. As 1038^{b}1 the substrate and the essence and the compound of these are called substance, so also is the universal. About two of these we have spoken; about the essence and about the substrate, of which we have said that it underlies in two senses, either 5 being a 'this'—which is the way in which an animal underlies its attributes—, or as the matter underlies the complete reality. The universal also is thought by some to be in the fullest sense a cause, and a principle; therefore let us attack the discussion of this point also. For it seems impossible that any universal term should be the name of a substance. For primary substance is that kind of substance which is peculiar to an individual, which does not belong to anything else; but the universal is 10 common, since that is called universal which naturally belongs to more than one thing. Of which individual then will this be the substance? Either of all or of none. But it cannot be the substance of all; and if it is to be the substance of one, this one will be the others also; for things whose substance is one and whose essence is one are themselves also one.

Further, substance means that which is not predicable of a subject, but the 15 universal is predicable of some subject always.

But perhaps the universal, while it cannot be substance in the way in which the essence is so, can be present in this, e.g. animal can be present in man and horse. Then clearly there is a formula of the universal. And it makes no difference even if

20   there is not a formula of everything that is in the substance; for none the less the universal will be the substance of something. Man is the substance of the individual man in whom it is present; therefore the same will happen again, for a substance, e.g. animal, must be the substance of that in which it is present as something peculiar to it. And further it is impossible and absurd that the 'this', i.e. the

25   substance, if it consists of parts, should not consist of substances nor of what is a 'this', but of quality; for that which is not substance, i.e. the quality, will then be prior to substance and to the 'this'. Which is impossible; for neither in formula nor in time nor in coming to be can the affections be prior to the substance; for then they would be separable from it. Further, in Socrates there will be a substance in a

30   substance, so that he will be the substance of two things. And in general it follows, if man and such things are substances, that none of the elements in their formulae is the substance of anything, nor does it exist apart from the species or in anything else; I mean, for instance, that no animal exists apart from the particular animals, nor does any other of the elements present in formulae exist apart.

If, then, we view the matter from these standpoints, it is plain that no universal

1039ᵃ1   attribute is a substance, and this is plain also from the fact that no common predicate indicates a 'this', but rather a 'such'. If not, many difficulties follow and especially the 'third man'.

The conclusion is evident also from the following consideration—that a substance cannot consist of substances present in it actually (for things that are thus

5   actually two are never actually one, though if they are *potentially* two, they can be one, e.g. the double line consists of two halves—potentially; for the *actualization* of the halves divides them from one another; therefore if the substance is one, it will not consist of substances present in it); and according to the argument which

10   Democritus states rightly; he says one thing cannot come from two nor two from one; for he identifies his indivisible magnitudes with substances. It is clear therefore that the same will hold good of number, if number is a synthesis of units, as is said by some; for two is either not one, or there is no unit present in it actually.

The consequence of this view involves a difficulty. If no substance can consist

15   of universals because a universal indicates a 'such', not a 'this', and if no composite substance can be composed of actual substances, every substance would be incomposite, so that there would not even be a formula of any substance. But it is thought by all and has been previously stated that it is either only, or primarily,

20   substance that can be defined; yet now it seems that not even substance can. There cannot, then, be a definition of anything; or rather in a sense there can be, and in a sense there cannot. And what we say will be plainer from what follows.

14 · It is clear also from these very facts what consequences confront those

25   who say the Ideas are substances and can exist apart, and at the same time make the Form consist of the genus and the differentiae. For if the Forms exist and animal is

present in man and horse, it is either one and the same in number, or different. (In formula it is clearly one; for he who states the formula unfolds the same formula in either case.) If there is a man-in-himself who is a 'this' and exists apart, the parts of 30 which he consists, e.g. animal and two-footed, must indicate a 'this' and be things existing apart and substances; therefore animal too must be of this sort.

Now if animal, which is in the horse and in man, is one and the same, as you are one and the same with yourself, how will the one in things that exist apart be 1039ᵇ1 one, and how will this animal escape being divided even from itself?

Further, if it is to share in two-footed and many-footed, an impossible conclusion follows; for contrary attributes will belong at the same time to it although it is one and a this. If it does not, what is the relation implied when one says the animal is two-footed or has feet? But perhaps these are put together and 5 are in contact, or are mixed. Yet all these are absurd.

But suppose the Form to be different in each species. Then there will be practically an infinite number of things whose *substance* is animal; for it is not by accident that man has animal for one of its elements. Further, animal-in-itself will be many. For the animal in each species will be the substance of the species; for it is not dependent on anything else; if it were, that other would be an element in man, i.e 10 would be the genus of man. And further all the elements of which man is composed will be Ideas. Now nothing can be the Idea of one thing and the substance of another; this is impossible. Each, then, of the Ideas present in the species of animals will be the ideal animal. Further, from what will these Ideas be derived; how will they be derived from the ideal animal? Or how can an Idea of animal whose essence 15 is simply animal exist apart from the ideal animal? Further, in the case of sensible things both these consequences and others still more absurd follow. If, then, these consequences are impossible, clearly there are not Forms of sensible things in the sense in which some maintain their existence.

15 · Since substance is of two kinds, the concrete thing and the formula (I 20 mean that one kind of substance is the formula taken with the matter, while another kind is the formula in its generality), substances in the former sense are capable of destruction (for they are capable also of generation), but there is no destruction of the formula in the sense that it is ever in course of being destroyed; for there is no generation of it (the being of house is not generated, but only the being of *this* 25 house), but without generation and destruction formulae are and are not; for it has been shown that no one produces nor makes these. For this reason, also, there is neither definition nor demonstration of sensible individual substances, because they have matter whose nature is such that they are capable both of being and of not being; for which reason all the individual instances of them are destructible. If then 30 demonstration is of necessary truths and definition involves knowledge, and if, just as knowledge cannot be sometimes knowledge and sometimes ignorance, but the state which varies thus is opinion, so too demonstration and definition cannot vary thus, but it is opinion that deals with that which can be otherwise than as it is, 1040ᵃ1 clearly there can neither be definition nor demonstration of sensible individuals. For

perishing things are obscure to those who have knowledge of them, when they have passed from our perception; and though the formulae remain in the soul unchanged,

5 there will no longer be either definition or demonstration. Therefore when one of those who aim at definition defines any individual, he must recognize that his definition may always be overthrown; for it is not possible to define such things.

Nor is it possible to define any Idea. For the Idea is, as its supporters say, an individual, and can exist apart; and the formula must consist of words; and he who

10 defines must not invent a word (for it would be unknown), but the established words are common to each of a number of things; these then must apply to something besides the thing defined; e.g. if one were defining you, he would say 'an animal which is lean' or 'white', or something else which will apply also to some one other than you. If any one were to say that perhaps all the attributes taken apart may

15 belong to many subjects, but together they belong only to this one, we must reply firstly that they belong also to both the elements, e.g. two-footed animal belongs to animal and to the two-footed. And where the elements are eternal this is even necessary, since the elements are prior to and parts of the compound; what is more, they can also exist apart, if 'man' can exist apart. For either neither or both can. If,

20 then, neither can, the genus will not exist apart from the species; but if it does, the differentia will also. Secondly, we must reply that they are prior in being; and things which are prior to others are not destroyed when the others are.

Again, if the Ideas consist of Ideas (as they must, since elements are simpler than the compound), it will be further necessary that the elements of which the Idea consists, e.g. animal and two-footed, should be predicated of many subjects. If not,

25 how will they be known? For there will then be an Idea which cannot be predicated of more subjects than one. But this is not thought possible—every Idea is thought to be capable of being shared.

As has been said, then, people do not realize that it is impossible to define in the case of eternal things, especially those which are unique, like the sun or the

30 moon. For they err not only by adding attributes after whose removal the sun would still exist, e.g. 'going round the earth' or 'night-hidden' (for from their view it follows that if it stands still or is visible, it will no longer be the sun; but it is strange if this is so; for 'the sun' means a certain *substance*); but also by the mention of attributes which can belong to another subject; e.g. if another thing with the stated attributes comes into existence, clearly it will be a sun; the formula therefore is

1040ᵇ1 general. But the sun was supposed to be an individual, like Cleon or Socrates. Why does not one of the supporters of the Ideas produce a definition of an Idea? It would become clear, if they tried, that what has now been said is true.

5   16 · Evidently even of the things that are thought to be substances, most are only potentialities,—e.g. the parts of animals (for none of them exists separately; and when they *are* separated, then they too exist, all of them, merely as matter) and earth and fire and air; for none of them is one, but they are like a heap before it is fused by heat and some one thing is made out of the bits. One might suppose

10 especially that the parts of living things and the corresponding parts of the soul are

both, i.e. exist both actually and potentially, because they have sources of movement in something in their joints; for which reason some animals live when divided. Yet all the parts must exist only potentially, when they are one and continuous by nature,—not by force or even by growing together, for such a   15
phenomenon is an abnormality.

Since the term 'unity' is used like the term 'being', and the substance of that which is one is one, and things whose substance is numerically one are numerically one, evidently neither unity nor being can be the substance of things, just as being an element or a principle cannot be the substance, but we seek *what* the principle is, that we may refer the thing to something more intelligible. Now of these things   20
being and unity are more substantial than principle or element or cause, but not even the former are substance, since in general nothing that is common is substance; for substance does not belong to anything but to itself and to that which has it, of which it is the substance. Further, that which is one cannot be in many things at the   25
same time, but that which is common is present in many things at the same time; so that clearly no universal exists apart from the individuals.

But those who say the Forms exist, in one respect are right, in saying the Forms exist apart, if they are substances; but in another respect they are not right, because they say the one *in* many is a Form. The reason for their doing this is that they   30
cannot say what are the substances of this sort, the imperishable substances which exist apart from the individual and sensible substances. They make them, then, the same in kind as the perishable things (for this kind of substance we know)—man himself and the horse itself, adding to the sensible things the word 'itself'. Yet even if we had not seen the stars, none the less, I suppose, would there be eternal   1041ª1
substances besides those which we knew; so that now also if we do not know what eternal substances there are, yet it is doubtless necessary that some should exist. Clearly, then, no universal term is the name of a substance, and no substance is composed of substances.   5

17 · We should say what, and what sort of thing, substance is, taking another starting-point; for perhaps from this we shall get a clear view also of that substance which exists apart from sensible substances. Since, then, substance is a principle and a cause, let us attack it from this standpoint. The 'why' is always   10
sought in this form—'why does one thing attach to another?' For to inquire why the musical man is a musical man, is either to inquire—as we have said—why the man is musical, or it is something else. Now 'why a thing is itself' is doubtless a meaningless inquiry; for the fact or the existence of the thing must already be   15
evident (e.g. that the moon is eclipsed), but the fact that a thing is itself is the single formula and the single cause to all such questions as why the man is man, or the musical musical, unless one were to say that each thing is inseparable from itself; and its being one just meant this. This, however, is common to all things and is a short and easy way with the question. But we *can* inquire why man is an animal of   20
such and such a nature. Here, then, we are evidently not inquiring why he who is a man is a man. We are inquiring, then, why something is predicable of something;

that it is predicable must be clear; for if not, the inquiry is an inquiry into nothing.
25 E.g. why does it thunder?—why is sound produced in the clouds? Thus the inquiry
is about the predication of one thing of another. And why are certain things, i.e.
stones and bricks, a house? Plainly we are seeking the cause. And this is the essence
(to speak abstractly), which in some cases is that for the sake of which, e.g. perhaps
30 in the case of a house or a bed, and in some cases is the first mover; for this also is a
cause. But while the efficient cause is sought in the case of genesis and destruction,
the final cause is sought in the case of being also.

The object of the inquiry is most overlooked where one term is not expressly
1041^{b}1 predicated of another (e.g. when we inquire why man is), because we do not
distinguish and do not say definitely 'why do these parts form this whole'? But we
must distinguish the elements before we begin to inquire; if not, it is not clear
whether the inquiry is significant or unmeaning. Since we must know the existence
5 of the thing and it must be given, clearly the question is *why* the matter is some
individual thing, e.g. why are these materials a house? Because that which was the
essence of a house is present. And why is this individual thing, or this body in this
state, a man? Therefore what we seek is the cause, i.e. the form, by reason of which
the matter is some definite thing; and this is the substance of the thing. Evidently,
then, in the case of simple things no inquiry nor teaching is possible; but we must
10 inquire into them in a different way.

As regards that which is compounded out of something so that the whole is
one—not like a heap, however, but like a syllable,—the syllable is not its elements,
ba is not the same as *b* and *a*, nor is flesh fire and earth; for when they are dissolved
15 the wholes, i.e. the flesh and the syllable, no longer exist, but the elements of the
syllable exist, and so do fire and earth. The syllable, then, is something—not only its
elements (the vowel and the consonant) but also something else; and the flesh is not
only fire and earth or the hot and the cold, but also something else. Since, then, that
20 something must be either an element or composed of elements, if it is an element the
same argument will again apply; for flesh will consist of this and fire and earth and
something still further, so that the process will go on to infinity; while if it is a
compound, clearly it will be a compound not of one but of many (or else it will itself
be that one), so that again in this case we can use the same argument as in the case
25 of flesh or of the syllable. But it would seem that this is something, and not an
element, and that it is the cause which makes *this* thing flesh and *that* a syllable.
And similarly in all other cases. And this is the substance of each thing; for this is
the primary cause of its being; and since, while some things are not substances, as
many as are substances are formed naturally and by nature, their substance would
30 seem to be this nature, which is not an element but a principle. An *element* is that
into which a thing is divided and which is present in it as matter, e.g. *a* and *b* are the
elements of the syllable.

BOOK VIII (H)

1 · We must draw our conclusions from what has been said, and sum up our results, and put the finishing touch to our inquiry. We have said that the causes, principles, and elements of substances are the object of our search. And some substances are recognized by all thinkers, but some have been advocated by particular schools. Those generally recognized are the natural substances, i.e. fire, earth, water, air, &c., the simple bodies; secondly, plants and their parts, and animals and the parts of animals; and finally the heavens and the parts of the heavens. Some particular schools say that Forms and the objects of mathematics are substances. And it follows from our arguments that there are other substances, the essence and the substratum. Again, in another way the genus seems more substantial than the species, and the universal than the particulars. And with the universal and the genus the Ideas are connected; it is in virtue of the same argument that they are thought to be substances. And since the essence is substance, and the definition is a formula of the essence, for this reason we have discussed definition and essential predication. Since the definition is a formula, and a formula has parts, we had to consider with respect to the notion of part, what are parts of the substance and what are not, and whether the same things are also parts of the definition. Further, then, neither the universal nor the genus is a substance; we must inquire later into the Ideas and the objects of mathematics; for some say these exist apart from sensible substances.

But now let us resume the discussion of the generally recognized substances. These are the sensible substances, and sensible substances all have matter. The substratum is substance, and this is in one sense the matter (and by matter I mean that which, not being a 'this' actually, is potentially a 'this'), and in another sense the formula or form (which being a 'this' can be separately formulated), and thirdly the complex of matter and form, which alone is generated and destroyed, and is, without qualification, capable of separate existence; for of substances in the sense of formulae some are separable and some are not.

But clearly matter also is substance; for in all the opposite changes that occur there is something which underlies the changes, e.g. in respect of place that which is now here and again elsewhere, and in respect of increase that which is now of one size and again less or greater, and in respect of alteration that which is now healthy and again diseased; and similarly in respect of substance there is something that is now being generated and again being destroyed, and now underlies the process as a 'this' and again underlies it as the privation of positive character. In this last change the others are involved. But in either one or two of the others this is not involved; for it is not necessary if a thing has matter for change of place that it should also have matter for generation and destruction.

2 · The difference between becoming in the unqualified sense and becoming in a qualified sense has been stated in the *Physics*. Since the substance which exists as substratum and as matter is generally recognized, and this is that which exists

10 potentially, it remains for us to say what is the substance, in the sense of *actuality*, of sensible things. Democritus seems to think there are three kinds of difference between things; the underlying body, the matter, is one and the same, but they differ either in rhythm, i.e. shape, or in turning, i.e. position, or in inter-contact, i.e.

15 order. But evidently there are many differences; for instance, some things are characterized by the mode of composition of their matter, e.g. the things formed by mixture, such as honey-water; and others by being bound together, e.g. a bundle; and others by being glued together, e.g. a book; and others by being nailed together, e.g. a casket; and others in more than one of these ways; and others by position, e.g.

20 the threshold and the lintel (for these differ by being placed in a certain way); and others by time, e.g. dinner and breakfast; and others by place, e.g. the winds; and others by the affections proper to sensible things, e.g. hardness and softness, density and rarity, dryness and wetness; and some things by some of these qualities, others

25 by them all, and in general some by excess and some by defect. Clearly then the word 'is' has just as many meanings; a thing is a threshold because it lies in such and such a position, and its being means its lying in that position, while being ice means having been solidified in such and such a way. And the being of some things will be defined by *all* these qualities, because some parts of them are mixed, others are

30 fused, others are bound together, others are solidified, and others possess the other differentiae; e.g. the hand or the foot. We must grasp, then, the kinds of differentiae (for these will be the principles of the being of things), e.g. the things characterized by the more and the less, or by the dense and the rare, and by other such qualities;

35 for all these are characterized by excess and defect. And everything that is characterized by shape or by smoothness and roughness, is determined by the straight and the curved. And for other things their being will mean their being

1043ᵃ1 mixed, and their not being will mean the opposite. It is clear then from these facts that if its substance is the cause of each thing's being, we must seek in these differentiae the cause of the being of each of these things. Now none of these differentiae is substance, even when coupled with matter, yet in each there is

5 something analogous to substance; and as in substances that which is predicated of the matter is the actuality itself, in all other definitions also it is what most resembles full actuality. E.g. if we had to define a threshold, we should say 'wood or stone in such and such a position', and a house we should define as 'bricks and timbers in such and such a position' (or we may name that for the sake of which as well in some cases), and if we define ice we say 'water frozen or solidified in such

10 and such a way', and harmony is 'such and such a blending of high and low'; and similarly in all other cases.

Obviously then the actuality or the formula is different when the matter is different; for in some cases it is the juxtaposition, in others the mixing, and in others some other of the attributes we have named. And so, in defining, those who define a

15 house as stones, bricks, and timbers, are speaking of the potential house, for these are the matter; but those who define it as a covering for bodies and chattels, or add some other similar differentia, speak of the actuality; and those who combine both of these speak of the third kind of substance, which is composed of matter and form.

20 For the formula that gives the differentiae seems to be an account of the form and

the actuality, while that which gives the components is rather an account of the matter. And the same is true with regard to the definitions which Archytas used to accept; for they are accounts of the combined form and matter. E.g. what is still weather? Absence of motion in a large extent of air; air is the matter, and absence of motion is the actuality and substance. What is a calm? Smoothness of sea; the material substratum is the sea, and the actuality or form is smoothness. It is 25 obvious then, from what has been said, what sensible substance is and how it exists—one kind of it as matter, another as form or actuality; while the third kind is that which is composed of these two.

3 . We must not forget that sometimes it is not clear whether a name means the composite substance, or the actuality or form, e.g. whether 'house' is a sign for 30 the composite thing, 'a covering consisting of bricks and stones laid thus and thus', or for the actuality or form, 'a covering', and whether a line is twoness in length or twoness, and whether an animal is a soul in a body or a soul. For soul is the substance or actuality of some body; but animal might be applied to both, not that 35 both are definable by one formula but because they refer to the same thing. But this question, while important for another purpose, is of no importance for the inquiry into sensible substance; for the essence certainly attaches to the form and the 1043^{b}1 actuality. For soul and to be soul are the same, but to be man and man are not the same, unless indeed the soul is to be called man; and thus on one interpretation the thing is the same as its essence, and on another it is not.

If we consider we find that the syllable is not produced by the letters and 5 juxtaposition, nor is the house bricks and juxtaposition. And this is right; for the juxtaposition or mixing is not produced by those things of which it is the juxtaposition or mixing. And the same is true in the other cases, e.g. if the threshold is characterized by its position, the position is not produced by the threshold, but rather the latter is produced by the former. Nor is man animal and biped, but there 10 must be something besides these, if these are matter,—something which is neither an element in the whole nor produced by an element, but is the substance, which people eliminate and state the matter. If then this is the cause of the thing's being, and if the cause of its being is its substance, they cannot be stating the substance itself.

This, then, must either be eternal or it must be destructible without being ever 15 in course of being destroyed, and must have come to be without ever being in course of coming to be. But it has been proved and explained elsewhere that no one makes or generates the form, but it is a 'this' that is made, i.e. the complex of form and matter that is generated. Whether the substances of destructible things can exist apart, is not yet at all clear; except that obviously this is impossible in some cases—in the case of things which cannot exist apart from the individual instances, 20 e.g. house or utensil. Perhaps neither these things themselves, nor any of the other things which are not formed by nature, are substances at all; for one might say that the nature in natural objects is the only substance to be found in destructible things.

Therefore the difficulty which was raised by the school of Antisthenes and

25 other such uneducated people has a certain appropriateness. They stated that the 'what' cannot be defined (for the definition so called is a long formula); but of what *sort* a thing, e.g. silver, is, they thought it possible to explain, not saying what it is but that it is like tin. Therefore one kind of substance can be defined and formulated, i.e. the composite kind, whether it be the object of sense or of reason;

30 but the primary parts of which this consists cannot be defined, since a definitory formula predicates something of something, and one part of the definition must play the part of matter and the other that of form.

It is also obvious that, if all substances are in a sense numbers, they are so in this sense and not, as some say as numbers of units. For definition is a sort of

35 number; for it is divisible, and into indivisible parts (for definitory formulae are not infinite), and number also is of this nature. And as, when one of the parts of which a number consists has been taken from or added to the number, it is no longer the same number, but a different one, even if it is the very smallest part that has been

1044ᵃ1 taken away or added, so the definition and the essence will no longer remain when anything has been taken away or added. And the number must have something in virtue of which it is one thing, while our opponents cannot say if it is one (for either

5 it is not one but a sort of heap, or if it is, we ought to say what it is that makes one out of many); and the definition is one, but similarly they cannot say what makes *it* one. And this is natural; for the same reason is applicable, and substance is one in the sense which we have explained, and not, as some say, by being a sort of unit or point; each is a complete reality and a definite nature. And as number does not admit of

10 the more and the less, neither does substance, in the sense of form, but if any substance does, it is only the substance which involves matter. Let this then suffice for an account of the generation and destruction of so-called substances—in what sense it is possible and in what sense impossible—and of the reduction of things to number.

15   4 · Regarding material substance we must not forget that even if all things have the same primary constituent or constituents, and if the same matter serves as starting-point for their generation, yet there is a matter proper to each, e.g. the sweet or the fat of phlegm, and the bitter, or something else, of bile; though perhaps

20 these have the same constituent. And there come to be several matters for the same thing, when the one matter is matter for the other, e.g. phlegm comes from the fat and from the sweet, if the fat comes from the sweet; and it comes from bile by analysis of the bile into its ultimate matter. For one thing comes from another in two senses, either because it will be found at a later stage of development, or because it is produced if the other is analysed into its original constituents. When

25 the matter is one, different things may be produced owing to difference in the moving cause, e.g. from wood may be made both a chest and a bed. But *some* different things must have their matter different, e.g. a saw could not be made of wood, nor is this in the power of the moving cause; for it could not make a saw of

30 wool or of wood. But if, as a matter of fact, the same thing can be made of different material, clearly the art, i.e. the moving principle, is the same; for if both the matter and the moving principle were different, the product would be too.

When one inquires what is the cause, one should, as causes are spoken of in several senses, state all the possible causes. E.g. what is the material cause of man? The menstrual fluid. What is the moving cause? The *semen*. The formal cause? His essence. The final cause? His end. But perhaps the latter two are the same.—We must state the *proximate* causes. What is the material cause? Not fire or earth, but the matter peculiar to the thing.

Regarding *generable* natural substances, *if* the causes are really these and of this number and we have to learn the causes, we must inquire thus, if we are to inquire rightly. But in the case of natural but *eternal* substances another account must be given. For perhaps some have no matter, or not matter of this sort but only such as can be moved in respect of place. Nor does matter belong to those things which exist by nature but are not substances; their substratum is the *substance*. E.g. what is the cause of an eclipse? What is its matter? There is none; the *moon* is that which suffers eclipse. What is the moving cause which extinguishes the light? The earth. The final cause perhaps does not exist. The formal principle is the definitory formula, but this is obscure if it does not include the cause. E.g. what is eclipse? Deprivation of light. But if we add 'by interposition of the earth', this is the formula which includes the cause. In the case of sleep it is not clear what it is that proximately has this affection. Surely the animal, it will be said. Yes, but the animal in virtue of what, i.e. what is the proximate subject? The heart or some other part. Next, by what is it produced? Next, what is the affection—that of the proximate subject, not of the whole animal? Shall we say that it is immobility of such and such a kind? Yes, but to what process in the proximate subject is this due?

5 · Since some things are and are not, without coming to be and ceasing to be, e.g. points, if they can be said to *be,* and in general forms (for it is not white that comes to be, but the wood comes to be white, if everything that comes to be comes from something and comes to be something), not all contraries can come from one another, but it is in different senses that a white man comes from a black man, and white comes from black. Nor has everything matter, but only those things which come to be and change into one another. Those things which, without ever being in course of changing, are or are not, have no matter.

There is difficulty in the question how the matter of each thing is related to its contrary states. E.g. if the body is potentially healthy, and disease is contrary to health, is it potentially both? And is water potentially wine and vinegar? We answer that it is the matter of one in virtue of its positive state and its form, and of the other in virtue of the privation of its positive state and the corruption of it contrary to its nature. It is also hard to say why wine is not said to be the matter of vinegar nor potentially vinegar (though vinegar is produced from it), and why the living man is not said to be potentially dead. In fact they are not, but the corruptions in question are accidental, and it is the matter of the animal that is itself in virtue of its corruption the potency and matter of a corpse, and it is water that is the matter of vinegar. For the one comes from the other as night from day. And *all* things which change thus into one another must be reduced to their matter, e.g. if from a corpse is

1044ᵇ1

5

10

15

20

25

30

35

1045ᵃ1

5 produced an animal, the corpse is first reduced to its matter, and only then becomes an animal; and vinegar is first reduced to water, and only then becomes wine.

6 · To return to the difficulty which has been stated with respect to definitions and numbers, what is the cause of the unity of each of them? In the case of all things which have several parts and in which the whole is not, as it were, a 10 mere heap, but the totality is something besides the parts, there is a cause of unity; for as regards material things contact is the cause in some cases, and in others viscidity or some other such quality. And a definition is a formula which is one not by being connected together, like the *Iliad,* but by dealing with one object.—What 15 then is it that makes man one; why is he one and not many, e.g. animal—biped, especially if there are, as some say, an ideal animal and an ideal biped? Why are not those Ideas the ideal man, so that men would exist by participation not in man, nor in one Idea, but in two, animal and biped? And in general man would be not one but 20 more than one thing, animal and biped.

Clearly, then, if people proceed thus in their usual manner of definition and speech, they cannot explain and solve the difficulty. But if, as we say, one element is matter and another is form, and one is potentially and the other actually, the 25 question will no longer be thought a difficulty. For this difficulty is the same as would arise if 'round bronze' were the definition of cloak; for this name would be a sign of the definitory formula, so that the question is, what is the cause of the unity of round and bronze? The difficulty disappears, because the one is matter, the other 30 form. What then is the cause of this—the reason why that which was potentially is actually,—what except, in the case of things which are generated, the agent? For there is no other reason why the potential sphere becomes actually a sphere, but this was the essence of either. Of matter some is the object of reason, some of sense, and 35 part of the formula is always matter and part is actuality, e.g. the circle is a figure which is plane. But of the things which have no matter, either for reason or for 1045ᵇ1 sense, each is by its nature essentially a kind of unity, as it is essentially a kind of being—a 'this', a quality, or a quantity. And so neither 'existent' nor 'one' is present in definitions, and an essence is by its very nature a kind of unity as it is a kind of being. This is why none of these has any reason outside itself for being one, nor for 5 being a kind of being; for each is by its nature a kind of being and a kind of unity, not as being in the genus 'being' or 'one' nor in the sense that being and unity can exist apart from particulars.

Owing to the difficulty about unity some speak of participation, and raise the question, what is the cause of participation and what is it to participate; and others 10 speak of communion, as Lycophron says knowledge is a communion of knowing with the soul; and others say life is a composition or connexion of soul with body. Yet the same account applies to all cases; for being healthy will be either a communion or a connexion or a composition of soul and health, and the fact that the 15 bronze is a triangle will be a composition of bronze and triangle, and the fact that a thing is white will be a composition of surface and whiteness.—The reason is that people look for a unifying formula, and a difference, between potentiality and actuality. But, as has been said, the proximate matter and the form are one and the same thing, the one potentially, the other actually. Therefore to ask the cause of their being one is like asking the cause of unity in general; for each thing is a unity, 20 and the potential and the actual are somehow one. Therefore there is no other cause here unless there is something which caused the movement from potentiality into actuality. And all things which have *no* matter are *without qualification* essentially unities.

BOOK IX (Θ)

1 · We have treated of that which *is* primarily and to which all the other categories of being are referred—i.e. of substance. For it is in virtue of the formula of substance that the others are said to be—quantity and quality and the like; for all 30 will be found to contain the formula of substance, as we said in the first part of our work. And since 'being' is in one way divided into 'what', quality, and quantity, and is in another way distinguished in respect of potentiality and fulfillment, and of function, let us discuss potentiality and fulfillment. First let us explain potentiality 35 in the strictest sense, which is, however, not the most useful for our present purpose. For potentiality and actuality extend further than the mere sphere of motion. But 1046ᵃ1 when we have spoken of this first kind, we shall in our discussions of actuality explain the other kinds of potentiality.

We have pointed out elsewhere that 'potentiality' and the word 'can' have 5 several senses.[1] Of these we may neglect all the potentialities that are so called homonomously. For some are called so by analogy, as in geometry; and we say things can be or cannot be because in some definite way they are or are not.

But all potentialities that conform to the same type are starting points, and are called potentialities in reference to one primary kind, which is a starting-point of 10 change in another thing or in the thing itself *qua* other. For one kind is a potentiality for being acted on, i.e. the principle in the very thing acted on, which makes it capable of being changed and acted on by another thing or by itself regarded as other; and another kind is a state of insusceptibility to change for the worse and to destruction by another thing or by the thing itself *qua* other, i.e. by a principle of change. In all these definitions is contained the formula of potentiality in the 15 primary sense.—And again these so-called potentialities are potentialities either of acting merely or of being acted on, or of acting or being acted on *well,* so that even in the formulae of the latter the formulae of the prior kinds of potentiality are somehow contained.

Obviously, then, in a sense the potentiality of acting and of being acted on is one (for a thing may be capable either because it can be acted on or because 20 something else can be acted on by it), but in a sense the potentialities are different.

---

[1]See V (Δ) 12, where 'δύναμις' was translated 'capacity'.

For the one is in the thing acted on; it is because it contains a certain motive principle, and because even the matter is a motive principle, that the thing acted on is acted on, one thing by one, another by another; for that which is oily is
25   inflammable, and that which yields in a particular way can be crushed; and similarly in all other cases. But the other potentiality is in the agent, e.g. heat and the art of building are present, one in that which can produce heat and the other in the man who can build. And so in so far as a thing is an organic unity, it cannot be acted on by itself; for it is one and not two different things. And want of potentiality,
30   or powerlessness, is the privation which is contrary to potentiality of this sort, so that every potentiality belongs to the same subject and refers to the same process as a corresponding want of potentiality. Privation has several senses; for it means that which has not a certain quality and that which might naturally have it but has not got it, either in general of when it might naturally have it, and either in some particular way, e.g. when it *completely* fails to have it, or when it in any degree fails to have it. And in certain cases if things which naturally have a quality lose it by
35   violence, we say they suffer privation.

2 · Since some such principles are present in soulless things, and others in
1046ᵇ1   things possessed of soul, and in soul and in the rational part of the soul, clearly some potentialities will be non-rational and some will be accompanied by reason. This is why all arts, i.e. all productive forms of knowledge, are potentialities; they are principles of change in another thing or in the artist himself considered as other.
5   And each of those which are accompanied by reason is alike capable of contrary effects, but one non-rational power produces one effect; e.g. the hot is capable only of heating, but the medical art can produce both disease and health. The reason is that science is a rational formula, and the same rational formula explains a thing and its privation, only not in the same way; and in a sense it applies
10   to both, but in a sense it applies rather to the positive fact. Therefore such sciences must deal with contraries, but with one in virtue of their own nature and with the other not in virtue of their nature; for the rational formula applies to one object in virtue of that object's nature, and to the other, in a sense, accidentally. For it is by denial and removal that it explains the contrary; for the contrary is the primary
15   privation, and this is the entire removal of the positive term. Now since on the one hand contraries do not occur in the same thing, but on the other hand science is a potentiality which depends on the possession of a rational formula, and the soul possesses a principle of movement; therefore, on the other hand, the healthy produces only health and what can heat only heat and what can cool only cold, but the scientific man, on the other hand, produces both the contrary effects. For there
20   is a rational formula which applies to both, though not in the same way, and it is in a soul which possesses a principle of movement; so that the soul will start both processes from the same principle, applying them to the same object. And so the things whose potentiality is according to a rational formula act contrariwise to the things whose potentiality is non-rational; for the products of the former are included under one principle, the rational formula.

It is obvious also that the potentiality of merely doing a thing or having it done 25
to one is implied in that of doing it or having it done *well,* but the latter is not always
implied in the former: for he who does a thing well must do it, but he who does it
merely need not do it well.

3 · There are some who say, as the Megaric school does, that a thing can act
only when it is acting, and when it is not acting it cannot act, e.g. he who is not 30
building cannot build, but only he who is building, when he is building; and so in all
other cases. It is not hard to see the absurdities that attend this view.

For it is clear that on this view a man will not be a builder unless he is building
(for to be a builder is to be able to build), and so with the other arts. If, then, it is 35
impossible to have such arts if one has not at some time learnt and acquired them,
and it is then impossible not to have them if one has not sometime lost them (either
by forgetfulness or by some accident or by time; for it cannot be by the destruction 1047ª1
of the object itself, for that lasts for ever), a man will not have the art when he has
ceased to use it, and yet he may immediately build again; how then will he have got
the art? And similarly with regard to lifeless things; nothing will be either cold or
hot or sweet or perceptible at all if people are not perceiving it; so that the upholders 5
of this view will have to maintain the doctrine of Protagoras. But, indeed, nothing
will even have perception if it is not perceiving, i.e. exercising its perception. If,
then, that is blind which has not sight though it would naturally have it, when it
would naturally have it and when it still exists, the same people will be blind many
times in the day—and deaf too. 10

Again, if that which is deprived of potentiality is incapable, that which is not
happening will be incapable of happening; but he who says of that which is
incapable of happening that it is or will be will say what is untrue; for this is what
incapacity meant. Therefore these views do away with both movement and
becoming. For that which stands will always stand, and that which sits will always 15
sit; if it is sitting it will not get up; for that which cannot get up will be incapable of
getting up. But we cannot say this, so that evidently potentiality and actuality are
different; but these views make potentiality and actuality the same, so that it is no
small thing they are seeking to annihilate. 20

Therefore it is possible that a thing may be capable of being and not *be,* and
capable of not being and yet *be,* and similarly with the other kinds of predicate; it
may be capable of walking and yet not walk, or capable of not walking and yet walk.
And a thing is capable of doing something if there is nothing impossible in its having
the actuality of that of which it is said to have the capacity. I mean for instance, if a 25
thing is capable of sitting and it is open to it to sit, there will be nothing impossible in
its actually sitting; and similarly if it is capable of being moved or moving or of
standing or making to stand or of being or coming to be, or of not being or not
coming to be.

The word 'actuality', which we connect with fulfillment, has, strictly speaking, 30
been extended from movements to other things; for actuality in the strict sense is
identified with movement. And so people do not assign movement to non-existent

things, though they do assign some other predicates. E.g. they say that non-existent things are objects of thought and desire, but not that they are moved; and this because, while they do not actually exist, they would have to exist actually if they were moved. For of non-existent things some exist potentially; but they do not *exist*, because they do not exist in fulfillment.

1047ᵇ1

4 · If what we have described is the possible or a consequence of the possible, evidently it cannot be true to say 'this is capable of being but will not be',—a view which leads to the conclusion that there is nothing incapable of being. Suppose, for instance, that a man (one who did not understand the meaning of 'incapable of being') were to say that the diagonal of the square is capable of being measured but will not be measured, because a thing may be capable of being or coming to be, and yet not be or be about to be. But from the premises this necessarily follows, that if we actually suppose that which is not, but is capable of being, to be or to have come to be, there will be nothing impossible in this; but the result *will* be impossible, for the actual measuring of the diagonal is impossible. For the false and the impossible are not the same; that you are standing now is false, but not impossible.

At the same time it is clear that if, when A is, B must be, then, when A is possible, B also must be possible. For if B need not be possible, there is nothing to prevent its not being possible. Now let A be supposed possible. Then, when A is possible, nothing impossible would follow if A were supposed to be; and then B must of course be. But we supposed B to be impossible. Let it be impossible, then. If, then, B is impossible, A also must be so. But A was supposed possible; therefore B also is possible. If, then, A is possible, B also will be possible, if they were so related that if A is, B must be. If, then, A and B being thus related, B is not possible on this condition, A and B will not be related as was supposed. And if when A is possible, B must be possible, then if A is, B must also be. For to say that B must be possible, if A is possible, means that if A is both at the time when and in the way in which it was supposed capable of being, B also must then and in that way be.

5 · As all potentialities are either innate, like the senses, or come by practice, like the power of playing the flute, or by learning, like that of the arts, those which come by practice or by rational formula we must acquire by previous exercise, but this is not necessary with those which are not of this nature and which imply passivity.

1048ª1

Since that which is capable is capable of something and at some time and in some way—with all the other qualifications which must be present in the definition—, and since some things can work according to a rational formula and their potentialities involve a formula, while other things are non-rational and their potentialities are non-rational, and the former potentialities must be in a living thing, while the latter can be both in the living and in the lifeless; as regards potentialities of the latter kind, when the agent and the patient meet in the way appropriate to the potentiality in question, the one must act and the other be acted on, but with the former kind this is not necessary. For the non-rational potentialities are all productive of one effect each, but the rational produce contrary effects, so that they would produce contrary effects at the same time; but this is impossible. That which decides, then, must be something else; I mean by this, desire or choice. For whichever of two things the animal desires decisively, it will do, when it is in the circumstances appropriate to the potentiality in question and meets the passive object. Therefore everything which has a rational potentiality, when it desires that for which it has a potentiality and in the circumstances in which it has it, must do this. And it has the potentiality in question when the passive object is present and is in a certain state; if not it will not be able to act. To add the qualification 'if nothing external prevents it' is not further necessary; for it has the potentiality in so far as this is a potentiality of acting, and it is this not in all circumstances but on certain conditions, among which will be the exclusion of external hindrances; for these are barred by some of the positive qualifications. And so even if one has a rational wish, or an appetite, to do two things or contrary things at the same time, one cannot do them; for it is not on these terms that one has the potentiality for them, nor is it a potentiality for doing both at the same time, since one will do just the things which it is a potentiality for doing.

6 · Since we have treated of the kind of potentiality which is related to movement, let us discuss actuality, what and what sort of thing it is. In the course of our analysis it will also become clear, with regard to the potential, that we not only ascribe potentiality to that whose nature it is to move something else, either without qualification or in some particular way, but also use the word in another sense, in the pursuit of which we have discussed these previous senses. Actuality means the existence of the thing, not in the way which we express by 'potentially'; we say that potentially, for instance, a statue of Hermes is in the block of wood and the half-line is in the whole, because it might be separated out, and even the man who is not studying we call a man of science, if he is capable of studying. Otherwise, actually. Our meaning can be seen in the particular cases by induction, and we must not seek a definition of everything but be content to grasp the analogy,—that as that which is building is to that which is capable of building, so is the waking to the sleeping, and that which is seeing to that which has its eyes shut but has sight, and that which is shaped out of the matter to the matter, and that which has been wrought to the unwrought. Let actuality be defined by one member of this antithesis, and the potential by the other. But all things are not said in the *same sense* to exist actually, but only by analogy—as A is in B or to B, C is in D or to D; for some are as movement to potentiality, and the others as substance to some sort of matter.

The infinite and the void and all similar things are said to exist potentially and actually in a different sense from that in which many other things are said so to exist, e.g. that which sees or walks or is seen. For of the latter class these predicates can at some time be truly asserted without qualification; for the seen is so called sometimes because it is being seen, sometimes because it is capable of being seen. But the infinite does not exist potentially in the sense that it will ever actually have separate existence; its separateness is only in knowledge. For the fact that division never ceases to be possible gives the result that this actuality exists potentially, but not that it exists separately.

Since of the actions which have a limit none is an end but all are relative to the end, e.g. the process of making thin is of this sort, and the things themselves when one is making them thin are in movement in this way (i.e. without being already that at which the movement aims), this is not an action or at least not a complete one (for it is not an end); but that in which the end is present is an action. E.g. at the same time we are seeing and have seen, are understanding and have understood, are thinking and have thought: but it is not true that at the same time we are learning and have learnt, or are being cured and have been cured. At the same time we are living well and have lived well, and are happy and have been happy. If not, the process would have had sometime to cease, as the process of making thin ceases: but, as it is, it does not cease; we are living and have lived. Of these processes, then, we must call the one set movements, and the other actualities. For every movement is incomplete—making thin, learning, walking, building; these are movements, and incomplete movements. For it is not true that at the same time we are walking and have walked, or are building and have built, or are coming to be and have come to be—it is a different thing that is being moved and that has been moved, and that is moving and that has moved; but it is the same thing that at the same time has seen and is seeing, or is thinking and has thought. The latter sort of process, then, I call an actuality, and the former a movement.

7 · What and what sort of thing the actual is may be taken as explained by these and similar considerations. But we must distinguish when a thing is potentially and when it is not; for it is not at any and every time. E.g. is *earth* potentially a man? No—but rather when it has already become *seed*, and perhaps not even then, as not everything can be healed by the medical art or by chance, but there is a certain kind of thing which is capable of it, and only this is potentially healthy. And the definition of that which as a result of *thought* comes to be in fulfillment from having been potentially is that when it has been wished it comes to pass if nothing external hinders it, while the condition on the other side—viz. in that which is healed—is that nothing in it hinders the result. Similarly there is potentially a house, if nothing in the thing acted on—i.e. in the matter—prevents it from becoming a house, and if there is nothing which must be added or taken away or changed; this is potentially a house, and the same is true of all other things for which the source of their becoming is external. And in the cases in which the source of the becoming is in the very thing which suffers change, all those things are said to be potentially something else, which will be it of themselves if nothing external hinders them. E.g. the seed is not yet potentially a man; for it must further undergo a change in a foreign medium.[2] But when through its own motive principle it has already got such and such attributes, in this state it is already potentially a man;

---

[2] Omitting πεσεῖν.

while in the former state it needs another principle, just as earth is not yet potentially a statue, for it must change in order to become bronze.

It seems that when we call a thing not something else but 'of' that something (e.g. a casket is not wood but of wood, and wood is not earth but made of earth, and again perhaps in the same way earth is not something else but made of that something), that something is always potentially (in the full sense of that word) the thing which comes after it in this series. E.g. a casket is not earthen nor earth, but wooden; for wood is potentially a casket and is the matter of a casket, wood in general of a casket in general, and this particular wood of this particular casket. And if there is a first thing, which no longer is called after something else, and said to be of it, this is prime matter; e.g. if earth is airy and air is not fire but fiery, fire then is prime matter, not being a 'this'. For the subject and substratum differ by being or not being a 'this'; the substratum of *accidents* is an individual such as a man, i.e. body and soul, while the accident is something like musical or white. (The subject is called, when music is implanted in it, not music but musical, and the man is not whiteness but white, and not ambulation or movement but walking or moving,—as in the above examples of 'of' something.) Wherever this is so, then, the ultimate subject is a substance; but when this is not so but the predicate is a form or a 'this', the ultimate subject is matter and material substance. And it is only right that the 'of' something locution should be used with reference both to the matter and to the accidents; for both are indeterminates. We have stated, then, when a thing is to be said to be potentially and when it is not.

8 · We have distinguished the various senses of 'prior', and it is clear that actuality is prior to potentiality. And I mean by potentiality not only that definite kind which is said to be a principle of change in another thing or in the thing itself regarded as other, but in general every principle of movement or of rest. For nature also is in the same genus as potentiality; for it is a principle of movement—not, however, in something else but in the thing itself *qua* itself. To all such potentiality, then, actuality is prior both in formula and in substance; and in time it is prior in one sense, and in another not.

Clearly it is prior in formula; for that which is in the primary sense potential is potential because it is possible for it to become actual, e.g. I mean by 'capable of building' that which can build, and by 'capable of seeing' that which can see, and by 'visible' that which can be seen. And the same account applies to all other cases, so that the formula and the knowledge of the one must precede the knowledge of the other.

In time it is prior in this sense: the actual member of a species is prior to the potential member of the same species, though the individual is potential before it is actual. I mean that the matter and the seed and that which is capable of seeing, which are potentially a man and corn and seeing, but not yet actually so, are prior in time to this particular man who now exists actually, and to the corn and to the seeing subject; but they are posterior in time to other actually existing things, from

which they were produced. For from the potential the actual is always produced by
25 an actual thing, e.g. man by man, musician by musician; there is always a first
mover, and the mover already exists actually. We have said in our account of
substance that everything that is produced is something produced from something
and by something, and is the same in species as it.

30   This is why it is thought impossible to be a builder if one has built nothing or a
harpist if one has never played the harp; for he who learns to play the harp learns to
play it by playing it, and all other learners do similarly. And thence arose the
sophistical quibble, that one who does not know a science will be doing that which is
the object of the science; for he who is learning it does not know it. But since, of that
35 which is coming to be, some part must have come to be, and, of that which, in
general, is changing, some part must have changed (this is shown in the treatise on
1050ª1 movement), he who is learning must, it would seem, know some part of the science.
It is surely clear, then, in this way, that the actuality is in this sense also, viz. in
order of becoming and of time, prior to the potentiality.

    But it is also prior in substance; firstly, because the things that are posterior in
5 becoming are prior in form and in substance, e.g. man is prior to boy and human
being to seed; for the one already has its form, and the other has not. Secondly,
because everything that comes to be moves towards a principle, i.e. an end. For that
for the sake of which a thing is, is its principle, and the becoming is for the sake of
the end; and the actuality is the end, and it is for the sake of this that the potentiality
10 is acquired. For animals do not see in order that they may have sight, but they have
sight that they may see. And similarly men have the art of building that they may
build, and theoretical science that they may theorize; but they do not theorize that
they may have theoretical science, except those who are learning by practice; and
these do not theorize except in a limited sense, or else they have no need to theorize.[3]
15 Further, matter exists in a potential state, just because it may attain to its form; and
when it exists *actually,* then it is in its form.

    And the same holds good in cases in which the end is a movement, as well as in
all others. Therefore as teachers think they have achieved their end when they have
exhibited the pupil at work, so also does nature. For if this is not the case, we shall
20 have Pauson's Hermes over again; for it will be hard to say about the knowledge, as
about the statue, whether it is within or without. For the action is the end, and the
actuality is the action. Therefore even the *word* 'actuality' is derived from 'action',
and points to the fulfillment.

    And while in some cases the exercise is the ultimate thing (e.g. in sight the
25 ultimate thing is seeing, and no other product besides this results from sight), but
from some things a product follows (e.g. from the art of building there results a
house as well as the act of building), yet none the less the act is in the former case
the end and in the latter more of an end than the mere potentiality is. For the act of
building is the thing that is being built, and comes to be—and is—at the same time
as the house.

[3]Omitting ὅτι.

Where, then, the result is something apart from the exercise, the actuality is in   30
the thing that is being made, e.g. the act of building is in the thing that is being built
and that of weaving in the thing that is being woven, and similarly in all other cases,
and in general the movement is in the thing that is being moved; but when there is
no product apart from the actuality, the actuality is in the agents, e.g. the act of   35
seeing is in the seeing subject and that of theorizing in the theorizing subject and the
life is in the soul (and therefore well-being also; for it is a certain kind of life).   1050ᵇ1
Obviously, therefore, the substance or form is actuality. From this argument it is
obvious that actuality is prior in substance to potentiality; and as we have said, one
actuality always precedes another in time right back to the actuality of the   5
eternal prime mover.

But actuality is prior in a higher sense also; for eternal things are prior in
substance to perishable things, and no eternal thing exists potentially. The reason is
this. Every potentiality is at one and the same time a potentiality for the opposite;
for, while that which is not capable of being present in a subject cannot be present,
everything that is capable of being may possibly not be actual. That, then, which is   10
capable of being may either be or not be; the same thing, then, is capable both of
being and of not being. And that which is capable of not being may possibly not be;
and that which may possibly not be is perishable, either without qualification, or in
the precise sense in which it is said that it possibly may not be, i.e. either in respect   15
of place or quantity or quality; 'without qualification' means 'in substance'.
Nothing, then, which is without qualification imperishable is without qualification
potentially (though there is nothing to prevent its being potentially in some respect,
e.g. potentially of a certain quality or in a certain place); imperishable things, then,
exist actually. Nor can anything which is of *necessity* be potential; yet these things
are primary; for if these did not exist, nothing would exist. Nor does eternal
movement, if there be such, exist potentially; and, if there is an eternal mover, it is   20
not potentially in motion (except in respect of 'whence' and 'whither'; there is
nothing to prevent its having matter for this). Therefore the sun and the stars and
the whole heaven are ever active, and there is no fear that they may sometime stand
still, as the natural philosophers fear they may. Nor do they tire in this activity; for
movement does not imply for them, as it does for perishable things, the potentiality   25
for opposites, so that the continuity of the movement should be laborious; for it is
that kind of substance which is matter and potentiality, not actuality, that causes
this.

Imperishable things are imitated by those that are involved in change, e.g.
earth and fire. For these also are ever active; for they have their movement of   30
themselves and in themselves. But the other potentialities, according to the
distinction we have drawn above, are all potentialities for opposites; for that which
can move another in this way can also move it not in this way, i.e. if it acts according
to a rational formula. But the same *non-rational* potentialities can produce opposite
results only by their presence or absence.

If, then, there are any entities or substances such as the dialecticians say the   35
Ideas are, there must be something much more scientific than the Idea of science

1051ᵃ1 and something more mobile than the Idea of movement; for these will be more of the nature of actualities, while the Ideas are potentialities for these. Obviously, then, actuality is prior both to potentiality and to every principle of change.

9 . That the good actuality is better and more valuable than the good
5 potentiality is evident from the following argument. Everything of which we say that it can do something, is alike capable of contraries, e.g. that of which we say that it can be healthy is the same as that which can be ill, and has both potentialities at once; for one and the same potentiality is a potentiality for health and illness, for
10 rest and motion, for building and throwing down, for being built and being thrown down. The capacity for contraries is present at the same time; but contraries cannot be present at the same time, and the actualities also cannot be present at the same time, e.g. health and illness. Therefore one of them must be the good, but the
15 capacity is both the contraries alike, or neither; the actuality, then, is better. And in the case of bad things, the end or actuality must be worse than the potentiality; for that which can is both contraries alike.

Clearly, then, the bad does not exist apart from bad things; for the bad is in its nature posterior to the potentiality. And therefore we may also say that in the things
20 which are from the beginning, i.e. in eternal things, there is nothing bad, nothing defective, nothing perverted (for perversion is something bad).

It is by actualization also that geometrical relations are discovered; for it is by dividing the given figures that people discover them. If they had been already divided, the relations would have been obvious; but as it is the divisions are present only potentially. Why are the angles of the triangle equal to two right angles?
25 Because the angles about one point are equal to two right angles. If, then, the line parallel to the side had been already drawn, the theorem would have been evident to any one as soon as he saw the figure. Why is the angle in a semicircle in all cases a right angle? Because if three lines are equal—the two which form the base, and the perpendicular from the centre—the conclusion is evident at a glance to one who knows this premise.

Obviously, therefore, the potentially existing relations are discovered by being
30 brought to actuality (the reason being that thinking is the actuality of thought); so that potentiality is discovered from actuality (and therefore it is by an act of construction that people acquire the knowledge), though the single actuality is later in generation.

10 · The terms 'being' and 'non-being' are employed firstly with reference to the categories, and secondly with reference to the potentiality or actuality of these
1051ᵇ1 or their opposites, while being and non-being in the strictest sense are truth and falsity[4]. The condition of this in the objects is their being combined or separated, so that he who thinks the separated to be separated and the combined to be combined

[4]Ross excises 'in the strictest sense'.

has the truth, while he whose thought is in a state contrary to that of the objects is in error. This being so, when is what is called truth or falsity present, and when is it 5 not? We must consider what we mean by these terms. It is not because we think that you are white, that you *are* white, but because you are white we who say this have the truth. If, then, some things are always combined and cannot be separated, and others are always separated and cannot be combined, while others are capable 10 either of combination or of separation, being is being combined and one, and not being is being not combined but more than one; regarding contingent facts, then, the same opinion or the same statement comes to be false and true, and it is possible at one time to have the truth and at another to be in error; but regarding things that 15 cannot be otherwise opinions are not at one time true and at another false, but the same opinions are always true or always false.

With regard to *incomposites,* what is being or not being, and truth or falsity? A thing of this sort is not composite, so as to be when it is compounded, and not to be if it is separated, like the white wood or the incommensurability of the diagonal; nor 20 will truth and falsity be still present in the same way as in the previous cases. In fact, as truth is not the same in these cases, so also being is not the same; but truth or falsity is as follows—contact and assertion are truth (assertion not being the same as affirmation), and ignorance is non-contact. For it is not possible to be in *error* 25 regarding the question what a thing is, save in an accidental sense; and the same holds good regarding non-composite substances (for it is not possible to be in error about them). And they all exist actually, not potentially; for otherwise they would come to be and cease to be; but, as it is, being itself does not come to be (nor cease to be); for if it did it would have to come out of something. About the things, then, 30 which are essences and exist in actuality, it is not possible to be in error, but only to think them or not to think them. Inquiry about their 'what' takes the form of asking whether they are of such and such a nature or not.

As regards being in the sense of truth and not being in the sense of falsity, in one case there is truth if the subject and the attribute are really combined, and falsity if they are not combined; in the other case, if the object is existent it exists in a particular way, and if it does not exist in this way it does not exist at all; and truth 1052ª1 means thinking these objects, and falsity does not exist, nor error, but only ignorance,—and not an ignorance which is like blindness; for blindness is akin to a total absence of the faculty of thinking.

It is evident also that about unchangeable things there can be no error in respect of time, if we assume them to be unchangeable. E.g. if we suppose that the 5 triangle does not change, we shall not suppose that at one time its angles are equal to two right angles while at another time they are not (for that would imply change). It is possible, however, to suppose that one member of such a class has a certain attribute and another has not, e.g. while we may suppose that no even number is prime, we may suppose that some are and some are not. But regarding a single number not even this form of error is possible; for we cannot in this case suppose that one instance has an attribute and another has not; but whether our 10 judgement be true or false, it is implied that the fact is eternal.

BOOK X (I)

15   1 · We have said previously, in our distinction of the various meanings of words, that 'one' has several meanings; while it is used in many senses, the things that are primarily and of their own nature and not accidentally called one may be summarized under four heads. (1) There is the continuous, either in general, or
20 especially that which is continuous by nature and not by contact nor by bonds; and of these, those things have more unity and are prior, whose movement is more indivisible and simpler. (2) That which is a whole and has a certain shape and form is *one* in a still higher degree; and especially if a thing is of this sort by nature, and not by force like the things which are unified by glue or nails or by being tied
25 together, i.e. if it has in itself something which is the cause of its continuity. A thing is of this sort because its movement is one and indivisible in place and time; so that evidently if a thing has by nature a principle of movement that is of the first kind (i.e. local movement) and the first in that kind (i.e. circular movement), this is in the primary sense one extended thing. The things, then, which are in this way one are either continuous[1] or whole, and the other things that are one are those whose
30 formula is one. Of this sort are the things the thought of which is one, i.e. those the thought of which is indivisible; and it is indivisible if the thing is indivisible in kind or in number. (3) In number, then, the individual is indivisible, and (4) in kind, that which in intelligibility and in knowledge is indivisible, so that that which causes substances to be one must be one in the primary sense. 'One,' then, has all these
35 meanings—the naturally continuous, the whole, the individual, and the universal. And all these are one because in some cases the movement, in others the thought or
1052ᵇ1 the formula, is indivisible.

But it must be observed that the questions, what sort of things are said to be one, and on the other hand what it is to be one and what is the formula of it, should not be assumed to be the same. 'One' has all these meanings, and each of those
5   things to which one of these kinds of unity belongs will be one; but 'to be one' will sometimes mean being one of these things, and sometimes something else, which is even nearer to the *word* 'one', while these other things approximate to its force. This is also true of 'element' or 'cause', if one had both to specify the things of which it is predicable and to give the definition of the word. For in a sense fire is an element
10 (and doubtless 'the indefinite' or something else of the sort is by its own nature the element), but in a sense it is not; for it is not the same thing to be fire and to be an element, but while as a particular thing with a nature of its own fire is an element, the name 'element' means that it has this attribute, that there is something which is
15 made of it as a primary constituent. And so with 'cause' and 'one' and all such terms. For this reason to be one is to be indivisible (being essentially a 'this' and capable of existing apart either in place or in form or thought); or perhaps to be whole and indivisible; but it is especially to be the first measure of a kind, and above all of quantity; for it is from this that it has been extended to the other categories.

───────────────────

¹Retaining ἢ συνεχές.

For measure is that by which quantity is known; and quantity *qua* quantity is known 20
either by a 'one' or by a number, and all number is known by a 'one'. Therefore all
quantity *qua* quantity is known by the one, and that by which quantities are
primarily known is the one itself; and so the one is the starting-point of number *qua*
number. And hence in the other classes too 'measure' means that by which each is 25
first known, and the measure of each is a 'one'—in length, in breadth, in depth, in
weight, in speed. (Weight and speed are common to both contraries; for each of
them has two meanings,—'weight' means both that which has any amount of
gravity and that which has an excess of gravity, and 'speed' both that which has any
amount of movement and that which has an excess of movement; for even the slow 30
has a certain speed and the light a certain weight.)

In all these, then, the measure and starting-point is something one and
indivisible, since even in lines we treat as indivisible the line a foot long. For
everywhere we seek as the measure something one and indivisible; and this is that
which is simple either in quality or in quantity. Now where it is thought impossible 35
to take away or to add, there the measure is exact. Hence that of number is most
exact; for we posit the unit as absolutely indivisible; and in all other cases we imitate 1053ª1
this sort of measure. For in the case of a furlong or a talent or of anything large any
addition or subtraction might more easily escape our notice than in the case of
something smaller; so that the first thing from which, as far as our perception goes, 5
nothing can be subtracted, all men make the measure, whether of liquids or of
solids, whether of weight or of size; and they think they know the quantity when
they know it by means of this measure. And they know movement too by the simple
movement and the quickest; for this occupies least time. And therefore in
astronomy a 'one' of this sort is the starting-point and measure (for they assume the 10
movement of the heavens to be uniform and the quickest, and judge the others by
reference to it), and in music the quarter-tone (because it is the least interval) and
in speech the letter. And all these are one in this sense—not that 'one' is something
predicable in the same sense of all of these, but in the sense we have mentioned.

But the measure is not always one in number—sometimes there are several; 15
e.g. the quarter-tones (not to the ear, but as determined by the ratios) are two, and
the articulate sounds by which we measure are more than one, and the diagonal of
the square and its side are measured by two quantities, and so are all spatial
magnitudes. Thus, then, the one is the measure of all things, because we come to
know the elements in the substance by dividing the things either in respect of
quantity or in respect of kind. The one is indivisible just because the first of each 20
class of things is indivisible. But it is not in the same way that every 'one' is
indivisible, e.g. a foot and a unit; the latter is absolutely indivisible, while the former
must be placed among things which are undivided in perception, as has been said
already,—for doubtless every continuous thing is divisible.

The measure is always homogeneous with the thing measured; the measure of
spatial magnitudes is a spatial magnitude, and in particular that of length is a 25
length, that of breadth a breadth, that of articulate sounds an articulate sound, that
of weight a weight, that of units a unit. (For we must state the matter so, and not say

that the measure of numbers is a number; we ought indeed to say this if we were to use the corresponding form of words, but the supposition does not really correspond—it is as if one supposed that the measure of units is units, and not a
30   unit, for number is a plurality of units.)

Knowledge also, and perception, we call the measure of things, for the same reason, because we know something by them,—while as a matter of fact they are measured rather than measure other things. But it is with us as if some one else measured us and we came to know how big we are by seeing that he applied the cubit-measure a certain number of times to us. But Protagoras says man is the
1053ᵇ1   measure of all things, meaning really the man who knows or the man who perceives, and these because they have respectively knowledge and perception, which we say are the measures of objects. They are saying nothing, then, while appearing to be saying something remarkable. Evidently, then, being one in the strictest sense, if we
5   define it according to the meaning of the word, is a measure, and especially of quantity, and secondly of quality. And some things will be one if they are indivisible in quantity, and others if they are indivisible in quality; therefore that which is one is indivisible, either absolutely or *qua* one.

2 · With regard to the substance and nature of the one we must ask in which
10   of two ways it exists. This is the very question that we reviewed in our discussion of problems, viz. what the one is and how we must conceive of it, whether we must take the one itself as being a substance (as both the Pythagoreans say in earlier and Plato in later times), or there is, rather, an underlying nature and it is to be explained more intelligibly and more in the manner of the natural philosophers, of whom one
15   says the one is love, another says it is air, and another the indefinite.

If then no universal can be a substance, as has been said in our discussion of substance and being, and if being itself cannot be a substance in the sense of a one apart from the many (for it is common to the many), but is only a predicate, clearly
20   the one also cannot be a substance; for being and one are the most universal of all predicates. Therefore, on the one hand, classes are not certain entities and substances separable from other things; and on the other hand the one cannot be a class, for the same reasons for which being and substance cannot be classes.

Further, this must hold good in all categories alike. Now 'being' and 'unity'
25   have an equal number of meanings; so that since in the sphere of qualities the one is something definite—some entity—and similarly in the sphere of quantities, clearly we must also ask in general what unity is, as we must ask what being is, since it is not enough to say that its nature is just to be unity or being. But in colours the one is
30   a colour, e.g. white—the other colours are observed to be produced out of this and black, and black is the privation of white, as darkness of light. Therefore if all existent things were colours, existent things would have been a number, indeed, but of what? Clearly of colours; and the 'one' would have been a particular 'one', e.g.
35   white. And similarly if all existent things were tunes, they would have been a number, but a number of quarter-tones, and their substance would not have been number; and the one would have been something whose substance was not the one
1054ª1   but the quarter-tone. And similarly if all existent things had been articulate sounds,

they would have been a number of letters, and the one would have been a vowel. And if all existent things were rectilineal figures, they would have been a number of figures, and the one would have been the triangle. And the same argument applies to all other classes. Since, therefore, while there are numbers and a one both in affections and in qualities and in quantities and in movement, in all cases the number is a number of particular things and the one is one something, and its substance is not to be one, the same must be true of substances; for it is true of all cases alike. That the one, then, in every class is a definite thing, and in no case is its nature just this—viz. unity, is evident; but as in colours the one itself which we must seek is one colour, so too in substance the one itself is one substance.

And that in a sense unity means the same as being is clear from the fact that it follows the categories in as many ways, and is not comprised within any category, e.g. neither in substance nor in quality, but is related to them just as being is; and from the fact that in 'one man' nothing more is predicated than in 'man', just as being is nothing apart from substance or quality or quantity; and to be one is just to be a particular thing.

3 · The one and the many are opposed in several ways, of which one is the opposition of the one and plurality as indivisible and divisible; for that which is either divided or divisible is called a plurality, and that which is indivisible or not divided is called one. Now since opposition is of four kinds, and one of these two terms is privative in meaning, they must be contraries, and neither contradictory nor correlative. And the one gets its meaning and explanation from its contrary, the indivisible from the divisible, because plurality and the divisible is more perceptible than the indivisible, so that in formula plurality is prior to the indivisible, because of the conditions of perception. To the one belong, as we indicated graphically in our distinction of the contraries, the same and the like and the equal, and to plurality belong the other and the unlike and the unequal.

'The same' has several meanings: we sometimes mean 'the same numerically'; again, we call a thing the same if it is one both in formula and in number, e.g. you are one with yourself both in form and in matter; and again, if the formula of its primary substance is one, e.g. equal straight lines are the same, and so are equal and equal-angled quadrilaterals—there are many such, but in these equality constitutes unity.

Things are like if, not being absolutely the same, nor without difference in their compound substance, they are the same in form, e.g. the larger square is like the smaller, and unequal straight lines are like; they are like, but not absolutely the same. Other things are like, if, having the same form, and being things in which difference of degree is possible, they have no difference of degree. Other things, if they have a quality that is in form one and the same—e.g. whiteness—in a greater or less degree, are called like because their form is one. Other things are called like if the qualities they have in common are more numerous than those in which they differ—either the qualities in general or the prominent qualities, e.g. tin is like silver, *qua* white, and gold is like fire, *qua* yellow and red.

Evidently, then, 'other' and 'unlike' also have several meanings. And the other

15 in one sense is the opposite of the same (so that everything is either the same as or other than everything else). In another sense things are other unless both their matter and their formula are one (so that you are other than your neighbour). The other in the third sense is exemplified in the objects of mathematics. 'Other' or 'the same' can for this reason be predicated of everything with regard to everything else,—but only if the things are one and existent, for the other is not the

20 *contradictory* of the same; which is why it is not predicated of non-existent things (while 'not the same' *is* so predicated). It *is* predicated of all *existing* things; for if a thing is both existent and one, it is naturally either one or not one. The other, then, and the same are thus opposed.

But difference is not the same as otherness. For the other and that which it is other than need not be other in some definite respect (for everything that exists is

25 either other or the same), but that which is different from anything is different in some respect, so that there must be something identical whereby they differ. And this identical thing is genus or species; for all things that differ differ either in genus or in species, in genus if the things have not their matter in common and are not generated out of each other (i.e. if they belong to different figures of predication),

30 and in species if they have the same genus (the genus is that same thing which both the different things are said to be in respect of their substance). And contraries are different, and contrariety is a kind of difference. That we are right in this supposition is shown by induction. For they are all seen to be different; they are not merely other, but some are other in genus, and others are in the same line of

1055ᵃ1 predication, and therefore in the same genus, and the same in genus. We have distinguished elsewhere what sort of things are the same or other in genus.

4 · Since things which differ may differ from one another more or less, there

5 is also a greatest difference, and this I call contrariety. That contrariety is the greatest difference is made clear by induction. For things which differ in *genus* have no way to one another, but are too far distant and are not comparable; and for things that differ in *species* the extremes from which generation takes place are the contraries; and the distance between extremes—and therefore that between contraries— is the greatest.

10 But that which is greatest in each class is complete. For that is greatest which cannot be exceeded, and that is complete beyond which nothing can be found. For the complete difference marks the end (just as the other things which are called complete are so called because they have attained an end), and beyond the end there is nothing; for in everything it is the extreme and includes all else, and therefore

15 there is nothing beyond the end, and the complete needs nothing further. From this, then, it is clear that contrariety is complete difference; and as contraries are so called in several senses, their modes of completeness will answer to the various modes of contrariety which attach to them.

This being so, evidently one thing cannot have more than one contrary, for

20 neither can there be anything more extreme than the extreme, nor can there be more than two extremes for the one interval. And in general if contrariety is a

difference, and if a difference must be between two things, then the complete difference must be so too.

And the other definitions are also necessarily true of contraries. For in each case the complete difference is the greatest difference. We cannot get anything beyond it, whether the things differ in genus or in species; for it has been shown that there is *no* difference between anything and the things outside its *genus*; and among these things the complete difference is the greatest. And the things in the same genus which differ most are contraries; for the complete difference is the greatest difference among these. And the things in the same receptive material which differ most are contrary; for the matter is the same for contraries. And of the things which are dealt with by the same faculty the most different are contrary; for one science deals with one class of things, and in these the complete difference is the greatest.

The primary contrariety is that between state and privation—not every privation, however (for 'privation' has several meanings), but that which is complete. And the other contraries must be called so with reference to these, some because they possess these, others because they produce or tend to produce them, others because they are acquisitions or losses of these or of other contraries. Now if the kinds of opposition are contradiction and privation and contrariety and relation, and of these the first is contradiction, and contradiction admits of no intermediate, while contraries admit of one, clearly contradiction and contrariety are not the same. But privation is a kind of contradiction; for what suffers privation, either in general or in some determinate way, is either that which is quite incapable of having some attribute or that which, being of such a nature as to have it, has it not; here we have already a variety of meanings, which have been distinguished elsewhere. Privation, therefore, is a contradiction or incapacity which is determinate or taken along with the receptive material. This is the reason why, while contradiction does not admit of an intermediate, privation sometimes does; for everything is equal or not equal, but not everything is equal or unequal, or if it is, it is only within the sphere of that which is receptive of equality. If, then, the changes which happen to the matter start from the contraries, and proceed either from the form and the possession of the form or from a privation of the form or shape, clearly all contrariety is a privation. (But perhaps not all privation is contrariety, the reason being that that which suffers privation may suffer it in several ways.) For the extremes from which the changes proceed are contraries.

And this is obvious also by induction. For every contrariety involves, as one of its terms, a privation. But not all cases are alike; inequality is the privation of equality and unlikeness of likeness, and vice is the privation of excellence. But the cases differ as has been said; in one case we mean simply that the thing suffers privation, in another case that it does so at a certain time or in a certain part (e.g. at a certain age or in the proper part), or throughout. This is why in some cases there is something in between (there are men who are neither good nor bad), and in others there is not (a number must be either odd or even). Further, some contraries have their subject defined, others have not.—Therefore it is evident that one of the contraries is always privative; but it is enough if this is true of the first—i.e., the generic—contraries, e.g. the one and the many; for the others can be referred to these.

30   5 · Since one thing has one contrary, we might raise the question how the one is opposed to the many and the equal to the great and the small.—For if we use the word 'whether' only in an opposition, asking e.g. whether it is white or black, and whether it is white or not white (we do not ask whether it is a man or white, unless

35 we are proceeding on a prior assumption and asking e.g. whether it was Cleon or Socrates that came. But this is not necessary in any class of things. Yet even this is an extension from the case of opposites; for opposites alone cannot be present together; and we assume this incompatibility here in asking which of the two came;

1056ᵃ1 for if they might both have come, the question would have been absurd. But if they might, even so this falls just as much into an opposition—that of the one and the many, i.e. we ask whether both came or only one):—if, then, the question 'whether' is always concerned with opposites, and we can ask whether it is greater or less or

5 equal, what is the opposition between the greater and the less, and the equal? The equal is not contrary either to one alone or to both; for why should it be contrary to the greater rather than to the less? Further, the equal is contrary to the *unequal*. Therefore it will be contrary to more things than one. But if the unequal means the same as both the greater and the less together, the equal *will* be opposite to both

10 (and the difficulty supports those who say the unequal is a 'two'), but it follows that one thing has two contraries, which is impossible. Again, the equal is evidently intermediate between the great and the small, but no contrary is either observed to be intermediate, nor, from its definition, can be so; for it would not be a perfect contrary if it were intermediate between any two things, but rather it always has something intermediate between itself and something else.

15   It remains, then, that it is opposed either as negation or as privation. It cannot be opposite to one of the two; for why to the great rather than to the small? It is then the privative negation of both. Therefore also 'whether' is said with reference to both—not to one of the two (e.g. we ask whether it is greater or equal, or whether it

20 is equal or less); there are always three cases. But it is not a *necessary* privation; for not everything which is not greater or less is equal, but only the things which are of such a nature as to have these attributes. The equal, then, is that which is neither great nor small and is naturally fitted to be either great or small; and it is opposed to both as a privative negation (and therefore is also intermediate). And that which is

25 neither good nor bad is opposed to both, but has no name (for each of these has several meanings and the receptive material is not one); but that which is neither white nor black has more claim to a name. Yet even this has not one name, though the colours of which this negation is privately predicated are in a way limited; for

30 they must be either grey or yellow or something else of the kind. Therefore it is an incorrect criticism that is passed by those who think that all such phrases are used in the same way, so that that which is neither a shoe nor a hand would be intermediate between a shoe and a hand, since that which is neither good nor bad is intermediate between the good and the bad,—as if there must be an intermediate in all cases.

This result does not necessarily follow. For the combined denial of opposites applies 35
when there is an intermediate and a certain natural interval; but in the other case
there is no difference; for the things, the denials of which are combined, belong to 1056ᵇ1
different classes, so that the substratum is not one.

6 · We might raise similar questions about the one and the many. For if the
many are absolutely opposed to the one, certain impossible results follow. One will 5
then be few; for the many are opposed also to the few. Further, two will be many,
since the double is multiple, and double derives from two; therefore one will be few;
for what is that in comparison with which two are called many, except one and that
which is few? For there is nothing fewer. Further, if a lot and few are in plurality 10
what the long and the short are in length, and whatever is a lot is also many, and the
many are a lot (unless, indeed, there is a difference in the case of an easily-bounded
continuum), the few will be a plurality. Therefore one is a plurality, if it is few; and
this must be so, if two are many. But perhaps, while the many are in a sense said to 15
be a lot, it is with a difference, e.g. there is a lot of water, not many waters.

But 'many' is applied to the things that are divisible; in one sense it means a
plurality which is excessive either absolutely or relatively (while 'few' is similarly a
plurality which is deficient), and in another sense it means number, in which sense
alone it is opposed to the one. For we say 'one or many', just as if one were to say 20
'one and ones' or 'white thing and white things', or to compare the things that have
been measured with the measure. It is in this sense also that multiples are so called.
For each number is said to be many because it consists of ones and because each
number is measurable by one; and it is many as that which is opposed to one, not to
the few. In this sense, then, even two is many—not however in the sense of a 25
plurality which is excessive either relatively or absolutely; it is the *first* plurality.
But without qualification two is few; for it is the first plurality which is deficient.
(For this reason Anaxagoras was not right in leaving the subject with the statement
that all things were together, boundless both in multitude and in smallness—where
by 'and in smallness' he meant 'and in fewness'; for they could not have been 30
boundless in fewness.) For it is not one, as some say, but two, that make a few.

The one is opposed then to the many in numbers as measure to thing
measurable; and these are opposed as relatives which are not from their very nature
relative. We have distinguished elsewhere the two senses in which relatives are so 35
called—some as contraries, others as knowledge to thing known, a term being called
relative because another is relative to it. There is nothing to prevent one from being 1057ª1
fewer than something, e.g. than two; for if it is fewer, it is not therefore few.
Plurality is as it were the class to which number belongs; for number is plurality
measurable by one. And one and number are in a sense opposed, not as contrary, but
as we have said some relative terms are opposed; for inasmuch as one is measure and 5
the other measurable, they are opposed. This is why not everything that is one is a
number, i.e. if the thing is indivisible it is not a number. But though knowledge is
similarly spoken of as related to the knowable, the relation does not work out
similarly, for while knowledge might be thought to be the measure, and the

10 knowable the thing measured, the fact is that all knowledge is knowable, but not all that is knowable is knowledge, because in a sense knowledge is measured by the knowable.—Plurality is contrary neither to the few (the *many* being contrary to this as excessive plurality to plurality exceeded), nor to the one in every sense; but in one
15 sense they are contrary, as has been said, because the former is divisible and the latter indivisible, while in another sense they are relative (as knowledge is to the knowable), if plurality is number and the one is measure.

7 · Since contraries admit of an intermediate and in some cases have it, the intermediate must be composed of the contraries. For all intermediates are in the
20 same genus as the things between which they stand. For we call those things intermediates, into which that which changes must change first; e.g. if we were to pass from the highest string to the lowest by the shortest way, we should come sooner to the intermediate notes, and in colours if we are to pass from white to black,
25 we shall come sooner to crimson and gray than to black; and similarly in all other cases. But to pass from one genus to another genus (e.g. from colour to figure) is not possible except in an incidental way. Intermediates, then, must be in the same genus as one another and as the things they stand between.
30 But all intermediates stand between opposites of some kind; for only between these can change take place in virtue of their own nature. Therefore an intermediate is impossible between things which are not opposite; for then there would be change which was not from one opposite towards the other. Among opposites, contradictories admit of no middle term; for contradiction is this—an opposition, one or other
35 side of which must attach to anything whatever, i.e. which has no intermediate. Of other opposites, some are relative, others privative, others contrary. Of relative terms, those which are not contrary have no intermediate. The reason is that they are not in the same genus. For what intermediate could there be between knowledge
1057ᵇ1 and the knowable? But between great and small there *is* one.
If intermediates are in the same genus, as has been shown, and stand between contraries, they must be composed of these contraries. For either there will be a genus including the contraries or there will be none. And if there is a genus in such a
5 way that it is something prior to the contraries, the differentiae which constitute the contrary species of the genus will be contraries prior to the species; for species are composed of the genus and the differentiae. E.g. if white and black are contraries, and one is a piercing colour and the other a compressing colour, these differentiae—
10 piercing and compressing—are prior; so that these are prior contraries of one another (though indeed the species which differ by contrariety are more truly contrary). And the other species, i.e. the intermediates, must be composed of their genus and their differentiae. E.g. all colours which are between white and black
15 must be said to be composed of the genus (i.e. colour) and certain differentiae. But these differentiae will not be the primary contraries; otherwise every colour would be either white or black. They are different, then, from the primary contraries; and therefore they will be between the primary contraries; the primary differentiae are piercing and compressing. Therefore it is with regard to these contraries which do

not fall within a genus that we must first ask of what their intermediates are   20
composed. (For things which *are* in the same genus must be composed of terms in
which the genus is not an element, or else be themselves incomposite.) Now
contraries do not involve one another in their composition, and are therefore first
principles; but the intermediates are either all incomposite, or none of them. But
there is something compounded out of the contraries, which is such that there can
be a change from a contrary to it sooner than to the other contrary; for it will have
less of the quality in question than the one contrary and more than the other. This   25
also, then, will come between the contraries. All the other intermediates also,
therefore, are *composite*; for that which has more of a quality than one thing and
less than another is compounded somehow out of the things than which it is said to
have more and less respectively. And since there are no other things prior to the
contraries and homogeneous with the intermediates, all intermediates must be   30
compounded out of the contraries. Therefore all the inferior classes, both the
contraries and their intermediates, will be compounded out of the primary
contraries. Clearly, then, intermediates are all in the same genus and intermediate
between contraries and compounded out of the contraries.

8 · That which is other in species is other than something in something, and   35
this must belong to both; e.g. if it is an animal other in species, both are animals.
The things, then, which are other in species must be in the same genus. For by genus
I mean that one identical thing which is predicated of both and is differentiated in
no merely accidental way, whether conceived as matter or otherwise. For not only   1058ᵃ1
must the common nature attach to the different things, e.g. not only must both be
animals, but this very animal must also be different for each (e.g. in the one case
horse, in the other man), and therefore this common nature is specifically different
for the two things. One then will be in virtue of its own nature one sort of animal,   5
and the other another, e.g. one a horse and the other a man. This difference then
must be an otherness of the genus. For I give the name of 'difference in the genus' to
an otherness which makes the genus itself other.

This, then, will be a contrariety (as can be shown also by induction). For all
things are divided by opposites, and it has been proved that contraries are in the   10
same genus. For contrariety was seen to be complete difference; and every
difference in species is a difference from something in something; so that this is the
same for both and is their genus. (Hence also all contraries which are different in
species and not in genus are in the same line of predication, and other than one
another in the highest degree—for the difference is complete—, and cannot be   15
present along with one another.) The difference, then, is a contrariety.

This, then, is the meaning of calling two things other in species—that they are
contrary, being in the same genus and being indivisible (and those things are the
same in species, which have no contrariety, being indivisible); for in the process of
division contrarieties arise even in the intermediate stages before we come to the   20
indivisibles. Evidently, therefore, with reference to that which is called the genus,
none of the species which belong to the genus is either the same as it or other than it

in species (rightly so, for the matter is indicated by negation, and the genus is the matter of that of which it is called the genus, not in the sense in which we speak of the genus of the Heraclidae, but in that in which we speak of a genus in nature), nor
25 is it so with reference to things which are not in the same genus, but it will differ in genus from them, and in species from things in the same genus. For the difference between things which differ in species must be a contrariety; and this belongs only to things in the same genus.

9 · One might raise the question, why woman does not differ from man in
30 species, female and male being contrary, and their difference being a contrariety; and why a female and a male animal are not different in species, though this difference belongs to animal in virtue of its own nature, and not as whiteness or blackness does; both female and male belong to it *qua* animal. This question is
35 almost the same as the other, why one contrariety makes things different in species and another does not, e.g. 'with feet' and 'with wings' do, but whiteness and blackness do not. Perhaps it is because the former are modifications peculiar to the genus, and the latter are less so. And since one element is formula and one is matter,
1058ᵇ1 contrarieties which are in the formula make a difference in species, but those which are in the compound material thing do not make one. Therefore whiteness in a man, or blackness, does not make one, nor is there a difference in species between the
5 white man and the black man, not even if each of them be denoted by one word. For man plays the part of matter, and matter does not create a difference; for it does not make individual men species of man, though the flesh and the bones of which this man and that man consist are other. The compound thing is other, but not other in species, because in the formula there is contrariety, and man is the ultimate
10 indivisible kind. Callias is formula together with matter; white man, then, is so also, because Callias is white; man, then, is white only incidentally. Nor do a brazen and a wooden circle differ in species; and if a brazen triangle and a wooden circle differ in species, it is not because of the matter, but because there is a contrariety in the
15 formula. But does the matter not make things other in species, when it is other in a certain way, or is there a sense in which it does? For why is this horse other than this man in species, although their matter is included with their formulae? Doubtless because there is a contrariety in the *formula*. For while there is a contrariety also between white man and black horse, and it is a contrariety in species, it does not
20 depend on the whiteness of the one and the blackness of the other, since even if both had been white, yet they would have been other in species. And male and female are indeed modifications peculiar to animal, not however in virtue of its substance but in the matter, i.e. the body. This is why the same seed becomes female or male by being acted on in a certain way. We have stated, then, what it is to be other in
25 species, and why some things differ in species and others do not.

10 · Since contraries are other in form, and the perishable and the imperishable are contraries (for privation is a determinate incapacity), the perishable and the imperishable must be different in kind.

Now so far we have spoken of the general terms themselves, so that it might be thought not to be necessary that every imperishable thing should be different from   30 every perishable thing in form, just as not every white thing is different in form from every black thing. For the same thing can be both, even at the same time if it is a universal (e.g. man can be both white and black), and if it is an individual it can still be both; for the same man can be, though not at the same time, white and black. Yet white is contrary to black.   35
But while some contraries belong to certain things by accident (e.g. those now mentioned and many others), others cannot, and among these are both 'perishable'   1059ª1 and 'imperishable'. For nothing is by accident perishable. What is accidental is capable of not being present, but perishableness is one of the attributes that belong of necessity to the things to which they belong; or else one and the same thing may be perishable and imperishable, if perishableness is capable of not belonging to it.   5 Perishableness then must either be the substance or be present in the substance of each perishable thing. The same account holds good for imperishableness also; for both are attributes which are present of necessity. The characteristics, then, in respect of which and in direct consequence of which one thing is perishable and another imperishable, are opposite, so that the things must be different in kind.   10
Evidently, then, there cannot be Forms such as some maintain, for then one man would be perishable and another imperishable. Yet the Forms are said to be the same in form with the individuals and not homonymous; but things which differ in kind are further apart than those which differ in form.

BOOK XI (K)

1 · That Wisdom is a science of first principles, is evident from the introductory chapters in which we have raised objections to the statements of others about the first principles; but one might ask the question whether Wisdom is to be   20 conceived as one science or as several. If as one, it may be objected that one science always deals with contraries, but the first principles are not contrary. If it is not one, what are these sciences with which it is to be identified?
Further, is it the business of one science or of more to examine the first principles of demonstration? If of one, why of this rather than of any other? If of   25 more, which must these be said to be?
Further, does it investigate all substances or not? If not all, it is hard to say which; but if, being one, it investigates them all, it is doubtful how the same science can embrace several subject-matters.
Further, does it deal with substances only or also with their accidents? If in the   30 case of attributes demonstration is possible, in that of substances it is not. But if the two sciences are different, what is each of them and which is Wisdom? If we think

of it as demonstrative, the science of the *accidents* is Wisdom, but if as dealing with first principles, the science of *substances* claims the title.

35   But again the science we are looking for must not be supposed to deal with the causes which have been mentioned in the *Physics*. For it does not deal with the final cause (for this is the good, and this is found in the field of action and movement; and it is the first mover—for that is the nature of the end—but in the case of things unmovable there is no first mover), and in general it is hard to say whether the

1059ᵇ1   science we are now looking for deals with perceptible substances or not with them, but with certain others. If with others, it must deal either with the Forms or with the objects of mathematics. Now evidently the Forms do not exist. (But it is hard to say, even if one suppose them to exist, why the same is not true of the other things of

5   which there are Forms, as of the objects of mathematics. I mean that they place the objects of mathematics between the Forms and perceptible things, as a third class of things besides the Forms and the things in this world; but there is not a third man or horse besides the ideal and the individuals. If on the other hand it is not as they say,

10   with what sort of things must the mathematician be supposed to deal? Certainly not with the things in this world; for none of these is the sort of thing which the mathematical sciences inquire into.) Nor does the science which we are now seeking treat of the objects of mathematics; for none of them can exist separately. But again it does not deal with perceptible substances; for they are perishable.

15   In general we might raise the question, to which science it belongs to discuss the difficulties about the matter of the objects of mathematics. Neither to natural science (because the whole inquiry of the natural scientist is about the things that have in themselves a principle of movement and rest), nor yet to the science which inquires into demonstration and science; for *this* is just the subject which *it*

20   investigates. It remains then that it is the philosophy which we have set before ourselves that treats of those subjects.

One might discuss the question whether the science we are seeking should be said to deal with the principles which are by some called elements. All men suppose

25   these to be present in compound things; but it might be thought that the science we seek should treat rather of *universals;* for every formula and every science is of universals and not of particulars, so that as far as this goes it would deal with the highest classes. These would be being and unity; for these might most of all be supposed to contain all things that are, and to be most like principles because they

30   are first by nature; for if they perish all other things are destroyed with them; for all things *are* and are one. But inasmuch as, if one is to suppose them to be genera, they must be genera predicable of their differentiae, and no genus is predicable of any of its differentiae, in this way it would seem that we should not make them genera nor

35   principles. Further, if the simpler is more of a principle than the less simple, and the ultimate members of the genus are simpler than the genus (for they are indivisible, but the genera are divided into many and differing species), the species might seem to be the principles, rather than the genera. But inasmuch as the species are involved in the destruction of the genera, the genera are more like principles; for

1060ᵃ1   that which involves another in its destruction is a principle of it. These and others of the kind are the subjects that involve difficulties.

2 · Further, must we suppose something apart from individual things, or is it these that the science we are seeking treats of? But these are infinite in number. But the things that are apart from the individuals are genera or species; and the science 5 we now seek treats of neither of these. The reason why this is impossible has been stated. It is in general hard to say whether one must assume that there is a separable substance besides the sensible substances (i.e. the substances in this world), or that these are the real things and philosophy is concerned with them. For we seem to 10 seek another kind of substance, and this is our problem, i.e. to see if there is something which can exist apart by itself and belongs to no sensible thing.— Further, if there is another substance apart from sensible substances, which kinds of sensible substance must be supposed to have this corresponding to them? Why should one suppose men or horses to have it, and not the other animals or even all 15 lifeless things? On the other hand to set up other and eternal substances equal in number to the sensible and perishable substances would seem to fall beyond the bounds of probability.—But if the principle we now seek is not separable from corporeal things, what has a better claim to the name than matter? This, however, 20 does not exist in actuality, but exists in potency, and it would seem rather that the form or shape is a more important principle than this; but the form is perishable, so that there is no eternal substance at all which can exist apart and independent. But this is paradoxical; for such a principle and substance seems to exist and is sought by nearly all the best thinkers as something that exists; for how is there to be order 25 unless there is something eternal and independent and permanent?

Further, if there is a substance or principle of such a nature as that which we are now seeking, and if this is one for all things, and the same for eternal and for perishable things, it is hard to say why, if there is the same principle, some of the things that fall under the principle are eternal, and others are not eternal; this is 30 paradoxical. But if there is one principle of perishable and another of eternal things, we shall be in a like difficulty if the principle of perishable things as well is eternal; for why, if the principle is eternal, are not the things that fall under the principle also eternal? But if it is perishable it must have another principle, and that must 35 have yet another, and this will go on to infinity.

If on the other hand we set up what are thought to be the most unchangeable principles, being and unity, firstly, if each of these does not indicate a 'this' and a 1060ᵇ1 substance, how will they be separable and independent? Yet we expect the eternal and primary principles to be so. But if each of them does signify a 'this' and a substance, all things that are are substances; for being is predicated of all things 5 (and unity also of some); but that all things that are are substance is false. Further, how can they be right who say that the first principle is unity and this is substance, and generate number as the first product from unity and from matter, and assert that number is substance? How are we to think of two, and each of the other 10 numbers composed of units, as one? On this point neither do they say anything nor is it easy to say anything. But if we suppose lines or what comes after these (I mean the primary plane figures) to be principles, these at least are not separable substances, but sections and divisions—the former of surfaces, the latter of solids 15 (while points are sections and divisions of lines); and further they are limits of these same things; and all these are in other things and none is separable. Further, how are we to suppose that there is a substance of unity and the point? Every substance comes into being, but the point does not; for the point is a division.

20   A further difficulty is raised by the fact that all knowledge is of universals and of the 'such', but substance does not belong to universals, but is rather a 'this' and separable, so that if there is knowledge about the first principles, the question arises, how are we to suppose the first principle to be substance?

Further, is there anything apart from the compound thing (by which I mean 25 the matter and that which is joined with matter), or not? If not, all things that are in matter are perishable. But if there *is* something, it must be the form or shape. It is hard to determine in which cases this exists apart and in which it does not; for in some cases the form is evidently not separable, e.g. in the case of a house.

Further, are the principles the same in kind or in number? If they are one in 30 number, all things will be the same.

3 · Since the science of the philosopher treats of being *qua* being universally and not of some part of it, and 'being' has many senses and is not used in one only, it follows that if it is used homonymously and in virtue of no common nature, it does not fall under one science (for there is no one class in the case of such things); but if 35 it is used in virtue of some common nature, it will fall under one science. The term seems to be used in the way we have mentioned, like 'medical' and 'healthy'. For 1061ª1 each of these also we use in many senses; and each is used in this way because the former refers somehow to medical science and the latter to health. Other terms refer to other things, but each term refers to some one thing. For a prescription and a knife are called medical because the former proceeds from medical science, and 5 the latter is useful to it. And a thing is called healthy in the same way; one thing because it is indicative of health, another because it is productive of it. And the same is true in the other cases. Everything that is, then, is said to be in this same way; each thing is said to be because it is a modification of being *qua* being or a 10 permanent or a transient state or a movement of it, or something else of the sort. And since everything that is may be referred to some one common nature, each of the contrarieties also may be referred to the first differences and contrarieties of being, whether the first differences of being are plurality and unity or likeness and 15 unlikeness, or some other differences; let these be taken as already discussed. It makes no difference whether that which is be referred to being or to unity. For even if they are not the same but different, they are convertible; for that which is one is also somehow being, and that which is being is one.—But as every pair of contraries falls to be examined by one and the same science, and in each pair one term is the 20 privation of the other (though one might regarding some contraries raise the question, how they can be privatively related, viz. those which have an intermediate, e.g. unjust and just; in all such cases one must maintain that the privation is not of the whole formula, but of its extreme form; e.g. if a man is just who is by virtue of 25 some permanent disposition obedient to the laws, the unjust man need not have the whole formula denied of him, but will be in some respect deficient in obedience to

the laws, and in this respect the privation will attach to him; and similarly in all other cases); and since, as the mathematician investigates abstractions (for in his investigation he eliminates all the sensible qualities, e.g. weight and lightness, hardness and its contrary, and also heat and cold and the other sensible contrarieties, and leaves only the quantitative and continuous, sometimes in one, sometimes in two, sometimes in three dimensions, and the attributes of things *qua* quantitative and continuous, and does not consider them in any other respect, and examines the relative positions of some and the consequences of these, and the commensurability and incommensurability of others, and the ratios of others; but yet we say there is one and the same science of all these things—geometry), the same is true with regard to being (for the attributes of this in so far as it is being, and the contrarieties in it *qua* being, it is the business of no other science than *philosophy* to investigate; for to natural science one would assign the study of things not *qua* being, but rather *qua* sharing in movement; while dialectic and sophistic deal with the attributes of things that are, but not of things *qua* being, and not with being itself in so far as it is being);—therefore it remains that the *philosopher* studies the things we have named, in so far as they are being. Since all that is is said to be in virtue of one common character though the term has many meanings, and contraries are in the same case (for they are referred to the first contrarieties and differences of being), and things of this sort can fall under one science, the difficulty we stated at the beginning is solved,—I mean the question how there can be one science of things which are many and different in genus.

4 · Since even the mathematician uses the common axioms only in a special application, it must be the business of first philosophy to examine the principles of mathematics also. That when equals are taken from equals the remainders are equal, is common to all quantities, but mathematics marks off a part of its proper matter and studies it separately, e.g. lines or angles or numbers or some other kind of quality—not, however, *qua* being but in so far as each of them is continuous in one or two or three dimensions; but philosophy does not inquire about particular subjects in so far as each of them has such and such attributes, but considers each subject in relation to being *qua* being.—Natural science is in the same position as mathematics; for natural science studies the attributes and the principles of the things that are, *qua* moving and not *qua* being, whereas the primary science, we have said, deals with these only in so far as the underlying subjects are existent, and not in virtue of any other character. Therefore both natural science and mathematics must be regarded as *parts* of Wisdom.

5 · There is a principle in things, about which we cannot be deceived, but must always, on the contrary, recognize the truth,—viz. that the same thing cannot at one and the same time be and not be, or admit any other similar pair of opposites. About such matters there is no proof in the full sense, though there is proof *ad hominem*. For it is not possible to infer this truth itself from a more certain principle, yet this is necessary if there is to be proof of it without qualification. But

he who wants to prove to the asserter of opposites that he is wrong must get from him an admission which shall *be* identical with the principle that the same thing cannot both be and not be at one and the same time, but shall not *seem* to be identical: for thus alone can he demonstrate his thesis to the man who says that
10 opposite statements can be truly made about the same subject. Those, then, who are to join in argument with one another must to some extent understand one another; for if this does not happen how *can* they join in argument with one another? Therefore every word must be intelligible and signify something, and not many
15 things but only one; and if it signifies more than one thing, it must be made plain to which of these the word is being applied. He, then, who says this is and is not denies what he affirms, so that what the word signifies, he says it does not signify; and this is impossible. Therefore if 'this is' signifies something, one cannot truly assert the contradictory.

20   Further, if the word signifies something and this can be truly asserted of it, it necessarily *is* this; and it is not possible that that which is necessary should ever not be; it is not possible therefore to make the opposed assertions truly of the same subject. Further, if the affirmation is no more true than the negation, he who says
25 'man' will be no more right than he who says 'not-man'. It would seem also that in saying the man is not a horse we should be either more or not less right than in saying he is not a man, so that we shall be right in saying that the same person *is* a horse; for it was assumed to be possible to make opposite statements equally truly. It follows then that the same person is a man and a horse, or any other animal. While,
30 then, there is no proof of the axiom without qualification, there is a proof relatively to anyone who will make these suppositions. And perhaps if we had questioned Heraclitus himself in this way we might have forced him to confess that opposite statements can never be true of the same subjects. But, as it is, he adopted his opinion without understanding what his statement involved. But in any case if what
1062ᵇ1 is said by him is true, not even this itself is true—viz. that the same thing can at one and the same time both be and not be. For as, when the statements are separated, the affirmation is no more true than the negation, in the same way—the complex
5 statement being like one affirmation—the whole taken as an affirmation will be no more true than its negation. Further, if it is not possible to affirm anything truly, this itself will be false—the assertion that there is no true affirmation. But if a true
10 affirmation exists, this appears to refute what is said by those who raise such objections and utterly destroy rational discourse.

6 · The saying of Protagoras is like the views we have mentioned; he said that man is the measure of all things, meaning simply that that which seems to each man
15 assuredly is. If this is so, it follows that the same thing both is and is not, and is bad and good, and that the contents of all other opposite statements are true, because often a particular thing appears beautiful to some and ugly to others, and that
20 which appears to each man is the measure. This difficulty may be solved by considering the source of the opinion. It seems to have arisen in some cases from the doctrine of the natural philosophers, and in others from the fact that all men have

not the same views about the same things, but a particular thing appears pleasant to some and the contrary of pleasant to others.

That nothing comes to be out of that which is not, but everything out of that which is, is a doctrine common to nearly all the natural philosophers. Since, then, a thing can become not-white, having been perfectly white and in no respect not-white, that which becomes white must come from that which is not-white; so that a thing must come to be out of that which is not (so they argue), unless the same thing was at the beginning both not-white and white. But it is not hard to solve this difficulty; for we have said in the *Physics*[1] in what sense things that come to be come to be from that which is not, and in what sense from that which is.

But to lend oneself equally to the opinions and the fancies of disputing parties is foolish; for clearly one of them must be mistaken. And this is evident from what happens in sensation; for the same thing never appears sweet to some and bitter to others, unless in the one case the sense-organ which discriminates the aforesaid flavours has been perverted and injured. And if this is so the one party must be taken to be the measure, and the other must not. And I say the same of good and bad, and beautiful and ugly, and all other such qualities. For to maintain the view we are opposing is just like maintaining the truth of what appears to people who put their finger under their eye and make the object appear two instead of one, i.e. like saying that it is two (because it appears to be of that number) and again one (for to those who do not interfere with their eye the one object appears one).

In general, it is absurd to make the fact that the things of this earth are observed to change and never to remain in the same state, the basis of our judgements about the truth. For in pursuing the truth one must start from the things that are always in the same state and suffer no change. Such are the heavenly bodies; for these do not appear to be now of one nature and again of another, but are manifestly always the same and share in no change.

Further, if there is movement, and something moved, and everything is moved out of something and into something, it follows that that which is moved must first be in that out of which it is to be moved, and then not be in it, and move into the other and come to be in it, and that the contradictory statements are not true *at the same time,* as our opponents assert they are.

And if the things of this earth continuously flow and move in respect of quantity—if one were to suppose this, although it is not true—why should they not endure in respect of quality? For the assertion of contradictory statements about the same thing seems to have arisen largely from the belief that the quantity of bodies does not endure, so that the same thing both is and is not four cubits long. But the substance depends on quality, and this is of determinate nature, though quantity is indeterminate.

Further, when the doctor orders people to take some particular food, why do they take it? For why is this bread rather than not bread?—so that it would make no difference whether one ate or not. But as a matter of fact they take it, assuming

25

30

1063ᵃ1

5

10

15

20

25

30

that they know the truth about it and that what has been prescribed is bread. Yet they should not, if there were no fixed constant nature in sensible things, but all moved and flowed for ever.

35 Again, if we are always changing and never remain the same, what wonder is it if to us, as to the sick, things never appear the same? For to them also, because they 1063ᵇl are not in the same condition as when they were well, sensible qualities do not appear like; yet, for all that, the sensible things themselves need not share in any change, though they produce different, and not identical, sensations in the sick. And 5 the same must surely happen to the healthy if the aforesaid change takes place. But if we do not change but remain the same, there will be something that endures.

As for those to whom these difficulties are suggested by reason, it is not easy to solve the difficulties unless they will posit something and no longer demand a reason 10 for it; for it is thus that all reasoning and all proof is accomplished; if they posit nothing, they destroy discussion and all reasoning. Therefore with such men there is no reasoning. But as for those who are perplexed by the traditional difficulties, it is easy to meet them and to dissipate the causes of their perplexity. This is evident from what has been said.

15 It is manifest, therefore, from these arguments that contradictory statements cannot be truly made about the same subject at one time, nor can contrary statements, because every contrariety depends on privation. This is evident if we reduce the formulae of contraries to their principle.

20 Similarly, no intermediate between contraries can be predicated of one and the same subject. If the subject is white we shall be wrong in saying it is neither white nor black, for it would follow that it is and is not white; for the first of the two terms we have put together would be true of it, and this is the contradictory of white.

25 We could not be right, then, in accepting the views either of Heraclitus or of Anaxagoras. If we were, it would follow that contraries would be predicated of the same subject, for when Anaxagoras says a portion of everything is in everything, he says nothing is sweet any more than it is bitter, and so with any other pair of contraries, since in everything everything is present not potentially only, but 30 actually and separately. And similarly all statements cannot be false nor all true, both because of many other difficulties which might be deduced as arising from this position, and because if all are false it will not be true even to say all are false, and if 35 all are true it will not be false to say all are false.

7 · Every science seeks certain principles and causes for each of its 1064ᵃl objects—e.g. medicine and gymnastics and each of the other sciences, whether productive or mathematical. For each of these marks off a certain class of things for itself and busies itself about this as about something that exists and is—not however *qua* being; the science that does *this* is another distinct from these. Of the sciences 5 mentioned each gets somehow the 'what' in some class of things and tries to prove the other truths, whether loosely or accurately. Some get the 'what' through perception, others by hypothesis; so that it is clear from an induction of this sort that there is no *demonstration* of the substance, i.e. of the 'what'.

There is a science of nature, and evidently it must be different both from 10
practical and from productive science. For in the case of productive science the
principle of production is in the producer and not in the product, and is either an art
or some other capacity. And similarly in practical science the movement is not in
the thing done, but rather in the doers. But the science of the natural philosopher 15
deals with the things that have in *themselves* a principle of movement. It is clear
from these facts, then, that natural science must be neither practical nor productive,
but theoretical (for it must fall into one of these classes). And since each of the
sciences must somehow know the 'what' and use this as a principle, we must not fail 20
to observe how the natural philosopher should define things and how he must state
the formula of the substance—whether as akin to snub or rather to concave. For of
these the formula of the snub includes the matter of the thing, but that of the
concave is independent of the matter; for snubness is found in a nose, so that its 25
formula includes the nose—for the snub is a concave nose. Evidently then the
formula of flesh and the eye and the other parts must always be stated without
eliminating the matter.

Since there is a science of being *qua* being and capable of existing apart, we
must consider whether this is to be regarded as the same as natural science or rather 30
as different. Natural science deals with the things that have a principle of
movement in themselves; mathematics is theoretical, and *is* a science that deals
with things that are at rest, but its subjects cannot exist apart. Therefore about that
which can exist apart and is unmovable there is a science different from both of
these, if there *is* a substance of this nature (I mean separable and unmovable), as we 35
shall try to prove there is. And if there is such a kind of thing in the world, here must
surely be the divine, and this must be the first and most important principle.
Evidently, then, there are three kinds of theoretical sciences—natural science, 1064ᵇ1
mathematics, theology. The class of theoretical sciences is the best, and of these
themselves the last named is best; for it deals with the highest of existing things, and
each science is called better or worse in virtue of its proper object. 5

One might raise the question whether the science of being *qua* being is to be
regarded as universal or not. Each of the mathematical sciences deals with some one
determinate class of things, but universal mathematics applies alike to all. Now if
natural substances are the first of existing things, natural science must be the first 10
of sciences; but if there is another entity and substance, separable and unmovable,
the science of it must be different and prior to natural science, and universal
because it is prior.

8 · Since things are said to be, without qualification, in several ways, of 15
which one is being by accident, we must consider first that which is in this sense.
Evidently none of the traditional sciences busies itself about the accidental. For
neither does building consider what will happen to those who are to use the house
(e.g. whether they will have a painful life in it or not), nor does weaving, or 20
shoemaking, or the confectioner's art, do the like; but each of these sciences
considers only what is peculiar to it, i.e. its proper end. And as for the argument that

when he who is musical becomes lettered he will be both at once, not having been
25 both before; and that which is, not having always been, must have been coming to
be; therefore he must have been at once becoming musical and lettered,—this none
of the recognized sciences considers, but only sophistic; for this alone busies itself
about the accidental, so that Plato was not wrong when he said that the sophist
spends his time on non-being.
30 That a science of the accidental is not even possible, will be evident if we try to
see what the accidental really is. We say that everything either is always and of
necessity (necessity not in the sense of violence, but that which we appeal to in
35 demonstrations), or is for the most part, or is neither for the most part, nor always
and of necessity, but merely as it chances; e.g. there might be cold in the dog-days,
but this occurs neither always and of necessity, nor for the most part, though it
1065ᵃ1 might happen sometimes. The accidental, then, is what occurs, but not always nor
of necessity, nor for the most part. Now we have said what the accidental is, and it is
obvious why there is no science of such a thing; for all science is of that which is
5 always or for the most part, but the accidental is in neither of these classes.
Evidently there are not causes and principles of the accidental, of the same
kind as there are of what is in its own right; for if there were, everything would be of
necessity. If A is when B is, and B is when C is, and if C exists not by chance but of
10 necessity, that of which C was cause will exist of necessity, down to the last
mentioned of the things caused (but this was supposed to be accidental). Therefore
all things will be of necessity, and chance and the possibility of a thing's either
occurring or not occurring are removed entirely from the range of events. And if the
15 cause be supposed not to exist but to be coming to be, the same results will follow;
everything will occur of necessity. For tomorrow's eclipse will occur if A occurs, and
A if B occurs, and B if C occurs; and in this way if we subtract time from the limited
time between now and tomorrow we shall come sometime to the already existing
20 condition. Therefore since this exists, everything after this will occur of
necessity, so that all things occur of necessity.
As to that which is in the sense of being true or of being by accident, the *former*
depends on a combination in thought and is an affection of thought (which is the
reason why it is the principles, not of that which is in this sense, but of that which is
outside and can exist apart, that are sought); and the *latter* is not necessary but
25 indeterminate (I mean the accidental); and of such a thing the causes are unordered
and indefinite.
The 'for the sake of something' is found in events that happen by nature or as
the result of thought. It is chance when one of these events happens by accident. For
as a thing may exist, so it may be a cause, either by its own nature or by accident.
30 Chance is a cause accidentally among those of events that happen for the sake of
something which are in accordance with choice. Therefore chance and thought are
concerned with the same sphere; for choice cannot exist without thought. The
causes from which chance results might happen are indeterminate; therefore
chance is obscure to human calculation and is a cause by accident, but in the
unqualified sense a cause of nothing. It is good or bad luck when the result is good or
1065ᵇ1 evil; and prosperity or misfortune when the scale is large.

Since nothing accidental is prior to the essential, neither are accidental causes prior. If, then, chance or spontaneity is a cause of the heavens, reason and nature are causes before it.

9 · Some things exist only actually, some potentially, some potentially and 5 actually—some as beings, some as quantities, others in the other categories. There is no movement apart from things; for change is always according to the categories of being; and there is nothing common to these and in no one category; but each of the categories belongs to all its subjects in either of two ways (e.g. 'thisness'—for 10 one kind of it is form, and the other is privation; and as regards quality one kind is white and the other black, and as regards quantity one kind is complete and the other incomplete, and as regards spatial movement one is upwards and the other downwards, or one thing is light and another heavy); so that there are as many kinds of movement and change as of being. Each kind of thing being divided into the 15 potential and the fulfilled, I call the actuality of the potential as such, movement. That what we say is true, is plain from the following facts. When the buildable, in so far as we call it such, exists actually, it is being built, and this is the process of building. Similarly with learning, healing, and rolling, walking, leaping, ageing, ripening. Movement takes place when the fulfillment itself exists, and neither 20 earlier nor later. The fulfillment then, of that which is potentially, when it is fulfilled and actual, not *qua* itself, but *qua* movable, is movement. By *qua* I mean this: bronze is potentially a statue; but yet the fulfillment of bronze, *qua* bronze, is 25 not movement. For it is not the same to be bronze and to be a certain potentiality. If it were absolutely the same in its formula, the fulfillment of bronze would have been a movement. But it is not the same. This is evident in the case of contraries; for to be capable of health and to be capable of illness are not the same; for if they were, health and illness would have been the same. (It is that which underlies and is 30 healthy or sick, whether it is moisture or blood, that is one and the same.) And since they are not the same, as colour and the visible are not the same, it is the fulfillment of the potential *as such,* that is movement. Evidently it is this, and movement takes place when the fulfillment itself exists, and neither earlier nor later. For each thing is capable of being sometimes actual, sometimes not, e.g. the buildable *qua* 1066ª1 buildable; and the actuality of the buildable *qua* buildable is building. For the actuality is either this—building—or the house. But when the *house* exists, it is no longer buildable; the buildable is being built. The actuality then must be the 5 *building,* and the building is a movement. And the same account applies to all other movements.

That what we have said is right, is evident from what all others say about movement, and from the fact that it is not easy to define it otherwise. For firstly one cannot put it in another class. This is evident from what people say. Some call it 10 difference and inequality and the unreal; none of these, however, is necessarily moved, and further, change is not to these nor from these but rather from opposite to opposite. The reason why people put movement in these classes is that it is thought to be something indefinite, and the principles on one side of the list of contraries are indefinite because they are privative, for none of them is either a 'this' 15

or a 'such' or in any of the other categories. And the reason why movement is thought to be indefinite is that it cannot be classed either with the potentiality of things or with their actuality, for neither that which is capable of being of a certain
20   quantity, nor that which is actually of a certain quantity, is moved of necessity. And movement is thought to be an actuality, but incomplete; the reason is that the potential, whose actuality it is, is incomplete. And therefore it is hard to grasp what movement is; for it must be classed either with privation or with potentiality or with absolute actuality, but evidently none of these is possible. Therefore what remains is
25   that it must be what we said—actuality, i.e. actuality in the sense we have defined—which is hard to understand but capable of existing.

And evidently movement is in the movable; for it is the fulfillment of this by that which is capable of causing movement. And the actuality of that which is capable of causing movement is no other than that of the movable. For it must be
30   the fulfillment of both. For a thing is capable of causing movement because it *can* do this, and is a mover because it is *active;* but it is on the movable that it is capable of acting, so that the actuality of both alike is one, just as there is the same interval from one to two as from two to one, and as the ascent and the descent are one, but being them is not one; the case of the mover and the moved is similar.

35   **10** · The infinite is either that which is incapable of being traversed because it is not its nature to be traversed (as the voice is invisible), or that which admits only of incomplete traverse or scarcely admits of traverse, or that which, though it naturally admits of traverse, is not traversed or limited; further, a thing may be
1066ᵇ1   infinite in respect of addition or of subtraction or of both. The infinite cannot be a separate, independent thing. For if it is neither a spatial magnitude nor a plurality, but infinity itself is its substance and not an accident, it will be indivisible; for the
5   divisible is either magnitude or plurality. But if indivisible, it is not infinite, except as the voice is invisible; but people do not mean this, nor are we examining this sort of infinite, but the infinite as untraversable. Further, how can an infinite exist by itself, unless number and magnitude also exist by themselves,—since infinity is an attribute of these? Further, if the infinite is an accident of something else, it cannot
10   be *qua* infinite an element in things, as the invisible is not an element in speech, though the voice is invisible. And evidently the infinite cannot exist actually. For then any part of it that might be taken would be infinite; for to be infinite and the infinite are the same, if the infinite is substance and not predicated of a subject. Therefore it is either indivisible, or if it can be divided, it is divisible into infinite
15   parts; but the same thing cannot be many infinites, yet as a part of air is air, so a part of the infinite would be infinite, if the infinite is a substance and a principle. Therefore it must be inseparable and indivisible. But the actually infinite cannot be indivisible; for it must be a quantity. Therefore infinity belongs to a subject
20   incidentally. But if so, as we have said, it cannot be a principle, but rather that of which it is an accident—the air or the even number.

This inquiry is universal; but that the infinite is not among sensible things, is evident from the following argument. If the formula of body is that which is bounded by planes, there cannot be an infinite body either sensible or intelligible; nor a separate and infinite number, for number or that which has a number can be counted. The following considerations drawn from natural science make matters clear: the infinite can neither be composite nor simple. For it cannot be a composite body, since the elements are limited in multitude. For the contraries must be equal and no *one* of them must be infinite; for if one of the two bodies falls at all short of the other in capacity, the finite will be destroyed by the infinite. And that *each* should be infinite is impossible. For body is that which has extension in all directions, and the infinite is the boundlessly extended, so that the infinite body will be infinite in every direction. Nor can the infinite body be one and simple—neither, as some say, something which is apart from the elements, from which they generate these (for there is no such body apart from the elements; for everything can be resolved into that of which it consists, but no such thing is observed except the simple bodies), nor fire nor any other of the elements. For apart from the question how any of them could be infinite, the universe, even if it is finite, cannot either be or become one of them, as Heraclitus says all things sometime become fire. The same argument applies to the One, which the natural philosophers posit besides the elements. For everything changes from the contrary, e.g. from hot to cold.

Further, every sensible body is somewhere, and whole and part have the same proper place, e.g. the whole earth and part of the earth. Therefore if the infinite body is homogeneous, it will be unmovable or it will be always moving. But the latter is impossible; for why should it rather move down than up or anywhere else? E.g. if there is a clod, where will this move or rest? The proper place of the body which is homogeneous with it is infinite. Will the clod occupy the whole place, then? And how? When then is its rest or its movement? It will either rest everywhere, and then it cannot move; or it will move everywhere, and then it cannot be still. But if the infinite body has unlike parts, the proper places of the parts are unlike also, and, firstly, the body of the universe is not one except by contact, and, secondly, the parts will be either finite or infinite in kind. *Finite* they cannot be; for then those of one kind will be infinite and those of another will not (if the universe is infinite), e.g. fire or water would be infinite, but such an infinite part would be destruction to its contrary. But if the parts are *infinite* and simple, their places also are infinite and the elements will be infinite; and if this is impossible, and the places are finite, the universe also must be limited.

In general, there cannot be an infinite body and also a proper place for all bodies, if every sensible body has either weight or lightness. For it must move either towards the middle or upwards, and the infinite—either the whole or the half—cannot do either; for how will you divide it? Or how will part of the infinite be up and part down, or part extreme and part middle? Further, every sensible body is in a place, and there are six kinds of place, but these cannot exist in an infinite body. In general, if there cannot be an infinite place, there cannot be an infinite body; for that which is in a place is somewhere, and this means either up or down or in one of the other directions, and each of these is a limit.

The infinite is not the same in the sense that it is one thing whether exhibited in

magnitude or in movement or in time, but the posterior among these is called
35 infinite in virtue of its relation to the prior, i.e. a movement is called infinite in virtue
of the distance covered by the spatial movement or alteration or growth, and a time
is called infinite because of the movement which occupies it.

1067ᵇ1   11 · Of things which change, some change in an accidental sense, like that in
which the musical may be said to walk, and others are said, without qualification, to
change, because something in them changes, i.e. the things that change in parts; the
body becomes healthy, because the eye does. But there is something which is by its
5   own nature moved primarily, and this is the essentially movable. The same
distinction is found in the case of the mover; for it causes movement either in an
accidental sense or in respect of a part of itself or essentially. There is something
that primarily causes movement; and there is something that is moved, also the time
in which it is moved, and that from which and that into which it is moved. But the
10   forms and the affections and the place, which are the terminals of the movement of
moving things, are unmovable, e.g. knowledge or heat; it is not heat that is a
movement, but heating. Change which is not accidental is found not in all things,
but between contraries, and their intermediates, and between contradictories. We
may convince ourselves of this by induction.
15   That which changes changes either from subject into subject, or from
non-subject into non-subject, or from subject into non-subject, or from non-subject
into subject. (By subject I mean that which is expressed by an affirmative term.)
20   Therefore there must be three changes; for that from non-subject into non-subject is
not change; for the terms are neither contraries nor contradictories, because there is
no opposition. The change from non-subject into contradictory subject is generation—absolute change absolute generation, and partial change partial generation;
and the change from subject to non-subject is destruction—absolute change
absolute destruction, and partial change partial destruction. If, then, 'that which is
25   not' has several senses, and movement can attach neither to that which implies
putting together or separating, nor to that which implies potentiality and is opposed
to that which is without qualification (true, the not-white or not-good *can* be moved
incidentally, for the not-white might be a man; but that which is not a 'this' at all
30   can in no way be moved), that which is not cannot be moved, and if this is so,
generation cannot be movement; for that which is not *is* generated. For even if we
admit to the fullest that its generation is accidental, yet it is true to say that
not-being is predicable of that which is generated absolutely. (Similarly *rest* cannot
35   belong to that which is not.) These difficulties, then, follow, and also this, that
everything that is moved is in a place, but that which is not is not in a place; for then
it would be somewhere. Nor is destruction movement; for the contrary of movement
1068ᵃ1   is movement or rest, but the contrary of destruction is generation. Since every
movement is a change, and the kinds of change are the three named above, and of
these those in the way of generation and destruction are not movements, and these
are the changes from a thing to its contradictory, only the change from subject into
5   subject can be movement. And the subjects are either contrary or intermediate; for

even privation must be regarded as contrary, and is expressed by a positive term, e.g. 'naked' or 'toothless' or 'black'.

12 · If the categories are classified as substance, quality, place, acting or being acted on, relation, quantity, there must be three kinds of movement—of quality, of quantity, of place. There is no movement in respect of substance 10 (because there is nothing contrary to substance), nor in respect of relation (for it is possible that if one of two things changes, the other ceases to be true, though it does not change at all,—so that their movement is accidental), nor of agent and patient, nor of mover and moved, because there is no movement of movement nor generation 15 of generation, nor, in general, change of change. For there *might* be movement of movement in two senses; (1) movement may be the subject moved, as a man is moved because he changes from white to black,—so that in this way movement might be either heated or cooled or change its place or increase. But this is impossible; for change is not a subject. Or (2) some other subject may change from 20 a change into some other species of change (as a man changes from disease into health). But this also is not possible except incidentally. For every movement is change from something into something. (And so are generation and destruction; but they are changes into things opposed in *one* way, while movements are changes into 25 things opposed in another way.) A thing changes, then, at the same time from health into illness, and from this change itself into another. Clearly, then, if it has become ill, it will have changed into some change or other (for it may be at rest), and, further, into a determinate change each time; and that new change will be from something into something; therefore it will be the opposite change, that of growing 30 well. But this happens only incidentally, e.g. there is a change from the process of recollection to that of forgetting, only because that to which the process attaches is changing, now into a state of knowledge, now into one of ignorance.

Further, the process will go on to infinity, if there is to be change of change and generation of generation. For if the later is, so too must the earlier be—e.g. if the simple coming to be was once coming to be, that which was coming to be it was also 1068^{b}1 once coming to be; therefore that which was simply coming to be it was not yet in existence, but something which was coming to be coming to be it was already in existence. And this was once coming to be, so that then it was not yet coming to be. Now since of an infinite number of terms there is not a first, the first in this series will not exist, and therefore no following term will exist. Nothing, then, can either 5 come to be or move or change. Further, that which has a movement has also the contrary movement and rest, and that which comes to be also ceases to be. Therefore that which is coming to be is ceasing to be when it has come to be coming to be; for it cannot cease to be at the very time at which it is coming to be coming to be, nor after it has come to be; for that which is ceasing to be must *be*. Further, there must be a matter underlying that which comes to be and changes. What will it be, 10 then, that becomes movement or generation, as body or soul is that which suffers alteration? And what is it that they move into? For their movement must be the movement or coming to be of this from that to the other. How, then, can this

condition be fulfilled? There can be no learning of learning, and therefore no
15 generation of generation.

Since there is not movement either of substance or of relation or of activity and passivity, it remains that movement is in respect of quality and quantity and place; for each of these admits of contrariety. By quality I mean not that which is in the substance (for even the differentia is a quality), but the passive quality, in virtue of
20 which a thing is said to be acted on or to be incapable of being acted on. The unmovable is either that which is wholly incapable of being moved, or that which is moved with difficulty in a long time or begins slowly, or that which would naturally be moved and can be moved, but is not moving when and where and as it would naturally be moved. This alone among unmovables I describe as being at rest; for
25 rest is contrary to movement, so that it must be a privation in that which is receptive of movement.

Things which are in one primary place are *together,* and things which are in different places are *apart.* Things whose extremes are together *touch.* That at which the changing thing, if it changes continuously according to its nature, naturally arrives before it arrives at the extreme into which it is changing, is
30 *between.* That which is most distant in a straight line is *contrary in place.* That is *successive* which is after the beginning (the order being determined by position or form or in some other way) and has nothing of the same class between it and that which it succeeds, e.g. lines succeed a line, units a unit, or one house another house. (There is nothing to prevent a thing of some *other* class from being between.) For the successive succeeds something and is something later; one does not succeed two,
1069ᵃ1 nor the first day of the month the second. That which, being successive, touches, is *contiguous.* Since all change is between opposites, and these are either contraries or contradictories, and there is no middle term for contradictories, clearly that which
5 is *between* is between contraries. The *continuous* is a species of the contiguous; two things are called continuous when the limits of each, with which they touch and are kept together, become one and the same, so that plainly the continuous is found in the things out of which a unity naturally arises in virtue of their contact. And plainly the successive is primary for the successive does not necessarily touch, but
10 that which touches is successive. And if a thing is continuous, it touches, but if it touches, it is not necessarily continuous; and in things in which there is no touching, there is no organic unity. Therefore a point is not the same as a unit; for contact belongs to points, but not to units, which have only succession; and there is something between two of the former but not between two of the latter.

BOOK XII (Λ)

1 · Substance is the subject of our inquiry; for the principles and the causes we are seeking are those of substances. For if the universe is of the nature of a whole,
20 substance is its first part; and if it coheres by virtue of succession, on this view also substance is first, and is succeeded by quality, and then by quantity. At the same

time these latter are not even beings in the unqualified sense, but are quantities and movements—or else even the not-white and the not-straight would be; at least we say even these *are*, e.g. 'there is a not-white'. Further, none of the others can exist apart. And the old philosophers also in effect testify to this; for it was of substance 25 that they sought the principles and elements and causes. The thinkers of the present day tend to rank universals as substances (for genera are universals, and these they tend to describe as principles and substances, owing to the abstract nature of their inquiry); but the old thinkers ranked particular things as substances, e.g. fire and earth, but not what is common to both, body.

There are three kinds of substance—one that is sensible (of which one 30 subdivision is eternal and another is perishable, and which all recognize, as comprising e.g. plants and animals),—of this we must grasp the elements, whether one or many; and another that is immovable, and this certain thinkers assert to be capable of existing apart, some dividing it into two, others combining the Forms and the objects of mathematics into one class, and others believing only in the 35 mathematical part of this class. The former two kinds of substance are the subject of natural science (for they imply movement); but the third kind belongs to another 1069ᵇ1 science, if there is no principle common to it and to the other kinds.

Sensible substance is changeable. Now if change proceeds from opposites or from intermediate points, and not from all opposites (for the voice is not-white) but 5 from the contrary, there must be something underlying which changes into the contrary state; for the contraries do not change.

2 · Further, something persists, but the contrary does not persist; there is, then, some third thing besides the contraries, viz. the matter. Now since changes are of four kinds—either in respect of the essence or of the quality or of the quantity or of the place, and change in respect of the 'this' is simple generation and destruction, 10 and change in quantity is increase and diminution, and change in respect of an affection is alteration, and change in place is motion, changes will be from given states into those contrary to them in these several respects. The matter, then, which changes must be capable of both states. And since things are said to be in two ways, everything changes from that which is potentially to that which is actually, e.g. 15 from the potentially white to the actually white, and similarly in the case of increase and diminution. Therefore not only can a thing come to be, incidentally, out of that which is not, but also all things come to be out of that which is, but is potentially, 20 and is not actually. And this is the 'One' of Anaxagoras; for instead of 'all things were together' and the 'Mixture' of Empedocles and Anaximander and the account given by Democritus, it is better to say all things were together potentially but not actually. Therefore these thinkers seem to have had some notion of matter.

Now all things that change have matter, but different matter; and of eternal 25 things those which are not generable but are movable in space have matter—not matter for generation, however, but for motion from one place to another.

(One might raise the question from what sort of non-being generation proceeds; for things are said not to be in three ways.)

If, then, a thing exists potentially, still it is not potentially any and every thing,

but different things come from different things; nor is it satisfactory to say that all
30 things were together; for they differ in their matter, since otherwise why did an
infinity of things come to be, and not one thing? For Reason is one, so that if matter
also is one, that must have come to be in actuality what the matter was in
potentiality. The causes and the principles, then, are three, two being the pair of
contraries of which one is formula and form and the other is privation, and the third
being the matter.

35   3 · Next we must observe that neither the matter nor the form comes to
be—i.e. the proximate matter and form. For everything that changes is something
1070ᵃ1 and is changed by something and into something. That by which it is changed is the
primary mover; that which is changed, the matter; that into which it is changed, the
form. The process, then, will go on to infinity, if not only the bronze comes to be
round but also the round or the bronze comes to be; therefore there must be a stop at
some point.

Next we must observe that each substance comes into being out of something
5 synonymous. (Natural objects and other things are substances.) For things come
into being either by art or by nature or by chance or by spontaneity. Now art is a
principle of movement in something other than the thing moved, nature is a
principle in the thing itself (for man begets man), and the other causes are
privations of these two.

There are three kinds of substance—the matter, which is a 'this' by being
10 perceived (for all things that are characterized by contact and not by organic unity
are matter and substratum); the nature, a 'this' and a state that it moves towards;
and again, thirdly, the particular substance which is composed of these two, e.g.
Socrates or Callias. Now in some cases the 'this' does not exist apart from the
composite substance, e.g. the form of house does not so exist, unless the art of
15 building exists apart (nor is there generation and destruction of these forms, but it is
in another way that the house apart from its matter, and health, and all things of
art, exist and do not exist); but if it does it is only in the case of natural objects. And
so Plato was not far wrong when he said that there are as many Forms as there are
kinds of natural things (if there are Forms at all),—though not of such things[1] as
20 fire, flesh, head; for all these are matter, and the last matter is the matter of that
which is in the fullest sense substance. The moving causes exist as things preceding
the effects, but causes in the sense of formulae are simultaneous with their effects.
For when a man is healthy, then health also exists; and the shape of a bronze sphere
exists at the same time as the bronze sphere. But we must examine whether any
25 form also survives afterwards. For in some cases this may be so, e.g. the soul may be
of this sort—not all soul but the reason; for doubtless it is impossible that *all* soul
should survive. Evidently then there is no necessity, on this ground at least, for the
existence of the Ideas. For man is begotten by man, each individual by an
30 individual; and similarly in the arts; for the medical art is the formula of health.

[1]Reading ἀλλ' οὐ τούτων.

4 · The causes and the principles of different things are in a sense different, but in a sense, if one speaks universally and analogically, they are the same for all. For we might raise the question whether the principles and elements are different or the same for substances and for relatives, and similarly in the case of each of the categories. But it is paradoxical that they should be the same for all. For then from the same elements will proceed relatives and substances. What then will this common element be? For there is nothing common to and distinct from substance and the other things which are predicated; but the element is prior to the things of which it is an element. But again substance is not an element of relatives, nor is any of these an element of substance. Further, how can all things have the same elements? For none of the elements can be the same as that which is composed of the elements, e.g. *b* or *a* cannot be the same as *ba*. (None, therefore, of the intelligibles, e.g. unity or being, is an element; for these are predicable of each of the compounds as well.) None of the elements then would be either a substance or a relative; but it must be one or other. All things then have not the same elements.

Or, as we put it, in a sense they have and in a sense they have not; e.g. perhaps the elements of perceptible bodies are, as *form,* the hot, and in another sense the cold, which is the *privation;* and, as *matter,* that which directly and of itself is potentially these; and both these are substances and also the things composed of these, of which these are the principles (i.e. any unity which is produced out of the hot and the cold, e.g. flesh or bone); for the product must be different from the elements. These things then have the same elements and principles, but different things have different elements; and if we put the matter thus, all things have not the same elements, but analogically they have; i.e. one might say that there are three principles—the form, the privation, and the matter. But each of these is different for each class, e.g. in colour they are white, black, and surface. Again, there is light, darkness, and air; and out of these are produced day and night.

Since not only the elements present in a thing are causes, but also something external, i.e. the moving cause, clearly while principle and element are different both are causes, and principle is divided into these two kinds; and that which moves a thing or makes it rest is a principle and a substance. Therefore analogically there are three elements, and four causes and principles; but the elements are different in different things, and the primary moving cause is different for different things. Health, disease, body; the moving cause is the medical art. Form, disorder of a particular kind, bricks; the moving cause is the building art. And since the moving cause in the case of natural things is, for instance man, and in the products of thought it is the form or its contrary, there are in a sense three causes, while in a sense there are four. For the medical art is in some sense health, and the building art is the form of the house, and man begets man; further, besides these there is that which as first of all things moves all things.

5 · Some things can exist apart and some cannot, and it is the former that are substances. And therefore all things have the same causes, because, without substances, affections and movements do not exist. Further, these causes will probably be soul and body, or reason and desire and body.

And in yet another way, analogically identical things are principles, i.e.,
⁵ actuality and potency; but these also are not only different for different things but
also apply in different senses to them. For in some cases the same thing exists at one
time actually and at another potentially, e.g. wine or flesh or man does so. (And
these too fall under the above-named causes. For the form exists actually, if it can
exist apart, and so does the complex of form and matter, and the privation, e.g.
¹⁰ darkness or the diseased. But the matter exists potentially; for this is that which can
become both the actual things.) But the distinction of actuality and potentiality
applies differently to cases where the matter is not the same, in which cases the form
also is not the same but different; e.g. the cause of man is the elements in man (viz.
fire and earth as matter, and the peculiar form), and the external cause, whatever it
¹⁵ is, e.g. the father, and besides these the sun and its oblique course, which are neither
matter nor form nor privation nor of the same species with man, but moving
causes.

Further, one must observe that some causes can be expressed in universal
terms, and some cannot. The primary principles of all things are the actual primary
'this' and another thing which exists potentially. The universal causes, then, of
²⁰ which we spoke do not *exist*. For the *individual* is the source of the individuals. For
while man is the cause of man universally, there *is* no universal man; but Peleus is
the cause of Achilles, and your father of you, and this particular *b* of this particular
ba, though *b* in general is the cause of *ba* taken without qualification.

Again, if the causes of substances are causes of everything, still different
²⁵ things have different causes and elements, as was said; the causes of things that are
not in the same class, e.g. of colours, sounds, substances, and quantities, are
different except in an analogical sense; and those of things in the same species are
different, not in species, but in the sense that the causes of different individuals are
different, your matter and form and moving cause being different from mine, while
in their universal formula they are the same. And if we inquire what are the
³⁰ principles or elements of substances and relations and qualities—whether they are
the same or different, clearly when the terms 'principle' and 'element' are used in
several senses the principles and elements of all are the same, but when the senses
are distinguished the causes are not the same but different, except that in a special
sense the causes of all are the same. They are in a special sense the same, i.e. by
analogy, because matter, form, privation, and the moving cause are common to all
things; and the causes of substances may be treated as causes of all things in this
³⁵ sense, that when they are removed all things are removed; further, that which is first
in respect of fulfillment is the cause of all things. But in another sense there are
different first causes, viz. all the contraries which are neither stated as classes nor
spoken of in several ways; and, further, the matters of different things are different.
1071ᵇ1 We have stated, then, what are the principles of sensible things and how many they
are, and in what sense they are the same and in what sense different.

6 · Since there were three kinds of substance, two of them natural and one
unmovable, regarding the latter we must assert that it is necessary that there should

be an eternal unmovable substance. For substances are the first of existing things, 5
and if they are all destructible, all things are destructible. But it is impossible that
movement should either come into being or cease to be; for it must always have
existed. Nor can time come into being or cease to be; for there could not be a before
and an after if time did not exist. Movement also is continuous, then, in the sense in
which time is; for time is either the same thing as movement or an attribute of 10
movement. And there is no continuous movement except movement in place, and of
this only that which is circular is continuous.

But if there is something which is capable of moving things or acting on them,
but is not actually doing so, there will not be movement; for that which has a
capacity need not exercise it. Nothing, then, is gained even if we suppose eternal
substances, as the believers in the Forms do, unless there is to be in them some 15
principle which can cause movement; and even this is not enough, nor is another
substance besides the Forms enough; for if it does not *act,* there will be no
movement. Further, even if it acts, this will not be enough, if its substance is
potentiality; for there will not be *eternal* movement; for that which is potentially
may possibly not be. There must, then, be such a principle, whose very substance is 20
actuality. Further, then, these substances must be without matter; for they must be
eternal, at least if anything else is eternal. Therefore they must be actuality.

Yet there is a difficulty; for it is thought that everything that acts is able to act,
but that not everything that is able to act acts, so that the potentiality is prior. But if
this is so, nothing at all will exist; for it is possible for things to be capable of existing 25
but not yet to exist. Yet if we follow the mythologists who generate the world from
night, or the natural philosophers who say that all things were together, the same
impossible result ensues. For how will there be movement, if there is no actual
cause? Matter will surely not move itself—the carpenter's art must act on it; nor 30
will the menstrual fluids nor the earth set themselves in motion, but the seeds and
the semen must act on them.

This is why some suppose eternal actuality—e.g. Leucippus and Plato; for they
say there is always movement. But why and what this movement is they do not say,
nor, if the world moves in this way or that, do they tell us the cause of its doing so.
Now nothing is moved at random, but there must always be something present, e.g. 35
as a matter of fact a thing moves in one way by nature, and in another by force or
through the influence of thought or something else. Further, what sort of movement
is primary? This makes a vast difference. But again Plato, at least, cannot even say
what it is that he sometimes supposes to be the source of movement—that which 1072ᵃ1
moves itself; for the *soul* is later, and simultaneous with the heavens, according to
his account. To suppose potentiality prior to actuality, then, is in a sense right, and
in a sense not; and we have specified these senses.

That actuality is prior is testified by Anaxagoras (for his thought is actuality) 5
and by Empedocles in his doctrine of love and strife, and by those who say that there
is always movement, e.g. Leucippus.

Therefore chaos or night did not exist for any infinite time, but the same things
have always existed (either passing through a cycle of changes or in some other

way), since actuality is prior to potentiality. If, then, there is a constant cycle,
10 something must always remain, acting in the same way. And if there is to be
generation and destruction, there must be something else which is always acting in
different ways. This must, then, act in one way in virtue of itself, and in another in
virtue of something else—either of a third agent, therefore, or of the first. But it
must be in virtue of the first. For otherwise this again causes the motion both of the
15 third agent and of the second. Therefore it is better to say the first. For it was the
cause of eternal movement; and something else is the cause of variety, and evidently
both together are the cause of eternal variety. This, accordingly, is the character
which the motions actually exhibit. What need then is there to seek for other
principles?

7 · Since this is a possible account of the matter, and if it were not true, the
20 world would have proceeded out of night and 'all things together' and out of
non-being, these difficulties may be taken as solved. There is, then, something
which is always moved with an unceasing motion, which is motion in a circle; and
this is plain not in theory only but in fact. Therefore the first heavens must be
eternal. There is therefore also something which moves them. And since that which
25 is moved and moves is intermediate, there is a mover² which moves without being
moved, being eternal, substance, and actuality. And the object of desire and the
object of thought move in this way; they move without being moved. The primary
objects of desire and of thought are the same. For the apparent good is the object of
appetite, and the real good is the primary object of wish. But desire is consequent on
opinion rather than opinion on desire; for the thinking is the starting-point. And
30 thought is moved by the object of thought, and one side of the list of opposites is in
itself the object of thought; and in this, substance is first, and in substance, that
which is simple and exists actually. (The one and the simple are not the same; for
'one' means a measure, but 'simple' means that the thing itself has a certain
35 nature.) But the good, also, and that which is in itself desirable are on this same side
of the list; and the first in any class is always best, or analogous to the best.
1072ᵇ1 That that for the sake of which is found among the unmovables is shown by
making a distinction; for that for the sake of which is both that *for* which and that
towards which, and of these the one is unmovable and the other is not. Thus it
produces motion by being loved, and it moves the other moving things. Now if
something is moved it is capable of being otherwise than as it is. Therefore if the
5 actuality of the heavens is primary motion, then in so far as they are in motion, in
this respect they are capable of being otherwise,—in place, even if not in substance.
But since there is something which moves while itself unmoved, existing actually,
this can in no way be otherwise than as it is. For motion in space is the first of the
kinds of change, and motion in a circle the first kind of spatial motion; and this the
10 first mover *produces*. The first mover, then, of necessity exists; and in so far as it is
necessary, it is good, and in this sense a first principle. For the necessary has all

²Reading κινοῦν μέσον, κινοῦν ἐστί.

these senses—that which is necessary perforce because it is contrary to impulse, that without which the good is impossible, and that which cannot be otherwise but is *absolutely* necessary.

On such a principle, then, depend the heavens and the world of nature. And its life is such as the best which we enjoy, and enjoy for but a short time. For it is ever in this state (which we cannot be), since its actuality is also pleasure. (And therefore waking, perception, and thinking are most pleasant, and hopes and memories are so because of their reference to these.) And thought in itself deals with that which is best in itself, and that which is thought in the fullest sense with that which is best in the fullest sense. And thought thinks itself because it shares the nature of the object of thought; for it becomes an object of thought in coming into contact with and thinking its objects, so that thought and object of thought are the same. For that which is *capable* of receiving the object of thought, i.e. the substance, is thought. And it is *active* when it *possesses* this object. Therefore the latter rather than the former is the divine element which thought seems to contain, and the act of contemplation is what is most pleasant and best. If, then, God is always in that good state in which we sometimes are, this compels our wonder; and if in a better this compels it yet more. And God *is* in a better state. And life also belongs to God; for the actuality of thought is life, and God is that actuality; and God's essential actuality is life most good and eternal. We say therefore that God is a living being, eternal, most good, so that life and duration continuous and eternal belong to God; for this *is* God.

Those who suppose, as the Pythagoreans and Speusippus do, that supreme beauty and goodness are not present in the beginning, because the beginnings both of plants and of animals are *causes,* but beauty and completeness are in the *effects* of these, are wrong in their opinion. For the seed comes from other individuals which are prior and complete, and the first thing is not seed but the complete being, e.g. we must say that before the seed there is a man,—not the man produced from the seed, but another from whom the seed comes.

It is clear then from what has been said that there is a substance which is eternal and unmovable and separate from sensible things. It has been shown also that this substance cannot have any magnitude, but is without parts and indivisible. For it produces movement through infinite time, but nothing finite has infinite power. And, while every magnitude is either infinite or finite, it cannot, for the above reason, have finite magnitude, and it cannot have infinite magnitude because there is no infinite magnitude at all. But it is also clear that it is impassive and unalterable; for all the other changes are posterior to change of place. It is clear, then, why the first mover has these attributes.

8 · We must not ignore the question whether we have to suppose one such substance or more than one, and if the latter, how many; we must also mention, regarding the opinions expressed by others, that they have said nothing that can even be clearly stated about the number of the substances. For the theory of Ideas has no special discussion of the subject; for those who believe in Ideas say the Ideas

20 are numbers, and they speak of numbers now as unlimited, now as limited by the number 10; but as for the reason why there should be just so many numbers, nothing is said with any demonstrative exactness.

We however must discuss the subject, starting from the presuppositions and distinctions we have mentioned. The first principle or primary being is not movable 25 either in itself or accidentally, but produces the primary eternal and single movement. And since that which is moved must be moved by something, and the first mover must be in itself unmovable, and eternal movement must be produced by something eternal and a single movement by a single thing, and since we see that besides the simple spatial movement of the universe, which we say the first and 30 unmovable substance produces, there are other spatial movements—those of the planets—which are eternal (for the body which moves in a circle is eternal and unresting; we have proved these points in the *Physics*[3]), each of *these* movements also must be caused by a substance unmovable in itself and eternal. For the nature 35 of the stars is eternal, being a kind of substance, and the mover is eternal and prior to the moved, and that which is prior to a substance must be a substance. Evidently, then, there must be substances which are of the same number as the movements of the stars, and in their nature eternal, and in themselves unmovable, and without 1073^{b}1 magnitude, for the reason before mentioned.

That the movers are substances, then, and that one of these is first and another second according to the same order as the movements of the stars, is evident. But in the number of movements we reach a problem which must be treated from the standpoint of that one of the mathematical sciences which is most akin to 5 philosophy—viz. of astronomy; for this science speculates about substance which is perceptible but eternal, but the other mathematical sciences, i.e. arithmetic and geometry, treat of no substance. That the movements are more numerous than the bodies that are moved, is evident to those who have given even moderate attention to 10 the matter; for each of the planets has more than one movement. But as to the actual number of these movements, we now—to give some notion of the subject— quote what some of the mathematicians say, that our thought may have some definite number to grasp; but, for the rest, we must partly investigate for ourselves, 15 partly learn from other investigators, and if those who study this subject form an opinion contrary to what we have now stated, we must esteem both parties indeed, but follow the more accurate.

Eudoxus supposed that the motion of the sun or of the moon involves, in either case, three spheres, of which the first is the sphere of the fixed stars, and the second 20 moves in the circle which runs along the middle of the zodiac, and the third in the circle which is inclined across the breadth of the zodiac; but the circle in which the moon moves is inclined at a greater angle than that in which the sun moves. And the motion of the planets involves, in each case, four spheres, and of these also the first and second are the same as the first two mentioned above(for the sphere of the 25 fixed stars is that which moves all the other spheres, and that which is placed

[3]*Physics* VIII 8–9.

beneath this and has its movement in the circle which bisects the zodiac is common to all), but the *poles* of the third sphere of each planet are in the circle which bisects the zodiac, and the motion of the fourth sphere is in the circle which is inclined at an angle to the equator of the third sphere; and the poles of the third spheres are 30 different for the other planets, but those of Venus and Mercury are the same.

Callippus made the position of the spheres the same as Eudoxus did, but while he assigned the same number as Eudoxus did to Jupiter and to Saturn, he thought two more spheres should be added to the sun and two to the moon, if we were to 35 explain the phenomena, and one more to each of the other planets.

But it is necessary, if all the spheres combined are to explain the phenomena, 1074ª1 that for each of the planets there should be other spheres (one fewer than those hitherto assigned) which counteract those already mentioned and bring back to the same position the first sphere of the star which in each case is situated below the star in question; for only thus can all the forces at work produce the motion of the 5 planets. Since, then, the spheres by which the planets themselves are moved are eight and twenty-five, and of these only those by which the lowest-situated planet is moved need not be counteracted, the spheres which counteract those of the first two planets will be six in number, and the spheres which counteract those of the next four planets will be sixteen, and the number of all the spheres—those which move 10 the planets and those which counteract these—will be fifty-five. And if one were not to add to the moon and to the sun the movements we mentioned, all the spheres will be forty-nine in number.⁴

Let this then be taken as the number of the spheres, so that the unmovable 15 substances and principles may reasonably be taken as just so many; the assertion of *necessity* must be left to more powerful thinkers.

If there can be no spatial movement which does not conduce to the moving of a star, and if further every being and every substance which is immune from change and in virtue of itself has attained to the best must be considered an end, there can 20 be no other being apart from these we have named, but this must be the number of the substances. For if there are others, they will cause change as being an end of movement; but there *cannot* be other movements besides those mentioned. And it is reasonable to infer this from a consideration of the bodies that are moved; for if everything that moves is for the sake of that which is moved, and every movement 25 belongs to something that is moved, no movement can be for the sake of itself or of another movement, but all movements must be for the sake of the stars. For if a movement is to be for the sake of a movement, this latter also will have to be for the sake of something else; so that since there cannot be an infinite regress, the end of every movement will be one of the divine bodies which move through the heaven. 30

Evidently there is but one heaven. For if there are many heavens as there are many men, the moving principles, of which each heaven will have one, will be one in form but in number many. But all things that are many in number have matter. (For one and the same formula applies to *many* things, e.g. the formula of man; but

⁴Reading ἐννέα for ἑπτά.

35   Socrates is *one*.) But the primary essence has not matter; for it is fulfillment. So the
     unmovable first mover is one both in formula and in number; therefore also that
     which is moved always and continuously is one alone; therefore there is one heaven
     alone.

1074ᵇ1   Our forefathers in the most remote ages have handed down to us their posterity
     a tradition, in the form of a myth, that these substances are gods and that the divine
     encloses the whole of nature. The rest of the tradition has been added later in
5   mythical form with a view to the persuasion of the multitude and to its legal and
     utilitarian expediency; they say these gods are in the form of men or like some of the
     other animals, and they say other things consequent on and similar to these which
     we have mentioned. But if we were to separate the first point from these additions
     and take it alone—that they thought the first substances to be gods—we must
10   regard this as an inspired utterance, and reflect that, while probably each art and
     science has often been developed as far as possible and has again perished, these
     opinions have been preserved like relics until the present. Only thus far, then, is the
     opinion of our ancestors and our earliest predecessors clear to us.

15   9 . The nature of the divine thought involves certain problems; for while
     thought is held to be the most divine of phenomena, the question what it must be in
     order to have that character involves difficulties. For if it thinks nothing, what is
     there here of dignity? It is just like one who sleeps. And if it thinks, but this depends
     on something else, then (as that which is its substance is not the act of thinking, but
20   a capacity) it cannot be the best substance; for it is through thinking that its value
     belongs to it. Further, whether its substance is the faculty of thought or the act of
     thinking, what does it think? Either itself or something else; and if something else,
     either the same always or something different. Does it matter, then, or not, whether
     it thinks the good or any chance thing? Are there not some things about which it is
25   incredible that it should think? Evidently, then, it thinks that which is most divine
     and precious, and it does not change; for change would be change for the worse, and
     this would be already a movement. First, then, if it is not the act of thinking but a
     capacity, it would be reasonable to suppose that the continuity of its thinking is
30   wearisome to it. Secondly, there would evidently be something else more precious
     than thought, viz. that which is thought. For both thinking and the act of thought
     will belong even to one who has the worst of thoughts. Therefore if this ought to be
     avoided (and it ought, for there are even some things which it is better not to see
     than to see), the act of thinking cannot be the best of things. Therefore it must be
     itself that thought thinks (since it is the most excellent of things), and its thinking is
     a thinking on thinking.

35   But evidently knowledge and perception and opinion and understanding have
     always something else as their object, and themselves only by the way. Further, if
     thinking and being thought are different, in respect of which does goodness belong
     to thought? For being an act of thinking and being an object of thought are not the
1075ᵃ1   same. We answer that in some cases the knowledge is the object. In the productive
     sciences (if we abstract from the matter) the substance in the sense of essence, and

in the theoretical sciences the formula or the act of thinking, *is* the object. As, then, thought and the object of thought are not different in the case of things that have not matter, they will be the same, i.e. the thinking will be one with the object of its thought.

A further question is left—whether the object of the thought is composite; for 5 if it were, thought would change in passing from part to part of the whole. We answer that everything which has not matter is indivisible. As human thought, or rather the thought of composite objects, is in a certain period of time (for it does not possess the good at this moment or at that, but its best, being something *different* from it, is attained only in a whole period of time), so throughout eternity is the thought which has *itself* for its object. 10

10 · We must consider also in which of two ways the nature of the universe contains the good or the highest good, whether as something separate and by itself, or as the order of the parts. Probably in both ways, as an army does. For the good is found both in the order and in the leader, and more in the latter; for he does not depend on the order but it depends on him. And all things are ordered together 15 somehow, but not all alike,—both fishes and fowls and plants; and the world is not such that one thing has nothing to do with another, but they are connected. For all are ordered together to one end. (But it is as in a house, where the freemen are least at liberty to act as they will, but all things or most things are already ordained for 20 them, while the slaves and the beasts do little for the common good, and for the most part live at random; for this is the sort of principle that constitutes the nature of each.) I mean, for instance, that all must at least come to be dissolved into their elements, and there are other functions similarly in which all share for the good of the whole.

We must not fail to observe how many impossible or paradoxical results 25 confront those who hold different views from our own, and what are the views of the subtler thinkers, and which views are attended by fewest difficulties. All make all things out of contraries. But neither 'all things' nor 'out of contraries' is right; nor do they tell us how the things in which the contraries are present can be made out of the 30 contraries; for contraries are not affected by one another. Now for us this difficulty is solved naturally by the fact that there is a third factor. These thinkers however make one of the two contraries matter; this is done for instance by those who make the unequal matter for the equal, or the many matter for the one. But this also is refuted in the same way; for the matter which is one is contrary to nothing. Further, all things, except the one, will, on the view we are criticizing, partake of evil; for the 35 bad is itself one of the two elements. But the other school does not treat the good and the bad even as principles; yet in all things the good is in the highest degree a principle. The school we first mentioned is right in saying that it is a principle, but *how* the good is a principle they do not say—whether as end or as mover or as 1075^{b}1 form.

Empedocles also has a paradoxical view; for he identifies the good with love. But this is a principle both as mover (for it brings things together) and as matter

(for it is part of the mixture). Now even if it happens that the same thing is a
5   principle both as matter and as mover, still *being* them is not the same. In which
respect then is love a principle? It is paradoxical also that strife should be
imperishable; strife is for him the nature of the bad.

Anaxagoras makes the good a motive principle; for thought moves things, but
moves them for the sake of something, which must be something other than it,
10   except according to *our* way of stating the case; for the medical art is in a sense
health. It is paradoxical also not to suppose a contrary to the good, i.e. to thought.
But all who speak of the contraries make no use of the contraries, unless we bring
their views into shape. And why some things are perishable and others imperishable, no one tells us; for they make all existing things out of the same principles.
15   Further, some make existing things out of the non-existent; and others to avoid the
necessity of this make all things one.

Further, why should there always be becoming, and what is the cause of
becoming?—this no one tells us. And those who suppose two principles must
suppose another, a superior principle, and so must those who believe in the Forms;
for why did things come to participate, or why do they participate, in the Forms?
And all other thinkers are confronted by the necessary consequence that there is
20   something contrary to Wisdom, i.e. to the highest knowledge; but *we* are not. For
there is nothing contrary to that which is primary (for all contraries have matter
and are potentially); and the ignorance which is contrary would lead us to a
contrary object; but what is primary has no contrary.

Again, if besides sensible things no others exist, there will be no first principle,
25   no order, no becoming, no heavenly bodies, but each principle will have a principle
before it, as in the accounts of the mythologists and all the natural philosophers. But
if the Forms or the numbers are to exist, they will be causes of nothing; or if not that,
at least not of movement.

Further, how is extension, i.e. a *continuum,* to be produced out of unextended
30   parts? For number will not, either as mover or as form, produce a *continuum.* But
again there cannot be any contrary that is also a productive or moving principle; for
it would be possible for it not to be. Or at least its action would be posterior to its
capacity. The world then would not be eternal. But it is; one of these premises, then,
must be denied. And we have said how this must be done. Further, in virtue of what
35   the numbers, or the soul and the body, or in general the form and the thing, are
one—of this no one tells us anything; nor can any one tell, unless he says, as we do,
that the mover makes them one. And those who say mathematical number is first
and go on to generate one kind of substance after another and give different
1076ª1   principles for each, make the substance of the universe a series of episodes (for one
substance has no influence on another by its existence or non-existence), and they
give us many principles; but the world must not be governed badly.

'The rule of many is not good; let there be one ruler.'[5]

---

[5]*Iliad* II 204.

BOOK XIII (M)

1 · We have stated what is the substance of sensible things, dealing in the treatise on physics with matter, and later with the substance which has actual existence. Now since our inquiry is whether there is or is not besides the sensible 10 substances any which is immovable and eternal, and, if there is, what it is, we must first consider what is said by others, so that, if there is anything which they say wrongly, we may not be liable to the same objections, while, if there is any opinion common to them and us, we shall not quarrel with ourselves on that account; for one 15 must be content to state some points better than one's predecessors, and others no worse.

Two opinions are held on this subject; it is said that the objects of mathematics—i.e. numbers and lines and the like—are substances, and again that the Ideas are substances. And since some recognize these as two different classes—the Ideas and the mathematical numbers—and some recognize both as having one nature, 20 while some others say that the mathematical substances are the only substances, we must consider first the objects of mathematics, not qualifying them by any other characteristic—not asking, for instance, whether they are Ideas or not, or whether they are the principles and substances of existing things or not, but only whether as 25 the objects of mathematics they exist or not, and if they do, how they exist; then after this we must separately consider the Ideas themselves in a general way, and only as far as systematic treatment demands; for most of what we have to say has been repeatedly stated in popular works. And the greater part of our account must attack the inquiry already mentioned, viz. whether the substances and the princi- 30 ples of existing things are numbers and Ideas; for after the discussion of the Ideas this remains as a third inquiry.

If the objects of mathematics exist, then they must exist either in sensible objects, as some say, or separate from sensible objects (and this also is said by some), or if they exist in neither of these ways, either they do not exist, or they exist 35 in some other way. So that the subject of our discussion will be not whether they exist but how they exist.

2 · That it is impossible for mathematical objects to exist *in* sensible things and at the same time that the doctrine in question is a fanciful one, has been said already in our discussion of difficulties,—the reasons being that it is impossible for 1076ᵇ1 two solids to be in the same place, and that according to the same argument all the other powers and characteristics also should exist in sensible things—none of them existing separately. This we have said already. But, further, it is obvious that on this theory it is impossible for any body whatever to be divided; for it would have to be 5 divided at a plane, and the plane at a line, and the line at a point, so that if the point cannot be divided, neither can the line, and if the line cannot, neither can the plane nor the solid. What difference then does it make whether sensible things are of this kind, or, without being so themselves, have such things in them? The result will be 10

the same; if the sensible things are divided the others will be divided too, or else not even the sensible things can be divided.

But, again, it is not possible that such entities should exist *separately*. For if besides the sensible solids there are to be other solids which are separate from them and prior to the sensible solids, it is plain that besides the planes also there must be other and separate planes and points and lines; for consistency requires this. But if these exist, again besides the planes and lines and points of the mathematical solid there must be others which are separate. For the incomposite is prior to the compound; and if there are, prior to the sensible bodies, bodies which are not sensible, by the same argument the planes which exist by themselves must be prior to those which are in the motionless solids. Therefore these will be planes and lines other than those that exist along with the separate mathematical solids; for the latter exist along with the mathematical solids, while the others are prior to the mathematical solids. Again, there will be, belonging to these planes, lines, and prior to them there will have to be, by the same argument, other lines and points; and prior to these points in the prior lines there will have to be other points, though there will be no others prior to these. Now the accumulation becomes absurd; for we find ourselves with one set of solids apart from the sensible solids; three sets of planes apart from the sensible planes—those which exist apart from the sensible planes, and those in the mathematical solids, and those which exist apart from those in the mathematical solids; four sets of lines, and five sets of points. With which of these, then, will the mathematical sciences deal? Certainly not with the planes and lines and points in the motionless solid; for science always deals with what is prior. And the same account will apply also to numbers; for there will be another set of units apart from each set of points, and also apart from each set of realities, from the objects of sense and again from those of thought; so that there will be various classes of mathematical numbers.

1077ᵃ1   Again, how is it possible to solve the questions which we enumerated in our discussion of difficulties? For besides the sensible things there will be, on similar principles, the things with which astronomy and those with which geometry deals; but how is it possible that a heaven and its parts—or indeed anything which has movement—should exist apart from the sensible heaven? Similarly also the objects of optics and harmonics will exist apart; for there will be voice and sight besides the sensible or individual voices and sights. Therefore it is plain that the other senses as well, and the other objects of sense, will exist apart; for why should one set of them do so and another not? And if this is so, animals also will exist apart, since the senses will.

Again, there are certain mathematical theorems of a universal character, extending beyond these substances. Here then we shall have another substance intermediate between, and separate from, the Ideas and the intermediates,—a substance which is neither number nor points nor spatial magnitude nor time. And if this is impossible, plainly it is also impossible that the *former* substances should exist separate from sensible things.

And, in general, conclusions contrary alike to the truth and to the usual views follow, if one supposes the objects of mathematics to exist thus as separate entities. For if they exist thus they must be prior to sensible spatial magnitudes, but in truth they must be posterior; for the incomplete spatial magnitude is in the order of generation prior, but in the order of substance posterior, as the lifeless is to the living.

Again, what in the world[1] will make mathematical magnitudes one? For things   20
in our perceptible world are one in virtue of soul, or of a part of soul, or of something else, reasonably enough; when these are not present, the thing is a plurality, and splits up into parts. But in the case of the objects of mathematics, which are divisible and are quantities, what is the cause of their being one and holding together?

Again, the modes of generation of the objects of mathematics show that we are right. For the dimension first generated is length, then comes breadth, lastly depth,   25
and the process is complete. If, then, that which is posterior in the order of generation is prior in the order of substance, body will be prior to the plane and the line. And in *this* way also it is more complete and more whole, because it can become animate. How, on the other hand, could a line or a plane be animate? The supposition passes the power of our senses.   30

Again, body is a sort of substance; for it already has in a sense completeness. But how can lines be substances? Neither as a form or shape, as the soul perhaps is, nor as matter, like body; for we have no experience of anything that can be put together out of lines or planes or points, while if these had been a sort of material   35
substance, we should have observed things which could be put together out of them.

Grant that they are prior in formula. Still not all things which are prior in   1077ᵇ1
formula are prior in substance. For those things are prior in substance which when separated from other things continue to exist, but those are prior in formula out of whose formulae the formulae of other things are compounded; and these two properties are not co-extensive. For if attributes, such as moving or white, do not exist apart from their substances, the white is prior to the white man in formula, but   5
not in substance. For it cannot exist separately, but is always along with the compound thing; and by the compound thing I mean the white man. Therefore it is plain that neither is the result of abstraction prior nor that which is produced by   10
adding posterior; for it is by adding to the white that we speak of the white man.

It has, then, been sufficiently pointed out that the objects of mathematics are not substances in a higher sense than bodies are, and that they are not prior to sensibles in being, but only in formula, and that they cannot in any way exist separately. But since they could not exist *in* sensibles either, it is plain that they   15
either do not exist at all or exist in a special way and therefore do not exist without qualification. For 'exist' has many senses.

3 · Just as the universal part of mathematics deals not with objects which exist separately, apart from magnitudes and from numbers, but with magnitudes

---

¹Reading ποτ᾽ for πότ᾽.

20 and numbers, not however *qua* such as to have magnitude or to be divisible, clearly it is possible that there should also be both formulae and demonstrations about sensible magnitudes, not however *qua* sensible but *qua* possessed of certain definite qualities. For as there are many formulae about things merely considered as in motion, apart from the essence of each such thing and from their accidents, and as it

25 is not therefore necessary that there should be either something in motion separate from sensibles, or a separate substance in the sensibles, so too in the case of moving things there will be formulae and sciences which treat them not *qua* moving but only *qua* bodies, or again only *qua* planes, or only *qua* lines, or *qua* divisibles, or *qua*

30 indivisibles having position, or only *qua* indivisibles.

Thus since it is true to say without qualification that not only things which are separable but also things which are inseparable exist—for instance, that moving things exist,—it is true also to say, without qualification, that the objects of mathematics exist, and with the character ascribed to them by mathematicians. And it is true to say of the other sciences too, without qualification, that they deal

35 with such and such a subject—not with what is accidental to it (e.g. not with the white, if the white thing is healthy, and the science has the healthy as its subject),

1078ª1 but with that which is the subject of each science—with the healthy if it treats things *qua* healthy, with man if *qua* man. So too is it with geometry; if its subjects happen to be sensible, though it does not treat them *qua* sensible, the mathematical sciences will not for that reason be sciences of sensibles—nor, on the other hand, of other things separate from sensibles.

5 Many properties attach to things in virtue of their own nature as possessed of some such property; e.g. there are attributes peculiar to the animal *qua* female or *qua* male, yet there is no female nor male separate from animals. And so also there are attributes which belong to things merely as lengths or as planes. And in proportion as we are dealing with things which are prior in formula and simpler, our

10 knowledge will have more accuracy, i.e. simplicity. Thus a science which abstracts from the magnitude of things is more precise than one which takes it into account; and a science is most precise if it abstracts from movement, but if it takes account of movement, it is most precise if it deals with the primary movement, for this is the simplest; and of this again uniform movement is the simplest form. The same account may be given of harmonics and optics; for neither considers its objects *qua*

15 light-ray or *qua* voice, but *qua* lines and numbers; but the latter are attributes proper to the former. And mechanics too proceeds in the same way. Thus if we suppose things separated from their attributes and make any inquiry concerning them as such, we shall not for this reason be in error, any more than when one draws

20 a line on the ground and calls it a foot long when it is not; for the error is not included in the propositions.

Each question will be best investigated in this way—by supposing separate what is not separate, as the arithmetician and the geometer do. For a man *qua* man is one indivisible thing; and the arithmetician supposes one indivisible thing, and

25 then considers whether any attribute belongs to a man *qua* indivisible. But the geometer treats him neither *qua* man nor *qua* indivisible, but as a solid. For

evidently the attributes which would have belonged to him even if he had not been indivisible, can belong to him apart from these attributes. Thus, then, geometers speak correctly—they talk about existing things, and their subjects do exist; for being has two forms—it exists not only in fulfillment but also as matter.   30

Now since the good and the beautiful are different (for the former always implies conduct as its subject, while the beautiful is found also in motionless things), those who assert that the mathematical sciences say nothing of the beautiful or the good are in error. For these sciences say and prove a very great deal about them; for if they do not expressly mention them, but prove attributes which are their results or   35 their formulae, it is not true to say that they tell us nothing about them. The chief forms of beauty are order and symmetry and definiteness, which the mathematical   1078ᵇ1 sciences demonstrate in a special degree. And since these (e.g. order and definiteness) are obviously causes of many things, evidently these sciences must treat this sort of cause also (i.e. the beautiful) as in some sense a cause. But we shall   5 speak more plainly elsewhere about these matters.

4 · So much then for the objects of mathematics; we have said that they exist and in what sense they exist, and in what sense they are prior and in what sense not prior. Now, regarding the Ideas, we must first examine the ideal theory by itself, not connecting it in any way with the nature of numbers, but treating it in the form in   10 which it was originally understood by those who first maintained the existence of Ideas. The supporters of the ideal theory were led to it because they were persuaded of the truth of the Heraclitean doctrine that all sensible things are ever passing away, so that if knowledge or thought is to have an object, there must be some other   15 and permanent entities, apart from those which are sensible; for there can be no knowledge of things which are in a state of flux. Socrates occupied himself with the excellences of character, and in connection with them became the first to raise the problem of universal definitions—for of the natural scientists, only Democritus touched on the matter and defined, after a fashion, the hot and the cold; while the   20 Pythagoreans had before this treated of a few things, whose formulae they connected with numbers—e.g. opportunity, justice, or marriage. But it was natural that Socrates should seek the essence. For he was seeking to deduce, and the essence is the starting-point of deductions. For there was as yet none of the dialectical power   25 which enables people even without knowledge of the essence to speculate about contraries and inquire whether the same science deals with contraries. For two things may be fairly ascribed by Socrates—inductive arguments and universal definition, both of which are concerned with the starting-point of science. But Socrates did not make the universals or the definitions exist apart; his successors,   30 however, gave them separate existence, and this was the kind of thing they called Ideas.

Therefore it followed for them, almost by the same argument, that there must be Ideas of all things that are spoken of universally, and it was almost as if a man wished to count certain things, and while they were few thought he would not be   35 able to count them, but made them more and then counted them; for the Forms are

almost more numerous than the groups of sensible things, yet it was in seeking the
1079ᵃ1 causes of sensible things that they proceeded from these to the Forms. For to each
set of substances there answers a Form which has the same name and exists apart
from the substances, and so also in the other categories there is one character
common to many individuals, whether these be sensible or eternal.

5   Again, of the ways in which it is proved that the Forms exist, none is
convincing; for from some no inference necessarily follows, and from some it follows
that there are Forms even of things of which they think there are no Forms.

For according to the arguments from the sciences there will be Forms of all
things of which there are sciences, and according to the argument that there is one
attribute common to many things there will be Forms even of negations, and
according to the argument that thought has an object when the individual object
10 has perished, there will be Forms of perishable things; for we can have an image of
these. Again, of the most accurate arguments, some lead to Ideas of relations, of
which they say there is no independent class, and others involve the difficulty of the
third man. And in general the arguments for the Forms destroy that for whose
15 existence the assertors of Forms are more anxious than for the existence of the
Ideas; for it follows that not the dyad but number is first, and the relative is prior to
that and prior to the self-dependent—and besides this there are all the other points
on which certain people, by following out the opinions held about the Forms, have
come into conflict with the principles of the theory.

Again, according to the assumption on which the belief in the Ideas rests, there
20 will be Forms not only of substances but also of many other things; for the concept is
single, not only in the case of substances, but also in that of non-substances, and
there are sciences of other things than substance; and a thousand other such
conclusions also follow. But according to the necessities of the case and the opinions
25 about the Forms, if they can be shared in there must be Ideas of substances only.
For they are not shared in incidentally, but each Form must be shared in as
something not predicated of a subject. (E.g. if a thing shares in the double itself, it
30 shares also in eternal, but incidentally; for the double happens to be eternal.)
Therefore the Forms will be substance. And the same names indicate substance in
this and in the ideal world (or what will be the meaning of saying that there is
something apart from the particulars—the one over many?). And if the Ideas and
the things that share in them have the same Form, there will be something common:
35 for why should 2 be one and the same in all the perishable 2's, or in the 2's which are
many but eternal, and not the same in the 2 itself as in the individual 2? But if they
1079ᵇ1 have not the same Form, they will have only the name in common, and it is as if one
were to call both Callias and a piece of wood 'man', without observing any
community between them.

But if we are to suppose that in other respects the common formulae apply to
5 the Forms, e.g. that plane figure and the other parts of the formula apply to the
circle itself, but that what it is must be added, we must inquire whether this is not
absolutely empty. For to what will this be added? To 'centre' or to 'plane' or to all
the parts of the formula? For all the elements in the substance are Ideas, e.g. animal

and two-footed. Further, the added notion must be an Idea, like plane, a definite
entity which will be present as genus in all its species.   10

5 · Above all one might discuss the question what on earth the Forms
contribute to sensible things, either to those that are eternal or to those which come
into being and cease to be; for they cause neither movement nor any change in them. 15
But again they help in no way towards the *knowledge* of other things (for they are
not even the substance of these, else they would have been in them), nor towards
their being, at least if they are not *in* the individuals which share in them—for in
that case they might be thought perhaps to be causes, as white is for the white thing
in which it is mixed. But this argument, which was used first by Anaxagoras, and   20
later by Eudoxus in his discussion of difficulties and by certain others, is too easily
upset; for it is easy to collect many insuperable objections to such a view.
      But further all other things cannot come from the Forms in any of the ways
that are usually suggested. And to say that they are patterns and the other things   25
share in them is to use empty words and poetical metaphors. For what is it that
works, looking to the Ideas? And any thing can both be and come into being without
being copied from something else, so that, whether Socrates exists or not, a man like
Socrates might come to be. And evidently this might be so even if Socrates were   30
eternal. And there will be several patterns of the same thing, and therefore several
Forms, e.g. animal and two-footed, and also man-himself, will be Forms of man.
Again, the Forms are patterns not only of sensible things, but of things-themselves
also, e.g. the genus is the pattern of the species of the genus; therefore the same
thing will be pattern and copy.   35
      Again, it might be thought impossible that substance and that whose substance
it is should exist apart; how, therefore, could the Ideas, being substances of things, 1080ª1
exist apart?
      In the *Phaedo*² it is stated in this way—that the Forms are causes both of being
and of becoming. Yet though the Forms exist, still things do not come into being,
unless there is something to move them; and many other things come into being (e.g.   5
a house or a ring), of which they say there are no Forms. Clearly therefore even the
things of which they say there are Ideas can both be and come into being owing to
such causes as produce the things just mentioned, and not owing to the Forms. But
regarding the Ideas it is possible, both in this way and by more abstract and more
accurate arguments, to collect many objections like those we have considered.   10

6 · Since we have discussed these points, it is well to consider again the
results regarding numbers which confront those who say that numbers are
separable substances and first causes of things. If number is a real thing and its   15
substance is nothing other than just number, as some say, it follows that either there
is a first in it and a second, each being different in kind, and³ this is true of the units

---

²*Phaedo* 100D.
³Omitting ἤ.

without qualification, and any unit is non-comparable with any unit, or they are all
20 directly successive, and any of them is comparable with any, as they say is the case
with mathematical number; for in mathematical number no unit is in any way
different from another. Or some units must be comparable and some not, e.g. 2 is
25 first after 1, and then comes 3 and then the other numbers, and the units in each
number are comparable, e.g. those in the first 2 with one another, and those in the
first 3 with one another, and so with the other numbers; but the units in the 2 itself
are not comparable with those in the 3 itself; and similarly in the case of the other
30 successive numbers. Therefore while mathematical number is counted thus—after
1, 2 (which consists of another 1 besides the former 1), and 3 (which consists of
another 1 besides these two), and the other numbers similarly, ideal number is
counted thus—after 1, a distinct 2 which does not include the first 1, and a 3 which
35 does not include the 2, and the other numbers similarly. Or one kind of number is
like the first that was named, one like that which the mathematicians speak of, and
that which we have named last must be a third kind.

1080ᵇ1   Again, these numbers must either be separable from things, or not separable
but in sensible things (not however in the way which we first considered, but in the
sense that sensible things consist of numbers which are present in them)—either
some of them and not others, or all of them.
5   These are of necessity the only ways in which the numbers can exist. And of
those who say that the 1 is the beginning and substance and element of all things,
and that number is formed from the 1 and something else, almost every one has
described number in one of these ways; only no one has said *all* the units are
10 incomparable. And this has happened reasonably enough; for there can be no way
besides those mentioned. Some say both kinds of number exist, that which has a
before and after being identical with the Ideas, and mathematical number being
different from the Ideas and from sensible things, and both being separable from
15 sensible things; and others say mathematical number alone exists, as the first of
realities, separate from sensible things.
     Now the Pythagoreans, also, believe in one kind of number—the mathemati-
cal; only they say it is not separate but sensible substances are formed out of it. For
they construct the whole universe out of numbers—only not numbers consisting of
20 abstract units; they suppose the units to have spatial magnitude. But how the first 1
was constructed so as to have magnitude, they seem unable to say.
     Another thinker says the first kind of number, that of the Forms, alone exists,
and some say mathematical number is identical with this.
     The case of lines, planes, and solids is similar. For some think that those which
25 are the objects of mathematics are different from those which come after the Ideas;
and of those who express themselves otherwise some speak of the objects of
mathematics and in a mathematical way—viz. those who do not make the Ideas
numbers nor say that Ideas exist; and others speak of the objects of mathematics,
but not mathematically; for they say that neither is every spatial magnitude
divisible into magnitudes, nor do any two units make 2. All who say the 1 is an
30 element and principle of things suppose numbers to consist of abstract units, except

the Pythagoreans; but *they* suppose the numbers to have magnitude, as has been said before. It is clear from this statement, then, in how many ways numbers may be described, and that all the ways have been mentioned; and all are impossible, but   35 some perhaps more than others.

7 . First let us inquire if the units are comparable or non-comparable, and if non-comparable, in which of the two ways we distinguished. For it is possible that   1081ᵃ1 any unit is non-comparable with any, and it is possible that those in the ideal 2 are non-comparable with those in the ideal 3, and, generally, that those in each primary number are non-comparable with one another. If all units are comparable and   5 without difference, we get mathematical number and this alone, and the Ideas cannot be the numbers. For what sort of number will the ideal man or animal or any other Form be? There is one Idea of each thing, e.g. one of ideal man and another one of ideal animal; but the similar and undifferentiated numbers are infinitely   10 many, so that *this* 3 is no more the ideal man than any other 3. But if the Ideas are not numbers, neither can they exist at all. For from what principles will the Ideas come? *Number* comes from the 1 and the indefinite dyad, and the principles and the elements are said to be principles and elements of number, and the Ideas cannot be   15 ranked as either prior or posterior to the numbers.

But if the units are non-comparable, and non-comparable in the sense that none is comparable with any other, number of this sort cannot be mathematical number; for mathematical number consists of undifferentiated units, and the truths   20 proved of it suit this character. Nor can it be ideal number. For 2 will not come first after 1 and the indefinite dyad, and be followed directly by the successive numbers, as we say '2, 3, 4' (for the units in the ideal 2 are generated at the same time, whether, as the first holder of the theory said, from unequals—coming into being when these were equalized—or in some other way).[4] Besides, if one unit is to be   25 prior to the other, it will be prior to the 2 composed of these; for when there is one thing prior and another posterior, the compound of these will be prior to one and posterior to the other.

Again, since the ideal 1 is first, and then there is a 1 which is first among the others and next after the ideal 1, and again a third which is next after the second   30 and next but one after the first 1, the units must be prior to the numbers by which they are named in counting, e.g. there will be a third unit in 2 before 3 exists, and a fourth and a fifth in 3 before the numbers 4 and 5 exist.—None of these thinkers   35 has said the units are non-comparable in this way, but according to their principles even this way is reasonable, though in truth it is impossible. For it is reasonable that   1081ᵇ1 the units should have priority and posteriority if there is a first unit and a first 1, and the 2's also if there is a first 2; for after the first it is reasonable and necessary that there should be a second, and if a second, a third, and so with the others   5 successively. (And to say both at the same time, that a *unit* is first and another unit is second after the ideal 1, and that a 2 is first after it, is impossible.) But they make

---

[4]Retaining ἔπειτα.

a first unit and 1, but not a second and a third, and a first 2, but not a second and a third.

10   Clearly, also, it is not possible, if all the units are non-comparable, that there should be an ideal 2 and 3; and similarly in the case of the other numbers. For whether the units are undifferentiated or each differs from each, number must be
15   counted by addition, e.g. 2 by adding another one to the one, 3 by adding another one to the two, and 4 similarly. This being so, numbers cannot be generated, as they generate them, from the dyad and the 1; for 2 becomes part of 3, and 3 of 4, and the
20   same happens in the case of the succeeding numbers, but for them 4 came from the first 2 and the indefinite 2,—which makes it two 2's *other* than the ideal 2; if not, the ideal 2 will be a part of 4 and one other 2 will be added. And similarly 2 will
25   consist of the ideal 1 and another 1; but if this is so, the other element cannot be an indefinite 2; for it generates a unit, but not a definite 2. Again, besides the ideal 3 and the ideal 2 how can there be other 3's and 2's? And how do they consist of prior
30   and posterior units? All these doctrines are absurd and fiction, and there cannot be a first 2 and then an ideal 3. Yet there must, if the 1 and the indefinite dyad are to be the elements. But if the results are impossible, it is also impossible that these are the principles.

    If the units, then, are differentiated, each from each, these results and others
35   similar to these follow of necessity. But if those in different numbers are differentiated, but those in the same number are alone undifferentiated from one
1082ª1   another, even so the difficulties that follow are no less. E.g. in the ideal 10 there are ten units, and the 10 is composed both of them and of two 5's. But since the ideal 10 is not any chance number nor composed of any chance 5's—or, for that matter,
5   units—the units in this 10 must differ. For if they do not differ, neither will the 5's of which the 10 consists differ; but since they differ, the units also will differ. But if they differ, will there be no other 5's in the 10 but only these two, or will there be
10   others? If there are not, this is paradoxical; and if there are, what sort of 10 will consist of them? For there is no other 10 in the 10 but itself. But it is also necessary that the 4 should not consist of any chance 2's; for the indefinite 2, as they say, took the definite 2 and made two 2's; for its nature was to double what it took.

15   Again, as to the 2 being a thing apart from the two units, and the 3 a thing apart from the three units, how is this possible? Either by one's sharing in the other, as white man is different from white and man (for it shares in these), or when one is a differentia of the other, as man is different from animal and two-footed. Again,
20   some things are one by contact, some by intermixture, some by position; none of which relations can belong to the units of which the 2 or the 3 consists; but as two men are not a unity apart from both, so must it be with the units. And their being
25   indivisible will make no difference to them; for points are indivisible, but yet a pair of them is nothing apart from the two.

    But this consequence also we must not forget, that it follows that there are prior and posterior 2's, and similarly with the other numbers. For let the 2's in the 4
30   be simultaneous; yet these are prior to those in the 8, and as the 2 generated them, they generated the 4's in the ideal 8. Therefore if the first 2 is an Idea, these 2's also

will be Ideas. And the same account applies to the units; for the units in the first 2 generate the four in 4, so that all the units come to be Ideas and an Idea will be 35 composed of Ideas. Clearly therefore those things also, of which these are Ideas, will be composite, e.g. one might say that animals are composed of animals, if there are 1082ᵇ1 Ideas of them.

In general, to differentiate the units in any way is an absurd fiction; and by a fiction I mean that which is brought in forcibly to suit a hypothesis. For neither in quantity nor in quality do we see unit differing from unit, and number must be 5 either equal or unequal—all number but especially that which consists of abstract units—so that if one number is neither greater nor less than another, it is equal; but what is equal and in no wise differentiated we take to be the same when we are speaking of numbers. If not, even the 2's in the ideal 10 will be differentiated though they are equal; for what reason will the man who says they are not differentiated be 10 able to allege?

Again, if every unit plus another unit makes two, a unit from the ideal 2 and one from the ideal 3 will make a 2. Now this consists of differentiated units; and will it be prior to the 3 or posterior? It rather seems that it must be prior; for one of the 15 units is simultaneous with the 3, and the other is simultaneous with the 2. And we, for our part, suppose that in general 1 and 1, whether the things are equal or unequal, is 2, e.g. the good and the bad, or a man and a horse; but those who hold these views say that not even two *units* are 2.

If the number of the ideal 3 is not greater than that of the 2, this is surprising; 20 and if it is, clearly there is a number in it equal to the 2, so that this is not different from the ideal 2. But this is not possible, if there is a first and a second number. Nor will the Ideas be numbers. For in this particular point they are right who claim that the units must be different, if there are to be Ideas, as has been said before. For the 25 Form is unique; but if the units are not different, the 2's and the 3's also will not be different. Therefore they must say that when we count thus—'1, 2,' we do not add to the previous number; for if we do, neither will the numbers be generated from the 30 indefinite dyad, nor can a number be an Idea; for one Idea will be in another, and all the Forms will be parts of one Form. Therefore with a view to their hypothesis they are right, but absolutely they are wrong; for their view is very destructive, since they will admit that this question itself affords some difficulty—whether, when we count and say '1, 2, 3,' we count by addition or by partitions. But we do both; therefore it is 35 absurd to refer this to so great a difference of substance.

8 · First of all it is well to determine what is the differentia of a 1083ª1 number—and of a unit, if it has a differentia. Units must differ either in quantity or in quality; and neither of these seems to be possible. But number *qua* number differs in quantity. And if the units also differed in quantity, number would differ from 5 number, though equal in number of units. Again, are the first units greater or smaller, and do the later ones increase or diminish? All these are irrational suppositions. But neither can they differ in quality. For no attribute can attach to them; for even to numbers quality is said to belong *after* quantity. Again, quality 10

could not come to them either from the 1 or from the dyad; for the former has no quality, and the latter gives *quantity;* for its nature is to cause things to be many. If

15 the facts are really otherwise, they should above all state this at the beginning and determine if possible, regarding the differentia of the unit, why it must exist; otherwise, what do they mean by it?

Evidently then, if the Ideas are numbers, the units cannot all be comparable,

20 nor can they be non-comparable in either of the two ways. But neither is the way in which some others speak about numbers correct. These are those who do not think there are Ideas, either without qualification or as identified with certain numbers, but think the objects of mathematics exist and the numbers are the first of real

25 things, and the ideal 1 is the starting-point of them. It is paradoxical that there should be a 1 which is first of 1's, as they say, but not a 2 which is first of 2's, nor a 3 of 3's; for the same reasoning applies to all. If, then, the facts with regard to number are so, and one supposes mathematical number alone to exist, the 1 is not the

30 starting point. For this sort of 1 must differ from the other units; and if this is so, there must also be a 2 which is first of 2's, and similarly with the other successive numbers. But if the 1 is the starting-point, the truth about the numbers must rather

35 be what Plato used to say, and there must be a first 2 and 3, and the numbers must not be comparable with one another. But if on the other hand one supposes this, many impossible results, as we have said, follow. But either this or the other must be

1083ᵇ1 the case, so that if neither is, number cannot exist separately.

It is evident from this that the third view is the worst,—that ideal and mathematical number is the same. For two mistakes evidently meet in the one

5 opinion. (1) Mathematical number cannot be of this sort, but the holder of this view has to spin it out by making suppositions peculiar to himself. And (2) he must also admit all the consequences that confront those who speak of numbers as Forms.

The doctrine of the Pythagoreans in one way affords fewer difficulties than those before named, but in another way has others peculiar to itself. For not

10 thinking of number as capable of existing separately removes many of the impossible consequences; but that bodies should be composed of numbers, and that this should be mathematical number, is impossible. For it is not true to speak of indivisible magnitudes; and however much there might be magnitudes of this sort,

15 units at least have no magnitude; and how can a magnitude be composed of indivisibles? But arithmetical number, at least, consists of abstract units, while these thinkers identify number with real things; at any rate they apply their propositions to bodies as if they consisted of those numbers.

20 If then it is necessary, if number is a self-subsistent real thing, that it should be conceived in one of these ways which have been mentioned, and if it cannot be conceived in any of these, evidently number has no such nature as those who make it separable construct for it.

Again, does each unit come from the great and the small, equalized, or one

25 from the small, another from the great? If the latter, neither does each thing contain all the elements, nor are the units without difference; for in one there is the great and in another the small, which is contrary in its nature to the great. Again, how is it with the units in the ideal 3? There is one over. But perhaps it is for this

reason that they give the ideal 1 the middle place in odd numbers. But if each of the two units consists of both the great and the small, equalized, how will the 2, which is   30 one thing, consist of the great and the small? Or how will it differ from the unit? Again, the unit is prior to the 2; for when it is destroyed the 2 is destroyed. It must, then, be the Idea of an Idea since it is prior to an Idea, and it must have come into being before it. From what, then? Not from the indefinite dyad, for *its* function was   35 to double.

Again, number must be either infinite or finite; for these thinkers think of number as capable of existing separately, so that it is not possible that neither of   1084ª1 those alternatives should be true. Clearly it cannot be *infinite;* for infinite number is neither odd nor even, but the generation of numbers is always the generation either of an odd or of an even number,—when 1 operates in one way on an even number, an odd number is produced, and when 2 (or an odd number) operates in the other   5 way, the numbers got from 1 by doubling (or the other even numbers) are produced. Again, if every Idea is an Idea of something, and the numbers are Ideas, infinite number will be an Idea of something, either of some sensible thing or of something else. Yet this is not possible in view of their hypothesis any more than it is reasonable in itself, if they conceive of the Ideas as they do.   10

But if number is *finite,* how far does it go? With regard to this not only the fact but the reason should be stated. But if number goes only up to 10, as some say, firstly the Forms will soon run short; e.g. if 3 is man-in-himself, what number will be the horse-in-itself? The numbers which are Ideas of the several things go up to 10. It   15 must, then, be one of the numbers within these limits; for it is these that are substances and Ideas. Yet they will run short; for the various kinds of animal will exceed them. At the same time it is clear that if in this way the 3 is the Idea of man, the other 3's are so also (for those in the same number are similar), so that there will   20 be an infinite number of men, and if each 3 is an Idea, each of the men will be man-in-himself, and if not, they will at least be men. And if the smaller number is part of the greater (being number of such a sort that the units in the same number are comparable), then if the ideal 4 is an Idea of something, e.g. of horse or of white, man will be a part of horse, if man is 2. It is paradoxical also that there should be an   25 Idea of 10, but not of 11, nor of the succeeding numbers. Again, there both are and come to be certain things of which there are no Forms; why, then, are there not Forms of them also? We infer that the Forms are not causes. Again, it is paradoxical if the number-series up to 10 is more of a real thing and a Form than 10   30 itself. There is no generation of the former as one thing, and there is of the latter. But they try to form a theory on the assumption that the series of numbers up to 10 is a complete series. At least they generate other things—the void, proportion, the odd, and the others of this kind—within the 10. For some things, e.g. movement, rest, good, bad, they assign to the principles, and the others to the numbers. This is   35 why they identify 1 with the odd; for if the odd implied 3, how would 5 be odd? Again, magnitudes and all such things are explained without going beyond a definite number, e.g. the first indivisible line, then the 2, then the others up to   1084ᵇ1 10.

Again, if number can exist separately, one might ask which is prior—1, or 2 or

3? Inasmuch as the number is composite, 1 is prior, but inasmuch as the universal
5 and the form is prior, the number is prior; for each of the units is part of the number
as its matter, and the number acts as form. And in a sense the right angle is prior to
the acute, because it is definite and in virtue of its formula; but in a sense the acute
is prior, because it is a part and the right angle is divided into acute angles. As
matter, then, the acute angle and the element and the unit are prior, but as regards
10 the form and the substance (in the sense of the formula), the right angle, and the
whole consisting of the matter and the form, are prior; for the compound thing is
nearer the form and the object of the formula, but in generation it is later. How then
is 1 the starting-point? Because it is not divisible, they say. But both the universal,
15 and the particular or the element, are indivisible; but in different ways, one in
formula and the other in time. In which way then is 1 the starting-point? As has
been said, the right angle is thought to be prior to the acute, and the acute to the
right, and each is one. They make 1 the starting-point in both ways. But this is
impossible. For one kind of starting-point is the form or substance, the other the
20 part or matter. For each is in a way one—in truth, each unit exists potentially (at
least if the number is a unity and not like a heap, i.e. if different numbers consist of
different units, as they say), but not actually.

The cause of the mistake they fell into is that they conducted their inquiry at
the same time from the standpoint of mathematics and from that of universal
25 formulae, so that from the former standpoint they treated unity, their first
principle, as a point; for the unit is a point without position. They put things
together out of the smallest parts, as some others have done. Therefore the unit
becomes the matter of numbers and at the same time prior to 2; and again posterior,
30 2 being treated as a whole, a unity, and a form. But because their inquiry was
universal they treated the unity which can be predicated of a number, as in this
sense also a part of the number. But these characteristics cannot belong at the same
time to the same thing.

If the ideal 1 must be merely without position[5] (for it differs in nothing from
other 1's except that it is the starting-point), and the 2 is divisible but the unit is not,
35 the unit must be more like the ideal 1. But if so, *it* must be more like the unit than
the 2; therefore each of the units must be prior to the 2. But they deny this; at least
1085ᵃ1 they generate the 2 first. Again, if the ideal 2 is a unity and the ideal 3 is one also,
both form a 2. From what, then, is this 2 produced?

9 · Since there is not contact in numbers, but the units between which there
5 is nothing, e.g. those in 2 or in 3, are successive, one might ask whether they succeed
the ideal 1 or not, and whether, of the terms that succeed it, 2 or either of the units
in 2 is prior.

Similar difficulties occur with regard to the classes of things posterior to
number,—the line, the plane, and body. For some construct these out of the forms
10 of great and small; e.g. lines from long and short, planes from broad and narrow;

---

⁵Ross marks this clause as corrupt.

masses from deep and shallow; which are forms of great and small. And the principle of these which answers to the 1 different men describe in different ways. And in these also the impossibilities, the fictions, and the contradictions of all probability are seen to be innumerable. For they are severed from one another, unless the principles of these imply one another in such a way that the broad and narrow is also long and short; but if this is so, the plane will be a line and the solid a plane. Again, how will angles and figures and such things be explained? And the same happens as in regard to number; for these things are attributes of magnitude, but magnitude does not *consist* of these, any more than the line consists of straight and curved, or solids of smooth and rough.

All these cases share a difficulty which occurs with regard to species of a genus, when one posits the universals, viz. whether it is the ideal animal or something other than the ideal animal that is in animals. True, if the universal is not separable, this will present no difficulty; but if the 1 and the numbers are separable, as those who express these views say, it is not easy to solve the difficulty, if one may call the impossible 'not easy'. For when we apprehend the unity in 2, or in general in a number, do we apprehend a thing-in-itself or something else?

Some, then, generate magnitudes from matter of this sort, others from the point—and the point is thought by them to be not 1 but something like 1—and from other matter like plurality, but not identical with it; about which principles none the less the same difficulties occur. For if the matter is one, line and plane and solid will be the same; for from the same elements will come one and the same thing. But if the matters are more than one, and there is one for the line and a second for the plane and another for the solid, they either imply one another or not, so that the same results will follow even so; for either the plane will not contain a line or it will be a line.

Again, how number can consist of the one and plurality, they make no attempt to explain; at least as they state the case, the same objections arise as confront those who construct number out of the one and the indefinite dyad. For the one view generates number from the universally predicated plurality, and not from a particular plurality; and the other generates it from a particular plurality, but the first; for 2 is said to be a first plurality. Therefore there is practically no difference, but the same difficulties will follow,—is it intermixture or position or fusion or generation? and so on. Above all one might press the question, if each unit is one, what does it come from? Certainly each is not the one-in-itself. It must, then, come from the one-in-itself and plurality, or a part of plurality. To say that the unit is a plurality is impossible, for it is indivisible; and to generate it from a part of plurality involves many other objections; for each of the parts must be indivisible (or it will be a plurality and the unit will be divisible) and the elements will not be the one and *plurality;* for the single units do not come from plurality and the one. Again, the holder of this view does nothing but produce another number; for his plurality of indivisibles is a number. Again, we must inquire, in view of this theory also, whether the number is infinite or finite. For there was at first, as it seems, a finite plurality, from which and from the one comes the finite number of units. And plurality in itself is different from infinite plurality; what sort of plurality, then, is the element which co-operates with the one?

One might inquire similarly about the point, i.e. the element out of which they make magnitudes. For surely this is not the one and only point; at any rate, then, let them say out of what each of the other points is formed. Certainly not of some *distance* together with the point-in-itself. Nor again can *parts* of a distance be indivisible parts, as the parts of plurality out of which the units are said to be made are indivisible; for number consists of indivisibles, but magnitudes do not.

All these objections and others of the sort make it evident that number and magnitudes cannot exist apart from things. Again, the fact that the chief thinkers disagree about numbers is a sign that it is the incorrectness of the alleged facts themselves that brings confusion into the theories. For those who make the objects of mathematics alone exist apart from sensible things, seeing the difficulty about the Forms and their fictitiousness, abandoned ideal number and posited mathematical. But those who wished to make the Forms at the same time numbers, but did not see, if one assumed these principles, how mathematical number was to exist apart from ideal, made ideal and mathematical number the same—in *name*, since in *fact* mathematical number is destroyed; for they state hypotheses peculiar to themselves and not those of mathematics. But he who first supposed that the Forms exist and that the Forms are numbers and that the objects of mathematics exist, naturally separated the two. Therefore it turns out that all of them are right in some respect, but on the whole not right. And they themselves confirm this, for their statements conflict. The cause is that their hypotheses and their principles are false. And it is hard to make a good case out of bad materials, according to Epicharmus: 'as soon as 'tis said, 'tis seen to be wrong.' But regarding numbers the questions we have raised and the conclusions we have reached are sufficient; for he who is already convinced might be further convinced by a longer discussion, but one not yet convinced would not come any nearer to conviction.

But regarding the first principles and the primary causes and elements, the views expressed by those who discuss only sensible substance have been partly stated in the *Physics*, and partly do not belong to the present inquiry; but the views of those who say there are other substances besides the sensible must be discussed next after those we have been mentioning. Since, then, some say that the Ideas and the numbers are such substances, and that the elements of these are elements and principles of real things, we must inquire regarding these what they say and in what sense they say it.

Those who posit numbers only, and these mathematical, must be considered later; but as regards those who believe in the Ideas one might survey at the same time their way of thinking and the difficulties into which they fall. For they at the same time treat the Ideas as universal, and again as separable and individual. That this is not possible has been shown before. The reason why those who say substances are universal combined these two views in one, is that they did not make them identical with sensible things. They thought that the sensible particulars were in a state of flux and none of them remained, but that the universal was apart from these and different. And Socrates gave the impulse to this theory, as we said before, by means of his definitions, but he did not *separate* them from the particulars; and in this he thought rightly, in not separating them. This is plain from the results; for without the universal it is not possible to get knowledge, but the separation is the cause of the objections that arise with regard to the Ideas. His successors, treating it as necessary, if there are to be substances besides the sensible and transient substances, that they must be separable, had no others, but gave separate existence to these universally predicated substances, so that it followed that universals and individuals were almost the same sort of thing. This in itself, then, would be one difficulty in the view we have mentioned.

10 · Let us now mention a point which presents a certain difficulty both to those who believe in the Ideas and to those who do not, and which was stated at the beginning among the problems. If we do not suppose substances to be separate, and in the way in which particular things are said to be separate, we shall destroy that sort of substance which we wish to maintain; but if we conceive substances to be separable, how are we to conceive their elements and their principles?

If they are individual and not universal, real things will be just of the same number as the elements, and the elements will not be knowable. For let the syllables in speech be substances, and their elements elements of substances; then there must be only one *ba* and one of each of the syllables, if they are not universal and the same in form but each is one in number and a 'this' and not homonymous (and again they suppose each thing-in-itself to be one). And if the syllables are unique, so are the parts of which they consist; there will not, then, be more *a*'s than one, nor more than one of any of the other elements, on the same principle on which none of the syllables can exist in the plural number. But if this is so, there will not be other things existing besides the elements, but only the elements. Again, the elements will not be even knowable; for they are not universal, and knowledge is of universals. This is clear both from demonstrations and from definitions; for we do not conclude that this triangle has its angles equal to two right angles, unless every triangle has its angles equal to two right angles, nor that this man is an animal, unless every man is an animal.

But if the principles are universal either the substances composed of them are universal too, or non-substance will be prior to substance; for the universal is not a substance, and the element or principle is universal, and the element or principle is prior to the things of which it is the principle or element.

All these difficulties follow naturally, when they make the Ideas out of elements and claim that there are separate unities apart from the substances which have the same form. But if, e.g., in the case of the elements of speech, the *a*'s and the *b*'s may quite well be many and there need be no ideal *a* and ideal *b* besides the many, there may be, as far as this goes, an infinite number of similar syllables. The statement that all knowledge is universal, so that the principles of things must also be universal and not separate substances, presents indeed, of all the points we have mentioned, the greatest difficulty, but yet the statement is in a sense true, although

15   in a sense it is not. For knowledge, like knowing, is spoken of in two ways—as
potential and as actual. The potentiality, being, as matter, universal and indefinite,
deals with the universal and indefinite; but the actuality, being definite, deals with a
definite object,—being a 'this', it deals with a 'this'. But *per accidens* sight sees
20   universal colour, because this individual colour which it sees is colour; and this
individual *a* which the grammarian investigates is an *a*. For if the principles must be
universal, what is derived from them must also be universal, as in demonstrations;
and if this is so, there will be nothing capable of separate existence—i.e. no
25   substance. But evidently in a sense knowledge is universal, and in a sense it is not.

BOOK XIV (N)

1 · Regarding this kind of substance, what we have said must be taken as
30   sufficient. All philosophers make the first principles contraries: as in natural things,
so also in the case of unchangeable substances. But since there cannot be anything
prior to the first principle of all things, the principle cannot be the principle as being
something else. To suggest this is like saying that the white is the first principle, not
qua anything else but *qua* white, but yet that it is predicable of a subject, and is
35   white as being something else; for then that subject will be prior. But all things are
generated from contraries as belonging to an underlying subject; a subject, then,
1087ᵇ1   must be present in the case of contraries, if anywhere. All contraries, then, are
always predicable of a subject, and none can exist apart. But appearances suggest
that there is nothing contrary to substance, and argument confirms this. No
contrary, then, is the first principle of all things in the full sense; the first principle is
something different.
5   But these thinkers make one of the contraries matter, some making the
unequal—which they take to be the essence of plurality—matter for the one, which
is the equal,[1] and others making plurality matter for the one. (The former generate
numbers out of the dyad of the unequal, i.e. of the great and small, and the other
thinker we have referred to generates them out of plurality, while according to both
it is generated *by* the substance of one.) For even the philosopher who says the
10   unequal and one are the elements, and the unequal is a dyad composed of the great
and small, treats the unequal, or the great and the small, as being one, and does not
draw the distinction that they are one in formula, but not in number. But they do
not describe rightly even the principles which they call elements, for some name the
15   great and the small with the one and treat these three as elements of numbers, two
being matter, one form; while others name the many and few, because the great and
the small are more appropriate in their nature to magnitude than to number; and
others name rather the universal character common to these—that which exceeds
and that which is exceeded. None of these varieties of opinion makes any difference

---

[1]Retaining τῷ ἴσῳ.

to speak of, in view of some of the consequences; they affect only the abstract objections, which these thinkers take care to avoid because their own demonstra- 20 tions are abstract,—with this exception, that if the exceeding and the exceeded are the principles, and not the great and the small, consistency requires that number should come from the elements before 2 does; for both are more universal than 2, as the exceeding and exceeded are more universal. But as it is, they say one of these 25 things but do not say the other. Others oppose the different and the other to the one, and others oppose plurality to the one. But if, as they claim, things consist of contraries, and to the one either there is nothing contrary, or if there must be something it is plurality, and the unequal is contrary to the equal and the different to the same and the other to the thing itself, those who oppose the one to plurality 30 have most claim to plausibility, but even their view is inadequate, for the one would on their view be a few; for plurality is opposed to fewness, and the many to the few.

'One' evidently means a measure. And in every case it is some underlying thing with a distinct nature of its own, e.g. in the scale a quarter-tone, in magnitude a finger or a foot or something of the sort, in rhythms a beat or a syllable; and 35 similarly in weight it is a definite weight; and in the same way in all cases, in qualities a quality, in quantities a quantity (and the measure is indivisible, in the 1088ᵃ1 former case in kind, and in the latter to the sense); which implies that the one is not, in any instance, in itself a substance. And this is reasonable; for the one means the measure of some plurality, and number means a measured plurality and a plurality 5 of measures. Thus it is natural that one is not a number; for the measure is not measures, but both the measure and the one are starting-points. The measure must always be something predicable of all alike, e.g. if the things are horses, the measure is horse, and if they are men, man. If they are a man, a horse, and a god, the 10 measure is perhaps living beings, and the number of them will be a number of living beings. If the things are man and white and walking, these will scarcely have a number, because all belong to a subject which is one and the same in number, yet the number of these will be a number of classes, or of some equivalent term.

Those who treat the unequal as one thing, and the dyad as an indefinite 15 compound of great and small, say what is very far from being probable or possible. For these are modifications and accidents, rather than substrata, of numbers and magnitudes—the many and few of number, and the great and small of magni- tude—like even and odd, smooth and rough, straight and curved. Again, apart from 20 this mistake, the great and the small, and the like, must be relative to something; but the relative is least of all things a real thing or substance, and is posterior to quality and quantity; and the relatives are accidents of quantity, as was said, but not 25 its matter, since there is something else both for relative in general and for its parts and kinds. For there is nothing either great or small, many or few, or, in general, relative, which is many or few, great or small, or relative without being so as something else. A sign that the relative is least of all a substance and a real thing is the fact that it alone has no proper generation or destruction or movement, as in 30 quantity there is increase and diminution, in quality alteration, in place locomotion, in substance simple generation and destruction. The relative has no proper change; for, without changing, a thing will be now greater and now less or equal, if that with which it is compared has changed in quantity. And the matter of each thing, and therefore of substance, must be that which is potentially of the nature in question; but the relative is neither potentially nor actually substance. It is strange, then, or rather impossible, to make non-substance an element in, and prior to, substance; for all the categories are posterior. Again, the elements are not predicated of the things of which they are elements, but many and few are predicated both apart and together of number, and long and short of the line, and both broad and narrow apply to the plane. If there is a plurality, then, of which the one term, viz. few, is always predicated, e.g. 2 (which cannot be many for if it were many, 1 would be few), there must be also one which is absolutely many, e.g. 10 is many (if there is no number which is greater than 10), or 10,000. How then, in view of this, can number consist of few and many? Either both ought to be predicated of it, or neither; but according to the present account only the one *or* the other is predicated.

2 · We must inquire generally, whether eternal things can consist of elements. If they do, they will have matter; for everything that consists of elements is composite. Since, then, a thing must have come into being out of that of which it consists (and if it is eternal, then if it *had* come into being it would have done so in that way), and since everything comes to be what it comes to be out of that which is it potentially (for it could not have come to be out of that which had not this capacity, nor could it consist of such elements), and since the potential can be either actual or not,—this being so, however everlasting number or anything else that has matter is, it must be capable of not existing, just like anything which is a single day or any number of years old; if this is capable of not existing, so is that which has lasted for a time so long that it has no limit. They cannot, then, be eternal, since that which is capable of not existing is not eternal, as we had occasion to show in another context. If that which we are now saying is true universally—that no substance is eternal unless it is actuality, and if the elements are matter that underlies substance, no eternal substance can have elements present in it, of which it consists.

There are some who describe the element which acts with the one as the indefinite dyad, and object to the unequal, reasonably enough, because of the ensuing difficulties; but they have got rid only of those objections which inevitably arise from the treatment of the unequal, i.e. the relative, as an element; those which arise apart from this opinion must confront even these thinkers, whether it is ideal number, or mathematical, that they construct out of those elements.

There are many causes which led them off into these explanations, and especially the fact that they framed the difficulty in an old-fashioned way. For they thought that all things that are would be one—viz. Being itself, if one did not join issue with and refute the saying of Parmenides:[2]

For never will this be proved, that things that are not are.

2 Frag. 7 Diels-Kranz.

They thought it necessary to prove that that which is not is; for thus—of that 5
which is and something else—could the things that are be composed, if they are
many.

But firstly, if 'being' has many senses (for it means sometimes substance,
sometimes quality, sometimes quantity, and at other times the other categories),
what sort of one are all the things that are, if non-being is to be supposed not to be?
Is it the substances that are one, or the affections and the other categories as well, or 10
everything—so that the 'this' and the 'such' and the 'so much' and the other
categories that indicate each some one thing will all be one? But it is strange, or
rather impossible, that a single nature should bring it about that part of that which
is is a 'this', part a 'such', part a 'so much', part somewhere.

Secondly, of what sort of non-being and being do the things that are consist? 15
For 'non-being' also has many senses, since 'being' has; and not being a man means
not being a certain 'this', not straight not being of a certain quality, not three cubits
long not being of a certain quantity. From what sort of being and non-being, then,
do the things that are come to be many? He means by the non-being, the union of 20
which with being makes the things that are many, the false and the character of
falsity. This is also why it was said that we must assume something that is false, as
geometers assume the line which is not a foot long to be a foot long. But this cannot
be so. For neither do geometers assume anything false (for the proposition in 25
question is extraneous to the inference), nor are the things that are, generated from
or resolved into non-being in this sense. But since non-being in the various cases has
as many senses as there are categories, and besides this the false is said not to be and
so is the potential, generation proceeds from the *latter*, man from that which is not
man but potentially man, and white from that which is not white but potentially 30
white, and this whether it is one thing that is generated or many.

The question evidently is, how being in the sense of *substances* is many; for the
things that are generated are numbers and lines and bodies. It is strange to inquire
how being in the sense of essence is many, and not how either qualities or quantities
are many. For surely the indefinite dyad or the great and the small are not a cause
of there being two kinds of white or many colours or flavors or shapes; for then these 1089^{b}1
also would be numbers and units. But if they had attacked this point, they would
have seen the cause of the plurality in substances also; for the cause is the same or
analogous. This aberration is the reason also why in seeking the opposite of being
and the one, from which and being and the one the things that are proceed, they 5
posited the relative (i.e. the unequal), which is neither the contrary nor the
contradictory of these, but is one kind of being as substance and quality are.

They should have inquired also how relatives are many and not one. But as it is,
they inquire how there are many units besides the first 1, but do not go on to inquire 10
how there are many unequals besides *the* unequal. Yet they use them and speak of
great and small, many and few (from which proceed numbers), long and short
(from which proceeds the line), broad and narrow (from which proceeds the plane),
deep and shallow (from which proceed solids); and they speak of yet more kinds of
relatives. What is the reason, then, why there is a plurality of these? 15

It is necessary, as we say, to presuppose for each thing that which is it

potentially; and the holder of these views further declared what that is which is potentially a 'this' and a substance but is not in itself being—viz. that it is the relative (as if he had said the qualitative), which is neither potentially the one or
20 being, nor the contradictory of the one nor of being, but one among beings. And it was much more necessary, as we said, if he was inquiring how beings are many, not to inquire about those in the same category—how there are many substances or many qualities—but how beings as a whole are many; for some are substances, some modifications, some relations. In the categories other than substance there is
25 another matter to give us pause, viz. how can there be many? For since they are not separable, qualities and quantities are many only because their substrate becomes and is many. Yet there *ought* to be a matter for each category; only it cannot be separable from substances. But in the case of a 'this', it is possible to explain how the
30 'this' is many things, unless a thing is to be treated as both a 'this' and a general character. The difficulty arising from these facts is rather this, how there are actually many substances and not one.

But further, if the 'this' and the quantitative are not the same, we are not told how and why the things that are are many, but how quantities are many. For all
35 number means a quantity, and so does the unit, unless it means merely a measure or the indivisible in quantity. If then the quantitative and essence are different, we are
1090ᵃ1 not told whence or how essence is many; but if any one says they are the same, he has to face many inconsistencies.

One might fix one's attention also on the question, regarding the numbers,—what justifies the belief that they exist. To the believer in the Ideas they provide a
5 cause for existing things, since each number is an Idea, and the Idea is to other things somehow or other the cause of their being; for let this supposition be granted them. But as for him who does not hold this view because he sees the inherent objections to the Ideas (so that it is not for this reason that he posits numbers), but
10 who posits *mathematical* number, why must we believe his statement that such number exists, and of what use is such number to other things? Neither does he who says it exists maintain that it is the cause of anything (he rather says it is a thing in itself), nor is it observed to be the cause of anything; for the theorems of
15 arithmeticians will all be found true even of sensible things, as was said.

3 · Those who suppose the Ideas to exist and to be numbers, take each to be one thing by setting each out apart from the many—so that they try at least to explain somehow why numbers exist. Since their reasons, however, are neither conclusive nor in themselves possible, one must not, on this account at least, assert
20 the existence of number. But the Pythagoreans, because they saw many attributes of numbers belonging to sensible bodies, supposed real things to be numbers—not separable numbers, however, but numbers of which real things consist. But why? Because the attributes of numbers are present in a musical scale and in the heavens
25 and in many other things. But those who say that mathematical number alone exists cannot according to their hypotheses say anything of this sort; indeed, they used to say that those numbers could not be objects of the sciences. But we maintain that

they are, as we said before. And it is evident that the objects of mathematics do not exist apart; for if they existed apart their attributes would not have been present in bodies. The Pythagoreans in this point are open to no objection; but in that they construct natural bodies out of numbers, things that have lightness and weight out of things that have not weight or lightness, they seem to speak of another heaven and other bodies, not of the sensible. But those who make number separable assume that it exists and is separable because the axioms would not be true of sensible things, while the statements of mathematics *are* true and delight the soul; and similarly with the magnitudes of mathematics. It is evident, then, both that our contrary theory will say the contrary of this, and that the difficulty we raised just now, why if numbers are in no way present in sensible things their attributes are present in sensible things, is solved for those who hold our views.

There are some who, because the point is the limit and extreme of the line, the line of the plane, and the plane of the solid, think there must be real things of this sort. We must therefore examine this argument too, and see whether it is not remarkably weak. For extremes are not substances, but rather all these things are mere limits. For even walking, and movement in general, has a limit, so that on their theory this will be a 'this' and a substance. But that is absurd. Even if they are substances, they will all be the substances of particular sensible things; for it is to these that the argument applied. Why then should they be capable of existing apart?

Again, if we are not too easily satisfied, we may, regarding all number and the objects of mathematics, press this difficulty, that they contribute nothing to one another, the prior to the posterior; for if number did not exist, none the less magnitudes would exist for those who maintain the existence of the objects of mathematics only, and if magnitudes did not exist, soul and sensible bodies would exist. But the phenomena show that nature is not a series of episodes, like a bad tragedy. The believers in the Ideas escape this difficulty; for they construct magnitudes out of matter and number, lines out of 2, planes doubtless out of 3, solids out of 4, or they use other numbers, which makes no difference. But will these magnitudes be Ideas, or what is their manner of existence, and what do they contribute to things? These contribute nothing, as the objects of mathematics contribute nothing. But not even is any theorem true of them, unless we want to change mathematics and invent doctrines of our own. But it is not hard to assume any random hypotheses and spin out a long string of conclusions. These thinkers, then, are wrong in this way, in wanting to unite the objects of mathematics with the Ideas.

And those who first posited two kinds of number, that of the Forms and the other which is mathematical, neither have said nor can say in the least how mathematical number is to exist and of what it is to consist. For they place it between ideal and sensible number. If it consists of the great and small, it will be the same as the other—ideal number. (And from what other[3] great and small can he

---

[3]Reading ἐξ ἄλλου δὲ τίνος.

1091ᵃ1   produce magnitudes?) And if he names some other element, he will be making his
elements rather many. And if the principle of each of the two kinds of number is a 1,
unity will be something common to these. And we must inquire how the one is these
many things, while at the same time *number,* according to him, cannot be generated
5   except from one and the indefinite dyad.

All this is absurd, and conflicts both with itself and with the probabilities, and
we seem to see in it Simonides' 'long story'; for the long story comes into play, like
those which slaves tell, when men have nothing sound to say. And the very
10   elements—the great and the small—seem to cry out against the violence that is
done to them; for they cannot in any way generate numbers other than those got
from 1 by doubling.

It is strange also to attribute generation to eternal things, or rather this is one
of the things that are impossible. There need be no doubt whether the Pythagoreans
15   attribute generation to them or not; for they obviously say that when the one had
been constructed, whether out of planes or of surface or of seed or of elements which
they cannot express, immediately the nearest part of the unlimited began to be
drawn in and limited by the limit. But since they are constructing a world and wish
to speak the language of natural science, it is fair to make some explanation of their
20   account of nature, but to let them off from the present inquiry; for we are
investigating the principles at work in *unchangeable* things, so that it is numbers of
this kind whose genesis we must study.

4 . These thinkers say there is no generation of the odd number, which
evidently implies that there *is* generation of the even; and some say the even is
25   produced first from unequals—the great and the small—when these are equalized.
The inequality, then, must belong to them *before* they are equalized. If they had
always been equalized, they would not have been unequal before; for there is
nothing before that which is always. Therefore evidently they are not giving their
account of the generation of numbers merely as a theoretical account.
30   A difficulty, and a reproach to any one who finds it *no* difficulty, are contained
in the question how the elements and the principles are related to the good and the
beautiful; the difficulty is this, whether any of the elements is such a thing as we
mean by the good itself and the best, or this is not so, but these are later in origin.
The mythologists seem to agree with some thinkers of the present day, who answer
the question in the negative, and say that both the good and the beautiful appear
35   only when nature has made some progress. This they do to avoid a real
objection which confronts those who say, as some do, that the one is a first principle.
1091ᵇ1   (The objection arises not from their ascribing goodness to the first principle as an
attribute, but from their making the one a principle—and a principle in the sense of
an element—and generating number from the one.) And the old poets agree with
5   this inasmuch as they say that not those who are first in time, e.g. Night and
Heaven or Chaos or Ocean, reign and rule, but Zeus. These poets, however, speak
thus only because they think of the rulers of the world as changing; for those of them
who combine two characters in that they do not use mythical language throughout,

e.g. Pherecydes and some others, make the original generating agent the Best, and 10
so do the Magi, and some of the later sages also, e.g. Empedocles and Anaxagoras,
of whom one made friendship an element, and the other made thought a principle.
Of those who maintain the existence of the unchangeable substances some say the
one itself is the good itself; but they thought its substance lay mainly in its unity.

This, then, is the problem,—which of the two ways of speaking is right. It 15
would be strange if to that which is primary and eternal and most self-sufficient this
very quality—self-sufficiency and self-maintenance—belongs primarily in some
other way than *as a good*. But indeed it can be for no other reason indestructible or
self-sufficient than because its nature is good. Therefore to say that the first
principle is good is probably correct; but that this principle should be the one or, if 20
not that, an element, and an element of numbers, is impossible. Powerful objections
arise, to avoid which some have given up the theory (viz. those who agree that the
one is a first principle and element, but only of *mathematical* number). For all the
units become identical with species of good, and there is a great profusion of goods. 25
Again, if the Forms are numbers, all the Forms are identical with species of good.
But let a man assume Ideas of anything he pleases. If these are Ideas only of goods,
the Ideas will not be substances; but if the Ideas are also Ideas of substances, all
animals and plants and all things that share in Ideas will be good. 30

These absurdities follow, and it also follows that the contrary element, whether
it is plurality or the unequal, i.e. the great and small, is the bad-itself. (Hence one
thinker avoided attaching the good to the one, because it would necessarily follow,
since generation is from contraries, that badness is the fundamental nature of
plurality; others say inequality is the nature of the bad.) It follows, then, that all 35
things partake of the bad except one—the one itself, and that numbers partake of it
in a more undiluted form than magnitudes, and that the bad is the space in which 1092ᵃ1
the good is realized, and that it partakes in and desires that which tends to destroy
it; for contrary tends to destroy contrary. And if, as we said, the matter is that which
is potentially each thing, e.g. that of actual fire is that which is potentially fire, the
bad will be just the potentially good. 5

All these objections, then, follow, partly because they make every principle an
element, partly because they make contraries principles, partly because they make
the one a principle, partly because they treat the numbers as the first substances,
and as capable of existing apart, and as Forms.

5 · If, then, it is equally impossible not to put the good among first principles
and to put it among them in this way, evidently the principles are not being correctly 10
described, nor are the first substances. Nor do we conceive the matter correctly if
we compare the principles of the universe to that of animals and plants, on the
ground that the more complete always comes from the indefinite and incomplete—
which is what leads this thinker to say that this is also true of the first principles of
reality, so that the one itself is not even an existing thing. For here too the principles 15
from which these come are complete; for it is a man that produces a man, and the
seed is not first.

It is strange, also, to generate place simultaneously with the mathematical solids (for place is peculiar to the individual things, and hence they are separable in
20 place, but mathematical objects are nowhere), and to say that they must be somewhere, but not say what the place is.

Those who say that the things that are come from elements and that the first of things that are are the numbers, should have first distinguished the senses in which one thing comes from another, and then said in which sense number comes from its elements.

By intermixture? But not everything is capable of intermixture, and that
25 which is produced by it is different, and on this view the one will not be separate or a distinct entity; but they want it to be so.

By juxtaposition, like a syllable? But then the elements must have position; and he who thinks of the one and plurality must think of them apart; number then will be this—a unit *and* plurality, or the one *and* the unequal.

Coming from certain things means in one sense that these are still to be found
30 in the product and in another that they are not; in which sense does number come from these elements? Only things that are generated can come from elements which are present in them. Does number come from its elements as from seed? But nothing can come from that which is indivisible. Does it come from its contrary, its contrary not persisting? But all things that come in this way come also from something else which does persist. Since, then, one thinker places the 1 as contrary
1092ᵇ1 to plurality, and another places it as contrary to the unequal, treating the 1 as equal, number is treated as coming from contraries. There will then be something else that persists, from which and from one contrary the compound is or has come to be. Again, why in the world do the other things that come from contraries, or that have contraries, perish (even when all of the contrary is used to produce them), while
5 number does not? Nothing is said about this. Yet whether present or not present in the compound the contrary destroys it, e.g. strife destroys the mixture (yet it should not; for it is not to that that it is contrary).

Once more, it has in no sense been determined in which way numbers are the causes of substances and of being—whether as limits (as points are of magnitudes).
10 This is how Eurytus decided what was the number of what (e.g. of man, or of horse), viz. by imitating the figures of living things with pebbles, as some people bring numbers into the forms of triangle and square. Or is it because harmony is a ratio of
15 numbers, and so is man and everything else? But how are the attributes—white and sweet and hot—numbers? Evidently the numbers are not the substance nor causes of the form; for the ratio is the substance, while the number is the matter. E.g. the substance of flesh or bone is number only in this way, 'three parts of fire and two of earth.' And a number, whatever it is, is always a number of certain things, either
20 of fire or earth or of units; but the substance is that there is so much of one thing to so much of another in the mixture; and this is no longer a number but a ratio of mixture of numbers, whether these are corporeal or of any other kind.

Number, then, whether number in general or the number which consists of abstract units, is neither the cause as agent, nor the matter, nor the formula and form of things. Nor, of course, is it that for the sake of which. 25

6 · One might also raise the question what the good is that things get from numbers because their composition is expressible by a number, either by one which is easily calculable or by an odd number. For in fact honey-water is no more wholesome if it is mixed in the proportion of three times three, but it would do more good if it were in no particular ratio but well diluted than if it were numerically 30 expressible but strong. Again, the ratios of mixtures are expressed by the *adding* of numbers, not by mere numbers, e.g. it is three parts to two, not three times two. For the same genus must underlie things that are multiplied together; therefore the product 1 × 2 × 3 must be measurable by 1, and 4 × 5 × 7 by 4, and therefore all products into which the same factor enters must be measurable by that factor. The number of fire, then, cannot be 2 × 5 × 3 × 7, and at the same time that of water 1093ᵃ1 2 × 3.

If all things must share in number, it must follow that many things are the same, and the same number must belong to one thing and to another. Is number the cause, then, and does the thing exist because of its number, or is this not certain? E.g. the motions of the sun have a number, and again those of the moon, and so do 5 the life and prime of each animal. Why, then, should not some of these numbers be squares, some cubes, and some equal, others double? There is no reason why they should not, and indeed they must be comprised within these descriptions, since all things were assumed to share in number and things that differed might fall under 10 the same number. Therefore if the same number had belonged to certain things, these would have been the same as one another, since they would have had the same form of number; e.g. sun and moon would have been the same. But why are these numbers causes? There are seven vowels, the scale has seven strings, the Pleiades are seven, at seven animals lose their teeth (at least some, though some do not), and 15 the champions who fought against Thebes were seven. Is it then because the number is what it is, that the champions were seven or the Pleias consists of seven stars? Surely the champions were seven because there were seven gates or for some other reason, and the Pleias *we* count as seven, as we count the Bear as twelve, while other peoples count more stars in both. They even say that Ξ, Ψ, and Z are concords, and 20 because there are three concords, the double consonants also are three. They quite neglect the fact that there might be a thousand such letters; for one sign might be attached to ΓΡ. But if they say that each of these three is equal to two of the other letters, and no other is so, and if the cause is that there are three parts of the mouth and one letter is applied to Σ in each, it is for this reason that there are only three, not because the concords are three; since as a matter of fact the concords are more 25 than three, but of double consonants there cannot be more. These people are like the old Homeric scholars, who see small resemblances but neglect great ones. Some say that there are many such cases, e.g. that the middle strings are represented by nine and eight, and that the epic verse has seventeen syllables, which is equal in number

to the two strings; and the scansion is, in the right half of the line nine syllables, and   109
in the left eight. And they say that the distance in the letters from alpha to omega is
equal to that from the lowest note of the flute to the highest, and that the number of
this note is equal to that of the whole system of the heavens. We must observe that
5   no one could find difficulty either in stating such analogies or in finding them in
eternal things, since they can be found even in perishable things.

But the celebrated characteristics of numbers and their contraries, and
generally the mathematical relations, if we view them as some do, making them
10 causes of nature, seem to escape us; for none of them is a cause in any of the senses
that have been distinguished in reference to the first principles. Yet if mathematical
objects be conceived as these thinkers conceive them, evidently goodness is
predicable of them, and the odd, the straight, the equal-by-equal, and the powers of
certain numbers, are in the column of the beautiful. For the seasons and a particular
15 number go together; and the other agreements that they collect from the theorems
of mathematics all have this meaning. Hence they are like coincidences. For they
are accidents, but appropriate to one another, and one by analogy. For in each
category of being an analogous term is found—as the straight line is in length, so is
20 the plane in surface, perhaps the odd in number, and the white in colour.

Again, it is not the *ideal* numbers that are the causes of musical phenomena
and the like (for equal ideal numbers differ from one another in form; for even the
units do); so that we need not assume Ideas for this reason at least.

These, then, are the results of the theory, and yet more might be brought
25 together. The fact that they have much trouble with the generation of ideal
numbers and can in no way make a system of them, seems to indicate that the
objects of mathematics are not separable from sensible things, as some say, and that
they are not the first principles.

NICOMACHEAN ETHICS

W. D. Ross
revised by J. O. Urmson

BOOK I

1 · Every art and every inquiry, and similarly every action and choice, is   1094ª1
thought to aim at some good; and for this reason the good has rightly been declared
to be that at which all things aim. But a certain difference is found among ends;
some are activities, others are products apart from the activities that produce them.
Where there are ends apart from the actions, it is the nature of the products to be   5
better than the activities. Now, as there are many actions, arts, and sciences, their
ends also are many; the end of the medical art is health, that of shipbuilding a
vessel, that of strategy victory, that of economics wealth. But where such arts fall
under a single capacity—as bridle-making and the other arts concerned with the   10
equipment of horses fall under the art of riding, and this and every military action
under strategy, in the same way other arts fall under yet others—in all of these the
ends of the master arts are to be preferred to all the subordinate ends; for it is for the   15
sake of the former that the latter are pursued. It makes no difference whether the
activities themselves are the ends of the actions, or something else apart from the
activities, as in the case of the sciences just mentioned.

2 · If, then, there is some end of the things we do, which we desire for its own
sake (everything else being desired for the sake of this), and if we do not choose
everything for the sake of something else (for at that rate the process would go on to   20
infinity, so that our desire would be empty and vain), clearly this must be the good
and the chief good. Will not the knowledge of it, then, have a great influence on life?
Shall we not, like archers who have a mark to aim at, be more likely to hit upon
what we should? If so, we must try, in outline at least, to determine what it is, and   25
of which of the sciences or capacities it is the object. It would seem to belong to the
most authoritative art and that which is most truly the master art. And politics
appears to be of this nature; for it is this that ordains which of the sciences should be
studied in a state, and which each class of citizens should learn and up to what point   1094ᵇ1
they should learn them; and we see even the most highly esteemed of capacities to
fall under this, e.g. strategy, economics, rhetoric; now, since politics uses the rest of

TEXT: I. Bywater, OCT, Oxford, 1894

5   the sciences, and since, again, it legislates as to what we are to do and what we are to abstain from, the end of this science must include those of the others, so that this end must be the good for man. For even if the end is the same for a single man and for a state, that of the state seems at all events something greater and more complete both to attain and to preserve; for though it is worth while to attain the end

10   merely for one man, it is finer and more godlike to attain it for a nation or for city-states. These, then, are the ends at which our inquiry, being concerned with politics, aims.

3 · Our discussion will be adequate if it has as much clearness as the subject-matter admits of; for precision is not to be sought for alike in all discussions, any more than in all the products of the crafts. Now fine and just actions, which political

15   science investigates, exhibit much variety and fluctuation, so that they may be thought to exist only by convention, and not by nature. And goods also exhibit a similar fluctuation because they bring harm to many people; for before now men have been undone by reason of their wealth, and others by reason of their courage. We must be content, then, in speaking of such subjects and with such premises to

20   indicate the truth roughly and in outline, and in speaking about things which are only for the most part true and with premises of the same kind to reach conclusions that are no better. In the same spirit, therefore, should each of our statements be *received;* for it is the mark of an educated man to look for precision in each class of

25   things just so far as the nature of the subject admits: it is evidently equally foolish to accept probable reasoning from a mathematician and to demand from a rhetorician demonstrative proofs.

Now each man judges well the things he knows, and of these he is a good judge. And so the man who has been educated in a subject is a good judge of that subject,

1095ªl   and the man who has received an all-round education is a good judge in general. Hence a young man is not a proper hearer of lectures on political science; for he is in-experienced in the actions that occur in life, but its discussions start from these and are about these; and, further, since he tends to follow his passions, his study will

5   be vain and unprofitable, because the end aimed at is not knowledge but action. And it makes no difference whether he is young in years or youthful in character; the defect does not depend on time, but on his living and pursuing each successive object as passion directs. For to such persons, as to the incontinent, knowledge brings no

10   profit; but to those who desire and act in accordance with a rational principle knowledge about such matters will be of great benefit.

These remarks about the student, the way in which our statements should be received, and the purpose of the inquiry, may be taken as our preface.

4 · Let us resume our inquiry and state, in view of the fact that all knowledge

15   and choice aims at some good, what it is that we say political science aims at and what is the highest of all goods achievable by action. Verbally there is very general agreement; for both the general run of men and people of superior refinement say that it is happiness, and identify living well and faring well with being happy;

but with regard to what happiness is they differ, and the many do not give the same   20
account as the wise. For the former think it is some plain and obvious thing, like
pleasure, wealth, or honour; they differ, however, from one another—and often
even the same man identifies it with different things, with health when he is ill, with
wealth when he is poor; but, conscious of their ignorance, they admire those who   25
proclaim some great thing that is above their comprehension. Now some thought
that apart from these many goods there is another which is good in itself and causes
the goodness of all these as well. To examine all the opinions that have been held
would no doubt be somewhat fruitless: it is enough to examine those that are most
prevalent or that seem to have some reason in their favour.   30

Let us not fail to notice, however, that there is a difference between arguments
from and those to the first principles. For Plato, too, was right in raising this
question and asking, as he used to do, 'are we on the way from or to the first
principles?' There is a difference, as there is in a race-course between the course
from the judges to the turning-point and the way back. For, while we must begin   1095ᵇ1
with what is familiar, things are so in two ways—some to us, some without
qualification. Presumably, then, *we* must begin with things familiar to *us*. Hence
any one who is to listen intelligently to lectures about what is noble and just and,
generally, about the subjects of political science must have been brought up in good   5
habits. For the facts are the starting-point, and if they are sufficiently plain to him,
he will not need the reason as well; and the man who has been well brought up has or
can easily get starting-points. And as for him who neither has nor can get them, let
him hear the words of Hesiod:[1]

> Far best is he who knows all things himself;   10
> Good, he that hearkens when men counsel right;
> But he who neither knows, nor lays to heart
> Another's wisdom, is a useless wight.

5 · Let us, however, resume our discussion from the point at which we
digressed. To judge from the lives that men lead, most men, and men of the most
vulgar type, seem (not without some reason) to identify the good, or happiness, with   15
pleasure; which is the reason why they love the life of enjoyment. For there are, we
may say, three prominent types of life—that just mentioned, the political, and
thirdly the contemplative life. Now the mass of mankind are evidently quite slavish
in their tastes, preferring a life suitable to beasts, but they get some reason for their   20
view from the fact that many of those in high places share the tastes of
Sardanapallus. But people of superior refinement and of active disposition identify
happiness with honour; for this is, roughly speaking, the end of the political life. But
it seems too superficial to be what we are looking for, since it is thought to depend on
those who bestow honour rather than on him who receives it, but the good we divine to   25
be something of one's own and not easily taken from one. Further, men seem to
pursue honour in order that they may be assured of their merit; at least it is by men

---

[1]*Works and Days* 293–7.

of practical wisdom that they seek to be honoured, and among those who know them, and on the ground of their excellence; clearly, then, according to them, at any
30   rate, excellence is better. And perhaps one might even suppose this to be, rather than honour, the end of the political life. But even this appears somewhat incomplete; for possession of excellence seems actually compatible with being asleep, or with lifelong inactivity, and, further, with the greatest sufferings and
1096ª1   misfortunes; but a man who was living so no one would call happy, unless he were maintaining a thesis at all costs. But enough of this; for the subject has been sufficiently treated even in ordinary discussions. Third comes the contemplative
5   life, which we shall consider later.

The life of money-making is one undertaken under compulsion, and wealth is evidently not the good we are seeking; for it is merely useful and for the sake of something else. And so one might rather take the aforenamed objects to be ends; for they are loved for themselves. But it is evident that not even these are ends—
10   although many arguments have been thrown away in support of them. Let us then dismiss them.

6 · We had perhaps better consider the universal good and discuss thoroughly what is meant by it, although such an inquiry is made an uphill one by the fact that the Forms have been introduced by friends of our own. Yet it would perhaps be thought to be better, indeed to be our duty, for the sake of maintaining
15   the truth even to destroy what touches us closely, especially as we are philosophers; for, while both are dear, piety requires us to honour truth above our friends.

The men who introduced this doctrine did not posit Ideas of classes within which they recognized priority and posteriority (which is the reason why they did not maintain the existence of an Idea embracing all numbers); but things are called
20   good both in the category of substance and in that of quality and in that of relation, and that which is *per se*, i.e. substance, is prior in nature to the relative (for the latter is like an offshoot and accident of what is); so that there could not be a common Idea set over all these goods. Further, since things are said to be good in as many ways as they are said to be (for things are called good both in the category of
25   substance, as God and reason, and in quality, e.g. the virtues, and in quantity, e.g. that which is moderate, and in relation, e.g. the useful, and in time, e.g. the right opportunity, and in place, e.g. the right locality and the like), clearly the good cannot be something universally present in all cases and single; for then it would not have been predicated in all the categories but in one only. Further, since of the
30   things answering to one Idea there is one science, there would have been one science of all the goods; but as it is there are many sciences even of the things that fall under one category, e.g. of opportunity (for opportunity in war is studied by strategy and in disease by medicine), and the moderate in food is studied by medicine and in exercise by the science of gymnastics. And one might ask the question, what in the world they *mean* by 'a thing itself', if in man himself and in a particular man the
1096ᵇ1   account of man is one and the same. For in so far as they are men, they will in no

respect differ; and if this is so, neither will there be a difference in so far as they are good. But again it will not be good any the more for being eternal, since that which lasts long is no whiter than that which perishes in a day. The Pythagoreans seem to give a more plausible account of the good, when they place the one in the column of 5 goods; and it is they that Speusippus seems to have followed.

But let us discuss these matters elsewhere; an objection to what we have said, however, may be discerned in the fact that the Platonists have not been speaking about *all* goods, and that the goods that are pursued and loved for themselves are 10 called good by reference to a single Form, while those which tend to produce or to preserve these somehow or to prevent their contraries are called so by reference to these, and in a different sense. Clearly, then, goods must be spoken of in two ways, and some must be good in themselves, the others by reason of these. Let us separate, then, things good in themselves from things useful, and consider whether the former 15 are called good by reference to a single Idea. What sort of goods would one call good in themselves? Is it those that are pursued even when isolated from others, such as intelligence, sight, and certain pleasures and honours? Certainly, if we pursue these also for the sake of something else, yet one would place them among things good in themselves. Or is nothing other than the Idea good in itself? In that case the Form 20 will be empty. But if the things we have named are also things good in themselves, the account of the good will have to appear as something identical in them all, as that of whiteness is identical in snow and in white lead. But of honour, wisdom, and pleasure, just in respect of their goodness, the accounts are distinct and diverse. The 25 good, therefore, is not something common answering to one Idea.

But then in what way are things called good? They do not seem to be like the things that only chance to have the same name. Are goods one, then, by being derived from one good or by all contributing to one good, or are they rather one by analogy? Certainly as sight is in the body, so is reason in the soul, and so on in other cases. But perhaps these subjects had better be dismissed for the present; for perfect 30 precision about them would be more appropriate to another branch of philosophy. And similarly with regard to the Idea; even if there is some one good which is universally predicable of goods or is capable of separate and independent existence, clearly it could not be achieved or attained by man; but we are now seeking something attainable. Perhaps, however, some one might think it worth while to have knowledge of it with a view to the goods that *are* attainable and achievable; for 1097ᵃ1 having this as a sort of pattern we shall know better the goods that are good for us, and if we know them shall attain them. This argument has some plausibility, but seems to clash with the procedure of the sciences; for all of these, though they aim at some good and seek to supply the deficiency of it, leave on one side the knowledge of 5 *the* good. Yet that all the exponents of the arts should be ignorant of, and should not even seek, so great an aid is not probable. It is hard, too, to see how a weaver or a carpenter will be benefited in regard to his own craft by knowing this 'good itself', or how the man who has viewed the Idea itself will be a better doctor or general 10 thereby. For a doctor seems not even to study health in this way, but the health of man, or perhaps rather the health of a particular man; for it is individuals that he is healing. But enough of these topics.

15 **7** · Let us again return to the good we are seeking, and ask what it can be. It seems different in different actions and arts; it is different in medicine, in strategy, and in the other arts likewise. What then is the good of each? Surely that for whose sake everything else is done. In medicine this is health, in strategy victory, in
20 architecture a house, in any other sphere something else, and in every action and choice the end; for it is for the sake of this that all men do whatever else they do. Therefore, if there is an end for all that we do, this will be the good achievable by action, and if there are more than one, these will be the goods achievable by action.

So the argument has by a different course reached the same point; but we must
25 try to state this even more clearly. Since there are evidently more than one end, and we choose some of these (e.g. wealth, flutes, and in general instruments) for the sake of something else, clearly not all ends are complete ends; but the chief good is evidently something complete. Therefore, if there is only one complete end, this will be what we are seeking, and if there are more than one, the most complete of these
30 will be what we are seeking. Now we call that which is in itself worthy of pursuit more complete than that which is worthy of pursuit for the sake of something else, and that which is never desirable for the sake of something else more complete than the things that are desirable both in themselves and for the sake of that other thing, and therefore we call complete without qualification that which is always desirable in itself and never for the sake of something else.

Now such a thing happiness, above all else, is held to be; for this we choose
1097ᵇ1 always for itself and never for the sake of something else, but honour, pleasure, reason, and every excellence we choose indeed for themselves (for if nothing resulted from them we should still choose each of them), but we choose them also
5 for the sake of happiness, judging that through them we shall be happy. Happiness, on the other hand, no one chooses for the sake of these, nor, in general, for anything other than itself.

From the point of view of self-sufficiency the same result seems to follow; for the complete good is thought to be self-sufficient. Now by self-sufficient we do not mean that which is sufficient for a man by himself, for one who lives a solitary life,
10 but also for parents, children, wife, and in general for his friends and fellow citizens, since man is sociable by nature. But some limit must be set to this; for if we extend our requirement to ancestors and descendants and friends' friends we are in for an infinite series. Let us examine this question, however, on another occasion; the
15 self-sufficient we now define as that which when isolated makes life desirable and lacking in nothing; and such we think happiness to be; and further we think it most desirable of all things, without being counted as one good thing among others—if it were so counted it would clearly be made more desirable by the addition of even the least of goods; for that which is added becomes an excess of goods, and of goods the

greater is always more desirable. Happiness, then, is something complete and   20
self-sufficient, and is the end of action.

Presumably, however, to say that happiness is the chief good seems a platitude,
and a clearer account of what it is is still desired. This might perhaps be given, if we
could first ascertain the function of man. For just as for a flute-player, a sculptor, or   25
any artist, and, in general, for all things that have a function or activity, the good
and the 'well' is thought to reside in the function, so would it seem to be for man, if
he has a function. Have the carpenter, then, and the tanner certain functions or
activities, and has man none? Is he naturally functionless? Or as eye, hand, foot,   30
and in general each of the parts evidently has a function, may one lay it down that
man similarly has a function apart from all these? What then can this be? Life
seems to be common even to plants, but we are seeking what is peculiar to man. Let   1098^{a}1
us exclude, therefore, the life of nutrition and growth. Next there would be a life of
perception, but *it* also seems to be common even to the horse, the ox, and every
animal. There remains, then, an active life of the element that has a rational
principle (of this, one part has such a principle in the sense of being obedient to one,
the other in the sense of possessing one and exercising thought); and as this too can   5
be taken in two ways, we must state that life in the sense of activity is what we
mean; for this seems to be the more proper sense of the term. Now if the function of
man is an activity of soul in accordance with, or not without, rational principle, and
if we say a so-and-so and a good so-and-so have a function which is the same in kind,
e.g. a lyre-player and a good lyre-player, and so without qualification in all cases,   10
eminence in respect of excellence being added to the function (for the function of a
lyre-player is to play the lyre, and that of a good lyre-player is to do so well): if this is
the case, [and we state the function of man to be a certain kind of life, and this to be
an activity or actions of the soul implying a rational principle, and the function of a
good man to be the good and noble performance of these, and if any action is well
performed when it is performed in accordance with the appropriate excellence: if   15
this is the case,]² human good turns out to be activity of soul in conformity with
excellence, and if there are more than one excellence, in conformity with the best
and most complete.

But we must add 'in a complete life'. For one swallow does not make a summer,
nor does one day; and so too one day, or a short time, does not make a man blessed
and happy.

Let this serve as an outline of the good; for we must presumably first sketch it   20
roughly, and then later fill in the details. But it would seem that any one is capable
of carrying on and articulating what has once been well outlined, and that time is a
good discoverer or partner in such a work; to which facts the advances of the arts are
due; for any one can add what is lacking. And we must also remember what has   25
been said before, and not look for precision in all things alike, but in each class of
things such precision as accords with the subject-matter, and so much as is

---

²Excised by Bywater.

appropriate to the inquiry. For a carpenter and a geometer look for right angles in
30   different ways; the former does so in so far as the right angle is useful for his work,
while the latter inquires what it is or what sort of thing it is; for he is a spectator of
the truth. We must act in the same way, then, in all other matters as well, that our
main task may not be subordinated to minor questions. Nor must we demand the
1098ᵇ1   cause in all matters alike; it is enough in some cases that the *fact* be well established,
as in the case of the first principles; the fact is a primary thing or first principle.
Now of first principles we see some by induction, some by perception, some by a
certain habituation, and others too in other ways. But each set of principles we must
5   try to investigate in the natural way, and we must take pains to determine them
correctly, since they have a great influence on what follows. For the beginning is
thought to be more than half of the whole, and many of the questions we ask are
cleared up by it.

8 · We must consider it, however, in the light not only of our conclusion and
10   our premises, but also of what is commonly said about it; for with a true view all the
facts harmonize, but with a false one they³ soon clash. Now goods have been divided
into three classes, and some are described as external, others as relating to soul or to
body; and we call those that relate to soul most properly and truly goods. But we are
15   positing actions and activities relating to soul.⁴ Therefore our account must be
sound, at least according to this view, which is an old one and agreed on by
philosophers. It is correct also in that we identify the end with certain actions and
activities; for thus it falls among goods of the soul and not among external goods.
20   Another belief which harmonizes with our account is that the happy man lives well
and fares well; for we have practically defined happiness as a sort of living and
faring well. The characteristics that are looked for in happiness seem also, all of
excellence, some with practical wisdom, others with a kind of philosophic wisdom,
25   others with these, or one of these, accompanied by pleasure or not without pleasure;
while others include also external prosperity. Now some of these views have been
held by many men and men of old, others by a few persons; and it is not probable
that either of these should be entirely mistaken, but rather that they should be right
in at least some one respect or even in most respects.
30   With those who identify happiness with excellence or some one excellence our
account is in harmony; for to excellence belongs activity in accordance with
excellence. But it makes, perhaps, no small difference whether we place the chief
good in possession or in use, in state or in activity. For the state may exist without
1099ª1   producing any good result, as in a man who is asleep or in some other way quite
inactive, but the activity cannot; for one who has the activity will of necessity be
acting, and acting well. And as in the Olympic Games it is not the most beautiful
and the strongest that are crowned but those who compete (for it is some of these
5   that are victorious), so those who act rightly win the noble and good things in life.

³Omitting τἀληθές.
⁴Omitting ψυχικάς.

Their life is also in itself pleasant. For pleasure is a state of soul, and to each   5
man that which he is said to be a lover of is pleasant; e.g. not only is a horse pleasant
to the lover of horses, and a spectacle to the lover of sights, but also in the same way   10
just acts are pleasant to the lover of justice and in general excellent acts to the lover
of excellence. Now for most men their pleasures are in conflict with one another
because these are not by nature pleasant, but the lovers of what is noble find
pleasant the things that are by nature pleasant; and excellent actions are such, so
that these are pleasant for such men as well as in their own nature. Their life,
therefore, has no further need of pleasure as a sort of adventitious charm, but has its   15
pleasure in itself. For, besides what we have said, the man who does not rejoice in
noble actions is not even good; since no one would call a man just who did not enjoy
acting justly, nor any man liberal who did not enjoy liberal actions; and similarly in   20
all other cases. If this is so, excellent actions must be in themselves pleasant. But
they are also *good* and *noble*, and have each of these attributes in the highest
degree, since the good man judges well about these attributes and he judges in the
way we have described. Happiness then is the best, noblest, and most pleasant thing,
and these attributes are not severed as in the inscription at Delos—   25

> Most noble is that which is justest, and best is health;
> But pleasantest is it to win what we love.

For all these properties belong to the best activities; and these, or one—the best—of   30
these, we identify with happiness.

Yet evidently, as we said, it needs the external goods as well; for it is
impossible, or not easy, to do noble acts without the proper equipment. In many
actions we use friends and riches and political power as instruments; and there are   1099^{b}1
some things the lack of which takes the lustre from blessedness, as good birth,
satisfactory children, beauty; for the man who is very ugly in appearance or ill-born
or solitary and childless is hardly happy, and perhaps a man would be still less so if
he had thoroughly bad children or friends or had lost good children or friends by   5
death. As we said, then, happiness seems to need this sort of prosperity in addition;
for which reason some identify happiness with good fortune, though others identify
it with excellence.

9 · For this reason also the question is asked, whether happiness is to be
acquired by learning or by habituation or some other sort of training, or comes in   10
virtue of some divine providence or again by chance. Now if there is *any* gift of the
gods to men, it is reasonable that happiness should be god-given, and most surely
god-given of all human things inasmuch as it is the best. But this question would
perhaps be more appropriate to another inquiry; happiness seems, however, even if
it is not god-sent but comes as a result of excellence and some process of learning or   15
training, to be among the most godlike things; for that which is the prize and end of
excellence seems to be the best thing and something godlike and blessed.

It will also on this view be very generally shared; for all who are not maimed as
regards excellence may win it by a certain kind of study and care. But if it is better

20   to be happy thus than by chance, it is reasonable that the facts should be so, since everything that depends on the action of nature is by nature as good as it can be, and similarly everything that depends on art or any cause, and especially if it depends on the best of all causes. To entrust to chance what is greatest and most noble would be a very defective arrangement.

25   The answer to the question we are asking is plain also from the definition[5]; for it has been said to be a certain kind of activity of soul. Of the remaining goods, some are necessary and others are naturally co-operative and useful as instruments. And this will be found to agree with what we said at the outset; for we stated the end of

30   political science to be the best end, and political science spends most of its pains on making the citizens to be of a certain character, viz. good and capable of noble acts.

It is natural, then, that we call neither ox nor horse nor any other of the

1100ᵃ1   animals happy; for none of them is capable of sharing in such activity. For this reason also a boy is not happy; for he is not yet capable of such acts, owing to his age; and boys who are called happy are being congratulated by reason of the hopes we have for them. For there is required, as we said, not only complete excellence but

5   also a complete life, since many changes occur in life, and all manner of chances, and the most prosperous may fall into great misfortunes in old age, as is told of Priam in the Trojan Cycle; and one who has experienced such chances and has ended wretchedly no one calls happy.

10   **10 ·** Must no one at all, then, be called happy while he lives; must we, as Solon says, see the end? Even if we are to lay down this doctrine, is it also the case that a man is happy when he is *dead*? Or is not this quite absurd, especially for us

15   who say that happiness is an activity? But if we do not call the dead man happy, and if Solon does not mean this, but that one can then safely *call* a man blessed as being at last beyond evils and misfortunes, this also affords matter for discussion; for both evil and good are thought to exist for a dead man, as much as for one who is alive but

20   not aware of them; e.g. honours and dishonours and the good or bad fortunes of children and in general of descendants. And this also presents a problem; for though a man has lived blessedly up to old age and has had a death worthy of his life, many

25   reverses may befall his descendants—some of them may be good and attain the life they deserve, while with others the opposite may be the case; and clearly too the degrees of relationship between them and their ancestors may vary indefinitely. It would be odd, then, if the dead man were to share in these changes and become at one time happy, at another wretched; while it would also be odd if the fortunes of

30   the descendants did not for *some* time have *some* effect on the happiness of their ancestors.

But we must return to our first difficulty; for perhaps by a consideration of it our present problem might be solved. Now if we must see the end and only then call a man blessed, not as being blessed but as having been so before, surely it is odd that when he is happy the attribute that belongs to him is not to be truly predicated of

---

[5] Omitting κατ᾽ ἀρετήν.

him because we do not wish to call living men happy, on account of the changes that   1100ᵇ1
may befall them, and because we have assumed happiness to be something
permanent and by no means easily changed, while a single man may suffer many
turns of fortune's wheel. For clearly if we were to follow his fortunes, we should
often call the same man happy and again wretched, making the happy man out to be   5
a 'chameleon and insecurely based'. Or is this following his fortunes quite wrong?
Success or failure in life does not depend on these, but human life, as we said, needs
these as well, while excellent activities or their opposites are what determine   10
happiness or the reverse.

The question we have now discussed confirms our definition. For no function of
man has so much permanence as excellent activities (these are thought to be more
durable even than knowledge), and of these themselves the most valuable are more   15
durable because those who are blessed spend their life most readily and most
continuously in these; for this seems to be the reason why we do not forget them.
The attribute in question, then, will belong to the happy man, and he will be happy
throughout his life; for always, or by preference to everything else, he will do and
contemplate what is excellent, and he will bear the chances of life most nobly and   20
altogether decorously, if he is 'truly good' and 'foursquare beyond reproach'.

Now many events happen by chance, and events differing in importance; small
pieces of good fortune or of its opposite clearly do not weigh down the scales of life
one way or the other, but a multitude of great events if they turn out well will make   25
life more blessed (for not only are they themselves such as to add beauty to life, but
the way a man deals with them may be noble and good), while if they turn out ill
they crush and maim blessedness; for they both bring pain with them and hinder
many activities. Yet even in these nobility shines through, when a man bears with   30
resignation many great misfortunes, not through insensibility to pain but through
nobility and greatness of soul.

If activities are, as we said, what determines the character of life, no blessed
man can become miserable; for he will never do the acts that are hateful and mean.
For the man who is truly good and wise, we think, bears all the chances of life   1101ᵃ1
becomingly and always makes the best of circumstances, as a good general makes
the best military use of the army at his command and a shoemaker makes the best
shoes out of the hides that are given him; and so with all other craftsmen. And if this   5
is the case, the happy man can never become miserable—though he will not reach
blessedness, if he meet with fortunes like those of Priam.

Nor, again, is he many-coloured and changeable; for neither will he be moved
from his happy state easily or by any ordinary misadventures, but only by many   10
great ones, nor, if he has had many great misadventures, will he recover his
happiness in a short time, but if at all, only in a long and complete one in which he
has attained many splendid successes.

Why then should we not say that he is happy who is active in conformity with
complete excellence and is sufficiently equipped with external goods, not for some   15
chance period but throughout a complete life? Or must we add 'and who is destined
to live thus and die as befits his life'? Certainly the future is obscure to us, while
happiness, we claim, is an end and something in every way final. If so, we shall call

20 blessed those among living men in whom these conditions are, and are to be, fulfilled—but blessed *men*. So much for these questions.

11 · That the fortunes of descendants and of all a man's friends should not affect his happiness at all seems a very unfriendly doctrine, and one opposed to the opinions men hold; but since the events that happen are numerous and admit of all
25 sorts of difference, and some come more near to us and others less so, it seems a long—indeed an endless—task to discuss each in detail; a general outline will perhaps suffice. If, then, as some of a man's own misadventures have a certain weight and influence on life while others are, as it were, lighter, so too there are
30 differences among the misadventures of all our friends, and it makes a difference whether the various sufferings befall the living or the dead (much more even than whether lawless and terrible deeds are presupposed in a tragedy or done on the stage), this difference also must be taken into account; or rather, perhaps, the fact that doubt is felt whether the dead share in any good or evil. For it seems, from these
1101ᵇ1 considerations, that even if anything whether good or evil penetrates to them, it must be something weak and negligible, either in itself or for them, or if not, at least it must be such in degree and kind as not to make happy those who are not happy
5 nor to take away their blessedness from those who are. The good or bad fortunes of friends, then, seem to have some effects on the dead, but effects of such a kind and degree as neither to make the happy unhappy nor to produce any other change of the kind.

10 12 · These questions having been answered, let us consider whether happiness is among the things that are praised or rather among the things that are prized; for clearly it is not to be placed among *potentialities*. Everything that is praised seems to be praised because it is of a certain kind and is related somehow to something else; for we praise the just or brave man and in general both the good
15 man and excellence itself because of the actions and functions involved, and we praise the strong man, the good runner, and so on, because he is of a certain kind and is related in a certain way to something good and important. This is clear also from the praises of the gods; for it seems absurd that the gods should be referred to
20 our standard, but this is done because praise involves a reference, as we said, to something else. But if praise is for things such as we have described, clearly what applies to the best things is not praise, but something greater and better, as is indeed obvious; for what we do to the gods and the most godlike of men is to call them
25 blessed and happy. And so too with good things; no one praises happiness as he does justice, but rather calls it blessed, as being something more divine and better.
    Eudoxus also seems to have been right in his method of advocating the supremacy of pleasure; he thought that the fact that, though a good, it is not praised
30 indicated it to be better than the things that are praised, and that this is what God and the good are; for by reference to these all other things are judged. Praise is appropriate to excellence; for as a result of excellence men tend to do noble deeds (*encomia* are bestowed on acts, whether of the body or of the soul—but perhaps nicety in these matters is more proper to those who have made a study of encomia);

but to us it is clear from what has been said that happiness is among the things that 1102^a1
are prized and complete. It seems to be so also from the fact that it is a first
principle; for it is for the sake of this that we all do everything else, and the first
principle and cause of goods is, we claim, something prized and divine.

13 · Since happiness is an activity of soul in accordance with complete 5
excellence, we must consider the nature of excellence; for perhaps we shall thus see
better the nature of happiness. The true student of politics, too, is thought to have
studied this above all things; for he wishes to make his fellow citizens good and
obedient to the laws. As an example of this we have the lawgivers of the Cretans and 10
the Spartans, and any others of the kind that there may have been. And if this
inquiry belongs to political science, clearly the pursuit of it will be in accordance
with our original plan. But clearly the excellence we must study is human
excellence; for the good we were seeking was human good and the happiness human 15
happiness. By human excellence we mean not that of the body but that of the soul;
and happiness also we call an activity of soul. But if this is so, clearly the student of
politics must know somehow the facts about soul, as the man who is to heal the eyes
must know about the whole body also; and all the more since politics is more prized 20
and better than medicine; but even among doctors the best educated spend much
labour on acquiring knowledge of the body. The student of politics, then, must study
the soul, and must study it with these objects in view, and do so just to the extent
which is sufficient for the questions we are discussing; for further precision is
perhaps something more laborious than our purposes require. 25
Some things are said about it, adequately enough, even in the discussions
outside our school, and we must use these; e.g. that one element in the soul is
irrational and one has a rational principle. Whether these are separated as the parts
of the body or of anything divisible are, or are distinct by definition but by nature 30
inseparable, like convex and concave in the circumference of a circle, does not affect
the present question.
Of the irrational element one division seems to be widely distributed, and
vegetative in its nature, I mean that which causes nutrition and growth; for it is this
kind of power of the soul that one must assign to all nurslings and to embryos, and 1102^b1
this same power to full-grown creatures; this is more reasonable than to assign some
different power to them. Now the excellence of this seems to be common to all and
not specifically human; for this part or faculty seems to function most in sleep, while
goodness and badness are least manifest in sleep (whence comes the saying that the 5
happy are not better off than the wretched for half their lives; and this happens
naturally enough, since sleep is an inactivity of the soul in that respect in which it is
called good or bad), unless perhaps to a small extent some of the movements
actually penetrate, and in this respect the dreams of good men are better than those 10
of ordinary people. Enough of this subject, however; let us leave the nutritive faculty
alone, since it has by its nature no share in human excellence.
There seems to be also another irrational element in the soul—one which in a
sense, however, shares in a rational principle. For we praise the reason of the
continent man and of the incontinent, and the part of their soul that has reason, 15

since it urges them aright and towards the best objects; but there is found in them also another natural element beside reason, which fights against and resists it. For exactly as paralysed limbs when we choose to move them to the right turn on the contrary to the left, so is it with the soul; the impulses of incontinent people move in
20 contrary directions. But while in the body we see that which moves astray, in the soul we do not. No doubt, however, we must none the less suppose that in the soul too there is something beside reason, resisting and opposing it. In what sense it is
25 distinct from the other elements does not concern us. Now even this seems to have a share in reason, as we said; at any rate in the continent man it obeys reason—and presumably in the temperate and brave man it is still more obedient; for in them it speaks, on all matters, with the same voice as reason.

Therefore the irrational element also appears to be two-fold. For the vegetative
30 element in no way shares in reason, but the appetitive and in general the desiring element in a sense shares in it, in so far as it listens to and obeys it; this is the sense in which we speak of paying heed to one's father or one's friends, not that in which we speak of 'the rational' in mathematics.[6] That the irrational element is in some sense persuaded by reason is indicated also by the giving of advice and by all reproof and
1103ª1 exhortation. And if this element also must be said to have reason, that which has reason also will be twofold, one subdivision having it in the strict sense and in itself, and the other having a tendency to obey as one does one's father.

Excellence too is distinguished into kinds in accordance with this difference;
5 for we say that some excellences are intellectual and others moral,[7] philosophic wisdom and understanding and practical wisdom being intellectual, liberality and temperance moral. For in speaking about a man's character we do not say that he is wise or has understanding but that he is good-tempered or temperate; yet we praise the wise man also with respect to his state; and of states we call those which merit
10 praise excellences.

BOOK II

1 · Excellence, then, being of two kinds, intellectual and moral, intellectual
15 excellence in the main owes both its birth and its growth to teaching (for which reason it requires experience and time), while moral excellence comes about as a result of habit, whence also its name is one that is formed by a slight variation from the word for 'habit'.[8] From this it is also plain that none of the moral excellences
20 arises in us by nature; for nothing that exists by nature can form a habit contrary to its nature. For instance the stone which by nature moves downwards cannot be habituated to move upwards, not even if one tries to train it by throwing it up ten thousand times; nor can fire be habituated to move downwards, nor can anything

---

[6] Λόγον ἔχειν means (i) 'possess reason', (ii) 'pay heed to', 'obey', (iii) 'be rational' (in the mathematical sense).
[7] 'Moral', here and hereafter, is used in the archaic sense of 'pertaining to character or *mores*'.
[8] ἠθική from ἔθος.

else that by nature behaves in one way be trained to behave in another. Neither by nature, then, nor contrary to nature do excellences arise in us; rather we are adapted by nature to receive them, and are made perfect by habit.   25

Again, of all the things that come to us by nature we first acquire the potentiality and later exhibit the activity (this is plain in the case of the senses; for it was not by often seeing or often hearing that we got these senses, but on the contrary we had them before we used them, and did not come to have them by using them);   30 but excellences we get by first exercising them, as also happens in the case of the arts as well. For the things we have to learn before we can do, we learn by doing, e.g. men become builders by building and lyre-players by playing the lyre; so too we become just by doing just acts, temperate by doing temperate acts, brave by doing   1103ᵇ1 brave acts.

This is confirmed by what happens in states; for legislators make the citizens good by forming habits in them, and this is the wish of every legislator; and those who do not effect it miss their mark, and it is in this that a good constitution differs   5 from a bad one.

Again, it is from the same causes and by the same means that every excellence is both produced and destroyed, and similarly every art; for it is from playing the lyre that both good and bad lyre-players are produced. And the corresponding statement is true of builders and of all the rest; men will be good or bad builders as a   10 result of building well or badly. For if this were not so, there would have been no need of a teacher, but all men would have been born good or bad at their craft. This, then, is the case with the excellences also; by doing the acts that we do in our transactions with other men we become just or unjust, and by doing the acts that we   15 do in the presence of danger, and being habituated to feel fear or confidence, we become brave or cowardly. The same is true of appetites and feelings of anger; some men become temperate and good-tempered, others self-indulgent and irascible, by behaving in one way or the other in the appropriate circumstances. Thus, in one   20 word, states arise out of like activities. This is why the activities we exhibit must be of a certain kind; it is because the states correspond to the differences between these. It makes no small difference, then, whether we form habits of one kind or of another from our very youth; it makes a very great difference, or rather *all* the   25 difference.

2 · Since, then, the present inquiry does not aim at theoretical knowledge like the others (for we are inquiring not in order to know what excellence is, but in order to become good, since otherwise our inquiry would have been of no use), we must examine the nature of actions, namely how we ought to do them; for these   30 determine also the nature of the states that are produced, as we have said. Now, that we must[9] act according to right reason is a common principle and must be assumed—it will be discussed later, i.e. both what it is, and how it is related to the other excellences. But this must be agreed upon beforehand, that the whole account   1104ª1 of matters of conduct must be given in outline and not precisely, as we said at the

[9]Reading πράττειν δεῖν.

very beginning that the accounts we demand must be in accordance with the subject-matter; matters concerned with conduct and questions of what is good for us have no fixity, any more than matters of health. The general account being of this nature, the account of particular cases is yet more lacking in exactness; for they do not fall under any art or set of precepts, but the agents themselves must in each case consider what is appropriate to the occasion, as happens also in the art of medicine or of navigation.

But though our present account is of this nature we must give what help we can. First, then, let us consider this, that it is the nature of such things to be destroyed by defect and excess, as we see in the case of strength and of health (for to gain light on things imperceptible we must use the evidence of sensible things); both excessive and defective exercise destroys the strength, and similarly drink or food which is above or below a certain amount destroys the health, while that which is proportionate both produces and increases and preserves it. So too is it, then, in the case of temperance and courage and the other excellences. For the man who flies from and fears everything and does not stand his ground against anything becomes a coward, and the man who fears nothing at all but goes to meet every danger becomes rash; and similarly the man who indulges in every pleasure and abstains from none becomes self-indulgent, while the man who shuns every pleasure, as boors do, becomes in a way insensible; temperance and courage, then, are destroyed by excess and defect, and preserved by the mean.

But not only are the sources and causes of their origination and growth the same as those of their destruction, but also the sphere of their activity will be the same; for this is also true of the things which are more evident to sense, e.g. of strength; it is produced by taking much food and undergoing much exertion, and it is the strong man that will be most able to do these things. So too is it with the excellences; by abstaining from pleasures we become temperate, and it is when we have become so that we are most able to abstain from them; and similarly too in the case of courage; for by being habituated to despise things that are terrible and to stand our ground against them we become brave, and it is when we have become so that we shall be most able to stand our ground against them.

3 · We must take as a sign of states the pleasure or pain that supervenes on acts; for the man who abstains from bodily pleasures and delights in this very fact is temperate, while the man who is annoyed at it is self-indulgent, and he who stands his ground against things that are terrible and delights in this or at least is not pained is brave, while the man who is pained is a coward. For moral excellence is concerned with pleasures and pains; it is on account of pleasure that we do bad things, and on account of pain that we abstain from noble ones. Hence we ought to have been brought up in a particular way from our very youth, as Plato says, so as both to delight in and to be pained by the things that we ought; for this is the right education.

Again, if the excellences are concerned with actions and passions, and every passion and every action is accompanied by pleasure and pain, for this reason also excellence will be concerned with pleasures and pains. This is indicated also by the fact that punishment is inflicted by these means; for it is a kind of cure, and it is the nature of cures to be effected by contraries.

Again, as we said but lately, every state of soul has a nature relative to and concerned with the kind of things by which it tends to be made worse or better; but 20 it is by reason of pleasures and pains that men become bad, by pursuing and avoiding these—either the pleasures and pains they ought not or when they ought not or as they ought not, or by going wrong in one of the other similar ways that reason can distinguish. Hence men even define the excellences as certain states of impassivity and rest; not well, however, because they speak absolutely, and do not 25 say 'as one ought' and 'as one ought not' and 'when one ought or ought not', and the other things that may be added. We assume, then, that this kind of excellence tends to do what is best with regard to pleasures and pains, and badness does the contrary.

The following facts also may show us that they are concerned with these same things. There being three objects of choice and three of avoidance, the noble, the 30 advantageous, the pleasant, and their contraries, the base, the injurious, the painful, about all of these the good man tends to go right and the bad man to go wrong, and especially about pleasure; for this is common to the animals, and also it accompanies all objects of choice; for even the noble and the advantageous appear pleasant. 1105ª1

Again, it has grown up with us all from our infancy; this is why it is difficult to rub off this passion, engrained as it is in our life. And we measure even our actions, some of us more and others less, by pleasure and pain. For this reason, then, our 5 whole inquiry must be about these; for to feel delight and pain rightly or wrongly has no small effect on our actions.

Again, it is harder to fight with pleasure than with anger, to use Heraclitus' phrase, but both art and excellence are always concerned with what is harder; for even the good is better when it is harder. Therefore for this reason also the whole 10 concern both of excellence and of political science is with pleasures and pains; for the man who uses these well will be good, he who uses them badly bad.

That excellence, then, is concerned with pleasures and pains, and that by the acts from which it arises it is both increased and, if they are done differently, 15 destroyed, and that the acts from which it arose are those in which it actualizes itself—let this be taken as said.

4 · The question might be asked, what we mean by saying that we must become just by doing just acts, and temperate by doing temperate acts; for if men do just and temperate acts, they are already just and temperate, exactly as, if they do 20 what is grammatical or musical they are proficient in grammar and music.

Or is this not true even of the arts? It is possible to do something grammatical either by chance or under the guidance of another. A man will be proficient in grammar, then, only when he has both done something grammatical and done it grammatically; and this means doing it in accordance with the grammatical 25 knowledge in himself.

Again, the case of the arts and that of the excellences are not similar; for the products of the arts have their goodness in themselves, so that it is enough that they

should have a certain character, but if the acts that are in accordance with the excellences have themselves a certain character it does not follow that they are done
30 justly or temperately. The agent also must be in a certain condition when he does them; in the first place he must have knowledge, secondly he must choose the acts, and choose them for their own sakes, and thirdly his action must proceed from a
1105ᵇ1 firm and unchangeable character. These are not reckoned in as conditions of the possession of the arts, except the bare knowledge; but as a condition of the possession of the excellences, knowledge has little or no weight, while the other conditions count not for a little but for everything, i.e. the very conditions which result from often doing just and temperate acts.

5   Actions, then, are called just and temperate when they are such as the just or the temperate man would do; but it is not the man who does these that is just and temperate, but the man who also does them *as* just and temperate men do them. It is well said, then, that it is by doing just acts that the just man is produced, and by
10 doing temperate acts the temperate man; without doing these no one would have even a prospect of becoming good.

But most people do not do these, but take refuge in theory and think they are being philosophers and will become good in this way, behaving somewhat like
15 patients who listen attentively to their doctors, but do none of the things they are ordered to do. As the latter will not be made well in body by such a course of treatment, the former will not be made well in soul by such a course of philosophy.

5 · Next we must consider what excellence is. Since things that are found in
20 the soul are of three kinds—passions, faculties, states—excellence must be one of these. By passions I mean appetite, anger, fear, confidence, envy, joy, love, hatred, longing, emulation, pity, and in general the feelings that are accompanied by pleasure or pain; by faculties the things in virtue of which we are said to be capable
25 of feeling these, e.g. of becoming angry or being pained or feeling pity; by states the things in virtue of which we stand well or badly with reference to the passions, e.g. with reference to anger we stand badly if we feel it violently or too weakly, and well if we feel it moderately; and similarly with reference to the other passions.

Now neither the excellences nor the vices are *passions*, because we are not
30 called good or bad on the ground of our passions, but are so called on the ground of our excellences and our vices, and because we are neither praised nor blamed for our passions (for the man who feels fear or anger is not praised, nor is the man who
1106ª1 simply feels anger blamed, but the man who feels it in a certain way), but for our excellences and our vices we *are* praised or blamed.

Again, we feel anger and fear without choice, but the excellences are choices or involve choice. Further, in respect of the passions we are said to be moved, but in
5 respect of the excellences and the vices we are said not to be moved but to be disposed in a particular way.

For these reasons also they are not *faculties*; for we are neither called good nor bad, nor praised nor blamed, for the simple capacity of feeling the passions; again, we have the faculties by nature, but we are not made good or bad by nature; we have
10 spoken of this before.

If, then, the excellences are neither passions nor faculties, all that remains is that they should be *states*.

Thus we have stated what excellence is in respect of its genus.

6 · We must, however, not only describe it as a state, but also say what sort of state it is. We may remark, then, that every excellence both brings into good condition the thing of which it is the excellence and makes the work of that thing be done well; e.g. the excellence of the eye makes both the eye and its work good; for it is by the excellence of the eye that we see well. Similarly the excellence of the horse makes a horse both good in itself and good at running and at carrying its rider and at awaiting the attack of the enemy. Therefore, if this is true in every case, the excellence of man also will be the state which makes a man good and which makes him do his own work well.

How this is to happen we have stated already, but it will be made plain also by the following consideration of the nature of excellence. In everything that is continuous and divisible it is possible to take more, less, or an equal amount, and that either in terms of the thing itself or relatively to us; and the equal is an intermediate between excess and defect. By the intermediate in the object I mean that which is equidistant from each of the extremes, which is one and the same for all men; by the intermediate relatively to us that which is neither too much nor too little—and this is not one, nor the same for all. For instance, if ten is many and two is few, six is intermediate, taken in terms of the object; for it exceeds and is exceeded by an equal amount; this is intermediate according to arithmetical proportion. But the intermediate relatively to us is not to be taken so; if ten pounds are too much for a particular person to eat and two too little, it does not follow that the trainer will order six pounds; for this also is perhaps too much for the person who is to take it, or too little—too little for Milo, too much for the beginner in athletic exercises. The same is true of running and wrestling. Thus a master of any art avoids excess and defect, but seeks the intermediate and chooses this—the intermediate not in the object but relatively to us.

If it is thus, then, that every art does its work well—by looking to the intermediate and judging its works by this standard (so that we often say of good works of the art that it is not possible either to take away or to add anything, implying that excess and defect destroy the goodness of works of art, while the mean preserves it; and good artists, as we say, look to this in their work), and if, further, excellence is more exact and better than any art, as nature also is, then it must have the quality of aiming at the intermediate. I mean moral excellence; for it is this that is concerned with passions and actions, and in these there is excess, defect, and the intermediate. For instance, both fear and confidence and appetite and anger and pity and in general pleasure and pain may be felt both too much and too little, and in both cases not well; but to feel them at the right times, with reference to the right objects, towards the right people, with the right aim, and in the right way, is what is both intermediate and best, and this is characteristic of excellence. Similarly with regard to actions also there is excess, defect, and the intermediate. Now excellence is concerned with passions and actions, in which excess is a form of failure, and so is defect, while the intermediate is praised and is a form of success; and both these things are characteristics of excellence. Therefore excellence is a kind of mean, since it aims at what is intermediate.

Again, it is possible to fail in many ways (for evil belongs to the class of the unlimited, as the Pythagoreans conjectured, and good to that of the limited), while to succeed is possible only in one way (for which reason one is easy and the other difficult—to miss the mark easy, to hit it difficult); for these reasons also, then, excess and defect are characteristic of vice, and the mean of excellence;

For men are good in but one way, but bad in many.

Excellence, then, is a state concerned with choice, lying in a mean relative to us, this being determined by reason and in the way in[10] which the man of practical wisdom would determine it. Now it is a mean between two vices, that which depends on excess and that which depends on defect; and again it is a mean because the vices respectively fall short of or exceed what is right in both passions and actions, while excellence both finds and chooses that which is intermediate. Hence in respect of its substance and the account which states its essence is a mean, with regard to what is best and right it is an extreme.

But not every action nor every passion admits of a mean; for some have names that already imply badness, e.g. spite, shamelessness, envy, and in the case of actions adultery, theft, murder; for all of these and suchlike things imply by their names that they are themselves bad, and not the excesses or deficiencies of them. It is not possible, then, ever to be right with regard to them; one must always be wrong. Nor does goodness or badness with regard to such things depend on committing adultery with the right woman, at the right time, and in the right way, but simply to do any of them is to go wrong. It would be equally absurd, then, to expect that in unjust, cowardly, and self-indulgent action there should be a mean, an excess, and a deficiency; for at that rate there would be a mean of excess and of deficiency, an excess of excess, and a deficiency of deficiency. But as there is no excess and deficiency of temperance and courage because what is intermediate is in a sense an extreme, so too of the actions we have mentioned there is no mean nor any excess and deficiency, but however they are done they are wrong; for in general there is neither a mean of excess and deficiency, nor excess and deficiency of a mean.

7 · We must, however, not only make this general statement, but also apply it to the individual facts. For among statements about conduct those which are general apply more widely, but those which are particular are more true, since conduct has to do with individual cases, and our statements must harmonize with the facts in these cases. We may take these cases from the diagram. With regard to feelings of fear and confidence courage is the mean; of the people who exceed, he who exceeds in fearlessness has no name (many of the states have no name), while the man who exceeds in confidence is rash, and he who exceeds in fear and falls short in confidence is a coward. With regard to pleasures and pains—not all of them, and not so much with regard to the pains—the mean is temperance, the

---

[10]Reading ὡς ἄν.

excess self-indulgence. Persons deficient with regard to the pleasures are not often found; hence such persons also have received no name. But let us call them 'insensible'.

With regard to giving and taking of money the mean is liberality, the excess and the defect prodigality and meanness. They exceed and fall short in contrary ways to one another:[11] the prodigal exceeds in spending and falls short in taking, while the mean man exceeds in taking and falls short in spending. (At present we are giving a mere outline or summary, and are satisfied with this; later these states will be more exactly determined.) With regard to money there are also other dispositions—a mean, magnificence (for the magnificent man differs from the liberal man; the former deals with large sums, the latter with small ones), an excess, tastelessness and vulgarity, and a deficiency, niggardliness; these differ from the states opposed to liberality, and the mode of their difference will be stated later.

With regard to honour and dishonour the mean is proper pride, the excess is known as a sort of empty vanity, and the deficiency is undue humility; and as we said liberality was related to magnificence, differing from it by dealing with small sums, so there is a state similarly related to proper pride, being concerned with small honours while that is concerned with great. For it is possible to desire small honours[12] as one ought, and more than one ought, and less, and the man who exceeds in his desires is called ambitious, the man who falls short unambitious, while the intermediate person has no name. The dispositions also are nameless, except that that of the ambitious man is called ambition. Hence the people who are at the extremes lay claim to the middle place; and we ourselves sometimes call the intermediate person ambitious and sometimes unambitious, and sometimes praise the ambitious man and sometimes the unambitious. The reason of our doing this will be stated in what follows; but now let us speak of the remaining states according to the method which has been indicated.

With regard to anger also there is an excess, a deficiency, and a mean. Although they can scarcely be said to have names, yet since we call the intermediate person good-tempered let us call the mean good temper; of the persons at the extremes let the one who exceeds be called irascible, and his vice irascibility, and the man who falls short an inirascible sort of person, and the deficiency inirascibility.

There are also three other means, which have a certain likeness to one another, but differ from one another: for they are all concerned with intercourse in words and actions, but differ in that one is concerned with truth in this sphere, the other two with pleasantness; and of this one kind is exhibited in giving amusement, the other in all the circumstances of life. We must therefore speak of these too, that we may the better see that in all things the mean is praiseworthy, and the extremes neither praiseworthy nor right, but worthy of blame. Now most of these states also have no names, but we must try, as in the other cases, to invent names ourselves so that we may be clear and easy to follow. With regard to truth, then, the intermediate is a

10

15

20

25

30

1108ᵃ1

5

10

15

---

[11] Reading ἐναντίως δὲ αὐτοῖς.
[12] Reading μικρᾶς τιμῆς.

20   truthful sort of person and the mean may be called truthfulness, while the pretence which exaggerates is boastfulness and the person characterized by it a boaster, and that which understates is mock modesty and the person characterized by it mock-modest. With regard to pleasantness in the giving of amusement the intermediate person is ready-witted and the disposition ready wit, the excess is
25   buffoonery and the person characterized by it a buffoon, while the man who falls short is a sort of boor and his state is boorishness. With regard to the remaining kind of pleasantness, that which is exhibited in life in general, the man who is pleasant in the right way is friendly and the mean is friendliness, while the man who exceeds is an obsequious person if he has no end in view, a flatterer if he is aiming at his own advantage, and the man who falls short and is unpleasant in all circumstances is a
30   quarrelsome and surly sort of person.

There are also means in the passions and concerned with the passions; since shame is not an excellence, and yet praise is extended to the modest man. For even in these matters one man is said to be intermediate, and another to exceed, as for instance the bashful man who is ashamed of everything; while he who falls short or is not ashamed of anything at all is shameless, and the intermediate person is
1108ᵇ1   modest. Righteous indignation is a mean between envy and spite, and these states are concerned with the pain and pleasure that are felt at the fortunes of our neighbours; the man who is characterized by righteous indignation is pained at undeserved good fortune, the envious man, going beyond him, is pained at all good
5   fortune, and the spiteful man falls so far short of being pained that he even rejoices. But these states there will be an opportunity of describing elsewhere; with regard to justice, since it has not one simple meaning, we shall, after describing the other states, distinguish its two kinds and say how each of them is a mean; and similarly
10   we shall treat also of the rational excellences.

8 · There are three kinds of disposition, then, two of them vices, involving excess and deficiency and one an excellence, viz. the mean, and all are in a sense opposed to all; for the extreme states are contrary both to the intermediate state and
15   to each other, and the intermediate to the extremes; as the equal is greater relatively to the less, less relatively to the greater, so the middle states are excessive relatively to the deficiencies, deficient relatively to the excesses, both in passions and in actions. For the brave man appears rash relatively to the coward, and cowardly
20   relatively to the rash man; and similarly the temperate man appears self-indulgent relatively to the insensible man, insensible relatively to the self-indulgent, and the liberal man prodigal relatively to the mean man, mean relatively to the prodigal. Hence also the people at the extremes push the intermediate man each over to the
25   other, and the brave man is called rash by the coward, cowardly by the rash man, and correspondingly in the other cases.

These states being thus opposed to one another, the greatest contrariety is that of the extremes to each other, rather than to the intermediate; for these are further from each other than from the intermediate, as the great is further from the small
30   and the small from the great than both are from the equal. Again, to the intermediate some extremes show a certain likeness, as that of rashness to courage

and that of prodigality to liberality; but the extremes show the greatest unlikeness to each other; now contraries are defined as the things that are furthest from each other, so that things that are further apart are more contrary.

To the mean in some cases the deficiency, in some the excess is more opposed; 1109ª1 e.g. it is not rashness, which is an excess, but cowardice, which is a deficiency, that is more opposed to courage, and not insensibility, which is a deficiency, but self-indulgence, which is an excess, that is more opposed to temperance. This happens from two reasons, one being drawn from the thing itself; for because one 5 extreme is nearer and liker to the intermediate, we oppose not this but rather its contrary to the intermediate. E.g., since rashness is thought liker and nearer to courage, and cowardice more unlike, we oppose rather the latter to courage; for 10 things that are further from the intermediate are thought more contrary to it. This, then, is one cause, drawn from the thing itself; another is drawn from ourselves; for the things to which we ourselves more naturally tend seem more contrary to the intermediate. For instance, we ourselves tend more naturally to pleasures, and 15 hence are more easily carried away towards self-indulgence than towards propriety. We describe as contrary to the mean, then, the states into which we are more inclined to lapse; and therefore self-indulgence, which is an excess, is the more contrary to temperance.

9 · That moral excellence is a mean, then, and in what sense it is so, and that 20 it is a mean between two vices, the one involving excess, the other deficiency, and that it is such because its character is to aim at what is intermediate in passions and in actions, has been sufficiently stated. Hence also it is no easy task to be good. For in everything it is no easy task to find the middle, e.g. to find the middle of a circle is 25 not for every one but for him who knows; so, too, any one can get angry—that is easy—or give or spend money; but to do this to the right person, to the right extent, at the right time, with the right aim, and in the right way, *that* is not for every one, nor is it easy; that is why goodness is both rare and laudable and noble.

Hence he who aims at the intermediate must first depart from what is the more 30 contrary to it, as Calypso advises—

Hold the ship out beyond that surf and spray.[13]

For of the extremes one is more erroneous, one less so; therefore, since to hit the mean is hard in the extreme, we must as a second best, as people say, take the least of the evils; and this be done best in the way we describe. 1109ᵇ1

But we must consider the things towards which we ourselves also are easily carried away; for some of us tend to one thing, some to another; and this will be recognizable from the pleasure and the pain we feel. We must drag ourselves away to the contrary extreme; for we shall get into the intermediate state by drawing well 5 away from error, as people do in straightening sticks that are bent.

Now in everything the pleasant or pleasure is most to be guarded against; for we do not judge it impartially. We ought, then, to feel towards pleasure as the elders

---

[13]*Odyssey* XII 219.

10   of the people felt towards Helen, and in all circumstances repeat their saying; for if
we dismiss pleasure thus we are less likely to go astray. It is by doing this, then, (to
sum the matter up) that we shall best be able to hit the mean.

But this is no doubt difficult, and especially in individual cases; for it is not
15   easy to determine both how and with whom and on what provocation and how long
one should be angry; for we too sometimes praise those who fall short and call them
good-tempered, but sometimes we praise those who get angry and call them manly.
The man, however who deviates little from goodness is not blamed, whether he do so
in the direction of the more or of the less, but only the man who deviates more
20   widely; for *he* does not fail to be noticed. But up to what point and to what extent a
man must deviate before he becomes blameworthy it is not easy to determine by
reasoning, any more than anything else that is perceived by the senses; such things
depend on particular facts, and the decision rests with perception. So much, then,
makes it plain that the intermediate state is in all things to be praised, but that we
25   must incline sometimes towards the excess, sometimes towards the deficiency; for so
shall we most easily hit the mean and what is right.

BOOK III

30   1 · Since excellence is concerned with passions and actions, and on voluntary
passions and actions praise and blame are bestowed, on those that are involuntary
forgiveness, and sometimes also pity, to distinguish the voluntary and the involuntary is presumably necessary for those who are studying excellence and useful also
for legislators with a view to the assigning both of honours and of punishments.

Those things, then, are thought involuntary, which take place under compul-
1110ᵃ1   sion or owing to ignorance; and that is compulsory of which the moving principle is
outside, being a principle in which nothing is contributed by the person who acts or
is acted upon, e.g. if he were to be carried somewhere by a wind, or by men who had
him in their power.

But with regard to the things that are done from fear of greater evils or for
5   some noble object (e.g. if a tyrant were to order one to do something base, having
one's parents and children in his power, and if one did the action they were to be
saved, but otherwise would be put to death), it may be debated whether such actions
are involuntary or voluntary. Something of the sort happens also with regard to the
throwing of goods overboard in a storm; for in the abstract no one throws goods
10   away voluntarily, but on condition of its securing the safety of himself and his crew
any sensible man does so. Such actions, then, are mixed, but are more like voluntary
actions; for they are worthy of choice at the time when they are done, and the end of
an action is relative to the occasion. Both the terms, then, 'voluntary' and
'involuntary', must be used with reference to the moment of action. Now the man
15   acts voluntarily; for the principle that moves the instrumental parts of the body in
such actions is in him, and the things of which the moving principle is in a man
himself are in his power to do or not to do. Such actions, therefore, are voluntary,

but in the abstract perhaps involuntary; for no one would choose any such act in itself.

For such actions men are sometimes even praised, when they endure something base or painful in return for great and noble objects gained; in the opposite case they are blamed, since to endure the greatest indignities for no noble end or for a trifling end is the mark of an inferior person. On some actions praise indeed is not bestowed, but forgiveness is, when one does what he ought not under pressure which overstrains human nature and which no one could withstand. But some acts, perhaps, we cannot be forced to do, but ought rather to face death after the most fearful sufferings; for the things that forced Euripides' Alcmaeon to slay his mother seem absurd. It is difficult sometimes to determine what should be chosen at what cost, and what should be endured in return for what gain, and yet more difficult to abide by our decisions; for as a rule what is expected is painful, and what we are forced to do is base, whence praise and blame are bestowed on those who have been compelled or have not.

What sort of acts, then, should be called compulsory? We answer that without qualification actions are so when the cause is in the external circumstances and the agent contributes nothing. But the things that in themselves are involuntary, but now and in return for these gains are worthy of choice, and whose moving principle is in the agent, are in themselves involuntary, but now and in return for these gains voluntary. They are more like voluntary acts; for actions are in the class of particulars, and the particular acts here are voluntary. What sort of things are to be chosen in return for what it is not easy to state; for there are many differences in the particular cases.

But if some one were to say that pleasant and noble objects have a compelling power, forcing us from without, all acts would be for him compulsory; for it is for these objects that all men do everything they do. And those who act under compulsion and unwillingly act with pain, but those who do acts for their pleasantness and nobility do them with pleasure; it is absurd to make external circumstances responsible, and not oneself, as being easily caught by such attractions, and to make oneself responsible for noble acts but the pleasant objects responsible for base acts. The compulsory, then, seems to be that whose moving principle is outside, the person compelled contributing nothing.

Everything that is done by reason of ignorance is *non*-voluntary; it is only what produces pain and regret that is *in*voluntary. For the man who has done something owing to ignorance, and feels not the least vexation at his action, has not acted voluntarily, since he did not know what he was doing, nor yet involuntarily, since he is not pained. Of people, then, who act by reason of ignorance he who regrets is thought an involuntary agent, and the man who does not regret may, since he is different, be called a non-voluntary agent; for, since he differs from the other, it is better that he should have a name of his own.

Acting by reason of ignorance seems also to be different from acting *in* ignorance; for the man who is drunk or in a rage is thought to act as a result not of ignorance but of one of the causes mentioned, yet not knowingly but in ignorance.

Now every wicked man is ignorant of what he ought to do and what he ought to

abstain from, and error of this kind makes men unjust and in general bad; but the
30 term 'involuntary' tends to be used not if a man is ignorant of what is to his advantage—for it is not ignorance in choice that makes action involuntary (it makes men wicked), nor ignorance of the universal (for *that* men are *blamed*), but ignorance of particular circumstances of the action and the objects with which it is
1111ᵃ1 concerned. For it is on these that both pity and forgiveness depend, since the person who is ignorant of any of these acts involuntarily.

Perhaps it is just as well, therefore, to determine their nature and number. A man may be ignorant, then, of who he is, what he is doing, what or whom he is acting on, and sometimes also what (e.g. what instrument) he is doing it with, and to
5 what end (e.g. for safety), and how he is doing it (e.g. whether gently or violently). Now of all of these no one could be ignorant unless he were mad, and evidently also he could not be ignorant of the agent; for how could he not know himself? But of what he is doing a man might be ignorant, as for instance people say 'it slipped out of their mouths as they were speaking',¹⁴ or 'they did not know it was a secret', as
10 Aeschylus said of the mysteries, or a man might say he 'let it go off when he merely wanted to show its working', as the man did with the catapult. Again, one might think one's son was an enemy, as Merope did, or that a pointed spear had a button on it, or that a stone was pumice-stone; or one might give a man a draught to save him, and really kill him; or one might want to touch a man, as people do in sparring,
15 and really strike him. The ignorance may relate, then, to any of these things, i.e. of the circumstances of the action, and the man who was ignorant of any of these is thought to have acted involuntarily, and especially if he was ignorant on the most important points; and these are thought to be what¹⁵ he is doing and with what aim.
20 Further,¹⁶ the doing of an act that is called involuntary in virtue of ignorance of this sort must be painful and involve regret.

Since that which is done under compulsion or by reason of ignorance is involuntary, the voluntary would seem to be that of which the moving principle is in the agent himself, he being aware of the particular circumstances of the action.
25 Presumably acts done by reason of anger or appetite are not rightly called involuntary. For in the first place, on that showing none of the other animals will act voluntarily, nor will children; and secondly, is it meant that we do not do voluntarily *any* of the acts that are due to appetite or anger, or that we do the noble acts voluntarily and the base acts involuntarily? Is not this absurd, when one and the same thing is the cause? But it would surely be odd to describe as involuntary the
30 things one ought to desire; and we ought both to be angry at certain things and to have an appetite for certain things, e.g. for health and for learning. Also what is involuntary is thought to be painful, but what is in accordance with appetite is thought to be pleasant. Again, what is the difference in respect of involuntariness between errors committed upon calculation and those committed in anger? Both
1111ᵇ1 are to be avoided, but the irrational passions are thought not less human than reason

¹⁴Reading λέγοντας . . . αὐτούς.
¹⁵Reading δοκεῖ ὃ καὶ οὗ ἕνεκα.
¹⁶Reading δέ.

is, and therefore also the actions which proceed from anger or appetite are the man's actions. It would be odd, then, to treat them as involuntary.

2 · Both the voluntary and the involuntary having been delimited, we must next discuss choice; for it is thought to be most closely bound up with excellence and   5
to discriminate characters better than actions do.

Choice, then, seems to be voluntary, but not the same thing as the voluntary; the latter extends more widely. For both children and the other animals share in voluntary action, but not in choice, and acts done on the spur of the moment we describe as voluntary, but not as chosen.   10

Those who say it is appetite or anger or wish or a kind of opinion do not seem to be right. For choice is not common to irrational creatures as well, but appetite and anger are. Again, the incontinent man acts with appetite, but not with choice; while the continent man on the contrary acts with choice, but not with appetite. Again,   15
appetite is contrary to choice, but not appetite to appetite. Again, appetite relates to the pleasant and the painful, choice neither to the painful nor to the pleasant.

Still less is it anger; for acts due to anger are thought to be less than any other objects of choice.

But neither is it wish, though it seems near to it; for choice cannot relate to   20
impossibles, and if any one said he chose them he would be thought silly; but there may be a wish even for impossibles, e.g. for immortality. And wish may relate to things that could in no way be brought about by one's own efforts, e.g. that a particular actor or athlete should win in a competition; but no one chooses such things, but only the things that he thinks could be brought about by his own efforts.   25
Again, wish relates rather to the end, choice to what contributes to the end; for instance, we wish to be healthy, but we choose the acts which will make us healthy, and we wish to be happy and say we do, but we cannot well say we choose to be so; for, in general, choice seems to relate to the things that are in our own power.   30

For this reason, too, it cannot be opinion; for opinion is thought to relate to all kinds of things, no less to eternal things and impossible things than to things in our own power; and it is distinguished by its falsity or truth, not by its badness or goodness, while choice is distinguished rather by these.

Now with opinion in general perhaps no one really says it is identical. But it is   1112ᵃ1
not identical even with any kind of opinion; for by choosing what is good or bad we are men of a certain character, which we are not by holding certain opinions. And we choose to get or avoid something good or bad, but we have opinions about what a thing is or whom it is good for or how it is good for him; we can hardly be said to opine to get or avoid anything. And choice is praised for being related to the right   5
object rather than for being rightly related to it, opinion for being truly related to its object. And we choose what we best know to be good, but we opine what we do not know at all; and it is not the same people that are thought to make the best choices and to have the best opinions, but some are thought to have fairly good opinions, but   10
by reason of vice to choose what they should not. If opinion precedes choice or

accompanies it, that makes no difference; for it is not this that we are considering, but whether it is *identical* with some kind of opinion.

What, then, or what kind of thing is it, since it is none of the things we have mentioned? It seems to be voluntary, but not all that is voluntary to be an object of
15   choice. Is it, then, what has been decided on by previous deliberation? For choice involves reason and thought. Even the name seems to suggest that it is what is chosen before other things.[17]

3 · Do we deliberate about everything, and is everything a possible subject of deliberation, or is deliberation impossible about some things? We ought presum-
20   ably to call not what a fool or a madman would deliberate about, but what a sensible man would deliberate about, a subject of deliberation. Now about eternal things no one deliberates, e.g. about the universe or the incommensurability of the diagonal and the side of a square. But no more do we deliberate about the things that involve movement but always happen in the same way, whether of necessity or by nature or
25   from any other cause, e.g. the solstices and the risings of the stars; nor about things that happen now in one way, now in another, e.g. droughts and rains; nor about chance events, like the finding of treasure. But we do not deliberate even about all human affairs; for instance, no Spartan deliberates about the best constitution for
30   the Scythians. For none of these things can be brought about by our own efforts.

We deliberate about things that are in our power and can be done; and these are in fact what is left. For nature, necessity, and chance are thought to be causes, and also thought and everything that depends on man. Now every class of men deliberates about the things that can be done by their own efforts. And in the case of
1112^b1   exact and self-contained sciences there is no deliberation, e.g. about the letters of the alphabet (for we have no doubt how they should be written); but the things that are brought about by our own efforts, but not always in the same way, are the things about which we deliberate, e.g. questions of medical treatment or of money-making.
5   And we do so more in the case of the art of navigation than in that of gymnastics, inasmuch as it has been less exactly worked out, and again about other things in the same ratio, and more also in the case of the arts than in that of the sciences; for we have more doubt about the former. Deliberation is concerned with things that happen in a certain way for the most part, but in which the event is obscure, and
10   with things in which it is indeterminate. We call in others to aid us in deliberation on important questions, distrusting ourselves as not being equal to deciding.

We deliberate not about ends but about what contributes to ends. For a doctor does not deliberate whether he shall heal, nor an orator whether he shall convince, nor a statesman whether he shall produce law and order, nor does any one else
15   deliberate about his end. Having set the end they consider how and by what means it is to be attained; and if it seems to be produced by several means they consider by which it is most easily and best produced, while if it is achieved by one only they consider how it will be achieved by this and by what means *this* will be achieved, till they come to the first cause, which in the order of discovery is last. For the person

---

[17]'προαίρεσις' connected with 'πρὸ ἐτέρων αἱρετόν'.

who deliberates seems to inquire and analyse in the way described as though he   20
were analysing a geometrical construction (not all inquiry appears to be deliberation—for instance mathematical inquiries—but all deliberation is inquiry), and
what is last in the order of analysis seems to be first in the order of becoming. And if
we come on an impossibility, we give up the search, e.g. if we need money and this   25
cannot be got; but if a thing appears possible we try to do it. By 'possible' things I
mean things that might be brought about by our own efforts; and these in a sense
include things that can be brought about by the efforts of our friends, since the
moving principle is in ourselves. The subject of investigation is sometimes the
instruments, sometimes the use of them; and similarly in the other cases—
sometimes the means, sometimes the mode of using it or the means of bringing it   30
about. It seems, then, as has been said, that man is a moving principle of actions;
now deliberation is about the things to be done by the agent himself, and actions are
for the sake of things other than themselves. For the end cannot be a subject of
deliberation, but only what contributes to the ends; nor indeed can the particular
facts be a subject of it, as whether this is bread or has been baked as it should; for   1113ᵃ1
these are matters of perception. If we are to be always deliberating, we shall have to
go on to infinity.

The same thing is deliberated upon and is chosen, except that the object of
choice is already determinate, since it is that which has been decided upon as a
result of deliberation that is the object of choice. For every one ceases to inquire how   5
he is to act when he has brought the moving principle back to himself and to the
ruling part of himself; for this is what chooses. This is plain also from the ancient
constitutions, which Homer represented; for the kings announced their choices to
the people. The object of choice being one of the things in our own power which is   10
desired after deliberation, choice will be deliberate desire of things in our own
power; for when we have decided as a result of deliberation, we desire in accordance
with our deliberation.

We may take it, then, that we have described choice in outline, and stated the
nature of its objects and the fact that it is concerned with what contributes to the
ends.

4 · That *wish* is for the end has already been stated; some think it is for the   15
good, others for the apparent good. Now those who say that the good is the object of
wish must admit in consequence that that which the man who does not choose
aright wishes for is not an object of wish (for if it is to be so, it must also be good; but
it was, if it so happened, bad); while those who say the apparent good is the object of   20
wish must admit that there is no natural object of wish, but only what seems so to
each man. Now different things appear so to different people, and, if it so happens,
even contrary things.

If these consequences are unpleasing, are we to say that absolutely and in truth
the good is the object of wish, but for each person the apparent good; that that
which is in truth an object of wish is an object of wish to the good man, while any   25
chance thing may be so to the bad man, as in the case of bodies also the things that

are in truth wholesome are wholesome for bodies which are in good condition, while for those that are diseased other things are wholesome—or bitter or sweet or hot or 30 heavy, and so on; since the good man judges each class of things rightly, and in each the truth appears to him? For each state of character has its own ideas of the noble and the pleasant, and perhaps the good man differs from others most by seeing the truth in each class of things, being as it were the norm and measure of them. In most things the error seems to be due to pleasure; for it appears a good when it is not. We 1113ᵇ1 therefore choose the pleasant as a good, and avoid pain as an evil.

5 · The end, then, being what we wish for, the things contributing to the end what we deliberate about and choose, actions concerning the latter must be 5 according to choice and voluntary. Now the exercise of the excellences is concerned with these. Therefore excellence also is in our own power, and so too vice. For where it is in our power to act it is also in our power not to act, and *vice versa;* so that, if to act, where this is noble, is in our power, not to act, which will be base, will also be in 10 our power, and if not to act, where this is noble, is in our power, to act, which will be base, will also be in our power. Now if it is in our power to do noble or base acts, and likewise in our power not to do them, and this was what being good or bad meant, then it is in our power to be virtuous or vicious.

15 The saying that 'no one is voluntarily wicked nor involuntarily blessed' seems to be partly false and partly true; for no one is involuntarily blessed, but wickedness *is* voluntary. Or else we shall have to dispute what has just been said, at any rate, and deny that man is a moving principle or begetter of his actions as of children. But 20 if these facts are evident and we cannot refer actions to moving principles other than those in ourselves, the acts whose moving principles are in us must themselves also be in our power and voluntary.

Witness seems to be borne to this both by individuals in their private capacity and by legislators themselves; for these punish and take vengeance on those who do wicked acts (unless they have acted under compulsion or as a result of ignorance for 25 which they are not themselves responsible), while they honour those who do noble acts, as though they meant to encourage the latter and deter the former. But no one is encouraged to do the things that are neither in our power nor voluntary; it is assumed that there is no gain in being persuaded not to be hot or in pain or hungry or the like, since we shall experience these feelings none the less. Indeed, we punish 30 a man for his very ignorance, if he is thought responsible for the ignorance, as when penalties are doubled in the case of drunkenness; for the moving principle is in the man himself, since he had the power of not getting drunk and his getting drunk was the cause of his ignorance. And we punish those who are ignorant of anything in the 1114ᵃ1 laws that they ought to know and that is not difficult, and so too in the case of anything else that they are thought to be ignorant of through carelessness; we assume that it is in their power not to be ignorant, since they have the power of taking care.

But perhaps a man is the kind of man not to take care. Still they are themselves by their slack lives responsible for becoming men of that kind, and men are 5 themselves responsible for being unjust or self-indulgent, in that they cheat or spend their time in drinking bouts and the like; for it is activities exercised on particular objects that make the corresponding character. This is plain from the case of people training for any contest or action; they practise the activity the whole time. Now not to know that it is from the exercise of activities on particular objects that states of character are produced is the mark of a thoroughly senseless person. Again, it is 10 irrational to suppose that a man who acts unjustly does not wish to be unjust or a man who acts self-indulgently to be self-indulgent. But if without being ignorant a man does the things which will make him unjust, he will be unjust voluntarily. Yet it does not follow that if he wishes he will cease to be unjust and will be just. For neither does the man who is ill become well on those terms—although[18] he may, 15 perhaps, be ill voluntarily, through living incontinently and disobeying his doctors. In that case it was *then* open to him not to be ill, but not now, when he has thrown away his chance, just as when you have let a stone go it is too late to recover it; but yet it was in your power to throw it, since the moving principle was in you. So, too, to the unjust and to the self-indulgent man it was open at the beginning not to become 20 men of this kind, and so they are such voluntarily; but now that they have become so it is not possible for them not to be so.

But not only are the vices of the soul voluntary, but those of the body also for some men, whom we accordingly blame; while no one blames those who are ugly by nature, we blame those who are so owing to want of exercise and care. So it is, too, with respect to weakness and infirmity; no one would reproach a man blind from 25 birth or by disease or from a blow, but rather pity him, while every one would blame a man who was blind from alcoholism or some other form of self-indulgence. Of vices of the body, then, those in our own power are blamed, those not in our power are not. And if this be so, in the other cases also the vices that are blamed must be in 30 our own power.

Now some one may say that all men aim at the apparent good, but have no control over how things appear to him; but the end appears to each man in a form 1114^b1 answering to his character. We reply that if each man is somehow responsible for the state he is in, he will also be himself somehow responsible for how things appear; but if not, no one is responsible for his own evildoing, but everyone does evil acts through ignorance of the end, thinking that by these he will get what is best, and the 5 aiming at the end is not self-chosen but one must be born with an eye, as it were, by which to judge rightly and choose what is truly good, and he is well endowed by nature who is well endowed with this. For it is what is greatest and most noble, and what we cannot get or learn from another, but must have just such as it was when 10 given us at birth, and to be well and nobly endowed with this will be complete and true natural endowment. If this is true, then, how will excellence be more voluntary than vice? To both men alike, the good and the bad, the end appears and is fixed by nature or however it may be, and it is by referring everything else to this that men 15 do whatever they do.

Whether, then, it is not by nature that the end appears to each man such as it does appear, but something also depends on him, or the end is natural but because

[18]Reading καίτοι εἰ.

the good man does the rest voluntarily excellence is voluntary, vice also will be none
20   the less voluntary; for in the case of the bad man there is equally present that which
depends on himself in his actions even if not in his end. If, then, as is asserted, the
excellences are voluntary (for we are ourselves somehow part-causes of our states of
character, and it is by being persons of a certain kind that we assume the end to be
25   so and so), the vices also will be voluntary; for the same is true of them.

With regard to the excellences in *general* we have stated their genus in outline,
viz. that they are means and that they are states, and that they tend by their own
nature to the doing of the acts by which they are produced, and that they are in our
30   power and voluntary, and act as right reason prescribes. But actions and states are
not voluntary in the same way; for we are masters of our actions from the beginning
right to the end, if we know the particular facts, but though we control the
1115ᵃ1   beginning of our states the gradual progress is not obvious, any more than it is in
illnesses; because it was in our power, however, to act in this way or not in this way,
therefore the states are voluntary.

Let us take up the several excellences, however, and say which they are and
what sort of things they are concerned with and how they are concerned with them;
5   at the same time it will become plain how many they are. And first let us speak of
courage.

6 · That it is a mean with regard to fear and confidence has already been
made evident; and plainly the things we fear are terrible things, and these are, to
speak without qualification, evils; for which reason people even define fear as
10   expectation of evil. Now we fear all evils, e.g. disgrace, poverty, disease, friendless-
ness, death, but the brave man is not thought to be concerned with all; for to fear
some things is even right and noble, and it is base not to fear them—e.g. disgrace;
who fears this is good and modest, and he who does not is shameless. He is, however,
15   by some people called brave, by an extension of the word; for he has in him
something which is like the brave man, since the brave man also is a fearless person.
Poverty and disease we perhaps ought not to fear, nor in general the things that do
not proceed from vice and are not due to a man himself. But not even the man who is
fearless of these is brave. Yet we apply the word to him also in virtue of a similarity;
20   for some who in the dangers of war are cowards are liberal and are confident in face
of the loss of money. Nor is a man a coward if he fears insult to his wife and children
or envy or anything of the kind; nor brave if he is confident when he is about to be
flogged. With what sort of terrible things, then, is the brave man concerned? Surely
25   with the greatest; for no one is more likely than he to stand his ground against what
is dreadful. Now death is the most terrible of all things; for it is the end, and nothing
is thought to be any longer either good or bad for the dead. But the brave man would
not seem to be concerned even with death in *all* circumstances, e.g. at sea or in
disease. In what circumstances, then? Surely in the noblest. Now such deaths are
30   those in battle; for these take place in the greatest and noblest danger. And this
agrees with the ways in which honours are bestowed in city-states and at the courts
of monarchs. Properly, then, he will be called brave who is fearless in face of a noble
death, and of all emergencies that involve death; and the emergencies of war are in

the highest degree of this kind. Yet at sea also, and in disease, the brave man is fearless, but not in the same way as the seamen; for he has given up hope for safety, and is disliking the thought of death in this shape, while they are hopeful because of their experience. At the same time, we show courage in situations where there is the opportunity of showing prowess or where death is noble; but in these forms of death neither of these conditions is fulfilled.

7 . What is terrible is not the same for all men; but we say there are things terrible even beyond human strength. These, then, are terrible to every one—at least to every sensible man; but the terrible things that are *not* beyond human strength differ in magnitude and degree, and so too do the things that inspire confidence. Now the brave man is as dauntless as man may be. Therefore, while he will fear even the things that are not beyond human strength, he will fear them as he ought and as reason directs, and[19] he will face them for the sake of what is noble; for this is the end of excellence. But it is possible to fear these more, or less, and again to fear things that are not terrible as if they were. Of the faults that are committed one consists in fearing what one should not, another in fearing as we should not, another in fearing when we should not, and so on; and so too with respect to the things that inspire confidence. The man, then, who faces and who fears the right things and with the right aim, in the right way and at the right time, and who feels confidence under the corresponding conditions, is brave; for the brave man feels and acts according to the merits of the case and in whatever way reason directs. Now the end of every activity is conformity to the corresponding state. This is true, therefore, of the brave man as well as of others. But courage is noble.[20] Therefore the end also is noble; for each thing is defined by its end. Therefore it is for a noble end that the brave man endures and acts as courage directs.

Of those who go to excess he who exceeds in fearlessness has no name (we have said previously that many states have no names), but he would be a sort of madman or insensible person if he feared nothing, neither earthquakes nor the waves, as they say the Celts do not; while the man who exceeds in confidence about what really is terrible is rash. The rash man, however, is also thought to be boastful and only a pretender to courage; at all events, as the brave man *is* with regard to what is terrible, so the rash man wishes to *appear;* and so he imitates him in situations where he can. Hence also most of them are a mixture of rashness and cowardice; for, while in these situations they display confidence, they do not hold their ground against what is really terrible. The man who exceeds in fear is a coward; for he fears both what he ought not and as he ought not, and all the similar characterizations attach to him. He is lacking also in confidence; but he is more conspicuous for his excess of fear in painful situations. The coward, then, is a despairing sort of person; for he fears everything. The brave man, on the other hand, has the opposite disposition; for confidence is the mark of a hopeful disposition. The coward, the rash man, and the brave man, then, are concerned with the same objects but are differently disposed towards them; for the first two exceed and fall short, while the

---

[19]Reading ὡς ὁ λόγος, ὑπομενεῖ τε.
[20]Reading ἀνδρείῳ δή · ἡ δ' ἀνδρεία.

third holds the middle, which is the right, position; and rash men are precipitate, and wish for dangers beforehand but draw back when they are in them, while brave men are keen in the moment of action, but quiet beforehand.

As we have said, then, courage is a mean with respect to things that inspire confidence or fear, in the circumstances that have been stated; and it chooses or endures things because it is noble to do so, or because it is base not to do so. But to die to escape from poverty or love or anything painful is not the mark of a brave man, but rather of a coward; for it is softness to fly from what is troublesome, and such a man endures death not because it is noble but to fly from evil.

8 · Courage, then, is something of this sort, but the name is also applied to five other kinds. (1) First comes political courage; for this is most like true courage. Citizens seem to face dangers because of the penalties imposed by the laws and the reproaches they would otherwise incur, and because of the honours they win by such action; and therefore those peoples seem to be bravest among whom cowards are held in dishonour and brave men in honour. This is the kind of courage that Homer depicts, e.g. in Diomede and in Hector:

First will Polydamas be to heap reproach on me then;[21]

and

For Hector one day 'mid the Trojans shall utter his vaulting harangue:
"Afraid was Tydeides, and fled from my face,"[22]

This kind of courage is most like that which we described earlier, because it is due to excellence; for it is due to shame and to desire of a noble object (i.e. honour) and avoidance of disgrace, which is ignoble. One might rank in the same class even those who are compelled by their rulers; but they are inferior, inasmuch as they act not from shame but from fear, and to avoid not what is disgraceful but what is painful; for their masters compel them, as Hector does:

But if I shall spy any dastard that cowers far from the fight,
Vainly will such an one hope to escape from the dogs.[23]

And those who give them their posts, and beat them if they retreat, do the same, and so do those who draw them up with trenches or something of the sort behind them; all of these apply compulsion. But one ought to be brave not under compulsion but because it is noble to be so.

(2) Experience with regard to particular facts is also thought to be courage; this is indeed the reason why Socrates thought courage was knowledge. Other people exhibit this quality in other dangers, and soldiers exhibit it in the dangers of war; for there seem to be many empty alarms in war, of which these have had the most comprehensive experience; therefore they seem brave, because the others do not know the nature of the facts. Again, their experience makes them most capable

[21]*Iliad* XXII 100.
[22]*Iliad* VIII 148.
[23]See *Iliad* II 391; XV 348.

of doing without being done to, since they can use their arms and have the kind that   10
are likely to be best both for doing and for not being done to; therefore they fight
like armed men against unarmed or like trained athletes against amateurs; for in
such contests too it is not the bravest men that fight best, but those who are
strongest and have their bodies in the best condition. Soldiers turn cowards,   15
however, when the danger puts too great a strain on them and they are inferior in
numbers and equipment; for they are the first to fly, while citizen-forces die at their
posts, as in fact happened at the temple of Hermes. For to the latter flight is
disgraceful and death is preferable to safety on those terms; while the former from   20
the very beginning faced the danger on the assumption that they were stronger, and
when they know the facts they fly, fearing death more than disgrace; but the brave
man is not that sort of person.

(3) Passion also is sometimes reckoned as courage; those who act from passion,
like wild beasts rushing at those who have wounded them, are thought to be brave,   25
because brave men also are passionate; for passion above all things is eager to rush
on danger, and hence Homer's 'put strength into his passion' and 'aroused their
spirit and passion' and 'bitter spirit in his nostrils' and 'his blood boiled'.[24] For all
such expressions seem to indicate the stirring and onset of passion. Now brave men   30
act for the sake of the noble, but passion aids them; while wild beasts act under the
influence of pain; for they attack because they have been wounded or because they
are afraid, since if they are in a forest they do not come near one. Thus they are not
brave because, driven by pain and passion, they rush on danger without foreseeing   35
any of the perils, since at that rate even asses would be brave when they are hungry;
for blows will not drive them from their food; and lust also makes adulterers do   1117ª1
many daring things. [Those creatures are not brave, then, which are driven on to
danger by pain or passion.][25] The courage that is due to passion seems to be the most
natural, and to be courage if choice and aim be added.   5

Men, then, as well as beasts, suffer pain when they are angry, and are pleased
when they exact their revenge; those who fight for these reasons, however, are
pugnacious but not brave; for they do not act for the sake of the noble nor as reason
directs, but from feeling; they have, however, something akin to courage.

(4) Nor are sanguine people brave; for they are confident in danger only   10
because they have conquered often and against many foes. Yet they closely
resemble brave men, because both are confident; but brave men are confident for
the reasons stated earlier, while these are so because they think they are the
strongest and can suffer nothing. (Drunken men also behave in this way; they
become sanguine). When their adventures do not succeed, however, they run away;   15
but it was the mark of a brave man to face things that are, and seem, terrible for a
man, because it is noble to do so and disgraceful not to do so. Hence also it is
thought the mark of a braver man to be fearless and undisturbed in sudden alarms
than to be so in those that are foreseen; for it must have proceeded more from a state
of character, because less from preparation; for acts that are foreseen may be   20

[24]See *Iliad* V 470; XI 11; XVI 529; *Odyssey* XXIV 318.
[25]Excised in Bywater.

chosen by calculation and reason, but sudden actions in accordance with one's state of character.

(5) People who are ignorant also appear brave, and they are not far removed from those of a sanguine temper, but are inferior inasmuch as they have no self-reliance while these have. Hence also the sanguine hold their ground for a time; but those who have been deceived fly if they know or suspect that things are different as happened to the Argives when they fell in with the Spartans and took them for Sicyonians.

9 . We have, then, described the character both of brave men and of those who are thought to be brave.

Though courage is concerned with confidence and fear, it is not concerned with both alike, but more with the things that inspire fear; for he who is undisturbed in face of these and bears himself as he should towards these is more truly brave than the man who does so towards the things that inspire confidence. It is for facing what is painful, then, as has been said, that men are called brave. Hence also courage involves pain, and is justly praised; for it is harder to face what is painful than to abstain from what is pleasant. Yet the end which courage sets before it would seem to be pleasant, but to be concealed by the attending circumstances, as happens also in athletic contests; for the end at which boxers aim is pleasant—the crown and the honours—but the blows they take are distressing to flesh and blood, and painful, and so is their whole exertion; and because the blows and the exertions are many the end, which is but small, appears to have nothing pleasant in it. And so, if the case of courage is similar, death and wounds will be painful to the brave man and against his will, but he will face them because it is noble to do so or because it is base not to do so. And the more he is possessed of excellence in its entirety and the happier he is, the more he will be pained at the thought of death; for life is best worth living for such a man, and he is knowingly losing the greatest goods, and this is painful. But he is none the less brave, and perhaps all the more so, because he chooses noble deeds of war at that cost. It is not the case, then, with all the excellences that the exercise of them is pleasant, except in so far as it reaches its end. But it is quite possible that the best soldiers may be not men of this sort but those who are less brave but have no other good; for these are ready to face danger, and they sell their life for trifling gains.

So much, then, for courage; it is not difficult to grasp its nature in outline, at any rate, from what has been said.

10 . After courage let us speak of temperance; for these seem to be the excellences of the irrational parts. We have said that temperance is a mean with regard to pleasures (for it is less, and not in the same way, concerned with pains); self-indulgence also is manifested in the same sphere. Now, therefore, let us determine with what sort of pleasures they are concerned. We may assume the distinction between bodily pleasures and those of the soul, such as love of honour and love of learning; for the lover of each of these delights in that of which he is a

lover, the body being in no way affected, but rather the mind; but men who are concerned with such pleasures are called neither temperate nor self-indulgent. Nor, again, are those who are concerned with the other pleasures that are not bodily; for those who are fond of hearing and telling stories and who spend their days on anything that turns up are called gossips, but not self-indulgent, nor are those who are pained at the loss of money or of friends. 1118ᵃ1

Temperance must be concerned with bodily pleasures, but not all even of these; for those who delight in objects of vision, such as colours and shapes and painting, are called neither temperate nor self-indulgent; yet it would seem possible to delight 5 even in these either as one should or to excess or to a deficient degree.

And so too is it with objects of hearing; no one calls those who delight extravagantly in music or acting self-indulgent, nor those who do so as they ought temperate.

Nor do we apply these names to those who delight in odour, unless it be incidentally; we do not call those self-indulgent who delight in the odour of apples or 10 roses or incense, but rather those who delight in the odour of unguents or of dainty dishes; for self-indulgent people delight in these because these remind them of the objects of their appetite. And one may see even other people, when they are hungry, delighting in the smell of food; but to delight in this kind of thing is the mark of the 15 self-indulgent man; for these are objects of appetite to him.

Nor is there in animals other than man any pleasure connected with these senses except incidentally. For dogs do not delight in the scent of hares, but in the eating of them, but the scent told them the hares were there; nor does the lion delight in the lowing of the ox, but in eating it; but he perceived by the lowing that it 20 was near, and therefore appears to delight in the lowing; and similarly he does not delight because he sees 'a stag or a wild goat',²⁶ but because he is going to make a meal of it. Temperance and self-indulgence, however, are concerned with the kind of pleasures that the other animals share in, which therefore appear slavish and 25 brutish; these are touch and taste. But even of taste they appear to make little or no use; for the business of taste is the discriminating of flavours, which is done by wine-tasters and people who season dishes; but they hardly take pleasure in making these discriminations, or at least self-indulgent people do not, but in the actual 30 enjoyment, which in all cases comes through touch, both in the case of food and in that of drink and in that of sexual intercourse. This is why a certain gourmand prayed that his throat might become longer than a crane's, implying that it was the contact that he took pleasure in. Thus the sense with which self-indulgence is 1118ᵇ1 connected is the most widely shared of the senses; and self-indulgence would seem to be justly a matter of reproach, because it attaches to us not as men but as animals. To delight in such things, then, and to love them above all others, is brutish. For even of the pleasures of touch the most liberal have been eliminated, 5 e.g. those produced in the gymnasium by rubbing and by the consequent heat; for the contact characteristic of the self-indulgent man does not affect the whole body but only certain parts.

²⁶*Iliad* III 24.

11 · Of the appetites some seem to be common, others to be peculiar to individuals and acquired; e.g. the appetite for food is natural, since every one who is without it craves for food or drink, and sometimes for both, and for love also (as Homer says) if he is young and lusty; but not every one craves for this or that kind of nourishment or love, nor for the same things. Hence such craving appears to be our very own. Yet it has of course something natural about it; for different things are pleasant to different kinds of people, and some things are more pleasant to every one than chance objects. Now in the natural appetites few go wrong, and only in one direction, that of excess; for to eat or drink whatever offers itself till one is surfeited is to exceed the natural amount, since natural appetite is the replenishment of one's deficiency. Hence these people are called belly-gods, this implying that they fill their belly beyond what is right. It is people of entirely slavish character that become like this. But with regard to the pleasures peculiar to individuals many people go wrong and in many ways. For while the people who are fond of so and so are so called because they delight either in the wrong things, or more than most people do, or in the wrong way, the self-indulgent exceed in all three ways; they both delight in some things that they ought not to delight in (since they are hateful), and if one ought to delight in some of the things they delight in, they do so more than one ought and than most men do.

Plainly, then, excess with regard to pleasures is self-indulgence and is culpable; with regard to pains one is not, as in the case of courage, called temperate for facing them or self-indulgent for not doing so, but the self-indulgent man is so called because he is pained more than he ought at not getting pleasant things (even his pain being caused by pleasure), and the temperate man is so called because he is not pained at the absence of what is pleasant and at his abstinence from it.

The self-indulgent man, then, craves for all pleasant things or those that are most pleasant, and is led by his appetite to choose these at the cost of everything else; hence he is pained both when he fails to get them and when he is craving for them (for appetite involves pain); but it seems absurd to be pained for the sake of pleasure. People who fall short with regard to pleasures and delight in them less than they should are hardly found; for such insensibility is not human. Even the other animals distinguish different kinds of food and enjoy some and not others; and if there is any one who finds nothing pleasant and nothing more attractive than anything else, he must be something quite different from a man; this sort of person has not received a name because he hardly occurs. The temperate man occupies a middle position with regard to these objects. For he neither enjoys the things that the self-indulgent man enjoys most—but rather dislikes them—nor in general the things that he should not, nor anything of this sort to excess, nor does he feel pain or craving when they are absent, or does so only to a moderate degree, and not more than he should, nor when he should not, and so on; but the things that, being pleasant, make for health or for good condition, he will desire moderately and as he should, and also other pleasant things if they are not hindrances to these ends, or contrary to what is noble, or beyond his means. For he who neglects these conditions loves such pleasures more than they are worth, but the temperate man is not that sort of person, but the sort of person that right reason prescribes.

12 · Self-indulgence is more like a voluntary state than cowardice. For the former is actuated by pleasure, the latter by pain, of which the one is to be chosen and the other to be avoided; and pain upsets and destroys the nature of the person who feels it, while pleasure does nothing of the sort. Therefore self-indulgence is more voluntary. Hence also it is more a matter of reproach; for it is easier to become   25 accustomed to its objects, since there are many things of this sort in life, and the process of habituation to them is free from danger, while with terrible objects the reverse is the case. But cowardice would seem to be voluntary in a different degree from its particular manifestations; for it is itself painless, but in these we are upset by pain, so that we even throw down our arms and disgrace ourselves in other ways;   30 hence our acts are even thought to be done under compulsion. For the self-indulgent man, on the other hand, the particular acts are voluntary (for he does them with craving and desire), but the whole state is less so; for no one craves to be self-indulgent.

The name self-indulgence is applied also to childish faults; for they bear a certain resemblance to what we have been considering. Which is called after which,   1119ᵇ1 makes no difference to our present purpose; plainly, however, the later is called after the earlier. The transference of the name seems not a bad one; for that which desires what is base and which develops quickly ought to be kept in a chastened condition,[27] and these characteristics belong above all to appetite and to the child,   5 since children in fact live at the beck and call of appetite, and it is in them that the desire for what is pleasant is strongest. If, then, it is not going to be obedient and subject to the ruling principle, it will go to great lengths; for in an irrational being the desire for pleasure is insatiable and tries every source of gratification, and the exercise of appetite increases its innate force, and if appetites are strong and violent they even expel the power of calculation. Hence they should be moderate and few,   10 and should in no way oppose reason—and this is what we call an obedient and chastened state—and as the child should live according to the direction of his tutor, so the appetitive element should live according to reason. Hence the appetitive element in a temperate man should harmonize with reason; for the noble is the mark   15 at which both aim, and the temperate man craves for the things he ought, as he ought, and when he ought; and this is what reason directs.

Here we conclude our account of temperance.

BOOK IV

1 · Let us speak next of liberality. It seems to be the mean with regard to wealth; for the liberal man is praised not in respect of military matters, nor of those in respect of which the temperate man is praised, nor of judicial decisions, but with regard to the giving and taking of wealth, and especially in respect of giving. Now   25 by wealth we mean all the things whose value is measured by money. Further,

---

[27]ἀκόλαστος ('self-indulgent') is connected with κολάζειν ('chasten,' 'punish').

prodigality and meanness are excesses and defects with regard to wealth; and meanness we always impute to those who care more than they ought for wealth, but

30 we sometimes apply the word 'prodigality' in a complex sense; for we call those men prodigals who are incontinent and spend money on self-indulgence. Hence also they are thought the poorest characters; for they combine more vices than one. Therefore the application of the word to them is not its proper use; for a 'prodigal' means a

1120ᵃ1 man who has a single evil quality, that of wasting his substance; since a prodigal is one who is being ruined by his own fault, and the wasting of substance is thought to be a sort of ruining of oneself, life being held to depend on possession of substance.

This, then, is the sense in which we take prodigality. Now the things that have

5 a use may be used either well or badly; and riches is a useful thing; and everything is used best by the man who has the excellence concerned with it; riches, therefore, will be used best by the man who has the excellence concerned with wealth; and this is the liberal man. Now spending and giving seem to be the using of wealth; taking

10 and keeping rather the possession of it. Hence it is more the mark of the liberal man to give to the right people than to take from the right sources and not to take from the wrong. For it is more characteristic of excellence to do good than to have good done to one, and more characteristic to do what is noble than not to do what is base; and it is not hard to see that giving implies doing good and doing what is noble, and

15 taking implies having good done to one or not acting basely. And gratitude is felt towards him who gives, not towards him who does not take, and praise also is bestowed more on him. It is easier, also, not to take than to give; for men are apter to give away their own too little than to take what is another's. Givers, too, are called

20 liberal; but those who do not take are not praised for liberality but rather for justice; while those who take are hardly praised at all. And the liberal are almost the most loved of all excellent characters, since they are useful; and this depends on their giving.

Now excellent actions are noble and done for the sake of the noble. Therefore the liberal man will give for the sake of the noble, and rightly; for he will give to the

25 right people, the right amounts, and at the right time, with all the other qualifications that accompany right giving; and that too with pleasure or without pain; for that which is excellent is pleasant or free from pain—least of all will it be painful. But he who gives to the wrong people or not for the sake of the noble but for some other cause, will be called not liberal but by some other name. Nor is he liberal

30 who gives with pain; for he would prefer the wealth to the noble act, and this is not characteristic of a liberal man. But no more will the liberal man take from wrong sources; for such taking is not characteristic of the man who sets no store by wealth. Nor will he be a ready asker; for it is not characteristic of a man who confers benefits to accept them lightly. But he will take from the right sources, e.g. from his

1120ᵇ1 own possessions, not as something noble but as a necessity, that he may have something to give. Nor will he neglect his own property, since he wishes by means of this to help others. And he will refrain from giving to anybody and everybody, that he may have something to give to the right people, at the right time, and where it is

5 noble to do so. It is highly characteristic of a liberal man also to go to excess in giving, so that he leaves too little for himself; for it is the nature of a liberal man not

to look to himself. The term 'liberality' is used relatively to a man's substance; for liberality resides not in the multitude of the gifts but in the state of the giver, and this is relative to the giver's substance.[28] There is therefore nothing to prevent the man who gives less from being the more liberal man, if he has less to give. Those are 10 thought to be more liberal who have not made their wealth but inherited it; for in the first place they have no experience of want, and secondly all men are fonder of their own productions, as are parents and poets. It is not easy for the liberal man to be rich, since he is not apt either at taking or at keeping, but at giving away, and 15 does not value wealth for its own sake but for the sake of giving. Hence comes the charge that is brought against fortune, that those who deserve riches most get it least. But it is not unreasonable that it should turn out so; for he cannot have wealth, any more than anything else, if he does not take pains to have it. Yet he will not give 20 to the wrong people nor at the wrong time, and so on; for he would no longer be acting in accordance with liberality, and if he spent on these objects he would have nothing to spend on the right objects. For, as has been said, he is liberal who spends according to his substance and on the right objects; and he who exceeds is prodigal. Hence we do not call despots prodigal; for it is thought not easy for them to give and 25 spend beyond the amount of their possessions. Liberality, then, being a mean with regard to giving and taking of wealth, the liberal man will both give and spend the right amounts and on the right objects, alike in small things and in great, and that 30 with pleasure; he will also take the right amounts and from the right sources. For, the excellence being a mean with regard to both, he will do both as he ought; for right taking accompanies right giving, and wrong taking is contrary to it, and accordingly those that accompany each other are present together in the same man, while the contrary kinds evidently are not. But if he happens to spend in a manner 1121ª1 contrary to what is right and noble, he will be pained, but moderately and as he ought; for it is the mark of excellence both to be pleased and to be pained at the right objects and in the right way. Further, the liberal man is easy to deal with in money matters; for he can be got the better of, since he sets no store by money, and is more 5 annoyed if he has not spent something that he ought than pained if he has spent something that he ought not, and does not agree with Simonides.

The prodigal errs in these respects also; for he is neither pleased nor pained at the right things or in the right way; this will be more evident as we go on. We have said that prodigality and meanness are excesses and deficiencies, and in two things, 10 in giving and in taking; for we include spending under giving. Now prodigality exceeds in giving and not taking, and falls short in taking, while meanness falls short in giving, and exceeds in taking, except in small things. 15

The characteristics of prodigality are not often combined; for it is not easy to give to all if you take from none; private persons soon exhaust their substance with giving, and it is to these that the name of prodigals is applied—though a man of this sort would seem to be in no small degree better than a mean man. For he is easily 20 cured both by age and by poverty, and thus he may move towards the middle state. For he has the characteristics of the liberal man, since he both gives and refrains

---

[28]Omitting δίδωσιν.

from taking, though he does neither of these in the right manner or well. Therefore if he were brought to do so by habituation or in some other way, he would be liberal; for he will then give to the right people, and will not take from the wrong sources. This is why he is thought to have not a bad character; it is not the mark of a wicked or ignoble man to go to excess in giving and not taking, but only of a foolish one. The man who is prodigal in this way is thought much better than the mean man both for the aforesaid reasons and because he benefits many while the other benefits no one, not even himself.

But most prodigal people, as has been said, also take from the wrong sources, and are in this respect mean. They become apt to take because they wish to spend and cannot do this easily; for their possessions soon run short. Thus they are forced to provide means from some other source. At the same time, because they care nothing for honour, they take recklessly and from any source; for they have an appetite for giving, and they do not mind how or from what source. Hence also their giving is not liberal; for it is not noble, nor does it aim at nobility, nor is it done in the right way; sometimes they make rich those who should be poor, and will give nothing to people of respectable character, and much to flatterers or those who provide them with some other pleasure. Hence also most of them are self-indulgent; for they spend lightly and waste money on their indulgences, and incline towards pleasures because they do not live with a view to what is noble.

The prodigal man, then, turns into what we have described if he is left untutored, but if he is treated with care he will arrive at the intermediate and right state. But meanness is both incurable (for old age and every disability is thought to make men mean) and more innate in men than prodigality; for most men are fonder of getting money than of giving. It also extends widely, and is multiform, since there seem to be many kinds of meanness.

For it consists in two things, deficiency in giving and excess in taking, and is not found complete in all cases but is sometimes divided: some men go to excess in taking, others fall short in giving. Those who are called by such names as 'miserly', 'close', 'stingy', all fall short in giving, but do not covet the possessions of others nor wish to get them. In some this is due to a sort of honesty and avoidance of what is disgraceful (for some seem, or at least profess, to hoard their money for this reason, that they may not some day be forced to do something disgraceful; to this class belong the cheeseparer and every one of the sort; he is so called from his excess of unwillingness to give anything); while others again keep their hands off the property of others from fear, on the ground that it is not easy, if one takes the property of others oneself, to avoid having one's own taken by them; they are therefore content neither to take nor to give.

Others again exceed in respect of taking by taking anything and from any source, e.g. those who ply sordid trades, pimps and all such people, and those who lend small sums and at high rates. For all of these take more than they ought and from wrong sources. What is common to them is evidently sordid love of gain; they all put up with a bad name for the sake of gain, and little gain at that. For those who make great gains but from wrong sources, and not the right gains, e.g. despots when they sack cities and spoil temples, we do not call mean but rather wicked, impious, and unjust. But the gamester and the footpad belong to the class of the mean, since they have a sordid love of gain. For it is for gain that both of them ply their craft and endure the disgrace of it, and the one faces the greatest dangers for the sake of the 10 booty, while the other makes gain from his friends, to whom he ought to be giving. Both, then, since they are willing to make gain from wrong sources, are sordid lovers of gain; therefore all such forms of taking are mean.

And it is natural that meanness is described as the contrary of liberality; for not only is it a greater evil than prodigality, but men err more often in this direction 15 than in the way of prodigality as we have described it.

So much, then, for liberality and the opposed vices.

2 · It would seem proper to discuss magnificence next. For this also seems to be an excellence concerned with wealth; but it does not like liberality extend to all 20 the actions that are concerned with wealth, but only to those that involve expenditure; and in these it surpasses liberality in scale. For, as the name itself suggests, it is a fitting expenditure involving largeness of scale. But the scale is relative; for the expense of equipping a trireme is not the same as that of heading a sacred embassy. It is what is fitting, then, in relation to the agent, and to the 25 circumstances and the object. The man who in small or middling things spends according to the merits of the case is not called magnificent (e.g. the man who can say 'many a gift I gave the wanderer'),[29] but only the man who does so in great things. For the magnificent man is liberal, but the liberal man is not necessarily magnificent. The deficiency of this state is called niggardliness, the excess 30 vulgarity, lack of taste, and the like, which do not go to excess in the amount spent on right objects, but by showy expenditure in the wrong circumstances and the wrong manner; we shall speak of these vices later.

The magnificent man is like an artist; for he can see what is fitting and spend large sums tastefully. For, as we said at the beginning, a state is determined by its 1122^b1 activities and by its objects. Now the expenses of the magnificent man are large and fitting. Such, therefore, are also his results; for thus there will be a great expenditure and one that is fitting to its result. Therefore the result should be worthy of the expense, and the expense should be worthy of the result, or should 5 even exceed it. And the magnificent man will spend such sums for the sake of the noble; for this is common to the excellences. And further he will do so gladly and lavishly; for nice calculation is a niggardly thing. And he will consider how the result can be made most beautiful and most becoming rather than for how much it can be produced and how it can be produced most cheaply. It is necessary, then, that 10 the magnificent man be also liberal. For the liberal man also will spend what he ought and as he ought; and it is in these matters that the greatness implied in the name of the magnificent man—his bigness, as it were—is manifested, since liberality is concerned with these matters; and at an equal expense he will produce a more magnificent result. For a possession and a result have not the same excellence. The most valuable possession is that which is worth most, e.g. gold, but the most 15

----

[29]*Odyssey* XVII 420.

valuable result is that which is great and beautiful (for the contemplation of such a thing inspires admiration, and so does magnificence); and the excellence of a result[30] involves magnitude. Magnificence is an attribute of expenditures of the kind
20 which we call honourable, e.g. those connected with the gods—votive offerings, buildings, and sacrifices—and similarly with any form of religious worship, and all those that are proper objects of public-spirited ambition, as when people think they ought to equip a chorus or a trireme, or entertain the city, in a brilliant way. But in all cases, as has been said, we have regard to the agent as well and ask who he is and
25 what means he has; for the expenditure should be worthy of his means, and suit not only the result but also the producer. Hence a poor man cannot be magnificent, since he has not the means with which to spend large sums fittingly; and he who tries is a fool, since he spends beyond what can be expected of him and what is proper, but it is *right* expenditure that is excellent. But great expenditure is
30 becoming to those who have suitable means to start with, acquired by their own efforts or from ancestors or connexions, and to people of high birth or reputation, and so on; for all these things bring with them greatness and prestige. Primarily, then, the magnificent man is of this sort, and magnificence is shown in expenditures
35 of this sort, as has been said; for these are the greatest and most honourable. Of *private* occasions of expenditure the most suitable are those that take place once for
1123ᵃ1 all, e.g. a wedding or anything of the kind, or anything that interests the whole city or the people of position in it, and also the receiving of foreign guests and the sending of them on their way, and gifts and countergifts; for the magnificent man
5 spends not on himself but on public objects, and gifts bear some resemblance to votive offerings. A magnificent man will also furnish his house suitably to his wealth (for even a house is a sort of public ornament), and will spend by preference on those works that are lasting (for these are the most beautiful), and on every class of things he will spend what is becoming; for the same things are not suitable for
10 gods and for men, nor in a temple and in a tomb. And since each expenditure may be great of its kind, and what is most magnificent absolutely is great expenditure on a great object, but what is magnificent *here* is what is great in *these* circumstances, and greatness in the work differs from greatness in the expense (for the most
15 beautiful ball or bottle is magnificent as a gift to a child, but the price of it is small and mean),—therefore it is characteristic of the magnificent man, whatever kind of result he is producing, to produce it magnificently (for such a result is not easily surpassed) and to make it worthy of the expenditure.

Such, then, is the magnificent man; the man who goes to excess and is vulgar
20 exceeds, as has been said, by spending beyond what is right. For on small objects of expenditure he spends much and displays a tasteless showiness; e.g. he gives a club dinner on the scale of a wedding banquet, and when he provides the chorus for a comedy he brings them on to the stage in purple, as they do at Megara. And all such
25 things he will do not for the sake of the noble but to show off his wealth, and because he thinks he is admired for these things, and where he ought to spend much he spends little and where little, much. The niggardly man on the other hand will fall

---

[30]Omitting ἡ μεγαλοπρέπεια.

short in everything, and after spending the greatest sums will spoil the beauty of the result for a trifle, and whatever he is doing he will hesitate and consider how he may spend least, and lament even that, and think he is doing everything on a bigger scale   30 than he ought.

These states, then, are vices; yet they do not bring *disgrace* because they are neither harmful to one's neighbour nor very unseemly.

3 · Pride seems even from its name to be concerned with great things; what sort of great things, is the first question we must try to answer. It makes no difference whether we consider the state or the man characterized by it. Now the   1123^{b}1 man is thought to be proud who thinks himself worthy of great things, being worthy of them; for he who does so beyond his deserts is a fool, but no excellent man is foolish or silly. The proud man, then, is the man we have described. For he who is worthy of little and thinks himself worthy of little is temperate, but not proud; for   5 pride implies greatness, as beauty implies a good-sized body, and little people may be neat and well-proportioned but cannot be beautiful. On the other hand, he who thinks himself worthy of great things, being unworthy of them, is vain; though not every one who thinks himself worthy of more than he really is worthy of is vain. The man who thinks himself worthy of less than he is really worthy of is unduly humble,   10 whether his deserts be great or moderate, or his deserts be small but his claims yet smaller. And the man whose deserts are great would seem *most* unduly humble; for what would he have done if they had been less? The proud man, then, is an extreme in respect of the greatness of his claims, but a mean in respect of the rightness of them; for he claims what is in accordance with his merits, while the others go to   15 excess or fall short.

If, then, he deserves and claims great things, and above all the greatest things, he will be concerned with one thing in particular. Desert is relative to external goods; and the greatest of these, we should say, is that which we render to the gods, and which people of position most aim at, and which is the prize appointed for the noblest deeds; and this is honour; that is surely the greatest of external goods.   20 Honours and dishonours, therefore, are the objects with respect to which the proud man is as he should be. And even apart from argument it is with honour that proud men appear to be concerned; for it is honour that they chiefly claim, but in accordance with their deserts. The unduly humble man falls short both in comparison with his own merits and in comparison with the proud man's claims.   25 The vain man goes to excess in comparison with his own merits, but does not exceed the proud man's claims.

Now the proud man, since he deserves most, must be good in the highest degree; for the better man always deserves more, and the best man most. Therefore the truly proud man must be good. And greatness in every excellence would seem to   30 be characteristic of a proud man. And it would be most unbecoming for a proud man to fly from danger, swinging his arms by his sides, or to wrong another; for to what end should he do disgraceful acts, he to whom nothing is great? If we consider him point by point we shall see the utter absurdity of a proud man who is not good.

Nor, again, would he be worthy of honour if he were bad; for honour is the prize of
1124ª1   excellence and it is to the good that it is rendered. Pride, then, seems to be a sort of
crown of the excellences; for it makes them greater, and it is not found without
them. Therefore it is hard to be truly proud; for it is impossible without nobility and
5   goodness of character. It is chiefly with honours and dishonours, then, that the
proud man is concerned; and at honours that are great and conferred by good men
he will be moderately pleased, thinking that he is coming by his own or even less
than his own; for there can be no honour that is worthy of perfect excellence, yet he
will at any rate accept it since they have nothing greater to bestow on him; but
10   honour from casual people and on trifling grounds he will utterly despise, since it is
not this that he deserves, and dishonour too, since in his case it cannot be just. In the
first place, then, as has been said, the proud man is concerned with honours; yet he
will also bear himself with moderation towards wealth and power and all good or
15   evil fortune, whatever may befall him, and will be neither over-joyed by good
fortune nor over-pained by evil. For not even about honour does he care much,[31]
although it is the greatest thing (for power and wealth are desirable for the sake of
honour—at least those who have them wish to get honour by means of them); and
for him to whom even honour is a little thing the others must be so too. Hence proud
20   men are thought to be disdainful.

The goods of fortune also are thought to contribute towards pride. For men
who are well-born are thought worthy of honour, and so are those who enjoy power
or wealth; for they are in a superior position, and everything that has a superiority in
something good is held in greater honour. Hence even such things make men
prouder; for they are honoured by some for having them; but in truth the good man
25   alone is to be honoured; he, however, who has both advantages is thought the more
worthy of honour. But those who without excellence have such goods are neither
justified in making great claims nor entitled to the name of 'proud'; for these things
imply perfect excellence. Disdainful and insolent, however, even those who have
1124ᵇ1   such goods become. For without excellence it is not easy to bear gracefully the goods
of fortune; and, being unable to bear them, and thinking themselves superior to
others, they despise others and themselves do what they please. They imitate the
proud man without being like him, and this they do where they can; so they do not
5   act excellently, but they do despise others. For the proud man despises justly (since
he thinks truly), but the many do so at random.

He does not run into trifling dangers, nor is he fond of danger, because he
honours few things; but he will face great dangers, and when he is in danger he is
unsparing of his life, knowing that there are conditions on which life is not worth
having. And he is the sort of man to confer benefits, but he is ashamed of receiving
10   them; for the one is the mark of a superior, the other of an inferior. And he is apt to
confer greater benefits in return; for thus the original benefactor besides being paid
will incur a debt to him, and will be the gainer by the transaction. They seem also to
remember any service they have done, but not those they have received (for he who
receives a service is inferior to him who has done it, but the proud man wishes to be

[31]Omitting ὡς.

superior), and to hear of the former with pleasure, of the latter with displeasure; 15
this, it seems, is why Thetis did not mention to Zeus the services she had done him,
and why the Spartans did not recount their services to the Athenians, but those they
had received. It is a mark of the proud man also to ask for nothing or scarcely
anything, but to give help readily, and to be dignified towards people who enjoy
high position and good fortune, but unassuming towards those of the middle class;
for it is a difficult and lofty thing to be superior to the former, but easy to be so to 20
the latter, and a lofty bearing over the former is no mark of ill-breeding, but among
humble people it is as vulgar as a display of strength against the weak. Again, it is
characteristic of the proud man not to aim at the things commonly held in honour,
or the things in which others excel; to be sluggish and to hold back except where
great honour as a great result is at stake, and to be a man of few deeds, but of great 25
and notable ones. He must also be open in his hate and in his love (for to conceal
one's feelings is a mark of timidity), and must care more for truth than for what
people will think, and must speak and act openly; for he is free of speech because he
is contemptuous, and he is given to telling the truth, except when he speaks in irony 30
to the vulgar. He must be unable to make his life revolve round another, unless it be
a friend; for this is slavish, and for this reason all flatterers are servile and people 1125ᵃ1
lacking in self-respect are flatterers. Nor is he given to admiration; for nothing to
him is great. Nor is he mindful of wrongs; for it is not the part of a proud man to
have a long memory, especially for wrongs, but rather to overlook them. Nor is he a 5
gossip; for he will speak neither about himself nor about another, since he cares not
to be praised nor for others to be blamed; nor again is he given to praise; and for the
same reason he is not an evil-speaker, even about his enemies, except from
haughtiness. With regard to necessary or small matters he is least of all men given
to lamentation or the asking of favours; for it is the part of one who takes such 10
matters seriously to behave so with respect to them. He is one who will possess
beautiful and profitless things rather than profitable and useful ones; for this is
more proper to a character that suffices to itself.

Further, a slow step is thought proper to the proud man, a deep voice, and a
level utterance; for the man who takes few things seriously is not likely to be
hurried, nor the man who thinks nothing great to be excited, while a shrill voice and 15
a rapid gait are the results of hurry and excitement.

Such, then, is the proud man; the man who falls short of him is unduly humble,
and the man who goes beyond him is vain. Now these too are not thought to be bad
(for they are not evil-doers), but only mistaken. For the unduly humble man, being
worthy of good things, robs himself of what he deserves, and seems to have 20
something bad about him from the fact that he does not think himself worthy of
good things, and seems also not to know himself; else he would have desired the
things he was worthy of, since these were good. Yet such people are not thought to
be fools, but rather unduly retiring. Such an estimate, however, seems actually to
make them worse; for each class of people aims at what corresponds to its worth, 25
and these people stand back even from noble actions and undertakings, deeming
themselves unworthy, and from external goods no less. Vain people, on the other
hand, are fools and ignorant of themselves, and that manifestly; for, not being

worthy of them, they attempt honourable undertakings, and then are found out; and
30 they adorn themselves with clothing and outward show and such things, and wish
their strokes of good fortune to be made public, and speak about them as if they
would be honoured for them. But undue humility is more opposed to pride than
vanity is; for it is both commoner and worse.

Pride, then, is concerned with honour on the grand scale, as has been said.

1125ᵇ1 4 · There seems to be in the sphere of honour also, as was said in our first
remarks on the subject, an excellence which would appear to be related to pride as
liberality is to magnificence. For neither of these has anything to do with the grand
5 scale, but both dispose us as is right with regard to middling and unimportant
objects; as in getting and giving of wealth there is a mean and an excess and defect,
so too honour may be desired more than is right, or less, or from the right sources
and in the right way. We blame both the ambitious man as aiming at honour more
than is right and from wrong sources, and the unambitious man as not choosing to
10 be honoured even for noble reasons. But sometimes we praise the ambitious man as
being manly and a lover of what is noble, and the unambitious man as being
moderate and temperate as we said in our first treatment of the subject. Evidently,
since people are said to be fond of such and such in more than one way, we do not
15 assign the term 'ambition'³² always to the same thing, but when we praise the
quality we think of the man who loves honour more than most people, and when we
blame it we think of him who loves it more than is right. The mean being without a
name, the extremes seem to dispute for its place as though that were vacant. But
where there is excess and defect, there is also an intermediate; now men desire
20 honour both more than they should and less; therefore it is possible also to do so as
one should; at all events this is the state that is praised, being an unnamed mean in
respect of honour. Relatively to ambition it seems to be unambitiousness, and
relatively to unambitiousness it seems to be ambition, while relatively to both it
seems in a sense to be both. This appears to be true of the other excellences also. But
25 in this case the extremes seem to be opposed because the mean has not received a
name.

5 · Good temper is a mean with respect to anger; the middle state being
unnamed, and the extremes almost without a name as well, we place good temper in
the middle position, though it inclines towards the deficiency, which is without a
30 name. The excess might be called a sort of irascibility. For the passion is anger,
while its causes are many and diverse.

The man who is angry at the right things and with the right people, and,
further, as he ought, when he ought, and as long as he ought, is praised. This will be
the good-tempered man, then, since good temper is praised. For the good-tempered
man tends to be unperturbed and not to be led by passion, but to be angry in the
manner, at the things, and for the length of time, that reason dictates; but he is

---

³²'Ambitious' translates φιλότιμος, a compound of the form 'fond-of-such-and-such,' φιλοτοιοῦτος.

thought to err rather in the direction of deficiency; for the good-tempered man is   1126ᵃ1
not revengeful, but rather tends to forgive.

The deficiency, whether it is a sort of inirascibility or whatever it is, is blamed.
For those who are not angry at the things they should be are thought to be fools, and
so are those who are not angry in the right way, at the right time, or with the right   5
persons; for such a man is thought not to feel things nor to be pained by them, and,
since he does not get angry, he is thought unlikely to defend himself; and to endure
being insulted and to put up with insults to one's friends is slavish.

The excess can be manifested in all the points (for one can be angry with the
wrong persons, at the wrong things, more than is right, too quickly, or too long); yet   10
all are not found in the same person. Indeed they could not; for evil destroys even
itself, and if it is complete becomes unbearable. Now *hot-tempered* people get
angry quickly and with the wrong persons and at the wrong things and more than is
right, but their anger ceases quickly—which is the best point about them. This   15
happens to them because they do not restrain their anger but retaliate openly owing
to their quickness of temper, and then their anger ceases. By reason of excess
choleric people are quick-tempered and ready to be angry with everything and on
every occasion; whence their name. *Sulky* people are hard to appease, and retain
their anger long; for they repress their passion. But it ceases when they retaliate; for   20
revenge relieves them of their anger, producing in them pleasure instead of pain. If
this does not happen they retain their burden; for owing to its not being obvious no
one even reasons with them, and to digest one's anger in oneself takes time.[33] Such
people are most troublesome to themselves and to their dearest friends. We call   25
bad-tempered those who are angry at the wrong things, more than is right, and
longer, and cannot be appeased until they inflict vengeance or punishment.

To good temper we oppose the excess rather than the defect; for not only is it
commoner (since revenge is the more human), but bad-tempered people are worse   30
to live with.

What we have said before is plain also from what is said; for it is not easy to
define how, with whom, at what, and how long one should be angry, and at what
point right action ceases and wrong begins. For the man who strays a little from the   35
path, either towards the more or towards the less, is not blamed; since sometimes we
praise those who exhibit the deficiency, and call them good-tempered, and   1126ᵇ1
sometimes we call angry people manly, as being capable of ruling. How far,
therefore, and how a man must stray before he becomes blameworthy, it is not easy
to determine by reason; for the decision depends on the particular facts and on
perception. But so much at least is plain, that the middle state is praiseworthy—   5
that in virtue of which we are angry with the right people, at the right things, in the
right way, and so on, while the excesses and defects are blameworthy—slightly so if
they are present in a low degree, more if in a higher degree, and very much if in a
high degree. Evidently, then, we must cling to the middle state.—Enough of the
states relative to anger.   10

[33]Reading δεῖται.

6 · In gatherings of men, in social life and the interchange of words and deeds, some men are thought to be obsequious, viz. those who to give pleasure praise everything and never oppose, but think they should give no pain to the people they
15 meet; while those who, on the contrary, oppose everything and care not a whit about giving pain are called churlish and contentious. That the states we have named are culpable is plain enough, and that the middle state is laudable—that in virtue of which a man will put up with, and will resent, the right things and in the right way;
20 but no name has been assigned to it, though it most resembles friendship. For the man who corresponds to this middle state is very much what, with affection added, we call a good friend. But the state in question differs from friendship in that it implies no passion or affection for one's associates; since it is not by reason of loving or hating that such a man takes everything in the right way, but by being a man of a
25 certain kind. For he will behave so alike towards those he knows and those he does not know, towards intimates and those who are not so, except that in each of these cases too he will behave as is befitting; for it is not proper to have the same care for intimates and for strangers, nor again to pain them in the same ways. Now we have said generally that he will associate with people in the right way; but it is by reference to what is noble and expedient that he will aim at either[34] giving pain or at
30 contributing pleasure. For he seems to be concerned with the pleasures and pains of social life; and wherever it is not noble, or is harmful, for him to contribute pleasure, he will refuse, and will choose rather to give pain; also if his acquiescence in another's action would bring disgrace, and that in a high degree, or injury, on the
35 agent, while his opposition brings a little pain, he will not acquiesce but will decline. He will associate differently with people in high station and with ordinary people,
1127ª1 with closer and more distant acquaintances, and so too with regard to all other differences, rendering to each class what is befitting, and while for its own sake he chooses to contribute pleasure, and avoids the giving of pain, he will be guided by
5 the consequences, if these are greater, i.e. the noble and the expedient. For the sake of a great future pleasure, too, he will inflict small pains.

The man who attains the mean, then, is such as we have described, but has not received a name; of those who contribute pleasure, the man who aims at being pleasant with no ulterior object is obsequious, but the man who does so in order that he may get some advantage in the direction of money or the things that money buys
10 is a flatterer; while the man who quarrels with everything is, as has been said, churlish and contentious. And the extremes seem to be opposed to each other because the mean is without a name.

7 · The mean for boastfulness[35] is found in almost the same sphere; and this also is without a name. It will be no bad plan to describe these states as well; for we
15 shall both know the facts about character better if we go through them in detail, and we shall be convinced that the excellences are means if we see this to be so in all cases. In the field of social life those who make the giving of pleasure or pain their

---

[34]Reading τοῦ ἢ λυπεῖν.
[35]Omitting Bywater's καὶ εἰρωνείας.

object in associating with others have been described; let us now describe those who pursue truth or falsehood alike in words and deeds and in the claims they put   20
forward. The boastful man, then, is thought to be apt to claim the things that bring repute, when he has not got them, or to claim more of them than he has, and the mock-modest man on the other hand to disclaim what he has or belittle it, while the man who observes the mean is one who calls a thing by its own name, being truthful both in life and in word, owning to what he has, and neither more nor less. Now each   25
of these courses may be adopted either with or without an object. But each man speaks and acts and lives in accordance with his character, if he is *not* acting for some object. And falsehood is in itself mean and culpable, and truth noble and worthy of praise. Thus the truthful man is another case of a man who, being in the   30
mean, is worthy of praise, and both forms of untruthful man are culpable, and particularly the boastful man.

Let us discuss them both, but first of all the truthful man. We are not speaking of the man who keeps faith in his agreements, i.e. in the things that pertain to justice or injustice (for this would belong to another excellence), but the man who in the 1127^b1
matters in which nothing of this sort is at stake is true both in word and in life because his character is such. But such a man would seem to be as a matter of fact equitable. For the man who loves truth, and is truthful where nothing is at stake, will still more be truthful where something is at stake; he will avoid falsehood as   5
something base, seeing that he avoided it even for its own sake; and such a man is worthy of praise. He inclines rather to understate the truth; for this seems in better taste because exaggerations are wearisome.

He who claims more than he has with no ulterior object is a contemptible sort   10
of fellow (otherwise he would not delight in falsehood), but seems futile rather than bad; but if he does it for an object, he who does it for the sake of reputation or honour is (for a boaster[36]) not very much to be blamed, but he who does it for money, or the things that lead to money, is an uglier character (it is not the capacity that makes the boaster, but the choice; for it is in virtue of his state and by being a man of a certain kind that he is a boaster); as one man is a liar because he enjoys the   15
lie itself, and another because he desires reputation or gain. Now those who boast for the sake of reputation claim such qualities as win praise or congratulation, but those whose object is gain claim qualities which are of value to one's neighbours and one's lack of which is not easily detected, e.g. the powers of a seer, a sage, or a   20
physician. For this reason it is such things as these that most people claim and boast about; for in them the above-mentioned qualities are found.

Mock-modest people, who understate things, seem more attractive in character; for they are thought to speak not for gain but to avoid parade; and here too it is qualities which bring reputation that they disclaim, as Socrates used to do. Those   25
who disclaim trifling and obvious qualities are called humbugs and are more contemptible; and sometimes this seems to be boastfulness, like the Spartan dress; for both excess and great deficiency are boastful. But those who use understatement with moderation and understate about matters that do not very much force   30

[36]Reading ὡς γ᾽ ἀλαζών.

themselves on our notice seem attractive. And it is the boaster that seems to be opposed to the truthful man; for he is the worse character.

8 · Since life includes rest as well, and in this is included leisure and amusement, there seems here also to be a kind of intercourse which is tasteful; there is such a thing as saying—and again listening to—what one should and as one should. The kind of people one is speaking or listening to will also make a difference. Evidently here also there is both an excess and a deficiency as compared with the mean. Those who carry humour to excess are thought to be vulgar buffoons, striving after humour at all costs, and aiming rather at raising a laugh than at saying what is becoming and at avoiding pain to the object of their fun; while those who can neither make a joke themselves nor put up with those who do are thought to be boorish and unpolished. But those who joke in a tasteful way are called ready-witted, which implies a sort of readiness to turn this way and that; for such sallies are thought to be movements of the character, and as bodies are discriminated by their movements, so too are characters. The ridiculous side of things is not far to seek, however, and most people delight more than they should in amusement and in jesting, and so even buffoons are called ready-witted because they are found attractive; but that they differ from the ready-witted man, and to no small extent, is clear from what has been said.

To the middle state belongs also tact; it is the mark of a tactful man to say and listen to such things as befit a good and well-bred man; for there are some things that it befits such a man to say and to hear by way of jest, and the well-bred man's jesting differs from that of a vulgar man, and the joking of an educated man from that of an uneducated. One may see this even from the old and the new comedies; to the authors of the former indecency of language was amusing, to those of the latter innuendo is more so; and these differ in no small degree in respect of propriety. Now should we define the man who jokes well by his saying what is not unbecoming to a well-bred man, or by his not giving pain, or even giving delight, to the hearer? Or is the latter, at any rate, itself indefinite, since different things are hateful or pleasant to different people? The kind of jokes he will listen to will be the same; for the kind he can put up with are also the kind he seems to make. There are, then, jokes he will not make; for the jest is a sort of abuse, and there are things that lawgivers forbid us to abuse; and they should, perhaps, have forbidden us even to make a jest of such. The refined and well-bred man, therefore, will be as we have described, being as it were a law to himself.

Such, then, is the man who observes the mean, whether he be called tactful or ready-witted. The buffoon, on the other hand, is the slave of his sense of humour, and spares neither himself nor others if he can raise a laugh, and says things none of which a man of refinement would say, and to some of which he would not even listen. The boor, again, is useless for such social intercourse; for he contributes nothing and finds fault with everything. But relaxation and amusement are thought to be a necessary element in life.

The means in life that have been described, then, are three in number, and are

all concerned with an interchange of words and deeds of some kind. They differ,   5
however, in that one is concerned with truth, and the other two with pleasantness.
Of those concerned with pleasure, one is displayed in jests, the other in the general
social intercourse of life.

9 · Shame should not be described as an excellence; for it is more like a   10
passion than a state. It is defined, at any rate, as a kind of fear of disrepute and
produces an effect similar to that[37] produced by fear of danger; for people who feel
disgraced blush, and those who fear death turn pale. Both, therefore, seem to be in a
sense bodily conditions, which is thought to be characteristic of passion rather than   15
of a state.
    The passion is not becoming to every age, but only to youth. For we think
young people should be prone to shame because they live by passion and therefore
commit many errors, but are restrained by shame; and we praise young people who
are prone to this passion, but an older person no one would praise for being prone to   20
the sense of disgrace, since we think he should not do anything that need cause this
sense. For the sense of disgrace is not even characteristic of a good man, since it is
consequent on bad actions (for such actions should not be done; and if some actions
are disgraceful in very truth and others only according to common opinion, this
makes no difference; for neither class of actions should be done, so that no disgrace
should be felt); and it is a mark of a bad man even to be such as to do any disgraceful   25
action. To be so constituted as to feel disgraced if one does such an action, and for
this reason to think oneself good, is absurd; for it is for voluntary actions that shame
is felt, and the good man will never voluntarily do bad actions. But shame may be
said to be conditionally a good thing; *if* a good man did such actions, he would feel   30
disgraced; but the excellences are not subject to such a qualification. And if
shamelessness—not to be ashamed of doing base actions—is bad, that does not
make it good to be ashamed of doing such actions. Continence too is not virtue, but a
mixed sort of state; this will be shown later. Now, however, let us discuss justice.   35

BOOK V

1 · With regard to justice and injustice we must consider what kind of
actions they are concerned with, what sort of mean justice is, and between what
extremes the just act is intermediate. Our investigation shall follow the same course   5
as the preceding discussions.
    We see that all men mean by justice that kind of state which makes people
disposed to do what is just and makes them act justly and wish for what is just; and   10
similarly by injustice that state which makes them act unjustly and wish for what is
unjust. Let us too, then, first lay this down as a rough sketch. For the same is not
true of the sciences and the faculties as of states. For it seems that the same faculty

---

[37]Reading καὶ ἀποτελεῖ τι.

or science deals with contraries; but a state of character which is one of two contraries does *not* produce the contrary results; e.g. as a result of health we do not

15　do what is the opposite of healthy, but only what is healthy; for we say a man walks healthily, when he walks as a healthy man would.

Now often one contrary state is recognized from its contrary, and often states are recognized from the subjects that exhibit them; for if good condition is known,

20　bad condition also becomes known, and good condition is known from the things that are in good condition, and they from it. If good condition is firmness of flesh, it is necessary both that bad condition should be flabbiness of flesh and that the wholesome should be that which causes firmness in flesh. And it follows for the most

25　part that if one contrary is ambiguous the other also will be ambiguous; e.g. if 'just' is so, that 'unjust' will be so too.

Now 'justice' and 'injustice' seem to be ambiguous, but because the homonymy is close, it escapes notice and is not obvious as it is, comparatively, when the meanings are far apart, e.g. (for here the difference in outward form is great) as the

30　homonymy in the use of *kleis* for the collar-bone of an animal and for that with which we lock a door. Let us then ascertain the different ways in which a man may be said to be unjust. Both the lawless man and the grasping and unequal man are thought to be unjust, so that evidently both the law-abiding and the equal man will

1129ᵇ1　be just. The just, then, is the lawful and the equal, the unjust the unlawful and the unequal.

Since the unjust man is grasping, he must be concerned with goods—not all goods, but those with which prosperity and adversity have to do, which taken absolutely are always good, but for a particular person are not always good. (Men

5　pray for and pursue the same[38] things; but they should not, but should pray that the things that are good absolutely may also be good for them, and should choose the things that are good for them.) The unjust man does not always choose the greater, but also the less—in the case of things bad absolutely; but because the lesser evil is itself thought to be in a sense good, and graspingness is directed at the good,

10　therefore he is thought to be grasping. And he is unequal; for this contains and is common to both.

Since the lawless man was seen to be unjust and the law-abiding man just, evidently all lawful acts are in a sense just acts; for the acts laid down by the legislative art are lawful, and each of these, we say, is just. Now the laws in their

15　enactments on all subjects aim at the common advantage either of all or of the best or of those who hold power, or something of the sort; so that in one sense we call those acts just that tend to produce and preserve happiness and its components for the political society. And the law bids us do both the acts of a brave man (e.g. not to

20　desert our post or take to flight or throw away our arms), and those of a temperate man (e.g. not to commit adultery or outrage), and those of a good-tempered man (e.g. not to strike another or speak evil), and similarly with regard to the other excellences and forms of wickedness, commanding some acts and forbidding others;

---

[38]Reading ταὐτά.

and the rightly-framed law does this rightly, and the hastily conceived one less   25
well.

This form of justice, then is complete excellence—not absolutely, but in
relation to others. And therefore justice is often thought to be the greatest of
excellences and 'neither evening nor morning star' is so wonderful; and proverbially
'in justice is every excellence comprehended'. And it is complete excellence in its   30
fullest sense, because it is the actual exercise of complete excellence. It is complete
because he who possesses it can exercise his excellence towards others too and not
merely by himself; for many men can exercise excellence in their own affairs, but
not in their relations to excellence. This is why the saying of Bias is thought to be   1130ª1
true, that 'rule will show the man'; for a ruler is necessarily in relation to other men
and a member of a society. For this same reason justice, alone of the excellences, is
thought to be another's good, because it is related to others; for it does what is
advantageous to another, either a ruler or a partner. Now the worst man is he who   5
exercises his wickedness both towards himself and towards his friends, and the best
man is not he who exercises his excellence towards himself but he[39] who exercises it
towards another; for this is a difficult task. Justice in this sense, then, is not part of
excellence but excellence entire, nor is the contrary injustice a part of vice but vice   10
entire. What the difference is between excellence and justice in this sense is plain
from what we have said; they are the same but being them is not the same; what, as
a relation to others, is justice is, as a certain kind of state without qualification,
excellence.

2 · But at all events what we are investigating is the justice which is a *part* of
excellence; for there is a justice of this kind, as we maintain. Similarly it is with   15
injustice in the particular sense that we are concerned.

That there is such a thing is indicated by the fact that while the man who
exhibits in action for the other forms of wickedness acts unjustly but not graspingly
(e.g. the man who throws away his shield through cowardice or speaks harshly
through bad temper or fails to help a friend with money through meanness), when a
man acts graspingly he often exhibits none of these vices,—no, nor all together, but   20
certainly wickedness of some kind (for we blame him) and injustice. There is, then,
another kind of injustice which is a part of injustice in the wide sense, and
something unjust which answers to a part of what is unjust in the wide sense of
contrary to the law. Again, if one man commits adultery for the sake of gain and
makes money by it, while another does so at the bidding of appetite though he loses   25
money and is penalized for it, the latter would be held to be self-indulgent rather
than grasping while the former is unjust, but not self-indulgent; evidently,
therefore, he is unjust by reason of his making gain by his act. Again, all other
unjust acts are ascribed invariably to some particular kind of wickedness, e.g.
adultery to self-indulgence, the desertion of a comrade in battle to cowardice,   30

[39]Reading ἀλλ' ὅ.

physical violence to anger; but if a man makes gain, his action is ascribed to no form of wickedness but injustice. Evidently, therefore, there is apart from injustice in the wide sense another, particular, injustice which shares the name and nature of the first, because its definition falls within the same genus; for the force of both lies in a relation to others but the one is concerned with honour or money or safety—or that which includes all these, if we had a single name for it—and its motive is the pleasure that arises from gain; while the other is concerned with all the objects with which the good man is concerned.

It is clear, then, that there is more than one kind of justice, and that there is one which is distinct from excellence entire; we must try to grasp what and what sort of thing it is.

The unjust has been divided into the unlawful and the unequal, and the just into the lawful and the equal. To the unlawful answers the afore-mentioned sort of injustice. But since the unequal and the unlawful are not the same, but are different as a part is from its whole (for all that is unequal is unlawful, but not all that is unlawful is unequal), the unjust and injustice are not the same as but different from the former kind, as part from whole; for injustice in this sense is a part of injustice in the wide sense, and similarly justice in the one sense of justice in the other. Therefore we must speak also about particular justice and particular injustice, and similarly about the just and the unjust. The justice, then, which answers to the whole of excellence and the corresponding injustice, one being the exercise of excellence as a whole, and the other that of vice as a whole towards others, we may leave on one side. And how the just and the unjust which answer to these are to be distinguished is evident; for practically the majority of the acts commanded by the law are those which are prescribed from the point of view of excellence taken as a whole; for the law bids us practise every excellence and forbids us to practise any vice. And the things that tend to produce excellence taken as a whole are those of the acts prescribed by the law which have been prescribed with a view to education for the common good. But with regard to the education of the individual as such, which makes him without qualification a good man, we must determine later whether this is the function of the political art or of another; for perhaps it is not the same in every case to be a good man and a good citizen.

Of particular justice and that which is just in the corresponding sense, one kind is that which is manifested in distributions of honour or money or the other things that fall to be divided among those who have a share in the constitution (for in these it is possible for one man to have a share either unequal or equal to that of another), and another kind is that which plays a rectifying part in transactions. Of this there are two divisions; of transactions some are voluntary and others involuntary— voluntary such transactions as sale, purchase, usury, pledging, lending, depositing, letting (they are called voluntary because the origin of these transactions is voluntary), while of the involuntary some are clandestine, such as theft, adultery, poisoning, procuring, enticement of slaves, assassination, false witness, and others

are violent, such as assault, imprisonment, murder, robbery with violence, mutilation, abuse, insult.

3 · Since the unjust man is unequal and the unjust act unequal, it is clear   10
that there is also an intermediate for the unequal. And this is the equal; for in any
kind of action in which there is a more and a less there is also what is equal. If, then,
the unjust be unequal, the just is equal, as all men suppose it to be, even apart from
argument. And since the equal is intermediate, the just will be an intermediate.
Now equality implies at least two things. The just, then, must be both intermediate   15
and equal and relative (i.e. for certain persons). And *qua* intermediate it must be
between certain things (which are respectively greater and less); *qua* equal, it
involves *two* things; *qua* just, it is for certain people. The just, therefore, involves at
least four terms; for the persons for whom it is in fact just are two, and the things in
which it is manifested, the objects, are two. And the same equality will exist   20
between the persons and between the things concerned; for as the latter—the things
concerned—are related, so are the former; if they are not equal, they will not have
what is equal, but this is the origin of quarrels and complaints—when either equals
have and are awarded unequal shares, or unequals equal shares. Further, this is
plain from the fact that awards should be according to merit; for all men agree that
what is just in distribution must be according to merit in some sense, though they do   25
not all specify the same sort of merit, but democrats identify it with the status of
freeman, supporters of oligarchy with wealth (or with noble birth), and supporters
of aristocracy with excellence.
    The just, then, is a species of the proportionate (proportion being not a
property only of the kind of number which consists of abstract units, but of number   30
in general). For proportion is equality of ratios, and involves four terms at least
(that discrete proportion involves four terms is plain, but so does continuous
proportion, for it uses one term as two and mentions it twice; e.g. as the line A is to   1131^{b}1
the line B, so is the line B to the line C; the line B, then, has been mentioned twice, so
that if the line B be assumed twice, the proportional terms will be four); and the
just, too, involves at least four terms, and the ratio is the same—for there is a similar
distinction between the persons and between the things. As the term A, then, is to B,   5
so will C be to D, and therefore, *alternando,* as A is to C, B will be to D. Therefore
also the whole is in the same ratio to the whole; and this coupling the distribution
effects, and, if the terms are so combined, effects justly. The conjunction, then, of
the term A with C and of B with D is what is just in distribution, and this species of   10
the just is intermediate, and the unjust is what violates the proportion; for the
proportional is intermediate, and the just is proportional. (Mathematicians call this
kind of proportion geometrical; for it is in geometrical proportion that it follows that
the whole is to the whole as either part is to the corresponding part.) This proportion
is not continuous; for we cannot get a single term standing for a person and a   15
thing.

This, then, is what the just is—the proportional; the unjust is what violates the proportion. Hence one term becomes too great, the other too small, as indeed happens in practice; for the man who acts unjustly has too much, and the man who is unjustly treated too little, of what is good. In the case of evil the reverse is true; for the lesser evil is reckoned a good in comparison with the greater evil, since the lesser evil is rather to be chosen than the greater, and what is worthy of choice is good, and what is worthier of choice a greater good.

This, then, is one species of the just.

4 · The remaining one is the rectificatory, which arises in connexion with transactions both voluntary and involuntary. This form of the just has a different specific character from the former. For the justice which distributes common possessions is always in accordance with the kind of proportion mentioned above (for in the case also in which the distribution is made from common funds it will be according to the same ratio which the funds put into the business bear to one another); and the injustice opposed to this kind of justice is that which violates the proportion. But the justice in transactions is a sort of equality indeed, and the injustice a sort of inequality; not according to that kind of proportion, however, but according to arithmetical proportion. For it makes no difference whether a good man has defrauded a bad man or a bad man a good one, nor whether it is a good or a bad man that has committed adultery; the law looks only to the distinctive character of the injury, and treats the parties as equal, if one is in the wrong and the other is being wronged, and if one inflicted injury and the other has received it. Therefore, this kind of injustice being an inequality, the judge tries to equalize it; for in the case also in which one has received and the other has inflicted a wound, or one has slain and the other been slain, the suffering and the action have been unequally distributed; but the judge tries to equalize things by means of the penalty, taking away from the gain of the assailant. For the term 'gain' is applied generally to such cases, even if it be not a term appropriate to certain cases, e.g. to the person who inflicts a wound—and 'loss' to the sufferer; at all events when the suffering has been estimated, the one is called loss and the other gain. Therefore the equal is intermediate between the greater and the less, but the gain and the loss are respectively greater and less in contrary ways; more of the good and less of the evil are gain, and the contrary is loss; intermediate between them is, as we saw, the equal, which we say is just; therefore corrective justice will be the intermediate between loss and gain. This is why, when people dispute, they take refuge in the judge; and to go to the judge is to go to justice; for the nature of the judge is to be a sort of animate justice; and they seek the judge as an intermediate, and in some states they call judges mediators, on the assumption that if they get what is intermediate they will get what is just. The just, then, is an intermediate, since the judge is so. Now the judge restores equality; it is as though there were a line divided into unequal parts, and he took away that by which the greater segment exceeds the

half, and added it to the smaller segment. And when the whole has been equally divided, then they say they have their own—i.e. when they have got what is equal. It is for this reason also that it is called just (δίκαιον), because it is a division into two 30 parts (δίχα), just as if one were to call it δίχαιον; and the judge (δικαστής) is one who bisects (διχαστής). The equal is intermediate between the greater and the lesser according to arithmetical proportion.[40] For when something is subtracted from one of two equals and added to the other, the other is in excess by these two; since if what was taken from the one had not been added to the other, the latter would have been in excess by one only. It therefore exceeds the intermediate by one, and the 1132^{b}1 intermediate exceeds by one that from which something was taken. By this, then, we shall recognize both what we must substract from that which has more, and what we must add to that which has less; we must add to the latter that by which the intermediate exceeds it, and subtract from the greatest that by which it exceeds the 5 intermediate. Let the lines AA, BB, CC be equal to one another; from the line AA let the segment AE have been subtracted, and to the line CC let the segment CD have been added, so that the whole line DCC exceeds the line EA by the segment CD and the segment CF; therefore it exceeds the line BB [And this is true of the other arts also; for they would have been destroyed if what the patient suffered had 10 not been just what the agent did, and of the same amount and kind.][41] by the segment CD. These names, both loss and gain, have come from voluntary exchange; for to have more than one's own is called gaining, and to have less than one's original share is called losing, e.g. in buying and selling and in all other matters in 15 which the law has left people free to make their own terms; but when they get neither more nor less but just what belongs to themselves, they say that they have their own and that they neither lose nor gain.

Therefore the just is intermediate between a sort of gain and a sort of loss, viz. those which are involuntary; it consists in having an equal amount before and after 20 the transaction.

5 · Some think that *reciprocity* is without qualification just, as the Pythagoreans said; for they defined justice without qualification as reciprocity. Now reciprocity fits neither distributive nor rectificatory justice—yet people *want* even the justice of Rhadamanthus to mean this: 25

Should a man suffer what he did, right justice would be done

—for in many cases they are not in accord; e.g. if an official has inflicted a wound, he should not be wounded in return, and if someone has wounded an official, he ought not to be wounded only but punished in addition. Further, there is a great 30 difference between a voluntary and an involuntary act. But in associations for

---

[40]In the MSS, and in Bywater, this sentence occurs after '. . . what is equal,' line 29.
[41]Excised in Bywater: see 1133^{a}14–16.

exchange this sort of justice does hold men together—reciprocity in accordance with a proportion and not on the basis of equality. For it is by proportionate requital that the city holds together. Men seek to return either evil for evil—and if they cannot do so, think their position mere slavery—or good for good—and if they cannot do so there is no exchange, but it is by exchange that they hold together. This is why they give a prominent place to the temple of the Graces—to promote the requital of services; for this is characteristic of grace—we should serve in return one who has shown grace to us, and should another time take the initiative in showing it.

Now proportionate return is secured by cross-conjunction. Let A be a builder, B a shoemaker, C a house, D a shoe. The builder, then, must get from the shoemaker the latter's work, and must himself give him in return his own. If, then, first there is proportionate equality of goods, and then reciprocal action takes place, the result we mention will be effected. If not, the bargain is not equal, and does not hold; for there is nothing to prevent the work of the one being better than that of the other; they must therefore be equated. (And this is true of the other arts also; for they would have been destroyed if what the patient suffered had not been just what the agent did, and of the same amount and kind.) For it is not two doctors that associate for exchange, but a doctor and a farmer, or in general people who are different and unequal; but these must be equated. This is why all things that are exchanged must be somehow commensurable. It is for this end that money has been introduced, and it becomes in a sense an intermediate; for it measures all things, and therefore the excess and the defect—how many shoes are equal to a house or to a given amount of food. The number of shoes exchanged for a house [or for a given amount of food]⁴² must therefore correspond to the ratio of builder to shoemaker. For if this be not so, there will be no exchange and no intercourse. And this proportion will not be effected unless the goods are somehow equal. All goods must therefore be measured by some one thing, as we said before. Now this unit is in truth demand, which holds all things together (for if men did not need one another's goods at all, or did not need them equally, there would be either no exchange or not the same exchange); but money has become by convention a sort of representative of demand; and this is why it has the name 'money' (νόμισμα)—because it exists not by nature but by law (νόμος) and it is in our power to change it and make it useless. There will, then, be reciprocity when the terms have been equated so that as farmer is to shoemaker, the amount of the shoemaker's work is to that of the farmer's work. But we must not bring them into a figure of proportion when they have already exchanged (otherwise one extreme will have both excesses), but when they still have their own goods. Thus they are equals and associates just because this equality can be effected in their case. Let A be a farmer, C food, B a shoemaker, D his product equated to C. If it had not been possible for reciprocity to be thus effected, there

---

⁴²Excised by Ramsauer.

would have been no association of the parties. That demand holds things together as a single unit is shown by the fact that when men do not need one another, i.e. when neither needs the other or one does not need the other, they do not exchange, as we do when some one wants what one has oneself, e.g. when people permit the exportation of corn in exchange for wine. This equation therefore must be   10 established. And for the future exchange—that if we do not need a thing now we shall have it if ever we do need it—money is as it were our surety; for it must be possible for us to get what we want by bringing the money. Now the same thing happens to money itself as to goods—it is not always worth the same; yet it tends to be steadier. This is why all goods must have a price set on them; for then there will always be exchange, and if so, association. Money, then, acting as a measure, makes   15 goods commensurate and equates them; for neither would there have been association if there were not exchange, nor exchange if there were not equality, nor equality if there were not commensurability. Now in truth it is impossible that things differing so much should become commensurate, but with reference to demand they may become so sufficiently. There must, then, be a unit, and that fixed   20 by agreement (for which reason it is called money); for it is this that makes all things commensurate, since all things are measured by money. Let A be a house, B ten minae, C a bed. A is half of B, if the house is worth five minae or equal to them; the bed, C, is a tenth of B; it is plain, then, how many beds are equal to a house, viz.   25 five. That exchange took place thus because there was money is plain; for it makes no difference whether it is five beds that exchange for a house, or the money value of five beds.

We have now defined the unjust and the just. These having been marked off from each other, it is plain that just action is intermediate between acting unjustly   30 and being justly treated; for the one is to have too much and the other to have too little. Justice is a kind of mean, but not in the same way as the other excellences, but because it relates to an intermediate amount, while injustice relates to the extremes. And justice is that in virtue of which the just man is said to be a doer, by choice, of   1134ᵃ1 that which is just, and one who will distribute either between himself and another or between two others not so as to give more of what is desirable to himself and less to his neighbour (and conversely with what is harmful), but so as to give what is equal   5 in accordance with proportion; and similarly in distributing between two other persons. Injustice on the other hand is similarly related to the unjust, which is excess and defect, contrary to proportion, of the useful or hurtful. For which reason injustice is excess and defect, viz. because it is productive of excess and defect—in one's own case excess of what is in its own nature useful and defect of what is   10 hurtful, while in the case of others it is as a whole like what it is in one's own case, but proportion may be violated in either direction. In the unjust act to have too little is to be unjustly treated; to have too much is to act unjustly.

Let this be taken as our account of the nature of justice and injustice, and   15 similarly of the just and the unjust in general.

6 · Since acting unjustly does not necessarily imply being unjust, we must ask what sort of unjust acts imply that the doer is unjust with respect to each type of injustice, e.g. a thief, an adulterer, or a brigand. Surely the answer does not turn on the difference between these types. For a man might even lie with a woman knowing who she was, but the origin of this act might be not choice but passion. He acts unjustly, then, but is not unjust; e.g. a man is not a thief, yet he stole, nor an adulterer, yet he committed adultery; and similarly in all other cases.

Now we have previously stated how the reciprocal is related to the just; but we must not forget that what we are looking for is not only what is just without qualification but also political justice. This is found among men who share their life with a view to self-sufficiency, men who are free and either proportionately or arithmetically equal, so that between those who do not fulfil this condition there is no political justice but justice in a special sense and by analogy. For justice exists only between men whose mutual relations are governed by law; and law exists for men between whom there is injustice; for legal justice is the discrimination of the just and the unjust. And between men between whom there is injustice there is also unjust action (though there is not injustice between all between whom there is unjust action), and this is assigning too much to oneself of things good in themselves and too little of things evil in themselves. This is why we do not allow a *man* to rule, but law,[43] because a man behaves thus in his own interests and becomes a tyrant. The magistrate on the other hand is the guardian of justice, and, if of justice, then of equality also. And since he is assumed to have no more than his share, if he is just (for he does not assign to himself more or what is good in itself, unless such a share is proportional to his merits—so that it is for others that he labours, and it is for this reason that men, as we stated previously, say that justice is another's good), therefore a reward must be given him, and this is honour, and privilege; but those for whom such things are not enough become tyrants.

The justice of a master and that of a father are not the same as this, though they are like it; for there can be no injustice in the unqualified sense towards things that are one's own, but a man's chattel, and his child until it reaches a certain age and sets up for itself, are as it were part of himself, and no one chooses to hurt himself (for which reason there can be no injustice towards oneself). Therefore the justice or injustice of citizens is not manifested in these relations; for it was as we saw according to law, and between people naturally subject to law, and these as we saw are people who have an equal share in ruling and being ruled. Hence justice can more truly be manifested towards a wife than towards children and chattels, for the former is household justice; but even this is different from political justice.

7 · Of political justice part is natural, part legal,—natural, that which everywhere has the same force and does not exist by people's thinking this or that;

---

[43]Reading νόμον for λόγον ('reason').

legal, that which is originally indifferent, but when it has been laid down is not   20
indifferent, e.g. that a prisoner's ransom shall be a mina, or that a goat and not two
sheep shall be sacrificed, and again all the laws that are passed for particular cases,
e.g. that sacrifice shall be made in honour of Brasidas, and the provisions of decrees.
Now some think that all justice is of this sort, because that which is by nature is
unchangeable and has everywhere the same force (as fire burns both here and in   25
Persia), while they see change in the things recognized as just. This, however, is not
true in this unqualified way, but is true in a sense; or rather, with the gods it is
perhaps not true at all, while with us there is something that is just even by nature,
yet all of it is changeable; but still some is by nature, some not by nature. It is   30
evident which sort of thing, among things capable of being otherwise, is by nature,
and which is not but is legal and conventional, assuming that both are equally
changeable. And in all other things the same distinction will apply; by nature the
right hand is stronger, yet it is possible that all men should come to be
ambidextrous. The things which are just by virtue of convention and expediency are   1135ᵃ1
like measures; for wine and corn measures are not everywhere equal, but larger in
wholesale and smaller in retail markets. Similarly, the things which are just not by
nature but by human enactment are not everywhere the same, since constitutions
also are not the same, though there is but one which is everywhere by nature the   5
best.

Of things just and lawful each is related as the universal to its particulars; for
the things that are done are many, but of *them* each is one, since it is universal.

There is a difference between the act of injustice and what is unjust, and
between the act of justice and what is just; for a thing is unjust by nature or by
enactment; and this very thing, when it has been done, is an act of injustice, but   10
before it is done is not yet this but is unjust. So, too, with an act of justice (though
the general term is rather 'just action', and 'act of justice' is applied to the
correction of the act of injustice).

Each of these must later be examined separately with regard to the nature and
number of its species and the nature of the things with which it is concerned.   15

8 · Acts just and unjust being as we have described them, a man acts
unjustly or justly whenever he does such acts voluntarily; when involuntarily, he
acts neither unjustly nor justly except in an incidental way; for he does things which
happen to be just or unjust. Whether an act is or is not one of injustice (or of justice)
is determined by its voluntariness or involuntariness; for when it is voluntary it is   20
blamed, and at the same time is then an act of injustice; so that there will be things
that are unjust but not yet acts of injustice, if voluntariness be not present as well.
By the voluntary I mean, as has been said before, any of the things in a man's own
power which he does with knowledge, i.e. not in ignorance either of the person acted
on or of the instrument used or of the end that will be attained (e.g. whom he is   25
striking, with what, and to what end), each such act being done not incidentally nor

under compulsion (e.g. if you take my hand and strike someone else with it, I do not act voluntarily; for the act was not in my power). The person struck may be the striker's father, and the striker may know that it is a man or one of the persons present, but not know that it is his father; a similar distinction may be made in the case of the end, and with regard to the whole action. Therefore that which is done in ignorance, or though not done in ignorance is not in the agent's power, or is done under compulsion, is involuntary (for many natural processes, even, we knowingly both perform and experience, none of which is either voluntary or involuntary; e.g. growing old or dying). But in the case of unjust and just acts alike the injustice or justice may be only incidental; for a man might return a deposit unwillingly and from fear, and then he must not be said either to do what is just or to act justly, except in an incidental way. Similarly the man who under compulsion and unwillingly fails to return the deposit must be said to act unjustly, and to do what is unjust, only incidentally. Of voluntary acts we do some by choice, others not by choice; by choice those which we do after deliberation, not by choice those which we do without previous deliberation. Thus there are three kinds of injury in transactions; those done in ignorance are *mistakes* when the person acted on, the act, the instrument, or the end is other than the agent supposed; the agent thought either that he was not hitting any one or that he was not hitting with this missile or not hitting this person or to this end, but a result followed other than that which he thought likely (e.g. he threw not with intent to wound but only to prick), or the person hit or the missile was other than he supposed. Now when the injury takes place contrary to reasonable expectation, it is a *misadventure*. When it is not contrary to reasonable expectation but does not imply vice, it is a *mistake* (for a man makes a mistake when the ignorance[44] originates in him, but is the victim of accident when its origin lies outside him). When he acts with knowledge but not after deliberation, it is an *act of injustice*—e.g. the acts due to anger or to other passions necessary or natural to man; for when men do such harmful and mistaken acts they act unjustly, and the acts are acts of injustice, but this does not imply that the doers are unjust or wicked; for the injury is not due to vice. But when a man acts from choice, he is an *unjust man* and a vicious man.

Hence acts proceeding from anger are rightly judged not to be done of malice aforethought; for it is not the man who acts in anger but he who enraged him that starts the mischief. Again, the matter in dispute is not whether the thing happened or not, but its justice; for it is apparent injustice that occasions anger. For they do not dispute about the occurrence of the act—as in commercial transactions where one of the two parties *must* be vicious—unless they do so owing to forgetfulness; but, agreeing about the fact, they dispute on which side justice lies (whereas a man who has deliberately injured another cannot help knowing that he has done so), so that the one thinks he is being treated unjustly and the other disagrees.

[44]Reading ἀγνοίας for αἰτίας.

But if a man harms another by choice, he acts unjustly; and *these* are the acts   1136ª1
of injustice which imply that the doer is an unjust man, provided that the act
violates proportion or equality. Similarly, a man *is just* when he acts justly by
choice; but he *acts justly* if he merely acts voluntarily.

Of involuntary acts some are forgivable, others not. For the mistakes which   5
men make not only in ignorance but also from ignorance are forgivable, while those
which men do not from ignorance but (though they do them *in* ignorance) owing to
a passion which is neither natural nor such as man is liable to, are not forgivable.

9 · Assuming that we have sufficiently defined the suffering and doing of   10
injustice, it may be asked whether there is any truth in Euripides' paradoxical
words:

> 'I slew my mother, that's my tale in brief.'
> 'Were you both willing, or unwilling both?'

Is it truly possible to be voluntarily treated unjustly, or is all suffering of injustice   15
involuntary, as all unjust action is voluntary? And is all suffering of injustice of the
latter kind or else all of the former, or is it sometimes voluntary, sometimes
involuntary? So, too, with the case of being justly treated; all just action is
voluntary, so that it is reasonable that there should be a similar opposition in either
case—that both being unjustly and being justly treated should be either alike   20
voluntary or alike involuntary. But it would be thought paradoxical even in the case
of being justly treated, if it were always voluntary; for some are non-voluntarily
treated justly. One might raise this question also, whether every one who has
suffered what is unjust is being unjustly treated, or on the other hand it is with
suffering as with acting. In both it is possible to partake of justice incidentally, and   25
similarly (it is plain) of injustice; for to do what is unjust is not the same as to act
unjustly, nor to suffer what is unjust as to be treated unjustly, and similarly in the
case of acting justly and being justly treated; for it is impossible to be unjustly
treated if the other does not act unjustly, or justly treated unless he acts justly. Now   30
if to act unjustly is simply to harm some one voluntarily, and 'voluntarily' means
'knowing the person acted on, the instrument, and the manner of one's acting', and
the incontinent man voluntarily harms himself, not only will he voluntarily be
unjustly treated but it will be possible to treat oneself unjustly. (This also is one of   1136ᵇ1
the questions in doubt, whether a man can treat himself unjustly.) Again, a man
may voluntarily, owing to incontinence, be harmed by another who acts voluntarily,
so that it would be possible to be voluntarily treated unjustly. Or is our definition
incorrect; must we to 'harming another, with knowledge both of the person acted on,
of the instrument, and of the manner' add 'contrary to the wish of the person acted
on'? Then a man may be voluntarily harmed and voluntarily suffer what is unjust,   5
but no one is voluntarily treated unjustly; for no one wishes to be unjustly treated,

not even the incontinent man. He acts contrary to his wish; for no one *wishes* for what he does not think to be good, but the incontinent man does *do* things that he does not think he ought to do. Again, one who gives what is his own, as Homer says

10   Glaucus gave Diomede

> Armour of gold for brazen, the price of a hundred beeves for nine,[45]

is not unjustly treated; for though to give is in his power, to be unjustly treated is not, but there must be some one to treat him unjustly. It is plain, then, that being unjustly treated is not voluntary.

15   Of the questions we intended to discuss two still remain for discussion: whether it is the man who has assigned to another more than his deserts that acts unjustly, or he who has the excessive share, and whether it is possible to treat oneself unjustly. The questions are connected; for if the former alternative is possible and the distributor acts unjustly and not the man who has the excessive share, then if a man assigns more to another than to himself, knowingly and voluntarily, he treats

20   himself unjustly; which is what modest people seem to do, since the virtuous man tends to take less than his share. Or does this statement too need qualification? For he perhaps gets more than his share of some other good, e.g. of honour or of intrinsic nobility. Again, the question is solved by applying the distinction we applied to unjust action; for he suffers nothing contrary to his own wish, so that he is not

25   unjustly treated as far as this goes, but at most only suffers harm.

It is plain too that the distributor acts unjustly, but not always the man who has the excessive share; for it is not he to whom what is unjust appertains that acts unjustly, but he to whom it appertains to do the unjust act voluntarily, i.e. the person in whom lies the origin of the action, and this lies in the distributor not in the receiver. Again, since things are said to do things in different senses, and there is a

30   sense in which lifeless things, or a hand, or a servant who obeys an order, may be said to slay, he who gets an excessive share does not act unjustly; though he does what is unjust.

Again, if the distributor gave his judgment in ignorance, he does not act unjustly in respect of legal justice, and his judgment is not unjust in this sense, but in a sense it *is* unjust (for legal justice and primary justice are different); but if with

1137ᵃ1   knowledge he judged unjustly, he is himself aiming at an excessive share either of gratitude or of revenge. As much, then, as if he were to share in the unjust act, the man who has judged unjustly for these reasons has got too much; for, assigning the land on that condition, he received not land but money.

5   Men think that acting unjustly is in their power, and therefore that being just is easy. But it is not; to lie with one's neighbour's wife, to wound another, to deliver a bribe, is easy and in our power, but to do these things as a result of a certain state of character is neither easy nor in our power. Similarly to know what is just and what

10   is unjust requires, men think, no great wisdom, because it is not hard to understand the matters dealt with by the laws (though these are not the things that are just,

---

[45]*Iliad* VI 236.

except incidentally); but how actions must be done and distributions effected in order to be just, to know *this* is a greater achievement than knowing what is good for the health; though even there, while it is easy to know that honey, wine, hellebore, cautery, and the use of the knife are so, to know how, to whom, and when there 15 should be applied with a view to producing health, is no less an achievement than that of being a physician. Again, for this very reason men think that acting unjustly is characteristic of the just man no less than of the unjust, because he would be not less but even more capable of doing each of these acts; for he could lie with a woman or wound a neighbour; and the brave man could throw away his shield and turn to 20 flight in this direction or in that. But to play the coward or to act unjustly consists not in doing these things, except incidentally, but in doing them as the result of a certain state of character, just as to practise medicine and to heal consists not in applying or not applying the knife, in using or not using medicines, but in doing so in 25 a certain way.

Just acts occur between people who participate in things good in themselves and can have too much or too little of them; for some beings (e.g. presumably the gods) cannot have too much of them, and to others, those who are incurably bad, not even the smallest share in them is beneficial but all such goods are harmful, while to others they are beneficial up to a point; therefore justice is essentially something 30 human.

10 · Our next subject is equity and the equitable, and their respective relations to justice and the just. For on examination they appear to be neither absolutely the same nor generically different; and while we sometimes praise what is equitable and the equitable man (so that we apply the name by way of praise even to instances of the other virtues, instead of 'good', meaning by 'more equitable'[46] 1137ᵇ1 that a thing is better), at other times, when we reason it out, it seems strange if the equitable, being something different from the just, is yet praiseworthy; for either the just or the equitable is not good,[47] if they are different; or, if both are good, they 5 are the same.

These, then, are pretty much the considerations that give rise to the problem about the equitable; they are all in a sense correct and not opposed to one another; for the equitable, though it is better than one kind of justice, yet is just, and it is not as being a different class of thing that it is better than the just. The same thing, then, is just and equitable, and while both are good the equitable is superior. What 10 creates the problem is that the equitable is just, but not the legally just but a correction of legal justice. The reason is that all law is universal but about some things it is not possible to make a universal statement which will be correct. In those cases, then, in which it is necessary to speak universally, but not possible to do so 15 correctly, the law takes the usual case, though it is not ignorant of the possibility of error. And it is none the less correct; for the error is not in the law nor in the

---

[46]Reading τῷ ἐπιεικέστερον.
[47]Omitting οὐ δίκαιον.

legislator but in the nature of the thing, since the matter of practical affairs is of this
20 kind from the start. When the law speaks universally, then, and a case arises on it
which is not covered by the universal statement, then it is right, when the legislator
fails us and has erred by over-simplicity, to correct the omission—to say what the
legislator himself would have said had he been present, and would have put into his
law if he had known. Hence the equitable is just, and better than one kind of
25 justice—not better than absolute justice but better than the error that arises from
the absoluteness of the statement. And this is the nature of the equitable, a
correction of law where it is defective owing to its universality. In fact this is the
reason why all things are not determined by law, viz. that about some things it is
impossible to lay down a law, so that a decree is needed. For when the thing is
30 indefinite the rule also is indefinite, like the lead rule used in making the Lesbian
moulding; the rule adapts itself to the shape of the stone and is not rigid, and so too
the decree is adapted to the facts.

It is plain, then, what the equitable is, and that it is just and is better than one
kind of justice. It is evident also from this who the equitable man is; the man who
chooses and does such acts, and is no stickler for justice in a bad sense but tends to
1138ª1 take less than his share though he has the law on his side, is equitable, and this state
is equity, which is a sort of justice, and not a different state.

11 · Whether a man can treat himself unjustly or not, is evident from what
5 has been said. For one class of just acts are those acts in accordance with any
excellence which are prescribed by the law; e.g. the law does not command a man to
kill himself, and what it does not command it forbids. Again, when a man in
violation of the law harms another (otherwise than in retaliation) voluntarily, he
acts unjustly, and a voluntary agent is one who knows both the person he is affecting
and the instrument; and he who through anger voluntarily stabs himself does this
10 contrary to right reason, and this the law does not allow; therefore he is acting
unjustly. But towards whom? Surely towards the state, not towards himself. For he
suffers voluntarily, but no one is voluntarily treated unjustly. This is also the reason
why the state punishes; a certain loss of civil rights attaches to the man who destroys
himself, on the ground that he is treating the state unjustly.

Further, in the sense in which the man who acts unjustly is unjust only and not
15 bad all round, it is not possible to treat oneself unjustly (this is different from the
former sense; the unjust man in one sense of the term is wicked in a particularized
way just as the coward is, not in the sense of being wicked all round, so that his
unjust act does not manifest wickedness in general). For that would imply the
possibility of the same thing's having been subtracted from and added to the same
20 thing at the same time; but this is impossible—the just and the unjust always
involve more than one person. Further, unjust action is voluntary and done by
choice, and is prior (for the man who because he has suffered does the same in
return is not thought to act unjustly); but if a man harms himself he suffers and
does the same things *at the same time*. Further, a man could be voluntarily treated

unjustly. Besides, no one acts unjustly without committing particular acts of injustice; but no one can commit adultery with his own wife or housebreaking on his   25 own house or theft on his own property.

In general, the question 'can a man treat himself unjustly?' is solved also by the distinction we applied to the question 'can a man be voluntarily treated unjustly?'

(It is evident too that both are bad, being unjustly treated and acting unjustly; for the one means having less and the other having more than the intermediate   30 amount, which plays the part here that the healthy does in the medical art, and that good condition does in the art of bodily training. But still acting unjustly is the worse, for it involves vice and is blameworthy—involves vice which is either of the complete and unqualified kind or almost so (for not all voluntary unjust action implies injustice), while being unjustly treated does not involve vice and injustice. In itself, then, being unjustly treated is less bad, but there is nothing to prevent its being incidentally a greater evil. But theory cares nothing for this; it calls pleurisy a   1138ᵇ1 more serious mischief than a stumble; yet the latter may become incidentally the more serious, if the fall due to it leads to your being taken prisoner or put to death by   5 the enemy.)

Metaphorically and in virtue of a certain resemblance there is a justice, not indeed between a man and himself, but between certain parts of him; yet not every kind of justice but that of master and servant or that of husband and wife. For these are the ratios in which the part of the soul that has reason stands to the irrational part; and it is with a view to these parts that people also think a man can be unjust to   10 himself, viz. because these parts are liable to suffer something contrary to their desires; there is therefore thought to be a mutual justice between them as between ruler and ruled.

Let this be taken as our account of justice and the other, i.e. the moral, excellences.

BOOK VI

1 · Since we have previously said that one ought to choose that which is intermediate, not the excess nor the defect, and that the intermediate is determined by the dictates of reason, let us discuss this. In all the states we have mentioned, as   20 in all other matters, there is a mark to which the man who possesses reason looks, and heightens or relaxes his activity accordingly, and there is a standard which determines the mean states which we say are intermediate between excess and defect, being in accordance with right reason. But such a statement, though true, is   25 by no means illuminating; for in all other pursuits which are objects of knowledge it is indeed true to say that we must not exert ourselves nor relax our efforts too much nor too little, but to an intermediate extent and as right reason dictates; but if a man

30   had only this knowledge he would be none the wiser—e.g. we should not know what sort of medicines to apply to our body if some one were to say 'all those which the medical art prescribes, and which agree with the practice of one who possesses the art'. Hence it is necessary with regard to the states of the soul also not only that this true statement should be made, but also that it should be determined what right reason is and what is the standard that fixes it.

1139ᵃ1   We divided the excellences of the soul and said that some are excellences of character and others of intellect. Now we have discussed the moral excellences; with regard to the others let us express our view as follows, beginning with some remarks about the soul. We said before that there are two parts of the soul—that which possesses reason and that which is irrational; let us now draw a similar

5   distinction within the part which possesses reason. And let it be assumed that there are two parts which possess reason—one by which we contemplate the kind of things whose principles cannot be otherwise, and one by which we contemplate variable things; for where objects differ in kind the part of the soul answering to

10   each of the two is different in kind, since it is in virtue of a certain likeness and kinship with their objects that they have the knowledge they have. Let one of these parts be called the scientific and the other the calculative; for to deliberate and to calculate are the same thing, but no one deliberates about what cannot be

15   otherwise. Therefore the calculative is one part of the faculty which possesses reason. We must, then, learn what is the best state of each of these two parts; for this is the excellence of each.

2 · The excellence of a thing is relative to its proper function. Now there are three things in the soul which control action and truth—sensation, thought, desire. Of these sensation originates no action; this is plain from the fact that beasts

20   have sensation but no share in action.

What affirmation and negation are in thinking, pursuit and avoidance are in desire; so that since moral excellence is a state concerned with choice, and choice is deliberate desire, therefore both the reasoning must be true and the desire right, if

25   the choice is to be good, and the latter must pursue just what the former asserts. Now this kind of intellect and of truth is practical; of the intellect which is contemplative, not practical nor productive, the good and the bad state are truth and falsity (for this is the function of everything intellectual); while of the part

30   which is practical and intellectual the good state is truth in agreement with right desire.

The origin of action—its efficient, not its final cause—is choice, and that of choice is desire and reasoning with a view to an end. This is why choice cannot exist either without thought and intellect or without a moral state; for good action and its

35   opposite cannot exist without a combination of intellect and character. Intellect itself, however, moves nothing, but only the intellect which aims at an end and is

1139ᵇ1   practical; for this rules the productive intellect as well, since every one who makes makes for an end, and that which is made is not an end in the unqualified sense (but only relative to something, i.e. of something)—only that which is *done* is that; for good action is an end, and desire aims at this. Hence choice is either desiderative thought or intellectual desire, and such an origin of action is a man. (Nothing that is 5 past is an object of choice, e.g. no one chooses to have sacked Troy; for no one *deliberates* about the past, but about what is future and contingent, while what is past is not capable of not having taken place; hence Agathon is right in saying

> For this alone is lacking even to God, 10
> To make undone things that have once been done.)

The function of both the intellectual parts, then, is truth. Therefore the states that are most strictly those in respect of which each of these parts will reach truth are the excellences of the two parts.

3 · Let us begin, then, from the beginning, and discuss these states once more. Let it be assumed that the states by virtue of which the soul possesses truth by 15 way of affirmation or denial are five in number, i.e. art, knowledge, practical wisdom, philosophic wisdom, comprehension; for belief and opinion may be mistaken.

Now what *knowledge* is, if we are to speak exactly and not follow mere similarities, is plain from what follows. We all suppose that what we know is not 20 capable of being otherwise; of things capable of being otherwise we do not know, when they have passed outside our observation, whether they exist or not. Therefore the object of knowledge is of necessity. Therefore it is eternal; for things that are of necessity in the unqualified sense are all eternal; and things that are eternal are ungenerated and imperishable. Again, every science is thought to be capable of 25 being taught, and its object of being learned. And all teaching starts from what is already known, as we maintain in the *Analytics*[50] also; for it proceeds sometimes through induction and sometimes by deduction. Now induction is of first principles[51] and of the universal and deduction proceeds *from* universals. There are therefore principles from which deduction proceeds, which are not reached by 30 deduction; it is therefore by induction that they are acquired. Knowledge, then, is a state of capacity to demonstrate, and has the other limiting characteristics which we specify in the *Analytics;* for it is when a man believes in a certain way and the principles are known to him that he has knowledge, since if they are not better known to him than the conclusion, he will have his knowledge only incidentally. 35

Let this, then, be taken as our account of knowledge.

4 · Among things that can be otherwise are included both things made and 1140ª1 things done; making and acting are different (for their nature we treat even the discussions outside our school as reliable); so that the reasoned state of capacity to act is different from the reasoned state of capacity to make. Nor[52] are they included 5 one in the other; for neither is acting making nor is making acting. Now since building is an art and is essentially a reasoned state of capacity to make, and there is

---

[50]*Posterior Analytics* I 1.   [51]Reading ἀρχῆς.   [52]Omitting διό.

neither any art that is not such a state nor any such state that is not an art, *art* is
10   identical with a state of capacity to make, involving a true course of reasoning. All
art is concerned with coming into being, i.e. with contriving and considering how
something may come into being which is capable of either being or not being, and
whose origin is in the maker and not in the thing made; for art is concerned neither
with things that are, or come into being, by necessity, nor with things that do so in
15   accordance with nature (since these have their origin in themselves). Making and
acting being different, art must be a matter of making, not of acting. And in a sense
chance and art are concerned with the same objects; as Agathon says, 'art loves
20   chance and chance loves art'. Art, then, as has been said, is a state concerned with
making, involving a true course of reasoning, and lack of art on the contrary is a
state concerned with making, involving a false course of reasoning; both are
concerned with what can be otherwise.

5 · Regarding *practical wisdom* we shall get at the truth by considering who
25   are the persons we credit with it. Now it is thought to be a mark of a man of
practical wisdom to be able to deliberate well about what is good and expedient for
himself, not in some particular respect, e.g. about what sorts of thing conduce to
health or to strength, but about what sorts of thing conduce to the good life in
general. This is shown by the fact that we credit men with practical wisdom in some
particular respect when they have calculated well with a view to some good end
30   which is one of those that are not the object of any art. Thus in general the man who
is capable of deliberating has practical wisdom. Now no one deliberates about
things that cannot be otherwise nor about things that it is impossible for him to do.
Therefore, since knowledge involves demonstration, but there is no demonstration
of things whose first principles can be otherwise (for all such things might actually
1140ᵇ1   be otherwise), and since it is impossible to deliberate about things that are of
necessity, practical wisdom cannot be knowledge nor art; not knowledge because
that which can be done is capable of being otherwise, not art because action and
making are different kinds of thing. It remains, then, that it is a true and reasoned
5   state of capacity to act with regard to the things that are good or bad for man. For
while making has an end other than itself, action cannot; for good action itself is its
end. It is for this reason that we think Pericles and men like him have practical
wisdom, viz. because they can see what is good for themselves and what is good for
10   men in general; we consider that those can do this who are good at managing
households or states. (This is why we call temperance by this name; we imply that it
preserves one's practical wisdom.⁵³ Now what it preserves is a belief of the kind we
have described. For it is not any and every belief that pleasant and painful objects
destroy and pervert, e.g. the belief that the triangle has or has not its angles equal to
15   two right angles, but only beliefs about what is to be done. For the principles of the
things that are done consist in that for the sake of which they are to be done; but the
man who has been ruined by pleasure or pain forthwith fails to see any such

---

⁵³Σωφροσύνη connected with σώζειν τὴν φρόνησιν.

principle—to see that for the sake of this or because of this he ought to choose and do whatever he chooses and does; for vice is destructive of the principle.)

Practical wisdom, then, must be a reasoned and true state of capacity to act   20
with regard to human goods. But further, while there is such a thing as excellence in art, there is no such thing as excellence in practical wisdom; and in art he who errs willingly is preferable, but in practical wisdom, as in the excellences he is the reverse. Plainly, then, practical wisdom is an excellence and not an art. There being   25
two parts of the soul that possess reason, it must be the excellence of one of the two, i.e. of that part which forms opinions; for opinion is about what can be otherwise, and so is practical wisdom. But yet it is not only a reasoned state; this is shown by the fact that a state of that sort may be forgotten but practical wisdom cannot.   30

6 · Knowledge is belief about things that are universal and necessary, and there are principles of everything that is demonstrated and of all knowledge (for knowledge involves reasoning). This being so, the first principle of what is known cannot be an object of knowledge, of art, or of practical wisdom; for that which can be known can be demonstrated, and art and practical wisdom deal with things that   1141ᵃ1
can be otherwise. Nor are these first principles the objects of wisdom, for it is a mark of the wise man to have *demonstration* about some things. If, then, the states by which we have truth and are never deceived about things that cannot—or can—be otherwise are knowledge, practical wisdom, philosophic wisdom, and   5
comprehension, and it cannot be any of the three (i.e. practical wisdom, scientific knowledge, or philosophic wisdom), the remaining alternative is that it is comprehension that grasps the first principles.

7 · *Wisdom* in the arts we ascribe to their most finished exponents, e.g. to Phidias as a sculptor and to Polyclitus as a maker of statues, and here we mean   10
nothing by wisdom except excellence in art; but we think that some people are wise in general, not in some particular field or in any other limited respect, as Homer says in the *Margites*,

Him did the gods make neither a digger nor yet a ploughman   15
Nor wise in anything else.

Therefore wisdom must plainly be the most finished of the forms of knowledge. It follows that the wise man must not only know what follows from the first principles, but must also possess truth about the first principles. Therefore wisdom must be comprehension combined with knowledge—knowledge of the highest objects which has received as it were its proper completion.

For it would be strange to think that the art of politics, or practical wisdom, is   20
the best knowledge, since man is not the best thing in the world. Now if what is healthy or good is different for men and for fishes, but what is white or straight is always the same, any one would say that what is wise is the same but what is practically wise is different; for it is to that which observes well the various matters   25
concerning itself that one ascribes practical wisdom, and it is to this that one will

entrust such matters. This is why we say that some even of the lower animals have practical wisdom, viz. those which are found to have a power of foresight with regard to their own life. It is evident also that wisdom and the art of politics cannot
30 be the same; for if the state of mind concerned with a man's own interests is to be called wisdom, there will be many wisdoms; there will not be one concerned with the good of all animals (any more than there is one art of medicine for all existing things), but a different wisdom about the good of each species.

But if the argument be that man is the best of the animals, this makes no difference; for there are other things much more divine in their nature even than
1141ᵇ1 man, e.g., most conspicuously, the bodies of which the heavens are framed. From what has been said it is plain, then, that wisdom is knowledge, combined with comprehension, of the things that are highest by nature. This is why we say Anaxagoras, Thales, and men like them have wisdom but not practical wisdom,
5 when we see them ignorant of what is to their own advantage, and why we say that they know things that are remarkable, admirable, difficult, and divine, but useless; viz. because it is not human goods that they seek.

Practical wisdom on the other hand is concerned with things human and things about which it is possible to deliberate; for we say this is above all the work of the
10 man of practical wisdom, to deliberate well, but no one deliberates about things that cannot be otherwise, nor about things which have not an end, and that a good that can be brought about by action. The man who is without qualification good at deliberating is the man who is capable of aiming in accordance with calculation at the best for man of things attainable by action. Nor is practical wisdom concerned
15 with universals only—it must also recognize the particulars; for it is practical, and practice is concerned with particulars. This is why some who do not know, and especially those who have experience, are more practical than others who know; for if a man knew that light meats are digestible and wholesome, but did not know which sorts of meat are light, he would not produce health, but the man who knows
20 that chicken is wholesome is more likely to produce health.

Now practical wisdom is concerned with action; therefore one should have both forms of it, or the latter in preference to the former. Here, too, there must be a controlling kind.

8 · Political wisdom and practical wisdom are the same state of mind, but to be them is not the same. Of the wisdom concerned with the city, the practical
25 wisdom which plays a controlling part is legislative wisdom, while that which is related to this as particulars to their universal is known by the general name 'political wisdom'; this has to do with action and deliberation, for a decree is a thing to be carried out in the form of an individual act. This is why the exponents of this art are alone said to take part in politics; for these alone do things as manual labourers do things.
30 Practical wisdom also is identified especially with that form of it which is concerned with a man himself—with the individual; and this is known by the general name 'practical wisdom'; of the other kinds one is called household

management, another legislation, the third politics, and of the last one part is called deliberative and the other judicial. Now knowing what is good for oneself will be one kind of knowledge, but is very different from the other kinds; and the man who knows and concerns himself with his own interests is thought to have practical wisdom, while politicians are thought to be busybodies; hence the words of Euripides,

> But how could I be wise, who might at ease,
> Numbered among the army's multitude,
> Have had an equal share?. . .
> For those who aim too high and do too much. . . .

Those who think thus seek their own good, and consider that one ought to do so. From this opinion, then, has come the view that such men have practical wisdom; yet perhaps one's own good cannot exist without household management, nor without a form of government. Further, how one should order one's own affairs is not clear and needs inquiry.

What has been said is confirmed by the fact that while young men become geometricians and mathematicians and wise in matters like these, it is thought that a young man of practical wisdom cannot be found. The cause is that such wisdom is concerned not only with universals but with particulars, which become familiar from experience, but a young man has no experience, for it is length of time that gives experience; indeed one might ask this question too, why a boy may become a mathematician, but not a wise man or a natural scientist. Is it because the objects of mathematics exist by abstraction, while the first principles of these other subjects come from experience, and because young men have no conviction about the latter but merely use the proper language, while the essence of mathematical objects is plain enough to them?

Further, error in deliberation may be either about the universal or about the particular; we may fail to know either that all water that weighs heavy is bad, or that this particular water weighs heavy.

That practical wisdom is not knowledge is evident; for it is, as has been said, concerned with the ultimate particular fact, since the thing to be done is of this nature. It is opposed, then, to comprehension; for comprehension is of the definitions, for which no reason can be given, while practical wisdom is concerned with the ultimate particular, which is the object not of knowledge but of perception—not the perception of qualities peculiar to one sense but a perception akin to that by which we perceive that the particular figure before us is a triangle; for in that direction too there will be a limit. But this is rather perception than practical wisdom, though it is another kind of perception.

9 · There is a difference between inquiry and deliberation; for deliberation is a particular kind of inquiry. We must grasp the nature of excellence in deliberation as well—whether it is a form of knowledge, or opinion, or skill in conjecture, or some other kind of thing. It is not *knowledge;* for men do not inquire about the

1142ᵇ1 things they know about, but good deliberation is a kind of deliberation, and he who deliberates inquires and calculates. Nor is it *skill in conjecture;* for this both involves no reasoning and is something that is quick in its operation, while men deliberate a long time, and they say that one should carry out quickly the
5 conclusions of one's deliberation, but should deliberate slowly. Again, *readiness of mind* is different from excellence in deliberation; it is a sort of skill in conjecture. Nor again is excellence in deliberation *opinion* of any sort. But since the man who deliberates badly makes a mistake, while he who deliberates well does so correctly, excellence in deliberation is clearly a kind of correctness, but neither of knowledge
10 nor of opinion; for there is no such thing as correctness of knowledge (since there is no such thing as error of knowledge), and correctness of opinion is truth; and at the same time everything that is an object of opinion is already determined. But again excellence in deliberation involves reasoning. The remaining alternative, then, is that it is *correctness of thinking;* for this is not yet assertion, since, while opinion is not inquiry but already assertion, the man who is deliberating, whether he does so
15 well or ill, is searching for something and calculating.

But excellence in deliberation is a certain correctness of deliberation; hence we must first inquire what deliberation is and what it is about. And, there being more than one kind of correctness, plainly excellence in deliberation is not any and every kind; for the incontinent man and the bad man will reach as a result of his calculation what he sets himself to do,[54] so that he will have deliberated correctly,
20 but he will have got for himself a great evil. Now to have deliberated well is thought to be a good thing; for it is this kind of correctness of deliberation that is excellence in deliberation, viz. that which tends to attain what is good. But it is possible to attain even good by a false deduction and to attain what one ought to do but not by the right means, the middle term being false; so that this too is not yet excellence in
25 deliberation—this state in virtue of which one attains what one ought but not by the right means. Again it is possible to attain it by long deliberation while another man attains it quickly. Therefore in the former case we have not yet got excellence in deliberation, which is rightness with regard to the expedient—rightness in respect both of the conclusion, the manner, and the time. Further it is possible to have deliberated well either in the unqualified sense or with reference to a particular end.
30 Excellence in deliberation in the unqualified sense, then, is that which succeeds with reference to what is the end in the unqualified sense, and excellence in deliberation in a particular sense is that which succeeds relatively to a particular end. If, then, it is characteristic of men of practical wisdom to have deliberated well, excellence in deliberation will be correctness with regard to what conduces to the end of which practical wisdom is the true apprehension.

10 · Understanding, also, and goodness of understanding, in virtue of which
1143ᵃ1 men are said to be men of understanding or of good understanding, are neither entirely the same as opinion or knowledge (for at that rate all men would have been

---

[54]Reading δεῖν for ἰδεῖν.

men of understanding), nor are they one of the particular sciences, such as medicine, the science of things connected with health, or geometry, the science of spatial magnitudes. For understanding is neither about things that are always and are unchangeable, nor about any and every one of the things that come into being, but about things which may become subjects of questioning and deliberation. Hence it is about the same objects as practical wisdom; but understanding and practical wisdom are not the same. For practical wisdom issues commands, since its end is what ought to be done or not to be done; but understanding only judges. (Understanding is identical with goodness of understanding, men of understanding with men of good understanding.) Now understanding is neither the having nor the acquiring of practical wisdom; but as learning is called understanding when it means the exercise of the faculty of knowledge, so 'understanding' is applicable to the exercise of the faculty of opinion for the purpose of judging of what some one else says about matters with which practical wisdom is concerned—and of judging soundly; for 'well' and 'soundly' are the same thing. And from this has come the use of the name 'understanding' in virtue of which men are said to be of good understanding, viz. from the application of the word to learning; for we often call learning understanding.

11 · What is called judgement, in virtue of which men are said to be forgiving[55] and to have judgement, is the right discrimination of the equitable. This is shown by the fact that we say the equitable man is above all others a man of forgiveness and identify equity with forgiveness about certain facts. And forgiveness is judgement which discriminates what is equitable and does so correctly; and correct judgement is that which judges what is true.

Now all the states we have considered converge, as might be expected, on the same point; for when we speak of judgement and understanding and practical wisdom and comprehension we credit the same people with possessing judgement and comprehension and with having practical wisdom and understanding. For all these faculties deal with ultimates, i.e. with particulars; and being a man of understanding and of good judgement or of forgiveness consists in being able to judge about the things with which practical wisdom is concerned; for the equities are common to all good men in relation to other men. Now all things which have to be done are included among particulars or ultimates; for not only must the man of practical wisdom know particular facts, but understanding and judgement are also concerned with things to be done, and these are ultimates. And comprehension is concerned with the ultimates in both directions; for both the primary definitions and the ultimates are objects of comprehension and not of argument, and in demonstrations comprehension grasps the unchangeable and primary definitions, while in practical reasonings it grasps the last and contingent fact, i.e. the second proposition. For these are the starting-points of that for the sake of which, since the

5   universals are reached from the particulars; of these therefore we must have
perception, and this is comprehension.

This is why these states are thought to be natural endowments—why, while no
one is thought to be wise by nature, people are thought to have by nature
judgement, understanding, and comprehension. This is shown by the fact that we
think our powers correspond to our time of life, and that a particular age brings with
it comprehension and judgement; this implies that nature is the cause. [Hence
10   comprehension is both beginning and end; for demonstrations are from these and
about these.][56] Therefore we ought to attend to the undemonstrated sayings and
opinions of experienced and older people or of people of practical wisdom not less
than to demonstrations; for because experience has given them an eye they see
aright.

15   We have stated, then, what practical wisdom and wisdom are, and with what
each of them is concerned, and we have said that each is the excellence of a different
part of the soul.

12 · Difficulties might be raised as to the utility of these qualities of mind.
For wisdom will contemplate none of the things that will make a man happy (for it
20   is not concerned with any coming into being), and though practical wisdom has *this*
merit, for what purpose do we need it? Practical wisdom is the quality of mind
concerned with things just and noble and good for man, but these are the things
which it is the mark of a *good* man to do, and we are none the more able to act for
25   *knowing* them if the excellences are states, just as we are none the better able to act
for knowing the things that are healthy and sound, in the sense not of producing but
of issuing from the state of health; for we are none the more able to act for having
the art of medicine or of gymnastics. But if we are to say that it is useful[57] not for the
sake of this but for the sake of becoming good, practical wisdom will be of no use to
30   those who *are* good; but again it is of no use to those who are not;[58] for it will make
no difference whether they have practical wisdom themselves or obey others who
have it, and it would be enough for us to do what we do in the case of health; though
we wish to become healthy, yet we do not learn the art of medicine. Besides this, it
would be thought strange if practical wisdom, being inferior to wisdom, is to be put
in authority over it, as seems to be implied by the fact that the art which produces
35   anything rules and issues commands about that thing.

These, then, are the questions we must discuss; so far we have only stated the
difficulties.

1144ª1   Now first let us say that in themselves these states must be worthy of choice
because they are the excellences of the two parts of the soul respectively, even if
neither of them produces anything.

Secondly, they do produce something, not as the art of medicine produces
health, however, but as health produces health; so does wisdom produce happiness;

---

[56]Bywater thinks that this sentence has been misplaced.
[57]Reading χρήσιμον for φρόνιμον.   [58]Reading οὖσιν for ἔχουσιν.

for, being a part of excellence entire, by being possessed and by actualizing itself it   5
makes a man happy.

Again, the function of man is achieved only in accordance with practical
wisdom as well as with moral excellence; for excellence makes the aim right, and
practical wisdom the things leading to it. (Of the fourth part of the soul—the
nutritive—there is no such excellence; for there is nothing which it is in its power to   10
do or not to do.)

With regard to our being none the more able to do because of our practical
wisdom what is noble and just, let us begin a little further back, starting with the
following principle. As we say that some people who do just acts are not necessarily
just, i.e. those who do the acts ordained by the laws either unwillingly or owing to   15
ignorance or for some other reason and not for the sake of the acts themselves
(though, to be sure, they do what they should and all the things that the good man
ought), so is it, it seems, that in order to be good one must be in a certain state when
one does the several acts, i.e. one must do them as a result of choice and for the sake
of the acts themselves. Now excellence makes the choice right, but the question of   20
the things which should naturally be done to carry out our choice belongs not to
excellence but to another faculty. We must devote our attention to these matters
and give a clearer statement about them. There is a faculty which is called
cleverness; and this is such as to be able to do the things that tend towards the mark   25
we have set before ourselves, and to hit it. Now if the mark be noble, the cleverness
is laudable, but if the mark be bad, the cleverness is mere villainy; hence we call
clever both men of practical wisdom and villains.[59] Practical wisdom is not the
faculty, but it does not exist without this faculty. And this eye of the soul acquires
its formed state not without the aid of excellence as has been said and is plain; for   30
inferences which deal with acts to be done are things which involve a starting-point,
viz. 'since the end, i.e. what is best, is of such and such a nature', whatever it may be
(let it for the sake of argument be what we please); and this is not evident except to
the good man; for wickedness perverts us and causes us to be deceived about the   35
starting-points of action. Therefore it is evident that it is impossible to be practically
wise without being good.

13 · We must therefore consider excellence also once more; for virtue too is   1144ᵇ1
similarly related; as practical wisdom is to cleverness—not the same, but like it—so
is natural excellence to excellence in the strict sense. For all men think that each
type of character belongs to its possessors in some sense by nature; for from the very
moment of birth we are just or fitted for self-control or brave or have the other   5
moral qualities; but yet we seek something else as that which is good in the strict
sense—we seek for the presence of such qualities in another way. For both children
and brutes have the natural dispositions to these qualities, but without thought
these are evidently hurtful. Only we seem to see this much, that, while one may be   10
led astray by them, as a strong body which moves without sight may stumble badly

---

[59]Reading τοὺς πανούργους.

because of its lack of sight, still, if a man once acquires thought that makes a difference in action; and his state, while still like what it was, will then be excellence in the strict sense. Therefore, as in the part of us which forms opinions there are two
15   types, cleverness and practical wisdom, so too in the moral part there are two types, natural excellence and excellence in the strict sense, and of these the latter involves practical wisdom. This is why some say that all the excellences are forms of practical wisdom, and why Socrates in one respect was on the right track while in another he went astray; in thinking that all the excellences were forms of practical
20   wisdom he was wrong, but in saying they implied practical wisdom he was right. This is confirmed by the fact that even now all men, when they define excellence, after naming the state and its objects add 'that (state) which is in accordance with the right reason'; now the right reason is that which is in accordance with practical wisdom. All men, then, seem somehow to divine that this kind of state is excellence,
25   viz. that which is in accordance with practical wisdom. But we must go a little further. For it is not merely the state in accordance with right reason, but the state that implies the *presence* of right reason, that is excellence; and practical wisdom is right reason about such matters. Socrates, then, thought the excellences were forms of reason (for he thought they were, all of them, forms of knowledge), while we think they *involve* reason.
30   It is clear, then, from what has been said, that it is not possible to be good in the strict sense without practical wisdom, nor practically wise without moral excellence. But in this way we may also refute the dialectical argument whereby it might be contended that the excellences exist in separation from each other; the same man, it might be said, is not best equipped by nature for all the excellences, so that
35   he will have already acquired one when he has not yet acquired another. This is possible in respect of the natural excellences, but not in respect of those in respect of
1145ª1   which a man is called without qualification good; for with the presence of the one quality, practical wisdom, will be given all the excellences. And it is plain that, even if it were of no practical value, we should have needed it because it is the excellence of the part of us in question; plain too that the choice will not be right without
5   practical wisdom any more than without excellence; for the one determines the end and the other makes us do the things that lead to the end.
    But again it is not *supreme* over wisdom, i.e. over the superior part of us, any more than the art of medicine is over health; for it does not use it but provides for its coming into being; it issues orders, then, for its sake, but not to it. Further, to
10   maintain its supremacy would be like saying that the art of politics rules the gods because it issues orders about all the affairs of the state.

BOOK VII

15   1 · Let us now make a fresh beginning and point out that of moral states to be avoided there are three kinds—vice, incontinence, brutishness. The contraries of two of these are evident—one we call excellence, the other continence; to brutish-

ness it would be most fitting to oppose superhuman excellence, something heroic
and divine, as Homer has represented Priam saying of Hector that he was very   20
good,

> For he seemed not, he,
> The child of a mortal man, but as one that of God's seed came.[60]

Therefore if, as they say, men become gods by excess of excellence, of this kind must
evidently be the state opposed to the brutish state; for as a brute has no vice or   25
excellence, so neither has a god; his state is higher than excellence, and that of a
brute is a different kind of state from vice.

Now, since it is rarely that a godlike man is found—to use the epithet of the
Spartans, who when they admire any one highly call him a 'godlike man'—so too
the brutish type is rarely found among men, it is found chiefly among foreigners,   30
but some brutish qualities are also produced by disease or deformity; and we also
call by this evil name those who surpass ordinary men in vice. Of this kind of
disposition, however, we must later make some mention, while we have discussed
vice before; we must now discuss incontinence and softness (or effeminacy), and   35
continence and endurance; for we must treat each of the two neither as identical
with excellence or wickedness, nor as a different genus. We must, as in all other   1145ᵇ1
cases, set the phenomena before us and, after first discussing the difficulties, go on
to prove, if possible, the truth of all the reputable opinions about these affections or,   5
failing this, of the greater number and the most authoritative; for if we both resolve
the difficulties and leave the reputable opinions undisturbed, we shall have proved
the case sufficiently.

Now both continence and endurance are thought to be included among things
good and praiseworthy, and both incontinence and softness among things bad and
blameworthy; and the same man is thought to be continent and ready to abide by   10
the result of his calculations, or incontinent and ready to abandon them. And the
incontinent man, knowing that what he does is bad, does it as a result of passion,
while the continent man, knowing that his appetites are bad, does not follow them
because of his reason. The temperate man all men call continent and disposed to
endurance, while the continent man some maintain to be always temperate but   15
others do not; and some call the self-indulgent man incontinent and the incontinent
man self-indulgent indiscriminately, while others distinguish them. The man of
practical wisdom, they sometimes say, cannot be incontinent, while sometimes they
say that some who are practically wise and clever *are* incontinent. Again men are
said to be incontinent with respect to anger, honour, and gain.—These, then, are the   20
things that are said.

2 · Now we may ask what kind of right belief is possessed by the man who
behaves incontinently. That he should behave so when he has knowledge, some say
is impossible; for it would be strange—so Socrates thought—if when knowledge
was in a man something else could master it and drag it about like a slave. For

---

[60]*Iliad* XXIV 258.

25 *Socrates* was entirely opposed to the view in question, holding that there is no such thing as incontinence; no one, he said, acts against what he believes best—people act so only by reason of ignorance. Now this view contradicts the plain phenomena, and we must inquire about what happens to such a man; if he acts by reason of ignorance, what is the manner of his ignorance? For that the man who behaves

30 incontinently does not, before he gets into this state, *think* he ought to act so, is evident. But there are *some* who concede certain of Socrates' contentions but not others; that nothing is stronger than knowledge they admit, but not that no one acts contrary to what has seemed to him the better course, and therefore they say that

35 the incontinent man has not knowledge when he is mastered by his pleasures, but opinion. But *if* it is opinion and not knowledge, if it is not a strong belief that resists

1146ᵃ1 but a weak one, as in men who hesitate, we forgive their failure to stand by such convictions against strong appetites; but we do not forgive wickedness, nor any of the other blameworthy states. It is then *practical wisdom* whose resistance is

5 mastered? That is the strongest of all states. But this is absurd; the same man will be at once practically wise and incontinent, but *no one* would say that it is the part of a practically wise man to do willingly the basest acts. Besides, it has been shown before that the man of practical wisdom is one who will *act* (for he is a man concerned with the individual facts) and who has the other excellences.

10   Further, if continence involves having strong and bad appetites, the temperate man will not be continent nor the continent man temperate; for a temperate man will have neither excessive nor bad appetites. But the continent man *must;* for if the appetites are good, the state that restrains us from following them is bad, so that not

15 all continence will be good; while if they are weak and not bad, there is nothing admirable in resisting them, and if they are weak and bad, there is nothing great in resisting these either.

Further, if continence makes a man ready to stand by any and every opinion, it is bad, i.e. if it makes him stand even by a false opinion; and if incontinence makes a man apt to abandon any and every opinion, there will be a good incontinence, of which Sophocles' Neoptolemus in the *Philoctetes* will be an instance; for he is to be

20 praised for not standing by what Odysseus persuaded him to do, because he is pained at telling a lie.

Further, the sophistic argument presents a difficulty; for, because they want to produce paradoxical results to show how clever they are, when they succeed the resulting inference presents a difficulty (for thought is bound fast when it will not rest because the conclusion does not satisfy it, and cannot advance because it cannot

25 refute the argument). There is an argument from which it follows that folly coupled with incontinence is excellence; for a man does the opposite of what he believes owing to incontinence, but believes what is good to be evil and something that he

30 should not do, and in consequence he will do what is good and not what is evil.

Further, he who on conviction does and pursues and chooses what is pleasant would be thought to be better than one who does so as a result not of calculation but of incontinence; for he is easier to cure since he may be persuaded to change his mind. But to the incontinent man may be applied the proverb 'when water chokes, what is one to wash it down with?' If he had been persuaded of the rightness of what he does, he would have desisted when he was persuaded to change his mind; but now he acts in spite of his being persuaded of something quite different. 1146^b1

Further, if incontinence and continence are concerned with any and every kind of object, who is it that is incontinent in the unqualified sense? No one has all the forms of incontinence, but we say some people are incontinent without qualifica- 5 tion.

3 · Of some such kind are the difficulties that arise; some of these points must be refuted and the others left in possession of the field; for the solution of the difficulty is the discovery of the truth. We must consider first, then, whether incontinent people act knowingly or not, and in what sense knowingly; then with what sorts of object the incontinent and the continent man may be said to be concerned (i.e. whether with any and every pleasure and pain or with certain 10 determinate kinds), and whether the continent man and the man of endurance are the same or different; and similarly with regard to the other matters germane to this inquiry. The starting-point of our investigation is the question whether the continent man and the incontinent are differentiated by their objects or by their 15 attitude, i.e. whether the continent man is incontinent simply by being concerned with such and such objects, or, instead, by his attitude, or, instead of that, by both these things; the second question is whether incontinence and continence are concerned with any and every object or not. The man who is incontinent in the unqualified sense is neither concerned with any and every object, but with precisely those with which the self-indulgent man is concerned, nor is he characterized by 20 being simply related to these (for then his state would be the same as self-indulgence), but by being related to them in a certain way. For the one is led on in accordance with his own choice, thinking that he ought always to pursue the present pleasure; while the other does not think so, but yet pursues it.

As for the suggestion that it is true opinion and not knowledge against which we act incontinently, that makes no difference to the argument; for some people 25 when in a state of opinion do not hesitate, but think they know exactly. If, then, it is owing to their weak conviction those who have opinion are more likely to act against their belief than those who know, there will be no difference between knowledge and opinion; for some men are no less convinced of what they think than others of what 30 they know; as is shown by the case of Heraclitus. But since we use the word 'know' in two senses (for both the man who has knowledge but is not using it and he who is using it are said to know), it *will* make a difference whether, when a man does what he should not, he has the knowledge but is not exercising it, or *is* exercising it; for the latter seems strange, but not the former.

Further, since there are two kinds of propositions, there is nothing to prevent a 1147^a1 man's having both and acting against his knowledge, provided that he is using only the universal and not the particular; for it is particular acts that have to be done. And there are also two kinds of universal; one is predicable of the agent, the other of the object; e.g. 'dry food is good for every man', and 'I am a man', or 'such and such 5 food is dry'; but whether this food is such and such, of this the incontinent man either has not or is not exercising the knowledge. There will, then, be, firstly, an enormous difference between these manners of knowing, so that to know in one way would not seem anything strange, while to know in the other way would be extraordinary.

10   And further the possession of knowledge in another sense than those just named is something that happens to men; for within the case of having knowledge but not using it we see a difference of state, admitting of the possibility of having knowledge in a sense and yet not having it, as in the instance of a man asleep, mad, or drunk. But now this is just the condition of men under the influence of passions;

15   for outbursts of anger and sexual appetites and some other such passions, it is evident, actually alter our bodily condition, and in some men even produce fits of madness. It is plain, then, that incontinent people must be said to be in a similar condition to these. The fact that men use the language that flows from knowledge proves nothing; for even men under the influence of these passions utter scientific

20   proofs and verses of Empedocles, and those who have just begun to learn can string together words, but do not yet know; for it has to become part of themselves, and that takes time; so that we must suppose that the use of language by men in an incontinent state means no more than its utterance by actors on the stage.

Again, we may also view the cause as follows with reference to the facts of

25   nature. The one opinion is universal, the other is concerned with the particular facts, and here we come to something within the sphere of perception; when a single opinion results from the two, the soul must in one type of case affirm the conclusion, while in the case of opinions concerned with production it must immediately act (e.g. if everything sweet ought to be tasted, and this is sweet, in the sense of being

30   one of the particular sweet things, the man who can act and is not restrained must at the same time actually act accordingly). When, then, the universal opinion is present in us restraining us from tasting, and there is also the opinion that everything sweet is pleasant, and that this is sweet (now this is the opinion that is active), and when appetite happens to be present in us, the one opinion bids us avoid the object, but appetite leads us towards it (for it can move each of our bodily parts);

1147ᵇ1 so that it turns out that a man behaves incontinently under the influence (in a sense) of reason and opinion, and of opinion not contrary in itself, but only incidentally— for the appetite is contrary not the opinion—to right reason. It also follows that this is the reason why the lower animals are not incontinent, viz. because they have no

5   universal beliefs but only imagination and memory of particulars.

The explanation of how the ignorance is dissolved and the incontinent man regains his knowledge, is the same as in the case of the man drunk or asleep and is not peculiar to this condition; we must go to the students of natural science for it. Now, the last proposition both being an opinion about a perceptible object, and

10   being what determines our actions, this a man either has not when he is in the state of passion, or has it in the sense in which having knowledge did not mean knowing but only talking, as a drunken man may utter the verses of Empedocles. And because the last term is not universal nor equally an object of knowledge with the

universal term, the position that Socrates sought to establish actually seems to result; for it is not what is thought to be knowledge proper that the passion overcomes[61] (nor is it this that is dragged about as a result of the passion), but perceptual knowledge.

This must suffice as our answer to the question of whether men can act incontinently when they know or not, and in what sense they know.

4 · We must next discuss whether there is any one who is incontinent without qualification, or all men who are incontinent are so in a particular sense, and if so, with what sort of objects. That both continent persons and persons of endurance, and incontinent and soft persons, are concerned with pleasures and pains, is evident.

Now of the things that produce pleasure some are necessary, while others are worthy of choice in themselves but admit of excess, the bodily causes of pleasure being necessary (by such I mean both those concerned with food and those concerned with sexual intercourse, i.e. the bodily matters with which we defined self-indulgence and temperance as being concerned), while the others are not necessary but worthy of choice in themselves (e.g. victory, honour, wealth, and good and pleasant things of this sort). This being so, those who go to excess with reference to the latter, contrary to the right reason which is in themselves, are not called incontinent simply, but incontinent with the qualification 'in respect of money, gain, honour, or anger',—not simply incontinent, on the ground that they are different from incontinent people and are called incontinent by reason of a resemblance. (Compare the case of Man, who won a contest at the Olympic games; in his case the general formula of man differed little from the one peculiar to *him*, but yet it *was* different.) This is shown by the fact that incontinence either without qualification or in some particular respect is blamed not only as a fault but as a kind of vice, while none of the others is so blamed.

But of the people who are incontinent with respect to bodily enjoyments, with which we say the temperate and the self-indulgent man are concerned, he who pursues the excesses of things pleasant—and shuns those of things painful, of hunger and thirst and heat and cold and all the objects of touch and taste—not by choice but contrary to his choice and his judgement, is called incontinent, not with the qualification 'in respect of this or that', e.g. of anger, but without qualification. This is confirmed by the fact that men are called soft with regard to these pleasures, but not with regard to any of the others. And for this reason we group together the incontinent and the self-indulgent, the continent and the temperate man—but not any of these other types—because they are concerned somehow with the same pleasures and pains; but although these are concerned with the same objects, they are not similarly related to them, but some of them choose them while the others do not choose them.

This is why we should describe as self-indulgent rather the man who without

15

20

25

30

1148ᵃ1

5

10

15

---

[61]Reading περιγίνεται for παρούσης γίνεται.

20 appetite or with but a slight appetite pursues the excesses and avoids moderate pains, than the man who does so because of his strong appetites; for what would the former do, if he had in addition a vigorous appetite, and a violent pain at the lack of the necessary objects?

Now of appetites and pleasures some belong to the class of things generically noble and good—for some pleasant things are by nature worthy of choice—while 25 others are contrary to these, and others are intermediate, to adopt our previous distinction, e.g. wealth, gain, victory, honour. And with reference to all objects whether of this or of the intermediate kind men are not blamed for being affected by them, for desiring and loving them, but for doing so in a certain way, i.e. for going to excess. (This is why all those who contrary to reason either are mastered by or pursue one of the objects which are naturally noble and good, e.g. those who busy 30 themselves more than they ought about honour or about children and parents—for these too are goods, and those who busy themselves about them are praised; but yet there is an excess even in them—if like Niobe one were to fight even against the 1148^{b}1 gods, or were to be as much devoted to one's father as Satyrus nicknamed 'the filial', who was thought to be very silly on this point.) There is no wickedness, then, with regard to these objects, for the reason named, viz. because each of them is by nature a thing worthy of choice for its own sake; yet excesses in respect of them are bad and to be avoided. Similarly there is no incontinence with regard to them; for 5 incontinence is not only to be avoided but is also a thing worthy of blame; but owing to a similarity in the passion people apply the name incontinence, adding in each case what it is in respect of, as we may describe as a bad doctor or a bad actor one whom we should not call bad, simply. As, then, is the case we do not apply the term 10 without qualification because each of these conditions is not badness but only analogous to it, so it is clear that in the other case also that alone must be taken to be incontinence and continence which is concerned with the same objects as temperance and self-indulgence, but we apply the term to anger by virtue of a resemblance; and this is why we say with a qualification 'incontinent in respect of anger' as we say 'incontinent in respect of honour, or of gain'.

15 5 · Some things are pleasant by nature, and of these some are so without qualification, and others are so with reference to particular classes either of animals or of men; while others are not pleasant by nature, but some of them become so by reason of deformities, and others by reason of habits, and others by reason of bad natures. This being so it is possible with regard to each of the latter kinds to discover 20 similar states; I mean the brutish states, as in the case of the female who, they say, rips open pregnant women and devours the infants, or of the things in which some of the tribes about the Black Sea that have gone savage are said to delight—in raw meat or in human flesh, or in lending their children to one another to feast upon—or of the story of Phalaris.

25 These states are brutish, but others arise as a result of disease (or, in some cases, of madness, as with the man who sacrificed and ate his mother, or with the slave who ate the liver of his fellow), and others are morbid states resulting from

custom,[62] e.g. the habit of plucking out the hair or of gnawing the nails, or even coals or earth, and in addition to these paederasty; for these arise in some by nature and in others, as in those who have been the victims of lust from childhood, from habit.   30

Now those in whom nature is the cause of such a state no one would call incontinent, any more than one would apply the epithet to women because of the passive part they play in copulation; nor would one apply it to those who are in a morbid condition as a result of habit. To have these various types of habit is beyond the limits of vice, as brutishness is too; for a man who has them to master or be 1149^a1 mastered by them is not simple incontinence but that which is so by analogy, as the man who is in this condition in respect of fits of anger is to be called incontinent in respect of that feeling, but not incontinent.

For every excessive state whether of folly, of cowardice, of self-indulgence, or   5 of bad temper, is either brutish or morbid; the man who is by nature apt to fear everything, even the squeak of a mouse, is cowardly with a brutish cowardice, while the man who feared a weasel did so in consequence of disease; and of foolish people those who by nature are thoughtless and live by their senses alone are brutish, like   10 some races of the distant foreigners, while those who are so as a result of disease (e.g. of epilepsy) or of madness are morbid. Of these characteristics it is possible to have some only at times, and not to be mastered by them, e.g. Phalaris may have restrained a desire to eat the flesh of a child or an appetite for unnatural sexual pleasure; but it is also possible to be mastered, not merely to have the feelings. Thus,   15 as the wickedness which is on the human level is called wickedness simply, while that which is not is called wickedness not simply but with the qualification 'brutish' or 'morbid', in the same way it is plain that some incontinence is brutish and some morbid, while only that which corresponds to *human* self-indulgence is incontinence   20 simply.

That incontinence and continence, then, are concerned only with the same objects as self-indulgence and temperance and that what is concerned with other objects is a type distinct from incontinence, and called incontinence by a metaphor and not simply, is plain.

6 · That incontinence in respect of anger is less disgraceful than that in respect of the appetites is what we will now proceed to see. Anger seems to listen to   25 reason to some extent, but to mishear it, as do hasty servants who run out before they have heard the whole of what one says, and then muddle the order, or as dogs bark if there is but a knock at the door, before looking to see if it is a friend; so anger by reason of the warmth and hastiness of its nature, though it hears, does not hear   30 an order, and springs to take revenge. For reason or imagination informs us that we have been insulted or slighted, and anger, reasoning as it were that anything like this must be fought against, boils up straightway; while appetite, if reason or perception merely says that an object is pleasant, springs to the enjoyment of it. Therefore anger obeys reason in a sense, but appetite does not. It is therefore more 1149^b1

<hr>

[62]Omitting ἤ.

disgraceful; for the man who is incontinent in respect of anger is in a sense conquered by reason, while the other is conquered by appetite and not by reason.

Further, we forgive people more easily for following natural desires, since we forgive them more easily for following such appetites as are common to all men, and in so far as they are common; now anger and bad temper are more natural than the appetites for excess, i.e. for unnecessary objects. Take for instance the man who defended himself on the charge of striking his father by saying 'yes, but *he* struck *his* father, and *he* struck *his*, and' (pointing to his child) 'this boy will strike *me* when he is a man; it runs in the family'; of the man who when he was being dragged along by his son bade him stop at the doorway, since he himself had dragged his father only as far as that.

Further, those who are more given to plotting against others are more unjust. Now a passionate man is not given to plotting, nor is anger itself—it is open; but the nature of appetite is illustrated by what the poets call Aphrodite, 'guile-weaving daughter of Cyprus', and by Homer's words about her 'embroidered girdle':

And the whisper of wooing is there,
Whose subtlety stealeth the wits of the wise, how prudent soe'er.[63]

Therefore if this form of incontinence is more unjust and disgraceful than that in respect of anger, it is both incontinence without qualification and in a sense vice.

Further, no one commits wanton outrage with a feeling of pain, but every one who acts in anger acts with pain, while the man who commits outrage acts with pleasure. If, then, those acts at which it is most just to be angry are more unjust, the incontinence which is due to appetite is the more unjust; for there is no wanton outrage involved in anger.

Plainly, then, the incontinence concerned with appetite is more disgraceful than that concerned with anger, and continence and incontinence are concerned with bodily appetites and pleasures; but we must grasp the differences among the latter themselves. For, as has been said at the beginning, some are human and natural both in kind and in magnitude, others are brutish, and others are due to deformities and diseases. Only with the first of these are temperance and self-indulgence concerned; this is why we call the lower animals neither temperate nor self-indulgent except by a metaphor, and only if some one kind[64] of animals exceeds another as a whole in wantonness, destructiveness, and omnivorous greed; these have no power of choice or calculation, but they *are* departures from what is natural as, among men, madmen are. Now brutishness is less evil than vice, though more alarming; for it is not that the better part has been perverted, as in man,—they *have* no better part. Thus it is like comparing a lifeless thing with a living in respect of badness; for the badness of that which has no source of movement is always less hurtful, and thought is a source. Thus it is like comparing injustice with an unjust man. Each is in some sense worse; for a bad man will do ten thousand times as much evil as a brute.

[63]*Iliad* XIV 214.
[64]Reading τι for τινι.

7 . With regard to the pleasures and pains and appetites and aversions arising through touch and taste, to which both self-indulgence and temperance were 10 formerly narrowed down, it is possible to be in such a state as to be defeated even by those of them which most people master, or to master even those by which most people are defeated; among these possibilities, those relating to pleasures are incontinence and continence, those relating to pains softness and endurance. The state of most people is intermediate, even if they lean more towards the worse 15 states.

Now, since some pleasures are necessary while others are not, and are necessary up to a point while the excesses of them are not, nor the deficiencies, and this is equally true of appetites and pains, the man who pursues the excesses of things pleasant, or pursues to excess necessary objects, and[65] does so by choice, for 20 their own sake and not at all for the sake of any result distinct from them, is self-indulgent; for such a man is of necessity without regrets, and therefore incurable, since a man without regrets cannot be cured. The man who is deficient is the opposite; the man who is intermediate is temperate. Similarly, there is the man who avoids bodily pains not because he is defeated by them but by choice. (Of those who do not *choose* such acts, one kind of man is led to them as a result of the 25 pleasure involved, another because he avoids the pain arising from the appetite, so that these types differ from one another. Now any one would think worse of a man if with no appetite or with weak appetite he were to do something disgraceful, than if he did it under the influence of powerful appetite, and worse of him if he struck a blow not in anger than if he did it in anger; for what would he have done if he *had* 30 been strongly affected? This is why the self-indulgent man is worse than the incontinent.) Of the states named, then, the latter is rather a kind of softness; the former is self-indulgence. While to the incontinent man is opposed the continent, to the soft is opposed the man of endurance; for endurance consists in resisting, while continence consists in conquering, and resisting and conquering are different, as not 35 being beaten is different from winning; this is why continence is also more worthy of choice than endurance. Now the man who is defective in respect of resistance to the 1150[b]1 things which most men both resist and resist successfully is soft and effeminate; for effeminacy too is a kind of softness; such a man trails his cloak to avoid the pain of lifting it, and plays the invalid without thinking himself wretched, though the man 5 he imitates is a wretched man.

The case is similar with regard to continence and incontinence. For if a man is defeated by violent and excessive pleasures or pains, there is nothing wonderful in that; indeed we are ready to forgive him if he has resisted, as Theodectes' Philoctetes does when bitten by the snake, or Carcinus' Cercyon in the *Alope,* and 10 as people who try to restrain their laughter burst out in a guffaw, as happened to Xenophantus. But it is surprising if a man is defeated by and cannot resist pleasures or pains which most men can hold out against, when this is not due to heredity or disease, like the softness that is hereditary with the kings of the Scythians, or that 15 which distinguishes the female sex from the male.

[65]Reading καθ' ὑπερβολήν, καί.

The lover of amusement, too, is thought to be self-indulgent, but is really soft. For amusement is a relaxation, since it is a rest; and the lover of amusement is one of the people who go to excess in this.

Of incontinence one kind is impetuosity, another weakness. For some men after deliberating fail, owing to their passion, to stand by the conclusions of their deliberation, others because they have not deliberated are led by their passion; since some men (just as people who first tickle others are not tickled themselves), if they have first perceived and seen what is coming and have first roused themselves and their calculative faculty, are not defeated by their passion, whether it be pleasant or painful. It is keen and excitable people that suffer especially from the impetuous form of incontinence; for the former because of their quickness and the latter because of the violence of their passions do not wait on reason, because they are apt to follow their imagination.

8 · The self-indulgent man, as was said, has no regrets; for he stands by his choice; but any incontinent man is subject to regrets. This is why the position is not as it was expressed in the formulation of the problem, but the self-indulgent man is incurable and the incontinent man curable; for wickedness is like a disease such as dropsy or consumption, while incontinence is like epilepsy; the former is a permanent, the latter an intermittent badness. And generally incontinence and vice are different in kind; vice is unconscious of itself, incontinence is not (of incontinent men themselves, those who become beside themselves are better than those who possess reason but do not abide by it, since the latter are defeated by a weaker passion, and do not act without previous deliberation like the others); for the incontinent man is like the people who get drunk quickly and on little wine, i.e. on less than most people.

Evidently, then, incontinence is not vice (though perhaps it is so in a qualified sense); for incontinence is contrary to choice while vice is in accordance with choice; not but what they are similar in respect of the actions they lead to; as in the saying of Demodocus about the Milesians, 'the Milesians are not without sense, but they do the things that senseless people do', so too incontinent people are not unjust but they will do unjust acts.

Now, since the incontinent man is apt to pursue, not on conviction, bodily pleasures that are excessive and contrary to right reason, while the self-indulgent man is convinced because he is the sort of man to pursue them, it is on the contrary the former that is easily persuaded to change his mind, while the latter is not. For excellence and vice respectively preserve and destroy the first principle, and in actions that for the sake of which is the first principle, as the hypotheses are in mathematics; neither in that case is it reason that teaches the first principles, nor is it so here—excellence either natural or produced by habituation is what teaches right opinion about the first principle. Such a man as this, then, is temperate; his contrary is the self-indulgent.

But there is a sort of man who is carried away as a result of passion and contrary to right reason—a man whom passion masters so that he does not act according to right reason, but does not master to the extent of making him ready to believe that he ought to pursue such pleasures without reserve; this is the incontinent man, who is better than the self-indulgent man, and not bad without qualification; for the best thing in him, the first principle, is preserved. And 25 contrary to him is another kind of man, he who abides by his convictions and is not carried away, at least as a result of passion. It is evident from these considerations that the latter is a good state and the former a bad one.

9 . Is the man continent who abides by any and every reasoning and any and every choice, or the man who abides by the right choice, and is he incontinent who 30 abandons any and every choice and any and every reasoning, or he who abandons the reasoning that is not false and the choice that is right? this is how we put it before our statement of the problem. Or is it incidentally any and every choice but *per se* the true reasoning and the right choice by which the one abides and the other does not? If any one chooses or pursues this for the sake of that, *per se* he pursues and 1151^b1 chooses the latter, but incidentally the former. But when we speak without qualification we mean what is *per se*. Therefore in a sense the one abides by, and the other abandons, any and every opinion; but without qualification, the true opinion.

There are some who are apt to abide by their opinion, who are called 5 strong-headed, viz. those who are hard to persuade and are not easily persuaded to change; these have in them something like the continent man, as the prodigal is in a way like the liberal man and the rash man like the confident man; but they are different in many respects. For it is to passion and appetite that the one will not yield, since on occasion the continent man *will* be easy to persuade; but it is to 10 reason that the others refuse to yield, for they do form appetites and many of them are led by their pleasures. Now the people who are strong-headed are the opinionated, the ignorant, and the boorish—the opinionated being influenced by pleasure and pain; for they delight in the victory they gain if they are not persuaded to change, and are pained if their decisions become null and void as decrees 15 sometimes do; so that they are more like the incontinent than the continent man.

But there are some who fail to abide by their resolutions, not as a result of incontinence, e.g. Neoptolemus in Sophocles' *Philoctetes;* yet it was for the sake of pleasure that he did not stand fast—but a noble pleasure; for telling the truth was noble to him, but he had been persuaded by Odysseus to tell the lie. For not every 20 one who does anything for the sake of pleasure is either self-indulgent or bad or incontinent, but he who does it for a disgraceful pleasure.

Since there is also a sort of man who takes less delight than he should in bodily things, and does not abide by reason, he who is intermediate between him and the incontinent man is the continent man; for the incontinent man fails to abide by 25 reason because he delights too much in them, and this man because he delights in them too little; while the continent man abides by it and does not change on either account. Now if continence is good, both the contrary states must be bad, as they

30 actually appear to be; but because the other extreme is seen in few people and seldom, as temperance is thought to be contrary only to self-indulgence, so is continence to incontinence.

Since many names are applied analogically, it is by analogy that we have come to speak of the continence of the temperate man; for both the continent man and the temperate man are such as to do nothing contrary to reason for the sake of the 1152ª1 bodily pleasures, but the former has and the latter has not bad appetites, and the latter is such as not to feel pleasure contrary to reason, while the former is such as to feel pleasure but not to be led by it. And the incontinent and the self-indulgent man 5 are also like one another; they are different, but both pursue bodily pleasures—the latter, however, also thinking that he ought to do so, while the former does not think this.

10 · Nor can the same man have practical wisdom and be incontinent; for it has been shown that a man is at the same time practically wise, and good in respect of character. Further, a man has practical wisdom not by knowing only but by acting; but the incontinent man is unable to act—there is, however, nothing to 10 prevent a clever man from being incontinent; this is why it is sometimes actually thought that some people have practical wisdom but are incontinent, viz. because cleverness and practical wisdom differ in the way we have described in our first discussions, and are near together in respect of their reasoning, but differ in respect of their choice—nor yet is the incontinent man like the man who knows and is 15 contemplating a truth, but like the man who is asleep or drunk. And he acts voluntarily (for he acts in a sense with knowledge both of what he does and of that for the sake of which he does it), but is not wicked since his choice is good; so that he is half-wicked. And he is not unjust; for he does not act of malice aforethought; of the two types of incontinent man the one does not abide by the conclusions of his deliberation, while the excitable man does not deliberate at all. And thus the 20 incontinent man is like a city which passes all the right decrees and has good laws, but makes no use of them, as in Anaxandrides' jesting remark,

'The city willed it, that cares nought for laws';

but the wicked man is like a city that uses its laws, but has wicked laws to use.

25 Now incontinence and continence are concerned with that which is in excess of the state characteristic of most men; for the continent man abides by his resolutions more and the incontinent man less than most men can.

Of the forms of incontinence, that of excitable people is more curable than that of those who deliberate but do not abide by their decisions, and those who are incontinent through habituation are more curable than those in whom incontinence 30 is innate; for it is easier to change a habit than to change one's nature; even habit is hard to change just because it is like nature, as Evenus says:

I say that habit's but long practice, friend,
And this becomes men's nature in the end.

We have now stated what continence, incontinence, endurance, and softness are, and how these states are related to each other.

11 · The study of pleasure and pain belongs to the province of the political [1152ᵇ1]
philosopher; for he is the architect of the end, with a view to which we call one thing bad and another good without qualification. Further, it is one of our necessary tasks to consider them; for not only did we lay it down that moral excellence and vice are 5 concerned with pains and pleasures, but most people say that happiness involves pleasure; this is why the blessed man is called by a name derived from a word meaning enjoyment.[66]

Now some people think that no pleasure is a good, either in itself or incidentally, since the good and pleasure are not the same; others think that some 10 pleasures are good but that most are bad. Again there is a third view, that even if all pleasures are goods, yet the best thing cannot be pleasure. The reasons given for the view that pleasure is not a good at all are (a) that every pleasure is a perceptible process to a natural state, and that no process is of the same kind as its end, e.g. no process of building of the same kind as a house. (b) A temperate man avoids 15 pleasures. (c) A man of practical wisdom pursues what is free from pain, not what is pleasant. (d) The pleasures are a hindrance to thought, and the more so the more one delights in them, e.g. in sexual pleasure; for no one could think of anything while absorbed in this. (e) There is no art of pleasure; but every good is the product of some art. (f) Children and the brutes pursue pleasures. The reasons for the view 20 that not all pleasures are good are that (a) there are pleasures that are actually base and objects of reproach, and (b) there are harmful pleasures; for some pleasant things are unhealthy. The reason for the view that the best thing is not pleasure is that pleasure is not an end but a process.

12 · These are pretty much the things that are said. That it does not follow from these grounds that pleasure is not a good, or even the chief good, is plain from 25 the following considerations. First, since that which is good may be so in either of two senses (one thing good simply and another good for a particular person), natural constitutions and states, and therefore also movements and processes, will be correspondingly divisible. Of those which are thought to be bad some will be bad without qualification but not bad for a particular person, but worthy of his choice, and some will not be worthy of choice even for a particular person, but only at a 30 particular time and for a short period, though not without qualification; while others are not even pleasures, but seem to be so, viz. all those which involve pain and whose end is curative, e.g. the processes that go on in sick persons.

Further, one kind of good being activity and another being state, the processes that restore us to our natural state are only incidentally pleasant; for that matter the activity at work in the appetites for them is the activity of so much of our state and 35 nature as has remained unimpaired; for there are actually pleasures that involve *no*

[66] μακάριος from χαίρειν.

1153ᵃ1   pain or appetite (e.g. those of contemplation), the nature in such a case not being defective at all. That the others are incidental is indicated by the fact that men do not enjoy the same things[67] when their nature is in its settled state as they do when it is being replenished, but in the former case they enjoy the things that are pleasant without qualification, in the latter the contraries of these as well; for then they enjoy
5   even sharp and bitter things, none of which is pleasant either by nature or without qualification. Nor, then, are the pleasures; for as pleasant things differ, so do the pleasures arising from them.

Again, it is not necessary that there should be something else better than pleasure, as some say the end is better than the process; for pleasures are not
10   processes nor do they all involve process—they are activities and ends; nor do they arise when we are becoming something, but when we are exercising some faculty; and not all pleasures have an end different from themselves, but only the pleasures of persons who are being led to the completing of their nature. This is why it is not right to say that pleasure is a perceptible process, but it should rather be called
15   activity of the natural state, and instead of 'perceptible' 'unimpeded'. It is thought to be a[68] process just because they think it is in the strict sense *good;* for they think that activity is a process which it is not.

The view that pleasures are bad because some pleasant things are unhealthy is like saying that healthy things are bad because some healthy things are bad for the pocket; both are bad in the respect mentioned, but they are not *bad* for *that*
20   reason—indeed, contemplation itself is sometimes injurious to health.

Neither practical wisdom or any state is impeded by the pleasure arising from it; it is foreign pleasures that impede, for the pleasures arising from contemplation and learning will make us contemplate and learn all the more.

The fact that no pleasure is the product of any art arises naturally enough;
25   there is no art of any other activity either, but only of the capacity; though for that matter the arts of the perfumer and the cook *are* thought to be arts of pleasure.

The arguments that the temperate man avoids pleasure and that the man of practical wisdom pursues the painless life, and that children and the brutes pursue pleasure, are all refuted by the same consideration. We have pointed out in what
30   sense pleasures are good without qualification and in what sense some are not good; now both the brutes and children pursue pleasures of the latter kind (and the man of practical wisdom pursues tranquil freedom from that kind), viz. those which imply appetite and pain, i.e. the bodily pleasures (for it is these that are of this nature) and the excesses of them, in respect of which the self-indulgent man is self-indulgent.
35   This is why the temperate man avoids these pleasures; for even he has pleasures of his own.

1153ᵇ1   13 · But further it is agreed that pain is bad and to be avoided; for some pain is without qualification bad, and other pain is bad because it is in some respect an impediment to us. Now the contrary of that which is to be avoided, *qua* something

[67]Omitting ἡδεῖ.
[68]Retaining τις for τισιν.

to be avoided and bad, is good. Pleasure, then, is necessarily a good. For the answer of Speusippus, that it is just as the greater is contrary both to the less and to the equal, is not successful; since he would not say that pleasure is essentially a species of evil.

And if certain pleasures are bad, that does not prevent the best thing from being some pleasure—just as knowledge might be, though certain kinds of knowledge are bad. Perhaps it is even necessary, if each state has unimpeded activities, that whether the activity (if unimpeded) of all our states or that of some one of them is happiness, this should be the thing most worthy of our choice; and this activity is a pleasure. Thus the chief good would be some pleasure, though most pleasures might perhaps be bad without qualification. And for this reason all men think that the happy life is pleasant and weave pleasure into happiness—and reasonably too; for no activity is complete when it is impeded, and happiness is a complete thing; this is why the happy man needs the goods of the body and external goods, i.e. those of fortune, viz. in order that he may not be impeded in these ways. Those who say that the victim on the rack or the man who falls into great misfortunes is happy if he is good, are, whether they mean to or not, talking nonsense. Now because we need fortune as well as other things, some people think good fortune the same thing as happiness; but it is not that, for even good fortune itself when in excess is an impediment, and perhaps should then be no longer called good fortune; for its limit is fixed by reference to happiness.

And indeed the fact that all things, both brutes and men, pursue pleasure in an indication of its being somehow the chief good:

No voice is wholly lost that many peoples. . . .[69]

But since no one nature or state either is or is thought the best for all, neither do all pursue the same pleasure; yet all pursue pleasure. And perhaps they actually pursue not the pleasure they think they pursue nor that which they would say they pursue, but the same pleasure; for all things have by nature something divine in them. But the bodily pleasures have appropriated the name both because we oftenest steer our course for them and because all men share in them; thus because they alone are familiar, men think there are no others.

It is evident also that if pleasure and activity is not a good, it will not be the case that the happy man lives a pleasant life; for to what end should he need pleasure, if it is not a good but the happy man may even live a painful life? For pain is neither an evil nor a good, if pleasure is not; why then should he avoid it?

Therefore, too, the life of the good man will not be pleasanter than that of any one else, if his activities are not more pleasant.

14 · With regard to the bodily pleasures, those who say that *some* pleasures are very much to be chosen, viz. the noble pleasures, but not the bodily pleasures, i.e. those with which the self-indulgent man is concerned, must consider why,[70]

---

[69]Hesiod, *Works and Days* 763.
[70]Placing a comma after ἀκόλαστος.

then, the contrary pains are bad. For the contrary of bad is good. Are the necessary pleasures good in the sense in which even that which is not bad is good? Or are they good up to a point? Is it that where you have states and processes of which there cannot be too much, there cannot be too much of the corresponding pleasure, and that where there can be too much of the one there can be too much of the other also? 15 Now there can be too much of bodily goods, and the bad man is bad by virtue of pursuing the excess, not by virtue of pursuing the necessary pleasures (for *all* men enjoy in some way or other both dainty foods and wines and sexual intercourse, but not all men do so as they ought). The contrary is the case with pain; for he does not 20 avoid the excess of it, he avoids it altogether; for the alternative to excess of pleasure is not pain, except to the man who pursues this excess.

Since we should state not only the truth, but also the cause of error—for this contributes towards producing conviction, since when a reasonable explanation is 25 given of why the false view appears true, this tends to produce belief in the true view—therefore we must state why the bodily pleasures appear the more worthy of choice. Firstly, then, it is because they expel pain; owing to the excesses of pain men pursue excessive and in general bodily pleasure as being a cure for the pain. Now 30 curative agencies produce intense feeling—which is the reason why they are pursued—because they show up against the contrary pain. (Indeed pleasure is thought not to be good for these two reasons, as has been said, viz. that some of them are activities belonging to a bad nature—either congenital, as in the case of a brute, or due to habit, i.e. those of bad men; while others are meant to cure a defective nature, and it is better to be in a healthy state than to be getting into it, but these 1154ᵇ1 arise during the process of being made complete and are therefore only incidentally good.) Further, they are pursued because of their violence by those who cannot enjoy other pleasures. At all events some people[71] manufacture thirsts for themselves. When these are harmless, the practice is irreproachable; when they are 5 hurtful, it is bad. For they have nothing else to enjoy, and, besides, a neutral state is painful to many people because of their nature. For animals are always toiling, as the students of natural science also testify, saying that sight and hearing are painful; but we have become used to this, as they maintain. Similarly, while, in 10 youth, people are, owing to the growth that is going on, in a situation like that of drunken men, and youth is pleasant, on the other hand people of excitable nature always need relief; for even their body is ever in torment owing to its special composition, and they are always under the influence of violent desire; but pain is driven out both by the contrary pleasure, and by any chance pleasure if it be strong; 15 and for these reasons they become self-indulgent and bad. But the pleasures that do not involve pains do not admit of excess; and these are among the things pleasant by nature and not incidentally. By things pleasant incidentally I mean those that act as cures (for because as a result people are cured, through some action of the part that remains healthy, for this reason the process is thought pleasant); things naturally 20 pleasant are those that stimulate the action of the healthy nature.

[71]Reading τινές.

There is no one thing that is always pleasant, because our nature is not simple but there is another element in us as well, inasmuch as we are perishable creatures, so that if the one element does something, this is unnatural to the other nature, and when the two elements are evenly balanced, what is done seems neither painful nor pleasant; for if the nature of anything were simple, the same action would always be most pleasant to it. This is why God always enjoys a single and simple pleasure; for there is not only an activity of movement but an activity of immobility, and pleasure is found more in rest than in movement. But 'change in all things is sweet', as the poet says,[72] because of some vice; for as it is the vicious man that is changeable, so the nature that needs change is vicious; for it is not simple nor good.

We have now discussed continence and incontinence, and pleasure and pain, both what each is and in what sense some of them are good and others bad; it remains to speak of friendship.

BOOK VIII

1 · After what we have said, a discussion of friendship would naturally follow, since it is an excellence or implies excellence, and is besides most necessary with a view to living. For without friends no one would choose to live, though he had all other goods; even rich men and those in possession of office and of dominating power are thought to need friends most of all; for what is the use of such prosperity without the opportunity of beneficence, which is exercised chiefly and in its most laudable form towards friends? Or how can prosperity be guarded and preserved without friends? The greater it is, the more exposed is it to risk. And in poverty and in other misfortunes men think friends are the only refuge. It helps the young, too, to keep from error; it aids older people by ministering to their needs and supplementing the activities that are failing from weakness; those in the prime of life it stimulates to noble actions—'two going together'—for with friends men are more able both to think and to act. Again, parent seems by nature to feel it for offspring and offspring for parent, not only among men but among birds and among most animals; it is felt mutually by members of the same race, and especially by men, whence we praise lovers of their fellow men. We may see even in our travels how near and dear every man is to every other. Friendship seems too to hold states together, and lawgivers to care more for it than for justice; for unanimity seems to be something like friendship, and this they aim at most of all, and expel faction as their worst enemy; and when men are friends they have no need of justice, while when they are just they need friendship as well, and the truest form of justice is thought to be a friendly quality.

But it is not only necessary but also noble; for we praise those who love their

[72]Euripides, *Orestes* 234.

30   friends, and it is thought to be a fine thing to have many friends; and again we think
it is the same people that are good men and are friends.

Not a few things about friendship are matters of debate. Some define it as a
kind of likeness and say like people are friends, whence come the sayings 'like to
like', 'birds of a feather flock together', and so on; others on the contrary say 'two of
1155ᵇ1   a trade never agree'. On this very question they inquire more deeply and in a more
scientific fashion, Euripides saying that 'parched earth loves the rain, and stately
heaven when filled with rain loves to fall to earth', and Heraclitus that 'it is what
5   opposes that helps' and 'from different tones comes the fairest tune' and 'all things
are produced through strife'; while Empedocles, as well as others, expresses the
opposite view that like aims at like. The scientific problems we may leave alone (for
they do not belong to the present inquiry); let us examine those which are human
10   and involve character and feeling, e.g. whether friendship can arise between any
two people or people cannot be friends if they are wicked, and whether there is one
species of friendship or more than one. Those who think there is only one because it
admits of degrees have relied on an inadequate indication; for even things different
15   in species admit of degree. We have discussed this matter previously.

2 · The kinds of friendship may perhaps be cleared up if we first come to
know the object of love. For not everything seems to be loved but only the lovable,
and this is good, pleasant, or useful; but it would seem to be that by which some
20   good or pleasure is produced that is useful, so that it is the good and the pleasant
that are lovable as ends. Do men love, then, *the* good, or what is good for *them?*
These sometimes clash. So too with regard to the pleasant. Now it is thought that
each loves what is good for himself, and that the good is without qualification
25   lovable, and what is good for each man is lovable for him; but each man loves not
what is good for him but what seems good. This however will make no difference; we
shall just have to say that this is that which seems lovable. Now there are three
grounds on which people love; of the love of lifeless objects we do not use the word
'friendship'; for it is not mutual love, nor is there a wishing of good to the other (for
30   it would surely be ridiculous to wish wine well; if one wishes anything for it, it is that
it may keep, so that one may have it oneself); but to a friend we say we ought to wish
what is good for his sake. But to those who thus wish good we ascribe only goodwill,
if the wish is not reciprocated; goodwill when it *is* reciprocal being friendship. Or
must we add 'when it is recognized'? For many people have goodwill to those whom
1156ᵃ1   they have not seen but judge to be good or useful; and one of these might return this
feeling. These people seem to bear goodwill to each other; but how could one call
them friends when they do not know their mutual feelings? To be friends, then, they
must be mutually recognized as bearing goodwill and wishing well to each other for
5   one of the aforesaid reasons.

3 · Now these reasons differ from each other in kind; so therefore, do the
corresponding forms of love and friendship. There are therefore three kinds of
friendship, equal in number to the things that are lovable; for with respect to each

there is a mutual and recognized love, and those who love each other wish well to each other in that respect in which they love one another. Now those who love each   10 other for their utility do not love each other for themselves but in virtue of some good which they get from each other. So too with those who love for the sake of pleasure; it is not for their character that men love ready-witted people, but because they find them pleasant. Therefore those who love for the sake of utility love for the sake of what is good for *themselves,* and those who love for the sake of pleasure do   15 so for the sake of what is pleasant to *themselves,* and not in so far as the other is the person loved but in so far as he is useful or pleasant. And thus these friendships are only incidental; for it is not as being the man he is that the loved person is loved, but as providing some good or pleasure. Such friendships, then, are easily dissolved, if the parties do not remain like themselves; for if the one party is no longer pleasant or   20 useful the other ceases to love him.

Now the useful is not permanent but is always changing. Thus when the motive of the friendship is done away, the friendship is dissolved, inasmuch as it existed only for the ends in question. This kind of friendship seems to exist chiefly between old people (for at that age people pursue not the pleasant but the useful)   25 and, of those who are in their prime or young, between those who pursue utility. And such people do not live much with each other either; for sometimes they do not even find each other pleasant; therefore they do not need such companionship unless they are useful to each other; for they are pleasant to each other only in so far as they rouse in each other hopes of something good to come. Among such friendships   30 people also class the friendship of host and guest. On the other hand the friendship of young people seems to aim at pleasure; for they live under the guidance of emotion, and pursue above all what is pleasant to themselves and what is immediately before them; but with increasing age their pleasures become different. This is why they quickly become friends and quickly cease to be so; their friendship changes with the object that is found pleasant, and such pleasure alters quickly.   1156ᵇ1 Young people are amorous too; for the greater part of the friendship of love depends on emotion and aims at pleasure; this is why they fall in love and quickly fall out of love, changing often within a single day. But these people do wish to spend their days and lives together; for it is thus that they attain the purpose of their   5 friendship.

Perfect friendship is the friendship of men who are good, and alike in excellence; for these wish well alike to each other *qua* good, and they are good in themselves. Now those who wish well to their friends for their sake are most truly·   10 friends; for they do this by reason of their own nature and not incidentally; therefore their friendship lasts as long as they are good—and excellence is an enduring thing. And each is good without qualification and to his friend, for the good are both good without qualification and useful to each other. So too they are pleasant; for the good are pleasant both without qualification and to each other, since to each his own   15 activities and others like them are pleasurable, and the actions of the good *are* the same or like. And such a friendship is as might be expected lasting since there meet in it all the qualities that friends should have. For all friendship is for the sake of

20   good or of pleasure—good or pleasure either in the abstract or such as will be
enjoyed by him who has the friendly feeling—and is based on a certain
resemblance; and to a friendship of good men all the qualities we have named
belong in virtue of the nature of the friends themselves; for in the case of this kind of
friendship the other qualities also are alike in both friends, and that which is good
without qualification is also without qualification pleasant, and these are the most
lovable qualities. Love and friendship therefore are found most and in their best
form between such men.

25   But it is natural that such friendships should be infrequent; for such men are
rare. Further, such friendship requires time and familiarity; as the proverb says,
men cannot know each other till they have 'eaten salt together'; nor can they admit
each other to friendship or be friends till each has been found lovable and been
30   trusted by each. Those who quickly show the marks of friendship to each other wish
to be friends, but are not friends unless they both are lovable and know the fact; for
a wish for friendship may arise quickly, but friendship does not.

      4 · This kind of friendship, then is complete both in respect of duration and
in all other respects, and in it each gets from each in all respects the same as, or
something like what, he gives; which is what ought to happen between friends.
1157ᵃ1   Friendship for the sake of pleasure bears a resemblance to this kind; for good people
too are pleasant to each other. So too does friendship for the sake of utility; for the
good are also useful to each other. Among men of these sorts too, friendships are
most permanent when the friends get the same thing from each other (e.g.
5   pleasure), and not only that but also from the same source, as happens between
ready-witted people, not as happens between lover and beloved. For these do not
take pleasure in the same things, but the one in seeing the beloved and the other in
receiving attentions from his lover; and when the bloom of youth is passing the
friendship sometimes passes too (for the one finds no pleasure in the sight of the
10   other, and the other gets no attentions from the first); but many lovers on the other
hand are constant, if familiarity has led them to love each other's characters, these
being alike. But those who exchange not pleasure but utility in their love are both
less truly friends and less constant. Those who are friends for the sake of utility part
15   when the advantage is at an end; for they were lovers not of each other but of
profit.
      For the sake of pleasure or utility, then, even bad men may be friends of each
other, or good men of bad, or one who is neither good nor bad may be a friend to any
sort of person, but for their own sake clearly only good men can be friends; for bad
men do not delight in each other unless some advantage come of the relation.
20   The friendship of the good too alone is proof against slander; for it is not easy to
trust any one's talk about a man who has long been tested by oneself; and it is
among good men that trust and the feeling that he would never wrong me and all the
other things that are demanded in true friendship are found. In the other kinds of
25   friendship, however, there is nothing to prevent these evils arising.
      For men apply the name of friends even to those whose motive is utility, in

which sense states are said to be friendly (for the alliances of states seem to aim at advantage), and to those who love each other for the sake of pleasure, in which sense children are called friends. Therefore we too ought perhaps to call such people friends, and say that there are several kinds of friendship—firstly and in the proper   30
sense that of good men *qua* good, and by similarity the other kinds; for it is in virtue of something good and something similar that they are friends, since even the pleasant is good for the lovers of pleasure. But these two kinds of friendship are not often united, nor do the same people become friends for the sake of utility and of pleasure; for things that are only incidentally connected are not often coupled   35
together.

Friendship being divided into these kinds; bad men will be friends for the sake   1157ᵇ1
of pleasure or of utility, being in this respect like each other, but good men will be friends for their own sake, i.e. in virtue of their goodness. These, then, are friends without qualification; the others are friends incidentally and through a resemblance to these.

5 · As in regard to the excellences some men are called good in respect of a   5
state, others in respect of an activity, so too in the case of friendship; for those who live together delight in each other and confer benefits on each other, but those who are asleep or locally separated are not performing, but are disposed to perform, the activities of friendship; distance does not break off the friendship absolutely, but   10
only the activity of it. But if the absence is lasting, it seems actually to make men forget their friendship; hence the saying 'out of sight, out of mind'. Neither old people nor sour people seem to make friends easily; for there is little that is pleasant in them, and no one can spend his days with one whose company is painful, or not   15
pleasant, since nature seems above all to avoid the painful and to aim at the pleasant. Those, however, who approve of each other but do not live together seem to be well-disposed rather than actual friends. For there is nothing so characteristic of friends as living together (since while it is people who are in need that desire   20
benefits, even those who are blessed desire to spend their days together; for solitude suits such people least of all); but people cannot live together if they are not pleasant and do not enjoy the same things, as friends who are companions seem to do.

The truest friendship, then, is that of the good, as we have frequently said; for   25
that which is without qualification good or pleasant seems to be lovable and desirable, and for each person that which is good or pleasant to him; and the good man is lovable and desirable to the good man for both these reasons. Now it looks as if love were a passion, friendship a state; for love may be felt just as much towards lifeless things, but mutual love involves choice and choice springs from a state; and   30
men wish well to those whom they love, for their sake, not as a result of passion but as a result of a state. And in loving a friend men love what is good for themselves; for the good man in becoming a friend becomes a good to his friend. Each, then, both loves what is good for himself, and makes an equal return in goodwill and in pleasantness; for friendship is said to be equality, and both of these are found most   1158ᵃ1
in the friendship of the good.

6 · Between sour and elderly people friendship arises less readily, inasmuch as they are less good-tempered and enjoy companionship less; for these are thought to be the greatest marks of friendship and most productive of it. This is why, while young men become friends quickly, old men do not; it is because men do not become friends with those in whom they do not delight; and similarly sour people do not quickly make friends either. But such men may bear goodwill to each other; for they wish one another well and aid one another in need; but they are hardly *friends* because they do not spend their days together nor delight in each other, and these are thought the greatest marks of friendship.

One cannot be a friend to many people in the sense of having friendship of the complete type with them, just as one cannot be in love with many people at once (for love is a sort of excess, and it is the nature of such only to be felt towards one person); and it is not easy for many people at the same time to please the same person very greatly, or perhaps even to be good for him. One must, too, acquire some experience of the other person and become familiar with him, and that is very hard. But with a view to utility or pleasure it is possible that many people should please one; for many people are useful or pleasant, and these services take little time.

Of these two kinds that which is for the sake of pleasure is the more like friendship, when both parties get the same things from each other and delight in each other or in the same things, as in the friendships of the young; for generosity is more found in such friendships. Friendship based on utility is for the commercially minded. People who are blessed, too, have no need of useful friends, but do need pleasant friends; for they wish to live with others, and, though they can endure for a short time what is painful, no one could put up with it continuously, nor even with the Good itself if it were painful to him; this is why they look out for friends who are pleasant. Perhaps they should look out for friends who, being pleasant, are also good, and good for them too; for so they will have all the characteristics that friends should have.

People in positions of authority seem to have friends who fall into distinct classes; some people are useful to them and others are pleasant, but the same people are rarely both; for they seek neither those whose pleasantness is accompanied by excellence nor those whose utility is with a view to noble objects, but in their desire for pleasure they seek for ready-witted people, and their other friends they choose as being clever at doing what they are told, and these characteristics are rarely combined. Now we have said that the good man is at the same time pleasant and useful; but such a man does not become the friend of one who surpasses him, unless he is surpassed also in excellence; if this is not so, he does not establish equality by being proportionally exceeded. But such men are not so easy to find.

1158^{b}1   However that may be, the aforesaid friendships involve equality; for the friends get the same things from one another and wish the same things for one another, or exchange one thing for another, e.g. pleasure for utility; we have said, however, that they are both less truly friendships and less permanent. But it is from

their likeness and their unlikeness to the same thing that they are thought both to be 5
and not to be friendships. It is by their likeness to the friendship of excellence that
they seem to be friendships (for one of them involves pleasure and the other utility,
and these characteristics belong to the friendship of excellence as well); while it is
because the friendship of excellence is proof against slander and lasting, while these
quickly change (besides differing from the former in many other respects), that 10
they appear *not* to be friendships; i.e. it is because of their unlikeness to the
friendship of excellence.

7 · But there is another kind of friendship, viz. that which involves an
inequality, e.g. that of father to son and in general of elder to younger, that of man
to wife and in general that of ruler to subject. And these friendships differ also from
each other; for it is not the same that exists between parents and children and 15
between rulers and subjects, nor is even that of father to son the same as that of son
to father, nor that of husband to wife the same as that of wife to husband. For the
excellence and the function of each of these is different, and so are the reasons for
which they love; the love and the friendship are therefore different also. Each party,
then, neither gets the same from the other, nor ought to seek it; but when children 20
render to parents what they ought to render to those who brought them into the
world, and parents render what they should to their children, the friendship of such
persons will be lasting and excellent. In all friendships implying inequality the love
also should be proportional, i.e. the better should be more loved than he loves, and so 25
should the more useful, and similarly in each of the other cases; for when the love is
in proportion to the merit of the parties, then in a sense arises equality, which is held
to be characteristic of friendship.

But equality does not seem to take the same form in acts of justice and in
friendship; for in acts of justice what is equal in the primary sense is that which is in 30
proportion to merit, while quantitative equality is secondary, but in friendship
quantitative equality is primary and proportion to merit secondary. This becomes
clear if there is a great interval in respect of excellence or vice or wealth or anything
else between the parties; for then they are no longer friends, and do not even expect
to be so. And this is most manifest in the case of the gods; for they surpass us most
decisively in all good things. But it is clear also in the case of kings; for with them, 1159ª1
too, men who are much their inferiors do not expect to be friends; nor do men of no
account expect to be friends with the best or wisest men. In such cases it is not
possible to define exactly up to what point friends can remain friends; for much can
be taken away and friendship remain, but when one party is removed to a great
distance, as God is, the possibility of friendship ceases. This is in fact the origin of 5
the question whether friends really wish for their friends the greatest goods, e.g.
that of being gods; since in that case their friends will no longer be friends to them,
and therefore will not be good things for them (for friends *are* good things). Now if
we were right in saying that friend wishes good to friend for his sake, his friend must
remain the sort of being he is, whatever that may be; therefore it is for him only so 10

long as he remains a man that he will wish the greatest goods. But perhaps not *all* the greatest goods; for it is for himself most of all that each man wishes what is good.

8 · Most people seem, owing to ambition, to wish to be loved rather than to love; which is why most men love flattery; for the flatterer is a friend in an inferior
15   position, or pretends to be such and to love more than he is loved; and being loved seems to be akin to being honoured, and this is what most people aim at. But it seems to be not for its own sake that people choose honour, but incidentally. For most people enjoy being honoured by those in positions of authority because of their
20   hopes (for they think that if they want anything they will get it from them; and therefore they delight in honour as a token of favour to come); while those who desire honour from good men, and men who know, are aiming at confirming their own opinion of themselves; they delight in honour, therefore, because they believe in their own goodness on the strength of the judgement of those who speak about them.
25   In being loved, on the other hand, people delight for its own sake; whence it would seem to be better than being honoured, and friendship to be desirable in itself. But it seems to lie in loving rather than in being loved, as is indicated by the delight mothers take in loving; for some mothers hand over their children to be brought up, and so long as they know their fate they love them and do not seek to be loved in
30   return (if they cannot have both), but seem to be satisfied if they see them prospering; and they themselves love their children even if these owing to their ignorance give them nothing of a mother's due. Now since friendship depends more on loving, and it is those who love their friends that are praised, loving seems to be the characteristic excellence of friends, so that it is only those in whom this is found
1159ᵇ1   in due measure that are lasting friends, and only their friendship that endures.
It is in this way more than any other that even unequals can be friends; they can be equalized. Now equality and likeness are friendship, and especially the likeness of those who are like in excellence; for being steadfast in themselves they
5   hold fast to each other, and neither ask nor give base services, but (one may say) even prevent them; for it is characteristic of good men neither to go wrong themselves nor to let their friends do so. But wicked men have no steadfastness (for they do not even stay similar to themselves), but become friends for a short time
10   because they delight in each other's wickedness. Friends who are useful or pleasant last longer; i.e. as long as they provide each other with enjoyments or advantages. Friendship for utility's sake seems to be that which most easily exists between contraries, e.g. between poor and rich, between ignorant and learned; for what a man actually lacks he aims at, and he gives something else in return. Under this
15   head, too, one might bring lover and beloved, beautiful and ugly. This is why lovers sometimes seem ridiculous, when they demand to be loved as they love; if they are equally lovable their claim can perhaps be justified, but when they have nothing lovable about them it is ridiculous. Perhaps, however, contrary does not even aim at
20   contrary in its own nature, but only incidentally, the desire being for what is intermediate; for that is what is good, e.g. it is good for the dry not to become wet

but to come to the intermediate state, and similarly with the hot and in all other cases. These subjects we may dismiss; for they are indeed somewhat foreign to our inquiry.

9 . Friendship and justice seem, as we have said at the outset of our 25 discussion, to be concerned with the same objects and exhibited between the same persons. For in every community there is thought to be some form of justice, and friendship too; at least men address as friends their fellow-voyagers and fellow-soldiers, and so too those associated with them in any other kind of community. And the extent of their association is the extent of their friendship, as it is the extent to 30 which justice exists between them. And the proverb 'what friends have is common property' expresses the truth; for friendship depends on community. Now brothers and comrades have all things in common, but the others have definite things in common—some more things, others fewer; for of friendships, too, some are more and others less truly friendships. And the claims of justice differ too; the duties of parents to children and those of brothers to each other are not the same, nor those of 1160ª1 comrades and those of fellow-citizens, and so, too, with the other kinds of friendship. There is a difference, therefore, also between the acts that are unjust towards each of these classes of associates, and the injustice increases by being exhibited towards those who are friends in a fuller sense; e.g. it is a more terrible thing to defraud a comrade than a fellow citizen, more terrible not to help a brother 5 than a stranger, and more terrible to wound a father than any one else. And the demands of justice also naturally increase with the friendship, which implies that friendship and justice exist between the same persons and have an equal extension.

Now all forms of community are like parts of the political community; for men journey together with a view to some particular advantage, and to provide 10 something that they need for the purposes of life; and it is for the sake of advantage that the political community too seems both to have come together originally and to endure, for this is what legislators aim at, and they call just that which is to the common advantage. Now the other communities aim at some particular advantage, e.g. sailors at what is advantageous on a voyage with a view to making money or 15 something of the kind, fellow-soldiers at what is advantageous in war, whether it is wealth or victory or the taking of a city that they seek, and members of tribes and demes act similarly. [Some communities seem to arise for the sake of pleasure, viz. religious guilds and social clubs; for these exist respectively for the sake of offering 20 sacrifice and of companionship. But all these seem to fall under the political community; for it aims not at present advantage but at what is advantageous for life as a whole],[73] offering sacrifices and arranging gatherings for the purpose, and assigning honours to the gods, and providing pleasant relaxations for themselves. 25 For the ancient sacrifices and gatherings seem to take place after the harvest as a sort of first fruits, because it was at these seasons that people had most leisure. All the communities, then, seem to be parts of the political community; and the particular kinds of friendship will correspond to the particular kinds of community. 30

[73]Excised by Cook Wilson.

10 · There are three kinds of constitution, and an equal number of deviation-forms—perversions, as it were, of them. The constitutions are monarchy,
aristocracy, and thirdly that which is based on a property qualification, which it
35 seems appropriate to call timocratic, though most people usually call it polity. The
best of these is monarchy, the worst timocracy. The deviation from monarchy is
1160ᵇ1 tyranny; for both are forms of one-man rule, but there is the greatest difference
between them; the tyrant looks to his own advantage, the king to that of his subjects.
For a man is not a king unless he is sufficient to himself and excels his subjects in all
5 good things; and such a man needs nothing further; therefore he will not look to his
own interests but to those of his subjects; for a king who is not like that would be a
mere titular king. Now tyranny is the very contrary of this; the tyrant pursues his
own good. And it is clearer in the case of tyranny that it is the worst deviation-form;
10 but it is the contrary of the best that is worst. Monarchy passes over into tyranny;
for tyranny is the evil form of one-man rule and the bad king becomes a tyrant.
Aristocracy passes over into oligarchy by the badness of the rulers, who distribute
contrary to merit what belongs to the city—all or most of the good things to
15 themselves, and office always to the same people, paying most regard to wealth;
thus the rulers are few and are bad men instead of the most worthy. Timocracy
passes over into democracy; for these are coterminous, since timocracy too tends to
involve a mass of people, and all who have the property qualification count as equal.
Democracy is the least bad of the deviations; for in its case the form of constitution
is but a slight deviation. These then are the changes to which constitutions are most
subject; for these are the smallest and easiest transitions.

One may find resemblances to the constitutions and, as it were, patterns of
them even in households. For the association of a father with his sons bears the form
25 of monarchy, since the father cares for his children; and this is why Homer calls
Zeus 'father'; it is the ideal of monarchy to be paternal rule. But among the Persians
the rule of the father is tyrannical; they use their sons as slaves. Tyrannical too is the
30 rule of a master over slaves; for it is the advantage of the master that is brought
about in it. Now this seems to be a correct form of government, but the Persian type
is perverted; for the modes of rule appropriate to different relations are diverse. The
association of man and wife seems to be aristocratic; for the man rules in
accordance with merit, and in those matters in which a man should rule, but the
35 matters that befit a woman he hands over to her. If the man rules in everything the
relation passes over into oligarchy; for he does this contrary to merit and not *qua*
1161ª1 better. Sometimes, however, women rule, because they are heiresses; so their rule is
not in virtue of excellence but due to wealth and power, as in oligarchies. The
association of brothers is like timocracy; for they are equal, except in so far as they
5 differ in age; hence if they differ *much* in age, the friendship is no longer of the
fraternal type. Democracy is found chiefly in masterless dwellings (for here every
one is on an equality), and in those in which the ruler is weak and every one has
licence to do as he pleases.

10   11 · Each of the constitutions may be seen to involve friendship just in so far
as it involves justice. The friendship between a king and his subjects depends on an

excess of benefits conferred; for he confers benefits on his subjects if being a good man he cares for them with a view to their well-being, as a shepherd does for his sheep (whence Homer called Agamemnon 'shepherd of the peoples'). Such too is 15 the friendship of a father, though this exceeds the other in the greatness of the benefits conferred; for he is responsible for the existence of his children, which is thought the greatest good, and for their nurture and upbringing. These things are ascribed to ancestors as well. Further, by nature a father tends to rule over his sons, ancestors over descendants, a king over his subjects. These friendships imply superiority of one party over the other, which is why parents are honoured. The 20 justice therefore that exists between persons so related is not the same but proportioned to merit; for that is true of the friendship as well. The friendship of man and wife, again, is the same that is found in an aristocracy; for it is in accordance with excellence—the better gets more of what is good, and each gets what befits him; and so, too, with the justice in these relations. The friendship of 25 brothers is like that of comrades; for they are equal and of like age, and such persons are for the most part like in their feelings and their character. Like this, too, is the friendship appropriate to timocratic government; for the citizens tend to be equal and fair; therefore rule is taken in turn, and on equal terms; and the friendship appropriate here will correspond.

But in the deviation-forms, as justice hardly exists, so too does friendship. It 30 exists least in the worst form; in tyranny there is little or no friendship. For where there is nothing common to ruler and ruled, there is not friendship either, since there is not justice; e.g. between craftsman and tool, soul and body, master and slave; the latter in each case is benefited by that which uses it, but there is no 1161^{b}1 friendship nor justice towards lifeless things. But neither is there friendship towards a horse or an ox, nor to a slave *qua* slave. For there is nothing common to the two parties; the slave is a living tool and the tool a lifeless slave. *Qua* slave then, one cannot be friends with him. But *qua* man one can; for there seems to be some justice 5 between any man and any other who can share in a system of law or be a party to an agreement; therefore there can also be friendship with him in so far as he is a man. Therefore while in tyrannies friendship and justice hardly exist, in democracies they exist more fully; for where the citizens are equal they have much in common. 10

12 · Every form of friendship, then, involves association, as has been said. One might, however, mark off from the rest both the friendship of kindred and that of comrades. Those of fellow-citizens, fellow-tribesmen, fellow-voyagers, and the like are more like mere friendships of association; for they seem to rest on a sort of 15 compact. With them we might class the friendship of host and guest.

The friendship of kinsmen itself, while it seems to be of many kinds, appears to depend in every case on paternal friendship; for parents love their children as being a part of themselves, and children their parents as being something originating from them. Now parents know their offspring better than their children know that they 20 are their children, and the originator is more attached to his offspring than the offspring to their begetter; for the product belongs to the producer (e.g. a tooth or hair or anything else to him whose it is), but the producer does not belong to the

product, or belongs in a less degree. And the length of time produces the same
25   result; parents love their children as soon as these are born, but children love their
parents only after time has elapsed and they have acquired understanding or
perception. From these considerations it is also plain why mothers love more than
fathers do. Parents, then, love their children as themselves (for their issue are by
virtue of their separate existence a sort of other selves), while children love their
30   parents as being born of them, and brothers love each other as being born of the
same parents; for their identity with them makes them identical with each other
(which is the reason why people talk of 'the same blood', 'the same stock', and so
on). They are, therefore, in a sense the same thing, though in separate individuals.
Two things that contribute greatly to friendship are a common upbringing and
similarity of age; for 'two of an age take to each other', and familiarity makes for
comradeship; whence the friendship of brothers is akin to that of comrades. And
1162ª1   cousins and other kinsmen are attached by derivation from brothers, viz. by being
derived from the same parents. They come to be closer together or farther apart by
virtue of the nearness or distance of the original ancestor.

The friendship of children to parents, and of men to gods, is a relation to them
5   as to something good and superior; for they have conferred the greatest benefits,
since they are the causes of their being and of their nourishment, and of their
education from their birth; and this kind of friendship possesses pleasantness and
utility also, more than that of strangers, inasmuch as their life is lived more in
10   common. The friendship of brothers has the characteristics found in that of
comrades (and especially when these are good), and in general between people who
are like each other, inasmuch as they belong more to each other and start with a love
for each other from their very birth, and inasmuch as those born of the same parents
and brought up together and similarly educated are more akin in character; and the
test of time has been applied most fully and convincingly in their case.
15   Between other kinsmen friendly relations are found in due proportion.
Between man and wife friendship seems to exist by nature; for man is naturally
inclined to form couples—even more than to form cities, inasmuch as the household
is earlier and more necessary than the city, and reproduction is more common to
20   man than with the animals. With the other animals the union extends only to this
point, but human beings live together not only for the sake of reproduction but also
for the various purposes of life; for from the start the functions are divided, and
those of man and woman are different; so they help each other by throwing their
peculiar gifts into the common stock. It is for these reasons that both utility and
25   pleasure seem to be found in this kind of friendship. But this friendship may be
based also on excellence, if the parties are good; for each has its own excellence and
they will delight in the fact. And children seem to be a bond of union (which is the
reason why childless people part more easily); for children are a good common to
both and what is common holds them together.
30   How man and wife and in general friend and friend ought mutually to behave
seems to be the same question as how it is just for them to behave; for a man does not
seem to have the same duties to a friend, a stranger, a comrade, and a schoolfel-
low.

13 · There are three kinds of friendship, as we said at the outset of our inquiry, and in respect of each some are friends on an equality and others by virtue of a superiority (for not only can equally good men become friends but a better man can make friends with a worse, and similarly in friendships of pleasure or utility the friends may be equal or unequal in the benefits they confer). This being so, equals must effect the required equalization on a basis of equality in love and in all other respects, while unequals must render what is in proportion to their superiority or inferiority.

Complaints and reproaches arise either only or chiefly in the friendship of utility, and this is only to be expected. For those who are friends on the ground of excellence are anxious to do well by each other (since that is a mark of excellence and of friendship), and between men who are emulating each other in this there cannot be complaints or quarrels; no one is offended by a man who loves him and does well by him—if he is a person of nice feeling he takes his revenge by doing well by the other. And the man who excels will not complain of his friend, since he gets what he aims at; for each man desires what is good. Nor do complaints arise much even in friendships of pleasure; for both get at the same time what they desire, if they enjoy spending their time together; and even a man who complained of another for *not* affording him pleasure would seem ridiculous, since it is in his power not to spend his days with him.

But the friendship of utility is full of complaints; for as they use each other for their own interests they always want to get the better of the bargain, and think they have got less than they should, and blame their partners because they do not get all they want and deserve; and those who do well by others cannot help them as much as those whom they benefit want.

Now it seems that, as justice is of two kinds, one unwritten and the other legal, one kind of friendship of utility is moral and the other legal. And so complaints arise most of all when men do not dissolve the relation in the spirit of the same type of friendship in which they contracted it. The *legal* type is that which is on fixed terms; its purely commercial variety is on the basis of immediate payment, while the more liberal variety allows time but stipulates for a definite *quid pro quo*. In this variety the debt is clear and not ambiguous, but in the postponement it contains an element of friendliness; and so some states do not allow suits arising out of such agreements, but think men who have bargained on a basis of credit ought to be content. The *moral* type is not on fixed terms; it makes a gift, or does whatever it does, as to a friend; but one expects to receive as much or more, as having not given but lent; and if a man is worse off when the relation is dissolved than he was when it was contracted he will complain. This happens because all or most men, while they wish for what is noble, choose what is advantageous; now it is noble to do well by another without a view to repayment, but it is the receiving of benefits that is advantageous.

Therefore if we can we should return the equivalent of what we have received (for we must not make a man our friend against his will; we must recognize that we were mistaken at the first and took a benefit from a person we should not have taken it from—since it was not from a friend, nor from one who did it just for the sake of

5 acting so—and we must settle up just as if we had been benefited on fixed terms).
Indeed, one would agree to repay if one could (if one could not, even the giver would
not have expected one to do so); therefore if it is possible we must repay. But at the
outset we must consider the man by whom we are being benefited and on what
terms he is acting, in order that we may accept the benefit on these terms, or else
decline it.

10   It is disputable whether we ought to measure a service by its utility to the
receiver and make the return with a view to that, or by the beneficence of the giver.
For those who have received say they have received from their benefactors what
meant little to the latter and what they might have got from others—minimizing
the service; while the givers, on the contrary, say it was the biggest thing they had,

15 and what could not have been got from others, and that it was given in times of
danger or similar need. Now if the friendship is one that aims at *utility,* surely the
advantage to the receiver is the measure. For it is he that asks for the service, and
the other man helps him on the assumption that he will receive the equivalent; so the
assistance has been precisely as great as the advantage to the receiver, and therefore

20 he must return as much as he has received, or even more (for that would be nobler).
In friendships based on *excellence* on the other hand, complaints do not arise, but
the choice of the doer is a sort of measure; for in choice lies the essential element of
excellence and character.

14 · Differences arise also in friendship based on superiority for each
25 expects to get more out of them, but when this happens the friendship is dissolved.
Not only does the better man think he ought to get more, since more should be
assigned to a good man, but the more useful similarly expects this; they say a useless
man should not get as much as they should, since it becomes an act of public service

30 and not a friendship if the proceeds of the friendship do not answer to the worth of
the benefits conferred. For they think that, as in a commercial partnership those
who put more in get more out, so it should be in friendship. But the man who is in a
state of need and inferiority makes the opposite claim; they think it is the part of a
good friend to help those who are in need; what, they say, is the use of being the
friend of a good man or a powerful man, if one is to get nothing out of it?

1163ᵇ1   At all events it seems that each party is justified in his claim, and that each
should get more out of the friendship than the other—not more of the same thing,
however, but the superior more honour and the inferior more gain; for honour is the
prize of excellence and of beneficence, while gain is the assistance required by
inferiority.

5   It seems to be so in constitutional arrangements also; the man who contributes
nothing good to the common stock is not honoured; for what belongs to the public is
given to the man who benefits the public, and honour does belong to the public. It is
not possible to get wealth from the common stock and at the same time honour. For
no one puts up with the smaller share in *all* things; therefore to the man who loses in

10 wealth they assign honour and to the man who is willing to be paid, wealth, since the
proportion to merit equalizes the parties and preserves the friendship, as we have
said.

This then is also the way in which we should associate with unequals; the man who is benefited in respect of wealth or excellence must give honour in return, repaying what he can. For friendship asks a man to do what he can, not what is 15 proportional to the merits of the case; since that cannot always be done, e.g. in honours paid to the gods or to parents; for no one could ever return to them the equivalent of what he gets, but the man who serves them to the utmost of his power is thought to be a good man.

This is why it would not seem open to a man to disown his father (though a father may disown his son); being in debt, he should repay, but there is nothing by 20 doing which a son will have done the equivalent of what he has received, so that he is always in debt. But creditors can remit a debt; and a father can therefore do so too. At the same time it is thought that presumably no one would repudiate a son who was not far gone in wickedness; for apart from the natural friendship it is human nature not to reject assistance. But the son, if he *is* wicked, will naturally avoid 25 aiding his father, or not be zealous about it; for most people wish to get benefits, but avoid doing them, as a thing unprofitable.—So much for these questions.

BOOK IX

1 · In all friendships between dissimilars it is, as we have said, proportion that equalizes the parties and preserves the friendship; e.g. in the political form of friendship the shoemaker gets a return for his shoes in proportion to his worth, and the weaver and the rest do the same. Now here a common measure has been 1164ª1 provided in the form of money, and therefore everything is referred to this and measured by this; but in the friendship of lovers sometimes the lover complains that his excess of love is not met by love in return (though perhaps there is nothing lovable about him), while often the beloved complains that the lover who formerly 5 promised everything now performs nothing. Such incidents happen when the lover loves the beloved for the sake of pleasure while the beloved loves the lover for the sake of utility, and they do not both possess the qualities expected of them. If these be the objects of the friendship it is dissolved when they do not get the things that formed the motives of their love; for each did not love the other person himself but 10 the qualities he had, and these were not enduring; that is why the friendships also are transient. But the love of characters, as has been said, endures because it is self-dependent. Differences arise when what they get is something different and not what they desire; for it is like getting nothing at all when we do not get what we aim at; compare the story of the person who made promises to a lyre-player, promising 15 him the more, the better he sang, but in the morning, when the other demanded the fulfilment of his promises, said that he had given pleasure for pleasure. Now if this had been what each wanted, all would have been well; but if the one wanted enjoyment but the other gain, and the one has what he wants while the other has not, the terms of the association will not have been properly fulfilled; for what each 20

in fact wants is what he attends to, and it is for the sake of that that he will give what he has.

But who is to fix the worth of the service; he who makes the offer or he who has got the advantage? At any rate the one who offers seems to leave it to him. This is what they say Protagoras used to do; whenever he taught anything whatsoever, he bade the learner assess the value of the knowledge, and accepted the amount so fixed. But in such matters some men approve of the saying 'let a man have his fixed reward'.[74]

Those who get the money first and then do none of the things they said they would, owing to the extravagance of their promises, naturally find themselves the objects of complaint; for they do not fulfil what they agreed to. The sophists are perhaps compelled to do this because no one would give money for the things they *do* know. These people then, if they do not do what they have been paid for, are naturally made the objects of complaint.

But where there is *no* contract of service, those who offer something for the sake of the other party cannot (as we have said) be complained of (for that is the nature of the friendship of excellence), and the return to them must be made on the basis of their choice (for it is choice that is the characteristic thing in a friend and in excellence). And so too, it seems, should one make a return to those with whom one has studied philosophy; for their worth cannot be measured against money, and they can get no honour which will balance their services, but still it is perhaps enough, as it is with the gods and with one's parents, to give them what one can.

If the gift was not of this sort, but was made on conditions, it is no doubt preferable that the return made should be one that seems fair to both parties, but if this cannot be achieved, it would seem not only necessary that the person who gets the first service should fix the reward, but also just; for if the other gets in return the equivalent of the advantage the beneficiary has received, or the price he would have paid for the pleasure, he will have got what is fair as from the other.

We see this happening too with things put up for sale, and in some places there are laws providing that no actions shall arise out of voluntary contracts, on the assumption that one should settle with a person whom one has trusted, in the spirit in which one bargained with him. The law holds that it is more just that the person to whom credit was given should fix the terms than that the person who gave credit should do so. For most things are not assessed at the same value by those who have them and those who want them; each class values highly what is its own and what it is offering; yet the return is made on the terms fixed by the receiver. But no doubt the receiver should assess a thing not at what it seems worth when he has it, but at what he assessed it at before he had it.

2 · A further problem is set by such questions as, whether one should in all things give the preference to one's father and obey him, or whether when one is ill one should trust a doctor, and when one has to elect a general should elect a man of

[74]Hesiod, *Works and Days* 370.

military skill; and similarly whether one should render a service by preference to a   25
friend or to a good man, and should show gratitude to a benefactor or oblige a
friend, if one cannot do both.

   Surely all questions are hard to decide with precision. For they admit of many
variations of all sorts in respect both of the magnitude of the service and of its
nobility and necessity. But that we should not give the preference in all things to the   30
same person is plain enough; and we must for the most part return benefits rather
than oblige friends, as we must pay back a loan to a creditor rather than make one to
a friend. But perhaps even this is not always true; e.g. should a man who has been
ransomed out of the hands of brigands ransom his ransomer in return, whoever he
may be (or pay him if he has not been captured but requests payment), or should he   1165ᵃ1
ransom his father? It would seem that he should ransom his father in preference
even to himself. As we have said, then, generally the debt should be paid, but if the
gift is exceedingly noble or exceedingly necessary, one should defer to these
considerations. For sometimes it is not even fair to return the equivalent of what one   5
has received, when the one man has done a service to one whom he knows to be good,
while the other makes a return to one whom he believes to be bad. For that matter,
one should sometimes not lend in return to one who has lent to oneself; for the one
person lent to a good man, expecting to recover his loan, while the other has no hope
of recovering from one who is believed to be bad. Therefore if the facts really are so,   10
the demand is not fair; and if they are not, but people think they are, they would be
held to be doing nothing strange in refusing. As we have often pointed out, then,
discussions about feelings and actions have just as much definiteness as their
subject-matter.

   That we should not make the same return to every one, nor give a father the
preference in everything, as one does not sacrifice everything to Zeus, is plain   15
enough; but since we ought to render different things to parents, brothers,
comrades, and benefactors, we ought to render to each class what is appropriate and
becoming. And this is what people seem in fact to do; to marriages they invite their
kinsfolk; for these have a part in the family and therefore in the doings that affect
the family; and at funerals also they think that kinsfolk, before all others, should   20
meet, for the same reason. And it would be thought that in the matter of food we
should help our parents before all others, since we owe our own nourishment to
them, and it is more noble to help in this respect the authors of our being even before
ourselves; and honour too one should give to one's parents as one does to the gods,
but not any and every honour; for one should not give the same honour to one's   25
father and one's mother, nor again should one give them the honour due to a wise
man or to a general, but the honour due to a father, or again to a mother. To all
older persons, too, one should give honour appropriate to their age, by rising to
receive them and finding seats for them and so on; while to comrades and brothers
one should allow freedom of speech and common use of all things. To kinsmen, too,   30
and fellow-tribesmen and fellow-citizens and to every other class one should always
try to assign what is appropriate, and to compare the claims of each class with
respect to nearness of relation and to excellence or usefulness. The comparison is

easier when the persons belong to the same class, and more laborious when they are
35   different. Yet we must not on *that* account shrink from the task, but decide the
question as best we can.

3 · Another question that arises is whether friendships should or should not
1165^b1   be broken off when the other party does not remain the same. Perhaps we may say
that there is nothing strange in breaking off a friendship based on utility or
pleasure, when our friends no longer have these attributes. For it was of these
attributes that we were the friends; and when these have failed it is reasonable to
love no longer. But one might complain of another if, when he loved us for our
5   usefulness or pleasantness, he pretended to love us for our character. For, as we said
at the outset, most differences arise between friends when they are not friends in the
spirit in which they think they are. So when a man has made a mistake and has
thought he was being loved for his character, when the other person was doing
10   nothing of the kind, he must blame himself; but when he has been deceived by the
pretences of the other person, it is just that he should complain against his
deceiver—and with more justice than one does against people who counterfeit the
currency, inasmuch as the wrongdoing is concerned with something more valuable.

But if one accepts another man as good, and he becomes bad and is seen to do
so, must one still love him? Surely it is impossible, since not everything can be loved,
15   but only what is good. What is evil neither can nor should be loved; for one should
not be a lover of evil, nor become like what is bad; and we have said that like is dear
to like. Must the friendship, then, be forthwith broken off? Or is this not so in all
cases, but only when one's friends are incurable in their wickedness? If they are
capable of being reformed one should rather come to the assistance of their
20   character or their property, inasmuch as this is better and more characteristic of
friendship. But a man who breaks off such a friendship would seem to be doing
nothing strange; for it was not to a man of this sort that he was a friend; when his
friend has changed, therefore, and he is unable to save him, he gives him up.

But if one friend remained the same while the other became better and far
outstripped him in excellence, should the latter treat the former as a friend? Surely
25   he cannot. When the interval is great this becomes most plain, e.g. in the case of
childish friendships; if one friend remained a child in intellect while the other
became a fully developed man, how could they be friends when they neither
approved of the same things nor delighted in and were pained by the same things?
For not even with regard to each other will their tastes agree, and without this (as
30   we saw) they cannot be friends; for they cannot live together. But we have discussed
these matters.

Should he, then, behave no otherwise towards him than he would if he had
never been his friend? Surely he should keep a remembrance of their former
intimacy, and as we think we ought to oblige friends rather than strangers, so to
35   those who have been our friends we ought to make some allowance for our former
friendship, when the breach has not been due to excess of wickedness.

4 · Friendly relations with one's neighbours, and the marks by which   1166ᵃ1
friendships are defined, seem to have proceeded from a man's relations to himself.
For men think a friend is one who wishes and does what is good, or seems so, for the
sake of his friend, or one who wishes his friend to exist and live, for his sake; which   5
mothers do to their children, and friends do who have come into conflict. And others
think a friend is one who lives with and has the same tastes as another, or one who
grieves and rejoices with his friend; and this too is found in mothers most of all. It is
by some one of these characteristics that friendship too is defined.

Now each of these is true of the good man's relation to himself (and of all other   10
men in so far as they think themselves good; excellence and the good man seem, as
has been said, to be the measure of every class of things). For his opinions are
harmonious, and he desires the same things with all his soul; and therefore he wishes
for himself what is good and what seems so, and does it (for it is characteristic of the   15
good man to exert himself for the good), and does so for his own sake (for he does it
for the sake of the intellectual element in him, which is thought to be the man
himself); and he wishes himself to live and be preserved, and especially the element
by virtue of which he thinks. For existence is good to the good man, and each man
wishes himself what is good, while no one chooses to possess the whole world if he   20
has first to become some one else (for that matter, even now God possesses the
good); he wishes for this only on condition of being whatever he is; and the element
that thinks would seem to be the individual man, or to be so more than any other
element in him. And such a man wishes to live with himself; for he does so with
pleasure, since the memories of his past acts are delightful and his hopes for the   25
future are good, and therefore pleasant. His mind is well stored too with subjects of
contemplation. And he grieves and rejoices, more than any other, with himself; for
the same thing is always painful, and the same thing always pleasant, and not one
thing at one time and another at another; he has, so to speak, nothing to regret.

Therefore, since each of these characteristics belongs to the good man in   30
relation to himself, and he is related to his friend as to himself (for his friend is
another self), friendship too is thought to be one of these attributes, and those who
have these attributes to be friends. Whether there is or is not friendship between a
man and himself is a question we may dismiss for the present; there would seem to
be friendship in so far as he is two or more, to judge from what has been said, and
from the fact that the extreme of friendship is likened to one's love for oneself.   1166ᵇ1

But the attributes named seem to belong even to the majority of men, poor
creatures though they may be. Are we to say then that in so far as they are satisfied
with themselves and think they are good, they share in these attributes? Certainly
no one who is thoroughly bad and impious has these attributes, or even seems to do   5
so. They hardly belong even to inferior people; for they are at variance with
themselves, and have appetites for some things and wishes for others. This is true,
for instance, of incontinent people; for they choose, instead of the things they
themselves think good, things that are pleasant but hurtful; while others again,
through cowardice and laziness, shrink from doing what they think best for   10
themselves. And those who have done many terrible deeds and are hated for their

wickedness even shrink from life and destroy themselves. And wicked men seek for people with whom to spend their days, and shun themselves; for they remember
15   many a grievous deed, and anticipate others like them, when they are by themselves, but when they are with others they forget. And having nothing lovable in them they have no feeling of love to themselves. Therefore also such men do not rejoice or grieve with themselves; for their soul is rent by faction, and one element in it by
20   reason of its wickedness grieves when it abstains from certain acts, while the other part is pleased, and one draws them this way and the other that, as if they were pulling them in pieces. If a man cannot at the same time be pained and pleased, at all events after a short time he is pained *because* he was pleased, and he could have wished that these things had not been pleasant to him; for bad men are laden with regrets.

25   Therefore the bad man does not seem to be amicably disposed even to himself, because there is nothing in him to love; so that if to be thus is the height of wretchedness, we should strain every nerve to avoid wickedness and should endeavour to be good; for so one may be both friendly to oneself and a friend to another.

30   5 · Goodwill is a friendly sort of relation, but is not *identical* with friendship; for one may have goodwill both towards people whom one does not know, and without their knowing it, but not friendship. This has indeed been said already. But goodwill is not even friendly feeling. For it does not involve intensity or desire, whereas these accompany friendly feeling; and friendly feeling implies intimacy while goodwill may arise of a sudden, as it does towards competitors in a contest; we
1167ª1   come to feel goodwill for them and to share in their wishes, but we would not *do* anything with them; for, as we said, we feel goodwill suddenly and love them only superficially.

    Goodwill seems, then, to be a beginning of friendship, as the pleasure of the eye is the beginning of love. For no one loves if he has not first been delighted by the
5   form of the beloved, but he who delights in the form of another does not, for all that, love him, but only does so when he also longs for him when absent and craves for his presence; so too it is not possible for people to be friends if they have not come to feel goodwill for each other, but those who feel goodwill are not for all that friends; for they only *wish* well to those for whom they feel goodwill, and would not do anything
10   with them nor take trouble for them. And so one might by an extension of the term say that goodwill is inactive friendship, though when it is prolonged and reaches the point of intimacy it becomes friendship—not the friendship based on utility nor that based on pleasure; for goodwill too does not arise on those terms. The man who has received a benefit bestows goodwill in return for what has been done to him, and in
15   doing so is doing what is just; while he who wishes some one to prosper because he hopes for enrichment through him seems to have goodwill not to him but rather to himself, just as a man is not a friend to another if he cherishes him for the sake of some use to be made of him. In general, goodwill arises on account of some excellence and worth, when one man seems to another beautiful or brave or
20   something of the sort, as we pointed out in the case of competitors in a contest.

6 · Unanimity also seems to be a friendly relation. For this reason it is not identity of opinion; for that might occur even with people who do not know each other; nor do we say that people who have the same views on any and every subject are unanimous, e.g. those who agree about the heavenly bodies (for unanimity 25 about these is not a friendly relation), but we do say that a city is unanimous when men have the same opinion about what is to their interest, and choose the same actions, and do what they have resolved in common. It is about things to be done, therefore, that people are said to be unanimous, and, among these, about matters of consequence and in which it is possible for both or all parties to get what they want; 30 e.g. a city is unanimous when all its citizens think that the offices in it should be elective, or that they should form an alliance with Sparta, or that Pittacus should be their ruler—at a time when he himself was also willing to rule. But when each of two people wishes himself to have the thing in question, like the captains in the *Phoenissai,* they are in a state of faction; for it is not unanimity when each of two parties thinks of the same thing, whatever that may be, but only when they think of the same thing in relation to the same person, e.g. when both the common people and those of the better class wish the best men to rule; for thus do all get what they 1167ᵇ1 aim at. Unanimity seems, then, to be political friendship, as indeed it is commonly said to be; for it is concerned with things that are to our interest and have an influence on our life.

Now such unanimity is found among good men; for they are unanimous both in 5 themselves and with one another, being, so to say, of one mind (for the wishes of such men are constant and not at the mercy of opposing currents like a strait of the sea), and they wish for what is just and what is advantageous, and these are the objects of their common endeavour as well. But bad men cannot be unanimous except to a small extent, any more than they can be friends, since they aim at 10 getting more than their share of advantages, while in labour and public service they fall short of their share; and each man wishing for advantage to himself criticizes his neighbour and stands in his way; for if people do not watch it carefully the common interest is soon destroyed. The result is that they are in a state of faction, putting compulsion on each other but unwilling themselves to do what is just. 15

7 · Benefactors are thought to love those they have benefited, more than those who have been well treated love those that have treated them well, and this is discussed as though it were paradoxical. Most people think it is because the latter are in the position of debtors and the former of creditors; and therefore as, in the 20 case of loans, debtors wish their creditors did not exist, while creditors actually take care of the safety of their debtors, so it is thought that benefactors wish the objects of their action to exist since they will then get their gratitude, while the beneficiaries take no interest in making this return. Epicharmus would perhaps declare that they 25 say this because they 'look at things on their bad side', but it is quite like human nature; for most people are forgetful, and are more anxious to be well treated than to treat others well. But the cause would seem to be more deeply rooted in the nature of things; the case of those who have lent money is not even analogous. For they

30   have no friendly feeling to their debtors, but only a wish that they may be kept safe
with a view to what is to be got from them; while those who have done a service to
others feel friendship and love for those they have served even if these are not of any
use to them and never will be. This is what happens with craftsmen too; every man
loves his own handiwork better than he would be loved by it if it came alive; and this
1168ª1   happens perhaps most of all with poets; for they have an excessive love for their own
poems, doting on them as if they were their children. This is what the position of
benefactors is like; for that which they have treated well is their handiwork, and
5   therefore they love this more than the handiwork does its maker. The cause of this is
that existence is to all men a thing to be chosen and loved, and that we exist by
virtue of activity (i.e. by living and acting), and that the handiwork *is* in a sense, the
producer in activity; he loves his handiwork, therefore, because he loves existence.
And this is rooted in the nature of things; for what he is in potentiality, his
handiwork manifests in activity.

10   At the same time to the benefactor that is noble which depends on his action, so
that he delights in the object of his action, whereas to the patient there is nothing
noble in the agent, but at most something advantageous, and this is less pleasant
and lovable. What *is* pleasant is the activity of the present, the hope of the future,
the memory of the past; but most pleasant is that which depends on activity, and
15   similarly this is most lovable. Now for a man who has made something his work
remains (for the noble is lasting), but for the person acted on the utility passes away.
And the memory of noble things is pleasant, but that of useful things is not likely to
be pleasant, or is less so; though the reverse seems true of expectation.
Further, love is like activity, being loved like passivity; and loving and its
20   concomitants are attributes of those who are the more active.
Again, all men love more what they have won by labour; e.g. those who have
made their money love it more than those who have inherited it; and to be well
treated seems to involve no labour, while to treat others well is a laborious task.
25   These are the reasons, too, why mothers are fonder of their children than fathers;
bringing them into the world costs them more pains, and they know better that the
children are their own. This last point, too, would seem to apply to benefactors.

8 · The question is also debated, whether a man should love himself most, or
some one else. People criticize those who love themselves most, and call them
30   self-lovers, using this as an epithet of disgrace, and a bad man seems to do
everything for his own sake, and the more so the more wicked he is—and so men
reproach him, for instance, with doing nothing of his own accord—while the good
man acts for honour's sake, and the more so the better he is, and acts for his friend's
sake, and sacrifices his own interest.
But the facts clash with these arguments, and this is not surprising. For men
1168ᵇ1   say that one ought to love best one's best friend, and a man's best friend is one who
wishes well to the object of his wish for his sake, even if no one is to know of it; and
these attributes are found most of all in a man's attitude towards himself, and so are
5   all the other attributes by which a friend is defined; for, as we have said, it is from

this relation that all the characteristics of friendship have extended to others. All the proverbs, too, agree with this, e.g. 'a single soul', and 'what friends have is common property', and 'friendship is equality', and 'charity begins at home'; for all these marks will be found most in a man's relation to himself; he is his own best friend and therefore ought to love himself best. It is therefore a reasonable question, which of the two views we should follow; for both are plausible. 10

Perhaps we ought to mark off such arguments from each other and determine how far and in what respects each view is right. Now if we grasp the sense in which each party uses the phrase 'lover of self', the truth may become evident. Those who use the term as one of reproach ascribe self-love to people who assign to themselves 15 the greater share of wealth, honours, and bodily pleasures; for these are what most people desire, and busy themselves about as though they were the best of all things, which is the reason, too, why they become objects of competition. So those who are grasping with regard to these things gratify their appetites and in general their feelings and the irrational element of the soul; and most men are of this nature thus 20 the epithet has taken its meaning from the prevailing type of self-love, which is a bad one); it is just, therefore, that men who are lovers of self in this way are reproached for being so. That it is those who give themselves the preference in regard to objects of this sort that most people usually call lovers of self is plain; for if a man were always anxious that he himself, above all things, should act justly, 25 temperately, or in accordance with any other of the excellences, and in general were always to try to secure for himself the honourable course, no one will call such a man a lover of self or blame him.

But such a man would seem more than the other a lover of self; at all events he assigns to himself the things that are noblest and best, and gratifies the most 30 authoritative element in himself and in all things obeys this; and just as a city or any other systematic whole is most properly identified with the most authoritative element in it, so is a man; and therefore the man who loves this and gratifies it is most of all a lover of self. Besides, a man is said to have or not to have self-control according as his intellect has or has not the control, on the assumption that this is the man himself; and the things men have done from reason are thought most properly their own acts and voluntary acts. That this is the man himself, then, or is $1169^{a}1$ so more than anything else, is plain, and also that the good man loves most this part of him. Whence it follows that he is most truly a lover of self, of another type than that which is a matter of reproach, and as different from that as living according to reason is from living as passion dictates, and desiring what is noble from desiring 5 what seems advantageous. Those, then, who busy themselves in an exceptional degree with noble actions all men approve and praise; and if *all* were to strive towards what is noble and strain every nerve to do the noblest deeds, everything would be as it should be for the common good, and every one would secure for 10 himself the goods that are greatest, since excellence is the greatest of goods.

Therefore the good man should be a lover of self (for he will both himself profit by doing noble acts, and will benefit his fellows), but the wicked man should not; for he will hurt both himself and his neighbours, following as he does evil passions. For

15 the wicked man, what he does clashes with what he ought to do, but what the good man ought to do he does; for the intellect always chooses what is best for itself, and the good man obeys his intellect. It is true of the good man too that he does many acts for the sake of his friends and his country, and if necessary dies for them; for he

20 will throw away both wealth and honours and in general the goods that are objects of competition, gaining for himself nobility; since he would prefer a short period of intense pleasure to a long one of mild enjoyment, a twelvemonth of noble life to many years of humdrum existence, and one great and noble action to many trivial

25 ones. Now those who die for others doubtless attain this result; it is therefore a great prize that they choose for themselves. They will throw away wealth too on condition that their friends will gain more; for while a man's friend gains wealth he himself achieves nobility; he is therefore assigning the greater good to himself. The same too

30 is true of honour and office; all these things he will sacrifice to his friend; for this is noble and laudable for himself. Rightly then is he thought to be good, since he chooses nobility before all else. But he may even give up actions to his friend; it may be nobler to become the cause of his friend's acting than to act himself. In all the actions, therefore, that men are praised for, the good man is seen to assign to

1169ᵇ1 himself the greater share in what is noble. In this sense, then, as has been said, a man should be a lover of self; but in the sense in which most men are so, he ought not.

9 · It is also disputed whether the happy man will need friends or not. It is said that those who are blessed and self-sufficient have no need of friends; for they

5 have the things that are good, and therefore being self-sufficient they need nothing further while a friend, being another self, furnishes what a man cannot provide by his own effort; whence the saying 'when fortune is kind, what need of friends?'[75] But it seems strange, when one assigns all good things to the happy man, not to assign

10 friends, who are thought the greatest of external goods. And if it is more characteristic of a friend to do well by another than to be well done by, and to confer benefits is characteristic of the good man and of excellence, and it is nobler to do well by friends than by strangers, the good man will need people to do well by. This is why the question is asked whether we need friends more in prosperity or in

15 adversity, on the assumption that not only does a man in adversity need people to confer benefits on him, but also those who are prospering need people to do well by. Surely it is strange, too, to make the blessed man a solitary; for no one would choose to possess all good things on condition of being alone, since man is a political creature and one whose nature is to live with others. Therefore even the happy man lives with others; for he has the things that are by nature good. And plainly it is

20 better to spend his days with friends and good men than with strangers or any chance persons. Therefore the happy man needs friends.

What then is it that the first party means, and in what respect is it right? Is it that most men identify friends with useful people? Of such friends indeed the

---

[75]Euripides, *Orestes* 667.

blessed man will have no need, since he already has the things that are good; nor will he need those whom one makes one's friends because of their pleasantness, or he will need them only to a small extent (for his life, being pleasant, has no need of adventitious pleasure); and because he does not need *such* friends he is thought not to need friends. 25

But that is surely not true. For we have said at the outset that happiness is an activity; and activity plainly comes into being and is not present at the start like a piece of property. If happiness lies in living and being active, and the good man's activity is virtuous and pleasant in itself, as we have said at the outset, and if a thing's being one's own is one of the attributes that make it pleasant, and if we can contemplate our neighbours better than ourselves and their actions better than our own, and if the actions of virtuous men who are their friends are pleasant to good men (since these have both the attributes that are naturally pleasant)—if this be so, the blessed man will need friends of this sort, since he chooses to contemplate worthy actions and actions that are his own, and the actions of a good man who is his friend have both these qualities. 30   1170ᵃ1

Further, men think that the happy man ought to live pleasantly. Now if he were a solitary, life would be hard for him; for by oneself it is not easy to be continuously active; but with others and towards others it is easier. With others therefore his activity will be more continuous, being in itself pleasant, as it ought to be for the man who is blessed; for a good man *qua* good delights in excellent actions and is vexed at vicious ones, as a musical man enjoys beautiful tunes but is pained at bad ones. A certain training in excellence arises also from the company of the good, as Theognis remarks. 5   10

If we look deeper into the nature of things, a virtuous friend seems to be naturally desirable for a virtuous man. For that which is good by nature, we have said, is for the virtuous man good and pleasant in itself. Now life is defined in the case of animals by the power of perception, in that of man by the power of perception or thought; and a power is referred to the corresponding activity, which is the essential thing; therefore life seems to be essentially perceiving or thinking. And life is among the things that are good and pleasant in themselves, since it is determinate and the determinate is of the nature of the good; and that which is good by nature is also good for the virtuous man (which is the reason why life seems pleasant to all men); but we must not apply this to a wicked and corrupt life nor to a life spent in pain; for such a life is indeterminate, as are its attributes. The nature of pain will become plainer in what follows. But if life itself is good and pleasant (which it seems to be, from the very fact that all men desire it, and particularly those who are good and blessed; for to such men life is most .desirable, and their existence is the most blessed; and if he who sees perceives that he sees, and he who hears, that he hears, and he who walks, that he walks, and in the case of all other activities similarly there is something which perceives that we are active, so that if we perceive, we perceive that we perceive, and if we think, that we think; and if to perceive that we perceive or think is to perceive that we exist (for existence was defined as perceiving or thinking); and if perceiving that one lives is one of the 15   20   25   30   1170ᵇ1

things that are pleasant in themselves (for life is by nature good, and to perceive
what is good present in oneself is pleasant); and if life is desirable, and particularly
so for good men, because to them existence is good and pleasant (for they are
5 pleased at the consciousness of what is in itself good); and if as the virtuous man is to
himself, he is to his friend also (for his friend is another self):—then as his own
existence is desirable for each man, so, or almost so, is that of his friend. Now his
existence was seen to be desirable because he perceived his own goodness, and such
10 perception is pleasant in itself. He needs, therefore, to be conscious of the existence
of his friend as well, and this will be realized in their living together and sharing in
discussion and thought; for this is what living together would seem to mean in the
case of man, and not, as in the case of cattle, feeding in the same place.

If, then, existence is in itself desirable for the blessed man (since it is by its
15 nature good and pleasant), and that of his friend is very much the same, a friend will
be one of the things that are desirable. Now that which is desirable for him he must
have, or he will be deficient in this respect. The man who is to be happy will
therefore need virtuous friends.

20   10 · Should we, then, make as many friends as possible, or—as in the case of
hospitality it is thought to be suitable advice, that one should be 'neither a man of
many guests nor a man with none'[76]—will that apply to friendship as well; should a
man neither be friendless nor have an excessive number of friends?

To friends made with a view to *utility* this saying would seem thoroughly
25 applicable; for to do services to many people in return is a laborious task and life is
not long enough for its performance. Therefore friends in excess of those who are
sufficient for our own life are superfluous, and hindrances to the noble life; so that
we have no need of them. Of friends made with a view to *pleasure,* also, few are
enough, as a little seasoning in food is enough.

But as regards *good* friends, should we have as many as possible, or is there a
30 limit to the number of one's friends, as there is to the size of a city? You cannot
make a city of ten men, and if there are a hundred thousand it is a city no longer.
But the proper number is presumably not a single number, but anything that falls
1171ᵃ1 between certain fixed points. So for friends too there is a fixed number—perhaps
the largest number with whom one can live together (for that, we found, is thought
to be most characteristic of friendship); and that one cannot live with many people
and divide oneself up among them is plain. Further, they too must be friends of one
5 another, if they are all to spend their days together; and it is a hard business for this
condition to be fulfilled with a large number. It is found difficult, too, to rejoice and
to grieve in an intimate way with many people, for it may likely happen that one has
at once to be merry with one friend and to mourn with another. Presumably, then, it
is well not to seek to have as many friends as possible, but as many as are enough for
10 the purpose of living together; for it would seem actually impossible to be a great

---

[76]Hesiod, *Works and Days* 715.

friend to many people. This is why one cannot love several people; love tends to be a sort of excess friendship, and that can only be felt towards one person; therefore great friendship too can only be felt towards a few people. This seems to be confirmed in practice; for we do not find many people who are friends in the comradely way of friendship, and the famous friendships of this sort are always   15 between two people. Those who have many friends and mix intimately with them all are thought to be no one's friend, except in the way proper to fellow-citizens, and such people are also called obsequious. In the way proper to fellow-citizens, indeed, it is possible to be the friend of many and yet not be obsequious but a genuinely good man; but one cannot have with many people the friendship based on excellence and on the character of our friends themselves, and we must be content if we find even a   20 few such.

11 · Do we need friends more in good fortune or in bad? They are sought after in both; for while men in adversity need help, in prosperity they need people to live with and to make the objects of their beneficence; for they wish to do well by others. Friendship, then, is more necessary in bad fortune, and so it is useful friends   25 that one wants in this case; but it is more noble in good fortune, and so we also seek for good men as our friends, since it is more desirable to confer benefits on these and to live with these. For the very presence of friends is pleasant both in good fortune and also in bad, since grief is lightened when friends sorrow with us. Hence one   30 might ask whether they share as it were our burden, or—without that happening— their presence by its pleasantness, and the thought of their grieving with us, make our pain less. Whether it is for these reasons or for some other that our grief is lightened, is a question that may be dismissed; at all events what we have described appears to take place.

But their presence seems to contain a mixture of various factors. The very seeing of one's friends is pleasant, especially if one is in adversity, and becomes a   1171^b1 safeguard against grief (for a friend tends to comfort us both by the sight of him and by his words, if he is tactful, since he knows our character and the things that please or pain us); but to see him pained at our misfortunes is painful; for every one shuns   5 being a cause of pain to his friends. For this reason people of a manly nature guard against making their friends grieve with them, and, unless he be exceptionally insensible to pain, such a man cannot stand the pain that ensues for his friends, and in general does not admit fellow-mourners because he is not himself given to mourning; but women and womanly men enjoy sympathisers in their grief, and love   10 them as friends and companions in sorrow. But in all things one obviously ought to imitate the better type of person.

On the other hand, the presence of friends in our *prosperity* implies both a pleasant passing of our time and the thought of their pleasure at our own good fortune. For this cause it would seem that we ought to summon our friends readily   15 to share our good fortunes (for the beneficent character is a noble one), but summon them to our bad fortunes with hesitation; for we ought to give them as little a share as possible in our evils—whence the saying 'enough is *my* misfortune'. We should summon friends to us most of all when they are likely by suffering a few inconveniences to do us a great service.

20 Conversely, it is fitting to go unasked and readily to the aid of those in adversity (for it is characteristic of a friend to render services, and especially to those who are in need and have not demanded them; such action is nobler and pleasanter for both persons); but when our friends are prosperous we should join readily in their activities (for they need friends for these too), but be tardy in 25 coming forward to be the objects of their kindness; for it is not noble to be keen to receive benefits. Still, we must no doubt avoid getting the reputation of kill-joys by repulsing them; for that sometimes happens.

The presence of friends, then, seems desirable in all circumstances.

12 · Does it not follow, then, that, as for lovers the sight of the beloved is the 30 thing they love most, and they prefer this sense to the others because on it love depends most for its being and for its origin, so for friends the most desirable thing is living together? For friendship is a partnership, and as a man is to himself, so is he to his friend; now in his own case the perception of his existence is desirable, and so therefore is that of his friend's, and the activity of this perception is produced when 1172ᵃ1 they live together, so that it is natural that they aim at this. And whatever existence means for each class of men, whatever it is for whose sake they value life, in *that* they wish to occupy themselves with their friends; and so some drink together, others dice together, others join in athletic exercises and hunting, or in the study of 5 philosophy, each class spending their days together in whatever they love most in life; for since they wish to live with their friends, they do and share in those things as far as they can.[77] Thus the friendship of bad men turns out an evil thing (for because of their instability they unite in bad pursuits, and besides they become evil by 10 becoming like each other), while the friendship of good men is good, being augmented by their companionship; and they are thought to become better too by their activities and by improving each other; for from each other they take the mould of the characteristics they approve—whence the saying 'noble deeds from 15 noble men'[78]—So much, then, for friendship; our next task must be to discuss pleasure.

BOOK X

1 · After these matters we ought perhaps next to discuss pleasure. For it is 20 thought to be most intimately connected with our human nature, which is the reason why in educating the young we steer them by the rudders of pleasure and pain; it is thought, too, that to enjoy the things we ought and to hate the things we

[77]Reading ὡς οἶόν τε for οἶς οἴονται συζῆν.
[78]Theognis, 35.

ought has the greatest bearing on excellence of character. For these things extend right through life, with a weight and power of their own in respect both to excellence and to the happy life, since men choose what is pleasant and avoid what is painful; 25 and such things, it will be thought, we should least of all omit to discuss, especially since they admit of much dispute. For some say pleasure is the good, while others, on the contrary, say it is thoroughly bad—some no doubt being persuaded that the facts are so, and others thinking it has a better effect on our life to exhibit pleasure 30 as a bad thing even if it is not; for most people (they think) incline towards it and are the slaves of their pleasures, for which reason they ought to lead them in the opposite direction, since thus they will reach the middle state. But surely this is not correct. For arguments about matters concerned with feelings and actions are less 35 reliable than facts: and so when they clash with the facts of perception they are despised, and discredit the truth as well; if a man who runs down pleasure is once 1172ᵇ1 seen to be aiming at it, his inclining towards it is thought to imply that it is all worthy of being aimed at; for most people are not good at drawing distinctions. True arguments seem, then, most useful, not only with a view to knowledge, but with a 5 view to life also; for since they harmonize with the facts they are believed, and so they stimulate those who understand them to live according to them.—Enough of such questions; let us proceed to review the opinions that have been expressed about pleasure.

2 · Eudoxus thought pleasure was the good because he saw all things, both rational and irrational, aiming at it, and because in all things that which is the 10 object of choice is what is excellent, and that which is most the object of choice the greatest good; thus the fact that all things moved towards the same object indicated that this was for all things the chief good (for each thing, he argued, finds its own good, as it finds its own nourishment); and that which is good for all things and at which all aim was *the* good. His arguments were credited more because of the 15 excellence of his character than for their own sake; he was thought to be remarkably temperate, and therefore it was thought that he was not saying what he did say as a friend of pleasure, but that the facts really were so. He believed that the same conclusion followed no less plainly from a study of the contrary of pleasure; pain was in itself an object of aversion to all things, and therefore its contrary must be similarly an object of choice. And again that is most an object of choice which we 20 choose not because or for the sake of something else, and pleasure is admittedly of this nature; for no one asks to what end he is pleased, thus implying that pleasure is in itself an object of choice. Further, he argued that pleasure when added to any good, e.g. to just or temperate action, makes it more worthy of choice, and that it is 25 only by itself that the good can be increased.

This argument seems to show it to be one of the goods, and no more a good than any other; for every good is more worthy of choice along with another good than taken alone. And so it is by an argument of this kind that Plato[79] proves the

---

[79] See *Philebus* 60BE.

good *not* to be pleasure; he argues that the pleasant life is more desirable with
30   wisdom than without, and that if the mixture is better, pleasure is not the good; for
the good cannot become more desirable by the addition of anything to it. Now it is
clear that nothing else either can be the good if it is made more desirable by the
addition of any of the things that are good in themselves. What, then, is there that
satisfies this criterion, which at the same time we can participate in? It is something
of this sort that we are looking for.

1173ᵃ1   Those who object that that at which all things aim is not necessarily good are
talking nonsense. For we say that that which everyone thinks really is so; and the
man who attacks this belief will hardly have anything more credible to maintain
instead. If it is senseless creatures that desire the things in question, there might be
something in what they say; but if intelligent creatures do so as well, what sense can
there be in this view? But perhaps even in inferior creatures there is some natural
5   good stronger than themselves which aims at their proper good.

Nor does the argument about the contrary of pleasure seem to be correct. They
say that if pain is an evil it does not follow that pleasure is a good; for evil is opposed
to evil and at the same time both are opposed to the neutral state—which is correct
enough but does not apply to the things in question. For if both belonged to the class
10   of evils they ought both to be objects of aversion, while if they belonged to the class
of neutrals neither should be or they should both be equally so; but in fact people
evidently avoid the one as evil and choose the other as good; that then must be the
nature of the opposition between them.

3 · Nor again, if pleasure is not a quality, does it follow that it is not a good;
15   for the activities of excellence are not qualities either, nor is happiness.

They say, however, that the good is determinate, while pleasure is indeterminate, because it admits of degrees. Now if it is from the feeling of pleasure that they
judge thus, the same will be true of justice and the other excellences in respect of
which we plainly say that people of a certain character are so more or less, and act
20   more or less in accordance with these excellences; for people may be more just or
brave, and it is possible also to act justly or temperately more or less. But if their
judgement is based on the various pleasures, surely they are not stating the cause, if
in fact some pleasures are unmixed and others mixed. Again, just as health admits
25   of degrees without being indeterminate, why should not pleasure? The same
proportion is not found in all things, nor a single proportion always in the same
thing, but it may be relaxed and yet persist up to a point, and it may differ in degree.
The case of pleasure also may therefore be of this kind.

Again, they assume that the good is complete while movements and comings
30   into being are incomplete and try to exhibit pleasure as being a movement and a
coming into being. But they do not seem to be right, nor does it seem to be a
movement.[80] For speed and slowness are thought to be proper to every movement, if

---

[80]Reading κίνησις.

not in itself (as e.g. that of the heavens) then in relation to something else; but of pleasure neither of these things is true. For while we may *become* pleased quickly as we may become angry quickly, we cannot *be* pleased quickly, not even in relation to   1173ᵇ1 some one else, while we *can* walk, or grow, or the like, quickly. While, then, we can change quickly or slowly into a state of pleasure, we cannot quickly exhibit the activity of pleasure, i.e. be pleased. Again, how can it be a coming into being? It is not thought that any chance thing can come out of any chance thing, but that a   5 thing is dissolved into that out of which it comes into being; and pain would be the destruction of that of which pleasure is the coming into being.

They say, too, that pain is the lack of that which is according to nature, and pleasure is replenishment. But these experiences are bodily. If then pleasure is replenishment with that which is according to nature, that which feels pleasure will   10 be that in which the replenishment takes place, i.e. the body; but that is not thought to be the case; therefore the replenishment is not pleasure, though one might be pleased when replenishment was taking place, just as one would be pained if one was being operated on. This opinion seems to be based on the pains and pleasures connected with nutrition; on the fact that when people have been short of food and have felt pain beforehand they are pleased by the replenishment. But this does not   15 happen with all pleasures; for the pleasures of learning and, among the sensuous pleasures, those of smell, and also many sounds and sights, and memories and hopes, do not presuppose pain. Of what then will these be the coming into being? There has not been lack of anything of which they could be the replenishment.   20

In reply to those who bring forward the disgraceful pleasures one may say that these are not pleasant; if things are pleasant to people of vicious constitution, we must not suppose that they are also pleasant to others than these, just as we do not reason so about the things that are wholesome or sweet or bitter to sick people, or ascribe whiteness to the things that seem white to those suffering from a disease of   25 the eye. Or one might answer thus—that the pleasures are desirable, but not from *these* sources, as wealth is desirable, but not as the reward of betrayal, and health, but not at the cost of eating anything and everything. Or perhaps pleasures differ in kind; for those derived from noble sources are different from those derived from base sources, and one cannot get the pleasure of the just man without being just, nor   30 that of the musical man without being musical, and so on.

The fact, too, that a friend is different from a flatterer seems to make it plain that pleasure is not a good or that pleasures are different in kind; for the one is thought to consort with us with a view to the good, the other with a view to our pleasure, and the one is reproached for his conduct while the other is praised on the ground that he consorts with us for different ends. And no one would choose to live   1174ᵃ1 with the intellect of a child throughout his life, however much he were to be pleased at the things that children are pleased at, nor to get enjoyment by doing some most disgraceful deed, though he were never to feel any pain in consequence. And there are many things we should be keen about even if they brought no pleasure, e.g.   5 seeing, remembering, knowing, possessing the excellences. If pleasures necessarily

do accompany these, that makes no odds; we should choose these even if no pleasure resulted. It seems to be clear, then, that neither is pleasure the good nor is all
10   pleasure desirable, and that some pleasures *are* desirable in themselves, differing in kind or in their sources from the others. So much for the things that are said about pleasure and pain.

4 . What pleasure is, or what kind of thing it is, will become plainer if we take up the question again from the beginning. Seeing seems to be at any moment
15   complete, for it does not lack anything which coming into being later will complete its form; and pleasure also seems to be of this nature. For it is a whole, and at no time can one find a pleasure whose form will be completed if the pleasure lasts longer. For this reason, too, it is not a movement. For every movement (e.g. that of
20   building) takes time and is for the sake of an end, and is complete when it has made what it aims at. It is complete, therefore, only in the whole time or at the final moment. In their parts and during the time they occupy, all movements are incomplete, and are different in kind from the whole movement and from each other. For the fitting together of the stones is different from the fluting of the column, and these are both different from the making of the temple; and the making
25   of the temple is complete (for it lacks nothing with a view to the end proposed), but the making of the base or of the triglyph is incomplete; for each is the making of a part. They differ in kind, then, and it is not possible to find at any and every time a movement complete in form, but if at all, only in the whole time. So, too, in the case
30   of walking and all other movements. For if locomotion is a movement from here to there, it, too, has differences in kind—flying, walking, leaping, and so on. And not only so, but in walking itself there are such differences; for the whence and whither are not the same in the whole racecourse and in a part of it, nor in one part and in another, nor is it the same thing to traverse this line and that; for one traverses not
1174^{b}1   only a line but one which is in a place, and this one is in a different place from that. We have discussed movement with precision in another work, but it seems that it is not complete at any and every time, but that the many movements are incomplete
5   and different in kind, since the whence and whither give them their form. But of pleasure the form is complete at any and every time. Plainly, then, pleasure and movement must be different from each other, and pleasure must be one of the things that are whole and complete. This would seem to be the case, too, from the fact that it is not possible to move otherwise than in time, but it *is* possible to be pleased; for that which takes place in a moment is a whole.

From these considerations it is clear, too, that these thinkers are not right in
10   saying there is a movement or a coming into being *of* pleasure.[81] For these cannot be ascribed to all things, but only to those that are divisible and not wholes; there is no coming into being of seeing nor of a point nor of a unit, nor is any of these a movement or coming into being; therefore there is none of pleasure either; for it is a whole.

Since every sense is active in relation to its object, and a sense which is in good

---

[81]Reading τῆς ἡδονῆς.

condition acts completely in relation to the most beautiful of its objects (for   15
complete activity seems to be especially of this nature; whether we say that *it* is
active, or the organ in which it resides, may be assumed to be immaterial), it follows
that in the case of each sense the best activity is that of the best-conditioned organ in
relation to the finest of its objects. And this activity will be the most complete and
pleasant. For, while there is pleasure in respect of any sense, and in respect of   20
thought and contemplation no less, the most complete is pleasantest, and that of a
well-conditioned organ in relation to the worthiest of its objects is the most
complete; and the pleasure completes the activity. But the pleasure does not
complete it in the same way as the object perceived and the faculty of perception, if
they are good, do—just as health and the doctor are not in the same way the cause   25
of a man's being healthy. (That pleasure is produced in respect to each sense is
plain; for we speak of sights and sounds as pleasant. It is also plain that it arises
most of all when both the sense is at its best and it is active in reference to an object
which corresponds; when both object and perceiver are of the best there will always   30
be pleasure, since the requisite agent and patient are both present.) Pleasure
completes the activity not as the inherent state does, but as an end which supervenes
as the bloom of youth does on those in the flower of their age. So long, then, as both
the intelligible or sensible object and the discriminating or contemplative faculty
are as they should be, the pleasure will be involved in the activity; for when both the   1175ᵃ1
passive and the active factor are unchanged and are related to each other in the
same way, the same result naturally follows.

How, then, is it that no one is continuously pleased? Is it that we grow weary?
Certainly all human things are incapable of continuous activity. Therefore pleasure
also is not continuous; for it accompanies activity. Some things delight us when they   5
are new, but later do so less, for the same reason; for at first the mind is in a state of
stimulation and intensely active about them, as people are with respect to their
vision when they look hard at a thing, but afterwards our activity is not of this kind,
but has grown relaxed; for which reason the pleasure also is dulled.   10

One might think that all men desire pleasure because they all aim at life; life is
an activity, and each man is active about those things and with those faculties that
he loves most; e.g. the musician is active with his hearing in reference to tunes, the
student with his mind in reference to theoretical questions, and so on in each case;   15
now pleasure completes the activities, and therefore life, which they desire. It is
with good reason, then, that they aim at pleasure too, since for everyone it completes
life, which is desirable. But whether we choose life for the sake of pleasure or
pleasure for the sake of life is a question we may dismiss for the present. For they
seem to be bound up together and not to admit of separation, since without activity   20
pleasure does not arise, and every activity is completed by pleasure.

5 · For this reason pleasures seem, too, to differ in kind. For things different
in kind are, we think, completed by different things (we see this to be true both of
natural objects and of things produced by art, e.g. animals, trees, a painting, a   25
sculpture, a house, an implement); and, similarly, we think that activities differing

in kind are completed by things differing in kind. Now the activities of thought differ from those of the senses, and among themselves, in kind; so, therefore, do the pleasures that complete them.

This may be seen, too, from the fact that each of the pleasures is bound up with the activity it completes. For an activity is intensified by its proper pleasure, since each class of things is better judged of and brought to precision by those who engage in the activity with pleasure; e.g. it is those who enjoy geometrical thinking that become geometers and grasp the various propositions better, and, similarly, those who are fond of music or of building, and so on, make progress in their proper function by enjoying it; and the pleasures intensify the activities, and what intensifies a thing is proper to it, but things different in kind have properties different in kind.

This will be even more apparent from the fact that activities are hindered by pleasures arising from other sources. For people who are fond of playing the flute are incapable of attending to arguments if they overhear some one playing the flute, since they enjoy flute-playing more than the activity in hand; so the pleasure connected with flute-playing destroys the activity concerned with argument. This happens, similarly, in all other cases, when one is active about two things at once; the more pleasant activity drives out the other, and if it is much more pleasant does so all the more, so that one even ceases from the other. This is why when we enjoy anything very much we do not throw ourselves into anything else, and do one thing only when we are not much pleased by another; e.g. in the theatre the people who eat sweets do so most when the actors are poor. Now since activities are made precise and more enduring and better by their proper pleasure, and injured by alien pleasures, evidently the two kinds of pleasure are far apart. For alien pleasures do pretty much what proper pains do, since activities are destroyed by their proper pains; e.g. if a man finds writing or doing sums unpleasant and painful, he does not write, or does not do sums, because the activity is painful. So an activity suffers contrary effects from its proper pleasures and pains, i.e. from those that supervene on it in virtue of its own nature. And alien pleasures have been stated to do much the same as pain; they destroy the activity, only not to the same degree.

Now since activities differ in respect of goodness and badness, and some are worthy to be chosen, others to be avoided, and others neutral, so, too, are the pleasures; for to each activity there is a proper pleasure. The pleasure proper to a worthy activity is good and that proper to an unworthy activity bad; just as the appetites for noble objects are laudable, those for base objects culpable. But the pleasures involved in activities are more proper to them than the desires; for the latter are separated both in time and in nature, while the former are close to the activities, and so hard to distinguish from them that it admits of dispute whether the activity is not the same as the pleasure. (Still, pleasure does not seem to *be* thought or perception—that would be strange; but because they are not found apart they appear to some people the same.) As activities are different, then, so are the corresponding pleasures. Now sight is superior to touch in purity, and hearing and smell to taste; the pleasures, therefore, are similarly superior, and those of thought superior to these, and within each of the two kinds some are superior to others.

Each animal is thought to have a proper pleasure, as it has a proper function; viz. that which corresponds to its activity. If we survey them species by species, too, this will be evident; horse, dog, and man have different pleasures, as Heraclitus says 'asses would prefer sweepings to gold';[82] for food is pleasanter than gold to asses. So the pleasures of creatures different in kind differ in kind, and it is plausible to suppose that those of a single species do not differ. But they vary to no small extent, in the case of men at least; the same things delight some people and pain others, and are painful and odious to some, and pleasant to and liked by others. This happens, too, in the case of sweet things; the same things do not seem sweet to a man in a fever and a healthy man—nor hot to a weak man and one in good condition. The same happens in other cases. But in all such matters that which appears to the good man is thought to be really so. If this is correct, as it seems to be, and excellence and the good man as such are the measure of each thing, those also will be pleasures which appear so to him, and those things pleasant which he enjoys. If the things he finds tiresome seem pleasant to some one, that is nothing surprising; for men may be ruined and spoilt in many ways; but the things are not pleasant, but only pleasant to these people and to people in this condition. Those which are admittedly disgraceful plainly should not be said to be pleasures, except to a perverted taste; but of those that are thought to be good what kind of pleasure or what pleasure should be said to be that proper to man? Is it not plain from the corresponding activities? The pleasures follow these. Whether, then, the complete and blessed man has one or more activities, the pleasures that complete these will be said in the strict sense to be pleasures proper to man, and the rest will be so in a secondary and fractional way, as are the activities.

6 · Now that we have spoken of the excellences, the forms of friendship, and the varieties of pleasure, what remains is to discuss in outline the nature of happiness, since this is what we state the end of human nature to be. Our discussion will be the more concise if we first sum up what we have said already. We said, then, that it is not a state; for if it were it might belong to some one who was asleep throughout his life, living the life of a plant, or, again, to some one who was suffering the greatest misfortunes. If these implications are unacceptable, and we must rather class happiness as an activity, as we have said before, and if some activities are necessary and desirable for the sake of something else, while others are so in themselves, evidently happiness must be placed among those desirable in themselves, not among those desirable for the sake of something else; for happiness does not lack anything, but is self-sufficient. Now those activities are desirable in themselves from which nothing is sought beyond the activity. And of this nature excellent actions are thought to be; for to do noble and good deeds is a thing desirable for its own sake.

Pleasant amusements also are thought to be of this nature; we choose them not for the sake of other things; for we are injured rather than benefited by them, since we are led to neglect our bodies and our property. But most of the people who are

[82]Frag. 9 Diels-Kranz.

deemed happy take refuge in such pastimes, which is the reason why those who are ready-witted at them are highly esteemed at the courts of tyrants; they make
15   themselves pleasant companions in the tyrant's favourite pursuits, and that is the sort of man they want. Now these things are thought to be of the nature of happiness because people in despotic positions spend their leisure in them, but perhaps such people prove nothing; for excellence and thought, from which good activities flow, do not depend on despotic position; nor, if these people, who have
20   never tasted pure and generous pleasure, take refuge in the bodily pleasures, should these for that reason be thought more desirable; for boys, too, think the things that are valued among themselves are the best. It is to be expected, then, that, as different things seem valuable to boys and to men, so they should to bad men and to
25   good. Now, as we have often maintained, those things are both valuable and pleasant which are such to the good man; and to each man the activity in accordance with his own state is most desirable, and, therefore, to the good man that which is in accordance with excellence. Happiness, therefore, does not lie in amusement; it would, indeed, be strange if the end were amusement, and one were
30   to take trouble and suffer hardship all one's life in order to amuse oneself. For, in a word, everything that we choose we choose for the sake of something else—except happiness, which is an end. Now to exert oneself and work for the sake of amusement seems silly and utterly childish. But to amuse oneself in order that one may exert oneself, as Anacharsis puts it, seems right; for amusement is a sort of relaxation, and we need relaxation because we cannot work continuously. Relaxa-
1177ª1   tion, then, is not an end; for it is taken for the sake of activity.

The happy life is thought to be one of excellence; now an excellent life requires exertion, and does not consist in amusement. And we say that serious things are better than laughable things and those connected with amusement, and that the
5   activity of the better of any two things— whether it be two parts or two men— is the better; but the activity of the better is *ipso facto* superior and more of the nature of happiness. And any chance person—even a slave—can enjoy the bodily pleasures no less than the best man; but no one assigns to a slave a share in happiness—unless he assigns to him also a share in human life. For happiness does not lie in such
10   occupations, but, as we have said before, in excellent activities.

7 · If happiness is activity in accordance with excellence, it is reasonable that it should be in accordance with the highest excellence; and this will be that of the best thing in us. Whether it be intellect or something else that is this element which
15   is thought to be our natural ruler and guide and to take thought of things noble and divine, whether it be itself also divine or only the most divine element in us, the activity of this in accordance with its proper excellence will be complete happiness. That this activity is contemplative we have already said.

Now this would seem to be in agreement both with what we said before and
20   with the truth. For this activity is the best (since not only is intellect the best thing in us, but the objects of intellect are the best of knowable objects); and, secondly, it is the most continuous, since we can contemplate truth more continuously than we can

do anything. And we think happiness has pleasure mingled with it, but the activity of wisdom is admittedly the pleasantest of excellent activities; at all events philosophy is thought to offer pleasures marvellous for their purity and their 25
enduringness, and it is to be expected that those who know will pass their time more pleasantly than those who inquire. And the self-sufficiency that is spoken of must belong most to the contemplative activity. For while a wise man, as well as a just man and the rest, needs the necessaries of life, when they are sufficiently equipped with things of that sort the just man needs people towards whom and with whom he 30
shall act justly, and the temperate man, the brave man, and each of the others is in the same case, but the wise man, even when by himself, can contemplate truth, and the better the wiser he is; he can perhaps do so better if he has fellow-workers, but still he is the most self-sufficient. And this activity alone would seem to be loved for 1177^{b}1
its own sake; for nothing arises from it apart from the contemplating, while from practical activities we gain more or less apart from the action. And happiness is thought to depend on leisure; for we are busy that we may have leisure, and make 5
war that we may live in peace. Now the activity of the practical excellences is exhibited in political or military affairs, but the actions concerned with these seem to be unleisurely. Warlike actions are completely so (for no one chooses to be at war, or provokes war, for the sake of being at war; any one would seem absolutely 10
murderous if he were to make enemies of his friends in order to bring about battle and slaughter); but the action of the statesman is also unleisurely, and—apart from the political action itself—aims at despotic power and honours, or at all events happiness, for him and his fellow citizens—a happiness different from political action, and evidently sought as being different. So if among excellent actions 15
political and military actions are distinguished by nobility and greatness, and these are unleisurely and aim at an end and are not desirable for their own sake, but the activity of intellect, which is contemplative, seems both to be superior in worth and to aim at no end beyond itself, and to have its pleasure proper to itself (and this 20
augments the activity), and the self-sufficiency, leisureliness, unweariedness (so far as this is possible for man), and all the other attributes ascribed to the blessed man are evidently those connected with this activity, it follows that this will be the complete happiness of man, if it be allowed a complete term of life (for none of the 25
attributes of happiness is *in*complete).

But such a life would be too high for man; for it is not in so far as he is man that he will live so, but in so far as something divine is present in him; and by so much as this is superior to our composite nature is its activity superior to that which is the exercise of the other kind of excellence. If intellect is divine, then, in comparison 30
with man, the life according to it is divine in comparison with human life. But we must not follow those who advise us, being men, to think of human things, and, being mortal, of mortal things, but must, so far as we can, make ourselves immortal, and strain every nerve to live in accordance with the best thing in us; for even if it be small in bulk, much more does it in power and worth surpass everything. This would 1178^{a}1
seem, too, to be each man himself, since it is the authoritative and better part of him. It would be strange, then, if he were to choose not the life of himself but that of

5 something else. And what we said before will apply now; that which is proper to each thing is by nature best and most pleasant for each thing; for man, therefore, the life according to intellect is best and pleasantest, since intellect more than anything else *is* man. This life therefore is also the happiest.

8 · But in a secondary degree the life in accordance with the other kind of
10 excellence is happy; for the activities in accordance with this befit our human estate. Just and brave acts, and other excellent acts, we do in relation to each other, observing what is proper to each with regard to contracts and services and all manner of actions and with regard to passions; and all of these seem to be human. Some of them seem even to arise from the body, and excellence of character to be in
15 many ways bound up with the passions. Practical wisdom, too, is linked to excellence of character, and this to practical wisdom, since the principles of practical wisdom are in accordance with the moral excellences and rightness in the moral excellences is in accordance with practical wisdom. Being connected with the
20 passions also, the moral excellences must belong to our composite nature; and the excellences of our composite nature are human; so, therefore, are the life and the happiness which correspond to these. The excellence of the intellect is a thing apart; we must be content to say this much about it, for to describe it precisely is a task greater than our purpose requires. It would seem, however, also to need external
25 equipment but little, or less than moral excellence does. Grant that both need the necessaries, and do so equally, even if the statesman's work is the more concerned with the body and things of that sort; for there will be little difference there; but in what they need for the exercise of their activities there will be much difference. The liberal man will need money for the doing of his liberal deeds, and the just man too
30 will need it for the returning of services (for wishes are hard to discern, and even people who are not just pretend to wish to act justly); and the brave man will need power if he is to accomplish any of the acts that correspond to his excellence, and the temperate man will need opportunity; for how else is either he or any of the others to be recognized? It is debated, too, whether the choice or the deed is more essential to excellence, which is assumed to involve both; it is surely clear that its
1178ᵇ1 completion involves both; but for deeds many things are needed, and more, the greater and nobler the deeds are. But the man who is contemplating the truth needs no such thing, at least with a view to the exercise of his activity; indeed they are, one
5 may say, even hindrances, at all events to his contemplation; but in so far as he is a man and lives with a number of people, he chooses to do excellent acts; he will therefore need such aids to living a human life.

But that complete happiness is a contemplative activity will appear from the following consideration as well. We assume the gods to be above all other beings
10 blessed and happy; but what sort of actions must we assign to them? Acts of justice? Will not the gods seem absurd if they make contracts and return deposits, and so on? Acts of a brave man, then, confronting dangers and running risks because it is noble to do so? Or liberal acts? To whom will they give? It will be strange if they are
15 really to have money or anything of the kind. And what would their temperate acts

be? Is not such praise tasteless, since they have no bad appetites? If we were to run through them all, the circumstances of action would be found trivial and unworthy of gods. Still, every one supposes that they *live* and therefore that they are active; we cannot suppose them to sleep like Endymion. Now if you take away from a living ²⁰ being action, and still more production, what is left but contemplation? Therefore the activity of God, which surpasses all others in blessedness, must be contemplative; and of human activities, therefore, that which is most akin to this must be most of the nature of happiness.

This is indicated, too, by the fact that the other animals have no share in happiness, being completely deprived of such activity. For while the whole life of the ²⁵ gods is blessed, and that of men too in so far as some likeness of such activity belongs to them, none of the other animals is happy, since they in no way share in contemplation. Happiness extends, then, just so far as contemplation does, and those to whom contemplation more fully belongs are more truly happy, not ³⁰ accidentally, but in virtue of the contemplation; for this is in itself precious. Happiness, therefore, must be some form of contemplation.

But, being a man, one will also need external prosperity; for our nature is not self-sufficient for the purpose of contemplation, but our body also must be healthy and must have food and other attention. Still, we must not think that the man who is to be happy will need many things or great things, merely because he cannot be 1179ᵃ1 blessed without external goods; for self-sufficiency and action do not depend on excess, and we can do noble acts without ruling earth and sea; for even with moderate advantages one can act excellently (this is manifest enough; for private ⁵ persons are thought to do worthy acts no less than despots—indeed even more); and it is enough that we should have so much as that; for the life of the man who is active in accordance with excellence will be happy. Solon, too, was perhaps sketching well the happy man when he described him as moderately furnished with externals but ¹⁰ as having done (as Solon thought) the noblest acts, and lived temperately; for one can with but moderate possessions do what one ought. Anaxagoras also seems to have supposed the happy man not to be rich nor a despot, when he said that he would not be surprised if the happy man were to seem to most people a strange ¹⁵ person; for they judge by externals, since these are all they perceive. The opinions of the wise seem, then, to harmonize with our arguments. But while even such things carry some conviction, the truth in practical matters is discerned from the facts of life; for these are the decisive factor. We must therefore survey what we have ²⁰ already said, bringing it to the test of the facts of life, and if it harmonizes with the facts we must accept it, but if it clashes with them we must suppose it to be mere theory. Now he who exercises his intellect and cultivates it seems to be both in the best state and most dear to the gods. For if the gods have any care for human affairs, as they are thought to have, it would be reasonable both that they should delight in ²⁵ that which was best and most akin to them (i.e. intellect) and that they should reward those who love and honour this most, as caring for the things that are dear to them and acting both rightly and nobly. And that all these attributes belong most of all to the wise man is manifest. He, therefore, is the dearest to the gods. And he who ³⁰ is that will presumably be also the happiest; so that in this way too the wise man will more than any other be happy.

9 . If these matters and the excellences, and also friendship and pleasure, have been dealt with sufficiently in outline, are we to suppose that our programme has reached its end? Surely, as is said, where there are things to be done the end is not to survey and recognize the various things, but rather to do them; with regard to excellence, then, it is not enough to know, but we must try to have and use it, or try any other way there may be of becoming good. Now if arguments were in themselves enough to make men good, they would justly, as Theognis says, have won very great rewards, and such rewards should have been provided; but as things are, while they seem to have power to encourage and stimulate the generous-minded among the young, and to make a character which is gently born, and a true lover of what is noble, ready to be possessed by excellence, they are not able to encourage the many to nobility and goodness. For these do not by nature obey the sense of shame, but only fear, and do not abstain from bad acts because of their baseness but through fear of punishment; living by passion they pursue their own pleasures and the means to them, and avoid the opposite pains, and have not even a conception of what is noble and truly pleasant, since they have never tasted it. What argument would remould such people? It is hard, if not impossible, to remove by argument the traits that have long since been incorporated in the character; and perhaps we must be content if, when all the influences by which we are thought to become good are present, we get some tincture of excellence.

Now some think that we are made good by nature, others by habituation, others by teaching. Nature's part evidently does not depend on us, but as a result of some divine causes is present in those who are truly fortunate; while argument and teaching, we may suspect, are not powerful with all men, but the soul of the student must first have been cultivated by means of habits for noble joy and noble hatred, like earth which is to nourish the seed. For he who lives as passion directs will not hear argument that dissuades him, nor understand it if he does; and how can we persuade one in such a state to change his ways? And in general passion seems to yield not to argument but to force. The character, then, must somehow be there already with a kinship to excellence, loving what is noble and hating what is base.

But it is difficult to get from youth up a right training for excellence if one has not been brought up under right laws; for to live temperately and hardily is not pleasant to most people, especially when they are young. For this reason their nurture and occupations should be fixed by law; for they will not be painful when they have become customary. But it is surely not enough that when they are young they should get the right nurture and attention; since they must, even when they are grown up, practise and be habituated to them, we shall need laws for this as well, and generally speaking to cover the whole of life; for most people obey necessity rather than argument, and punishments rather than what is noble.

This is why some think that legislators ought to stimulate men to excellence and urge them forward by the motive of the noble, on the assumption that those who have been well advanced by the formation of habits will attend to such influences; and that punishments and penalties should be imposed on those who disobey and are of inferior nature, while the incurably bad should be completely banished. A good man (they think), since he lives with his mind fixed on what is noble, will submit to 10 argument, while a bad man, whose desire is for pleasure, is corrected by pain like a beast of burden. This is, too, why they say the pains inflicted should be those that are most opposed to the pleasures such men love.

However that may be, if (as we have said) the man who is to be good must be well trained and habituated, and go on to spend his time in worthy occupations and 15 neither willingly nor unwillingly do bad actions, and if this can be brought about if men live in accordance with a sort of intellect and right order, provided this has force,—if this be so, the paternal command indeed has not the required force or compulsive power (nor in general has the command of one man, unless he be a king 20 or something similar), but the law *has* compulsive power, while it is at the same time an account proceeding from a sort of practical wisdom and intellect. And while people hate *men* who oppose their impulses, even if they oppose them rightly, the law in its ordaining of what is good is not burdensome.

In the Spartan state alone, or almost alone, the legislator seems to have paid 25 attention to questions of nurture and occupations; in most states such matters have been neglected, and each man lives as he pleases, Cyclops-fashion, 'to his own wife and children dealing law'.[83] Now it is best that there should be a public and proper care for such matters; but if they are neglected by the community it would seem 30 right for each man to help his children and friends towards excellence, and that they should be able or at least choose, to do this.[84]

It would seem from what has been said that he can do this better if he makes himself capable of legislating. For public care is plainly effected by laws, and good care by good laws; whether written or unwritten would seem to make no difference, 1180[b]1 nor whether they are laws providing for the education of individuals or of groups—any more than it does in the case of music or gymnastics and other such pursuits. For as in cities laws and character have force, so in households do the injunctions and the habits of the father, and these have even more because of the tie 5 of blood and the benefits he confers; for the children start with a natural affection and disposition to obey. Further, individual education has an advantage over education in common, as individual medical treatment has; for while in general rest and abstinence from food are good for a man in a fever, for a particular man they may not be; and a boxer presumably does not prescribe the same style of fighting to 10 all his pupils. It would seem, then, that the detail is worked out with more precision if the care is particular to individuals; for each person is more likely to get what suits his case.

But individuals[85] can be best cared for by a doctor or gymnastic instructor or

[83]*Odyssey* IX 114.
[84]Placing καὶ δρᾶν αὐτὸ δύνασθαι after συμβάλλεσθαι.
[85]Reading καθ' ἕνα.

any one else who has the universal knowledge of what is good for every one or for
people of a certain kind (for the sciences both are said to be, and are, concerned with
what is common); not but what some particular detail may perhaps be well looked
after by an unscientific person, if he has studied accurately in the light of experience
what happens in each case, just as some people seem to be their own best doctors,
though they could give no help to any one else. None the less, it will perhaps be
agreed that if a man does wish to become master of an art or science he must go to
the universal, and come to know it as well as possible; for, as we have said, it is with
this that the sciences are concerned.

And surely he who wants to make men, whether many or few, better by his
care must try to become capable of legislating, if it is through laws that we can
become good. For to get anyone whatever—anyone who is put before us—into the
right condition is not for the first chance comer; if anyone can do it, it is the man
who knows, just as in medicine and all other matters which give scope for care and
practical wisdom.

Must we not, then, next examine whence or how one can learn how to
legislate? Is it, as in all other cases, from statesmen? Certainly it was thought to be
a part of statesmanship. Or is a difference apparent between statesmanship and the
other sciences and faculties? In the others the same people are found offering to
teach the faculties and practising them, e.g. doctors or painters; but while the
sophists profess to teach politics, it is practised not by any of them but by the
politicians, who would seem to do so by dint of a certain faculty and experience
rather than of thought; for they are not found either writing or speaking about such
matters (though it were a nobler occupation perhaps than composing speeches for
the law-courts and the assembly), nor again are they found to have made statesmen
of their own sons or any other of their friends. But it was to be expected that they
should if they could; for there is nothing better than such a skill that they could have
left to their cities, or could choose to have for themselves, or, therefore, for those
dearest to them. Still, experience seems to contribute not a little; else they could not
have become politicians by familiarity with politics; and so it seems that those who
aim at knowing about the art of politics need experience as well.

But those of the sophists who profess the art seem to be very far from teaching
it. For, to put the matter generally, they do not even know what kind of thing it is
nor what kinds of things it is about; otherwise they would not have classed it as
identical with rhetoric or even inferior to it, nor have thought it easy to legislate by
collecting the laws that are thought well of; they say it is possible to select the best
laws, as though even the selection did not demand intelligence and as though right
judgement were not the greatest thing, as in matters of music. For while people
experienced in any department judge rightly the works produced in it, and
understand by what means or how they are achieved, and what harmonizes with
what, the inexperienced must be content if they do not fail to see whether the work
has been well or ill made—as in the case of painting. Now laws are as it were the
works of the political art; how then can one learn from them to be a legislator, or
judge which are best? Even medical men do not seem to be made by a study of

text-books. Yet people try, at any rate, to state not only the treatments, but also how particular classes of people can be cured and should be treated—distinguishing the various states; but while this seems useful to experienced people, to the ignorant it is valueless. Surely, then, while collections of laws, and of constitutions also, may be serviceable to those who can study them and judge what is good or bad and what enactments suit what circumstances, those who go through such collections without a practised faculty will not have right judgement (unless it be spontaneous), though they may perhaps become more intelligent in such matters.

Now our predecessors have left the subject of legislation to us unexamined; it is perhaps best, therefore, that we should ourselves study it, and in general study the question of the constitution, in order to complete to the best of our ability the philosophy of human nature. First, then, if anything has been said well in detail by earlier thinkers, let us try to review it; then in the light of the constitutions we have collected let us study what sorts of influence preserve and destroy states, and what sorts preserve or destroy the particular kinds of constitution, and to what causes it is due that some are well and others ill administered. When these have been studied we shall perhaps be more likely to see which constitution is best, and how each must be ordered, and what laws and customs it must use. Let us make a beginning of our discussion.

MAGNA MORALIA*

St. G. Stock

BOOK I

1 · Since our purpose is to speak about matters to do with character, we must
1181ᵃ25 first inquire of what character is a branch. To speak concisely, then, it would seem
to be a branch of nothing else than statecraft. For it is not possible to act at all in
affairs of state unless one is of a certain kind, to wit, good. Now to be good is to
1181ᵇ25 possess the excellences. If therefore one is to act successfully in affairs of state, one
must be of a good character. The treatment of character then is, as it seems, a
branch and starting-point of statecraft. And as a whole it seems to me that the
subject ought rightly to be called, not Ethics, but Politics.
1182ᵃ1 We must therefore, as it seems, speak first about excellence, both what it is and
from what it comes. For it is perhaps of no use to know excellence without
understanding how or from what it is to arise. We must not limit our inquiry to
5 knowing what it is, but extend it to how it is to be produced. For we wish not only to
know but also ourselves to be such; and this will be impossible for us, unless we know
from what and how it is to be produced. Of course, it is indispensable to know what
excellence is (for it is not easy to know the source and manner of its production, if
10 one does not know what it is, any more than in the sciences); but we ought to be
aware also of what others have said before us on this subject.

Pythagoras first attempted to speak about excellence, but not successfully; for
by referring the excellences to numbers he submitted the excellences to a treatment
which was not proper to them. For justice is not a square number.

15 After him came Socrates, who spoke better and further about this subject, but
even he was not successful. For he used to make the excellences sciences, and this is
impossible. For the sciences all involve reason, and reason is to be found in the
intellectual part of the soul. So that all the excellences, according to him, are to be
20 found in the rational part of the soul. The result is that in making the excellences
sciences he is doing away with the irrational part of the soul, and is thereby doing

TEXT: F. Susemihl, Teubner, Leipzig, 1884

away also both with passion and character; so that he has not been successful in this respect in his treatment of the excellences.

After this Plato divided the soul into the rational and the irrational part—and in this he was right—assigning appropriate excellences to each. So far so good. But after this he went astray. For he mixed up excellence with the treatment of the good, which cannot be right, not being appropriate. For in speaking about the truth of things he ought not to have discoursed upon excellence; for there is nothing common to the two. 25 30

The above-mentioned, then, have touched upon the subject so far and in the way above described. The next thing will be to see what we ought to say ourselves upon the subject.

First of all, then, we must see that every science and capacity has an end, and that too a good one; for no science or capacity exists for the sake of evil. Since then in every capacity the end is good, it is plain that the end of the best will be the best good. But statecraft is the best capacity, so that the end of this will be the good.[1] It is about good, then, as it seems, that we must speak, and about good not without qualification, but relatively to ourselves. For we have not to do with the good of the Gods. To speak about that is a different matter, and the inquiry is foreign to our present purpose. It is therefore about the good of the state that we must speak. 35 1182ᵇ1 5

But we must make a distinction here. About good in what sense of the term have we to speak? For the word is not univocal. For 'good' is used either of what is best in the case of each being, that is, what is desirable because of its own nature, or of that by partaking in which all other things are good, that is, the Idea of Good. 10

Are we, then, to speak of the Idea of Good? Or not of that, but of good as the element common to all goods? For this would seem to be different from the Idea. For the Idea is a thing apart and by itself, whereas the common element exists in all: it therefore is not identical with what is apart. For that which is apart and whose nature it is to be by itself cannot possibly exist in all. Are we then to speak about this indwelling good? Surely not! And why? Because the common element is that which is got by definition or by induction. Now the aim of defining is to state the substance of each thing, either what good is[2] or what evil is, or whatever else it may be. But the definition states that whatever thing is of such a kind as to be desirable for its own sake is good in all cases. And the common element in all goods is much the same as the definition. And the definition says what is good, whereas no science or capacity whatsoever states of its own end that it is good, but it is the province of another capacity to speculate as to this (for neither the physician nor the mason says that health or a house is good, but that one thing produces health, and how it produces it, and another thing a house). It is evident then that neither has statecraft to do with the common element of good. For it is itself only one science among the rest, and we have seen that it is not the business of any capacity or science to talk of this as end. It is not therefore the business of statecraft to speak of the common element of good corresponding to the definition. 15 20 25 30

¹Reading τἀγαθόν.   ²Reading ὅ τι for ὅτι, twice.

But neither has it to speak of the common element as arrived at by induction. Why so? Because when we wish to prove some particular good, we either prove by defining that the same description applies to the good and to the thing which we wish to prove to be good, or else have recourse to induction; for instance, when we 1183ᵃ1 wish to prove that magnanimity is a good, we say that justice is a good and courage is a good, and so of the excellences generally, and that magnanimity is an excellence, so that magnanimity also is a good. Neither then will statecraft have to speak of the common good arrived at by induction, because the same impossible 5 consequences will ensue in this case as in that of the common good conformable to the definition. For here also one will be saying that the end is good. It is clear therefore that what it has to speak about is the best good, and the best in the sense of the best for us.

And generally one can see that it is not the part of any one science or capacity to consider the question of good in general. Why so? Because good occurs in all the 10 categories—in that of substance, quality, quantity, time, relation, and generally in all. But what is good at a given time is known in medicine by the doctor, in navigation by the pilot, and in each art by the expert in that art. For it is the doctor 15 who knows when one ought to amputate, and the pilot when one ought to sail. And in each art each expert will know the time of the good which concerns himself. For neither will the doctor know the time of the good in navigation nor the pilot that in medicine. It follows then from this point of view also that we have not to speak about the common good; for time is common to all the arts. Similarly the relative good and 20 the good which corresponds to other categories is common to all, and it does not belong to any capacity or science to speak of what is good in each at a given time, nor, we may add, is it the part of statecraft to speak about the common element of good. Our subject then is the good, in the sense of the best, and that the best for us.

25   Perhaps when one wishes to prove something, one ought not to employ illustrations that are not manifest, but to illustrate the obscure by the manifest, and the things of mind by the things of sense; for the latter are more manifest. When, therefore, one undertakes to speak about the good, one ought not to speak about the Idea. And yet they think it quite necessary, when they are speaking about the good, 30 to speak about the Idea. For they say that it is necessary to speak about what is most good, and the thing-itself in each kind has the quality of that kind in the highest degree, so that the Idea will be the most good, as they think. Possibly there is truth in such a contention; but all the same the science or capacity of statecraft, about which we are now speaking, does not inquire about this good, but about that which 35 is good for us. [For no science or capacity pronounces its end to be good, so that statecraft does not do so either.]³ Hence it does not concern itself to speak about the good in the sense of the Idea.

But, it may be said, one may employ this good as a first principle to start from in speaking about particular goods. Even this is not correct. For the first principles

³Excised by Susemihl.

that one assumes ought to be appropriate. How absurd it would be if, when one _{1183ᵇ1} wished to prove that the three angles of a triangle are equal to two right angles, one were to assume as a principle that the soul is immortal! For it is not appropriate, and the first principle ought to be appropriate and connected. As a matter of fact, one can prove that the three angles of a triangle are equal to two right angles quite as 5 well without the immortality of the soul. In the same way in the case of goods, one can speculate about the rest without the Ideal Good. Hence such a good is not an appropriate principle.⁴

Neither was Socrates right in making the excellences sciences. For he used to think that nothing ought to be in vain, but from the excellences being sciences he 10 met with the result that the excellences were in vain. Why so? Because in the case of the sciences, as soon as one knows what the science is, it results that one is scientific (for any one who knows what medicine is is forthwith a physician, and so with the other sciences). But this result does not follow in the case of the excellences. For any 15 one who knows what justice is is not forthwith just, and similarly in the case of the rest. It follows then that the excellences are actually in vain and that they are not sciences.

2 · Now that we have settled these points, let us try to say in how many senses the term 'good' is used. For goods may be divided into the honourable, the 20 praiseworthy, and capacities. By the honourable I mean such a thing as the divine, the more excellent (for instance, soul, intellect), the more ancient, the first principle, and so on. For those things are honourable which attract honour, and all such things as these are attended with honour. Excellence then also is a thing that is honourable, at least when some one has become a good man in consequence of it; for 25 already such a one has come into the form of excellence. Other goods are praiseworthy, as excellences; for praise is bestowed in consequence of the actions which are prompted by them. Others are capacities—for instance, office, wealth, strength, beauty; for these are things which the good man can use well and the bad man ill. Hence such goods are called capacities. Goods indeed they are (for 30 everything is judged by the use made of it by the good man, not by that of the bad); and it is incidental to these same goods that fortune is the cause of their production. For from fortune comes wealth, and also office, and generally all the things which 35 rank as capacities. The fourth and last class of goods is that which is preservative and productive of good, as exercise of health, and other things of that sort.

But goods admit of another division, to wit, some goods are everywhere and absolutely desirable, and some are not. For instance, justice and the other excellences are everywhere and absolutely desirable, but strength, and wealth, and 1184ª1 power, and the like, are not so everywhere nor absolutely.

Again, take another division. Some goods are ends and some are not; for instance, health is an end, but the means to health are not ends: and wherever things stand in this relation, the end is always better; for instance, health is better 5

---

⁴Text uncertain.

than the means to health, and without exception, always and universally, that thing is better for the sake of which the rest are.

Again, among ends themselves the complete is always better than the incomplete. A complete good is one the presence of which leaves us in need of nothing; an incomplete good is one which may be present while yet we need something further; for instance, we may have justice and yet need many things besides, but when we have happiness we need nothing more. This then is the best thing of which we are in search, which is the complete end. The complete end then is the good and end of goods.

The next point is how we are to look for the best good. Is it itself to be reckoned in with other goods? Surely that is absurd. For the best is the complete end, and the complete end, roughly speaking, would seem to be nothing else than happiness, and happiness we regard as made up of many goods; so that if, in looking for the best, you reckon in itself also, it will be better than itself, because it is itself the best thing. For instance, take the means to health, and health, and raise the question which is the best of all these. The answer is that health is the best. If then this is the best of all, it is also better than itself; so that an absurdity ensues. Perhaps then this is not the way in which we ought to look for the best. Are the other goods then to be separated from it?[5] Is not this also absurd? For happiness is composed of certain goods. But to raise the question whether a given thing is better than its own components is absurd. For happiness is not something else apart from these, but just these.

But perhaps the right method of inquiry may be by comparison of the best somewhat as follows. I.e., by comparing happiness itself, which is made up of these goods, with others which are not contained in it, would this be the right way of inquiring into the best thing? But the best of which we are now in search is not of a simple nature. For instance, one might say that wisdom is the best of all goods when they are compared one by one. But perhaps this is not the way in which we ought to seek for the best good. For it is the complete good we are in search of, and wisdom by itself is not complete. It is not, therefore, the best in this sense, nor in this way, of which we are in search.

1184^b1　　3 · After this, then, goods admit of another division. For some goods are in the soul—for instance, the virtues; some in the body—for instance, health, beauty; and some outside of us—wealth, office, honour, and such like. Of these those in the soul are best. But the goods in the soul are divided into three—wisdom, excellence, and pleasure.

Now we come to happiness, which we all declare to be, and which seems in fact to be, the end of goods and the most complete thing, and this we maintain to be identical with[6] doing well and living well. But the end is not single but twofold. For the end of some things is the activity and use itself—for instance, of sight; and the using is more desirable than the having; for the using is the end. For no one would

<hr>

[5]Reading αὐτό for αὐτοῦ.　　[6]Reading τῷ for τό.

care to have sight, if he were destined never to see, but always to have his eyes shut. And the same with hearing and the like. When then a thing may be both used and had, the using is always better and more desirable than the having. For the use and 15 exercise are the end, whereas the having is with a view to the using.

Next, then, if one examines this point in the case of all the sciences, he will see that it is not one that makes a house and another that makes a good house, but simply the art of housebuilding; and what the housebuilder makes, that same thing 20 his excellence enables him to make well. Similarly in all other cases.

4 . After this, then, we see that it is by nothing else than soul that we live. Excellence is in the soul. We maintain that the soul and the excellence of the soul do the same thing. But excellence in each thing does that well of which it is the 25 excellence, and, among the other functions of the soul, it is by it we live. It is therefore owing to the excellence of the soul that we shall live well. But to live well and do well, we say, is nothing else than being happy. Being happy, then, and happiness, consist in living well, and living well is living in accordance with the excellences. This, then, is the end and happiness and the best thing. Happiness 30 therefore will consist in a kind of use and activity. For we found that where there was having and using, the use and exercise are the end. Now excellence is a habit of the soul. And there is such a thing as the exercise and use of it;[7] so that the end will be its activity and use. Happiness therefore will consist in living in accordance with 35 the excellences. Since then the best good is happiness, and this is the end, and the complete end is an activity,[8] it follows that it is by living in accordance with the excellences that we shall be happy and shall have the best good.   1185ᵃ1

Since, then, happiness is a complete good and end, we must not fail to observe that it will be found in that which is complete. For it will not be found in a child (for a child is not happy), but in a man; for he is complete. Nor will it be found in an incomplete, but in a complete, period. And a complete period of time will be as long 5 as a man lives. For it is rightly said among the many that one ought to judge of the happy man in the longest time of his life, on the assumption that what is complete ought to be in a complete period and a complete person. But that it is an activity can be seen also from the following consideration. For supposing some one to be asleep 10 all his life, we should hardly consent to call such a man happy. Life indeed he has, but life in accordance with the excellences he has not, and it was in this that we made the activity to consist.

The topic that is next about to be treated of is neither very intimately connected with our main subject nor yet quite alien from it. I mean, since there is, as 15 it seems, a part of the soul whereby we are nourished, which we call nutritive (for it is reasonable to suppose that this exists; at all events we see that stones are incapable of being nourished, so that it is evident that to be nourished is a property of living things; and, if so, the soul will be the cause of it; but none of these parts of the soul will be the cause of nourishment, to wit, the rational or spirited or 20

---

[7] Omitting τῶν ἀρετῶν.   [8] Reading ἐνέργεια.

appetitive, but something else besides these, to which we can apply no more appropriate name than 'nutritive'), one might say, 'Very well, has this part of the soul also an excellence? For if it has, it is plain that we ought to act with this also. For happiness is the exercise of complete excellence'. Now, whether there is or is not an excellence of this part is another question; but, if there is, it has no activity. For those things which have no impulse will not have any activity either; and there does not seem to be any impulse in this part, but it seems to be on a par with fire. For that also will consume whatever you throw in, but if you do not throw anything in, it has no impulse to get it. So it is also with this part of the soul; for, if you throw in food, it nourishes, but, if you fail to throw in food, it has no impulse to nourish. Hence it has no activity, being devoid of impulse. So that this part in no way co-operates towards happiness.

After this, then, we must say what excellence is, since it is the exercise of this which is happiness. Speaking generally, then, excellence is the best state. But perhaps it is not sufficient to speak thus generally, but it is necessary to define more clearly.

1185ᵇ1   5 · First, then, we ought to speak about the soul in which it resides, not to say what the soul is (for to speak about that is another matter), but to divide it in outline. Now the soul is, as we say, divided into two parts, the rational and the irrational. In the rational part, then, there resides wisdom, readiness of wit, philosophy, aptitude to learn, memory, and so on; but in the irrational those which are called the excellences—temperance, justice, courage, and such other states of character as are held to be praiseworthy. For it is in respect of these that we are called praiseworthy; but no one is praised for the excellences of the rational part. For no one is praised for being philosophical or for being wise, or generally on the ground of anything of that sort. Nor indeed is the irrational part praised, except in so far as it is capable of subserving or actually subserves the rational part.

Moral excellence[9] is destroyed by defect and excess. Now, that defect and excess destroy can be seen from perceptible instances, and we must use what we can see as evidence for what we cannot see. For one can see this at once in the case of gymnastic exercises. If they are overdone, the strength is destroyed, while if they are deficient, it is so also. And the same is the case with food and drink. For if too much is taken health is destroyed, and also if too little, but by the right proportion strength and health are preserved. The same is the case with temperance and courage and the rest of the excellences. For if you make a man too fearless, so as not even to fear the gods, he is not brave but mad, but if you make him afraid of everything, he is a coward. To be brave, then, a man must not either fear everything or nothing. The same things, then, both increase and destroy excellence. For undue and indiscriminate fears destroy, and so does the lack of fear about anything at all. And courage has to do with fears, so that moderate fears increase courage. Courage, then, is both increased and destroyed by the same things. For men are

---

[9] I.e. excellence of character.

liable to this effect owing to fears. And the same holds true of the other excellences.

6 · In addition, excellence may also be determined by pleasure and pain. For it is owing to pleasure that we commit base actions, and owing to pain that we 35 abstain from noble ones. And generally it is not possible to achieve excellence or vice without pain and pleasure. Excellence then has to do with pleasures and pains.

Moral excellence gets its name as follows, if etymology has any bearing upon truth, as perhaps it has. 'Character ($\tilde{\eta}\theta o\varsigma$)' derives from 'custom ($\H{\epsilon}\theta o\varsigma$)'; for it is 1186ª1 called moral ($\eta\theta\iota\kappa\H{\eta}$) excellence because it is the result of accustoming. Whereby it is evident that no one of the excellences of the irrational part springs up in us by nature. For nothing that is by nature becomes other by custom. For instance, a stone, and heavy things in general, naturally go downwards. If any one, then, throws 5 them up repeatedly, and tries to accustom them to go up, all the same they never would go up, but always down. Similarly in all other such cases.

7 · After this, then, as we wish to say what excellence is, we must know what are the things that there are in the soul. They are these—feelings, capacities, states; 10 so that it is evident that excellence will be some one of these. Now feelings are anger, fear, hate, regret, emulation, pity, and the like, which are usually attended by pain or pleasure. Capacities are those things in virtue of which we are said to be capable of these feelings; for instance, those things in virtue of which we are capable 15 of feeling anger or pain or pity, and so on. States are those things in virtue of which we stand in a good or bad relation to these feelings; for instance, towards being angered: if we are angry overmuch, we stand in a bad relation towards anger, whereas if we are not angry at all where we ought to be, in that case also we stand in a bad relation towards anger.

The mean state, then, is neither to be pained overmuch nor to be absolutely 20 insensible. When, then, we stand thus, we are in a good disposition. And similarly as regards other like things. For good temper and gentleness are in a mean between anger and insensibility to anger. Similarly in the case of boastfulness and mock-humility. For to pretend to more than one has shows boastfulness, while to 25 pretend to less shows mock-humility. The mean state, then, between these is truthfulness.

8 · Similarly in all other cases. For this is what marks the state, to stand in a good or bad relation towards these feelings, and to stand in a good relation towards them is to incline neither towards the excess nor towards the defect. The state, then, 30 which implies a good relation is directed towards the mean of such things, in respect of which we are called praiseworthy, whereas that which implies a bad relation inclines towards excess or defect.

Since, then, excellence is a mean of these feelings, and the feelings are either

pains or pleasures or impossible apart from pain or pleasure, it is evident from this
35   that excellence has to do with pains and pleasures.

But there are other feelings, as one might think, in the case of which the vice
does not lie in any excess or defect; for instance, adultery and the adulterer. The
1186ᵇ1   adulterer is not the man who corrupts free women too much; but both this and
anything else of the kind which is comprised under the pleasure of intemperance,
whether[10] it be something in the way of excess or of defect, is blamed.

9 · After this, then, it is perhaps necessary to have it stated what is opposed
5   to the mean, whether it is the excess or the defect. For to some means the defect is
opposed and to some the excess; for instance, to courage it is not rashness, which is
the excess, that is opposed, but cowardice, which is the defect; and to temperance,
which is a mean between intemperance and insensibility to pleasures, it does not
10   seem that insensibility, which is the defect, is opposed, but intemperance, which is
the excess. But both are opposed to the mean, excess and defect. For the mean is in
defect of the excess and in excess of the defect. Hence it is that prodigals call the
15   liberal illiberal, while the illiberal call the liberal prodigals, and the rash and
headlong call the brave cowards, while cowards call the brave headlong and mad.

There would seem to be two reasons for our opposing the excess or the defect to
the mean. Either people look at the matter from the point of view of the thing itself,
20   to see which is nearer to, or further from, the mean; for instance, in the case of
liberality, whether prodigality or illiberality is further from it. For prodigality
would seem more to be liberality than illiberality is. Illiberality, then, is further off.
But things which are further distant from the mean would seem to be more opposed
25   to it. From the point of view, then, of the thing itself the defect presents itself as
more opposed. But there is also another way, to wit, those things are more opposed
to the mean to which we have a greater natural inclination. For instance, we have a
greater natural inclination to be intemperate than sober in our conduct. The
tendency, therefore, occurs rather towards the things to which nature inclines us;
and the things to which we have a greater tendency are more opposed; and our
30   tendency is towards intemperance rather than towards sobriety; so that the excess
of the mean will be the more opposed; for intemperance is the excess in the case of
temperance.

What excellence is, then, has been examined (for it seems to be a mean of the
feelings, so that it will be necessary for the man who is to obtain credit for his
35   character to observe the mean with regard to each of the feelings; for which reason
it is a difficult matter to be good; for to seize the mean in anything is a difficult
matter; for instance, any one can draw a circle, but to fix upon the mean point in it is
187ᵃ1   hard; and in the same way to be angry indeed is easy, and so is the opposite of this,
but to be in the mean is hard; and generally in each of the feelings one can see that
what surrounds the mean is easy, but the mean is hard, and this is the point for
which we are praised; for which reason the good is rare).

[10]Omitting ἤ.

Since, then, excellence has been spoken of . . .[11] we must next inquire whether   5
it is possible of attainment or is not, but, as Socrates said, to be good or bad does not
rest with us to come about. For if, he says, one were to ask any one whatever
whether he would wish to be just or unjust, no one would choose injustice. Similarly
in the case of courage and cowardice, and so on always with the rest of the   10
excellences. And it is evident that any who are bad will not be bad voluntarily; so
that it is evident that neither will they be voluntarily good.

Such a statement is not true. For why does the lawgiver forbid the doing of
wrong acts, and bid the doing of right and good ones? And why does he appoint a   15
penalty for wrong acts, if one does them, and for right acts, if one fails to do them?
Yet it would be absurd to legislate about those things which are not in our power to
do. But, as it seems, it is in our power to be good or bad.

Again, we have evidence in the praise and blame that are accorded. For there is
praise for excellence and blame for vice. But praise and blame are not bestowed   20
upon things involuntary. So it is evident that it is equally in our power to do good
and bad acts.

They used also to employ some such comparison as this in their desire to show
that it is not voluntary. For why, they say, when we are ill or ugly, does no one blame   25
us for things of this sort? But this is not true. For we do blame people for things of
this sort, when we think that they themselves are the causes of being ill or of their
having their body in a bad state, on the assumption that there is voluntary action
even there. It seems, then, that there is voluntariness in being excellent and
vicious.

10 · One can see this still more clearly from the following considerations.   30
Every natural kind is given to begetting a being like itself, i.e. plants and animals;
for both are apt to beget. And they are given to beget from their first principles—for
instance, the tree from the seed; for this is a kind of principle. And what follows the
principles stands thus: as are the principles, so is what comes from the principles.   35

This can be seen more clearly in matters of geometry. For there also, when
certain principles are assumed, as are the principles, so are what follow the
principles; for instance, if the triangle has its angles equal to two right angles, and
the quadrilateral to four, then according as the triangle changes, so does the   1187[b]1
quadrilateral share in its changes (for it is convertible), and if the quadrilateral has
not its angles equal to four right angles, neither will the triangle have its angles
equal to two right angles.

11 · So, then, and in the like way with this, is it in the case of man. For since
man is apt to produce things, he tends to produce the actions which he does from   5
certain principles. How else could it be? For we do not say that any of the things
without life acts, nor any other of the things with life, except men. It is evident, then,
that man is the begetter of his acts.

---

[11]There is a lacuna in the text.

10   Since, then, we see that the acts change, and we never do the same things, and the acts have been brought into being from certain principles, it is evident that, since the acts change, the principles from which the acts proceed also change, as we said in our comparison was the case with geometrical properties.

15   Now the principle of an act, whether good or bad, is choice and wish, and all that accords with reason. It is evident, then, that these also change. But we change in our actions voluntarily. So that the principle also, choice, changes voluntarily. So

20   that it is plain that it will be in our power to be either good or bad.

Perhaps, then, some one may say, 'Since it is in my power to be just and good, if I wish I shall be the best of all men'. This, of course, is not possible. Why so? Because in the case of the body it is not so either. For if one wishes to bestow attention upon his body, it does not follow that he will have the best body that any

25   one has. For it is necessary not merely for attention to be bestowed, but also for the body to be beautiful and good by nature. He will then have his body better, but best of all men, No. And so we must suppose it to be also in the case of soul. For he who

30   chooses to be best will not be so, unless nature also be presupposed; better, however, he will be.

12 · Since, then, it appears that to be good is in our power, it is necessary next to say what the voluntary is. For this is what chiefly determines excellence, to wit, the voluntary. Roughly speaking, that is voluntary which we do when not under

35   compulsion. But perhaps we ought to speak more clearly about it.

What prompts us to action is desire; and desire has three forms—appetite, passion, wish.

First of all, then, we must inquire into the act which is in accordance with appetite. Is that voluntary or involuntary? That it is involuntary would not seem to

1188ᵃ1   be the case. Why so? And on what ground? Because wherever we do not act voluntarily, we act under compulsion, and all acts done under compulsion are attended with pain, whereas acts due to appetite are attended with pleasure, so that on this way of looking at the matter acts due to appetite will not be involuntary, but voluntary.

5   But, again, there is another argument opposed to this, which makes its appeal to incontinence. No one, it is maintained, does evil voluntarily, knowing it to be evil. But yet the incontinent, knowing that what he does is bad, nevertheless does it, and does it in accordance with appetite; he is not therefore acting voluntarily; therefore

10   he is under compulsion. There again the same answer will meet this argument. For if the act is in accordance with appetite, it is not of compulsion; for appetite is attended with pleasure, and acts due to pleasure are not of compulsion.

There is another way in which this may be made plain—I mean, that the incontinent acts voluntarily. For those who commit injustice do so voluntarily, and

15   the incontinent are unjust and act unjustly. So that the incontinent man will voluntarily commit his acts of incontinence.

13 · But, again, there is another argument opposed to this, which maintains

that it is not voluntary. For the self-restrained man voluntarily performs his acts of self-restraint. For he is praised, and people are praised for voluntary acts. But if that which is in accordance with appetite is voluntary, that which runs counter to 20 appetite is involuntary. But the man of self-restraint acts contrary to his appetite. So that the man of self-restraint will not be self-restrained voluntarily. But this conclusion does not commend itself. Therefore the act which is in accordance with appetite is not voluntary.

Again, the same thing holds of acts prompted by passion. For the same arguments apply as to appetite, so that they will cause the difficulty. For it is 25 possible to be incontinent or continent of anger.

Among the desires in our division we have still to inquire about wish, whether it is voluntary. Now the incontinent wish for the time being the things to which their impulse is directed. Therefore the incontinent perform their bad acts with their own wish. But no one voluntarily does evil, knowing it to be evil. But the incontinent 30 man, knowing evil to be evil, does it with his own wish. Therefore he is not a voluntary agent, and wish therefore is not a voluntary thing. But this argument annuls incontinence and the incontinent man. For if he is not a voluntary agent, he is not blameworthy. But the incontinent is blameworthy. Therefore he is a voluntary agent. Therefore wish is voluntary. 35

Since, then, certain arguments seem opposed, we must speak more clearly about the voluntary.

14 · Before doing so, however, we must speak about force and about necessity. Force may occur even in the case of things without life. For things 1188ᵇ1 without life have each their proper place assigned to them—to fire the upper region and to earth the lower. It is, however, possible to force a stone to go up and fire to go down. It is also possible to apply force to an animal; for instance, when a horse is 5 galloping straight ahead, one may take hold of him and divert his course. Now whenever the cause of men's doing something contrary to their nature or contrary to their wish is outside of them, we will say that they are forced to do what they do. But when the cause is in themselves, we will not in that case say that they are forced. Otherwise the incontinent man will have his answer ready, in denying that he is bad. 10 For he will say that he is forced by his appetite to perform the bad acts.

15 · Let this, then, be our definition of what is due to force—those things of which the cause by which men are forced to do them is external (but where the cause is internal and in themselves there is no force).

But now we must speak about necessity and the necessary. The term 15 'necessary' must not be used in all circumstances nor in every case—for instance, of what we do for the sake of pleasure. For if one were to say 'I was necessitated by pleasure to debauch my friend's wife', he would be a strange person. For 'necessary' does not apply to everything, but only to externals; for instance, whenever a man receives some damage by way of alternative to some other greater, when compelled 20 by circumstances. For instance, 'I found it necessary to hurry my steps to the country; otherwise I should have found my stock destroyed'. Such, then, are the cases in which we have the necessary.

25   16 · But since the voluntary lies in no impulse, there will remain what proceeds from thought. For the involuntary is what is done from necessity or from force, and, thirdly, what is not accompanied by thought. This is plain from facts. For whenever a man has struck or killed a man, or has done something of that sort
30   without having thought about it beforehand, we say that he has acted involuntarily, implying that the voluntariness lies in the having thought about it. For instance, they say that once a woman gave a love-potion to somebody; then the man died from the effects of the love-potion, and the woman was put on trial before the Areopagus; on her appearance she was acquitted, just for the reason that she did not do it with
35   design. For she gave it in love, but missed her mark; hence it was not held to be voluntary, because in giving the love-potion she did not give it with the thought of killing. In that case, therefore, the voluntary falls under the head of what is accompanied with thought.

1189ª1   17 · It now remains for us to inquire into choice. Is choice desire or is it not? Now desire is found in the lower animals, but not choice; for choice is attended with reason, and none of the lower animals has reason. Therefore it will not be desire.
5   Is it then wish? Or is it not this either? For wish is concerned even with the impossible; for instance, we wish that we may live for ever, but we do not choose it. Again, choice is not concerned with the end but with what contributes to the end; for instance, no one chooses to be in health, but we choose what leads to health, e.g.
10   walking, running; but we wish for the ends. For we wish to be in health. So that it is evident in this way also that wish and choice are not the same thing.

But choice seems to be what its name suggests; I mean, we choose one thing instead of another; for instance, the better instead of the worse. Whenever, then, we
15   take the better in exchange for the worse as a matter of choice, there the term 'to choose' would seem to be appropriate.

Since, then, choice is none of these things, can it be thought that constitutes choice? Or is this not so either? For we entertain many thoughts and opinions in our
20   minds. Do we then choose whatever we think? Or is this not so? For often we think about things in India, but it does not follow that we choose them. Choice therefore is not thought either.

Since, then, choice is not any of these singly, and these are the things that there are in the soul, choice must result from the combination of some of them.
25   Since, then, choice, as was said before, is concerned with the goods that contribute to the end and not with the end, and with the things that are possible to us, and with such as afford ground for controversy as to whether this or that is desirable, it is evident that one must have thought and deliberated about them beforehand; then when a thing appears best to us after having thought it over, there
30   ensues an impulse to act, and it is when we act in this way that we are held to act on choice.

Since, then, choice is a deliberate desire attended with thought, the voluntary is not necessarily done by choice. For there are many acts which we do voluntarily before thinking and deliberating about them; for instance, we sit down and stand up, and do many other things of the same sort voluntarily but without having 35 thought about them, whereas every act done by choice was found to be attended with thought. The voluntary, therefore, is not necessarily done by choice, but the act 1189ᵇ1 done by choice is voluntary; for if we choose to do anything after deliberation, we act voluntarily. And a few legislators, even, appear to distinguish the voluntary act from the act done by choice as being something different, in making the penalties that they appoint for voluntary acts less than for those that are done by choice. 5

Choice, then, lies in matters of action, and in those in which it is in our power to do or not to do, and to act in this way or not in this way, and where we can know the reason why.

But the reason why is not always of the same kind. For in geometry, when one says that the quadrilateral has its angles equal to four right angles, and one asks the 10 reason why, one says, 'Because the triangle has its angles equal to two right angles'. Now in such cases they reached the reason why from a definite principle; but in matters of action, with which choice has to do, it is not so (for there is no definite principle laid down), but if one asks, 'Why did you do this?' the answer is, 'Because 15 it was the only thing possible', or 'Because it was better so'. It is from the consequences themselves, according as they appear to be better, that one chooses, and these are the reason why.

Hence in such matters the deliberation is as to the how, but not so in the sciences. For no one deliberates how he ought to write the name Archicles, because 20 it is a settled matter how one ought to write the name Archicles. The error, then, does not arise in the thought, but in the act of writing. For where the error is not in the thought, neither do people deliberate about those things. But wherever there is an indefiniteness about the how, there error comes in.

Now there is the element of indefiniteness in matters of action, and in those 25 matters in which the errors are two-fold. We err, then, in matters of action and in what pertains to the excellences in the same way. For in aiming at excellence we err in the natural directions. For there is error both in defect and in excess, and we are carried in both these directions through pleasure and pain. For it is owing to 30 pleasure that we do base deeds, and owing to pain that we abstain from noble ones.

18 · Again, thought is not like the senses; for instance, with sight one could not do anything else than see, nor with hearing anything else than hear. So also we do not deliberate whether we ought to hear with hearing or see. But thought is not like this, but it is able to do one thing and others also. That is why deliberation 1190ᵃ1 comes in there.

The error, then, in the choice of goods is not about the ends (for as to these all are at one in their judgement, for instance, that health is a good), but only about those which lead to the ends; for instance, whether a particular food is good for 5 health or not. The chief cause of our going wrong in these matters is pleasure and pain; for we avoid the one and choose the other.

Since, then, it has been settled in what error takes place and how, it remains to ask what it is that excellence aims at. Does it aim at the end or at what contributes 10 to the end? for instance, at what is right or at what contributes to it?

How, then, is it with science? Does it belong to the science of housebuilding to design the end rightly, or to see what contributes to it? For if the design is right—I mean, to make a beautiful house—it is no other than the housebuilder who will 15 discover and provide what contributes to it. And similarly in the case of all the other sciences.

So, then, it would seem to be also in the case of excellence, that its aim is rather the end, which it must design rightly, than what contributes to the end. And no one else will provide the materials for this or discover what is needed to contribute to it. And it is reasonable to suppose that excellence should have this in view. For both 20 design and execution always belong to that with which the origination of the best lies. Now there is nothing better than excellence; for it is for its sake that all other things are, and the origination looks to this, and the contributory factors are rather for the sake of it; now the end seems to be a kind of principle, and everything is for 25 the sake of it. But this will be as it ought to be. So that it is plain also in the case of excellence, since it is the best mode of causation, that it aims at the end rather than at what contributes to the end.

19 · Now the end of excellence is the right. This, then, is what excellence aims at rather than the things from which it will be produced. But it has to do also 30 with these. But to make these its whole concern is manifestly absurd. For perhaps in painting one might be a good imitator and yet not be praised, if one does not make it his aim to imitate the best subjects. This, therefore, is quite the business of excellence, to design the right.

Why, then, someone may say, did we say before that the activity was better 35 than the corresponding state, whereas now we are assigning to excellence as nobler not the material for activity, but something in which there is no activity? Yes, but 1190ᵇ1 now also we assert this just the same, that the activity is better than the state. For his fellow men in viewing the good man judge him from his acts, owing to its not being possible to make clear the choice which each has, since if it were possible to 5 know how the judgement of each man stands towards the right, he would have been thought good even without acting.

But since we reckoned up certain means of the feelings, we must say with what sort of feelings they are concerned.

20 · . . .¹² Since, then, courage has to do with feelings of confidence and fear, 10 we must examine with what sort of fears and confidences it has to do. If, then, any

---

¹²There is a lacuna in the text.

one is afraid of losing his property, is he a coward? And if any one is confident about these matters, is he brave? Surely not! And in the same way if one is afraid of or confident about illness, one ought not to say that the man who fears is a coward or that the man who does not fear is brave. It is not, therefore, in such fears and confidences as these that courage consists. Nor yet in such as follow; for instance, if 15 one is not afraid of thunder or lightning or any other superhuman terror, he is not brave but a sort of madman. It is with human fears and confidences, then, that the brave man has to do; I mean to say that anyone who is confident under circumstances in which most people or all are afraid, is a brave man.   20

These points having been settled, we must inquire, since there are many ways in which men are brave, which is the brave man. For you may have a man who is brave from experience, like soldiers. For they know, owing to experience, that in such a place or time or condition it is impossible to suffer any damage. But the man 25 who knows these things and for this reason stands his ground against the enemy is not brave; for if none of these things is the case, he does not stand his ground. Hence one ought not to call those brave whose courage is due to experience. Nor indeed was Socrates right in asserting that courage was knowledge. For knowledge becomes knowledge by getting experience from custom. But of those whose 30 endurance is due to experience we do not say, nor would men in general say, that they are brave. Courage, therefore, will not consist in knowledge.

But again, on the other hand, there are some who are brave from the opposite of experience. For those who have no experience of the probable results are free from fear owing to their inexperience. Neither, then, must we call these brave.

Again, there are others who appear brave owing to their passions; for instance, those who are in love or are inspired by the gods. We must not call these brave either. For if their passion is taken away, they are not brave any more, whereas the 1191ᵃ1 truly brave man must always be brave. Hence one would not call wild beasts like boars brave, owing to their defending themselves when they have been pained by a wound, nor ought the brave man to be brave through passion.

Again, there is another form of courage, which we may call civic; for instance, 5 if men endure dangers out of shame before their fellow citizens, and so appear to be brave. In illustration of this we may take the way in which Homer has represented Hector as saying—

Then were Polydamas first to pile reproaches upon me;[13]

for which reason he thinks that he ought to fight. We must not call this sort courage 10 either. For the same definition will apply to each of these. For he whose courage does not endure on the deprivation of something cannot properly be considered brave; if, then, I take away the shame owing to which he was brave, he will no longer be brave.

There is yet another way of appearing brave, namely, through hope and anticipation of good. We must not say that these are brave either, since it appears 15

[13]*Iliad* XXII 100.

absurd to call those brave who are of such a character and under such circumstances.

No one, then, of the above kinds must be put down as brave.

We have then to ask who is to be so put down, and who is the brave man. Broadly speaking, then, it is he who is brave owing to none of the things above-mentioned, but owing to his thinking it to be right, and who acts bravely whether any one is present or not.

Not, indeed, that courage arises in one entirely without passion and impulse. But the impulse must proceed from reason and be directed to the right. He, then, who is carried by a rational impulse to face danger for the sake of right, being free from fear about these things, is brave; and these are the things with which courage has to do.

When we say 'free from fear', it is not to be understood that the brave man feels no fear at all. For such a person is not brave, for whom nothing at all has any terrors. For in that way a stone and other things without life would be brave. But it is necessary that while he feels fear he should still face the danger; for if he faces it without feeling fear, he will not be brave.

Further, according to the distinction that we made above, it is not concerned with all fears and dangers, but only with those which threaten existence. Moreover, not at any and every time, but when the fears and the dangers are near. For if one is void of fear with regard to a danger that is ten years off, it does not follow that he is brave. For some are confident owing to its being far away, but, if they come near it, are ready to die with fear. Such, then, are courage and the brave man.

21 · Temperance is a mean between intemperance and insensibility to pleasures. For temperance and generally every excellence is the best state, and the best state lies in the attainment of the best thing, and the best thing is the mean between excess and defect; for people are blameworthy on both grounds, both on that of excess and on that of defect. So that, since the mean is best, temperance will be a mean state between intemperance and insensibility. These, then, are the vices between which it will be a mean.

Temperance is concerned with pleasures and pains, but not with all, nor with those that have to do with all objects. For one is not intemperate if one takes pleasure in beholding a painting or a statue or something of that sort, and in the same way not so in the case of hearing or smell; but only in the pleasures which have to do with touch and taste.

Nor yet with regard to these will a man be temperate who is in such a state as not to be affected at all by any pleasures of this sort (for such a person is devoid of feeling), but rather he who feels them and yet does not let himself be led away into enjoying them to excess and regarding everything else as of secondary consideration; and, we must add, the man who acts for the sake of right and nothing else. . . .[14] For whoever abstains from the excess of such pleasures either from fear or some other such motive is not temperate. For neither do we call the other animals

---

[14]There is a lacuna in the text.

temperate except man, because there is not reason in them whereby they test and choose the right. For every excellence is concerned with and aims at the right. So 20 temperance will be concerned with pleasures and pains, and these those that occur in touch and taste.

22 · Next to this we must speak about the definition and sphere of gentleness. Gentleness, then, is in a mean between irascibility and a want of anger. And generally the excellences seem to be a kind of means. One can show that they 25 are so in this way as well. For if the best is in the mean, and excellence is the best state excellence will be the mean. But it will be more plain as we inquire into them separately. For since he is irascible who gets angry with everybody and under all 30 circumstances and to too great an extent, and such a one is blameworthy (for one ought not to be angry with everybody nor at everything nor under all circumstances and always, nor yet again ought one to be in such a state as never to be angry with anybody; for this character also is blameworthy, as being insensible), since then both he who is in the excess is blameworthy and he who is in the defect, the man who 35 is in the mean between them will be gentle and praiseworthy. For neither he who is in defect in anger nor he who is in excess is praiseworthy, but he who stands in a mean with regard to these things. He is gentle; and gentleness will be a mean state with regard to these feelings.

23 · Liberality is a mean state between prodigality and illiberality. Feelings of this sort have to do with property. The prodigal is he who spends on wrong objects 1192ᵃ1 and more than he ought and at wrong times, while the illiberal man, in the opposite way to him, is he who does not spend on right objects and as much as he ought and when he ought. And both these characters are blameworthy. And one of them is 5 characterized by defect and the other by excess. The liberal man, therefore, since he is praiseworthy, will be in a mean between them. Who, then, is he? He who spends on right objects and right amounts and at right times.

24 · There are several forms of illiberality; for instance, we call some people *niggards* and *cheese-parers,* and *lovers of base gain,* and *petty.* Now all these fall 10 under the head of illiberality. For evil is multiform, but good uniform; for instance, health is single, but disease has many shapes. In the same way excellence is single, but vice has many shapes. For all these characters are blameworthy in relation to property.
　　Is it, then, the business of the liberal man also to get and procure property? 15 Surely not! That sort of thing is not the business of any excellence at all. It is not the business of courage to make weapons, but of something else, but it is the business of this when it has got them to make a right use of them; and so in the case of temperance and the other excellences. This, then, is not the business of liberality, but rather of the art of procuring property. 20

25 · Greatness of soul is a mean between vanity and littleness of soul, and it has to do with honour and dishonour, not with honour from the many but with that

from the good, or at any rate[15] more with the latter. For the good will bestow honour
25 with knowledge and good judgement. He will wish then rather to be honoured by
those who know as he does himself that he deserves honour. For he will not be
concerned with every honour, but with the best, and with the good that is
honourable and ranks as a principle. Those, then, who are despicable and bad, but
30 who deem themselves worthy of great things, and besides that think that they ought
to be honoured, are vain. But those who deem themselves worthy of less than befits
them are men of little soul. The man, therefore, who is in the mean between these is
he who neither deems himself worthy of less honour than is befitting to him, nor of
greater than he deserves, nor of all. And he is the man of great soul. So that it is
35 evident that greatness of soul is a mean between vanity and littleness of soul.

26 · Magnificence is a mean between ostentation and shabbiness. Now
magnificence has to do with expenses which are proper to be incurred by a man of
1192ᵇ1 eminence. Whoever therefore spends on the wrong occasions is ostentatious; for
instance, one who feasts his dinner-club as though he were giving a wedding-
banquet is ostentatious (for the ostentatious man is the sort of person who shows off
5 his own means on the wrong occasion). But the shabby man is the opposite of this,
who fails to make a great expenditure when he ought; or if, without going to that
length, when, for instance, he is spending money on a wedding-feast or the
mounting of a play, he does it in an unworthy and deficient way—such a person is
shabby. Magnificence from its very name shows itself to be such as we are
10 describing. For since it spends the great amount on the fitting occasion, it is rightly
called magnificence. Magnificence, then, since it is praiseworthy, is a mean
between defect and excess with regard to proper expenses on the right occasions.
But there are, as people think, more kinds of magnificence than one; for
15 instance, people say, 'his gait was magnificent', and there are of course other uses of
the term 'magnificent' in a metaphorical, not in a strict sense. For it is not in those
things that magnificence lies, but in those which we have mentioned.

27 · Righteous indignation is a mean state between enviousness and malice.
For both these states are blameworthy, but the man who shows righteous indigna-
20 tion is praiseworthy. Now righteous indignation is a kind of pain with regard to
good things which are found to attach to the undeserving. The man, then, who feels
righteous indignation is he who is apt to feel pain at such things. And this same
person again will feel pain, if he sees a man faring ill, who does not deserve it.
Righteous indignation, then, and the person who feels it, are perhaps of this sort,
25 but the envious man is the opposite of this. For he will feel pain without distinction,
whether one deserves the good fortune or not. In the same way the malicious man
will be pleased at ill-fortune, whether deserved or undeserved. Not so with the man
who feels righteous indignation, but he is in the mean between these.

[15]Reading ἢ μᾶλλον γε δή.

28 · Dignity is in a mean between pride and complaisance, and has to do   30
with social intercourse. For the proud man is inclined not to meet or talk to anybody
(but his name seems to be given to him from his character; for it means
self-pleasing, from his gratifying himself); but the complaisant is ready to associate
with every one under all circumstances and in all places. Neither of these characters   35
is praiseworthy; but the dignified man, being in the mean between them, is
praiseworthy. For he does not lay himself out to please everybody, but only those
who are worthy, nor yet nobody, for he does so to these same.

29 · Modesty is a mean between shamelessness and bashfulness, and it has   1193ᵃ1
to do with deeds and words. For the shameless man is he who says and does anything
on any occasion or before any people; but the bashful man is the opposite of this,
who is afraid to say or do anything before anybody (for such a man is incapacitated   5
for action, who is bashful about everything); but modesty and the modest man are a
mean between these. For he will not say and do anything under any circumstances,
like the shameless man, nor, like the bashful man, be afraid on every occasion and
under all circumstances, but will say and do what he ought, where he ought, and   10
when he ought.

30 · Wit is a mean state between buffoonery and boorishness, and it is
concerned with jests. For the buffoon is he who thinks fit to jest at every one and
everything, and the boor is he who neither thinks fit to make jests nor to have them
made at him, but gets angry. But the witty man is midway between these, who   15
neither jests at all persons and under all circumstances, nor on the other hand is a
boor. But wit is of two sorts. For both he who is able to jest in good taste and he who
can stand being jested at may be called a man of wit. Such, then, is wit.

31 · Friendliness is a mean state between flattery and unfriendliness, and it   20
has to do with acts and words. For the flatterer is he who adds more than is proper
and true, while the unfriendly man is hostile and detracts from the truth. Neither of
them, then, can rightly be praised, but the friendly man is between the two. For he
will not add more than the facts, nor praise what is not proper, nor on the other hand   25
will he represent things as less than they are, nor oppose in all cases contrary to what
he thinks. Such, then, is the friendly man.

32 · Truthfulness is a mean between self-depreciation and boastfulness. It
has to do with words, but not with all words. For the boaster is he who pretends to
have more than he has, or to know what he does not know; while the self-   30
depreciator, on the other hand, lays claim to less than he really has and does not
declare what he knows, but tries to hide his knowledge. But the truthful man will do
neither of these things. For he will not pretend either to more than he has or less, but
will say that he has and knows what as a matter of fact he does have and does   35
know.
Whether, then, these are excellences or not is another question. But that they

are means of the above-mentioned states is plain. For those who live according to them are praised.

33 · It remains to speak about justice—what it is, in what, and about what. First, then, if we could fix upon what justice is. Justice is twofold, of which one kind is legal justice. For people say that what the law commands is just. Now the law commands us to act bravely and temperately, and generally to perform the actions which come under the head of the excellences. For which reason also, they say, justice appears to be a kind of complete excellence. For if the things which the law commands us to do are just, and the law ordains what is in accordance with all excellences, it follows that he who abides by legal justice will be completely good, so that the just man and justice are a kind of complete excellence.

The just, then, in one sense is in these things and about these things. But it is not the just in this sense, nor the justice which deals with these things, of which we are in search. For in respect of just conduct of this sort it is possible to be just when one is alone (for the temperate and the brave and the self-controlled is each of them so when alone). But what is just towards one's neighbour is different from the legal justice that has been spoken of. For in things just towards one's neighbour it is not possible to be just when alone. But it is the just in this sense of which we are in search, and the justice which has to do with these things.

The just, then, in relation to one's neighbour is, speaking generally, the equal. For the unjust is the unequal. For when people assign more of the goods to themselves and less of the evils, this is unequal, and in that case they think that injustice is done and suffered. It is evident, therefore, that since injustice implies unequal things, justice and the just will consist in an equality of contracts. So that it is evident that justice will be a mean between excess and defect, between too much and too little. For the unjust man by doing wrong has more, and his victim by being wronged has less; but the mean between these is just. And the mean is equal. So that the equal between more and less will be just, and he will be just who wishes to have what is equal. But the equal implies two things at least. To be equal therefore in relation to one's neighbour is just, and a man of this sort will be just.

Since, then, justice consists in just and equal dealing and in a mean, we must notice that the just is said to be just as between certain persons, and the equal is a relation between certain persons, and the mean is a mean for certain persons; so that justice and the just will have relation to certain persons and be between certain persons.

Since, then, the just is equal, the proportionally equal will be just. Now proportion implies four terms at least; for as A is to B, C is to D. For instance, it is proportional that he who has much should contribute much, and that he who has little should contribute little; again, in the same way, that he who has worked much should receive much, and that he who has worked little should receive little. But as the man who has worked is to the man who has not worked, so is the much to the little; and as the man who has worked is to the much, so is the man who has not worked to the little. Plato also seems to employ proportional justice in his *Republic*.

For the farmer, he says, produces food, and the housebuilder a house, and the weaver a cloak, and the shoemaker a shoe. Now the farmer gives the housebuilder food, and the housebuilder gives the farmer a house; and in the same way all the rest 10 exchange their products for those of others. And this is the proportion. As the farmer is to the housebuilder, so is the housebuilder to the farmer. In the same way with the shoemaker, the weaver, and all the rest, the same proportion holds towards 15 one another. And this proportion holds the republic together. So that the just seems to be the proportional. For the just holds republics together, and the just is the same thing as the proportional.

But since the work which the housebuilder produces is of more value than that of the shoemaker, and the shoemaker had to exchange his work with the 20 housebuilder, but it was not possible to get a house for shoes; under these circumstances they had recourse to using something for which all these things are purchasable, to wit silver, which they called money, and to effecting their mutual exchanges by each paying the worth of each product, and thereby holding the political communion together. 25

Since, then, the just is in those things and in what was mentioned before, the justice which is concerned with these things will be an habitual impulse attended with choice about and in these things.

Reciprocation also is just; not, however, as the Pythagoreans maintained. For they thought that it was just that a man should suffer in return what he had done. 30 But this cannot be the case in relation to all persons. For the same thing is not just for a servant as for a freeman. For if the servant has struck the freeman, it is not just that he should merely be struck in return, but many times. And reciprocal justice, also consists in proportion. For as the freeman is to the slave in being 35 superior, so is retaliation to aggression. It will be the same with one freeman in relation to another. For it is not just, if a man has knocked out somebody's eye, merely that he should have his own knocked out, but that he should suffer more, if he is to observe the proportion. For he was the first to begin and did a wrong, and is in the wrong in both ways, so that the acts of injustice are proportional, and for him 1194^b1 to suffer more than he did is just.

But since the term 'just' is used in more senses than one, we must determine what kind of justice it is about which our inquiry is.

There is, then, a sort of justice, as they say, for a servant as against his master, 5 and a son as against his father. But the just in these cases would seem to be homonymous with political justice (for the justice about which we are inquiring is political justice); for this above all consists in equality (for citizens are a sort of partners, and tend to be on a par by nature, though they differ in character), but a 10 son against his father or a servant against his master would not seem to have any justice at all, any more than my foot or my hand has any justice against me, and in the same way with each of the members. The same, then, would seem to be the case with the son as against his father. For the son is, as it were, a part of his father, except when he has already attained to the position of a man and has been separated 15 from him; then he is the equal and peer of his father. Now citizens are supposed to

be on that footing. And in the same way neither has a servant any justice as against
his master for the same reason. For the servant is a part of his master. Or if he has
20 any justice against him, it is in the way of economic justice. But this is not what we
are in search of, but political justice; for political justice seems to lie in equality and
similarity. Though, indeed, the justice that there is in the partnership between wife
and husband comes near to political justice. For the wife is inferior to the husband,
25 but more intimately connected with him, and partakes in a way more of equality,
because their life is an approximation to political society, so that justice between
man and wife is more than any other like that between citizens. Since, then, the just
is that which is found in political society, justice also and the just man will be
concerned with the politically just.
30 Things are just either by nature or by law. But we must not regard the natural
as being something which cannot by any possibility change; for even the things
which are by nature partake of change. I mean, for instance, if we were all to
practice always throwing with the left hand, we should become ambidextrous. But
35 still by nature left is left, and the right is none the less naturally superior to the left
hand, even if we do everything with the left as we do with the right. Nor because
things change does it follow that they are not by nature. But if for the most part and
for the greater length of time the left continues thus to be left and the right right,
1195ᵃ1 this is by nature. The same is the case with things just by nature. Do not suppose
that, if things change owing to our use, there is not therefore a natural justice;
because there is. For that which continues for the most part can plainly be seen to be
naturally just. As to what we establish for ourselves and practise, that is thereby
5 just, and we call it just according to law. Natural justice, then, is better than legal.
But what we are in search of is political justice. Now the politically just is the legal,
not the natural.
The unjust and the unjust act might seem to be the same, but they are not. For
10 the unjust is that which is determined by law; for instance, it is unjust to steal a
deposit, but the unjust act is the actual doing of something unjustly. And in the
same way the just is not the same as a just act. For the just is what is determined by
law, but a just act is the doing of just deeds.
When, therefore, have we the just, and when not? Generally speaking, when
15 one acts in accordance with choice and voluntarily (what was meant by the
voluntary has been stated by us above), and when one does so knowing the person,
the means, and the end, those are the conditions of a just act. In the very same way
the unjust man will be he who knows the person, the means, and the end. But when
without knowing any of these things one has done something that is unjust, one is
20 not unjust oneself, but unfortunate. For if a man has slain his father under the idea
that he was slaying an enemy, though he has done something that is unjust, still he
is not doing injustice to anybody, but is unfortunate.
The possibility, then, of not committing injustice when one does things that are
unjust lies in being ignorant of what was mentioned a little above, viz. when one
does not know whom one is hurting, nor with what, nor to what end. But we must
25 now define the ignorance, and say how the ignorance must arise if a man is not to be
doing an injustice to the person whom he hurts. Let this, then, be the definition.

When the ignorance is the cause of his doing something, he does not do this voluntarily, so that he does not commit injustice; but when he is himself the cause of his ignorance and does something in accordance with the ignorance of which he is himself the cause, then he is guilty of injustice, and such a person will justly be 30 called unjust. Take for instance people who are drunk. Those who are drunk and have done something bad commit injustice. For they are themselves the causes of their ignorance. For they need not have drunk so much as not to know that they were beating their father. Similarly with the other sorts of ignorance which are due to men themselves, the people who commit injustice from them are unjust. But 35 where they are not themselves the causes, but their ignorance is the cause of their doing what they do, they are not unjust. This sort of ignorance is that which comes from nature; for instance, children strike their parents in ignorance, but the 1195ᵇ1 ignorance which is in them, being due to nature, does not make the children be called unjust owing to this conduct. For it is ignorance which is the cause of their behaving thus, and they are not themselves causes of their ignorance, for which reason they are not called unjust either.

But how about being injured? Can a man be injured voluntarily? Surely not. 5 We do indeed voluntarily perform just and unjust acts, but we cannot be said to be injured voluntarily. For we avoid being punished, so that it is evident that we would not voluntarily let ourselves be injured. For no one voluntarily endures to be hurt. Now to be injured is to be hurt.

Yes, but there are some who, when they ought to have an equal share, give way 10 to others, so that if, as we have seen, to have the equal is just, and to have less is to be injured, and a man voluntarily has less, it follows, it is maintained, that he is injured voluntarily. But from the following consideration it is evident, on the other hand, that this is not so. For all who accept less get compensation for it in the way of honour, or praise, or glory, or friendship, or something of that sort. But he who takes 15 compensation of some kind for what he forgoes cannot be said to be injured; and if he is not injured, then he is not injured voluntarily.

Yet again, those who get less and are injured in so far as they do not get what is equal, pride and plume themselves on such things, for they say, 'Though I might have had my share, I did not take it, but gave way to an elder' or 'to a friend'. But no 20 one prides himself on being injured. But if they do not pride themselves upon suffering acts of injustice and do pride themselves upon such things, it follows generally that they will not be injured by thus getting less. And if they are not injured, then they will not be injured voluntarily.

But as against these and the like arguments[16] we have a counter-argument in 25 the case of the incontinent man. For the incontinent man hurts himself by doing bad acts, and these acts he does voluntarily; he therefore hurts himself knowingly, so that he is voluntarily injured by himself. But here if we add a distinction, it will impede the force of the argument. And the distinction is this, that no one wishes to 30 be injured. The incontinent man does with his own wish what is prompted by his incontinence, so that he injures himself; he therefore wishes to do to himself what is

---

[16]Reading τοὺς τοιούτους λόγους.

bad. But no one wishes to be injured, so that even the incontinent man will not voluntarily be doing an injury to himself.

35 But here again one might perhaps raise a difficulty. Is it possible for a man to be unjust to himself? Judging from the incontinent man it would seem possible. 1196ª1 And, again, in this way. If it is just to do those things which the law ordains to be done, he who does not do these is committing injustice; and if when he does not do them to him to whom the law commands, he is doing an injustice to that person, but the law commands one to be temperate, to possess property, to take care of one's body, and all other such things, then he who does not do these things is doing an 5 injustice to himself. For it is not possible to refer such acts of injustice to anyone else.

But these statements can hardly be true, nor is it possible for a man to be unjust to himself. For it is not possible for the same man at the same time to have more and less, nor at once to act voluntarily and involuntarily. But yet he who does 10 injustice, in so far as he does it, has more, and he who suffers it, in so far as he suffers it, has less. If therefore a man does injustice to himself, it is possible for the same man at the same time to have more and less. But this is impossible. It is not therefore possible for a man to be unjust to himself.

Again, he who does injustice does it voluntarily, and he who suffers it suffers it involuntarily, so that, if it is possible for a man to be unjust to himself, it would be 15 possible at the same time to do something involuntarily and voluntarily. But this is impossible. So in this way also it is not possible for a man to be unjust to himself.

Again, one might look at the question from the point of view of particular acts of injustice. Whenever men commit injustice, it is either by stealing a deposit, or 20 committing adultery, or thieving, or doing some other particular act of injustice; but no one ever robbed himself of a deposit, or committed adultery with his own wife, or stole his own property; so that if the commission of injustice lies in such things, and it is not possible to do any of them to oneself, it will not be possible to commit injustice against oneself.

25 Or if so, it will not be an act of injustice of the political, but rather of the economic type. For the soul being divided into several parts has in itself a better and a worse, so that if there is any act of injustice within the soul, it will be done by the parts against one another. Now we distinguished the economic act of injustice by its 30 being directed against the better or worse, so that in this sense a man may be unjust or just to himself. But this is not what we are investigating, but the political act of injustice. So that in such acts of injustice as form the subject of our inquiry, it is not possible for a man to commit injustice against himself.

Which of the two, again, commits injustice, and with which of the two does the 35 act of injustice lie, when a man has anything unjustly? Is it not with him who has judged and made the award, as in the games? For he who takes the palm from the president who has adjudged it to him is not committing injustice, even if it be wrongly awarded to him; but without doubt it is he who has judged badly and given 1196ᵇ1 it who commits injustice. And he is in a way committing injustice, while in a way he is not. For in that he has not judged what is really and naturally just, he is committing an injustice, while in that he has judged what appears to him to be just, he is not committing an injustice.

34 · Now since we have spoken about the excellences in general, saying what they are and in what and about what, and about each of them in particular, how we must do the best in accordance with right reason, to say no more than this, namely, 'to act in accordance with right reason', would be much the same as if one were to say that health would be best secured if one were to adopt the means of health. Such a statement is unilluminating. I shall have it said to me, 'Explain what are the means of health'. So also in the case of reason, 'What is reason and which is right reason?'

Perhaps it is necessary first of all to make a division of that in which reason is found. A distinction, indeed, was made in outline about soul before, how one part of it is possessed of reason, while there is another part of the soul that is irrational. But the part of the soul which is possessed of reason has two divisions, of which one is the deliberative faculty, the other the faculty by which we know. That they are different from one another will be evident from their subject-matter. For as colour and flavour and sound and smell are different from one another, so also nature has rendered the senses whereby we perceive them different (for sound we recognize by hearing, flavour by taste, and colour by sight), and in like manner we must suppose it to be the same with all other things. When, then, the subject-matters are different, we must suppose that the parts of the soul whereby we recognize these are also different. Now there is a difference between the object of thought and the object of sense; and these we recognize by soul. The part of the soul, therefore, which is concerned with objects of sense will be different from that which is concerned with objects of thought. But the faculty of deliberation and choice has to do with objects of sense that are liable to change, and generally all that is subject to generation and destruction. For we deliberate about those things which depend upon us and our choice to do or not to do, about which there is deliberation and choice as to whether to do them or not. And these are sensible objects which are in process of change. So that the part of the soul in which choice resides will correspond to sensible objects.

These points having been settled, we must go on as follows. The question is one of truth, and the subject of our inquiry is how the truth stands, and we have to do with knowledge, wisdom, intuition, philosophy, belief. What, then, is the object of each of these?

Now knowledge deals with the object of knowledge, and this through a process accompanied with demonstration and reason, but wisdom with matters of action, in which there is choice and avoidance, and it is in our power to do or not to do.

When things are made and done, that which makes and that which does them are not the same. For the arts of making have some other end beyond the making; for instance, beyond housebuilding, since that is the art of making a house, there is a house as its end beyond the making, and similarly in the case of carpentry and the

other arts of making; but in the processes of doing there is no other end beyond the
10   doing; for instance, beyond playing the harp there is no other end, but just this is the
end, the activity and the doing. Wisdom, then, is concerned with doing and things
done, but art with making and things made; for it is in things made rather than in
things done that artistic contrivance is displayed.

So that wisdom will be a state of choosing and doing things which it is in our
15   own power to do or not to do, so far as they are of actual importance to welfare.
Wisdom is an excellence, it would seem, not a science. For the wise are praiseworthy, and praise is bestowed on excellence. Again, every science has its excellence,
but wisdom has no excellence, but, as it seems, is itself an excellence.

20   Intuition has to do with the first principles of things intelligible and real. For
knowledge has to do with things that admit of demonstration, but the principles are
indemonstrable, so that it will not be knowledge but intuition that is concerned with
the principles.

Philosophy is compounded of knowledge and intuition. For philosophy has to
25   do both with the principles and with what can be proved from the principles, with
which knowledge deals. In so far, then, as it deals with the principles, it itself
partakes of intuition, but in so far as it deals with demonstrative conclusions from
the principles, it partakes of knowledge. So that it is evident that philosophy is
compounded of intuition and knowledge, so that it will deal with the same things
with which intuition and knowledge do.

30   Belief is that whereby we are left in doubt about all things as to whether they
are in a particular way or not.

Are wisdom and philosophy the same thing? Surely not! For philosophy has to
do with things that can be demonstrated and are eternally the same, but wisdom has
35   not to do with these, but with things that undergo change. I mean, for instance,
straight or crooked or convex and the like are always what they are, but things
expedient do not follow this analogy, so as never to change into anything else; they
do change, and a given thing is expedient now, but not to-morrow, to this man but
1197ᵇ1   not to that, and is expedient in this way, but not in that way. Now wisdom has to do
with things expedient, but philosophy not. Therefore philosophy and wisdom are not
the same.

Is philosophy an excellence or not? It can become plain to us that it is an
5   excellence by merely looking at wisdom. For if wisdom is, as we maintain, the
excellence of one of the two rational parts, and wisdom is inferior to philosophy (for
its objects are inferior; for philosophy has to do with the eternal and the divine, as
we maintain, but wisdom with what is expedient for man), if, then, the inferior thing
is an excellence, it is reasonable that the better should be an excellence, so that it is
10   evident that philosophy is an excellence.

What is intelligence, and with what is it concerned? The sphere of intelligence
is the same as that of wisdom, having to do with matters of action. For the
intelligent man is doubtless so called from his capacity for deliberation, and in that
he judges and sees a thing rightly. But his judgement is about small things and on
15   small occasions. Intelligence, then, and the intelligent man are a part of wisdom and

the wise man, and cannot be found apart from these; for you cannot separate the intelligent from the wise man.

The case would seem to be the same with cleverness. For cleverness and the clever man are not wisdom and the wise man; the wise man, however, is clever, 20 hence cleverness co-operates in a way with wisdom. But the bad man also is called clever; for instance, Mentor was thought to be clever, but he was not wise. For it is the part of the wise man and of wisdom to aim at the best things, and always to choose and do these, but it is the part of cleverness and the clever man to consider by 25 what means each object of action may be effected, and to provide these. Such, then, would seem to be the province and sphere of the clever man.

It may raise a question and cause surprise that, when speaking of character and dealing with a department of state-craft, we are speaking about philosophy. Perhaps the reason is, firstly, that the inquiry about it will not appear foreign to our 30 subject, if it is an excellence, as we maintain. Again, it is perhaps the part of the philosopher to glance also at subjects adjacent to his main interest. And it is necessary, when we are speaking about the contents of soul, to speak about them all; now philosophy is also in soul; so that we are not going beyond our proper subject in 35 speaking about soul.[17]

But as cleverness is to wisdom, so it would seem to be in the case of all the excellences. What I mean is that there are excellences which spring up even by nature in different persons, a sort of impulses in the individual, apart from reason, to courageous and just conduct and the like behaviour; and there are also 1198ª1 excellences due to custom and choice. But the excellences that are accompanied with reason, when they supervene, are completely praiseworthy.

Now this natural excellence which is unaccompanied by reason, so long as it remains apart from reason, is of little account, and falls short of being praised, but 5 when added to reason and choice, it makes complete excellence. Hence also the natural impulse to excellence co-operates with reason and is not apart from reason. Nor, on the other hand, are reason and choice quite completed as excellence without the natural impulse.

Hence Socrates was not speaking correctly when he said that excellence was 10 reason, thinking that it was no use doing brave and just acts, unless one did them from knowledge and rational choice. This was why he said that excellence was reason. Herein he was not right, but the men of the present day say better; for they say that excellence is doing what is good in accordance with right reason. Even they, indeed, are not right. For one might do what is just without any choice at all or 15 knowledge of the good, but from an irrational impulse, and yet do this rightly and in accordance with right reason (I mean he may have acted in the way that right reason would command); but all the same, this sort of conduct does not merit praise. But it is better to say, according to our definition , that it is the accompaniment by 20 reason of the impulse to good. For that is excellence and that is praiseworthy.

The question might be raised whether wisdom is an excellence or not. It will be

---

[17]Text uncertain.

evident, however, from the following consideration that it is an excellence. For if justice and courage and the rest of the excellences, because they lead to the doing of
25 right, are also praiseworthy, it is evident that wisdom will also be among the things that are praiseworthy and that rank as excellences. For wisdom also has an impulse towards those acts which courage has an impulse to do. For, speaking generally,
30 courage acts as wisdom ordains, so that if it is itself praiseworthy for doing what wisdom ordains, wisdom will be in a complete degree both praiseworthy and an excellence.

But whether wisdom is practical or not one might see from this, namely, by looking at the sciences, for instance at housebuilding. For there is, as we say, in
35 housebuilding one person who is called an architect, and another, who is subordinate to him, a housebuilder; and he is capable of making a house. But the architect also, inasmuch as he made the house, is capable of making a house. And the case is the same in all the other productive arts, in which there is a
1198ᵇ1 master-craftsman and his subordinate. The master-craftsman therefore also will be capable of making something, and that the same thing which his subordinate is capable of making. If, then, the analogy holds in the case of the excellences, as is likely and reasonable, wisdom also will be practical. For all the excellences are
5 practical, and wisdom is a kind of master-craftsman of them. For as it shall ordain, so the excellences and good men act. Since then the excellences are practical, wisdom also will be practical.

But does this hold sway over all things in the soul, as is held and also
10 questioned? Surely not! For it would not seem to do so over what is superior to itself; for instance, it does not hold sway over philosophy. But, it is said, this has charge of all, and is supreme in issuing commands. But perhaps it holds the same position as the steward in the household. For he is supreme over all and manages everything. But it does not follow that he holds sway over all; instead of that he is procuring
15 leisure for the master, in order that he may not be hindered by necessary cares and so shut out from doing something that is noble and befitting. So and in like manner with him wisdom is, as it were, a kind of steward of philosophy, and is procuring leisure for it and for the doing of its work, by subduing the passions and keeping
20 them in order.

BOOK II

25 1 · After this we must inquire into equity. What is it? And what is its field and sphere? Equity and the equitable man is he who is inclined to take less than his legal rights. There are matters in which it is impossible for the lawgiver to enter into exact details in defining, and where he has to content himself with a general statement. When, then, a man gives way in these matters, and chooses those things
30 which the lawgiver would have wished indeed to determine in detail, but was not able to, such a man is equitable. It is not the way with him to take less than what is

just absolutely; for he does not fall short of what is naturally and really just, but only of what is legally just in matters which the law left undetermined for want of power.

2 · Considerateness and the considerate man have to do with the same things as equity, with points of justice that have been omitted by the lawgiver owing to the 35 inexactness of his definitions. The considerate man criticizes the omissions of the lawgiver, and knows that, though things have been omitted by the lawgiver, they are nevertheless just. Such is the considerate man. Now considerateness is not found 1199ᵃ1 apart from equity. To the considerate man it belongs to judge, and to the equitable man to act in accordance with the judgement.

3 · Good counsel is concerned with the same things as wisdom (dealing with matters of action which concern choice and avoidance), and it is not found apart 5 from wisdom. For wisdom leads to the doing of these things, while good counsel is a state or disposition or something of that sort, which leads to the attainment of the best and most expedient in matters of action. Hence things that turn out right spontaneously do not seem to form the subject of good counsel. For where there is no 10 reason which is on the look-out for what is best, you would not in that case say that a man to whom something turned out as it should be was well counselled, but lucky. For things that go right without the judgement of reason are due to good luck.

Is it in the part of the just man to put himself on a level with everybody in his intercourse (I mean in the way of becoming all things to all men)? Surely not. For 15 this would seem to be the part of a flatterer and obsequious person. But to suit his intercourse to the worth of each, this would seem to be the part of the man who is absolutely just and good.

Here is also a difficulty that might be raised. If doing injustice is hurting somebody voluntarily and with full knowledge of the person and the manner and the 20 end, and harm and injustice are in and concerned with good things, it follows that the doer of injustice and the unjust man will know what kind of things are good and what bad. But to know about these things is a peculiar property of the wise man and of wisdom. The absurdity then follows that wisdom, which is the greatest good, is 25 attendant upon the unjust man. Surely it will not be thought that wisdom is attendant upon the unjust man. For the unjust man does not discern and is not able to judge between what is good in itself and what is good for him, but makes a mistake. But this is the province of wisdom, to be able to take a right view of these 30 things (just as in matters of medicine we all know what is absolutely wholesome and what is productive of health, that hellebore and an aperient and surgery and cautery are wholesome and productive of health, and yet we do not possess the science of medicine), for without it we no longer know what is good in particular cases, just as 35 the doctor knows for whom a given thing is good and when and in what disposition; for herein the science of medicine displays itself. Now we may know things that are absolutely wholesome, and yet not have the science of medicine attendant upon us; and the same is the case with the unjust man. That in an absolute sense autocracy 1199ᵇ1 and government and power are good, he knows; but whether they are good for him or not, or when, or in what condition, that is what he does not also know. But this is just the business of wisdom, so that wisdom does not attend upon the unjust man. For the goods which he chooses and for which he commits injustice are what are absolutely good, not what are good for him. For wealth and office are good absolutely, but for him perhaps they are not good; for by obtaining wealth and office he will do much evil to himself and his friends, for he will not be able to make a right use of office.

Here also is a point which presents a difficulty and suggest inquiry. Can justice be done to a bad man or not? For if injustice consists in hurt, and hurt in the deprivation of goods, it would seem not to hurt him. For the goods which he supposes to be good for him are not really so. For office and wealth will hurt the bad man who is not able to make a right use of them. If then they will hurt him by their presence, he who deprives him of these would seem to be doing him an injustice. This kind of argument indeed will appear a paradox to the many. For all think that they are able to use office and power and wealth, but they are not right in this supposition. This is made plain by the lawgiver. For the lawgiver does not allow all to hold office, but there is a standard of age and means which must be possessed by him who is to hold office, implying that it is not possible for every one to do so. If then some one were to make it a grievance that he does not hold office or that he is not allowed to steer the ship. the answer would be, 'Well, you have nothing in your soul of a kind which will enable you to hold office or steer the ship'. In the case of the body we see that those cannot be in good health who apply to themselves things that are absolutely good, but if a man is to have his bad body in health, he must first apply to it water and a low diet. And when a man has his soul in a vicious state, in order that he may not work any ill must we not withhold him from wealth and office and power and things of that sort generally, the more so as soul is easier to move and more ready to change than body? For as the man whose body was bad was fit to be dieted in that way, so the man whose soul is bad is fit to live thus, without having any things of this sort.

This also presents a difficulty. For instance, when it is not possible at the same time to do brave and just acts, which is one to do? Now in the case of the natural excellences we said that there existed only the impulse to right without reason; but he who has choice has it in reason and the rational part. So that as soon as choice is present, complete excellence will be there, which we said was accompanied by wisdom, but not without the natural impulse to right. Nor will one excellence run counter to another, for its nature is to obey the dictates of reason, so that it inclines to that to which reason leads. For it is this which chooses the better. For the other excellences do not come into existence without wisdom, nor is wisdom complete without the other excellences, but they co-operate in a way with one another, attending upon wisdom.

No less will the following present itself as a difficulty. Is it in the case of the excellences as it is in the case of the other goods, whether external or bodily? For these when they run to excess make men worse; for instance, when wealth becomes great it makes men supercilious and disagreeable. And so also with the other goods—office, honour, beauty, stature. Is it, then, thus in the case of excellence also, so that, if one comes to have justice or courage to excess, he will be worse? Surely not! But, it will be said, from excellence comes honour, and when honour becomes great, it makes men worse, so that it is evident that excellence when progressing to a great extent will make men worse. For excellence is the cause of honour, so that excellence also, if it becomes great, will make men worse. Surely this cannot be true! For excellence, though it may have many other functions, as it has, has this among the most special, to be able to make a right use of these and the like goods when they are there. If therefore the good man on there coming to him high honour or high office shall not make a right use of these, it shows that he is not a good man. Therefore neither honour nor office will make the good man worse, so that neither will excellence. But generally, since it was laid down by us at the start that the excellences are mean states, it follows that the more any state is an excellence, the more it is a mean; so that not only will excellence as it becomes great not make a man worse, but it will make him better. For the mean in question was found to be the mean between excess and defect in the passions. So much then for these matters.

4 · After this we must make a new start and speak about self-control and incontinence. But as the excellence and the vice are themselves of a strange nature, so the discussion which will ensue about them must necessarily be strange also. For this excellence is not like the rest. For in the rest reason and passion have an impulse towards the same objects and are not opposed to one another, but in the case of this reason and passion are opposed to one another.

There are three things in the soul in respect of which we are called bad—vice, incontinence, brutality. About excellence and vice, then, their nature and their sphere, we have spoken above; but now we must speak about incontinence and brutality.

5 · Brutality is a kind of excessive vice. For when we see some one utterly degraded, we say that he is not even a man but a brute, implying that there is a vice of brutality. Now the excellence opposed to this is without a name, but this sort of thing is above man, a kind of heroic and divine excellence. But this excellence is without a name, because excellence does not belong to god. For god is superior to excellence and it is not in the way of excellence that his goodness lies. For, if it were, excellence would be better than god. For this reason the excellence which is opposed to the vice of brutality is without a name. But the usual antithesis to this kind of vice is divine and superhuman excellence. For as the vice of brutality transcends man, so also does the excellence opposed to it.

6 · But with regard to incontinence and self-control we must first state the difficulties and the arguments which run counter to appearances, in order that, having viewed the matter together from the point of view of the difficulties and

counter-arguments, and having examined these, we may see the truth about them so far as possible; for it will be more easy to see the truth in that way.

25 Now Socrates the elder used to reject and deny incontinence altogether, saying that no one would choose evil who knew it to be such. But the incontinent seems, while knowing things to be bad, to choose them all the same, letting himself be led by passion. Owing to such considerations he did not think that there was 30 incontinence. But there he was wrong. For it is absurd that conviction of the truth of this argument should lead to the rejection of what credibly occurs. For men do display incontinence, and do things which they themselves know to be bad.

Since, then, there is such a thing as incontinence, does the incontinent possess some knowledge whereby he views and examines his bad acts? But, again, this 35 would not seem so. For it would be strange that the strongest and surest thing in us should be vanquished by anything. For knowledge is of all things in us the most permanent and the most constraining. So that this argument again runs counter to there being knowledge.[18]

Is it then not knowledge, but opinion? But if the incontinent man has opinion, 1201ᵃ1 he will not be blameworthy. For if he does something bad with respect to which he has no exact knowledge but only an opinion, one would make allowances for his siding with pleasure and doing what is bad, if he does not know for certain that it is bad, but only has an opinion; and those for whom we make allowances we do not 5 blame. So that the incontinent, if he only has opinion, will not be to blame. But he is to blame. Such arguments then land us in difficulties. For some denied knowledge on the ground of absurd consequences, and others again denied opinion on the ground that there were absurd consequences from that also.

10 Here is another difficulty that might be raised. It is held that the temperate man is also self-controlled. Will this involve the temperate man's having vehement appetites? If then he is to be self-controlled, it will be necessary for him to have vehement appetites (for you would not speak of a man as self-controlled who masters moderate appetites); but if he is to have vehement appetites, in that case he 15 will not be temperate (for the temperate is he who does not display appetite or feeling at all).

The following considerations again present a difficulty. For it results from the statements that the incontinent man is sometimes praiseworthy and the self-controlled man blameworthy. For let it be supposed, it may be said, that some one has gone wrong in his reasoning, and let it appear to him as the result of his 20 reasoning that which is right is wrong, but let appetite lead him to the right; then reason indeed will forbid his doing it, but being led by appetite he does it (for such we found was the incontinent man); he will therefore do what is right, supposing that appetite leads him thereto (but reason will try to hinder him; for let it be 25 supposed that he is mistaken in his reasoning about right); it follows that he will be incontinent and yet be praiseworthy; for in so far as he does what is right, he is praiseworthy. The result then is a paradox.

---

[18]Retaining ἐναντιοῦται τῷ μὴ εἶναι.

Again, on the other hand, let his reason be mistaken, and let what is right not seem to him to be so, but let appetite lead him to the right. Now he is self-controlled who, though he has an appetite for a thing, yet does not act upon it owing to reason; therefore if his reason is wrong it will hinder him from doing what he has an appetite for;[19] therefore it hinders him from doing what is right (for to that we supposed that his appetite led him); but he who fails to do what is right, when it is his duty to do it, is blameworthy; therefore the man of self-control will sometimes be blameworthy. In this way then also the result is a paradox.

A difficulty might also be raised as to whether incontinence and the incontinent man display themselves in and about everything, for instance, property and honour and anger and glory (for people seem to be incontinent with regard to all these things), or whether they do not, but incontinence has a certain definite sphere.

The above, then, are the points which present a difficulty; but it is necessary to solve these difficulties. First, then, that which is connected with knowledge. For it appeared to be an absurdity that one who possessed knowledge should cast it from him or fall away from it. But the same reasoning applies also to opinion; for it makes no difference whether it is opinion or knowledge. For if opinion is intensely firm and unalterable by persuasion, it will not differ from knowledge, opinion carrying with it the belief that things are as he opines them to be; for instance, Heraclitus of Ephesus has this sort of opinion about his own opinions.

But there is no paradox in the incontinent man's doing something bad, whether he has knowledge or opinion such as we describe. For there are two ways of knowing, one of which is the possessing knowledge (for we say that one knows when he possesses knowledge), the other is putting the knowledge into operation. He then who possesses the knowledge of right, but does not operate with it, is incontinent. When, then, he does not operate with this knowledge, it is nothing surprising that he should do what is bad, though he possesses the knowledge. For the case is the same as that of sleepers. For they, though they possess the knowledge, nevertheless in their sleep both do and suffer many disgusting things. For the knowledge is not operative in them. So it is in the case of the incontinent. For he seems like one asleep and does not operate with his knowledge. Thus, then, is the difficulty solved. For the difficulty was whether the incontinent man expels his knowledge or falls away from it, both of which appear paradoxical.

But, again, the thing may be made manifest in this way: as we said in the *Analytics* deduction depends on two propositions, and of these the first is universal, while the second is subsumed under it and is particular. For instance, I know how to cure any one with a fever, this man has a fever: therefore I know how to cure this man.

Now there are things which I know with the knowledge of the universal, but not with that of the particular. Here then also mistake becomes possible to the man who possesses the knowledge: for instance I know how to cure any one with a fever, but I do not know if this man has a fever. Similarly then in the case of the

---

[19]Text uncertain.

incontinent man who possesses the knowledge the same mistake will arise. For it is
35 possible for the incontinent man to possess the knowledge of the universal, that such
and such things are bad and hurtful, but yet not to know that these particular things
are bad, so that while possessing knowledge in this way he will go wrong; for he has
the universal knowledge, but not the particular. Neither, then, in this way is it at all
1202ᵃ1 a surprising result in the case of the incontinent man, that he who has the knowledge
should do something bad.

For it is so in the case of persons who are drunk. For those who are drunk, when
the intoxication has passed off, are themselves again. Reason was not expelled from
them, nor was knowledge, but it was overcome by the intoxication; and when they
5 have got rid of the intoxication, they are themselves again. So, then, it is with the
incontinent. His passion gains the mastery and brings his reasoning to a standstill.
But when the passion, like the intoxication, has been got rid of, he is himself again.

There was another argument touching incontinence which presented a difficulty as seeming to show that the incontinent man will sometimes be praiseworthy,
10 and the self-controlled man blameworthy. But this is not the case. For the man who
is deceived in his reason is neither continent nor incontinent, but only he who
possesses right reason and thereby judges of right and wrong, and it is the man who
disobeys this kind of reason who is incontinent, while he who obeys it and is not led
15 by his appetites is self-controlled. If a man does not think it disgraceful to strike his
father and has a desire to strike him, but abstains from doing so, he is not a man of
self-control. So that, since there is neither self-control nor incontinence in such
cases, neither will incontinence be praiseworthy or self-control blameworthy in the
way that was thought.

There are forms of incontinence which are morbid and others which are due to
20 nature. For instance, such as these are morbid. There are some people who pluck
their hairs and nibble them. If one masters this ᵢpleasure, then, he is not
praiseworthy, nor blameworthy if he fails to do so, or not very much. As an instance
of incontinence due to nature we may take the story of a son who was brought to
trial in court for beating his father, and who defended himself by saying, 'Why, he
25 did so to his own father'—and he was acquitted, for the judges thought that his
going wrong was due to nature. If, then, one were to master the impulse to beat his
father, he is not praiseworthy. It is not, then, such forms of incontinence or
continence as these of which we are now in search, but those for which we are called
blameworthy or praiseworthy without qualification.

30 Of goods some are external, as wealth, office, honour, friends, glory; others
necessary and concerned with the body, for instance, touch and taste, and bodily
pleasures.[20] He, then, who is incontinent with respect to these, would appear to be
incontinent without qualification. And the incontinence of which we are in search
would seem to be concerned with just these. And the difficulty was about the sphere
35 of incontinence. As regards honour, then, a man is not incontinent without
qualification; for he who is incontinent with regard to honour is praised in a way, as

---

[20]Transposing καὶ ἡδοναὶ σωματικαί to follow γεῦσις.

being ambitious. And generally when we call a man incontinent in the case of such things we do it with some addition, incontinent 'as regards honour or glory or anger'. But when a man is incontinent without qualification, we do not add the sphere, it being assumed in his case, and being manifest without the addition, what the sphere is. For he who is incontinent without qualification has to do with the pleasures and pains of the body.

1202ᵇ1

It is evident also from the following consideration that incontinence has to do with these things. For since the incontinent man is blameworthy, the subject-matter of his incontinence ought also to be blameworthy. Now honour and glory and office and riches, and the other things with respect to which people are called incontinent, are not blameworthy, whereas bodily pleasures are blameworthy. Therefore, reasonably enough, the man who is concerned with these more than he ought is called incontinent in the complete sense.

5

Among the so-called incontinences with respect to other things that which is concerned with anger is the most blameworthy. But which is more blameworthy, this or incontinence with regard to pleasures? Now incontinence with regard to anger resembles servants who are eager to minister to one's needs. For they, when the master says 'Give me', are carried away by their eagerness, and before they hear what they ought to give, give something, and give the wrong thing. For often, when they ought to give a book, they give a pen. Something like this is the case with the man who cannot control his anger. For passion, as soon as it hears the first mention of injury, is impelled to take vengeance, without waiting to hear whether it ought or ought not, or not so vehemently. This sort of impulse, then, to anger, which appears to be incontinence of anger, is not greatly to be blamed, but the impulse to pleasure is blameworthy. For this latter differs from the former owing to the injunction of reason to abstain, which it nevertheless acts against; for which reason it is more blameworthy than incontinence due to anger. For incontinence due to anger is a pain (for no one feels anger without being pained), but that which is due to appetite is attended with pleasure, for which reason it is more blameworthy. For incontinence due to pleasure seems to involve wantonness.

10

15

20

25

Are self-control and endurance the same thing? Surely not! For self-control has to do with pleasures and the man of self-control is he who masters pleasures, but endurance has to do with pains. For the man of endurance is he who endures and undergoes pains. Again, lack of self-control and softness are not the same thing. For softness and the soft person is he who does not undergo pains—not all of them, but such as any one else would undergo, if he had to; whereas the incontinent man is he who is not able to endure pleasures, but succumbs to them and lets himself be led by them.

30

35

Again, there is another character who is called intemperate. Is the intemperate, then, the same as the incontinent? Surely not! For the intemperate is the kind of man who thinks that what he does is best and most expedient for himself, and who has no reason opposing the things which appear pleasant to himself, whereas the incontinent does possess reason which opposes his going in pursuit of those things to which his appetite leads.

1203ᵃ1

5

But which is the more curable, the intemperate or the incontinent? On first sight, indeed, it might seem that it is not the incontinent. The intemperate, it may be urged, is more easy to cure; for if reason could be engendered in him, to teach him that things are bad, he will leave off doing them; but the incontinent man has

10 reason, and yet acts as he does, so that such a person would seem to be incurable. But on the other hand which is in the worse condition, he who has no good at all, or he who has some good joined with these evils? Plainly the former, the more so inasmuch as it is the more valuable part that is in a bad condition. The incontinent man, then, does possess a good in his reason being right, while the intemperate does

15 not. Again, reason is the principle in each. Now in the incontinent the principle, which is the most valuable thing, is in a good condition, but in the intemperate in a bad; so that the intemperate will be worse than the incontinent. Again, like the vice of brutality of which we spoke, you cannot see it in a beast, but only in a human

20 being (for brutality is a name for excessive vice). Why so? Just because a beast has in it no bad principle. Now the principle is reason. For which would do more evil, a lion, or Dionysius or Phalaris or Clearchus, or some of those wicked men? Plainly the latter. For their having in them a bad principle contributes greatly to their

25 powers of mischief, but in the beast there is no principle at all. In the intemperate, then, there is a bad principle. For inasmuch as he does bad acts and reason assents to these, and it seems to him that he ought to do these things, there is in him a principle which is not a sound one. Hence the incontinent would seem to be better than the intemperate.

30 There are two species of incontinence, one in the way of precipitancy and want of forethought, a kind that comes on suddenly (for instance, when we see a beautiful woman, we are at once affected in some way, and from the affection there ensues an impulse to do something which perhaps we ought not), the other a sort of weakness, but attended with reason which warns against action. Now the former would not seem to be very blameworthy. For this kind occurs even in the good, in those who are

1203ᵇ1 of warm temperament and of a rich natural endowment; but the other in the cold and atrabilious, and such are blameworthy. Again, one may avoid being affected by fortifying oneself beforehand with the thought, 'There will come a pretty woman, so one must control oneself'. So that, if he has fortified himself beforehand with a thought of this kind, he whose incontinence is due to the suddenness of the

5 impression will not be affected at all, nor do anything wrong. But he who knows indeed from reason that he ought not, but gives in to pleasure and succumbs to it, is more blameworthy. The good man would never become incontinent in that way, and fortification by reason would be no cure for it. For this is the guide within the man,

10 and yet he does not obey it, but gives in to pleasure, and succumbs with a sort of weakness.

Whether the temperate man is self-controlled was raised as a difficulty above, but now let us speak of it. Yes, the temperate man is also self-controlled. For the man of self-control is not merely he who, when he has appetites in him, represses

15 these owing to reason, but also he who is of such a kind that, though he has not appetites in him, he would repress them, if they did arise. But it is he who has not

bad desires and who has his reason right with respect to these things who is temperate, while the man of self-control is he who has bad desires and who has his reason right with regard to these things; so that self-control will go along with temperance, and the temperate will be self-controlled, but not the self-controlled 20 temperate. For the temperate is he who does not feel passion, while the self-controlled man is he who does feel passion, or is capable of feeling it, but subdues it. But neither of these is actually the case with the temperate. Hence the self-controlled is not temperate.

But is the intemperate incontinent or the incontinent intemperate? Or does neither follow on the other? For the incontinent is he whose reason fights with his 25 passions, but the intemperate is not of this sort, but he who in doing base deeds has the consent of his reason. Neither then is the intemperate like the incontinent nor the incontinent like the intemperate. Further, the intemperate is worse than the incontinent. For what comes by nature is harder to cure than what results from 30 custom (for the reason why custom is held to be so strong is that it turns things into nature). The intemperate, then, is in himself the kind of man who is bad by nature, owing to which, and as a result of which, the reason in him is bad. But not so the incontinent. It is not true of him that his reason is not good because he is himself such (for he would have to be bad, if he were of himself by nature such as the bad). The incontinent, then, seems to be bad by custom, but the intemperate by nature. 1204ª1 Therefore the intemperate is the harder to cure. For one custom is dislodged by another, but nothing will dislodge nature.

But seeing that the incontinent is the kind of man who knows and is not 5 deceived in his reason, while the wise man also is of the same kind, who views everything by right reason, is it possible for the wise man to be incontinent? Surely not! For though one might raise the foregoing difficulties, yet if we keep consistent with our former statements, the wise man will not be incontinent. For we said that the wise man was not merely he in whom right reason exists, but he who also does 10 what appears in accordance with right reason to be best. Now if the wise man does what is best, the wise man will not be incontinent; but an incontinent man may be clever. For we distinguished above between the clever and the wise as being different. For though their spheres are the same, yet the one does what he ought and 15 the other does not. It is possible, then, for the clever man to be incontinent (for he does not succeed in doing what he ought), but it is not possible for the wise man to be incontinent.

7 · After this we must speak about pleasure, since our discussion is on the subject of happiness, and all think that happiness is either pleasure and living 20 pleasantly, or not without pleasure. Even those who feel disgust at pleasure, and do not think that pleasure ought to be reckoned among goods, at least add the absence of pain; now to live without pain borders on pleasure. Therefore we must speak about pleasure, not merely because other people think that we ought, but because it 25 is actually indispensable for us to do so. For since our discussion is about happiness, and we have defined and declare happiness to be an exercise of excellence in a

complete life, and excellence has to do with pleasure and pain, it is indispensable to
30 speak about pleasure, since happiness is not apart from pleasure.

First, then, let us mention the reasons which some people give for thinking that one ought not to regard pleasure as part of good. First, they say that pleasure is a becoming, and that a becoming is something incomplete, but that the good never
35 occupies the place of the incomplete. Secondly, that there are some bad pleasures, whereas the good is never to be found in badness. Again, that it is found in all, both in the bad man and in the good, and in beasts wild and tame; but the good is unmixed
1204ᵇ1 with the bad and not promiscuous. And that pleasure is not the best thing, whereas the good is the best thing. And that it is an impediment to right action, and what tends to impede right cannot be good.

First, then, we must address ourselves to the first argument, that about
5 becoming, and must endeavour to dispose of this on the ground of its not being true. For, to begin with, not every pleasure is a becoming. For the pleasure which results from thought is not a becoming, nor that which comes from hearing and seeing and smelling. For it is not the effect of deficiency, as in the other cases; for instance,
10 those of eating and drinking. For these are the result of defect and excess, owing to the fulfilment of a deficiency or the relief of an excess; which is why they are held to be a becoming. Now defect and excess are pain. There is therefore pain wherever there is a becoming of pleasure. But in the case of seeing and hearing and smelling
15 there is no previous pain. For no one in taking pleasure in seeing or smelling was affected with pain beforehand. Similarly in the case of thought. One may speculate on something with pleasure without having felt any pain beforehand. So that there may be a pleasure which is not a becoming. If then pleasure, as their argument maintained, is not a good for this reason, namely, that is a becoming, but there is
20 some pleasure which is not a becoming, this pleasure may be good.

But generally no pleasure is a becoming. For even the pleasures of eating and drinking are not becomings, but there is a mistake on the part of those who say that these pleasures are becomings. For they think that pleasure is a becoming because it
25 ensues on the application of the remedy; but it is not. For there being a part of the soul with which we feel pleasure, this part of the soul acts and moves simultaneously with the application of the things which we need, and its movement and action are pleasure. Owing, then, to that part of the soul acting simultaneously with the
30 application, or owing to its activity, they think that pleasure is a becoming, from the application being visible, but the part of the soul invisible. It is like thinking that man is body, because this is perceptible by sense, while the soul is not; but the soul also exists. So it is also in this case; for there is a part of the soul with which we feel
35 pleasure, which acts along with the application. Therefore no pleasure is a becoming.

And it is, they say, a conscious restoration to a normal state. But there is pleasure without such restoration to a normal state. For restoration means the
1205ᵃ1 filling up of what by nature is deficient but it is possible, as we maintain, to feel pleasure without any deficiency. For deficiency is pain, and we say that there is pleasure without pain and prior to pain. So that pleasure will not be a restoration of

a deficiency. For in such pleasures there is no deficiency. So that if the reason for thinking that pleasure is not a good was because it is a becoming, and it is found that no pleasure is a becoming, pleasure may be a good.   5

But next it is maintained that some pleasures are not good. One can get a comprehensive view of this point as follows. Since we maintain that good is mentioned in all the categories (in that of substance and relation and quantity and time and generally in all), this much is plain at once. Every activity of good is attended with a certain pleasure, so that, since good is in all the categories, pleasure also will be in all;[21] so that since the goods and pleasure are in these, and the pleasure that comes from the goods is pleasure, every pleasure will be good.   10   15

At the same time it is manifest from this that pleasures differ in kind. For the categories are different in which pleasure is. For it is not as in the sciences, for instance grammar or any other science whatever. For if Lampros possesses the science of grammar, he as a grammarian will be disposed by this knowledge of grammar in the same way as any one else who possesses the science; there will not be two different sciences of grammar, that in Lampros and that in Ileus. But in the case of pleasure it is not so. For the pleasure which comes from drunkenness and that which comes from the commerce of the sexes do not dispose in the same way. Therefore pleasures would seem to differ in kind.   20   25

But another reason why pleasure was held by them not to be good was because some pleasures are bad. But this sort of objection and this kind of judgement is not peculiar to pleasure, but applies also to nature and knowledge. For there is such a thing as a bad nature, for example that of worms and beetles and of ignoble creatures generally, but it does not follow that nature is a bad thing. In the same way there are bad branches of knowledge, for instance the mechanical; nevertheless it does not follow that knowledge is a bad thing, but both knowledge and nature are good in kind. For just as one must not form one's views of the quality of a sculptor from his failures and bad workmanship, but from his successes, so one must not judge of the quality of knowledge or nature or of anything else from the bad, but from the good.   30   35

In the same way pleasure is good in kind, though there are bad pleasures—of that we ourselves are as well aware as any one. For since the natures of creatures differ in the way of bad and good, for instance that of man is good, but that of a wolf or some other beast bad, and in like manner there is one nature of a horse, another of a man, an ass, or a dog, and since pleasure is a restoration of each to its own nature from that which runs counter to it, it follows that this will be appropriate, that the bad nature should have the bad pleasure. For the thing is not the same for a horse and a man, any more than for any of the rest. But since their natures are different, their pleasures also are different. For pleasure, as we saw, is a restoration, and the restoration, they maintain, restores to nature, so that the restoration of the bad nature is bad, and that of the good, good.   1205ᵇ1   5   10

But those who assert that pleasure is not a good thing are in much the same

---

[21]Reading ἐν ἀπάσαις for ἀγαθόν.

15 case as those who, not knowing nectar, think that the gods drink wine, and that there is nothing more delightful than this. But this is owing to their ignorance. In much the same case are all those who assert that all pleasures are becoming, and therefore not a good. For owing to their not knowing other than bodily pleasures, and seeing these to be becomings and not good, for this reason they think in general

20 that pleasure is not a good.

Since, then, there are pleasures both of a nature undergoing restoration and also of one in its normal state, for instance of the former the satisfactions which follow upon deficiency, but of a nature in its normal state the pleasures of sight, hearing, and so on, the activities of the nature in its normal state will be better—for

25 the pleasures of both kinds are activities. It is evident, then, that the pleasures of sight, hearing, and thought will be best, since the bodily pleasures result from a satisfaction.

Again, this was also said by way of showing that it is not a good, that what

30 exists in all and is common to all is not good. Such an objection might seem to be appropriate in the case of a man who covets honour and is actuated by that feeling. For the man who is covetous of honour is one who wishes to be sole possessor of something and by some such means to surpass all others; so he thinks that, if pleasure is to be a good, it too must be something of this sort. Surely this is not so, but, on the contrary, it would seem to be a good for this reason, that all things aim at

35 it. For it is the nature of all things to aim at the good, so that, if all things aim at pleasure, pleasure must be good in kind.

1206ᵃ1 Again, it was denied that pleasure is a good on the ground that it is an impediment. But their asserting it to be an impediment seems to arise from a wrong view of the matter. For the pleasure that comes from the performance of the action is not an impediment; if, however, it be a different pleasure, it is an impediment; for

5 instance, the pleasure of intoxication is an impediment to action; but on this principle one kind of knowledge will be a hindrance to another, for one cannot exercise both at once. But why is knowledge not good, if it produces the pleasure that comes from knowledge? And will that pleasure be an impediment? Surely not; but it will intensify the action. For the pleasure is an incentive to increased action, if

10 it comes from the action itself. For suppose the good man to be doing his acts of excellence, and to be doing them pleasantly; will he not much more exert himself in the action? And if he acts with pleasure, he will be good, but if he does the right with pain, he is not good. For pain attends upon what is due to compulsion, so that if

15 one is pained at doing right, he is acting under compulsion; and he who acts under compulsion is not good.

But indeed it is not possible to perform excellent acts without pain or pleasure. The middle state does not exist. Why so? Because excellence implies feeling, and

20 feeling pain or pleasure, and there is nothing intermediate. It is evident, then, that excellence is either attended with pain or with pleasure. Now if one does the right with pain he is not good. So that excellence will not be attended with pain. Therefore with pleasure. Not only, then, is pleasure not an impediment, but it is actually an incentive to action, and generally excellence cannot exist without the

25 pleasure that comes from it.

There was another argument, to the effect that there is no science which produces pleasure. But this is not true either. For cooks and garland-makers and perfumers are engaged in the production of pleasure. But indeed the other sciences do not have pleasure as their end, but the end is with pleasure and not without it; there is, therefore, a science productive of pleasure.   30

Again, there was another argument, that it is not the best thing. But in that way and by the like reasoning you will reject the particular excellences too. For courage is not the best thing. Is it, therefore, not a good? Surely this is absurd! And the same with the rest. Neither, then, is pleasure not a good simply because it is not   35 the best thing.

To pass on, a difficulty of the following kind might be raised in the case of the excellences. I mean, since the reason sometimes masters the passions (for we say so in the case of the man of self-control), and the passions again conversely master the reason (as happens in the case of the incontinent), since, then, the irrational part of the soul, being vicious, masters the reason, which is well-disposed (for the $1206^{b}1$ incontinent man is of this kind), the reason in like manner, being in a bad condition, will master the passions, which are well-disposed and have their proper excellence, and if this should be the case, the result will be a bad use of excellence (for the   5 reason being in a bad condition and using excellence will use it badly); now such a result would appear paradoxical.

This difficulty it is easy to answer and resolve from what has been said by us before about excellence. For we assert that there is excellence when reason being in a good condition is commensurate with the passions, these possessing their proper   10 excellence, and the passions with the reason; for in such a condition they will accord with one another, so that reason should always ordain what is best, and the passions being well disposed find it easy to carry out what reason ordains. If, then, the reason is in a bad condition, and the passions not, there will not be excellence owing to the   15 failure of reason (for excellence consists in both). So that it is not possible to make a bad use of excellence.

Speaking generally, it is not the case, as others think, that reason is the principle and guide to excellence, but rather the feelings. For there must first be produced in us (as indeed is the case) an irrational impulse to the right, and then   20 later on reason must put the question to the vote and decide it. One may see this from the case of children and those who live without reason. For in these, apart from reason, there spring up, first, impulses of the feelings towards right, and reason supervening later and giving its vote the same way is the cause of right action. But if   25 they have received from reason the principle that leads to right, the feelings do not necessarily follow and consent thereto, but often oppose it. Hence a right disposition of the feelings seems to be the principle that leads to excellence rather than the reason.

8 · Since our discussion is about happiness, it will be connected with the   30 preceding to speak about good fortune. For the majority think that the happy must be the fortunate life, or not apart from good fortune, and perhaps they are right in thinking so. For it is not possible to be happy without external goods, over which

35 fortune is supreme. Therefore we must speak about good fortune, saying generally who the fortunate man is, and what is his province and his sphere.

First, then, one may raise difficulties by having recourse to the following considerations. One would not say of fortune that it is nature. For what nature is the cause of, that she produces for the most part or without exception,[22] but this is never

1207ᵃ1 the case with fortune—her effects are disorderly and as it may chance; this is why we speak of chance in the case of such things.

Neither would one identify it with any mind or right reason. For here more than ever is there order and uniformity, but not chance. Hence, where there is most

5 of mind and reason, there is least chance, and where there is most chance, there is there least mind.

Can it be, then, that good fortune is a sort of care of the gods? Surely it will not be thought to be this! For we suppose that, if god is the disposer of such things, he assigns both good and evil in accordance with desert, whereas chance and the things of chance do really occur as it may chance. But if we assign such a dispensation to

10 god, we shall be making him a bad judge or else unjust. And this is not befitting to god.

And yet outside of these there is no other position which one can assign to fortune, so that it is plain that it must be one of these. Now mind and reason and knowledge seem to be a thing utterly foreign to it. And yet neither would the care and providence of god seem to be good fortune, owing to its being found also in the

15 bad, though it is not likely that god would have a care of the bad.

Nature, then, is left as being most connected with good fortune. And good fortune and fortune generally displays itself in things that are not in our own power,

20 and of which we are not masters nor able to bring them about. For which reason no one calls the just man, in so far as he is just, fortunate, nor yet the brave man, nor any other excellent character. For these things are in our power to have or not to have. But it is just in such things as follow that we shall speak more appropriately of good fortune. For we do call the well-born fortunate, and generally the man who

25 possesses such kinds of goods of which he is not himself the controller.

But all the same even there good fortune would not seem to be used in its strict sense. But there are more meanings than one of the term 'fortunate'. For we call a man fortunate to whom it has befallen to achieve some good beyond his own calculation, and him who has made a gain when he ought reasonably to have

30 incurred a loss. Good fortune, then, consists in some good accruing beyond expectation, and in escaping some evil that might reasonably have been expected. But good fortune would seem to consist to a greater extent and more properly in the obtaining of good. For the obtaining of good would seem to be in itself a piece of

35 good fortune, while the escaping evil is a piece of good fortune accidentally.

Good fortune, then, is nature without reason. For the fortunate man is he who apart from reason has an impulse to good things and obtains these, and this comes from nature. For there is in the soul by nature something of this sort whereby we are

---

[22]Transposing ἀεί to follow ἐπὶ τὸ πολὺ ἤ.

impelled, not under the guidance of reason, towards things for which we are well fitted. And if one were to ask a man in this state, 'Why does it please you to do so'?—he would say, 'I don't know, except that it does please me', being in the same condition as those who are inspired by religious frenzy; for they also have an impulse to do something apart from reason.

1207ᵇ1

We cannot call good fortune by a proper name of its own, but we often say that it is a cause, though cause is not a suitable name for it. For a cause and its effect are different, and what is called a cause contains no reference to an impulse which attains good, in the way either of avoiding evil or on the other hand of obtaining good, when not thinking to obtain it. Good fortune, then, in this sense is different from the former, and this seems to result from the way in which things fall out, and to be good fortune accidentally. So that, if this also is to be called good fortune, at all events the other sort has a more intimate connexion with happiness, namely, that wherein the principle of impulse towards the attainment of goods is in the man himself.

5

10

15

Since, then, happiness cannot exist apart from external goods, and these result from good fortune, as we said just now, it follows that it will work along with happiness. So much then about good fortune.

9 · But since we have spoken about each of the excellences in detail, it remains to sum up the particulars under one general statement. There is a phrase, then, which is not badly used of the completely good man, namely, 'nobility and goodness'. For he is noble and good, they say, when he is completely good. For it is in the case of excellence that they use the expression 'noble and good'; for instance, they say that the just man is noble and good, the brave man, the temperate, and generally in the case of the excellences. Since, then, we make a dual division, and say that some things are noble and others good, and that some goods are absolutely good and others not so, calling noble such things as the excellences and the actions which spring from them, and good, office, wealth, glory, honour, and the like, the noble and good man is he to whom the things that are absolutely good are good, and the things that are absolutely noble are noble. For such a man is noble and good. But he to whom things absolutely good are not good is not noble and good, any more than he would be thought to be in health to whom the things that are absolutely healthy are not healthy. For if the accession of wealth and office were to hurt anybody, they would not be desirable, but he will wish to have for himself such things as will not hurt him. But he who is of such a nature as to shrink from having anything good would not seem to be noble and good. But he for whom the possession of all good things is good and who is not spoilt by them, as, for instance, by wealth and power, such a man is noble and good.

20

25

30

35

1208ᵃ1

10 · But about acting rightly in accordance with the excellences something indeed has been said, but not enough. For we said that it was acting in accordance with right reason. But possibly one might be ignorant as to this very point, and

5

might ask, 'What is acting in accordance with right reason? And where is right reason'? To act, then, in accordance with right reason is when the irrational part of the soul does not prevent the rational from displaying its own activity. For then the action will be in accordance with right reason. For seeing that in the soul we have a worse and a better part and the worse is always for the sake of the better, as in the case of body and soul the body is for the sake of the soul, and we shall say that we have our body in a good state, when its state is such as not to hinder, but actually to help and take part in inciting towards the soul accomplishing its own work (for the worse is for the sake of the better, to aid the better in its work); when, then, the passions do not hinder the mind from performing its own work, then you will have what is done in accordance with right reason.

Yes, but perhaps some one may say, 'In what state must the passions be so as not to act as a hindrance, and when are they in this state? For I do not know', This sort of thing is not easy to put into words, any more than the doctor finds it so. But when he has given orders that barley-gruel shall be administered to a patient in a fever, and you say to him, 'But how am I to know when he has a fever?'—he replies, 'When you see him pale'. 'But how am I to know when he is pale'? There the doctor ... says,[23] 'Well, if you can't perceive that much yourself, it's no good talking to you any more'. The same thing applies in like manner to all such subjects. And the case is the same with regard to recognizing the passions. For one must contribute something oneself towards the perception.

But perhaps one might raise the following sort of question also, 'If I really know these things, shall I then be happy'? For they think they must be; whereas it is not so. For none of the other sciences transmits to the learner the use and exercise, but only the faculty. So in this case also the knowing of these things does not transmit the use (for happiness is an activity, as we maintain), but the faculty, nor does happiness consist in the knowledge of what produces it, but comes from the use of these means. Now the use and exercise of these it is not the business of this treatise to impart, any more than any other science imparts the use of anything, but only the faculty.

11 · In addition to all that has gone before, it is necessary to speak about friendship, saying what it is, and what are its circumstances and sphere. For since we see that it is co-extensive with life and presents itself on every occasion, and that it is a good, we must embrace it also in our view of happiness.

First, then, perhaps it will be as well to go through the difficulties and questions that are raised about it. Does friendship exist among the like, as is thought and said? For 'Jackdaw sits by jackdaw', as the proverb has it, and

> Unto the like God ever brings the like.[24]

There is a story also of a dog that used always to sleep upon the same tile, and how Empedocles, on being asked, 'Why does the dog sleep on the same tile'? said,

---

[23]Text uncertain.
[24]See *Odyssey* XVII 218.

'Because the dog has something that is like the tile', implying that it was owing to the likeness that the dog resorted to it.

But again, on the other hand, some people think that friendship occurs rather 15 among opposites. Take the line:

Earth loves the shower, what time the plain is dry.

It is the opposite, they say, that loves to be friends with the opposite; for among the like there is no room for friendship. For the like, they say, has no need of the like, and more to the same effect.

Again, is it hard or easy to become a friend? Flatterers, at all events, who 20 quickly gain a footing of close attendance, are not friends, though they appear to be.

Further, such difficulties as the following are raised. Will the good man be a friend to the bad? Or will he not? For friendship implies fidelity and steadfastness, and the bad man is not at all of this character. And will one bad man be a friend to 25 another? Or will this not be the case either?

First, then, we must determine what kind of friendship we are in search of. For there is, people think, a friendship towards god and towards things without life, but here they are wrong. For friendship, we maintain, exists only where there can be a return of affection, but friendship towards god does not admit of love being returned, nor at all of loving. For it would be strange if one were to say that he loved 30 Zeus. Neither is it possible to have affection returned by lifeless objects, though there is a love for such things, for instance wine or something else of that sort. Therefore it is not love towards god of which we are in search, nor love towards things without life, but love towards things with life, that is, where there can be a 35 return of affection.

If, then, one were to inquire next what is the lovable, it is none other than the good. Now there is a difference between the lovable and what is to be loved, as between the desirable and what is to be desired. For that is desirable which is absolutely good, but that is to be desired by each which is good for him; so also that 1209ᵃ1 which is absolutely good is lovable, but that is to be loved which is good for oneself, so that what is to be loved is lovable, but the lovable is not to be loved.

Here, then, we see the source of the difficulty as to whether the good man is a friend to the bad man or not. For what is good for oneself is in a way attached to the 5 good, and so is that which is to be loved to the lovable, and it depends as a consequence upon the good that it should be pleasant and that it should be useful. Now the friendship of the good lies in their loving one another; and they love one another in so far as they are lovable; and they are lovable in so far as they are good. 'The good man, then', it will be replied, 'will not be a friend to the bad'. Yes he will. 10 For since the good had as its consequence the useful and the pleasant, in so far as, though bad, he is pleasant, so far he is a friend; again, being useful, then so far as he is useful, so far is he a friend. But this sort of friendship will not depend upon lovableness. For the good, we saw, was lovable, but the bad man is not lovable. 15 Rather such a friendship will depend on a man's being one who is to be loved. For springing from the perfect friendship which exists among the good there are also these forms of friendship, that which refers to the pleasant and that which refers to the useful. He, then, whose love is based on the pleasant does not love with the love which is based on the good, nor does he whose friendship is based upon the useful.

20   And these forms of friendship, that of the good, the pleasant, and the useful, are not indeed the same, nor yet absolutely different from one another, but hang in a way from the same point. Just so we call a knife surgical, a man surgical, and knowledge

25   surgical. They are not called so in the same way, but the knife is called surgical from being useful in surgery, and the man from his being able to produce health, and the knowledge from its being cause and principle. Similarly, the forms of friendship are not all called so in the same way, the friendship of the good which is based on the good, the friendship depending on pleasure, and that depending on

30   utility. Nor yet is it a mere case of homonymy, but, while they are not actually the same, they have still in a way the same sphere and the same origin. If, therefore, some one were to say, 'He whose love is prompted by pleasure is not a friend to so-and-so; for his friendship is not based on the good', he is having recourse to the friendship of the virtuous, which is a compound of all these, of the good and the

35   pleasant and the useful, so that it is true that he is not a friend in respect of that friendship, but only in respect of the friendship depending on the pleasant or the useful.

Will the good man then be a friend to the good, or will he not? For the like, it is urged, has no need of the like. An argument of this sort is on the look-out for the

1209ᵇ1   friendship based on utility; for if they are friends in so far as the one has need of the other, they are in the friendship which is based on utility. But the friendship which is based on utility has been distinguished from that which is based on excellence or on pleasure. It is likely, then, that the good should be much more friends; for they

5   have all the qualifications for friendship, the good and the pleasant and the useful. But the good may also be a friend to the bad; for it may be that he is a friend in so far as he is pleasant. And the bad also to the bad; for it may be that they are friends in so far as they have the same interest. For we see this as a matter of fact, that, when persons have the same interest, they are friends owing to that interest, so that

10   there will be nothing to prevent the bad also having to some extent the same interest.

Now friendship among the good, which is founded on excellence and the good, is naturally the surest, the most abiding, and the finest form. For excellence, to which the friendship is due, is unchangeable, so that it is natural that this form of

15   friendship should be unchangeable, whereas interest is never the same. Hence the friendship which rests on interest is never secure, but changes along with the interest; and the same with the friendship which rests on pleasure. The friendship, then, of the best men is that which arises from excellence, but that of the common run of men depends upon utility, while that which rests on pleasure is found among vulgar and commonplace persons.

20   When people find their friends bad, the result is complaint and expressions of surprise; but it is nothing extraordinary. For when friendship has taken its start

from pleasure, and this is why they are friends, or from interest, so soon as these fail the friendship does not continue. Very often the friendship does remain, but a man treats his friend badly, owing to which there are complaints; but neither is this   25 anything out of the way. For your friendship with this man was not from the first founded on excellence, so that it is not extraordinary that he should do nothing of what excellence requires. The complaints, then, are unreasonable. Having formed their friendship with a view to pleasure, they think they ought to have the kind which is due to excellence; but that is not possible. For the friendship of pleasure   30 and interest does not depend on excellence. Having entered then into a partnership in pleasure, they expect excellence, but there they are wrong. For excellence does not follow upon pleasure and utility, but both these follow upon excellence. For it would be strange not to suppose that the good are the most pleasant to one another. For even the bad, as Euripides says, are pleasant to one another. 'The bad man is   35 fused into one with the bad'. For excellence does not follow upon pleasure, whereas pleasure does follow upon excellence.

But is it necessary that there should be pleasure in the friendship of the good? Or is it not? It would be strange indeed to say that it is not. For if you deprive them of the quality of being pleasant to one another, they will procure other friends, who   1210ᵃ1 are pleasant, to live with, for in view of that there is nothing more important than being pleasant. It would be curious then not to think that the good ought above all others to live in common one with another; and this cannot be without the element of pleasure. It will be necessary, then, as it seems, for them above all to be   5 pleasant.

But since friendships have been divided into three species, and in the case of these the question was raised whether friendship takes place in equality or in inequality, the answer is that it may depend on either. For that which implies likeness is the friendship of the good, and complete friendship; but that which implies unlikeness is the friendship of utility. For the poor man is a friend to the rich owing to his own lack of what the wealthy man has in abundance, and the bad man   10 to the good for the same reason. For owing to his lack of excellence he is for this reason a friend to him from whom he thinks he will get it. Among the unequal then there arises friendship based on utility. So that Euripides says,

Earth loves the shower, what time the plain is dry,

intimating that the friendship of utility has place between these as opposites. For if   15 you like to set down fire and water as the extreme opposites, these are useful to one another. For fire, they say, if it has not moisture, perishes, as this provides it with a kind of nutriment, but that to such an extent as it can get the better of; for if you make the moisture too great, it will obtain the mastery, and will cause the fire to go   20 out, but if you supply it in moderation, it will be of service to it. It is evident, then, that friendship based on utility occurs among things the most opposite.

All the forms of friendship, both those in equality and those in inequality, are referred to the three in our division. But in all the forms of friendship there is a difference that arises between the partners when they are not on a level in love or in   25 benefaction or in service, or whatever else of the kind it may be. For when one exerts himself energetically, and the other is in defect, there is complaint and blame on the score of the defect. Not but that the defect on the part of the one is plain to see in the case of such persons as have the same end in view in their friendship; for instance, if

30 both are friends to one another on the ground of utility or of pleasure or of excellence. If, then, you do me more good than I do you, I do not even dispute that you ought to be loved more by me; but in a friendship where we are not friends with

35 the same object, there is more room for differences. For the defect on one side or the other is not manifest. For instance, if one is a friend for pleasure and the other for interest, that is where the dispute will arise. For he who is superior in utility does not think the pleasure a fair exchange for the utility, and he who is more pleasant does

1210ᵇ1 not think that he receives in the utility an adequate return for the pleasure which bestows. Hence differences are more likely to arise in such kinds of friendship.

When men are friends on an unequal footing, those who are superior in wealth or anything of that sort do not think that they themselves ought to love, but think

5 that they ought to be loved by their inferiors. But it is better to love than to be loved. For to love is a pleasurable activity and a good, whereas from being loved there results no activity to the object of the love. Again, it is better to know than to be

10 known; for to be known and to be loved attach even to things without life, but to know and to love to things with life. Again, to be inclined to benefit is better than not; now he who loves is inclined to benefit, just in so far as he loves, but this is not the case with him who is loved, in so far as he is loved.

But owing to ambition men wish rather to be loved than to love, because of

15 there being a certain superiority in being loved. For he who is loved has always a superiority in pleasure or wealth or excellence, and the ambitious man reaches out after superiority. And those who are in a position of superiority do not think that they themselves ought to love, since they make a return to those who love them, in those things in which they are superior. And again the others are inferior to them, for which reason the superiors do not think they themselves ought to love but to be

20 loved. But he who is deficient in wealth or pleasures or excellence admires him who has a superiority in these things, and loves him owing to his getting these things or thinking that he will get them.

Now such friendships arise from sympathy, that is, from wishing good to some one. But the friendship which takes place in these cases has not all the required

25 attributes. For often we wish good to one person and like to live with another. But ought we to say that these things are characteristics of friendship or of complete friendship which is founded on excellence? For in that friendship all these things are contained; for there is none other with whom we should wish to live (for

30 pleasantness and usefulness and excellence are attributes of the good man), and it is to him that we should most wish good, and to live and to live well we should wish to none other than he.

Whether a man can have friendship for and towards himself may be omitted for the present, but we shall speak of it later. But all the things that we wish for a

35 friend we wish for ourselves. For we wish to live along with ourselves (though that is

perhaps unavoidable), and to live well, and to live, and the wishing of the good applies to none so much. Further, we are most sympathetic with ourselves; for if we meet with a defeat or fall into any kind of misfortune, we are at once grieved. So looking at the matter in this way it would seem that there is friendship towards oneself. In speaking then of such things as sympathy and living well and so on we are referring either to friendship towards ourselves or to complete friendship. For all these things are found in both. For the living together and the wish for a thing's existence and for its well-being and all the rest are found in these.

1211ᵃ1

5

Further, it may perhaps be thought that wherever justice is possible, there friendship may exist too. Hence there are as many species of friendship as there are of just dealing. Now there can be justice between a foreigner and a citizen, between a slave and his master, between one citizen and another, between son and father, between wife and husband, and generally every form of association has its separate form of friendship. But the firmest of friendships would seem to be that with a foreigner; for they have no common aim about which to dispute, as is the case with fellow-citizens; for when these dispute with one another for the priority, they do not remain friends.

10

15

It will be in place now to speak about this, whether there is friendship towards oneself or not. Since then we see, as we said just a little above, that the act of loving is recognized from the particulars, and it is to ourselves that we should most wish the particulars (the good, and existence, and well-being; and we are most sympathetic with ourselves, and we most wish to live along with ourselves); therefore, if friendship is known from the particulars, and we should wish the particulars to belong to ourselves, it is plain that there is friendship towards ourselves, just as we maintained that there is injustice towards oneself. Though, indeed, as it takes one person to inflict and another to receive an injury, while each individual is the same person, it appeared for that reason that there was no injustice towards oneself. It is possible, however, as we said on examining the parts of the soul, when these, as they are more than one, are not in agreement, that then there should be injustice towards oneself. In the same way then there would seem to be friendship towards oneself. For the friend being, according to the proverb—when we wish to describe a very great friend, we say 'my soul and his are one'; since then the parts of the soul are more than one, then only will the soul be one, when the reason and the passions are in accord with one another (for so it will be one): so that when it has become one there will be friendship towards oneself. And this friendship towards oneself will exist in the good man; for in him alone the parts of the soul are in proper relation to one another owing to their not being at variance, since the bad man is never a friend to himself, for he is always at odds with himself. At all events the incontinent man, when he has done something to which pleasure prompts, not long afterwards repents and reviles himself. It is the same with the bad man in other vices. For he is always fighting with and opposing himself.

20

25

30

35

1211ᵇ1

There is also a friendship in equality; for instance, that of comrades is on an equality in respect of number and capacity of good (for neither of them deserves to have a greater share of goods either in number or capacity or size, but what is equal;

5

for comrades are supposed to be a kind of equals). But that between father and son
is on an inequality, and that between ruler and subject, between worse and better,
10   between wife and husband, and generally in all cases where there is one who
occupies the position of worse or better in friendship. This friendship in inequality
indeed, is proportional. For in giving of good no one would ever give an equal share
to the better and the worse, but always a greater to the one who was superior. And
15   this is the proportionally equal. For the worse with a less good is in a kind of way
equal to the better with a greater.

12 · Among all the above-mentioned forms of friendship love is in a way
strongest in that which is based on kindred, and more particularly in the relation of
20   father to son. Now why is it that the father loves the son more than the son the
father? Is it, as some say rightly enough as regards the many, because the father has
been a kind of benefactor to the son, and the son owes him a return for the benefit?
Now this cause would seem to hold good in the friendship which is based on utility.
25   But as we see it to be in the sciences, so it is here also. What I mean is that in some
the end and the activity are the same, and there is not any other end beyond the
activity; for instance, to the flute-player the activity and end are the same (for to
30   play the flute is both his end and his activity); but not to the art of housebuilding
(for it has a different end beyond the activity); now friendship is a sort of activity,
and there is not any other end beyond the act of loving, but just this. Now the father
is always in a way more active owing to the son being a kind of production of his
35   own. And this we see to be so in the other cases also. For all feel a sort of kindness
towards what they have themselves produced. The father, then, feels a sort of
kindness towards the son as being his own production, led on by memory and by
hope. This is why the father loves the son more than the son the father.
There are other things which are called and are thought to be forms of
1212ᵃ1   friendship, about which we must inquire whether they are friendship. For instance,
goodwill is thought to be friendship. Now, speaking absolutely, goodwill would
seem not to be friendship (for towards many persons and on many occasions we
entertain a feeling of goodwill either from seeing or hearing some good about them.
Does it follow then that we are friends? Surely not! For if some one felt goodwill
5   towards Darius, when he was alive among the Persians, as some one may have done,
it did not follow that he had a friendship towards Darius); but goodwill would seem
to be sometimes the beginning of friendship, and goodwill may become friendship if,
where one has the power to do good, there be added the wish to do it for the sake of
the person towards whom the goodwill is felt. But goodwill implies character and is
10   relative to it. For no one is said to have a goodwill towards wine or towards anything
else without life that is good or pleasant, but if any one be of a good character,
goodwill is felt towards him. And goodwill is not separate from friendship, but acts
in the same sphere. This is why it is thought to be friendship.
Unanimity borders close on friendship, if the kind of unanimity that you take is
15   that which is strictly so called. For if one entertains the same notions as Empedocles
and has the same views about the elements as he, is he unanimous with Empedo-

cles? Surely not! Since the same thing would have to hold in any like case. For to begin with, the sphere of unanimity is not matters of thought but matters of action, and herein it is not in so far as they think the same, but in so far as in addition to thinking the same they choose to do the same about what they think. For if both think to rule, but each of them thinks that he is to be ruler, are they therefore unanimous? Surely not. But if I wish to be ruler myself, and he wishes me to be so, then it is that we are unanimous. Unanimity, then, is found in matters of action coupled with the wish for the same thing. It is therefore the establishment of the same ruler in matters of action that is the sphere of unanimity in the strict sense. 20 25

13 · Since there is, as we maintain, such a thing as friendship towards oneself, will the good man be a lover of self or not? Now the lover of self is he who does everything for his own sake in matters of advantage. The bad man is a lover of self (for he does everything for his own sake), but not the good man. For the reason why he is a good man is because he does so and so for the sake of another; hence he is not a lover of self. But it is true that all feel an impulse towards things that are good, and think that they themselves ought to have these in the highest degree. This is most apparent in the case of wealth and rule. Now the good man will resign these to another, not on the ground that it does not become him in the highest degree to have them, but if he sees that another will be able to make more use of these than he; but other men will not do this owing to ignorance (for they do not think they might make a bad use of such goods) or else owing to the ambition of ruling. But the good man will not be affected in either of these ways. Hence he is not a lover of self as regards such goods at least; but, if at all, in respect of the noble. For this is the only thing in which he will not resign his share, but in respect of things useful and pleasant he will. In the choice, then, of things in accordance with the noble he will display his love of self, but in the choice which we describe as being prompted by the useful and the pleasant it is not he who will do so, but the bad man. 30 35 1212^{b}1 5

14 · Will the good man love himself most of all or not? In a way he will love himself most and in a way not. For since we say that the good man will resign goods in the way of utility to his friend, he will be loving his friend more than himself. Yes; but his resignation of such goods implies that he is compassing the noble for himself in resigning these to his friend. In a way, therefore, he is loving his friend more than himself, and in a way he is loving himself most. In respect of the useful he is loving his friend, but in respect of the noble and good he is loving himself most; for he is compassing these for himself as being noblest. He is therefore a lover of good, not a lover of self. For, if he does love himself, it is only because he is good. But the bad man is a lover of self. For he has nothing in the way of nobility for which he should love himself, but apart from these grounds he will love himself qua self. Hence it is he who will be called a lover of self in the strict sense. 10 15 20

15 · It will come next to speak about self-sufficingness and the self-sufficing man. Will the self-sufficing man require friendship too? Or will he not, but will he 25

be sufficient to himself as regards that also? For even the poets have such sayings as these—

What need of friends, when Heaven bestows the good?[25]

Whence also the difficulty arises, whether he who has all the goods and is
30   self-sufficing will need a friend too? Or is it then that he will need him most? For to whom will he do good? Or with whom will he live? For surely he will not live alone. If, then, he will need these things, and these are not possible without friendship, the self-sufficing man will need friendship too. Now the analogy that is generally
35   derived from god in discussions is not right there, nor will it be useful here. For if god is self-sufficing and has need of none, it does not follow that we shall need no one. For we hear this kind of thing said about god. Seeing that god, so it is said, possesses all goods and is self-sufficing, what will he do? We can hardly suppose that he will sleep. It follows, we are told, that he will contemplate something; for
1213ᵃ1   this is the noblest and the most appropriate employment. What, then, will he contemplate? For if he is to contemplate anything else, it must be something better than himself that he will contemplate. But this is absurd, that there should be anything better than god. Therefore he will contemplate himself. But this also is
5   absurd. For if a human being surveys himself, we censure him as stupid. It will be absurd therefore, it is said, for god to contemplate himself. As to what god is to contemplate, then, we may let that pass. But the self-sufficingness about which we are conducting our inquiry is not that of god but of man, the question being whether
10   the self-sufficing man will require friendship or not. If, then, when one looked upon a friend one could see the nature and attributes of the friend, . . .[26] such as to be a second self, at least if you make a very great friend, as the saying has it, 'Here is another Heracles, a dear other self'. Since then it is both a most difficult thing, as some of the sages have said, to attain a knowledge of oneself, and also a most
15   pleasant (for to know oneself is pleasant)—now we are not able to see what we are from ourselves (and that we cannot do so is plain from the way in which we blame others without being aware that we do the same things ourselves; and this is the effect of favour or passion, and there are many of us who are blinded by these things
20   so that we judge not aright); as then when we wish to see our own face, we do so by looking into the mirror, in the same way when we wish to know ourselves we can obtain that knowledge by looking at our friend. For the friend is, as we assert, a second self. If, then, it is pleasant to know oneself, and it is not possible to know this
25   without having some one else for a friend, the self-sufficing man will require friendship in order to know himself.

Again, if it is a fine thing, as it is, to do good when one has the goods of fortune, to whom will he do good? And with whom will he live? For surely he will not spend his time alone; for to live with some one is pleasant and necessary. If, then, these
1213ᵇ1   things are fine and pleasant and necessary, and these things cannot be without friendship, the self-sufficing man will need friendship too.

---

[25]Euripides, *Orestes* 667.
[26]There is a lacuna in the text.

16 · Should one acquire many friends or few? They ought neither to be absolutely many nor yet few. For if they are many, it is difficult to apportion one's   5 love to each. For in all other things also the weakness of our nature incapacitates us from reaching far. For we do not see far with our eyes, but if you set the object too far off, the sight fails owing to the weakness of nature; and the case is the same with hearing and with all other things alike. Failing, then, to show love through   10 incapacity one would, not unjustly, incur accusations, and would not be a friend, as one would be loving only in name; but this is not what friendship means. Again, if they are many, one can never be quit of grief. For if they are many, it is always likely that something unfortunate will occur to one at least of them, and when these   15 things take place grief is unavoidable. Nor yet, on the other hand, should one have few, only one or two, but a number commensurate with one's circumstances and one's own impulse to love.

17 · After this we must inquire how one ought to treat a friend. This inquiry does not present itself in every friendship, but in that in which friends are most liable to bring complaints against one another. They do not do this so much in the   20 other cases; for instance, in the friendship between father and son there is no complaint such as the claim that we hear made in some forms of friendship, 'As I to you, so you to me', failing which there is in those cases grave complaint. But between unequal friends equality is not expected, and the relation between father and son is on a footing of inequality, as is also that between wife and husband, or   25 between servant and master, and generally between the worse and the better. They will therefore not have complaints of this sort. But it is between equal friends and in a friendship of that sort that a complaint of this kind arises. So we must inquire how we ought to treat a friend in the friendship between friends who are on a footing of   30 equality.

EUDEMIAN ETHICS

J. Solomon

BOOK I

1214ª1   1 · The man who stated his judgement in the god's precinct in Delos made an inscription on the propylaeum to the temple of Leto, in which he separated from one another the good, the beautiful, and the pleasant as not all properties of the same
5   thing; he wrote, 'Most beautiful is what is most just, but best is health, and pleasantest the obtaining of what one desires'. But let us disagree with him; for happiness is at once the most beautiful and best of all things and also the pleasantest.
10   Now about each thing and kind there are many views that are disputed and need investigation; of these some concern knowledge only, some the acquisition of things and the performance of acts as well. About those which involve speculative philosophy only we must at a suitable opportunity say what is relevant to that study.
15   But first we must consider in what the good life consists and how it is to be acquired, whether all who receive the epithet 'happy' become so by nature (as we become tall, short, or of different complexions), or by teaching (happiness being a sort of science), or by some sort of discipline—for men acquire many qualities neither by
20   nature nor by teaching but by habituation, bad qualities if they are habituated to the bad, good if to the good. Or do men become happy in none of these ways, but either—like those possessed by nymphs or deities—through a sort of divine influence, being as it were inspired, or through chance? For many declare happiness
25   to be identical with good luck.
That men, then, possess happiness through all or some or one of these causes is evident; for practically all events come under these principles—for all acts arising from intelligence may be included among acts that arise from knowledge. Now to
30   be happy, to live blissfully and beautifully, must consist mainly in three things, which seem most desirable; for some say practical wisdom is the greatest good, some excellence, and some pleasure. Some also dispute about the magnitude of the contribution made by each of these elements to happiness, some declaring the
1214ᵇ1   contribution of one to be greater, some that of another—these regarding wisdom as a greater good than excellence, those the opposite, while others regard pleasure as a

TEXT: F. Susemihl, Teubner, Leipzig, 1884

greater good than either; and some consider the happy life to be compounded of all or of two of these, while others hold it to consist in one of them alone.   5

2 · First then about these things we must enjoin every one that has the power to live according to his own choice to set up for himself some object for the good life to aim at (whether honour or reputation or wealth or culture), with reference to which he will then do all his acts, since not to have one's life organized in view of   10 some end is a mark of much folly. Then above all we must first define to ourselves without hurry or carelessness in which of our belongings the happy life is lodged, and what are the indispensable conditions of its attainment—for health is not the same as the indispensable conditions of health; and so it is with many other things,   15 so that the good life and its indispensable conditions are not identical. Of such things some are not peculiar to health or even to life, but common—to speak broadly—to all dispositions and actions, e.g. without breathing or being awake or having the power of movement we could enjoy neither good nor evil; but some are   20 peculiar to each kind of thing, and these it is specially important to observe; e.g. the eating of meat and walking after meals are more peculiarly the indispensable conditions of a good physical state than the more general conditions mentioned above. For herein is the cause of the disputes about happy living, its nature and   25 causes; for some take to be elements in happiness what are merely its indispensable conditions.

3 · To examine then all the views held about happiness is superfluous, for children, sick people, and the insane all have views, but no sane person would   30 dispute over them; for such persons need not argument but years in which they may change, or else medical or political correction—for medicine, no less than whipping, is a correction. Similarly we have not to consider the views of the multitude (for they talk without consideration about almost everything, and most about happi-   1215ᵃ1 ness); for it is absurd to apply argument to those who need not argument but experience. But since every study has its special problems, evidently there are such relating to the best life and best existence; it is well to examine these opinions, for a   5 disputant's refutation of what is opposed to his arguments is a demonstration of the argument itself.

Further, it is proper not to neglect these considerations, especially with a view to that at which all inquiry should be directed, viz. the causes that enable us to share in the good and noble life—if any one finds it invidious to call it the blessed   10 life—and with a view to the hope we may have of attaining each good. For if the good life consists in what is due to fortune or nature, it would be something that many cannot hope for, since its acquisition is not in their power, nor attainable by their care or activity; but if it depends on the individual and his personal acts being   15 of a certain character, then the supreme good would be both more general and more divine, more general because more would be able to possess it, more divine because happiness would then be the prize offered to those who make themselves and their acts of a certain character.

20   4 · Most of the doubts and difficulties raised will become clear, if we define well what we ought to think happiness to be, whether it consists merely in having a soul of a certain character—as some of the sages and older writers thought—or whether the man must indeed be of a certain character, but it is even more
25 necessary that his acts should be of a certain character.

Now if we make a division of the kinds of life, some do not even pretend to this sort of well-being, being only pursued for the sake of what is necessary, e.g. those concerned with vulgar arts, or with commercial or servile occupations—by vulgar I
30 mean arts pursued only with a view to reputation, by servile those which are sedentary and wage-earning, by commercial those connected with selling in markets and selling in shops. But there are also three goods directed to a happy employment of life, those which we have above called the three greatest of human
35 goods, excellence, wisdom, and pleasure. We thus see that there are three lives which all those choose who have power, viz. the lives of the political man, the
1215ᵇ1 philosopher, the voluptuary; for of these the philosopher intends to occupy himself with wisdom and contemplation of truth, the political man with noble acts (i.e. those springing from excellence), the voluptuary with bodily pleasures. Therefore
5 each calls a different person happy, as was indeed said before. Anaxagoras of Clazomenae being asked, 'Who was the happiest of men'? answered, 'None of those you suppose, but one who would appear a strange being to you', because he saw that
10 the questioner thought it impossible for one not great and beautiful or rich to deserve the epithet 'happy', while he himself perhaps thought that the man who lived painlessly and pure of injustice or else engaged in some divine contemplation was really, as far as a man may be, blessed.

15   5 · About many other things it is difficult to judge well, but most difficult about that on which judgement seems to all easiest and the knowledge of it in the power of any man—viz. what of all that is found in living is desirable, and what, if attained, would satisfy our desire. For there are many consequences of life that
20 make men fling away life, such as disease, excessive pain, storms, so that it is clear that, if one were given the power of choice, not to be born at all would, as far at least as these reasons go, have been desirable. Further, the life we lead as children is not desirable,[1] for no one in his senses would consent to return again to this. Further,
25 many incidents involving neither pleasure nor pain or involving pleasure but not of a noble kind are such that, as far as they are concerned, non-existence is preferable to life. And generally, if one were to bring together all that all men do and experience but not willingly because not for its own sake, and were to add to this an existence of
30 infinite duration, one would none the more on account of these experiences choose existence rather than non-existence. But further, neither for the pleasure of eating or that of sex, if all the other pleasures were removed that knowing or seeing or any other sense provides men with, would any man value existence, unless he were
35 utterly servile, for it is clear that to the man making this choice there would be no

[1] Omitting τίς.

difference between being born a brute and a man; at any rate the ox in Egypt, which
they reverence as Apis, in most of such matters has more power than many   1216ᵃ1
monarchs. We may say the same of the pleasure of sleeping. For what is the
difference between sleeping an unbroken sleep from one's first day to one's last, say
for a thousand or any number of years, and living the life of a plant? Plants at any   5
rate seem to possess this sort of existence, and similarly children; for children, too,
continue having their nature from their first coming into being in their mother's
womb, but sleep the entire time. It is clear then from these considerations that men,
though they look, fail to see what is well-being, what is the good in life.   10

And so they tell us that Anaxagoras answered a man who was raising problems
of this sort and asking why one should choose rather to be born than not by saying
'for the sake of viewing the heavens and the whole order of the universe'. He, then,
thought the choice of life for the sake of some sort of knowledge to be precious; but   15
those who felicitate Sardanapallus or Smindyrides the Sybarite or any other of
those who live the voluptuary's life, these seem all to place happiness in the feeling
of pleasure. But others would rather choose excellent deeds than wisdom or sensual   20
pleasures; at any rate some choose these not only for the sake of reputation, but even
when they are not going to win credit by them; but most 'political' men are not truly
so called; they are not in truth 'political', for the 'political' man is one who chooses   25
noble acts for their own sake, while most take up the 'political' life for the sake of
money and greed.

From what has been said, then, it is clear that all connect happiness with one or
other of three lives, the 'political', the philosophic, and the voluptuary's. Now
among these the nature and quality and sources of the pleasure of the body and   30
sensual enjoyment are clear, so that we have not to inquire what such pleasures are,
but whether they tend to happiness or not and how they tend, and whether—
supposing it right to attach to the noble life certain pleasures—it is right to attach
these, or whether some other sort of participation in these is a necessity, but the   35
pleasures through which men rightly think the happy man to live pleasantly and not
merely painlessly are different.

But about these let us inquire later. First let us consider excellence and
wisdom, the nature of each, and whether they are parts of the good life either in
themselves or through the actions that arise from them, since all—or at least all
important thinkers—connect happiness with these.   1216ᵇ1

Socrates, then, the elder, thought the knowledge of excellence to be the end,
and used to inquire what is justice, what bravery and each of the parts of virtue; and   5
his conduct was reasonable, for he thought all the excellences to be kinds of
knowledge, so that to know justice and to be just came simultaneously; for the
moment that we have learned geometry or building we are builders and geometers.
Therefore he inquired what excellence is, not how or from what it arises. This is   10
correct with regard to theoretical knowledge, for there is no other part of astronomy
or physics or geometry except knowing and contemplating the nature of the things
which are the subjects of those sciences; though nothing prevents them from being   15
in an incidental way useful to us for much that we cannot do without. But the end of

the productive sciences is different from science and knowledge, e.g. health from medical science, law and order (or something of the sort) from political science.
20 Now to know anything that is noble is itself noble; but regarding excellence, at least, not to know what it is, but to know out of what it arises is most precious. For we do not wish to know what bravery is but to be brave, nor what justice is but to be just, just as we wish to be in health rather than to know what being in health is, and to
25 have our body in good condition rather than to know what good condition is.

6 · About all these matters we must try to get conviction by arguments, using the phenomena as evidence and illustration. It would be best that all men should clearly concur with what we are going to say, but if that is unattainable, then that
30 all should in some way at least concur. And this if converted they will do, for every man has some contribution to make to the truth, and with this as a starting-point we must give some sort of proof about these matters. For by advancing from true but obscure judgements he will arrive at clear ones, always exchanging the usual
35 confused statement for more real knowledge. Now in every inquiry there is a difference between philosophic and unphilosophic argument; therefore we should not think even in political philosophy that the sort of consideration which not only makes the nature of the thing evident but also its cause is superfluous; for such consideration is in every inquiry the truly philosophic method. But this needs much
1217ᵃ1 caution. For there are some who, through thinking it to be the mark of a philosopher to make no arbitrary statement but always to give a reason, often unawares give reasons foreign to the subject and idle—this they do sometimes from ignorance,
5 sometimes because they are charlatans—by which reasons even men experienced and able to act are trapped by those who neither have nor are capable of having practical and constructive intelligence. And this happens to them from want of culture; for inability in regard to each matter to distinguish reasonings appropriate
10 to the subject from those foreign to it is want of culture. And it is well to criticize separately the explanation and the conclusion both because of what has just been said, viz. that one should attend not merely to what is inferred by argument, but often attend more to the phenomena—whereas now when men are unable to see a flaw in the argument they are compelled to believe what has been said—and
15 because often that which seems to have been shown by argument is true indeed but not for the cause which the argument assigns; for one may prove truth by means of falsehood, as is clear from the *Analytics*.

7 · After these further preliminary remarks let us start on our discourse from what we have called the first confused judgements, and then² seek to discover a
20 clear judgement about the nature of happiness. Now this is admitted to be the greatest and best of human goods—we say human, for there might perhaps be a happiness peculiar to some superior being, e.g. a god; for of the other animals, which
25 are inferior in their nature to men, none have a right to the epithet 'happy'; for no

²Reading ἔπειτα for ἐπὶ τό.

horse, bird, or fish is happy, nor anything the name of which does not imply some share of a divine element in its nature; but in virtue of some other sort of participation in good things some have a better existence, some a worse.

But we must see later that this is so. At present we say that of goods some are within the range of human action, some not; and this we say because some things—and therefore also some good things—are incapable of change, yet these are perhaps as to their nature the best. Some things, again, are within the range of action, but only to beings superior to us. But since 'within the range of action' is an ambiguous phrase—for both that for the sake of which we act and the things we do for its sake have to do with practice and thus we put among things within the range of action both health and wealth and the acts done for the sake of these ends, i.e. health-giving conduct and money-bringing conduct—it is clear that we must regard happiness as the best of what is within the range of action for man.

8 · We must then examine what is the best, and in how many senses we use the word. The answer is principally contained in three views. For men say that the good *per se* is the best of all things, the good *per se* being that whose property is to be the original good and the cause by its presence in other things of their being good; both of which attributes belong to the Idea of good (I mean by 'both' that of being the original good and also the cause of other things being good by its presence in them); for good is predicated of this Idea most truly (other things being good by participation in and likeness to this); and this is the original good, for the destruction of that which is participated in involves also the destruction of that which participates in the Idea, and is named from its participation in it. But this is the relation of the first to the later, so that the Idea of good is the good *per se;* for this is also (they say) separable from what participates in it, like all other Ideas.

The discussion, however, of this view belongs necessarily to another inquiry and a more abstract one, for arguments that are at once destructive and general belong to no other science. But if we must speak briefly about these matters, we say first that it is to speak abstractly and idly to assert that there is an Idea whether of good or of anything whatever—this has been considered in many ways both in our popular and in our philosophic discussions. Next, however much there are Ideas and in particular an Idea of good, they are perhaps useless with a view to a good life and to action. For the good has many senses, as numerous as those of being. For being, as we have divided it in other works, signifies now what a thing is, now quality, now quantity, now time, and again some of it consists in being changed and in changing; and the good is found in each of these modes, in substance as mind and God, in quality as justice, in quantity as moderation, in time as opportunity, while as examples of it in change, we have that which teaches and that which is being taught. As then being is not one in all that we have just mentioned, so neither is good; nor is there one science either of being or of the good; not even things named good in the same category are the objects of a single science, e.g. opportunity or moderation; but one science studies one kind of opportunity or moderation, and another another: e.g. opportunity and moderation in regard to food are studied by medicine and

gymnastics, in military matters by the art of strategy, and similarly with other sorts
1218ª1 of action, so that it can hardly be the province of one science to study the good *per se*.

Further, in things having an earlier and a later, there is no common element beyond, and, further, separable from, them, for then there would be something prior to the first; for the common and separable element would be prior, because with its
5 destruction the first would be destroyed as well; e.g. if the double is the first of the multiples, then the universal multiple cannot be separable, for it would be prior to the double³ . . . if the common element turns out to be the Idea, as it would be if one
10 made the common element separable: for if justice is good, and so also is bravery, there is then, they say, a good *per se,* for which they add '*per se*' to the general definition; but what could this mean except that it is eternal and separable? But what is white for many days is no whiter than that which is white for a single day; so the good will not be more good by being eternal. Hence the common good is not
15 identical with the Idea, for the common good belongs to all.

But we should show the nature of the good *per se* in the opposite way to that now used. For now from what is not agreed to possess the good they demonstrate the things admitted to be good, e.g. from numbers they demonstrate that justice and health are goods, for they are arrangements and numbers, and it is assumed that
20 goodness is a property of numbers and units because unity is the good itself. But they ought, from what are admitted to be goods, e.g. health, strength, and temperance, to demonstrate that beauty is present even more in the changeless; for all these things are order and rest; but if so, then the changeless is still more beautiful, for it has these attributes still more. And it is a bold way to demonstrate
25 that unity is the good *per se* to say that numbers have desire; for no one says distinctly how they desire, but the saying is altogether too unqualified. And how can one suppose that there is desire where there is no life? One should consider seriously about this and not assume without reasons what it is not easy to believe even with
30 reasons. And to say that all existing things desire some one good is not true; for each seeks its own special good, the eye vision, the body health, and so on.

There are then these difficulties in the way of there being a good *per se;*
35 further, it would be useless to political philosophy, which, like all others, has its particular good, e.g. as gymnastic has good bodily condition.

[Further, there is the argument written in the discourse—that the Idea itself of good is useful to no art or to all arts in the same way. Further, it is not practicable.]⁴ And similarly neither is good as a universal either the good *per se* (for it might
1218ᵇ1 belong even to a small good) or practicable; for medicine does not consider how to procure an attribute that may be an attribute of *anything,* but how to procure health; and so each of the other arts. But 'good' is ambiguous, and there is in it a
5 noble part, and part is practicable but the rest not so. The sort of good that is practicable is an object aimed at, but not the good in things unchanging.

It is clear, then, that neither the Idea of good nor the good as universal is the

---

³Susemihl marks a lacuna.   ⁴Excised by Susemihl.

good *per se* that we are actually seeking; for the one is unchanging and not practical, and the other though changing is still not practical. But the object aimed at as end is best, and the cause of all that comes under it, and first of all goods. This 10 then would be the good *per se,* the end of all human action. And this would be what comes under the master-art of all, which is politics, economics, and wisdom; for these mental habits differ from all others by their being of this nature; whether they 15 differ from one another must be stated later. And that the end is the cause of all that comes under it, the method of teaching shows; for the teacher first defines the end and thence shows of each of the other things that it is good; for the end aimed at is the cause. E.g. since to be in health is so and so, so and so must needs be what conduces to it; the health-giving is the efficient cause of health and yet[5] only of its 20 actual existence; it is not the cause of health being good. Further, no one demonstrates that health is good (unless he is a sophist and no doctor, but one who produces deceptive arguments from inappropriate considerations), any more than any other principle.

We must now consider, making a fresh start, in how many senses the good as 25 the end of man, the best in the field of action, is the best of all, since this is best.

BOOK II

1 · After this let us start from a new beginning and speak about what follows from it. All goods are either outside or in the soul, and of these those in the soul are more desirable; this distinction we make even in our popular discussions. For wisdom, excellence, and pleasure are in the soul, and some or all of these seem to all 35 to be the end. But of the contents of the soul some are states or faculties, others activities and movements.

Let this then be assumed, and also that excellence is the best state or condition or faculty of all things that have a use and work. This is clear by induction; for in all 1219ª1 cases we lay this down: e.g. a garment has an excellence, for it has a work and use, and the best state of the garment is its excellence. Similarly a vessel, house, or anything else has an excellence; therefore so also has the soul, for it has a work. And 5 let us assume that the better state has the better work; and as the states are to one another, so let us assume the corresponding works to be to one another. And the work of anything is its end; it is clear, therefore, from this that the work is better than the state; for the end is best, as being end: for we assumed the best, the final 10 stage, to be the end for the sake of which all else exists. That the work, then, is better than the state or condition is plain.

But 'work' has two senses; for some things have a work beyond mere employment, as building has a house and not the act of building, medicine health 15 and not the act of curing and restoring to health; while the work of other things is just their employment, e.g. of vision seeing and of mathematical science contemplation. Hence, necessarily, in those whose work is their employment the employment is more valuable than the state.

Having made these distinctions, we say that the work of a thing is also the work
20 of its excellence, only not in the same sense, e.g. a shoe is the work both of the art of cobbling and of the action of cobbling. If, then, the art of cobbling and the good cobbler have an excellence, their work is a good shoe: and similarly with everything else.

Further, let the work of the soul be to produce living, this[6] consisting in
25 employment and being awake—for slumber is a sort of inactivity and rest. Therefore, since the work must be one and the same both for the soul and for its excellence, the work of the excellence of the soul would be a good life. This, then, is the complete good, which (as we saw) was happiness. And it is clear from our assumptions (for these were that happiness was the best of things, and ends and the
30 best goods were in the soul; it is itself either a state or an activity . . .),[7] and since the activity is better than the state, and the best activity than the best state, and excellence is the best state, that the activity of the excellence of the soul is the best thing. But happiness, we saw, was the best of things; therefore happiness is the
35 activity of a good soul. But since happiness was something complete, and living is either complete or incomplete and so also excellence—one excellence being a whole, the other a part—and the activity of what is incomplete is itself incomplete, therefore happiness would be the activity of a complete life in accordance with complete excellence.

And that we have rightly stated its genus and definition common opinions
1219ᵇ1 prove. For to do well and to live well is held to be identical with being happy, but each of these—living and doing—is an employment, an activity; for the practical life is one of using or employing, e.g. the smith produces a bridle, the good horseman uses it.

We find confirmation also in the common opinion that we cannot ascribe
5 happiness to an existence of a single day, or to a child, or to each of the ages of life; and therefore Solon's advice holds good, never to call a man happy when living, but only when his life is ended. For nothing incomplete is happy, not being whole.

Further, praise is given to excellence because of its actions, but to actions something higher than praise, the encomium. And we crown the actual winners, not
10 those who have the power to win but do not actually win. Further, our judging the character of a man by his acts is a confirmation. Further, why is happiness not praised? Surely because other things are praised owing to this, either by their having reference to it or by their being parts of it. Therefore felicitation, praise, and
15 encomium differ; for encomium is discourse relative to the particular act, praise declares the general nature of the man, but felicitation is for the end. This clears up the difficulty sometimes raised—why for half their lives the good are no better than

---

[6]Reading τοῦτο for τοῦ.   [7]Susemihl marks a lacuna.

the bad, for all are alike when asleep; the cause is that sleep is an inactivity, not an activity of the soul. Therefore, even if there is some other part of the soul, e.g. the vegetative, its excellence is not a part of entire excellence, any more than the excellence of the body is; for in sleep the vegetative part is more active, while the perceptive and the appetitive are incomplete in sleep. But as far as they do to some extent partake of movement, even the visions of the good are better than those of the bad, except so far as they are caused by disease or bodily defect. 25

After this we must consider the soul. For excellence belongs to the soul and essentially so. But since we are looking for human excellence, let it be assumed that the parts of the soul partaking of reason are two, but that they partake not in the same way, but the one by its natural tendency to command, the other by its natural tendency to obey and listen; if there is a part without reason in some other sense, let it be disregarded. It makes no difference whether the soul is divisible or indivisible, so long as it has different faculties, namely those mentioned above, just as the curved includes the concave and the convex, or, again, the straight and the white, yet the straight is not white except incidentally and is not the same in substance.[8]

We also neglect any other part of the soul that there may be, e.g. the vegetative, for the above-mentioned parts are peculiar to the human soul; therefore the excellences of the nutritive part and that concerned with growth are not those of man. For, if we speak of him *qua* man, he must have the power of reasoning, a governing principle,[9] action; but reason governs not reason, but desire and the passions; he must then have these parts. And just as general good condition of the body is compounded of the partial excellences, so also is the excellence of the soul, *qua* end.

But of excellence there are two species, the moral[10] and the intellectual. For we praise not only the just but also the intelligent and the wise. For we assumed that what is praiseworthy is either the excellence or its work, and these are not activities, but have activities. But since the intellectual excellences involve reason, they belong to that rational part of the soul which governs the soul by its possession of reason, while the moral belong to the part which is irrational but by its nature obedient to the part possessing reason; for we do not describe the character of a man by saying that he is wise or clever, but by saying that he is gentle or bold.

After this we must first consider moral excellence, its nature, its parts—for our inquiry has been forced back on this—and how it is produced. We must make our search as all do in other things—they search having something to start with; so here, by means of true but indistinct judgements, we should always try to attain to what is true and distinct. For we are now in the condition of one who describes health as the best condition of the body, or Coriscus as the darkest man in the market-place; for what either of these is we do not know, but yet for the attainment of knowledge of either it is worth while to be in this condition. First, then, let it be laid down that the best state is produced by the best means, and that with regard to everything the best is done from the excellence of that thing (e.g. the exercises and food are best which

[8]Reading οὐσίᾳ τὸ αὐτό.   [9]Retaining καί.
[10]'Moral' translates ἠθικός: the word should be taken in the sense 'concerned with character'.

25 produce a good condition of body, and from such a condition men best perform exercises). Further, that every condition is produced and destroyed by some sort of application of the same things, e.g. health from food, exercises, and weather. This is clear from induction. Excellence too, then, is that sort of condition which is
30 produced by the best movements in the soul, and from which are produced the soul's best works and feelings; and by the same things, if they happen in one way, it is produced, but if they happen in another, it is destroyed. The employment of excellence is relative to the same things by which it is increased and destroyed, and it puts us in the best attitude towards them. A proof that both excellence and
35 badness are concerned with the pleasant and the painful is that punishment being cure and operating through opposites, as the cure does in everything else, acts through these.

2 · That moral excellence, then, is concerned with the pleasant and the painful is clear. But since the character, being as its name indicates something that
1220ᵇ1 grows by habit[11]—and that which is under guidance other than innate is trained to a habit by frequent movement of a particular kind—is the active principle present after this process, but in things inanimate we do not see this (for even if you throw a stone upwards ten thousand times, it will never go upward except by compulsion),—
5 consider, then, character to be this, viz. a quality in accordance with governing reason belonging to the irrational part of the soul which is yet able to obey the reason. Now we have to state in respect of what part of the soul we have character of this or that kind.[12] It will be in respect of the faculties of passion, in virtue of which men are spoken of as subject to passion, and in respect of the habits, in virtue of which men are described, in reference to those passions, either as feeling them in
10 some way or as not feeling them. After this comes the division made in . . .[13] into the passions, faculties, and habits. By passions I mean such as anger, fear, shame, sensual desire—in general, all that is usually followed of itself by sensuous pleasure
15 or pain. Quality does not depend on these—they are merely experienced—but on the faculties. By faculty I mean that in virtue of which men who act from their passions are called after them, e.g. are called irascible, insensible, amorous, bashful, shameless. And habits are the causes through which these faculties belong to us either in a reasonable way or the opposite, e.g. bravery, temperance, cowardice,
20 intemperance.

3 · After these distinctions we must notice that in everything continuous and divisible there is excess, deficiency and the mean, and these in relation to one another or in relation to us, e.g. in the gymnastic or medical arts, in those of building
25 and navigation, and in any sort of action, alike scientific and non-scientific, skilled and unskilled. For motion is continuous, and action is motion. In all cases the mean in relation to us is the best; for this is as knowledge and reason direct us. And this
30 everywhere also makes the best habit. This is clear both by induction and by

---

[11]ἦθος ('character') from ἔθος ('habit').
[12]Reading ποι᾽ ἄττα for ποιότης τά.   [13]Text uncertain.

reasoning. For opposites destroy one another, and extremes are opposite both to one another and to the mean; for the mean is to either extreme the other extreme, e.g. the equal is greater to the less, but less to the greater. Therefore moral excellence must have to do with the mean and be a sort of mean. We must then notice what sort   35
of mean excellence is and about what sort of means; let each be taken from the list by way of illustration, and studied:

irascibility	lack of feeling	gentleness
foolhardiness	cowardice	bravery
shamelessness	shyness	modesty 1221ª1
intemperance	insensibility	temperance
envy	(unnamed)	righteous indignation
gain	loss	the just
lavishness	meanness	liberality 5
boastfulness	self-depreciation	sincerity
habit of flattery	habit of dislike	friendliness
servility	stubbornness	dignity
[luxuriousness	submission to evils	endurance][14]
vanity	meanness of spirit	greatness of spirit 10
extravagance	pettiness	magnificence
[cunning	simplicity	wisdom][15]

These and similar are the passions that occur in the soul; they receive their names, some from being excesses, some from being defects. For the irascible is one   15
who is angry more than he ought to be, and more quickly, and with more people than he ought; the unfeeling is deficient in regard to persons, occasions, and manner. The man who fears neither what, nor when, nor as he ought is foolhardy; the man who fears what he ought not, and on the wrong occasions, and in the wrong manner is cowardly. . . . similarly, intemperate . . .[16] one prone to sensual desire and   20
exceeding in all possible ways, while he who is deficient and does not feel desire even so far as is good for him and in accordance with nature, but is as much without feeling as a stone, is insensible. The man who makes profit from any source is greedy of gain; the man who makes it from none, or perhaps few, is a waster. The braggart is one who pretends to more than he possesses, the self-depreciator is one   25
who pretends to less. The man who is more ready than is proper to join in praise is a flatterer; the man who is less ready is grudging. To act in everything so as to give another pleasure is servility, but to give pleasure seldom and reluctantly is stubbornness. [Further, one who can endure no pain, even if it is good for him, is soft; one who can endure all pain alike has no name literally applicable to him, but   30
by metaphor is called hard, patient, or ready of submission.][17] The vain man is he who thinks himself worthy of more than he is, while the poor-spirited thinks himself worthy of less. Further, the lavish is he who exceeds, the mean is he who is deficient, in every sort of expenditure. Similar are the stingy and the purse-proud; the latter   35

[14]Excised by Susemihl.   [15]Excised by Susemihl.
[16]Susemihl marks lacunae.   [17]Excised by Susemihl.

exceeds what is fitting, the former falls short of it. [The rogue aims at gain in any way and from any source; the simple not even from the right source.]¹⁸ A man is envious when he feels pain at the sight of prosperity more often than he ought, for even those who deserve prosperity cause when prosperous pain to the envious; the opposite character has not so definite a name: he is one who shows excess in not grieving even at the prosperity of the undeserving, but accepts all, as gluttons accept all food, while his opposite is impatient through envy.

It is superfluous to add to the definition that the particular relations to each thing should not be accidental; for no art, theoretical or productive, uses such additions to its definitions in speech or action; the addition is merely directed against logical quibbles against the arts. Take the above then, as simple definitions, which will be made more accurate when we speak of the opposite habits.

But of these states themselves there are species with names differing according as the excess is in time, in degree, or in the object provoking the state: e.g. one is quick-tempered through feeling anger quicker than one ought, irascible and passionate through feeling it more, bitter through one's tendency to retain one's anger, violent and abusive through the punishments one inflicts from anger . . .¹⁹ Epicures, gluttons, drunkards are so named from having a tendency contrary to reason to indulgence in one or the other kind of nutriment.

Nor must we forget that some of the faults mentioned cannot be taken to depend on the manner of action, if manner means excess of passion: e.g. the adulterer is not so called from his excessive intercourse with married women; 'excess' is inapplicable here, but the act is simply in itself wicked; the passion and its character are expressed in the same word. Similarly with assault. Hence men dispute the liability of their actions to be called by these names; they say that they had intercourse but did not commit adultery (for they acted ignorantly or by compulsion), or that they gave a blow but committed no assault; and so they defend themselves against all other similar charges.

4 · Having got so far, we must next say that, since there are two parts of the soul, the excellences are divided correspondingly, those of the rational part being the intellectual, whose function is truth, whether about a thing's nature or genesis, while the others belong to the part irrational but appetitive—for not any and every part of the soul, supposing it to be divisible, is appetitive. Necessarily, then, the character must be bad or good by its pursuit or avoidance of certain pleasures and pains. This is clear from our classification of the passions, powers, and states; for the powers and states are powers and states of the passions, and the passions are distinguished by pain and pleasure. So that for these reasons and also because of our previous propositions it follows that all moral excellence has to do with pleasures and pains. For by whatever things a soul tends to become better or worse, it is with regard to and in relation to these things that it finds pleasure. But we say men are bad through pleasures and pains, either by the pursuit and avoidance of improper

¹⁸Excised by Susemihl.   ¹⁹Susemihl marks a lacuna.

pleasures or pains or by their pursuit in an improper way. Therefore all readily define the excellences as insensibility or immobility as regards pleasures and pains, and vices as constituted by the opposites of these.   5

5 · But since we have assumed that excellence is that sort of habit from which men have a tendency to do the best actions, and through which they are in the best disposition towards what is best; and best is what is in accordance with right reason, and this is the mean between excess and defect relative to us; it would follow   10 that moral excellence is a mean relative to each individual himself, and is concerned with certain means in pleasures and pains, in the pleasant and the painful. The mean will sometimes be in pleasures (for there too is excess and defect), sometimes in pains, sometimes in both. For he who is excessive in his feeling of delight exceeds   15 in the pleasant, but he who exceeds in his feeling of pain, in the painful—and this either absolutely or with reference to some standard, e.g. when he differs from the majority of men; but the good man feels as he ought. But since there is a habit in consequence of which its possessor will in some cases admit the excess, in others the defect of the same thing, it follows that as these acts are opposed to one another and   20 to the mean, so the habits will also be opposed to one another and to excellence.

It happens, however, that sometimes all these oppositions will be clearer, sometimes those on the side of excess, sometimes those on the side of defect. And the reason for the difference is that the unlikeness or likeness to the mean is not always   25 of the same kind, but in one case one might change quicker from the excess to the middle habit, sometimes from the defect, and the person further distant seems more opposed; e.g. in regard to the body excess in exercise is healthier than defect, and nearer to the mean, but in food defect is healthier than excess. And so of those states   30 of choice which tend to training now some, now others, will show a greater tendency to health in case of the two acts of choice—now those good at work, now those good at abstemiousness; and he who is opposed to the moderate and the reasonable will be the man who avoids exercise, not both; and in the case of food the self-indulgent   35 man, not the man who starves himself. And the reason is that from the start our nature does not diverge in the same way from the mean as regards all things; we are less inclined to exercise, and more inclined to indulgence. So it is too with regard to the soul. We regard, then, as the habit opposed to the mean, that towards which both ourselves and men in general are more inclined—the other extreme, as though   40 not existent, escapes our notice, being unperceived because of its rarity. Thus we oppose anger to gentleness, and the irascible to the gentle. Yet there is also excess in   1222ᵇ1 the direction of gentleness and readiness to be reconciled, and the repression of anger when one is struck. But the men prone to this are few, and all incline more to the opposite extreme; there is none of the spirit of reconciliation[20] in anger.

And since we have reached a list of the habits in regard to the several passions,   5 with their excesses and defects, and the opposite habits in virtue of which men are as

---

[20]Reading καταλλακτικόν.

right reason directs them to be—(what right reason is, and with an eye to what standard we are to fix the mean, must be considered later)—it is clear that all the
10 moral excellences and vices have to do with excesses and defects of pleasures and pains, and that pleasures and pains arise from the above-mentioned habits and passions. But the best habit is that which is the mean in respect of each class of things. It is clear then that all, or at least some, of the excellences will be connected with means.

15   6 · Let us, then, take another starting-point for the succeeding inquiry. Every substance is by nature a sort of principle; therefore each can produce many similar to itself, as man man, animals in general animals, and plants plants. But in addition to this man alone of animals is also the source of certain actions; for no
20 other animal would be said to act. Such principles, which are primary sources of movements, are called principles in the strict sense, and most properly such as have necessary results; God is doubtless a principle of this kind. The strict sense of 'principle' is not to be found among principles without movement, e.g. those of
25 mathematics, though by analogy we use the name there also. For there, too, if the principle should change, practically all that is proved from it would alter; but its consequences do not change themselves, one being destroyed by another, except by destroying the assumption and, by its refutation, proving the truth. But man is the source of a kind of movement, for action is movement. But since, as elsewhere, the
30 source or principle is the cause of all that exists or arises through it, we must take the same view as in demonstrations. For if, supposing the triangle to have its angles equal to two right angles, the quadrilateral must have them equal to four right angles, it is clear that the property of the triangle is the cause of this last. And if the
35 triangle should change, then so must the quadrilateral, having six right angles if the triangle has three, and eight if it has four: but if the former does not change but remains as it was before, so must the quadrilateral.

The necessity of what we are endeavouring to show is clear from the *Analytics*; at present we can neither affirm nor deny anything with precision except just this.

Supposing there were no further cause for the triangle's having the above
40 property, then the triangle would be a sort of principle or cause of all that comes later. So that if anything existent may have the opposite to its actual qualities, so of
1223ᵃ1 necessity may its principles. For what results from the necessary is necessary; but the results of the contingent might be the opposite of what they are; what depends on men themselves forms a great portion of contingent matters, and men themselves are the sources of such contingent results. So that it is clear that all the acts of which
5 man is the principle and controller may either happen or not happen, and that their happening or not happening—those at least of whose existence or non-existence he has the control—depends on him. But of what it depends on him to do or not to do, he is himself the cause; and what he is the cause of depends on him. And since
10 excellence and badness and the acts that spring from them are respectively praised or blamed—for we do not give praise or blame for what is due to necessity, or chance, or nature, but only for what we ourselves are causes of; for what another is

the cause of, for that he bears the blame or praise—it is clear that excellence and badness have to do with matters where the man himself is the cause and source of his acts. We must then ascertain of what actions he is himself the source and cause. 15 Now, we all admit that of acts that are voluntary and done from the choice of each man he is the cause, but of involuntary acts he is not himself the cause; and all that he does from choice he clearly does voluntarily. It is clear then that excellence and badness have to with voluntary acts. 20

7 . We must then ascertain what is the voluntary and the involuntary, and what is choice, since by these excellence and badness are defined. First we must consider the voluntary and involuntary. Of three things it would seem to be one, agreement with either desire, or choice, or thought—that is, the voluntary would 25 agree, the involuntary would be contrary to one of these. But again, desire is divided into three sorts, wish, anger, and sensual appetite. We have, then, to distinguish these, and first to consider the case of agreement with sensual appetite.

Now all that is in agreement with sensual appetite would seem to be voluntary; for all the involuntary seems to be forced, and what is forced is painful, and so is all 30 that men do and suffer from compulsion—as Evenus says, 'all to which we are compelled is unpleasant'. So that if an act is painful it is forced on us, and if forced it is painful. But all that is contrary to sensual appetite is painful—for such appetite is for the pleasant—and therefore forced and involuntary; what then agrees with 35 sensual appetite is voluntary; for these two are opposites. Further, all wickedness makes one more unjust, and incontinence seems to be wickedness, the incontinent being the sort of man that acts in accordance with his appetite and contrary to his reason, and shows his incontinence when he acts in accordance with his appetite; but to act unjustly is voluntary, so that the incontinent will act unjustly by acting 1223ᵇ1 according to his appetite; he will then act voluntarily, and what is done according to appetite is voluntary. Indeed, it would be absurd that those who become incontinent should be more just.

From these considerations, then, the act done from appetite would seem voluntary, but from the following the opposite: what a man does voluntarily he 5 wishes, and what he wishes to do he does voluntarily. But no one wishes what he thinks to be bad; but surely the man who acts incontinently does not do what he wishes, for to act incontinently is to act through appetite contrary to what the man thinks best; whence it results that the same man acts at the same time both voluntarily and involuntarily; but this is impossible. Further, the continent will do a 10 just act, and more so than incontinence; for continence is an excellence, and excellence makes men more just. Now one acts continently whenever he acts against his appetite in accordance with his reason. So that if to act justly is voluntary as to act unjustly is—for both these seem to be voluntary, and if the one is, so must the 15 other be—but action contrary to appetite is involuntary, then the same man will at the same time do the same thing voluntarily and involuntarily.

The same argument may be applied to anger; for there is thought to be a continence and incontinence of anger just as there is of appetite; and what is

20   contrary to our anger is painful, and the repression is forced, so that if the forced is
involuntary, all acts done out of anger would be voluntary. Heraclitus, too, seems to
be regarding the strength of anger when he says that the restraint of it is
painful—'It is hard', he says, 'to fight with anger; for it gives its life for what it
25   desires'. But if it is impossible for a man voluntarily and involuntarily to do the same
thing[21] at the same time in regard to[22] the same part of the act, then what is done
from wish is more voluntary than that which is done from appetite or anger; and a
proof of this is that we do many things voluntarily without anger or desire.

It remains then to consider whether to act from wish and to act voluntarily are
30   identical. But this too seems impossible. For we assumed and all admit that
wickedness makes men more unjust, and incontinence seems a kind of wickedness.
But the opposite will result from the hypothesis above; for no one wishes what he
thinks bad, but does it when he becomes incontinent. If, then, to commit injustice is
voluntary, and the voluntary is what agrees with wish, then when a man becomes
35   incontinent he will be no longer committing injustice, but will be more just than
before he became incontinent. But this is impossible. That the voluntary then is not
action in accordance with desire, nor the involuntary action in opposition to it, is
clear.

8 · But again, that action in accordance with, or in opposition to, choice is
not the true description of the voluntary and involuntary is clear from the following
considerations: it has been shown that the act in agreement with wish was not
1224ª1   involuntary, but rather that all that one wishes is voluntary, though it has only been
shown that one may do voluntarily what one does not wish. But we do many things
from wish suddenly, but no one chooses an act suddenly.

5   But if, as we saw, the voluntary must be one of these three—action according
either to desire, choice, or thought, and it is not two of these, the remaining
alternative is that the voluntary consists in action with some kind of thought.
Advancing a little further, let us close our delimitation of the voluntary and the
10   involuntary. To act on compulsion or not on compulsion seems connected with these
terms; for we say that the enforced is involuntary, and all the involuntary is
enforced: so that first we must consider the action done on compulsion, its nature
and its relation to the voluntary and the involuntary. Now the enforced and the
necessary, force and necessity, seem opposed to the voluntary and to persuasion in
15   the case of acts done. Generally, we speak of enforced action and necessity even in
the case of inanimate things; for we say that a stone moves upwards and fire
downwards on compulsion and by force; but when they move according to their
natural internal tendency, we do not call the act one due to force; nor do we call it
voluntary either; there is no name for this antithesis; but when they move contrary
20   to this tendency, then we say they move by force. So, too, among things living and
among animals we often see things suffering and acting from force, when something
from without moves them contrary to their own internal tendency. Now in the

---

[21]Reading αὐτό for αὐτόν.   [22]Reading ἅμα κατά.

inanimate the moving principle is simple, but in the animated there is more than one principle; for desire and reason do not always agree. And so with the other animals   25 the action on compulsion is simple (just as in the inanimate), for they have not desire and reason opposing one another, but live by desire; but man has both, that is at a certain age, to which we attribute also the power of action; for we do not use this term of the child, nor of the brute, but only of the man who has come to act from reason.

So the compulsory act seems always painful, and no one acts from force and   30 yet with pleasure. Hence there arises much dispute about the continent and incontinent, for each of them acts with two tendencies mutually opposed, so that (as the expression goes) the continent forcibly drags himself from the pleasant appetites (for he feels pain in dragging himself away against the resistance of   35 desire), while the incontinent forcibly drags himself contrary to his reason. But still the latter seems less to be in pain; for appetite is for the pleasant, and this he follows with delight; so that the incontinent rather acts voluntarily and not from force,   1224^{b}1 because he acts without pain. But persuasion is opposed to force and necessity, and the continent goes towards what he is persuaded of, and so proceeds not from force but voluntarily. But appetite leads without persuading, being devoid of reason. We have, then, shown that these alone seem to act from force and involuntarily, and why they seem to, viz. from a certain likeness to the enforced action, in virtue of which we attribute enforced action also to the inanimate. Yet if we add the addition   5 made in our definition, there also the statement becomes untrue. For it is only when something external moves a thing, or brings it to rest against its own internal tendency, that we say this happens by force; otherwise we do not say that it happens by force. But in the continent and the incontinent it is the present internal tendency that leads them, for they have both tendencies. So that neither acts on compulsion   10 nor by force, but, as far at least as the above goes, voluntarily. For the external moving principle, that hinders or moves in opposition to the internal tendency, is what we call necessity, e.g. when we strike someone with the hand of one whose wish and appetite alike resist; but when the principle is from within, there is no force. Further, there is both pleasure and pain in both; for the continent feels pain   15 now in acting against his appetite, but has the pleasure of hope, i.e. that he will be presently benefited, or even the pleasure of being actually at present benefited because he is in health; while the incontinent is pleased at getting through his incontinency what he desires, but has a pain of expectation, thinking that he is doing   20 ill. So that to say that both act from compulsion is not without reason, the one sometimes acting involuntarily owing to his desire, the other owing to his reason; these two, being separated, are thrust out by one another. Whence men apply the language to the soul as a whole, because we see something like the above in the   25 elements of the soul. Now of the parts of the soul this may be said; but the soul as a whole, whether in the continent or the incontinent, acts voluntarily, and neither acts on compulsion, but one of the elements in them does, since by nature we have both. For reason is in them by nature, because if growth is permitted and not maimed, it   30 will be there; and appetite, because it accompanies and is present in us from birth.

But these are practically the two marks by which we define the natural—it is either that which is found with us as soon as we are born, or that which comes to us if growth is allowed to proceed regularly, e.g. grey hair, old age, and so on. So that
35 either acts contrary to nature, and yet, broadly speaking, according to nature, but not the same nature. The puzzles then about the continent and incontinent are these—do both, or one of them, act on compulsion, so that they act involuntarily or else at the same time both on compulsion and voluntarily; that is, if the compulsory is involuntary, both voluntarily and involuntarily? And it is tolerably clear from the
1225ᵃ1 above how these puzzles are to be met.

In another way, too, men are said to act by force and compulsion without any disagreement between reason and desire in them, viz. when they do what they
5 consider both painful and bad, but they are threatened with whipping, imprisonment, or death, if they do not do it. Such acts they say they did on compulsion. Or shall we deny this, and say that all do the act itself voluntarily? For they had the power to abstain from doing it, and to submit to the suffering. Again perhaps one might say that some such acts were voluntary and some not. For of the acts that a
10 man does without wishing them some he has the power to do or abstain from doing; these he always does voluntarily and not by force; but those in which he has not this power, he does by force in a sense (but not absolutely), because he does not choose the very thing he does, but the purpose for which it is done, since there is a difference, too, in this. For if a man were to murder another so as not to be caught at
15 blind man's buff he would be laughed at if he were to say that he acted by force, and on compulsion; there ought to be some greater and more painful evil that he would suffer if he did not commit the murder. For then he will act on compulsion and by force, or at least not by nature, when he does something evil for the sake of good, or release from a greater evil; then he will at least act involuntarily, for such acts are
20 not subject to his control. Hence, many regard love, anger in some cases, and natural conditions as involuntary, as being too strong for nature; we pardon them as things capable of overpowering nature. A man would more seem to act from force and involuntarily if he acted to escape violent than if to escape gentle pain, and generally if to escape pain than if to get pleasure. For that which depends on
25 him—and all turns on this—is what his nature is able to bear; what it is not, what is not under the control of his natural desire or reason, that does not depend on him. Therefore those who are inspired and prophesy, though their act is one of thought, we still say have it not in their own power either to say what they said, or to do what
30 they did. And so of acts done through appetite. So that some thoughts and passions do not depend on us, nor the acts[23] following such thoughts and reasonings, but, as Philolaus said, some arguments are too strong for us.

So that if the voluntary and involuntary had to be considered in reference to the presence of force as well as from other points of view, let this be our final
15 distinction. Nothing obscures the idea of the voluntary so much . . . as though they act from force and yet voluntarily.[24]

---

[23] Reading καὶ αἱ πράξεις for ἢ πράξεις.   [24] The text is uncertain.

9 · Since we have finished this subject, and we have found the voluntary not to be defined either by desire or by choice, it remains to define it as that which depends on thought. The voluntary, then, seems opposed to the involuntary, and to act with knowledge of the person acted on, instrument and aim—for sometimes one knows the object, e.g. as father, but not that the aim of the act is to kill, not to save, as in the case of Pelias's daughters; or knows the object to be a drink but takes it to be a philtre or wine when it was really hemlock—seems opposed to action in ignorance of the person, instrument, or thing, if, that is, the action is essentially the effect of ignorance. All that is done owing to ignorance, whether of person, instrument, or thing, is involuntary; the opposite therefore is voluntary. All, then, that a man does—it being in his power to abstain from doing it—not in ignorance and owing to himself must needs be voluntary; this is what voluntariness is. But all that he does in ignorance and owing to his ignorance, he does involuntarily. But since science or knowledge is of two sorts, one the possession, the other the use of knowledge, the man who has but does not use knowledge may in a sense be justly called ignorant, but in another sense not justly, e.g. if he had not used his knowledge owing to carelessness. Similarly, one might be blamed for not having the knowledge, if it were something easy or necessary and he does not have it because of carelessness or pleasure or pain. This, then, we must add to our definition.

Such, then, is the completion of our distinction of the voluntary and the involuntary.

10 · Let us next speak about choice, first raising various difficulties about it. For one might doubt to what genus it belongs and in which to place it, and whether the voluntary and the chosen are or are not the same. Now some insist that choice is either opinion or desire, and the inquirer might well think that it is one or the other, for both are found accompanying it. Now that it is not desire is plain; for then it would be either wish, appetite, or anger, for none desires without having experienced one of these feelings. But anger and appetite belong also to the brutes while choice does not; further, even those who are capable of both the former often choose without either anger or appetite; and when they are under the influence of those passions they do not choose but remain unmoved by them. Further, anger and appetite always involve pain, but we often choose without pain. But neither are wish and choice the same; for we often wish for what we know is impossible, e.g. to rule all mankind or to be immortal, but no one chooses such things unless ignorant of the impossibility, nor does he even choose what is possible, generally, if he does not think it in his power to do or to abstain from doing it. So that this is clear, that the object of choice must be one of the things in our own power. Similarly, choice is not an opinion nor, generally, what one thinks; for the object of choice was something in one's power and many things may be thought that are not in our power, e.g. that the diagonal is commensurable. Further, choice is not either true or false. Nor yet is choice identical with our opinion about matters of practice which are in our own power, as when we think that we ought to do or not to do something. This argument applies to wish as well as to opinion; for no one chooses an end, but things that

1225ᵇ1

5

10

15

20

25

30

35

1226ᵃ1

5

contribute to an end, e.g. no one chooses to be in health, but to walk or to sit for the
10 purpose of keeping well; no one chooses to be happy but to make money or run risks
for the purpose of being happy. And in general, in choosing we show both what we
choose and for what we choose it, the latter being that for which we choose
something else, the former that which we choose for something else. But it is the end
that we specially *wish for,* and we *think* we ought to be healthy and happy. So that
15 it is clear through this that choice is different both from opinion and from wish; for
wish and opinion pertain especially to the end, but choice does not.

It is clear, then, that choice is not wish, or opinion, or judgement simply. But in
what does it differ from these? How is it related to the voluntary? The answer to
20 these questions will also make it clear what choice is. Of possible things, then, there
are some such that we can deliberate about them, while about others we cannot. For
some things are possible, but the production of them is not in our power, some being
25 due to nature, others to other causes; and about these none would attempt to
deliberate except in ignorance. But about others, not only existence and non-
existence is possible, but also human deliberation;[25] these are things the doing or not
doing of which is in our own power. Therefore, we do not deliberate about the
affairs of the Indians nor how the circle may be squared; for the first are not in *our*
30 power, the second is wholly beyond the power of action; but we do not even
deliberate about all things that may be done and that are in our power (by which it
is clear that choice is not opinion simply), though the matters of choice and action
belong to the class of things in our own power. One might then raise the
35 problem—why do doctors deliberate about matters within their science, but not
grammarians? The reason is that error may occur in two ways (either in reasoning
or in perception when we are engaged in the very act), and in medicine one may go
wrong in both ways, but in grammar one can do so only in respect of the perception
1226ᵇ1 and action, and if they inquired about this there would be no end to their inquiries.
Since then choice is[26] neither opinion nor wish singly nor yet both (for no one
chooses suddenly, though he thinks he ought to act, and wishes, suddenly), it must
5 be compounded of both, for both are found in a man choosing. But we must
ask—how compounded out of these? The very name is some indication. For choice
is not simply picking but picking one thing before another; and this is impossible
without consideration and deliberation; therefore choice arises out of deliberate
opinion.

10 Now about the end no one deliberates (this being fixed for all), but about that
which tends to it—whether this or that tends to it, and—supposing this or that
resolved on—how it is to be brought about. All consider this till they have brought
the beginning of the process to a point in their own power. If then, no one chooses
15 without some preparation, without some deliberation whether it is better or worse to
do so and so, and if, of the things which contribute to an end, and which may or may
not come about, we deliberate about those which are in our power, then it is clear
that choice is a deliberate desire for something in one's own power; for we all

---

²⁵Ignoring Susemihl's indication of a lacuna.   ²⁶Omitting ἐστι.

deliberate about what we choose, but we do not choose all that we deliberate about. I call it deliberate when deliberation is the source and cause of the desire, and the man desires because of the deliberation. Therefore in the other animals choice does not exist, nor in man at every age or in every condition; for there is not deliberation or judgement on the ground of an act; but it is quite possible that many animals have an opinion whether a thing is to be done or not; only thinking with deliberation is impossible to them. For the deliberating part of the soul is that which observes a cause of some sort; and the object of an action is one of the causes; for we call cause that owing to which a thing comes about; but the purpose of a thing's existence or production is what we specially call its cause, e.g. of walking, the fetching of things, if this is the purpose for which one walks. Therefore, those who have no aim fixed have no inclination to deliberate. So that since, if a man of himself and not through ignorance does or abstains from that which is in his power to do or abstain from, he acts or abstains voluntarily, but we do many such things without deliberation or premeditation, it follows that all that has been chosen is voluntary, but not all the voluntary is chosen, and that all that is according to choice is voluntary, but not all that is voluntary is according to choice.[27] And at the same time it is clear from this that those legislators define well who enact that some states of feeling are to be considered voluntary, some involuntary, and some premeditated; for if they are not thoroughly accurate, at least they approximate to the truth. But about this we will speak in our investigation of justice; meanwhile, it is clear that choice is not simply wish or simply opinion, but opinion and desire together when following as a conclusion from deliberation.

But since in deliberating one always deliberates for the sake of some end, and he who deliberates has always an aim by reference to which he judges what is expedient, no one deliberates about the end; this is the starting-point and assumption, like the assumptions in theoretical science (we have spoken about this briefly in the beginning of this work and minutely in the *Analytics*). Everyone's inquiry, whether made with or without art, is about what tends to the end, e.g. whether they shall go to war or not, when this is what they are deliberating about. But the cause or object will come first, e.g. wealth, pleasure, or anything else of the sort that happens to be our object. For the man deliberating deliberates if he has considered, from the point of view of the end, what[28] conduces to bringing the end within his own action, or what he at present can do towards the object. But the object or end is always something good by nature, and men deliberate about its partial constituents, e.g. the doctor whether he is to give a drug, or the general where he is to pitch his camp. To them the absolutely best end is good. But contrary to nature and by perversion[29] not the good but the apparent good is the end. And the reason is that some things cannot be used for anything but what their nature determines, e.g. sight; for one can see nothing but what is visible, nor hear anything but what is audible. But science enables us to do what does not belong to that science; for the

20

25

30

35

1227ᵃ1

5

10

15

20

25

---

[27] Reading ἑκούσια (Susemihl's ἀκούσια is a misprint).
[28] Omitting Susemihl's ἤ.   [29] Reading διὰ στροφήν.

same science is not similarly related to health and disease, but naturally to the former, contrary to nature to the latter. And similarly wish is of the good naturally, but of the bad contrary to nature, and by nature one wishes the good, but contrary
30   to nature and through perversion[30] the bad as well.

But further, the corruption and perversion of a thing does not tend to anything at random but to the contrary or the intermediate between it and the contrary. For out of this province one cannot go, since error leads not to anything at random but to the contrary of truth where there is a contrary, and to that contrary which is
35   according to the appropriate science contrary. Therefore, the error and the resulting choice must deviate from the mean towards the opposite—and the opposite of the mean is excess or defect. And the cause is pleasantness or painfulness; for we are so constituted that the pleasant appears good to the soul and the more pleasant better, while the painful appears bad and the more painful worse. So that from this also it is
1227ᵇ1   clear that excellence and badness have to do with pleasures and pains; for they have to do with objects of choice, and choice has to do with the good and bad or what seems such, and pleasure and pain naturally seem such.
5   It follows then, since moral excellence is itself a mean and wholly concerned with pleasures and pains, and badness lies in excess or defect and is concerned with the same matters as excellence, that moral excellence is a habit tending to choose the mean in relation to us in things pleasant and painful, in regard to which,
10   according as one is pleased or pained, men are said to have a definite sort of character; for one is not said to have a special sort of character merely for liking what is sweet or what is bitter.

11 · These distinctions having been made, let us say whether excellence makes the choice correct and the end right so that a man chooses for the right end,
15   or whether (as some say) it makes the reason so. But what does this is continence, for this preserves the reason. But excellence and continence differ. We must speak later about them, since those who think that excellence makes the reason right, do so for this cause—namely, that continence is of this nature and continence is one of the things we praise. Now that we have discussed preliminary questions let us state
20   our view.[31] It is possible for the aim to be right, but for a man to go wrong in what contributes to that aim; and again the aim may be mistaken, while the things leading to it are right; or both may be mistaken. Does then excellence make the aim, or the things that contribute to that aim? We say the aim, because this is not
25   attained by inference or reasoning. Let us assume this as starting-point. For the doctor does not ask whether one ought to be in health or not, but whether one ought to walk or not; nor does the trainer ask whether one ought to be in good condition or not, but whether one should wrestle or not. And similarly no art asks questions about the end; for as in theoretical sciences the assumptions are our starting-points,
30   so in the productive the end is starting-point and assumed. E.g. we reason that since this body is to be made healthy, therefore so and so must be found in it if health is to

---

[30]Reading διὰ στροφήν.   [31]Reading λέγωμεν.

be had—just as in geometry we argue, if the angles of the triangle are equal to two right angles, then so and so must be the case. The end aimed at is, then, the starting-point of our thought, the end of our thought the starting-point of action. If, then, of all correctness either reason or excellence is the cause, if reason is not the cause, then the end (but not the things contributing to it) must owe its rightness to   35 excellence. But the end is the object of the action; for all choice is of something and for the sake of some object. The object, then, is the mean, and excellence is the cause of this by choosing the object. Still choice is not of this but of the things done for the sake of this. To hit on these things—I mean what ought to be done for the sake of the object—belongs to another faculty; but of the rightness of the end of   1228ª1 the choice the cause is excellence. And therefore it is from a man's choice that we judge his character—that is from the object for the sake of which he acts, not from the act itself. Similarly, badness brings it about that we choose the opposite object. If, then, a man, having it in his power to do the honourable and abstain from the   5 base, does the opposite, it is clear that this man is not good. Hence, it follows that both excellence and badness are voluntary; for there is no necessity to do what is wicked. Therefore badness is blamable and excellence praiseworthy. For the involuntary if base or bad is not blamable, if good is not praiseworthy, but only the   10 voluntary. Further, we praise and blame all men with regard to their choice rather than their acts (though activity is more desirable than excellence), because men may do bad acts under compulsion, but no one chooses them under compulsion. Further, it is only because it is not easy to see the nature of a man's choice that we   15 are forced to judge of his character by his acts. The activity then is more desirable, but the choice is more praiseworthy. And this both follows from our assumptions and is in agreement with the phenomena.

BOOK III

1 · That there are mean states, then, in the excellences, and that these are states of choice, and that the opposite states are vices and what these are, has been stated in its universal form. But let us take them individually and speak of them in   25 order; and first let us speak of bravery. All are practically agreed that the brave man is concerned with fears and that bravery is one of the excellences. We distinguished also in the table foolhardiness and fear as contraries; in a sense they are, indeed, opposed to one another. Clearly, then, those named after these habits   30 will be similarly opposed to one another, i.e. the coward, for he is so called from fearing more than he ought and being less confident than he ought, and the foolhardy man, who is so called for fearing less than he ought and being more confident than he ought. (Hence they have names cognate to those of the qualities,   35 e.g. 'foolhardy' is cognate to 'foolhardiness'.) So that since bravery is the best habit in regard to fear and confidence, and one should be neither like the foolhardy (who are defective in one way, excessive in another) nor like the cowards (of whom the same may be said, only not about the same objects, but inversely, for they are   1228ᵇ1

defective in confidence and excessive in fear), it is clear that the middle habit between foolhardiness and cowardice is bravery, for this is the best.

The brave man seems to be in general fearless, the coward prone to fear; the
5 latter fears many things and few, great things and small, and intensely and quickly, while his opposite fears either not at all or slightly and reluctantly and seldom, and great things only. The brave man endures even what is very frightening, the coward not even what is slightly frightening. What, then, does the brave man endure? First,
10 is it the things that appear frightening to himself or to another? If the latter, his bravery would be no considerable matter. But if it is the things that he himself fears, then he must find many things frightening—frightening things[32] being things that cause fear to those who find them frightening, great fear if very frightening, slight
15 fear if slightly frightening. Then it follows that the brave man feels much and serious fear; but on the contrary bravery seemed to make a man fearless, fearlessness consisting in fearing few things if any, and in fearing slightly and with reluctance. But perhaps we use 'frightening'—like 'pleasant' and 'good'—in two senses. Some things are pleasant or good absolutely, others to a particular person
20 pleasant or good—but absolutely bad and not pleasant, e.g. what is useful to the wicked or pleasant to children as such; and similarly the frightening is either absolutely such or such to a particular person. What, then, a coward as such fears is
25 not frightening to anyone or but slightly so; but what is frightening to the majority of men or to human nature, that we call absolutely frightening. But the brave man shows himself fearless towards these and endures such things, they being to him frightening in one sense but in another not—frightening to him *qua* man, but not frightening to him except slightly so, or not at all, *qua* brave. These things, however,
30 are frightening, for they are so to the majority of men. This is the reason, by the way, why the habit of the brave man is praised; his condition is analogous to that of the strong or healthy. For these are what they are, not because, in the case of the one, no toil, or in the case of the other, no extreme, crushes them, but because they are either unaffected absolutely or affected only to a slight extent by the things that
35 affect the many or the majority. The sick, then, and the weak and the cowardly are affected by the common affections, as well as by others, only more quickly and to a greater extent than the many, . . .[33] and further, by the things that affect the many they are wholly unaffected or but slightly affected.

But it is still questioned whether anything is frightening to the brave man,
1229ª1 whether he would not be incapable of fear. May we not allow him to be capable of it in the way above mentioned? For bravery consists in following reason, and reason bids one choose the noble. Therefore the man who endures the frightening from any other cause than this is either out of his wits or foolhardy; but the man who does so for the sake of the noble is alone fearless and brave. The coward, then, fears even
5 what he ought not, the foolhardy is confident even when he ought not to be; the brave man both fears and is confident when he ought to be and is in this sense a mean, for he is confident or fears as reason bids him. But reason does not bid a man

---

[32]Omitting μεγάλα καί, and reading φοβερά. ⟨τὰ δὲ φοβερὰ⟩ φόβον.
[33]Susemihl marks a lacuna.

to endure what is very painful or destructive unless it is noble; now the foolhardy man is confident about such things even if reason does not bid him be so, while the coward is not confident even if it does; the brave man alone is confident about them   10 only if reason bids him.

There are five kinds of courage, so named for a certain analogy between them; for they all endure the same things but not for the same reasons. One is a civic courage, due to the sense of shame; another is military, due to experience and knowledge, not (as Socrates said[34]) of what is fearful, but of the resources they have   15 to meet what is fearful. The third kind is due to inexperience and ignorance; it is that which makes children and madmen face objects moving towards them and take hold of snakes. Another kind is due to hope, which makes those who have often been fortunate, or those who are drunk, face dangers—for wine makes them sanguine.   20 Another kind is due to irrational feeling, e.g. love or anger; for a man in love is rather foolhardy than timid, and faces many dangers, like him who slew the tyrant in Metapontum or the man of whom stories are told in Crete. Similar is the action of anger or passion, for passion is beside itself. Hence wild boars are thought to be   25 brave though they are not really so, for they behave as such when beside themselves, but at other times are unpredictable like foolhardy men. But still the bravery of passion is above all natural (passion is invincible, and therefore children are excellent fighters); civic courage is the effect of law. But in truth none of these   30 forms is courage, though all are useful for encouragement in danger.

So far we have spoken of the frightening generally; now it is best to distinguish further. In general, then, whatever is productive of fear is called frightening, and this is all that causes destructive pain. For those who expect some other pain may   35 perhaps have another pain and other emotions but not fear, e.g. if a man foresees that he will suffer the pain of envy or of jealousy or of shame. But fear only occurs in connexion with the expectation of pains whose nature is to be destructive to life. Therefore men who are very effeminate as to some things are brave, and some who   1229^{b}1 are hard and enduring are cowards. Indeed, it is thought practically the special mark of bravery to take up a certain attitude towards death and the pain of it. For if a man were so constituted as to be patient as reason requires towards heat and cold   5 and similar not dangerous pains, but weak and timid about death, not for any other feeling, but just because it means destruction, while another was soft in regard to these but unaffected in regard to death, the former would seem cowardly, the latter   10 brave; for we speak of danger also only in regard to such objects of fear as bring near to us that which will cause such destruction; when this seems close, then we speak of danger.

The objects of fear, then, in regard to which we call a man brave are, as we have said, those which appear capable of causing destructive pain, but only when they appear near and not far off, and are of such magnitude, real or apparent, as is   15 not out of proportion to man, for some things must appear frightening and must perturb any man. For just as things hot and cold and certain other powers are too

---

[34]See Plato, *Protagoras* 360D.

20 strong for us and the conditions of the human body, so it may be with regard to the emotions of the soul.

The cowardly, then, and the foolhardy are misled by their habits; for to the coward what is not frightening seems frightening, and what is slightly frightening greatly so, while in the opposite way, to the foolhardy man the frightening seems 25 safe and the very frightening but slightly so; but the brave man thinks things what they truly are. Therefore, if a man faces the frightening through ignorance (e.g. if a man faces in the transport of madness the attack of a thunderbolt), he is not brave nor yet if, knowing the magnitude of the danger, he faces it through passion—as the Celts take up their arms to go to meet the waves; in general, all the bravery of 30 foreigners involves passion. But some face danger also for other pleasures—for passion is not without a certain pleasure, involving as it does the hope of vengeance. But still, whether a man faces death for this or some other pleasure or to flee from greater evils, he would not justly be called brave. For if dying were pleasant, the 35 profligate would have often died because of his incontinence, just as now—since what causes death is pleasant though not death itself—many knowingly incur death through their incontinence, but none of them would be thought brave even if they do it with perfect readiness to die. Nor is a man brave if he seeks death to avoid trouble, 1230ᵃ1 as many do; to use Agathon's words: 'Bad men too weak for toil are in love with death,' And so the poets narrate that Chiron, because of the pain of his wound, prayed for death and release from his immortality. Similarly, all who face dangers 5 owing to experience are not really brave; this is what, perhaps, most soldiers do. For the truth is the exact opposite of what Socrates thought; he held that bravery was knowledge. But those who know how to ascend masts are confident not because they 10 know what is frightening but because they know how to help themselves in dangers. Nor is all that makes men fight more boldly courage; for then, as Theognis puts it, strength and wealth would be bravery—'every man' (he says) 'is daunted by poverty'. Obviously some, though cowards, face dangers because of their experience, because they do not think them dangers, as they know how to help themselves; 15 and a proof of this is that, when they think they can get no help and the danger is close at hand, they no longer face it. But of all brave men of this sort, it is those who face danger because of shame who would most seem to be brave, as Homer says 20 Hector faced the danger from Achilles—'and shame seized Hector'; and, again, 'Polydamas will be the first to taunt me'.³⁵ Such bravery is civic. But the true bravery is neither this nor any of the others, but like them, as is also the bravery of brutes which from passion run to meet the blow. For a man ought to hold his ground though frightened, not because he will incur disrepute, nor through anger, nor 25 because he does not expect to be killed or has powers by which to protect himself; for in that case he will not even think that there is anything to be feared. But since all excellence implies choice—we have said before what this means and that it makes a man choose everything for the sake of some end, and that the end is the noble–it is 30 clear that bravery, because it is an excellence, will make a man face what is

---

³⁵*Iliad* XXII 100.

frightening for some end, so that he does it neither through ignorance—for his excellence rather makes him judge correctly—nor for pleasure, but because the act is noble; since, if it is not noble but frantic, he does not face the danger, for that would be disgraceful. In regard, then, to what things bravery is a mean state, between what, and why, and the meaning of the frightening, we have now spoken 35 tolerably adequately for our present purpose.

2 · After this we must try to draw certain distinctions regarding profligacy and temperance. 'Profligate' has many senses. A man is profligate when he has not been corrected or cured (just as what has not been cut is uncut), and of such men, some are capable, others incapable of correction; just as the uncut includes both 1230ᵇ1 what cannot be cut and what can be but has not been cut; and so with 'profligate'. For it is both that which by its nature refuses correction, and that which is of a nature to accept but has not yet received correction for the faults in regard to which 5 the temperate man acts rightly—e.g. children. For we give them the same name as the profligate, but because of this latter kind of profligacy. And, further, it is in different senses that we give the name to those hard to cure and to those whom it is quite impossible to cure through correction. Profligacy, then, having many senses, it is clear that it has to do with certain pleasures and pains, and that the forms differ 10 from one another and from other states by the kind of attitude towards these; we have already stated how, in the use of the word 'profligacy', we apply it to various states by analogy. As to those who from insensibility are unmoved by these same pleasures, some call them insensible, while others describe them as such by other 15 names; but this state is not very familiar or common because all rather err in the opposite direction, and it is congenital to all to be overcome by and to be sensible to such pleasures. It is the state chiefly of such as the rustics introduced on the stage by comic writers, who keep aloof from even moderate and necessary pleasures. 20

But since temperance has to do with pleasures, it must also have to do with certain appetites; we must, then, ascertain which. For the temperate man does not exhibit his temperance in regard to all appetites and all pleasures, but about the objects, as it seems, of two senses, taste and touch, or rather really about those of 25 touch alone. For his temperance is shown not in regard to visual pleasure in the beautiful (so long as it is unaccompanied by sexual appetite) or visual pain at the ugly; nor, again, in regard to the pleasure or pain of the ear at harmony or discord; nor, again, in regard to olfactory pleasure or pain at pleasant or disagreeable odours. Nor is a man called profligate for feeling or want of feeling in regard to such 30 matters. For instance, if one sees a beautiful statue, or horse, or human being, or hears singing, without any accompanying wish for eating, drinking, or sexual indulgence, but only with the wish to see the beautiful and to hear the singers, he would not be thought profligate any more than those who were charmed by the 35 Sirens. Temperance and profligacy have to do with those two senses whose objects are alone felt by and give pleasure and pain to brutes as well; and these are the senses of taste and touch, the brutes seeming insensible to the pleasures of practically all the other senses alike, e.g. harmony or beauty; for they obviously 1231ᵃ1 have no feeling worth mentioning at the mere sight of the beautiful or the hearing of the harmonious, except, perhaps, in some marvellous instances. And with regard to pleasant and disagreeable odours it is the same, though all their senses are sharper than ours. They do, indeed, feel pleasure at certain odours; but these gladden them accidentally and not of their own nature. By those enjoyed not of their own nature I mean those that give us pleasure owing to expectation and memory, e.g. the pleasure from the scent of foods and drinks; for these we enjoy because of a different pleasure, that of eating or drinking; the odours enjoyed for their own nature are such as those of flowers (therefore Stratonicus neatly remarked that these smell beautifully, food, etc., pleasantly). Indeed, the brutes are not excited over every pleasure connected with taste, e.g. not over those which are felt in the tip of the tongue, but only over those that are felt in the gullet, the sensation being one of touch rather than of taste. Therefore gluttons pray not for a long tongue but for the gullet of a crane, as did Philoxenus, the son of Eryxis. Therefore, broadly, we should regard profligacy as concerned with objects of touch. Similarly it is with such pleasures that the profligate man is concerned. For drunkenness, gluttony, lecherousness, gormandizing, and all such things are concerned with the above-mentioned senses; and these are the parts into which we divide profligacy. But in regard to the pleasures of sight, hearing, and smell, no one is called profligate if he is in excess, but we blame without considering disgraceful such faults, and all in regard to which we do not speak of men as continent; the incontinent are neither profligate nor temperate.

The man, then, so constituted as to be deficient in the pleasures in which all must in general partake and rejoice is insensible (or whatever else we ought to call him); the man in excess is profligate. For all naturally take delight in these objects and conceive appetites for them, and neither are nor are called profligate; for they neither exceed by rejoicing more than is right when they get them, nor by feeling greater pain than they ought when they miss them; nor are they insensible, for they are not deficient in the feeling of joy or pain, but rather in excess.

But since there is excess and defect in regard to these things, there is clearly also a mean, and this state is the best and opposed to both of the others; so that if the best state about the objects with which the profligate is concerned is temperance, temperance would be the mean state in regard to the above-mentioned sensible pleasures, the mean between profligacy and insensibility, the excess being profligacy and the defect either nameless or expressed by the names we have suggested. More accurate distinctions about the class of pleasures will be drawn in what is said later about continence and incontinence.

3 · In the same way we must ascertain what is gentleness and irascibility. For we see that the gentle is concerned with the pain that arises from anger, being characterized by a certain attitude towards this. We have given in our list as opposed to the passionate, irascible, and savage—all such being names for the same state—the slavish and the stupid. For these are pretty much the names we apply to those who are not moved to anger even when they ought, but take insults easily and

are tolerant of contempt—for slowness to anger is opposed to quickness, violence to quietness, long persistence in that feeling of pain which we call anger to short. And since there is here, as we have said there is elsewhere, excess and defect—for the irascible is one that feels anger more quickly, to a greater degree, and for a longer time, and when he ought not, and at what he ought not, and frequently, while the slavish is the opposite—it is clear that there is a mean to this inequality. Since, then, both the above-mentioned habits are wrong, it is clear that the mean state between them is good; for he is neither too soon nor too late, and does not feel anger when he ought not, nor feel no anger when he ought. So that since in regard to these emotions the best condition is gentleness, gentleness would be a mean state, and the gentle a mean between the irascible and the slavish.

4 · Also magnanimity, magnificence, and liberality are mean states—liberality being shown in the acquisition or expenditure of wealth. For the man who is more pleased than he ought to be with every acquisition and more pained than he ought to be at every expenditure is illiberal; he who feels less of both than he ought is lavish; he who feels both as he ought is liberal. (By 'as he ought', both in this and in the other cases, I mean 'as right reason directs'.) But since the two former show their nature respectively by excess and defect—and where there are extremes, there is also a mean and that is best, a single best for each kind of action—liberality must be the mean between lavishness and meanness in regard to the acquisition and expenditure of wealth. I take wealth and the art of wealth in two senses; the art in one sense being the proper use of one's property (say of a shoe or a coat), in the other an accidental mode of using it—not the use of a shoe for a weight, but, say, the selling of it or letting it out for money; for here too the shoe is used. Now the lover of money is a man eager for actual money, which is a sign of possession taking the place of the accidental use of other possessions. But the illiberal man may even be lavish in the accidental pursuit of wealth, for it is in the natural pursuit of it that he aims at increase. The lavish runs short of necessaries; but the liberal man gives his superfluities. There are also species of these genera which exceed or fall short as regards parts of the subject-matter of liberality, e.g. the sparing, the skinflint, the grasper at disgraceful gain, are all illiberal; the sparing is characterized by his refusal to spend, the grasper at disgraceful gain by his readiness to accept anything, the skinflint by his strong feeling over small amounts, while the man who has the sort of injustice that involves meanness is a false reckoner and cheat. And similarly one class of spendthrift is a waster by his disorderly expenditure, the other a fool who cannot bear the pain of calculation.

5 · As to magnanimity we must define its specific nature from the qualities that we ascribe to the magnanimous. For just as with other things, in virtue of their nearness and likeness up to a certain point, their divergence beyond that point escapes notice, so it is with magnanimity. Therefore, sometimes men really opposite lay claim to the same character, e.g. the lavish to that of the liberal, the self-willed to that of the dignified, the foolhardy to that of the brave. For they are

concerned with the same things, and are up to a certain point contiguous; thus the brave man and the foolhardy man are alike ready to face danger—but the former in one way, the latter in another; and these ways differ greatly. Now, we assert that the magnanimous man, as is indicated by the name we apply to him, is characterized by
30 a certain greatness of soul and faculty; and so he seems like the dignified and the magnificent man, since[36] magnanimity seems to accompany all the excellences. For to distinguish correctly great goods from small is laudable. Now, those goods are thought great which are pursued by the man of the best habit in regard to what
35 seem to be pleasures;[37] and magnanimity is the best habit. But every special excellence correctly distinguishes the greater from the less among its objects, as the wise man and excellence would direct, so that all the excellences seem to go with this one of magnanimity, or this with all the excellences.

Further, it seems characteristic of the magnanimous man to be disdainful;
1232ᵇ1 each excellence makes one disdainful of what is esteemed great contrary to reason (e.g. bravery disdains dangers of this kind—for it considers it disgraceful to hold[38] them great; and numbers are not always fearful: so the temperate disdains many great pleasures, and the liberal wealth). But this characteristic seems to belong to
5 the magnanimous man because he cares about few things only, and those great, and not because someone else thinks them so. The magnanimous man would consider rather what one good man thinks than many ordinary men, as Antiphon after his condemnation said to Agathon when he praised his defence of himself. Contempt seems particularly the special characteristic of the magnanimous man; and, again,
10 as regards honour, life, and wealth—about which mankind seems to care—he values none of them except honour. He would be pained if denied honour, and if ruled by one undeserving. He delights most of all when he obtains honour.

In this way he would seem to contradict himself; for to be[39] concerned above all
15 with honour, and yet to disdain the multitude and[40] reputation, are inconsistent. So we must first distinguish. For honour, great or small, is of two kinds; for it may be given by a crowd of ordinary men or by those worthy of consideration; and, again, there is a difference according to the ground on which honour is given. For it is
20 made great not merely by the number of those who give the honour or by their quality, but also by its being precious; but in reality, power and all other goods are precious and worthy of pursuit only if they are truly great, so that there is no excellence without greatness; therefore every excellence, as we have said, makes a man magnanimous in regard to the object with which that excellence is concerned.
25 But still there is a single excellence, magnanimity, alongside of the other excellences, and he who has this must be called in a special sense magnanimous. But since some goods are precious and some as we distinguished earlier, and of such goods some are in truth great and some small, and of these some men are worthy
30 and think themselves so, among these we must look for the magnanimous man. There must be four different kinds of men. For a man may be worthy of great goods

---

³⁶Reading ὅτι for ὅτε.   ³⁷Reading δοκοῦντα for τοιαῦτα.
³⁸Reading μέγα γὰρ ἡγεῖσθαι.   ³⁹Reading τό for τῷ.   ⁴⁰Retaining καί.

and think himself worthy of them, and again there may be small goods and a man worthy of them and thinking himself worthy; and we may have the opposites in regard to either kind of goods; for there may be a man worthy of small who thinks himself worthy of great and esteemed goods; and, again, one worthy of great but   35 thinking himself worthy only of small. He then who is worthy of the small but thinks himself worthy of the great is blameable; for it is stupid and not noble that he should obtain out of proportion to his worth: the man also is blameable who being worthy of great goods, because he possesses the gifts that make a man worthy, does not think himself worthy to share in them. There remains then the opposite of these two—the   1233ª1 man who is worthy of great goods and thinks himself worthy of them, such being his disposition; he is the mean between the other two and is praiseworthy. Since, then, in respect of the choice and use of honour and the other esteemed goods, the best   5 condition is magnanimity, and we define the magnanimous man as being this, and not as being concerned with things useful; and since this mean is the most praiseworthy state, it is clear that magnanimity is a mean. But of the opposites, as shown in our list, the quality consisting in thinking oneself worthy of great goods   10 when not worthy is vanity—for we give the name of vain to those who think themselves worthy of great things though they are not; but the quality of not thinking oneself worthy of great things though one is, we call mean-spiritedness— for it is held to be the mark of the mean-spirited not to think himself worthy of anything great though he possesses that for which he would justly be deemed worthy of it; hence, it follows that magnanimity is a mean between vanity and   15 mean-spiritedness. The fourth of the sorts of men we have distinguished is neither wholly blameable nor yet magnanimous, not having to do with anything that possesses greatness, for he neither is worthy nor thinks himself worthy of great goods; therefore, he is not opposite to the magnanimous man; yet to be worthy and think oneself worthy of small goods might seem opposite to being worthy and   20 thinking oneself worthy of great ones. But such a man is not opposite to the magnanimous man, for he is not to be blamed (his habit being what reason directs); he is, in fact, similar in nature to the magnanimous man; for both think themselves worthy of what they really are worthy of. He might become magnanimous, for of whatever he is worthy of he will think himself worthy. But the mean-spirited man   25 who, possessed of great and honourable qualities, does not think himself worthy of great goods—what would he do if he deserved only small? Either[41] he would think himself worthy of great goods and thus be vain, or else of still smaller than he has. Therefore, no one would call a man mean-spirited because, being an alien in a city, he does not claim to govern but submits, but only one who does not, being well born and thinking power a great thing.   30

6 · The magnificent man is not concerned with any and every action or choice, but with expenditure—unless we use the name metaphorically; without expense there cannot be magnificence. It is the fitting in ornament, but ornament is

---

[41]Reading ἤ for εἰ, and ignoring Susemihl's lacuna.

35 not to be got out of ordinary expenditure, but consists in surpassing the merely necessary. The man, then, who tends to choose in great expenditure the fitting magnitude, and desires this sort of mean, and with a view to this sort of pleasure, is magnificent; the man whose inclination is to something larger than necessary but

1233ᵇ1 out of harmony, has no name, though he is near to those called by some tasteless and showy: e.g. if a rich man, spending money on the marriage of a favourite, thinks it sufficient to make such arrangements as one makes to entertain those who drink to the Good Genius, he is shabby; while one who receives guests of this sort in the way

5 suited to a marriage feast resembles the showy man, if he does it neither for the sake of reputation nor to gain power; but he who entertains suitably and as reason directs, is magnificent; for what looks well is the suitable; nothing unsuitable is fitting. And what one does should be fitting. For in what is fitting is involved suitability both to the object[42] (e.g. one thing is fitting for a servant's, another for a

10 favourite's wedding) and to the entertainer both in extent and kind, e.g. people thought that the mission conducted by Themistocles to the Olympian games was not fitting to him because of his previous low station, but would have been to Cimon. But the man who is indifferent to questions of suitability is in none of the above classes.

15 Similarly with liberality; for a man may be neither liberal nor illiberal.

7 · In general of the other blameable or praiseworthy qualities of character some are excesses, others defects, others means, but of feelings, e.g. the envious man and the man who rejoices over another's misfortunes. For, to consider the habits to

20 which they owe their names, envy is pain felt at deserved good fortune, while the feeling of the man who rejoices at misfortunes has itself no name,[43] but such a man shows his nature by[44] rejoicing over undeserved ill fortune. Between them is the man inclined to righteous indignation, the name given by the ancients to pain felt at

25 either good or bad fortune if undeserved, or to joy felt at them if deserved. Hence they make righteous indignation (νέμεσις) a god. Shame is a mean between shamelessness and shyness; for the man who thinks of no one's opinion is shameless, he who thinks of everyone's alike is shy, he who thinks only of that of apparently

30 good men is modest. Friendliness is a mean between animosity and flattery; for the man who readily accommodates himself in all respects to another's desires is a flatterer; the man who opposes every desire is prone to enmity; the man who neither accommodates himself to nor resists everyone's pleasure, but only accommodates himself to what seems to be best, is friendly. Dignity is a mean between self-will and

35 too great obligingness; for the contemptuous man who lives with no consideration for another is self-willed; the man who adapts his whole life to another and is submissive to everybody is too obliging; but he who acts thus in certain cases but not in others, and only to those worthy, is dignified. The sincere and simple, or, as he is

1234ᵃ1 called, straightforward man, is a mean between the dissembler and the boaster. For

---

[42]The text of this clause is uncertain. [43]Omitting ἐπὶ τό. [44]Reading ἐστι τῷ for ἐπὶ τό.

the man who knowingly and falsely depreciates himself is a dissembler; the man who exalts himself is a boaster; the man who represents himself as he is, is sincere, and in the Homeric phrase honest; in general the one loves truth, the other a lie. Wittiness also is a mean, the witty man being a mean between the rustic and the   5 buffoon. For just as the squeamish differs from the omnivorous in that the one takes little or nothing and that with reluctance, while the other accepts everything readily, so is the rustic related to the vulgar buffoon; the one accepts nothing comic without difficulty, the other takes all easily and with pleasure. Neither attitude is   10 right; one ought to accept some things and not others, as reason directs—and the man who does this is witty. The proof is the usual one; wittiness of this kind, supposing we do not use the word in some transferred sense, is the best habit, and the mean is praiseworthy, and the extremes blameable. But wit being of two kinds—one being delight in the comic, even when directed against one's self, if it be   15 really comic, like a jest, the other being the faculty of producing such things—the two sorts differ from one another but both are means. For the man who can[45] produce what a good judge will be pleased at, even if the joke is against himself, will   20 be midway between the vulgar and the frigid man; this definition is better than that which merely requires the thing said to be not painful to the person mocked, no matter what sort of man he is; one ought rather to please the man who is in the mean, for he is a good judge.

All these mean states are praiseworthy without being excellences, nor are their opposites vices—for they do not involve choice. All of them occur in the   25 classifications of affections, for each is an affection. But since they are natural, they tend to the natural excellences; for, as will be said later, each excellence is found both naturally and also otherwise, viz. as including thought. Envy then tends to   30 injustice (for the acts arising from it affect another), righteous indignation to justice, shame to temperance—whence some even put temperance into this genus. The sincere and the false are respectively sensible and foolish.

But the mean is more opposed to the extremes than these to one another, because the mean is found with neither, but the extremes often with one another,   1234^{b}1 and sometimes the same people are at once cowardly and foolhardy, or lavish in some ways, illiberal in others, and in general are lacking in uniformity in a bad sense—for if they lack uniformity in a good sense, men of the mean type are produced; since, in a way, both extremes are present in the mean.   5

The opposition between the mean and the extremes does not seem to be alike in both cases; sometimes the opposition is that of the excessive extreme, sometimes that of the defective, and the causes are the two first given—rarity, e.g. of those insensible to pleasures, and the fact that the error to which we are most prone seems the more opposed to the mean. There is a third reason, namely, that the more like   10 seems less opposite, e.g. foolhardiness to bravery, lavishness to liberality.

We have, then, spoken sufficiently about the other praiseworthy excellences; we must now speak of justice.

[45]Reading ὁ δυνάμενος.

BOOK VII

1 · Friendship, what it is and of what nature, who is a friend, and whether
20 friendship has one or many senses (and if many, how many), and, further, how we
should treat a friend, and what is justice in friendship—all this must be examined
not less than any of the things that are noble and desirable in character. For it is
thought to be the special business of the political art to produce friendship, and men
say that excellence is useful because of this, for those who are unjustly treated by
25 one another cannot be friends to one another. Further, all say that justice and
injustice are specially exhibited towards friends; the same man seems both good and
a friend, and friendship seems a sort of moral habit; and if one wishes to make men
not wrong one another, one should[46] make them friends, for genuine friends do not
30 act unjustly. But neither will men act unjustly if they are just; therefore justice and
friendship are either the same or not far different.

Further, men believe a friend to be among the greatest of goods, and
friendlessness and solitude to be most terrible, because all life and voluntary
1235ᵃ1 association is with friends; for we spend our days with our family, kinsmen, or
comrades, children, parents, or wife. The private justice practised to friends
depends on ourselves alone, while justice towards all others is determined by the
laws, and does not depend on us.

Many questions are raised about friendship. There is the view of those who
5 include the external world and give the term an extended meaning; for some think
that like is friend to like, whence the saying 'how God ever draws like to like'; or the
saying 'crow to crow'; or 'thief knows thief, and wolf wolf'. The physicists even
10 systematize the whole of nature on the principle that like goes to like—whence
Empedocles said that the dog sat on the tile because it was most like it. Some, then,
describe a friend thus, but others say that opposites are friends; for they say the
15 loved and desired is in every case a friend, but the dry does not desire the dry but the
moist—whence the sayings, 'Earth loves the rain', and 'in all things change is
pleasant'; but change is change to an opposite. And like hates like, for 'potter is
jealous of potter', and animals nourished from the same source are enemies. Such,
20 then, is the discrepancy between these views; for some think the like a friend, and
the opposite an enemy—'the less is ever the enemy of the more, and begins a day of
hate'; and, further, the places of contraries are separate, but friendship seems to
25 bring together. But others think opposites are friends, and Heraclitus blames the
poet who wrote 'may strife perish from among gods and men'; for (says he) there
could not be harmony without the low and the high note, nor living things without
male and female, two opposites. There are, then, these two views about friendship;
30 and they are too general and far removed. There are other views that come nearer to
and are more suitable to the phenomena. Some think that bad men cannot be
friends but only the good; while others think it strange that mothers should not love

---

[46]Reading ἀλλήλους, δεῖ φίλους.

their own children. (Even among the brutes we find such friendship; at least they choose to die for their children.) Some, again, think that we only regard the useful   35 as a friend, their proof being that all pursue the useful, but the useless, even in themselves, they throw away (as old Socrates said, citing the case of our spittle, hairs, and nails), and that we cast off useless parts, and in the end at death our very body, the corpse being useless; but those who have a use for it keep it, as in Egypt.   1235ᵇ1 Now all these things seem opposed to one another; for the like is useless to the like, and contrariety is furthest removed from likeness, and the contrary is not useless to   5 its contrary, for contraries destroy one another. Further, some think it easy to acquire a friend, others a very rare thing to recognize one, and impossible without misfortune; for all wish to seem friends to the prosperous. But others would have us distrust even those who remain with us in misfortune, alleging that they are deceiving us and making pretence, that by giving their company to us when we are   10 in misfortune they may obtain our friendship when we are again prosperous.

2 · We must, then, find a method that will best explain the views held on these topics, and also put an end to difficulties and contradictions. And this will happen if the contrary views are seen to be held with some show of reason; such a   15 view will be most in harmony with the phenomena; and both the contradictory statements will in the end stand, if what is said is true in one sense but untrue in another.

Another puzzle is whether the good or the pleasant is the object of love. For if we love what we *desire*—and love is of this kind, for 'none is a lover but one who ever   20 loves'—and if desire is for the pleasant, in this way the object of love would be the pleasant; but if it is what we *wish for,* then it is the good—the good and the pleasant being different.

About all these and the other cognate questions we must attempt to gain clear distinctions, starting from the following principle. The desired and the wished for is   25 either the good or the apparent good. Now this is why the pleasant is desired, for it is an apparent good; for some think it such, and to some it appears such, though they do not think so. For appearance and opinion do not reside in the same part of the soul. It is clear, then, that we love both the good and the pleasant.

This being settled, we must make another assumption. Of the good some is   30 absolutely good, some good to a particular man, though not absolutely; and the same things are at once absolutely good and absolutely pleasant. For we say that what is advantageous to a body in health is absolutely good for a body, but not what is good for a sick body, such as drugs and the knife. Similarly, things absolutely   35 pleasant to a body are those pleasant to a healthy and unaffected body, e.g. seeing in light, not in darkness, though the opposite is the case to one with ophthalmia. And the pleasanter wine is not that which is pleasant to one whose tongue has been spoilt by inebriety (for they⁴⁷ add vinegar to it), but that which is pleasant to sensation   1236ª1 unspoiled. So with the soul; what is pleasant not to children or brutes, but to the

---

⁴⁷Omitting οὔτε.

adult, is really pleasant; at least, when we remember both we choose the latter. And
5 as the child or brute is to the adult man, so are the bad and foolish to the good and
sensible. To these, that which suits their habit is pleasant, and that is the good and
noble.

Since, then, 'good' has many meanings—for one thing we call good because its
nature is such, and another because it is profitable and useful—and further, the
pleasant is in part absolutely pleasant and absolutely good, and in part pleasant to a
10 particular individual and apparently good; just as in the case of inanimate things we
may choose and love a thing for either of these reasons, so in the case of a man loving
one man because of his character or because of excellence, another because he is
profitable and useful, another because he is pleasant, and for pleasure. So a man
15 becomes a friend when he is loved and returns that love, and this is recognized by
the two men in question.

There must, then, be three kinds of friendship, not all being so named for one
thing or as species of one genus, nor yet having the same name quite by mere
accident. For all the senses are related to one which is the primary, just as is the case
with the word 'medical'; for we speak of a medical soul, body, instrument, or act,
20 but properly the name belongs to that primarily so called. The primary is that of
which the definition is contained in the definition of all;[48] e.g. a medical instrument
is one that a medical man would use, but the definition of the contained is not
implied in that of 'medical man'. Everywhere, then, we seek for the primary. But
because the universal is primary, they also take the primary to be universal, and this
25 is an error. And so they are not able to do justice to all the phenomena of friendship;
for since one definition will not suit all, they think there are no other friendships; but
the others are friendships, only not similarly so. But they, finding the primary
friendship will not suit, assuming it would be universal if really primary, deny that
the other friendships even are friendships; whereas there are many species of
30 friendship; this was part of what we have already said, since we have distinguished
the three senses of friendship—one due to excellence, another to usefulness, a third
to pleasantness.

Of these the friendship based on usefulness is that of the majority; men love
35 one another because of their usefulness and to the extent of this; so we have the
proverb 'Glaucus, a helper is a friend so long as[49] he fights', and 'the Athenians no
longer know the Megarians'. But the friendship based on pleasure is that of the
young, for they are sensitive to pleasure; therefore also their friendship easily
changes; for with a change in their characters as they grow up there is also a change
1236ᵇ1 in their pleasures. But the friendship based on excellence is that of the best men.

It is clear from this that the primary friendship, that of good men, is a mutual
returning of love and choice. For what is loved is dear to him who loves it, but a man
5 loving in return is dear to the man loved. This friendship, then, is peculiar to man,
for he alone perceives another's choice. But the other friendships are found also
among the brutes where utility is in some degree present, both between tame

[48]Reading πᾶσιν for ἡμῖν.   [49]Reading τόσσον φίλος ἔστε.

animals and men, and between animals themselves, as in the case mentioned by
Herodotus of the friendship between the sandpiper and the crocodile, and the
coming together and parting of birds that soothsayers speak of. The bad may be   10
friends to one another on the ground both of usefulness and of pleasure; but some
deny them to be friends, because there is not the primary friendship between them;
for a bad man will injure a bad man, and those who are injured by one another do
not love one another; but in fact they do love, only not with the primary friendship.   15
Nothing prevents their loving with the other kinds; for owing to pleasure they put up
with each other's injury, so long as[50] they are incontinent. But those whose love is
based on pleasure do not seem to be friends, when we look carefully, because their
friendship is not of the primary kind, being unstable, while that is stable; it is,
however, as has been said, a friendship, only not the primary kind but derived from   20
it. To speak, then, of friendship in the primary sense only is to do violence to the
phenomena, and makes one assert paradoxes; but it is impossible for all friendships
to come under one definition. The only alternative left is that in a sense there is only
one friendship, the primary; but in a sense all kinds are friendship, not as possessing
a common name accidentally without being specially related to one another, nor yet   25
as falling under one species, but rather as in relation to one and the same thing.

But since the same thing is at the same time absolutely good and absolutely
pleasant (if nothing interferes), and the genuine friend is absolutely the friend in the
primary sense, and such is the man desirable for himself (and he must be such; for
the man to whom[51] one wishes good to happen for himself, one must also desire to   30
exist), the genuine friend is also absolutely pleasant; hence any sort of friend is
thought pleasant. Again, one ought rather to distinguish further, for the subject
needs reflection. Do[52] we love what is good for ourselves or what is good absolutely?
and is actual loving attended with pleasure, so that the loved object is pleasant, or   35
not? For the two must be harmonized. For what is not absolutely good, but
perhaps[53] bad, is something to avoid, and what is not good for one's self is nothing to
one; but what is sought is that the absolutely good should be good in the further
sense of being good to the individual. For the absolutely good is absolutely desirable,   1237ᵃ1
but for each individual his own; and these must agree. Excellence brings about this
agreement, and the political art exists to make them agree for those to whom as yet
they do not. . . .[54] And one who is a human being is ready and on the road for this
(for by nature that which is absolutely good is good to him), and man rather than   5
woman, and the gifted rather than the ungifted; but the road is through pleasure;
what is noble must be pleasant. But when these two disagree a man cannot yet be
perfectly good, for incontinence may arise; for it is in the disagreement of the good
with the pleasant in the passions that incontinence occurs.

So that since the primary friendship is grounded on excellence, friends of this   10
sort will be themselves absolutely good, and this not because they are useful, but in
another way. For good to the individual and the absolutely good are two, and as with

---

[50]Reading ἕως for ὡς.   [51]Reading ᾧ for ὡς.   [52]Reading ἔχει γὰρ ἐπίστασιν πότερον.
[53]Reading ἄν πως for ἀπλῶς.   [54]Susemihl marks a lacuna.

the profitable so with habits. For the absolutely profitable differs from what is
15 profitable to an individual, as[55] taking exercise does from taking drugs. So that the
habit called human excellence is of two kinds, for we will assume man to be one of
the things excellent by nature; for the excellence of the naturally excellent is an
absolute good, but the excellence of that which is not thus good only to it. Similarly,
then, with the pleasant. For here one must pause and examine whether friendship
can exist without pleasure, how such a friendship differs from other friendship, and
20 on which of the two—goodness or pleasure—the loving depends, whether one loves
a man because he is good even if not pleasant, and in any case not for his
pleasantness. Now, loving having two senses, does actual love seem to involve
pleasure because activity is good? It is clear that just as in science what we have
recently contemplated and learnt is most perceptible because of its pleasantness, so
25 also is the recognition of the familiar, and the same account applies to both.
Naturally, at least, the absolutely good is absolutely pleasant, and pleasant to those
to whom it is good. From which it at once follows that like takes pleasure in like, and
that nothing is so pleasant to man as man; and if this is so even before they are
perfect, it is clear it must be so when they are perfect; and the good man is perfect.
30 But if active loving is a mutual choice with pleasure in each other's acquaintance, it
is clear that in general the primary friendship is a reciprocal choice of the absolutely
good and pleasant because it is good and pleasant; and this friendship is the habit
from which such choice springs. For its function is an activity, and this is not
35 external, but in the one who feels love. But the function of every faculty is external;
for it is in something different or in one's self *qua* different. Therefore to love is to
feel pleasure, but not to be loved; for to be loved is the activity of what is lovable, but
to love is the activity of friendship also; and the one is found only in the animate, the
other also in the inanimate, for even inanimate things are loved. But since active
1237ᵇ1 loving is to treat the loved[56] *qua* loved, and the friend is loved by the friend *qua*
friend and not *qua* musician or doctor, the pleasure coming from him merely as
being himself is the pleasure of friendship; for he loves the object as himself and not
for being someone else. So that if he does not rejoice in him for being good the
5 primary friendship does not exist, nor should any of his incidental qualities hinder
more than his goodness gives pleasure. For if[57] a man has an unpleasant odour he is
left. For he must be content with goodwill without actual association.[58] This then is
primary friendship, and all admit it to be friendship. It is through it that the other
friendships seem friendships to some, but are doubted to be such by others. For
10 friendship seems something stable, and this alone is stable. For a formed decision is
stable, and where we do not act quickly or easily, we get the decision right. There is
no stable friendship without confidence, but confidence needs time. One must then
15 make trial, as Theognis says, 'You cannot know the mind of man or woman till you
have tried them as you might cattle'. Nor is a friend made except through time; they
do indeed wish to be friends, and such a state easily passes muster as friendship. For

---

[55]Reading αὐτῷ, οἷον τό for τὸ καλὸν τοιοῦτον.   [56]Reading τῷ φιλουμένῳ.
[57]Reading ἀ for τί.
[58]Reading ἀγαπητὸν γὰρ τὸ εὐνοεῖν, συζῆν δὲ μή.

when men are eager to be friends, by performing every friendly service to one
another they think they not merely wish to be, but are friends. But it happens with   20
friendship as with other things; as man is not in health merely because he wishes to
be so, neither are men at once friends as soon as they wish to be friends. The proof is
that men in this condition, without having made trial of one another, are easily
made enemies; wherever each has allowed the other to test him, they are not easily   25
made enemies; but where they have not, they will be persuaded whenever those who
try to break up the friendship produce evidence. It is clear at the same time that this
friendship does not exist between the bad, for the bad man feels distrust and is
malignant to all, measuring others by himself. Therefore the good are more easily
deceived unless experience has taught them distrust. But the bad prefer natural   30
goods to a friend and none of them loves a man so much as things; therefore they are
not friends. The proverbial 'community among friends' is not found among them;
the friend is made a part of things, not things regarded as part of the friend. The
primary friendship then is not found towards many, for it is hard to test many men,   35
for one would have to live with each. Nor should one choose a friend like a garment.
Yet in all things it seems the mark of a sensible man to choose the better of two
alternatives; and if one has used the worse garment for a long time and not the
better, the better is to be chosen, but not in place of an old friend one of whom you
do not know whether he is better. For a friend is not to be had without trial nor in a   1238ᵃ1
single day, but there is need of time and so 'the bushel of salt' has become
proverbial. He must also be not merely good absolutely but good for you, if the
friend is to be a friend to you. For a man is good absolutely by being good, but a   5
friend by being good for another, and absolutely good and a friend when these two
attributes are combined so that what is absolutely good is good for the other, or[59]
else not absolutely good for the good man, but good to another in the sense of useful.
But the need of active loving also prevents one from being at the same time a friend
to many; for one cannot be active towards many at the same time.   10
    From these facts then it is clear that it is correctly said that friendship is a
stable thing, just as happiness is a thing sufficient in itself. It has been rightly said,
'for nature is stable but not wealth', but it is still better to say 'excellence' than
'nature'; and Time is said to show the friend, and bad fortune rather than good   15
fortune. For then it is clear that the goods of friends are common (for friends alone
instead of things naturally good and evil—which are the matters with which good
and bad fortune are concerned—choose a man rather than the existence of some of
those things and the non-existence of others). But misfortune shows those who are
not really friends, but friends only for some utility. But time reveals both sorts; for   20
even the useful man does not show his usefulness quickly, as the pleasant man does
his pleasantness; yet the absolutely pleasant is not quick to show himself either. For
men are like wines and meats; the pleasantness of them shows itself quickly, but if it
continues longer it is unpleasant and not sweet, and so it is with men. For the   25
absolutely pleasant must be determined as such by the end it realizes and the time

---

[59]Reading τοῦτο τῷ ἄλλῳ ἢ καί.

for which it continues pleasant. Even the vulgar would admit this, judging not[60] merely according to results but in the way in which, speaking of a drink, they call it sweeter. For this is unpleasant not[61] for the result but from not being continuous, though it deceives us at the start.

30 The first friendship then—by reason of which the others get the name—is that based on excellence and due to the pleasure of excellence, as has been said before; the other kinds occur also in children, brutes, and bad men; whence the sayings, 'like is pleased with like' and 'bad adheres to bad from pleasure'. For the bad may

35 be pleasant to one another, not *qua* bad or *qua* neither good nor bad, but (say) as both being musicians, or the one fond of music and the other a musician, and inasmuch as all have some good in them, and in this way they harmonize with one another. Further, they might be useful and profitable to one another, not absolutely

1238^b1 but in relation to their choice, or in virtue of some neutral characteristic. Also a good man may be a friend to a bad, the bad being of use to the good in relation to the good man's existing choice, the good to the incontinent in relation to his existing

5 choice, and to the bad in relation to his natural choice. And he will wish for his friend what is good, the absolutely good absolutely, and conditionally what is good for the friend, so far as poverty or illness is of advantage to him—and these for the sake of absolute goods; taking a medicine is an instance, for that no one wishes,[62] but wishes only for some particular purpose. Further, a good man and a bad man may

10 be friends in the way in which those not good might be friends to one another. A man might be pleasant, not as bad but as partaking in some common property, e.g. as being musical, or again, so far as there is something good in all (for which reason some might be glad to associate even with the good), or in so far as they suit each individual; for all have something of the good.

15 3 · These then are three kinds of friendship; and in all of them the word friendship implies a kind of equality. For even those who are friends through excellence are mutually friends by a sort of equality of excellence.

But another variety is the friendship of superiority to inferiority, e.g. as the excellence of a god is superior to that of a man (for this is another kind of

20 friendship)—and in general that of ruler to subject; just as justice in this case is different, for here it is a proportional equality, not numerical equality. Into this class falls the relation of father to son and of benefactor to beneficiary; and there are varieties of these again, e.g. there is a difference between the relation of father

25 to son, and of husband to wife, the latter being that of ruler to subject, the former that of benefactor to beneficiary. In these varieties there is not at all, or at least not in equal degree, the return of love for love. For it would be ridiculous to accuse a god because the love one receives in return from him is not equal to the love given him, or for the subject to make the same complaint against his ruler. For the part of a ruler is to receive not to give love, or at least to give love in a different way. And the

30 pleasure[63] of the man who needs nothing over his own possessions or child, and that

---

[60]Retaining οὐκ for ὅτι. [61]Reading οὐ διά.
[62]Ignoring Susemihl's lacuna. [63]Omitting οὐδέν.

of him who lacks over what comes to him, are not the same. Similarly also with those who are friends through use or pleasure, some are on an equal footing with each other, in others there is the relation of superiority and inferiority. Therefore those who think themselves to be on the former footing find fault if the other is not equally useful to and a benefactor of them; and similarly with regard to pleasure. 35 This is obvious in the case of lover and beloved; for this is frequently a cause of strife between them. The lover does not perceive that the passion in each has not the same reason; therefore . . .[64] a lover would not say such things. But they think that there is the same reason for the passion of each.

4 · There being, then, as has been said, three kinds of friendship—based on 1239ª1 excellence, utility, and pleasantness—these again are subdivided each into two, one kind based on equality, the other on superiority. Both are friendships, but only those between whom there is equality are friends; it would be absurd for a man to be the 5 friend of a child, yet certainly he loves and is loved by him. Sometimes the superior ought to be loved, but if he loves, he is reproached for loving one undeserving; for measurement is made by the worth of the friends and a sort of equality. Some then, owing to inferiority in age, do not deserve to receive an equal love, and others because of excellence or birth or some other such superiority possessed by the other 10 person. The superior ought to[65] claim either not to return the love or not to return it in the same measure, whether in the friendship of utility, pleasure, or excellence. Where the superiority is small, disputes naturally arise; for the small is in some cases of no account, e.g. in weighing wood, though not in weighing gold. But men 15 judge wrongly what is small; for their own good by its nearness seems great, that of another by its distance small. But when the difference is excessive, then not even those affected seek to make out that their love should be returned or equally returned, e.g. as if a man were to claim this from a god. It is clear then that men are friends when on an equality with each other, but we may have return of love without 20 their being friends. And it is clear why men seek the friendship of superiority rather than that of equality; for in the former they obtain both love and superiority. Therefore with some the flatterer is more valued than the friend, for he procures the appearance of both love and superiority for the object of his flattery. The ambitious 25 are especially of this kind; for to be an object of admiration involves superiority. By nature some grow up loving, and others ambitious; the former is one who delights rather in loving than in being loved, the other tends to be fond of honour. He, then, who delights in being loved and admired really loves superiority; the other, the 30 loving, is fond of the pleasure of loving. This by his mere activity of loving he must have;[66] for to be loved is an accident; one may be loved without knowing it, but not love. Loving, rather than being loved, depends on lovingness; being loved rather depends on the nature of the object of love. And here is a proof. The friend would 35 choose, if both were not possible, rather to know than to be known, as we see women do when allowing others to adopt their children, e.g. Antiphon's Andromache. For

---

[64]The text at this point is corrupt.   [65]Reading δεῖ for ἀεί.   [66]Reading ἀνάγκη ἐνεργοῦντι.

wishing to be known seems to be felt on one's own account and in order to get, not to do, some good; but wishing to know is felt in order that one may do and love. 1239ᵇ1 Therefore we praise those who persist in their love towards the dead; for they know but are not known. That, then, there are several sorts of friendship, that they are three in number, and what are the differences between being loved and having love returned, and between friends on an equality and friends in a relation of superiority and inferiority, has now been stated.

5 · But since 'friendly' is also used more universally, as was indeed said at the beginning, by those who take in extraneous considerations—some saying that the like is friendly, and some the contrary,—we must speak also of the relation of these friendships to those previously mentioned. The like is brought both under the pleasant and under the good, for the good is simple, but the bad various in form; and the good man is ever like himself and does not change in character; but the bad and the foolish are quite different in the evening from what they were in the morning. Therefore unless the bad come to some agreement, they are not friends to one another but are parted; but unstable friendship is not friendship. So thus the like is friendly, because the good is like; but it may also be friendly because of pleasure; for those like one another have the same pleasures, and everything too is by nature pleasant to itself. Therefore the voices, habits, and company of those of the same species are pleasantest to each side, even in the animals other than man; and in this way it is possible for even the bad to love one another: 'pleasure glues the bad to the bad'.

But opposites are friendly through usefulness; for the like is useless to itself; therefore master needs slave, and slave master; man and woman need one another, and the opposite is pleasant and desired *qua* useful, not as included in the end but as contributing towards it. For when a thing has obtained what it desires, it has reached its end and no longer desires the opposite, e.g. heat does not desire cold, nor dryness moisture. Yet in a sense the love of the contrary is love of the good; for the opposites desire one another because of the mean; they desire one another like tallies because thus out of the two arises a single mean. Further, the love is accidentally of the opposite, but *per se* of the mean, for opposites desire not one another but the mean. For if over-chilled they return to the mean by being warmed, and if over-warmed by being chilled. And so with everything else. Otherwise they are ever desiring, never in the mean states; but that which is in the mean delights without desire in what is naturally pleasant, while the others delight in all that puts them out of their natural condition. This kind of relation then is found also among inanimate things; but love occurs when the relation is found among the living. Therefore some delight in what is unlike themselves, the austere in the witty, the energetic in the lazy; for they reduce each other to the mean state. Accidentally, then, as has been said, opposites are friendly, because of the good.

The number then of kinds of friendship, and the different senses in which we speak of 'friends' and of persons as 'loving' and 'loved', both where this constitutes friendship and where it does not, have now been stated.

6 · The question whether a man is a friend to himself or not requires much inquiry. For some think that every man is above all a friend to himself; and they use this friendship as a canon by which to test his friendship to all other friends. If we look to argument and to the properties usually thought characteristic of friends, then the two kinds of friendship are in some of these respects opposed to one another, but in others alike. For this friendship—that to oneself—is, in a way, friendship by analogy, not absolutely. For loving and being loved require two separate individuals. Therefore a man is a friend to himself rather in the sense in which we have described the incontinent and continent as willing or unwilling, namely in the sense that the parts of his soul are in a certain relation to each other; and all problems of this sort have a similar explanation, e.g. whether a man can be a friend or enemy to himself, and whether a man can wrong himself. For all these relations require two separate individuals; so far then as the soul is two, these relations can in a sense belong to it; so far as these two are not separate, the relations cannot belong to it.

By a man's attitude to himself the other modes of friendship, under which we are accustomed to consider friendship in this discourse, are determined. For a man seems to us a friend, who wishes the good or what he thinks to be such to someone, not on his own account but for the sake of that other; or, in another way, if he wishes for another man existence—even if he is not bestowing goods[67]—on that other's account and not on his own, he would seem most of all to be a friend to him. And in yet another manner he would be a friend to him whom he wishes to live with merely for the sake of his company and for no other reason; thus fathers wish the existence of their sons, but prefer to live with others. Now these various ways of friendship are discordant with one another. For some think they are not loved, unless the other wishes them this or that good, some unless their existence or their society is desired. Further, to sorrow with the sorrowing, for no other reason than their sorrow, we shall regard as love (e.g. slaves grieve with their masters because their masters when in trouble are cruel to them, not for the sake of the masters themselves)—as mothers feel towards their children, and birds that share one another's pains. For the friend wants, if possible, not merely to feel pain along with his friend, but to feel the same pain, e.g. to feel thirsty when he is thirsty, if that could be, as closely as possible. The same words are applicable to joy, which, if felt for no other reason than that the other feels joy, is a sign of friendship. Further, we say about friendship such things as that friendship is equality, and true friends a single soul. All such phrases point back to the single individual; for a man wishes good to himself[68] in this fashion; for no one benefits himself for some further reason . . .[69] for he who shows that he loves seems to want to be loved, not to love. And wishing the existence above all of the friend, living with him, sharing his joy and his grief, unity of soul with the friend, the impossibility of even living without one another, and the dying together are characteristic of a single individual. (For such is the condition of the individual and he perhaps takes pleasure in his own company.) All these characters we find in

10

15

20

25

30

35

1240ᵇ1

5

10

---

[67]Omitting μὴ τῷ τὸ εἶναι.   [68]Reading αὐτῷ for αὐτῷ.   [69]Text corrupt.

the relation of the good man to himself. In the bad man, e.g. the incontinent, there is variance, and for this reason it seems possible for a man to be at enmity with
15 himself; but so far as he is single and indivisible, he is an object of desire to himself. Such is the good man, the man whose friendship is based on excellence, for the wicked man is not one but many, in the same day other than himself and fickle. So that a man's friendship for himself is at bottom friendship towards the good; for because a man is in a sense like himself, single, and good for himself, so far he is a
20 friend and object of desire to himself. And this is natural to man; but the bad man is unnatural. The good man never finds fault with himself at the moment of his act, like the incontinent, nor the later with the earlier man, like the penitent, nor the earlier with the later, like the liar. Generally, if it is necessary to distinguish as the
25 sophists do, he is related to himself as Coriscus to good Coriscus. For it is clear that some identical portion of them is good; for when they blame themselves, they kill themselves. But every one seems good to himself. But the man that is good absolutely, seeks to be a friend to himself, as has been said, since he has within him
30 two parts which by nature desire to be friends and which it is impossible to tear apart. Therefore in the case of man each is thought to be the friend of himself; but not so with the other animals; e.g. the horse is himself to himself. . .[70] therefore not a friend. Nor are children, till they have attained the power of choice; for already then the mind is at variance with the appetite. One's friendship to oneself resembles the
35 friendship arising from kinship; for neither bond can be dissolved by one's own power; but even if they quarrel, the kinsmen remain kinsmen; and so the man remains one so long as he lives.

The various senses then of loving, and how all friendships reduce to the primary kind, is clear from what has been said.

1241ᵃ1   7 · It is appropriate to the inquiry to study agreement of feeling and kindly feeling; for some identify these, and others think they cannot exist apart. Now kindly feeling is not altogether different from friendship, nor yet the same; for when we distinguish friendship according to its three sorts, kindly feeling is found neither
5 in the friendship of usefulness nor in that of pleasure. For if one wishes well to the other because that is useful to oneself, one would be so wishing not for the object's sake, but for his own; but goodwill seems like. . .[71] to be not goodwill for him who feels the goodwill, but for him towards whom it is felt. Now if goodwill existed in the friendship towards the pleasant, then men would feel goodwill towards things
10 inanimate. So that it is clear that goodwill is concerned with the friendship that depends on character; but goodwill shows itself in merely wishing, friendship in also doing what one wishes. For goodwill is the beginning of friendship; every friend has goodwill, but not all who have goodwill are friends. He who has goodwill only is like a man at the beginning, and therefore it is the beginning of friendship, not friendship itself . . .[72]
15   For friends seem to agree in feeling, and those who agree in feeling seem to be

[70]Susemihl marks a lacuna.   [71]Susemihl marks a lacuna.   [72]Susemihl marks a lacuna.

friends. Friendly agreement is not about all things, but only about things that may be done by those in agreement and about what relates to their common life. Nor is it agreement merely in thought or merely in desire, for it is possible to know one thing and desire the opposite,[73] as in the incontinent the motives disagree, nor if[74] a man agrees with another in choice, does he necessarily agree in desire. Agreement is only found in the case of good men; at least, bad men when they choose and desire the same things[75] harm one another. Agreement, like friendship, does not appear to have a single meaning; but still in its primary and natural form it is good; and so the bad cannot agree; the agreement of the bad, when they choose and desire the same things, is something different. And the two parties must so desire the same thing that it is possible for both to get what they desire; for if they desire that which cannot belong to both, they will quarrel; but those in agreement will not quarrel. There is agreement when the two parties make the same choice as to who is to rule, who to be ruled, meaning by 'the same', not that each one should choose himself, but that both should choose the same person. Agreement is the friendship of fellow citizens. So much then about agreement and goodwill.

8 · It is disputed why benefactors are more fond of the benefited than the benefited of their benefactors. The opposite seems to be just. One might suppose it happens from consideration of utility and what is profitable to oneself; for the benefactor has a debt due to him, while the benefited has to repay a debt. This, however, is not all; the reason is partly the general natural principle—activity is more desirable. There is the same relation between the effect and the activity, the benefited being as it were an effect or creation of the benefactor. Hence in animals their strong feeling for their children both in begetting them and in preserving them afterwards. And so fathers love their children—and still more mothers—more than they are loved by them. And these again love their own children more than their parents, because nothing is so good as activity; in fact, mothers love more than fathers because they think the children to be more their own creation; for the amount of work is measured by the difficulty, and the mother suffers more in birth. So much then for friendship towards oneself and among more than one.

9 · But justice seems to be a sort of equality and friendship also involves equality, if the saying is not wrong that 'love is equality'. Now constitutions are all of them a particular form of justice; for a constitution is a partnership, and every partnership rests on justice, so that whatever be the number of species of friendship, there are the same of justice and partnership; these all border on one another, and the species of one have differences akin to those of the other. But since there is the same relation between soul and body, artisan and tool, and master and slave, between each of these pairs there is no partnership; for they are not two, but the first term in each is one, and the second a part of this one. Nor is the good to be divided between the two, but that of both belongs to the one for the sake of which the pair

---

[73]Reading νοεῖν καὶ for τὸ κινοῦν.   [74]Reading οὐδ' εἰ for οὐ δεῖ.   [75]Reading ταὐτά for ταῦτα.

exists. For the body is the soul's natural tool, while the slave is as it were a part and detachable tool of the master, the tool being a sort of inanimate slave.

25 The other partnerships are a part of the civic partnership, e.g. those of the phratries and priestly colleges[76] or pecuniary partnerships.[77] All constitutions are found together in the household, both the true and the corrupt forms, for the same thing is true in constitutions as of harmonies. The government of the children by the 30 father is royal, the relation of husband and wife aristocratic, the relation of brothers that of a commonwealth; the corruptions of these three are tyranny, oligarchy, and democracy. The forms of justice then are also so many in number.

But since equality is either numerical or proportional, there will be various species of justice, friendship, and partnership; on numerical equality rests the 35 democratic partnership, and the friendship of comrades—both being measured by the same standard, on proportional the aristocratic[78] and the royal. For the same thing is not just for the superior and the inferior; what is proportional is just. Such is the friendship between father and child; and the same sort of thing may be seen in partnerships.

1242ª1   **10** · We speak of friendships of kinsmen, comrades, partners, the so-called 'civic friendship'. That of kinsmen has more than one species, that of brothers and that of father and sons. There is the friendship based on proportion, as that of the father to his children, and that based on mere number, e.g. that of brothers, for this 5 latter resembles the friendship of comrades; for here too age gives certain privileges. Civic friendship has been established mainly in accordance with utility; for men seem to have come together because each is not sufficient for himself, though they would have come together anyhow for the sake of living in company. Only the civic 10 friendship and its parallel corruption are not merely friendships, but the partnership is that of friends; other friendships rest on the relation of superiority. The justice belonging to the friendship of those useful to one another is pre-eminently justice, for it is civic or political justice. The concurrence of the saw and the art that uses it is of another sort; for it is not for some end common to both—it is like instrument 15 and soul—but for the sake of the user. It is true that the tool itself[79] receives attention, and it is just that it should receive it, for its function, that is; for it exists for the sake of its function. . . .[80] And the essence of a gimlet is twofold, but more properly it is its activity, namely boring holes. In this class come the body and a slave, as has been said before.

To inquire, then, how to behave to a friend is to look for a particular kind of 20 justice, for generally all justice is in relation to a friend. For justice involves a number of individuals who are partners, and the friend is a partner either in family or in one's scheme of life. For man is not merely a political but also a household-maintaining animal, and his unions are not, like those of the other animals, confined to certain times, and formed with any chance partner, whether male or female; but 25 . . .[81] man has a tendency to partnership with those to whom he is by nature akin.

---

[76]Reading ὀργέων.   [77]Omitting ἔτι πολιτεῖαι.   [78]Omitting ἀρίστη.
[79]Reading αὐτὸ τό for τοῦτο.   [80]Susemihl marks a lacuna.   [81]Text corrupt.

There would, then, be partnership and a kind of justice, even if there were no state; and the household is a kind of friendship; the relation, indeed, of master and servant is that of an art and its tools, a soul and its body; and these are not friendships, nor forms of justice, but something similar to justice; just as health is not justice, but something similar. But the friendship of man and wife is a friendship based on utility, a partnership; that of father and son is the same as that of god to man, of the benefactor to the benefited, and in general of the natural ruler to the natural subject. That of brothers to one another is eminently that of comrades, inasmuch as it involves equality[82]—'for I was not declared a bastard brother to him; but the same Zeus, my king, was called the father of both of us'.[83] For this is the language of men that seek equality. Therefore in the household first we have the sources and springs of friendship, of political organization, and of justice.

But since there are three sorts of friendship, based on excellence, utility, and pleasantness respectively, and two varieties of each of these—for each of them may imply either superiority or equality—and the justice involved in these is clear from the debates that have been held on it, in a friendship between superior and inferior the claim for proportion takes different forms, the superior's claim being one for inverse proportion, i.e. as he is to the inferior, so should what he receives from the inferior be to what the inferior receives from him, he being in the position of ruler to subject; if he cannot get that, he demands at least numerical equality. For so it is in the other associations, the two members enjoying an equality sometimes of number, sometimes of ratio. For if they contributed numerically equal sums of money, they divide an equal amount, and by an equal number; if not equal sums, then they divide proportionally. But the inferior inverts this proportion and joins crosswise. But in this way the superior would seem to come off the worse, and friendship and partnership to be a gratuitous burden. Equality must then be restored and proportion created by some other means; and this means is honour, which by nature belongs to a ruler or god in relation to a subject. The profit and the honour must be equated.

But civic friendship is that resting on equality; it is based on utility; and just as cities are friends to one another, so in the like way are citizens. 'The Athenians no longer know the Megarians'; nor do citizens one another, when they are no longer useful to one another, and the friendship is merely a temporary one for a particular exchange of goods. There is here, too, the relation of ruler and subject which is neither the natural relation, nor that involved in kingship, but each is ruler and ruled in turn; nor is it either's purpose to act with the free beneficence of a god, but that he may share equally in the good and in the burdensome service. Civic friendship, then, claims to be one based on equality. But of the friendship of utility there are two kinds, the strictly legal and the moral. Civic friendship looks to equality and to the object as sellers and buyers do; hence the proverb 'a fixed wage for a friend'. When, then, this civic friendship proceeds by contract, it is of the legal kind; but when each of the two parties leaves the return for his services to be fixed by the other, we have the moral friendship, that of comrades. Therefore recrimina-

---

[82]Reading ἦ κατ' ἰσότητα.   [83]Sophocles, frag. 684 Nauck.

tion is very frequent in this sort of friendship; and the reason is that it is unnatural; for friendships based on utility and based on excellence are different; but these wish to have both together, associating together really for the sake of utility, but

1243ᵃ1   representing their friendship as moral, like that of good men; pretending to trust one another they make out their friendship to be not merely legal. For in general there are more recriminations in the useful friendship than in either of the other two (for excellence is not given to recrimination, and pleasant friends having got what they wanted, and given what they had, are done with it; but useful friends do not dissolve

5   their association at once, if their relations are not merely legal but those of comrades); still the legal form of useful friendship is free from recrimination. The legal association is dissolved by a money-payment (for it measures equality in money), but the moral is dissolved by voluntary consent. Therefore in some countries the law forbids lawsuits for voluntary transactions between those who

10   associate thus as friends, and rightly; for good men do not have bonds of justice with one another; and such as these have dealings with one another as good and trustworthy men. In this kind of friendship it is uncertain how either will recriminate on the other, seeing that they trust each other not in a limited legal way but on the basis of their characters.

     It is a further problem on which of two grounds we are to determine what is

15   just, whether by looking to the amount of service rendered, or to what was its character for the recipient; for, to borrow the language of Theognis, the service may be 'Small to thee, O goddess, but great to me'. Or the opposite may happen, as in the

20   saying, 'this is sport to you but death to me'. Hence, as we have said, come recriminations. For the benefactor claims a return on the ground of having done a great service, because he has done it at the request of the other, or with some other plea of the great value of the benefit to the other's interest, saying nothing about what it was to himself; while the recipient insists on its value to the benefactor, not

25   on its value to himself. Sometimes the receiver inverts the position, insisting how little the benefit has turned out to him, while the doer insists on its great magnitude to *him*, e.g. if at considerable risk one has benefited another to the extent of a drachma, the one insists on the greatness of the risk, the other on the smallness of the money, just as in the repayment of money—for there the dispute is on this

30   point—the one claims the value of it when it was lent, the other concedes only the value of it now when it is returned, unless they have made an explicit provision in the contract. Civic friendship, then, looks to the agreement and the thing, moral friendship to the choice; here then we have a truer justice, and a friendly justice. The reason for the quarrel is that moral friendship is more noble, but useful

35   friendship more necessary; men start, then, by proposing to be moral friends, i.e. friends through excellence; but as soon as some private interest arises, they show clearly they were not so. For the multitude aim at the noble only when they have

1243ᵇ1   plenty of everything else; and at noble friendship similarly. So that it is clear what distinctions should be drawn in these matters. If the two are moral friends, we must look to see if the choice of each is equal; and then nothing more should be claimed by either from the other. But if their friendship is of the useful or civic kind, we must consider what would have been profitable lines for an agreement. And if one declares that they are friends on one basis, but the other on the other, it is not honourable, if one ought to *do* something in return, merely to use fine language; and so too, in the other cases; but since they have not declared their friendship a moral friendship, someone must be made judge, so that neither cheats the other by a false pretence; and so each must put up with his luck. But that moral friendship is based on choice is clear, since even if after receiving great benefits one does not repay them through inability, but repays only to the extent of his ability, he acts honourably; and a god is satisfied at getting sacrifices as good as our power allows. But a seller of goods will not be satisfied if the buyer says he cannot pay more; nor will a lender of money.

Recriminations are common in dissimilar friendships, where action and reaction are not in the same straight line; and it is not easy to see what is just. For it is hard to measure by just this one unit different directions; we find this in the relation of lovers, for there the one pursues the other as a pleasant person, in order to live with him, while the latter seeks the other at times for his utility. When the love is over, one changes as the other changes. Then they calculate the *quid pro quo;*[84] thus Python and Pammenes quarrelled; and so do teacher and pupil (for knowledge and money have no common measure), and so Herodicus the doctor quarrelled with a patient who paid him only a small fee; such too was the case of the king and the lyre-player; the former regarded his associate as pleasant, the latter his as useful; and so the king, when he had to pay, chose to regard himself as an associate of the pleasant kind, and said that just as the player had given him pleasure by singing, so he had given the player pleasure by his promise. But it is clear here too how one should decide; the measurement must be by one measure, only here not by a term but by a ratio; we must measure by proportion, just as one measures in the associations of citizens. For how is a cobbler to have dealings with a farmer unless one equates the work of the two by proportion? So to all whose exchanges are not of the same for the same, proportion is the measure, e.g. if the one complains that he has given wisdom, and the other that he has given money, we must measure first the ratio of wisdom to wealth, and then what has been given for each. For if the one gives half of the lesser, and the other does not give even a small fraction of the greater object, it is clear that the latter does injustice. Here, too, there may be a dispute at the start, if one party pretends they have come together for use, and the other denies this and alleges that they have met from some other kind of friendship.

11 · As regards the good man who is loved for his excellence, we must consider whether we ought to render useful services and help to him, or to one who makes a return and has power. This is the same problem as whether we ought rather to benefit a friend or a virtuous man. For if the friend is also good, there is perhaps no great difficulty, if one does not exaggerate the one quality and minimize the

---

[84]Reading τί ἀντὶ τίνος for παντί τινος.

other, making him very much of a friend, but not much of a good man. But in other cases many problems arise, e.g. if the one has been but will no longer remain so, and the other will be but is not yet what he is going to be, or the one was but is not, and the other is but has not been and will not be . . .[85] But the other is a harder question.

10 For perhaps Euripides is right in saying, 'A word is your just pay for a word, but a deed for him who has given deeds'.[86] And one must not do everything for one's father, but there are some things also one should do for one's mother, though a father is the better of the two. For, indeed, even to Zeus we do not sacrifice all

15 things, nor does he have all honours but only some. Perhaps, then, there are things which should be rendered to the useful friend and others to the good one; e.g. because a man gives you food and what is necessary, you need not give him your society; nor, therefore, need you give the man to whom you grant your society that which not he but the useful friend gives. Those who doing this give all to the object of their love, when they ought not, are worthless.

20   And the various definitions of friendship that we give in our discourses all belong to friendship in some sense, but not to the same friendship. To the useful friend applies the fact that one wishes what is good for him, and to a benefactor, and in fact to any kind of friend[87]—for this definition does not distinguish the class of friendship; to another we should wish existence, of another we should wish the society, to the friend on the basis of pleasure sympathy in joy and grief is the proper

25 gift. All these definitions are appropriate to some friendship, but none to a single unique thing, friendship. Hence there are many definitions, and each appears to belong to a single thing, viz. friendship, though really it does not, e.g. the purpose to maintain the friend's existence. For the superior friend and benefactor wishes[88] the existence of that which he has made, and to him who has given one existence one

30 ought to give it in return, but not necessarily one's society; that gift is for the pleasant friend.

Some friends wrong one another; they love rather the things than the possessor of them; and so they love the persons much as they choose wine because it is pleasant, or wealth because it is useful; for wealth is more useful than its owner. Therefore he should not be indignant, as if he had preferred his wealth to him as to

35 something inferior. But the other side complain in turn; for they now look to find in him a good man, when before they looked for one pleasant or useful.

1244ᵇ1   12 · We must also consider about independence and friendship, and the relations they have to one another. For one might doubt whether, if a man be in all respects independent, he will have a friend, if one seeks a friend from want and the

5 good man is perfectly independent.[89] If the possessor of excellence is happy, why should he need a friend? For the independent man neither needs useful people nor

---

⁸⁵Susemihl marks a lacuna.   ⁸⁶Frag. 882 Nauck.
⁸⁷Reading ὁποίῳ δή for ὁποῖος δεῖ.   ⁸⁸Ignoring Susemihl's lacuna.
⁸⁹Ignoring Susemihl's lacuna, placing a comma after τούτῳ φίλος, and putting a full stop after αὐταρκέστατος.

people to cheer him, nor society; his own society is enough for him. This is most
plain in the case of a god; for it is clear that, needing nothing, he will not need a
friend, nor have one, supposing that he does not need one.[90] So that the happiest   10
man will least need a friend, and only as far as it is impossible for him to be
independent. Therefore the man who lives the best life must have fewest friends,
and they must always be becoming fewer, and he must show no eagerness for men to
become his friends, but despise not merely the useful but even men desirable for
society. But surely this makes it all the clearer that the friend is not for use or help,   15
but that the friend through excellence[91] is the only friend. For when we need
nothing, then we all seek others to share our enjoyment, those whom we may benefit
rather than those who will benefit us. And we judge better when independent than
when in want, and most of all we then seek friends worthy to be lived with. But as to   20
this problem, we must see if we have not been partially right, and partially missed
the truth owing to our illustration. It will be clear if we ascertain what is life in its
active sense and as end. Clearly, it is perception and knowledge , and therefore life
in society is perception and knowledge in common. And self-perception and   25
self-knowledge is most desirable to every one, and hence the desire of living is
congenital in all; for living must be regarded as a kind of knowledge. If then we were
to cut off and abstract mere knowledge and its opposite[92]—this passes unnoticed in   30
the argument as we have given it, but in fact need not remain unnoticed—there
would be no difference between this and another's knowing instead of oneself; and
this is like another's living instead of oneself. Now naturally the perception and
knowledge of oneself is more desirable. For we must take two things into
consideration, that life is desirable and also that the good is, and thence that it is   35
desirable that such a nature should belong to oneself[93] as belongs to them. If, then,
of such a pair of corresponding series there is always one series of the desirable, and   1245ª1
the known and the perceived are in general constituted by their participation in the
nature of the determined; so that to wish to perceive one's self is to wish oneself to be
of a certain definite character,—since, then, we are not in ourselves possessed of   5
each of such characters, but only by participation in these qualities in perceiving
and knowing—for the perceiver becomes perceived in that way and in that respect
in which he first perceives, and according to the way in which and the object which
he perceives; and the knower becomes known in the same way—therefore it is for
this reason that one always desires to live, because one always desires to know; and
this is because he himself wishes to be the object known. The choice to live with   10
others might seem, from a certain point of view, silly—(first, in the case of things
common also to the other animals, e.g. eating together, drinking together; for what
is the difference between doing these things in the neighbourhood of others or apart
from them, if you take away speech? But even to share in speech of a casual kind   15
does not make the case different. Further, for friends who are self-dependent
neither teaching nor learning is possible; for if one learns, he is not as he should be:

---

[90]Reading μηθενὸς δεομένῳ for οὔτε μηθὲν δεσπότου.
[91]Reading ὁ δι' ἀρετήν.   [92]Ignoring Susemihl's lacuna.   [93]Reading αὐτοῖς for αὐτὸ τοῖς.

and if he teaches, his friend is not; and likeness is friendship)—but surely it is obviously so, and all of us find greater pleasure in sharing good things with friends
20   as far as these come to each—I mean the greatest good one can share; but to some it falls to share in bodily delights, to others in artistic contemplation, to others in philosophy. And the friend must be present too; whence the proverb, 'distant friends are a burden', so that men must not be at a distance from one another when there is
25   friendship between them. Hence sensuous love seems like friendship; for the lover aims at the society of his beloved, but not as ideally he ought, but in a merely sensuous way.

The argument, then, says what we have before mentioned, raising difficulties; but the facts are as we saw later, so that it is clear that the objector is in a way misleading us. We must see the truth from what follows: a friend wants to be, in the
30   words of the proverb, 'another Heracles', 'a second self'; but he is severed from his friend, and it is hard to find in two people the characteristics of a single individual. But though a friend is by nature what is most akin to his friend, one man is like another in body, and another like him in soul, and one like him in one part of the body or soul, and another like him in another. But none the less does a friend wish to
35   be as it were a separate self. Therefore, to perceive a friend must be in a way to perceive one's self and to know a friend to know one's self. So that even the vulgar forms of pleasure and life in the society of a friend are naturally pleasant (for perception of the friend always takes place at the same time), but still more the communion in the diviner pleasures. And the reason is, that it is always pleasanter
1245ᵇ1   to see one's self enjoying the superior good. And this is sometimes a passion, sometimes an action, sometimes something else. But if it is pleasant for a man himself to live well and also his friend, and in their common life to engage in mutually helpful activity, their partnership surely would be above all in things included in the end. Therefore, men should contemplate in common and feast in
5   common, only not on the pleasures of food or on necessary pleasures; such society does not[94] seem to be true society, but sensuous enjoyment. But the end which each can attain is that in which he desires the society of another; if that is not possible, men desire to benefit and be benefited by friends in preference to others. Thus it is
10   clear that friends ought to live together, that all wish this above all things, and that the happiest and best man tends especially to do so. But that the contrary appeared as the conclusion of the argument was also reasonable, since the argument said what was true. For it is because of the comparison of the two cases that the solution is not found, the case compared being in itself truly enough stated. For because a
15   god is not such as to need a friend, we claim the same of the man who resembles a god. But by this reasoning the virtuous man will not even think; for the perfection of a god is not in this, but in being superior to thinking of anything beside himself. The reason is, that with us welfare involves a something beyond us, but the deity is his own well-being.
20   As to our seeking and praying for many friends, while we say that the man who

---

[94]Reading τοιαῦται γὰρ οὐχ ὁμιλίαι.

has many friends has no friend, both are correct. For if it is possible to live with and share the perceptions of many at the same time, it is most desirable that these should be as numerous as possible; but since this is most difficult, the activity of joint perception must exist among fewer. So that it is not only hard to get many friends—for testing is necessary—but also to use them when you have got them.   25

Sometimes we wish the object of our love to be happy away from us, sometimes to share the same fortune as ourselves; the wish to be together is characteristic of friendship. For if the two can both be together and be happy, all choose this; but if they cannot be both, then we choose as the mother of Heracles might have chosen,   30 i.e. that her son should be a god rather than in her company but a serf to Eurystheus. One might say something like the jesting remark of the Laconian, when some one bade him in a storm to summon the Dioscuri.

It appears to be the mark of one who loves to keep the object of his love from sharing in hardships, but of the beloved to wish to share them; the conduct of both is   35 reasonable. For nothing ought to be so painful to a friend as not to see his friend, but it is thought that he ought not to choose what is for his own interest. Therefore men keep their friends from participation in their calamities; their own suffering is enough, that they may not show themselves studying their own interest, and choosing joy at the cost of a friend's pain, . . .[95] again, being relieved by not bearing   1246ª1 their troubles alone. But since both well-being and participation are desirable, it is clear that participation with a smaller good is more desirable than to enjoy a greater good in solitude. But since the weight to be attached to participation is not   5 ascertained, men differ, and some think that participation in all things at once is the mark of friendship, e.g. they say that it is better to dine together than separately, though having the same food; yet others would not wish it. And since if one takes extreme cases . . . they agree that they suffer great adversity together or great good fortune apart . . .[96] We have something similar in the case of ill-fortune. For   10 sometimes we wish our friends to be absent and we wish to give them no pain, when they are not going to be of any use to us; at another time we find it pleasantest for them to be present. But this contradiction is quite reasonable. For this happens in consequence of what we have mentioned above, and because we often simply avoid the sight of a friend in pain or in bad condition, as we should the sight of ourselves so   15 placed; yet to see a friend is as pleasant as anything can be (because of the above-mentioned cause), and to see him not ill if you are ill yourself. So that whichever of these two is the pleasanter decides us whether to wish the friend present or not. This also happens, for the same reason, in the case of the worse sort   20 of men; for they are most anxious that their friends should not fare well nor even exist if they themselves have to fare badly.[97] Therefore some kill the objects of their love with themselves. For they think that if the objects of their love are to survive they would perceive their own trouble more acutely, just as one who remembered that once he had been happy would feel it more than if he thought himself to be   25 always unhappy . . .[98]

---

[95]Susemihl marks a lacuna.   [96]Susemihl marks two lacunae.
[97]Reading ἂν ἀνάγκη for ἀνάγκαι.   [98]Susemihl marks a lacuna.

13[99] · Here one might raise a question. One can use each thing both for its natural purpose and otherwise, and either *per se* or again *per accidens*, as, for instance, one might use the eye for seeing, and also for falsely seeing by squinting,

30 so that one thing appears as two. Both these uses are due to the eye being an eye, but it was possible to use the eye in another way—*per accidens*, e.g. if one could sell or eat it.[100] Knowledge may be used similarly; it is possible to use it truly or to do what is wrong, e.g. when a man voluntarily writes incorrectly, thus using knowledge as ignorance, like a person using his hand as a foot—dancing-girls sometimes use the

35 foot as a hand and the hand as a foot. If, then, all the excellences are kinds of knowledge, one might use justice also as injustice, and so one would be unjust and do unjust actions from justice, as ignorant things may be done from knowledge. But

1246ᵇ1 if this is impossible, it is clear that the excellences are not species of knowledge. And even if ignorance cannot proceed from knowledge, but only error and the doing of the same things as proceed from ignorance, it must be remembered that from justice one will not act as from injustice. But since practical wisdom is knowledge

5 and something true, it may behave like knowledge; one might act foolishly though possessed of wisdom, and commit the errors of the foolish. But if the use of each thing as such were single, then in so acting men would still be acting wisely. Over other kinds of knowledge, then, there is something superior that diverts them; but how can there be any knowledge that diverts the highest knowledge of all? There is

10 no longer any knowledge to do this. But neither can excellence do it, for wisdom *uses* that; for the excellence of the ruling part uses that of the subject. Then what will it be? Perhaps the position is like that of incontinence, which is said to be a vice of the irrational part of the soul, and the incontinent man who has reason but is

15 intemperate. But if so, supposing appetite to be strong it will twist him and he will draw the opposite conclusion. Or is it obvious[101] that if there is excellence in the irrational part, but ignorance in the rational, they are transformed? Thus it will be possible to use justice unjustly[102] and badly, and wisdom foolishly—and therefore the opposite uses will also be possible. For it is absurd that vice occurring sometimes

20 in the irrational part should twist the excellence in the rational part and make the man ignorant, but that excellence in the irrational part, when ignorance is present in the rational, should not divert the latter and make the man judge wisely and as is right, and again, wisdom in the rational part should not make the intemperance in the irrational part act temperately. This seems the very essence of continence. And

25 therefore we shall also get wise action arising out of ignorance. But all these consequences are absurd, especially that of acting wisely out of ignorance, for we certainly do not see this in any other case, e.g. intemperance does not pervert one's medical or grammatical knowledge. But at any rate we may say that not[103]

30 ignorance, if opposite, (for it has no superiority), but excellence is rather related in

---

[99]Susemihl begins a new book here, so that VII 13–15 become VIII 1–3.
[100]The text is uncertain.
[101]Reading ἤ ἔστι δῆλον for ἤ**σφι** δῆλον.
[102]Reading τ' οὐ for τό.
[103]Reading οὐ for ὁ.

this way to vice in general. For whatever the just man can do, the unjust can do; and in general powerlessness is covered by power. And so it is clear that wisdom and excellence go together, and that those are states of someone else,[104] and the Socratic saying that nothing is stronger than wisdom is right. But when Socrates said this of knowledge he was wrong. For wisdom is an excellence and not a species of 35 knowledge, but another kind of cognition. . . .[105]

14 · But since not only wisdom and excellence produce well-doing, but we say also that the fortunate do well, thus assuming that good fortune produces well-doing and the same results as knowledge, we must inquire whether it is or is not 1247ª1 by nature that one man is fortunate, another not, and what is the truth about these things. For that there are fortunate men we see, who though foolish are often successful in matters controlled by fortune. Again, in matters involving art, chance 5 too largely enters, e.g. strategy and navigation. Does their success, then, arise from some mental condition, or do they effect fortunate results not because of their own qualities at all (at present men take the latter view, regarding them as having some special natural endowment); does nature, rather, make men with different qualities 10 so that they differ from birth; as some are blue-eyed and some black-eyed because they have some particular part of a particular nature,[106] so are some lucky and others unlucky? For that they do not succeed through wisdom is clear, for wisdom is not irrational but can give a reason why it acts as it does; but they could not say why they succeed; that would be art. Further, it is clear that they succeed though foolish, 15 and not about other things—that would not be strange at all, e.g. Hippocrates was a geometer, but in other respects was thought silly and foolish, and once on a voyage was robbed of much money by the customs-collectors at Byzantium, owing to his silliness, as we are told—but foolish in the very business in which they are lucky. 20 For in navigation not the cleverest are the most fortunate, but it is as in throwing dice, where one throws nothing, another throws a high score, according to his natural luck. Or is it because he is loved, as the phrase is, by a god, success being something coming from without, as a worse-built vessel often sails better, not owing 25 to itself but because it has a good pilot? So, the fortunate man has a good pilot, namely, the divinity. But it is absurd that a god or divinity should love such a man and not the best and most wise of men. If, then, success must be due either to nature or intelligence or some sort of protection, and the latter two causes are out of the 30 question, then the fortunate must be so by nature. But, on the other hand, nature is the cause of what is always or for the most part so, fortune the opposite. If, then, it is thought that unexpected success is due to chance, but that, if it *is* through chance that one is fortunate, the cause of his fortune is not the sort of cause that produces always or usually the same result—further, if a person succeeds or fails because he 35 is a certain sort of man, just as a man sees badly because he is blue-eyed, then it follows that not fortune but nature is the cause; the man then is not fortunate but

---

[104]Reading ἀγαθοί, ἐκεῖναι δ' ἄλλου.   [105]Susemihl marks a lacuna.
[106]Reading τῷ τοδὶ τοιονδὶ ἔχειν.

rather naturally gifted. So we must say that the people we call fortunate are not so through fortune; therefore they are not fortunate, for those goods only are in the 1247ᵇ1 disposal of fortune of which good fortune is the cause.

But if this is so, shall we say that fortune does not exist at all, or that it exists but is not a cause? No, it must both exist and be a cause. It will, then, also cause good or evil to certain people. But whether it is to be wholly removed, and we ought 5 to say that nothing happens by chance, but *do* say that chance is a cause simply because, though there is some other cause, we do not see it (and therefore, in defining chance, some make it a cause incalculable to human reasoning, taking it to be a genuine reality)—this would be matter for another inquiry. But since we see people who are fortunate once only, why should they not be fortunate a second 10 time? Because they succeed once, they do so again. The cause is the same. Then this cannot be a matter of chance. But when the same event follows from indefinite and undetermined antecedents, it will be good or evil, but there will not be the science that comes by experience of it, since otherwise some would have learned to be lucky, 15 or even—as Socrates said—all the sciences would have been kinds of good luck. What, then, prevents such things happening to a man often in succession, not because they should, but as, say, dice might continually throw a lucky number? But again, are there not in the soul impulses, some from reason and others from 20 irrational desire, the latter being the earlier? For if the desire arising from appetite for the pleasant is natural, everything would by nature march towards the good. If, then, some have a natural endowment—as musical[107] people, though they have not learned to sing, are fortunately endowed in this way—and move without reason in the direction[108] given them by their nature, and desire that which they ought at the 25 time and in the manner they ought, such men are successful, even if they are foolish and irrational, just as the others will sing[109] well though not able to teach singing. And such men are fortunate, namely those who generally succeed without the aid of reason. Men, then, who are fortunate will be so by nature. Perhaps, however, 'good fortune' is a phrase with several senses. For some things are done from impulse and 30 are due to choice, and others not, but the opposite; and if, in the former cases, they succeed where they seem to have reasoned badly, we say that they have been lucky; and again, in the latter cases, if they wished for a different good than they got.[110] Men who are lucky in the former way, then, may be fortunate by nature, for the 35 impulse and the desire was for the right object and succeeded, but the reasoning was silly; and people in this case, when it happens that their reasoning seems incorrect but desire is the cause of their reasoning, are saved by the rightness of their desire;[111] but on another occasion a man reasons again in this way owing to appetite and turns out unfortunate.

But in the other cases how can the good luck be due to a natural goodness in 248ª1 desire and appetite? But surely the good fortune and chance spoken of here and in the other case are the same, or else there is more than one sort of good fortune, and

---

[107]Reading ὠδικοί for ἄδικοι.   [108]Reading ᾗ ἡ φύσις.   [109]Reading ᾄσονται for ἔσονται.
    [110]Reading ἐβούλοντο ἄλλο ἢ ἔλαβον.
    [111]Reading τυχῇ, ἡ δ' αὐτοῦ αἰτία οὖσα, αὕτη.

chance is of two kinds.[112] But since we see some men lucky contrary to all knowledge and right reasonings, it is clear that the cause of luck must be something different from these. But is it luck or not by which[113] a man desires what and when he ought, 5 though for him[114] human reasoning could not lead to this? For that is not altogether unreasonable, nor is the desire natural, though it is misled by something. The man, then, is thought to have good luck, because luck is the cause of things contrary to reason, and this is contrary to reason (for it is contrary to knowledge and the 10 universal). But probably it does not spring from chance, but seems so for the above reason. So that this argument shows not that good luck is due to nature, but that not all who seem to be lucky are successful owing to chance, but rather owing to nature; nor does it show that fortune is not the cause of anything, but only not of all 15 that it seems to be the cause of. This, however, one might question: whether fortune is the cause of just this, viz. desiring what and when one ought. But will it not in this case be the cause of everything, even of thought and deliberation? For one does not deliberate after previous deliberation which itself presupposed deliberation, but there is some starting-point; nor does one think after thinking previously to 20 thinking, and so ad infinitum. Thought, then, is not the starting-point of thinking nor deliberation of deliberation. What, then, can be the starting-point except chance? Thus everything would come from chance. Perhaps there is a starting-point with none other outside it, and this can act in this sort of way by being such as it is. The object of our search is this—what is the commencement of movement in the 25 soul? The answer is clear: as in the universe, so in the soul, it is god. For in a sense the divine element in us moves everything. The starting-point of reasoning is not reasoning, but something greater. What, then, could be greater even than knowledge and intellect but god? For excellence is an instrument of the intellect. And for this reason, as I said a while ago,[115] those are called fortunate who, whatever they 30 start on,[116] succeed in it without being good at reasoning. And deliberation is of no advantage to them, for they have in them a principle that is better than intellect and deliberation, while the others have not this but have intellect; they have inspiration, but they cannot deliberate. For, though lacking reason, they succeed, and like the prudent and wise, their divination is speedy; and we must mark off as included in it 35 all but the judgement that comes from reasoning;[117] in some cases it is due to experience, in others to habituation in the use of reflection; and both experience and habituation use god. This quality sees well the future and the present, and these[118] are the men in whom the reasoning-power is relaxed. Hence we have the melancholic men, the dreamers of what is true. For the moving principle seems to become stronger when the reasoning-power is relaxed. So the blind remember 1248ᵇ1 better, being freed from concern with the visible, since their memory is stronger. It is clear, then, that there are two kinds of good luck, the one divine—and so the lucky seem to succeed owing to god—, the other natural. Men of this sort seem to succeed

---

[112]Placing καὶ τύχη διττή after εὐτυχίαι.   [113]Reading ᾗ for ἤ.
[114]Reading ᾧ for **το.   [115]Omitting οἱ.
[116]Reading οἳ οἱ.   [117]Text uncertain.   [118]Reading οὗτοι for οὗτος.

5 in following their impulse, the others to succeed contrary to their impulse; both are irrational, but the one is persistent good luck, the other not.

15 · About each excellence by itself we have already spoken; now since we have distinguished their natures separately, we must describe clearly the excellence
10 that arises out of the combination of them, what we have already called nobility-and-goodness. That he who truly deserves this denomination must have the separate excellences is clear; it cannot be otherwise with other things either, for no one is healthy in his entire body and yet healthy in no part of it, but the most numerous
15 and important parts, if not all, must be in the same condition as the whole. Now goodness and nobility-and-goodness differ not only in name but also in themselves. For all goods have ends which are to be chosen for their own sake. Of these, we call
20 noble those which, existing all of them for their own sake, are praised. For these are those which are the source of praised acts and are themselves praised, such as justice itself and just acts; also temperate acts,[119] for temperance is praised, but health is not praised, for its effect is not; nor vigorous action, for vigour is not. These
25 are good but not praised. Induction makes this clear about the rest, too. A good man, then, is one for whom the natural goods are good. For the goods men fight for and think the greatest—honour, wealth, bodily excellences, good fortune, and
30 power—are naturally good, but may be to some hurtful because of their dispositions. For neither the foolish nor the unjust nor the intemperate would get any good from the employment of them, any more than an invalid from the food of a healthy man, or one weak and maimed from the equipment of one in health and sound in all limbs. A man is noble and good because those goods which are noble are possessed
35 by him for themselves, and because he practises the noble and for its own sake, the noble being the excellences and the acts that proceed from excellence. There is also the civic disposition, such as the Laconians have, and others like them might have; its nature would be something like this—there are some who think one should have excellence but only for the sake of the natural goods, and so such men are good (for
1249ª1 the natural goods are good for them), but they have not nobility and goodness. For it is not true of them that they acquire the noble for itself, that they choose acts good and noble at once[120]—more than this, that what is not noble by nature but good by
5 nature is noble to them; for objects are noble when a man's motives for acting and choosing them are noble, because to the noble and good man the naturally good is noble—for what is just is noble, justice is proportion to merit, and he merits these things; or what is fitting is noble, and to him these things—wealth, high birth, and
10 power—are fitting. So that to the noble and good man things profitable are also noble; but to the many the profitable and the noble do not coincide, for things absolutely good are not good for them as they are for the good man; to the noble and good man they are also noble, for he does many noble deeds by reason of them.[121] But the man
15 who thinks he ought to have the excellences for the sake of external goods does deeds that are noble only *per accidens*. Nobility and goodness, then, is perfect excellence.

---

[119]Reading αἱ σώφρονες.   [120]Reading καλὰ κἀγαθά for καλοὶ κἀγαθοί.
[121]Reading δι᾽ αὐτά.

About pleasure, too, we have spoken, what it is and in what sense good; we have said that the absolutely pleasant is also noble, and the absolutely good pleasant. But pleasure only arises in action; therefore the truly happy man will also live most pleasantly: that this should be so is no idle demand of man.

But since the doctor has a standard by reference to which he distinguishes what is healthy for the body from what is not, and with reference to which each thing up to a certain point ought to be done and is healthy,[122] while if less or more is done health is the result no longer, so in regard to actions and choice of what is naturally good but not praiseworthy, the good man should have a standard both of disposition and of choice and avoidance with regard to excess or deficiency of wealth and good fortune, the standard being—as above said—as reason directs; this corresponds to saying in regard to diet that the standard should be as medical science and its reason direct. But this, though true, is not illuminating. One must, then, here as elsewhere, live with reference to the ruling principle and with reference to the formed habit and[123] the activity of the ruling principle, as the slave must live with reference to that of the master, and each of us by the rule proper to him. But since man is by nature composed of a ruling and a subject part, each of us should live according to the governing element within himself—but this is ambiguous, for medical science governs in one sense, health in another, the former existing for the latter. And so it is with the theoretic faculty; for god is not an imperative ruler, but is the end with a view to which wisdom issues its commands (the word 'end' is ambiguous, and has been distinguished elsewhere), for *god* needs nothing. What choice, then, or possession of the natural goods—whether bodily goods, wealth, friends, or other things—will most produce the contemplation of god, that choice or possession is best; this is the noblest standard, but any that through deficiency or excess hinders one from the contemplation and service of god is bad; this a man possesses in his soul, and this is the best standard for the soul—to perceive the irrational part of the soul, as such, as little as possible.

So much, then, for the standard of nobility and goodness and the object of the absolute goods.

20

1249ᵇ1

5

10

15

20

25

---

[122]Reading ὑγιεινόν for εὖ ὑγιαῖνον.   [123]Reading καί for κατά.

ON VIRTUES AND
VICES **

J. Solomon

^{1249ª25} 1 · The noble is the object of praise, the base of blame: at the head of what is noble stand the excellences, at the head of what is base the vices; the excellences, then, are objects of praise, but so also are the causes of the excellences and their
³⁰ accompaniments and results, the opposites are objects of blame.

If in agreement with Plato we take the soul to have three parts, then wisdom is
^{1249ᵇ25} the excellence of the rational, gentleness and bravery of the passionate, temperance and continence of the appetitive; and of the soul as a whole, justice, liberality, and magnanimity. Folly is the vice of the rational, irascibility and cowardice of the
^{1250ª1} passionate, intemperance and incontinence of the appetitive; and of the soul as a whole, injustice, illiberality, and small-mindedness.

2 · Wisdom is an excellence of the rational part capable of procuring all that
⁵ tends to happiness. Gentleness is an excellence of the passionate part, through which men become difficult to stir to anger. Bravery is an excellence of the passionate part, through which men are difficult to scare by apprehension of death. Temperance is an excellence of the appetitive part, by which men cease to desire
¹⁰ bad sensual pleasures. Continence is an excellence of the appetitive part, by which men check by thinking the appetite that rushes to bad pleasures. Justice is an excellence of the soul that distributes to each according to his desert. Liberality is an excellence of the soul ready to spend on noble objects. Magnanimity is an excellence of the soul, by which men are able to bear good and bad fortune, honour
¹⁵ and dishonour.

3 · Folly is a vice of the rational part, causing evil living. Irascibility is a vice of the passionate part, through which men are easily stirred to anger. Cowardice is a vice of the passionate part, through which men are scared by apprehensions,
²⁰ especially such as relate to death. Intemperance is a vice of the appetitive part, by which men become desirous of bad sensual pleasures. Incontinence is a vice of the appetitive part, through which one chooses bad pleasures, though reason opposes

TEXT: F. Susemihl, Teubner, Leipzig, 1884

this. Injustice is a vice of the soul, through which men become covetous of more than   25
they deserve. Illiberality is a vice of the soul, through which men aim at gain from
every source. Small-mindedness is a vice of the soul, which makes men unable to
bear alike good and bad fortune, alike honour and dishonour.

4 · To wisdom belongs right deliberation, right judgement as to what is good   30
and bad and all in life that is to be chosen and avoided, noble use of all the goods
that belong to us, correctness in social intercourse, the grasping of the right
moment, the sagacious use of word and deed, the possession of experience of all that
is useful. Memory, experience, tact, good judgement, sagacity—each of these either   35
arises from wisdom or accompanies it. Or possibly some of them are, as it were,
subsidiary causes of wisdom (such as experience and memory), while others are, as
it were, parts of it, e.g. good judgement and sagacity.

To gentleness belongs the power to bear with moderation accusations and[1]   40
slights, not to rush hastily to vengeance, not to be easily stirred to anger, to be
without bitterness or contentiousness in one's character, to have in one's soul
quietude and steadfastness.

To bravery belongs slowness to be scared by apprehensions of death, to be of
good courage in dangers and bold in facing risks, and to choose a noble death rather   1250[b]1
than preservation in some base way, and to be the cause of victory. Also it belongs to
bravery to labour, to endure, and to play the man. And there accompanies it
readiness to dare, high spirits, and confidence; and further, fondness for toil and   5
endurance.

To temperance belongs absence of admiration for the enjoyment of bodily
pleasures, absence of desire for all base sensual enjoyment, fear of ill-repute, an
ordered course of life, alike in small things and in great. And temperance is   10
accompanied by discipline, orderliness, shame, caution.

5 · To continence belongs the power to restrain by reason the appetite when
it rushes to base enjoyment of pleasures, endurance, steadfastness under natural
want and pain.   15

To justice belongs the capacity to distribute to each his deserts, to preserve
ancestral customs and laws and also the written law, to be truthful in matters of
importance, to observe one's agreements. First among acts of justice come those
towards the gods, then those to deified spirits, then those towards one's country and   20
parents, then those towards the departed: amongst these comes piety, which is
either a part of justice or an accompaniment of it. Also justice is accompanied by
purity, truth, trust, and hatred of wickedness.

To liberality it belongs to be profuse of money on praiseworthy objects, to be   25
generous in spending on a proper purpose, to be helpful and kind in disputed
matters,[2] and not to take from improper sources. The liberal man is also clean in his
dress and house, ready to provide himself with what is not strictly necessary but

---

[1]Omitting μετρίας.   [2]Omitting Susemihl's καὶ φιλάνθρωπον.

30 beautiful and enjoyable without profit, inclined to keep all animals that have anything peculiar or marvellous about them. Liberality is accompanied by a suppleness and ductility of disposition, by kindness, by pitifulness, by love for friends, for strangers, for what is noble.

35 It belongs to magnanimity to bear nobly good and bad fortune, honour and dishonour; not to admire luxury or attention or power or victory in contests, but to have a sort of depth and greatness of soul. The magnanimous is one who neither

40 values living highly nor is fond of life, but is in disposition simple and noble, one who can be injured and is not prompt to avenge himself. The accompaniments of magnanimity are simpleness, nobleness, and truth.

6 · To folly it belongs to judge things badly, to deliberate badly, to be bad in social intercourse, to use badly present goods, to think erroneously about what is
1251ᵃ1 good and noble as regards life. Folly is accompanied by ignorance, inexperience, incontinence, tactlessness, shortness of memory.

Of irascibility there are three species—promptness to anger, peevishness,
5 sullenness. It is the mark of the irascible man to be unable to bear small slights or defeats, to be ready to punish, prompt at revenge, easily moved to anger by any chance word or deed. The accompaniments of irascibility are a disposition easily excited, ready changes of feeling, attention to small matters, vexation at small
10 things, and all these rapid and on slight occasion.

To cowardice it belongs to be easily moved by chance fears, especially if relating to death or maiming of the body, and to suppose preservation in any manner to be better than a noble death. Its accompaniments are softness,
15 unmanliness, despair, love of life. Beneath it, however, is a sort of caution of disposition and slowness to quarrel.

To intemperance it belongs to choose the enjoyments of hurtful and base pleasures, to suppose that those living in such pleasures are in the highest sense happy, to love laughter, jeering, wit, and levity in word and deed. Its accompani-
20 ments are indiscipline, shamelessness, disorder, luxury, ease, negligence, contempt, dissipation.

To incontinence it belongs to choose the enjoyment of pleasures though reason forbids, to partake of them none the less though believing it to be better not to
25 partake of them, and while thinking one ought to do what is noble and profitable still to abstain from these for the sake of pleasures. The accompaniments of incontinence are effeminacy, negligence, and generally the same as those of intemperance.

30 7 · Of injustice there are three species—impiety, greed, outrage. Impiety is wrong-doing towards gods, deified spirits, the departed, one's parents, and one's country. Greed is wrong-doing in regard to agreements, claiming a share of the object in dispute beyond one's deserts. Outrage occurs when in providing pleasure
35 for oneself one brings shame on others, whence Evenus says of it: 'That which while gaining nothing still wrongs another'. It belongs to injustice to violate ancestral

customs and laws, to disobey enactments and rulers, to lie, to commit perjury, to violate agreements and pledges. The accompaniments of injustice are quibbling, boasting, unsociability, pretence, malignity, unscrupulousness.   1251^b1

Of illiberality there are three species, pursuit of disgraceful gain, parsimony, stinginess: pursuit of disgraceful gain, in so far as such men seek gain from all   5
sources and think more of the profit than of the shame; parsimony, in so far as they are unready to spend money on a suitable purpose; stinginess, in so far as, while spending, they spend in small sums and badly, and are more hurt than profited from not spending in season. It belongs to illiberality to value money above everything,   10
and to think no reproach can ever attach to what yields a profit. The life of the illiberal man is servile, suited to a slave, and sordid, remote from ambition and liberality. The accompaniments of illiberality are pettiness, sullenness, small-   15
mindedness, self-humiliation, lack of measure, ignobility, misanthropy.

It belongs to small-mindedness to be able to bear neither honour nor dishonour, neither good nor ill fortune, but to grow braggart when honoured, to be elated at small prosperities, to be unable to bear even the smallest deprivation of honour, to regard any ill-success whatever as a great misfortune, to complain and to   20
be impatient over everything. Further, the small-minded man is such as to call every slight an outrage and a dishonour, even such as are inflicted through ignorance or forgetfulness. The accompaniments of small-mindedness are pettiness, grumbling, hopelessness, self-humiliation.   25

8 · In general it belongs to excellence to make the condition of the soul good, using quiet and ordered motions and in agreement with itself throughout all its parts: whence the condition of a good soul seems a pattern of a good political constitution. It belongs also to excellence to do good to the worthy, to love the good;   30
not to be prompt either to chastise or seek vengeance, but to be complaisant, kindly, and forgiving. Its accompaniments are worth, equity, indulgence, good hope, and further all such qualities as love of home, love of friends, love of comrades, love of   35
strangers, love of men, love of the noble: all these qualities are among the laudable. The marks of vice are the opposites, and its accompaniments the opposites; and all these marks and accompaniments of vice belong to the class of the blameable.

POLITICS

B. Jowett

BOOK I

1252a1 1 · Every state is a community of some kind, and every community is established with a view to some good; for everyone always acts in order to obtain that which they think good. But, if all communities aim at some good, the state or political community, which is the highest of all, and which embraces all the rest, aims at good in a greater degree than any other, and at the highest good.

Some people think that the qualifications of a statesman, king, householder, and master are the same, and that they differ, not in kind, but only in the number of their subjects. For example, the ruler over a few is called a master; over more, the manager of a household; over a still larger number, a statesman or king, as if there were no difference between a great household and a small state. The distinction which is made between the king and the statesman is as follows: When the government is personal, the ruler is a king; when, according to the rules of the political science, the citizens rule and are ruled in turn, then he is called a statesman.

But all this is a mistake, as will be evident to any one who considers the matter according to the method which has hitherto guided us. As in other departments of science, so in politics, the compound should always be resolved into the simple elements or least parts of the whole. We must therefore look at the elements of which the state is composed, in order that we may see in what the different kinds of rule differ from one another, and whether any scientific result can be attained about each one of them.

2 · He who thus considers things in their first growth and origin, whether a state or anything else, will obtain the clearest view of them. In the first place there must be a union of those who cannot exist without each other; namely, of male and female, that the race may continue (and this is a union which is formed, not of choice, but because, in common with other animals and with plants, mankind have a natural desire to leave behind them an image of themselves), and of natural ruler and subject, that both may be preserved. For that which can foresee by the exercise

TEXT: A. Dreizehnter, Munich, 1970

of mind is by nature lord and master, and that which can with its body give effect to such foresight is a subject, and by nature a slave; hence master and slave have the same interest. Now nature has distinguished between the female and the slave. For she is not niggardly, like the smith who fashions the Delphian knife for many uses; she makes each thing for a single use, and every instrument is best made when intended for one and not for many uses. But among barbarians no distinction is made between women and slaves, because there is no natural ruler among them: they are a community of slaves, male and female. That is why the poets say,— 1252^b1

It is meet that Hellenes should rule over barbarians;

as if they thought that the barbarian and the slave were by nature one.

Out of these two relationships the first thing to arise is the family, and Hesiod 10 is right when he says,—

First house and wife and an ox for the plough,

for the ox is the poor man's slave. The family is the association established by nature for the supply of men's everyday wants, and the members of it are called by Charondas, 'companions of the cupboard', and by Epimenides the Cretan, 'compan- 15 ions of the manger'. But when several families are united, and the association aims at something more than the supply of daily needs, the first society to be formed is the village. And the most natural form of the village appears to be that of a colony from the family, composed of the children and grandchildren, who are said to be 'suckled with the same milk'. And this is the reason why Hellenic states were originally governed by kings; because the Hellenes were under royal rule before they came together, as the barbarians still are. Every family is ruled by the eldest, 20 and therefore in the colonies of the family the kingly form of government prevailed because they were of the same blood. As Homer says:

Each one gives law to his children and to his wives.

For they lived dispersedly, as was the manner in ancient times. That is why men say that the Gods have a king, because they themselves either are or were in ancient 25 times under the rule of a king. For they imagine not only the forms of the Gods but their ways of life to be like their own.

When several villages are united in a single complete community, large enough to be nearly or quite self-sufficing, the state comes into existence, originating in the bare needs of life, and continuing in existence for the sake of a good life. And 30 therefore, if the earlier forms of society are natural, so is the state, for it is the end of them, and the nature of a thing is its end. For what each thing is when fully developed, we call its nature, whether we are speaking of a man, a horse, or a family. Besides, the final cause and end of a thing is the best, and to be self-sufficing 1253^a1 is the end and the best.

Hence it is evident that the state is a creation of nature, and that man is by nature a political animal. And he who by nature and not by mere accident is without a state, is either a bad man or above humanity; he is like the

Tribeless, lawless, heartless one,

5   whom Homer denounces—the natural outcast is forthwith a lover of war; he may be compared to an isolated piece at draughts.

Now, that man is more of a political animal than bees or any other gregarious animals is evident. Nature, as we often say, makes nothing in vain, and man is the
10 only animal who has the gift of speech. And whereas mere voice is but an indication of pleasure or pain, and is therefore found in other animals (for their nature attains to the perception of pleasure and pain and the intimation of them to one another, and no further), the power of speech is intended to set forth the
15 expedient and inexpedient, and therefore likewise the just and the unjust. And it is a characteristic of man that he alone has any sense of good and evil, of just and unjust, and the like, and the association of living beings who have this sense makes a family and a state.

Further, the state is by nature clearly prior to the family and to the individual,
20 since the whole is of necessity prior to the part; for example, if the whole body be destroyed, there will be no foot or hand, except homonymously, as we might speak of a stone hand; for when destroyed the hand will be no better than that. But things are defined by their function and power; and we ought not to say that they are the same when they no longer have their proper quality, but only that they are
25 homonymous. The proof that the state is a creation of nature and prior to the individual is that the individual, when isolated, is not self-sufficing; and therefore he is like a part in relation to the whole. But he who is unable to live in society, or who has no need because he is sufficient for himself, must be either a beast or a god: he is
30 no part of a state. A social instinct is implanted in all men by nature, and yet he who first founded the state was the greatest of benefactors. For man, when perfected, is the best of animals, but, when separated from law and justice, he is the worst of all; since armed injustice is the more dangerous, and he is equipped at birth with arms,
35 meant to be used by intelligence and excellence, which he may use for the worst ends. That is why, if he has not excellence, he is the most unholy and the most savage of animals, and the most full of lust and gluttony. But justice is the bond of men in states; for the administration of justice, which is the determination of what is just, is the principle of order in political society.

1253ᵇ1   **3** · Seeing then that the state is made up of households, before speaking of the state we must speak of the management of the household. The parts of household management correspond to the persons who compose the household, and a complete household consists of slaves and freemen. Now we should begin by
5   examining everything in its fewest possible elements; and the first and fewest possible parts of a family are master and slave, husband and wife, father and children. We have therefore to consider what each of these three relations is and ought to be:—I mean the relation of master and servant, the marriage relation (the
10 conjunction of man and wife has no name of its own), and thirdly, the paternal relation (this also has no proper name). And there is another element of a

household, the so-called art of getting wealth, which, according to some, is identical with household management, according to others, a principal part of it; the nature of this art will also have to be considered by us.

Let us first speak of master and slave, looking to the needs of practical life and also seeking to attain some better theory of their relation than exists at present. For some are of the opinion that the rule of a master is a science, and that the management of a household, and the mastership of slaves, and the political and royal rule, as I was saying at the outset, are all the same. Others affirm that the rule of a master over slaves is contrary to nature, and that the distinction between slave and freeman exists by convention only, and not by nature; and being an interference with nature is therefore unjust.

4 · Property is a part of the household, and the art of acquiring property is a part of the art of managing the household; for no man can live well, or indeed live at all, unless he is provided with necessaries. And as in the arts which have a definite sphere the workers must have their own proper instruments for the accomplishment of their work, so it is in the management of a household. Now instruments are of various sorts; some are living, others lifeless; in the rudder, the pilot of a ship has a lifeless, in the look-out man, a living instrument; for in the arts the servant is a kind of instrument. Thus, too, a possession is an instrument for maintaining life. And so, in the arrangement of the family, a slave is a living possession, and property a number of such instruments; and the servant is himself an instrument for instruments. For if every instrument could accomplish its own work, obeying or anticipating the will of others, like the statues of Daedalus, or the tripods of Hephaestus, which, says the poet,

of their own accord entered the assembly of the Gods;

if, in like manner, the shuttle would weave and the plectrum touch the lyre, chief workmen would not want servants, nor masters slaves. Now the instruments commonly so called are instruments of production, whilst a possession is an instrument of action. From a shuttle we get something else besides the use of it, whereas of a garment or of a bed there is only the use. Further, as production and action are different in kind, and both require instruments, the instruments which they employ must likewise differ in kind. But life is action and not production, and therefore the slave is the minister of action. Again, a possession is spoken of as a part is spoken of; for the part is not only a part of something else, but wholly belongs to it; and this is also true of a possession. The master is only the master of the slave; he does not belong to him, whereas the slave is not only the slave of his master, but wholly belongs to him. Hence we see what is the nature and office of a slave; he who is by nature not his own but another's man, is by nature a slave; and he may be said to be another's man who, being a slave, is also a possession. And a possession may be defined as an instrument of action, separable from the possessor.

5 · But is there any one thus intended by nature to be a slave, and for whom

such a condition is expedient and right, or rather is not all slavery a violation of nature?

20   There is no difficulty in answering this question, on grounds both of reason and of fact. For that some should rule and others be ruled is a thing not only necessary, but expedient; from the hour of their birth, some are marked out for subjection, others for rule.

    And there are many kinds both of rulers and subjects (and that rule is the
25 better which is exercised over better subjects—for example, to rule over men is better than to rule over wild beasts; for the work is better which is executed by better workmen, and where one man rules and another is ruled, they may be said to have a work); for in all things which form a composite whole and which are made up
30 of parts, whether continuous or discrete, a distinction between the ruling and the subject element comes to light. Such a duality exists in living creatures, originating from nature as a whole; even in things which have no life there is a ruling principle, as in a musical mode. But perhaps this is matter for a more popular investigation. A living creature consists in the first place of soul and body, and of these two, the one
35 is by nature the ruler and the other the subject. But then we must look for the intentions of nature in things which retain their nature, and not in things which are corrupted. And therefore we must study the man who is in the most perfect state both of body and soul, for in him we shall see the true relation of the two; although
1254ᵇ1 in bad or corrupted natures the body will often appear to rule over the soul, because they are in an evil and unnatural condition. At all events we may firstly observe in living creatures both a despotical and a constitutional rule; for the soul rules the
5 body with a despotical rule, whereas the intellect rules the appetites with a constitutional and royal rule. And it is clear that the rule of the soul over the body, and of the mind and the rational element over the passionate, is natural and expedient; whereas the equality of the two or the rule of the inferior is always
10 hurtful. The same holds good of animals in relation to men; for tame animals have a better nature than wild and all tame animals are better off when they are ruled by man; for then they are preserved. Again, the male is by nature superior, and the female inferior; and the one rules, and the other is ruled; this principle, of necessity,
15 extends to all mankind. Where then there is such a difference as that between soul and body, or between men and animals (as in the case of those whose business is to use their body, and who can do nothing better), the lower sort are by nature slaves,
20 and it is better for them as for all inferiors that they should be under the rule of a master. For he who can be, and therefore is, another's, and he who participates in reason enough to apprehend, but not to have, is a slave by nature. Whereas the lower animals cannot even apprehend reason;[1] they obey their passions. And indeed the use made of slaves and of tame animals is not very different; for both with their
25 bodies minister to the needs of life. Nature would like to distinguish between the bodies of freemen and slaves, making the one strong for servile labour, the other
30 upright, and although useless for such services, useful for political life in the arts

---

[1] Reading λόγου.

both of war and peace. But the opposite often happens—that some have the souls and others have the bodies of freemen. And doubtless if men differed from one another in the mere forms of their bodies as much as the statues of the Gods do from men, all would acknowledge that the inferior class should be slaves of the superior. And if this is true of the body, how much more just that a similar distinction should exist in the soul? But the beauty of the body is seen, whereas the beauty of the soul is not seen. It is clear, then, that some men are by nature free, and others slaves, and that for these latter slavery is both expedient and right.

6 · But that those who take the opposite view have in a certain way right on their side, may be easily seen. For the words slavery and slave are used in two senses. There is a slave or slavery by convention as well as by nature. The convention is a sort of agreement—the convention by which whatever is taken in war is supposed to belong to the victors. But this right many jurists impeach, as they would an orator who brought forward an unconstitutional measure: they detest the notion that, because one man has the power of doing violence and is superior in brute strength, another shall be his slave and subject. Even among philosophers there is a difference of opinion. The origin of the dispute, and what makes the views invade each other's territory, is as follows: in some sense excellence, when furnished with means, has actually the greatest power of exercising force: and as superior power is only found where there is superior excellence of some kind, power seems to imply excellence, and the dispute to be simply one about justice (for it is due to one party identifying[2] justice with goodwill, while the other identifies it with the mere rule of the stronger). If these views are thus set out separately, the other views have no force or plausibility against the view that the superior in excellence ought to rule, or be master. Others, clinging, as they think, simply to a principle of justice (for convention is a sort of justice), assume that slavery in accordance with the custom of war is just, but at the same moment they deny this. For what if the cause of the war be unjust? And again, no one would ever say that he is a slave who is unworthy to be a slave. Were this the case, men of the highest rank would be slaves and the children of slaves if they or their parents chanced to have been taken captive and sold. That is why people do not like to call themselves slaves, but confine the term to foreigners. Yet, in using this language, they really mean the natural slave of whom we spoke at first; for it must be admitted that some are slaves everywhere, others nowhere. The same principle applies to nobility. People regard themselves as noble everywhere, and not only in their own country, but they deem foreigners noble only when at home, thereby implying that there are two sorts of nobility and freedom, the one absolute, the other relative. The Helen of Theodectes says:

Who would presume to call me servant who am on both sides sprung
from the stem of the Gods?

What does this mean but that they distinguish freedom and slavery, noble and

---

[2]Reading τὸ . . . εὔνοιαν δοκεῖν.

1255ᵇ1 humble birth, by the two principles of good and evil? They think that as men and animals beget men and animals, so from good men a good man springs. Nature intends to do this often but cannot.

5 We see then that there is some foundation for this difference of opinion, and that all are not either slaves by nature or freemen by nature, and also that there is in some cases a marked distinction between the two classes, rendering it expedient and right for the one to be slaves and the others to be masters: the one practising obedience, the others exercising the authority and lordship which nature intended
10 them to have. The abuse of this authority is injurious to both; for the interests of part and whole, of body and soul, are the same, and the slave is a part of the master, a living but separated part of his bodily frame. Hence, where the relation of master and slave between them is natural they are friends and have a common interest, but
15 where it rests merely on convention and force the reverse is true.

7 · The previous remarks are quite enough to show that the rule of a master is not a constitutional rule, and that all the different kinds of rule are not, as some affirm, the same as each other. For there is one rule exercised over subjects who are by nature free, another over subjects who are by nature slaves. The rule of a household is a monarchy, for every house is under one head: whereas constitutional
20 rule is a government of freemen and equals. The master is not called a master because he has science, but because he is of a certain character, and the same remark applies to the slave and the freeman. Still there may be a science for the master and a science for the slave. The science of the slave would be such as the man
25 of Syracuse taught, who made money by instructing slaves in their ordinary duties. And such a knowledge may be carried further, so as to include cookery and similar menial arts. For some duties are of the more necessary, others of the more honourable sort; as the proverb says, 'slave before slave, master before master'. But
30 all such branches of knowledge are servile. There is likewise a science of the master, which teaches the use of slaves; for the master as such is concerned, not with the acquisition, but with the use of them. Yet this science is not anything great or wonderful; for the master need only know how to order that which the slave must
35 know how to execute. Hence those who are in a position which places them above toil have stewards who attend to their households while they occupy themselves with philosophy or with politics. But the art of acquiring slaves, I mean of justly acquiring them, differs both from the art of the master and the art of slave, being a species of hunting or war. Enough of the distinction between master and slave.

1256ᵃ1 8 · Let us now inquire into property generally, and into the art of getting wealth, in accordance with our usual method, for a slave has been shown to be a part of property. The first question is whether the art of getting wealth is the same as the
5 art of managing a household or a part of it, or instrumental to it; and if the last, whether in the way that the art of making shuttles is instrumental to the art of weaving, or in the way that the casting of bronze is instrumental to the art of the statuary, for they are not instrumental in the same way, but the one provides tools

and the other material; and by material I mean the substratum out of which any work is made; thus wool is the material of the weaver, bronze of the statuary. Now it is easy to see that the art of household management is not identical with the art of   10 getting wealth, for the one uses the material which the other provides. For the art which uses household stores can be no other than the art of household management. There is, however, a doubt whether the art of getting wealth is a part of household management or a distinct art. If the getter of wealth has to consider whence wealth   15 and property can be procured, but there are many sorts of property and riches, then are husbandry, and the care and provision of food in general, parts of the art of household management or distinct arts? Again, there are many sorts of food, and therefore there are many kinds of lives both of animals and men; they must all have   20 food, and the differences in their food have made differences in their ways of life. For of beasts, some are gregarious, others are solitary; they live in the way which is best adapted to sustain them, accordingly as they are carnivorous or herbivorous or   25 omnivorous: and their habits are determined for them by nature with regard to their ease and choice of food. But the same things are not naturally pleasant to all of them; and therefore the lives of carnivorous or herbivorous animals further differ among themselves. In the lives of men too there is a great difference. The laziest are   30 shepherds, who lead an idle life, and get their subsistence without trouble from tame animals; their flocks having to wander from place to place in search of pasture, they are compelled to follow them, cultivating a sort of living farm. Others support   35 themselves by hunting, which is of different kinds. Some, for example, are brigands, others, who dwell near lakes or marshes or rivers or a sea in which there are fish, are fishermen, and others live by the pursuit of birds or wild beasts. The greater number obtain a living from the cultivated fruits of the soil. Such are the modes of   40 subsistence which prevail among those whose industry springs up of itself, and whose food is not acquired by exchange and retail trade—there is the shepherd, the   1256ᵇ1 husbandman, the brigand, the fisherman, the hunter. Some gain a comfortable maintenance out of two employments, eking out the deficiencies of one of them by another: thus the life of a shepherd may be combined with that of a brigand, the life   5 of a farmer with that of a hunter. Other modes of life are similarly combined in any way which the needs of men may require. Property, in the sense of a bare livelihood, seems to be given by nature herself to all, both when they are first born, and when   10 they are grown up. For some animals bring forth, together with their offspring, so much food as will last until they are able to supply themselves; of this the vermiparous or oviparous animals are an instance; and the viviparous animals have up to a certain time a supply of food for their young in themselves, which is called milk. In like manner we may infer that, after the birth of animals, plants exist for   15 their sake, and that the other animals exist for the sake of man,[3] the tame for use and food, the wild, if not all, at least the greater part of them, for food, and for the provision of clothing and various instruments. Now if nature makes nothing   20 incomplete, and nothing in vain, the inference must be that she has made all

---

[3]Retaining ζῷα τῶν ἀνθρώπων.

animals for the sake of man. And so, from one point of view, the art of war is a natural art of acquisition, for the art of acquisition includes hunting, an art which we ought to practise against wild beasts, and against men who, though intended by
25 nature to be governed, will not submit; for war of such a kind is naturally just.

Of the art of acquisition then there is one kind which by nature is a part of the management of a household, in so far as the art of household management must either find ready to hand, or itself provide, such things necessary to life, and useful
30 for the community of the family or state, as can be stored. They are the elements of true riches; for the amount of property which is needed for a good life is not unlimited, although Solon in one of his poems says that

No bound to riches has been fixed for man.

But there is a boundary fixed, just as there is in the other arts; for the instruments of
35 any art are never unlimited, either in number or size, and riches may be defined as a number of instruments to be used in a household or in a state. And so we see that there is a natural art of acquisition which is practised by managers of households and by statesmen, and the reason for this.

40   9 . There is another variety of the art of acquisition which is commonly and rightly called an art of wealth-getting, and has in fact suggested the notion that
1257ᵃ1 riches and property have no limit. Being nearly connected with the preceding, it is often identified with it. But though they are not very different, neither are they the same. The kind already described is given by nature, the other is gained by
5 experience and art.

Let us begin our discussion of the question with the following considerations. Of everything which we possess there are two uses: both belong to the thing as such, but not in the same manner, for one is the proper, and the other the improper use of
10 it. For example, a shoe is used for wear, and is used for exchange; both are uses of the shoe. He who gives a shoe in exchange for money or food to him who wants one, does indeed use the shoe as a shoe, but this is not its proper use, for a shoe is not made to be an object of barter. The same may be said of all possessions, for the art
15 of exchange extends to all of them, and it arises at first from what is natural, from the circumstance that some have too little, others too much. Hence we may infer that retail trade is not a natural part of the art of getting wealth; had it been so, men would have ceased to exchange when they had enough. In the first community,
20 indeed, which is the family, this art is obviously of no use, but it begins to be useful when the society increases. For the members of the family originally had all things in common; later, when the family divided into parts, the parts shared in many things, and different parts in different things, which they had to give in exchange
25 for what they wanted, a kind of barter which is still practised among barbarous nations who exchange with one another the necessaries of life and nothing more; giving and receiving wine, for example, in exchange for corn, and the like. This sort of barter is not part of the wealth-getting art and is not contrary to nature, but is
30 needed for the satisfaction of men's natural wants. The other form of exchange

grew, as might have been inferred, out of this one. When the inhabitants of one country became more dependent on those of another, and they imported what they needed, and exported what they had too much of, money necessarily came into use. For the various necessaries of life are not easily carried about, and hence men agreed to employ in their dealings with each other something which was intrinsi- 35 cally useful and easily applicable to the purposes of life, for example, iron, silver, and the like. Of this the value was at first measured simply by size and weight, but in process of time they put a stamp upon it, to save the trouble of weighing and to 40 mark the value.

When the use of coin had once been discovered, out of the barter of necessary 1257^b1 articles arose the other art of wealth-getting, namely, retail trade; which was at first probably a simple matter, but became more complicated as soon as men learned by experience whence and by what exchanges the greatest profit might be made. Originating in the use of coin, the art of getting wealth is generally thought to be 5 chiefly concerned with it, and to be the art which produces riches and wealth, having to consider how they may be accumulated. Indeed, riches is assumed by many to be only a quantity of coin, because the arts of getting wealth and retail trade are concerned with coin. Others maintain that coined money is a mere sham, a 10 thing not natural, but conventional only, because, if the users substitute another commodity for it, it is worthless, and because it is not useful as a means to any of the necessities of life, and, indeed, he who is rich in coin may often be in want of necessary food. But how can that be wealth of which a man may have a great abundance and yet perish with hunger, like Midas in the fable, whose insatiable 15 prayer turned everything that was set before him into gold?

Hence men seek after a better notion of riches and of the art of getting wealth, and they are right. For natural riches and the natural art of wealth-getting are a different thing; in their true form they are part of the management of a household; 20 whereas retail trade is the art of producing wealth, not in every way, but by exchange. And it is thought to be concerned with coin; for coin is the unit of exchange and the limit of it. And there is no bound to the riches which spring from this art of wealth-getting. As in the art of medicine there is no limit to the pursuit of 25 health, and as in the other arts there is no limit to the pursuit of their several ends, for they aim at accomplishing their ends to the uttermost (but of the means there is a limit, for the end is always the limit), so, too, in this art of wealth-getting there is no limit of the end, which is riches of the spurious kind, and the acquisition of 30 wealth. But the art of wealth-getting which consists in household management, on the other hand, has a limit;[4] the unlimited acquisition of wealth is not its business. And, therefore, from one point of view, all riches must have a limit; nevertheless, as a matter of fact, we find the opposite to be the case; for all getters of wealth increase their hoard of coin without limit. The source of the confusion is the near connexion 35 between the two kinds of wealth-getting; in both, the instrument is the same, although the use is different, and so they pass into one another; for each is a use of

<hr>

[4]Reading αὖ for οὖ.

the same property, but with a difference: accumulation is the end in the one case, but there is a further end in the other. Hence some persons are led to believe that getting wealth is the object of household management, and the whole idea of their lives is that they ought either to increase their money without limit, or at any rate not to lose it. The origin of this disposition in men is that they are intent upon living only, and not upon living well; and, as their desires are unlimited, they also desire that the means of gratifying them should be without limit. Those who do aim at a good life seek the means of obtaining bodily pleasures; and, since the enjoyment of these appears to depend on property, they are absorbed in getting wealth: and so there arises the second species of wealth-getting. For, as their enjoyment is in excess, they seek an art which produces the excess of enjoyment; and, if they are not able to supply their pleasures by the art of getting wealth, they try other causes, using in turn every faculty in a manner contrary to nature. The quality of courage, for example, is not intended to make wealth, but to inspire confidence; neither is this the aim of the general's or of the physician's art; but the one aims at victory and the other at health. Nevertheless, some men turn every quality or art into a means of getting wealth; this they conceive to be the end, and to the promotion of the end they think all things must contribute.

Thus, then, we have considered the art of wealth-getting which is unnecessary, and why men want it; and also the necessary art of wealth-getting, which we have seen to be different from the other, and to be a natural part of the art of managing a household, concerned with the provision of food, not, however, like the former kind, unlimited, but having a limit.

10 · And we have found the answer to our original question, Whether the art of getting wealth is the business of the manager of a household and of the statesman or not their business?—viz. that wealth is presupposed by them. For as political science does not make men, but takes them from nature and uses them, so too nature provides them with earth or sea or the like as a source of food. At this stage begins the duty of the manager of a household, who has to order the things which nature supplies—he may be compared to the weaver who has not to make but to use wool, and to know, too, what sort of wool is good and serviceable or bad and unserviceable. Were this otherwise, it would be difficult to see why the art of getting wealth is a part of the management of a household and the art of medicine not; for surely the members of a household must have health just as they must have life or any other necessity. The answer is that as from one point of view the master of the house and the ruler of the state have to consider about health, from another point of view not they but the physician has to; so in one way the art of household management, in another way the subordinate art, has to consider about wealth. But, strictly speaking, as I have already said, the means of life must be provided beforehand by nature; for the business of nature is to furnish food to that which is born, and the food of the offspring is always what remains over of that from which it is produced. That is why the art of getting wealth out of fruits and animals is always natural.

There are two sorts of wealth-getting, as I have said; one is a part of household management, the other is retail trade: the former is necessary and honourable, while that which consists in exchange is justly censured; for it is unnatural, and a 1258ᵇ1 mode by which men gain from one another. The most hated sort, and with the greatest reason, is usury, which makes a gain out of money itself, and not from the natural object of it. For money was intended to be used in exchange, but not to increase at interest. And this term interest, which means the birth of money from 5 money, is applied to the breeding of money because the offspring resembles the parent. That is why of all modes of getting wealth this is the most unnatural.

11 · Enough has been said about the theory of wealth-getting; we will now proceed to the practical part. Such things may be studied by a free man, but will 10 only be practised from necessity. The useful parts of wealth-getting are, first, the knowledge of live-stock—which are most profitable, and where, and how—as for example, what sort of horses or sheep or oxen or any other animals are most likely to give a return. A man ought to know which of these pay better than others, and 15 which pay best in particular places, for some do better in one place and some in another. Secondly, husbandry, which may be either tillage or planting, and the keeping of bees and of fish, or fowl, or of any animals which may be useful to man. 20 These are the divisions of the true or proper art of wealth-getting and come first. Of the other, which consists in exchange, the first and most important division is commerce (of which there are three kinds—ship-owning, the conveyance of goods, exposure for sale—these again differing as they are safer or more profitable), the second is usury, the third, service for hire—of this, one kind is employed in the 25 mechanical arts, the other in unskilled and bodily labour. There is still a third sort of wealth-getting intermediate between this and the first or natural mode which is partly natural, but is also concerned with exchange, viz. the industries that make their profit from the earth, and from things growing from the earth which, although 30 they bear no fruit, are nevertheless profitable; for example, the cutting of timber and all mining. The art of mining itself has many branches, for there are various kinds of things dug out of the earth. Of the several divisions of wealth-getting I now speak generally; a minute consideration of them might be useful in practice, but it 35 would be tiresome to dwell upon them at greater length now.

Those occupations are most truly arts in which there is the least element of chance; they are the meanest in which the body is most maltreated, the most servile in which there is the greatest use of the body, and the most illiberal in which there is the least need of excellence.

Works have been written upon these subjects by various persons; for example, by Chares the Parian, and Apollodorus the Lemnian, who have treated of Tillage 1259ᵃ1 and Planting, while others have treated of other branches; anyone who cares for such matters may refer to their writings. It would be well also to collect the scattered stories of the ways in which individuals have succeeded in amassing a 5 fortune; for all this is useful to persons who value the art of getting wealth. There is the anecdote of Thales the Milesian and his financial scheme, which involves a

principle of universal application, but is attributed to him on account of his reputation for wisdom. He was reproached for his poverty, which was supposed to
10 show that philosophy was of no use. According to the story, he knew by his skill in the stars while it was yet winter that there would be a great harvest of olives in the coming year; so, having a little money, he gave deposits for the use of all the olive-presses in Chios and Miletus, which he hired at a low price because no one bid
15 against him. When the harvest-time came, and many were wanted all at once and of a sudden, he let them out at any rate which he pleased, and made a quantity of money. Thus he showed the world that philosophers can easily be rich if they like, but that their ambition is of another sort. He is supposed to have given a striking
20 proof of his wisdom, but, as I was saying, his scheme for getting wealth is of universal application, and is nothing but the creation of a monopoly. It is an art often practised by cities when they are in want of money; they make a monopoly of provisions.

There was a man of Sicily, who, having money deposited with him, bought up
25 all the iron from the iron mines; afterwards, when the merchants from their various markets came to buy, he was the only seller, and without much increasing the price he gained 200 per cent. Which when Dionysius heard, he told him that he might
30 take away his money, but that he must not remain at Syracuse, for he thought that the man had discovered a way of making money which was injurious to his own interests. He made the same discovery as Thales; they both contrived to create a monopoly for themselves. And statesmen as well ought to know these things; for a state is often as much in want of money and of such schemes for obtaining it as a
35 household, or even more so; hence some public men devote themselves entirely to finance.

12 · Of household management we have seen that there are three parts— one is the rule of a master over slaves, which has been discussed already, another of a father, and the third of a husband. A husband and father, we saw, rules over wife
1259ᵇ1 and children, both free, but the rule differs, the rule over his children being a royal, over his wife a constitutional rule. For although there may be exceptions to the order of nature, the male is by nature fitter for command than the female, just as the elder and full-grown is superior to the younger and more immature. But in most
5 constitutional states the citizens rule and are ruled by turns, for the idea of a constitutional state implies that the natures of the citizens are equal, and do not differ at all. Nevertheless, when one rules and the other is ruled we endeavour to create a difference of outward forms and names and titles of respect, which may be illustrated by the saying of Amasis about his foot-pan. The relation of the male to
10 the female is always of this kind. The rule of a father over his children is royal, for he rules by virtue both of love and of the respect due to age, exercising a kind of royal power. And therefore Homer has appropriately called Zeus 'father of Gods and men', because he is the king of them all. For a king is the natural superior of his
15 subjects, but he should be of the same kin or kind with them, and such is the relation of elder and younger, of father and son.

13 · Thus it is clear that household management attends more to men than to the acquisition of inanimate things, and to human excellence more than to the excellence of property which we call wealth, and to the excellence of freemen more than to the excellence of slaves. A question may indeed be raised, whether there is any excellence at all in a slave beyond those of an instrument and of a servant— whether he can have the excellences of temperance, courage, justice, and the like; or whether slaves possess only bodily services. And, whichever way we answer the question, a difficulty arises; for, if they have excellence, in what will they differ from freemen? On the other hand, since they are men and share in rational principle, it seems absurd to say that they have no excellence. A similar question may be raised about women and children, whether they too have excellences; ought a woman to be temperate and brave and just, and is a child to be called temperate, and intemperate, or not? So in general we may ask about the natural ruler, and the natural subject, whether they have the same or different excellences. For if a noble nature is equally required in both, why should one of them always rule, and the other always be ruled? Nor can we say that this is a question of degree, for the difference between ruler and subject is a difference of kind, which the difference of more and less never is. Yet how strange is the supposition that the one ought, and that the other ought not, to have excellence! For if the ruler is intemperate and unjust, how can he rule well? if the subject, how can he obey well? If he is licentious and cowardly, he will certainly not do what is fitting. It is evident, therefore, that both of them must have a share of excellence, but varying as natural subjects also vary among themselves. Here the very constitution of the soul has shown us the way; in it one part naturally rules, and the other is subject, and the excellence of the ruler we maintain to be different from that of the subject—the one being the excellence of the rational, and the other of the irrational part. Now, it is obvious that the same principle applies generally, and therefore almost all things rule and are ruled according to nature. But the kind of rule differs—the freeman rules over the slave after another manner from that in which the male rules over the female, or the man over the child; although the parts of the soul are present in all of them, they are present in different degrees. For the slave has no deliberative faculty at all; the woman has, but it is without authority, and the child has, but it is immature. So it must necessarily be supposed to be with the excellences of character also; all should partake of them, but only in such manner and degree as is required by each for the fulfilment of his function. Hence the ruler ought to have excellence of character in perfection, for his function, taken absolutely, demands a master artificer, and reason is such an artificer; the subjects, on the other hand, require only that measure of excellence which is proper to each of them. Clearly, then, excellence of character belongs to all of them; but the temperance of a man and of a woman, or the courage and justice of a man and of a woman, are not, as Socrates maintained, the same; the courage of a man is shown in commanding, of a woman in obeying. And this holds of all other excellences, as will be more clearly seen if we look at them in detail, for those who say generally that excellence consists in a good disposition of the soul, or in doing rightly, or the like, only deceive themselves. Far

better than such definitions is the mode of speaking of those who, like Gorgias, enumerate the excellences. All classes must be deemed to have their special attributes; as the poet says of women,

30   Silence is a woman's glory,

but this is not equally the glory of man. The child is imperfect, and therefore obviously his excellence is not relative to himself alone, but to the perfect man and to his teacher, and in like manner the excellence of the slave is relative to a master. Now we determined that a slave is useful for the wants of life, and therefore he will

35 obviously require only so much excellence as will prevent him from failing in his function through cowardice or lack of self-control. Someone will ask whether, if what we are saying is true, excellence will not be required also in the artisans, for they often fail in their work through the lack of self-control. But is there not a great

40 difference in the two cases? For the slave shares in his master's life; the artisan is less closely connected with him, and only attains excellence in proportion as he

1260ᵇ1 becomes a slave. The meaner sort of mechanic has a special and separate slavery; and whereas the slave exists by nature, not so the shoemaker or other artisan. It is manifest, then, that the master ought to be the source of such excellence in the

5 slave, and not a mere possessor of the art of mastership which trains the slave in his functions. That is why they are mistaken who forbid us to converse with slaves and say that we should employ command only, for slaves stand even more in need of admonition than children.

So much for this subject; the relations of husband and wife, father and child,

10 their several excellences, what in their intercourse with one another is good, and what is evil, and how we may pursue the good and escape the evil, will have to be discussed when we speak of the different forms of government. For, inasmuch as every family is a part of a state, and these relationships are the parts of a family, and the excellence of the part must have regard to the excellence of the whole, women

15 and children must be trained by education with an eye to the constitution, if the excellences of either of them are supposed to make any difference in the excellences of the state. And they must make a difference: for the children grow up to be

20 citizens, and half the free persons in a state are women.

Of these matters, enough has been said; of what remains, let us speak at another time. Regarding, then, our present inquiry as complete, we will make a new beginning. And, first, let us examine the various theories of a perfect state.

BOOK II

25 1 · Our purpose is to consider what form of political community is best of all for those who are most able to realize their ideal of life. We must therefore examine not only this but other constitutions, both such as actually exist in well-governed

30 states, and any theoretical forms which are held in esteem, so that what is good and useful may be brought to light. And let no one suppose that in seeking for something

beyond them we are anxious to make a sophistical display at any cost; we only
undertake this inquiry because all the constitutions which now exist are faulty.   35
    We will begin with the natural beginning of the subject. The members of a
state must either have all things or nothing in common, or some things in common
and some not. That they should have nothing in common is clearly impossible, for
the constitution is a community, and must at any rate have a common place—one
city will be in one place, and the citizens are those who share in that one city. But   1261ᵃ1
should a well-ordered state have all things, as far as may be, in common, or some
only and not others? For the citizens might conceivably have wives and children and   5
property in common, as Socrates proposes in the *Republic* of Plato. Which is better,
our present condition, or one conforming to the law laid down in the *Republic?*

    2 · There are many difficulties in the community of women. And the   10
principle on which Socrates rests the necessity of such an institution evidently is not
established by his arguments. Further, as a means to the end which he ascribes to
the state, the scheme, taken literally, is impracticable, and how we are to interpret it
is nowhere precisely stated. I am speaking of the supposition from which the
argument of Socrates proceeds, that it is best for the whole state to be as unified as   15
possible. Is it not obvious that a state may at length attain such a degree of unity as
to be no longer a state?—since the nature of a state is to be a plurality, and in
tending to greater unity, from being a state, it becomes a family, and from being a
family, an individual; for the family may be said to be more one than the state, and   20
the individual than the family. So that we ought not to attain this greatest unity
even if we could, for it would be the destruction of the state. Again, a state is not
made up only of so many men, but of different kinds of men; for similars do not
constitute a state. It is not like a military alliance. The usefulness of the latter   25
depends upon its quantity even where there is no difference in quality (for mutual
protection is the end aimed at), just as a greater weight depresses the scale more (in
like manner, a state differs from a nation, when the nation has not its population
organized in villages, but lives an Arcadian sort of life); but the elements out of
which a unity is to be formed differ in kind. That is why the principle of reciprocity,   30
as I have already remarked in the *Ethics,* is the salvation of states. Even among
freemen and equals this is a principle which must be maintained, for they cannot all
rule together, but must change at the end of a year or some other period of time or in
some order of succession. The result is that upon this plan they all govern; just as if   35
shoemakers and carpenters were to exchange their occupations, and the same
persons did not always continue shoemakers and carpenters. And since it is better
that this should be so in politics as well, it is clear that while there should be
continuance of the same persons in power where this is possible, yet where this is not
possible by reason of the natural equality of the citizens, and at the same time it is   1261ᵇ1
just that all should share in the government (whether to govern be a good thing or a
bad),—in these cases this is imitated.[1] Thus the one party rules and the others are
ruled in turn, as if they were no longer the same persons. In like manner when they   5
hold office there is a variety in the offices held. Hence it is evident that a city is not

¹The text is uncertain.

by nature one in that sense which some persons affirm; and that what is said to be
the greatest good of cities is in reality their destruction; but surely the good of things
10 must be that which preserves them. Again, from another point of view, this extreme
unification of the state is clearly not good; for a family is more self-sufficing than an
individual, and a city than a family, and a city only comes into being when the
community is large enough to be self-sufficing. If then self-sufficiency is to be
15 desired, the lesser degree of unity is more desirable than the greater.

3 · But, even supposing that it were best for the community to have the
greatest degree of unity, this unity is by no means proved to follow from the fact of
all men saying 'mine' and 'not mine' at the same instant of time, which, according
20 to Socrates, is the sign of perfect unity in a state. For the word 'all' is ambiguous. If
the meaning be that every individual says 'mine' and 'not mine' at the same time,
then perhaps the result at which Socrates aims may be in some degree accomplished; each man will call the same person his own son and the same person his own
wife, and so of his property and of all that falls to his lot. This, however, is not the
25 way in which people would speak who had their wives and children in common; they
would say 'all' but not 'each'. In like manner their property would be described as
belonging to them, not severally but collectively. There is an obvious fallacy in the
term 'all': like some other words, 'both', 'odd', 'even', it is ambiguous, and even in
30 abstract argument becomes a source of logical puzzles. That all persons call the
same thing mine in the sense in which each does so may be a fine thing, but it is
impracticable; or if the words are taken in the other sense, such a unity in no way
conduces to harmony. And there is another objection to the proposal. For that
which is common to the greatest number has the least care bestowed upon it. Every-
35 one thinks chiefly of his own, hardly at all of the common interest; and only when he
is himself concerned as an individual. For besides other considerations, everybody is
more inclined to neglect something which he expects another to fulfil; as in families
many attendants are often less useful than a few. Each citizen will have a thousand
1262ᵃ1 sons who will not be his sons individually, but anybody will be equally the son of
anybody, and will therefore be neglected by all alike. Further, upon this principle,
every one will use the word 'mine' of one who is prospering or the reverse, however
small a fraction he may himself be of the whole number; the same boy will be my
son, so and so's son, the son of each of the thousand, or whatever be the number of
5 the citizens; and even about this he will not be positive; for it is impossible to know
who chanced to have a child, or whether, if one came into existence, it has survived.
But which is better—for each to say 'mine' in this way, making a man the same
relation to two thousand or ten thousand citizens, or to use the word 'mine' as it is
now used in states? For usually the same person is called by one man his own son
10 whom another calls his own brother or cousin or kinsman—blood relation or
connexion by marriage—either of himself or of some relation of his, and yet another
his clansman or tribesman; and how much better is it to be the real cousin of
somebody than to be a son after Plato's fashion! Nor is there any way of preventing
15 brothers and children and fathers and mothers from sometimes recognizing one

another; for children are born like their parents, and they will necessarily be finding indications of their relationship to one another. Geographers declare such to be the fact; they say that in part of Upper Libya, where the women are common, 20 nevertheless the children who are born are assigned to their respective fathers on the ground of their likeness. And some women, like the females of other animals—for example, mares and cows—have a strong tendency to produce offspring resembling their parents, as was the case with the Pharsalian mare called Honest Wife.

4 · Other difficulties, against which it is not easy for the authors of such a 25 community to guard, will be assaults and homicides, voluntary as well as involuntary, quarrels and slanders, all of which are most unholy acts when committed against fathers and mothers and near relations, but not equally unholy when there is no relationship. Moreover, they are much more likely to occur if the relationship is 30 unknown than if it is known and, when they have occurred, the customary expiations of them can be made if the relationship is known, but not otherwise. Again, how strange it is that Socrates, after having made the children common, should hinder lovers from carnal intercourse only, but should permit love and 35 familiarities between father and son or between brother and brother, than which nothing can be more unseemly, since even without them love of this sort is improper. How strange, too, to forbid intercourse for no other reason than the violence of the pleasure, as though the relationship of father and son or of brothers with one another made no difference. 40

This community of wives and children seems better suited to the husbandmen than to the guardians, for if they have wives and children in common, they will be bound to one another by weaker ties, as a subject class should be, and they will 1262^{b}1 remain obedient and not rebel. In a word, the result of such a law would be just the opposite of that which good laws ought to have, and the intention of Socrates in making these regulations about women and children would defeat itself. For 5 friendship we believe to be the greatest good of states and what best preserves them against revolutions; and Socrates particularly praises the unity of the state which seems and is said by him to be created by friendship. But the unity which he 10 commends would be like that of the lovers in the *Symposium*, who, as Aristophanes says, desire to grow together in the excess of their affection, and from being two to become one, in which case one or both would certainly perish. Whereas in a state having women and children common, love will be diluted; and the father will 15 certainly not say 'my son', or the son 'my father'. As a little sweet wine mingled with a great deal of water is imperceptible in the mixture, so, in this sort of community, the idea of relationship which is based upon these names will be lost; there is no reason why the so-called father should care about the son, or the son about the 20 father, or brothers about one another. Of the two qualities which chiefly inspire regard and affection—that a thing is your own and that it is precious—neither can exist in such a state as this.

Again, the transfer of children as soon as they are born from the rank of 25 husbandmen or of artisans to that of guardians, and from the rank of guardians into

a lower rank, will be very difficult to arrange; the givers or transferrers cannot but know whom they are giving and transferring, and to whom. And the previously
30 mentioned assaults, unlawful loves, homicides, will happen more often among them; for they will no longer call the members of the class they have left brothers, and children, and fathers, and mothers, and will not, therefore, be afraid of committing
35 any crimes by reason of consanguinity. Touching the community of wives and children, let this be our conclusion.

5 . Next let us consider what should be our arrangements about property: should the citizens of the perfect state have their possessions in common or not?
40 This question may be discussed separately from the enactments about women and children. Even supposing that the women and children belong to individuals, according to the custom which is at present universal, may there not be an
1263ª1 advantage in having and using possessions in common? E.g. (1) the soil may be appropriated, but the produce may be thrown for consumption into the common
5 stock; and this is the practice of some nations. Or (2), the soil may be common, and may be cultivated in common, but the produce divided among individuals for their private use; this is a form of common property which is said to exist among certain foreigners. Or (3), the soil and the produce may be alike common.
When the husbandmen are not the owners, the case will be different and easier
10 to deal with; but when they till the ground for themselves the question of ownership will give a world of trouble. If they do not share equally in enjoyments and toils, those who labour much and get little will necessarily complain of those who labour
15 little and receive or consume much. But indeed there is always a difficulty in men living together and having all human relations in common, but especially in their having common property. The partnerships of fellow-travellers are an example to the point; for they generally fall out over everyday matters and quarrel about any trifle which turns up. So with servants: we are most liable to take offence at those
20 with whom we most frequently come into contact in daily life.
These are only some of the disadvantages which attend the community of property; the present arrangement, if improved as it might be by good customs and
25 laws, would be far better, and would have the advantages of both systems. Property should be in a certain sense common, but, as a general rule, private; for, when everyone has a distinct interest, men will not complain of one another, and they will make more progress, because everyone will be attending to his own business. And
30 yet by reason of goodness, and in respect of use, 'Friends', as the proverb says, 'will have all things common'. Even now there are traces of such a principle, showing that it is not impracticable, but, in well-ordered states, exists already to a certain extent and may be carried further. For, although every man has his own property, some things he will place at the disposal of his friends, while of others he shares the
35 use with them. The Lacedaemonians, for example, use one another's slaves, and horses, and dogs, as if they were their own; and when they lack provisions on a journey, they appropriate what they find in the fields throughout the country. It is clearly better that property should be private, but the use of it common; and the

special business of the legislator is to create in men this benevolent disposition. Again, how immeasurably greater is the pleasure, when a man feels a thing to be his own; for surely the love of self is a feeling implanted by nature and not given in vain, 1263ᵇ1 although selfishness is rightly censured; this, however, is not the mere love of self, but the love of self in excess, like the miser's love of money; for all, or almost all, men love money and other such objects in a measure. And further, there is the greatest pleasure in doing a kindness or service to friends or guests or companions, 5 which can only be rendered when a man has private property. These advantages are lost by excessive unification of the state. The exhibition of two excellences, besides, is visibly annihilated in such a state: first, temperance towards women (for it is an honourable action to abstain from another's wife for temperance sake); secondly, 10 liberality in the matter of property. No one, when men have all things in common, will any longer set an example of liberality or do any liberal action; for liberality consists in the use which is made of property.

Such legislation may have a specious appearance of benevolence; men readily 15 listen to it, and are easily induced to believe that in some wonderful manner everybody will become everybody's friend—especially when someone is heard denouncing the evils now existing in states, suits about contracts, convictions for perjury, flatteries of rich men and the like, which are said to arise out of the 20 possession of private property. These evils, however, are due not to the absence of communism but to wickedness. Indeed, we see that there is much more quarrelling among those who have all things in common, though there are not many of them 25 when compared with the vast numbers who have private property.

Again, we ought to reckon not only the evils from which the citizens will be saved, but also the advantages which they will lose. The life which they are to lead appears to be quite impracticable. The error of Socrates must be attributed to the 30 false supposition from which he starts. Unity there should be, both of the family and of the state, but in some respects only. For there is a point at which a state may attain such a degree of unity as to be no longer a state, or at which, without actually ceasing to exist, it will become an inferior state, like harmony passing into unison, or 35 rhythm which has been reduced to a single foot. The state, as I was saying, is a plurality, which should be united and made into a community by education; and it is strange that the author of a system of education which he thinks will make the state virtuous, should expect to improve his citizens by regulations of this sort, and not by 40 philosophy or by customs and laws, like those which prevail at Sparta and Crete respecting common meals, whereby the legislator has made property common. Let us remember that we should not disregard the experience of ages; in the multitude 1264ᵃ1 of years these things, if they were good, would certainly not have been unknown; for almᴖst everything has been found out, although sometimes they are not put together; in other cases men do not use the knowledge which they have. Great light would be thrown on this subject if we could see such a form of government in the 5 actual process of construction; for the legislator could not form a state at all without distributing and dividing its constituents into associations for common meals, and into phratries and tribes. But all this legislation ends only in forbidding agriculture to the guardians, a prohibition which the Lacedaemonians try to enforce already. 10

But, indeed, Socrates has not said, nor is it easy to decide, what in such a community will be the general form of the state. The citizens who are not guardians are the majority, and about them nothing has been determined: are the husband-
15 men, too, to have their property in common? Or is each individual to have his own? and are their wives and children to be individual or common? If, like the guardians, they are to have all things in common, in what do they differ from them, or what will they gain by submitting to their government? Or upon what principle would they
20 submit, unless indeed the governing class adopt the ingenious policy of the Cretans, who give their slaves the same institutions as their own, but forbid them gymnastic exercises and the possession of arms. If, on the other hand, the inferior classes are to be like other cities in respect of marriage and property, what will be the form of the
25 community? Must it not contain two states in one, each hostile to the other? He makes the guardians into a mere occupying garrison, while the husbandmen and artisans and the rest are real citizens. But if so the suits and quarrels, and all the evils which Socrates affirms to exist in other states, will exist equally among them.
30 He says indeed that, having so good an education, the citizens will not need many laws, for example laws about the city or about the markets; but then he confines his education to the guardians. Again, he makes the husbandmen owners of the property upon condition of their paying a tribute. But in that case they are likely to
35 be much more unmanageable and conceited than the Helots, or Penestae, or slaves in general. And whether community of wives and property be necessary for the lower equally with the higher class or not, and the questions akin to this, what will be the education, form of government, laws of the lower class, Socrates has nowhere determined: neither is it easy to discover this, nor is their character of small importance if the common life of the guardians is to be maintained.

1264ᵇ1   Again, if Socrates makes the women common, and retains private property, the men will see to the fields, but who will see to the house? And who will do so if the agricultural class have both their property and their wives in common? Once more:
5 it is absurd to argue, from the analogy of animals, that men and women should follow the same pursuits, for animals have not to manage a household. The government, too, as constituted by Socrates, contains elements of danger; for he makes the same persons always rule. And if this is often a cause of disturbance
10 among the meaner sort, how much more among high-spirited warriors? But that the persons whom he makes rulers must be the same is evident; for the gold which the God mingles in the souls of men is not at one time given to one, at another time to another, but always to the same: as he says, God mingles gold in some, and silver in others, from their very birth; but brass and iron in those who are meant to be
15 artisans and husbandmen. Again, he deprives the guardians even of happiness, and says that the legislator ought to make the whole state happy. But the whole cannot be happy unless most, or all, or some of its parts enjoy happiness. In this respect
20 happiness is not like the even principle in numbers, which may exist only in the whole, but in neither of the parts; not so happiness. And if the guardians are not happy, who are? Surely not the artisans, or the common people. The Republic of
25 which Socrates discourses has all these difficulties, and others quite as great.

6 · The same, or nearly the same, objections apply to Plato's later work, the *Laws*, and therefore we had better examine briefly the constitution which is therein described. In the *Republic*, Socrates has definitely settled in all a few questions only; such as the community of women and children, the community of property, and the constitution of the state. The population is divided into two classes—one of husbandmen, and the other of warriors; from this latter is taken a third class of counsellors and rulers of the state. But Socrates has not determined whether the husbandmen and artisans are to have a share in the government, and whether they, too, are to carry arms and share in the military service, or not. He certainly thinks that the women ought to share in the education of the guardians, and to fight by their side. The remainder of the work is filled up with digressions foreign to the main subject, and with discussions about the education of the guardians. In the *Laws* there is hardly anything but laws; not much is said about the constitution. This, which he had intended to make more of the ordinary type, he gradually brings round to the other form. For with the exception of the community of women and property, he supposes everything to be the same in both states; there is to be the same education; the citizens of both are to live free from servile occupations, and there are to be common meals in both. The only difference is that in the *Laws*, the common meals are extended to women, and the warriors number 5000, but in the *Republic* only 1000.

The discourses of Socrates are never commonplace; they always exhibit grace and originality and thought; but perfection in everything can hardly be expected. We must not overlook the fact that the number of 5000 citizens, just now mentioned, will require a territory as large as Babylon, or some other huge site, if so many persons are to be supported in idleness, together with their women and attendants, who will be a multitude many times as great. In framing an ideal we may assume what we wish, but should avoid impossibilities.

It is said that the legislator ought to have his eye directed to two points—the people and the country. But neighbouring countries also must not be forgotten by him, firstly because the state for which he legislates is to have a political and not an isolated life. For a state must have such a military force as will be serviceable against her neighbours, and not merely useful at home. Even if such a life is not accepted, either for individuals or states, still a city should be formidable to enemies, whether invading or retreating.

There is another point: Should not the amount of property be defined in some way which differs from this by being clearer? For Socrates says that a man should have so much property as will enable him to live temperately, which is only a way of saying to live well; this is too general a conception. Further, a man may live temperately and yet miserably. A better definition would be that a man must have so much property as will enable him to live not only temperately but liberally; if the two are parted, liberality will combine with luxury; temperance will be associated with toil. For liberality and temperance are the only eligible qualities which have to do with the use of property. A man cannot use property with mildness or courage, but temperately and liberally he may; and therefore the practice of these

excellences is inseparable from property. There is an absurdity, too, in equalizing
40   the property and not regulating the number of citizens; the population is to remain
unlimited, and he thinks that it will be sufficiently equalized by a certain number of
marriages being unfruitful, however many are born to others, because he finds this
1265ᵇ1   to be the case in existing states. But greater care will be required than now; for
among ourselves, whatever may be the number of citizens, the property is always
distributed among them, and therefore no one is in want; but, if the property were
5   incapable of division as in the *Laws,* the supernumeraries, whether few or many,
would get nothing. One would have thought that it was even more necessary to limit
population than property; and that the limit should be fixed by calculating the
10   chances of mortality in the children, and of sterility in married persons. The neglect
of this subject, which in existing states is so common, is a never-failing cause of
poverty among the citizens; and poverty is the parent of revolution and crime.
Pheidon the Corinthian, who was one of the most ancient legislators, thought that
the families and the number of citizens ought to remain the same, although
15   originally all the lots may have been of different sizes; but in the *Laws* the opposite
principle is maintained. What in our opinion is the right arrangement will have to be
explained hereafter.

    There is another omission in the *Laws*: Socrates does not tell us how the rulers
20   differ from their subjects; he only says that they should be related as the warp and
the woof, which are made out of different wools. He allows that a man's whole
property may be increased fivefold, but why should not his land also increase to a
25   certain extent? Again, will the good management of a household be promoted by his
arrangement of homesteads? for he assigns to each individual two homesteads in
separate places, and it is difficult to live in two houses.

    The whole system of government tends to be neither democracy nor oligarchy,
but something in a mean between them, which is usually called a polity, and is
composed of the heavy-armed soldiers. Now, if he intended to frame a constitution
30   which would suit the greatest number of states, he was very likely right, but not if he
meant to say that this constitutional form came nearest to his first state; for many
would prefer the Lacedaemonian, or, possibly, some other more aristocratic
government. Some, indeed, say that the best constitution is a combination of all
35   existing forms, and they praise the Lacedaemonian because it is made up of
oligarchy, monarchy, and democracy, the king forming the monarchy, and the
council of elders the oligarchy, while the democratic element is represented by the
Ephors; for the Ephors are selected from the people. Others, however, declare the
Ephorate to be a tyranny, and find the element of democracy in the common meals
1266ª1   and in the habits of daily life. In the *Laws* it is maintained that the best constitution
is made up of democracy and tyranny, which are either not constitutions at all, or
are the worst of all. But they are nearer the truth who combine many forms; for the
5   constitution is better which is made up of more numerous elements. The constitution proposed in the *Laws* has no element of monarchy at all; it is nothing but
oligarchy and democracy, leaning rather to oligarchy. This is seen in the mode of
appointing magistrates; for although the appointment of them by lot from among

those who have been already selected combines both elements, the way in which the rich are compelled by law to attend the assembly and vote for magistrates or discharge other political duties, while the rest may do as they like, and the endeavour to have the greater number of the magistrates appointed out of the richer classes and the highest officers selected from those who have the greatest incomes, both these are oligarchical features. The oligarchical principle prevails also in the choice of the council, for all are compelled to choose, but the compulsion extends only to the choice out of the first class, and of an equal number out of the second class and out of the third class, but not in this latter case to all the voters but to those from the third or fourth class; and the selection of candidates out of the fourth class is only compulsory on the first and second. Then, from the persons so chosen, he says that there ought to be an equal number of each class selected. Thus a preponderance will be given to the better sort of people, who have the larger incomes, because some of the lower classes, not being compelled, will not vote. These considerations, and others which will be adduced when the time comes for examining similar constitutions, tend to show that states like Plato's should not be composed of democracy and monarchy. There is also a danger in electing the magistrates out of a body who are themselves elected; for, if but a small number choose to combine, the elections will always go as they desire. Such is the constitution which is described in the *Laws*.

7 · Other constitutions have been proposed; some by private persons, others by philosophers and statesmen, which all come nearer to established or existing ones than either of Plato's. No one else has introduced such novelties as the community of women and children, or public tables for women: other legislators begin with what is necessary. In the opinion of some, the regulation of property is the chief point of all, that being the question upon which all revolutions turn. This danger was recognized by Phaleas of Chalcedon, who was the first to affirm that the citizens of a state ought to have equal possessions. He thought that in a new colony the equalization might be accomplished without difficulty, not so easily when a state was already established; and that then the shortest way of compassing the desired end would be for the rich to give and not to receive marriage portions, and for the poor not to give but to receive them.

Plato in the *Laws* was of the opinion that, to a certain extent, accumulation should be allowed, forbidding, as I have already observed, any citizen to possess more than five times the minimum qualification. But those who make such laws should remember what they are apt to forget—that the legislator who fixes the amount of property should also fix the number of children; for, if the children are too many for the property, the law must be broken. And, besides the violation of the law, it is a bad thing that many from being rich should become poor; for men of ruined fortunes are sure to stir up revolutions. That the equalization of property exercises an influence on political society was clearly understood even by some of the old legislators. Laws were made by Solon and others prohibiting an individual from possessing as much land as he pleased; and there are other laws in states which

forbid the sale of property: among the Locrians, for example, there is a law that a
20 man is not to sell his property unless he can prove unmistakably that some
misfortune has befallen him. Again, there have been laws which enjoin the
preservation of the original lots. Such a law existed in the island of Leucas, and the
abrogation of it made the constitution too democratic, for the rulers no longer had
the prescribed qualification. Again, where there is equality of property, the amount
25 may be either too large or too small, and the possessor may be living either in luxury
or penury. Clearly, then, the legislator ought not only to aim at the equalization of
properties, but at moderation in their amount. Further, if he prescribe this
moderate amount equally to all, he will be no nearer the mark; for it is not the
30 possessions but the desires of mankind which require to be equalized, and this is
impossible, unless a sufficient education is provided by the laws. But Phaleas will
probably reply that this is precisely what he means; and that, in his opinion, there
ought to be in states, not only equal property, but equal education. Still he should
35 tell us what will be the character of his education; there is no use in having one and
the same for all, if it is of a sort that predisposes men to avarice, or ambition, or
both. Moreover, civil troubles arise, not only out of the inequality of property, but
out of the inequality of honour, though in opposite ways. For the common people
1267ᵃ1 quarrel about the inequality of property, the higher class about the equality of
honour; as the poet says,

                    The bad and good alike in honour share.

        There are crimes for which the motive is want; and for these Phaleas expects to
find a cure in the equalization of property, which will take away from a man the
temptation to be a robber, because he is hungry or cold. But want is not the sole
5 incentive to crime; men also wish to enjoy themselves and not to be in a state of
desire—they wish to cure some desire, going beyond the necessities of life, which
preys upon them; indeed this is not the only reason—they may desire to enjoy
pleasures unaccompanied with pain, and therefore they commit crimes.
        Now what is the cure of these three disorders? Of the first, moderate
10 possessions and occupation; of the second, habits of temperance; as to the third, if
any desire pleasures which depend on themselves, they will find the satisfaction of
their desires nowhere but in philosophy; for all other pleasures we are dependent on
others. The fact is, that the greatest crimes are caused by excess and not by
necessity. Men do not become tyrants in order that they may not suffer cold; and
15 hence great is the honour bestowed, not on him who kills a thief, but on him who
kills a tyrant. Thus we see that the institutions of Phaleas avail only against petty
crimes.
        There is another objection to them. They are chiefly designed to promote the
internal welfare of the state. But the legislator should consider also its relation to
neighbouring nations, and to all who are outside of it. The government must be
20 organized with a view to military strength; and of this he has said not a word. And so
with respect to property: there should not only be enough to supply the internal
wants of the state, but also to meet dangers coming from without. The property of

the state should not be so large that more powerful neighbours may be tempted by 25
it, while the owners are unable to repel the invaders; nor yet so small that the state is
unable to maintain a war even against states of equal power, and of the same
character. Phaleas has not laid down any rule; but we should bear in mind that
abundance of wealth is an advantage. The best limit will probably be, that a more
powerful neighbour must have no inducement to go to war with you by reason of the 30
excess of your wealth, but only such as he would have had if you had possessed less.
There is a story that Eubulus, when Autophradates was going to besiege Atarneus,
told him to consider how long the operation would take, and then reckon up the cost
which would be incurred in the time. 'For', said he, 'I am willing for a smaller sum
than that to leave Atarneus at once.' These words of Eubulus made an impression 35
on Autophradates, and he desisted from the siege.

The equalization of property is one of the things that tend to prevent the
citizens from quarrelling. Not that the gain in this direction is very great. For the
nobles will be dissatisfied because they think themselves worthy of more than an
equal share of honours; and this is often found to be a cause of sedition and
revolution. And the avarice of mankind is insatiable; at one time two obols was pay 1267^b1
enough; but now, when this sum has become customary, men always want more and
more without end; for it is of the nature of desire to be unlimited, and most men live
only for the gratification of it. The beginning of reform is not so much to equalize 5
property as to train the nobler sort of natures not to desire more, and to prevent the
lower from getting more; that is to say, they must be kept down, but not ill-treated.
Besides, the equalization proposed by Phaleas is imperfect; for he only equalizes 10
land, whereas a man may be rich also in slaves, and cattle, and money, and in the
abundance of what are called his movables. Now either all these things must be
equalized, or some limit must be imposed on them, or they must all be let alone. It
would appear that Phaleas is legislating for a small city only, if, as he supposes, all
the artisans are to be public slaves and not to form a supplementary part of the body 15
of citizens. But if there is a law that artisans are to be public slaves, it should only
apply to those engaged on public works, as at Epidamnus, or at Athens on the plan
which Diophantus once introduced.

From these observations any one may judge how far Phaleas was wrong or 20
right in his ideas.

8 · Hippodamus, the son of Euryphon, a native of Miletus, the same who
invented the art of planning cities, and who also laid out the Piraeus—a strange
man, whose fondness for distinction led him into a general eccentricity of life, which
made some think him affected (for he would wear flowing hair and expensive 25
ornaments; but these were worn on a cheap but warm garment both in winter and
summer); he, besides aspiring to be an adept in the knowledge of nature, was the
first person not a statesman who made inquiries about the best form of government. 30

The city of Hippodamus was composed of 10,000 citizens divided into three
parts—one of artisans, one of husbandmen, and a third of armed defenders of the

state. He also divided the land into three parts, one sacred, one public, the third
35   private:—the first was set apart to maintain the customary worship of the gods, the
second was to support the warriors, the third was the property of the husbandmen.
He also divided laws into three classes, and no more, for he maintained that there
are three subjects of lawsuits—insult, injury, and homicide. He likewise instituted
40   a single final court of appeal, to which all causes seeming to have been improperly
decided might be referred; this court he formed of elders chosen for the purpose. He
1268ª1   was further of the opinion that the decisions of the courts ought not to be given by
the use of a voting pebble, but that everyone should have a tablet on which he might
not only write a simple condemnation, or leave the tablet blank for a simple
acquittal; but, if he partly acquitted and partly condemned, he was to distinguish
5   accordingly. To the existing law he objected that it obliged the judges to be guilty of
perjury, whichever way they voted. He also enacted that those who discovered
anything for the good of the state should be honoured, and he provided that the
children of citizens who died in battle should be maintained at public expense, as if
10   such an enactment had never been heard of before, yet it actually exists at Athens
and in other places. As to the magistrates, he would have them all elected by the
people, that is, by the three classes already mentioned, and those who were elected
were to watch over the interests of the public, of strangers, and of orphans. These
15   are the most striking points in the constitution of Hippodamus. There is not much
else.
        The first of these proposals to which objection may be taken is the threefold
division of the citizens. The artisans, and the husbandmen, and the warriors, all
have a share in the government. But the husbandmen have no arms, and the artisans
20   neither arms nor land, and therefore they become all but slaves of the warrior class.
That they should share in all the offices is an impossibility; for generals and
guardians of the citizens, and nearly all the principal magistrates, must be taken
from the class of those who carry arms. Yet, if the two other classes have no share in
25   the government, how can they be loyal citizens? It may be said that those who have
arms must necessarily be masters of both the other classes, but this is not so easily
accomplished unless they are numerous; and if they are, why should the other
classes share in the government at all, or have power to appoint magistrates?
30   Further, what use are farmers to the city? Artisans there must be, for these are
wanted in every city, and they can live by their craft, as elsewhere; and the
husbandmen, too, if they really provided the warriors with food, might fairly have a
share in the government. But in the republic of Hippodamus they are supposed to
35   have land of their own, which they cultivate for their private benefit. Again, as to
this common land out of which the soldiers are maintained, if they are themselves to
be the cultivators of it, the warrior class will be identical with the husbandmen,
although the legislator intended to make a distinction between them. If, again, there
are to be other cultivators distinct both from the husbandmen, who have land of
40   their own, and from the warriors, they will make a fourth class, which has no place
in the state and no share in anything. Or, if the same persons are to cultivate their
own lands, and those of the public as well, they will have a difficulty in supplying

the quantity of produce which will maintain two households:[2] and why, in this case,   1268ᵇ1
should there be any division, for they might find food themselves and give to the
warriors from the same land and the same lots? There is surely a great confusion in
all this.

Neither is the law to be commended which says that the judges, when a simple   5
issue is laid before them, should make a distinction in their judgement; for the judge
is thus converted into an arbitrator. Now, in an arbitration, although the arbitrators
are many, they confer with one another about the decision; but in courts of law this
is impossible, and, indeed, most legislators take pains to prevent the judges from   10
holding any communication with one another. Again, will there not be confusion if
the judge thinks that damages should be given, but not so much as the suitor
demands? He asks, say, for twenty minae, and the judge allows him ten minae (or in
general the suitor asks for more and the judge allows less), while another judge
allows five, another four minae. In this way they will go on splitting up the damages,   15
and some will grant the whole and others nothing: how is the final reckoning to be
taken? Again, no one contends that he who votes for a simple acquittal or
condemnation perjures himself, if the indictment has been laid in an unqualified
form; and this is just, for the judge who acquits does not decide that the defendant   20
owes nothing, but that he does not owe the twenty minae. He only is guilty of
perjury who thinks that the defendant ought not to pay twenty minae, and yet
condemns him.

To honour those who discover anything which is useful to the state is a proposal
which has a specious sound, but cannot safely be enacted by law, for it may
encourage informers, and perhaps even lead to political commotions. This question   25
involves another. It has been doubted whether it is or is not expedient to make any
changes in the laws of a country, even if another law be better. Now, if all changes
are inexpedient, we can hardly assent to the proposal of Hippodamus; for, under
pretence of doing a public service, a man may introduce measures which are really   30
destructive to the laws or to the constitution. But, since we have touched upon this
subject, perhaps we had better go a little into detail, for, as I was saying, there is a
difference of opinion, and it may sometimes seem desirable to make changes. Such
changes in the other arts and sciences have certainly been beneficial; medicine, for
example, and gymnastics, and every other art and craft have departed from   35
traditional usage. And, if politics be an art, change must be necessary in this as in
any other art. That improvement has occurred is shown by the fact that old customs
are exceedingly simple and barbarous. For the ancient Hellenes went about armed   40
and bought their brides from each other. The remains of ancient laws which have
come down to us are quite absurd; for examples, at Cumae there is a law about   1269ª1
murder, to the effect that if the accuser produce a certain number of witnesses from
among his own kinsmen, the accused shall be held guilty. Again, men in general
desire the good, and not merely what their fathers had. But the primaeval
inhabitants, whether they were born of the earth or were the survivors of some   5

²Reading οἰκίαις

destruction, may be supposed to have been no better than ordinary or even foolish people among ourselves (such is certainly the tradition concerning the earth-born men); and it would be ridiculous to rest contented with their notions. Even when laws have been written down, they ought not always to remain unaltered. As in
10 other sciences, so in politics, it is impossible that all things should be precisely set down in writing; for enactments must be universal, but actions are concerned with particulars. Hence we infer that sometimes and in certain cases laws should be changed; but when we look at the matter from another point of view, great caution would seem to be required. For the habit of lightly changing the laws is an evil, and,
15 when the advantage is small, some errors both of lawgivers and rulers had better be left; the citizen will not gain so much by making the change as he will lose by the habit of disobedience. The analogy of the arts is false; a change in a law is a very
20 different thing from a change in an art. For the law has no power to command obedience except that of habit, which can only be given by time, so that a readiness to change from old to new laws enfeebles the power of the law. Even if we admit that the laws are to be changed, are they all to be changed, and in every state? And are
25 they to be changed by anybody who likes, or only by certain persons? These are very important questions; and therefore we had better reserve the discussion of them to a more suitable occasion.

9 · In the governments of Lacedaemon and Crete, and indeed in all
30 governments, two points have to be considered: first, whether any particular law is good or bad, when compared with the perfect state; secondly, whether it is or is not consistent with the idea and character which the lawgiver has set before his citizens. That in a well-ordered state the citizens should have leisure and not have to provide
35 for their daily wants is generally acknowledged, but there is a difficulty in seeing how this leisure is to be attained. The Thessalian Penestae have often risen against their masters, and the Helots in like manner against the Lacedaemonians, for whose misfortunes they are always lying in wait. Nothing, however, of this kind has as yet happened to the Cretans; the reason probably is that the neighboring cities, even
1269ᵇ1 when at war with one another, never form an alliance with rebellious serfs, rebellions not being for their interest, since they themselves have a dependent population. Whereas all the neighbours of the Lacedaemonians, whether Argives, Messenians, or Arcadians, were their enemies. In Thessaly, again, the original
5 revolt of the slaves occurred because the Thessalians were still at war with the neighbouring Achaeans, Perrhaebians and Magnesians. Besides, if there were no other difficulty, the treatment or management of slaves is a troublesome affair; for, if not kept in hand, they are insolent, and think that they are as good as their
10 masters, and, if harshly treated, they hate and conspire against them. Now it is clear that when these are the results the citizens of a state have not found out the secret of managing their subject population.

Again, the license of the Lacedaemonian women defeats the intention of the Spartan constitution, and is adverse to the happiness of the state. For, a husband
15 and a wife being each a part of every family, the state may be considered as about

equally divided into men and women; and, therefore, in those states in which the condition of the women is bad, half the city may be regarded as having no laws. And this is what has actually happened at Sparta; the legislator wanted to make the   20 whole state hardy, and he has carried out his intention in the case of the men, but he has neglected the women, who live in every sort of intemperance and luxury. The consequence is that in such a state wealth is too highly valued, especially if the citizens fall under the dominion of their wives, after the manner of most warlike   25 races, except the Celts and a few others who openly approve of male homosexuality. The old mythologer would seem to have been right in uniting Ares and Aphrodite, for all warlike races are prone to the love either of men or of women. This was   30 exemplified among the Spartans in the days of their greatness; many things were managed by their women. But what difference does it make whether women rule, or the rulers are ruled by women? The result is the same. Even in regard to boldness, which is of no use in daily life, and is needed only in war, the influence of the   35 Lacedaemonian women has been most mischievous. The evil showed itself in the Theban invasion, when, unlike the women in other cities, they were utterly useless and caused more confusion than the enemy. This license of the Lacedaemonian women existed from the earliest times, and was only what might be expected. For, during the wars of the Lacedaemonians, first against the Argives, and afterwards   1270ᵃ1 against the Arcadians and Messenians, the men were long away from home, and, on the return of peace, they gave themselves into the legislator's hand, already prepared by the discipline of a soldier's life (in which there are many elements of   5 excellence), to receive his enactments. But, when Lycurgus, as tradition says, wanted to bring the women under his laws, they resisted, and he gave up the attempt. These then are the causes of what then happened, and this defect in the constitution is clearly to be attributed to them. We are not, however, considering   10 what is or is not to be excused, but what is right or wrong, and the disorder of the women, as I have already said, not only gives an air of indecorum to the constitution considered in itself, but tends in a measure to foster avarice.

The mention of avarice naturally suggests a criticism on the inequality of   15 property. While some of the Spartan citizens have quite small properties, others have very large ones: hence the land has passed into the hands of a few. And this is due also to faulty laws; for, although the legislator rightly holds up to shame the sale or purchase of an inheritance, he allows anybody who likes to give or bequeath it.   20 Yet both practices lead to the same result. And nearly two-fifths of the whole country are held by women; this is owing to the number of heiresses and to the large dowries which are customary. It would surely have been better to have given no   25 dowries at all, or, if any, but small or moderate ones. As the law now stands, a man may bestow his heiress on any one whom he pleases, and, if he die intestate, the privilege of giving her away descends to his heir. Hence, although the country is able to maintain 1500 cavalry and 30,000 hoplites, the whole number of Spartan   30 citizens fell below 1000. The result proves the faulty nature of their laws respecting property; for the city sank under a single defeat; the want of men was their ruin. There is a tradition that, in the days of their ancient kings, they were in the habit of

35 giving the rights of citizenship to strangers, and therefore, in spite of their long
wars, no lack of population was experienced by them; indeed, at one time Sparta is
said to have numbered not less than 10,000 citizens. Whether this statement is true
or not, it would certainly have been better to have maintained their numbers by the
equalization of property. Again, the law which relates to the procreation of children
1270ᵇ1 is adverse to the correction of this inequality. For the legislator, wanting to have as
many Spartans as he could, encouraged the citizens to have large families; and
there is a law at Sparta that the father of three sons shall be exempt from military
service, and he who has four from all the burdens of the state. Yet it is obvious that,
5 if there were many children, the land being distributed as it is, many of them must
necessarily fall into poverty.

The Lacedaemonian constitution is defective also in respect of the Ephorate.
This magistracy has authority in the highest matters, but the Ephors are chosen
10 from the whole people, and so the office is apt to fall into the hands of very poor
men, who, being badly off, are open to bribes. There have been many examples at
Sparta of this evil in former times; and quite recently, in the matter of the Andrians,
certain of the Ephors who were bribed did their best to ruin the state. And so great
15 and tyrannical is their power, that even the kings have been compelled to court
them, so that, in this way as well, together with the royal office the whole
constitution has deteriorated, and from being an aristocracy has turned into a
democracy. The Ephorate certainly does keep the state together; for the people are
contented when they have a share in the highest office, and the result, whether due
20 to the legislator or to chance, has been advantageous. For if a constitution is to be
permanent, all the parts of the state must wish that it should exist and these
arrangements be maintained. This is the case at Sparta, where the kings desire its
permanence because they have due honour in their own persons; the nobles because
25 they are represented in the council of elders (for the office of elder is a reward of
excellence); and the people, because all are eligible for the Ephorate. The election of
Ephors out of the whole people is perfectly right, but ought not to be carried on in
the present fashion, which is too childish. Again, they have the decision of great
causes, although they are quite ordinary men, and therefore they should not
30 determine them merely on their own judgement, but according to written rules, and
to the laws. Their way of life, too, is not in accordance with the spirit of the
constitution—they have a deal too much license; whereas, in the case of the other
citizens, the excess of strictness is so intolerable that they run away from the law
35 into the secret indulgence of sensual pleasures.

Again, the council of elders is not free from defects. It may be said that the
elders are good men and well trained in manly virtue; and that, therefore, there is an
advantage to the state in having them. But that judges of important causes should
hold office for life is a disputable thing, for the mind grows old as well as the body.
1271ᵃ1 And when men have been educated in such a manner that even the legislator
himself cannot trust them, there is real danger. Many of the elders are well known
to have taken bribes and to have been guilty of partiality in public affairs. And
5 therefore they ought not to be non-accountable; yet at Sparta they are so. All

magistracies are accountable to the Ephors. But this prerogative is too great for them, and we maintain that the control should be exercised in some other manner. Further, the mode in which the Spartans elect their elders is childish; and it is 10 improper that the person to be elected should canvass for the office; the worthiest should be appointed, whether he chooses or not. And here the legislator clearly indicates the same intention which appears in other parts of his constitution; he would have his citizens ambitious, and he has reckoned upon this quality in the 15 election of the elders; for no one would ask to be elected if he were not. Yet ambition and avarice, almost more than any other passions, are the motives of voluntary injustices.

Whether kings are or are not an advantage to states, I will consider at another 20 time; they should at any rate be chosen, not as they are now, but with regard to their personal life and conduct. The legislator himself obviously did not suppose that he could make them really good men; at least he shows a great distrust of their virtue. For this reason the Spartans used to join enemies with them in the same embassy, 25 and the quarrels between the kings were held to preserve the state.

Neither did the first introducer of the common meals, called 'phiditia', regulate them well. The entertainment ought to have been provided at public cost, as in Crete; but among the Lacedaemonians everyone is expected to contribute, and 30 some of them are too poor to afford the expense; thus the intention of the legislator is frustrated. The common meals were meant to be a democratic institution, but the existing manner of regulating them is the reverse of democratic. For the very poor can scarcely take part in them; and, according to ancient custom, those who cannot 35 contribute are not allowed to retain their rights of citizenship.

The law about the Spartan admirals has often been censured, and with justice; it is a source of dissension, for the kings are perpetual generals, and this office of admiral is but the setting up of another king.

The charge which Plato brings, in the *Laws,* against the intention of the 1271ᵇ1 legislator, is likewise justified; the whole constitution has regard to one part of excellence only—the excellence of the soldier, which gives victory in war. So long as they were at war, therefore, their power was preserved, but when they had attained empire they fell, for of the arts of peace they knew nothing, and have never engaged 5 in any employment higher than war. There is another error, equally great, into which they have fallen. Although they truly think that the goods for which men contend are to be acquired by excellence rather than by vice, they err in supposing 10 that these goods are to be preferred to the excellence which gains them.

Again, the revenues of the state are ill-managed; there is no money in the treasury, although they are obliged to carry on great wars, and they are unwilling to pay taxes. The greater part of the land being in the hands of Spartans, they do not look closely into one another's contributions. The result which the legislator has 15 produced is the reverse of beneficial; for he has made his city poor, and his citizens greedy.

Enough respecting the Spartan constitution, of which these are the principal defects.

20   10 · The Cretan constitution nearly resembles the Spartan, and in some few points is quite as good; but for the most part less perfect in form. The older constitutions are generally less elaborate than the later, and the Lacedaemonian is said to be, and probably is, in a very great measure, a copy of the Cretan. According

25   to tradition, Lycurgus, when he ceased to be the guardian of King Charillus, went abroad and spent most of his time in Crete. For the two countries are nearly connected; the Lyctians are a colony of the Lacedaemonians, and the colonists,

30   when they came to Crete, adopted the constitution which they found existing among the inhabitants. Even to this day the Perioeci are governed by the original laws which Minos is supposed to have enacted. The island seems to be intended by nature for dominion in Hellas, and to be well situated; it extends right across the sea, around which nearly all the Hellenes are settled; and while one end is not far from

35   the Peloponnese, the other almost reaches to the region of Asia about Triopium and Rhodes. Hence Minos acquired the empire of the sea, subduing some of the islands

40   and colonizing others; at last he invaded Sicily, where he died near Camicus.

The Cretan institutions resemble the Lacedaemonian. The Helots are the

1272ª1   husbandmen of the one, the Perioeci of the other, and both Cretans and Lacedaemonians have common meals, which were anciently called by the Lacedaemonians not 'phiditia' but 'andria'; and the Cretans have the same word, the use of which proves that the common meals originally came from Crete. Further, the two

5   constitutions are similar; for the office of the Ephors is the same as that of the Cretan Cosmi, the only difference being that whereas the Ephors are five, the Cosmi are ten in number. The elders, too, answer to the elders in Crete, who are termed by the Cretans the council. And the kingly office once existed in Crete, but

10   was abolished, and the Cosmi have now the duty of leading them in war. All classes share in the ecclesia, but it can only ratify the decrees of the elders and the Cosmi.

The common meals of Crete are certainly better managed than the Lacedae

15   monian; for in Lacedaemon every one pays so much per head, or, if he fails, the law, as I have already explained, forbids him to exercise the rights of citizenship. But in Crete they are of a more popular character. There, of all the fruits of the earth the cattle raised on the public lands, and of the tribute which is paid by the Perioeci, one

20   portion is assigned to the gods and to the service of the state, and another to the common meals, so that men, women, and children are all supported out of a common stock. The legislator has many ingenious ways of securing moderation in eating, which he conceives to be a gain; he likewise encourages the separation of men from women, lest they should have too many children, and the companionship

25   of men with one another—whether this is a good or bad thing I shall have an opportunity of considering at another time. Thus that the Cretan common meals are better ordered than the Lacedaemonian there can be no doubt.

On the other hand, the Cosmi are even a worse institution than the Ephors, of which they have all the evils without the good. Like the Ephors, they are any chance

30   persons, but in Crete this is not counterbalanced by a corresponding political advantage. At Sparta everyone is eligible, and the body of the people, having a share in the highest office, want the constitution to be permanent. But in Crete the

Cosmi are elected out of certain families, and not out of the whole people, and the elders out of those who have been Cosmi.   35
     The same criticism may be made about the Cretan, which has been already made about the Lacedaemonian affairs. Their unaccountability and life tenure is too great a privilege, and their arbitrary power of acting upon their own judgement, and dispensing with written law, is dangerous. It is no proof of the goodness of the institution that the people are not discontented at being excluded from it. For there   40
is no profit to be made out of the office as out of the Ephorate, since, unlike the Ephors, the Cosmi, being in an island, are removed from temptation.   1272^{b}1
     The remedy by which they correct the evil of this institution is an extraordinary one, suited rather to a dynasty than to a constitutional state. For the Cosmi are often expelled by a conspiracy of their own colleagues, or of private individuals; and they are allowed also to resign before their term of office has expired. Surely all   5
matters of this kind are better regulated by law than by the will of man, which is a very unsafe rule. Worst of all is the suspension of the office of Cosmi, a device to which the nobles often have recourse when they will not submit to justice. This shows that the Cretan government, although possessing some of the characteristics   10
of a constitutional state, is really a dynasty.
     The nobles have a habit, too, of setting up a chief; they get together a party among the common people and their own friends and then quarrel and fight with one another. What is this but the temporary destruction of the state and dissolution of society? A city is in a dangerous condition when those who are willing are also   15
able to attack her. But, as I have already said, the island of Crete is saved by her situation; distance has the same effect as the prohibition of strangers. This is the reason why the Perioeci are contented in Crete, whereas the Helots are perpetually revolting. For the Cretans have no foreign dominions and, when lately foreign   20
invaders found their way into the island, the weakness of the Cretan constitution was revealed. Enough of the government of Crete.

     11 · The Carthaginians are also considered to have an excellent form of government, which differs from that of any other state in several respects, though it   25
is in some very like the Lacedaemonian. Indeed, all three states—the Lacedaemonian, the Cretan, and the Carthaginian—nearly resemble one another, and are very different from any others. Many of the Carthaginian institutions are excellent. The superiority of their constitution is proved by the fact that the common people   30
remains loyal to the constitution; the Carthaginians have never had any rebellion worth speaking of, and have never been under the rule of a tyrant.
     Among the points in which the Carthaginian constitution resembles the Lacedaemonian are the following:—The common tables of the clubs answer to the Spartan phiditia, and their magistracy of the 104 to the Ephors; but, whereas the Ephors are any chance persons, the magistrates of the Carthaginians are elected according to merit—this is an improvement. They have also their kings and their   35
council of elders, who correspond to the kings and elders of Sparta. Their kings, unlike the Spartan, are not always of the same family, nor that an ordinary one, but

if there is some distinguished family they are selected out of it and not appointed by seniority—this is far better. Such officers have great power, and therefore, if they are persons of little worth, do a great deal of harm, and they have already done harm at Lacedaemon.

Most of the defects or deviations from the perfect state, for which the Carthaginian constitution would be censured, apply equally to all the forms of government which we have mentioned. But of the deflections from aristocracy and constitutional government, some incline more to democracy and some to oligarchy. The kings and elders, if unanimous, may determine whether they will or will not bring a matter before the people, but when they are not unanimous, the people decide on such matters as well. And whatever the kings and elders bring before the people is not only heard but also determined by them, and anyone who likes may oppose it; now this is not permitted in Sparta and Crete. That the magistracies of five who have under them many important matters should be co-opted, that they should choose the supreme council of 100, and should hold office longer than other magistrates (for they are virtually rulers both before and after they hold office)— these are oligarchical features; their being without salary and not elected by lot, and any similar points, such as the practice of having all suits tried by the magistrates, and not some by one class and some by another, as at Lacedaemon, are characteristic of aristocracy. The Carthaginian constitution deviates from aristocracy and inclines to oligarchy, chiefly on a point where popular opinion is on their side. For men in general think that magistrates should be chosen not only for their merit, but for their wealth: a man, they say, who is poor cannot rule well—he has not the leisure. If, then, election of magistrates for their wealth be characteristic of oligarchy, and election for merit of aristocracy, there will be a third form under which the constitution of Carthage is comprehended; for the Carthaginians choose their magistrates, and particularly the highest of them—their kings and generals— with an eye both to merit and to wealth.

But we must acknowledge that, in thus deviating from aristocracy, the legislator has committed an error. Nothing is more absolutely necessary than to provide that the highest class, not only when in office, but when out of office, should have leisure and not disgrace themselves in any way; and to this his attention should be first directed. Even if you must have regard to wealth, in order to secure leisure, yet it is surely a bad thing that the greatest offices, such as those of kings and generals, should be bought. The law which allows this abuse makes wealth of more account than excellence, and the whole state becomes avaricious. For, whenever the chiefs of the state deem anything honourable, the other citizens are sure to follow their example; and, where excellence has not the first place, there aristocracy cannot be firmly established. Those who have been at the expense of purchasing their places will be in the habit of repaying themselves; and it is absurd to suppose that a poor and honest man will be wanting to make gains, and that a lower stamp of man who has incurred a great expense will not. That is why they should rule who are able to rule best. And even if the legislator does not care to protect the good from poverty, he should at any rate secure leisure for them when in office.

It would seem also to be a bad principle that the same person should hold many offices, which is a favourite practice among the Carthaginians, for one business is better done by one man. The legislator should see to this and should not appoint the 10 same person to be a flute-player and a shoemaker. Hence, where the state is large, it is more in accordance both with constitutional and with democratic principles that the offices of state should be distributed among many persons. For, as I said, this arrangement is fairer to all, and any action familiarized by repetition is better and 15 sooner performed. We have a proof in military and naval matters; the duties of command and of obedience in both these services extend to all.

The government of the Carthaginians is oligarchical, but they successfully escape the evils of oligarchy by being wealthy, sending out one portion of the people after another to the cities. This is their panacea and the means by which they give 20 stability to the state. This is the result of chance but it is the legislator who should be able to provide against revolution. As things are, if any misfortune occurred, and the bulk of the subjects revolted, there would be no way of restoring peace by legal methods.

Such is the character of the Lacedaemonian, Cretan, and Carthaginian 25 constitutions, which are justly celebrated.

12 · Of those who have treated of governments, some have never taken any part at all in public affairs, but have passed their lives in a private station; about most of them, what was worth telling has been already told. Others have been 30 lawgivers, either in their own or in foreign cities, whose affairs they have administered; and of these some have only made laws, others have framed constitutions; for example, Lycurgus and Solon did both. Of the Lacedaemonian 35 constitution I have already spoken. As to Solon, he is thought by some to have been a good legislator, who put an end to the exclusiveness of the oligarchy, emancipated the people, established the ancient Athenian democracy, and harmonized the different elements of the state. According to their view, the council of Areopagus 40 was an oligarchical element, the elected magistracy, aristocratic, and the courts of law, democratic. The truth seems to be that the council and the elected magistracy existed before the time of Solon, and were retained by him, but that he formed the 1274ª1 courts of law out of all the citizens, thus creating the democracy, which is the very reason why he is sometimes blamed. For in giving the supreme power to the law courts, which are elected by lot, he is thought to have destroyed the non-democratic 5 element. When the law courts grew powerful, to please the people who were now playing the tyrant the old constitution was changed into the existing democracy. Ephialtes and Pericles curtailed the power of the Areopagus; Pericles also instituted the payment of the juries, and thus every demagogue in turn increased the power of 10 the democracy until it became what we now see. All this seems, however, to be the result of circumstances, and not to have been intended by Solon. For the people, having been instrumental in gaining the empire of the sea in the Persian War, began to get a notion of itself, and followed worthless demagogues, whom the better class opposed. Solon, himself, appears to have given the Athenians only that power of 15

electing to offices and calling to account the magistrates which was absolutely necessary; for without it they would have been in a state of slavery and enmity to the government. All the magistrates he appointed from the notables and the men of

20 wealth, that is to say, from the pentacosiomedimni, or from the class called zeugitae, or from a third class of so-called knights. The fourth class were labourers who had no share in any magistracy.

Mere legislators were Zaleucus, who gave laws to the Epizephyrian Locrians, and Charondas, who legislated for his own city of Catana, and for the other

25 Chalcidian cities in Italy and Sicily. Some people attempt to make out that Onomacritus was the first person who had any special skill in legislation, and that he, although a Locrian by birth, was trained in Crete, where he lived in the exercise of his prophetic art; that Thales was his companion, and that Lycurgus and

30 Zaleucus were disciples of Thales, as Charondas was of Zaleucus. But their account is quite inconsistent with chronology.

There was also Philolaus, the Corinthian, who gave laws to the Thebans. This Philolaus was one of the family of the Bacchiadae, and a lover of Diocles, the Olympic victor, who left Corinth in horror of the incestuous passion which his

35 mother Halcyone had conceived for him, and retired to Thebes, where the two friends together ended their days. The inhabitants still point out their tombs, which are in full view of one another, but one is visible from the Corinthian territory, the

40 other not. Tradition says the two friends arranged them thus, Diocles out of horror at his misfortunes, so that the land of Corinth might not be visible from his tomb;

1274^{b}1 Philolaus that it might. This is the reason why they settled at Thebes, and so Philolaus legislated for the Thebans, and, besides some other enactments, gave them laws about the procreation of children, which they call the 'Laws of Adoption'.

5 These laws were peculiar to him, and were intended to preserve the number of the lots.

In the legislation of Charondas there is nothing distinctive, except the suits against false witnesses. He is the first who instituted denunciation for perjury. His laws are more exact and more precisely expressed than even those of our modern legislators.

10 (Characteristic of Phaleas is the equalization of property; of Plato, the community of women, children, and property, the common meals of women, and the law about drinking, that the sober shall be masters of the feast; also the training of soldiers to acquire by practice equal skill with both hands, so that one should be as useful as the other.)

15 Draco has left laws, but he adapted them to a constitution which already existed, and there is no peculiarity in them which is worth mentioning, except the greatness and severity of the punishments.

Pittacus, too, was only a lawgiver, and not the author of a constitution; he has a law which is peculiar to him, that, if a drunken man do something wrong, he shall be

20 more heavily punished than if he were sober; he looked not to the excuse which might be offered for the drunkard, but only to expediency, for drunken more often than sober people commit acts of violence.

Androdamas of Rhegium gave laws to the Chalcidians of Thrace. Some of them relate to homicide, and to heiresses; but there is nothing distinctive in   25 them.

And here let us conclude our inquiry into the various constitutions which either actually exist, or have been devised by theorists.

BOOK III

1 · He who would inquire into the essence and attributes of various kinds of government must first of all determine what a state is. At present this is a disputed question. Some say that the state has done a certain act; others, not the state, but   35 the oligarchy or the tyrant. And the legislator or statesman is concerned entirely with the state, a government being an arrangement of the inhabitants of a state. But a state is composite, like any other whole made up of many parts—these are the   40 citizens, who compose it. It is evident, therefore, that we must begin by asking, Who is the citizen, and what is the meaning of the term? For here again there may be a 1275^a1 difference of opinion. He who is a citizen in a democracy will often not be a citizen in an oligarchy. Leaving out of consideration those who have been made citizens, or   5 who have obtained the name of citizen in any other accidental manner, we may say, first, that a citizen is not a citizen because he lives in a certain place, for resident aliens and slaves share in the place; nor is he a citizen who has legal rights to the extent of suing and being sued; for this right may be enjoyed under the provisions of   10 a treaty. Resident aliens in many places do not possess even such rights completely, for they are obliged to have a patron, so that they do but imperfectly participate in the community, and we call them citizens only in a qualified sense, as we might apply the term to children who are too young to be on the register, or to old men who   15 have been relieved from state duties. Of these we do not say quite simply that they are citizens, but add in the one case that they are not of age, and in the other, that they are past the age, or something of that sort; the precise expression is immaterial, for our meaning is clear. Similar difficulties to those which I have mentioned may be raised and answered about disfranchised citizens and about exiles. But the citizen whom we are seeking to define is a citizen in the strictest sense, against whom no such exception can be taken, and his special characteristic is that he   20 shares in the administration of justice, and in offices. Now of offices some are discontinuous, and the same persons are not allowed to hold them twice, or can only   25 hold them after a fixed interval; others have no limit of time—for example, the office of juryman or member of the assembly. It may, indeed, be argued that these are not magistrates at all, and that their functions give them no share in the government. But surely it is ridiculous to say that those who have the supreme power do not govern. Let us not dwell further upon this, which is a purely verbal   30 question; what we want is a common term including both juryman and member of the assembly. Let us, for the sake of distinction, call it 'indefinite office', and we will

assume that those who share in such office are citizens. This is the most comprehensive definition of a citizen, and best suits all those who are generally so called.

35   But we must not forget that things of which the underlying principles differ in kind, one of them being first, another second, another third, have, when regarded in this relation, nothing, or hardly anything, worth mentioning in common. Now we see that governments differ in kind, and that some of them are prior and that others 1275ᵇ1   are posterior; those which are faulty or perverted are necessarily posterior to those which are perfect. (What we mean by perversion will be hereafter explained.) The citizen then of necessity differs under each form of government; and our definition 5   is best adapted to the citizen of a democracy; but not necessarily to other states. For in some states the people are not acknowledged, nor have they any regular assembly, but only extraordinary ones; and law-suits are distributed by sections among the magistrates. At Lacedaemon, for instance, the Ephors determine suits 10   about contracts, which they distribute among themselves, while the elders are judges of homicide, and other causes are decided by other magistrates. A similar principle prevails at Carthage; there certain magistrates decide all causes. We may, indeed, modify our definition of the citizen so as to include these states. In them it is 15   the holder of a definite, not an indefinite office, who is juryman and member of the assembly, and to some or all such holders of definite offices is reserved the right of deliberating or judging about some things or about all things. The conception of the citizen now begins to clear up.

He who has the power to take part in the deliberative or judicial administration 20   of any state is said by us to be a citizen of that state; and, speaking generally, a state is a body of citizens sufficing for the purposes of life.

2 · But in practice a citizen is defined to be one of whom both the parents are citizens (and not just one, i.e. father or mother); others insist on going further back; 25   say to two or three or more ancestors. This is a short and practical definition; but there are some who raise the further question of how this third or fourth ancestor came to be a citizen. Gorgias of Leontini, partly because he was in a difficulty, partly in irony, said that mortars are what is made by the mortar-makers, and the citizens of Larissa are those who are made by the magistrates; for it is their trade to 30   'make Larissaeans'. Yet the question is really simple, for, if according to the definition just given they shared in the government, they were citizens. This is a better definition than the other. For the words, 'born of a father or mother who is a citizen', cannot possibly apply to the first inhabitants or founders of a state.

There is a greater difficulty in the case of those who have been made citizens 35   after a revolution, as by Cleisthenes at Athens after the expulsion of the tyrants, for he enrolled in tribes many metics, both strangers and slaves. The doubt in these cases is, not who is, but whether he who is ought to be a citizen; and there will still be 1276ᵃ1   a further doubt, whether he who ought not to be a citizen, is one in fact, for what ought not to be is what is false. Now, there are some who hold office, and yet ought not to hold office, whom we describe as ruling, but ruling unjustly. And the citizen was defined by the fact of his holding some kind of rule or office—he who holds a certain sort of office fulfils our definition of a citizen. It is evident, therefore, that the citizens about whom the doubt has arisen must be called citizens.   5

3 . Whether they ought to be so or not is a question which is bound up with the previous inquiry. For a parallel question is raised respecting the state, whether a certain act is or is not an act of the state; for example, in the transition from an oligarchy or a tyranny to a democracy. In such cases persons refuse to fulfil their contracts or any other obligations, on the ground that the tyrant and not the state,   10 contracted them; they argue that some constitutions are established by force, and not for the sake of the common good. But this would apply equally to democracies, and then the acts of the democracy will be neither more nor less acts of the state in   15 question than those of an oligarchy or of a tyranny. This question runs up into another:—on what principle shall we ever say that the state is the same, or different? It would be a very superficial view which considered only the place and   20 the inhabitants (for the soil and the population may be separated, and some of the inhabitants may live in one place and some in another). This, however, is not a very serious difficulty; we need only remark that the word 'state' is ambiguous.

It is further asked: When are men, living in the same place, to be regarded as a   25 single city—what is the limit? Certainly not the wall of the city, for you might surround all Peloponnesus with a wall. Babylon, we may say, is like this, and every city that has the compass of a nation rather than a city; Babylon, they say, had been taken for three days before some part of the inhabitants become aware of the fact.   30 This difficulty may, however, with advantage be deferred to another occasion; the statesman has to consider the size of the state, and whether it should consist of more than one race or not.

Again, shall we say that while the race of inhabitants remains the same, the   35 city is also the same, although the citizens are always dying and being born, as we call rivers and fountains the same, although the water is always flowing away and more coming? Or shall we say that the generations of men, like the rivers, are the same, but that the state changes? For, since the state is a partnership, and is a   1276^b1 partnership of citizens in a constitution, when the form of the government changes, and becomes different, then it may be supposed that the state is no longer the same, just as a tragic differs from a comic chorus, although the members of both may be   5 identical. And in this manner we speak of every union or composition of elements as different when the form of their composition alters; for example, a scale containing the same sounds is said to be different, accordingly as the Dorian or the Phrygian mode is employed. And if this is true it is evident that the sameness of the state   10 consists chiefly in the sameness of the constitution, and it may be called or not called by the same name, whether the inhabitants are the same or entirely different. It is quite another question, whether a state ought or ought not to fulfil engagements when the form of government changes.   15

4 . There is a point nearly allied to the preceding: Whether the excellence of a good man and a good citizen is the same or not. But before entering on this discussion, we must certainly first obtain some general notion of the excellence of

20 the citizen. Like the sailor, the citizen is a member of a community. Now, sailors have different functions, for one of them is a rower, another a pilot, and a third a look-out man, a fourth is described by some similar term; and while the precise
25 definition of each individual's excellence applies exclusively to him, there is, at the same time, a common definition applicable to them all. For they have all of them a common object, which is safety in navigation. Similarly, one citizen differs from another, but the salvation of the community is the common business of them all.
30 This community is the constitution; the excellence of the citizen must therefore be relative to the constitution of which he is a member. If, then, there are many forms of government, it is evident that there is not one single excellence of the good citizen which is perfect excellence. But we say that the good man is he who has one single excellence which is perfect excellence. Hence it is evident that the good citizen need
35 not of necessity possess the excellence which makes a good man.

The same question may also be approached by another road, from a consideration of the best constitution. If the state cannot be entirely composed of good men, and yet each citizen is expected to do his own business well, and must therefore have excellence, still, inasmuch as all the citizens cannot be alike, the excellence of the
1277ª1 citizen and of the good man cannot coincide. All must have the excellence of the good citizen—thus, and thus only, can the state be perfect; but they will not have the excellence of a good man, unless we assume that in the good state all the citizens must be good.

5 Again, the state, as composed of unlikes, may be compared to the living being: as the first elements into which a living being is resolved are soul and body, as soul is made up of rational principle and appetite, the family of husband and wife, property of master and slave, so of all these, as well as other dissimilar elements, the state is
10 composed; and therefore the excellence of all the citizens cannot possibly be the same, any more than the excellence of the leader of a chorus is the same as that of the performer who stands by his side. I have said enough to show why the two kinds of excellence cannot be absolutely the same.

But will there then be no case in which the excellence of the good citizen and the excellence of the good man coincide? To this we answer that the good *ruler* is a
15 good and wise man, but the citizen need not be wise. And some persons say that even the education of the ruler should be of a special kind; for are not the children of kings instructed in riding and military exercises? As Euripides says:

No subtle arts for me, but what the state requires.

20 As though there were a special education needed for a ruler. If the excellence of a good ruler is the same as that of a good man, and we assume further that the subject is a citizen as well as the ruler, the excellence of the good citizen and the excellence of the good man cannot be absolutely the same, although in some cases they may; for the excellence of a ruler differs from that of a citizen. It was the sense of this difference which made Jason say that 'he felt hungry when he was not a tyrant',
25 meaning that he could not endure to live in a private station. But, on the other hand, it may be argued that men are praised for knowing both how to rule and how to obey, and he is said to be a citizen of excellence who is able to do both well. Now if

we suppose the excellence of a good man to be that which rules, and the excellence of the citizen to include ruling and obeying, it cannot be said that they are equally worthy of praise. Since, then, it is sometimes thought that the ruler and the ruled must learn different things and not the same, but that the citizen must know and share in them both, the inference is obvious. There is, indeed, the rule of a master, which is concerned with menial offices—the master need not know how to perform these, but may employ others in the execution of them: the other would be degrading; and by the other I mean the power actually to do menial duties, which vary much in character and are executed by various classes of slaves, such, for example, as handicraftsmen, who, as their name signifies, live by the labour of their hands—under these the mechanic is included. Hence in ancient times, and among some nations, the working classes had no share in the government—a privilege which they only acquired under extreme democracy. Certainly the good man and the statesman and the good citizen ought not to learn the crafts of inferiors except for their own occasional use; if they habitually practise them, there will cease to be a distinction between master and slave.

But there is a rule of another kind, which is exercised over freemen and equals by birth—a constitutional rule, which the ruler must learn by obeying, as he would learn the duties of a general of cavalry by being under the orders of a general of cavalry, or the duties of a general of infantry by being under the orders of a general of infantry, and by having had the command of a regiment and of a company. It has been well said that he who has never learned to obey cannot be a good commander. The excellence of the two is not the same, but the good citizen ought to be capable of both; he should know how to govern like a freeman, and how to obey like a freeman—these are the excellences of a citizen. And, although the temperance and justice of a ruler are distinct from those of a subject, the excellence of a good man will include both; for the excellence of the good man who is free and also a subject, e.g. his justice, will not be one but will comprise distinct kinds, the one qualifying him to rule, the other to obey, and differing as the temperance and courage of men and women differ. For a man would be thought a coward if he had no more courage than a courageous woman, and a woman would be thought loquacious if she imposed no more restraint on her conversation than the good man; and indeed their part in the management of the household is different, for the duty of the one is to acquire, and of the other to preserve. Practical wisdom is the only excellence peculiar to the ruler: it would seem that all other excellences must equally belong to ruler and subject. The excellence of the subject is certainly not wisdom, but only true opinion; he may be compared to the maker of the flute, while his master is like the flute-player or user of the flute.

From these considerations may be gathered the answer to the question, whether the excellence of the good man is the same as that of the good citizen, or different, and how far the same, and how far different.

5 · There still remains one more question about the citizen: Is he only a true citizen who has a share of office, or is the mechanic to be included? If they who hold no office are to be deemed citizens, not every citizen can have this excellence; for

this man is a citizen. And if none of the lower class are citizens, in which part of the state are they to be placed? For they are not resident aliens, and they are not foreigners. May we not reply, that as far as this objection goes there is no more absurdity in excluding them than in excluding slaves and freedmen from any of the above-mentioned classes? It must be admitted that we cannot consider all those to be citizens who are necessary to the existence of the state; for example, children are not citizens equally with grown-up men, who are citizens absolutely, but children, not being grown up, are only citizens on a certain assumption. In ancient times, and among some nations, the artisan class *were* slaves or foreigners, and therefore the majority of them are so now. The best form of state will not admit them to citizenship; but if they are admitted, then our definition of the excellence of a citizen will not apply to every citizen, nor to every free man as such, but only to those who are freed from necessary services. The necessary people are either slaves who minister to the wants of individuals, or mechanics and labourers who are the servants of the community. These reflections carried a little further will explain their position; and indeed what has been said already is of itself, when understood, explanation enough.

Since there are many forms of government there must be many varieties of citizens, and especially of citizens who are subjects; so that under some governments the mechanic and the labourer will be citizens, but not in others, as, for example, in so-called aristocracies, if there are any, in which honours are given according to excellence and merit; for no man can practise excellence who is living the life of a mechanic or labourer. In oligarchies the qualification for office is high, and therefore no labourer can ever be a citizen; but a mechanic may, for an actual majority of them are rich. At Thebes there was a law that no man could hold office who had not retired from business for ten years. But in many states the law goes to the length of admitting aliens; for in some democracies a man is a citizen though his mother only be a citizen; and a similar principle is applied to illegitimate children among many. Nevertheless they make such people citizens because of the dearth of legitimate citizens (for they introduce this sort of legislation owing to lack of population); so when the number of citizens increases, first the children of a male or a female slave are excluded; then those whose mothers only are citizens; and at last the right of citizenship is confined to those whose fathers and mothers are both citizens.

Hence, as is evident, there are different kinds of citizens; and he is a citizen in the fullest sense who shares in the honours of the state. Compare Homer's words 'like some dishonoured stranger';[1] he who is excluded from the honours of the state is no better than an alien. But when this exclusion is concealed, then its object is to deceive their fellow inhabitants.

As to the question whether the excellence of the good man is the same as that of the good citizen, the considerations already adduced prove that in some states the good man and the good citizen are the same, and in others different. When they are

---

[1] *Iliad* IX 648.

the same it is not every citizen who is a good man, but only the statesman and those who have or may have, alone or in conjunction with others, the conduct of public affairs.   5

6 · Having determined these questions, we have next to consider whether there is only one form of government or many, and if many, what they are, and how many, and what are the differences between them.

A constitution is the arrangement of magistracies in a state, especially of the highest of all. The government is everywhere sovereign in the state, and the   10 constitution is in fact the government. For example, in democracies the people are supreme, but in oligarchies, the few; and, therefore, we say that these two constitutions also are different: and so in other cases.

First, let us consider what is the purpose of a state, and how many forms of rule   15 there are by which human society is regulated. We have already said, in the first part of this treatise, when discussing household management and the rule of a master, that man is by nature a political animal. And therefore, men, even when they do not require one another's help, desire to live together; not but that they are   20 also brought together by their common interests in so far as they each attain to any measure of well-being. This is certainly the chief end, both of individuals and of states. And mankind meet together and maintain the political community also for   25 the sake of mere life (in which there is possibly some noble element so long as the evils of existence do not greatly overbalance the good). And we all see that men cling to life even at the cost of enduring great misfortune, seeming to find in life a natural sweetness and happiness.   30

There is no difficulty in distinguishing the various kinds of rule; they have been often defined already in our popular discussions. The rule of a master, although the slave by nature and the master by nature have in reality the same interests, is nevertheless exercised primarily with a view to the interest of the master, but   35 accidentally considers the slave, since, if the slave perish, the rule of the master perishes with him. On the other hand, the government of a wife and children and of a household, which we have called household management, is exercised in the first instance for the good of the governed or for the common good of both parties, but essentially for the good of the governed, as we see to be the case in medicine,   1279ª1 gymnastic, and the arts in general, which are only accidentally concerned with the good of the artists themselves. For there is no reason why the trainer may not sometimes practise gymnastics, and the helmsman is always one of the crew. The trainer or the helmsman considers the good of those committed to his care. But,   5 when he is one of the persons taken care of, he accidentally participates in the advantage, for the helmsman is also a sailor, and the trainer becomes one of those in training. And so in politics: when the state is framed upon the principle of equality and likeness, the citizens think that they ought to hold office by turns. Formerly, as   10 is natural, everyone would take his turn of service; and then again, somebody else would look after his interest, just as he, while in office, had looked after theirs. But nowadays, for the sake of the advantage which is to be gained from the public

revenues and from office, men want to be always in office. One might imagine that
15   the rulers, being sickly, were only kept in health while they continued in office; in
that case we may be sure that they would be hunting after places. The conclusion is
evident: that governments which have a regard to the common interest are
constituted in accordance with strict principles of justice, and are therefore true
20   forms; but those which regard only the interest of the rulers are all defective and
perverted forms, for they are despotic, whereas a state is a community of freemen.

7 · Having determined these points, we have next to consider how many
forms of government there are, and what they are; and in the first place what are the
25   true forms, for when they are determined the perversions of them will at once be
apparent. The words constitution and government have the same meaning, and the
government, which is the supreme authority in states, must be in the hands of one,
or of a few, or of the many. The true forms of government, therefore, are those in
which the one, or the few, or the many, govern with a view to the common interest;
but governments which rule with a view to the private interest, whether of the one,
30   or of the few, or of the many, are perversions. For the members of a state, if they are
truly citizens, ought to participate in its advantages. Of forms of government in
which one rules, we call that which regards the common interest, kingship; that in
35   which more than one, but not many, rule, aristocracy; and it is so called, either
because the rulers are the best men, or because they have at heart the best interests
of the state and of the citizens. But when the many administer the state for the
common interest, the government is called by the generic name—a constitution.
And there is a reason for this use of language. One man or a few may excel in
1279ᵇ1   excellence; but as the number increases it becomes more difficult for them to attain
perfection in every kind of excellence, though they may in military excellence, for
this is found in the masses. Hence in a constitutional government the fighting-men
have the supreme power, and those who possess arms are the citizens.
Of the above-mentioned forms, the perversions are as follows:—of kingship,
5   tyranny; of aristocracy, oligarchy; of constitutional government, democracy. For
tyranny is a kind of monarchy which has in view the interest of the monarch only;
oligarchy has in view the interest of the wealthy; democracy, of the needy: none of
10   them the common good of all.

8 · But there are difficulties about these forms of government, and it will
therefore be necessary to state a little more at length the nature of each of them. For
he who would make a philosophical study of the various sciences, and is not only
concerned with practice, ought not to overlook or omit anything, but to set forth the
15   truth in every particular. Tyranny, as I was saying, is monarchy exercising the rule
of a master over the political society; oligarchy is when men of property have the
government in their hands; democracy, the opposite, when the indigent, and not the
20   men of property, are the rulers. And here arises the first of our difficulties, and it
relates to the distinction just drawn. For democracy is said to be the government of
the many. But what if the many are men of property and have the power in their

hands? In like manner oligarchy is said to be the government of the few; but what if   25
the poor are fewer than the rich, and have the power in their hands because they are
stronger? In these cases the distinction which we have drawn between these
different forms of government would no longer hold good.

Suppose, once more, that we add wealth to the few and poverty to the many,
and name the governments accordingly—an oligarchy is said to be that in which the
few and the wealthy, and a democracy that in which the many and the poor are the   30
rulers—there will still be a difficulty. For, if the only forms of government are the
ones already mentioned, how shall we describe those other governments also just
mentioned by us, in which the rich are the more numerous and the poor are the
fewer, and both govern in their respective states?

The argument seems to show that, whether in oligarchies or in democracies,   35
the number of the governing body, whether the greater number, as in a democracy,
or the smaller number, as in an oligarchy, is an accident due to the fact that the rich
everywhere are few, and the poor numerous. But if so, there is a misapprehension of
the causes of the difference between them. For the real difference between
democracy and oligarchy is poverty and wealth. Wherever men rule by reason of   1280ª1
their wealth, whether they be few or many, that is an oligarchy, and where the poor
rule, that is a democracy. But in fact the rich are few and the poor many; for few are
well-to-do, whereas freedom is enjoyed by all, and wealth and freedom are the   5
grounds on which the two parties claim power in the state.

9 . Let us begin by considering the common definitions of oligarchy and
democracy, and what is oligarchical and democratic justice. For all men cling to
justice of some kind, but their conceptions are imperfect and they do not express the   10
whole idea. For example, justice is thought by them to be, and is, equality—not,
however, for all, but only for equals. And inequality is thought to be, and is, justice;
neither is this for all, but only for unequals. When the persons are omitted, then men
judge erroneously. The reason is that they are passing judgement on themselves,   15
and most people are bad judges in their own case. And whereas justice implies a
relation to persons as well as to things, and a just distribution, as I have already said
in the *Ethics,* implies the same ratio between the persons and between the things,
they agree about the equality of the things, but dispute about the equality of the
persons, chiefly for the reason which I have just given—because they are bad   20
judges in their own affairs; and secondly, because both the parties to the argument
are speaking of a limited and partial justice, but imagine themselves to be speaking
of absolute justice. For the one party, if they are unequal in one respect, for example
wealth, consider themselves to be unequal in all; and the other party, if they are
equal in one respect, for example free birth, consider themselves to be equal in all.
But they leave out the capital point. For if men met and associated out of regard to   25
wealth only, their share in the state would be proportioned to their property, and the
oligarchical doctrine would then seem to carry the day. It would not be just that he
who paid one mina should have the same share of a hundred minae, whether of the   30
principal or of the profits, as he who paid the remaining ninety-nine. But a state

exists for the sake of a good life, and not for the sake of life only: if life only were the object, slaves and brute animals might form a state, but they cannot, for they have no share in happiness or in a life based on choice. Nor does a state exist for the sake

35 of alliance and security from injustice, nor yet for the sake of exchange and mutual intercourse; for then the Tyrrhenians and the Carthaginians, and all who have commercial treaties with one another, would be the citizens of one state. True, they have agreements about imports, and engagements that they will do no wrong to one

1280ᵇ1 another, and written articles of alliance. But there are no magistracies common to the contracting parties; different states have each their own magistracies. Nor does one state take care that the citizens of the other are such as they ought to be, nor see that those who come under the terms of the treaty do no wrong or wickedness at all, but only that they do no injustice to one another. Whereas, those who care for good

5 government take into consideration political excellence and defect. Whence it may be further inferred that excellence must be the care of a state which is truly so called, and not merely enjoys the name: for without this end the community becomes a mere alliance which differs only in place from alliances of which the

10 members live apart; and law is only a convention, 'a surety to one another of justice', as the sophist Lycophron says, and has no real power to make the citizens good and just.

15   This is obvious; for suppose distinct places, such as Corinth and Megara, to be brought together so that their walls touched, still they would not be one city, not even if the citizens had the right to intermarry, which is one of the rights peculiarly characteristic of states. Again, if men dwelt at a distance from one another, but not so far off as to have no intercourse, and there were laws among them that they

20 should not wrong each other in their exchanges, neither would this be a state. Let us suppose that one man is a carpenter, another a farmer, another a shoemaker, and so on, and that their number is ten thousand: nevertheless, if they have nothing in common but exchange, alliance, and the like, that would not constitute a state. Why is this? Surely not because they are at a distance from one another; for even

25 supposing that such a community were to meet in one place, but that each man had a house of his own, which was in a manner his state, and that they made alliance with one another, but only against evil-doers; still an accurate thinker would not deem this to be a state, if their intercourse with one another was of the same character after as before their union. It is clear then that a state is not a mere

30 society, having a common place, established for the prevention of mutual crime and for the sake of exchange. These are conditions without which a state cannot exist; but all of them together do not constitute a state, which is a community of families and aggregations of families in well-being, for the sake of a perfect and self-

35 sufficing life. Such a community can only be established among those who live in the same place and intermarry. Hence there arise in cities family connexions, brotherhoods, common sacrifices, amusements which draw men together. But these are created by friendship, for to choose to live together is friendship. The end of the state is the good life, and these are the means towards it. And the state is the union

1281ᵃ1 of families and villages in a perfect and self-sufficing life, by which we mean a happy and honourable life.

Our conclusion, then, is that political society exists for the sake of noble actions, and not of living together. Hence they who contribute most to such a society have a greater share in it than those who have the same or a greater freedom or nobility of birth but are inferior to them in political excellence; or than those who exceed them in wealth but are surpassed by them in excellence. 5

From what has been said it will be clearly seen that all the partisans of different forms of government speak of a part of justice only. 10

10 · There is also a doubt as to what is to be the supreme power in the state:—Is it the multitude? Or the wealthy? Or the good? Or the one best man? Or a tyrant? Any of these alternatives seems to involve disagreeable consequences. If the poor, for example, because they are more in number, divide among themselves the property of the rich—is not this unjust? No, by heaven (will be the reply), for the supreme authority justly willed it. But if this is not extreme injustice, what is? Again, when in the first division all has been taken, and the majority divide anew the property of the minority, is it not evident, if this goes on, that they will ruin the state? Yet surely, excellence is not the ruin of those who possess it, nor is justice destructive of a state; and therefore this law of confiscation clearly cannot be just. If it were, all the acts of a tyrant must of necessity be just; for he only coerces other men by superior power, just as the multitude coerce the rich. But is it just then that the few and the wealthy should be the rulers? And what if they, in like manner, rob and plunder the people—is this just? If so, the other case will likewise be just. But there can be no doubt that all these things are wrong and unjust. 15 / 20 / 25

Then ought the good to rule and have supreme power? But in that case everybody else, being excluded from power, will be dishonoured. For the offices of a state are posts of honour; and if one set of men always hold them, the rest must be deprived of them. Then will it be well that the one best man should rule? That is still more oligarchical, for the number of those who are dishonoured is thereby increased. Someone may say that it is bad in any case for a man, subject as he is to all the accidents of human passion, to have the supreme power, rather than the law. But what if the law itself be democratic or oligarchical, how will that help us out of our difficulties? Not at all; the same consequences will follow. 30 / 35

11 · Most of these questions may be reserved for another occasion. The principle that the multitude ought to be in power rather than the few best might seem to be solved and to contain some difficulty and perhaps even truth.[2] For the many, of whom each individual is not a good man, when they meet together may be better than the few good, if regarded not individually but collectively, just as a feast to which many contribute is better than a dinner provided out of a single purse. For each individual among the many has a share of excellence and practical wisdom, and when they meet together, just as they become in a manner one man, who has many feet, and hands, and senses, so too with regard to their character and thought. Hence the many are better judges than a single man of music and poetry; for some 40 / 1281ᵇ1 / 5

understand one part, and some another, and among them they understand the
10 whole. There is a similar combination of qualities in good men, who differ from any
individual of the many, as the beautiful are said to differ from those who are not
beautiful, and works of art from realities, because in them the scattered elements
are combined, although, if taken separately, the eye of one person or some other
15 feature in another person would be fairer than in the picture. Whether this principle
can apply to every democracy, and to all bodies of men, is not clear. Or rather, by
heaven, in some cases it is impossible to apply; for the argument would equally hold
20 about brutes; and wherein, it will be asked, do some men differ from brutes? But
there may be bodies of men about whom our statement is nevertheless true. And if
so, the difficulty which has been already raised, and also another which is akin to
it—viz. what power should be assigned to the mass of freemen and citizens, who are
25 not rich and have no personal merit—are both solved. There is still a danger in
allowing them to share the great offices of state, for their folly will lead them into
error, and their dishonesty into crime. But there is a danger also in not letting them
share, for a state in which many poor men are excluded from office will necessarily
30 be full of enemies. The only way of escape is to assign to them some deliberative and
judicial functions. For this reason Solon and certain other legislators give them the
power of electing to offices, and of calling the magistrates to account, but they do
35 not allow them to hold office singly. When they meet together their perceptions are
quite good enough, and combined with the better class they are useful to the state
(just as impure food when mixed with what is pure sometimes makes the entire
mass more wholesome than a small quantity of the pure would be), but each
individual, left to himself, forms an imperfect judgement. On the other hand, the
popular form of government involves certain difficulties. In the first place, it might
40 be objected that he who can judge of the healing of a sick man would be one who
could himself heal his disease, and make him whole—that is, in other words, the
1282ᵃ1 physician; and so in all professions and arts. As, then, the physician ought to be
called to account by physicians, so ought men in general to be called to account by
their peers. But physicians are of three kinds:—there is the ordinary practitioner,
and there is the master physician, and thirdly the man educated in the art: in all arts
5 there is such a class; and we attribute the power of judging to them quite as much as
to professors of the art. Secondly, does not the same principle apply to elections?
For a right election can only be made by those who have knowledge; those who know
geometry, for example, will choose a geometrician rightly, and those who know how
10 to steer, a pilot; and, even if there be some occupations and arts in which private
persons share in the ability to choose, they certainly cannot choose better than those
who know. So that, according to this argument, neither the election of magistrates,
nor the calling of them to account, should be entrusted to the many. Yet possibly
15 these objections are to a great extent met by our old answer, that if the people are
not utterly degraded, although individually they may be worse judges than those
who have special knowledge, as a body they are as good or better. Moreover, there
are some arts whose products are not judged of solely, or best, by the artists
themselves, namely those arts whose products are recognized even by those who do

not possess the art; for example, the knowledge of the house is not limited to the 20
builder only; the user, or, in other words, the master, of the house will actually be a
better judge than the builder, just as the pilot will judge better of a rudder than the
carpenter, and the guest will judge better of a feast than the cook.

This difficulty seems now to be sufficiently answered, but there is another akin
to it. That inferior persons should have authority in greater matters than the good 25
would appear to be a strange thing, yet the election and calling to account of the
magistrates is the greatest of all. And these, as I was saying, are functions which in
some states are assigned to the people, for the assembly is supreme in all such
matters. Yet persons of any age, and having but a small property qualification, sit in 30
the assembly and deliberate and judge, although for the great officers of state, such
as treasurers and generals, a high qualification is required. This difficulty may be
solved in the same manner as the preceding, and the present practice of democracies
may be really defensible. For the power does not reside in the juryman, or
counsellor, or member of the assembly, but in the court, and the council, and the 35
assembly, of which the aforesaid individuals—counsellor, assemblyman, juryman—are only parts or members. And for this reason the many may claim to have a
higher authority than the few; for the people, and the council, and the courts consist
of many persons, and their property collectively is greater than the property of one 40
or of a few individuals holding great offices. But enough of this.

The discussion of the first question shows nothing so clearly as that laws, when 1282ᵇ1
good, should be supreme; and that the magistrate or magistrates should regulate
those matters only on which the laws are unable to speak with precision owing to the
difficulty of any general principle embracing all particulars. But what are good laws 5
has not yet been clearly explained; the old difficulty remains. The goodness or
badness, justice or injustice, of laws varies of necessity with the constitutions of
states. This, however, is clear, that the laws must be adapted to the constitutions. 10
But, if so, true forms of government will of necessity have just laws, and perverted
forms of government will have unjust laws.

12 · In all sciences and arts the end is a good, and the greatest good and in
the highest degree a good in the most authoritative of all—this is the political 15
science of which the good is justice, in other words, the common interest. All men
think justice to be a sort of equality; and to a certain extent they agree with what we
have said in our philosophical works about ethics. For they say that what is just is 20
just *for* someone and that it should be equal for equals. But there still remains a
question: equality or inequality of what? Here is a difficulty which calls for political
speculation. For very likely some persons will say that offices of state ought to be
unequally distributed according to superior excellence, in whatever respect, of the
citizen, although there is no other difference between him and the rest of the 25
community; for those who differ in any one respect have different rights and claims.
But, surely, if this is true, the complexion or height of a man, or any other
advantage, will be a reason for his obtaining a greater share of political rights. The
error here lies upon the surface, and may be illustrated from the other arts and 30

sciences. When a number of flute-players are equal in their art, there is no reason why those of them who are better born should have better flutes given to them; for they will not play any better on the flute, and the superior instrument should be
35 reserved for him who is the superior artist. If what I am saying is still obscure, it will be made clearer as we proceed. For if there were a superior flute-player who was far inferior in birth and beauty, although either of these may be a greater good than the
40 art of flute-playing and may excel flute-playing in a greater ratio than he excels the others in his art, still he ought to have the best flutes given to him, unless the
1283ª1 advantages of wealth and birth contribute to excellence in flute-playing, which they do not. Moreover, upon this principle any good may be compared with any other.
5 For if a given height[3] may be measured against wealth and against freedom, height in general may be so measured. Thus if A excels in height more than B in excellence, even if excellence in general excels height still more, all goods will be comparable; for if a certain amount is better than some other, it is clear that some other will be equal. But since no such comparison can be made, it is evident that
10 there is good reason why in politics men do not ground their claim to office on every sort of inequality. For if some be slow, and others swift, that is no reason why the one should have little and the others much; it is in gymnastic contests that such excellence is rewarded. Whereas the rival claims of candidates for office can only be
15 based on the possession of elements which enter into the composition of a state. And therefore the well-born, or free-born, or rich, may with good reason claim office; for holders of offices must be freemen and tax-payers: a state can be no more composed entirely of poor men than entirely of slaves. But if wealth and freedom are necessary
20 elements, justice and valour are equally so; for without the former qualities a state cannot exist at all, without the latter not well.

13 · If the existence of the state is alone to be considered, then it would seem that all, or some at least, of these claims are just; but, if we take into account a good
25 life, then, as I have already said, education and excellence have superior claims. As, however, those who are equal in one thing ought not to have an equal share in all, nor those who are unequal in one thing to have an unequal share in all, it is certain that all forms of government which rest on either of these principles are perversions.
30 All men have a claim in a certain sense, as I have already admitted, but not all have an absolute claim. The rich claim because they have a greater share in the land, and land is the common element of the state; also they are generally more trustworthy in contracts. The free claim under the same title as the well-born; for they are nearly
35 akin. For the well-born are citizens in a truer sense than the low-born, and good birth is always valued in a man's own home. Another reason is, that those who are sprung from better ancestors are likely to be better men, for good birth is excellence of race. Excellence, too, may be truly said to have a claim, for justice has been acknowledged by us to be a social excellence, and it implies all others. Again, the
40 many may urge their claim against the few; for, when taken collectively, and

---

[3]Omitting συμβάλλοιτο.

compared with the few, they are stronger and richer and better. But, what if the good, the rich, the well-born, and the other classes who make up a state, are all living together in the same city, will there, or will there not, be any doubt who shall rule?—No doubt at all in determining who ought to rule in each of the above-mentioned forms of government. For states are characterized by differences in their governing bodies—one of them has a government of the rich, another of the good, and so on. But a difficulty arises when all these elements coexist. How are we to decide? Suppose the good to be very few in number: may we consider their numbers in relation to their duties, and ask whether they are enough to administer the state, or so many as will make up a state? Objections may be urged against all the aspirants to political power. For those who found their claims on wealth or family might be thought to have no basis of justice; on this principle, if any one person were richer than all the rest, it is clear that he ought to be ruler of them. In like manner he who is very distinguished by his birth ought to have the superiority over all those who claim on the ground that they are free-born. In an aristocracy a like difficulty occurs about excellence; for if one citizen is better than the other members of the government, however good they may be, he too, upon the same principle of justice, should rule over them. And if the people are to be supreme because they are stronger than the few, then if one man, or more than one, but not a majority, is stronger than the many, they ought to rule, and not the many.

All these considerations appear to show that none of the principles on which men claim to rule and to hold all other men in subjection to them are right. To those who claim to be masters of the government on the ground of their excellence or their wealth, the many might fairly answer that they themselves are often better and richer than the few—I do not say individually, but collectively. And another problem which is sometimes put forward may be met in a similar manner. Some persons doubt whether the legislator who desires to make the justest laws ought to legislate with a view to the good of the better or of the many, when the case which we have mentioned occurs. Now what is right must be construed as equally right, and what is equally right is to be considered with reference to the advantage of the state, and the common good of the citizens. And a citizen is one who shares in governing and being governed. He differs under different forms of government, but in the best state he is one who is able and chooses to be governed and to govern with a view to the life of excellence.

If, however, there be some one person, or more than one, although not enough to make up the full complement of a state, whose excellence is so pre-eminent that the excellence or the political capacity of all the rest admit of no comparison with his or theirs, he or they can be no longer regarded as part of a state; for justice will not be done to the superior, if he is reckoned only as the equal of those who are so far inferior to him in excellence and in political capacity. Such a man may truly be deemed a God among men. Hence we see that legislation is necessarily concerned only with those who are equal in birth and in capacity; and that for men of pre-eminent excellence there is no law—they are themselves a law. Anyone would be ridiculous who attempted to make laws for them: they would probably retort

1283ᵇ1

5

10

15

20

25

30

35

40

1284ᵃ1

5

10

15

what, in the fable of Antisthenes, the lions said to the hares, when in the council of
the beasts the latter began haranguing and claiming equality for all. And for this
reason democratic states have instituted ostracism; equality is above all things their
aim, and therefore they ostracized and banished from the city for a time those who
20   seemed to predominate too much through their wealth, or the number of their
friends, or through any other political influence. Mythology tells us that the
Argonauts left Heracles behind for a similar reason; the ship Argo would not take
25   him because she feared that he would have been too much for the rest of the crew.
That is why those who denounce tyranny and blame the counsel which Periander
gave to Thrasybulus cannot be held altogether just in their censure. The story is that
Periander, when the herald was sent to ask counsel of him, said nothing, but only cut
30   off the tallest ears of corn till he had brought the field to a level. The herald did not
know the meaning of the action, but came and reported what he had seen to
Thrasybulus, who understood that he was to cut off the principal men in the state;
and this is a policy not only expedient for tyrants or in practice confined to them, but
35   equally necessary in oligarchies and democracies. Ostracism is a measure of the
same kind, which acts by disabling and banishing the most prominent citizens.
Great powers do the same to whole cities and nations, as the Athenians did to the
40   Samians, Chians, and Lesbians; no sooner had they obtained a firm grasp of the
empire, than they humbled their allies contrary to treaty; and the Persian king has
1284ᵇ1   repeatedly crushed the Medes, Babylonians, and other nations, when their spirit has
been stirred by the recollection of their former greatness.

The problem is a universal one, and equally concerns all forms of government,
5   true as well as false; for, although perverted forms with a view to their own interests
may adopt this policy, those which seek the common interest do so likewise. The
same thing may be observed in the arts and sciences; for the painter will not allow
10   the figure to have a foot which, however beautiful, is not in proportion, nor will the
ship-builder allow the stern or any other part of the vessel to be unduly large, any
more than the chorus-master will allow anyone who sings louder or better than all
the rest to sing in the choir. Monarchs, too, may practise compulsion and still live in
15   harmony with their cities, if their own government is for the interest of the state.
Hence where there is an acknowledged superiority the argument in favour of
ostracism is based upon a kind of political justice. It would certainly be better that
the legislator should from the first so order his state as to have no need of such a
remedy. But if the need arises, the next best thing is that he should endeavour to
20   correct the evil by this or some similar measure. The principle, however, has not
been fairly applied in states; for, instead of looking to the good of their own
constitution, they have used ostracism for factious purposes. It is true that under
perverted forms of government, and from their special point of view, such a measure
25   is just and expedient, but it is also clear that it is not absolutely just. In the perfect
state there would be great doubts about the use of it, not when applied to excess in
strength, wealth, popularity, or the like, but when used against someone who is
pre-eminent in excellence—what is to be done with him? People will not say that
30   such a man is to be expelled and exiled; on the other hand, he ought not to be a

subject—that would be as if mankind should claim to rule over Zeus, dividing his offices among them. The only alternative is that all should happily obey such a ruler, according to what seems to be the order of nature, and that men like him should be kings in their state for life.

14 · The preceding discussion, by a natural transition, leads to the consider-   35
ation of kingship, which we say is one of the true forms of government. Let us see whether in order to be well governed a state or country should be under the rule of a king or under some other form of government; and whether monarchy, although good for some, may not be bad for others. But first we must determine whether there is one species of kingship or many. It is easy to see that there are many, and   1285ª1
that the manner of government is not the same in all of them.

Of kingships according to law, the Lacedaemonian is thought to be the best example; but there the royal power is not absolute, except when the kings go on an   5
expedition, and then they take the command. Matters of religion are likewise committed to them. The kingly office is in truth a kind of generalship, sovereign and perpetual. The king has not the power of life and death, except in certain cases, as for instance, in ancient times, he had it when upon a campaign, by right of force. This custom is described in Homer. For Agamemnon puts up with it when he is   10
attacked in the assembly, but when the army goes out to battle he has the power even of life and death. Does he not say: 'When I find a man skulking apart from the battle, nothing shall save him from the dogs and vultures, for in my hands is death'?[4]

This, then, is one form of kingship—a generalship for life; and of such   15
kingships some are hereditary and others elective.

There is another sort of monarchy not uncommon among foreigners, which nearly resembles tyranny. But this is both legal and hereditary. For foreigners, being more servile in character than Hellenes, and Asiatics than Europeans, do not   20
rebel against a despotic government. Such kingships have the nature of tyrannies because the people are by nature slaves; but there is no danger of their being overthrown, for they are hereditary and legal. For the same reason, their guards are such as a king and not such as a tyrant would employ, that is to say, they are   25
composed of citizens, whereas the guards of tyrants are mercenaries. For kings rule according to law over voluntary subjects, but tyrants over involuntary; and the one are guarded by their fellow-citizens, the others are guarded against them.

These are two forms of monarchy, and there was a third which existed in ancient Hellas, called an Aesymnetia. This may be defined generally as an elective   30
tyranny, which, like foreign monarchy, is legal, but differs from it in not being hereditary. Sometimes the office was held for life, sometimes for a term of years, or until certain duties had been performed. For example, the Mytilenaeans once   35
elected Pittacus leader against the exiles, who were headed by Antimenides and Alcaeus the poet. And Alcaeus himself shows in one of his banquet odes that they

[4]*Iliad* II 391–393.

chose Pittacus tyrant, for he reproaches his fellow-citizens for 'having made the
1285ᵇ1   low-born Pittacus tyrant of the spiritless and ill-fated city, with one voice shouting
his praises'.

These forms of government have always had the character of tyrannies,
because they possess despotic power; but inasmuch as they are elective and
acquiesced in by their subjects, they are kingly.

5   There is a fourth species of kingly monarchy—that of the heroic times—which
was hereditary and legal, and was exercised over willing subjects. For the first
chiefs were benefactors of the people in arts or arms; they either gathered them into
a community, or procured land for them; and thus they became kings of voluntary
subjects, and their power was inherited by their descendants. They took the
10   command in war and presided over the sacrifices, except those which required a
priest. They also decided law-suits either with or without an oath; and when they
swore, the form of the oath was the stretching out of their sceptre. In ancient times
their power extended continuously to all things in city and country and across the
15   border; but at a later date they relinquished several of these privileges, and others
the people took from them, until in some states nothing was left to them but the
sacrifices; and where they retained more of the reality they had only the right of
leadership in war beyond the border.

20   These, then, are the four kinds of kingship. First the monarchy of the heroic
ages; this was exercised over voluntary subjects, but limited to certain functions; the
king was a general and a judge, and had the control of religion. The second is that of
foreigners, which is an hereditary despotic government in accordance with law. A
25   third is the power of the so-called Aesymnete; this is an elective tyranny. The fourth
is the Lacedaemonian, which is in fact a generalship, hereditary and perpetual.
These four forms differ from one another in the manner which I have described.

There is a fifth form of kingly rule in which one man has the disposal of all, just
30   as each nation or each state has the disposal of public matters; this form
corresponds to the control of a household. For as household management is the
kingly rule of a house, so kingly rule is the household management of a city, or of a
nation, or of many nations.

35   15 · Of these forms we need only consider two, the Lacedaemonian and the
absolute royalty; for most of the others lie in a region between them, having less
power than the last, and more than the first. Thus the inquiry is reduced to two
points: first, is it advantageous to the state that there should be a perpetual general,
and if so, should the office be confined to one family, or open to the citizens in turn?
1286ᵃ1   Secondly, is it well that a single man should have the supreme power in all things?
The first question falls under the head of laws rather than of constitutions; for
perpetual generalship might equally exist under any form of government, so that
5   this matter may be dismissed for the present. The other kind of kingship is a sort of
constitution; this we have now to consider, and to run over the difficulties involved
in it. We will begin by inquiring whether it is more advantageous to be ruled by the
best man or by the best laws.

The advocates of kingship maintain that the laws speak only in general terms, 10
and cannot provide for circumstances; and that for any science to abide by written
rules is absurd. In Egypt the physician is allowed to alter his treatment after the
fourth day, but if sooner, he takes the risk. Hence it is clear that a government
acting according to written laws is plainly not the best. Yet surely the ruler cannot 15
dispense with the general principle which exists in law; and that is a better ruler
which is free from passion than that in which it is innate. Whereas the law is
passionless, passion must always sway the heart of man. Yes, it may be replied, but 20
then on the other hand an individual will be better able to deliberate in particular
cases.

The best man, then, must legislate, and laws must be passed, but these laws
will have no authority when they miss the mark, though in all other cases retaining
their authority. But when the law cannot determine a point at all, or not well, should 25
the one best man or should all decide? According to our present practice assemblies
meet, sit in judgement, deliberate, and decide, and their judgements all relate to
individual cases. Now any member of the assembly, taken separately, is certainly
inferior to the wise man. But the state is made up of many individuals. And as a
feast to which all the guests contribute is better than a banquet furnished by a single 30
man, so a multitude is a better judge of many things than any individual.

Again, the many are more incorruptible than the few; they are like the greater
quantity of water which is less easily corrupted than a little. The individual is liable
to be overcome by anger or by some other passion, and then his judgement is
necessarily perverted; but it is hardly to be supposed that a great number of persons
would all get into a passion and go wrong at the same moment. Let us assume that 35
they are the freemen, and that they never act in violation of the law, but fill up the
gaps which the law is obliged to leave. Or, if such virtue is scarcely attainable by the
multitude, we need only suppose that the majority are good men and good citizens,
and ask which will be the more incorruptible, the one good ruler, or the many who
are all good? Will not the many? But, you will say, there may be factions among 1286ᵇ1
them, whereas the one man is not divided against himself. To which we may answer
that their character is as good as his. If we call the rule of many men, who are all of
them good, aristocracy, and the rule of one man kingship, then aristocracy will be 5
better for states than kingship, whether the government is supported by force or not,
provided only that a number of men equal in excellence can be found.

The first governments were kingships, probably for this reason, because of old,
when cities were small, men of eminent excellence were few. Further, they were 10
made kings because they were benefactors, and benefits can only be bestowed by
good men. But when many persons equal in merit arose, no longer enduring the
pre-eminence of one, they desired to have a commonwealth, and set up a
constitution. The ruling class soon deteriorated and enriched themselves out of the
public treasury; riches became the path to honour, and so oligarchies naturally grew 15
up. These passed into tyrannies and tyrannies into democracies; for love of gain in
the ruling classes was always tending to diminish their number, and so to strengthen
the masses, who in the end set upon their masters and established democracies.

20   Since cities have increased in size, no other form of government appears to be any longer even easy to establish.

Even supposing the principle to be maintained that kingly power is the best thing for states, how about the family of the king? Are his children to succeed him?

25   If they are no better than anybody else, that will be mischievous. But perhaps the king, though he might, will not hand on his power to his children? That, however, is hardly to be expected, and is too much to ask of human nature. There is also a difficulty about the force which he is to employ; should a king have guards about

30   him by whose aid he may be able to coerce the refractory? If not, how will he administer his kingdom? Even if he is the lawful sovereign who does nothing arbitrarily or contrary to law, still he must have some force wherewith to maintain the law. In the case of a limited monarchy there is not much difficulty in answering

35   this question; the king must have such force as will be more than a match for one or more individuals, but not so great as that of the people. The ancients observed this principle when they gave guards to anyone whom they appointed Aesymnete or tyrant. Thus, when Dionysius asked the Syracusans to allow him guards, somebody advised that they should give him only such a number.

1287ª1   16 · At this place in the discussion there impends the inquiry respecting the king who acts solely according to his own will; he has now to be considered. The so-called kingship according to law, as I have already remarked, is not a form of government, for under all governments, as, for example, in a democracy or

5   aristocracy, there may be a general holding office for life, and one person is often made supreme over the administration of a state. A magistracy of this kind exists at Epidamnus, and also at Opus, but in the latter city has a more limited power. Now,

10   absolute monarchy, or the arbitrary rule of a sovereign over all the citizens, in a city which consists of equals, is thought by some to be quite contrary to nature; it is argued that those who are by nature equals must have the same natural right and worth, and that for unequals to have an equal share, or for equals to have an unequal share, in the offices of state, is as bad as for different bodily constitutions to

15   have the same food and clothing. That is why it is thought to be just that among equals everyone be ruled as well as rule, and therefore that all should have their turn. We thus arrive at law; for an order of succession implies law. And the rule of

20   the law, it is argued, is preferable to that of any individual. On the same principle, even if it be better for certain individuals to govern, they should be made only guardians and ministers of the law. For magistrates there must be—this is admitted; but then men say that to give authority to any one man when all are equal is unjust. There may indeed be cases which the law seems unable to determine, but

25   such cases a man could not determine either. But the law trains officers for this express purpose, and appoints them to determine matters which are left undecided by it, to the best of their judgement. Further, it permits them to make any amendment of the existing laws which experience suggests. Therefore he who bids the law rule may be deemed to bid God and Reason alone rule, but he who bids man

30   rule adds an element of the beast; for desire is a wild beast, and passion perverts the minds of rulers, even when they are the best of men. The law is reason unaffected by

desire. We are told that a patient should call in a physician; he will not get better if he is doctored out of a book. But the parallel of the arts is clearly not in point; for the physician does nothing contrary to rule from motives of friendship; he only cures a   35
patient and takes a fee; whereas magistrates do many things from spite and partiality. And, indeed, if a man suspected the physician of being in league with his enemies to destroy him for a bribe, he would rather have recourse to the book. But
certainly physicians, when they are sick, call in other physicians, and training-   1287ᵇ1
masters, when they are in training, other training-masters, as if they could not judge truly about their own case and might be influenced by their feelings. Hence it is evident that in seeking for justice men seek for the mean, for the law is the mean.
Again, customary laws have more weight, and relate to more important matters,   5
than written laws, and a man may be a safer ruler than the written law, but not safer than the customary law.

Again, it is by no means easy for one man to superintend many things; he will have to appoint a number of subordinates, and what difference does it make   10
whether these subordinates always existed or were appointed by him because he needed them? If, as I said before, the good man has a right to rule because he is better, still two good men are better than one: this is the old saying,

> two going together,

and the prayer of Agamemnon,

> would that I had ten such counsellors!   15

And even now there are magistrates, for example judges, who have authority to decide some matters which the law is unable to determine, since no one doubts that the law would command and decide in the best manner whatever it could. But some things can, and other things cannot, be comprehended under the law, and this is the origin of the vexed question whether the best law or the best man should rule. For   20
matters of detail about which men deliberate cannot be included in legislation. Nor does anyone deny that the decision of such matters must be left to man, but it is argued that there should be many judges, and not one only. For every ruler who has   25
been trained by the law judges well; and it would surely seem strange that a person should see better with two eyes, or hear better with two ears, or act better with two hands or feet, than many with many; indeed, it is already the practice of kings to make to themselves many eyes and ears and hands and feet. For they make   30
colleagues of those who are the friends of themselves and their governments. They must be friends of the monarch and of his government; if not his friends, they will not do what he wants; but friendship implies likeness and equality; and, therefore, if he thinks that his friends ought to rule, he must think that those who are equal to himself and like himself ought to rule equally with himself. These are the principal   35
controversies relating to monarchy.

17 · But may not all this be true in some cases and not in others? for there is by nature both a justice and an advantage appropriate to the rule of a master,

another to kingly rule, another to constitutional rule; but there is none naturally
40 appropriate to tyranny, or to any other perverted form of government; for these
come into being contrary to nature. Now, to judge at least from what has been said,
1288ª1 it is manifest that, where men are alike and equal, it is neither expedient nor just
that one man should be lord of all, whether there are laws, or whether there are no
laws, but he himself is in the place of law. Neither should a good man be lord over
good men, nor a bad man over bad; nor, even if he excels in excellence, should he
5 have a right to rule, unless in a particular case, at which I have already hinted, and
to which I will once more recur. But first of all, I must determine what natures are
suited for government by a king, and what for an aristocracy, and what for a
constitutional government.

A people who are by nature capable of producing a race superior in the
excellence needed for political rule are fitted for kingly government; and a people
10 submitting to be ruled as freemen by men whose excellence renders them capable of
political command are adapted for an aristocracy: while the people who are suited
for constitutional freedom are those among whom there naturally exists a warlike
multitude. In the former case the multitude is capable of being ruled by men whose
excellence is appropriate to political command; in the latter case the multitude is
15 able to rule and to obey in turn by a law which gives office to the well-to-do
according to their desert. But when a whole family, or some individual, happens to
be so pre-eminent in excellence as to surpass all others, then it is just that they
should be the royal family and supreme over all, or that this one citizen should be
king. For, as I said before, to give them authority is not only agreeable to that notion
20 of justice which the founders of all states, whether aristocratic, or oligarchical, or
again democratic, are accustomed to put forward (for these all recognize the claim
of superiority, although not the same superiority), but accords with the principle
25 already laid down. For surely it would not be right to kill, or ostracize, or exile such
a person, or require that he should take his turn in being governed. The whole is
naturally superior to the part, and he who has this pre-eminence is in the relation of
a whole to a part. But if so, the only alternative is that he should have the supreme
power, and that mankind should obey him, not in turn, but always. These are the
30 conclusions at which we arrive respecting kingship and its various forms, and this is
the answer to the question, whether it is or is not advantageous to states, and to
which, and how.

18 · We maintain that the true forms of government are three, and that the
35 best must be that which is administered by the best, and in which there is one man,
or a whole family, or many persons, excelling all the others together in excellence,
and both rulers and subjects are fitted, the one to rule, the others to be ruled, in such
a manner as to attain the most desirable life. We showed at the commencement of
our inquiry that the excellence of the good man is necessarily the same as the
excellence of the citizen of the perfect state. Clearly then in the same manner, and
by the same means through which a man becomes truly good, he will frame a state
1288ᵇ1 that is to be ruled by an aristocracy or by a king, and the same education and the

same habits will be found to make a good man and a man fit to be a statesman or king.

Having arrived at these conclusions, we must proceed to speak of the perfect state, and describe how it comes into being and is established.

So if we are to inquire in the appropriate way about it, we must. . . .   5

BOOK IV

1 · In all arts and sciences which embrace the whole of any subject, and do   10
not come into being in a fragmentary way, it is the province of a single art or science to consider all that appertains to a single subject. For example, the art of gymnastics considers not only the suitableness of different modes of training to different bodies, but what sort is the best (for the best must suit that which is by nature best and best   15
furnished with the means of life), and also what common form of training is adapted to the great majority of men. And if a man does not desire the best habit of body, or the greatest skill in gymnastics, which might be attained by him, still the trainer or the teacher of gymnastics should be able to impart any lower degree of either. The same principle equally holds in medicine and ship-building, and the making of   20
clothes, and in the arts generally.

Hence it is obvious that government too is the subject of a single science, which has to consider what government is best and of what sort it must be, to be most in accordance with our aspirations, if there were no external impediment, and also what kind of government is adapted to particular states. For the best is often unattainable, and therefore the true legislator and statesman ought to be acquaint-   25
ed, not only with that which is best in the abstract, but also with that which is best relatively to circumstances. We should be able further to say how a state may be constituted under any given conditions; both how it is originally formed and, when formed, how it may be longest preserved; the supposed state neither having the best   30
constitution nor being provided even with the conditions necessary for the best, nor being the best under the circumstances, but of an inferior type.

We ought, moreover, to know the form of government which is best suited to states in general; for political writers, although they have excellent ideas, are often   35
unpractical. We should consider, not only what form of government is best, but also what is possible and what is easily attainable by all. There are some who would have none but the most perfect; for this many natural advantages are required. Others,   40
again, speak of a more attainable form, and, although they reject the constitution under which they are living, they extol some one in particular, for example the Lacedaemonian. Any change of government which has to be introduced should be   1289ᵃ1
one which men, starting from their existing constitutions, will be both willing and able to adopt, since there is quite as much trouble in the reformation of an old constitution as in the establishment of a new one, just as to unlearn is as hard as to   5
learn. And therefore, in addition to the qualifications of the statesman already

mentioned, he should be able to find remedies for the defects of existing constitutions, as has been said before. This he cannot do unless he knows how many forms of government there are. It is often supposed that there is only one kind of democracy and one of oligarchy. But this is a mistake; and, in order to avoid such mistakes, we
10 must ascertain what differences there are in the constitutions of states, and in how many ways they are combined. The same political insight will enable a man to know which laws are the best, and which are suited to different constitutions; for the laws are, and ought to be, framed with a view to the constitution, and not the constitution
15 to the laws. A constitution is the organization of offices in a state, and determines what is to be the governing body, and what is the end of each community. But laws are not to be confounded with the principles of the constitution; they are the rules according to which the magistrates should administer the state, and proceed against
20 offenders. So that we must know the varieties, and the number of varieties, of each form of government, if only with a view to making laws. For the same laws cannot be equally suited to all oligarchies or to all democracies, since there is certainly
25 more than one form both of democracy and of oligarchy.

2 · In our original discussion about governments we divided them into three true forms: kingly rule, aristocracy, and constitutional government, and three
30 corresponding perversions—tyranny, oligarchy, and democracy. Of kingly rule and of aristocracy we have already spoken, for the inquiry into the perfect state is the same thing as the discussion of the two forms thus named, since both imply a
35 principle of excellence provided with external means. We have already determined in what aristocracy and kingly rule differ from one another, and when the latter should be established. In what follows we have to describe the so-called constitutional government, which bears the common name of all constitutions, and the other forms, tyranny, oligarchy, and democracy.

It is obvious which of the three perversions is the worst, and which is the next in badness. That which is the perversion of the first and most divine is necessarily the
1289ᵇ1 worst. And just as a royal rule, if not a mere name, must exist by virtue of some great personal superiority in the king, so tyranny, which is the worst of governments, is necessarily the farthest removed from a well-constituted form; oligarchy is little better, for it is a long way from aristocracy, and democracy is the most tolerable of the three.

5 A writer who preceded me has already made these distinctions, but his point of view is not the same as mine. For he lays down the principle that when all the constitutions are good (the oligarchy and the rest being virtuous), democracy is the worst, but the best when all are bad. Whereas we maintain that they are in any case
10 defective, and that one oligarchy is not to be accounted better than another, but only less bad.

Not to pursue this question further at present, let us begin by determining how many varieties of constitution there are (since of democracy and oligarchy there are
15 several); what constitution is the most generally acceptable, and what is preferable in the next degree after the perfect state; and besides this what other there is which

is aristocratic and well-constituted, and at the same time adapted to states in general; and of the other forms of government we must ask to what people each is suited. For democracy may meet the needs of some better than oligarchy, and conversely. In the next place we have to consider in what manner a man ought to proceed who desires to establish some one among these various forms, whether of democracy or of oligarchy; and lastly, having briefly discussed these subjects to the best of our power, we will endeavour to ascertain the modes of ruin and preservation both of constitutions generally and of each separately, and to what causes they are to be attributed.

3 · The reason why there are many forms of government is that every state contains many elements. In the first place we see that all states are made up of families, and in the multitude of citizens there must be some rich and some poor, and some in a middle condition; the rich possess heavy armour, and the poor not. Of the common people, some are farmers, and some traders, and some artisans. There are also among the notables differences of wealth and property—for example, in the number of horses which they keep, for they cannot afford to keep them unless they are rich. And therefore in old times the cities whose strength lay in their cavalry were oligarchies, and they used cavalry in wars against their neighbours; as was the practice of the Eretrians and Chalcidians, and also of the Magnesians on the river Mæander, and of other peoples in Asia. Besides differences of wealth there are differences of rank and merit, and there are some other elements which were mentioned by us when in treating of aristocracy we enumerated the essentials of a state. Of these elements, sometimes all, sometimes the lesser, and sometimes the greater number, have a share in the government. It is evident then that there must be many forms of government, differing in kind, since the parts of which they are composed differ from each other in kind. For a constitution is an organization of offices, which all the citizens distribute among themselves, according to the power which different classes possess (for example the rich or the poor), or according to some principle of equality which includes both. There must therefore be as many forms of government as there are modes of arranging the offices, according to the superiorities and the differences of the parts of the state.

There are generally thought to be two principal forms: as men say of the winds that there are but two, north and south, and that the rest of them are only variations of these, so of governments there are said to be only two forms—democracy and oligarchy. For aristocracy is considered to be a kind of oligarchy, as being the rule of a few, and the so-called constitutional government to be really a democracy, just as among the winds we make the west a variation of the north, and the east of the south wind. Similarly of musical modes there are said to be two kinds, the Dorian and the Phrygian; the other arrangements of the scale are comprehended under one or other of these two. About forms of government this is a very favourite notion. But in either case the better and more exact way is to distinguish, as I have done, the one or two which are true forms, and to regard the others as perversions, whether of the most perfectly attempered or of the best form of government: the more taut and more overpowering are oligarchical, and the more relaxed and gentler are democratic.

30   4 · It must not be assumed, as some are fond of saying, that democracy is simply that form of government in which the greater number are sovereign, for in oligarchies, and indeed in every government, the majority rules; nor again is oligarchy that form of government in which a few are sovereign. Suppose the whole

35   population of a city to be 1300, and that of these 1000 are rich, and do not allow the remaining 300 who are poor, but free, and in all other respects their equals, a share of the government—no one will say that this is a democracy. In like manner, if the poor were few and the masters of the rich who outnumber them, no one would ever call such a government, in which the rich majority have no share of office, an

1290ᵇ1   oligarchy. Therefore we should rather say that democracy is the form of government in which the free are rulers, and oligarchy in which the rich; it is only an accident that the free are the many and the rich are the few. Otherwise a government in which the offices were given according to stature, as is said to be the

5   case in Ethiopia, or according to beauty, would be an oligarchy; for the number of tall or good-looking men is small. And yet oligarchy and democracy are not sufficiently distinguished merely by these two characteristics of wealth and freedom. Both of them contain many other elements, and therefore we must carry our analysis further, and say that the government is not a democracy in which the

10   freemen, being few in number, rule over the many who are not free, as at Apollonia on the Ionian Gulf, and at Thera (for in each of these states the nobles, who were also the earliest settlers, held office, although they were but a few out of many). Neither is it a democracy when the rich have the government because they exceed

15   in number; as was the case formerly at Colophon, where the bulk of the inhabitants were possessed of large property before the Lydian War. But the form of government is a democracy when the free, who are also poor and the majority, govern, and an oligarchy when the rich and the noble govern, they being at the same

20   time few in number.

I have said that there are many forms of government, and have explained to what causes the variety is due. Why there are more than those already mentioned, and what they are, and whence they arise, I will now proceed to consider, starting from the principle already admitted, which is that every state consists, not of one,

25   but of many parts. If we were going to speak of the different species of animals, we should first of all determine the organs which are indispensable to every animal, as for example some organs of sense and the instruments of receiving and digesting food, such as the mouth and the stomach, besides organs of locomotion. Assuming now that there are only so many kinds of organs, but that there may be differences

30   in them—I mean different kinds of mouths, and stomachs, and perceptive and locomotive organs—the possible combinations of these differences will necessarily furnish many varieties of animals. (For animals cannot be the same which have different kinds of mouths or of ears.) And when all the combinations are exhausted,

35   there will be as many sorts of animals as there are combinations of the necessary

organs. The same, then, is true of the forms of government which have been described; states, as I have repeatedly said, are composed, not of one, but of many elements. One element is the food-producing class, who are called farmers; a second, the class of artisans who practise the arts without which a city cannot exist—of these arts some are absolutely necessary, others contribute to luxury or to the grace of life. The third class is that of traders, and by traders I mean those who are engaged in buying and selling, whether in commerce or in retail trade. A fourth class is that of labourers. The military make up the fifth class, and they are as necessary as any of the others, if the country is not to be the slave of every invader. For how can a state which has any title to the name be of a slavish nature? The state is independent and self-sufficing, but a slave is the reverse of independent. Hence we see that this subject, though ingeniously, has not been satisfactorily treated in the *Republic*. Socrates says that a state is made up of four sorts of people who are absolutely necessary; these are a weaver, a farmer, a shoemaker, and a builder; afterwards, finding that they are not enough, he adds a smith, and again a herdsman, to look after the necessary animals; then a merchant, and then a retail trader. All these together form the complement of the first state, as if a state were established merely to supply the necessaries of life, rather than for the sake of the good, or stood equally in need of shoemakers and of farmers. But he does not admit into the state a military class until the country has increased in size, and is beginning to encroach on its neighbour's land, whereupon they go to war. Yet even amongst his four original citizens, or whatever be the number of those whom he associates in the state, there must be some one who will dispense justice and determine what is just. And as the soul may be said to be more truly part of an animal than the body, so the higher parts of states, that is to say, the warrior class, the class engaged in the administration of justice, and that engaged in deliberation, which is the special business of political understanding—these are more essential to the state than the parts which minister to the necessaries of life. Whether their several functions are the functions of different citizens, or of the same—for it may often happen that the same persons are both soldiers and farmers—is immaterial to the argument. The higher as well as the lower elements are to be equally considered parts of the state, and if so, the military element at any rate must be included. There are also the wealthy who minister to the state with their property; these form the seventh class. The eighth class is that of public servants and of administrators; for the state cannot exist without rulers. And therefore some must be able to take office and to serve the state, either always or in turn. There only remains the class of those who deliberate and who judge between disputants; we were just now distinguishing them. If the presence of all these elements, and their fair and equitable organization, is necessary to states, then there must also be persons who have the ability of statesmen. Different functions appear to be often combined in the same individual; for example, the soldier may also be a farmer, or an artisan; or, again the counsellor a judge. And all claim to possess political ability, and think that they are quite competent to fill most offices. But the same persons cannot be rich and poor at the same time. For this reason the rich and the poor are especially regarded as parts of a

1291ª1

5

10

15

20

25

30

35

40

1291ᵇ1

5

10 state. Again, because the rich are generally few in number, while the poor are many, they appear to be antagonistic, and as the one or the other prevails they form the government. Hence arises the common opinion that there are two kinds of government—democracy and oligarchy.

I have already explained that there are many forms of constitution, and to
15 what causes the variety is due. Let me now show that there are different forms both of democracy and oligarchy, as will indeed be evident from what has preceded. For both in the common people and in the notables various classes are included; of the common people, one class are farmers, another artisans; another traders, who are
20 employed in buying and selling; another are the sea-faring class, whether engaged in war or in trade, as ferrymen or as fishermen. (In many places any one of these classes forms quite a large population; for example, fishermen at Tarentum and Byzantium, crews of triremes at Athens, merchant seamen at Aegina and Chios,
25 ferrymen at Tenedos.) To the classes already mentioned may be added day-labourers, and those who, owing to their needy circumstances, have no leisure, or those who are not of free birth on both sides; and there may be other classes as well. The notables again may be divided according to their wealth, birth, excellence,
30 education, and similar differences.

Of forms of democracy first comes that which is said to be based strictly on equality. In such a democracy the law says that it is just for the poor to have no more advantage than the rich; and that neither should be masters, but both equal. For if
35 liberty and equality, as is thought by some, are chiefly to be found in democracy, they will be best attained when all persons alike share in the government to the utmost. And since the people are the majority, and the opinion of the majority is decisive, such a government must necessarily be a democracy. Here then is one sort of democracy. There is another, in which the magistrates are elected according to a
40 certain property qualification, but a low one; he who has the required amount of property has a share in the government, but he who loses his property loses his
1292ª1 rights. Another kind is that in which all the citizens who are under no disqualification share in the government, but still the law is supreme. In another, everybody, if he be only a citizen, is admitted to the government, but the law is supreme as before. A fifth form of democracy, in other respects the same, is that in which not the law,
5 but the multitude, have the supreme power, and supersede the law by their decrees. This is a state of affairs brought about by the demagogues. For in democracies which are subject to the law the best citizens hold the first place, and there are no
10 demagogues; but where the laws are not supreme, there demagogues spring up. For the people becomes a monarch, and is many in one; and the many have the power in their hand, not as individuals, but collectively. Homer says that 'it is not good to have a rule of many',[1] but whether he means this corporate rule, or the rule of many
15 individuals, is uncertain. At all events this sort of democracy, which is now a monarchy, and no longer under the control of law, seeks to exercise monarchical sway, and grows into a despot; the flatterer is held in honour; this sort of democracy

---

[1]*Iliad* II 204.

is to other democracies what tyranny is to other forms of monarchy. The spirit of both is the same, and they alike exercise a despotic rule over the better citizens. The decrees of the one correspond to the edicts of the tyrant; and the demagogue is to the one what the flatterer is to the other. Both have great power—the flatterer with the tyrant, the demagogue with democracies of the kind which we are describing. The demagogues make the decrees of the people override the laws, by referring all things to the popular assembly. And therefore they grow great, because the people have all things in their hands, and they hold in their hands the votes of the people, who obey them. Further, those who have any complaint to bring against the magistrates say, 'let the people be judges'; the people are happy to accept the invitation; and so the authority of every office is undermined. Such a democracy is fairly open to the objection that it is not a constitution at all; for where the laws have no authority, there is no constitution. The law ought to be supreme over all, and the magistracies should judge of particulars, and only this[2] should be considered a constitution. So that if democracy be a real form of government, the sort of system in which all things are regulated by decrees is clearly not even a democracy in the true sense of the word, for decrees relate only to particulars.

These then are the different kinds of democracy.

5 · Of oligarchies, too, there are different kinds: one where the property qualification for office is such that the poor, although they form the majority, have no share in the government, yet he who acquires a qualification may obtain a share. Another sort is when there is a qualification for office, but a high one, and the vacancies in the governing body are filled by co-optation. If the election is made out of all the qualified persons, a constitution of this kind inclines to an aristocracy, if out of a privileged class, to an oligarchy. Another sort of oligarchy is when the son succeeds the father. There is a fourth form, likewise hereditary, in which the magistrates are supreme and not the law. Among oligarchies this is what tyranny is among monarchies, and the last-mentioned form of democracy among democracies; and in fact this sort of oligarchy receives the name of a dynasty.

These are the different sorts of oligarchies and democracies. It should, however, be remembered that in many states the constitution which is established by law, although not democratic, owing to the education and habits of the people may be administered democratically, and conversely in other states the established constitution may incline to democracy, but may be administered in an oligarchical spirit. This most often happens after a revolution; for governments do not change at once; at first the dominant party are content with encroaching a little upon their opponents. The laws which existed previously continue in force, but the authors of the revolution have the power in their hands.

6 · From what has been already said we may safely infer that there are these many democracies and oligarchies. For it is necessary that either all the classes

---

[2]Reading ταύτην for τήν.

25 whom we mentioned must share in the government, or some only and not others. When the class of farmers and of those who possess moderate fortunes have the supreme power, the government is administered according to law. For the citizens being compelled to live by their labour have no leisure; and so they set up the authority of the law, and attend assemblies only when necessary. They all obtain a

30 share in the government when they have acquired the qualification which is fixed by the law; hence all who have acquired the property qualification are admitted to a share in the constitution. For the absolute exclusion of any class would be oligarchical; but leisure cannot be provided for them unless there are revenues to support them. This is one sort of democracy, and these are the causes which give

35 birth to it. Another kind is based on the distinction which naturally comes next in order; in this, everyone to whose birth there is no objection is eligible, but actually shares in the government only if he can find leisure. Hence in such a democracy the supreme power is vested in the laws, because the state has no means of paying the citizens. A third kind is when all freemen have a right to share in the government, but do not actually share, for the reason which has been already given; so that in this

1293ª1 form again the law must rule. A fourth kind of democracy is that which comes latest in the history of states. For when cities have far outgrown their original size, and their revenues have increased, all the citizens have a place in the government, through the great preponderance of the multitude; and they all, including the poor

5 who receive pay, and therefore have leisure to exercise their rights, share in the administration. Indeed, when they are paid, the common people have the most leisure, for they are not hindered by the care of their property, which often fetters the rich, who are thereby prevented from taking part in the assembly or in the

10 courts, and so the state is governed by the poor, who are a majority, and not by the laws. Such and so many are the kinds of democracy, and they grow out of these necessary causes.

Of oligarchies, one form is that in which the majority of the citizens have some property, but not very much; and this is the first form, which allows to anyone who

15 obtains the required amount the right of sharing in the government. The sharers in the government being a numerous body, it follows that the law must govern, and not individuals. For in proportion as they are further removed from a monarchical form of government, and in respect of property have neither so much as to be able to live without attending to business, nor so little as to need state support, they must admit

20 the rule of law and not claim to rule themselves. But if the men of property in the state are fewer than in the former case, and own more property, there arises a second form of oligarchy. For the stronger they are, the more power they claim, and having this object in view, they themselves select those of the other classes who are

25 to be admitted to the government; but, not being as yet strong enough to rule without the law, they make the law represent their wishes. When this power is intensified by a further diminution of their numbers and increase of their property, there arises a third and further stage of oligarchy, in which the governing class keep the offices in their own hands, and the law ordains that the son shall succeed the

30 father. When, again, the rulers have great wealth and numerous friends, this sort of

family despotism approaches a monarchy; individuals rule and not the law. This is the fourth sort of oligarchy, and is analogous to the last sort of democracy.

7 · There are still two forms besides democracy and oligarchy; one of them is universally recognized and included among the four principal forms of government, which are said to be monarchy, oligarchy, democracy, and the so-called aristocracy. But there is also a fifth, which retains the generic name of constitutional government; this is not common, and therefore has not been noticed by writers who attempt to enumerate the different kinds of government; like Plato, in their books about the state, they recognize four only. The term 'aristocracy' is rightly applied to the form of government which is described in the first part of our treatise; for that only can be rightly called aristocracy which is a government formed of the best men absolutely, and not merely of men who are good relative to some hypothesis. In the perfect state the good man is absolutely the same as the good citizen; whereas in other states the good citizen is only good relatively to his own form of government. But there are some states differing from oligarchies and also differing from the so-called constitutional government; these are termed aristocracies, and in them magistrates are certainly chosen both according to their wealth and according to their merit. Such a form of government differs from each of the two just now mentioned, and is termed an aristocracy. For indeed in states which do not make excellence the aim of the community, men of merit and reputation for excellence may be found. And so where a government has regard to wealth, excellence, and the populace, as at Carthage, that is aristocracy; and also where it has regard only to two out of the three, as at Lacedaemon, to excellence and the populace, and the two principles of democracy and excellence temper each other. There are these two forms of aristocracy in addition to the first and perfect state, and there is a third form, viz. the constitutions which incline more than the so-called constitutional government towards oligarchy.

8 · I have yet to speak of the so-called polity and of tyranny. I put them in this order, not because a polity or constitutional government is to be regarded as a perversion any more than the above-mentioned aristocracies. The truth is, that they all fall short of the most perfect form of government, and so they are reckoned among perversions, and the really perverted forms are perversions of these, as I said in the original discussion. Last of all I will speak of tyranny, which I place last in the series because I am inquiring into the constitutions of states, and this is the very reverse of a constitution.

Having explained why I have adopted this order, I will proceed to consider constitutional government; of which the nature will be clearer now that oligarchy and democracy have been defined. For polity or constitutional government may be described generally as a fusion of oligarchy and democracy; but the term is usually applied to those forms of government which incline towards democracy, and the term aristocracy to those which incline towards oligarchy, because birth and education are commonly the accompaniments of wealth. Moreover, the rich already

possess the external advantages the want of which is a temptation to crime, and
40 hence they are called noblemen and gentlemen. And inasmuch as aristocracy seeks
to give predominance to the best of the citizens, people say also of oligarchies that
1294ª1 they are composed of noblemen and gentlemen. Now it appears to be an impossible
thing that the state which is governed not by the best citizens but by the worst
should be well-governed, and equally impossible that the state which is ill-governed
should be governed by the best. But we must remember that good laws, if they are
not obeyed, do not constitute good government. Hence there are two parts of good
5 government; one is the actual obedience of citizens to the laws, the other part is the
goodness of the laws which they obey; they may obey bad laws as well as good. And
there may be a further subdivision; they may obey either the best laws which are
attainable to them, or the best absolutely.

The distribution of offices according to excellence is a special characteristic of
10 aristocracy, for the principle of an aristocracy is excellence, as wealth is of an
oligarchy, and freedom of a democracy. In all of them there of course exists the
right of the majority, and whatever seems good to the majority of those who share in
the government has authority, whether in an oligarchy, an aristocracy or a
15 democracy. Now in most states the form called polity exists, for the fusion goes no
further than the attempt to unite the freedom of the poor and the wealth of the rich,
who commonly take the place of the noble. But as there are three grounds on which
20 men claim an equal share in the government, freedom, wealth, and excellence (for
the fourth, what is called good birth, is the result of the two last, being only ancient
wealth and excellence), it is clear that the admixture of the two elements, that is to
say, of the rich and poor, is to be called a polity or constitutional government; and
the union of the three is to be called aristocracy, and more than any other form of
25 government, except the true and ideal, has a right to this name.

Thus far I have shown the existence of forms of states other than monarchy,
democracy, and oligarchy, and what they are, and in what aristocracies differ from
one another, and polities from aristocracies—that the two latter are not very unlike
is obvious.

30   9 · Next we have to consider how by the side of oligarchy and democracy the
so-called polity or constitutional government springs up, and how it should be
organized. The nature of it will be at once understood from a comparison of
oligarchy and democracy; we must ascertain their different characteristics, and
35 taking a portion from each, fit the two together, like the parts of a tally-stick. Now
there are three modes in which fusions of government may be effected. In the first
mode we must combine the laws made by both governments, say concerning the
administration of justice. In oligarchies they impose a fine on the rich if they do not
serve as judges, and to the poor they give no pay; but in democracies they give pay to
40 the poor and do not fine the rich. Now the union of these two modes is a common or
middle term between them, and is therefore characteristic of a constitutional
1294ᵇ1 government, for it is a combination of both. This is one mode of uniting the two
elements. Or a mean may be taken between the enactments of the two: thus

democracies require no property qualification, or only a small one, from members of the assembly, oligarchies a high one; here neither of these is the common term, but a mean between them. There is a third mode, in which something is borrowed from the oligarchical and something from the democratic principle. For example, the appointment of magistrates by lot is thought to be democratic, and the election of them oligarchical; democratic again when there is no property qualification, oligarchical when there is. In the aristocratic or constitutional state, one element will be taken from each—from oligarchy the principle of electing to offices, from democracy the disregard of qualification. Such are the various modes of combination.

There is a true union of oligarchy and democracy when the same state may be termed either a democracy or an oligarchy; those who use both names evidently feel that the fusion is complete. Such a fusion there is also in the mean; for both extremes appear in it. The Lacedaemonian constitution, for example, is often described as a democracy, because it has many democratic features. In the first place the youth receive a democratic education. For the sons of the poor are brought up with the sons of the rich, who are educated in such a manner as to make it possible for the sons of the poor to be educated like them. A similar equality prevails in the following period of life, and when the citizens are grown up to manhood the same rule is observed; there is no distinction between the rich and poor. In like manner they all have the same food at their public tables, and the rich wear only such clothing as any poor man can afford. Again, the people elect to one of the two greatest offices of state, and in the other they share; for they elect the Senators and share in the Ephoralty. By others the Spartan constitution is said to be an oligarchy, because it has many oligarchical elements. That all offices are filled by election and none by lot, is one of these oligarchical characteristics; that the power of inflicting death or banishment rests with a few persons is another; and there are others. In a well attempered polity there should appear to be both elements and yet neither; also the government should rely on itself, and not on foreign aid, and on itself not through the good will of a majority[3]—they might be equally well-disposed when there is a vicious form of government—but through the general willingness of all classes in the state to maintain the constitution.

Enough of the manner in which a constitutional government, and in which the so-called aristocracies, ought to be framed.

10 · Of the nature of tyranny I have still to speak, in order that it may have its place in our inquiry (since even tyranny is reckoned by us to be a form of government), although there is not much to be said about it. I have already in the former part of this treatise discussed royalty or kingship according to the most usual meaning of the term, and considered whether it is or is not advantageous to states, and what kind of royalty should be established, and from what source, and how.

When speaking of royalty we also spoke of two forms of tyranny, which are both according to law, and therefore easily pass into royalty. Among Barbarians

---

[3]Omitting ἔξωθεν.

there are elected monarchs who exercise a despotic power; despotic rulers were also elected in ancient Greece, called Aesymnetes. These monarchies, when compared with one another, exhibit certain differences. And they are, as I said before, royal,
15   in so far as the monarch rules according to law over willing subjects; but they are tyrannical in so far as he is despotic and rules according to his own fancy. There is also a third kind of tyranny, which is the most typical form, and is the counterpart of
20   the perfect monarchy. This tyranny is just that arbitrary power of an individual which is responsible to no one, and governs all alike, whether equals or betters, with a view to its own advantage, not to that of its subjects, and therefore against their will. No freeman willingly endures such a government.

The kinds of tyranny are such and so many, and for the reasons which I have given.

25   11 · We have now to inquire what is the best constitution for most states, and the best life for most men, neither assuming a standard of excellence which is above ordinary persons, nor an education which is exceptionally favoured by nature and circumstances, nor yet an ideal state which is an aspiration only, but having
30   regard to the life in which the majority are able to share, and to the form of government which states in general can attain. As to those aristocracies, as they are called, of which we were just now speaking, they either lie beyond the possibilities of the greater number of states, or they approximate to the so-called constitutional government, and therefore need no separate discussion. And in fact the conclusion
35   at which we arrive respecting all these forms rests upon the same grounds. For if what was said in the *Ethics* is true, that the happy life is the life according to excellence lived without impediment, and that excellence is a mean, then the life which is in a mean, and in a mean attainable by everyone, must be the best. And the same principles of excellence and badness are characteristic of cities and of
1295ᵇ1 constitutions; for the constitution is so to speak the life of the city.

Now in all states there are three elements: one class is very rich, another very poor, and a third in a mean. It is admitted that moderation and the mean are best,
5   and therefore it will clearly be best to possess the gifts of fortune in moderation; for in that condition of life men are most ready to follow rational principle. But he who greatly excels in beauty, strength, birth, or wealth, or on the other hand who is very poor, or very weak, or of very low status, finds it difficult to follow rational principle. Of these two the one sort grow into violent and great criminals, the others
10   into rogues and petty rascals. And two sorts of offences correspond to them, the one committed from violence, the other from roguery [Again, the middle class is least likely to shrink from rule, or to be over-ambitious for it],[4] both of which are injuries to the state. Again, those who have too much of the goods of fortune, strength,
15   wealth, friends, and the like, are neither willing nor able to submit to authority. The evil begins at home; for when they are boys, by reason of the luxury in which they are brought up, they never learn, even at school, the habit of obedience. On the

---

[4]Excised by Dreizehnter.

other hand, the very poor, who are in the opposite extreme, are too degraded. So that the one class cannot obey, and can only rule despotically; the other knows not how to command and must be ruled like slaves. Thus arises a city, not of freemen, but of masters and slaves, the one despising, the other envying; and nothing can be more fatal to friendship and good fellowship in states than this: for good fellowship springs from friendship; when men are at enmity with one another, they would rather not even share the same path. But a city ought to be composed, as far as possible, of equals and similars; and these are generally the middle classes. Wherefore the city which is composed of middle-class citizens is necessarily best constituted in respect of the elements of which we say the fabric of the state naturally consists. And this is the class of citizens which is most secure in a state, for they do not, like the poor, covet other men's goods; nor do others covet theirs, as the poor covet the goods of the rich; and as they neither plot against others, nor are themselves plotted against, they pass through life safely. Wisely then did Phocylides pray—'Many things are best in the mean; I desire to be of a middle condition in my city'.

Thus it is manifest that the best political community is formed by citizens of the middle class, and that those states are likely to be well-administered in which the middle class is large, and stronger if possible than both the other classes, or at any rate than either singly; for the addition of the middle class turns the scale, and prevents either of the extremes from being dominant. Great then is the good fortune of a state in which the citizens have a moderate and sufficient property; for where some possess much, and the others nothing, there may arise an extreme democracy, or a pure oligarchy; or a tyranny may grow out of either extreme—either out of the most rampant democracy, or out of an oligarchy; but it is not so likely to arise out of the middle constitutions and those akin to them. I will explain the reason for this hereafter, when I speak of the revolutions of states. The mean condition of states is clearly best, for no other is free from faction; and where the middle class is large, there are least likely to be factions and dissensions. For a similar reason large states are less liable to faction than small ones, because in them the middle class is large; whereas in small states it is easy to divide all the citizens into two classes who are either rich or poor, and to leave nothing in the middle. And democracies are safer and more permanent than oligarchies, because they have a middle class which is more numerous and has a greater share in the government; for when there is no middle class, and the poor are excessive in number, troubles arise, and the state soon comes to an end. A proof of the superiority of the middle class is that the best legislators have been of a middle condition; for example, Solon, as his own verses testify; and Lycurgus, for he was not a king; and Charondas, and almost all legislators.

These considerations will help us to understand why most governments are either democratic or oligarchical. The reason is that the middle class is seldom numerous in them, and whichever party, whether the rich or the common people, transgresses the mean and predominates, draws the constitution its own way, and thus arises either oligarchy or democracy. There is another reason—the poor and

the rich quarrel with one another, and whichever side gets the better, instead of
30   establishing a just or popular government, regards political supremacy as the prize
of victory, and the one party sets up a democracy and the other an oligarchy.
Further, both the parties which had the supremacy in Greece looked only to the
interest of their own form of government, and established in states, the one,
35   democracies, and the other, oligarchies; they thought of their own advantage, and of
the advantage of the other states not at all. For these reasons the middle form of
government has rarely, if ever, existed, and among a very few only. One man alone
of all who ever ruled in Greece was induced to give this middle constitution to states.
1296ᵇ1   But it has now become a habit among the citizens of states not even to care about
equality; all men are seeking for dominion, or, if conquered, are willing to submit.

What then is the best form of government, and what makes it the best, is
evident; and of other constitutions, since we say that there are many kinds of
democracy and many of oligarchy, it is not difficult to see which has the first and
5   which the second or any other place in the order of excellence, now that we have
determined which is the best. For that which is nearest to the best must of necessity
be better, and that which is further from the mean worse, if we are judging
absolutely and not relatively to given conditions: I say 'relatively to given
10   conditions', since a particular government may be preferable, but another form may
be better for some people.

12 · We have now to consider what and what kind of government is suitable
to what and what kind of men. I may begin by assuming, as a general principle
15   common to all governments, that the portion of the state which desires the
permanence of the constitution ought to be stronger than that which desires the
reverse. Now every city is composed of quality and quantity. By quality I mean
freedom, wealth, education, good birth, and by quantity, superiority of numbers.
20   Quality may exist in one of the classes which make up the state, and quantity in the
other. For example, the meanly-born may be more in number than the well-born, or
the poor than the rich, yet they may not so much exceed in quantity as they fall
short in quality; and therefore there must be a comparison of quantity and quality.
25   Where the number of the poor exceeds a given proportion, there will naturally be a
democracy, varying in form with the sort of people who compose it in each case. If,
for example, the farmers exceed in number, the first form of democracy will then
30   arise; if the artisans and labouring class, the last; and so with the intermediate
forms. But where the rich and the notables exceed in quality more than they fall
short in quantity, there oligarchy arises, similarly assuming various forms according to the kind of superiority possessed by the oligarchs.
35   The legislator should always include the middle class in his government; if he
makes his laws oligarchical, let him look to the middle class; if he makes them
democratic, he should equally by his laws try to attach this class to the state. There
only can the government ever be stable where the middle class exceeds one or both
1297ª1   of the others, and in that case there will be no fear that the rich will unite with the
poor against the rulers. For neither of them will ever be willing ᵗo serve the other,

and if they look for some form of government more suitable to both, they will find none better than this, for the rich and the poor will never consent to rule in turn, because they mistrust one another. The arbiter is always the one most trusted, and he who is in the middle is an arbiter. The more perfect the admixture of the political elements, the more lasting will be the constitution. Many even of those who desire to form aristocratic governments make a mistake, not only in giving too much power to the rich, but in attempting to cheat the people. There comes a time when out of a false good there arises a true evil, since the encroachments of the rich are more destructive to the constitution than those of the people.

13 · The devices by which oligarchies deceive the people are five in number; they relate to the assembly; the magistracies; the courts of law; the use of arms; and gymnastic exercises. The assemblies are thrown open to all, but either the rich only are fined for non-attendance, or a much larger fine is inflicted upon them. As to the magistracies, those who are qualified by property cannot decline office upon oath, but the poor may. In the law-courts the rich, and the rich only, are fined if they do not serve, the poor are let off with impunity, or, as in the laws of Charondas, a larger fine is inflicted on the rich, and a smaller one on the poor. In some states all citizens who have registered themselves are allowed to attend the assembly and to try causes; but if after registration they do not attend either in the assembly or at the courts, heavy fines are imposed upon them. The intention is that through fear of the fines they may avoid registering themselves, and then they cannot sit in the law-courts or in the assembly. Concerning the possession of arms, and gymnastic exercises, they legislate in a similar spirit. For the poor are not obliged to have arms, but the rich are fined for not having them; and in like manner no penalty is inflicted on the poor for non-attendance at the gymnasium, and consequently, having nothing to fear, they do not attend, whereas the rich are liable to a fine, and therefore they take care to attend.

These are the devices of oligarchical legislators, and in democracies they have counter-devices. They pay the poor for attending the assemblies and the law-courts, and they inflict no penalty on the rich for non-attendance. It is obvious that he who would duly mix the two principles should combine the practice of both, and provide that the poor should be paid to attend, and the rich fined if they do not attend, for then all will take part; if there is no such combination, power will be in the hands of one party only. The government should be confined to those who carry arms. As to the property qualification, no absolute rule can be laid down, but we must see what is the highest qualification sufficiently comprehensive to secure that the number of those who have the rights of citizens exceeds the number of those excluded. Even if they have no share in office, the poor, provided only that they are not outraged or deprived of their property, will be quiet enough.

But to secure gentle treatment for the poor is not an easy thing, since a ruling class is not always humane. And in time of war the poor are apt to hesitate unless they are fed; when fed, they are willing enough to fight. In some states the government is vested, not only in those who are actually serving, but also in those

who have served; among the Malians, for example, the governing body consisted of
the latter, while the magistrates were chosen from those actually on service. And
the earliest government which existed among the Greeks, after the overthrow of the
kingly power, grew up out of the warrior class, and was originally taken from the
knights (for strength and superiority in war at that time depended on cavalry;
indeed, without discipline, infantry are useless, and in ancient times there was no
military knowledge or tactics, and therefore the strength of armies lay in their
cavalry). But when cities increased and the heavy-armed grew in strength, more
had a share in the government; and this is the reason why the states which we call
constitutional governments have been hitherto called democracies. Ancient constitutions, as might be expected, were oligarchical and royal; their population being
small they had no considerable middle class; the people were weak in numbers and
organization, and were therefore more content to be governed.

I have explained why there are various forms of government, and why there are
more than is generally supposed; for democracy, as well as other constitutions, has
more than one form: also what their differences are, and whence they arise, and
what is the best form of government, speaking generally, and to whom the various
forms of government are best suited; all this has now been explained.

14 · Having thus gained an appropriate basis of discussion we will proceed
to speak of the points which follow next in order. We will consider the subject not
only in general but with reference to particular constitutions. All constitutions have
three elements, concerning which the good lawgiver has to regard what is expedient
for each constitution. When they are well-ordered, the constitution is well-ordered,
and as they differ from one another, constitutions differ. There is one element which
deliberates about public affairs; secondly that concerned with the magistracies—
the questions being, what they should be, over what they should exercise authority,
and what should be the mode of electing to them; and thirdly that which has judicial
power.

The deliberative element has authority in matters of war and peace, in making
and unmaking alliances; it passes laws, inflicts death, exile, confiscation, elects
magistrates and audits their accounts. These powers must be assigned either all to
all the citizens or all to some of them (for example, to one or more magistracies, or
different causes to different magistracies), or some of them to all, and others of
them only to some. That all things should be decided by all is characteristic of
democracy; this is the sort of equality which the people desire. But there are various
ways in which all may share in the government; they may deliberate, not all in one
body, but by turns, as in the constitution of Telecles the Milesian. There are other
constitutions in which the boards of magistrates meet and deliberate, but come into
office by turns, and are elected out of the tribes and the very smallest divisions of the
state, until every one has obtained office in his turn. The citizens, on the other hand,
are assembled only for the purposes of legislation, and to consult about the
constitution, and to hear the edicts of the magistrates. In another variety of
democracy the citizens form one assembly, but meet only to elect magistrates, to

pass laws, to advise about war and peace, and to make scrutinies. Other matters are referred severally to special magistrates, who are elected by vote or by lot out of all the citizens. Or again, the citizens meet about election to offices and about 25 scrutinies, and deliberate concerning war or alliances while other matters are administered by the magistrates, who, as far as is possible, are elected by vote. I am speaking of those magistracies in which special knowledge is required. A fourth form of democracy is when all the citizens meet to deliberate about everything, and the magistrates decide nothing, but only make the preliminary inquiries; and that is 30 the way in which the last form of democracy, corresponding, as we maintain, to the close family oligarchy and to tyranny, is at present administered. All these modes are democratic.

On the other hand, that some should deliberate about all is oligarchical. This again is a mode which, like the democratic, has many forms. When the deliberative 35 class being elected out of those who have a moderate qualification are numerous and they respect and obey the prohibitions of the law without altering it, and any- one who has the required qualification shares in the government, then, just because of this moderation, the oligarchy inclines towards polity. But when only selected individuals and not the whole people share in the deliberations of the state, then, 1298ᵇ1 although, as in the former case, they observe the law, the government is a pure oligarchy. Or, again, when those who have the power of deliberation are self- elected, and son succeeds father, and they and not the laws are supreme—the government is of necessity oligarchical. Where, again, particular persons have 5 authority in particular matters—for example, when the whole people decide about peace and war and hold scrutinies, but the magistrates regulate everything else, and they are elected by vote or by lot—there the government is an aristocracy or a constitutional government. And if some questions are decided by magistrates elected by vote, and others by magistrates elected by lot, either absolutely or out of select candidates, or elected partly by vote, partly by lot—these practices are partly characteristic of an aristocratic government, and partly of a pure constitutional 10 government.

These are the various forms of the deliberative body; they correspond to the various forms of government. And the government of each state is administered according to one or other of the principles which have been laid down. Now it is for the interest of democracy, according to the most prevalent notion of it (I am speaking of that extreme form of democracy in which the people are supreme even 15 over the laws), with a view to better deliberation to adopt the custom of oligarchies respecting courts of law. For in oligarchies the rich who are wanted to be judges are compelled to attend under pain of a fine, whereas in democracies the poor are paid to attend. And this practice of oligarchies should be adopted by democracies in their public assemblies, for they will advise better if they all deliberate together, the 20 people with the notables and the notables with the people. It is also a good plan that those who deliberate should be elected by vote or by lot in equal numbers out of the different classes; and that if the people greatly exceed in number those who have political training, pay should not be given to all, but only to as many as would

25 balance the number of the notables, or that the number in excess should be eliminated by lot. But in oligarchies either certain persons should be co-opted from the mass, or a class of officers should be appointed such as exist in some states, who are termed Probuli and guardians of the law; and the citizens should occupy
30 themselves exclusively with matters on which they have previously deliberated; for in that way the people will have a share in the deliberations of the state, but will not be able to disturb the principles of the constitution. Again, in oligarchies either the people ought to accept the measures of the government, or not to pass anything contrary to them; or, if all are allowed to share in counsel, the decision should rest
35 with the magistrates. The opposite of what is done in constitutional governments should be the rule in oligarchies; the veto of the majority should be final, their assent not final, but the proposal should be referred back to the magistrates. Whereas in constitutional governments they take the contrary course; the few have the negative, not the affirmative power; the affirmation of everything rests with the multitude.

1299ᵃ1   These, then, are our conclusions respecting the deliberative, that is, the supreme element in states.

15 · Next we will proceed to consider the distribution of offices; this, too, being a part of politics concerning which many questions arise:—What shall their
5 number be? Over what shall they preside, and what shall be their duration? Sometimes they last for six months, sometimes for less; sometimes they are annual, whilst in other cases offices are held for still longer periods. Shall they be for life or for a long term of years; or, if for a short term only, shall the same persons hold them
10 over and over again, or once only? Also about the appointment to them—from whom are they to be chosen, by whom, and how? We should first be in a position to say what are the possible varieties of them, and then we may proceed to determine which are suited to different forms of government. But what are to be included
15 under the term 'offices'? That is a question not quite so easily answered. For a political community requires many officers; and not every one who is chosen by vote or by lot is to be regarded as a ruler. In the first place there are the priests, who must be distinguished from political officers; masters of choruses and heralds, even ambassadors, are elected by vote. Some duties of superintendence again are
20 political, extending either to all the citizens in a single sphere of action, like the office of the general who superintends them when they are in the field, or to a section of them only, like the inspectorships of women or of youth. Other offices are concerned with household management, like that of the corn measurers who exist in many states and are elected officers. There are also menial offices which the rich
25 have executed by their slaves. Speaking generally, those are to be called offices to which the duties are assigned of deliberating about certain measures and of judging and commanding, especially the last; for to command is the especial duty of a magistrate. But the question is not of any importance in practice; no one has ever
30 brought into court the meaning of the word, although such problems have a speculative interest.

What kinds of offices, and how many, are necessary to the existence of a state, and which, if not necessary, yet conduce to its well-being, are much more important considerations, affecting all constitutions, but more especially small states. For in great states it is possible, and indeed necessary, that every office should have a special function; where the citizens are numerous, many may hold office. And so it happens that some offices a man holds a second time only after a long interval, and others he holds once only; and certainly every work is better done which receives the sole and not the divided attention of the worker. But in small states it is necessary to combine many offices in a few hands, since the small number of citizens does not admit of many holding office—for who will there be to succeed them? And yet small states at times require the same offices and laws as large ones; the difference is that the one want them often, the others only after long intervals. Hence there is no reason why the care of many offices should not be imposed on the same person, for they will not interfere with each other. When the population is small, offices should be like the spits which also serve to hold a lamp. We must first ascertain how many magistrates are necessary in every state, and also how many are not exactly necessary, but are nevertheless useful, and then there will be no difficulty in seeing what offices can be combined in one. We should also know over which matters several local tribunals are to have jurisdiction, and in which cases authority should be centralized: for example, should one person keep order in the market and another in some other place, or should the same person be responsible everywhere? Again, should offices be divided according to the subjects with which they deal, or according to the persons with whom they deal: I mean to say, should one person see to good order in general, or one look after the boys, another after the women, and so on? Further, under different constitutions, should the magistrates be the same or different? For example, in democracy, oligarchy, aristocracy, monarchy, should there be the same magistrates, although they are elected not out of equal or similar classes of citizens, but differently under different constitutions—in aristocracies, for example, they are chosen from the educated, in oligarchies from the wealthy, and in democracies from the free—or are there certain differences in the offices answering to them as well, and may the same be suitable to some, but different offices to others? For in some states it may be convenient that the same office should have a more extensive, in other states a narrower sphere. Special offices are peculiar to certain forms of government—for example that of Probuli, which is not a democratic office, although a council is democratic. There must be some body of men whose duty is to prepare measures for the people in order that they may not be diverted from their business; when these are few in number, the state inclines to an oligarchy: or rather the Probuli must always be few, and are therefore an oligarchical element. But when both institutions exist in a state, the Probuli are a check on the council; for the counsellor is a democratic element, but the Probuli are oligarchical. Even the power of the council disappears when democracy has taken that extreme form in which the people themselves are always meeting and deliberating about everything. This the case when the members of the assembly receive abundant pay; for they have nothing to do and are always holding

35

1299ᵇ1

5

10

15

20

25

30

35

1300ᵃ1

assemblies and deciding everything for themselves. A magistracy which controls the
5   boys or the women, or any similar office, is suited to an aristocracy rather than to a
democracy; for how can the magistrates prevent the wives of the poor from going
out of doors? Neither is it an oligarchical office; for the wives of the oligarchs are
too grand.

10   Enough of these matters. I will now inquire into appointments to offices. The
varieties depend on three terms, and the combinations of these give all possible
modes: first, who appoints? secondly, from whom? and thirdly, how? Each of these
15   three admits of two varieties. For either all the citizens, or only some, appoint.
Either the magistrates are chosen out of all or out of some who are distinguished
either by a property qualification, or by birth, or excellence, or for some special
reason, as at Megara only those were eligible who had returned from exile and
fought together against the democracy. They may be appointed either by vote or by
20   lot. Again, these several varieties may be coupled, I mean that some officers may be
elected by some, others by all, and some again out of some, and others out of all, and
some by vote and others by lot. Each variety of these terms admits of four modes.

          For either all may appoint from all by vote, or all from all by lot, or all from
some by vote, or all from some by lot. Again, if it is only some who appoint, they
25   may do so from all by vote or from all by lot or from some by vote or from some by
lot. And if from all, either by sections, as, for example, by tribes, and wards, and
phratries, until all the citizens have been gone through; or the citizens may be in all
cases eligible indiscriminately; or sometimes in one way, sometimes in the other—I
30   mean, from all by vote in some cases, by lot in others. Thus the modes that arise,
apart from the two couplings, number twelve. Of these systems two are popular,
that all should appoint from all by vote or by lot— or by both, some of the offices by
lot, others by vote. That all should not appoint at once, but should appoint from all
35   or from some either by lot or by vote or by both, or appoint to some offices from all
and to others from some ('by both' meaning to some offices by lot, to others by
vote), is characteristic of a polity. [And that some should appoint from all, to some
offices by vote, to others by lot or by both—some by lot, others by vote—is
oligarchical; and it is more oligarchical to appoint by both. And to appoint to some
offices from all, to others from some, is characteristic of a polity with a leaning
1300ᵇ1   towards aristocracy— or to appoint some by vote, others by lot.]⁵ That some should
appoint from some is oligarchical— even that some should appoint from some by
lot (and if this does not actually occur, it is none the less oligarchical in character),
or that some should appoint from some by both. That some should appoint from all,
and that sometimes all should appoint from some, by vote, is aristocratic.

5   These are the different modes of constituting magistrates, and these correspond to different forms of government:—which are proper to which, or how they
ought to be established, will be evident when we determine the nature of their
10   powers. By powers I mean such powers as a magistrate exercises over the revenue or
in defence of the country; for there are various kinds of power: the power of the

---

⁵Excised by Dreizehnter. The text is uncertain throughout this paragraph.

general, for example, is not the same as that which regulates contracts in the market.

Of the three parts of government the judicial remains to be considered, and this we shall divide on the same principle. There are three points on which the varieties of law-courts depend: the persons from whom they are appointed, the matters with which they are concerned, and the manner of their appointment. I mean, are the judges taken from all, or from some only? how many kinds of law-courts are there? are the judges chosen by vote or by lot?

First, let me determine how many kinds of law-courts there are. They are eight in number: one is the court of audits or scrutinies; a second takes cognizance of ordinary offences against the state; a third is concerned with treason against the constitution; the fourth determines disputes respecting penalties, whether raised by magistrates or by private persons; the fifth decides the more important civil cases; the sixth tries cases of homicide, which are of various kinds, premeditated, involuntary, and cases in which the guilt is confessed but the justice is disputed; and there may be a fourth court in which murderers who have fled from justice are tried after their return, such as the Court of Phreatto is said to be at Athens. But cases of this sort rarely happen at all even in large cities. The different kinds of homicide may be tried either by the same or by different courts. There are courts for strangers:— of these there are two subdivisions, one for the settlement of their disputes with one another, the other for the settlement of disputes between them and the citizens. And besides all these there must be courts for small suits about sums of a drachma up to five drachmas, or a little more, which have to be determined, but do not require many judges.

Nothing more need be said of these small suits, nor of the courts for homicide and for strangers:—I would rather speak of political cases, which, when misManaged, create division and disturbances in constitutions.

Now if all the citizens judge, in all the different cases which I have distinguished, they may be appointed by vote or by lot, or sometimes by lot and sometimes by vote. Or when a single class of causes are tried, the judges who decide them may be appointed, some by vote, and some by lot. These then are the four modes of appointing judges from the whole people, and there will be likewise four modes, if they are elected from a part only; for they may be appointed from some by vote and judge in all causes; or they may be appointed from some by lot and judge in all causes; or they may be elected in some cases by vote, and in some cases taken by lot, or some courts, even when judging the same causes, may be composed of members some appointed by vote and some by lot. These modes, then, as was said, answer to those previously mentioned.

Once more, the modes of appointment may be combined; I mean, that some may be chosen out of the whole people, others out of some, some out of both; for example, the same tribunal may be composed of some who were elected out of all, and of others who were elected out of some, either by vote or by lot or by both.

In how many forms law-courts can be established has now been considered. The first form, viz. that in which the judges are taken from all the citizens, and in

which all causes are tried, is democratic; the second, which is composed of a few only who try all causes, oligarchical; the third, in which some courts are taken from
15   all classes, and some from certain classes only, aristocratic and constitutional.

BOOK V

1 · The design which we proposed to ourselves is now nearly completed. Next
20   in order follow the causes of revolution in states, how many, and of what nature they are; what modes of destruction apply to particular states, and out of what, and into what they mostly change; also what are the modes of preservation in states generally, or in a particular state, and by what means each state may be best preserved: these questions remain to be considered.
25   In the first place we must assume as our starting-point that in the many forms of government which have sprung up there has always been an acknowledgement of justice and proportionate equality, although mankind fail in attaining them, as indeed I have already explained. Democracy, for example, arises out of the notion that those who are equal in any respect are equal in all respects; because men are
30   equally free, they claim to be absolutely equal. Oligarchy is based on the notion that those who are unequal in one respect are in all respects unequal; being unequal, that is, in property, they suppose themselves to be unequal absolutely. The democrats think that as they are equal they ought to be equal in all things; while the oligarchs,
35   under the idea that they are unequal, claim too much, which is one form of inequality. All these forms of government have a kind of justice, but, tried by an absolute standard, they are faulty; and, therefore, both parties, whenever their share in the government does not accord with their preconceived ideas, stir up revolution. Those who excel in excellence have the best right of all to rebel (for they
1301^{b}1   alone can with reason be deemed absolutely unequal), but then they are of all men the least inclined to do so. There is also a superiority which is claimed by men of rank; for they are thought noble because they spring from wealthy and excellent
5   ancestors. Here then, so to speak, are opened the very springs and fountains of revolution; and hence arise two sorts of changes in governments; the one affecting the constitution, when men seek to change from an existing form into some other, for example, from democracy into oligarchy, and from oligarchy into democracy, or
10   from either of them into constitutional government or aristocracy, and conversely; the other not affecting the constitution, when, without disturbing the form of government, whether oligarchy, or monarchy, or any other, they try to get the administration into their own hands. Further, there is a question of degree; an
15   oligarchy, for example, may become more or less oligarchical, and a democracy more or less democratic; and in like manner the characteristics of the other forms of government may be more or less strictly maintained. Or the revolution may be directed against a portion of the constitution only, e.g., the establishment or overthrow of a particular office: as at Sparta it is said that Lysander attempted to

overthrow the monarchy, and king Pausanias, the ephoralty. At Epidamnus, too,   20
the change was partial. For instead of phylarchs or heads of tribes, a council was
appointed; but to this day the magistrates are the only members of the ruling class
who are compelled to go to the Heliaea when an election takes place, and the office   25
of the single archon was another oligarchical feature. Everywhere inequality is a
cause of revolution, but an inequality in which there is no proportion—for instance,
a perpetual monarchy among equals; and always it is the desire for equality which
rises in rebellion.

Now equality is of two kinds, numerical and proportional; by the first I mean   30
sameness or equality in number or size; by the second, equality of ratios. For
example, the excess of three over two is numerically equal to the excess of two over
one; whereas four exceeds two in the same ratio in which two exceeds one, for two is
the same part of four that one is of two, namely, the half. As I was saying before,   35
men agree that justice in the abstract is proportion, but they differ in that some
think that if they are equal in any respect they are equal absolutely, others that if
they are unequal in any respect they should be unequal in all. Hence there are two
principal forms of government, democracy and oligarchy; for good birth and
excellence are rare, but wealth and numbers are more common. In what city shall   1302ᵃ1
we find a hundred persons of good birth and of excellence? whereas the rich
everywhere abound. That a state should be ordered, simply and wholly, according to
either kind of equality, is not a good thing; the proof is the fact that such forms of
government never last. They are originally based on a mistake, and, as they begin   5
badly, cannot fail to end badly. The inference is that both kinds of equality should
be employed; numerical in some cases, and proportionate in others.

Still democracy appears to be safer and less liable to revolution than oligarchy.
For in oligarchies there is the double danger of the oligarchs falling out among   10
themselves and also with the people; but in democracies there is only the danger of a
quarrel with the oligarchs. No dissension worth mentioning arises among the people
themselves. And we may further remark that a government which is composed of
the middle class more nearly approximates to democracy than to oligarchy, and is
the safest of the imperfect forms of government.   15

2 · In considering how dissensions and political revolutions arise, we must
first of all ascertain the beginnings and causes of them which affect constitutions
generally. They may be said to be three in number; and we have now to give an
outline of each. We want to know what is the state of mind and what are the motives 20
of those who make them and whence arise political disturbances and quarrels. The
universal and chief cause of this revolutionary feeling has been already mentioned;
viz. the desire for equality, when men think that they are equal to others who have   25
more than themselves; or, again, the desire for inequality and superiority, when
conceiving themselves to be superior they think that they have not more but the
same or less than their inferiors; pretensions which may or may not be just. Inferiors
revolt in order that they may be equal, and equals that they may be superior. Such is 30
the state of mind which creates revolutions. The motives for making them are the

desire for gain and honour, or the fear of dishonour and loss; the authors of them want to divert punishment or dishonour from themselves or their friends. The causes and reasons of revolutions, whereby men are themselves affected in the way
35   described, and about the things which I have mentioned, viewed in one way may be regarded as seven, and in another as more than seven. Two of them have been already noticed; but they act in a different manner, for men are excited against one another by the love of gain and honour—not, as in the case which I have just
1302ᵇ1   supposed, in order to obtain them for themselves, but at seeing others, justly or unjustly, monopolising them. Other causes are insolence, fear, excessive predominance, contempt, disproportionate increase in some part of the state; causes of another sort are election intrigues, carelessness, neglect about trifles, dissimilarity of elements.

5   3 . What share insolence and avarice have in creating revolutions, and how they work, is plain enough. When the magistrates are insolent and grasping they conspire against one another and also against the constitution from which they derive their power, making their gains either at the expense of individuals or of the
10   public. It is evident, again, what an influence honour exerts and how it is a cause of revolution. Men who are themselves dishonoured and who see others obtaining honours rise in rebellion; the honour or dishonour when undeserved is unjust; and
15   just when awarded according to merit. Again, superiority is a cause of revolution when one or more persons have a power which is too much for the state and the power of the government; this is a condition of affairs out of which there tends to arise a monarchy, or a family oligarchy. And therefore, in some places, as at Athens and Argos, they have recourse to ostracism. But how much better to provide from
20   the first that there should be no such pre-eminent individuals instead of letting them come into existence and then finding a remedy.
         Another cause of revolution is fear. Either men have committed wrong, and are afraid of punishment, or they are expecting to suffer wrong and are desirous of anticipating their enemy. Thus at Rhodes the notables conspired against the people
25   through fear of the suits that were brought against them. Contempt is also a cause of insurrection and revolution; for example, in oligarchies—when those who have no share in the state are the majority, they revolt, because they think that they are the stronger. Or, again, in democracies, the rich despise the disorder and anarchy of the
30   state; at Thebes, for example, where, after the battle of Oenophyta, the bad administration of the democracy led to its ruin. At Megara the fall of the democracy was due to a defeat occasioned by disorder and anarchy. And at Syracuse the democracy aroused contempt before the tyranny of Gelo arose; at Rhodes, before the insurrection.
         Political revolutions also spring from a disproportionate increase in any part of
35   the state. For as a body is made up of many members, and every member ought to grow in proportion so that symmetry may be preserved, but it loses its nature if the foot is four cubits long and the rest of the body two spans; and, should the abnormal increase be one of quality as well as of quantity, it may even take the form of

another animal: even so a state has many parts, of which some one may often grow   1303ª1
imperceptibly; for example, the number of poor in democracies and in constitutional states. And this disproportion may sometimes happen by an accident, as at
Tarentum, from a defeat in which many of the notables were slain in a battle with
the Iapygians just after the Persian War, the constitutional government in   5
consequence becoming a democracy; or as was the case at Argos, where the Argives,
after their army had been cut to pieces on the seventh day of the month by
Cleomenes the Lacedaemonian, were compelled to admit to citizenship some of
their serfs; and at Athens, when, after frequent defeats of their infantry at the time
of the Peloponnesian War, the notables were reduced in number, because the   10
soldiers had to be taken from the roll of citizens. Revolutions arise from this cause
as well, in democracies as in other forms of government, but not to so great an
extent. When the rich grow numerous or properties increase, the form of government changes into an oligarchy or a government of families. Forms of government
also change—sometimes even without revolution, owing to election contests, as at
Heraea (where, instead of electing their magistrates, they took them by lot, because   15
the electors were in the habit of choosing their own partisans); or owing to
carelessness, when disloyal persons are allowed to find their way into the highest
offices, as at Oreum, where, upon the accession of Heracleodorus to office, the
oligarchy was overthrown, and changed by him into a constitutional and democratic   20
government.

Again, the revolution may be facilitated by the slightness of the change; I
mean that a great change may sometimes slip into the constitution through neglect
of a small matter; at Ambracia, for instance, the qualification for office, small at
first, was eventually reduced to nothing. For the Ambraciots thought that a small
qualification was much the same as none at all.

Another cause of revolution is difference of races which do not at once acquire   25
a common spirit; for a state is not the growth of a day, any more than it grows out of
a multitude brought together by accident. Hence the reception of strangers in
colonies, either at the time of their foundation or afterwards, has generally
produced revolution; for example, the Achaeans who joined the Troezenians in the
foundation of Sybaris, becoming later the more numerous, expelled them; hence the   30
curse fell upon Sybaris. At Thurii the Sybarites quarrelled with their fellow-
colonists; thinking that the land belonged to them, they wanted too much of it and
were driven out. At Byzantium the new colonists were detected in a conspiracy, and
were expelled by force of arms; the people of Antissa, who had received the Chian
exiles, fought with them, and drove them out; and the Zancleans, after having   35
received the Samians, were driven by them out of their own city. The citizens of
Apollonia on the Euxine, after the introduction of a fresh body of colonists, had a
revolution; the Syracusans, after the expulsion of their tyrants, having admitted
strangers and mercenaries to the rights of citizenship, quarrelled and came to   1303ᵇ1
blows; the people of Amphipolis, having received Chalcidian colonists, were nearly
all expelled by them.

Now, in oligarchies the masses make revolution under the idea that they are

5 unjustly treated, because, as I said before, they are equals, and have not an equal
share, and in democracies the notables revolt, because they are not equals, and yet
have only an equal share.

Again, the situation of cities is a cause of revolution when the country is not
naturally adapted to preserve the unity of the state. For example, the Chytians at
10 Clazomenae did not agree with the people of the island; and the people of Colophon
quarrelled with the Notians; at Athens, too, the inhabitants of the Piraeus are more
democratic than those who live in the city. For just as in war the impediment of a
ditch, however small, may break a regiment, so every cause of difference makes a
15 breach in a city. The greatest opposition is confessedly that of excellence and
badness; next comes that of wealth and poverty; and there are other antagonistic
elements, greater or less, of which one is this difference of place.

4 · In revolutions the occasions may be trifling, but great interests are at
stake. Even trifles are most important when they concern the rulers, as was the case
20 of old at Syracuse; for the Syracusan constitution was once changed by a
love-quarrel of two young men, who were in the government. The story is that while
one of them was away from home his beloved was gained over by his companion,
25 and he to revenge himself seduced the other's wife. They then drew the members of
the ruling class into their quarrel and so split all the people into portions. We learn
from this story that we should be on our guard against the beginnings of such evils,
and should put an end to the quarrels of chiefs and mighty men. The mistake lies in
the beginning—as the proverb says—'Well begun is half done'; so an error at the
30 beginning, though quite small, bears the same ratio to the errors in the other parts.
In general, when the notables quarrel, the whole city is involved, as happened in
Hestiaea after the Persian War. The occasion was the division of an inheritance;
one of two brothers refused to give an account of their father's property and the
35 treasure which he had found: so the poorer of the two quarrelled with him and
enlisted in his cause the popular party, the other, who was very rich, the wealthy
classes.

At Delphi, again, a quarrel about a marriage was the beginning of all the
1304ᵃ1 troubles which followed. In this case the bridegroom, fancying some occurrence to
be of evil omen, came to the bride, and went away without taking her. Whereupon
her relations, thinking that they were insulted by him, put some of the sacred
treasure among his offerings while he was sacrificing, and then slew him,
pretending that he had been robbing the temple. At Mytilene, too, a dispute about
5 heiresses was the beginning of many misfortunes, and led to the war with the
Athenians in which Paches took their city. A wealthy citizen, named Timophanes,
left two daughters; Dexander, another citizen, wanted to obtain them for his sons;
but he was rejected in his suit, whereupon he stirred up a revolution, and instigated
the Athenians (of whom he was representative) to interfere. A similar quarrel about
10 an heiress arose at Phocis between Mnaseas the father of Mnason, and Euthycrates
the father of Onomarchus; this was the beginning of the Sacred War. A marriage-
quarrel was also the cause of a change in the government of Epidamnus. A certain
man betrothed his daughter to a person whose father, having been made a

magistrate, fined the father of the girl, and the latter, stung by the insult, conspired   15
with the unenfranchised classes to overthrow the state.

Governments also change into oligarchy or into democracy or into a constitutional government because the magistrates, or some other section of the state,
increase in power or renown. Thus at Athens the reputation gained by the court of
the Areopagus, in the Persian War, seemed to tighten the reins of government. On   20
the other hand, the victory of Salamis, which was gained by the common people who
served in the fleet, and won for the Athenians the empire due to command of the
sea, strengthened the democracy. At Argos, the notables, having distinguished   25
themselves against the Lacedaemonians in the battle of Mantinea, attempted to put
down the democracy. At Syracuse, the people, having been the chief authors of the
victory in the war with the Athenians, changed the constitutional government into
democracy. At Chalcis, the people, uniting with the notables, killed Phoxus the   30
tyrant, and then seized the government. At Ambracia, the people, in like manner,
having joined with the conspirators in expelling the tyrant Periander, transferred
the government to themselves. And generally, it should be remembered that those
who have secured power to the state, whether private citizens, or magistrates, or   35
tribes, or any other part or section of the state, are apt to cause revolutions. For
either envy of their greatness draws others into rebellion, or they themselves, in
their pride of superiority, are unwilling to remain on a level with others.

Revolutions also break out when opposite parties, e.g. the rich and the people,   1304^{b}1
are equally balanced, and there is little or no middle class; for, if either party were
manifestly superior, the other would not risk an attack upon them. And for this
reason, those who are eminent in excellence usually do not stir up insurrections,
being always a minority. Such in general are the beginnings and causes of the   5
disturbances and revolutions to which every form of government is liable.

Revolutions are effected in two ways, by force and by fraud. Force may be
applied either at the time of making the revolution or afterwards. Fraud, again, is of
two kinds; for sometimes the citizens are deceived into acquiescing in a change of   10
government, and afterwards they are held in subjection against their will. This was
what happened in the case of the Four Hundred, who deceived the people by telling
them that the king would provide money for the war against the Lacedaemonians,
and, having cheated the people, still endeavoured to retain the government. In other   15
cases the people are persuaded at first, and afterwards, by a repetition of the
persuasion, their goodwill and allegiance are retained. The revolutions which affect
constitutions generally spring from the above-mentioned causes.

5 · And now, taking each constitution separately, we must see what follows
from the principles already laid down.   20

Revolutions in democracies are generally caused by the intemperance of
demagogues, who either in their private capacity lay information against rich men
until they compel them to combine (for a common danger unites even the bitterest
enemies), or coming forward in public stir up the people against them. The truth of
this remark is proved by a variety of examples. At Cos the democracy was   25
overthrown because wicked demagogues arose, and the notables combined. At

Rhodes the demagogues not only provided pay for the multitude, but prevented them from making good to the trierarchs the sums which had been expended by them; and they, in consequence of the suits which were brought against them, were
30 compelled to combine and put down the democracy. The democracy at Heraclea was overthrown shortly after the foundation of the colony by the injustice of the demagogues, which drove out the notables, who came back in a body and put an end
35 to the democracy. Much in the same manner the democracy at Megara was overturned; there the demagogues drove out many of the notables in order that they might be able to confiscate their property. At length the exiles, becoming numerous, returned, and, engaging and defeating the people, established the oligarchy. The same thing happened with the democracy of Cyme, which was overthrown by
1305ª1 Thrasymachus. And we may observe that in most states the changes have been of this character. For sometimes the demagogues, in order to curry favour with the people, wrong the notables and so force them to combine—either they make a
5 division of their property, or diminish their incomes by the imposition of public services, and sometimes they bring accusations against the rich so that they may have their wealth to confiscate.

Of old, the demagogue was also a general, and then democracies changed into tyrannies. Most of the ancient tyrants were originally demagogues. They are not so
10 now, but they were then; and the reason is that they were generals and not orators, for oratory had not yet come into fashion. Whereas in our day, when the art of rhetoric has made such progress, the orators lead the people, but their ignorance of military matters prevents them from usurping power; at any rate instances to the
15 contrary are few and slight. Tyrannies were more common formerly than now, for this reason also, that great power was placed in the hands of individuals; thus a tyranny arose at Miletus out of the office of the Prytanis, who had supreme authority in many important matters. Moreover, in those days, when cities were not
20 large, the people dwelt in the fields, busy at their work; and their chiefs, if they possessed any military talent, seized the opportunity, and winning the confidence of the masses by professing their hatred of the wealthy, they succeeded in obtaining the tyranny. Thus at Athens Peisistratus led a faction against the men of the plain,
25 and Theagenes at Megara slaughtered the cattle of the wealthy, which he found by the river side, where they had put them to graze. Dionysius, again, was thought worthy of the tyranny because he denounced Daphnaeus and the rich; his enmity to the notables won for him the confidence of the people. Changes also take place from the ancient to the latest form of democracy; for where there is a popular election of
30 the magistrates and no property qualification, the aspirants for office get hold of the people, and contrive at last even to set them above the laws. A more or less complete cure for this state of things is for the separate tribes, and not the whole people, to elect the magistrates.
35   These are the principal causes of revolutions in democracies.

6 · There are two patent causes of revolutions in oligarchies: first, when the oligarchs oppress the people, for then anybody is good enough to be their champion,

especially if he be himself a member of the oligarchy, as Lygdamis at Naxos, who afterwards came to be tyrant. But revolutions which commence outside the 1305^{b}1 governing class may be further subdivided. Sometimes, when the government is very exclusive, the revolution is brought about by persons of the wealthy class who are excluded, as happened at Massalia and Istros and Heraclea, and other cities. 5 Those who had no share in the government created a disturbance, until first the elder brothers, and then the younger, were admitted; for in some places father and son, in others, elder and younger brothers, do not hold office together. At Massalia 10 the oligarchy became more like a constitutional government, but at Istros ended in a democracy, and at Heraclea was enlarged to 600. At Cnidos, again, the oligarchy underwent a considerable change. For the notables fell out among themselves, because only a few shared in the government; there existed among them the rule already mentioned, that father and son could not hold office together, and, if there were several brothers, only the eldest was admitted. The people took advantage of 15 the quarrel, and choosing one of the notables to be their leader, attacked and conquered the oligarchs, who were divided, and division is always a source of weakness. The city of Erythrae, too, in old times was ruled, and ruled well, by the 20 Basilidae, but the people took offence at the narrowness of the oligarchy and changed the constitution.

Of internal causes of revolutions in oligarchies one is the personal rivalry of the oligarchs, which leads them to play the demagogue. Now, the oligarchical demagogue is of two sorts: either he practises upon the oligarchs themselves (for, although the oligarchy are quite a small number, there may be a demagogue among 25 them, as at Athens Charicles' party won power by courting the Thirty, that of Phrynichus by courting the Four Hundred); or the oligarchs may play the demagogue with the people. This was the case at Larissa, where the guardians of the citizens endeavoured to gain over the people because they were elected by them; 30 and such is the fate of all oligarchies in which the magistrates are elected, as at Abydos, not by the class in which they belong, but by the heavy-armed or by the people, although they may be required to have a high qualification, or to be members of a political club; or, again, where the law-courts are composed of persons outside the government, the oligarchs flatter the people in order to obtain a decision in their own favour, and so they change the constitution; this happened at Heraclea 35 in Pontus. Again, oligarchies change whenever any attempt is made to narrow them; for then those who desire equal rights are compelled to call in the people. Changes in the oligarchy also occur when the oligarchs waste their private property by extravagant living; for then they want to innovate, and either try to make themselves tyrants, or install some one else in the tyranny, as Hipparinus did 1306^{a}1 Dionysius at Syracuse, and as at Amphipolis a man named Cleotimus introduced Chalcidian colonists, and when they arrived, stirred them up against the rich. For a like reason in Aegina the person who carried on the negotiation with Chares endeavoured to revolutionize the state. Sometimes a party among the oligarchs try 5 directly to create a political change; sometimes they rob the treasury, and then either the thieves or, as happened at Apollonia in Pontus, those who resist them in

10   their thieving quarrel with the rulers. But an oligarchy which is at unity with itself is not easily destroyed from within; of this we may see an example at Pharsalus, for there, although the rulers are few in number, they govern a large city, because they have a good understanding among themselves.

Oligarchies, again, are overthrown when another oligarchy is created within 15   the original one, that is to say, when the whole governing body is small and yet they do not all share in the highest offices. Thus at Elis the governing body was a small senate; and very few ever found their way into it, because the senators were only ninety in number, and were elected for life and out of certain families in a manner 20   similar to the Lacedaemonian elders. Oligarchy is liable to revolutions alike in war and in peace; in war because, not being able to trust the people, the oligarchs are compelled to hire mercenaries, and the general who is in command of them often ends in becoming a tyrant, as Timophanes did at Corinth; or if there are more generals than one they make themselves into a junta. Sometimes the oligarchs, 25   fearing this danger, give the people a share in the government because their services are necessary to them. And in time of peace, from mutual distrust, the two parties hand over the defence of the state to the army and to an arbiter between the two factions, who often ends the master of both. This happened at Larissa when Simos 30   the Aleuad had the government, and at Abydos in the days of Iphiades and the political clubs. Revolutions also arise out of marriages or lawsuits which lead to the overthrow of one party among the oligarchs by another. Of quarrels about 35   marriages I have already mentioned some instances; another occurred at Eretria, where Diagoras overturned the oligarchy of the knights because he had been wronged about a marriage. A revolution at Heraclea, and another at Thebes, both arose out of decisions of law-courts upon a charge of adultery; in both cases the punishment was just, but executed in the spirit of party, at Heraclea upon Eurytion, 1306ᵇ1   and at Thebes upon Archias; for their enemies were jealous of them and so had them pilloried in the agora. Many oligarchies have been destroyed by some members of the ruling class taking offence at their excessive despotism; for 5   example, the oligarchy at Cnidus and at Chios.

Changes of constitutional governments, and also of oligarchies which limit the office of counsellor, judge, or other magistrate to persons having a certain money qualification, often occur by accident. The qualification may have been originally 10   fixed according to the circumstances of the time, in such a manner as to include in an oligarchy a few only, or in a constitutional government the middle class. But after a time of prosperity, whether arising from peace or some other good fortune, the same property becomes many times as valuable, and then everybody partici- 15   pates in every office; this happens sometimes gradually and insensibly, and sometimes quickly. These are the causes of changes and revolutions in oligarchies.

We must remark generally, both of democracies and oligarchies, that they sometimes change, not into the opposite forms of government, but only into another 20   variety of the same class; I mean to say, from those forms of democracy and oligarchy which are regulated by law into those which are arbitrary, and converse- ly.

7 · In aristocracies revolutions are stirred up when a few only share in the honours of the state; a cause which has been already shown to affect oligarchies; for an aristocracy is a sort of oligarchy, and, like an oligarchy, is the government of a 25 few, although few not for the same reason; hence the two are often confused. And revolutions will be most likely to happen, and must happen, when the mass of the people are of the high-spirited kind, and have a notion that they are as good as their rulers. Thus at Lacedaemon the so-called Partheniae, who were the sons of the 30 Spartan peers, attempted a revolution, and, being detected, were sent away to colonize Tarentum. Again, revolutions occur when great men who are at least of equal excellence are denied honours by those higher in office, as Lysander was by the kings of Sparta; or, when a brave man is excluded from the honours of the state, like Cinadon, who conspired against the Spartans in the reign of Agesilaus; or, 35 again, when some are very poor and others very rich, a state of society which is most often the result of war, as at Lacedaemon in the days of the Messenian War; this is proved from the poem of Tyrtaeus, entitled 'Good Order'; for he speaks of certain 1307ª1 citizens who were ruined by the war and wanted to have a redistribution of the land. Again, revolutions arise when an individual who is great, and might be greater, wants to rule alone, as, at Lacedaemon, Pausanias, who was general in the Persian War, or like Hanno at Carthage. 5

Constitutional governments and aristocracies are commonly overthrown owing to some deviation from justice in the constitution itself; the cause of the downfall is, in the former, the ill-mingling of the two elements democracy and oligarchy; in the latter, of the three elements, democracy, oligarchy, and excellence, but especially democracy and oligarchy. For to combine these is the endeavour of constitutional 10 governments; and most of the so-called aristocracies have a like aim, but differ from polities in the mode of combination; hence some of them are more and some less permanent. Those which incline more to oligarchy are called aristocracies, and 15 those which incline to democracy constitutional governments. And therefore the latter are the safer of the two; for the greater the number, the greater the strength, and when men are equal they are contented. But the rich, if the constitution gives them power, are apt to be insolent and avaricious; and, in general, whichever way 20 the constitution inclines, in that direction it changes as either party gains strength, a constitutional government becoming a democracy, an aristocracy an oligarchy. But the process may be reversed, and aristocracy may change into democracy. This happens when the poor, under the idea that they are being wronged, force the 25 constitution to take an opposite form. In like manner constitutional governments change into oligarchies. The only stable principle of government is equality according to merit, and for every man to enjoy his own.

What I have just mentioned actually happened at Thurii, where the qualification for office, at first high, was therefore reduced, and the magistrates increased in number. The notables had previously acquired the whole of the land contrary to 30 law; for the government tended to oligarchy, and they were able to encroach. . . .[1]

---

[1] Dreizehnter marks a lacuna.

But the people, who had been trained by war, soon got the better of the guards kept by the oligarchs, until those who had too much gave up their land.

Again, since all aristocratic governments incline to oligarchy, the notables are apt to be grasping; thus at Lacedaemon, where property tends to pass into few hands, the notables can do too much as they like, and are allowed to marry whom they please. The city of Locri was ruined by a marriage connexion with Dionysius, but such a thing could never have happened in a democracy, or in a well-balanced aristocracy.

I have already remarked that in all states revolutions are occasioned by trifles. In aristocracies, above all, they are of a gradual and imperceptible nature. The citizens begin by giving up some part of the constitution, and so with greater ease the government change something else which is a little more important, until they have undermined the whole fabric of the state. At Thurii there was a law that generals should only be re-elected after an interval of five years, and some young men who were popular with the soldiers of the guard for their military prowess, despising the magistrates and thinking that they would easily gain their purpose, wanted to abolish this law and allow their generals to hold perpetual commands; for they well knew that the people would be glad enough to elect them. Whereupon the magistrates who had charge of these matters, and who are called councillors, at first determined to resist, but they afterwards consented, thinking that, if only this one law was changed, no further inroad would be made on the constitution. But other changes soon followed which they in vain attempted to oppose; and the state passed into the hands of the revolutionists, who established a dynastic oligarchy.

All constitutions are overthrown either from within or from without; the latter, when there is some government close at hand having an opposite interest, or at a distance, but powerful. This was exemplified by the Athenians and the Lacedaemonians; the Athenians everywhere put down the oligarchies, and the Lacedaemonians the democracies.

I have now explained what are the chief causes of revolutions and dissensions in states.

8 · We have next to consider what means there are of preserving constitutions in general, and in particular cases. In the first place it is evident that if we know the causes which destroy constitutions, we also know the causes which preserve them; for opposites produce opposites, and destruction is the opposite of preservation.

In all well-balanced governments there is nothing which should be more jealously maintained than the spirit of obedience to law, more especially in small matters; for transgression creeps in unperceived and at last ruins the state, just as the constant recurrence of small expenses in time eats up a fortune. The expense does not take place all at once, and therefore is not observed; the mind is deceived, as in the fallacy which says that 'if each part is little, then the whole is little'. And this is true in one way, but not in another, for the whole and the all are not little, although they are made up of littles.

In the first place, then, men should guard against the beginning of change, and in the second place they should not rely upon the political devices of which I have already spoken, invented only to deceive the people, for they are proved by experience to be useless. Further, we note that oligarchies as well as aristocracies may last, not from any inherent stability in such forms of government, but because the rulers are on good terms both with the unenfranchised and with the governing classes, not maltreating any who are excluded from the government, but introducing into it the leading spirits among them. They should never wrong the ambitious in a matter of honour, or the common people in a matter of money; and they should treat one another and their fellow-citizens in a spirit of equality. The equality which the friends of democracy seek to establish for the multitude is not only just but likewise expedient among equals. Hence, if the governing class are numerous, many democratic institutions are useful; for example, the restriction of the tenure of offices to six months, so that all those who are of equal rank may share in them. Indeed, a group of equals is a kind of democracy, and therefore demagogues are very likely to arise among them, as I have already remarked. The short tenure of office prevents oligarchies and aristocracies from falling into the hands of families; it is not easy for a person to do any great harm when his tenure of office is short, whereas long possession begets tyranny in oligarchies and democracies. For the aspirants to tyranny are either the principal men of the state, who in democracies are demagogues and in oligarchies members of ruling houses, or those who hold great offices, and have a long tenure of them.

Constitutions are preserved when their destroyers are at a distance, and sometimes also because they are near, for the fear of them makes the government keep in hand the constitution. Wherefore the ruler who has a care of the constitution should invent terrors, and bring distant dangers near, in order that the citizens may be on their guard, and, like sentinels in a night-watch, never relax their attention. He should endeavour too by help of the laws to control the contentions and quarrels of the notables, and to prevent those who have not hitherto taken part in them from catching the spirit of contention. No ordinary man can discern the beginning of evil, but only the true statesman.

As to the change produced in oligarchies and constitutional governments by the alternation of the qualification, when this arises, not out of any variation in the qualification but only out of the increase of money, it is well to compare the new valuation of property with that of past years, annually in those cities in which the census is taken annually, and in larger cities every third or fifth year. If the whole is many times greater or many times less than when the ratings recognized by the constitution were fixed, there should be power given by law to raise or lower the qualification as the amount is greater or less. Where this is not done a constitutional government passes into an oligarchy, and an oligarchy is narrowed to a rule of families; or in the opposite case constitutional government becomes democracy, and oligarchy either constitutional government or democracy.

It is a principle common to democracy, oligarchy, and every other form of government not to allow the disproportionate increase of any citizen, but to give

moderate honour for a long time rather than great honour for a short time. For men
are easily spoilt; not every one can bear prosperity. But if this rule is not observed, at
any rate the honours which are given all at once should be taken away by degrees
and not all at once. Especially should the laws provide against any one having too
much power, whether derived from friends or money; if he has, he should be sent
clean out of the country. And since innovations creep in through the private life of
individuals also, there ought to be a magistracy which will have an eye to those
whose life is not in harmony with the government, whether oligarchy or democracy
or any other. And for a like reason an increase of prosperity in any part of the state
should be carefully watched. The proper remedy for this evil is always to give the
management of affairs and offices of state to opposite elements; such opposites are
the good and the many, or the rich and the poor. Another way is to combine the poor
and the rich in one body, or to increase the middle class: thus an end will be put to
the revolutions which arise from inequality.

But above all every state should be so administered and so regulated by law
that its magistrates cannot possibly make money. In oligarchies special precautions
should be used against this evil. For the people do not take any great offence at
being kept out of the government—indeed they are rather pleased than otherwise at
having leisure for their private business—but what irritates them is to think that
their rulers are stealing the public money; then they are doubly annoyed; for they
lose both honour and profit. If office brought no profit, then and then only could
democracy and aristocracy be combined; for both notables and people might have
their wishes gratified. All would be able to hold office, which is the aim of
democracy, and the notables would be magistrates, which is the aim of aristocracy.
And this result may be accomplished when there is no possibility of making money
out of the offices; for the poor will not want to have them when there is nothing to be
gained from them—they would rather be attending to their own concerns; and the
rich, who do not want money from the public treasury, will be able to take them; and
so the poor will keep to their work and grow rich, and the notables will not be
governed by the lower class. In order to avoid peculation of the public money, the
transfer of the revenue should be made at a general assembly of the citizens, and
duplicates of the accounts deposited with the different brotherhoods, companies,
and tribes. And honours should be given by law to magistrates who have the
reputation of ruling without gain. In democracies the rich should be spared; not only
should their property not be divided, but their incomes also, which in some states
are taken from them imperceptibly, should be protected. It is a good thing to
prevent the wealthy citizens, even if they are willing, from undertaking expensive
and useless public services, such as the giving of choruses, torch-races, and the like.
In an oligarchy, on the other hand, great care should be taken of the poor, and
lucrative offices should go to them; if any of the wealthy classes insult them, the
offender should be punished more severely than if he had wronged one of his own
class. Provision should be made that estates pass by inheritance and not by gift, and
no person should have more than one inheritance; for in this way properties will be
equalized, and more of the poor rise to wealth. It is also expedient both in a

democracy and in an oligarchy to assign to those who have less share in the government (i.e. to the rich in a democracy and to the poor in an oligarchy) an equality or preference in all but the principal offices of state. The latter should be   30
entrusted chiefly or only to members of the governing class.

9 . There are three qualifications required in those who have to fill the highest offices—first of all, loyalty to the established constitution; then the greatest   35
administrative capacity; and excellence and justice of the kind proper to each form of government; for, if what is just is not the same in all governments, the quality of justice must also differ. There may be a doubt, however, when all these qualities do not meet in the same person; suppose, for example, a good general is a bad man and   1309^{b}1
not a friend to the constitution, and another man is loyal and just, which should we choose? In making the election ought we not to consider two points? what qualities are common, and what are rare. Thus in the choice of a general, we should regard his experience rather than his excellence; for few have military experience, but   5
many have excellence. In any office of trust or stewardship, on the other hand, the opposite rule should be observed; for more excellence than ordinary is required in the holder of such an office, but the necessary knowledge is of a sort which all men possess.

It may, however, be asked what a man wants with excellence if he has   10
political ability and is loyal, since these two qualities alone will make him do what is for the public interest. But may not men have both of them and yet be deficient in self-control?—If, knowing and loving their own interests, they do not always attend to them, may they not be equally negligent of the interests of the public?

Speaking generally, we may say that whatever legal enactments are held to be for the interest of various constitutions, all these preserve them. And the great   15
preserving principle is the one which has been repeatedly mentioned—to have a care that the loyal citizens should be stronger than the disloyal. Neither should we forget the mean, which at the present day is lost sight of in perverted forms of government; for many practices which appear to be democratic are the ruin of   20
democracies, and many which appear to be oligarchical are the ruin of oligarchies. Those who think that all excellence is to be found in their own party principles push matters to extremes; they do not consider that disproportion destroys a state. A nose which varies from the ideal of straightness to a hook or snub may still be of good shape and agreeable to the eye; but if the excess is very great, all symmetry is lost,   25
and the nose at last ceases to be a nose at all on account of some excess in one direction or defect in the other; and this is true of every other part of the human body. The same law of proportion equally holds in states. Oligarchy or democracy,   30
although a departure from the most perfect form, may yet be a good enough government, but if any one attempts to push the principles of either to an extreme, he will begin by spoiling the government and end by having none at all. Therefore the legislator and the statesman ought to know what democratic measures save and   35
what destroy a democracy, and what oligarchical measures save or destroy an oligarchy. For neither the one nor the other can exist or continue to exist unless both

rich and poor are included in it. If equality of property is introduced, the state must of necessity take another form; for when by laws carried to excess one or other 1310ᵃ1 element in the state is ruined, the constitution is ruined.

There is an error common both to oligarchies and to democracies:—in the latter the demagogues, when the multitude are above the law, are always cutting 5 the city in two by quarrels with the rich, whereas they should always profess to be maintaining their cause; just as in oligarchies the oligarchs should profess to maintain the cause of the people, and should take oaths the opposite of those which they now take. For there are cities in which they swear—'I will be an enemy to the 10 people, and will devise all the harm against them which I can'; but they ought to exhibit and to entertain the very opposite feeling; in the form of their oath there should be an express declaration—'I will do no wrong to the people'.

But of all the things which I have mentioned that which most contributes to the permanence of constitutions is the adaptation of education to the form of government, and yet in our own day this principle is universally neglected. The best laws, 15 though sanctioned by every citizen of the state, will be of no avail unless the young are trained by habit and education in the spirit of the constitution, if the laws are democratic, democratically, or oligarchically, if the laws are oligarchical. For there may be a want of self-discipline in states as well as in individuals. Now, to have been 20 educated in the spirit of the constitution is not to perform the actions in which oligarchs or democrats delight, but those by which the existence of an oligarchy or of a democracy is made possible. Whereas among ourselves the sons of the ruling class in an oligarchy live in luxury, but the sons of the poor are hardened by exercise 25 and toil, and hence they are both more inclined and better able to make a revolution. And in democracies of the more extreme type there has arisen a false idea of freedom which is contradictory to the true interests of the state. For two principles are characteristic of democracy, the government of the majority and freedom. Men 30 think that what is just is equal; and that equality is the supremacy of the popular will; and that freedom means doing what one likes. In such democracies every one lives as he pleases, or in the words of Euripides, 'according to his fancy'. But this is all wrong; men should not think it slavery to live according to the rule of the 35 constitution; for it is their salvation.

I have now discussed generally the cause of the revolution and destruction of states, and the means of their preservation and continuance.

10 · I have still to speak of monarchy, and the causes of its destruction and preservation. What I have said already respecting forms of constitutional govern- 1310ᵇ1 ment applies almost equally to royal and to tyrannical rule. For royal rule is of the nature of an aristocracy, and a tyranny is a compound of oligarchy and democracy 5 in their most extreme forms; it is therefore most injurious to its subjects, being made up of two evil forms of government, and having the perversions and errors of both. These two forms of monarchy are contrary in their very origin. The appointment of 10 a king is the resource of the better classes against the people, and he is elected by them out of their own number, because either he himself or his family excel in excellence and excellent actions; whereas a tyrant is chosen from the people to be

their protector against the notables, and in order to prevent them from being injured. History shows that almost all tyrants have been demagogues who gained the favour of the people by their accusation of the notables. At any rate this was the manner in which the tyrannies arose in the days when cities had increased in power. Others which were older originated in the ambition of kings wanting to overstep the limits of their hereditary power and become despots. Others again grew out of the class which were chosen to be chief magistrates; for in ancient times the people who elected them gave the magistrates, whether civil or religious, a long tenure. Others arose out of the custom which oligarchies had of making some individual supreme over the highest offices. In any of these ways an ambitious man had no difficulty, if he desired, in creating a tyranny, since he had the power in his hands already, either as king or as one of the officers of state. Thus Pheidon at Argos and several others were originally kings, and ended by becoming tyrants; Phalaris, on the other hand, and the Ionian tyrants, acquired the tyranny by holding great offices. Whereas Panaetius at Leontini, Cypselus at Corinth, Peisistratus at Athens, Dionysius at Syracuse, and several others who afterwards became tyrants, were at first demagogues.

And so, as I was saying, royalty ranks with aristocracy, for it is based upon merit, whether of the individual or of his family, or on benefits conferred, or on these claims with power added to them. For all who have obtained this honour have benefited, or had in their power to benefit, states and nations; some, like Codrus, have prevented the state from being enslaved in war; others, like Cyrus, have given their country freedom, or have settled or gained a territory, like the Lacedaemonian, Macedonian, and Molossian kings. The idea of a king is to be a protector of the rich against unjust treatment, of the people against insult and oppression. Whereas a tyrant, as has often been repeated, has no regard to any public interest, except as conducive to his private ends; his aim is pleasure, the aim of a king, honour. Therefore they differ also in their excesses; the tyrant accumulates riches, the king seeks what brings honour. And the guards of a king are citizens, but of a tyrant mercenaries.

That tyranny has all the vices both of democracy and oligarchy is evident. As of oligarchy so of tyranny, the end is wealth (for by wealth only can the tyrant maintain his guard and his luxury). Both mistrust the people, and therefore deprive them of their arms. Both agree too in injuring the people and driving them out of the city and dispersing them. From democracy tyrants have borrowed the art of making war upon the notables and destroying them secretly or openly, or of exiling them because they are rivals and stand in the way of their power; and also because plots against them are contrived by men of this class, who either want to rule or to escape subjection. Hence Periander advised Thrasybulus by cutting off the tops of the tallest ears of corn, meaning that he must always put out of the way the citizens who overtop the rest. And so, as I have already intimated, the beginnings of change are the same in monarchies as in forms of constitutional government; subjects attack their sovereigns out of fear or contempt, or because they have been unjustly treated by them. And of injustice the most common form is insult, another is confiscation of property.

The ends sought by conspiracies against monarchies, whether tyrannies or
royalties, are the same as the ends sought by conspiracies against other forms of
30   government. Monarchs have great wealth and honour, which are objects of desire to
all mankind. The attacks are made sometimes against their lives, sometimes against
the office; where the sense of insult is the motive, against their lives. Any sort of
insult (and there are many) may stir up anger, and when men are angry, they
35   commonly act out of revenge, and not from ambition. For example, the attempt
made upon the Peisistratidae arose out of the public dishonour offered to the sister
of Harmodius and the insult to himself. He attacked the tyrant for his sister's sake,
and Aristogeiton joined in the attack for the sake of Harmodius. A conspiracy was
also formed against Periander, the tyrant of Ambracia, because, when drinking
1311ᵇ1   with a favourite youth, he asked him whether by this time he was not with child by
him. Philip, too, was attacked by Pausanias because he permitted him to be insulted
by Attalus and his friends, and Amyntas the Little, by Derdas, because he boasted
5   of having enjoyed his youth. Evagoras of Cyprus, again, was slain by the eunuch to
revenge an insult; for his wife had been carried off by Evagoras's son. Many
conspiracies have originated in shameful attempts made by sovereigns on the
persons of their subjects. Such was the attack of Crataeas upon Archelaus; he had
always hated his intercourse with the king, and so, when Archelaus, having
10   promised him one of his two daughters in marriage, did not give him either of them,
but broke his word and married the elder to the king of Elymeia, when he was hard
pressed in a war against Sirrhas and Arrhabaeus, and the younger to his own son
Amyntas, under the idea that Amyntas would then be less likely to quarrel with his
15   son by Cleopatra—Crataeas made this slight a pretext for attacking Archelaus,
though even a less reason would have sufficed, for the real cause of the estrange-
ment was the disgust which he felt at his sexual subjection. And from a like motive
Hellanocrates of Larissa conspired with him; for when Archelaus, who was his
lover, did not fulfil his promise of restoring him to his country, he thought that
20   the intercourse between them had originated, not in sexual desire, but in the wish to
insult him. Pytho, too, and Heracleides of Aenos, slew Cotys in order to avenge their
father, and Adamas revolted from Cotys in revenge for the wanton outrage which
he had committed in castrating him when a child.

Many, too, enraged by blows inflicted on the person which they deemed an
25   insult, have either killed or attempted to kill officers of state and royal princes by
whom they have been injured. Thus, at Mytilene, Megacles and his friends attacked
and slew the Penthilidae, as they were going about and striking people with clubs.
At a later date Smerdis, who had been beaten and torn away from his wife by
30   Penthilus, slew him. In the conspiracy against Archelaus, Decamnichus stimulated
the fury of the assassins and led the attack; he was enraged because Archelaus had
delivered him to Euripides to be scourged; for the poet had been irritated at some
remark made by Decamnichus on the foulness of his breath. Many other examples
35   might be cited of murders and conspiracies which have arisen from similar
causes.

Fear is another motive which, as we have said, has caused conspiracies as well in monarchies as in more popular forms of government. Thus Artapanes conspired against Xerxes and slew him, fearing that he would be accused of hanging Darius against his orders—he having been under the impression that Xerxes would forget what he had said in the middle of a meal, and that the offence would be forgiven.

Another motive is contempt, as in the case of Sardanapalus, whom someone saw carding wool with his women, if the story-tellers say truly; and the tale may be true, if not of him, of someone else. Dion attacked the younger Dionysius because he despised him, and saw that he was equally despised by his own subjects, and that he was always drunk. Even the friends of a tyrant will sometimes attack him out of contempt; for the confidence which he reposes in them breeds contempt, and they think that they will not be found out. The expectation of success is likewise a sort of contempt; the assailants are ready to strike, and think nothing of the danger, because they seem to have the power in their hands. Thus generals of armies attack monarchs; as, for example, Cyrus attacked Astyages, despising the effeminacy of his life, and believing that his power was worn out. Thus again, Seuthes the Thracian conspired against Amadocus, whose general he was.

And sometimes men are actuated by more than one motive, like Mithridates, who conspired against Ariobarzanes, partly out of contempt and partly from the love of gain.

Bold natures, placed by their sovereigns in a high military position, are most likely to make the attempt in the expectation of success; for courage is emboldened by power, and the union of the two inspires them with the hope of an easy victory.

Attempts of which the motive is ambition arise in a different way as well as in those already mentioned. There are men who will not risk their lives in the hope of gains and honours however great, but who nevertheless regard the killing of a tyrant simply as an extraordinary action which will make them famous and notable in the world; they wish to acquire, not a kingdom, but a name. It is rare, however, to find such men; he who would kill a tyrant must be prepared to lose his life if he fails. He must have the resolution of Dion, who, when he made war upon Dionysius, took with him very few troops, saying 'that whatever measure of success he might attain would be enough for him, even if he were to die the moment he landed; such a death would be welcome to him'. But this is a temper to which few can attain.

Once more, tyrannies, like all other governments, are destroyed from without by some opposite and more powerful form of government. That such a government will have the will to attack them is clear; for the two are opposed in principle; and all men, if they can, do what they want to. Democracy is antagonistic to tyranny, on the principle of Hesiod, 'Potter hates Potter', because they are nearly akin, for the extreme form of democracy is tyranny; and royalty and aristocracy are both alike opposed to tyranny, because they are constitutions of a different type. And therefore the Lacedaemonians put down most of the tyrannies, and so did the Syracusans during the time when they were well governed.

Again, tyrannies are destroyed from within, when the reigning family are divided among themselves, as that of Gelo was, and more recently that of Dionysius; in the case of Gelo because Thrasybulus, the brother of Hiero, flattered the son of

1312ª1

5

10

15

20

25

30

35

1312ᵇ1

5

10

Gelo and led him into excesses in order that he might rule in his name. Whereupon the family got together a party to get rid of Thrasybulus and save the tyranny; but those of the people who conspired with them seized the opportunity and drove them all out. In the case of Dionysius, Dion, his own relative, attacked and expelled him with the assistance of the people; he afterwards perished himself.

There are two chief motives which induce men to attack tyrannies—hatred and contempt. Hatred of tyrants is inevitable, and contempt is also a frequent cause of their destruction. Thus we see that most of those who have acquired, have retained their power, but those who have inherited, have lost it, almost at once; for, living in luxurious ease, they have become contemptible, and offer many opportunities to their assailants. Anger, too, must be included under hatred, and produces the same effects. It is often even more ready to strike—the angry are more impetuous in making an attack, for they do not follow rational principle. And men are very apt to give way to their passions when they are insulted. To this cause is to be attributed the fall of the Peisistratidae and of many others. Hatred is more reasonable, for anger is accompanied by pain, which is an impediment to reason, whereas hatred is painless.

In a word, all the causes which I have mentioned as destroying the last and most unmixed form of oligarchy, and the extreme form of democracy, may be assumed to affect tyranny; indeed the extreme forms of both are only tyrannies distributed among several persons. Kingly rule is little affected by external causes, and is therefore lasting; it is generally destroyed from within. And there are two ways in which the destruction may come about; when the members of the royal family quarrel among themselves, and when the kings attempt to administer the state too much after the fashion of a tyranny, and to extend their authority contrary to the law. Royalties do not now come into existence; where such forms of government arise, they are rather monarchies or tyrannies. For the rule of a king is over voluntary subjects, and he is supreme in all important matters; but in our own day men are more upon an equality, and no one is so immeasurably superior to others as to represent adequately the greatness and dignity of the office. Hence mankind will not, willingly, endure it, and any one who obtains power by force or fraud is at once thought to be a tyrant. In hereditary monarchies a further cause of destruction is the fact that kings often fall into contempt, and, although possessing not tyrannical power, but only royal dignity, are apt to outrage others. Their overthrow is then readily effected; for there is an end to the king when his subjects do not want to have him, but the tyrant lasts, whether they like him or not.

The destruction of monarchies is to be attributed to these and the like causes.

11 · And they are preserved, to speak generally, by the opposite causes; or, if we consider them separately, royalty is preserved by the limitation of its powers. The more restricted the functions of kings, the longer their power will last unimpaired; for then they are more moderate and not so despotic in their ways; and they are less envied by their subjects. This is the reason why the kingly office has lasted so long among the Molossians. And for a similar reason it has continued

among the Lacedaemonians, because there it was always divided between two, and 25
afterwards further limited by Theopompus in various respects, more particularly by
the establishment of the Ephoralty. He diminished the power of the kings, but
established on a more lasting basis the kingly office, which was thus made in a
certain sense not less, but greater. There is a story that when his wife once asked 30
him whether he was not ashamed to leave to his sons a royal power which was less
than he had inherited from his father, 'No indeed', he replied, 'for the power which I
leave to them will be more lasting'.

As to tyrannies, they are preserved in two quite opposite ways. One of them is
the old traditional method in which most tyrants administer their government. Of 35
such arts Periander of Corinth is said to have been the great master, and many
similar devices may be gathered from the Persians in the administration of their
government. There are firstly the prescriptions mentioned some distance back, for
the preservation of a tyranny, in so far as this is possible; viz. that the tyrant should 40
lop off those who are too high; he must put to death men of spirit; he must not allow
common meals, clubs, education, and the like; he must be upon his guard against 1313^{b}1
anything which is likely to inspire either courage or confidence among his subjects;
he must prohibit schools or other meetings for discussion, and he must take every
means to prevent people from knowing one another (for acquaintance begets 5
mutual confidence). Further, he must compel all persons staying in the city to
appear in public and live at his gates; then he will know what they are doing: if they
are always kept under, they will learn to be humble. In short, he should practise
these and the like Persian and barbaric arts, which all have the same object. A 10
tyrant should also endeavour to know what each of his subjects says or does, and
should employ spies, like the 'female detectives' at Syracuse, and the eavesdroppers
whom Hiero was in the habit of sending to any place of resort or meeting; for the 15
fear of informers prevents people from speaking their minds, and if they do, they are
more easily found out. Another art of the tyrant is to sow quarrels among the
citizens; friends should be embroiled with friends, the people with the notables, and
the rich with one another. Also he should impoverish his subjects; he thus provides
against the maintenance of a guard by the citizens, and the people, having to keep 20
hard at work, are prevented from conspiring. The Pyramids of Egypt afford an
example of this policy; also the offerings of the family of Cypselus, and the building
of the temple of Olympian Zeus by the Peisistratidae, and the great Polycratean
monuments at Samos; all these works were alike intended to occupy the people and 25
keep them poor. Another practice of tyrants is to multiply taxes, after the manner of
Dionysius at Syracuse, who contrived that within five years his subjects should
bring into the treasury their whole property. The tyrant is also fond of making war
in order that his subjects may have something to do and be always in want of a
leader. And whereas the power of a king is preserved by his friends, the 30
characteristic of a tyrant is to distrust his friends, because he knows that all men
want to overthrow him, and they above all have the power to do so.

Again, the practices of the last and worst form of democracy are all found in
tyrannies. Such are the power given to women in their families in the hope that they

35 will inform against their husbands, and the licence which is allowed to slaves in
order that they may betray their masters; for slaves and women do not conspire
against tyrants; and they are of course friendly to tyrannies and also to democracies,
since under them they have a good time. For the people too would fain be a
monarch, and therefore by them, as well as by the tyrant, the flatterer is held in
40 honour; in democracies he is the demagogue; and the tyrant also has those who
associate with him in a humble spirit, which is a work of flattery.

1314ᵃ1   Hence tyrants are always fond of bad men, because they love to be flattered,
but no man who has the spirit of a freeman in him will lower himself by flattery;
good men love others, or at any rate do not flatter them. Moreover, the bad are
5 useful for bad purposes; 'nail knocks out nail', as the proverb says. It is characteristic of a tyrant to dislike every one who has dignity or independence; he wants to be
alone in his glory, but anyone who claims a like dignity or asserts his independence
encroaches upon his prerogative, and is hated by him as an enemy to his power.
Another mark of a tyrant is that he likes foreigners better than citizens, and lives
10 with them and invites them to his table; for the one are enemies, but the others enter
into no rivalry with him.

Such are the marks of the tyrant and the arts by which he preserves his power;
there is no wickedness too great for him. All that we have said may be summed up
15 under three heads, which answer to the three aims of the tyrant. These are, the
humiliation of his subjects, for he knows that a mean-spirited man will not conspire
against anybody: the creation of mistrust among them; for a tyrant is not
overthrown until men begin to have confidence in one another; and this is the reason
why tyrants are at war with the good; they are under the idea that their power is
20 endangered by them, not only because they will not be ruled despotically, but also
because they are loyal to one another, and to other men, and do not inform against
one another or against other men: the tyrant desires that his subjects shall be
incapable of action, for no one attempts what is impossible, and they will not
25 attempt to overthrow a tyranny if they are powerless. Under these three heads the
whole policy of a tyrant may be summed up, and to one or other of them all his ideas
may be referred: he sows distrust among his subjects; he takes away their power;
and he humbles them.

30 This then is one of the two methods by which tyrannies are preserved; and
there is another which proceeds upon an almost opposite principle of action. The
nature of this latter method may be gathered from a comparison of the causes which
destroy kingdoms, for as one mode of destroying kingly power is to make the office
35 of king more tyrannical, so the salvation of a tyranny is to make it more like the rule
of a king. But of one thing the tyrant must be careful; he must keep power enough to
rule over his subjects, whether they like him or not, for if he once gives this up he
gives up his tyranny. But though power must be retained as the foundation, in all
else the tyrant should act or appear to act in the character of a king. In the first
1314ᵇ1 place he should pretend concern for the public revenues, and not waste money in
making presents of a sort at which the common people get excited when they see
their hard-won earnings snatched from them and lavished on courtesans and

foreigners and artists. He should give an account of what he receives and of what he spends (a practice which has been adopted by some tyrants); for then he will seem to be a steward of the public rather than a tyrant; nor need he fear that, while he is the lord of the city, he will ever be in want of money. Such a policy is at all events much more advantageous for the tyrant when he goes from home, than to leave behind him a hoard, for then the garrison who remain in the city will be less likely to attack his power; and a tyrant, when he is absent from home, has more reason to fear the guardians of his treasure than the citizens, for the one accompany him, but the others remain behind. In the second place, he should be seen to collect taxes and to require public services only for state purposes, and so as to form a fund in case of war, and generally he ought to make himself the guardian and treasurer of them, as if they belonged, not to him, but to the public. He should appear, not harsh, but dignified, and when men meet him they should look upon him with reverence, and not with fear. Yet it is hard for him to be respected if he inspires no respect, and therefore whatever virtues he may neglect, at least he should maintain the character of a great soldier, and produce the impression that he is one. Neither he nor any of his associates should ever assault the young of either sex who are his subjects, and the women of his family should observe a like self-control towards other women; the insolence of women has ruined many tyrannies. In the indulgence of pleasures he should be the opposite of our modern tyrants, who not only begin at dawn and pass whole days in sensuality, but want other men to see them, so that they may admire their happy and blessed lot. In these things a tyrant should if possible be moderate, or at any rate should not parade his vices to the world; for a drunken and drowsy tyrant is soon despised and attacked; not so he who is temperate and wide awake. His conduct should be the very reverse of nearly everything which has been said before about tyrants. He ought to adorn and improve his city, as though he were not a tyrant, but the guardian of the state. Also he should appear to be particularly earnest in the service of the gods; for if men think that a ruler is religious and has a reverence for the gods, they are less afraid of suffering injustice at his hands, and they are less disposed to conspire against him, because they believe him to have the very gods fighting on his side. At the same time his religion must not be thought foolish. And he should honour men of merit, and make them think that they would not be held in more honour by the citizens if they had a free government. The honour he should distribute himself, but the punishment should be inflicted by officers and courts of law. It is a precaution which is taken by all monarchs not to make one person great; but if one, then two or more should be raised, that they may keep an eye on one another. If after all some one has to be made great, he should not be a man of bold spirit; for such dispositions are ever most inclined to strike. And if any one is to be deprived of his power, let it be diminished gradually, not taken from him all at once. The tyrant should abstain from all outrage; in particular from personal violence and from wanton conduct towards the young. He should be especially careful of his behaviour to men who are lovers of honour; for as the lovers of money are offended when their property is touched, so are the lovers of honour and the good when their honour is affected. Therefore a tyrant ought either not to commit

20   such acts at all; or he should be thought only to employ fatherly correction, and not to trample upon others—and his acquaintance with youth should be supposed to arise from desire, and not from the insolence of power, and in general he should compensate the appearance of dishonour by the increase of honour.

25   Of those who attempt assassination they are the most dangerous, and require to be most carefully watched, who do not care to survive, if they effect their purpose. Therefore special precaution should be taken about any who think that either they or those for whom they care have been insulted; for when men are led away by 30 passion to assault others they are regardless of themselves. As Heracleitus says, 'It is difficult to fight against anger; for a man will buy revenge with his soul'.

  And whereas states consist of two classes, of poor men and of rich, the tyrant should lead both to imagine that they are preserved and prevented from harming 35 one another by his rule, and whichever of the two is stronger he should attach to his government; for, having this advantage, he has no need either to emancipate slaves or to disarm the citizens; either party added to the force which he already has, will 40 make him stronger than his assailants.

  But enough of these details—what should be the general policy of the tyrant is 1315ᵇ1 obvious. He ought to show himself to his subjects in the light, not of a tyrant, but of a steward and a king. He should not appropriate what is theirs, but should be their guardian; he should be moderate, not extravagant in his way of life; he should win the notables by companionship, and the multitude by flattery. For then his rule will 5 of necessity be nobler and happier, because he will rule over better men whose spirits are not crushed, and who do not hate and fear him. His power too will be more lasting. His disposition will be virtuous, or at least half virtuous; and he will 10 not be wicked, but half wicked only.

12 · Yet no forms of government are so short-lived as oligarchy and tyranny. The tyranny which lasted longest was that of Orthagoras and his sons at Sicyon; this 15 continued for a hundred years. The reason was that they treated their subjects with moderation, and to a great extent observed the laws; and in various ways gained the favour of the people by the care which they took of them. Cleisthenes, in particular, was respected for his military ability. If report may be believed, he crowned the 20 judge who decided against him in the games; and, as some say, the sitting statue in the Agora of Sicyon is the likeness of this person. (A similar story is told of Peisistratus, who is said on one occasion to have allowed himself to be summoned and tried before the Areopagus.)

  Next in duration to the tyranny of Orthagoras was that of the Cypselidae at Corinth, which lasted seventy-three years and six months: Cypselus reigned thirty 25 years, Periander forty and a half, and Psammetichus the son of Gorgus three. Their continuance was due to similar causes: Cypselus was a popular man, who during the whole time of his rule never had a body-guard; and Periander, although he was a 30 tyrant, was a great soldier. Third in duration was the rule of the Peisistratidae at Athens, but it was interrupted; for Peisistratus was twice driven out, so that out of thirty-three years he reigned only seventeen; and his sons reigned

eighteen—altogether thirty-five years. Of other tyrannies, that of Hiero and Gelo 35
at Syracuse was the most lasting. Even this, however, was short, not more than
eighteen years in all; for Gelo continued tyrant for seven years, and died in the
eighth; Hiero reigned for ten years, and Thrasybulus was driven out in the eleventh
month. In fact, tyrannies generally have been of quite short duration.

I have now gone through almost all the causes by which constitutional 40
governments and monarchies are either destroyed or preserved.

In the *Republic* of Plato, Socrates treats of revolutions, but not well, for he 1316ª1
mentions no cause of change which peculiarly affects the first or perfect state. He
only says that the cause is that nothing is abiding, but all things change in a certain
cycle; and that the origin of the change consists in those numbers 'of which 4 and 3, 5
married with 5, furnish two harmonies' (he means when the number of this figure
becomes solid); he conceives that nature at certain times produces bad men who will
not submit to education; in which latter particular he may very likely be not far 10
wrong, for there may well be some men who cannot be educated and made virtuous.
But why is such a cause of change peculiar to his ideal state, and not rather common
to all states, or indeed, to everything which comes into being at all? And is it by the
agency of time, which, as he declares, makes all things change, that things which 15
did not begin together, change together? For example, if something has come into
being the day before the completion of the cycle, will it change with things that
came into being before? Further, why should the perfect state change into the
Spartan? For governments more often take an opposite form than one akin to them.
The same remark is applicable to the other changes; he says that the Spartan 20
constitution changes into an oligarchy, and this into a democracy, and this again
into a tyranny. And yet the contrary happens quite as often; for a democracy is even
more likely to change into an oligarchy than into a monarchy. Further, he never
says whether tyranny is, or is not, liable to revolutions, and if it is, what is the cause 25
of them, or into what form it changes. And the reason is, that he could not very well
have told: for there is no rule; according to him it should revert to the first and best,
and then there would be a complete cycle. But in point of fact a tyranny often
changes into a tyranny, as that at Sicyon changed from the tyranny of Myron into 30
that of Cleisthenes; into oligarchy, as the tyranny of Antileon did at Chalcis; into
democracy, as that of Gelo's family did at Syracuse; into aristocracy, as at
Carthage, and the tyranny of Charilaus in Lacedaemon. Often an oligarchy
changes into a tyranny, like most of the ancient oligarchies in Sicily; for example, 35
the oligarchy at Leontini changed into the tyranny of Panaetius; that at Gela into
the tyranny of Cleander; that at Rhegium into the tyranny of Anaxilaus; the same
thing has happened in many other states. And it is absurd to suppose that the state
changes into oligarchy merely because the ruling class are lovers and makers of 1316ᵇ1
money, and not because the very rich think it unfair that the very poor should have
an equal share in the government with themselves. Moreover, in many oligarchies
there are laws against making money in trade. But at Carthage, which is a 5
democracy, there is no such prohibition; and yet to this day the Carthaginians have
never had a revolution. It is absurd too for him to say that an oligarchy is two cities,

one of the rich, and the other of the poor. Is not this just as much the case in the
Spartan constitution, or in any other in which either all do not possess equal
10   property, or all are not equally good men? Nobody need be any poorer than he was
before, and yet the oligarchy may change all the same into a democracy, if the poor
form the majority; and a democracy may change into an oligarchy, if the wealthy
class are stronger than the people, and the one are energetic, the other indifferent.
15   Once more, although the causes of the change are very numerous, he mentions only
one, which is, that the citizens become poor through dissipation and debt, as though
he thought that all, or the majority of them, were originally rich. This is not true:
though it is true that when any of the leaders lose their property they are ripe for
revolution; but, when anybody else does, it is no great matter, and an oligarchy does
20   not even then more often pass into a democracy than into any other form of
government. Again, if men are deprived of the honours of state, and are wronged,
and insulted, they make revolutions, and change forms of government, even
although they have not wasted their substance because they might do what they
like—of which extravagance he declares excessive freedom to be the cause.
25   Finally, although there are many forms of oligarchies and democracies,
Socrates speaks of their revolutions as though there were only one form of either of
them.

BOOK VI

30   1 · We have now considered the varieties of the deliberative or supreme
power in states, and the various arrangements of law-courts and state offices, and
which of them are adapted to different forms of government. We have also spoken
35   of the destruction and preservation of constitutions, how and from what causes they
arise.
Of democracy and all other forms of government there are many kinds; and it
will be well to assign to them severally the modes of organization which are proper
and advantageous to each, adding what remains to be said about them. Moreover,
we ought to consider the various combinations of these modes themselves; for such
1317ª1   combinations make constitutions overlap one another, so that aristocracies have an
oligarchical character, and constitutional governments incline to democracies.
When I speak of the combinations which remain to be considered, and thus far
have not been considered by us, I mean such as these:—when the deliberative part
5   of the government and the election of officers is constituted oligarchically, and the
law-courts aristocratically, or when the courts and the deliberative part of the state
are oligarchical, and the election of offices aristocratic, or when in any other way
there is a want of harmony in the composition of a state.
10   I have shown already what forms of democracy are suited to particular cities,
and what forms of oligarchy to particular peoples, and to whom each of the other
forms of government is suited. Further, we must not only show which of these

governments is the best for each state, but also briefly proceed to consider how these
and other forms of government are to be established.   15

First of all let us speak of democracy, which will also bring to light the opposite
form of government commonly called oligarchy. For the purposes of this inquiry we
need to ascertain all the elements and characteristics of democracy, since from the
combinations of these the varieties of democratic government arise. There are   20
several of these differing from each other, and the difference is due to two causes.
One has been already mentioned—differences of population; for the popular
element may consist of farmers, or of artisans, or of labourers, and if the first of   25
these is added to the second, or the third to the two others, not only does the
democracy become better or worse, but its very nature is changed. A second cause
remains to be mentioned: the various properties and characteristics of democracy,
when variously combined, make a difference. For one democracy will have less and   30
another will have more, and another will have all of these characteristics. There is
an advantage in knowing them all, whether a man wishes to establish some new
form of democracy, or only to remodel an existing one. Founders of states try to   35
bring together all the elements which accord with the ideas of the several
constitutions; but this is a mistake of theirs, as I have already remarked when
speaking of the destruction and preservation of states. We will now set forth the
principles, characteristics, and aims of such states.

2 · The basis of a democratic state is liberty; which, according to the   40
common opinion of men, can only be enjoyed in such a state—this they affirm to be
the great end of every democracy. One principle of liberty is for all to rule and be   1317ᵇ1
ruled in turn, and indeed democratic justice is the application of numerical not
proportionate equality; whence it follows that the majority must be supreme, and   5
that whatever the majority approve must be the end and the just. Every citizen, it is
said, must have equality, and therefore in a democracy the poor have more power
than the rich, because there are more of them, and the will of the majority is
supreme. This, then, is one note of liberty which all democrats affirm to be the   10
principle of their state. Another is that a man should live as he likes. This, they say,
is the mark of liberty, since, on the other hand, not to live as a man likes is the mark
of a slave. This is the second characteristic of democracy, whence has arisen the
claim of men to be ruled by none, if possible, or, if this is impossible, to rule and be   15
ruled in turns; and so it contributes to the freedom based upon equality.

Such being our foundation and such the principle from which we start, the
characteristics of democracy are as follows:—the election of officers by all out of
all; and that all should rule over each, and each in his turn over all; that the   20
appointment to all offices, or to all but those which require experience and skill,
should be made by lot; that no property qualification should be required for offices,
or only a very low one; that a man should not hold the same office twice, or not
often, or in the case of few except military offices; that the tenure of all offices, or of
as many as possible, should be brief; that all men should sit in judgement, or that   25
judges selected out of all should judge, in all matters, or in most and in the greatest

and most important—such as the scrutiny of accounts, the constitution, and private contracts; that the assembly should be supreme over all causes, or at any rate over
30 the most important, and the magistrates over none or only over a very few. Of all magistracies, a council is the most democratic when there is not the means of paying all the citizens, but when they are paid even this is robbed of its power; for the people then draw all cases to themselves, as I said in the previous discussion. The
35 next characteristic of democracy is payment for services; assembly, law-courts, magistrates, everybody receives pay, when it is to be had; or when it is not to be had for all, then it is given to the law-courts and to the stated assemblies, to the council and to the magistrates, or at least to any of them who are compelled to have their meals together. [And whereas oligarchy is characterized by birth, wealth, and
40 education, the marks of democracy appear to be the opposite of these—low birth, poverty, mean employment.][1] Another characteristic is that no magistracy is
1318ᵃ1 perpetual, but if any such have survived some ancient change in the constitution it should be stripped of its power, and the holders should be elected by lot and no longer by vote. These are the points common to all democracies; but democracy and demos in their truest form are based upon the recognized principle of democratic
5 justice, that all should count equally; for equality implies that the poor should have no more share in the government than the rich, and should not be the only rulers, but that all should rule equally according to their numbers. And in this way men
10 think that they will secure equality and freedom in their state.

3 · Next comes the question, how is this equality to be obtained? Are we to assign to a thousand poor men the property qualifications of five hundred rich men? and shall we give the thousand a power equal to that of the five hundred? or, if this
15 is not to be the mode, ought we, still retaining the same ratio, to take equal numbers from each and give them the control of the elections and of the courts?—Which, according to the democratic notion, is the juster form of the constitution—this or one based on numbers only? Democrats say that justice is that to which the
20 majority agree, oligarchs that to which the wealthier class agree; in their opinion the decision should be given according to the amount of property. In both principles there is some inequality and injustice. For if justice is the will of the few, any one person who has more wealth than all the rest of the rich put together, ought, upon the oligarchical principle, to have the sole power—but this would be tyranny; or if
25 justice is the will of the majority, as I was before saying, they will unjustly confiscate the property of the wealthy minority. To find a principle of equality in which they both agree we must inquire into their respective ideas of justice.
Now they agree in saying that whatever is decided by the majority of the
30 citizens is to be deemed law. Granted, but not without some reserve; since there are two classes out of which a state is composed—the poor and the rich—that is to be deemed law, on which both or the greater part of both agree; and if they disagree, that which is approved by the greater number, and by those who have the higher qualification. For example, suppose that there are ten rich and twenty poor, and

[1]Excised by Dreizehnter.

some measure is approved by six of the rich and is disapproved by fifteen of the   35
poor, and the remaining four of the rich join with the party of the poor, and the
remaining five of the poor with that of the rich; in such a case the will of those whose
qualifications, when both sides are added up, are the greatest, should prevail. If they
turn out to be equal, there is no greater difficulty than at present, when, if the
assembly or the courts are divided, recourse is had to the lot, or to some similar   1318^{b}1
expedient. But, although it may be difficult in theory to know what is just and equal,
the practical difficulty of inducing those to forbear who can, if they like, encroach,
is far greater, for the weaker are always asking for equality and justice, but the
stronger care for none of these things.   5

4 · Of the four kinds of democracy, as was said in the previous discussion, the
best is that which comes first in order; it is also the oldest of them all. I am speaking
of them according to the natural classification of their inhabitants. For the best
material of democracy is an agricultural population; there is no difficulty in
forming a democracy where the mass of the people live by agriculture or tending of   10
cattle. Being poor, they have no leisure, and therefore do not often attend the
assembly, and having the necessaries of life they are always at work, and do not
covet the property of others. Indeed, they find their employment pleasanter than the
cares of government or office where no great gains can be made out of them, for the   15
many are more desirous of gain than of honour. A proof is that even the ancient
tyrannies were patiently endured by them, as they still endure oligarchies, if they
are allowed to work and are not deprived of their property; for some of them grow   20
quickly rich and the others are well enough off. Moreover, they have the power of
electing the magistrates and calling them to account; their ambition, if they have
any, is thus satisfied; and in some democracies, although they do not all share in the
appointment of offices, except through representatives elected in turn out of the
whole people, as at Mantinea—yet, if they have the power of deliberating, the   25
many are contented. Even this form of government may be regarded as a
democracy, and was such at Mantinea. Hence it is both expedient and customary in
the afore-mentioned type of democracy that all should elect to offices, and conduct
scrutinies, and sit in the law-courts, but that the great offices should be filled up by   30
election and from persons having a qualification; the greater requiring a greater
qualification, or, if there are no offices for which a qualification is required, then
those who are marked out by special ability should be appointed. Under such a form
of government the citizens are sure to be governed well (for the offices will always
be held by the best persons; the people are willing enough to elect them and are not
jealous of the good). The good and the notables will then be satisfied, for they will   35
not be governed by men who are their inferiors, and the persons elected will rule
justly, because others will call them to account. Every man should be responsible to
others, nor should anyone be allowed to do just as he pleases; for where absolute
freedom is allowed there is nothing to restrain the evil which is inherent in every   1319^{a}1
man. But the principle of responsibility secures that which is the greatest good in
states; the right persons rule and are prevented from doing wrong, and the people

5   have their due. It is evident that this is the best kind of democracy—and why?
because the people are drawn from a certain class. Some of the ancient laws of most
states were useful with a view to making the people husbandmen. They provided
either that no one should possess more than a certain quantity of land, or that, if he
did, the land should not be within a certain distance from the town or the acropolis.

10   Formerly in many states there was a law forbidding anyone to sell his original
allotment of land. There is a similar law attributed to Oxylus, which is to the effect
that there should be a certain portion of every man's land on which he could not
borrow money. A useful corrective to the evil of which I am speaking would be the

15   law of the Aphytaeans, who, although they are numerous, and do not possess much
land, are all of them farmers. For their properties are reckoned in the census, not
entire, but only in such small portions that even the poor may have more than the
amount required.

20   Next best to an agricultural, and in many respects similar, are a pastoral
people, who live by their flocks; they are the best trained of any for war, robust in

25   body and able to camp out. The people of whom other democracies consist are far
inferior to them, for their life is inferior; there is no room for excellence in any of
their employments, whether they be artisans or traders or labourers. Besides, people

30   of this class can readily come to the assembly, because they are continually moving
about in the city and in the agora; whereas farmers are scattered over the country
and do not meet or feel the same need of assembling together. Where the territory
also happens to extend to a distance from the city, there is no difficulty in making an

35   excellent democracy or constitutional government; for the people are compelled to
settle in the country, and even if there is a town population the assembly ought not
to meet, in democracies, when the country people cannot come. We have thus
explained how the first and best form of democracy should be constituted; it is clear
that the other or inferior sorts will deviate in a regular order, and the population

1319ᵇ1 which is excluded will at each stage be of a lower kind.
          The last form of democracy, that in which all share alike, is one which cannot
be borne by all states, and will not last long unless well regulated by laws and

5   customs. The more general causes which tend to destroy this or other kinds of
government have been pretty fully considered. In order to constitute such a
democracy and strengthen the people, the leaders have been in the habit of
including as many as they can, and making citizens not only of those who are
legitimate, but even of the illegitimate, and of those who have only one parent a

10   citizen, whether father or mother; for nothing of this sort comes amiss to such a
democracy. This is the way in which demagogues proceed. Whereas the right thing
would be to make no more additions when the number of the commonalty exceeds
that of the notables and of the middle class and not to go beyond this. When in

15   excess of this point, the constitution becomes disorderly, and the notables grow
excited and impatient of the democracy, as in the insurrection at Cyrene; for no
notice is taken of a little evil, but when it increases it strikes the eye. Measures like

20   those which Cleisthenes passed when he wanted to increase the power of the
democracy at Athens, or such as were taken by the founders of popular government

at Cyrene, are useful in the extreme form of democracy. Fresh tribes and brotherhoods should be established; the private rites of families should be restricted and converted into public ones; in short, every contrivance should be adopted which will mingle the citizens with one another and get rid of old connexions. Again, the measures which are taken by tyrants appear all of them to be democratic; such, for instance, as the licence permitted to slaves (which may be to a certain extent advantageous) and also to women and children, and the allowing everybody to live as he likes. Such a government will have many supporters, for most persons would rather live in a disorderly than in a sober manner.

5 · The mere establishment of a democracy is not the only or principal business of the legislator, or of those who wish to create such a state, for any state, however badly constituted, may last one, two, or three days; a far greater difficulty is the preservation of it. The legislator should therefore endeavour to have a firm foundation according to the principles already laid down concerning the preservation and destruction of states; he should guard against the destructive elements, and should make laws, whether written or unwritten, which will contain all the preservatives of states. He must not think the truly democratic or oligarchical measure to be that which will give the greatest amount of democracy or oligarchy, but that which will make them last longest. The demagogues of our own day often get property confiscated in the law-courts in order to please the people. Hence those who have the welfare of the state at heart should counteract them, and make a law that the property of the condemned should not be public and go into the treasury but be sacred. Thus offenders will be as much afraid, for they will be punished all the same, and the people, having nothing to gain, will not be so ready to condemn the accused. Care should also be taken that state trials are as few as possible, and heavy penalties should be inflicted on those who bring groundless accusations; for it is the practice to indict, not members of the popular party, but the notables, although the citizens ought to be all attached to the constitution as well, or at any rate should not regard their rulers as enemies.

Now, since in the last form of democracy the citizens are very numerous, and can hardly be made to assemble unless they are paid, and to pay them when there are no revenues presses hardly upon the notables (for the money must be obtained by a property-tax and confiscations and corrupt practices of the courts, things which have before now overthrown many democracies); where, I say, there are no revenues, the government should hold few assemblies, and the law-courts should consist of many persons, but sit for a few days only. This system has two advantages: first, the rich do not fear the expense, even though they are unpaid themselves when the poor are paid; and secondly, cases are better tried, for wealthy persons, although they do not like to be long absent from their own affairs, do not mind going for a few days to the law-courts. Where there are revenues the demagogues should not be allowed after their manner to distribute the surplus; the poor are always receiving and always wanting more and more, for such help is like water poured into a leaky cask. Yet the true friend of the people should see that they are not too poor,

for extreme poverty lowers the character of the democracy; measures therefore
35   should be taken which will give them lasting prosperity; and as this is equally the
interest of all classes, the proceeds of the public revenues should be accumulated
and distributed among its poor, if possible, in such quantities as may enable them to
1320ᵇ1 purchase a little farm, or, at any rate, make a beginning in trade or farming. And if
this benevolence cannot be extended to all, money should be distributed in turn
according to tribes or other divisions, and in the meantime the rich should pay the
fee for the attendance of the poor at the necessary assemblies; and should in return
be excused from useless public services. By administering the state in this spirit the
5   Carthaginians retain the affections of the people; their policy is from time to time to
send some of them into their dependent towns, where they grow rich. It is also
worthy of a generous and sensible nobility to divide the poor amongst them, and give
them the means of going to work. The example of the people of Tarentum is also
10   well deserving of imitation, for, by sharing the use of their own property with the
poor, they gain their good will. Moreover, they divide all their offices into two
classes, some of them being elected by vote, the others by lot; the latter, so that the
people may participate in them, and the former, so that the state may be better
administered. A like result may be gained by dividing the same offices, so as to have
15   two classes of magistrates, one chosen by vote, the other by lot.
    Enough has been said of the manner in which democracies ought to be
constituted.

6 · From these considerations there will be no difficulty in seeing what
20   should be the constitution of oligarchies. We have only to reason from opposites and
compare each form of oligarchy with the corresponding form of democracy.
    The first and best balanced of oligarchies is akin to a constitutional govern-
ment. In this there ought to be two standards of qualification; the one high, the
other low—the lower qualifying for the humbler yet indispensable offices and the
25   higher for the superior ones. He who acquires the prescribed qualification should
have the rights of citizenship. The number of those admitted should be such as will
make the entire governing body stronger than those who are excluded, and the new
citizen should be always taken out of the better class of the people. The principle,
30   narrowed a little, gives another form of oligarchy; until at length we reach the most
cliquish and tyrannical of them all, answering to the extreme democracy, which,
being the worst, requires vigilance in proportion to its badness. For as healthy
35   bodies and ships well provided with sailors may undergo many mishaps and survive
them, whereas sickly constitutions and rotten ill-manned ships are ruined by the
very least mistake, so do the worst forms of government require the greatest care.
1321ª1 The populousness of democracies generally preserves them (for number is to
democracy in the place of justice based on merit); whereas the preservation of an
oligarchy clearly depends on an opposite principle, viz. good order.

5   7 · As there are four chief divisions of the common people, farmers, artisans,
traders, labourers; so also there are four kinds of military forces—the cavalry, the

heavy infantry, the light-armed troops, the navy. When the country is adapted for
cavalry, then a strong oligarchy is likely to be established. For the security of the   10
inhabitants depends upon a force of this sort, and only rich men can afford to keep
horses. The second form of oligarchy prevails when the country is adapted to heavy
infantry; for this service is better suited to the rich than to the poor. But the
light-armed and the naval element are wholly democratic; and nowadays, where
they are numerous, if the two parties quarrel, the oligarchy are often worsted by   15
them in the struggle. A remedy for this state of things may be found in the practice
of generals who combine a proper contingent of light-armed troops with cavalry and
heavy-armed. And this is the way in which the poor get the better of the rich in civil
contests; being lightly armed, they fight with advantage against cavalry and heavy   20
infantry. An oligarchy which raises such a force out of the lower classes raises a
power against itself. And therefore, since the ages of the citizens vary and some are
older and some younger, the fathers should have their own sons, while they are still
young, taught the agile movements of light-armed troops; and these, when they   25
have been taken out of the ranks of the youth, should become light-armed warriors
in reality. The oligarchy should also yield a share in the government to the people,
either, as I said before, to those who have a property qualification, or, as in the case
of Thebes, to those who have abstained for a certain number of years from mean
employments, or, as at Massalia, to men of merit who are selected for their   30
worthiness, whether previously citizens or not. The magistracies of the highest rank,
which ought to be in the hands of the governing body, should have expensive duties
attached to them, and then the people will not desire them and will take no offence
at the privileges of their rulers when they see that they pay a heavy fine for their
dignity. It is fitting also that the magistrates on entering office should offer   35
magnificent sacrifices or erect some public edifice, and then the people who
participate in the entertainments, and see the city decorated with votive offerings
and buildings, will not desire an alteration in the government, and the notables will
have memorials of their munificence. This, however, is anything but the fashion of   40
our modern oligarchs, who are as covetous of gain as they are of honour; oligarchies
like theirs may be well described as petty democracies. Enough of the manner in   1321^{b}1
which democracies and oligarchies should be organized.

8 · Next in order follows the right distribution of offices, their number, their   5
nature, their duties, of which indeed we have already spoken. No state can exist not
having the necessary offices, and no state can be well administered not having the
offices which tend to preserve harmony and good order. In small states, as we have   10
already remarked, there must not be many of them, but in larger states there must
be a larger number, and we should carefully consider which offices may properly be
united and which separated.

First among necessary offices is that which has the care of the market; a
magistrate should be appointed to inspect contracts and to maintain order. For in
every state there must inevitably be buyers and sellers who will supply one another's   15
wants; this is the readiest way to make a state self-sufficient and so fulfill the

purpose for which men come together into one state. A second office of a similar
20 kind undertakes the supervision and embellishment of public and private buildings,
the maintaining and repairing of houses and roads, the prevention of disputes about
boundaries, and other concerns of a like nature. This is commonly called the office
25 of City-warden, and has various departments, which, in more populous towns, are
shared among different persons, one, for example, taking charge of the walls,
another of the fountains, a third of harbours. There is another equally necessary
office, and of a similar kind, having to do with the same matters outside the walls
30 and in the country—the magistrates who hold this office are called Wardens of the
country, or Inspectors of the woods. Besides these three there is a fourth office of
receivers of taxes, who have under their charge the revenue which is distributed
among the various departments; these are called Receivers or Treasurers. Another
35 officer registers all private contracts, and decisions of the courts, all public
indictments, and also all preliminary proceedings. This office again is sometimes
subdivided; but in some places a single officer is responsible for all these matters.
40 These officers are called Recorders or Sacred Recorders, Presidents, and the like.

     Next to these comes an office of which the duties are the most necessary and
also the most difficult, viz. that to which is committed the execution of punishments, or the exaction of fines from those who are posted up according to the
1322ᵃ1 registers; and also the custody of prisoners. The difficulty of this office arises out of
the odium which is attached to it; no one will undertake it unless great profits are to
be made, and anyone who does is loath to execute the law. Still the office is
5   necessary; for judicial decisions are useless if they take no effect; and if society
cannot exist without them, neither can it exist without the execution of them. It is
an office which, being so unpopular, should not be entrusted to one person, but
divided among several taken from different courts. In like manner an effort should
10 be made to distribute among different persons the writing up of those who are on the
register of public debtors. Some sentences should be executed by the magistrates
also, and in particular penalties due to the outgoing magistrates should be exacted
by the incoming ones; and as regards those due to magistrates already in office,
when one court has given judgement, another should exact the penalty; for example,
the wardens of the city should exact the fines imposed by the wardens of the agora,
and others again should exact the fines imposed by them. For penalties are more
15 likely to be exacted when less odium attaches to the exaction of them; but a double
odium is incurred when the judges who have passed also execute the sentence, and if
they are always the executioners, they will be the enemies of all.

     In many places, while one magistracy executes the sentence, another has the
20 custody of the prisoners, as, for example, 'the Eleven' at Athens. It is well to
separate off the jailorship also, and try by some device to render the office less
unpopular. For it is quite as necessary as that of the executioners; but good men do
all they can to avoid it, and worthless persons cannot safely be trusted with it; for
25 they themselves require a guard, and are not fit to guard others. There ought not
therefore to be a single or permanent officer set apart for this duty; but it should be
entrusted to the young, wherever they are organized into a band or guard, and
different magistrates acting in turn should take charge of it.

There are the indispensable officers, and should be ranked first—next in order 30
follow others, equally necessary, but of higher rank, and requiring great experience
and trustworthiness. Such are the offices to which are committed the guard of the
city, and other military functions. Not only in time of war but of peace their duty 35
will be to defend the walls and gates, and to muster and marshal the citizens. In
some states there are many such offices; in others there are a few only, while small
states are content with one; these officers are called generals or commanders.
Again, if a state has cavalry or light-armed troops or archers or a naval force, it will 1322ᵇ1
sometimes happen that each of these departments has separate officers, who are
called admirals, or generals of cavalry or of light-armed troops. And there are
subordinate officers called naval captains, and captains of light-armed troops and of
horse, having others under them—all these are included in the department of war. 5
Thus much of military command.

But since some, not to say all, of these offices handle the public money, there
must of necessity be another office which examines and audits them, and has no
other functions. Such officers are called by various names—Scrutineers, Auditors, 10
Accountants, Controllers. Besides all these offices there is another which is supreme
over them; for the same office often deals with rates and taxes, or presides, in a
democracy, over the assembly. For there must be a body which convenes the 15
supreme authority in the state. In some places they are called 'probuli', because
they hold previous deliberations, but in a democracy more commonly 'councillors'.
These are the chief political offices.

Another set of officers is concerned with the maintenance of religion; priests
and guardians see to the preservation and repair of the temples of the gods and to 20
other matters of religion. One office of this sort may be enough in small places, but
in larger ones there are a great many besides the priesthood; for example
superintendents of public worship, guardians of shrines, treasurers of the sacred 25
revenues. Nearly connected with these there are also the officers appointed for the
performance of the public sacrifices, except any which the law assigns to the priests;
such sacrifices derive their dignity from the public hearth of the city. They are
sometimes called archons, sometimes kings, and sometimes prytanes.

These, then, are the necessary offices, which may be summed up as follows: 30
offices concerned with matters of religion, with war, with the revenue and
expenditure, with the market, with the city, with the harbours, with the country;
also with the courts of law, with the records of contracts, with execution of
sentences, with custody of prisoners, with audits and scrutinies and accounts of 35
magistrates; lastly, there are those which preside over the public deliberations of the
state. There are likewise magistracies characteristic of states which are peaceful
and prosperous, and at the same time have a regard to good order: such as the
offices of guardians of women, guardians of the laws, guardians of children, and
directors of gymnastics; also superintendents of gymnastic and Dionysiac contests, 1323ª1
and of other similar spectacles. Some of these are clearly not democratic offices; for
example, the guardianships of women and children—the poor, not having any
slaves, must employ both their women and children as servants. 5

Once more: there are three offices according to whose directions the highest

magistrates are chosen in certain states—guardians of the law, probuli, councillors—of these, the guardians of the law are an aristocratic, the probuli an
10 oligarchical, the council a democratic, institution. Enough, in outline, of the
different kinds of offices.

BOOK VII

15   1 · He who would duly inquire about the best form of a state ought first to
determine which is the most eligible life; while this remains uncertain the best form
of the state must also be uncertain; for, in the natural order of things, those men
may be expected to lead the best life who are governed in the best manner of which
20 their circumstances admit. We ought therefore to ascertain, first of all, which is the
most generally eligible life, and then whether the same life is or is not best for the
state and for individuals.

Assuming that enough has been already said in discussions outside the school
concerning the best life, we will now only repeat what is contained in them.
Certainly no one will dispute the propriety of that partition of goods which
25 separates them into three classes, viz. external goods, goods of the body, and goods
of the soul, or deny that the happy man must have all three. For no one would
maintain that he is happy who has not in him a particle of courage or temperance or
30 justice or practical wisdom, who is afraid of every insect which flutters past him,
and will commit any crime, however great, in order to gratify his lust for meat or
drink, who will sacrifice his dearest friend for the sake of half a farthing, and is as
feeble and false in mind as a child or a madman. These propositions are almost
35 universally acknowledged as soon as they are uttered, but men differ about the
degree or relative superiority of this or that good. Some think that a very moderate
amount of excellence is enough, but set no limit to their desires for wealth, property,
power, reputation, and the like. To them we shall reply by an appeal to facts, which
40 easily prove that mankind does not acquire or preserve the excellences by the help of
external goods, but external goods by the help of the excellences, and that
1323ᵇ1 happiness, whether consisting in pleasure or excellence, or both, is more often found
with those who are most highly cultivated in their mind and in their character, and
have only a moderate share of external goods, than among those who possess
5 external goods to a useless extent but are deficient in higher qualities; and this is not
only a matter of experience, but, if reflected upon, will easily appear to be in
accordance with reason. For, whereas external goods have a limit, like any other
instrument, and all things useful are useful for a purpose, and where there is too
much of them they must either do harm, or at any rate be of no use, to their
10 possessors, every good of the soul, the greater it is, is also of greater use, if the
epithet useful as well as noble is appropriate to such subjects. No proof is required
to show that the best state of one thing in relation to another corresponds in degree

of excellence to the interval between the natures of which we say that these very states are states: so that, if the soul is more noble than our possessions or our bodies, both absolutely and in relation to us, it must be admitted that the best state of either has a similar ratio to the other. Again, it is for the sake of the soul that goods external and goods of the body are desirable at all, and all wise men ought to choose them for the sake of the soul, and not the soul for the sake of them.

Let us acknowledge then that each one has just so much of happiness as he has of excellence and wisdom, and of excellent and wise action. The gods are a witness to us of this truth, for they are happy and blessed, not by reason of any external good, but in themselves and by reason of their own nature. And herein of necessity lies the difference between good fortune and happiness; for external goods come of themselves, and chance is the author of them, but no one is just or temperate by or through chance. In like manner, and by a similar train of argument, the happy state may be shown to be that which is best and which acts rightly; and it cannot act rightly without doing right actions, and neither individual nor state can do right actions without excellence and wisdom. Thus the courage, justice, and wisdom of a state have the same form and nature as the qualities which give the individual who possesses them the name of just, wise or temperate.

Thus much may suffice by way of preface: for I could not avoid touching upon these questions, neither could I go through all the arguments affecting them; these are the business of another science.

Let us assume then that the best life, both for individuals and states, is the life of excellence, when excellence has external goods enough for the performance of good actions. If there are any who dispute our assertion, we will in this treatise pass them over, and consider their objections hereafter.

2 · There remains to be discussed the question, whether the happiness of the individual is the same as that of the state, or different. Here again there can be no doubt—no one denies that they are the same. For those who hold that the well-being of the individual consists in his wealth, also think that riches make the happiness of the whole state, and those who value most highly the life of a tyrant deem that city the happiest which rules over the greatest number; while they who approve an individual for his excellence say that the more excellent a city is, the happier it is. Two points here present themselves for consideration: first, which is the more desirable life, that of a citizen who is a member of a state, or that of an alien who has no political ties; and again, which is the best form of constitution or the best condition of a state, either on the supposition that political privileges are desirable for all, or for a majority only? Since the good of the state and not of the individual is the proper subject of political thought and speculation, and we are engaged in a political discussion, while the first of these two points has a secondary interest for us, the latter will be the main subject of our inquiry.

Now it is evident that that form of government is best in which every man, whoever he is, can act best and live happily. But even those who agree in thinking that the life of excellence is the most desirable raise a question, whether the life of business and politics is or is not more desirable than one which is wholly independent of external goods, I mean than a contemplative life, which by some is maintained to be the only one worthy of a philosopher. For these two lives—the life 30 of the philosopher and the life of the statesman—appear to have been preferred by those who have been most keen in the pursuit of excellence, both in our own and in other ages. Which is the better is a question of no small moment; for the wise man, 35 like the wise state, will necessarily regulate his life according to the best end. There are some who think that while a despotic rule over others is the greatest injustice, to exercise a constitutional rule over them, even though not unjust, is a great impediment to a man's individual well-being. Others take an opposite view; they maintain that the true life of man is the practical and political, and that every 1324ᵇ1 excellence admits of being practised, quite as much by statesmen and rulers as by private individuals. Others, again, are of the opinion that arbitrary and tyrannical rule alone makes for happiness; indeed, in some states the entire aim both of the laws and of the constitution is to give men despotic power over their neighbours. 5 And, therefore, although in most cities the laws may be said generally to be in a chaotic state, still, if they aim at anything, they aim at the maintenance of power: thus in Lacedaemon and Crete the system of education and the greater part of the 10 laws are framed with a view to war. And in all nations which are able to gratify their ambition military power is held in esteem, for example among the Scythians and Persians and Thracians and Celts. In some nations there are even laws tending to stimulate the warlike virtues, as at Carthage, where we are told that men obtain the 15 honour of wearing as many armlets as they have served campaigns. There was once a law in Macedonia that he who had not killed an enemy should wear a halter, and among the Scythians no one who had not slain his man was allowed to drink out of the cup which was handed round at a certain feast. Among the Iberians, a warlike nation, the number of enemies whom a man has slain is indicated by the number of 20 obelisks which are fixed in the earth round his tomb; and there are numerous practices among other nations of a like kind, some of them established by law and others by custom. Yet to a reflecting mind it must appear very strange that the statesman should be always considering how he can dominate and tyrannize over 25 others, whether they are willing or not. How can that which is not even lawful be the business of the statesman or the legislator? Unlawful it certainly is to rule without regard to justice, for there may be might where there is no right. The other arts and 30 sciences offer no parallel; a physician is not expected to persuade or coerce his patients, nor a pilot the passengers in his ship. Yet most men appear to think that the art of despotic government is statesmanship, and what men affirm to be unjust and inexpedient in their own case they are not ashamed of practising towards 35 others; they demand just rule for themselves, but where other men are concerned they care nothing about it. Such behaviour is irrational; unless the one party is, and the other is not, born to serve, in which case men have a right to command, not indeed all their fellows, but only those who are intended to be subjects; just as we 40 ought not to hunt men, whether for food or sacrifice, but only those animals which may be hunted for food or sacrifice, that is to say, such wild animals as are eatable.

And surely there may be a city happy in isolation, which we will assume to be 1325ª1
well-governed (for it is quite possible that a city thus isolated might be well-
administered and have good laws); but such a city would not be constituted with any
view to war or the conquest of enemies—all that sort of thing must be excluded. 5
Hence we see very plainly that warlike pursuits, although generally to be deemed
honourable, are not the supreme end of all things, but only means. And the good
lawgiver should inquire how states and races of men and communities may
participate in a good life, and in the happiness which is attainable by them. His 10
enactments will not be always the same; and where there are neighbours he will
have to see what sort of studies should be practised in relation to their several
characters, or how the measures appropriate in relation to each are to be adopted.
The end at which the best form of government should aim may be properly made a 15
matter of future consideration.

3 · Let us now address those who, while they agree that the life of excellence
is the most desirable, differ about the manner of practising it. For some renounce
political power, and think that the life of the freeman is different from the life of the 20
statesman and the best of all; but others think the life of the statesman best. The
argument of the latter is that he who does nothing cannot do well, and that acting
well is identical with happiness. To both we say: 'you are partly right and partly
wrong.' The first class are right in affirming that the life of the freeman is better
than the life of the despot; for there is nothing noble in having the use of a slave, in 25
so far as he is a slave; or in issuing commands about necessary things. But it is an
error to suppose that every sort of rule is despotic like that of a master over slaves,
for there is as great a difference between rule over freemen and rule over slaves as
there is between slavery by nature and freedom by nature, about which I have said 30
enough at the commencement of this treatise. And it is equally a mistake to place
inactivity above action, for happiness is activity, and the actions of the just and wise
are the realization of much that is noble.

But perhaps someone, accepting these premises, may still maintain that
supreme power is the best of all things, because the possessors of it are able to 35
perform the greatest number of noble actions. If so, the man who is able to rule,
instead of giving up anything to his neighbour, ought rather to take away his power;
and the father should care nothing for his son, nor the son for his father, nor friend
for friend; they should not bestow a thought on one another in comparison with this
higher object, for the best is the most desirable and 'acting well' is the best. There
might be some truth in such a view if we assume that robbers and plunderers attain 1325ᵇ1
the chief good. But this can never be; their hypothesis is false. For the actions of a
ruler cannot really be honourable, unless he is as much superior to other men as a
man is to a woman, or a father to his children, or a master to his slaves. And 5
therefore he who violates the law can never recover by any success, however great,
what he has already lost in departing from excellence. For equals the honourable
and the just consist in sharing alike, as is just and equal. But that the unequal should
be given to equals, and the unlike to those who are like, is contrary to nature, and

10   nothing which is contrary to nature is good. If, therefore, there is anyone superior in
     excellence and in the power of performing the best actions, he is the man we ought
     to follow and obey, but he must have the capacity for action as well as excellence.
         If we are right in our view, and happiness is assumed to be acting well, the
15   active life will be the best, both for every city collectively, and for individuals. Not
     that a life of action must necessarily have relation to others, as some persons think,
     nor are those ideas only to be regarded as practical which are pursued for the sake of
     practical results, but much more the thoughts and contemplations which are
20   independent and complete in themselves; since acting well, and therefore a certain
     kind of action, is an end, and even in the case of external actions the directing mind
     is most truly said to act. Neither, again, is it necessary that states which are cut off
     from others and choose to live alone should be inactive; for activity, as well as other
25   things, may take place by sections; there are many ways in which the sections of a
     state act upon one another. The same thing is equally true of every individual. If this
     were otherwise, the gods and the universe, who have no external actions over and
30   above their own energies, would be far enough from perfection. Hence it is evident
     that the same life is best for each individual, and for states and for mankind
     collectively.

     4 · Thus far by way of introduction. In what has preceded I have discussed
35   other forms of government; in what remains the first point to be considered is what
     should be the conditions of the ideal or perfect state; for the perfect state cannot
     exist without a due supply of the means of life. And therefore we must presuppose
     many purely imaginary conditions, but nothing impossible. There will be a certain
     number of citizens, a country in which to place them, and the like. As the weaver or
1326ᵃ1 shipbuilder or any other artisan must have the material proper for his work (and in
     proportion as this is better prepared, so will the result of his art be nobler), so the
     statesman or legislator must also have the materials suited to him.
5   First among the materials required by the statesman is population: he will
     consider what should be the number and character of the citizens, and then what
     should be the size and character of the country. Most persons think that a state in
10   order to be happy ought to be large; but even if they are right, they have no idea
     what is a large and what a small state. For they judge of the size of the city by the
     number of the inhabitants; whereas they ought to regard, not their number, but
     their power. A city too, like an individual, has a work to do; and that city which is
     best adapted to the fulfilment of its work is to be deemed greatest, in the same sense
15   of the word great in which Hippocrates might be called greater, not as a man, but as
     a physician, than some one else who was taller. And even if we reckon greatness by
     numbers, we ought not to include everybody, for there must always be in cities a
20   multitude of slaves and resident aliens and foreigners; but we should include those
     only who are members of the state, and who form an essential part of it. The number
     of the latter is a proof of the greatness of a city; but a city which produces numerous
     artisans and comparatively few soldiers cannot be great, for a great city is not the
25   same as a populous one. Moreover, experience shows that a very populous city can

rarely, if ever, be well governed; since all cities which have a reputation for good government have a limit of population. We may argue on grounds of reason, and the same result will follow. For law is order, and good law is good order; but a very great 30 multitude cannot be orderly: to introduce order into the unlimited is the work of a divine power—of such a power as holds together the universe. Beauty is realized in number and magnitude, and the state which combines magnitude with good order must necessarily be the most beautiful. To the size of states there is a limit, as there 35 is to other things, plants, animals, implements; for none of these retain their natural power when they are too large or too small, but they either wholly lose their nature, or are spoiled. For example, a ship which is only a span long will not be a ship at all, nor a ship a quarter of a mile long; yet there may be a ship of a certain size, either 1326ᵇ1 too large or too small, which will still be a ship, but bad for sailing. In like manner a state when composed of too few is not, as a state ought to be, self-sufficient; when of too many, though self-sufficient in all mere necessaries, as a nation may be, it is not a state, being almost incapable of constitutional government. For who can be the 5 general of such a vast multitude, or who the herald, unless he have the voice of a Stentor?

A state, then, only begins to exist when it has attained a population sufficient for a good life in the political community: it may indeed, if it somewhat exceeds this number, be a greater state. But, as I was saying, there must be a limit. What the 10 limit should be will be easily ascertained by experience. For both governors and governed have duties to perform; the special functions of a governor are to command and to judge. But if the citizens of a state are to judge and to distribute offices according to merit, then they must know each other's characters; where they 15 do not possess this knowledge, both the election to offices and the decision of lawsuits will go wrong. When the population is very large they are manifestly settled at haphazard, which clearly ought not to be. Besides, in an over-populous 20 state foreigners and resident aliens will readily acquire the rights of citizens, for who will find them out? Clearly then the best limit of the population of a state is the largest number which suffices for the purposes of life, and can be taken in at a single view. Enough concerning the size of a state. 25

5 · Much the same principle will apply to the territory of the state: everyone would agree in praising the territory which is most self-sufficient; and that must be the territory which can produce everything necessary, for to have all things and to want nothing is sufficiency. In size and extent it should be such as may enable the 30 inhabitants to live at once temperately and liberally in the enjoyment of leisure. Whether we are right or wrong in laying down this limit we will inquire more precisely hereafter, when we have occasion to consider what is the right use of property and wealth—a matter which is much disputed, because men are inclined 35 to rush into one of two extremes, some into meanness, others into luxury.

It is not difficult to determine the general character of the territory which is required (there are, however, some points on which military authorities should be 40 heard); it should be difficult of access to the enemy, and easy of egress to the

1327ª1 inhabitants. Further, we require that the land as well as the inhabitants of whom we were just now speaking should be taken in at a single view, for a country which is easily seen can be easily protected. As to the position of the city, if we could have
5 what we wish, it should be well situated in regard both to sea and land. This then is one principle, that it should be a convenient centre for the protection of the whole country: the other is, that it should be suitable for receiving the fruits of the soil, and also for the bringing in of timber and any other products that are easily
10 transported.

6 · Whether a communication with the sea is beneficial to a well-ordered state or not is a question which has often been asked. It is argued that the introduction of strangers brought up under other laws, and the increase of
15 population, will be adverse to good order; the increase arises from their using the sea and having a crowd of merchants coming and going, and is inimical to good government. Apart from these considerations, it would be undoubtedly better, both with a view to safety and to the provision of necessaries, that the city and territory
20 should be connected with the sea; the defenders of a country, if they are to maintain themselves against an enemy, should be easily relieved both by land and by sea; and even if they are not able to attack by sea and land at once, they will have less
25 difficulty in doing mischief to their assailants on one element, if they themselves can use both. Moreover, it is necessary that they should import from abroad what is not found in their own country, and that they should export what they have in excess; for a city ought to be a market, not indeed for others, but for herself.
Those who make themselves a market for the world only do so for the sake of
30 revenue, and if a state ought not to desire profit of this kind it ought not to have such an emporium. Nowadays we often see in countries and cities dockyards and harbours very conveniently placed outside the city, but not too far off; and they are
35 kept in dependence by walls and similar fortifications. Cities thus situated manifestly reap the benefit of intercourse with their ports; and any harm which is likely to accrue may be easily guarded against by the laws, which will pronounce and determine who may hold communication with one another, and who may not.
There can be no doubt that the possession of a moderate naval force is advantageous to a city; the city should be formidable not only to its own citizens but
1327ᵇ1 to some of its neighbours, or, if necessary, able to assist them by sea as well as by land. The proper number or magnitude of this naval force is relative to the
5 character of the state; for if her function is to take a leading part in politics, her naval power should be commensurate with the scale of her enterprises. The population of the state need not be much increased, since there is no necessity that the sailors should be citizens: the marines who have the control and command will
10 be freemen, and belong also to the infantry; and wherever there is a dense population of country people and farmers, there will always be sailors more than enough. Of this we see instances at the present day. The city of Heraclea, for
15 example, although small in comparison with many others, can man a considerable

fleet. Such are our conclusions respecting the territory of the state, its harbours, its towns, its relations to the sea, and its maritime power.

7 · Having spoken of the number of the citizens, we will proceed to speak of what should be their character. This is a subject which can be easily understood by anyone who casts his eye on the more celebrated states of Greece, and generally on the distribution of races in the habitable world. Those who live in a cold climate and in Europe are full of spirit, but wanting in intelligence and skill; and therefore they retain comparative freedom, but have no political organization, and are incapable of ruling over others. Whereas the natives of Asia are intelligent and inventive, but they are wanting in spirit, and therefore they are always in a state of subjection and slavery. But the Hellenic race, which is situated between them, is likewise intermediate in character, being high-spirited and also intelligent. Hence it continues free, and is the best-governed of any nation, and, if it could be formed into one state, would be able to rule the world. There are also similar differences in the different tribes of Greece; for some of them are of a one-sided nature, and are intelligent or courageous only, while in others there is a happy combination of both qualities. And clearly those whom the legislator will most easily lead to excellence may be expected to be both intelligent and courageous. Some say that the guardians should be friendly towards those whom they know, fierce towards those whom they do not know. Now, passion is the quality of the soul which begets friendship and enables us to love; notably the spirit within us is more stirred against our friends and acquaintances than against those who are unknown to us, when we think that we are despised by them; for which reason Archilochus, complaining of his friends, very naturally addresses his spirit in these words, 'For surely thou are plagued on account of friends.'

The power of command and the love of freedom are in all men based upon this quality, for passion is commanding and invincible. Nor is it right to say that the guardians should be fierce towards those whom they do not know, for we ought not to be out of temper with anyone; and a lofty spirit is not fierce by nature, but only when excited against evil-doers. And this, as I was saying before, is a feeling which men show most strongly towards their friends if they think they have received a wrong at their hands: as indeed is reasonable; for, besides the actual injury, they seem to be deprived of a benefit by those who owe them one. Hence the saying, 'Cruel is the strife of brethren', and again, 'They who love in excess also hate in excess'.

Thus we have nearly determined the number and character of the citizens of our state, and also the size and nature of their territory. I say 'nearly', for we ought not to require the same accuracy in theory as in the facts given by perception.

8 · As in other natural compounds the conditions of a composite whole are not necessarily organic parts of it, so in a state or in any other combination forming a unity not everything is a part which is a necessary condition. The members of an association have necessarily some one thing the same and common to all, in which

they share equally or unequally; for example, food or land or any other thing. But where there are two things of which one exists for the sake of the other, they have nothing in common except that the one receives what the other produces. Such, for example, is the relation in which workmen and tools stand to their work; the house and the builder have nothing in common, but the art of the builder is for the sake of the house. And so states require property, but property, even though living beings are included in it, is no part of a state; for a state is a community of equals, aiming at the best life possible. Now, whereas happiness is the highest good, being a realization and perfect practice of excellence, which some can attain, while others have little or none of it, the various qualities of men are clearly the reason why there are various kinds of states and many forms of government; for different men seek after happiness in different ways and by different means, and so make for themselves different modes of life and forms of government. We must see also how many things are indispensable to the existence of a state, for what we call the parts of a state will be found among the indispensable things. Let us then enumerate the functions of a state, and we shall easily elicit what we want.

First, there must be food; secondly, arts, for life requires many instruments; thirdly, there must be arms, for the members of a community have need of them, and in their own hands, too, in order to maintain authority both against disobedient subjects and against external assailants; fourthly, there must be a certain amount of revenue, both for internal needs, and for the purposes of war; fifthly, or rather first, there must be a care of religion, which is commonly called worship; sixthly, and most necessary of all, there must be a power of deciding what is for the public interest, and what is just in men's dealings with one another.

These are the services which every state may be said to need. For a state is not a mere aggregate of persons, but, as we say, a union of them sufficing for the purposes of life; and if any of these things is wanting, it is impossible that the community can be absolutely self-sufficient. A state then should be framed with a view to the fulfilment of these functions. There must be farmers to procure food, and artisans, and a warlike and a wealthy class, and priests, and judges to decide what is necessary and expedient.

9 · Having determined these points, we have in the next place to consider whether all ought to share in every sort of occupation. Shall every man be at once farmer, artisan, councillor, judge, or shall we suppose the several occupations just mentioned assigned to different persons? or, thirdly, shall some employments be assigned to individuals and others common to all? The same arrangement, however, does not occur in every constitution; as we were saying, all may be shared by all, or not all by all, but only some by some; and hence arise the differences of constitutions, for in democracies all share in all, in oligarchies the opposite practice prevails. Now, since we are here speaking of the best form of government, i.e. that under which the state will be most happy (and happiness, as has been already said, cannot exist without excellence), it clearly follows that in the state which is best governed and possesses men who are just absolutely, and not merely relatively to the

principle of the constitution, the citizens must not lead the life of artisans or tradesmen, for such a life is ignoble and inimical to excellence. Neither must they be farmers, since leisure is necessary both for the development of excellence and the 1329^a1 performance of political duties.

Again, there is in a state a class of warriors, and another of councillors, who advise about the expedient and determine matters of law, and these seem in an especial manner parts of a state. Now, should these two classes be distinguished, or 5 are both functions to be assigned to the same persons? Here again there is no difficulty in seeing that both functions will in one way belong to the same, in another, to different persons. To different persons in so far as these employments are suited to different primes of life, for the one requires wisdom and the other strength. But on the other hand, since it is an impossible thing that those who are able to use or to resist force should be willing to remain always in subjection, from 10 this point of view the persons are the same; for those who carry arms can always determine the fate of the constitution. It remains therefore that both functions should be entrusted by the ideal constitution to the same persons, not, however, at the same time, but in the order prescribed by nature, who has given to young men strength and to older men wisdom. Such a distribution of duties will be expedient 15 and also just, and is founded upon a principle of conformity to merit. Besides, the ruling class should be the owners of property, for they are citizens, and the citizens of a state should be in good circumstances; whereas artisans or any other class which is not a producer of excellence have no share in the state. This follows from 20 our first principle, for happiness cannot exist without excellence, and a city is not to be termed happy in regard to a portion of the citizens, but in regard to them all. And clearly property should be in their hands, since the farmers will of necessity be 25 slaves or barbarian country people.

Of the classes enumerated there remain only the priests, and the manner in which their office is to be regulated is obvious. No farmer or artisan should be appointed to it; for the gods should receive honour from the citizens only. Now since the body of the citizens is divided into two classes, the warriors and the councillors, 30 and it is fitting that the worship of the gods should be duly performed, and also a rest provided in their service for those who from age have given up active life, to the old men of these two classes should be assigned the duties of the priesthood.

We have shown what are the necessary conditions, and what the parts of a 35 state: farmers, artisans, and labourers of all kinds are necessary to the existence of states, but the parts of the state are the warriors and councillors. And these are distinguished severally from one another, the distinction being in some cases permanent, in others not.

10 · It is no new or recent discovery of political philosophers that the state ought to be divided into classes, and that the warriors should be separated from the 1329^b1 farmers. The system has continued in Egypt and in Crete to this day, and was established, as tradition says, by a law of Sesostris in Egypt and of Minos in Crete.

5   The institution of common tables also appears to be of ancient date, being in Crete as old as the reign of Minos, and in Italy far older. The Italian historians say that
10   there was a certain Italus king of Oenotria, from whom the Oenotrians were called Italians, and who gave the name of Italy to the promontory of Europe lying within the Scylletic and Lametic Gulfs, which are distant from one another only half a
15   day's journey. They say that this Italus converted the Oenotrians from shepherds into farmers, and besides other laws which he gave them, was the founder of their common meals; even in our day some who are derived from him retain this institution and certain other laws of his. On the side of Italy towards Tyrrhenia
20   dwelt the Opici, who are now, as of old, called Ausones; and on the side towards Iapygia and the Ionian Gulf, in the district called Siritis, the Chones, who are likewise of Oenotrian race. From this part of the world originally came the institution of common tables; the separation into castes from Egypt, for the reign of
25   Sesostris is of far greater antiquity than that of Minos. It is true indeed that these and many other things have been invented several times over in the course of ages, or rather times without number; for necessity may be supposed to have taught men the inventions which were absolutely required, and when these were provided, it was natural that other things which would adorn and enrich life should grow up by
30   degrees. And we may infer that in political institutions the same rule holds. Egypt witnesses to the antiquity of all these things, for the Egyptians appear to be of all people the most ancient; and they have laws and a regular constitution existing from time immemorial. We should therefore make the best use of what has been already
35   discovered, and try to supply defects.

     I have already remarked that the land ought to belong to those who possess arms and have a share in the government, and that the farmers ought to be a class distinct from them; and I have determined what should be the extent and nature of the territory. Let me proceed to discuss the distribution of the land, and the character of the agricultural class; for I do not think that property ought to be
1330ª1   common, as some maintain, but only that by friendly consent there should be a common use of it; and that no citizen should be in want of subsistence.

     As to common meals, there is a general agreement that a well-ordered city
5   should have them; and we will hereafter explain what are our own reasons for taking this view. They ought, however, to be open to all the citizens. And yet it is not easy for the poor to contribute the requisite sum out of their private means, and to provide also for their household. The expense of religious worship should likewise be
10   a public charge. The land must therefore be divided into two parts, one public and the other private, and each part should be subdivided, part of the public land being appropriated to the service of the gods, and the other part used to defray the cost of the common meals; while of the private land, part should be near the border, and the
15   other near the city, so that, each citizen having two lots, they may all of them have land in both places; there is justice and fairness in such a division and it tends to inspire unanimity among the people in their border wars. Where there is not this arrangement, some of them are too ready to come to blows with their neighbours,
20   while others are so cautious that they quite lose the sense of honour. For this reason there is a law in some places which forbids those who dwell near the border to take

part in public deliberations about wars with neighbours, on the ground that their interests will pervert their judgement. For the reasons already mentioned, then, the land should be divided in the manner described. The very best thing of all would be that the farmers should be slaves taken from among men who are not all of the same race and not spirited, for if they have no spirit they will be better suited for their work, and there will be no danger of their making a revolution. The next best thing would be that they should be barbarian country people, and of a like inferior nature; some of them should be the slaves of individuals, and employed on the private estates of men of property, the remainder should be the property of the state and employed on the common land. I will hereafter explain what is the proper treatment of slaves, and why it is expedient that liberty should be always held out to them as the reward of their services.

11 · We have already said that the city should be open to the land and to the sea, and to the whole country as far as possible. In respect of the place itself our wish would be that its situation should be fortunate in four things. The first, health—this is a necessity: cities which lie towards the east, and are blown upon by winds coming from the east, are the healthiest; next in healthiness are those which are sheltered from the north wind, for they have a milder winter. The site of the city should likewise be convenient both for political administration and for war. With a view to the latter it should afford easy egress to the citizens, and at the same time be inaccessible and difficult of capture to enemies. There should be a natural abundance of springs and fountains in the town, or, if there is a deficiency of them, great reservoirs may be established for the collection of rain-water, such as will not fail when the inhabitants are cut off from the country by war. Special care should be taken of the health of the inhabitants, which will depend chiefly on the healthiness of the locality and of the quarter to which they are exposed, and secondly, on the use of pure water; this latter point is by no means a secondary consideration. For the elements which we use most and oftenest for the support of the body contribute most to health, and among these are water and air. For this reason, in all wise states, if there is a want of pure water, and the supply is not all equally good, the drinking water ought to be separated from that which is used for other purposes.

As to strongholds, what is suitable to different forms of government varies: thus an acropolis is suited to an oligarchy or a monarchy, but a plain to a democracy; neither to an aristocracy, but rather a number of strong places. The arrangement of private houses is considered to be more agreeable and generally more convenient if the streets are regularly laid out after the modern fashion which Hippodamus introduced, but for security in war the antiquated mode of building, which made it difficult for strangers to get out of a town and for assailants to find their way in, is preferable. A city should therefore adopt both plans of building: it is possible to arrange the houses irregularly, as farmers plant their vines in what are called 'clumps'. The whole town should not be laid out in straight lines, but only certain quarters and regions; thus security and beauty will be combined.

As to walls, those who say that cities making any pretension to military virtue should not have them, are quite out of date in their notions; and they may see the cities which prided themselves on this fancy confuted by facts. True, there is little courage shown in seeking for safety behind a rampart when an enemy is similar in character and not much superior in number; but the superiority of the besiegers may be and often is too much both for ordinary human valour and for that which is found only in a few; and if they are to be saved and to escape defeat and outrage, the strongest wall will be the truest soldierly precaution, more especially now that missiles and siege engines have been brought to such perfection. To have no walls would be as foolish as to choose a site for a town in an exposed country, and to level the heights; or as if an individual were to leave his house unwalled, lest the inmates should become cowards. Nor must we forget that those who have their cities surrounded by walls may either take advantage of them or not, but cities which are unwalled have no choice.

If our conclusions are just, not only should cities have walls, but care should be taken to make them ornamental, as well as useful for warlike purposes, and adapted to resist modern inventions. For as the assailants of a city do all they can to gain an advantage, so the defenders should make use of any means of defence which have been already discovered, and should devise and invent others, for when men are well prepared no enemy even thinks of attacking them.

12 · As the walls are to be divided by guard-houses and towers built at suitable intervals, and the body of citizens must be distributed at common tables, the idea will naturally occur that we should establish some of the common tables in the guard-houses. These might be arranged as has been suggested; while the principal common tables of the magistrates will occupy a suitable place, and there also will be the buildings appropriated to religious worship except in the case of those rites which the law or the Pythian oracle has restricted to a special locality. The site should be a spot seen far and wide, which gives due elevation to excellence[1] and towers over the neighbourhood. Below this spot should be established an agora, such as that which the Thessalians call the 'freemen's agora'; from this all trade should be excluded, and no artisan, farmer, or any such person allowed to enter, unless he be summoned by the magistrates. It would be a pleasing use of the place, if the gymnastic exercises of the elder men were performed there. For in this noble practice different ages should be separated, and some of the magistrates should stay with the boys, while the grown-up men remain with the magistrates; for the presence of the magistrates is the best mode of inspiring true modesty and ingenuous fear. There should also be a traders' agora, distinct and apart from the other, in a situation which is convenient for the reception of goods both by sea and land.

But we must not forget another section of the citizens, viz. the priests, for whom public tables should likewise be provided in their proper place near the temples. The magistrates who deal with contracts, indictments, summonses, and the

---

[1]Text uncertain.

like, and those who have the care of the agora and of the city respectively, ought to   10
be established near an agora and some public place of meeting; the neighbourhood
of the traders' agora will be a suitable spot; the upper agora we devote to the life of
leisure, the other is intended for the necessities of trade.

The same order should prevail in the country, for there too the magistrates,
called by some 'Inspectors of Forests' and by others 'Wardens of the Country', must   15
have guard-houses and common tables while they are on duty; temples should also
be scattered throughout the country, dedicated some to gods and some to heroes.

But it would be a waste of time for us to linger over details like these. The
difficulty is not in imagining but in carrying them out. We may talk about them as   20
much as we like, but the execution of them will depend upon fortune. Therefore let
us say no more about these matters for the present.

13 · Returning to the constitution itself, let us seek to determine out of what
and what sort of elements the state which is to be happy and well-governed should   25
be composed. There are two things in which all well-being consists: one of them is
the choice of a right end and aim of action, and the other the discovery of the actions
which contribute towards it; for the means and the end may agree or disagree.   30
Sometimes the right end is set before men, but in practice they fail to attain it; in
other cases they are successful in all the contributory factors, but they propose to
themselves a bad end; and sometimes they fail in both. Take, for example, the art of
medicine; physicians do not always understand the nature of health, and also the   35
means which they use may not effect the desired end. In all arts and sciences both
the end and the means should be equally within our control.

The happiness and well-being which all men manifestly desire, some have the
power of attaining, but to others, from some accident or defect of nature, the
attainment of them is not granted; for a good life requires a supply of external 1332^a1
goods, in a less degree when men are in a good state, in a greater degree when they
are in a lower state. Others again, who possess the conditions of happiness, go
utterly wrong from the first in the pursuit of it. But since our object is to discover the
best form of government, that, namely, under which a city will be best governed,   5
and since the city is best governed which has the greatest opportunity of obtaining
happiness, it is evident that we must clearly ascertain the nature of happiness.

We maintain, and have said in the *Ethics,* if the arguments there adduced are
of any value, that happiness is the realization and perfect exercise of excellence, and
this not conditional, but absolute. And I use the term 'conditional' to express that   10
which is indispensable, and 'absolute' to express that which is good in itself. Take
the case of just actions; just punishments and chastisements do indeed spring from a
good principle, but they are good only because we cannot do without them—it
would be better that neither individuals nor states should need anything of the   15
sort—but actions which aim at honour and advantage are absolutely the best. The
conditional action is only the choice of a lesser evil; whereas these are the
foundation and creation of good. A good man may make the best even of poverty
and disease, and the other ills of life; but he can only attain happiness under the   20

opposite conditions (for this also has been determined in the *Ethics,* that the good man is he for whom, because he is excellent, the things that are absolutely good are good; it is also plain that his use of these goods must be excellent and in the absolute

25   sense good). This makes men fancy that external goods are the cause of happiness, yet we might as well say that a brilliant performance on the lyre was to be attributed to the instrument and not to the skill of the performer.

It follows then from what has been said that some things the legislator must find ready to his hand in a state, others he must provide. And therefore we can only

30   say: may our state be constituted in such a manner as to be blessed with the goods of which fortune disposes (for we acknowledge her power): whereas excellence and goodness in the state are not a matter of chance but the result of knowledge and choice. A city can be excellent only when the citizens who have a share in the government are excellent, and in our state all the citizens share in the government;

35   let us then inquire how a man becomes excellent. For even if we could suppose the citizen body to be excellent, without each of them being so, yet the latter would be better, for in the excellence of each the excellence of all is involved.

There are three things which make men good and excellent; these are nature,

40   habit, reason. In the first place, every one must be born a man and not some other animal; so, too, he must have a certain character, both of body and soul. But some

1332ᵇ1   qualities there is no use in having at birth, for they are altered by habit, and there are some gifts which by nature are made to be turned by habit to good or bad. Animals lead for the most part a life of nature, although in lesser particulars some

5   are influenced by habit as well. Man has reason, in addition, and man only. For this reason nature, habit, reason must be in harmony with one another; for they do not always agree; men do many things against habit and nature, if reason persuades them that they ought. We have already determined what natures are likely to be

10   most easily moulded by the hands of the legislator. All else is the work of education; we learn some things by habit and some by instruction.

14 · Since every political society is composed of rulers and subjects, let us consider whether the relations of one to the other should interchange or be

15   permanent. For the education of the citizens will necessarily vary with the answer given to this question. Now, if some men excelled others in the same degree in which gods and heroes are supposed to excel mankind in general (having in the first place a great advantage even in their bodies, and secondly in their minds), so that the

20   superiority of the governors was undisputed and patent to their subjects, it would clearly be better that once for all the one class should rule and the others serve. But since this is unattainable, and kings have no marked superiority over their subjects,

25   such as Scylax affirms to be found among the Indians, it is obviously necessary on many grounds that all the citizens alike should take their turn of governing and being governed. Equality consists in the same treatment of similar persons, and no government can stand which is not founded upon justice. For if the government is

30   unjust everyone in the country unites with the governed in the desire to have a revolution, and it is an impossibility that the members of the government can be so

numerous as to be stronger than all their enemies put together. Yet that governors should be better than their subjects is undeniable. How all this is to be effected, and in what way they will respectively share in the government, the legislator has to 35 consider. The subject has been already mentioned. Nature herself has provided the distinction when she made a difference between old and young within the same species, of whom she fitted the one to govern and the other to be governed. No one takes offence at being governed when he is young, nor does he think himself better than his governors, especially if he will enjoy the same privilege when he reaches the 40 required age.

We conclude that from one point of view governors and governed are identical, and from another different. And therefore their education must be the same and 1333ᵃ1 also different. For he who would learn to command well must, as men say, first of all learn to obey. As I observed in the first part of this treatise, there is one rule which is for the sake of the rulers and another rule which is for the sake of the ruled; the former is a despotic, the latter a free government. Some commands differ not in the 5 thing commanded, but in the intention with which they are imposed. That is why many apparently menial offices are an honour to the free youth by whom they are performed; for actions do not differ as honourable or dishonourable in themselves so 10 much as in the end and intention of them. But since we say that the excellence of the citizen and ruler is the same as that of the good man, and that the same person must first be a subject and then a ruler, the legislator has to see that they become good men, and by what means this may be accomplished, and what is the end of the 15 perfect life.

Now the soul of man is divided into two parts, one of which has a rational principle in itself, and the other, not having a rational principle in itself, is able to obey such a principle. And we call a man in any way good because he has the excellences of these two parts. In which of them the end is more likely to be found is 20 no matter of doubt to those who adopt our division; for in the world both of nature and of art the inferior always exists for the sake of the superior, and the superior is that which has a rational principle. This principle, too, in our ordinary way of making the division, is divided into two kinds, for there is a practical and a 25 speculative principle. This part, then, must evidently be similarly divided. And there must be a corresponding division of actions; the actions of the naturally better part are to be preferred by those who have it in their power to attain to two out of the three or to all, for that is always to everyone the most desirable which is the highest 30 attainable by him. The whole of life is further divided into two parts, business and leisure, war and peace, and of actions some aim at what is necessary and useful, and some at what is honourable. And the preference given to one or the other class of actions must necessarily be like the preference given to one or other part of the soul and its actions over the other; there must be war for the sake of peace, business for 35 the sake of leisure, things useful and necessary for the sake of things honourable. All these points the statesman should keep in view when he frames his laws; he should consider the parts of the soul and their functions, and above all the better and the end; he should also remember the diversities of human lives and actions. For

1333^b1   men must be able to engage in business and go to war, but leisure and peace are
better; they must do what is necessary and indeed what is useful, but what is
honourable is better. On such principles children and persons of every age which
requires education should be trained. Whereas even the Greeks of the present day

5   who are reputed to be best governed, and the legislators who gave them their
constitutions, do not appear to have framed their governments with a regard to the
best end, or to have given them laws and education with a view to all the excellences,

10   but in a vulgar spirit have fallen back on those which promised to be more useful
and profitable. Many modern writers have taken a similar view: they commend the
Lacedaemonian constitution, and praise the legislator for making conquest and war

15   his sole aim, a doctrine which may be refuted by argument and has long ago been
refuted by facts. For most men desire empire in the hope of accumulating the goods
of fortune; and on this ground Thibron and all those who have written about the

20   Lacedaemonian constitution have praised their legislator, because the Lacedaemonians, by being trained to meet dangers, gained great power. But surely they are
not a happy people now that their empire has passed away, nor was their legislator
right. How ridiculous is the result, if, while they are continuing in the observance of

25   his laws and no one interferes with them, they have lost the better part of life! These
writers further err about the sort of government which the legislator should
approve, for the government of freemen is nobler and implies more excellence than
despotic government. Neither is a city to be deemed happy or a legislator to be

30   praised because he trains his citizens to conquer and obtain dominion over their
neighbours, for there is great harm in this. On a similar principle any citizen who
could, should obviously try to obtain the power in his own state—the crime which

35   the Lacedaemonians accuse king Pausanias of attempting, although he had such
great honour already. No such principle and no law having this object is either
statesmanlike or useful or right. For the same things are best both for individuals
and for states, and these are the things which the legislator ought to implant in the
minds of his citizens. Neither should men study war with a view to the enslavement

40   of those who do not deserve to be enslaved; but first of all they should provide
against their own enslavement, and in the second place obtain empire for the good

1334^a1   of the governed, and not for the sake of exercising a general despotism, and in the
third place they should seek to be masters only over those who deserve to be slaves.
Facts, as well as arguments, prove that the legislator should direct all his military

5   and other measures to the provision of leisure and the establishment of peace. For
most of these military states are safe only while they are at war, but fall when they
have acquired their empire; like unused iron they lose their edge in time of peace.
And for this the legislator is to blame, he never having taught them how to lead the

10   life of peace.

15 · Since the end of individuals and of states is the same, the end of the best
man and of the best constitution must also be the same; it is therefore evident that
there ought to exist in both of them the excellences of leisure; for peace, as has been

15   often repeated, is the end of war, and leisure of toil. But leisure and cultivation may

be promoted not only by those excellences which are practised in leisure, but also by some of those which are useful to business. For many necessaries of life have to be supplied before we can have leisure. Therefore a city must be temperate and brave, and able to endure: for truly, as the proverb says, 'There is no leisure for 20 slaves,' and those who cannot face danger like men are the slaves of any invader. Courage and endurance are required for business and philosophy for leisure, temperance and justice for both, and more especially in times of peace and leisure, 25 for war compels men to be just and temperate, whereas the enjoyment of good fortune and the leisure which comes with peace tend to make them insolent. Those then who seem to be the best-off and to be in the possession of every good, have 30 special need of justice and temperance—for example, those (if such there be, as the poets say) who dwell in the Islands of the Blest; they above all will need philosophy and temperance and justice, and all the more the more leisure they have, living in the midst of abundance. There is no difficulty in seeing why the state that would be 35 happy and good ought to have these excellences. If it is disgraceful in men not to be able to use the goods of life, it is peculiarly disgraceful not to be able to use them in time of leisure—to show excellent qualities in action and war, and when they have peace and leisure to be no better than slaves. That is why we should not practise excellence after the manner of the Lacedaemonians. For they, while agreeing with 40 other men in their conception of the highest goods, differ from the rest of mankind in thinking that they are to be obtained by the practice of a single excellence. And 1334ᵇ1 since these goods and the enjoyment of them are greater than the enjoyment derived from the excellences . . .² and that for its own sake, is evident from what has been said; we must now consider how and by what means it is to be attained. 5

We have already determined that nature and habit and reason are required, and, of these, the proper nature of the citizens has also been defined by us. But we have still to consider whether the training of early life is to be that of reason or habit, for these two must accord, and when in accord they will then form the best of 10 harmonies. Reason may be mistaken and fail in attaining the highest ideal of life, and there may be a like influence of habit. Thus much is clear in the first place, that, as in all other things, birth implies an antecedent beginning, and that there are beginnings whose end is relative to a further end. Now, in men reason and mind are 15 the end towards which nature strives, so that the birth and training in custom of the citizens ought to be ordered with a view to them. In the second place, as the soul and body are two, we see also that there are two parts of the soul, the rational and the irrational, and two corresponding states—reason and appetite. And as the body is 20 prior in order of generation to the soul, so the irrational is prior to the rational. The proof is that anger and wishing and desire are implanted in children from their very birth, but reason and understanding are developed as they grow older. For this reason, the care of the body ought to precede that of the soul, and the training of the 25 appetitive part should follow: none the less our care of it must be for the sake of the reason, and our care of the body for the sake of the soul.

²Dreizehnter marks a lacuna.

16 · Since the legislator should begin by considering how the bodies of the children whom he is rearing may be as good as possible, his first care will be about marriage—at what age should his citizens marry, and who are fit to marry? In legislating on this subject he ought to consider the persons and the length of their life, that their procreative life may terminate at the same period, and that they may not differ in their bodily powers, as will be the case if the man is still able to beget children while the woman is unable to bear them, or the woman able to bear while the man is unable to beget, for from these causes arise quarrels and differences between married persons. Secondly, he must consider the time at which the children will succeed to their parents; there ought not to be too great an interval of age, for then the parents will be too old to derive any pleasure from their affection, or to be of any use to them. Nor ought they to be too nearly of an age; to youthful marriages there are many objections—the children will be lacking in respect for the parents, who will seem to be their contemporaries, and disputes will arise in the management of the household. Thirdly, and this is the point from which we digressed, the legislator must mould to his will the bodies of newly-born children. Almost all these objects may be secured by attention to one point. Since the time of generation is commonly limited within the age of seventy years in the case of a man, and of fifty in the case of a woman, the commencement of the union should conform to these periods. The union of male and female when too young is bad for the procreation of children; in all other animals the offspring of the young are small and ill-developed, and with a tendency to produce female children, and therefore also in man, as is proved by the fact that in those cities in which men and women are accustomed to marry young, the people are small and weak; in childbirth also younger women suffer more, and more of them die; some persons say that this was the meaning of the response once given to the Troezenians—the oracle really meant that many died because they married too young; it had nothing to do with the gathering of the harvest. It also conduces to temperance not to marry too soon; for women who marry early are apt to be wanton; and in men too the bodily frame is stunted if they marry while the seed is growing (for there is a time when the growth of the seed, also, ceases, or continues to but a slight extent). Women should marry when they are about eighteen years of age, and men at thirty-seven; then they are in the prime of life, and the decline in the powers of both will coincide. Further, the children, if their birth takes place soon, as may reasonably be expected, will succeed in the beginning of their prime, when the fathers are already in the decline of life, and have nearly reached their term of three-score years and ten.

Thus much of the age proper for marriage: the season of the year should also be considered; according to our present custom, people generally limit marriage to the season of winter, and they are right. The precepts of physicians and natural philosophers about generation should also be studied by the parents themselves; the physicians give good advice about the favourable conditions of the body, and the natural philosophers about the winds; of which they prefer the north to the south.

What constitution in the parent is most advantageous to the offspring is a subject which we will consider more carefully when we speak of the education of

children, and we will only make a few general remarks at present. The constitution 5
of an athlete is not suited to the life of a citizen, or to health, or to the procreation of
children, any more than the valetudinarian or exhausted constitution, but one which
is in a mean between them. A man's constitution should be inured to labour, but not
to labour which is excessive or of one sort only, such as is practised by athletes; he 10
should be capable of all the actions of a freeman. These remarks apply equally to
both parents.

Women who are with child should take care of themselves; they should take
exercise and have a nourishing diet. The first of these prescriptions the legislator
will easily carry into effect by requiring that they shall take a walk daily to some 15
temple, where they can worship the gods who preside over birth. Their minds,
however, unlike their bodies, they ought to keep quiet, for the offspring derive their
natures from their mothers as plants do from the earth.

As to the exposure and rearing of children, let there be a law that no deformed 20
child shall live. But as to an excess in the number of children, if the established
customs of the state forbid the exposure of any children who are born, let a limit be
set to the number of children a couple may have; and if couples have children in
excess, let abortion be procured before sense and life have begun; what may or may 25
not be lawfully done in these cases depends on the question of life and sensation.

And now, having determined at what ages men and women are to begin their
union, let us also determine how long they shall continue to beget and bear offspring
for the state; men who are too old, like men who are too young, produce children 30
who are defective in body and mind; the children of very old men are weakly. The
limit, then, should be the age which is the prime of their intelligence, and this in
most persons, according to the notion of some poets who measure life by periods of
seven years, is about fifty; at four or five years later, they should cease from having 35
families; and from that time forward only cohabit with one another for the sake of
health, or for some similar reason.

As to adultery, let it be held disgraceful, in general, for any man or woman to
be found in any way unfaithful when they are married, and called husband and
wife. If during the time of bearing children anything of the sort occur, let the guilty 1336ᵃ1
person be punished with a loss of privileges in proportion to the offence.

17 · After the children have been born, the manner of rearing them may be
supposed to have a great effect on their bodily strength. It would appear from the 5
example of animals, and of those nations who desire to create the military habit,
that the food which has most milk in it is best suited to human beings; but the less
wine the better, if they would escape diseases. Also all the motions to which children
can be subjected at their early age are very useful. But in order to preserve their
tender limbs from distortion, some nations have had recourse to mechanical 10
appliances which straighten their bodies. To accustom children to the cold from
their earliest years is also an excellent practice, which greatly conduces to health,
and hardens them for military service. Hence many barbarians have a custom of 15
plunging their children at birth into a cold stream; others, like the Celts, clothe

them in a light wrapper only. For human nature should be early habituated to endure all which by habit it can be made to endure; but the process must be gradual.
20   And children, from their natural warmth, may be easily trained to bear cold. Such care should attend them in the first stage of life.

The next period lasts to the age of five; during this no demand should be made
25   upon the child for study or labour, lest its growth be impeded; and there should be sufficient motion to prevent the limbs from being inactive. This can be secured, among other ways, by play, but the play should not be vulgar or tiring or effeminate.
30   The Directors of Education, as they are termed, should be careful what tales or stories the children hear, for all such things are designed to prepare the way for the business of later life, and should be for the most part imitations of the occupations which they will hereafter pursue in earnest. Those are wrong who in their *Laws*
35   attempt to check the loud crying and screaming of children, for these contribute towards their growth, and, in a manner, exercise their bodies. Straining the voice has a strengthening effect similar to that produced by the retention of the breath in
40   violent exertions. The Directors of Education should have an eye to their bringing up, and in particular should take care that they are left as little as possible with
1336ᵇ1   slaves. For until they are seven years old they must live at home; and therefore, even at this early age, it is to be expected that they should acquire a taint of meanness from what they hear and see. Indeed, there is nothing which the legislator should be
5   more careful to drive away than indecency of speech; for the light utterance of shameful words leads soon to shameful actions. The young especially should never be allowed to repeat or hear anything of the sort. A freemen who is found saying or doing what is forbidden, if he be too young as yet to have the privilege of reclining at
10   the public tables, should be disgraced and beaten, and an elder person degraded as his slavish conduct deserves. And since we do not allow improper language, clearly we should also banish pictures or speeches from the stage which are indecent. Let
15   the rulers take care that there be no image or picture representing unseemly actions, except in the temples of those gods at whose festivals the law permits even ribaldry, and whom the law also permits to be worshipped by persons of mature age on behalf of themselves, their children, and their wives. But the legislator should not allow
20   youth to be spectators of iambi or of comedy until they are of an age to sit at the public tables and to drink strong wine; by that time education will have armed them against the evil influences of such representations.

We have made these remarks in a cursory manner—they are enough for the
25   present occasion; but hereafter we will return to the subject and after a fuller discussion determine whether such liberty should or should not be granted, and in what way granted, if at all. Theodorus, the tragic actor, was quite right in saying
30   that he would not allow any other actor, not even if he were quite second-rate, to enter before himself, because the spectators grew fond of the voices which they first heard. And the same principle applies universally to association with things as well as with persons, for we always like best whatever comes first. And therefore youth should be kept strangers to all that is bad, and especially to things which suggest
35   vice or hate. When the five years have passed away, during the two following years

they must look on at the pursuits which they are hereafter to learn. There are two periods of life with reference to which education has to be divided, from seven to the age of puberty, and onwards to the age of twenty-one. The poets who divide ages by 40 sevens are in the main right: but we should observe the divisions actually made by nature; for the deficiencies of nature are what art and education seek to fill up. 1337ᵃ1

Let us then first inquire if any regulations are to be laid down about children, and secondly, whether the care of them should be the concern of the state or of 5 private individuals, which latter is in our own day the common custom, and in the third place, what these regulations should be.

BOOK VIII

1 · No one will doubt that the legislator should direct his attention above all 10 to the education of youth; for the neglect of education does harm to the constitution. The citizen should be moulded to suit the form of government under which he lives. For each government has a peculiar character which originally formed and which continues to preserve it. The character of democracy creates democracy, and the 15 character of oligarchy creates oligarchy; and always the better the character, the better the government.

Again, for the exercise of any faculty or art a previous training and habituation 20 are required; clearly therefore for the practice of excellence. And since the whole city has one end, it is manifest that education should be one and the same for all, and that it should be public, and not private—not as at present, when everyone looks after his own children separately, and gives them separate instruction of the 25 sort which he thinks best; the training in things which are of common interest should be the same for all. Neither must we suppose that anyone of the citizens belongs to himself, for they all belong to the state, and are each of them a part of the state, and the care of each part is inseparable from the care of the whole. In this 30 particular as in some others the Lacedaemonians are to be praised, for they take the greatest pains about their children, and make education the business of the state.

2 · That education should be regulated by law and should be an affair of state is not to be denied, but what should be the character of this public education, and how young persons should be educated, are questions which remain to be 35 considered. As things are, there is disagreement about the subjects. For men are by no means agreed about the things to be taught, whether we look to excellence or the best life. Neither is it clear whether education is more concerned with intellectual or with moral excellence. The existing practice is perplexing; no one knows on what 40 principle we should proceed—should the useful in life, or should excellence, or should the higher knowledge, be the aim of our training?—all three opinions have been entertained. Again, about the means there is no agreement; for different 1337ᵇ1 persons, starting with different ideas about the nature of excellence, naturally

disagree about the practice of it. There can be no doubt that children should be taught those useful things which are really necessary, but not all useful things; for 5 occupations are divided into liberal and illiberal; and to young children should be imparted only such kinds of knowledge as will be useful to them without making mechanics of them. And any occupation, art, or science, which makes the body or 10 soul or mind of the freeman less fit for the practice or exercise of excellence, is mechanical; wherefore we call those arts mechanical which tend to deform the body, and likewise all paid employments, for they absorb and degrade the mind. 15 There are also some liberal arts quite proper for a freeman to acquire, but only in a certain degree, and if he attends to them too closely, in order to attain perfection in them, the same harmful effects will follow. The object also which a man sets before him makes a great difference; if he does or learns anything for his own sake or for the sake of his friends, or with a view to excellence, the action will not appear 20 illiberal; but if done for the sake of others, the very same action will be thought menial and servile. The received subjects of instruction, as I have already remarked, are partly of a liberal and partly of an illiberal character.

3 · The customary branches of education are in number four; they are— reading and writing, gymnastic exercises, and music, to which is sometimes added 25 drawing. Of these, reading and writing and drawing are regarded as useful for the purposes of life in a variety of ways, and gymnastic exercises are thought to infuse courage. Concerning music a doubt may be raised—in our own day most men cultivate it for the sake of pleasure, but originally it was included in education, 30 because nature herself, as has been often said, requires that we should be able, not only to work well, but to use leisure well; for, as I must repeat once again, the first principle of all action is leisure. Both are required, but leisure is better than occupation and is its end; and therefore the question must be asked, what ought we 35 to do when at leisure? Clearly we ought not to be playing, for then play would be the end of life. But if this is inconceivable, and play is needed more amid serious occupations than at other times (for he who is hard at work has need of relaxation, and play gives relaxation, whereas occupation is always accompanied with exertion 40 and effort), we should introduce amusements only at suitable times, and they should be our medicines, for the emotion which they create in the soul is a 1338ᵃl relaxation, and from the pleasure we obtain rest. But leisure of itself gives pleasure and happiness and enjoyment of life, which are experienced, not by the busy man, but by those who have leisure. For he who is occupied has in view some end which he 5 has not attained; but happiness is an end, since all men deem it to be accompanied with pleasure and not with pain. This pleasure, however, is regarded differently by different persons, and varies according to the habit of individuals; the pleasure of the best man is the best, and springs from the noblest sources. It is clear then that 10 there are branches of learning and education which we must study merely with a view to leisure spent in intellectual activity, and these are to be valued for their own sake; whereas those kinds of knowledge which are useful in business are to be deemed necessary, and exist for the sake of other things. And therefore our fathers

admitted music into education, not on the ground either of its necessity or utility, for it is not necessary, nor indeed useful in the same manner as reading and writing, which are useful in money-making, in the management of a household, in the acquisition of knowledge and in political life, nor like drawing, useful for a more correct judgement of the works of artists, nor again like gymnastic, which gives health and strength; for neither of these is to be gained from music. There remains, then, the use of music for intellectual enjoyment in leisure; which is in fact evidently the reason of its introduction, this being one of the ways in which it is thought that a freeman should pass his leisure; as Homer says—

But he who alone should be called to the pleasant feast,

and afterwards he speaks of others whom he describes as inviting

The bard who would delight them all.

And in another place Odysseus says there is no better way of passing life than when men's hearts are merry and

The banqueters in the hall, sitting in order, hear the voice of the minstrel.

It is evident, then, that there is a sort of education in which parents should train their sons, not as being useful or necessary, but because it is liberal or noble. Whether this is of one kind only, or of more than one, and if so, what they are, and how they are to be imparted, must hereafter be determined. Thus much we are already in a position to say; for the ancients bear witness to us—their opinion may be gathered from the fact that music is one of the received and traditional branches of education. Further, it is clear that children should be instructed in some useful things—for example, in reading and writing—not only for their usefulness, but also because many other sorts of knowledge are acquired through them. With a like view they may be taught drawing, not to prevent their making mistakes in their own purchases, or in order that they may not be imposed upon in the buying or selling of articles, but perhaps rather because it makes them judges of the beauty of the human form. To be always seeking after the useful does not become free and exalted souls. Now it is clear that in education practice must be used before theory, and the body be trained before the mind; and therefore boys should be handed over to the trainer, who creates in them the proper habit of body, and to the wrestling-master, who teaches them their exercises.

4 · Of those states which in our own day seem to take the greatest care of children, some aim at producing in them an athletic habit, but they only injure their bodies and stunt their growth. Although the Lacedaemonians have not fallen into this mistake, yet they brutalize their children by laborious exercises which they think will make them courageous. But in truth, as we have often repeated, education should not be exclusively, or principally, directed to this end. And even if we suppose the Lacedaemonians to be right in their end, they do not attain it. For among barbarians and among animals courage is found associated, not with the

greatest ferocity, but with a gentle and lion-like temper. There are many races who
are ready enough to kill and eat men, such as the Achaeans and Heniochi, who both
live about the Black Sea; and there are other mainland tribes, as bad or worse, who
all live by plunder, but have no courage. It is notorious that the Lacedaemonians
themselves, while they alone were assiduous in their laborious drill, were superior to
others, but now they are beaten both in war and gymnastic exercises. For their
ancient superiority did not depend on their mode of training their youth, but only on
the circumstance that they trained them when their only rivals did not. Hence we
may infer that what is noble, not what is brutal, should have the first place; no wolf
or other wild animal will face a really noble danger; such dangers are for the brave
man. And parents who devote their children to gymnastics while they neglect their
necessary education, in reality make them mechanics; for they make them useful to
the art of statesmanship in one quality only, and even in this the argument proves
them to be inferior to others. We should judge the Lacedaemonians not from what
they have been, but from what they are; for now they have rivals who compete with
their education; formerly they had none.

It is an admitted principle that gymnastic exercises should be employed in
education, and that for children they should be of a lighter kind, avoiding severe diet
or painful toil, lest the growth of the body be impaired. The evil of excessive training
in early years is strikingly proved by the example of the Olympic victors; for not
more than two or three of them have gained a prize both as boys and as men; their
early training and severe gymnastic exercises exhausted their constitutions. When
boyhood is over, three years should be spent in other studies; the period of life which
follows may then be devoted to hard exercise and strict diet. Men ought not to
labour at the same time with their minds and with their bodies; for the two kinds of
labour are opposed to one another; the labour of the body impedes the mind, and the
labour of the mind the body.

5 · Concerning music there are some questions which we have already
raised; these we may now resume and carry further; and our remarks will serve as a
prelude to this or any other discussion of the subject. It is not easy to determine the
nature of music, or why anyone should have a knowledge of it. Shall we say, for the
sake of amusement and relaxation, like sleep or drinking, which are not good in
themselves, but are pleasant, and at the same time 'make care to cease', as
Euripides says? And for this end men also appoint music, and make use of all three
alike—sleep, drinking, music—to which some add dancing. Or shall we argue that
music conduces to excellence, on the ground that it can form our minds and
habituate us to true pleasures as our bodies are made by gymnastic to be of a certain
character? Or shall we say that it contributes to the enjoyment of leisure and
mental cultivation, which is a third alternative? Now obviously youths are not to be
instructed with a view to their amusement, for learning is no amusement, but is
accompanied with pain. Neither is intellectual enjoyment suitable to boys of that
age, for it is the end, and that which is imperfect cannot attain the end. But perhaps
it may be said that boys learn music for the sake of the amusement which they will
have when they are grown up. If so, why should they learn themselves, and not, like

the Persian and Median kings, enjoy the pleasure and instruction which is derived   35
from hearing others? (for surely persons who have made music the business and
profession of their lives will be better performers than those who practise only long
enough to learn). If they must learn music, on the same principle they should learn
cookery, which is absurd. And even granting that music may form the character,   40
the objection still holds: why should we learn ourselves? Why cannot we attain true
pleasure and form a correct judgement from hearing others, as the Lacedaemonians   1339^{b}1
do?—for they, without learning music, nevertheless can correctly judge, as they
say, of good and bad melodies. Or again, if music should be used to promote
cheerfulness and refined intellectual enjoyment, the objection still remains—why   5
should we learn ourselves instead of enjoying the performances of others? We may
illustrate what we are saying by our conception of the gods; for in the poets Zeus
does not himself sing or play on the lyre. Indeed we call professional performers
artisans; no freeman would play or sing unless he were intoxicated or in jest. But
these matters may be left for the present.   10

The first question is whether music is or is not to be a part of education. Of the
three things mentioned in our discussion, which does it produce—education or
amusement or intellectual enjoyment?—for it may be reckoned under all three, and
seems to share in the nature of all of them. Amusement is for the sake of relaxation,   15
and relaxation is of necessity sweet, for it is the remedy of pain caused by toil; and
intellectual enjoyment is universally acknowledged to contain an element not only
of the noble but of the pleasant, for happiness is made up of both. All men agree that
music is one of the pleasantest things, whether with or without song; as Musaeus   20
says,

> Song is to mortals of all things the sweetest.

Hence and with good reason it is introduced into social gatherings and entertainments, because it makes the hearts of men glad: so that on this ground alone we may
assume that the young ought to be trained in it. For innocent pleasures are not only   25
in harmony with the end of life, but they also provide relaxation. And whereas men
rarely attain the end, but often rest by the way and amuse themselves, not only with
a view to a further end, but also for the pleasure's sake, it may be well at times to let   30
them find a refreshment in music. It sometimes happens that men make amusement
the end, for the end probably contains some element of pleasure, though not any
ordinary pleasure; but they mistake the lower for the higher, and in seeking for the
one find the other, since every pleasure has a likeness to the end of action. For the   35
end is not desirable for the sake of any future good, nor do the pleasures which we
have described exist for the sake of any future good but of the past, that is to say,
they are the alleviation of past toils and pains. And we may infer this to be the   –
reason why men seek happiness from these pleasures. But music is pursued, not only   40
as an alleviation of past toil, but also as providing recreation. And who can say
whether, having this use, it may not also have a nobler one? In addition to this   1340^{a}1
common pleasure, felt and shared in by all (for the pleasure given by music is
natural, and therefore adapted to all ages and characters), may it not have also   5
some influence over the character and the soul? It must have such an influence if

characters are affected by it. And that they are so affected is proved in many ways, and not least by the power which the songs of Olympus exercise; for beyond
10 question they inspire enthusiasm, and enthusiasm is an emotion of the character of the soul. Besides, when men hear imitations, even apart from the rhythms and tunes themselves, their feelings move in sympathy. Since then music is a pleasure, and
15 excellence consists in rejoicing and loving and hating rightly, there is clearly nothing which we are so much concerned to acquire and to cultivate as the power of forming right judgements, and of taking delight in good dispositions and noble actions. Rhythm and melody supply imitations of anger and gentleness, and also of
20 courage and temperance, and of all the qualities contrary to these, and of the other qualities of character, which hardly fall short of the actual affections, as we know from our own experience, for in listening to such strains our souls undergo a change. The habit of feeling pleasure or pain at mere representations is not far removed
25 from the same feeling about realities; for example, if any one delights in the sight of a statue for its beauty only, it necessarily follows that the sight of the original will be pleasant to him. The objects of no other sense, such as taste or touch, have any
30 resemblance to moral qualities; in visible objects there is only a little, for there are figures which are of a moral character, but only to a slight extent, and all do not participate in the feeling about them. Again, figures and colours are not imitations, but signs, of character, indications which the body gives of states of feeling. The
35 connexion of them with morals is slight, but in so far as there is any, young men should be taught to look, not at the works of Pauson, but at those of Polygnotus, or any other painter or sculptor who expresses character. On the other hand, even in
40 mere melodies there is an imitation of character, for the musical modes differ essentially from one another, and those who hear them are differently affected by
1340ᵇ1 each. Some of them make men sad and grave, like the so-called Mixolydian, others enfeeble the mind, like the relaxed modes, another, again, produces a moderate and
5 settled temper, which appears to be the peculiar effect of the Dorian; the Phrygian inspires enthusiasm. The whole subject has been well treated by philosophical writers on this branch of education, and they confirm their arguments by facts. The same principles apply to rhythms; some have a character of rest, others of motion,
10 and of these latter again, some have a more vulgar, others a nobler movement. Enough has been said to show that music has a power of forming the character, and should therefore be introduced into the education of the young. The study is suited
15 to the stage of youth, for young persons will not, if they can help, endure anything which is not sweetened by pleasure, and music has a natural sweetness. There seems to be in us a sort of affinity to musical modes and rhythms, which makes some philosophers say that the soul is a harmony, others, that it possesses harmony.

20   6 · And now we have to determine the question which has been already raised, whether children should be themselves taught to sing and play or not. Clearly there is a considerable difference made in the character by the actual practice of the art. It is difficult, if not impossible, for those who do not perform to
25 be good judges of the performance of others. Besides, children should have something to do, and the rattle of Archytas, which people give to their children in

order to amuse them and prevent them from breaking anything in the house, was a capital invention, for a young thing cannot be quiet. The rattle is a toy suited to the infant mind, and education is a rattle or toy for children of a larger growth. We 30 conclude then that they should be taught music in such a way as to become not only critics but performers.

The question what is or is not suitable for different ages may be easily answered; nor is there any difficulty in meeting the objection of those who say that the study of music is mechanical. We reply in the first place, that they who are to be 35 judges must also be performers, and that they should begin to practise early, although when they are older they may be spared the execution; they must have learned to appreciate what is good and to delight in it, thanks to the knowledge which they acquired in their youth. As to the vulgarizing effect which music is 40 supposed to exercise, this is a question which we shall have no difficulty in determining when we have considered to what extent freemen who are being trained to political excellence should pursue the art, what melodies and what 1341ᵃ1 rhythms they should be allowed to use, and what instruments should be employed in teaching them to play; for even the instrument makes a difference. The answer to the objection turns upon these distinctions; for it is quite possible that certain methods of teaching and learning music do really have a degrading effect. It is 5 evident then that the learning of music ought not to impede the business of riper years, or to degrade the body or render it unfit for civil or military training, whether for bodily exercises at the time or for later studies.

The right measure will be attained if students of music stop short of the arts 10 which are practised in professional contests, and do not seek to acquire those fantastic marvels of execution which are now the fashion in such contests, and from these have passed into education. Let the young practise even such music as we have prescribed, only until they are able to feel delight in noble melodies and rhythms, and not merely in that common part of music in which every slave or child and even 15 some animals find pleasure.

From these principles we may also infer what instruments should be used. The flute, or any other instrument which requires great skill, as for example the harp, ought not to be admitted into education, but only such as will make men intelligent students of music or of the other parts of education. Besides, the flute is not an 20 instrument which is expressive of character; it is too exciting. The proper time for using it is when the performance aims not at instruction, but at the relief of the passions. And there is a further objection; the impediment which the flute presents to the use of the voice detracts from its educational value. The ancients therefore 25 were right in forbidding the flute to youths and freemen, although they had once allowed it. For when their wealth gave them a greater inclination to leisure, and they had loftier notions of excellence, being also elated with their success, both before and after the Persian War, with more zeal than discernment they pursued 30 every kind of knowledge, and so they introduced the flute into education. In Lacedaemon there was a choragus who led the chorus with a flute, and at Athens the instrument became so popular that most freemen could play upon it. The 35 popularity is shown by the tablet which Thrasippus dedicated when he furnished the chorus to Ecphantides. Later experience enabled men to judge what was or was not really conducive to excellence, and they rejected both the flute and several other old-fashioned instruments, such as the Lydian harp, the many-stringed lyre, the 'heptagon', 'triangle', 'sambuca', and the like—which are intended only to give pleasure to the hearer, and require extraordinary skill of hand. There is a meaning also in the myth of the ancients, which tells how Athene invented the flute and then threw it away. It was not a bad idea of theirs that the Goddess disliked the instrument because it made the face ugly; but with still more reason may we say that she rejected it because the acquirement of flute-playing contributes nothing to the mind, since to Athene we ascribe both knowledge and art.

Thus then we reject the professional instruments and also the professional mode of education in music (and by professional we mean that which is adopted in contests), for in this the performer practises the art, not for the sake of his own improvement, but in order to give pleasure, and that of a vulgar sort, to his hearers. For this reason the execution of such music is not the part of a freeman but of a paid performer, and the result is that the performers are vulgarized, for the end at which they aim is bad. The vulgarity of the spectator tends to lower the character of the music and therefore of the performers; they look to him—he makes them what they are, and fashions even their bodies by the movements which he expects them to exhibit.

7 · We have also to consider rhythms and modes, and their use in education. Shall we use them all or make a distinction? and shall the same distinction be made for those who practise music with a view to education, or shall it be some other? Now we see that music is produced by melody and rhythm, and we ought to know what influence these have respectively on education, and whether we should prefer excellence in melody or excellence in rhythm. But as the subject has been very well treated by many musicians of the present day, and also by philosophers who have had considerable experience of musical education, to these we would refer the more exact student of the subject; we shall only speak of it now after the manner of the legislator, stating the general principles.

We accept the division of melodies proposed by certain philosophers into melodies of character, melodies of action, and passionate or inspiring melodies, each having, as they say, a mode corresponding to it. But we maintain further that music should be studied, not for the sake of one, but of many benefits, that is to say, with a view to education, or purgation (the word 'purgation' we use at present without explanation, but when hereafter we speak of poetry, we will treat the subject with more precision); music may also serve for intellectual enjoyment, for relaxation and for recreation after exertion. It is clear, therefore, that all the modes must be employed by us, but not all of them in the same manner. In education the modes most expressive of character are to be preferred, but in listening to the performances of others we may admit the modes of action and passion also. For feelings such as pity and fear, or, again, enthusiasm, exist very strongly in some souls, and have more or less influence over all. Some persons fall into a religious frenzy, and we see them restored as a result of the sacred melodies—when they have

used the melodies that excite the soul to mystic frenzy—as though they had found 10
healing and purgation. Those who are influenced by pity or fear, and every
emotional nature, must have a like experience, and others in so far as each is
susceptible to such emotions, and all are in a manner purged and their souls
lightened and delighted. The melodies which purge the passions likewise give an 15
innocent pleasure to mankind. Such are the modes and the melodies in which those
who perform music at the theatre should be invited to compete. But since the
spectators are of two kinds—the one free and educated, and the other a vulgar
crowd composed of artisans, labourers, and the like—there ought to be contests and 20
exhibitions instituted for the relaxation of the second class also. And the music will
correspond to their minds; for as their minds are perverted from the natural state, so
there are perverted modes and highly strung and unnaturally coloured melodies. A
man receives pleasure from what is natural to him, and therefore professional 25
musicians may be allowed to practise this lower sort of music before an audience of
a lower type. But, for the purposes of education, as I have already said, those modes
and melodies should be employed which are expressive of character, such as the
Dorian, as we said before; though we may include any others which are approved by 30
philosophers who have had a musical education. The Socrates of the *Republic* is
wrong in retaining only the Phrygian mode along with the Dorian, and the more so
because he rejects the flute; for the Phrygian is to the modes what the flute is to 1342^{b}1
musical instruments—both of them are exciting and emotional. Poetry proves this,
for Bacchic frenzy and all similar emotions are most suitably expressed by the flute, 5
and are better set to the Phrygian than to any other mode. The dithyramb, for
example, is acknowledged to be Phrygian, a fact of which the connoisseurs of music
offer many proofs, saying, among other things, that Philoxenus, having attempted
to compose his *Mysians* as a dithyramb in the Dorian mode, found it impossible, 10
and fell back by the very nature of things into the more appropriate Phrygian. All
men agree that the Dorian music is the gravest and manliest. And whereas we say
that the extremes should be avoided and the mean followed, and whereas the Dorian 15
is a mean between the other modes, it is evident that our youth should be taught the
Dorian music.

Two principles have to be kept in view, what is possible, and what is becoming:
at these every man ought to aim. But even these are relative to age; the old, who 20
have lost their powers, cannot very well sing the high-strung modes, and nature
herself seems to suggest that their songs should be of the more relaxed kind. That is
why the musicians too blame Socrates, and with justice, for rejecting the relaxed
modes in education under the idea that they are intoxicating, not in the ordinary 25
sense of intoxication (for wine rather tends to excite men), but because they have no
strength in them. And so, with a view also to the time of life when men begin to grow
old, they ought to practise the gentler modes and melodies as well as the others, and, 30
further, any mode, such as the Lydian above all others appears to be, which is suited
to children of tender age, and possesses the elements both of order and of education.
Thus it is clear that education should be based upon three principles—the mean, the
possible, the becoming, these three.

ECONOMICS*

E. S. Forster

(Book III by G. C. Armstrong)

BOOK I

1343ª1   1 · The sciences of politics and economics differ not only as widely as a household and a city (the subject-matter with which they severally deal), but also in the fact that the science of politics involves a number of rulers, whereas the sphere of economics is a monarchy.

5   Now certain of the arts fall into sub-divisions, and it does not pertain to the same art to manufacture and to use the article manufactured, for instance, a lyre or pipes; but the function of political science is both to constitute a city in the beginning and also when it has come into being to make a right use of it. It is clear, therefore, that it must be the function of economic science too both to found a household and also to make use of it.

10   Now a city is an aggregate made up of households and land and property, self-sufficient with regard to a good life. This is clear from the fact that, if men cannot attain this end, the community is dissolved. Further, it is for this end that they associate together; and that for the sake of which any particular thing exists and has come into being is its substance. It is evident, therefore, that economics is
15   prior in origin to politics; for its function is prior, since a household is part of a city. We must therefore examine economics and see what its function is.

    2 · The parts of a household are man and property. But since the nature of any given thing is most quickly seen by taking its smallest parts, this would apply
20   also to a household. So, according to Hesiod, it would be necessary that there should be

First and foremost a house, a woman, and an ox for the plough . . . ,[1]

for the first point concerns subsistence, the second free men. We should have, therefore, to organize properly the association of husband and wife; and this involves providing what sort of a woman she ought to be.

TEXT: B. A. van Groningen and A. Wartelle, Budé, Paris, 1968
[1]*Works and Days,* 405.

In regard to property the first care is that which comes naturally. Now in the 25 course of nature the art of agriculture is prior, and next come those arts which extract the products of the earth, mining and the like. Agriculture ranks first because of its justice; for it does not take anything away from men, either with their consent, as do retail trading and the mercenary arts, or against their will, as do the warlike arts. Further, agriculture is natural; for by nature all derive their 1343ᵇl sustenance from their mother, and so men derive it from the earth. In addition to this it also conduces greatly to bravery; for it does not make men's bodies unserviceable, as do the illiberal arts, but it renders them able to lead an open-air life and work hard; furthermore it makes them adventurous against the foe, for 5 husbandmen are the only citizens whose property lies outside the fortifications.

3 · As regards the human part of the household, the first care is concerning a wife; for a common life is above all things natural to the female and to the male. For we have elsewhere laid down the principle that nature aims at producing many such forms of association, just as also it produces the various kinds of animals. But it is 10 impossible for the female to accomplish this without the male or the male without the female, so that their common life has necessarily arisen. Now in the other animals this intercourse is not based on reason, but depends on the amount of natural instinct which they possess and is entirely for the purpose of procreation. 15 But in the civilized and more intelligent animals the bond of unity is more complex (for in them we see more mutual help and goodwill and co-operation), above all in the case of man, because the female and the male co-operate to ensure not merely existence but a good life. And the production of children is not only a way of serving 20 nature but also of securing advantage; for the trouble which parents bestow upon their helpless children when they are themselves vigorous is repaid to them in old age when they are helpless by their children, who are then in their full vigour. At the same time also nature thus periodically provides for the perpetuation of mankind as a species, since she cannot do so individually. Thus the nature both of the man and 25 of the woman has been preordained by the will of heaven to live a common life. For they are distinguished in that the powers which they possess are not applicable to purposes in all cases identical, but in some respects their functions are opposed to one another though they all tend to the same end. For nature has made the one sex stronger, the other weaker, that the latter through fear may be the more cautious, 1344ªl while the former by its courage is better able to ward off attacks; and that the one may acquire possessions outside the house, the other preserve those within. In the performance of work, she made one sex able to lead a sedentary life and not strong enough to endure exposure, the other less adapted for quiet pursuits but well 5 constituted for outdoor activities; and in relation to offspring she has made both share in the procreation of children, but each render its peculiar service towards them, the woman by nurturing, the man by educating them.

4 · First, then, he must not do her any wrong; for thus a man is less likely himself to be wronged. This is inculcated by the general law, as the Pythagoreans 10

say, that one least of all should injure a wife as being 'a suppliant and taken from her hearth'. Now wrong inflicted by a husband is the formation of connexions outside his own house. As regards association, she ought not to need him when he is present or be incapacitated in his absence, but should be accustomed to be competent whether he is present or not. The saying of Hesiod is a good one:

> A man should marry a maiden, that habits discreet he may teach her.[2]

For dissimilarity of habits tends more than anything to destroy affection. As regards adornment, husband and wife ought not to approach one another with false affectation in their person any more than in their manners; for if the society of husband and wife requires such embellishment, it is no better than play-acting on the tragic stage.

5 · Of possessions, that which is the best and the worthiest subject of economics comes first and is most essential—I mean, man. It is necessary therefore first to provide oneself with good slaves. Now slaves are of two kinds, the overseer and the worker. And since we see that methods of education produce a certain character in the young, it is necessary when one has procured slaves to bring up carefully those to whom the higher duties are to be entrusted. The intercourse of a master with his slaves should be such as to allow them to be neither insolent nor uncontrolled. To the higher class of slaves he ought to give some share of honour, and to the workers abundance of nourishment. And since the drinking of wine makes even freemen insolent, and many nations even of freemen abstain therefrom (the Carthaginians, for instance, when they are on military service), it is clear that wine ought never to be given to slaves, or at any rate very seldom. Three things make up the life of a slave, work, punishment, and food. To give them food but no punishment and no work makes them insolent; and that they should have work and punishment but no food is tyrannical and destroys their efficiency. It remains therefore to give them work and sufficient food; for it is impossible to rule without offering rewards, and a slave's reward is his food. And just as all other men become worse when they get no advantage by being better and there are no rewards for virtue and vice, so also is it with servants. Therefore we must take careful notice and bestow or withhold everything, whether food or clothing or leisure or punishments, according to merit, in word and deed following the practice adopted by physicians in the matter of medicine, remembering at the same time that food is not medicine because it must be given continually.

The slave who is best suited for his work is the kind that is neither too cowardly nor too courageous. Slaves who have either of these characteristics are injurious to their owners; those who are too cowardly lack endurance, while the high-spirited are not easy to control. All ought to have a definite end in view; for it is just and beneficial to offer slaves their freedom as a prize, for they are willing to work when a prize is set before them and a limit of time is defined. One ought to bind slaves to

---

[2] *Works and Days,* 699.

one's service by letting them have children, and not to have many persons of the same race in a household, any more than in a state. One ought to provide sacrifices and pleasures more for the sake of slaves than for freemen; for in the case of the　20 former there are present more of the reasons why such things have been instituted.

6 · The householder has four roles in relation to wealth. He ought to be able to acquire it, and to guard it; otherwise there is no advantage in acquiring it, but it is a case of drawing water with a sieve, or the proverbial jar with a hole in it. Further,　25 he ought to be able to order his possessions aright and make a proper use of them; for it is for these purposes that we require wealth. The various kinds of property ought to be distinguished, and those which are productive ought to be more numerous than the unproductive, and the sources of income ought to be so distributed that they may not run a risk with all their possessions at the same time. For the preservation of wealth it is best to follow both the Persian and the Laconian　30 methods. The Attic system of economy is also useful; for they sell their produce and buy what they want, and thus there is not the need of a storehouse in the smaller establishments. The Persian system was that everything should be organized and that the master should superintend everything personally, as Dio said of Dionysius;　35 for no one looks after the property of others as well as he looks after his own, so that, as far as possible, a man ought to attend to everything himself. The sayings of the　1345ᵇ1 Persian and the Libyan may not come amiss; the former of whom, when asked what was the best thing to fatten a horse, replied, 'His master's eye', while the Libyan, when asked what was the best manure, answered, 'The master's foot-prints'. Some　5 things should be attended to by the master, others by his wife, according to the sphere allotted to each in the economy of the household. Inspections need only be made occasionally in small establishments, but should be frequent where overseers are employed. For good imitation is impossible unless a good example is set,　10 especially when trust is delegated to others; for unless the master is careful, it is impossible for his overseers to be careful. And since it is good for the formation of character and useful in the interests of economy, masters ought to rise earlier than their slaves and retire to rest later, and a house should never be left unguarded any more than a city, and when anything needs doing it ought not to be left undone,　15 whether it be day or night. There are occasions when a master should rise while it is still night; for this helps to make a man healthy and wealthy and wise. On small estates the Attic system of disposing of the produce is a useful one; but on large estates, where a distinction is made between yearly and monthly expenditure and　20 likewise between the daily and the occasional use of household appliances, such matters must be entrusted to overseers. Furthermore, a periodical inspection should be made, in order to ascertain what is still existing and what is lacking.

The house must be arranged both with a view to one's possessions and for the　25 health and well-being of its inhabitants. By possessions I mean the consideration of what is suitable for produce and clothing, and in the case of produce what is suitable for dry and what for moist produce, and amongst other possessions what is suitable for property whether animate or inanimate, for slaves and freemen, women and　30

men, strangers and citizens. With a view to well-being and health, the house ought to be airy in summer and sunny in winter. This would be best secured if it faces north and is not as wide as it is long. In large establishments a man who is no use for other purposes seems to be usefully employed as a doorkeeper to safeguard what is
1345ᵇ1 brought into and out of the house. For the ready use of household appliances the Laconian method is a good one; for everything ought to have its own proper place and so be ready for use and not require to be searched for.

BOOK II

1 · He who intends to practise economy aright ought to be fully acquainted with the places in which his labour lies and to be naturally endowed with good parts and by choice industrious and upright; for if he is lacking in any of these respects, he
10 will make many mistakes in the business which he takes in hand.

Now there are four kinds of economy, that of the king, that of the provincial governor, that of the city, and that of the individual. This is a broad method of division; and we shall find that the other forms of economy fall within it.
15 Of these that of the king is the most important and the simplest, . . . ,[3] that of the city is the most varied and the easiest, that of the individual the least important and the most varied. They must necessarily have most of their characteristics in common; but it is the points which are peculiar to each kind that we must consider. Let us therefore examine royal economy first. It is universal in its scope, but has
20 four special departments—the coinage, exports, imports, and expenditure. To take each of these separately: in regard to the coinage, I mean the question as to what coin should be struck and when; in the matter of exports and imports, what
25 commodities it will be advantageous to receive from the satraps in tax and dispose of and when; in regard to expenditure, what expenses ought to be curtailed and when, and whether one should pay what is expended in coin or in commodities which have an equivalent value.

Let us next take satrapic economy. Here we find six kinds of revenue—[from
30 land, from the peculiar products of the district, from merchandise, from taxes, from cattle, and from all other sources].[4] Of these the first and most important is that which comes from land (which some call tax on land-produce, others tithe); next in importance is the revenue from peculiar products, from gold, or silver, or copper, or anything else which is found in a particular locality; thirdly comes that derived from
1346ᵃ1 merchandise; fourthly, the revenue from the cultivation of the soil and from market-dues; fifthly, that which comes from cattle, which is called tax on animal produce or tithe; and sixthly, that which is derived from men, which is called the poll-tax or tax on artisans.

---

³van Groningen and Wartelle mark a lacuna here.
⁴Excised by van Groningen and Wartelle.

Thirdly, let us examine the economy of the city. Here the most important   5
source of revenue is from the peculiar products of the country, next comes that
derived from merchandise and customs, and lastly that which comes from the
ordinary taxes.

Fourthly and lastly, let us take individual economy. Here we find wide
divergences, because economy is not necessarily always practised with one aim in
view. It is the least important kind of economy, because the incomings and expenses   10
are small. Here the main source of revenue is the land, next other kinds of regular
activity, and thirdly investments of money.

Further, there is a consideration which is common to all branches of economy
and which calls for the most careful attention, especially in individual economy,   15
namely, that the expenditure must not exceed the income.

Now that we have mentioned the divisions of the subject, we must next
consider whether the satrapy or city with which we are dealing can produce all, or
the most important revenues which we have just distinguished; if it can, it should   20
use them. Next we must consider which sources of revenue do not exist at all but can
be introduced, or are at present small but can be augmented; and which of the
expenses at present incurred, and to what amount, can be dispensed with without
doing any harm to the whole.   25

We have now mentioned the various kinds of economy and their constituent
parts. We have further made a collection of all the methods that we conceived to be
worth mentioning, which men of former days have employed or cunningly devised
in order to provide themselves with money. For we conceived that this information   30
also might be useful; for a man will be able to apply some of these instances to such
business as he himself takes in hand.

2 · Cypselus, the Corinthian, having vowed to Zeus that, if he made himself
master of the city, he would dedicate to him all the property of the Corinthians,
ordered them to draw up a list of their possessions. When they had done so, he took a   1346ᵇ1
tenth part from each citizen and told them to trade with the remainder. As each
year came round, he did the same thing again, with the result that in ten years he
had all that he had consecrated to the god, while the Corinthians had acquired other   5
property.

Lygdamis, the Naxian, having driven certain men into exile, when no one was
willing to buy their possessions except at a low price, sold them to the exiles
themselves. And offerings belonging to them which were lying half finished in   10
certain workshops he sold to the exiles and any one else who wished to buy them,
allowing the name of the purchaser to be inscribed upon them.

The Byzantines being in need of money sold the sacred enclosures belonging to
the state. Those which were fertile they sold on lease, and those which were
unproductive in perpetuity. They treated in the same way the enclosures which
belonged to associations and clans and all which were situated on private estates; for   15
the owners of the rest of the property bought them at a high price. To the
associations they sold other lands, viz. the public lands round the gymnasium, or the   20

market-place, or the harbour; and they sold the places where markets were held at which various commodities were sold, and the rights over the sea-fisheries and the sale of salt, and . . .[5] of jugglers, and soothsayers, and druggists, and other such persons plied their trades; but they ordered them to pay over a third of their profits. And they sold the right of changing money to a single bank, and no one else might
25 either give money in exchange to anyone, or receive it in exchange from anyone, under penalty of forfeiting the money. And whereas there was a law amongst them that no one should have political rights who was not born of parents who were both citizens, being in want of money they passed a decree that a man who was sprung from a citizen on one side only should become a citizen if he paid down thirty minae.
30 And as they were suffering from want of food and lack of money, they made the ships from the Black Sea put in; but, as time went on, the merchants protested and so they paid them interest at ten per cent. and ordered those who purchased anything to pay the ten per cent. in addition to the price. And whereas certain
1347ª1 resident aliens had lent money on security of property, because these had not the right to hold property, they passed a decree that any one who wished could obtain a title to the property by paying a third of the loan to the state.

Hippias, the Athenian, put up for sale the parts of the upper rooms which
5 projected into the public streets, and the steps and fences in front of the houses, and the doors which opened outwards. The owners of the property therefore bought them, and a large sum was thus collected. He also declared the coinage then current in Athens to be base, and fixing a price for it ordered it to be brought to him; but
10 when they met to consider the striking of a new type of coin, he gave them back the same money again. And if anyone was about to equip a trireme or a division of cavalry or to provide a tragic chorus or incur expense on any other such state-service, he fixed a moderate fine and allowed him, if he liked, to pay this and be enrolled amongst those who had performed state services. He also ordered that a measure of barley, and another of wheat, and an obol should be brought to the
15 priestess of Athena-on-the-Acropolis on behalf of anyone who died, and that the same offering should be made by anyone to whom a child was born.

The Athenians who dwell in Potidaea, being in need of money to carry on war, ordered all the citizens to draw up a list of their property, each man enrolling not his
20 whole property collectively in his own deme, but each piece of property separately in the place where it was situated, in order that the poor might give in an assessment; anyone who possessed no property was to assess his own person at two minae. On the basis of this assessment they each contributed the amount enjoined.

25 Sosipolis of Antissa, when the city was in want of money, since the citizens were wont to celebrate the feast of Dionysus with great splendour and every year went to great expense in providing, amongst other things, very costly victims, persuaded them, when the festival was near at hand, to vow to Dionysus that they
30 would give double offerings the next year and collect and sell the dedications for the current year. Thus a substantial sum was collected for the needs of the moment.

---

[5]van Groningen and Wartelle mark a lacuna.

The people of Lampsacus, expecting a large fleet of triremes to come against them, ordered the dealers to sell a *medimnus* of barley-meal, of which the market price was four *drachmae,* at six *drachmae,* and a *chous* of oil, the price of which was three *drachmae,* at four *drachmae* and a half, and likewise wine and the other commodities. The individual seller thus received the old price, while the city gained the surplus and so was well provided with money.   1347[b]1

The people of Heraclea, when they were sending forty ships against the tyrants on the Bosporus, not being well provided with money, bought up from the merchants all their corn and oil and wine and the rest of their stores, fixing a date in   5 the future at which they were to make the payment. Now it suited the merchants better to sell their cargoes wholesale rather than retail. So the people of Heraclea, giving the soldiers two months' pay, took the provisions with them on board   10 merchant-vessels and put an official in charge of each of the ships. When they reached the enemies' territory, the soldiers bought up all the provisions from them. Thus money was collected before the generals had to pay the soldiers again, and so the same money was distributed time after time until they returned home.   15

When the Samians begged for money for their return home, the Lacedaemonians passed a decree that they would fast for one day, themselves and their domestics and their beasts of burden, and would give to the Samians the amount that each of them usually expended.

The Chalcedonians, having a large number of foreign mercenaries in their city,   20 owed them pay which they could not give them. They therefore proclaimed that if any citizen or resident alien had any right of seizure against any state or individual and wished to exercise it, they should give in their names. When many did so, they seized the ships which sailed into the Black Sea on a plausible pretext, and   25 appointed a time at which they promised to give an account of their captures. When a large sum of money had been collected they dismissed the soldiers and submitted themselves to trial for their reprisals, and the state out of its revenues made restitution to those who had been unjustly plundered.   30

When the people of Cyzicus were at variance and the popular party had gained the upper hand and the wealthy citizens had been imprisoned, they passed a decree, since they owed money to their soldiers, that they would not put their prisoners to death, but would exact money from them and send them into exile.

The Chians, who have a law that a public register of debts should be kept,   35 being in want of money decreed that debtors should pay their debts to the state and that the state should disburse the interest from its revenues to the creditors until   1348[a]1 they should be able to restore the principal.

Mausolus, tyrant of Caria, when the king of Persia sent and ordered him to pay his tribute, collected together the richest men in the country and told them that the   5 king was demanding the tribute, but he himself could not provide it. And certain men, who had been suborned to do so, immediately promised to contribute and named the amount that each would give. Upon this the wealthier men, partly through shame and partly from fear, promised and actually contributed far larger   10 sums.

On another occasion when he was in need of money, he called together the Mylassians and told them that this city of his, though it was their mother-city, was unfortified and that the king of Persia was marching against him. He therefore ordered the Mylassians each to contribute as much money as possible, saying that by what they paid now they would save the rest of their possessions. When a large contribution had been made, he kept the money and told them that at the moment the god would not allow them to build the wall.

Condalus, a governor under Mausolus, whenever during his passage through the country anyone brought him a sheep or a pig or a calf, used to make a record of the donor and the date and order him to take it back home and keep it until he returned. When he thought that sufficient time had elapsed, he used to ask for the animal which was being kept for him, and reckoned up and demanded the produce-tax on it as well. And any trees which projected over or fell into the royal roads he used to sell . . . the produce-taxes.[6] And if any soldier died, he demanded a drachma as a toll for the corpse passing the gates; and so he not only received money from this source, but also the officers could not deceive him as to the date of the soldier's death. Also, noticing that the Lycians were fond of wearing their hair long, he said that a dispatch had come from the king of Persia ordering him to send hair to make false fringes and that he was therefore commanded by Mausolus to cut off their hair. He therefore said that, if they would pay him a fixed poll-tax, he would have hair sent from Greece. They gladly gave him what he asked, and a large sum of money was collected from a great number of them.

Aristotle, the Rhodian, who was governor of Phocaea, was in want of money. Perceiving therefore that there were two parties amongst the Phocaeans, he made secret overtures to one party saying that the other faction was offering him money on condition that he would turn the scale in their favour, but that for his own part he would rather receive money from *them* and give the direction of affairs into their hands. When they heard this, those who were present immediately gave him the money, supplying him with all he asked for. He then went to the other party and showed them what he had received from their opponents; whereupon they also professed their willingness to give him an equal sum. So he took the money from both parties and reconciled them one with another. Also, noticing that there was much litigation among the citizens and that there were grievances of long standing among them owing to war, he established a court of law and proclaimed that unless they submitted their cases to judgement within a period which he appointed, there would be no further settlement of their former claims. Then getting control of a number of suits and of the cases which were subject to appeal with damages, and receiving money from both parties by other means, he collected a large sum.

The Clazomenians, when they were suffering from famine and were in want of money, decreed that private individuals who had any olive oil should lend it to the state, which would pay them interest. Now olives are abundant in this country. When the owners had lent them the oil, they hired ships and sent it to the marts from which their corn came, giving the value of the oil as a pledge. And when they

---

[6]van Groningen and Wartelle mark a lacuna.

owed pay to their soldiers to the amount of twenty talents and could not provide it, they paid the generals four talents a year as interest. But finding that they did not reduce the principal and that they were continually spending money to no purpose, they struck an iron coinage to represent a sum of twenty talents of silver, and then distributing it among the richest citizens in proportion to their wealth they received in exchange an equivalent sum in silver. Thus the individual citizens had money to disburse for their daily needs and the state was freed from debt. They then paid them interest out of their revenues and continually divided it up and distributed it in proper proportions, and called in the iron coinage.

The Selymbrians were once in need of money: they had a law which forbade the export of corn; when a famine occurred and they had a supply of last season's corn, they passed a decree that private persons should hand over their corn to the state at a fixed price, each reserving a year's supply; they then allowed anyone who wished to export his supply, fixing a price which they thought would give them a profit.

The people of Abydos, when their land was untilled owing to political dissensions and the resident aliens were paying them nothing because they still owed them money, passed a decree that anyone who was willing should lend money to the farmers in order that they might till the soil, providing that they should enjoy the first-fruits of the crop and that the others should have what remained.

The Ephesians, being in need of money, made a law that their women should not wear gold ornaments, but should lend to the state what they already possessed; and fixing the amount which was to be paid they allowed the name of any one who presented that sum to be inscribed as that of the dedicator on certain of the pillars in the temple.

Dionysius of Syracuse, wishing to collect money, called together an assembly and declared that Demeter had appeared to him and bade him bring the ornaments of the women to her temple. He had therefore, he said, done so with the ornaments of the women of his own household; and he demanded that everyone else should do the same, lest vengeance from the goddess should fall upon them. Anyone who refused would, he said, be guilty of sacrilege. When all had brought what they possessed through fear of the goddess and dread of Dionysius, after dedicating the ornaments to the goddess he then appropriated them, saying that they were lent to him by her. And when some time had elapsed and the women began wearing ornaments again, he ordered that any women who wished to wear jewellery of gold should dedicate a fixed sum in the temple.

And when he was intending to build triremes, he knew that he would be in want of money. He therefore called together an assembly and said that a certain city was to be betrayed to him and that he needed money for this purpose. He therefore asked the citizens to contribute two staters each; and they did so. He then let two or three days elapse, and pretending that he had failed in his attempt, after commending their generosity he gave every man his contribution back again. By this action he won the hearts of the citizens. And so they again contributed, thinking that they would receive their money back again; but he took the money and kept it for building his ships.

And when he was in need of money he struck a coinage of tin, and calling an assembly together he spoke at great length in favour of the money which had been
35 coined; and they, even against their will, decreed that everyone should regard any of it that he accepted as silver and not as tin.

1349ᵇ1 On another occasion, being in want of money, he asked the citizens to give him contributions; but they declared that they had nothing to give. Accordingly he brought out his own household goods and offered them for sale, as though compelled to do so by poverty. When the Syracusans bought them, he kept a record
5 of what each had bought, and when they had paid the price, he ordered each of them to bring back the articles which he had bought.

And when the citizens owing to the taxes could not keep cattle, he said that he had enough up to the present; those therefore who acquired cattle should now be free from a tax on them. But since many soon acquired a large number of cattle,
10 thinking that they could keep them without paying a tax on them, when he thought that a fitting moment had come he gave orders that they should assess their value and then imposed a tax. Accordingly the citizens, angry at having been deceived, slew their cattle and sold them. And when, to prevent this, he ordered them to kill only as many as were needed for daily use, they next devoted them for sacrifice to the gods. Dionysius then forbade them to sacrifice any female beast.

On another occasion when he was in need of money, he ordered all families of
15 orphans to enrol themselves; and when they⁷ had done so, he enjoyed their property until each came of age.

And after he had captured Rhegium he called an assembly of the inhabitants together and informed them that he would be quite justified in enslaving them, but under the circumstances he would let them go free if he received the amount which
20 he had spent on the war and three *minae* a head from all of them. The Rhegians then brought to light the wealth which before had been hidden, and the poor borrowed from the richer citizens and from foreigners and provided the sum which
25 he demanded. When he had received it from them he nevertheless sold them all as slaves, and seized all the treasures which had before been hidden and were now brought to light.

Also having borrowed money from the citizens under promise of repayment, when they demanded it back he ordered them to bring him whatever money any of them possessed, threatening them with death as the penalty if they failed to do so.
30 When the money had been brought, he issued it again after stamping it afresh so that each *drachma* had the value of two *drachmae,* and paid back the original debt and the money which they brought him on this occasion.⁸

And when he sailed against Tyrrhenia with a hundred ships he took much gold and silver and a considerable quantity of other ornaments of all kinds from the
35 temple of Leucothea. And knowing that the sailors too were keeping many things for themselves, he made a proclamation that everyone should bring him the half of
1350ᵃ1 what he had and might retain the other half; and he threatened with death anyone who failed to deliver up the half. The sailors, supposing that if they gave up the half

---

⁷Omitting ἄλλων.   ⁸Reading πρότερον ἀπέδωκε καὶ ὃ νῦν ἀνήνεγκαν.

they would be allowed undisturbed possession of the rest, did so; but Dionysius, when he had received it, ordered them to go back and bring him the other half.   5

The Mendaeans used the proceeds of their harbour customs and their other dues for the administration of their city, but did not exact the taxes on land and houses; but they kept a register of property-owners, and whenever they needed money, they paid as though they owed taxes. They thus profited during the time   10 which elapsed by having full use of the money without paying interest.

When they were at war with the Olynthians and needed money, seeing that they had slaves they decreed that a female and a male slave should be left to each citizen and the rest sold, so that private individuals might lend money to the state.   15

Callistratus the Athenian, when the harbour-dues in Macedonia were usually sold at twenty talents, made them fetch double that price. For, noticing that the richer men always bought them because it was necessary that the sureties provided for the twenty talents should be possessed of one talent, he proclaimed that anyone   20 who liked could purchase them and that sureties should be provided for only a third or any other proportion which each could guarantee.

Timotheus, the Athenian, when he was at war with the Olynthians, and in need of money, struck a bronze coinage and distributed it to the soldiers. When they protested, he told them that the merchants and retailers would all sell their goods on   25 the same terms as before. He then told the merchants, if they received any bronze money, to use it again to buy the commodities sent in for sale from the country and anything which was brought in as plunder, and said that, if they brought him any bronze money which they had left over, they should receive silver for it.

When he was making war in the neighbourhood of Corcyra and was in   30 difficulties, and the soldiers were demanding their pay and refusing to obey him and threatening to go over to the enemy, he called together an assembly and told them that no money could reach him owing to the stormy weather—though he had, he declared, such an abundance of supplies that he offered them as a free gift the three months' rations which they had already received. They, supposing that Timotheus   1350ᵇ1 would never have made such a valuable concession unless he really expected the money, kept silence about the pay; and he meanwhile achieved the objects which he had in view.

When he was besieging Samos he actually sold to the inhabitants the fruits and   5 the produce of their lands, and so had abundance of money to pay his soldiers. And when there was a shortage of provisions in the camp owing to the arrival of newcomers, he forbade the sale of corn ready ground, and of any smaller measure than a *medimnus,* and of any liquid in a smaller quantity than a *metreta.* Accordingly the commanders of divisions and companies bought up provisions   10 wholesale and distributed them to the soldiers, while the newcomers brought their own provisions with them and, when they departed, sold anything that they had left. The result was that the soldiers had an abundance of provisions.   15

Datames, the Persian, having soldiers under his command, could supply their daily needs from the enemy's country, but having no money to give them, and being requested to pay them, when the time came at which it was due he devised the following plan. He called together an assembly and told them that he had no lack of

20 money, but that it was in a certain place which he named. He therefore moved his
camp and started to march thither. Then when he was near the place, he went in
advance to it and took from the temples there all the embossed silver plate which
they contained. He then loaded his mules so that the silver plate was visible and they
looked as though they were carrying silver, and continued the march. The soldiers,
25 when they saw it, thought that the loads were all solid silver and were encouraged,
thinking that they would receive their pay. But Datames told them that he must go
to Amisus and have the silver minted. Now the journey to Amisus was one of many
days and exposed to the weather. So all this time he made use of the army, merely
30 giving them their rations.

He kept in his personal service all the skilled artificers in the army and the
retailers who carried on traffic in any commodity; and no one else was permitted to
do any of these things.

Chabrias, the Athenian, advised Taus, king of Egypt, when he was starting on
an expedition and was in need of money, to say to the priests that owing to the
expense some of the temples and the majority of the priests must be dispensed with.
1351ᵃ1 When the priests heard this, each wishing to retain his own temple and to remain a
priest himself, they offered him money. And when Taus had accepted money from
all of them, Chabrias advised him to order them to expend a tenth part of the
amount which they formerly spent on their temple and themselves, and to lend the
5 rest to him until the war against the king of Persia should come to an end. And he
advised him to fix the necessary amount and demand a contribution from each
household and likewise from each individual; and that, when corn was sold, the
buyer and the seller should give an obol for each *artabe* over and above the price;
and that he should demand the payment of a tenth part of the profits derived from
10 shipping and manufactures and any other form of industry. And he advised him,
when he was leaving the country on an expedition, to order that any unminted silver
or gold which anyone possessed should be brought to him: and when most people
15 brought it, he advised him to make use of it and to commend the lenders to the
provincial governors so that they might repay them out of the taxes.

Iphicrates, the Athenian, when Cotys had collected an army, provided him
with money in the following way. He advised him to order the men under his
20 command to sow land for him with three *medimni* of corn. The result of this was
that a great quantity of corn was collected. Accordingly he brought it down to the
markets and sold it, and thus gained an abundance of money.

Cotys, the Thracian, tried to borrow money from the Peirinthians so that he
25 might pay his soldiers; but the Peirinthians refused to give him any. He therefore
begged them at any rate to grant him some men from among their citizens to act as
a garrison for certain strongholds, in order that he might make full use of the
soldiers who were at present on duty there. To this request they promptly acceded,
thinking that they would thus obtain possession of these strongholds. But Cotys
30 threw into prison those who were sent and ordered the Peirinthians to recover them
by sending him the money which he wished to borrow from them.

Mentor, the Rhodian, having arrested Hermeias and seized his estates,
allowed the overseers whom Hermeias had appointed to retain their positions. But

when they all felt secure and took steps to recover anything which had been hidden   35
or deposited for safety elsewhere, he arrested them and deprived them of all they
had.

Memnon, the Rhodian, after making himself master of Lampsacus, was in   1351^b1
need of money. He therefore exacted a heavy tribute from the richest citizens,
telling them that they could collect it from the rest of the citizens. But when the
latter had contributed, he ordered them to lend him this sum as well, fixing a period   5
within which he would pay them back.

On another occasion when he was in need of money, he demanded contributions from them, saying that they should be repaid out of the revenues. They
therefore contributed, thinking that they would soon receive their money back. But
when the time was at hand for the payment of the revenues, he told them that he   10
needed these revenues as well, but would repay them later with interest.

He also excused himself from paying the rations and wages of those who were
serving under him for six days in the year, declaring that on these days they had no
watch to keep, no marching and no expenses, meaning the 'omitted' days.[9] As he   15
was already giving the soldiers their rations on the second day of the new month, he
thus passed over three days in the first month and five by the following month, and
so on till he reached a total of thirty days.

Charidemus of Orus, who held certain places in Aeolia, when Artabazus was   20
marching against him needed money to pay his soldiers. At first, then, the citizens
gave him contributions, but afterwards they declared that they had nothing left to
give. Charidemus then ordered the inhabitants of the place which he thought was
richest to send away to another place any coin or other valuable treasure which they
possessed, and he promised to give them an escort; at the same time it was clear that   25
he himself was also removing his valuables. When they had obeyed him, he led them
a little way outside the city and, after examining what they had, took all that he
needed and sent them back again. He also made a proclamation in the cities over
which he ruled that no one was to keep any arms in his house, the penalty for so   30
doing being a fine which he specified. He then took no further action and paid no
attention to the matter. The citizens, thinking that he had not meant the
proclamation to be taken seriously, continued to keep the arms which they
happened to possess. But Charidemus suddenly instituted a house to house search
and exacted the fine from those in whose houses he found any arms.   35

A certain Philoxenus, a Macedonian who was satrap of Caria, being in need of
money, said that he intended to celebrate the Dionysia, and he nominated the
richest of the Carians to defray the cost of the choruses and gave directions as to   1352^a1
what they had to supply. But seeing that they were annoyed, he sent to them
secretly and asked them what they were willing to give to be released from serving.
They declared their readiness to give considerably more than they thought it would
cost them, in order to be freed from the trouble and the neglect of their private   5
affairs which it would entail. Philoxenus accepted what they offered and put others
on the list, until he had received even more than he had wanted . . .[10]

[9]I.e. the six days 'omitted' from the year, one in each of the six 29-day months.
[10]The text is corrupt here.

Evaeses, the Syrian, being satrap of Egypt, discovering that the provincial
10   governors were on the point of revolting from him, summoned them to the palace
and hanged them all, and ordered that their relatives should be told that they were
in prison. Their relatives therefore severally began to negotiate on their behalf and
tried to buy the release of the captives. Evaeses made an agreement in each case
15   and, after receiving the sums for which he had stipulated, restored them to their
relatives—dead.

Cleomenes, an Alexandrian who was satrap of Egypt, when there was a severe
famine everywhere else while Egypt was less seriously affected, forbade the export
of corn, and when the provincial governors declared that they would not be able to
20   pay the tribute because corn could not be exported, he cancelled the prohibition, but
put a heavy tax on the corn. The result was that, if he did not . . .[11] he received a
large tax at the cost of a small exportation and the provincial governors lost their
excuse.

As he was sailing through the district in which the crocodile is regarded as a
deity, one of his slaves was carried off. He therefore summoned the priests and told
25   them that since he had been injured without provocation he intended to take
vengeance on the crocodiles, and gave orders to hunt them. The priests, in order that
their god might not be held in contempt, collected all the gold that they possessed
and presented it to him, with the result that he desisted.

30   When king Alexander commanded him to found a city near the Pharos and to
establish there the mart which was formerly held at Canopus, he sailed to Canopus
and told the priests and the owners of property there that he had come to transfer
them. The priests and inhabitants collected and gave him a sum of money to induce
35   him to leave their mart undisturbed. This he accepted and for the moment left them
alone, but afterwards, when he had the material for building ready, he sailed to
1352^{b}1   Canopus and demanded an excessive amount of money from them, which he said
represented the difference to him between having the mart near the Pharos and at
Canopus. And when they said that they would not be able to give him the money he
made them move their city.

And when he had sent someone to make a purchase and discovered that his
5   messenger had got what he wanted cheaply but intended to charge him an excessive
price, he told the friends of the purchaser that he had heard that he had made his
purchases at an excessive price and therefore he would go there himself; at the same
time with assumed wrath he railed against his stupidity. When they heard this they
10   told Cleomenes that he ought not to believe those who spoke against the messenger
until he came himself and rendered his account. When the purchaser arrived they
told him what Cleomenes had said; and he, wishing to make a good impression on
them and on Cleomenes, submitted the prices at which he had actually bought the
goods.

When corn was being sold in the country at ten *drachmae*, he summoned the
15   dealers and asked them at what price they would do business with him. They named
a lower price than that at which they were selling to the merchants. However, he

---

[11]van Groningen and Wartelle mark a lacuna.

ordered them to hand over their corn at the same price as they were selling to everyone else; and fixing the price of corn at thirty-two *drachmae* he then sold it himself.

He also called the priests together and told them that the expenditure on the temples in the country was excessive; consequently some of the temples and the majority of the priests must be abolished. The priests individually and collectively gave him the sacred treasures, thinking that he really intended to carry out his threat and because each wished that his own temple should be undisturbed and himself continue to be priest.

When Alexander was in the region of Babylon, Antimenes the Rhodian *hêmiolios* raised money in the following way. An ancient law existed in Babylonia that anything which was brought into the country should pay a duty of ten per cent., but no one ever enforced it. Antimenes, waiting till all the satraps and soldiers were expected and no small number of ambassadors and craftsmen . . .[12] and persons travelling on their own private affairs, and many gifts were being brought up, exacted the ten per cent. duty according to the existing law.

On another occasion, when providing the slaves who were to look after the camp, he commanded that any owner who wished should register the value which he put upon them, and they were to pay eight *drachmae* a year; if the slave ran away the owner was to receive the price which he had registered. Many slaves being registered, he amassed a considerable sum of money. And whenever any slave ran away he ordered the satrap of the country[13] in which the camp was situated to recover the runaway or else to pay the price to the owner.

Ophelas, the Olynthian, having appointed a superintendent over the province of Athribis, when the provincial governors of that district came to him and expressed their willingness to pay of their own accord a much larger sum and begged him to dismiss the superintendent whom he had just appointed, asked them if they would be able to pay what they promised; when they answered in the affirmative he left the superintendent at his post and bade him exact the amount of tribute which they themselves had assessed. Thus he did not think it right either to degrade the official whom he had appointed or to impose a heavier tribute upon them than they themselves had fixed, but at the same time he himself received a far larger amount of money.

Pythocles, the Athenian, recommended to the Athenians that the state should take the lead from the mines at Laurium out of private hands at the market price of two *drachmae* and that they should then themselves fix the price at six *drachmae* and so sell it.

Chabrias, when crews had been enrolled for a hundred and twenty ships and Taus only needed sixty, ordered the crews of the sixty ships which remained behind to supply those who sailed with two months' provisions, or else to sail themselves. They, wishing to attend to their own affairs, complied with his demand.

Antimenes ordered the satraps to keep the storehouses along the royal roads filled according to the custom of the country; but whenever an army or any other

---

[12]The text is corrupt here. [13]Reading τῆς γῆς.

body of men unaccompanied by the king passed along, he used to send one of his own men and sell the contents of the storehouses.

1353ᵇ1   Cleomenes, when the first day of the month was approaching and he had to give his soldiers their rations, purposely put back into harbour, and as the new month advanced he put out again and distributed the rations; he then left an 5   interval until the first day of the next month. The soldiers, therefore, because they had recently received their rations, kept quiet; and Cleomenes by passing over a month each year . . .¹⁴

Stabelbius, the Mysian, when he owed his soldiers pay, called the officers together¹⁵ and told them that he had no need of private soldiers but only of officers, 10   and that, when he did need soldiers, he would give each officer a sum of money and send him out to collect mercenaries, and that he would rather give the officers the pay which ought to go to the soldiers. He therefore ordered them each to send away their own levies out of the country. The officers, thinking that it would be an 15   opportunity to make money, dismissed the soldiers in accordance with his commands. But after a short interval he collected the officers together and told them that just as a flute player was no use without a chorus, so too officers were useless without private soldiers; he therefore ordered them to leave the country.

20   Dionysius, when he was making a round of the temples, whenever he saw a gold or silver table displayed, ordered that a libation should be poured out 'to good luck' and that the table should be carried off; and whenever he saw amongst the statues one which held out a wine cup, he would say, 'I accept your pledge', and order the statue to be carried away. And he used to strip the gold from the statues, 25   saying that he would give them others lighter and more fragrant; he then clad them with white garments and crowns of white poplar.

BOOK III¹⁶

1 · A good wife should be the mistress of her home, having under her care all that is within it, according to the rules we have laid down. She should allow none to enter without her husband's knowledge, dreading above all things the gossip of gadding women, which tends to poison the soul. She alone should have knowledge of what happens within, whilst if any harm is wrought by those from without, her husband will bear the blame. She must exercise control of the money spent on such festivities as her husband has approved, keeping well within the limit set by law upon expenditure, dress, and ornament; and remembering that beauty depends not on costliness of raiment, nor does abundance of gold so conduce to the excellence of a woman as self-control in all that she does, and her inclination towards an

---

¹⁴The text is corrupt.

¹⁵Reading ὁ Μυσός, ὀφείλων στρατιώταις μισθόν, συγκαλέσας τοὺς ἡγεμόνας.

¹⁶This book survives only in Latin translation; it is not included in Bekker's edition, so that the customary Bekker-references are absent. The English translation is adapted from that of G. C. Armstrong.

honourable and well-ordered life. For such adornment as this both elevates the mind and is a far surer warrant for the payment, to the woman herself in her old age and to her children after her, of the due meed of praise.

This, then, is the province over which a woman should be minded to bear an orderly rule; for it seems not fitting that a man should know all that passes within the house. But in all other matters, let it be her aim to obey her husband; giving no heed to public affairs, nor desiring any part in arranging the marriages of her children. Rather, when the time shall come to give or receive in marriage sons or daughters, let her even then hearken to her husband in all respects, and agreeing with him obey his behest; considering that it is less unseemly for him to deal with a matter within the house than it is for her to pry into those outside its walls. It is fitting that a woman of well-ordered life should consider that her husband's uses are as laws appointed for her own life by divine will, along with the marriage state and the fortune she shares. If she endures them with patience and gentleness, she will rule her home with ease; otherwise, not so easily. Hence not only when her husband is in prosperity and good report does it beseem her to be in agreement with him, and to render him the service he wills, but also in times of adversity. If, through sickness or fault of judgement, his good fortune fails, then must she show her quality, encouraging him ever with words of cheer and yielding him obedience in all fitting ways; only let her do nothing base or unworthy of herself, or remember any wrong her husband may have done her through distress of mind. Let her refrain from all complaint, nor charge him with the wrong, but rather attribute everything of this kind to sickness or ignorance or accidental errors. For the more sedulous her service herein, the fuller will be his gratitude when he is restored, and freed from his sickness; and if she has failed to obey him when he commanded aught that is amiss, the deeper will be his recognition when health returns. Hence, whilst careful to avoid obedience in such circumstances, in other respects she will serve him more assiduously than if she had been a bondwoman bought and taken home. For he has indeed bought her with a great price—with partnership in his life and in the procreation of children; than which things nought could be greater or more sacred. And besides all this, the wife who had only lived in company with a fortunate husband would not have had the like opportunity to show her true quality. For though there is no small merit in a right and noble use of prosperity, still the right endurance of adversity justly receives an honour greater by far. For only a great soul can live in the midst of trouble and wrong without itself committing any base act. And so, while praying that her husband may be spared adversity, if trouble should come it beseems the wife to consider that here a good woman wins her highest praise. Let her bethink herself how Alcestis would never have attained such renown nor Penelope have deserved all the high praises bestowed on her had not their husbands known adversity; whereas the troubles of Admetus and Ulysses have obtained for their wives a reputation that shall never die. For because in time of distress they proved themselves faithful and dutiful to their husbands, the gods have bestowed on them the honour they deserved. To find partners in prosperity is easy enough; but only the best women are ready to share in adversity. For all these reasons it is fitting that a woman should pay her husband an honour greater by far, nor feel shame on his account even when, as Orpheus says, Holy health of soul, and wealth, the child of a brave spirit, companion him no more.

2 · Such then is the pattern of the rules and ways of living which a good wife will observe. And the rules which a good husband will follow in treatment of his wife will be similar; seeing that she has entered his home as the partner of his life and his children; and that the offspring she leaves behind her will bear the names of their parents, her name as well as his. And what could be more sacred than this, or more desired by a man of sound mind, than to beget by a noble and honoured wife children who, as shepherds of their old age, shall be the most loyal and discreet guardians of their father and mother, and the preservers of the whole house? Rightly reared by father and mother, children will grow up virtuous, as those who have treated them piously and righteously deserve that they should; but without such education they will be flawed. For unless parents have given their children an example of how to live, the children in their turn will be able to offer a fair and specious excuse. Such parents will risk being rejected by their offspring for their evil lives, and thus bringing destruction upon their own heads.

Hence his wife's training should be the object of a man's unstinting care; that so far as is possible their children may spring from the noblest of stock. For the tiller of the soil spares no pains to sow his seed in the most fertile and best cultivated land, looking thus to obtain the fairest fruits; and to save it from devastation he is ready, if such be his lot, to fall in conflict with his foes, a death which men crown with the highest of praise. Seeing, then, that such care is lavished on the body's food, surely every care should be taken on behalf of our own children's mother and nurse, in whom is implanted the seed from which there springs a living soul. For it is only by this means that each mortal, successively produced, participates in immortality; and that petitions and prayers continue to be offered to ancestral gods. So that he who thinks lightly of this would seem also to be slighting the gods. Thus it is on behalf of the gods, in whose presence he offered sacrifice, that he led his wife home, promising to honour her far above all others except his parents.

Now a virtuous wife is best honoured when she sees that her husband is faithful to her, and has no preference for another woman, but before all others loves and trusts her and holds her as his own. And so much the more will the woman seek to be what he accounts her, if she perceives that her husband's affection for her is faithful and righteous, and she too will be faithful and righteous towards him. Hence a man of sound mind ought not to forget what honours are proper to his parents or what fittingly belong to his wife and children; so that rendering to each and all their own, he may obey the law of men and of gods. For the deprivation we feel most of all is that of the special honour which is our due; nor will abundant gifts of what belongs to others be welcome to him who is dispossessed of his own. Now to a wife nothing is of more value, nothing more rightfully her own, than honoured and faithful partnership with her husband. Hence it befits not a man of sound mind to bestow his person promiscuously, or have random intercourse with women; for otherwise the base-born will share in the rights of his lawful children, and his wife will be robbed of her honour due, and shame be attached to his sons.

3 . To all these matters, therefore, a man should give heed. And it is fitting that he should approach his wife in an honourable way, full of self-restraint and awe; and in his conversation with her, should use only the words of a right-minded man, suggesting only such acts as are themselves lawful and honourable; treating her with much self-restraint and trust, and passing over any trivial or unintentional errors she has committed. And if through ignorance she has done wrong, he should advise her of it without threatening, in a courteous and modest manner. Indifference and harsh reproof he must alike avoid. Between a courtesan and her lover, such tempers are allowed their course; between a free woman and her lawful spouse there should be a reverent and modest mingling of love and fear. For of fear there are two kinds. The fear which virtuous and honourable sons feel towards their fathers, and loyal citizens towards rightminded rulers, has for its companions reverence and modesty; but the other kind, felt by slaves for masters and by subjects for despots who treat them with injustice and wrong, is associated with hostility and hatred.

Reflecting on all this, a husband should choose the better course and secure the agreement, loyalty, and devotion of his wife, so that whether he himself is present or not, there may be no difference in her attitude towards him, since she realizes that they are alike guardians of the common interests; and so when he is away she may feel that to her no man is kinder or more virtuous or more truly hers than her own husband. And she will make this manifest from the beginning by her unfailing regard for the common welfare, novice though she may be in such matters. And if the husband learns first to master himself, he will thereby become his wife's best guide in all the affairs of life, and will teach her to follow his example. For Homer pays no honour either to affection or to fear where modesty is absent. Everywhere he bids affection be coupled with self-control and shame; whilst the fear he commends is such as Helen owns when she thus addresses Priam: "Beloved sire of my lord, it is fitting that I fear thee and dread thee and revere";[17] meaning that her love for him is mingled with fear and modest shame. And again, Ulysses speaks to Nausicaa in this manner: "Thou, lady, dost fill me with wonder and with fear."[18] For Homer believes that this is the feeling of a husband and wife for one another, and that if they so feel, it will be well with them both. For no one ever loves or admires or fears in this shamefaced way one of baser character; but such are the feelings towards one another of nobler souls and those by nature good; or of the inferior toward those they know to be their betters. Feeling thus toward Penelope, Ulysses remained faithful to her in his wanderings; whereas Agamemnon did wrong to his wife for the sake of Chryseis, declaring in open assembly that a base captive woman, and of alien race besides, was in no way inferior to Clytemnestra in womanly excellence. This was ill spoken of the mother of his children; nor was his connexion with the other a righteous one. How could it be, when he had but recently compelled her to be his concubine, and before he had any experience of her behaviour to him? Ulysses on the other hand, when the daughter of Atlas besought him to share her bed and board, and promised him immortality, could not bring himself even for the sake of immortality to betray the kindness and love and loyalty of his wife, deeming immortality purchased by unrighteousness to be the worst of all punishments. For it was only to save his comrades that he yielded his person to Circe; and in answer to her he even declared that in his eyes nothing could be more lovely than his native isle, rugged though it were; and prayed that he might die, if only he might look upon his mortal wife and son. So firmly did he keep troth with his wife; and received in return from her the like loyalty.

4 · Once again, in the words addressed by Ulysses to Nausicaa the poet makes clear the great honour in which he holds the virtuous companionship of man and wife in marriage. There he prays the gods to grant her a husband and a home; and between herself and her husband, precious unity of mind; provided that such unity be for righteous ends. For, says he, there is no greater blessing on earth than when husband and wife rule their home in harmony of mind and will. Moreover it is evident from this that the unity which the poet commends is no mutual subservience in each other's vices, but one that is rightfully allied with wisdom and understanding; for this is the meaning of the words "rule the house in harmony of mind." And he goes on to say that wherever such a love is found, it is a cause of sore distress to those who hate them and of delight to those that love them; while the truth of his words is most of all acknowledged by the happy pair. For when wife and husband are agreed about the best things in life, of necessity the friends of each will also be mutually agreed; and the strength which the pair gain will make them formidable to their enemies and helpful to their own. But when discord reigns between them, their friends too will disagree, while the pair themselves will realize most fully their weakness.

In all these precepts it is clear that the poet is teaching husband and wife to dissuade one another from whatever is evil and dishonourable, while unselfishly furthering to the best of their power one another's honourable and righteous aims. In the first place they will strive to perform all duty towards their parents, the husband towards those of his wife no less than towards his own, and she in her turn towards his. Their next duties are towards their children, their friends, their estate, and their entire household which they will treat as a common possession; each vying with the other in the effort to contribute most to the common welfare, and to excel in virtue and righteousness; laying aside arrogance, and ruling with justice in a kindly and unassuming spirit. And so at length, when they reach old age, and are freed from the duty of providing for others and from preoccupation with the pleasures and desires of youth, they will be able to give answer also to their children, if question arises which of them has contributed more good things to the common household store; and will be well assured that whatsoever of evil has befallen them is due to fortune, and whatsoever of good, to their own virtue. One who comes victorious through such question wins from heaven, as Pindar says, his chiefest reward; for "hope, and a soul filled with fair thoughts are supreme in the manifold mind of mortals"; and next, from his children the good fortune of being sustained by them in his old age. And therefore it behoves us to preserve throughout our lives a righteous attitude towards all gods and mortal men, to each individually, and to all in common; and not least towards our own wives and children and parents.

RHETORIC

W. Rhys Roberts

BOOK I

1354ª1   1 · Rhetoric is the counterpart of dialectic. Both alike are concerned with such things as come, more or less, within the general ken of all men and belong to no definite science. Accordingly all men make use, more or less, of both; for to a certain
5   extent all men attempt to discuss statements and to maintain them, to defend themselves and to attack others. Ordinary people do this either at random or through practice and from acquired habit. Both ways being possible, the subject can plainly be handled systematically, for it is possible to inquire the reason why some
10   speakers succeed through practice and others spontaneously; and everyone will at once agree that such an inquiry is the function of an art.

Now, the framers of the current treatises on rhetoric have constructed but a small portion of that art. The modes of persuasion are the only true constituents of the art: everything else is merely accessory. These writers, however, say nothing
15   about enthymemes, which are the substance of rhetorical persuasion, but deal mainly with non-essentials. The arousing of prejudice, pity, anger, and similar emotions has nothing to do with the essential facts, but is merely a personal appeal to the man who is judging the case. Consequently if the rules for trials which are
20   now laid down in some states—especially in well-governed states—were applied everywhere, such people would have nothing to say. All men, no doubt, *think* that the laws should prescribe such rules, but some, as in the court of Areopagus, give practical effect to their thoughts and forbid talk about non-essentials. This is sound law and custom. It is not right to pervert the judge by moving him to anger or envy
25   or pity—one might as well warp a carpenter's rule before using it. Again, a litigant has clearly nothing to do but to show that the alleged fact is so or is not so, that it has or has not happened. As to whether a thing is important or unimportant, just or unjust, the judge must surely refuse to take his instructions from the litigants: he
30   must decide for himself all such points as the law-giver has not already defined for him.

Now, it is of great moment that well-drawn laws should themselves define all the points they possibly can and leave as few as may be to the decision of the judges; and this for several reasons. First, to find one man, or a few men, who are sensible
1354ᵇ1   persons and capable of legislating and administering justice is easier than to find a

TEXT: R. Kassel, Berlin, 1976

large number. Next, laws are made after long consideration, whereas decisions in the courts are given at short notice, which makes it hard for those who try the case to satisfy the claims of justice and expediency. The weightiest reason of all is that the decision of the lawgiver is not particular but prospective and general, whereas members of the assembly and the jury find it *their* duty to decide on definite cases brought before them. They will often have allowed themselves to be so much influenced by feelings of friendship or hatred or self-interest that they lose any clear vision of the truth and have their judgement obscured by considerations of personal pleasure or pain. In general, then, the judge should, we say, be allowed to decide as few things as possible. But questions as to whether something has happened or has not happened, will be or will not be, is or is not, must of necessity be left to the judge, since the lawgiver cannot foresee them. If this is so, it is evident that anyone who lays down rules about other matters, such as what must be the contents of the 'introduction' or the 'narration' or any of the other divisions of a speech, is theorizing about non-essentials as if they belonged to the art. The only question with which these writers here deal is how to put the judge into a given frame of mind. About the orator's proper modes of persuasion they have nothing to tell us; nothing, that is, about how to gain skill in enthymemes.

Hence it comes that, although the same systematic principles apply to political as to forensic oratory, and although the former is a nobler business, and fitter for a citizen, than that which concerns the relations of private individuals, these authors say nothing about political oratory, but try, one and all, to write treatises on the way to plead in court. The reason for this is that in political oratory there is less inducement to talk about non-essentials. [Political oratory is less given to unscrupulous practices than forensic, but treats of wider issues.][1] In a political debate the man who is forming a judgement is making a decision about his own vital interests. There is no need, therefore, to prove anything except that the facts are what the supporter of a measure maintains they are. In forensic oratory this is not enough; to conciliate the listener is what pays here. It is other people's affairs that are to be decided, so that the judges, intent on their own satisfaction and listening with partiality, surrender themselves to the disputants instead of judging between them. Hence in many places, as we have said already, irrelevant speaking is forbidden in the law-courts: in the public assembly those who have to form a judgement are themselves well able to guard against that.

It is clear, then, that the technical study of rhetoric is concerned with the modes of persuasion. Now persuasion is a sort of demonstration (since we are most fully persuaded when we consider a thing to have been demonstrated); the orator's demonstration is an enthymeme, [and this is, in general, the most effective of the modes of persuasion];[1] the enthymeme is a sort of deduction (the consideration of deductions of all kinds, without distinction, is the business of dialectic, either of dialectic as a whole or of one of its branches): clearly, then, he who is best able to see how and from what elements a deduction is produced will also be best skilled in the enthymeme, when he has further learnt what its subject-matter is and in what

[1]Excised by Kassel.

respects it differs from the deductions of logic. For the true and the approximately
true are apprehended by the same faculty; it may also be noted that men have a
sufficient natural instinct for what is true, and usually do arrive at the truth. Hence
the man who makes a good guess at truth is likely to make a good guess at what is
reputable.

It has now been shown that the ordinary writers on rhetoric treat of
non-essentials; it has also been shown why they have inclined more towards the
forensic branch of oratory.

Rhetoric is useful because things that are true and things that are just have a
natural tendency to prevail over their opposites, so that if the decisions of judges are
not what they ought to be, the defeat must be due to the speakers themselves, and
they must be blamed accordingly. Moreover, before some audiences not even the
possession of the exactest knowledge will make it easy for what we say to produce
conviction. For argument based on knowledge implies instruction, and there are
people whom one cannot instruct. Here, then, we must use, as our modes of
persuasion and argument, notions possessed by everybody, as we observed in the
Topics[2] when dealing with the way to handle a popular audience. Further, we must
be able to employ persuasion, just as deduction can be employed, on opposite sides
of a question, not in order that we may in practice employ it in both ways (for we
must not make people believe what is wrong), but in order that we may see clearly
what the facts are, and that, if another man argues unfairly, we on our part may be
able to confute him. No other of the arts draws opposite conclusions: dialectic and
rhetoric alone do this. Both these arts draw opposite conclusions impartially.
Nevertheless, the underlying facts do not lend themselves equally well to the
contrary views. No; things that are true and things that are better are, by their
nature, practically always easier to prove and more persuasive. Again, it is absurd to
hold that a man ought to be ashamed of being unable to defend himself with his
limbs, but not of being unable to defend himself with rational speech, when the use
of rational speech is more distinctive of a human being than the use of his limbs.
And if it is objected that one who uses such power of speech unjustly might do great
harm, *that* is a charge which may be made in common against all good things except
excellence, and above all against the things that are most useful, as strength, health,
wealth, generalship. A man can confer the greatest of benefits by a right use of
these, and inflict the greatest of injuries by using them wrongly.

It is clear, then, that rhetoric is not bound up with a single definite class of
subjects, but is like dialectic; it is clear, also, that it is useful. It is clear, further, that
its function is not simply to succeed in persuading, but rather to discover the
persuasive facts in each case. In this it resembles all other arts. For example, it is not
the function of medicine simply to make a man quite healthy, but to put him as far
as may be on the road to health; it is possible to give excellent treatment even to
those who can never enjoy sound health. Furthermore, it is plain that it is the
function of one and the same art to discern the real and the apparent means of
persuasion, just as it is the function of dialectic to discern the real and the apparent

[2] See *Topics* 101ᵃ30.

deduction. What makes a man a sophist is not his abilities but his choices. In rhetoric, however, the term 'rhetorician' may describe either the speaker's knowledge of the art, or his choices. In dialectic a man is a sophist because he makes a certain kind of choice, a dialectician in respect not of his choices but of his abilities.

Let us now try to give some account of the systematic principles of rhetoric itself—of the right method and means of succeeding in the object we set before us. We must make as it were a fresh start, and before going further define what rhetoric is.

2 · Rhetoric may be defined as the faculty of observing in any given case the available means of persuasion. This is not a function of any other art. Every other art can instruct or persuade about its own particular subject-matter; for instance, medicine about what is healthy and unhealthy, geometry about the properties of magnitudes, arithmetic about numbers, and the same is true of the other arts and sciences. But rhetoric we look upon as the power of observing the means of persuasion on almost any subject presented to us; and that is why we say that, in its technical character, it is not concerned with any special or definite class of subjects.

Of the modes of persuasion some are technical, others non-technical. By the latter I mean such things as are not supplied by the speaker but are there at the outset—witnesses, evidence given under torture, written contracts, and so on. By the former I mean such as we can ourselves construct by means of the principles of rhetoric. The one kind has merely to be used, the other has to be invented.

Of the modes of persuasion furnished by the spoken word there are three kinds. The first kind depends on the personal character of the speaker; the second on putting the audience into a certain frame of mind; the third on the proof, or apparent proof, provided by the words of the speech itself. Persuasion is achieved by the speaker's personal character when the speech is so spoken as to make us think him credible. We believe good men more fully and more readily than others: this is true generally whatever the question is, and absolutely true where exact certainty is impossible and opinions are divided. This kind of persuasion, like the others, should be achieved by what the speaker says, not by what people think of his character before he begins to speak. It is not true, as some writers assume in their treatises on rhetoric, that the personal goodness revealed by the speaker contributes nothing to his power of persuasion; on the contrary, his character may almost be called the most effective means of persuasion he possesses. Secondly, persuasion may come through the hearers, when the speech stirs their emotions. Our judgements when we are pleased and friendly are not the same as when we are pained and hostile. It is towards producing these effects, as we maintain, that present-day writers on rhetoric direct the whole of their efforts. This subject will be treated in detail when we come to speak of the emotions. Thirdly, persuasion is effected through the speech itself when we have proved a truth or an apparent truth by means of the persuasive arguments suitable to the case in question.

There are, then, these three means of effecting persuasion. The man who is to

be in command of them must, it is clear, be able to reason logically, to understand human characters and excellences, and to understand the emotions—that is, to know what they are, their nature, their causes and the way in which they are
25 excited. It thus appears that rhetoric is an offshoot of dialectic and also of ethical studies. Ethical studies may fairly be called political; and for this reason rhetoric masquerades as political science, and the professors of it as political experts— sometimes from want of education, sometimes from ostentation, sometimes owing
30 to other human failings. As a matter of fact, it is a branch of dialectic and similar to it, as we said at the outset. Neither rhetoric nor dialectic is the scientific study of any one separate subject: both are faculties for providing arguments. This is
35 perhaps a sufficient account of their scope and of how they are related to each other.

[[With regard to the persuasion achieved by proof or apparent proof: just as in
1356ᵇ1 dialectic there is induction on the one hand and deduction or apparent deduction on the other, so it is in rhetoric. The example is an induction, the enthymeme is a deduction, and the apparent enthymeme is an apparent deduction; for I call a
5 rhetorical deduction an enthymeme, and a rhetorical induction an example.]]³ Everyone who effects persuasion through proof does in fact use either enthymemes or examples: there is no other way. And since everyone who proves anything at all is bound to use either deductions or inductions (and this is clear to us from the
10 *Analytics*), it must follow that each of the latter is the same as one of the former. The difference between example and enthymeme is made plain by the passages in the *Topics*⁴ where induction and deduction have already been discussed. When we base the proof of a proposition on a number of similar cases, this is induction in
15 dialectic, example in rhetoric; when it is shown that, certain propositions being true, a further and quite distinct proposition must also be true in consequence, whether universally or for the most part this is called deduction in dialectic, enthymeme in rhetoric. It is plain also that each of these types of oratory has its advantages. For
20 what has been said in the *Methodics* applies equally well here; in some oratorical styles examples prevail, in others enthymemes; and in like manner, some orators are better at the former and some at the latter. Speeches that rely on examples are as persuasive as the other kind, but those which rely on enthymemes excite the louder
25 applause. The reason for this, and their proper uses, we will discuss later. Our next step is to define the processes themselves more clearly.

What is persuasive is persuasive to someone; and something is persuasive either because it is directly self-evident or because it appears to be proved from other statements that are so. But none of the arts theorizes about individual cases.
30 Medicine, for instance, does not theorize about what will help to cure Socrates or Callias, but only about what will help to cure any or all of a given class of patients: this alone is subject to technique—individual cases are so infinitely various that no knowledge of them is possible. In the same way the theory of rhetoric is concerned not with what seems reputable to a given individual like Socrates or Hippias, but

---

³Kassel regards this passage as a later addition to the text by Aristotle himself.
⁴*Topics* I 12.

with what seems so to men of a given type; and this is true of dialectic also. Dialectic does not construct its deductions out of any haphazard materials, such as the fancies of crazy people, but out of materials that call for discussion; and rhetoric draws 1357ª1 upon the regular subjects of debate. The duty of rhetoric is to deal with such matters as we deliberate upon without arts or systems to guide us, in the hearing of persons who cannot take in at a glance a complicated argument, or follow a long chain of reasoning. The subjects of our deliberation are such as seem to present us with alternative possibilities: about things that could not have been, and cannot now 5 or in the future be, other than they are, nobody who takes them to be of this nature wastes his time in deliberation.

It is possible to form deductions and draw conclusions from the results of previous deductions; or, on the other hand, from premises which have not been thus proved, and at the same time are not reputable and so call for proof. Reasonings of 10 the former kind will necessarily be hard to follow owing to their length, for we assume an audience of untrained thinkers; those of the latter kind will fail to be persuasive, because they are based on premises that are not generally admitted or reputable.

The enthymeme and the example must, then, deal with what is for the most part capable of being otherwise, the example being an induction, and the 15 enthymeme a deduction. The enthymeme must consist of few propositions, fewer often than those which make up a primary deduction. For if any of these propositions is a familiar fact, there is no need even to mention it; the hearer adds it himself. Thus, to show that Dorieus has been victor in a contest for which the prize is a crown, it is enough to say 'For he has been victor in the Olympic games', without 20 adding 'And in the Olympic games the prize is a crown', a fact which everybody knows.

There are few facts of the necessary type that can form the basis of rhetorical deductions. Most of the things about which we make decisions, and into which we inquire, present us with alternative possibilities. For it is about our actions that we 25 deliberate and inquire, and all our actions have a contingent character; hardly any of them are determined by necessity. Again, conclusions that state what holds for the most part and is possible must be drawn from premises that do the same, just as necessary conclusions must be drawn from necessary premises; this too is clear to us from the *Analytics*.[5] It is evident, therefore, that the propositions forming the 30 basis of enthymemes, though some of them may be necessary, will in the main hold for the most part. Now the materials of enthymemes are probabilities and signs, so that each of the former must be the same as one of these. A probability is a thing 35 that happens for the most part—not, however, as some definitions would suggest, anything whatever that so happens, but only if it belongs to the class of what can turn out otherwise, and bears the same relation to that in respect of which it is probable as the universal bears to the particular. Of signs, one kind bears the same 1357ᵇ1 relation as the particular bears to the universal, the other the same as the universal bears to the particular. A necessary sign is an evidence, a non-necessary sign has no

---

[5]See *Prior Analytics* I 8; 12–14; 27.

5 specific name. By necessary signs I mean those on which deductions may be based; and this shows us why this kind of sign is called an evidence: when people think that what they have said cannot be refuted, they then think that they are bringing forward an evidence, meaning that the matter has now been demonstrated and 10 completed; for the word πέρας has the same meaning as the word τέκμαρ in the ancient tongue.[6] Now the one kind of sign (that which bears to the proposition it supports the relation of particular to universal) may be illustrated thus. Suppose it were said, 'The fact that Socrates was wise and just is a sign that the wise are just'. Here we certainly have a sign; but even though the proposition is true, the argument is refutable, since it does not form a deduction. Suppose, on the other 15 hand, it were said, 'The fact that he has a fever is a sign that he is ill', or, 'The fact that she is giving milk is a sign that she has lately borne a child'. Here we have the necessary kind of sign, the only kind that constitutes an evidence, since it is the only kind that, if true, is irrefutable. The other kind of sign, that which bears the relation of universal to particular, might be illustrated by saying, 'The fact that he breathes 20 fast is a sign that he has a fever'. This argument also is refutable, even if true, since a man may breathe hard without having a fever.

It has, then, been stated above what is the nature of a probability, of a sign, 25 and of an evidence, and what are the differences between them. In the *Analytics*[7] a more explicit description has been given of these points; it is there shown why some of these reasonings can be put into deductions and some cannot.

The example has already been described as one kind of induction; and the special nature of the subject-matter that distinguishes it from the other kinds has also been stated above. Its relation is not that of part to whole, nor whole to part, nor whole to whole, but of part to part, or like to like. When two statements are of the 30 same order, but one is more familiar than the other, the former is an example. The argument may, for instance, be that Dionysius, in asking as he does for a bodyguard, is scheming to make himself a despot. For in the past Peisistratus kept asking for a bodyguard in order to carry out such a scheme, and did make himself a despot as soon as he got it; and so did Theagenes at Megara; and in the same way all other instances known to the speaker are made into examples, in order to show what 35 is not yet known, that Dionysius has the same purpose in making the same request: all these being instances of the one general principle, that a man who asks for a 1358ᵃ1 bodyguard is scheming to make himself a despot. We have now described the sources of those means of persuasion which are popularly supposed to be demonstrative.

There is an important distinction between two sorts of enthymemes that has been wholly overlooked by almost everybody—one that also subsists between the 5 deductions treated of in dialectic. One sort of enthymeme really belongs to rhetoric; but the other sort really belongs to other arts and faculties, whether to those we already exercise or to those we have not yet acquired. Hence they are not noticed by

---

[6]'Evidence' renders τεκμήριον which Aristotle connects, *via* τέκμαρ, with πέρας and πεπερασμένος ('completed').
[7]*Prior Analytics* II 27.

the audience . . . and, touching on them more than is appropriate, they get away from them.[8] This statement will be clearer if expressed more fully. I mean that the proper subjects of dialectical and rhetorical deductions are the things with which we say the commonplaces are concerned, that is to say those that apply equally to questions of right conduct, natural science, politics, and many other things that have nothing to do with one another. Take, for instance, the commonplace concerned with 'the more or less'. On this it is equally easy to base a deduction or enthymeme about any of what nevertheless are essentially disconnected subjects— right conduct, natural science, or anything else whatever. But there are also those special commonplaces which are based on such propositions as apply only to particular groups or classes of things. Thus there are propositions about natural science on which it is impossible to base any enthymeme or deduction about ethics, and other propositions about ethics on which nothing can be based about natural science. The same principle applies throughout. The general commonplaces have no special subject-matter, and therefore will not increase our understanding of any particular class of things. On the other hand, the better the selection one makes of propositions suitable for special commonplaces the nearer one comes, unconsciously, to setting up a science that is distinct from dialectic and rhetoric. One may succeed in stating the required principles, but one's science will be no longer dialectic or rhetoric, but the science to which the principles thus discovered belong. Most enthymemes are in fact based upon these particular or special kinds; comparatively few on the common kind. As in the *Topics,* therefore, so in this work, we must distinguish, in dealing with the enthymemes, the kinds and the commonplaces on which they are to be founded. By kinds I mean the propositions peculiar to each several class of things, by commonplaces those common to all classes alike. We may begin with the kinds. But, first of all, let us classify rhetoric into its varieties. Having distinguished these we may deal with them one by one, and try to discover the elements of which each is composed, and the propositions each must employ.

3 · Rhetoric falls into three divisions, determined by the three classes of listeners to speeches. For of the three elements in speech-making—speaker, subject, and person addressed—it is the last one, the hearer, that determines the speech's end and object. The hearer must be either a judge, with a decision to make about things past or future, or an observer. A member of the assembly decides about future events, a juryman about past events [while those who merely decide on the orator's skill are observers].[9] From this it follows that there are three divisions of oratory—deliberative, forensic, and epideictic.

Deliberative speaking urges us either to do or not to do something: one of these two courses is always taken by private counsellors, as well as by men who address public assemblies. Forensic speaking either attacks or defends somebody: one or other of these two things must always be done by the parties in a case. Epideictic oratory either praises or censures somebody. These three kinds of rhetoric refer to three different kinds of time. The deliberative orator is concerned with the future: it

---

[8]Kassel marks a lacuna.   [9]Excised by Kassel.

15 is about things to be done hereafter that he advises, for or against. The party in a case at law is concerned with the past; one man accuses the other, and the other defends himself, with reference to things already done. The epideictic orator is, properly speaking, concerned with the present, since all men praise or blame in view of the state of things existing at the time, though they often find it useful also to 20 recall the past and to make guesses at the future.

Rhetoric has three distinct ends in view, one for each of its three kinds. The deliberative orator aims at establishing the expediency or the harmfulness of a proposed course of action; if he urges its acceptance, he does so on the ground that it will do good; if he urges its rejection, he does so on the ground that it will do harm; 25 and all other points, such as whether the proposal is just or unjust, honourable or dishonourable, he brings in as subsidiary and relative to this main consideration. Parties in a law-case aim at establishing the justice or injustice of some action, and they too bring in all other points as subsidiary and relative to this one. Those who praise or attack a man aim at proving him worthy of honour or the reverse, and they too treat all other considerations with reference to this one.

That the three kinds of rhetoric do aim respectively at the three ends we have 30 mentioned is shown by the fact that speakers will sometimes not try to establish anything else. Thus, the litigant will sometimes not deny that a thing has happened or that he has done harm. But that he is guilty of injustice he will never admit; otherwise there would be no need of a trial. So too, deliberative orators often make 35 any concession short of admitting that they are recommending their hearers to take an inexpedient course or not to take an expedient one. The question whether it is not *unjust* for a city to enslave its innocent neighbours often does not trouble them at all. In like manner those who praise or censure a man do not consider whether his 1359ª1 acts have been expedient or not, but often make it a ground of actual praise that he has neglected his own interest to do what was honourable. Thus they praise Achilles because he championed his fallen friend Patroclus, though he knew that this meant 5 death, and that otherwise he need not die: yet while to die thus was the nobler thing for him to do, the expedient thing was to live on.

It is evident from what has been said that it is these three subjects, more than any others, about which the orator must be able to have propositions at his command. Now the propositions of rhetoric are evidences, probabilities, and signs. Every kind of deduction is composed of propositions, and the enthymeme is a 10 deduction composed of the aforesaid propositions.

Since only possible actions, and not impossible ones, can ever have been done in the past or the present, and since things which have not occurred, or will not occur, also cannot have been done or be going to be done, it is necessary for the 15 deliberative, the forensic, and the epideictic speaker alike to be able to have at their command propositions about the possible and the impossible, and about whether a thing has or has not occurred, will or will not occur. Further, all men, in giving praise or blame, in urging us to accept or reject proposals for action, in accusing or defending, attempt not only to prove the points mentioned but also to show that the 20 good or the harm, the honour or disgrace, the justice or injustice, is great or small, either absolutely or relatively; and therefore it is plain that we must also have at our command propositions about greatness or smallness and the greater or the lesser—propositions both universal and particular. Thus, we must be able to say which is the greater or lesser good, the greater or lesser act of justice or injustice; 25 and so on.

Such, then, are the subjects regarding which we are inevitably bound to master the propositions relevant to them. We must now discuss each particular class of these subjects in turn, namely those dealt with in deliberative, in epideictic, and lastly in legal, oratory.

4 · First, then, we must ascertain what are the kinds of things, good or bad, 30 about which the deliberative orator offers counsel. For he does not deal with all things, but only with such as may or may not take place. Concerning things which exist or will exist inevitably, or which cannot possibly exist or take place, no counsel can be given. Nor, again, can counsel be given about the whole class of things which may or may not take place; for this class includes some good things that occur naturally, and some that occur by accident; and about these it is useless to offer 35 counsel. Clearly counsel can only be given on matters about which people can deliberate; matters, namely, that ultimately depend on ourselves, and which we have it in our power to set going. For we turn a thing over in our mind until we have 1359^{b}1 reached the point of seeing whether we can do it or not.

Now to enumerate and classify accurately the usual subjects of public business, and further to frame, as far as possible, true definitions of them, is a task which we must not attempt on the present occasion. For it does not belong to the art 5 of rhetoric, but to a more instructive art and a more real branch of knowledge; and as it is, rhetoric has been given a far wider subject-matter than strictly belongs to it. The truth is, as indeed we have said already, that rhetoric is a combination of the sciences of logic and of ethics; and it is partly like dialectic, partly like sophistical 10 reasoning. But the more we try to make either dialectic or rhetoric not, what they really are, practical faculties, but sciences, the more we shall inadvertently be destroying their true nature; for we shall be re-fashioning them and shall be passing into the region of sciences dealing with definite subjects rather than simply with 15 speeches. Even here, however, we will mention those points which it is of practical importance to distinguish, their fuller treatment falling to political science.

The main matters on which all men deliberate and on which deliberative speakers make speeches are five in number: ways and means, war and peace, 20 national defence, imports and exports, and legislation.

As to Ways and Means, then, the intending speaker will need to know the number and extent of the country's sources of revenue, so that, if any is being 25 overlooked, it may be added, and, if any is defective, it may be increased. Further, he should know all the expenditure of the country, in order that, if any part of it is superfluous, it may be abolished, or, if any is too large, it may be reduced. For men become richer not only by increasing their existing wealth but also by reducing their expenditure. A comprehensive view of these questions cannot be gained solely from 30 experience in home affairs; in order to advise on such matters a man must study the methods worked out in other lands.

35 As to Peace and War, he must know the extent of the military strength of his country, both actual and potential, and also the nature of that actual and potential strength; and further, what wars his country has waged, and how it has waged them. He must know these facts not only about his own country, but also about neighbouring countries; and also about countries with which war is likely, in order that peace may be maintained with those stronger than his own, and that his own 1360ᵃ1 may have power to make war or not against those that are weaker. He should know, too, whether the military power of another country is like or unlike that of his own; for this is a matter that may affect their relative strength. With that end in view he must, besides, have studied the wars of other countries as well as those of his own, 5 and the way they ended; similar causes are likely to have similar results.

With regard to National Defence he ought to know all about the methods of defence in actual use, and also the strength and character of the defensive force and the positions of the forts—this last means that he must be well acquainted with the 10 lie of the country—in order that a garrison may be increased if it is too small or removed if it is not wanted, and that the strategic points may be guarded with special care.

With regard to the Food Supply he must know what will meet the needs of his country; what kinds of food are produced at home and what imported; and what articles must be exported or imported. This last he must know in order that 15 agreements and commercial treaties may be made with the countries concerned. There are, indeed, two sorts of state to which he must see that his countrymen give no cause for offence, states stronger than his own, and states with which it is advantageous to trade.

But while he must, for security's sake, be able to take all this into account, he must before all things understand the subject of legislation; for it is on a country's 20 laws that its whole welfare depends. He must, therefore, know how many different forms of constitution there are; under what conditions each of these will prosper and by what circumstances, both proper and opposite, each of them tends to be destroyed. When I speak of destruction through proper circumstances I refer to the fact that all constitutions, except the best one of all, are destroyed both by not being 25 pushed far enough and by being pushed too far. Thus, democracy loses its vigour, and finally passes into oligarchy, not only when it is not pushed far enough, but also when it is pushed a great deal too far; just as the aquiline and the snub nose not only turn into normal noses by not being aquiline or snub enough, but also by being too violently aquiline or snub arrive at a condition in which they no longer look like 30 noses at all.

It is useful, in framing laws, not only to study the past history of one's own country, in order to understand which constitution is desirable for it now, but also to have a knowledge of the constitutions of other nations, and so to learn for what kinds of nation the various kinds of constitution are suited. From this we can see that books of travel are useful aids to legislation, since from these we may learn the

laws and customs of different races. The deliberative speaker will also find the   35
researches of historians useful. But all this is the business of political science and not
of rhetoric.

These, then, are the most important kinds of information which the deliberative speaker must possess. Let us now go back and state the premises from which he   1360ᵇ1
will have to argue in favour of adopting or rejecting measures regarding these and
other matters.

5 · It may be said that every individual man and all men in common aim at a
certain end which determines what they choose and what they avoid. This end, to   5
sum it up briefly, is happiness and its constituents. Let us, then, by way of
illustration only, ascertain what is in general the nature of happiness, and what are
the elements of its constituent parts. For all advice to do things or not to do them is
concerned with happiness and with the things that make for or against it; whatever   10
creates or increases happiness or some part of happiness, we ought to do; whatever
destroys or hampers happiness, or gives rise to its opposite, we ought not to do.

We may define happiness as prosperity combined with excellence; or as
independence of life; or as the secure enjoyment of the maximum of pleasure; or as a   15
good condition of property and body, together with the power of guarding one's
property and body and making use of them. That happiness is one or more of these
things, pretty well everybody agrees.

From this definition of happiness it follows that its constituent parts are:
good birth, plenty of friends, good friends, wealth, good children, plenty of children,
a happy old age, also such bodily excellences as health, beauty, strength,   20
large stature, athletic powers, together with fame, honour, good luck, and
excellence. A man cannot fail to be completely independent if he possesses these
internal and these external goods; for besides these there are no others to have.   25
(Goods of the soul and of the body are internal. Good birth, friends, money, and
honour are external.) Further, we think that he should possess resources and luck, in
order to make his life really secure. Let us now, then, try to ascertain what each of   30
these things is.

Now good birth in a race or a state means that its members are indigenous or
ancient; that its earliest leaders were distinguished men, and that from them have
sprung many who were distinguished for qualities that we admire.

The good birth of an individual may come either from the male or the female
side; it requires legitimacy on both sides, and implies that, as in the case of the state,   35
the founders of the line have been notable for excellence or wealth or something else
which is highly prized, and that many distinguished persons belong to the family,
men and women, young and old.

Possession of good children and of many children is clear enough. Applied to a   1361ᵃ1
community, they mean that its young men are numerous and of good quality: good
in regard to bodily excellences, such as stature, beauty, strength, athletic powers;
and also in regard to the excellences of the soul, which in a young man are
temperance and courage. Applied to an individual, they mean that his own children   5

are numerous and have the good qualities we have described. Both male and female are here included; the excellences of the latter are, in body, beauty and stature; in soul, self-command and an industry that is not sordid. Communities as well as
10 individuals should lack none of these perfections, in their women as well as in their men. Where, as among the Lacedaemonians, the state of women is bad, almost half of them are not happy.

The constituents of wealth are: plenty of coined money and territory; the ownership of numerous, large, and beautiful estates; also the ownership of
15 numerous and beautiful implements, live stock, and slaves. All these kinds of property are our own, are secure, gentlemanly, and useful. The useful kinds are those that are productive, the gentlemanly kinds are those that provide enjoyment. By 'productive' I mean those from which we get our income; by 'enjoyable', those from which we get nothing worth mentioning except the use of them. The criterion
20 of security is the ownership of property in such places and under such conditions that the use of it is in our power; and it is our own if it is in our own power to dispose of it or not. By 'disposing of it' I mean giving it away or selling it. Wealth as a whole consists in using things rather than in owning them; it is really the activity—that is,
25 the use—of property that constitutes wealth.

Fame means being respected by everybody, or having some quality that is desired by all men, or by most, or by the good, or by the wise.

Honour is the token of a man's being famous for doing good. It is chiefly and most properly paid to those who have already done good; but also to the man who
30 can do good in future. Doing good refers either to the preservation of life and the means of life, or to wealth, or to some other of the good things which it is hard to get either always or at that particular place or time—for many gain honour for things which seem small, but the place and the occasion account for it. The constituents of
35 honour are: sacrifices; commemoration, in verse or prose; privileges; grants of land; front seats at civic celebrations; state burial; statues; public maintenance; among foreigners, obeisances and giving place; and such presents as are among various bodies of men regarded as marks of honour. For a present is not only the bestowal of a piece of property, but also a token of honour; which explains why honour-loving as
1361ᵇ1 well as money-loving persons desire it. The present brings to both what they want; it is a piece of property, which is what the lovers of money desire; and it brings honour, which is what the lovers of honour desire.

The excellence of the body is health; that is, a condition which allows us, while keeping free from disease, to have the use of our bodies; for many people are healthy
5 in the way we are told Herodicus was; and these no one can congratulate on their health, for they have to abstain from everything or nearly everything that men do. Beauty varies with the time of life. In a young man beauty is the possession of a body fit to endure the exertion of running and of contests of strength; which means
10 that he is pleasant to look at; and therefore all-round athletes are the most beautiful, being naturally adapted both for contests of strength and for speed also. For a man in his prime, beauty is fitness for the exertion of warfare, together with a pleasant but at the same time formidable appearance. For an old man, it is to be strong

enough for such exertion as is necessary, and to be free from pain through escaping the ravages of old age. Strength is the power of moving something else at will; to do this, you must either pull, push, lift, pin, or grip it; thus you must be strong in all of those ways or at least in some. Excellence in size is to surpass ordinary people in height, thickness, and breadth by just as much as will not make one's movements slower in consequence. Athletic excellence of the body consists in size and strength; for the swift man is strong—he who can fling forward his legs in a certain way, and move them fast and far, is good at running; he who can grip and hold down is good at wrestling; he who can drive an adversary from his ground with the right blow is a good boxer; he who can do both the last is a good pancratiast, while he who can do all is an all-round athlete.

Happiness in old age is the coming of old age slowly and painlessly; for a man has not this happiness if he grows old either quickly, or tardily but painfully. It arises both from the excellences of the body and from good luck. If a man is not free from disease, or if he is not strong, he will not be free from suffering or pain; nor can he continue to live a long life unless he has good luck. There is, indeed, a capacity for long life that is quite independent of health or strength; for many people live long who lack the excellences of the body; but for our present purpose there is no use in going into the details of this.

The possession of many friends and the possession of good friends need no explanation; for we define a friend as one who will always try, for your sake, to do what he takes to be good for you. The man towards whom many feel thus has many friends; if these are worthy men, he has good friends.

Good luck is the acquisition or possession of all or most, or the most important, of those good things which are due to luck. Some of the things that are due to luck may also be due to artificial contrivance; but many are independent of art, as for example those which are due to nature—though, to be sure, things due to luck may actually be contrary to nature. Thus health may be due to artificial contrivance, but beauty and stature are due to nature. All such good things as excite envy are, as a class, the outcome of good luck. Luck is also the cause of good things that happen contrary to reasonable expectation: as when, for instance, all your brothers are ugly, but you are handsome yourself; or when you find a treasure that everybody else has overlooked; or when a missile hits the next man and misses you; or when you are the only man not to go to a place you have gone to regularly, while the others go there for the first time and are killed. All such things are reckoned pieces of good luck.

As to excellence, it is most closely connected with the subject of eulogy, and therefore we will wait to define it until we come to discuss that subject.

6 · It is now plain what our aims, future or actual, should be in urging, and what in deprecating, a proposal; the latter being the opposite of the former. Now the deliberative orator's aim is utility: deliberation seeks to determine not ends but the means to ends, i.e. what it is most useful to do. Further, utility is a good thing. We ought therefore to assure ourselves of the main facts about goodness and utility in general.

We may define a good thing as that which ought to be chosen for its own sake; or as that for the sake of which we choose something else; or as that which is sought after by all things, or by all things that have sensation or reason, or which will be sought after by any things that acquire reason; or as that which must be prescribed for a given individual by reason generally, or is prescribed for him by his individual reason, this being his individual good; or as that whose presence brings anything into a satisfactory and self-sufficing condition; or as self-sufficiency; or as what produces, maintains, or entails characteristics of this kind, while preventing and destroying their opposites (one thing may entail another in either of two ways—simultaneously, or subsequently. Thus learning entails knowledge subsequently, health entails life simultaneously. Things are productive of other things in three senses: first as being healthy produces health; secondly, as food produces health; and thirdly, as exercise does—i.e. it does so usually. All this being settled, we now see that both the acquisition of good things and the removal of bad things must be good; the latter entails freedom from the evil things simultaneously, while the former entails possession of the good things subsequently); or the acquisition of a greater in place of a lesser good, or of a lesser in place of a greater evil; for in proportion as the greater exceeds the lesser there is acquisition of good or removal of evil.[10] The excellences, too, must be something good; for it is by possessing these that we are in a good condition, and they tend to produce good works and good actions. They must be severally named and described elsewhere. Pleasure, again, must be a good thing, since it is the nature of all animals to aim at it. Consequently both pleasant and beautiful things must be good things, since the former are productive of pleasure, while of the beautiful things some are pleasant and some desirable in and for themselves.

The following is a more detailed list of things that must be good. Happiness, as being desirable in itself and sufficient by itself, and as being that for whose sake we choose all other things. Also justice, courage, temperance, magnanimity, magnificence, and all such qualities, as being excellences of the soul. Further, health, beauty, and the like, as being bodily excellences and productive of many other good things: for instance, health is productive both of pleasure and of life, and therefore is thought the greatest of goods, since these two things which it causes, pleasure and life, are two of the things most highly prized by ordinary people. Wealth, again; for it is the excellence of possession, and also productive of many other good things. Friends and friendship; for a friend is desirable in himself and also productive of many other good things. So, too, honour and reputation, as being pleasant, and productive of many other good things, and for the most part accompanied by the presence of the good things that cause them to be bestowed. The faculty of speech and action; since all such qualities are productive of what is good. Further—good parts, strong memory, receptiveness, quickness of intuition, and the like, for all such faculties are productive of what is good. Similarly, all the sciences and arts. And life; since, even if no other good were the result of life, it is desirable in itself. And justice, as the cause of good to the community.

---

[10]Reading τούτῳ for τούτου.

The above are pretty well all the things admittedly good. In dealing with things whose goodness is disputed, we may argue in the following ways:—That is good of which the contrary is bad. That is good the contrary of which is to the advantage of our enemies; for example, if it is to the particular advantage of our enemies that we should be cowards, clearly courage is of particular value to our countrymen. And generally, the contrary of that which our enemies desire, or of that at which they rejoice, is evidently valuable. Hence the passage beginning:

> Surely would Priam exult.[11]

This principle holds good for the most part, not always, since it may well be that our interest is sometimes the same as that of our enemies. Hence it is said that evils draw men together; that is, when the same thing is hurtful to them both.

Further: that which is not in excess is good, and that which is greater than it should be is bad. That also is good on which much labour or money has been spent; the mere fact of this makes it seem good, and such a good is assumed to be an end—an end reached through a long chain of means; and any end is a good. Hence the lines beginning:

> And for Priam a boast,[12]

and

> Oh, it were shame to have tarried so long[13]

and there is also the proverb about breaking the pitcher at the door.

That which most people seek after, and which is obviously an object of contention, is also a good; for, as has been shown, that is good which is sought after by everybody, and 'most people' seems pretty well to amount to 'everybody'. That which is praised is good, since no one praises what is not good. So, again, that which is praised by our enemies; for it is as though everyone were thereby agreeing. And that which is praised by those who have suffered—they would agree because it is evidently good. Similarly, those must be worthless whom their friends censure and their enemies do not. (For this reason the Corinthians conceived themselves to be insulted by Simonides when he wrote:

> Against the Corinthians hath Ilium no complaint.)

Again, that is good which has been distinguished by the favour of a discerning or virtuous man or woman, as Odysseus was distinguished by Athena, Helen by Theseus, Paris by the goddesses, and Achilles by Homer. And, generally speaking, all things are good which men choose to do; this will include the things already mentioned, and also whatever may be bad for their enemies or good for their friends, and at the same time practicable. Things are practicable in two senses: it is possible to do them, it is easy to do them. Things are done easily when they are done either without pain or quickly: the difficulty of an act lies either in its painfulness or

---

[11]Homer, *Iliad* I 255.   [12]*Iliad* II 160.   [13]*Iliad* II 298.

25 in the long time it takes. Again, a thing is good if it is as men wish; and they wish to have either no evil at all or at least a balance of good over evil. This last will happen where the penalty is either imperceptible or slight. Good, too, are things that are a man's very own, possessed by no one else, exceptional; for this increases the credit of having them. So are things which befit the possessors, such as whatever is

30 appropriate to their birth or capacity. And whatever they feel they ought to have but lack—such things may indeed be trifling, but none the less men deliberately make them the goal of their action. And things easily effected; for these are practicable (in the sense of being easy); such things are those in which everyone, or most people, or one's equals, or one's inferiors have succeeded. Good also are the things by which we shall gratify our friends or annoy our enemies; and the things

35 chosen by those whom we admire; and the things for which we are fitted by nature or experience, since we think we shall succeed more easily in these; and those in which no worthless man can succeed, for such things bring greater praise; and those which we do in fact desire, for what we desire is taken to be not only pleasant but

1363^{b}1 also better. Further, a man of a given disposition makes chiefly for the corresponding things: lovers of victory make for victory, lovers of honour for honour, money-loving men for money, and so with the rest. These, then, are the sources from which we must derive our means of persuasion about good and utility.

5   7 · Since, however, it often happens that people agree that two things are both useful but do not agree about which is the more so, the next step will be to treat of relative goodness and relative utility.

A thing which surpasses another may be regarded as being that other thing plus something more, and that other thing which is surpassed as being what is contained in the first thing. Now things are greater or more always in comparison

10 with something smaller or less, while they are great and small, much and little, in comparison with normal magnitude. The great is that which surpasses the normal, the small is that which is surpassed by the normal; and so with many and few.

Now we call 'good' what is desirable for its own sake and not for the sake of something else; that at which all things aim; what they would choose if they could

15 acquire understanding and practical wisdom; and that which tends to produce or preserve such goods, or is always accompanied by them; [Moreover, that for the sake of which things are done is the end (an end being that for the sake of which all else is done)]^{14} and for each individual that thing is a good which fulfils these conditions in regard to himself. It follows, then, that a greater number of goods is a greater good than one or than a smaller number, if that one or that smaller number

20 is included in the count; for then the larger number surpasses the smaller, and the smaller quantity is surpassed as being contained in the larger.

Again, if the largest member of one class surpasses the largest member of another, then the one class surpasses the other; and if one class surpasses another, then the largest member of the one surpasses the largest member of the other. Thus,

---

^{14}Excised by Kassel.

if the tallest man is taller than the tallest woman, then men in general are taller than 25
women. Conversely, if men in general are taller than women, then the tallest man is
taller than the tallest woman. For the superiority of class over class is proportionate
to the superiority possessed by their largest specimens. Again, where one good is
always accompanied by another, but does not always accompany it, it is greater
than the other, for the use of the second thing is implied in the use of the first. A 30
thing may be accompanied by another either simultaneously, or subsequently, or
potentially. Life accompanies health simultaneously (but not health life), knowledge accompanies the act of learning subsequently, cheating accompanies sacrilege
potentially, since a man who has committed sacrilege is always capable of cheating.
Again, when two things each surpass a third, that which does so by the greater
amount is the greater of the two; for it must surpass the less great as well. A thing
productive of a greater good is itself a greater good than that other. For that is what 35
being productive of something greater is. Likewise, that which is produced by a
greater good is itself a greater good; thus, if what is wholesome is more desirable
and a greater good than what gives pleasure, health too must be a greater good than
pleasure. Again, a thing which is desirable in itself is a greater good than a thing 1364ᵃ1
which is not desirable in itself, as for example bodily strength than what is
wholesome, since the latter is not pursued for its own sake, whereas the former is;
and this was our definition of the good. Again, if one of two things is an end, and the
other is not, the former is the greater good, as being chosen for its own sake and not
for the sake of something else; as, for example, exercise is a greater good than
physical well-being. And of two things that which stands less in need of other things 5
is the greater good, since it is more self-sufficing. (That which stands less in need of
others is that which needs either *fewer* or *easier* things.) And when one thing does
not exist or cannot come into existence without a second, while the second can exist
without the first, the second is the better. For that which does not need something
else is more self-sufficing than that which does, and presents itself as a greater good
for that reason. Again, that which is an origin of other things is a greater good than
that which is not, and that which is a cause is a greater good than that which is not; 10
the reason being the same in each case, namely that without a cause and an origin
nothing can exist or come into existence. Again, where there are two origins, what
arises from the greater is greater; and where there are two causes, what arises from
the greater cause is greater. And conversely, that origin or cause is itself the greater 15
which has the greater consequences. Now it is plain, from all that has been said,
that one thing may be shown to be greater than another from two opposite points of
view: it may appear the greater because it is an origin and the other thing is not, and
also because it is not an origin and the other thing is—on the ground that the end is
greater and is not an origin. So Leodamas, when accusing Callistratus, said that the
man who prompted the deed was more guilty than the doer, since it would not have 20
been done if he had not planned it. On the other hand, when accusing Chabrias he
said that the doer was worse than the prompter, since there would have been no deed
without some one to do it; men, said he, plot a thing only in order to carry it out.
    Further, what is rare is a greater good than what is plentiful. Thus, gold is a

25   better thing than iron, though less useful: it is harder to get, and therefore more
worth getting. In another way, the plentiful is a better thing than the rare, because
we can make more use of it. For what is often useful surpasses what is seldom
useful, whence the saying

The best of things is water.[15]

More generally: the hard thing is better than the easy, because it is rarer; and in
30   another way the easy thing is better than the hard, for it is as we wish it to be. That
is the greater good whose contrary is greater, and whose loss is greater. Excellence is
greater than non-excellence, badness than non-badness; for excellence, goodness
and badness are ends, which the mere absence of them cannot be. Further, if the
functions of things are nobler or baser, the things themselves are greater; and if the
badnesses and excellences are greater, their functions also are greater; for the
35   nature of results corresponds with that of their causes and origins and the nature of
causes and origins corresponds with that of their results. Moreover, those things are
greater goods, superiority in which is more desirable or more honourable. [[Thus,
keenness of sight is more desirable than keenness of smell, sight generally being
more desirable than smell generally; and similarly, unusually great love of friends
1364^b1   being more honourable than unusually great love of money, love of friends is more
honourable than love of money.]][16] Conversely, if one of two things is better or
nobler than the other, an unusual degree of that thing is better or nobler than an
unusual degree of the other. Again, one thing is more honourable or better than
5   another if it is more honourable or better to desire it; for greater desires have greater
objects; and for the same reason, if one thing is more honourable or better than
another, it is more honourable and better to desire it. Again, if one science is more
honourable and valuable than another, its objects are also more honourable and
valuable; as is the science, so is the reality that is its object, each science being
10   authoritative in its own sphere. So, also, the more valuable and honourable the
object of a science, the more valuable and honourable the science itself is in
consequence. Again, that which would be judged, or which has been judged, a
greater good, by all or most people of understanding, or by the majority of men, or
by the ablest, must be so; either without qualification, or in so far as they use their
understanding to form their judgement. This is indeed a general principle,
applicable to all other judgements also; not only the goodness of things, but their
15   essence, magnitude, and general nature are in fact just what knowledge and
understanding will declare them to be. Here the principle is applied to judgements
of goodness, since one definition of good was what beings that acquire understanding will choose in any given case; from which it clearly follows that that thing is
better which understanding declares to be so. That, again, is a better thing which
20   attaches to better men, either absolutely, or in virtue of their being better; as
courage is better than strength. And that is a greater good which would be chosen

---

¹⁵Pindar, *Olympian* I 1.
¹⁶Kassel marks this as a later addition by Aristotle himself.

by a better man, either absolutely, or in virtue of his being better: for instance, to suffer wrong rather than to do wrong, for that would be the choice of the juster man. Again, the pleasanter of two things is the better, since all things pursue pleasure, and things desire pleasurable sensation for its own sake; and these are two of the characteristics by which the good and the end have been defined. One pleasure is greater than another if it is more unmixed with pain, or more lasting. Again, the nobler thing is better than the less noble, since the noble is either what is pleasant or what is desirable in itself. And those things also are greater goods which men desire more earnestly to bring about for themselves or for their friends, whereas those things which they least desire to bring about are greater evils. And those things which are more lasting are better than those which are more fleeting, and the more secure than the less; the enjoyment of the lasting has the advantage of being longer, and that of the secure has the advantage of suiting our wishes, being there for us whenever we like. Further, in the case of co-ordinates and inflexions of the same stem, what is true of one is true of all. Thus if 'bravely' is more noble and desirable than 'temperately', then bravery is more desirable than temperance and being brave than being temperate. That, again, which is chosen by all is a greater good than that which is not, and that chosen by the majority than that chosen by the minority. For that which all desire is good, as we have said; and so, the more a thing is desired, the better it is. Further, that is the better thing which is considered so by competitors or enemies, or, again, by judges or those whom they judge. In the first two cases the decision is virtually that of everyone, in the last two that of authorities and experts. And sometimes what all share is the better thing, since it is a dishonour not to share in it; at other times, what none or few share is better, since it is rarer. The more praiseworthy things are, the nobler and therefore the better they are. So with the things that earn greater honours than others—honour is, as it were, a measure of value; and the things whose absence involves greater penalties; and the things that are greater than others admitted or believed to be great. Moreover, things look greater merely by being divided into their parts, since they then seem to surpass a greater number of things than before. Hence Homer says that Meleager was roused to battle by the thought of

All horrors that light on a folk whose city is ta'en of their foes,
When they slaughter the men, when the town is wasted with ravening flame,
When strangers are haling young children to thraldom.[17]

The same effect is produced by piling up facts in a climax after the manner of Epicharmus. The reason is partly the same as in the case of division (for combination too makes the impression of great superiority), and partly that the original thing appears to be the cause and origin of great results. And since a thing is greater when it is harder or rarer than other things, its superiority may be due to seasons, ages, places, times, or one's natural powers. When a man accomplishes something beyond his natural power, or beyond his years, or beyond the measure of

[17]See *Iliad* IX 592–4.

people like him, or in a special way, or at a special place or time, his deed will have a high degree of nobleness, goodness, and justice, or of their opposites. Hence the epigram on the victor at the Olympic games:

> In time past, bearing a yoke on my shoulders, of wood unshaven,
> I carried my loads of fish from Argos to Tegea town.

So Iphicrates used to extol himself by describing the low estate from which he had risen. Again, what is natural is better than what is acquired, since it is harder to come by. Hence the words of Homer:

> I have learnt from none but myself.[18]

And the greatest of a great thing is particularly good; as when Pericles in his funeral oration said that the country's loss of its young men in battle was as if the spring were taken out of the year. So with those things which are of service when the need is greater; for example, in old age and times of sickness. And of two things that which leads more directly to the end in view is the better. So too is that which is good for an individual than that which is good generally. Again, what *can* be got is better than what cannot, for it is good in a given case and the other thing is not. And what is an end of life is better than what is not, since ends are better than things close to the end. What aims at reality is better than what aims at appearance. We may define what aims at appearance as what a man will not choose if nobody is to know of his having it. This would seem to show that to receive benefits is more desirable than to confer them, since a man will choose the former even if nobody is to know of it, but it does not seem that he will choose the latter if nobody knows of it. What a man wants to *be* is better than what a man wants to *seem,* for in aiming at that he is aiming more at reality. Hence men say that justice is of small value, since it is more desirable to seem just than to be just, whereas with health it is not so. That is better than other things which is useful for a number of purposes; for example, that which promotes life, good life, pleasure, and noble conduct. For this reason wealth and health are thought to be of the highest value, as possessing all these advantages. Again, that is better than other things which is accompanied both with less pain and with actual pleasure; for here there is more than one advantage; and so here we have the good of feeling pleasure and also the good of not feeling pain. And of two good things that is the better whose addition to a third thing makes a better whole. Again, those things which we are seen to possess are better than those which we are not seen to possess, since the former have the air of reality. Hence being rich may be regarded as a greater good than seeming to be. That which is dearly prized is better than what is not—the sort of thing that some people have only one of, though others have more like it. Accordingly, blinding a one-eyed man inflicts worse injury than half-blinding a man with two eyes; for the one-eyed man has been robbed of what he dearly prized.

[18]*Odyssey* XXII 347.

The grounds on which we must base our persuasions, when we are speaking for   20
or against a proposal, have now been set forth more or less completely.

8 · The most important and effective qualification for success in persuading
audiences and speaking well on public affairs is to understand all the forms of
government and to discriminate their respective customs, institutions, and interests.
For all men are persuaded by considerations of their interest, and their interest lies   25
in the maintenance of the established order. Further, it rests with the supreme
authority to give authoritative decisions, and this varies with each form of
government; there are as many different supreme authorities as there are different
forms of government. The forms of government are four—democracy, oligarchy,
aristocracy, monarchy. The supreme right to judge and decide always rests,   30
therefore, with either a part or the whole of one or other of these governing
powers.

A democracy is a form of government under which the citizens distribute the
offices of state among themselves by lot, whereas under oligarchy there is a property
qualification, under aristocracy one of education. By education I mean that
education which is laid down by the law; for it is those who have been loyal to the   35
national institutions that hold office under an aristocracy. These are bound to be
looked upon as the best men, and it is from this fact that this form of government
has derived its name.[19] Monarchy, as the word implies, is the constitution in which
one man has authority over all. There are two forms of monarchy: kingship, which is   1366ª1
limited by prescribed conditions, and tyranny, which is not limited by anything.

We must also notice the ends which the various forms of government pursue,
since people choose such actions as will lead to the realization of their ends. The end
of democracy is freedom; of oligarchy, wealth; of aristocracy, the maintenance of   5
education and national institutions; of tyranny, the protection of the tyrant. It is
clear, then, that we must distinguish those particular customs, institutions, and
interests which tend to realize the end of each constitution, since men choose their
means with reference to their ends. But rhetorical persuasion is effected not only by
demonstrative but by ethical argument; it helps a speaker to convince us, if we   10
believe that he has certain qualities himself, namely, goodness, or goodwill towards
us, or both together. Similarly, we should know the character of each form of
government, for the special character of each is bound to provide us with our most
effective means of persuasion in dealing with it. We shall learn the qualities of
governments in the same way as we learn the qualities of individuals, since they are
revealed in their acts of choice; and these are determined by the end that inspires   15
them.

We have now considered the objects, present or future, at which we are to aim
when urging any proposal, and the grounds on which we are to base our persuasions
in favour of its utility, and the means and methods by which we shall gain a good   20
knowledge of the characters and institutions peculiar to the various forms of

[19]ἀριστοκρατία from ἄριστος ('best').

government—only, however, to the extent demanded by the present occasion; a detailed account of the subject has been given in the *Politics*.

9 · We have now to consider excellence and vice, the noble and the base, since these are the objects of praise and blame. In doing so, we shall at the same time be finding out how to make our hearers take the required view of our own characters—our second method of persuasion. The ways in which to make them trust the goodness of other people are also the ways in which to make them trust our own. Praise, again, may be serious or frivolous; nor is it always of a human or divine being but often of inanimate things, or of the humblest of the lower animals. Here too we must know on what grounds to argue, and must, therefore, now discuss the subject, though by way of illustration only.

The noble is that which is both desirable for its own sake and also worthy of praise; or that which is both good and also pleasant because good. If this is the noble, it follows that excellence must be noble, since it is both a good thing and also praiseworthy. Excellence is, according to the usual view, a faculty of providing and preserving good things; or a faculty of conferring many great benefits, and benefits of all kinds on all occasions. The parts of excellence are justice, courage, temperance, magnificence, magnanimity, liberality, gentleness, prudence, wisdom. If excellence is a faculty of beneficence, the highest kinds of it must be those which are most useful to others, and for this reason men honour most the just and the courageous, since courage is useful to others in war, justice both in war and in peace. Next comes liberality; liberal people let their money go instead of fighting for it, whereas other people care more for money than for anything else. Justice is the excellence through which everybody enjoys his own possessions in accordance with the law; its opposite is injustice, through which men enjoy the possessions of others in defiance of the law. Courage is the excellence that disposes men to do noble deeds in situations of danger, in accordance with the law and in obedience to its commands; cowardice is the opposite. Temperance is the excellence that disposes us to obey the law where physical pleasures are concerned; intemperance is the opposite. Liberality disposes us to spend money for others' good; illiberality is the opposite. Magnanimity is the excellence that disposes us to do good to others on a large scale; [its opposite is meanness of spirit].[20] Magnificence is the excellence productive of greatness in matters involving the spending of money. The opposites of these two are smallness of spirit and meanness respectively. Prudence is that excellence of the understanding which enables men to come to wise decisions about the relation to happiness of the goods and evils that have been previously mentioned.

The above is a sufficient account, for our present purpose, of excellence and vice in general, and of their various parts. As to further aspects of the subject, it is not difficult to discern the facts; it is evident that things productive of excellence are noble, as tending towards excellence; and also the effects of excellence, that is, the

[20]Excised by Kassel.

signs of its presence and the acts to which it leads. And since the signs of excellence
and such acts as it is the mark of a good man to do or have done to him, are noble, it
follows that all deeds or signs of courage, and everything done courageously, must   30
be noble things; and so with what is just and actions done justly. (Not, however,
things done to us; for in this alone of the excellences, justly does not always imply
nobly—when a man is punished, it is more shameful that this should be justly than   35
unjustly done to him.) The same is true of the other excellences. Again, those
actions are noble for which the reward is simply honour, or honour more than
money. So are those in which a man aims at something desirable for someone else's
sake; actions good absolutely, such as those a man does for his country without
thinking of himself; actions good in their own nature; actions that are not good
simply for the individual, since individual interests are selfish. Noble also are those   1367ª1
actions whose advantage may be enjoyed after death, as opposed to those whose
advantage is enjoyed during one's lifetime; for the latter are more likely to be for
one's own sake only. Also, all actions done for the sake of others, since these less
than other actions are done for one's own sake; and all successes which benefit
others and not oneself; and services done to one's benefactors, for this is just; and   5
good deeds generally, since they are not directed to one's own profit. And the
opposites of those things of which men feel ashamed, for men are ashamed of
saying, doing, or intending to do shameful things. So when Alcaeus said

> Something I fain would say to thee,
> Only shame restraineth me,   10

Sappho wrote

> If for things good and noble thou wert yearning,
> If to speak baseness were thy tongue not burning,
> No load of shame would on thine eyelids weigh;
> What thou with honour wishest thou wouldst say.

Those things, also, are noble for which men strive anxiously, without feeling fear;   15
for they feel thus about the good things which lead to fame. Again, one excellence or
action is nobler than another if it is that of a naturally finer being: thus a man's will
be nobler than a woman's. And those qualities are noble which give more pleasure to
other people than to their possessors; hence the nobleness of justice and just actions.
It is noble to avenge oneself on one's enemies and not to come to terms with them;   20
for requital is just, and the just is noble; and not to surrender is a sign of courage.
Victory, too, and honour belong to the class of noble things, since they are desirable
although they yield no fruits, and they prove our superiority in good qualities.
Things that deserve to be remembered are noble, and the more they deserve this, the
nobler they are. So are the things that continue even after death; [those which are   25
always attended by honour][21] those which are exceptional; and those which are
possessed by one person alone—these last are more readily remembered than

[21]Excised by Kassel.

others. So again are possessions that bring no profit, since they are more fitting than others for a gentleman. So are the distinctive qualities of a particular people, and the symbols of what it specially admires, like long hair in Sparta, where this is a mark of a free man, as it is not easy to perform any menial task when one's hair is long. Again, it is noble not to practise any sordid craft, since it is the mark of a free man not to live at another's beck and call. We are also to assume, when we wish either to praise a man or blame him, that qualities closely allied to those which he actually has are identical with them; for instance, that the cautious man is cold-blooded and treacherous, and that the stupid man is an honest fellow or the thick-skinned man a good-tempered one. We can always idealize any given man by drawing on the virtues akin to his actual qualities; thus we may say that the passionate and excitable man is frank; or that the arrogant man is superb or impressive. Those who run to extremes will be said to possess the corresponding good qualities; rashness will be called courage, and extravagance generosity. That will be what most people think; and at the same time this method enables an advocate to draw a misleading inference from the motive, arguing that if a man runs into danger needlessly, much more will he do so in a noble cause; and if a man is open-handed to anyone and everyone, he will be so to his friends also, since it is the extreme form of goodness to be good to everybody.

We must also take into account the nature of our particular audience when making a speech of praise; for, as Socrates used to say, it is not difficult to praise the Athenians to an Athenian audience.[22] If the audience esteems a given quality, we must say that our hero has that quality, no matter whether we are addressing Scythians or Spartans or philosophers. Everything, in fact, that is esteemed we are to represent as noble. After all, people regard the two things as much the same.

All actions are noble that are appropriate to the man who does them: if, for instance, they are worthy of his ancestors or of his own past career. For it makes for happiness, and is a noble thing, that he should add to the honour he already has. Even inappropriate actions are noble if they are better and nobler than the appropriate ones would be; for instance, if one who was just an average person when all went well becomes a hero in adversity, or if he becomes better and easier to get on with the higher he rises. Compare the saying of Iphicrates, 'Think what I was and what I am'; and the epigram on the victor at the Olympic games,

In time past, bearing a yoke on my shoulders, of wood unshaven;

and the encomium of Simonides,

A woman whose father, whose husband, whose brethren were princes all.

Since we praise a man for what he has actually done, and fine actions are distinguished from others by being chosen, we must try to prove that his acts are based on choice. This is all the easier if we can make out that he has often acted so before, and therefore we must assert coincidences and accidents to have been

---

[22]See Plato, *Menexenus* 235D.

chosen. Produce a number of good actions, all of the same kind, and people will think that they are signs of excellence and choice.

[23][[Praise is the expression in words of the eminence of a man's good qualities, and therefore we must display his actions as the product of such qualities; [Encomium refers to what he has actually done][24] the mention of accessories, such as good birth and education, merely helps to make our story credible—good fathers are likely to have good sons, and good training is likely to produce good character. [Hence it is only when a man has already done something that we bestow *encomiums* upon him.][25] Yet the actual deeds are evidence of the doer's character: even if a man has not actually done a given good thing, we shall bestow *praise* on him, if we are sure that he is the sort of man who *would* do it. [To call any one blest is the same thing as to call him happy; but these are not the same thing as to bestow praise and encomium upon him; the two latter are a part of calling happy, just as goodness is a part of happiness.][26]

To praise a man is in one respect akin to urging a course of action. The suggestions which would be made in the latter case become encomiums when differently expressed. Since we know what action or character is required, then, in order to express these facts as suggestions for action, we have to change and reverse our form of words. Thus the statement 'A man should be proud not of what he owes to fortune but of what he owes to himself', if put like this, amounts to a suggestion; to make it into praise we must put it thus, 'Since he is proud not of what he owes to fortune but of what he owes to himself'. Consequently, whenever you want to praise anyone, think what you would urge people to do; and when you want to urge the doing of anything, think what you would praise a man for having done. Since suggestion may or may not forbid an action, the praise into which we convert it must have one or other of two opposite forms of expression accordingly.[27]]]

There are, also, many useful ways of heightening the effect of praise. We must, for instance, point out that a man is the only one, or the first, or almost the only one who has done something, or that he has done it better than anyone else; all these distinctions are honourable. And we must, further, make much of the particular season and occasion of an action; and these must be used when the action was inappropriate. If a man has often achieved the same success, we must mention this; that is a strong point; he himself, and not luck, will then be given the credit. So, too, if it is on his account that observances have been devised and instituted to encourage or honour such achievements as his own [[and if the first encomium was made for him, as in the case of Hippolochus]],[28] as Harmodius and Aristogeiton had their statues put up in the market-place. And we may censure bad men for the opposite reason.

Again, if you cannot find enough to say of a man himself, you may pit him against others, which is what Isocrates used to do owing to his familiarity with

30

35

1368ᵃ1

5

10

15

20

---

[23]Kassel marks this and the following paragraph as a later addition by Aristotle himself.
[24]Excised by Kassel.   [25]Excised by Kassel.   [26]Excised by Kassel.
[27]The text of this sentence is uncertain.
[28]Marked by Kassel as a later addition by Aristotle himself.

forensic pleading. The comparison should be with famous men; that will strengthen your case; it is a noble thing to surpass men who are themselves great. It is only natural that methods of heightening the effect should be attached particularly to speeches of praise; they aim at proving superiority over others, and any such superiority is a form of nobleness. Hence if you cannot compare your hero with famous men, you should at least compare him with other people generally, since any superiority is held to reveal excellence. And, in general, of the lines of argument which are common to all speeches, this heightening of effect is most suitable for declamations, where we take the actions as admitted facts, and our business is simply to invest these with dignity and nobility. Examples are most suitable to deliberative speeches; for we judge of future events by divination from past events. Enthymemes are most suitable to forensic speeches; it is the past which, because of its obscurity, most admits of explanation and demonstration.

The above are the general lines on which all, or nearly all, speeches of praise or blame are constructed. We have seen the sort of thing we must bear in mind in making such speeches, and the materials out of which encomiums and censures are made. Knowing the above facts, we know their contraries; and it is out of these that speeches of censure are made.

10 · We have next to treat of Accusation and Defence, and to enumerate and describe the ingredients of the deductions used therein. There are three things we must ascertain—first, the nature and number of the incentives to wrong-doing; second, the state of mind of wrongdoers; third, the kind of persons who are wronged, and their condition. We will deal with these questions in order. But before that let us define the act of wrong-doing.

We may describe wrong-doing as injury voluntarily inflicted contrary to law. Law is either special or general. By special law I mean that written law which regulates the life of a particular community; by general law, all those unwritten principles which are supposed to be acknowledged everywhere. We do things voluntarily when we do them with knowledge and without constraint. (Not all voluntary acts are chosen but all chosen acts are done with knowledge—no one is ignorant of what he chooses.) The causes of our choosing harmful and wicked acts contrary to law are vice and incontinence. For the wrongs a man does to others will correspond to the bad quality or qualities that he himself possesses. Thus it is the mean man who will wrong others about money, the intemperate in matters of physical pleasure, the effeminate in matters of comfort, and the coward where danger is concerned [his terror makes him abandon those who are involved in the same danger].[29] The ambitious man does wrong for the sake of honour, the quick-tempered from anger, the lover of victory for the sake of victory, the embittered man for the sake of revenge, the stupid man because he has misguided notions of right and wrong, the shameless man because he does not mind what people think of him; and so with the rest—any wrong that anyone does to others corresponds to his particular faults of character.

---

[29]Excised by Kassel.

However, this subject has already been cleared up in part in our discussion of the excellences and will be further explained later when we treat of the emotions. We have now to consider the motives and states of mind of wrong-doers, and to whom they do wrong.

Let us first decide what sort of things people are trying to get or avoid when they set about doing wrong to others. For it is plain that the prosecutor must consider, out of all the aims that can ever induce us to do wrong to our neighbours, how many, and which, affect his adversary; while the defendant must consider how many, and which, do *not* affect him. Now every action of every person either is or is not due to that person himself. Of those not due to himself some are due to chance, the others to necessity; of these latter, again, some are due to compulsion, the others to nature. Consequently all actions that are not due to a man himself are due either to chance or to nature or to compulsion. All actions that *are* due to a man himself and caused by himself are due either to habit or to desire; and of the latter, some are due to rational desire, the others to irrational. Rational desire is wishing, and wishing is a desire for good—nobody wishes for anything unless he thinks it good. Irrational desire is twofold, viz. anger and appetite.

Thus every action must be due to one or other of seven causes: chance, nature, compulsion, habit, reasoning, anger, or appetite. It is superfluous further to distinguish actions according to the doers' ages, states, or the like; it is of course true that, for instance, young men do have hot tempers and strong appetites; still, it is not through youth that they act accordingly, but through anger or appetite. Nor, again, is action due to wealth or poverty; it is of course true that poor men, being short of money, do have an appetite for it, and that rich men, being able to command needless pleasures, do have an appetite for such pleasures: but here, again, their actions will be *due* not to wealth or poverty but to appetite. Similarly, with just men, and unjust men, and all others who are said to act in accordance with their states, their actions will really be due to one of the causes mentioned—either reasoning or emotion: due, indeed, sometimes to good dispositions and good emotions, and sometimes to bad; but that good qualities should be followed by good emotions, and bad by bad, is merely an accessory fact—it is no doubt true that the temperate man, for instance, because he is temperate, *is* always and at once attended by healthy opinions and appetites in regard to pleasant things, and the intemperate man by unhealthy ones. So we must ignore such distinctions. Still we must consider what kinds of actions and of people usually go together; for while there are no definite kinds of action associated with the fact that a man is fair or dark, tall or short, it does make a difference if he is young or old, just or unjust. And, generally speaking, all those accessory qualities that cause distinctions of human character are important: e.g. the sense of wealth or poverty, of being lucky or unlucky. This will be dealt with later—let us now deal first with the rest of the subject before us.

The things that happen by chance are all those whose cause cannot be determined, that have no purpose, and that happen neither always nor for the most part nor in any fixed way. The definition of chance shows just what they are. Those things happen by nature which have a fixed and internal cause; they take place uniformly, either always or for the most part. There is no need to discuss in exact detail the things that happen contrary to nature, nor to ask whether they happen in some sense naturally or from some other cause; it would seem that chance is indeed the cause of such events. Those things happen through compulsion which take place contrary to the desire or reason of the agents themselves. Acts are done from habit which men do because they have often done them before. Actions are due to reasoning when, in view of any of the goods already mentioned, they appear useful either as ends or as contributing to an end, and are performed for that reason—for intemperate men too perform a certain number of useful actions, but because they are pleasant and not because they are useful. To passion and anger are due all acts of revenge. Revenge and punishment are different things. Punishment is inflicted for the sake of the person punished; revenge for that of the punisher, to satisfy his feelings. (What anger is will be made clear when we come to discuss the emotions.) Appetite is the cause of all actions that appear pleasant. Things familiar and things habitual belong to the class of pleasant things; for there are many actions not naturally pleasant which men perform with pleasure, once they have become used to them. To sum up then, all actions due to ourselves either are or seem to be either good or pleasant. Moreover, as all actions due to ourselves are done voluntarily and actions not due to ourselves are done involuntarily, it follows that all voluntary actions must either be or seem to be either good or pleasant; for I reckon among goods escape from evils or apparent evils and the exchange of a greater evil for a less (since these things are in a sense desirable), and likewise I count among pleasures escape from painful or apparently painful things and the exchange of a greater pain for a less. We must ascertain, then, the number and nature of the things that are useful and pleasant. The useful has been previously examined in connexion with deliberative oratory; let us now proceed to examine the pleasant. Our various definitions must be regarded as adequate, even if they are not exact, provided they are clear.

11 · We may lay it down that pleasure is a movement, a movement by which the soul as a whole is consciously brought into its normal state of being; and that pain is the opposite. If this is what pleasure is, it is clear that the pleasant is what tends to produce this condition, while that which tends to destroy it, or to cause the soul to be brought into the opposite state, is painful. It must therefore be pleasant for the most part to move towards a natural state of being, particularly when a natural process has achieved the complete recovery of that natural state. Habits also are pleasant; for as soon as a thing has become habitual, it is virtually natural; habit is a thing not unlike nature; what happens often is akin to what happens always, natural events happening always, habitual events often. Again, that is pleasant which is not forced on us; for force is unnatural, and that is why what is compulsory is painful, and it has been rightly said

All that is done on compulsion is bitterness unto the soul.[30]

---

[30]Evenus, frag. 8 West.

So all acts of concentration, strong effort, and strain are necessarily painful; they all involve compulsion and force, unless we are accustomed to them, in which case it is custom that makes them pleasant. The opposites to these are pleasant; and hence ease, freedom from toil, relaxation, amusement, rest, and sleep belong to the class of pleasant things; for these are all free from any element of compulsion. Everything, too, is pleasant for which we have the appetite within us, since appetite is desire for pleasure. [[Of the appetites some are irrational, some associated with reason. By irrational I mean those which do not arise from any opinion held by the mind. Of this kind are those known as natural; for instance, those originating in the body, such as the appetite for nourishment, [namely hunger and thirst][31] and a separate kind of appetite answering to each kind of nourishment; and those connected with taste and sex and sensations of touch in general; and those of smell, hearing, and vision. Rational appetites are those which we are induced to have; there are many things we desire to see or get because we have been told of them and induced to believe them good.]][32] Further, pleasure is the consciousness through the senses of a certain kind of emotion; but imagination is a feeble sort of sensation, and there will always be in the mind of a man who remembers or expects something the imagination of what he remembers or expects. If this is so, it is clear that memory and expectation also, being accompanied by sensation, may be accompanied by pleasure. It follows that anything pleasant is either present and perceived, past and remembered, or future and expected, since we perceive present things, remember past ones, and expect future ones. Now the things that are pleasant to remember are not only those that, when actually present, *were* pleasant, but also some things that were not, provided that their results have subsequently proved noble and good. Hence the words

> Sweet 'tis when rescued to remember pain,[33]

and

> Even his griefs are a joy long after to one that remembers
> All that he wrought and endured.[34]

The reason for this is that it is pleasant even to be merely free from evil. The things it is pleasant to expect are those that when present are felt to afford us either great delight or great but not painful benefit. And in general, all the things that delight us when they are present also do so, for the most part, when we merely remember or expect them. Hence even being angry is pleasant—Homer said of wrath that

> Sweeter it is by far than the honeycomb dripping with
> sweetness—[35]

for no one grows angry with a person on whom there is no prospect of taking vengeance, and we feel comparatively little anger, or none at all, with those who are

---

[31]Excised by Kassel.   [32]Kassel marks this passage as a later addition by Aristotle himself.
[33]Euripides, frag. 133 Nauck.   [34]*Odyssey* XV 400.   [35]*Iliad* XVIII 109.

much our superiors in power. Some pleasant feeling is associated with most of our appetites; we are enjoying either the memory of a past pleasure or the expectation of a future one, just as persons down with fever, during their attacks of thirst, enjoy remembering the drinks they have had and looking forward to having more. So also a lover enjoys talking or writing about his loved one, or doing any little thing connected with him; all these things recall him to memory and make him as it were present to the eye of imagination. Indeed, it is always the first sign of love, that besides enjoying some one's presence, we remember him when he is gone; and we love when we actually feel pain because he is there no longer. Similarly there is an element of pleasure even in mourning and lamentation. There is grief, indeed, at his loss, but pleasure in remembering him and as it were seeing him before us in his deeds and in his life. We can well believe the poet when he says

He spake, and in each man's heart he awakened the love of lament.[36]

Revenge, too, is pleasant; it is pleasant to get anything that it is painful to fail to get, and angry people suffer extreme pain when they fail to get their revenge; but they enjoy the prospect of getting it. Victory also is pleasant, and not merely to the competitive but to everyone; the winner sees himself in the light of a champion, and everybody has a more or less keen appetite for being that. The pleasantness of victory implies of course that combative sports and intellectual contests are pleasant (since in these it often happens that someone wins) and also games like knucklebones, ball, dice, and draughts. And similarly with the serious sports; some of these become pleasant when one is accustomed to them; while others are pleasant from the first, like hunting with hounds, or indeed any kind of hunting. For where there is competition, there is victory. That is why forensic pleading and debating contests are pleasant to those who are accustomed to them and have the capacity for them. Honour and good repute are among the most pleasant things of all; they make a man see himself in the character of a fine fellow, especially when he is credited with it by people whom he thinks tell the truth. His neighbours are better judges than people at a distance; his associates and fellow-countrymen better than strangers; his contemporaries better than posterity; sensible persons better than foolish ones; a large number of people better than a small number: those of the former class, in each case, are the more likely to be truthful. Honour and credit bestowed by those whom you think much inferior to yourself—e.g. children or animals—you do not value: not for its own sake, anyhow: if you do value it, it is for some other reason. Friends belong to the class of pleasant things; it is pleasant to love—if you love wine, you certainly find it delightful; and it is pleasant to be loved, for this too makes a man see himself as the possessor of goodness, a thing that every being that has a feeling for it desires to possess: to be loved means to be valued for one's own personal qualities. To be admired is also pleasant, for the same reason as to be honoured is. Flattery and flatterers are pleasant: the flatterer is a man who, you believe, admires and likes you. To do the same thing often is pleasant, since, as

[36]*Iliad* XXIII 108; *Odyssey* IV 183.

we saw, anything familiar is pleasant. And to change is also pleasant: change means   25
an approach to nature, whereas invariable repetition of anything causes the
excessive prolongation of a settled condition: therefore, says the poet,

Change is in all things sweet.[37]

That is why what comes to us only at long intervals is pleasant, whether it be a
person or a thing; for it is a change from what we had before, and, besides, what   30
comes only at long intervals has the value of rarity. Learning things and wondering
at things are also pleasant for the most part; wondering implies the desire of
learning, so that the object of wonder is an object of desire; while in learning one is
brought into one's natural condition. [[Conferring and receiving benefits belong to
the class of pleasant things; to receive a benefit is to get what one desires; to confer a   1371[b]1
benefit implies both possession and superiority, both of which are things we try to
attain. It is because beneficent acts are pleasant that people find it pleasant to put
their neighbours straight again and to supply what they lack.]][38] Again, since
learning and wondering are pleasant, it follows that such things as acts of imitation   5
must be pleasant—for instance, painting, sculpture, poetry—and every product of
skilful imitation; this latter, even if the object imitated is not itself pleasant; for it is
not the object itself which here gives delight; the spectator draws inferences ('That
is a so-and-so') and thus learns something fresh. Dramatic turns of fortune and   10
hairbreadth escapes from perils are pleasant, because we feel all such things are
wonderful.

And since what is natural is pleasant, and things akin to each other seem
natural to each other, therefore all kindred and similar things are for the most part
pleasant to each other; for instance, one man, horse, or young person is pleasant to
another man, horse, or young person. Hence the proverbs 'mate delights mate', 'like   15
to like', 'beast knows beast', 'jackdaw to jackdaw', and the rest of them. But since
everything like and akin to oneself is pleasant, and since every man is himself more
like and akin to himself than anyone else is, it follows that all of us must be more or   20
less fond of ourselves. For all this resemblance and kinship is present particularly in
the relation of an individual to himself. And because we are all fond of ourselves, it
follows that what is our own is pleasant to all of us, as for instance our own deeds
and words. That is why we are for the most part fond of our flatterers, our lovers,
and honour; also of our children, for our children are our own work. It is also
pleasant to complete what is defective, for the whole thing thereupon becomes our   25
own work. [[And since power over others is very pleasant, it is pleasant to be thought
wise, for practical wisdom secures us power over others. (Scientific wisdom is the
knowledge of many wonderful things.)]][39] Again, since for the most part men are
ambitious, it must be pleasant to disparage our neighbours as well as to have power
over them.[40] It is pleasant for a man to spend his time over what he feels he can do   30

---

[37]Euripides, *Orestes* 234.
[38]Marked by Kassel as a later addition by Aristotle himself.
[39]Marked by Kassel as a later addition by Aristotle himself.
[40]Deleting the full stop after ἀναι.

best; just as the poet says,

> To that he bends himself,
> To that each day allots most time, wherein
> He is indeed the best part of himself.[41]

Similarly, since amusement and every kind of relaxation too belong to the class of pleasant things, it follows that ludicrous things are pleasant, whether men, words, or 1372ª1 deeds. We have discussed the ludicrous separately in the treatise on the *Art of Poetry.*

So much for the subject of pleasant things: by considering their opposites we can easily see what things are unpleasant.

12 . The above are the motives that make men do wrong to others; we are 5 next to consider the states of mind in which they do it, and the persons to whom they do it.

They must themselves suppose that the thing can be done, and done by them; and that they can do it without being found out, or that if they are found out they can escape being punished, or that if they are punished the disadvantage will be less than the gain for themselves or those they care for. The general subject of apparent 10 possibility and impossibility will be handled later on, since it is relevant to all kinds of speaking. But it may here be said that people think that they can themselves most easily do wrong to others without being punished for it if they possess eloquence, or practical ability, or much legal experience, or a large body of friends, or a great deal of money. Their confidence is greatest if they personally possess the advantages 15 mentioned; but even without them they are satisfied if they have friends or supporters or partners who do possess them: they can thus both commit their crimes and escape being found out and punished for committing them. They are also safe, they think, if they are on good terms with their victims or with the judges who try them. Their victims will in that case not be on their guard against being wronged, 20 and will make some arrangement with them instead of prosecuting; while their judges will favour them because they like them, either letting them off altogether or imposing light sentences. They are not likely to be found out if their appearance contradicts the charges that might be brought against them (for instance, a weakling is unlikely to be charged with violent assault, or a poor and ugly man with adultery), or if they act publicly and in the open (for nobody could at all suppose 25 that possible, and therefore no precautions are taken). The same is true of crimes so great and terrible that no man living could be suspected of them: here too no precautions are taken. For all men guard against ordinary offences, just as they guard against ordinary diseases; but no one takes precautions against an offence that nobody has ever yet committed. You feel safe, too, if you have either no enemies or a great many; if you have none, you expect not to be watched and 30 therefore not to be detected; if you have a great many, you will be watched, and therefore people will think you can never risk an attempt on them, and you can

---

[41]Euripides, frag. 183 Nauck.

defend your innocence by pointing out that you could never have taken such a risk. You may also trust to hide your crime by the way you do it or the place you do it in, or by some convenient means of disposal.

You may feel that even if you are found out you can stave off a trial, or have it postponed, or corrupt your judges: or that even if you are sentenced you can avoid paying damages, or can at least postpone doing so for a long time: or that you are so   35 badly off that you will have nothing to lose. You may feel that the gain to be got by wrong-doing is great or certain or immediate, and that the penalty is small or uncertain or distant. [[It may be that the advantage to be gained is greater than any $1372^{b}1$ possible retribution: as in the case of despotic power, as is thought.]][42] You may consider your crimes as bringing you solid profit, while their punishment is nothing more than being called bad names. Conversely, your crimes may bring you some credit (thus you may, incidentally, be avenging your father or mother, like Zeno),   5 whereas the punishment may amount to a fine, or banishment, or something of that sort. People may be led on to wrong others by either of these motives or feelings; but no man by both—they will affect people of quite opposite characters. You may be encouraged by having often escaped detection or punishment already; or by having often tried and failed; for in crime, as in war, there are men who will always refuse   10 to give up the struggle. You may get your pleasure on the spot and the pain later, or the gain on the spot and the loss later. That is what appeals to incontinent persons—and incontinence may be shown with regard to all the objects of desire. Conversely—what appeals to self-controlled and sensible people—the pain and loss may be immediate, while the pleasure and profit come later and last longer. You   15 may feel able to make it appear that your crime was due to chance, or to necessity, or to natural causes, or to habit: in fact, to put it generally, as if you had made a mistake rather than actually done wrong. You may be able to trust other people to judge you equitably. You may be stimulated by being in want: which may mean that you want necessaries, as poor people do, or that you want luxuries, as rich   20 people do. You may be encouraged by having a particularly good reputation, because that will save you from being suspected; or by having a particularly bad one, because nothing you are likely to do will make you more suspected.

The above, then, are the various states of mind in which a man sets about doing wrong to others. The kind of people to whom he does wrong, and the ways in which he does it, must be considered next. The people to whom he does it are those who have what he wants himself, whether this means necessities or luxuries and   25 materials for enjoyment. His victims may be far off or near at hand. If they are near, he gets his profit quickly; if they are far off, vengeance is slow, as those think who plunder the Carthaginians. They may be those who are trustful instead of being cautious and watchful, since all such people are easy to elude. Or those who are too easy-going to have enough energy to prosecute an offender. Or sensitive   30 people, who are not apt to show fight over questions of money. Or those who have been wronged already by many people, and yet have not prosecuted; such men must surely be the proverbial 'Mysian prey'. Or those who have either never or often been

[42]Marked by Kassel as a later addition by Aristotle himself.

wronged before; in neither case will they take precautions; if they have never been wronged they think they never will, and if they have often been wronged they feel that surely it cannot happen again. Or those whose character has been attacked in the past, or is exposed to attack in the future: they will be too much frightened of the judges to choose to prosecute, nor can they win their case if they do: this is true of those who are hated or unpopular. Another likely class of victim is those who their injurer can pretend have, themselves or through their ancestors or friends, treated badly, or intended to treat badly, the man himself, or his ancestors, or those he cares for; as the proverb says, 'wickedness needs but a pretext'. A man may wrong his enemies, because that is pleasant: he may equally wrong his friends, because that is easy. Then there are those who have no friends, and those who lack eloquence and practical capacity; these will either not attempt to prosecute, or they will come to terms, or failing that they will lose their case. There are those whom it does not pay to waste time in waiting for trial or damages, such as foreigners and small farmers; they will settle for a trifle, and always be ready to leave off. Also those who have themselves wronged others, either often, or in the same way as they are now being wronged themselves—for it is felt that next to no wrong is done to people when it is the same wrong as they have often themselves done to others: if, for instance, you assault a man who has been accustomed to behave with violence to others. So too with those who have done wrong to others, or have meant to, or mean to, or are likely to do so; there is something fine and pleasant in wronging such persons, it seems as though almost no wrong were done. Also those by doing wrong to whom we shall be gratifying our friends, or those we admire or love, or our masters, or in general the people by reference to whom we mould our lives. Also those whom we may wrong and yet be sure of equitable treatment. Also those against whom we have had any grievance, or any previous differences with them, as Callippus had when he behaved as he did to Dion: here too it seems as if almost no wrong were being done. Also those who are on the point of being wronged by others if we fail to wrong them ourselves, since here we feel we have no time left for thinking the matter over. So Aenesidemus is said to have sent the 'cottabus' prize to Gelon, who had just reduced a town to slavery, because Gelon had got there first and forestalled his own attempt. Also those by wronging whom we shall be able to do many righteous acts; for we feel that we can then easily cure the harm done. Thus Jason the Thessalian said that it is a duty to do some unjust acts in order to be able to do many just ones.

Among the kinds of wrong done to others are those that are done universally, or at least commonly: one expects to be forgiven for doing these. Also those that can easily be kept dark, as where things that can rapidly be consumed like eatables are concerned, or things that can easily be changed in shape, colour, or combination, or things that can easily be stowed away almost anywhere—portable objects that you can stow away in small corners, or things so like others of which you have plenty already that nobody can tell the difference. There are also wrongs of a kind that shame prevents the victim speaking about, such as outrages done to the women in his household or to himself or to his sons. Also those for which you would be thought very litigious to prosecute anyone—trifling wrongs, or wrongs for which people are usually excused.

The above is a fairly complete account of the circumstances under which men do wrong to others, of the sort of wrongs they do, of the sort of persons to whom they do them, and of their reasons for doing them.

13 · It will now be well to make a complete classification of just and unjust actions. We may begin by observing that they have been defined relatively to two kinds of law, and also relatively to two classes of persons. By the two kinds of law I mean particular law and universal law. Particular law is that which each community lays down and applies to its own members: this is partly written and partly unwritten. Universal law is the law of nature. For there really is, as everyone to some extent divines, a natural justice and injustice that is common to all, even to those who have no association or covenant with each other. It is this that Sophocles' Antigone clearly means when she says that the burial of Polyneices was a just act in spite of the prohibition: she means that it was just by nature.

> Not of to-day or yesterday it is,
> But lives eternal: none can date its birth.[43]

And so Empedocles, when he bids us kill no living creature, says that doing this is not just for some people while unjust for others,

> Nay, but, an all-embracing law, through the realms of the sky
> Unbroken it stretcheth, and over the earth's immensity.[44]

And Alcidamas says the same in his Messeniac Oration.

The actions that we ought to do or not to do have also been divided into two classes as affecting either the whole community or some one of its members. From this point of view we can perform just or unjust acts in either of two ways—towards one definite person, or towards the community. The man who is guilty of adultery or assault is doing wrong to some definite person; the man who avoids service in the army is doing wrong to the community.

Thus the whole class of unjust actions may be divided into two classes, those affecting the community, and those affecting one or more other persons. We will next, before going further, say what being wronged is. Since it has already been settled that doing a wrong must be voluntary, being wronged must consist in having an injury done to you by someone who does it voluntarily. In order to be wronged, a man must suffer actual harm and suffer it involuntarily. The various possible forms of harm are clearly explained by our previous separate discussion of goods and evils. We have also seen that a voluntary action is one where the doer knows what he is doing. We now see that every accusation must be of an action affecting either the community or some individual. The doer of the action must either know and act voluntarily or not know and act involuntarily. In the former case, he must be acting

1373^b1

5

10

15

20

25

30

35

---

[43]*Antigone* 456–7.   [44]Frag. 135 Diels-Kranz.

either from choice or from passion. (Anger will be discussed when we speak of the passions; the motives for crime and the state of mind of the criminal have already been discussed.) Now it often happens that a man will admit an act, but will not

1374ᵃ1 admit the prosecutor's label for the act nor the facts which that label implies. He will admit that he took a thing but not that he stole it; that he struck someone first, but not that he committed outrage; that he had intercourse with a woman, but not that he committed adultery; that he is guilty of theft, but not that he is guilty of

5 sacrilege, the object stolen not being consecrated; that he has encroached, but not that he has encroached on State lands; that he has been in communication with the enemy, but not that he has been guilty of treason. Here therefore we must be able to distinguish what is theft, outrage, or adultery, from what is not, if we are to be able to make the justice of our case clear, no matter whether our aim is to establish a man's guilt or to establish his innocence. Wherever such charges are brought

10 against a man, the question is whether he is or is not a wrong-doer and wicked. It is choice that constitutes wickedness and wrong-doing, and such names as outrage or theft imply choice as well as the mere action. A blow does not always amount to outrage, but only if it is struck with some such purpose as to insult the man struck or

15 gratify the striker himself. Nor does taking a thing without the owner's knowledge always amount to theft, but only if it is taken with the intention of keeping it and injuring the owner. And as with these charges, so with all the others.

We saw that there are two kinds of right and wrong conduct towards others, one provided for by written ordinances, the other by unwritten. We have now

20 discussed the kind about which the laws have something to say. The other kind has itself two varieties. First, there is the conduct that springs from exceptional goodness or badness, and is visited accordingly with censure and loss of honour, or with praise and increase of honour and decorations: for instance, gratitude to, or

25 requital of, our benefactors, readiness to help our friends, and the like. The second kind makes up for the defects of a community's written code of law. For equity is regarded as just; it is, in fact, the sort of justice which goes beyond the written law. Its existence partly is and partly is not intended by legislators; not intended, where they have noticed no defect in the law; intended, where they find themselves unable

30 to define things exactly, and are obliged to legislate universally where matters hold only for the most part; or where it is not easy to be complete owing to the endless possible cases presented, such as the kinds and sizes of weapons that may be used to inflict wounds—a lifetime would be too short to make out a complete list of these. If, then, a precise statement is impossible and yet legislation is necessary, the law

35 must be expressed in wide terms; and so, if a man has no more than a finger-ring on his hand when he lifts it to strike or actually strikes another man, he is guilty of a

1374ᵇ1 criminal act according to the written words of the law; but he is innocent really, and it is equity that declares him to be so. From this definition of equity it is plain what sort of actions, and what sort of persons, are equitable or the reverse. Equity must be

5 applied to forgivable actions; and it must make us distinguish between wrongdoings on the one hand, and mistakes, or misfortunes, on the other. (A misfortune is an act, not due to wickedness, that has unexpected results; a mistake is an act, also not due

to turpitude, that has results that might have been expected; a wrongdoing has results that might have been expected, but *is* due to turpitude.) Equity bids us be merciful to the weakness of human nature; to think less about the laws than about   10
the man who framed them, and less about what he said than about what he meant; not to consider the actions of the accused so much as his choice, nor this or that detail so much as the whole story; to ask not what a man is now but what he has   15
always or for the most part been. It bids us remember benefits rather than injuries, and benefits received rather than benefits conferred; to be patient when we are wronged; to settle a dispute by negotiation and not by force; to prefer arbitration to   20
litigation—for an arbitrator goes by the equity of a case, a judge by the law, and arbitration was invented with the express purpose of securing full power for equity.

The above may be taken as a sufficient account of the nature of equity.

14 · The worse of two acts of wrong done to others is that which is prompted by the worse disposition. Hence the most trifling acts may be the worst ones; as   25
when Callistratus charged Melanopus with having cheated the temple-builders of three consecrated half-obols. The converse is true of just acts. This is because the greater is here potentially contained in the less: there is no crime that a man who has stolen three consecrated half-obols would shrink from committing. Sometimes, however, the worse act is reckoned not in this way but by the greater harm that it   30
does. Or it may be because no punishment for it is severe enough to be adequate; or the harm done may be incurable—a difficult and even hopeless crime to defend;[45] or the sufferer may not be able to get his injurer legally punished, a fact that makes the harm incurable, since legal punishment and chastisement are the proper cure. Or again, the man who has suffered wrong may have inflicted some fearful punishment on himself; then the doer of the wrong ought in justice to receive a still more fearful   35
punishment. Thus Sophocles, when pleading for retribution to Euctemon, who had cut his own throat because of the outrage done to him, said he would not fix a   1375ᵃ1
penalty less than the victim had fixed for himself. Again, a man's crime is worse if he has been the first man, or the only man, or almost the only man, to commit it; or if it is by no means the first time he has made the same mistake; or if his crime has led to the thinking-out and invention of measures to prevent and punish similar crimes—thus in Argos a penalty is inflicted on a man on whose account a law is   5
passed, and also on those on whose account the prison was built; or if a crime is specially brutal, or specially deliberate; or if the report of it arouses more terror than pity. There are also such rhetorically effective ways of putting it as the following: that the accused has disregarded and broken not one but many solemn obligations like oaths, promises, pledges, or rights of intermarriage between   10
states—here the crime is worse because it consists of many crimes; and that the crime was committed in the very place where criminals are punished, as for example perjurers do—it is argued that a man who will commit a crime in a law-court would commit it anywhere. Further, the worse deed is that which involves the doer in

---

[45]The sense of this clause is obscure.

special shame; that whereby a man wrongs his benefactors—for he does more than
15   one wrong, by not merely doing them harm but failing to do them good; that which
breaks the unwritten laws of justice—the better sort of man will be just without
being forced to be so, and the written laws depend on force while the unwritten ones
do not. It may however be argued otherwise, that the crime is worse which breaks
the written laws; for the man who commits crimes for which terrible penalties are
20   provided will not hesitate over crimes for which no penalty is provided at all.—So
much, then, for the comparative badness of wrongdoing.

15 · There are also the so-called 'non-technical' means of persuasion; and we
must now take a cursory view of these, since they are specially characteristic of
forensic oratory. They are five in number: laws, witnesses, contracts, tortures,
oaths.

25   First, then, let us take laws and see how they are to be used in persuasion and
dissuasion, in accusation and defence. If the written law tells against our case,
clearly we must appeal to the universal law and to equity as being more just. We
must argue that the juror's oath 'I will give my verdict according to my honest
30   opinion' means that one will not simply follow the letter of the written law. We must
urge that the principles of equity are permanent and changeless, and that the
universal law does not change either, for it is the law of nature, whereas written laws
often do change. This is the bearing of the lines in Sophocles' *Antigone*, where
Antigone pleads that in burying her brother she had broken Creon's law, but not the
unwritten law:

1375ᵇ1   Not of today or yesterday they are;
                   Not I would fear the wrath of any man . . .[46]

We shall argue that justice indeed is true and profitable, but that sham justice is
not, and that consequently the written law is not, because it does not fulfil the
5   function of law. Or that justice is like silver, and must be assayed by the judges, if
the genuine is to be distinguished from the counterfeit. Or that the better man will
follow and abide by the unwritten law in preference to the written. Or perhaps that
the law in question contradicts some other highly-esteemed law, or even contradicts
10   itself. Thus it may be that one law will enact that all contracts must be held binding,
while another forbids us ever to make illegal contracts. Or if a law is ambiguous, we
shall turn it about and consider which construction best fits the interests of justice
or utility, and then follow that way of looking at it. Or if, though the law still exists,
15   the situation to meet which it was passed exists no longer, we must do our best to
prove this and to combat the law thereby. If however the written law supports our
case, we must urge that the oath 'to give my verdict according to my honest opinion'
is not meant to make the judges give a verdict that is contrary to the law, but to save
them from the guilt of perjury if they misunderstand what the law really means. Or
that no one chooses what is absolutely good, but everyone what is good for himself.

[46]*Antigone* 456, 458.

Or that not to use the laws is as bad as to have no laws at all. Or that, as in the other   20
arts, it does not pay to try to be cleverer than the doctor: for less harm comes from
the doctor's mistakes than from the growing habit of disobeying authority. Or that
trying to be cleverer than the laws is just what is forbidden by those codes of law
that are accounted best.—So far as the laws are concerned, the above discussion is   25
probably sufficient.

As to witnesses, they are of two kinds, the ancient and the recent; and these
latter, again, either do or do not share in the risks of the trial. By ancient witnesses I
mean the poets and all other notable persons whose judgements are known to all.
Thus the Athenians appealed to Homer as a witness about Salamis; and the men of   30
Tenedos not long ago appealed to Periander of Corinth in their dispute with the
people of Sigeum; and Cleophon supported his accusation of Critias by quoting the
elegiac verse of Solon, maintaining that discipline had long been slack in the family
of Critias, or Solon would never have written,

Pray thee, bid the red-haired Critias do what his father commands him.[47]

These witnesses are concerned with past events. As to future events we shall   1376ª1
also appeal to soothsayers: thus Themistocles quoted the oracle about 'the wooden
wall' as a reason for engaging the enemy's fleet. Further, proverbs are, as has been
said, one form of evidence. Thus if you are urging somebody not to make a friend of
an old man, you will appeal to the proverb,   5

Never show an old man kindness.

Or if you are urging that he who has made away with fathers should also make away
with their sons, quote,

Fool, who slayeth the father and leaveth his sons to avenge him.

Recent witnesses are well-known people who have expressed their opinions about
some disputed matter: such opinions will be useful support for subsequent disputants on the same points: thus Eubulus used in the law-courts against Chares   10
the reply Plato had made to Archibius, 'It has become the regular custom in this
country to admit that one is a scoundrel'. There are also those witnesses who share
the risk of punishment if their evidence is pronounced false. These are valid
witnesses to the fact that an action was or was not done, that something is or is not
the case; they are not valid witnesses to the quality of an action, to its being just or   15
unjust, useful or harmful. On such questions of *quality* the opinion of detached
persons does count. Most trustworthy of all are the ancient witnesses, since they
cannot be corrupted.

In dealing with the evidence of witnesses, the following are useful arguments.
If you have no witnesses on your side, you will argue that the judges must decide
from what is probable; that this is meant by 'giving a verdict in accordance with
one's honest opinion'; that probabilities cannot be bribed to mislead the court; and   20

[47]Frag. 22a West.

that probabilities are never convicted of perjury. If you *have* witnesses, and the other man has not, you will argue that probabilities cannot be put on their trial, and that we could do without the evidence of witnesses altogether if we need do no more than balance the pleas advanced on either side.

25

30

The evidence of witnesses may refer either to ourselves or to our opponent; and either to questions of fact or to questions of personal character: so, clearly, we need never be at a loss for useful evidence. For if we have no evidence of fact supporting our own case or telling against that of our opponent, at least we can always find evidence to prove our own worth or our opponent's worthlessness. Other arguments about a witness—that he is a friend or an enemy or neutral, or has a good, bad, or indifferent reputation, and any other such distinctions—we must construct from the same commonplaces as we use for enthymemes.

1376ᵇ1

5

10

15

20

25

30

Concerning contracts argument can be so far employed as to increase or diminish their importance and their credibility; we shall try to increase both if they tell in our favour, and to diminish both if they tell in favour of our opponent. Now for confirming or upsetting the credibility of contracts the procedure is just the same as for dealing with witnesses, for the credit to be attached to contracts depends upon the character of those who have signed them or have the custody of them. The contract being once admitted genuine, we must insist on its importance, if it supports our case. We may argue that a contract is a law, though of a special and limited kind; and that, while contracts do not of course make the law binding, the law does make any lawful contract binding, and that the law itself as a whole is a sort of contract, so that anyone who disregards or repudiates any contract is repudiating the law itself. Further, most business relations—those, namely, that are voluntary—are regulated by contracts, and if these lose their binding force, human intercourse ceases to exist. We need not go very deep to discover the other appropriate arguments of this kind. If, however, the contract tells against us and for our opponents, in the first place those arguments are suitable which we can use to fight a law that tells against us. We do not regard ourselves as bound to observe a bad law which it was a mistake ever to pass: and it is ridiculous to suppose that we are bound to observe a bad and mistaken contract. Again, we may argue that the duty of the judge as umpire is to decide what is just, and therefore he must ask where justice lies, and not what this or that document means. And that it is impossible to pervert justice by fraud or by force, since it is founded on nature, but a party to a contract may be the victim of either fraud or force. Moreover, we must see if the contract contravenes either universal law or any written law of our own or another country; and also if it contradicts any other previous or subsequent contract; arguing that the subsequent is the binding contract, or else that the previous one was right and the subsequent one fraudulent—whichever way suits us. Further, we must consider the question of utility, noting whether the contract is against the interest of the judges or not; and so on—these arguments are as obvious as the others.

Examination by torture is one form of evidence, to which great weight is often attached because it is in a sense compulsory. Here again it is not hard to point out the available grounds for magnifying its value, if it happens to tell in our favour, and arguing that it is the only form of evidence that is truthful; or, on the other hand, for refuting it if it tells against us and for our opponent, when we may say what is true of torture of every kind alike, that people under its compulsion lie just as often, sometimes persistently refusing to tell the truth, sometimes recklessly making a false charge in order to be let off sooner. We ought to be able to quote cases, familiar to the judges, in which this sort of thing has actually happened.

In regard to oaths, a fourfold division can be made. A man may either both offer and accept an oath, or neither, or one without the other—that is, he may offer an oath but not accept one, or accept an oath but not offer one. There is also the situation that arises when an oath has already been sworn either by himself or by his opponent.

If you refuse to offer an oath, you may argue that men do not hesitate to perjure themselves; and that if your opponent does swear, you lose your money, whereas, if he does not, you think the judges will decide against him; and that the risk of an unfavourable verdict is preferable, since you trust the judges and do not trust him.

If you refuse to accept an oath, you may argue that an oath is always paid for; that you would of course have taken it if you had been a rascal, since if you *are* a rascal you had better make something by it, and you would in that case have to swear in order to succeed. Thus your refusal, you argue, must be due to excellence, not to fear of perjury: and you may aptly quote the saying of Xenophanes, that it is no fair challenge when an impious man challenges a pious man—it is as if a strong man were to challenge a weakling to strike, or be struck by, him.

If you agree to accept an oath, you may argue that you trust yourself but not your opponent; and that (to invert the remark of Xenophanes) the fair thing is for the impious man to offer the oath and for the pious man to accept it; and that it would be monstrous if you yourself were unwilling to accept an oath in a case where you demand that the judges should do so before giving their verdict. If you wish to offer an oath, you may argue that piety disposes you to commit the issue to the gods; and that your opponent ought not to want other judges than himself, since you leave the decision with him; and that it is outrageous for your opponents to refuse to swear about this question, when they insist that others should do so.

Now that we see how we are to argue in each case separately, we see also how we are to argue when they occur in pairs, namely, when you are willing to accept the oath but not to offer it; to offer it but not to accept it; both to accept and to offer it; or to do neither. These are of course combinations of the cases already mentioned, and so your arguments also must be combinations of the arguments already mentioned.

If you have already sworn an oath that contradicts your present one, you must argue that it is not perjury, since perjury is a crime, and a crime must be a voluntary action, whereas actions due to the force or fraud of others are involuntary. You must further reason from this that perjury depends on the intention and not on the spoken words. But if it is your opponent who has already sworn an oath that contradicts his present one, you must say that if he does not abide by his oaths he is the enemy of society, and that this is the reason why men take an oath before administering the laws. 'Do my opponents insist that you, the judges, must abide by the oath you have sworn, and yet will not abide by their own oaths?' And there are other arguments which may be used to magnify the importance of the oath.

BOOK II

1 · We have now considered the materials to be used in supporting or opposing a measure, in pronouncing eulogies or censures, and for prosecution and defence. We have considered the opinions and propositions useful for persuasive arguments in these areas; for it is about these and on the basis of them that enthymemes are constructed, separately for each type of speech.

But since rhetoric exists to affect the giving of decisions—the hearers decide between one political speaker and another, and a legal verdict *is* a decision—the orator must not only try to make the argument of his speech demonstrative and worthy of belief; he must also make his own character look right and put his hearers, who are to decide, into the right frame of mind. Particularly in deliberative oratory, but also in lawsuits, it adds much to an orator's influence that his own character should look right and that he should be thought to entertain the right feelings towards his hearers; and also that his hearers themselves should be in just the right frame of mind. [[That the orator's own character should look right is particularly important in deliberative speaking: that the audience should be in the right frame of mind, in lawsuits.]][1] When people are feeling friendly and placable, they think one sort of thing; when they are feeling angry or hostile, they think either something totally different or the same thing with a different intensity: when they feel friendly to the man who comes before them for judgement, they regard him as having done little wrong, if any; when they feel hostile, they take the opposite view. Again, if they are eager for, and have good hopes of, a thing that will be pleasant if it happens, they think that it certainly will happen and be good for them; whereas if they are indifferent or annoyed, they do not think so.

There are three things which inspire confidence in the orator's own character—the three, namely, that induce us to believe a thing apart from any proof of it: good sense, excellence, and goodwill. False statements and bad advice are due to one or more of the following three causes. Men either form a false opinion through want of good sense; or they form a true opinion, but because of their moral badness do not say what they really think; or finally, they are both sensible and upright, but not well disposed to their hearers, and fail in consequence to recommend what they know to be the best course. These are the only possible cases. It follows that anyone who is thought to have all these good qualities will inspire trust in his audience. The

___

[1] Marked by Kassel as a later addition by Aristotle himself.

way to make ourselves thought to be sensible and good must be gathered from the analysis of goodness already given: the way to establish your own goodness is the same as the way to establish that of others. Goodwill and friendliness of disposition must form part of our discussion of the emotions. 20

The emotions are all those feelings that so change men as to affect their judgements, and that are also attended by pain or pleasure. Such are anger, pity, fear and the like, with their opposites. We must arrange what we have to say about each of them under three heads. Take, for instance, the emotion of anger: here we must discover what the state of mind of angry people is, who the people are with 25 whom they usually get angry, and on what grounds they get angry with them. It is not enough to know one or even two of these points; unless we know all three, we shall be unable to arouse anger in anyone. The same is true of the other emotions. So just as earlier in this work we drew up a list of propositions, let us now proceed in the same way to analyse the subject before us. 30

2 · Anger may be defined as a desire accompanied by pain, for a conspicuous revenge for a conspicuous slight at the hands of men who have no call to slight oneself or one's friends. If this is a proper definition of anger, it must always be felt towards some particular individual, e.g. Cleon, and not man in general. It must be felt because the other has done or intended to do something to him or one of his 1378ᵇ1 friends. It must always be attended by a certain pleasure—that which arises from the expectation of revenge. For it is pleasant to think that you will attain what you aim at, and nobody aims at what he thinks he cannot attain. Hence it has been well 5 said about wrath,

> Sweeter it is by far than the honeycomb dripping with sweetness,
> And spreads through the hearts of men.[2]

It is also attended by a certain pleasure because the thoughts dwell upon the act of vengeance, and the images then called up cause pleasure, like the images called up in dreams.

Now slighting is the actively entertained opinion of something as obviously of 10 no importance. We think bad things, as well as good ones, have serious importance; and we think the same of anything that tends to produce such things, while those which have little or no such tendency we consider unimportant. There are three kinds of slighting—contempt, spite, and insolence. Contempt is one kind of slighting: you feel contempt for what you consider unimportant, and it is just such 15 things that you slight. Spite is another kind; it is a thwarting another man's wishes, not to get something yourself but to prevent his getting it. The slight arises just from the fact that you do not aim at something for yourself: clearly you do not think that he can do you harm, for then you would be afraid of him instead of slighting him, 20 nor yet that he can do you any good worth mentioning, for then you would be anxious to make friends with him. Insolence is also a form of slighting, since it

[2]*Iliad* XVIII 109.

consists in doing and saying things that cause shame to the victim, not in order that
25   anything may happen to yourself, or because anything has happened to yourself,
but simply for the pleasure involved. (Retaliation is not insolence, but vengeance.)
The cause of the pleasure thus enjoyed by the insolent man is that he thinks himself
greatly superior to others when ill-treating them. That is why youths and rich men
are insolent; they think themselves superior when they show insolence. One sort of
30   insolence is to rob people of the honour due to them; you certainly slight them thus;
for it is the unimportant, for good or evil, that has no honour paid to it. So Achilles
says in anger:

> He hath taken my prize for himself and hath done me dishonour,

and

> Like an alien honoured by none,[3]

meaning that this is why he is angry. A man expects to be specially respected by his
1379ª1   inferiors in birth, in capacity, in goodness, and generally in anything in which he is
much their superior: as where money is concerned a wealthy man looks for respect
from a poor man; where speaking is concerned, the man with a turn for oratory
looks for respect from one who cannot speak; the ruler demands the respect of the
ruled, and the man who thinks he ought to be a ruler demands the respect of the
man whom he thinks he ought to be ruling. Hence it has been said

> Great is the wrath of kings, whose father is Zeus almighty,

5   and

> Yea, but his rancour abideth long afterward also,[4]

their great resentment being due to their great superiority. Then again a man looks
for respect from those who he thinks owe him good treatment, and these are the
people whom he has treated or is treating well, or means or has meant to treat well,
either himself, or through his friends, or through others at his request.

It will be plain by now, from what has been said, in what frame of mind, with
10   what persons, and on what grounds people grow angry. The frame of mind is that in
which any pain is being felt. In that condition, a man is always aiming at something.
Whether, then, another man opposes him either directly in any way, as by
preventing him from drinking when he is thirsty, or indirectly; whether someone
works against him, or fails to work with him, or otherwise vexes him while he is in
15   this mood, he is equally angry in all these cases. [Hence people who are afflicted by
sickness or poverty or love or thirst or any other unsatisfied desires are prone to
anger and easily roused: especially against those who slight their present distress.][5]
Thus a sick man is angered by disregard of his illness, a poor man by disregard of his
20   poverty, a man waging war by disregard of the war he is waging, a lover by
disregard of his love, and so in other cases too. Each man is predisposed, by the

---

[3]*Iliad* I 356; IX 648.   [4]*Iliad* II 196; I 82.   [5]Excised by Kassel.

emotion now controlling him, to his own particular anger. Further, we are angered if we happen to be expecting a contrary result; for a quite unexpected evil is specially painful, just as the quite unexpected fulfilment of our wishes is specially pleasant. Hence it is plain what seasons, times, conditions, and periods of life tend to stir men easily to anger, and where and when this will happen; and it is plain that the more we are under these conditions the more easily we are stirred.

These, then, are the frames of mind in which men are easily stirred to anger. The persons with whom we get angry are those who laugh, mock, or jeer at us, for such conduct is insolent. Also those who inflict injuries upon us that are marks of insolence. These injuries must be such as are neither retaliatory nor profitable to the doers; for then they will be felt to be due to insolence. Also those who speak ill of us, and show contempt for us, in connexion with the things we ourselves most care about: thus those who are eager to win fame as philosophers get angry with those who show contempt for their philosophy; those who pride themselves upon their appearance get angry with those who show contempt for their appearance; and so on in other cases. We feel particularly angry on this account if we suspect that we are in fact, or that people think we are, lacking completely or to any effective extent in the qualities in question. For when we are convinced that we excel in the qualities for which we are jeered at, we can ignore the jeering. Again, we are angrier with our friends than with other people, since we feel that our friends ought to treat us well and not badly. We are angry with those who have usually treated us with honour or regard, if a change comes and they behave to us otherwise; for we think that they feel contempt for us, or they would still be behaving as they did before. And with those who do not return our kindnesses or fail to return them adequately, and with those who oppose us though they are our inferiors; for all such persons seem to feel contempt for us—those who oppose us seem to think us inferior to themselves, and those who do not return our kindnesses seem to think that those kindnesses were conferred by inferiors. And we feel particularly angry with men of no account at all, if they slight us. For we have supposed that anger caused by the slight is felt towards people who are not justified in slighting us, and our inferiors are not thus justified. Again, we feel angry with friends if they do not speak well of us or treat us well; and still more, if they do the contrary; or if they do not perceive our needs, which is why Plexippus is angry with Meleager in Antiphon's play; for this want of perception shows that they are slighting us—we do not fail to perceive the needs of those for whom we care. Again, we are angry with those who rejoice at our misfortunes or simply keep cheerful in the midst of our misfortunes, since this shows that they either hate us or are slighting us. Also with those who are indifferent to the pain they give us: this is why we get angry with bringers of bad news. And with those who listen to stories about us or keep on looking at our weaknesses; this seems like either slighting us or hating us; for those who love us share in all our distresses and it must distress anyone to keep on looking at his own weaknesses. Further, with those who slight us before five classes of people: namely, our rivals, those whom we admire, those whom we wish to admire us, those for whom we feel reverence, those who feel reverence for us: if anyone slights us before such persons, we feel particularly angry. Again, we feel angry with those who slight us in connexion with what we are as honourable men bound to champion—our parents, children, wives, or subjects. And with those who do not return a favour, since such a slight is unjustifiable. Also with those who reply with humorous levity when we are speaking seriously, for such behaviour indicates contempt. And with those who treat us less well than they treat everybody else; it is another mark of contempt that they should think we do not deserve what everyone else deserves. Forgetfulness, too, causes anger, as when our own names are forgotten, trifling as this may be; since forgetfulness is felt to be another sign that we are being slighted; it is due to negligence, and to neglect us is to slight us.

The persons with whom we feel anger, the frame of mind in which we feel it, and the reasons why we feel it, have now all been set forth. Clearly the orator will have to speak so as to bring his hearers into a frame of mind that will dispose them to anger, and to represent his adversaries as open to such charges and possessed of such qualities as do make people angry.

3 · Since growing calm is the opposite of growing angry, and calmness the opposite of anger, we must ascertain in what frames of mind men are calm, towards whom they feel calm, and by what means they are made so. Growing calm may be defined as a settling down or quieting of anger. Now we get angry with those who slight us; and since slighting is a voluntary act, it is plain that we feel calm towards those who do nothing of the kind, or who do or seem to do it involuntarily. Also towards those who intended to do the opposite of what they did do. Also towards those who treat themselves as they have treated us: since no one can be supposed to slight himself. Also towards those who admit their fault and are sorry; since we accept their grief at what they have done as satisfaction, and cease to be angry. The punishment of servants shows this: those who contradict us and deny their offence we punish all the more, but we cease to be incensed against those who agree that they deserve their punishment. The reason is that it is shameless to deny what is obvious, and those who are shameless towards us slight us and show contempt for us: anyhow, we do not feel shame before those of whom we are thoroughly contemptuous. Also we feel calm towards those who humble themselves before us and do not gainsay us; we feel that they thus admit themselves our inferiors, and inferiors feel fear, and nobody can slight anyone so long as he feels afraid of him. That our anger ceases towards those who humble themselves before us is shown even by dogs, who do not bite people when they sit down. We also feel calm towards those who are serious when we are serious, because then we feel that we are treated seriously and not contemptuously. Also towards those who have done us more kindnesses than we have done them. Also towards those who pray to us and beg for mercy, since they humble themselves by doing so. Also towards those who do not insult or mock at or slight any one at all, or not any worthy person or anyone like ourselves. [[In general, the things that make us calm may be inferred by seeing what the opposites are of those that make us angry.]][6] We are not angry with people we

---

[6]Marked by Kassel as a later addition by Aristotle himself.

fear or respect; for while we are in these states we are not angry—you cannot be afraid of a person and also at the same time angry with him. Again, we feel no anger, or comparatively little, with those who have done what they did through anger; we do not feel that they have done it from a wish to slight us, for no one slights people when angry with them, since slighting is painless, and anger is painful. Nor do we grow angry with those who reverence us.

As to the frame of mind that makes people calm, it is plainly the opposite to that which makes them angry, as when they are amusing themselves or laughing or feasting; when they are feeling prosperous or successful or satisfied; when, in fine, they are enjoying freedom from pain, or inoffensive pleasure, or justifiable hope. Also when time has passed and their anger is no longer fresh, for time puts an end to anger. And vengeance previously taken on one person puts an end to even greater anger felt against another person. [[Hence Philocrates, being asked by someone, at a time when the public was angry with him, 'Why don't you defend yourself?' did right to reply, 'The time is not yet'. 'Why, when *is* the time?' 'When I see someone else calumniated'.]][7] For men become calm when they have spent their anger on somebody else. This happened in the case of Ergophilus: though the people were more irritated against him than against Callisthenes, they acquitted him because they had condemned Callisthenes to death the day before. Again, men become calm if they have convicted the offender; or if he has already suffered worse things than they in their anger would have themselves inflicted upon him; for they feel as if they were already avenged. Or if they feel that they themselves are in the wrong and are suffering justly, since men no longer think then that they are suffering without justification; and anger, as we have seen, means this. Hence we ought always to inflict a preliminary punishment in words: if that is done, even slaves are less aggrieved by the actual punishment. We also feel calm if we think that the offender will not see that he is punished on our account and because of the way he has treated us. This is plain from the definition. Hence the poet has well written:

> Say that it was Odysseus, sacker of cities,[8]

implying that Odysseus would not have been avenged unless the Cyclops perceived both by whom and for what he had been blinded. Consequently we do not get angry with anyone who cannot be aware of our anger, and we cease to be angry with people once they are dead, for we feel that the worst has been done to them, and that they will neither feel pain nor anything else that we in our anger aim at making them feel. And therefore the poet has well made Apollo say, in order to put a stop to the anger of Achilles against the dead Hector,

> For behold in his fury he doeth despite to the senseless clay.[9]

It is now plain that when you wish to calm others you must draw upon these commonplaces; you must put your hearers into the corresponding frame of mind,

35

1380[b]1

5

10

15

20

25

30

---

[7]Marked by Kassel as a later addition by Aristotle himself.
[8]*Odyssey* IX 504.
[9]*Iliad* XXIV 54.

and represent those with whom they are angry as formidable, or as worthy of reverence, or as benefactors, or as involuntary agents, or as much distressed at what they have done.

35   **4** · Let us now turn to friendship and enmity, and ask towards whom these feelings are entertained, and why. We will begin by defining friendship and friendly feeling. We may describe friendly feeling towards anyone as wishing for him what you believe to be good things, not for your own sake but for his, and being inclined, 1381ᵃ1   so far as you can, to bring these things about. [[A friend is one who feels thus and excites these feelings in return.]][10] Those who think they feel thus towards each other think themselves friends. This being assumed, it follows that your friend is the 5   sort of man who shares your pleasure in what is good and your pain in what is unpleasant, for your sake and for no other reason. This pleasure and pain of his will be the token of his good wishes for you, since we all feel glad at getting what we wish for, and pained at getting what we do not. Those, then, are friends to whom the same things are good and evil; [[and those who are, moreover, friendly or unfriendly 10   to the same people]][11] for in that case they must have the same wishes, and thus by wishing for each other what they wish for themselves, they show themselves each other's friends. Again, we feel friendly to those who have treated us well, either ourselves or those we care for; or if they have done so on a large scale, or readily, or at some particular crisis; provided it was for our own sake. And also to those who we 15   think *wish* to treat us well. And also to our friends' friends, and to those who like, or are liked by, those whom we like ourselves. And also to those who are enemies to those whose enemies we are, and dislike, or are disliked by, those whom we dislike. For all such persons think the things good which we think good, so that they wish 20   what is good for us; and this, as we saw, is what friends must do. And also to those who are willing to treat us well where money or our personal safety is concerned; and therefore we value those who are liberal and brave. And to just men—the just we consider to be those who do not live on others; which means those who work for their living, especially farmers and others who work with their own hands. We also 25   like temperate men, because they are not unjust to others; and, for the same reason, those who mind their own business. And also those whose friends we wish to be, if it is plain that they wish to be our friends: such are the good in respect of excellence, and those well thought of by everyone, by the best men, or by those whom we 30   admire or who admire us. And also those with whom it is pleasant to live and spend our days: such are the good-tempered, and those who are not too ready to show us our mistakes, and those who are not cantankerous or quarrelsome—such people are always wanting to fight us, and those who fight us we feel wish for the opposite of what we wish for ourselves—and those who have the tact to make and take a joke; for in both ways they have the same object in view as their neighbour, being able to 35   stand being made fun of as well as do it prettily themselves. And we also feel friendly towards those who praise such good qualities as we possess, and especially

---

[10]Marked by Kassel as a later addition by Aristotle himself.
[11]Marked by Kassel as a later addition by Aristotle himself.

if they praise the good qualities that we are not too sure we *do* possess. And towards those who are cleanly in their person, their dress, and all their way of life. And 1381ᵇ1 towards those who do not reproach us with what we have done amiss to them or they have done to help us, for both actions show a tendency to criticize us. And towards those who do not nurse grudges or store up grievances, but are always ready to make 5 friends again; for we take it that they will behave to us just as we find them behaving to everyone else. And towards those who are not slanderers and who are aware of neither their neighbours' bad points nor our own, but of our good ones only, as a good man always will be. And towards those who do not try to thwart us when we are angry or in earnest, which would mean being ready to fight us. And towards 10 those who have some serious feeling towards us, such as admiration for us, or belief in our goodness, or pleasure in our company; especially if they feel like this about qualities in us for which we especially wish to be admired, esteemed, or liked. And towards those who are like ourselves in character and occupation, provided they do 15 not get in our way or gain their living from the same source as we do—for then it will be a case of 'potter against potter'. And those who desire the same things as we desire, if it is possible for us both to share them together; otherwise the same trouble arises here too. And towards those with whom we are on such terms that, while we respect their opinions, we need not blush before them for doing what is conven- 20 tionally wrong; as well as towards those before whom we should be ashamed to do anything really wrong. Again, our rivals, and those whom we should like to envy us—though without ill-feeling—either we like these people or at least we wish them to like us. And we feel friendly towards those whom we help to secure good for themselves, provided we are not likely to suffer heavily by it ourselves. And those who feel as friendly to us when we are not with them as when we are—which is why 25 all men feel friendly towards those who are faithful to their dead friends. And, speaking generally, towards those who are really fond of their friends and do not desert them in trouble; of all good men, we feel most friendly to those who show their goodness as friends. Also towards those who are honest with us, including those who will tell us of their own weak points: it has just been said that with our 30 friends we are not ashamed of what is conventionally wrong, and if we do have this feeling, we do not love them; if therefore we do not have it, it looks as if we *did* love them. We also like those with whom we do not feel frightened or uncomfortable— nobody can like a man of whom he feels frightened. Friendship has various forms—comradeship, intimacy, kinship, and so on.

Things that cause friendship are: doing kindnesses; doing them unasked; and 35 not proclaiming the fact when they are done, which shows that they were done for our own sake and not for some other reason.

Enmity and hatred should clearly be studied by reference to their opposites. 1382ᵃ1 Enmity may be produced by anger or spite or calumny. Now whereas anger arises from offences against oneself, enmity may arise even without that; we may hate people merely because of what we take to be their character. Anger is always concerned with individuals—Callias or Socrates—whereas hatred is directed also 5 against classes: we all hate any thief and any informer. Moreover, anger can be

cured by time; but hatred cannot. The one aims at giving pain to its object, the other at doing him harm; the angry man wants his victims to feel; the hater does not mind
10 whether they feel or not. All painful things are felt; but the greatest evils, injustice and folly, are the least felt, since their presence causes no pain. And anger is accompanied by pain, hatred is not; the angry man feels pain, but the hater does not. Much may happen to make the angry man pity those who offend him, but the hater under no circumstances wishes to pity a man whom he has once hated; for the
15 one would have the offenders suffer for what they have done; the other would have them cease to exist.

It is plain from all this that we can prove people to be friends or enemies; if they are not, we can make them out to be so; if they claim to be so, we can refute their claim; and if they are disputing through anger or hatred, we can bring them to
20 whichever of these we prefer.

5 · Next, we show the things and persons of which, and the states of mind in which, we feel afraid. Fear may be defined as a pain or disturbance due to imagining some destructive or painful evil in the future. For there are some evils, e.g. wickedness or stupidity, the prospect of which does not frighten us: only such as amount to great pains or losses do. And even these only if they appear not remote
25 but so near as to be imminent: we do not fear things that are a very long way off; for instance, we all know we shall die, but we are not troubled thereby, because death is not close at hand. From this definition it will follow that fear is caused by whatever we feel has great power of destroying us, or of harming us in ways that tend to cause
30 us great pain. Hence the very indications of such things are terrible, making us feel that the terrible thing itself is close at hand; and this—the approach of what is terrible—is danger. Such indications are the enmity and anger of people who have power to do something to us; for it is plain that they have the will to do it, and so they are on the point of doing it. Also injustice in possession of power; for it is the unjust
1382ᵇ1 man's choice that makes him unjust. Also outraged excellence in possession of power; for it is plain that, when outraged, it always chooses to retaliate, and now it has the power to do so. Also fear felt by those who have the power to do something to us, since such persons are sure to be ready to do it. And since most men tend to be
5 bad—slaves to greed, and cowards in danger—it is, as a rule, a terrible thing to be at another man's mercy; and therefore, if we have done anything horrible, those in the secret terrify us with the thought that they may betray or desert us. And those who can do us wrong are terrible to us when we are liable to be wronged; for as a rule men do wrong to others whenever they have the power to do it. And those who
10 have been wronged, or believe themselves to be wronged, are terrible; for they are always looking out for their opportunity. Also those who have done people wrong, if they possess power, since they stand in fear of retaliation: we have already said that wickedness possessing power is terrible. Again, our rivals for a thing cause us fear when we cannot both have it at once; for we are always at war with such men. We
15 also fear those who are to be feared by stronger people than ourselves: if they can hurt those stronger people, still more can they hurt us; and, for the same reason, we

fear those whom those stronger people are actually afraid of. Also those who have destroyed people stronger than we are. Also those who are attacking people weaker than we are: either they are already formidable, or they will be so when they have thus grown stronger. Of those we have wronged, and of our enemies or rivals, it is not the passionate and outspoken whom we have to fear, but the quiet, dissembling, unscrupulous; since we never know when they are upon us, we can never be sure they are at a safe distance. All terrible things are more terrible if they give us no chance of retrieving a blunder—either no chance at all, or only one that depends on our enemies and not ourselves. Those things are also worse which we cannot, or cannot easily, help. Speaking generally, anything causes us to feel fear that when it happens to, or threatens, others causes us to feel pity.

The above are, roughly, the chief things that are terrible and are feared. Let us now describe the conditions under which we ourselves feel fear. If fear is associated with the expectation that something destructive will happen to us, plainly nobody will be afraid who believes nothing can happen to him; we shall not fear things that we believe cannot happen to us, nor people who we believe cannot inflict them upon us; nor shall we be afraid at times when we think ourselves safe from them. It follows therefore that fear is felt by those who believe something to be likely to happen to them, at the hands of particular persons, in a particular form, and at a particular time. People do not believe this when they are, or think they are, in the midst of great prosperity, and are in consequence insolent, contemptuous, and reckless—the kind of character produced by wealth, physical strength, abundance of friends, power; nor yet when they feel they have experienced every kind of horror already and have grown callous about the future, like men who are being flogged to death—if they are to feel the anguish of uncertainty, there must be some faint expectation of escape. This appears from the fact that fear sets us thinking what can be done, which of course nobody does when things are hopeless. Consequently, when it is advisable that the audience should be frightened, the orator must make them feel that they really are in danger of something, pointing out that it has happened to others who were stronger than they are, and is happening, or has happened, to people like themselves, at the hands of unexpected people, in an unexpected form, and at an unexpected time.

Having now seen the nature of fear, and of the things that cause it, and the various states of mind in which it is felt, we can also see what confidence is, about what things we feel it, and under what conditions. It is the opposite of fear, and what causes it is the opposite of what causes fear; it is, therefore, the imaginative expectation of the nearness of what keeps us safe and the absence or remoteness of what is terrible: it may be due either to the near presence of what inspires confidence or to the absence of what causes alarm. We feel it if we can take steps—many, or important, or both—to cure or prevent trouble; if we have neither wronged others nor been wronged by them; if we have either no rivals at all or no strong ones; if our rivals who are strong are our friends or have treated us well or been treated well by us; or if those whose interest is the same as ours are the more numerous party, or the stronger, or both.

25 As for our own state of mind, we feel confidence if we believe we have often succeeded and never suffered reverses, or have often met danger and escaped it safely. For there are two reasons why human beings face danger calmly: they may have no experience of it, or they may have means to deal with it: thus when in 30 danger at sea people may feel confident about what will happen either because they have no experience of bad weather, or because their experience gives them the means of dealing with it. We also feel confident whenever there is nothing to terrify other people like ourselves, or people weaker than ourselves, or people than whom we believe ourselves to be stronger—and we believe this if we have conquered them, or conquered others who are as strong as they are, or stronger. Also if we believe ourselves superior to our rivals in the number and importance of the advantages that 1383ᵇ1 make men formidable—plenty of money, men, friends, land, military equipment (of all, or the most important, kinds). Also if we have wronged no one, or not many, or 5 not those of whom we are afraid. And when we are being wronged; [[and generally, if our relations with the gods are satisfactory, as will be shown especially by signs and oracles]][12] for anger makes us confident and, anger is excited by our knowledge that we are not the wrongers but the wronged, and that the divine power is always supposed to be on the side of the wronged. Also when, at the outset of an enterprise, 10 we believe that we cannot fail, or that we shall succeed. So much for the causes of fear and confidence.

6 · Next we will explain the things that cause shame and shamelessness, and the persons before whom, and the states of mind under which they are felt. 15 Shame may be defined as pain or disturbance in regard to bad things, whether present, past, or future, which seem likely to involve us in discredit; and shamelessness as contempt or indifference in regard to these same bad things. If this definition be granted, it follows that we feel shame at such bad things as we think are disgraceful to ourselves or to those we care for. These evils are, in the first place, 20 those due to badness. Such are throwing away one's shield or taking to flight; for these bad things are due to cowardice. Also, withholding a deposit; for that is due to injustice. Also, having carnal intercourse with forbidden persons, at wrong times, or in wrong places; for these things are due to licentiousness. Also, making profit in petty or disgraceful ways, or out of helpless persons, e.g. the poor, or the 25 dead—whence the proverb 'He would pick a corpse's pocket'; for all this is due to low greed and meanness. Also, in money matters, giving less help than you might, or none at all, or accepting help from those worse off than yourself; so also borrowing when it will seem like begging; begging when it will seem like asking the return of a 30 favour; asking such a return when it will seem like begging; praising a man in order that it may seem like begging; and going on begging in spite of failure: all such actions are tokens of meanness. [[Again, praising people to their face is a mark of flattery.]][13] Also, praising extravagantly a man's good points and glozing over his

---

[12]Marked by Kassel as a later addition by Aristotle himself.
[13]Marked by Kassel as a later addition by Aristotle himself.

weaknesses, and showing extravagant sympathy with his grief when you are in his presence, and all that sort of thing; all this shows the disposition of a flatterer. Also, refusing to endure hardships that are endured by people who are older, more   1384ª1 delicately brought up, of higher rank, or generally less capable of endurance than ourselves; for all this shows effeminacy. Also, accepting benefits, especially accepting them often, from another man, and then abusing him for conferring them: all this shows a mean, ignoble disposition. Also, talking incessantly about   5 yourself, making loud professions, and appropriating the merits of others; for this is due to boastfulness. The same is true of the actions due to any of the other forms of badness of character, of the tokens of such badness, and the like: they are all disgraceful and shameless. Another sort of bad thing at which we feel shame is, lacking a share in the honourable things shared by everyone else, or by all or nearly   10 all who are like ourselves. By 'those like ourselves' I mean those of our own race or country or age or family, and generally those who are on our own level. Once we are on a level with others, it is a disgrace to be, say, less well educated than they are; and so with other advantages: all the more so, in each case, if it is seen to be our own fault: wherever we are ourselves to blame for our present, past, or future   15 circumstances, it follows at once that this is to a greater extent due to our badness. We are moreover ashamed of having done to us, having had done, or being about to have done to us acts that involve us in dishonour and reproach, e.g. when we submit to outrage (we yield to lust both voluntarily and involuntarily, to force involuntari-   20 ly), for unresisting submission to them is due to unmanliness or cowardice.

These things, and others like them, are what cause the feeling of shame. Now since shame is the imagination of disgrace, in which we shrink from the disgrace itself and not from its consequences, and we only care what opinion is held of us   25 because of the people who form that opinion, it follows that the people before whom we feel shame are those whose opinion of us matters to us. Such persons are: those who admire us, those whom we admire, those by whom we wish to be admired, those with whom we are competing, and those whose opinion of us we respect. We admire those, and wish those to admire us, who possess any good thing that is highly   30 esteemed; or from whom we are very anxious to get something that they are able to give us—as a lover feels. We compete with our equals. We respect, as true, the views of sensible people, such as our elders and those who have been well educated. And we feel more shame about a thing if it is done openly, before all men's eyes. Hence   35 the proverb, 'shame dwells in the eyes'. For this reason we feel most shame before those who will always be with us and those who notice what we do, since in both cases eyes are upon us. We also feel it before those not open to the same imputation   1384ᵇ1 as ourselves; for it is plain that their opinions about it are the opposite of ours. [[Also before those who are hard on anyone whose conduct they think wrong.]]¹⁴ For what a man does himself, he is said not to resent when his neighbours do it: so that of course he does resent their doing what he does not do himself. And before those who   5 are likely to tell everybody about you; not telling others is as good as not believing

---

¹⁴Marked by Kassel as a later addition by Aristotle himself.

you wrong. People are likely to tell others about you if you have wronged them, since they are on the look out to harm you; or if they speak evil of everybody, for those who attack the innocent will be still more ready to attack the guilty. And
10 before those whose main occupation is with their neighbours' failings—people like satirists and writers of comedy; these are really a kind of evil-speakers and tell-tales. And before those who have never yet known us come to grief, since their attitude to us has amounted to admiration so far: that is why we feel ashamed to refuse those a favour who ask one for the first time—we have not as yet lost credit with them. Such
15 are those who are just beginning to wish to be our friends; for they have seen our best side only (hence the appropriateness of Euripides' reply to the Syracusans); and such also are those among our old acquaintances who know nothing to our discredit. And we are ashamed not merely of the actual shameful conduct mentioned, but also of the signs of it: not merely, for example, of actual sexual
20 intercourse, but also of its signs; and not merely of disgraceful acts but also of disgraceful talk. Similarly we feel shame not merely in presence of the persons mentioned but also of those who will tell them what we have done, such as their servants or friends. And, generally, we feel no shame before those upon whose opinions we quite look down as untrustworthy (no one feels shame before small
25 children or animals); nor are we ashamed of the same things before intimates as before strangers, but before the former of what seem genuine faults, before the latter of what seem conventional ones.

The conditions under which we shall feel shame are these: first, having people related to us like those before whom we said we feel shame. These are, as was stated,
30 persons whom we admire, or who admire us, or by whom we wish to be admired, or from whom we desire some service that we shall not obtain if we forfeit their good opinion. These persons may be actually looking on (as Cydias represented them in his speech on land assignments in Samos, when he told the Athenians to imagine the Greeks to be standing all around them, actually seeing the way they voted and not
35 merely going to hear about it afterwards); or again they may be near at hand, or may be likely to find out about what we do. This is why in misfortune we do not wish
1385ᵃ1 to be seen by those who once wished themselves like us; for such a feeling implies admiration. And men feel shame when they have acts or exploits to their credit on which they are bringing dishonour, whether these are their own, or those of their ancestors, or those of other persons with whom they have some close connexion. Generally, we feel shame before those for whose own misconduct we should also feel
5 it—those already mentioned; those who take us as their models, e.g. those whose teachers or advisers we have been; or other people, it may be, like ourselves, whose rivals we are. For there are many things that shame before such people makes us do or leave undone. And we feel more shame when we are likely to be seen by, and go about under the eyes of, those who know of our disgrace. Hence, when Antiphon the
10 poet was to be flogged to death by order of Dionysius, and saw those who were to perish with him covering their faces as they went through the gates, he said 'Why do you cover your faces? Is it lest some of these spectators should see you to-morrow?'

So much for shame; to understand shamelessness, we need only consider the converse cases, and plainly we shall have all we need.   15

7 · To take kindness next: the definition of it will show us towards whom it is felt, why, and in what frames of mind. Kindness—under the influence of which a man is said to be kind—may be defined as helpfulness towards some one in need, not in return for anything, nor for the advantage of the helper himself, but for that of the person helped. Kindness is great if shown to one who is in great need, or who   20 needs what is important and hard to get, or who needs it at an important and difficult crisis; or if the helper is the only, the first, or the chief person to give the help. Desires constitute such needs; and in particular desires, accompanied by pain, for what is not being attained. The appetites are desires of this kind: sexual desire, for instance. Also those which arise during bodily injuries and in dangers; for appetite is active both in danger and in pain. Hence those who stand by us in poverty   25 or in banishment, even if they do not help us much, are yet really kind to us, because our need is great and the occasion pressing; for instance, the man who gave the mat in the Lyceum. The helpfulness must therefore meet, preferably, just this kind of need; and failing just this kind, some other kind as great or greater. We now see to   30 whom, why, and under what conditions kindness is shown; and these facts must form the basis of our arguments. We must show that the persons helped are, or have been, in such pain and need as has been described, and that their helpers gave, or are giving, the kind of help described, in the kind of need described. We can also see how to eliminate the idea of kindness and make our opponents appear unkind: we may maintain that they are being or have been helpful simply to promote their own   1385^{b}1 interest—this, as has been stated, is not kindness; or that their action was accidental, or was forced upon them; or that they were not doing a favour, but merely returning one, whether they know this or not—in either case the action is a mere return, and is therefore not a kindness even in the latter case. In considering this subject we must look at all the categories: an act may be an act of kindness   5 because it is a particular thing, it has a particular magnitude or quality, or is done at a particular time or place. As evidence of the want of kindness, we may point out that a smaller service had been refused to the man in need; or that the same service, or an equal or greater one, has been given to his enemies; these facts show that the service in question was not done for the sake of the person helped. Or we may point out that the thing desired was worthless and that the helper knew it: no one will   10 admit that he is in need of what is worthless.

8 · So much for kindness and unkindness. Let us now consider pity, asking ourselves what things excite pity, and for what persons, and in what states of our mind pity is felt. Pity may be defined as a feeling of pain at an apparent evil, destructive or painful, which befalls one who does not deserve it, and which we might expect to befall ourselves or some friend of ours, and moreover to befall us   15 soon. For if we are to feel pity we must obviously be capable of supposing that some evil may happen to us or some friend of ours, and moreover some such evil as is

stated in our definition or is more or less of that kind. It is therefore not felt by those completely ruined, who suppose that no further evil can befall them, since the worst has befallen them already; nor by those who imagine themselves immensely fortunate—their feeling is rather insolence, for when they think they possess all the good things of life, it is clear that the impossibility of evil befalling them will be included, this being one of the good things in question. Those who think evil *may* befall them are such as have already had it befall them and have safely escaped from it; elderly men, owing to their good sense and their experience; weak men, especially men inclined to cowardice; and also educated people, since these can take long views. Also those who have parents living, or children, or wives; for these are our own, and the evils mentioned above may easily befall them. And those who are neither moved by any courageous emotion such as anger or confidence (these emotions take no account of the future), nor by a disposition to insolence (insolent men, too, take no account of the possibility that something evil will happen to them), nor yet by great fear (panic-stricken people do not feel pity, because they are taken up with what is happening to themselves); only those feel pity who are between these two extremes. In order to feel pity we must also believe in the goodness of at least some people; if you think nobody good, you will believe that everybody deserves evil fortune. And, generally, we feel pity whenever we are in the condition of remembering that similar misfortunes have happened to us or ours, or expecting them to happen in future.

So much for the mental conditions under which we feel pity. What we pity is stated clearly in the definition. All unpleasant and painful things excite pity, and all destructive things; and all such evils as are due to chance, if they are serious. The painful and destructive evils are: death in its various forms, bodily injuries and afflictions, old age, diseases, lack of food. The evils due to chance are: friendless-ness, scarcity of friends (it is a pitiful thing to be torn away from friends and companions), deformity, weakness, mutilation; evil coming from a source from which good ought to have come; and the frequent repetition of such misfortunes. Also the coming of good when the worst has happened: e.g. the arrival of the Great King's gifts for Diopeithes after his death. Also that either no good should have befallen a man at all, or that he should not be able to enjoy it when it has.

The grounds, then, on which we feel pity are these or like these. The people we pity are: those whom we know, if only they are not very closely related to us—in that case we feel about them as if we were in danger ourselves. For this reason Amasis did not weep, they say, at the sight of his son being led to death, but did weep when he saw his friend begging: the latter sight was pitiful, the former terrible, and the terrible is different from the pitiful; it tends to cast out pity, and often helps to produce the opposite of pity. For we no longer feel pity when the danger is near ourselves. Also we pity those who are like us in age, character, disposition, social standing, or birth; for in all these cases it appears more likely that the same misfortune may befall us also. Here too we have to remember the general principle that what we fear for ourselves excites our pity when it happens to others. Further, since it is when the sufferings of others are close to us that they excite our pity (we

cannot remember what disasters happened a hundred centuries ago, nor look
forward to what will happen a hundred centuries hereafter, and therefore feel little   30
pity, if any, for such things): it follows that those who heighten the effect of their
words with suitable gestures, tones, appearance, and dramatic action generally, are
especially successful in exciting pity: they thus put the disasters before our eyes, and
make them seem close to us, just coming or just past. Anything that has just 1386^b1
happened, or is going to happen soon, is particularly piteous: so too therefore are the
signs of suffering—the garments and the like of those who have already suffered;
the words and the like of those actually suffering—of those, for instance, who are on
the point of death. For all this, because it seems close, tends to produce pity. Most   5
piteous of all is it when, in such times of trial, the victims are persons of noble
character, for their suffering is undeserved and it is set before our eyes.

9 . Most directly opposed to pity is the feeling called indignation. Pain at   10
unmerited good fortune is, in one sense, opposite to pain at unmerited bad fortune,
and is due to the same character. Both feelings are associated with good character;
it is our duty to feel sympathy and pity for unmerited distress, and to feel
indignation at unmerited prosperity; for whatever is undeserved is unjust, and that   15
is why we ascribe indignation even to the gods. It might indeed be thought that envy
is similarly opposed to pity, on the ground that envy is closely akin to indignation, or
even the same thing. But it is not the same. It is true that it also is a disturbing pain
excited by the prosperity of others. But it is excited not by the prosperity of the
undeserving but by that of people who are like us or equal with us. The two feelings   20
have this in common, that they must be due not to some untoward thing being likely
to befall ourselves, but only to what is happening to our neighbour. The feeling
ceases to be envy in the one case and indignation in the other, and becomes fear, if
the pain and disturbance are due to the prospect of something bad for ourselves as
the result of the other man's good fortune. The feelings of pity and indignation will   25
obviously be attended by the converse feelings of satisfaction. If you are pained by
the unmerited distress of others, you will be pleased, or at least not pained, by their
merited distress. Thus no good man can be pained by the punishment of parricides
or murderers. These are things we are bound to rejoice at, as we must at the   30
prosperity of the deserving; both these things are just, and both give pleasure to any
honest man, since he cannot help expecting that what has happened to a man like
him will happen to him too. All these feelings are associated with the same type of
character. And their contraries are associated with the contrary type; the man who
is delighted by others' misfortunes is identical with the man who envies others' 1387^a1
prosperity. For anyone who is pained by the occurrence or existence of a given thing
must be pleased by that thing's non-existence or destruction. We can now see that
all these feelings tend to prevent pity (though they differ among themselves, for the
reasons given), so that all are equally useful for neutralizing an appeal to pity.   5
We will first consider indignation—reserving the other emotions for subsequent discussion—and ask with whom, on what grounds, and in what states of mind
we may be indignant. These questions are really answered by what has been said

already. Indignation is pain caused by the sight of undeserved good fortune. It is, then, plain to begin with that there are some forms of good the sight of which cannot cause it. Thus a man may be just or brave, or acquire excellence: but we shall not be indignant with him for that reason, any more than we shall pity him for the contrary reason. Indignation is roused by the sight of wealth, power, and the like—by all those things, roughly speaking, which are deserved by good men and by those who possess the goods of nature—noble birth, beauty, and so on. Again, what is long established seems akin to what exists by nature; and therefore we feel more indignation at those possessing a given good if they have as a matter of fact only just got it and the prosperity it brings with it. The newly rich give more offence than those whose wealth is of long standing and inherited. The same is true of those who have office or power, plenty of friends, a fine family, etc. We feel the same when these advantages of theirs secure them others. For here again, the newly rich give us more offence by obtaining office through their riches than do those whose wealth is of long standing; and so in all other cases. The reason is that what the latter have is felt to be really their own, but what the others have is not: what appears to have been always what it is is regarded as real, and so the possessions of the newly rich do not seem to be really their own. Further, it is not any and every man that deserves any given kind of good; there is a certain correspondence and appropriateness in such things; thus it is appropriate for brave men, not for just men, to have fine weapons, and for men of family, not for parvenus, to make distinguished marriages. Indignation may therefore properly be felt when anyone gets what is not appropriate for him, though he may be a good man enough. It may also be felt when anyone sets himself up against his superior, especially against his superior in some particular respect—whence the lines

> Only from battle he shrank with Ajax, Telamon's son;
> Zeus had been angered with him, had he fought with a mightier one;[15]

but also, even apart from that, when the inferior in any sense contends with his superior; a musician, for instance, with a just man, for justice is a finer thing than music.

Enough has been said to make clear the grounds on which, and the persons against whom, indignation is felt—they are those mentioned, and others like them. As for the people who feel it; we feel it if we do ourselves deserve the greatest possible goods and moreover have them, for it is an injustice that those who are not our equals should have been held to deserve as much as we have. Or, secondly, we feel it if we are really good and honest people; our judgement is then sound, and we loathe any kind of injustice. Also if we are ambitious and eager to gain particular ends, especially if we are ambitious for what others are getting without deserving to get it. And, generally, if we think that we ourselves deserve a thing and that others do not, we are disposed to be indignant with those others so far as that thing is concerned. Hence servile, worthless, unambitious persons are not inclined to indignation, since there is nothing they can believe themselves to deserve.

---

[15]See *Iliad* XI 542.

From all this it is plain what sort of men those are at whose misfortunes,   15
distresses, or failures we ought to feel pleased, or at least not pained: by considering
the facts described we see at once what their contraries are. If therefore our speech
puts the judges in such a frame of mind as that indicated and shows that those who
claim pity on certain definite grounds do not deserve to secure pity but do deserve
not to secure it, it will be impossible for the judges to feel pity.   20

10 · To take envy next: we can see on what grounds, against what persons,
and in what states of mind we feel it. Envy is pain at the sight of such good fortune
as consists of the good things already mentioned; we feel it towards our equals; not
with the idea of getting something for ourselves, but because the other people have
it. We shall feel it if we have, or think we have, equals; and by 'equals' I mean equals   25
in birth, relationship, age, disposition, distinction, or wealth. We feel envy also if we
fall but a little short of having everything; which is why people in high place and
prosperity feel it—they think everyone else is taking what belongs to themselves.
Also if we are exceptionally distinguished for some particular thing, and especially   30
if that thing is wisdom or good fortune. Ambitious men are more envious than those
who are not. So also those who profess wisdom; they are ambitious to be thought
wise. Indeed, generally, those who aim at a reputation for anything are envious on
this particular point. And small-minded men are envious, for everything seems
great to them. The good things which excite envy have already been mentioned. The
deeds or possessions which arouse the love of reputation and honour and the desire   1388ᵃ1
for fame, and the various gifts of fortune, are almost all subject to envy; and
particularly if we desire the thing ourselves, or think we are entitled to it, or if
possession of it puts us a little above others, or a little below them. It is clear also
what kind of people we envy; that was included in what has been said already; we   5
envy those who are near us in time, place, age, or reputation. [[Hence the line:

Ay, kin can even be jealous of their kin.]]¹⁶

Also our fellow-competitors, who are indeed the people just mentioned—we do not
compete with men who lived a hundred centuries ago, or those not yet born, or those   10
who dwell near the Pillars of Hercules, or those whom, in our opinion or that of
others, we take to be far below us or far above us. So too we compete with those who
follow the same ends as ourselves: we compete with our rivals in sport or in love, and
generally with those who are after the same things; and it is therefore these whom   15
we are bound to envy beyond all others. Hence the saying, Potter against potter. We
also envy those whose possession of or success in a thing is a reproach to us: these are
our neighbours and equals; for it is clear that it is our own fault we have missed the
good thing in question; this annoys us, and excites envy in us. We also envy those
who have what we ought to have, or have got what we did have once. Hence old men   20
envy younger men, and those who have spent much envy those who have spent little
on the same thing. And men who have not got a thing, or not got it yet, envy those

---

¹⁶Marked by Kassel as a later addition by Aristotle himself. The quoted line
is Aeschylus, frag. 305 Nauck.

who have got it quickly. We can also see what things and what persons give pleasure to envious people, and in what states of mind they feel it: the states of mind in which 25 they feel pain are those under which they will feel pleasure in the contrary things. If therefore we ourselves with whom the decision rests are put into an envious state of mind, and those for whom our pity, or the award of something desirable, is claimed are such as have been described, it is obvious that they will win no pity from us.

11 · We will next consider emulation, showing in what follows its causes 30 and objects, and the state of mind in which it is felt. Emulation is pain caused by seeing the presence, in persons whose nature is like our own, of good things that are highly valued and are possible for ourselves to acquire; but it is felt not because others have these goods, but because we have not got them ourselves. It is therefore a good feeling felt by good persons, whereas envy is a bad feeling felt by bad 35 persons. Emulation makes us take steps to secure the good things in question, envy makes us take steps to stop our neighbour having them. Emulation must therefore 1388ᵇ1 tend to be felt by persons who believe themselves to deserve certain good things that they have not got. [[For no one aspires to things which appear impossible.]][17] It is accordingly felt by the young and by persons of lofty disposition. Also by those who possess such good things as are deserved by men held in honour—these are wealth, 5 abundance of friends, public office, and the like; on the assumption that they ought to be good men, they are emulous to gain such goods as ought, in their belief, to belong to men whose state of mind is good. Also by those whom all others think deserving. We also feel it about anything for which our ancestors, relatives, personal friends, race, or country are specially honoured, looking upon that thing as really 10 our own, and therefore feeling that we deserve to have it. Further, since all good things that are highly honoured are objects of emulation, excellence in its various forms must be such an object, and also all those good things that are useful and serviceable to others: for men honour those who are good, and also those who do them service. So with those good things our possession of which can give enjoyment to our neighbours—wealth and beauty rather than health. We can see, too, what 15 persons are the objects of the feeling. They are those who have these and similar things—those already mentioned, as courage, wisdom, public office. Holders of public office—generals, orators, and all who possess such powers—can do many people a good turn. Also those whom many people wish to be like; those who have 20 many acquaintances or friends; those whom many admire, or whom we ourselves admire; and those who have been praised and eulogized by poets or prose-writers. Persons of the contrary sort are objects of contempt: for the feeling and notion of contempt are opposite to those of emulation. Those who are such as to emulate or be 25 emulated by others are inevitably disposed to be contemptuous of all such persons as are subject to those bad things which are contrary to the good things that are the objects of emulation, despising them for just that reason. Hence we often despise the fortunate, when luck comes to them without their having those good things which are held in honour.

---

[17]Marked by Kassel as a later addition by Aristotle himself.

This completes our discussion of the means by which the several emotions may be produced or dissipated, and upon which depend the persuasive arguments 30 connected with the emotions.

12 · Let us now consider the various types of human character, in relation to the emotions, states of character, ages and fortunes. By emotions I mean anger, desire, and the like; these we have discussed already. By states of character I mean 35 excellences and vices; these also have been discussed already, as well as the various things that various types of men tend to choose and to do. By ages I mean youth, the prime of life, and old age. By fortune I mean birth, wealth, power, and their 1389ᵃ1 opposites—in fact, good fortune and ill fortune.

To begin with the youthful type of character. Young men have strong passions, and tend to gratify them indiscriminately. Of the bodily desires, it is the sexual by which they are most swayed and in which they show absence of 5 self-control. They are changeable and fickle in their desires, which are violent while they last, but quickly over: their impulses are keen but not deep-rooted, and are like sick people's attacks of hunger and thirst. They are hot-tempered and quick-tempered, and apt to give way to their anger; bad temper often gets the better of 10 them, for owing to their love of honour they cannot bear being slighted, and are indignant if they imagine themselves unfairly treated. While they love honour, they love victory still more; for youth is eager for superiority over others, and victory is one form of this. They love both more than they love money, which indeed they love very little, not having yet learnt what it means to be without it—this is the point of 15 Pittacus' remark about Amphiaraus. They look at the good side rather than the bad, not having yet witnessed many instances of wickedness. They trust others readily, because they have not yet often been cheated. They are sanguine; nature warms their blood as though with excess of wine; and besides that, they have as yet met 20 with few disappointments. Their lives are mainly spent not in memory but in expectation; for expectation refers to the future, memory to the past, and youth has a long future before it and a short past behind it: on the first day of one's life one has nothing at all to remember, and can only look forward. They are easily cheated, 25 owing to the sanguine disposition just mentioned. Their hot tempers and hopeful dispositions make them more courageous than older men are; the hot temper prevents fear, and the hopeful disposition creates confidence; we cannot feel fear so long as we are feeling angry, and any expectation of good makes us confident. They are shy, accepting the rules of society in which they have been trained, and not yet believing in any other standard of honour. They have exalted notions, because they 30 have not yet been humbled by life or learnt its necessary limitations; moreover, their hopeful disposition makes them think themselves equal to great things—and that means having exalted notions. They would always rather do noble deeds than useful ones: their lives are regulated more by their character than by reasoning; and 35 whereas reasoning leads us to choose what is useful, excellence leads us to choose what is noble. They are fonder of their friends and companions than older men are, because they like spending their days in the company of others, and have not yet 1389ᵇ1 come to value either their friends or anything else by their usefulness to themselves. All their mistakes are in the direction of doing things excessively and vehemently. They disobey Chilon's precept by overdoing everything; they love too much and hate too much, and the same with everything else. They think they know everything, and are always quite sure about it; this, in fact, is why they overdo everything. If they do wrong to others, it is because they mean to insult them, not to do them actual harm. They are ready to pity others, because they think everyone an honest man, or anyhow better than he is: they judge their neighbour by their own harmless natures, and so cannot think he deserves to be treated in that way. They are fond of fun and therefore witty, wit being well-bred insolence.

13 · Such, then, is the character of the young. The character of elderly men—men who are past their prime—may be said to be formed for the most part of elements that are the contrary of all these. They have lived many years; they have often been taken in, and often made mistakes; and life on the whole is a bad business. The result is that they are sure about nothing and under-do everything. They 'think', but they never 'know'; and because of their hesitation they always add a 'possibly' or a 'perhaps', putting everything this way and nothing positively. They are cynical; that is, they tend to put the worse construction on everything. Further, their experience makes them distrustful and therefore suspicious of evil. Consequently they neither love warmly nor hate bitterly, but following the hint of Bias they love as though they will some day hate and hate as though they will some day love. They are small-minded, because they have been humbled by life: their desires are set upon nothing more exalted or unusual than what will help them to keep alive. They are not generous, because money is one of the things they must have, and at the same time their experience has taught them how hard it is to get and how easy to lose. They are cowardly, and are always anticipating danger; unlike that of the young, who are warm-blooded, their temperament is chilly; old age has paved the way for cowardice; fear is, in fact, a form of chill. They love life; and all the more when their last day has come, because the object of all desire is something we have not got, and also because we desire most strongly that which we need most urgently. They are too fond of themselves; this is one form that small-mindedness takes. Because of this, they guide their lives too much by considerations of what is useful and too little by what is noble—for the useful is what is good for oneself, and the noble what is good absolutely. They are not shy, but shameless rather; caring less for what is noble than for what is useful, they feel contempt for what people may think of them. They lack confidence in the future; partly through experience—for most things go wrong, or anyhow turn out worse than one expects; and partly because of their cowardice. They live by memory rather than by hope; for what is left to them of life is but little as compared with the long past; and hope is of the future, memory of the past. This, again, is the cause of their loquacity; they are continually talking of the past, because they enjoy remembering it. Their fits of anger are sudden but feeble. Their sensual passions have either altogether gone or

have lost their vigour: consequently they do not feel their passions much, and their actions are inspired less by what they do feel than by the love of gain. Hence men at this time of life are often supposed to have a self-controlled character; the fact is   15 that their passions have slackened, and they are slaves to the love of gain. They guide their lives by reasoning more than by character; reasoning being directed to utility and character to excellence. If they wrong others, they mean to injure them, not to insult them. Old men may feel pity, as well as young men, but not for the same reason. Young men feel it out of kindness; old men out of weakness, imagining   20 that anything that befalls anyone else might easily happen to them, which, as we saw, is a thought that excites pity. Hence they are querulous, and not disposed to jesting or laughter—the love of laughter being the very opposite of querulousness.

Such are the characters of young men and elderly men. People always think well of speeches adapted to, and reflecting, their own character: and we can now see   25 how to compose our speeches so as to adapt both them and ourselves to our audiences.

14 · As for men in their prime, clearly we shall find that they have a character between that of the young and that of the old, free from the extremes of   30 either. They have neither that excess of confidence which amounts to rashness, nor too much timidity, but the right amount of each. They neither trust everybody nor distrust everybody, but judge people correctly. Their lives will be guided not by the sole consideration either of what is noble or of what is useful, but by both; neither by   1390^{b}1 parsimony nor by prodigality, but by what is fit and proper. So, too, in regard to anger and desire; they will be brave as well as temperate, and temperate as well as brave; these virtues are divided between the young and the old; the young are brave   5 but intemperate, the old temperate but cowardly. To put it generally, all the valuable qualities that youth and age divide between them are united in the prime of life, while all their excesses or defects are replaced by moderation and fitness. The body is in its prime from thirty to thirty-five; the mind about forty-nine.   10

15 · So much for the types of character that distinguish youth, old age, and the prime of life. We will now turn to those gifts of fortune by which human   15 character is affected. First let us consider good birth. Its effect on character is to make those who have it more ambitious; it is the way of all men who have something to start with to add to the pile, and good birth implies ancestral distinction. The well-born man will look down even on those who are as good as his own ancestors,   20 because any far-off distinction is greater than the same thing close to us, and better to boast about. Being well-born, which means coming of a fine stock, must be distinguished from nobility, which means being true to the family nature—a quality not usually found in the well-born, most of whom are poor creatures. In the generations of men as in the fruits of the earth, there is a varying yield; now and   25 then, where the stock is good, exceptional men are produced for a while, and then decadence sets in. A clever stock will degenerate towards the insane type of

30　character, like the descendants of Alcibiades or of the elder Dionysius; a steady stock towards the fatuous and torpid type, like the descendants of Cimon, Pericles, and Socrates.

16 · The type of character produced by wealth lies on the surface for all to see. Wealthy men are insolent and arrogant; their possession of wealth affects their
1391ª1　understanding; they feel as if they had every good thing that exists; wealth becomes a sort of standard of value for everything else, and therefore they imagine there is nothing it cannot buy. They are luxurious and ostentatious; luxurious, because of the luxury in which they live and the prosperity which they display; ostentatious and
5　vulgar, because, like other people's, their minds are regularly occupied with the object of their love and admiration, and also because they think that other people's idea of happiness is the same as their own. It is indeed quite natural that they should be affected thus; for if you have money, there are always plenty of people who come begging from you. Hence the saying of Simonides about wise men and rich men, in
10　answer to Hiero's wife, who asked him whether it was better to grow rich or wise. 'Why, rich', he said; 'for I see the wise men spending their days at the rich men's doors'. Rich men also consider themselves worthy to hold public office; for they consider they already have the things that give a claim to office. In a word, the type of character produced by wealth is that of a prosperous fool. There is indeed one
15　difference between the type of the newly-enriched and those who have long been rich: the newly-enriched have all the bad qualities mentioned in an exaggerated and worse form—to be newly-enriched means, so to speak, no education in riches. The wrongs they do others are not meant to injure their victims, but spring from insolence or self-indulgence, e.g. those that end in assault or in adultery.

20　　　17 · As to power, here too it may fairly be said that the type of character it produces is mostly obvious enough. Some elements in this type it shares with the wealthy type, others are better. Those in power are more ambitious and more manly in character than the wealthy, because they aspire to do the great deeds that their
25　power permits them to do. Responsibility makes them more serious: they have to keep paying attention to the duties their position involves. They are dignified rather than arrogant, for the respect in which they are held inspires them with dignity and therefore with moderation—dignity being a mild and becoming form of arrogance. If they wrong others, they wrong them not on a small but on a great scale.
30　　　Good fortune in certain of its branches produces the types of character belonging to the conditions just described, since these conditions are in fact more or less the kinds of good fortune that are regarded as most important. It may be added that good fortune leads us to gain all we can in the way of family happiness and
1391ᵇ1　bodily advantages. It does indeed make men more supercilious and more reckless; but there is one excellent quality that goes with it—piety, and respect for the divine power, in which they believe because of events which are really the result of chance.
　　　This account of the types of character that correspond to differences of age or

fortune may end here; for to arrive at the opposite types to those described, namely, those of the poor, the unfortunate, and the powerless, we have only to ask what the opposite qualities are.

18 · [[The use of persuasive speech is to lead to decisions. (When we know a thing, and have decided about it, there is no further use in speaking about it.) This is so even if one is addressing a single person and urging him to do or not to do something, as when we advise a man about his conduct or try to change his views: the single person is as much your judge as if he were one of many; we may say, without qualification, that anyone is your judge whom you have to persuade. Nor does it matter whether we are arguing against an actual opponent or against a mere proposition; in the latter case we still have to use speech and overthrow the opposing arguments, and we attack these as we should attack an actual opponent. Our principle holds good of epideictic speeches also; the audience for whom such a speech is put together is treated as the judge of it. Nevertheless, the only sort of person who can strictly be called a judge is the man who decides the issue in some matter of public controversy; for the issue concerns the facts under dispute or subject to deliberation.]][18] In the section on political oratory an account has already been given of the types of character that mark the different constitutions.

The manner and means of investing speeches with moral character may now be regarded as fully set forth.

Each of the main divisions of oratory has, we have seen, its own distinct goal. With regard to each division, we have noted the accepted views and propositions upon which we may base our arguments—for deliberative, for epideictic, and for forensic speaking. We have further determined completely by what means speeches may be invested with the required character. We are now to proceed to discuss the arguments common to *all* oratory. All orators are bound to use the topic of the possible and impossible; and to try to show that a thing has happened, or will happen in the future. Again, the topic of size is common to all oratory; all of us have to argue that things are bigger or smaller than they seem, whether we are making deliberative speeches, speeches of eulogy or attack, or prosecuting or defending in the law-courts. Having analysed these subjects, we will try to say what we can about the general principles of arguing by enthymeme and example, by the addition of which we may hope to complete the project with which we set out. Of the above-mentioned commonplaces, that concerned with amplification is—as has been already said—most appropriate to epideictic speeches; that concerned with the past, to forensic speeches, where the required decision is always about the past; that concerned with possibility and the future, to deliberative speeches.

19 · Let us first speak of the possible and impossible. It would seem to be the case that if it is possible for one of a pair of contraries to be or happen, then it is possible for the other: e.g. if a man can be cured, he can also fall ill; for any two

---

[18]Marked by Kassel as a later addition by Aristotle himself.

contraries are equally possible, in so far as they are contraries. That if of two similar things one is possible, so is the other. That if the harder of two things is possible, so is the easier. That if a thing can come into existence in a good and beautiful form, then it can come into existence generally; thus a house can exist more easily than a beautiful house. That if the beginning of a thing can occur, so can the end; for nothing impossible occurs or begins to occur; thus the commensurability of the diagonal of a square with its side neither occurs nor can begin to occur. That if the end is possible, so is the beginning; for all things that occur have a beginning. That if that which is posterior in essence or in order of generation can come into being, so can that which is prior: thus if a man can come into being, so can a boy, since the boy comes first in order of generation; and if a boy can, so can a man, for the man also is first. That those things are possible of which the love or desire is natural; for no one, as a rule, loves or desires impossibilities. That things which are the object of any kind of science or art are possible and exist or come into existence. That anything is possible the first step in whose production depends on men or things which we can compel or persuade to produce it, by our greater strength, our control of them, or our friendship with them. That where the parts are possible, the whole is possible; and where the whole is possible, the parts are usually possible. For if the slit in front, the toe-piece, and the upper leather can be made, then shoes can be made; and if shoes, then also the front slit and the toe-piece. That if a whole genus is a thing that can occur, so can the species; and if the species can occur, so can the genus: thus, if a sailing vessel can be made, so also can a trireme; and if a trireme, then a sailing vessel also. That if one of two things whose existence depends on each other is possible, so is the other; for instance, if double, then half, and if half, then double. That if a thing can be produced without art or preparation, it can be produced still more certainly by the careful application of art to it. Hence Agathon has said:

> To some things we by art must needs attain,
> Others by destiny or luck we gain.[19]

That if anything is possible to inferior, weaker, and stupider people, it is more so for their opposites; thus Isocrates said that it would be a strange thing if he could not discover a thing that Euthynus had found out. As for impossibility, we can clearly get what we want by taking the contraries of the arguments stated above.

Questions of past fact may be looked at in the following ways. First, that if the less likely of two things has occurred, the more likely must have occurred also. That if one thing that usually follows another has happened, then that other thing has happened; that, for instance, if a man has forgotten a thing, he has also once learnt it. That if a man had the power and the wish to do a thing, he has done it; for every one does do whatever he wants to do whenever he can do it, there being nothing to stop him. That, further, he has done the thing in question either if he intended it and nothing external prevented him; or if he had the power to do it and was angry at the

[19]Frag. 8 Nauck.

time; or if he had the power to do it and his heart was set upon it—for people, as a rule do what they long to do, if they can; bad people through lack of self-control; good people, because their hearts are set upon good things. Again, that if a thing was going to happen, it has happened; if a man was going to do something, he has done it, for it is likely that the intention was carried out. That if one thing has happened which naturally happens before another or with a view to it, the other has happened; for instance, if it has lightened, it has also thundered; and if an action has been attempted, it has been done. That if one thing has happened which naturally happens after another, or with a view to which that other happens, then that other (that which happens first, or happens with a view to this thing) has also happened; thus, if it has thundered it has also lightened, and if an action has been done it has been attempted. Of all these sequences some are inevitable and some merely usual. The arguments for the *non*-occurrence of anything can obviously be found by considering the opposites of those that have been mentioned.

How questions of future fact should be argued is clear from the same considerations: that a thing will be done if there is both the power and the wish to do it; or if along with the power to do it there is a craving for the result, or anger, or calculation, prompting it. That the thing will be done, in these cases,[20] if the man is actually setting about it, or even if he means to do it later—for usually what we mean to do happens rather than what we do not mean to do. That a thing will happen if another thing which naturally happens before it has already happened; thus, if it is clouding over, it is likely to rain. That if the means to an end have occurred, then the end is likely to occur; thus, if there is a foundation, there will be a house.

For arguments about the greatness and smallness of things, the greater and the lesser, and generally great things and small, what we have already said will show the line to take. In discussing deliberative oratory we have spoken about the relative greatness of various goods, and about the greater and lesser in general. Since therefore in each type of oratory the object under discussion is some kind of good—whether it is utility, nobleness, or justice—it is clear that every orator must obtain the materials of amplification through these channels. To go further than this, and try to establish abstract laws of greatness and superiority, is to argue without an object; in practical life, particular facts count more than generalizations.

Enough has now been said about these questions of possibility and the reverse, of past or future fact, and of the relative greatness or smallness of things.

20 · The special forms of oratorical argument having now been discussed, we have next to treat of those which are common to all kinds of oratory. These are of two main kinds, example and enthymeme; for a maxim is part of an enthymeme.

We will first treat of argument by example, for it has the nature of induction, which is the foundation of reasoning. This form of argument has two varieties; one

---

[20]The text is uncertain.

consisting in the mention of actual past facts, the other in the invention of facts by the speaker. Of the latter, again, there are two varieties, the illustrative parallel and
30   the fable (e.g. the fables of Aesop, or those from Libya). As an instance of the mention of actual facts, take the following. The speaker may argue thus: 'We must prepare for war against the king of Persia and not let him subdue Egypt. For Darius of old did not cross the Aegean until he had seized Egypt; but once he had seized it, he did cross. And Xerxes, again, did not attack us until he had seized Egypt; but
1393ᵇ1   once he had seized it, he did cross. If therefore the present king seizes Egypt, he also will cross, and therefore we must not let him'.

The illustrative parallel is the sort of argument Socrates used: e.g. 'Public
5   officials ought not to be selected by lot. That is like using the lot to select athletes, instead of choosing those who are fit for the contest; or using the lot to select a steersman from among a ship's crew, as if we ought to take the man on whom the lot falls, and not the man who knows most about it'.

Instances of the fable are that of Stesichorus about Phalaris, and that of Aesop
10   in defence of the popular leader. When the people of Himera had made Phalaris military dictator, and were going to give him a bodyguard, Stesichorus wound up a long talk by telling them the fable of the horse who had a field all to himself. Presently there came a stag and began to spoil his pasturage. The horse, wishing to
15   revenge himself on the stag, asked a man if he could help him to do so. The man said, 'Yes, if you will let me bridle you and get on to your back with javelins in my hand'. The horse agreed, and the man mounted; but instead of getting his revenge on the stag, the horse found himself the slave of the man. 'You too', said
20   Stesichorus, 'take care lest, in your desire for revenge on your enemies, you meet the same fate as the horse. By making Phalaris military dictator, you have already let yourselves be bridled. If you let him get on to your backs by giving him a bodyguard, from that moment you will be his slaves'.

Aesop, defending before the assembly at Samos a popular leader who was being tried for his life, told this story: A fox, in crossing a river, was swept into a hole
25   in the rocks; and, not being able to get out, suffered miseries for a long time through the swarms of fleas that fastened on her. A hedgehog, while roaming around, noticed the fox; and feeling sorry for her asked if he might remove the fleas. But the fox declined the offer; and when the hedgehog asked why, she replied, 'These fleas
30   are by this time full of me and not sucking much blood; if you take them away, others will come with fresh appetites and drink up all the blood I have left'. 'So, men of Samos', said Aesop, 'my client will do you no further harm; he is wealthy already.
1394ᵃ1   But if you put him to death, others will come along who are not rich, and their peculations will empty your treasury completely'.

Fables are suitable for addresses to popular assemblies; and they have one advantage—they are comparatively easy to invent, whereas it is hard to find parallels among actual past events. You will in fact frame them just as you frame
5   illustrative parallels: all you require is the power of thinking out your analogy, a power developed by intellectual training. But while it is easier to supply parallels by inventing fables, it is more valuable for the political speaker to supply them by

quoting what has actually happened, since in most respects the future will be like what the past has been.

Where we are unable to argue by enthymeme, we must try to demonstrate our point by this method of example, and to convince our hearers thereby. If we *can* argue by enthymeme, we should use our examples as subsequent supplementary evidence. They should not precede the enthymemes: that will give the argument an inductive air, which only rarely suits the conditions of speech-making. If they follow the enthymemes, they have the effect of witnesses giving evidence, and this always tells. For the same reason, if you put your examples first you must give a large number of them; if you put them last, a single one is sufficient; even a single witness will serve if he is a good one. It has now been stated how many varieties of argument by example there are, and how and when they are to be employed.

21 · We now turn to the use of maxims, in order to see upon what subjects and occasions, and for what kind of speaker, they will appropriately form part of a speech. This will appear most clearly when we have defined a maxim. It is a statement; not about a particular fact, such as the character of Iphicrates, but of a general kind; nor is it about any and every subject—e.g. 'straight is the contrary of curved' is not a maxim—but only about questions of practical conduct, courses of conduct to be chosen or avoided. Now an enthymeme is a deduction dealing with such practical subjects. It is therefore roughly true that the premisses or conclusions of enthymemes, considered apart from the rest of the argument, are maxims: e.g.

> Never should any man whose wits are sound
> Have his sons taught more wisdom than their fellows.

Here we have a maxim; add the reason or explanation, and the whole thing is an enthymeme; thus—

> It makes them idle; and therewith they earn
> Ill-will and jealousy throughout the city.[21]

Again,

> There is no man in all things prosperous,[22]

and

> There is no man among us all is free,

are maxims; but the latter, taken with what follows it, is an enthymeme—

> For all are slaves of money or of chance.[23]

From this definition of a maxim it follows that there are four kinds of maxims. In the first place, the maxim may or may not have a supplement. Proof is needed where

---

[21]Euripides, *Medea* 294–7. [22]id., frag. 661 Nauck. [23]id., *Hecuba* 864–5.

the statement is paradoxical or disputable; no supplement is wanted where the
10 statement contains nothing paradoxical, either because the view expressed is
already a known truth, e.g.

Chiefest of blessings is health for a man, as it seemeth to me,[24]

this being the general opinion; or because, as soon as the view is stated, it is clear at
15 a glance, e.g.

No love is true save that which loves for ever.[25]

Of the maxims that do have a supplement attached, some are part of an
enthymeme, e.g.

Never should any man whose wits are sound,

Others have the essential character of enthymemes, but are not stated as parts of
enthymemes; these latter are reckoned the best; they are those in which the reason
20 for the view expressed is simply implied, e.g.

O mortal man, nurse not immortal wrath.[26]

To say 'it is not right to nurse immortal wrath' is a maxim; the added words 'O
mortal man' give the reason. Similarly, with the words

25 Mortal creatures ought to cherish mortal, not immortal thoughts.[27]

What has been said has shown us how many kinds of maxim there are, and to what
subjects the various kinds are appropriate. They must not be given without
supplement if they express disputed or paradoxical views: we must, in that case,
either put the supplement first and make a maxim of the conclusion, e.g. you might
30 say, 'For my part, since both unpopularity and idleness are undesirable, I hold that
it is better not to be educated'; or you may say this first, and then add the previous
clause. Where a statement, without being paradoxical, is not obviously true, the
reason should be added as concisely as possible. In such cases both laconic and
1395ᵃ1 enigmatic sayings are suitable: thus one might say what Stesichorus said to the
Locrians, 'Insolence is better avoided, lest the cicadas chirp on the ground'.

The use of maxims is appropriate only to elderly men, and in handling subjects
in which the speaker is experienced. For a young man to use them is—like telling
5 stories—unbecoming; to use them in handling things in which one has no experience
is silly and ill-bred: a fact sufficiently proved by the special fondness of country
fellows for coining maxims, and their readiness to air them.

To declare a thing to be universally true when it is not is most appropriate
when working up feelings of horror and indignation in our hearers; especially by
10 way of preface, or after the facts have been proved. Even hackneyed and

---

[24]Epicharmus, frag. 19 Diels-Kranz.
[25]Euripides, *Troades* 1051.
[26]Frag. adesp. 79 Nauck.
[27]Epicharmus, frag. 20 Diels-Kranz.

commonplace maxims are to be used, if they suit one's purpose: just because they are commonplace, everyone seems to agree with them, and therefore they are taken for truth. Thus, anyone who is calling on his men to risk an engagement without obtaining favourable omens may quote:

> One omen of all is best, that we fight for our fatherland.[28]

Or, if he is calling on them to attack a stronger force—

> The War-God showeth no favour.[29]   15

Or, if he is urging people to destroy the innocent children of their enemies—

> Fool, who slayeth the father and leaveth his sons to avenge him.

Some proverbs are also maxims, e.g. 'An Attic neighbour.' You are not to avoid uttering maxims that contradict such sayings as have become public property (I mean such sayings as 'know thyself' and 'nothing in excess'), if doing so will raise   20
your hearers' opinion of your character, or convey an effect of strong emotion—e.g. an angry speaker might well say, 'It is not true that we ought to know ourselves: anyhow, if this man had known himself, he would never have thought himself fit for an army command.' It will raise people's opinion of our character to say, for   25
instance, 'We ought not to follow the saying that bids us treat our friends as future enemies: much better to treat our enemies as future friends.' Our choice should be implied partly by the very wording of our maxim. Failing this, we should add our reason: e.g. having said 'We should treat our friends, not as the saying advises, but as if they were going to be our friends always', we should add 'for the other behaviour is that of a traitor': or we might put it, 'I disapprove of that saying. A true   30
friend will treat his friend as if he were going to be his friend for ever'; and again, 'Nor do I approve of the saying "nothing in excess": we are bound to hate bad men excessively'.

One great advantage of maxims to a speaker is due to the want of intelligence   1395ᵇ1
in his hearers, who love to hear him succeed in expressing as a universal truth the opinions which they hold themselves about particular cases. I will explain what I mean by this, indicating at the same time how we are to hunt down the maxims required. The maxim, as has been already said, is a general statement, and people   5
love to hear stated in general terms what they already believe in some particular connexion: e.g. if a man happens to have bad neighbours or bad children, he will agree with any one who tells him, 'Nothing is more annoying than having neighbours', or 'Nothing is more foolish than to be the parent of children'. The orator has therefore to guess the subjects on which his hearers really hold views   10
already, and what those views are, and then must express, as general truths, these same views on these same subjects. This is one advantage of using maxims. There is another which is more important—it invests a speech with character. There is

<hr />

[28] *Iliad* XII 243.
[29] *Iliad* XVIII 309.

character in every speech in which the choice is conspicuous; and maxims always produce this effect, because the utterance of them amounts to a general declaration of what should be chosen; so that, if the maxims are sound, they display the speaker as a man of sound character. So much for the maxim—its nature, varieties, proper use, and advantages.

22 · We now come to the enthymemes, and will begin the subject with some general consideration of the proper way of looking for them, and then proceed to what is a distinct question, the commonplaces to be embodied in them. It has already been pointed out that the enthymeme is a deduction, and in what sense it is so. We have also noted the differences between it and the deduction of dialectic. Thus we must not carry its reasoning too far back, or the length of our argument will cause obscurity; nor must we put in all the steps that lead to our conclusion, or we shall waste words in saying what is manifest. It is this simplicity that makes the uneducated more effective than the educated when addressing popular audiences—makes them, as the poets[30] tell us, 'charm the crowd's ears more finely'. Educated men lay down broad general principles; uneducated men argue from common knowledge and draw obvious conclusions. We must not, therefore, start from any and every opinion, but only from those of definite groups of people—our judges or those whose authority they recognize; and there must, moreover, be no doubt in the minds of most, if not all, of our judges that the opinions put forward really are of this sort. We should also base our arguments upon what happens for the most part as well as upon what necessarily happens.

The first thing we have to remember is this. Whether our argument is made in a political gathering or in one of any other sort, we must know some, if not all, of the facts about the subject on which we are to speak and argue. Otherwise we can have no materials out of which to construct arguments. I mean, for instance, how could we advise the Athenians whether they should go to war or not, if we did not know their strength, whether it was naval or military or both, and how great it is; what their revenues amount to; who their friends and enemies are; what wars, too, they have waged, and with what success; and so on? Or how could we eulogize them if we knew nothing about the sea-fight at Salamis, or the battle of Marathon, or what they did for the Heracleidae, or any other facts like that? All eulogy is based upon the noble deeds—real or imaginary—that stand to the credit of those eulogized. On the same principle, invectives are based on facts of the opposite kind: the orator looks to see what base deeds—real or imaginary—stand to the discredit of those he is attacking, such as treachery to the cause of Hellenic freedom, or the enslavement of their gallant allies against the barbarians (Aegina, Potidaea), or any other misdeeds of this kind that are recorded against them. So, too, in a court of law: whether we are prosecuting or defending, we must pay attention to the existing facts of the case. It makes no difference whether the subject is the Lacedaemonians or the Athenians, a man or a god; we must do the same thing. Suppose it to be Achilles

----

[30]Cf. Euripides, *Hippolytus* 989.

whom we are to advise, to praise or blame, to accuse or defend; here too we must take the facts, real or imaginary; these must be our material, whether we are to praise or blame him for the noble or base deeds he has done, to accuse or defend him for his just or unjust treatment of others, or to advise him about what is or is not to his interest. The same thing applies to any subject whatever. Thus, in handling the question whether justice is or is not a good, we must start with the real facts about justice and goodness. We see, then, that this is the only way in which any one ever proves anything, whether his arguments are strictly cogent or not: not all facts can form his basis, but only those that bear on the matter in hand: nor, plainly, can proof be effected otherwise by means of the speech. Consequently, as appears in the *Topics,* we must first of all have by us a selection of arguments about questions that may arise and are suitable for us to handle; and then we must try to think out arguments of the same type for special needs as they emerge; not vaguely and indefinitely, but by keeping our eyes on the actual facts of the subject we have to speak on, and gathering in as many of them as we can that bear closely upon it; for the more actual facts we have at our command, the more easily we prove our case; and the more closely they bear on the subject, the more they will seem to belong to that speech only instead of being common. By 'common' I mean, for example, eulogy of Achilles because he is a human being or a demi-god, or because he joined the expedition against Troy: these things are true of many others, so that this kind of eulogy applies no better to Achilles than to Diomede. The special facts are those that are true of Achilles alone; such facts as that he slew Hector, the bravest of the Trojans, and Cycnus the invulnerable, who prevented all the Greeks from landing, and again that he was the youngest man who joined the expedition, and was not bound by oath to join it, and so on.

Here, then, we have our first principle of selection of enthymemes—that which refers to the commonplaces. We will now consider the elements of enthymemes. (By an element of an enthymeme I mean the same thing as a commonplace.) We will begin, as we must begin, by observing that there are two kinds of enthymemes. One kind proves some affirmative or negative proposition; the other kind disproves one. The difference between the two kinds is the same as that between refutation and deduction in dialectic. The probative enthymeme makes an inference from what is accepted, the refutative makes an inference to what is unaccepted.

We may now be said to have in our hands the commonplaces for the various *special* subjects that it is useful or necessary to handle, having selected the propositions suitable in various cases. We have, in fact, already ascertained the commonplaces applicable to enthymemes about good and evil, the noble and the base, justice and injustice, and also to those about types of character, emotions, and states of mind. Let us now lay hold of certain facts about the whole subject, considered from a different and more general point of view. In the course of our discussion we will take note of refutative and demonstrative commonplaces, and also of those used in what seem to be enthymemes, but are not, since they are not deductions at all. Having made all this clear, we will proceed to classify objections and refutations, showing how they can be brought to bear upon enthymemes.

30

1396^{b}1

5

10

15

20

25

30

1397^{a}1

5

23 · One probative commonplace is based upon consideration of the opposite of the thing in question. Observe whether that opposite has the opposite quality. If it has not, you refute the original proposition; if it has, you establish it. E.g. 'Temperance is beneficial; for licentiousness is hurtful'. Or, as in the Messenian speech, 'If war is the cause of our present troubles, peace is what we need to put things right again'.[31] Or—

> For if not even evil-doers should
> Anger us if they meant not what they did,
> Then can we owe no gratitude to such
> As were constrained to do the good they did us.[32]

Or—

> Since in this world liars may win belief,
> Be sure of the opposite likewise—that this world
> Hears many a true word and believes it not.[33]

Another commonplace is got by considering some modification of the key-word, and arguing that what can or cannot be said of the one, can or cannot be said of the other: e.g. 'just' does not always means 'beneficial', or 'justly' would always mean 'beneficially', whereas it is *not* desirable to be justly put to death.

Another is based upon correlative ideas. If it is true that one man *gave* noble or just treatment to another, you argue that the other must have *received* noble or just treatment; or that where it is right to command obedience, it must have been right to obey the command. Thus Diomedon, the tax-farmer, said of the taxes: 'If it is no disgrace for you to sell them, it is no disgrace for us to buy them'. Further, if 'well' or 'justly' is true of the person to whom a thing is done, you argue that it is true of the doer. But it is possible to draw a false conclusion here. It may be just that he should be treated in a certain way, and yet *not* just that he should be so treated by you. Hence you must ask yourself two distinct questions: Is it right that he should be thus treated? Is it right that you should thus treat him? and apply your results in whichever way is suitable. Sometimes in such a case the two answers differ: you may quite easily have a position like that in the *Alcmaeon* of Theodectes:

> And was there none to loathe thy mother's crime?

to which question Alcmaeon in reply says,

> Why, there are two things to examine here.

And when Alphesiboea asks what he means, he rejoins:

> They judged *her* fit to die, not *me* to slay her.

[[Again there is the lawsuit about Demosthenes and the men who killed Nicanor; as

---

[31]Alcidamas, frag. 2.   [32]Frag. adesp. 80 Nauck.   [33]Euripides, frag. 396 Nauck.

they were judged to have killed him justly, it was thought that he was killed justly. And in the case of the man who was killed at Thebes, the judges were requested to decide whether it was unjust that he should be killed, since if it was not, it was argued that it could not have been unjust to kill him.]][34]   10

Another is the *a fortiori*. Thus it may be argued that if even the gods are not omniscient, certainly human beings are not. The principle here is that, if a quality does not in fact exist where it is *more* likely to exist, it clearly does not exist where it is *less* likely. Again, the argument that a man who strikes his father also strikes his   15 neighbours follows from the principle that, if the less likely thing is true, the more likely thing is true also; for a man is less likely to strike his father than to strike his neighbours. The argument, then, may run thus. Or it may be urged that, if a thing is not true where it is more likely, or if it is true where it is less likely, etc.—according as we have to show that a thing *is* or is *not* true. This argument might also be used in a case of parity, as in the lines:

> Thou hast pity for *thy* sire, who has lost his sons:
> Hast none for Oeneus, whose brave son is dead?[35]   20

And, again, 'if Theseus did no wrong, neither did Paris'; or 'if the sons of Tyndareus did no wrong, neither did Paris'; or 'if Hector did well to slay Patroclus, Paris did well to slay Achilles'. And 'if other followers of an art are not bad men, neither are philosophers'. And 'if generals are not bad men because it often happens that they are condemned to death, neither are sophists'. And the remark that 'if each   25 individual among you ought to think of his own city's reputation, you ought all to think of the reputation of Greece as a whole'.

Another is based on considerations of time. Thus Iphicrates, in the case against Harmodius, said, 'if before doing the deed I had bargained that, if I did it, I should have a statue, you would have given me one. Will you not give me one now that I   *have* done the deed? You must not make promises when you are expecting a thing to   30 be done for you, and refuse to fulfil them when the thing has been done'. And, again, to induce the Thebans to let Philip pass through their territory into Attica, it was   1398ᵃ1 argued that 'if he had insisted on this before he helped them against the Phocians, they would have promised to do it. It is monstrous, therefore, that just because he threw away his advantage then, and trusted their honour, they should not let him pass through now'.

Another line is to apply to the other speaker what he has said against yourself. It is an excellent turn to give to a debate, as may be seen in the *Teucer*. It was employed by Iphicrates in his reply to Aristophon. 'Would *you*', he asked, 'take a   5 bribe to betray the fleet?' 'No', said Aristophon; and Iphicrates replied, 'Very good: if you, who are Aristophon, would not betray the fleet, would I, who am Iphicrates?' Only, it must be recognized beforehand that the other man is more likely than you are to commit the crime in question. Otherwise you will make yourself ridiculous; if

---

[34]Marked by Kassel as a later addition by Aristotle himself.
[35]Frag. adesp. 81 Nauck.

10   it is Aristeides who is prosecuting, you cannot say that sort of thing to him. The purpose is to discredit the prosecutor, who as a rule would have it appear that his character is better than that of the defendant, a pretension which it is desirable to upset. But the use of such an argument is in all cases ridiculous if you are attacking others for what you do or would do yourself, or are urging others to do what you neither do nor would do yourself.

15   Another is secured by defining your terms. Thus, 'What is the supernatural? Surely it is either a god or the work of a god. Well, anyone who believes that the work of a god exists, cannot help also believing that gods exist'. Or take the argument of Iphicrates, 'Goodness is true nobility; neither Harmodius nor Aristo-

20   geiton had any nobility before they did a noble deed'. He also argued that he himself was more akin to Harmodius and Aristogeiton than his opponent was. 'At any rate, my deeds are more akin to those of Harmodius and Aristogeiton than yours are'. Another example may be found in the *Alexander*. 'Everyone will agree that by incontinent people we mean those who are not satisfied with the enjoyment of one body'. A further example is to be found in the reason given by Socrates for

25   not going to the court of Archelaus. He said that 'one is insulted by being unable to requite benefits, as well as by being unable to requite injuries'. All the persons mentioned define their term and get at its essential meaning, and then use the result when reasoning on the point at issue.

Another is founded upon the various senses of a word. Such a word is 'sharp', as has been explained in the *Topics*.[36]

Another line is based upon logical division. Thus, 'All men do wrong from one

30   of three motives, A, B, or C: in my case A and B are out of the question, and even the accusers do not allege C'.

Another line is based upon induction. Thus from the case of the woman of Peparethus it might be argued that women everywhere can settle correctly the facts

1398ᵇ1   about their children. Another example of this occurred at Athens in the case between the orator Mantias and his son, when the boy's mother revealed the true facts: and yet another at Thebes, in the case between Ismenias and Stilbon, when Dodonis proved that it was Ismenias who was the father of her son Thettaliscus, and he was in consequence always regarded as being so. A further instance of induction

5   may be taken from the *Law* of Theodectes: 'If we do not hand over our horses to the care of men who have mishandled other people's horses, nor ships to those who have wrecked other people's ships, and if this is true of everything else alike, then men who have failed to secure other people's safety are not to be employed to secure our

10   own'. Another instance is the argument of Alcidamas: 'Everyone honours the wise. Thus the Parians have honoured Archilochus, in spite of his bitter tongue; the Chians Homer, though he was not their countryman; the Mytilenaeans Sappho, though she was a woman; the Lacedaemonians actually made Chilon a member of their senate, though they are the least literary of men; the inhabitants of Lampsacus

15   gave public burial to Anaxagoras, though he was an alien, and honour him even to

[36]See *Topics* 106ᵃ13, etc.

this day.' [[The Athenians became prosperous under Solon's laws and the Lacedaemonians under those of Lycurgus, while at Thebes no sooner did the leading men become philosophers than the country began to prosper.]][37]

Another is founded upon some decision already pronounced, whether on the same subject or on one like it or contrary to it. Such a proof is most effective if everyone has always decided thus; but if not everyone, then at any rate most people; or if all, or most, wise or good men have thus decided, or the actual judges of the present question, or those whose authority they accept, or anyone whose decision they cannot contradict because he has complete control over them, or those whom it is not seemly to contradict, as the gods, or one's father, or one's teachers. Thus Autocles said, when attacking Mixidemides, that it was a strange thing that the Dread Goddesses could without loss of dignity submit to the judgement of the Areopagus, and yet Mixidemides could not. Or as Sappho said, 'Death is an evil thing; the gods have so judged it, or they would die'. Or again as Aristippus said in reply to Plato when he spoke somewhat too dogmatically, as Aristippus thought: 'Well, anyhow, our *friend*', meaning Socrates, 'never spoke like that'. And Hegesippus, having previously consulted Zeus at Olympia, asked Apollo at Delphi 'whether his opinion was the same as his father's', implying that it would be shameful for him to contradict his father. Thus too Isocrates argued that Helen must have been a good woman, because Theseus decided that she was; and Paris a good man, because the goddesses chose him before all others; and Evagoras also, says Isocrates, was good, since when Conon met with his misfortune he betook himself to Evagoras without trying anyone else on the way.

Another consists in taking separately the parts of a subject. Such is that given in the *Topics*:[38] 'What *sort* of motion is the soul? for it must be this or that'. The *Socrates* of Theodectes provides an example: 'What temple has he profaned? What gods recognized by the state has he not honoured?'

Again, since it happens that any given thing usually has both good and bad conse·····ences, another line of argument consists in using those consequences as a reason for urging that a thing should or should not be done, for prosecuting or defending anyone, for eulogy or censure. E.g. education leads both to unpopularity, which is bad, and to wisdom, which is good. Hence you either argue, 'It is therefore not well to be educated, since it is not well to be unpopular,' or you answer, 'No, it is well to be educated, since it is well to be wise'. The *Art of Rhetoric* of Callippus is made up of this commonplace, with the addition of those of possibility and the others of that kind already described.

Another is used when we have to urge or discourage a course of action that may be done in either of two opposite ways, and have to apply the method just mentioned to both. The difference between this one and the last is that, whereas in the last any two things are contrasted, here the things contrasted are opposites. For instance, the priestess enjoined upon her son not to take to public speaking: 'For', she said, 'if you say what is right, men will hate you; if you say what is wrong, the

---

[37]Marked by Kassel as a later addition by Aristotle himself.   [38]See *Topics* 111^{b}5.

gods will hate you'. The reply might be, 'On the contrary, you *ought* to take to
public speaking: for if you say what is right, the gods will love you; if you say what is
25   wrong, men will love you'. This amounts to the proverbial 'buying the marsh with
the salt'. And this is 'bending back'—when each of two opposites has both a good
and a bad consequence opposite respectively to each other.

Another is this: the things people approve of openly are not those which they
30   approve of secretly: openly, their chief praise is given to justice and nobleness; but in
their hearts they prefer their own advantage. Try, in face of this, to establish the
point of view which your opponent has not adopted. This is the most effective of the
forms of argument that contradict common opinion.

Another line is that of rational correspondence. E.g. Iphicrates, when they
were trying to compel his son, a youth under the prescribed age, to perform one of
the state duties because he was tall, said 'If you count tall boys men, you will next be
1399ᵇ1   voting short men boys'. And Theodectes in his *Law* said, 'You make citizens of such
mercenaries as Strabax and Charidemus, as a reward of their merits; will you not
make exiles of such citizens as those who have done irreparable harm among the
5   mercenaries?'

Another line is the argument that if two results are the same their antecedents
are also the same. For instance, it was a saying of Xenophanes that to assert that the
gods had birth is as impious as to say that they die; the consequence of both
statements is that there is a time when the gods do not exist. This line of proof
assumes generally that the result of any given thing is always the same: e.g. 'you are
10   going to decide not about Isocrates, but about the value of the whole profession of
philosophy'. Or, 'to give earth and water' means slavery; or, 'to share in the
Common Peace' means obeying orders. We are to make either such assumptions or
their opposite, as suits us best.

Another is based on the fact that men do not always make the same choice on a
15   later as on an earlier occasion, but reverse their previous choice. E.g. the following
enthymeme: 'When we were exiles, we fought in order to return; now we have
returned, it would be strange to choose exile in order not to have to fight'. On one
occasion, that is, they chose to be true to their homes at the cost of fighting, and on
the other to avoid fighting at the cost of deserting their homes.

20   Another is the assertion that some possible motive for an event or state of
things is the real one: e.g. that a gift was given in order to cause pain by its
withdrawal. This notion underlies the lines:

> God gives to many great prosperity,
> Not of good will towards them, but to make
> The ruin of them more conspicuous.[39]

25   Or take the passage from the *Meleager* of Antiphon:

> To slay no boar, but to be witnesses
> Of Meleager's prowess unto Greece.[40]

---

[39]Frag. adesp. 82 Nauck.   [40]Frag. 2 Nauck.

Or the argument in the *Ajax* of Theodectes, that Diomede chose out Odysseus not to do him honour, but in order that his companion might be a lesser man than himself—such a motive for doing so is quite possible.   30

Another is common to forensic and deliberative oratory, namely, to consider inducements and deterrents, and the motives people have for doing or avoiding the actions in question. These are the conditions which make us bound to act if they are for us, and to refrain from action if they are against us: that is, we are bound to act if the action is possible, easy, and useful to ourselves or our friends or hurtful to our   35 enemies; this is true even if the action entails loss, provided the loss is outweighed by the solid advantage. These same arguments also form the materials for accusation   1400ª1 or defence—the deterrents being pointed out by the defence, and the inducements by the prosecution. This topic forms the whole *Art of Rhetoric* both of Pamphilus and of Callippus.

Another refers to things which are supposed to happen and yet seem   5 incredible. We may argue that people could not have believed them, if they had not been true or nearly true. And that they are the more likely to be true because they are incredible; for the things which men believe are either facts or probabilities: if, therefore, a thing that *is* believed is improbable and incredible, it must be true, since it is certainly not believed because it is at all probable or credible. An example is what Androcles of the deme Pitthus said in his arraignment of the law. The audience tried to shout him down when he observed that the laws required a law to   10 set them right. 'Why', he went on, 'fish need salt', improbable and incredible as this might seem for creatures reared in salt water; 'and olive-cakes need oil', incredible as it is that what produces oil should need it.

Another line is to refute our opponent's case by noting any disagreements: 15 first, in the case of our opponent [[if there is any disagreement among all his dates, ͺions, and statements]],[41] e.g. 'He says he is devoted to you, yet he conspired with the Thirty'; secondly, bearing on our own conduct, e.g. 'He says I am litigious, and yet he cannot prove that I have been engaged in a single lawsuit'; thirdly, referring to both of us together, e.g. '*He* has never even *lent* anyone a penny, but *I* have   20 *ransomed* quite a number of you'.

Another line that is useful for men and causes that have been really or seemingly slandered, is to show why the facts are not as supposed; pointing out that there is a reason for the false impression given. Thus a woman, who had palmed off her son on another woman, was thought to be the lad's mistress because she   25 embraced him; but when her action was explained the charge was shown to be groundless. Another example is from the *Ajax* of Theodectes, where Odysseus tells Ajax the reason why, though he is really braver than Ajax, he is not thought so.

Another is to show that if the *cause* is present, the *effect* is present, and if absent, absent. For cause and effect go together, and nothing can exist without a   30 cause. Thus Thrasybulus accused Leodamas of having had his name recorded as a criminal on the slab in the Acropolis, and of erasing the record in the time of the Thirty Tyrants: to which Leodamas replied, 'Impossible: for the Thirty would have   35

---

[41] Marked by Kassel as a later addition by Aristotle himself.

trusted me all the more if my quarrel with the commons had been inscribed on the slab'.

Another line is to consider whether the accused person can take or could have taken a better course than that which he is recommending or taking, or has taken. If so, it is clear that he is not guilty, since no one voluntarily and knowingly chooses what is bad. This argument is, however, fallacious, for it often becomes clear after the event how the action could have been done better, though before the event this was far from clear.

Another line is, when a contemplated action is inconsistent with any past action, to examine them both together. Thus, when the people of Elea asked Xenophanes if they should or should not sacrifice to Leucothea and mourn for her, he advised them not to mourn for her if they thought her a goddess, and not to sacrifice to her if they thought her a mortal woman.

Another line is to make previous mistakes the grounds of accusation or defence. Thus, in the *Medea* of Carcinus the accusers allege that Medea has slain her children; 'at all events', they say, 'they are not to be seen'—Medea having made the mistake of sending her children away. In defence she argues that it is not her children, but Jason, whom she would have slain; for it would have been a mistake on her part not to do this if she *had* done the other. This enthymematic commonplace and type forms the whole of the *Art of Rhetoric* in use before Theodorus.

Another line is to draw meanings from names. Sophocles, for instance, says,

> O steel in heart as thou art steel in name.[42]

This is common in praises of the gods. Thus, too, Conon called Thrasybulus *rash in counsel.* And Herodicus said of Thrasymachus, 'You are always *bold in battle'*; of Polus, 'you are always *a colt'*; and of the legislator Draco that his laws were those not of a human being but of *a dragon,* so savage were they. And, in Euripides, Hecuba says of Aphrodite,

> Her name and Folly's rightly begin alike,[43]

and Chaeremon writes:

> Pentheus—a name foreshadowing grief to come.[44]

The refutative enthymeme has a greater reputation than the demonstrative, because within a small space it works out two opposing arguments, and arguments put side by side are clearer to the audience. But of all deductions, whether refutative or demonstrative, those are most applauded of which we foresee the conclusions from the beginning, so long as they are not obvious at first sight—for part of the pleasure we feel is at our own intelligent anticipation; or those which we follow well enough to see the point of them as soon as the last word has been uttered.

1400[b]1

---

[42]Frag. 597 Nauck.
[43]*Troades* 990.
[44]Frag. 4 Nauck.

24 · Besides genuine deductions there may be deductions that look genuine but are not; and since an enthymeme is a deduction of a particular kind, it follows that, besides genuine enthymemes, there may be those that look genuine but are not.

Among the commonplaces that form the spurious enthymeme the first is that which arises from the particular words employed. One variety of this is when—as in dialectic, without having gone through any reasoning process, we make a final statement as if it were the conclusion of such a process, 'Therefore so-and-so is not true', 'Therefore also so-and-so must be true'—so too in enthymemes a compact and antithetical utterance passes for an enthymeme, such language being the proper province of enthymeme, so that it is seemingly the form of wording here that causes the illusion mentioned. In order to produce the effect of genuine reasoning by our form of wording it is useful to summarize the results of a number of previous reasonings: as 'some he saved—others he avenged—the Greeks he freed'. Each of these statements has been previously proved from other facts; but the collocation of them gives the impression of establishing some fresh conclusion.

Another variety is based on homonymy; e.g. the argument that the mouse must be a noble creature, since it gives its name to the most august of all religious rites—for such the Mysteries are. Or one may introduce, into a eulogy of the dog, the dog-star; or Pan, because Pindar said:

> O thou blessed one!
> Thou whom they of Olympus call
> The hound of manifold shape
> That follows the Mother of Heaven;[45]

or we may argue that, because there is much disgrace in there *not* being a dog about, there is honour in *being* a dog. Or that Hermes is readier than any other god to go shares, since we never say 'shares all round' except of him. Or that speech is a very excellent thing, since good men are not said to be worth money but to be worthy of esteem—the phrase 'worthy of esteem' also having the meaning of 'worth speech'.

Another line is to assert of the whole what is true of the parts, or of the parts what is true of the whole. A whole and its parts are supposed to be identical, though often they are not. You have therefore to adopt whichever of these two lines better suits your purpose. That is how Euthydemus argues; e.g. that anyone knows that there is a trireme in the Peiraeus, since he knows the separate details that make up this statement. There is also the argument that one who knows the letters knows the whole word, since the word is the same thing as the letters which compose it; or that, if a double portion of a certain thing is harmful to health, then a single portion must not be called wholesome, since it is absurd that two good things should make one bad thing. Put thus, the enthymeme is refutative; put as follows, demonstrative: 'For one good thing cannot be made up of two bad things'. The whole commonplace is

[45]Frag. 96 Snell.

fallacious. Again, there is Polycrates' saying that Thrasybulus put down thirty
35   tyrants, where the speaker adds them up one by one. Or the argument in the *Orestes*
of Theodectes, where the argument is from part to whole:

'Tis right that she who slays her lord should die.

'It is right, too, that the son should avenge his father. Very good: these two things
1401ᵇ1   are what Orestes has done'. Still, perhaps the two things, once they are put together,
do not form a right act. The fallacy might also be said to be due to omission, since
the speaker fails to say by whose hand a husband-slayer should die.

Another commonplace is the use of indignant language, whether to support
your own case or to overthrow your opponent's. We do this when we paint a
5   highly-coloured picture of the situation without having proved the facts of it: if the
defendant does so, he produces an impression of his innocence; and if the prosecutor
does,[46] he produces an impression of the defendant's guilt. Here there is no genuine
enthymeme: the hearer infers guilt or innocence, but no proof is given, and the
inference is fallacious accordingly.

10   Another line is to use a sign, which, again, yields no deduction. Thus, it might
be said that lovers are useful to their countries, since the love of Harmodius and
Aristogeiton caused the downfall of the tyrant Hipparchus. Or, again, that
Dionysius is a thief, since he is a vicious man—there is, of course, no deduction here;
not every vicious man is a thief, though every thief is a vicious man.

15   Another line relies on the accidental. An instance is what Polycrates says of the
mice, that they came to the rescue because they gnawed through the bowstrings. Or
it might be maintained that an invitation to dinner is a great honour, for it was
because he was *not* invited that Achilles was angered with the Greeks at Tenedos.
In fact, what angered him was the insult involved; it was a mere accident that this
was the particular form that the insult took.

20   Another is the argument from consequence. In the *Alexander,* for instance, it
is argued that Paris must have had a lofty disposition, since he despised society and
lived by himself on Mount Ida: because lofty people do this kind of thing, therefore
Paris too, we are to suppose, had a lofty soul. Or, if a man dresses fashionably and
roams around at night, he is a rake, since that is the way rakes behave. Another
25   similar argument points out that beggars sing and dance in temples, and that exiles
can live wherever they please, and that such privileges are at the disposal of those
we account happy; and therefore every one might be regarded as happy if only he
has those privileges. What matters, however, is the *circumstances* under which the
privileges are enjoyed. Hence this line too falls under the head of fallacies by
omission.

30   Another line consists in representing as causes things which are not causes, on
the ground that they happened along with or before the event in question. They
assume that, because B happens *after* A, it happens *because* of A. Politicians are
especially fond of taking this line. Thus Demades said that the policy of
Demosthenes was the cause of all the mischief, for after it the war occurred.

[46]Omitting ὅρση.

Another line consists in leaving out any mention of time and circumstances. 35
E.g. the argument that Paris was justified in taking Helen, since her father left her
free to choose: here the freedom was presumably not perpetual; it could only refer to
her first choice, beyond which her father's authority could not go. Or again, one
might say that to strike a free man is an act of wanton outrage; but it is not so in 1402ª1
every case—only when it is unprovoked.

Again, a spurious deduction may, as in eristical discussions, be based on the
confusion of the absolute with that which is not absolute. As, in dialectic, for
instance, it may be argued that what-is-not *is*, on the ground that what-is-not *is* 5
what-is-not; or that the unknown can be known, on the ground that it can be known
to *be* unknown: so also in rhetoric a spurious enthymeme may be based on the
confusion of some particular probability with absolute probability. Now no
particular probability is universally probable: as Agathon says,

> One might perchance say this was probable—   10
> That things improbable oft will hap to men.[47]

For what is improbable does happen, and therefore it is probable that improbable
things *will* happen. Granted this, one might argue that what is improbable is
probable. But this is not true absolutely. As, in eristic, the imposture comes from not
adding any clause specifying relationship or reference or manner; so here it arises 15
because the probability in question is not general but specific. It is of this
commonplace that Corax's *Art of Rhetoric* is composed. If the accused is not open
to the charge—for instance if a weakling is tried for violent assault—the defence is
that he was not likely to do such a thing. But if he *is* open to the charge—i.e. if he is
a *strong* man—the defence is still that he was not likely to do such a thing, since he 20
could be sure that people would think he *was* likely to do it. And so with any other
charge: the accused must be either open or not open to it: both seem probable, but
one is probable and the other not so absolutely but only in the way we have
described. This sort of argument illustrates what is meant by making the worse
argument seem the better. Hence people were right in objecting to the training 25
Protagoras undertook to give them. It was a fraud; the probability it handled was
not genuine but spurious, and has a place in no art except Rhetoric and Eristic.

25 · Enthymemes, genuine and apparent, have now been described; the next 30
subject is their refutation.

An argument may be refuted either by a counter-deduction or by bringing an
objection. It is clear that counter-deductions can be built up from the same
commonplaces; for the materials of deductions are reputable opinions, and such
opinions often contradict each other. Objections, as appears in the *Topics*,[48] may be 35
raised in four ways—either by directly attacking your opponent's own statement, or
by putting forward another statement like it, or by putting forward a statement
contrary to it, or by quoting previous decisions.

[47]Frag. 9 Nauck.
[48]See *Topics* VIII 10.

By 'attacking your opponent's own statement' I mean, for instance, this: if his enthymeme should assert that love is always good, the objection can be brought in two ways, either by making the general statement that all want is an evil, or by making the particular one that there would be no talk of Caunian love if there were not evil loves as well as good ones.

An objection from a contrary statement is raised when, for instance, the opponent's enthymeme having concluded that a good man does good to all his friends, you object, 'But a bad man does not do evil to all his friends'.

An example of an objection from a like statement is, the enthymeme having shown that ill-used men always hate their ill-users, to reply, 'But well-used men do not always love those who used them well'.

The decisions mentioned are those proceeding from well-known men; for instance, if the enthymeme employed has concluded that some allowance ought to be made for drunken offenders, since they did not know what they were doing, the objection will be, 'Pittacus, then, deserves no approval, or he would not have prescribed specially severe penalties for offences due to drunkenness'.

Enthymemes are based upon one or other of four things: probabilities, examples, evidences, signs. Enthymemes based upon probabilities are those which argue from what is, or is supposed to be, usually true. Enthymemes based upon example are those which proceed from one or more similar cases, arrive at a general proposition, and then argue deductively to a particular inference. Enthymemes based upon evidences are those which argue from the inevitable and invariable. Enthymemes based upon signs are those which argue from some universal or particular proposition, true or false.

Now as a probability is that which happens usually but not always, enthymemes founded upon probabilities can, it is clear, always be refuted by raising some objection. The refutation is not genuine but spurious; for it consists in showing not that your opponent's premiss is not probable, but only in showing that it is not inevitably true. Hence it is always in defence rather than in accusation that it is possible to gain an advantage by using this fallacy. For the accuser uses probabilities to prove his case: and to refute a conclusion as improbable is not the same thing as to refute it as not inevitable. Any argument based upon what usually happens is always open to objection: otherwise it would not happen usually and be a probability but hold always and be necessary. But the judges think, if the refutation takes this form, either that the accuser's case is not probable or that they must not decide it; which, as we said, is a false piece of reasoning. For they ought to decide by considering not merely what *must* be true but also what is *likely* to be true: this is, indeed, the meaning of 'giving a verdict in accordance with one's honest opinion'. Therefore it is not enough for the defendant to refute the accusation by proving that the charge is not *bound* to be true: he must do so by showing that it is not *likely* to be true. For this purpose his objection must state what is more usually true than the statement attacked. It may do so in either of two ways: either in respect of time or in respect of the facts. It will be most convincing if it does so in both respects; for if the thing in question happens *oftener* thus, the probability is greater.

Signs, and enthymemes based upon them, can be refuted even if the facts are correct, as was said at the outset. For we have shown in the *Analytics*[49] that every   5
sign is non-deductive.

Enthymemes depending on examples may be refuted in the same way as probabilities. If we have a single negative instance, the argument is refuted, in so far as it is proved not inevitable, even though the positive examples are more similar and more frequent. Otherwise, we must contend that the present case is dissimilar, or that its conditions are dissimilar, or that it is different in some way or other.   10

It will be impossible to refute evidences and enthymemes resting on them, by showing in any way that they are non-deductive: this, too, we see from the *Analytics*.[50] All we can do is to show that the fact alleged does not exist. If there is no doubt that it does, and that it is an evidence, refutation now becomes impossible;   15
for this is equivalent to a demonstration which is clear in every respect.

26 · Amplification and depreciation are not an element of enthymeme. By an element I mean the same thing as a commonplace; for an element is a commonplace embracing a large number of particular kinds of enthymeme. Amplification and depreciation are used to show that a thing is great or small; just   20
as there are other kinds used to show that a thing is good or bad, just or unjust, and anything else of the sort. All these things are the *subject-matter* of deductions and enthymemes; none of these is a commonplace for an enthymeme; no more, therefore, are amplification and depreciation.

Nor are refutative enthymemes a species. For it is clear that refutation consists   25
either in offering proof or in raising an objection, and that we prove the opposite of our adversary's statements. Thus, if he shows that a thing has happened, we show that it has not; if he shows that it has not happened, we show that it has. This, then, could not be the distinction, since the same means are employed by both parties,   30
enthymemes being adduced to show that the fact is or is not so-and-so. An objection, on the other hand, is not an enthymeme at all, but as was said in the *Topics*,[51] it consists in stating some opinion from which it will be clear that our opponent has not reasoned correctly or has made a false assumption.

Three points must be studied in making a speech; and we have now completed the account of examples, maxims, enthymemes, and in general the *thought-element*—the way to invent and refute arguments. We have next to discuss   1403b1
language and arrangement.

BOOK III

1 · In making a speech one must study three points: first, the means of   5
producing persuasion; second, the language; third, the proper arrangement of the various parts of the speech. We have already specified the sources of persuasion. We

[49]*Prior Analytics* II 27.   [50]*Prior Analytics* II 27.   [51]*Topics* I 10.

10 have shown that these are three in number; what they are; and why there are only these three; for persuasion is in every case effected either by working on the emotions of the judges themselves, by giving them the right impression of the speakers' character, or by proving the truth of the statements made.

Enthymemes also have been described, and the sources from which they should be derived; there being both special lines of argument for enthymemes and commonplaces.

15 Our next subject will be language. For it is not enough to know *what* we ought to say; we must also say it *as* we ought; much help is thus afforded towards producing the right impression of a speech. The first question to receive attention was naturally the one that comes first naturally—how persuasion can be produced

20 from the facts themselves. The second is how to set these facts out in language. A third would be the proper method of delivery; this is a thing that affects the success of a speech greatly; but hitherto the subject has been neglected. Indeed, it was long before it found a way into the arts of tragic drama and epic recitation: at first poets acted their tragedies themselves. It is plain that delivery has just as much to do with

25 oratory as with poetry. (In connexion with poetry, it has been studied by Glaucon of Teos among others.) It is, essentially, a matter of the right management of the voice to express the various emotions—of speaking loudly, softly, or between the two; of

30 high, low, or intermediate pitch; of the various rhythms that suit various subjects. These are the three things—volume of sound, modulation of pitch, and rhythm— that a speaker bears in mind. It is those who *do* bear them in mind who usually win prizes in the dramatic contests; and just as in drama the actors now count for more than the poets, so it is in the contests of public life, owing to the defects of our

35 political institutions. No systematic treatise upon the rules of delivery has yet been composed; indeed, even the study of language made no progress till late in the day.

1404ª1 Besides, delivery is—very properly—not regarded as an elevated subject of inquiry. Still, the whole business of rhetoric being concerned with appearances, we must pay attention to the subject of delivery, unworthy though it is, because we cannot do without it. The right thing in speaking really is that we should be satisfied not to

5 annoy our hearers, without trying to delight them: we ought in fairness to fight our case with no help beyond the bare facts; nothing, therefore, should matter except the proof of those facts. Still, as has been already said, other things affect the result considerably, owing to the defects of our hearers. The arts of language cannot help

10 having a small but real importance, whatever it is we have to expound to others: the way in which a thing is said does affect its intelligibility. Not, however, so much importance as people think. All such arts are fanciful and meant to charm the hearer. Nobody uses fine language when teaching geometry.

When the principles of delivery have been worked out, they will produce the same effect as on the stage. But only very slight attempts to deal with them have been made and by a few people, as by Thrasymachus in his 'Appeals to Pity'.

15 Dramatic ability is a natural gift, and can hardly be systematically taught. The principles of language can be so taught, and therefore we have men of ability in this direction too, who win prizes in their turn, as well as those speakers who excel in

delivery—speeches of the written kind owe more of their effect to their language than to their thought.

It was naturally the poets who first set the movement going; for words represent things, and they had also the human voice at their disposal, which of all our organs can best represent other things. Thus the arts of recitation and acting were formed, and others as well. Now it was because poets seemed to win fame through their fine language when their thoughts were simple enough, that language at first took a poetical colour, e.g. that of Gorgias. Even now most uneducated people think that poetical language makes the finest discourses. That is not true: the language of prose is distinct from that of poetry. This is shown by the state of things to-day, when even the language of tragedy has altered its character. Just as iambics were adopted, instead of tetrameters, because they are the most prose-like of all metres, so tragedy has given up all those words, not used in ordinary talk, which decorated the early drama and are still used by the writers of hexameter poems. It is therefore ridiculous to imitate a poetical manner which the poets themselves have dropped; and it is now plain that we have not to treat in detail the whole question of language, but may confine ourselves to that part of it which concerns our present subject, rhetoric. The other part of it has been discussed in the treatise on the *Art of Poetry*.

2 · We may, then, start from the observations there made, and the stipulation that language to be good must be clear, as is proved by the fact that speech which fails to convey a plain meaning will fail to do just what speech has to do. It must also be appropriate, avoiding both meanness and undue evaluation; poetical language is certainly free from meanness, but it is not appropriate to prose. Clearness is secured by using the words (nouns and verbs alike) that are current and ordinary. Freedom from meanness, and positive adornment too, are secured by using the other words mentioned in the *Art of Poetry*. Such variation makes the language appear more stately. People do not feel towards strangers as they do towards their own countrymen, and the same thing is true of their feeling for language. It is therefore well to give to everyday speech an unfamiliar air: people like what strikes them, and are struck by what is out of the way. In verse such effects are common, and there they are fitting: the persons and things there spoken of are comparatively remote from ordinary life; for even in poetry, it is not quite appropriate that fine language should be used by a slave or a very young man, or about very trivial subjects: even in poetry the style, to be appropriate, must sometimes be toned down, though at other times heightened. All the more so in prose, where the subject-matter is less exalted. We can now see that a writer must disguise his art and give the impression of speaking naturally and not artificially. Naturalness is persuasive, artificiality is the contrary; for our hearers are prejudiced and think we have some design against them, as if we were mixing their wines for them. It is like the difference between the quality of Theodorus' voice and the voices of all other actors: his really seems to be that of the character who is speaking, theirs do not. We can hide our purpose successfully by taking the single words of our composition from

25 the speech of ordinary life. This is done in poetry by Euripides, who was the first to show the way to his successors.

Language is composed of nouns and verbs. Nouns are of the various kinds considered in the treatise on poetry. Strange words, compound words, and invented
30 words must be used sparingly and on few occasions: on what occasions we shall state later. The reason for this restriction has been already indicated: they depart from what is suitable, in the direction of excess. In the language of prose, besides the regular and proper terms for things, metaphorical terms only can be used with advantage. This we gather from the fact that these two classes of terms, the proper
35 or regular and the metaphorical—these and no others—are used by everybody in conversation. We can now see that a good writer can produce a style that is distinguished without being obtrusive, and is at the same time clear, thus satisfying our definition of good oratorical prose. Words of ambiguous meaning are chiefly useful to enable the sophist to mislead his hearers. Synonyms are useful to the poet,
1405ª1 by which I mean words whose ordinary meaning is the same, e.g. πορεύεσθαι (*advancing*) and βαδίζειν (*proceeding*); these two are ordinary words and have the same meaning.

In the *Art of Poetry,* as we have already said, will be found definitions of these
5 kinds of words; a classification of metaphors; and mention of the fact that metaphor is of great value both in poetry and in prose. Prose-writers must, however, pay specially careful attention to metaphor, because their other resources are scantier than those of poets. Metaphor, moreover, gives style clearness, charm, and distinction as nothing else can: and it is not a thing whose use can be taught by one
10 man to another. Metaphors, like epithets, must be fitting, which means that they must fairly correspond to the thing signified: failing this, their inappropriateness will be conspicuous: the want of harmony between two things is emphasized by their being placed side by side. It is like having to ask ourselves what dress will suit an old man; certainly not the crimson cloak that suits a young man. And if you wish to pay
15 a compliment, you must take your metaphor from something better in the same line; if to disparage, from something worse. To illustrate my meaning: since opposites are in the same class, you do what I have suggested if you say that a man who begs prays, and a man who prays begs; for praying and begging are both varieties of
20 asking. So Iphicrates called Callias a mendicant priest instead of a torch-bearer, and Callias replied that Iphicrates must be uninitiated or he would have called him not a mendicant priest but a torch-bearer. Both are religious titles, but one is honourable and the other is not. Again, somebody calls actors hangers-on of Dionysus, but they call themselves artists: each of these terms is a metaphor, the one
25 intended to throw dirt at the actor, the other to dignify him. And pirates now call themselves purveyors. We can thus call a crime a mistake, or a mistake a crime. We can say that a thief took a thing, or that he plundered his victim. An expression like that of Euripides' Telephus,

30 King of the oar, on Mysia's coast he landed,[1]

---

[1] Frag. 705 Nauck.

is inappropriate; the word 'king' goes beyond the dignity of the subject, and so the art is *not* concealed. A metaphor may be amiss because the very syllables of the words conveying it fail to indicate sweetness of vocal utterance. Thus Dionysius the Brazen in his elegies calls poetry 'Calliope's screech'. Poetry and screeching are both, to be sure, vocal utterances. But the metaphor is bad, because the sounds of screeching, unlike those of poetry, are discordant and unmeaning. Further, in using metaphors to give names to nameless things, we must draw them not from remote but from kindred and similar things, so that the kinship is clearly perceived as soon as the words are said. Thus in the celebrated riddle

> I marked how a man glued bronze with fire to another man's body,[2]   1405ᵇ1

the process is nameless; but both it and gluing are a kind of application, and that is why the application of the cupping-glass is here called a 'gluing'. Good riddles do, in general, provide us with satisfactory metaphors; for metaphors imply riddles, and therefore a good riddle can furnish a good metaphor. Further, the materials of metaphors must be beautiful; and the beauty, like the ugliness, of all words may, as Licymnius says, lie in their sound or in their meaning. Further, there is a third consideration—one that upsets the fallacious argument of the sophist Bryson, that there is no such thing as foul language, because in whatever words you put a given thing your meaning is the same. This is untrue. One term may describe a thing more truly than another, may be more like it, and set it more intimately before our eyes. Besides, two different words will represent a thing in two different lights; so on this ground also one term must be held fairer or fouler than another. For both of two terms will indicate what *is* fair, or what *is* foul, but not simply their fairness or their foulness, or if so, at any rate not in an equal degree. The materials of metaphor must be beautiful to the ear, to the understanding, to the eye or some other physical sense. It is better, for instance, to say 'rosy-fingered morn', than 'crimson-fingered' or, worse still, 'red-fingered morn'. The epithets that we apply, too, may have a bad and ugly aspect, as when Orestes is called a mother-slayer; or a better one, as when he is called his father's avenger.[3] Simonides, when the victor in the mule-race offered him a small fee, refused to write him an ode, because, he said, it was so unpleasant to write odes to half-asses; but on receiving an adequate fee, he wrote

> Hail to you, daughters of storm-footed steeds,

though of course they were daughters of asses too. The same effect is attained by the use of diminutives, which make a bad thing less bad and a good thing less good. Take, for instance, the banter of Aristophanes in the *Babylonians* where he uses 'goldlet' for 'gold', 'cloaklet' for 'cloak', 'scofflet' for 'scoff', and 'plaguelet'. But alike in using epithets and in using diminutives we must be wary and must observe the mean.

3 · Frigidities in language may take any of four forms:—The misuse of compound words. Lycophron, for instance, talks of the 'many-visaged heaven'

---

[2]Cleobulina, frag. 1 West.   [3]Euripides, *Orestes* 1587–8.

above the 'giant-crested earth', and again the 'strait-pathed shore'; and Gorgias of
the 'pauper-poet flatterer' and 'oath-breaking and ever-oath-keeping'. Alcidamas
uses such expressions as 'the soul filling with rage and face becoming flame-
flushed', and 'he thought their enthusiasm would be issue-fraught' and 'issue-
fraught he made the persuasion of his words', and 'sombre-hued is the floor of the
sea'. The way all these words are compounded makes them, we feel, fit for verse
only. This, then, is one form in which bad taste is shown.

Another is the employment of strange words. For instance, Lycophron talks of
'the towering Xerxes' and 'spoliative Sciron', Alcidamas of 'a toy for poetry' and
'the witlessness of nature', and says 'whetted with the unmitigated temper of his
spirit'.

A third form is the use of long, unseasonable, or frequent epithets. It is
appropriate enough for a poet to talk of 'white milk', but in prose such epithets are
sometimes lacking in appropriateness or, when spread too thickly, plainly reveal the
author turning his prose into poetry. Of course we must use some epithets, since
they lift our style above the usual level and give it an air of distinction. But we must
aim at the due mean, or the result will be worse than if we took no trouble at all; we
shall get something actually bad instead of something merely not good. That is why
the epithets of Alcidamas seem so frigid; he does not use them as the seasoning of
the meat, but as the meat itself, so numerous and swollen and obtrusive are they.
For instance, he does not say 'sweat', but 'the moist sweat'; not 'to the Isthmian
games', but 'to the world-concourse of the Isthmian games'; not 'laws', but 'the laws
that are monarchs of states'; not 'at a run', but 'his heart impelling him to speed of
foot'; not 'a school of the Muses', but 'Nature's school of the Muses had he
inherited'; and so 'frowning care of heart', and 'achiever' not of 'popularity' but of
'universal popularity', and 'dispenser of pleasure to his audience', and 'he concealed
it' not 'with boughs' but 'with boughs of the forest trees', and 'he clothed' not 'his
body' but 'his body's nakedness', and 'his soul's desire was counter-imitative' (this
at one and the same time a compound and an epithet, so that it seems a poet's
effort), and 'so extravagant the excess of his wickedness'. We thus see how the
inappropriateness of such poetical language imports absurdity and frigidity into
speeches, as well as the obscurity that comes from all this verbosity—for when the
sense is plain, you only obscure and spoil its clearness by piling up words.

The ordinary use of compound words is where there is no term for a thing and
some compound can be easily formed, like 'pastime' ($\chi\rho o\nu o\tau\rho\iota\beta\hat{\epsilon}\iota\nu$); but if this is
much done, the prose character disappears entirely. We now see why the language
of compounds is just the thing for writers of dithyrambs, who love sonorous noises;
strange words for writers of epic poetry, which is a proud and stately affair; [and
metaphor for iambic verse, the metre which (as has been already said) is widely
used to-day.][4]

There remains the fourth region in which frigidity may be shown, metaphor.
Metaphors like other things may be inappropriate. Some are so because they are

[4]Excised by Kassel.

ridiculous; they are indeed used by comic as well as tragic poets. Others are too grand and theatrical; and these, if they are far-fetched, may also be obscure. For instance, Gorgias talks of 'events that are green and full of sap', and says 'foul was the deed you sowed and evil the harvest you reaped'. That is too much like poetry. Alcidamas, again, called philosophy 'a bulwark of the laws', and the *Odyssey* 'a goodly looking-glass of human life', and talked about 'offering no such toy to poetry': all these explanations fail, for the reasons given, to carry the hearer with them. The address of Gorgias to the swallow, when she had let her droppings fall on him as she flew overhead, is in the best tragic manner. He said, 'Nay, shame, O Philomela'. Considering her as a bird, you could not call her act shameful; considering her as a girl, you could; and so it was a good gibe to address her as what she was once and not as what she is.

4 · The simile also is a metaphor; the difference is but slight. When the poet says:

He leapt on the foe as a lion,[5]

this is a simile; when he says of him 'the lion leapt', it is a metaphor—here, since both are courageous, he has transferred to Achilles the name of 'lion'. Similes are useful in prose as well as in verse; but not often, since they are of the nature of poetry. They are to be employed just as metaphors are employed, since they are really the same thing except for the difference mentioned.

The following are examples of similes. Androtion said of Idrieus that he was like a terrier let off the chain, that flies at you and bites you—Idrieus too was savage now that he was let out of *his* chains. Theodamas compared Archidamus to a Euxenus who could not do geometry—a proportional simile, implying that Euxenus is an Archidamus who *can* do geometry. In Plato's *Republic* those who strip the dead are compared to curs which bite the stones thrown at them but do not touch the thrower; and there is the simile about the Athenian people, who are compared to a ship's captain who is strong but a little deaf; and the one about poets' verses, which are likened to persons who lack beauty but possess youthful freshness—when the freshness has faded the charm perishes, and so with verses when broken up into prose.[6] Pericles compared the Samians to children who take their pap but go on crying; and the Boeotians to holm-oaks, because they were ruining one another by civil wars just as one oak causes another oak's fall. Demosthenes said that the Athenian people were like sea-sick men on board ship. Again, Democrates compared the political orators to nurses who swallow the bit of food themselves and then smear the children's lips with the spittle. Antisthenes compared the lean Cephisodotus to frankincense, because it was his consumption that gave one pleasure. All these ideas may be expressed either as similes or as metaphors; those which succeed as metaphors will obviously do well also as similes,

---

[5]Cf. *Iliad* XX 164.
[6]*Republic* 469E, 488A, 601B.

and similes, with the explanation omitted, will appear as metaphors. But the proportional metaphor must always apply reciprocally to either of its co-ordinate terms. For instance, if a drinking bowl is the shield of Dionysus, a shield may fittingly be called the drinking-bowl of Ares.

5 · Such, then, are the ingredients of which speech is composed. The foundation of good style is correctness of language, which falls under five heads. First, the proper use of connecting words, and the arrangement of them in the natural sequence which some of them require. For instance, the connective μέν (e.g. ἐγὼ μέν) requires the correlative δέ (e.g. ὁ δέ). The answering word must be brought in before the first has been forgotten, and not be widely separated from it; nor, except in the few cases where this is appropriate, is another connective to be introduced before the one required. Consider the sentence, 'But I, as soon as he told me (for Cleon had come begging and praying), took them along and set out'. In this sentence many connecting words are inserted in front of the one required to complete the sense; and if there is a long interval, the result is obscurity. One merit, then, of good style lies in the right use of connecting words. The second lies in calling things by their own special names and not by vague general ones. The third is to avoid ambiguities; unless, indeed, you definitely desire to be ambiguous, as those do who have nothing to say but are pretending to mean something. Such people are apt to put that sort of thing into verse. Empedocles, for instance, by his long circumlocutions imposes on his hearers; these are affected in the same way as most people are when they listen to diviners, whose ambiguous utterances are received with nods of acquiescence—

Croesus by crossing the Halys will ruin a mighty realm.

Diviners use these vague generalities about the matter in hand because their predictions are thus, as a rule, less likely to be falsified. We are more likely to be right, in the game of 'odd and even', if we simply guess 'even' or 'odd' than if we guess at the actual number; and the oracle-monger is more likely to be right if he simply says that a thing will happen than if he says *when* it will happen, and therefore he refuses to add a definite date. All these ambiguities have the same sort of effect, and are to be avoided unless we have some such object as that mentioned. A fourth rule is to observe Protagoras' classification of nouns into masculine, feminine and neuter; for these distinctions also must be correctly given. 'Upon her arrival she said her say and departed (ἡ δ᾽ ἐλθοῦσα καὶ διαλεχθεῖσα ᾤχετο)'. A fifth rule is to express the singular and the plural by the correct wording, e.g. 'Having come, they struck me (οἱ δ᾽ ἐλθόντες ἔτυπτόν με)'.

It is a general rule that a written composition should be easy to read and therefore easy to deliver. This cannot be so where there are many connecting words or clauses, or where punctuation is hard, as in the writings of Heracleitus. To punctuate Heracleitus is no easy task, because we often cannot tell whether a particular word belongs to what precedes or what follows it. Thus, at the outset of his treatise he says, 'Though this truth is always men understand it not', where it is not clear to which of the two clauses the word 'always' belongs. Further, solecism will result if you annex to two terms a third which does not suit them both. Thus if you are talking of sound and colour 'perceive' will apply to both, 'see' will not. 20 Obscurity is also caused if, when you intend to insert a number of details, you do not first make your meaning clear; for instance, if you say, 'I meant, after telling him this, that, and the other thing, to set out', rather than something of this kind 'I meant to set out after telling him; then this, that, and the other thing occurred'. 25

6 · The following suggestions will help to give your language impressiveness. Describe a thing instead of naming it: do not say 'circle', but 'that surface which extends equally from the middle every way'. To achieve conciseness, do the opposite—put the name instead of the description. When mentioning anything ugly or unseemly, use its name if it is the description that is ugly, and describe it if it is 30 the name that is ugly. Represent things with the help of metaphors and epithets, being careful to avoid poetical effects. Use plural for singular, as in poetry, where one finds

Unto havens Achaean,[7]

though only one haven is meant, and

Here are my letter's many-leaved folds.[8]   35

Do not bracket two words under one article, but put one article with each; e.g. τῆς γυναικὸς τῆς ἡμετέρας. The reverse to secure conciseness; e.g. τῆς ἡμετέρας γυναικός. Use plenty of connecting words; conversely, to secure conciseness, dispense with connectives, while still preserving connexion; e.g. 'having gone and spoken', and 1408ᵃ1 'having gone, I spoke', respectively. And the practice of Antimachus, too, is useful—to describe a thing by mentioning attributes it does not possess; as he does in talking of Teumessus—

There is a little wind-swept knoll . . .

A subject can be developed indefinitely along these lines. You may apply this method of treatment by negation either to good or to bad qualities, according to 5 which your subject requires. It is from this source that the poets draw expressions such as the 'stringless' or 'lyreless' melody, thus forming epithets out of negations. This device is popular in proportional metaphors, as when the trumpet's note is called 'a lyreless melody'.

7 · Your language will be *appropriate* if it expresses emotion and character, 10 and if it corresponds to its subject. 'Correspondence to subject' means that we must neither speak casually about weighty matters, nor solemnly about trivial ones; nor must we add ornamental epithets to commonplace nouns, or the effect will be comic, as in the works of Cleophon, who can use phrases as absurd as 'O queenly 15

[7]Frag. adesp. 83 Nauck.   [8]Euripides, *Iphigenia in Tauris*, 727.

fig-tree'. To express emotion, you will employ the language of anger in speaking of outrage; the language of disgust and discreet reluctance to utter a word when speaking of impiety or foulness; the language of exultation for a tale of glory, and that of humiliation for a tale of pity; and so in all other cases.

20   This aptness of language is one thing that makes people believe in the truth of your story: their minds draw the false conclusion that you are to be trusted from the fact that others behave as you do when things are as you describe them; and therefore they take your story to be true, whether it is so or not. Besides, an emotional speaker always makes his audience feel with him, even when there is

25   nothing in his arguments; which is why many speakers try to overwhelm their audience by mere noise.

Furthermore, this way of proving your story by displaying these signs of its genuineness expresses your personal character. Each class of men, each type of disposition, will have its own appropriate way of letting the truth appear. Under 'class' I include differences of age, as boy, man, or old man; of sex, as man or woman; of nationality, as Spartan or Thessalian. By 'dispositions' I here mean those

30   dispositions only which determine the character of a man's life, for it is not every disposition that does this. If, then, a speaker uses the very words which are in keeping with a particular disposition, he will reproduce the corresponding character; for a rustic and an educated man will not say the same things nor speak in the same way. Again, some impression is made upon an audience by a device which speech-writers employ to nauseous excess, when they say 'Who does not know this?'

35   or 'It is known to everybody'. The hearer is ashamed of his ignorance, and agrees with the speaker, so as to have a share of the knowledge that everybody else possesses.

All the variations of oratorical style are capable of being used in season or out

1408^{b}1   of season. The best way to counteract any exaggeration is the well-worn device by which the speaker puts in some criticism of himself; for then people feel it must be all right for him to talk thus, since he certainly knows what he is doing. Further, it is better not to have everything always just corresponding to everything else—your

5   purpose will thus be hidden. I mean for instance, if your words are harsh, you should not extend this harshness to your voice and your countenance and have everything else in keeping. If you do, the artificial character of each detail becomes apparent; whereas if you adopt one device and not another, you are using art all the same and yet nobody notices it. (To be sure, if mild sentiments are expressed in harsh tones

10   and harsh sentiments in mild tones, you become comparatively unconvincing.) Compound words, fairly plentiful epithets, and strange words best suit an emotional speech. We forgive an angry man for talking about a wrong as 'heaven-high' or 'colossal'; and we excuse such language when the speaker has his hearers already in

15   his hands and has stirred them deeply either by praise or blame or anger or affection, as Isocrates, for instance, does at the end of his *Panegyric,* with his 'name and fame' and 'in that they brooked'. Men do speak in this strain when they are deeply stirred, and so, once the audience is in a like state of feeling, approval of course follows. This is why such language is fitting in poetry, which is an inspired

thing. This language, then, should be used either under stress of emotion, or
ironically, after the manner of Gorgias and of the passages in the *Phaedrus*.   20

8 · The form of a prose composition should be neither metrical nor destitute
of rhythm. The metrical form destroys the hearer's trust by its artificial appearance, and at the same time it diverts his attention, making him watch for metrical
recurrences, just as children catch up the herald's question, 'Whom does the   25
freedman choose as his advocate?', with the answer 'Cleon!' On the other hand,
unrhythmical language is too unlimited; we do not want the limitations of metre,
but some limitation we must have, or the effect will be vague and unsatisfactory.
Now it is number that limits all things; and it is the numerical limitation of the form
of a composition that constitutes rhythm, of which metres are definite sections.
Prose, then, is to be rhythmical, but not metrical, or it will become not prose   30
but verse. It should not even have too precise a prose rhythm, and therefore should
only be rhythmical to a certain extent.
Of the various rhythms, the heroic has dignity, but lacks the tones of the
spoken language. The iambic is the very language of ordinary people, so that in
common talk iambic lines occur oftener than any others: but in a speech we need   35
dignity and the power of taking the hearer out of his ordinary self. The trochee is too
much akin to wild dancing: we can see this in tetrameter verse, which is one of the   1409ª1
trochaic rhythms.
There remains the paean, which speakers began to use in the time of
Thrasymachus, though they had then no name to give it. The paean is a third class
of rhythm, closely akin to both the two already mentioned; it has in it the ratio of
three to two, whereas the other two kinds have the ratio of one to one, and two to one   5
respectively. Between the two last ratios comes the ratio of one-and-a-half to one,
which is that of the paean.
Now the other two kinds of rhythm must be rejected in writing prose, partly for
the reasons given, and partly because they are too metrical; and the paean must be
adopted, since from this alone of the rhythms mentioned no definite metre arises,
and therefore it is the least obtrusive of them. At present the same form of paean is   10
employed at the beginning as at the end of sentences, whereas the end should differ
from the beginning. There are two opposite kinds of paean, one of which is suitable
to the beginning of a sentence, where it is indeed actually used; this is the kind that
begins with a long syllable and ends with three short ones, as

$$\bar{\Delta}\alpha\bar{\lambda}o\breve{\gamma}\epsilon\breve{\nu}\breve{\epsilon}s \mid \bar{\epsilon}\breve{i}\tau\epsilon \ \Lambda\breve{\upsilon}\breve{\kappa}\breve{i} \mid \bar{\alpha}\bar{\nu},$$

and

$$\mathrm{X}\bar{\rho}\breve{\upsilon}\breve{\sigma}\breve{\epsilon}o\breve{\kappa}\acute{o}\mu \mid \bar{\alpha} \ "\mathrm{E}\bar{\kappa}\breve{\alpha}\tau\breve{\epsilon} \mid \pi\bar{\alpha}\breve{i} \ \Delta\breve{\iota}\acute{o}s$$ 15

The other paean begins, conversely, with three short syllables and ends with a long
one, as

$$\breve{\mu}\epsilon\tau\breve{\alpha} \ \breve{\delta}\grave{\epsilon} \ \gamma\bar{\alpha}\nu \mid \breve{\upsilon}\breve{\delta}\breve{\alpha}\tau\breve{\alpha} \ \tau' \ \bar{\omega}\kappa \mid \breve{\epsilon}\alpha\nu\breve{\delta}\nu \ \bar{\eta} \mid \phi\bar{\alpha}\bar{\nu}\breve{\iota}\sigma\epsilon \ \nu\bar{\upsilon}\xi.$$

This kind of paean makes a real close: a short syllable can give no effect of finality, and therefore makes the rhythm appear truncated. A sentence should break off
20　with the long syllable: the fact that it is over should be indicated not by the scribe, or by his full stop, but by the rhythm itself.

We have now seen that our language must be rhythmical and not destitute of rhythm, and what rhythms, in what particular shape, make it so.

9 · The language of prose must be either free-running, with its parts united
25　by nothing except the connecting words, like the preludes in dithyrambs; or compact and antithetical, like the strophes of the old poets. The free-running style is the ancient one, e.g. 'Herein is set forth the inquiry of Herodotus the Thurian'.[9] Every one used this method formerly; not many do so now. By 'free-running' style I
30　mean the kind that has no natural stopping-places, and comes to a stop only because there is no more to say of that subject. This style is unsatisfying just because it goes on indefinitely—one always likes to sight a stopping-place in front of one: it is only at the goal that men in a race faint and collapse; while they see the end of the course before them, they can keep going. Such, then, is the free-running kind of style; the
35　compact is that which is in periods. By a period I mean a portion of speech that has in itself a beginning and an end, being at the same time not too big to be taken in at
1409ᵇ1　a glance. Language of this kind is satisfying and easy to follow. It is satisfying, because it is just the reverse of indefinite; and moreover, the hearer always feels that he is grasping something and has reached some definite conclusion; whereas it is unsatisfactory to see nothing in front of you and get nowhere. It is easy to follow,
5　because it can easily be remembered; and this because language when in periodic form can be numbered, and number is the easiest of all things to remember. That is why verse, which is measured, is always more easily remembered than prose, which is not: the measures of verse can be numbered. The period must, further, not be completed until the sense is complete: it must not be capable of breaking off abruptly, as may happen with the following iambic lines

10　　　　　　　　Calydon's soil is this; of Pelops' land[10]

By a wrong division of the words the hearer may take the meaning to be the reverse of what it is: for instance, in the passage quoted, one might imagine that Calydon is in the Peloponnesus.

A period may be either divided into several members or simple. The period of several members is a portion of speech complete in itself, divided into parts, and
15　easily delivered at a single breath—as a whole, that is; not by fresh breath being taken at the division. A member is one of the two parts of such a period. By a 'simple' period, I mean that which has only one member. The members, and the whole periods, should be neither curt nor long. A member which is too short often
20　makes the listener stumble; he is still expecting the rhythm to go on to the limit his mind has fixed for it; and if meanwhile he is pulled back by the speaker's stopping,

---

⁹Herodotus I i.　　⁰Euripides, frag. 515 Nauck.

the shock is bound to make him, so to speak, stumble. If, on the other hand, you go on too long, you make him feel left behind, like people who pass beyond the boundary before turning back. So too if a period is too long you turn it into a speech, or something like a dithyrambic prelude. The result is much like the preludes that Democritus of Chios jeered at Melanippides for writing instead of antistrophic stanzas—

> He that sets traps for another man's feet
> Is like to fall into them first;
> And long-winded preludes do harm to us all,
> But the preluder catches it worst.

Which applies likewise to long-membered orators. Periods whose members are altogether too short are not periods at all; and the result is to bring the hearer down with a crash.

The periodic style which is divided into members is of two kinds. It is either simply divided, as in 'I have often wondered at the conveners of national gatherings and the founders of athletic contests';[11] or it is antithetical, where, in each of the two members, one of one pair of opposites is put along with one of another pair, or the same word is used to bracket two opposites, as 'They aided both parties—not only those who stayed behind but those who accompanied them: for the latter they acquired new territory larger than that at home, and to the former they left territory at home that was large enough'. Here the contrasted words are 'staying behind' and 'accompanying', 'enough' and 'larger'. So in the example, 'Both to those who want to acquire property and to those who desire to enjoy it', where 'enjoyment' is contrasted with 'acquisition'. Again, 'it often happens in such enterprises that the wise men fail and the fools succeed'; 'they were awarded the prize of valour immediately, and won the command of the sea not long afterwards'; 'to sail through the mainland and march through the sea, by bridging the Hellespont and cutting through Athos'; 'nature gave them their country and law took it away again'; 'some of them perished in misery, others were saved in disgrace'; 'Athenian citizens keep foreigners in their houses as servants, while the city of Athens allows her allies by thousands to live as the foreigner's slaves'; and 'to possess in life or to bequeath at death'. There is also what some one said about Peitholaus and Lycophron in a lawcourt, 'These men used to sell you when they were at home, and now they have come to you here and bought you'. All these passages have the structure described above. Such a form of speech is satisfying, because the significance of contrasted ideas is easily felt, especially when they are thus put side by side, and also because it has the effect of a logical argument; it is by putting two opposing conclusions side by side that you prove one of them false.

Such, then, is the nature of *antithesis*. *Parisosis* is making the two members of a period equal in length. *Paromoeosis* is making the extreme words of both members like each other. This must happen either at the beginning or at the end of

[11]This and the following quotations are from Isocrates' *Panegyricus.*

each member. If at the beginning, the resemblance must always be between whole words; at the end, between final syllables or inflexions of the same word or the same word repeated. Thus, at the beginning

$$\mathring{\alpha}\gamma\rho\grave{o}\nu\ \gamma\grave{\alpha}\rho\ \mathring{\epsilon}'\lambda\alpha\beta\epsilon\nu\ \mathring{\alpha}\rho\gamma\grave{o}\nu\ \pi\alpha\rho'\ \alpha\mathring{\upsilon}\tau o\mathring{\upsilon}^{12}$$

and

$$\delta\omega\rho\eta\tau o\acute{\iota}\ \tau'\ \mathring{\epsilon}\pi\acute{\epsilon}\lambda o\nu\tau o\ \pi\alpha\rho\acute{\alpha}\rho\rho\eta\tau o\acute{\iota}\ \tau'\ \mathring{\epsilon}\pi\acute{\epsilon}\epsilon\sigma\sigma\iota\nu.^{13}$$

At the end

30

$$\mathring{\omega}\acute{\eta}\theta\eta s\ \mathring{\alpha}\nu\ \alpha\mathring{\upsilon}\tau\grave{o}\nu\ o\mathring{\upsilon}\ \pi\alpha\iota\delta\acute{\iota}o\nu\ \tau\epsilon\tau o\kappa\acute{\epsilon}\nu\alpha\iota,\ \mathring{\alpha}\lambda\lambda'\ \alpha\mathring{\upsilon}\tau\grave{o}\nu\ \pi\alpha\iota\delta\acute{\iota}o\nu\ \gamma\epsilon\gamma o\nu\acute{\epsilon}\nu\alpha\iota,$$

and

$$\mathring{\epsilon}\nu\ \pi\lambda\acute{\epsilon}\iota\sigma\tau\alpha\iota s\ \delta\grave{\epsilon}\ \phi\rho o\nu\tau\grave{\iota}\sigma\iota\ \kappa\alpha\grave{\iota}\ \mathring{\epsilon}\nu\ \mathring{\epsilon}\lambda\alpha\chi\acute{\iota}\sigma\tau\alpha\iota s\ \mathring{\epsilon}\lambda\pi\acute{\iota}\sigma\iota\nu.$$

An example of inflexions of the same word is

$$\mathring{\alpha}'\xi\iota o s\ \delta\grave{\epsilon}\ \sigma\tau\alpha\theta\mathring{\eta}\nu\alpha\iota\ \chi\alpha\lambda\kappa o\mathring{\upsilon}s,\ o\mathring{\upsilon}\kappa\ \mathring{\alpha}'\xi\iota o s\ \mathring{\omega}\nu\ \chi\alpha\lambda\kappa o\mathring{\upsilon};$$

Of the same word repeated,

35

$$\sigma\grave{\upsilon}\ \delta'\ \alpha\mathring{\upsilon}\tau\grave{o}\nu\ \kappa\alpha\grave{\iota}\ \zeta\mathring{\omega}\nu\tau\alpha\ \mathring{\epsilon}'\lambda\epsilon\gamma\epsilon s\ \kappa\alpha\kappa\mathring{\omega}s\ \kappa\alpha\grave{\iota}\ \nu\mathring{\upsilon}\nu\ \gamma\rho\acute{\alpha}\phi\epsilon\iota s\ \kappa\alpha\kappa\mathring{\omega}s.$$

Of one syllable,

$$\tau\acute{\iota}\ \mathring{\alpha}\nu\ \mathring{\epsilon}'\pi\alpha\theta\epsilon s\ \delta\epsilon\iota\nu\acute{o}\nu,\ \epsilon\mathring{\iota}\ \mathring{\alpha}'\nu\delta\rho'\ \epsilon\mathring{\iota}\delta\epsilon s\ \mathring{\alpha}\rho\gamma\acute{o}\nu;$$

1410ᵇ1 It is possible for the same sentence to have all these features together—*antithesis, parison,* and *homoeoteleuton.* (The possible beginnings of periods have been pretty fully enumerated in the *Theodectea.*) There are also spurious antitheses, like that of Epicharmus—

5   There one time I as their guest did stay,
           And they were my hosts on another day.¹⁴

10 · We may now consider the above points settled, and pass on to say something about the way to devise lively and taking sayings. Their actual invention can only come through natural talent or long practice; but this treatise may indicate the way it is done. We may deal with them by enumerating the different kinds of them. We will begin by remarking that we all naturally find it agreeable to get hold

10 of new ideas easily: words express ideas, and therefore those words are the most agreeable that enable us to get hold of new ideas. Now strange words simply puzzle us; ordinary words convey only what we know already; it is from metaphor that we can best get hold of something fresh. When the poet calls old age 'a withered stalk',¹⁵ he conveys a new idea, a new fact, to us by means of the general notion of

---

¹²Aristophanes, frag. 649 Kock.   ¹³*Iliad* IX 526.
¹⁴Frag. 20a Diels-Kranz.   ¹⁵*Odyssey* XIV 213.

'lost bloom', which is common to both things. The similes of the poets do the same, 15
and therefore, if they are good similes, give an effect of brilliance. The simile, as has
been said before, is a metaphor, differing from it only in the way it is put; and just
because it is longer it is less attractive. Besides, it does not say outright that 'this' *is*
'that', and therefore the hearer is less interested in the idea. We see, then, that both
speech and reasoning are lively in proportion as they make us seize a new idea 20
promptly. For this reason people are not much taken either by obvious arguments
(using the word 'obvious' to mean what is plain to everybody and needs no
investigation), nor by those which puzzle us when we hear them stated, but only by
those which convey their information to us as soon as we hear them, provided we
had not the information already; or which the mind only just fails to keep up with. 25
These two kinds do convey to us a sort of information: but the obvious and the
obscure kinds convey nothing, either at once or later on. It is these qualities, then,
that, so far as the meaning of what is said is concerned, make an argument
acceptable. So far as the language is concerned, it is the antithetical form that
appeals to us, e.g. 'judging that the peace common to all the rest was a war upon 30
their own private interests',[16] where there is an antithesis between war and peace. It
is also good to use metaphorical words; but the metaphors must not be far-fetched,
or they will be difficult to grasp, nor obvious, or they will have no effect. The words,
too, ought to set the scene before our eyes; for events ought to be seen in progress
rather than in prospect. So we must aim at these three points: antithesis, metaphor, 35
and actuality.

Of the four kinds of metaphor the most taking is the proportional kind. Thus 1411ᵃ1
Pericles, for instance, said that the vanishing from their country of the young men
who had fallen in the war was 'as if the spring were taken out of the year'. Leptines,
speaking of the Lacedaemonians, said that he would not have the Athenians let
Greece 'lose one of her two eyes'. When Chares was pressing for leave to be 5
examined upon his share in the Olynthiac war, Cephisodotus was indignant, saying
that he wanted his examination to take place 'while he had his fingers upon the
people's throat'. The same speaker once urged the Athenians to march to Euboea,
'with Miltiades' decree as their rations'. Iphicrates, indignant at the truce made by 10
the Athenians with Epidaurus and the neighbouring sea-board, said that they had
stripped themselves of their travelling-money for the journey of war. Peitholaus
called the state-galley 'the people's big stick', and Sestos 'the corn-bin of the
Peiraeus'. Pericles bade his countrymen remove Aegina, 'that eyesore of the
Peiraeus'. And Moerocles said he was no more a rascal than was a certain 15
respectable citizen he named, 'whose rascality was worth over thirty per cent per
annum to him, instead of a mere ten like his own'. There is also the iambic line of
Anaxandrides about the way his daughters put off marrying—

My daughters' marriage-bonds are overdue. 20

Polyeuctus said of a paralytic man named Speusippus that he could not keep quiet,

---

[16]Isocrates, *Philippus* 73.

'though fortune had fastened him in the pillory of disease'. Cephisodotus called
warships 'painted millstones'. Diogenes the Dog called taverns 'the mess-rooms of
25   Attica'. Aesion said that the Athenians had 'emptied' their town into Sicily: this is a
graphic metaphor. 'Till all Hellas shouted aloud' may be regarded as a metaphor,
and a graphic one again. Cephisodotus bade the Athenians take care not to hold too
30   many 'parades'. Isocrates used the same word of those who 'parade' at the national
festivals. Another example occurs in the Funeral Speech: 'It is fitting that Greece
should cut off her hair beside the tomb of those who fell at Salamis, since her
freedom and their valour are buried in the same grave'. Even if the speaker here had
only said that it was right to weep when valour was being buried in their grave, it
would have been a metaphor, and a graphic one; but the coupling of 'their valour'
1411ᵇ1   and 'her freedom' presents a kind of antithesis as well. 'The course of my words',
said Iphicrates, 'lies straight through the middle of Chares' deeds': this is a
proportional metaphor, and the phrase 'straight through the middle' makes it
5   graphic. The expression 'to call in one danger to rescue us from another' is a graphic
metaphor. Lycoleon said, defending Chabrias, 'They did not respect even that
bronze statue of his that intercedes for him yonder'. This was a metaphor for the
moment, though it would not always apply; a vivid metaphor, however; Chabrias is
10   in danger, and his statue intercedes for him—that lifeless yet living thing which
records his services to his country. 'Practising in every way littleness of mind' is
metaphorical, for practising a quality implies increasing it. So is 'God kindled our
15   reason to be a lamp within our souls', for both reason and light reveal things. So is
'we are not putting an end to our wars, but only postponing them', for both literal
postponement and the making of such a peace as this apply to future action. So is
such a saying as 'This treaty is a far nobler trophy than those we set up on fields of
battle; they celebrate small gains and single successes; it celebrates our triumph in
the war as a whole'; for both trophy and treaty are signs of victory. So is 'A country
20   pays a heavy reckoning in being condemned by the judgement of mankind', for a
reckoning is damage deservedly incurred.

11 · It has already been mentioned that liveliness is got by using the
25   proportional type of metaphor and by making our hearers see things. We have still
to explain what we mean by their 'seeing things', and what must be done to effect
this. By 'making them see things' I mean using expressions that represent things as
in a state of activity. Thus, to say that a good man is 'four-square' is certainly a
metaphor; both the good man and the square are perfect; but the metaphor does not
suggest activity. On the other hand, in the expression 'with his vigour in full bloom'
there is a notion of activity; and so in 'But you must roam as free as a sacred
victim';[17] and in

30   Thereat up sprang the Hellenes to their feet,[18]

where 'up sprang' gives us activity as well as metaphor, for it at once suggests

---

[17]Isocrates, *Philippus* 10, 127
[18]Euripides, *Iphigenia in Aulis* 80.

swiftness. So with Homer's common practice of giving metaphorical life to lifeless things: all such passages are distinguished by the effect of activity they convey. Thus,

> Downward anon to the valley rebounded the boulder remorseless;

and

> The arrow flew;

and

> Flying on eagerly;

and

> Stuck in the earth, still panting to feed on the flesh of the heroes;   1412ª1

and

> And the point of the spear in its fury drove full through his breastbone.[19]

In all these examples the things have the effect of being active because they are made into living beings; shameless behaviour and fury and so on are all forms of activity. And the poet has attached these ideas to the things by means of proportional metaphors: as the stone is to Sisyphus, so is the shameless man to his   5
victim. In his famous similes, too, he treats inanimate things in the same way:

> Curving and crested with white, host following host without ceasing.[20]

Here he represents everything as moving and living; and activity is movement.

Metaphors must be drawn, as has been said already, from things that are   10
related to the original thing, and yet not obviously so related—just as in philosophy also an acute mind will perceive resemblances even in things far apart. Thus Archytas said that an arbitrator and an altar were the same, since the injured fly to both for refuge. Or you might say that an anchor and an overhead hook were the same, since both are in a way the same, only the one secures things from below and   15
the other from above. And to speak of states as 'levelled' is to identify two widely different things, the equality of a physical surface and the equality of political powers.

Liveliness is specially conveyed by metaphor, and by the further power of surprising the hearer; because the hearer expected something different, his acquisition of the new idea impresses him all the more. His mind seems to say, 'Yes,   20
to be sure; I never thought of that'. The liveliness of epigrammatic remarks is due to the meaning not being just what the words say: as in the saying of Stesichorus that 'the cicadas will chirp to themselves on the ground'. Well-constructed riddles are attractive for the same reason; a new idea is conveyed, and there is metaphorical

---

[19]*Odyssey* XI 598; *Iliad* XIII 587; IV 126; XI 574; XV 542.
[20]*Iliad* XIII 799.

25 expression. So with the 'novelties' of Theodorus. In these the thought is startling, and, as Theodorus puts it, does not fit in with the ideas you already have. They are like the burlesque words that one finds in the comic writers. The effect is produced even by jokes depending upon changes of the letters of a word; this too is a surprise. You find this in verse as well as in prose. The word which comes is not what the hearer imagined: thus

30   Onward he came, and his feet were shod with his—chilblains,

where one imagined the word would be 'sandals'. But the point should be clear the moment the words are uttered. Jokes made by altering the letters of a word consist in meaning, not just what you say, but something that gives a twist to the word used; e.g. the remark of Theodorus about Nicon the harpist, θράττει σε, where he pretends to mean θράττει σε,[21] and surprises us when we find he means something else. So you

1412ᵇ1 enjoy the point when you see it, though the remark will fall flat unless you are aware that Nicon is a Thracian. Or again: βούλει αὐτὸν πέρσαι. In both these cases the saying must fit the facts. This is also true of such lively remarks as the one to the effect that to the Athenians their empire (ἀρχή) of the sea was not the beginning

5 (ἀρχή) of their troubles, since they gained by it. Or the opposite one of Isocrates, that their empire (ἀρχή) was the beginning (ἀρχή) of their troubles. Either way, the speaker says something unexpected, the soundness of which is thereupon recognized. There would be nothing clever in saying empire is empire. Isocrates means more than that, and uses the word with a new meaning. So too with the former

10 saying, which denies that ἀρχή in one sense was ἀρχή in another sense. In all these jokes, whether a word is used in a second sense or metaphorically, the joke is good if it fits the facts. For instance, Ἀνάσχετος (proper name) οὐκ ἀνασχετός: where you say that what is so-and-so in one sense is not so-and-so in another; well, if the man is unpleasant, the joke fits the facts. Again, 'You should not be more a stranger than a

15 stranger'—or more than you should be. That is the same as: 'The stranger should not always be a stranger'. Here again is the use of one word in different senses. Of the same kind also is the much-praised verse of Anaxandrides:

          Death is most fit before you do
          Deeds that would make death fit for you.

This amounts to saying 'it is a fit thing to die when you are not fit to die', or 'it is a fit thing to die when death is not fit for you', i.e. when death is not the fit return for

20 what you are doing. The type of language employed is the same in all these examples; but the more briefly and antithetically such sayings can be expressed, the more taking they are, for antithesis impresses the new idea more firmly and brevity more quickly. They should always have either some personal application or some

25 merit of expression, if they are to be true without being common-place—two requirements not always satisfied simultaneously. Thus 'a man should die having done no wrong' is true but dull: 'the right man should marry the right woman' is also

---

[21]Text uncertain.

true but dull. No, there must be both good qualities together, as in 'it is fitting to die when you are not fit for death'. The more a saying has these qualities, the livelier it appears: if, for instance, its wording is metaphorical, metaphorical in the right way, antithetical, and balanced, and at the same time it gives an idea of activity.   30

Successful similes also, as has been said above, are in a sense metaphors, since they always involve two relations like the proportional metaphor. Thus: a shield, we say, is the 'drinking-bowl of Ares', and a bow is the 'chordless lyre'. This way of   1413ᵃ1 putting a metaphor is not 'simple', as it would be if we called the bow a lyre or the shield a drinking-bowl. There are 'simple' similes also: we may say that a flute-player is like a monkey, or that a short-sighted man's eyes are like a lamp-flame with water dropping on it, since both eyes and flame keep winking. A simile succeeds best when it is a converted metaphor, for it is possible to say that a   5 shield *is like* the drinking-bowl of Ares, or that a ruin *is like* a house in rags, and to say that Niceratus *is like* a Philoctetes stung by Pratys—the simile made by Thrasymachus when he saw Niceratus, who had been beaten by Pratys in a recitation competition, still going about unkempt and unwashed. It is in these respects that poets fail worst when they fail, and succeed best when they   10 succeed,

> Those legs of his curl just like parsley leaves;

and

> Just like Philammon struggling with his punch-ball.

These are all similes; and that similes are metaphors has been stated often already.

Proverbs, again, are metaphors from one species to another. Suppose, for   15 instance, a man to start some undertaking in hope of gain and then to lose by it later on, 'Here we have once more the man of Carpathus and his hare', says he. For both alike went through the said experience.

It has now been explained fairly completely how liveliness is secured and why it has the effect it has. Successful hyperboles are also metaphors, e.g. the one about   20 the man with a black eye, 'you would have thought he was a basket of mulberries'; here the 'black eye' is compared to a mulberry because of its colour, the exaggeration lying in the quantity of mulberries suggested. The phrase '*like* so-and-so' may introduce a hyperbole under the form of a simile. Thus

> *Just like* Philammon struggling with his punch-ball

is equivalent to '*you would have thought he was* Philammon struggling with his   25 punch-ball'; and

> Those legs of his curl *just like* parsley leaves

is equivalent to 'his legs are so curly that *you would have thought* they were not legs but parsley leaves'. Hyperboles are for young men to use; they show vehemence of character; [[and this is why angry people use them more than other people.   30

Not though he gave me as much as the dust or the sands of the sea . . .
But her, the daughter of Atreus' son, I never will marry,
Nay, not though she were fairer than Aphrodite the Golden,
Defter of hand than Athene . . .[22]]][23]

1413[b]1 [The Attic orators are particularly fond of this method of speech.][24] Consequently it does not suit an elderly speaker.

12 · It should be observed that each kind of rhetoric has its own appropriate style. The style of written prose is not that of spoken oratory, nor are those of
5 political and forensic speaking the same. Both written and spoken have to be known. To know the latter is to know how to speak good Greek. To know the former means that you are not obliged, as otherwise you are, to hold your tongue when you wish to communicate something to the general public.

The written style is the more finished: the spoken better admits of dramatic
10 delivery—alike the kind of oratory that reflects character and the kind that reflects emotion. Hence actors look out for plays written in the latter style, and poets for actors competent to act in such plays. Yet poets whose plays are meant to be read *are* read and circulated. Chaeremon, for instance, who is as finished as a professional speech-writer; and Licymnius among the dithyrambic poets. Com-
15 pared with those of others, the speeches of professional writers sound thin in actual contests. Those of the orators, on the other hand, look amateurish enough when they pass into the hands of a reader. This is just because they are so well suited for an actual tussle, and therefore contain many dramatic touches, which, being robbed of all dramatic rendering, fail to do their own proper work, and consequently look silly. Thus strings of unconnected words, and constant repetitions of words and phrases,
20 are very properly condemned in written speeches: but not in spoken speeches— speakers use them freely, for they have a dramatic effect. In this repetition there must be variety of tone, paving the way, as it were, to dramatic effect; e.g. 'This is the villain among you who deceived you, who cheated you, who meant to betray you
25 completely'. This is the sort of thing that Philemon the actor used to do in the *Old Men's Madness* of Anaxandrides, whenever he spoke the words 'Rhadamanthus and Palamedes', and also in the prologue to the *Saints* whenever he pronounced the pronoun 'I'. If one does not deliver such things cleverly, it becomes a case of 'the man who swallowed a poker'. So too with strings of unconnected words, e.g. 'I came
30 to him; I met him; I besought him'. Such passages must be *acted*, not delivered with the same quality and pitch of voice, as though they had only one idea in them. They have the further peculiarity of suggesting that a number of separate statements have been made in the time usually occupied by one. Just as the use of conjunctions makes many statements into a single one, so the omission of conjunctions acts in the reverse way and makes a single one into many. It thus makes everything more

---

[22]*Iliad* IX 385, 388–90.
[23]Marked by Kassel as a later addition by Aristotle himself.
[24]Excised by Kassel.

important: e.g. 'I came to him; I talked to him; I entreated him'—what a lot of facts!
the hearer thinks—'he paid no attention to anything I said'. This is the effect which
Homer seeks when he writes, 'Nireus likewise from Syme, Nireus, the son of
Aglaia, Nireus, the comeliest man'.[25] If many things are said about a man, his name
must be mentioned many times; and therefore people think that, if his name is
mentioned many times, many things have been said about him. So that Homer, by   5
means of this illusion, has made a great deal of Nireus, though he has mentioned
him only in this one passage, and has preserved his memory, though he nowhere
says a word about him afterwards.

Now the style of oratory addressed to public assemblies is really just like
scene-painting. The bigger the throng, the more distant is the point of view: so that,
in the one and the other, high finish in detail is superfluous and looks bad. The   10
forensic style is more highly finished; still more so is the style of language addressed
to a single judge, with whom there is very little room for rhetorical artifices, since he
can take the whole thing in better, and judge of what is to the point and what is not;
the struggle is less intense and so the judgement is undisturbed. This is why the
same speakers do not distinguish themselves in all these branches at once; high
finish is wanted least where dramatic delivery is wanted most, and here the speaker   15
must have a good voice, and above all, a strong one. It is epideictic oratory that is
most literary, for it is meant to be read; and next to it forensic oratory.

To analyse style still further, and add that it must be agreeable or magnificent,
is useless; for why should it have these traits any more than restraint, liberality, or   20
any other excellence of character? Obviously agreeableness will be produced by the
qualities already mentioned, if our definition of excellence of style has been correct.
For what other reason should style be clear, and not mean but appropriate? If it is
prolix, it is not clear; nor yet if it is curt. Plainly the middle way suits best. Again,   25
style will be made agreeable by the elements mentioned, namely by a good blending
of ordinary and unusual words, by the rhythm, and by the persuasiveness that
springs from appropriateness.

This concludes our discussion of style, both in its general aspects and in its
special applications to the various branches of rhetoric. We have now to deal with
arrangement.

13 · A speech has two parts. You must state your case, and you must prove   30
it. You cannot either state your case and omit to prove it, or prove it without having
first stated it; since any proof must be a proof of something, and the only use of a
preliminary statement is the proof that follows it. Of these two parts the first part is
called the statement of the case, the second part the argument, just as we   35
distinguish between problem and demonstration. The current division is absurd. For
narration surely is part of a forensic speech only: how in a political speech or a
speech of display can there be narration in the technical sense? or a reply to a
forensic opponent? or an epilogue in closely-reasoned speeches? Again, introduc-

[25]*Iliad* II 671–3.

tion, comparison of conflicting arguments, and recapitulation are only found in political speeches when there is a struggle between two policies. They *may* occur then; so may even accusation and defence, often enough; but they form no essential
5 part of a political speech. Even forensic speeches do not always need epilogues; not, for instance, a short speech, nor one in which the facts are easy to remember, the effect of an epilogue being always a reduction in the apparent length. It follows, then, that the only necessary parts of a speech are the statement and the argument. These are the essential features of a speech; and it cannot in any case have more than introduction, statement, argument, and epilogue. Refutation of the opponent is part of the arguments: so is comparison of the opponent's case with your own, for
10 that process is a magnifying of your own case and therefore a part of the arguments, since one who does this *proves* something. The introduction does nothing like this; nor does the epilogue—it merely reminds us of what has been said already. If we make such distinctions we shall end, like Theodorus and his followers, by distinguishing narration proper from 'post-narration' and 'pre-narration', and
15 refutation from 'final refutation'. But we ought only to bring in a new name if it indicates a real species with distinct specific qualities; otherwise, the practice is pointless and silly, like the way Licymnius invented names in his *Art of Rhetoric*— 'secundation', 'divagation', 'ramification'.

14 · The introduction is the beginning of a speech, corresponding to the
20 prologue in poetry and the prelude in flute-music; they are all beginnings, paving the way, as it were, for what is to follow. The musical prelude resembles the introduction to speeches of display; as flute-players play first some brilliant passage they know well and then fit it on to the opening notes of the piece itself, so in
25 speeches of display the writer should proceed in the same way; he should begin with what best takes his fancy, and then strike up his theme and lead into it; which is indeed what *is* always done. (Take as an example the introduction to the *Helen* of Isocrates—there is nothing in common between the eristics and Helen.) And here, even if you travel far from your subject, it is fitting, rather than that there should be sameness in the entire speech.
30 The usual subject for the introductions to speeches of display is some piece of praise or censure. Thus Gorgias writes in his *Olympic Speech,* 'You deserve widespread admiration, men of Greece', praising thus those who started the festival gatherings. Isocrates, on the other hand, censures them for awarding distinctions to
35 fine athletes but giving no prize for intellectual ability. Or one may begin with a piece of advice, thus: 'We ought to honour good men and so I myself am praising Aristeides' or 'We ought to honour those who are unpopular but not bad men, men whose good qualities have never been noticed, like Alexander son of Priam'. Here
1415ᵃ1 the orator gives advice. Or we may begin as speakers do in the law-courts; that is to say, with appeals to the audience to excuse us if our speech is about something paradoxical, difficult, or hackneyed; like Choerilus in the lines—

But now when allotment of all has been made . . .

Introductions to speeches of display, then, may be composed of some piece of 5
praise or censure, of advice to do or not to do something, or of appeals to the
audience; and you must choose between making these preliminary passages
connected or disconnected with the speech itself.

Introductions to forensic speeches, it must be observed, have the same value as
the prologues of dramas and the introductions to epic poems; the dithyrambic 10
prelude resembling the introduction to a speech of display, as

> For thee, and thy gifts, . . .[26]

In prologues, and in epic poetry, a foretaste of the theme is given, intended to inform
the hearers of it in advance instead of keeping their minds in suspense. Anything
vague puzzles them: so give them a grasp of the beginning, and they can hold fast to 15
it and follow the argument. So we find—

> Sing, O goddess of song, of the Wrath . . .

> Tell me, O Muse, of the hero . . .[27]

> Lead me to tell a new tale, how there came great warfare to Europe
> Out of the Asian land . . .

The tragic poets, too, let us know the pivot of their play; if not at the outset like
Euripides, at least somewhere in the prologue like Sophocles; 20

> [[Polybus was my father . . . ;]][28]

and so in comedy. This, then, is the most essential function and distinctive property
of the introduction, to show what the aim of the speech is; and therefore no
introduction ought to be employed where the subject is not long or intricate.

The other kinds of introduction employed are remedial in purpose, and may be 25
used in any type of speech. They are concerned with the speaker, the hearer, the
subject, or the speaker's opponent. Those concerned with the speaker himself or
with his opponent are directed to removing or exciting prejudice. But whereas the
defendant will begin by dealing with this sort of thing, the prosecutor will take quite
another line and deal with such matters in the closing part of his speech. The reason
for this is not far to seek. The defendant, when he is going to bring himself on the 30
stage, must clear away any obstacles, and therefore must begin by removing any
prejudice felt against him. But if you are to excite prejudice, you must do so at the
close, so that the judges may more easily remember what you have said.

The appeal to the hearer aims at securing his goodwill, and sometimes at 35
gaining his serious attention to the case—for gaining it is not always an advantage,
and speakers will often for that reason try to make him laugh.

You may use any means you choose to make your hearer receptive; among
others, giving him a good impression of your character, which always helps to

---

[26]Text uncertain.   [27]*Iliad* I 1; *Odyssey* I 1.
[28]Marked by Kassel as a later addition by Aristotle himself.

1415^b1 secure his attention. He will be ready to attend to anything that touches himself, and to anything that is important, surprising, or agreeable; and you should accordingly convey to him the impression that what you have to say is of this nature. If you wish to distract his attention, you should imply that the subject does not affect him, or is trivial or disagreeable. But observe, all this has nothing to do with
5 the speech itself. It merely has to do with the weak-minded tendency of the hearer to listen to what is beside the point. Where this tendency is absent, no introduction is wanted beyond a summary statement of your subject, to put a sort of head on the main body of your speech. Moreover, calls for attention, when required, may come
10 equally well in any part of a speech; in fact, the beginning of it is just where there is least slackness of interest; it is therefore ridiculous to put this kind of thing at the beginning, when every one is listening with most attention. Choose therefore any point in the speech where such an appeal is needed, and then say 'Now I beg you to note this point—it concerns you quite as much as myself'; or 'I will tell you that whose like you have never yet heard for terror'—or 'for wonder'. This is what
15 Prodicus called 'slipping in a bit of the fifty-drachma show-lecture for the audience whenever they began to nod'. It is plain that such introductions are addressed not to ideal hearers, but to hearers as we find them. The use of introductions to excite prejudice or to dispel misgivings is universal.

20 　　　　　　　[[My lord, I will not say that eagerly . . .

　　or

　　　　　　　Why all this preface?]]²⁹

Introductions are popular with those whose case is weak, or looks weak; it pays them to dwell on anything rather than the actual facts of it. That is why slaves, instead of answering the questions put to them, make indirect replies with long preambles.
25 The means of exciting in your hearers goodwill and various other feelings of the same kind have already been described. The poet finely says

　　　May I find in Phaeacian hearts, at my coming, goodwill and compassion;³⁰

and these are the two things we should aim at. In speeches of display we must make the hearer feel that the eulogy includes either himself or his family or his way of life
30 or something or other of the kind. For it is true, as Socrates says in the *Funeral Speech,* that 'the difficulty is not to praise the Athenians at Athens but at Sparta'.

　　　The introductions of political oratory will be made out of the same materials as those of the forensic kind, though the nature of political oratory makes them very rare. The subject is known already, and therefore the *facts* of the case need no
35 introduction; but you may have to say something on account of yourself or your opponents; or those present may be inclined to treat the matter either more or less seriously than you wish them to. You may accordingly have to excite or dispel some

²⁹Sophocles, *Antigone* 223; Euripides, *Iphigenia at Tauris* 1162. Marked by Kassel
as a later addition by Aristotle himself.
³⁰*Odyssey* VI 327.

prejudice, or to make the matter under discussion seem more or less important than before: for either of which purposes you will want an introduction. You may also want one to add elegance to your remarks, feeling that otherwise they will have a casual air, like Gorgias' eulogy of the Eleans, in which, without any preliminary sparring or fencing, he begins straight off with 'Happy city of Elis!' 1416ᵃ1

15 · In dealing with prejudice, one class of argument is that whereby you can dispel objectionable suppositions about yourself. It makes no practical 5 difference whether such a supposition has been put into words or not, so that this distinction may be ignored. Another commonplace is to meet any of the issues directly: to deny the alleged fact: or to say that you have done no harm, or none to him, or not as much as he says; or that you have done him no injustice, or not much; or that you have done nothing disgraceful, or nothing disgraceful enough to matter: these are the sort of questions on which the dispute hinges. Thus Iphicrates, 10 replying to Nausicrates, admitted that he had done the deed alleged, and that he had done Nausicrates harm, but not that he had done him wrong. Or you may admit the wrong, but balance it with other facts, and say that, if the deed harmed him, at any rate it was honourable; or that, if it gave him pain, at least it did him good; or something else like that. Another commonplace is to allege that your action was due to mistake, or bad luck, or necessity—as Sophocles said he was not trembling, as his 15 traducer maintained, in order to make people think him an old man, but because he could not help it; he would rather *not* be eighty years old. You may balance your motive against your actual deed; saying, for instance, that you did not mean to injure him but to do so-and-so; that you did not do what you are falsely charged with doing—the damage was accidental—'I should indeed be a detestable person if I had deliberately intended this result'. Another way is open when your calumniator, or 20 any of his connexions, is or has been subject to the same grounds for suspicion. Yet another, when others are subject to the same grounds for suspicion but are admitted to be in fact innocent of the charge: e.g. 'Must I be an adulterer because I am well-groomed? Then so-and-so must be one too'. Another, if other people have been calumniated by the same man or some one else, or, without being calumniated, have been suspected, like yourself now, and yet have been proved innocent. Another way 25 is to return calumny for calumny and say, 'It is monstrous to trust the man's statements when you cannot trust the man himself'. Another is when the question has been already decided. So with Euripides' reply to Hygiaenon, who, in the action for an exchange of properties, accused him of impiety in having written a line encouraging perjury— 30

My tongue hath sworn: no oath is on my soul.[31]

Euripides said that his opponent himself was guilty in bringing into the law-courts cases whose decision belonged to the Dionysiac contests. 'If I have not already answered for my words there, I am ready to do so if you choose to prosecute me there'. Another method is to denounce calumny, showing what an enormity it is,

[31]Euripides, *Hippolytus* 612.

35   and in particular that it raises false issues, and that it means a lack of confidence in
     the merits of the case. The argument from evidential circumstances is available for
1416ᵇ1 both parties: thus in the *Teucer* Odysseus says that Teucer is closely bound to
     Priam, since his mother Hesione was Priam's sister. Teucer replies that Telamon his
     father was Priam's enemy, and that he himself did not betray the spies to Priam.
     Another method, suitable for the calumniator, is to praise some trifling merit at
5   great length, and then attack some important failing concisely; or after mentioning
     a number of good qualities to attack one bad one that really bears on the question.
     This is the method of thoroughly skilful and unscrupulous prosecutors. By mixing
     up the man's merits with what is bad, they do their best to make use of them to
     damage him.
         There is another method open to both calumniator and apologist. Since a given
10   action can be done from many motives, the former must try to disparage it by
     selecting the worse motive of two, the latter to put the better construction on it.
     Thus one might argue that Diomedes chose Odysseus as his companion because he
     supposed Odysseus to be the best man for the purpose; and you might reply to this
     that it was, on the contrary, because he was the only hero so worthless that
15   Diomedes need not fear his rivalry.

16 · We may now pass from the subject of calumny to that of narration.

         Narration in epideictic oratory is not continuous but intermittent. There must,
     of course, be some survey of the actions that form the subject-matter of the speech.
     The speech is a composition containing two parts. One of these is not provided by
     the orator's art, viz. the actions themselves, of which the orator is in no sense author.
20   The other part is provided by his art, namely, the proof (where proof is needed) that
     the actions were done, the description of their quality or of their extent, or even all
     these three things together. Now the reason why sometimes it is not desirable to
     make the whole narrative continuous is that the case thus expounded is hard to keep
     in mind. Show, therefore, from one set of facts that your hero is, e.g. brave, and
     from other sets of facts that he is able, just, etc. A speech thus arranged is
25   comparatively simple, instead of being complicated and elaborate. You will have to
     recall well-known deeds among others; and because they are well-known, the hearer
     usually needs no narration of them; none, for instance, if your object is the praise of
     Achilles; we all know the facts of his life—what you have to do is to apply those
     facts. But if your object is the praise of Critias, you must narrate his deeds, which
     not many people know of. . .[32]
30   Nowadays it is said, absurdly enough, that the narration should be rapid.
     Remember what the man said to the baker who asked whether he was to make the
     cake hard or soft: 'What, can't you make it *right*?' Just so here. We are not to make
     long narrations, just as we are not to make long introductions or long arguments.
35   Here, again, rightness does not consist either in rapidity or in conciseness, but in the
     happy mean; that is, in saying just so much as will make the facts plain, or will lead

---

[32]Kassel marks a lacuna.

the hearer to believe that the thing has happened, or that the man has caused injury 1417ᵃ1
or wrong to some one, or that the facts are really as important as you wish them to
be thought: or the opposite facts to establish the opposite arguments.

You may also narrate as you go anything that does credit to yourself, e.g. 'I
kept telling him to do his duty and not abandon his children'; or discredit to your
adversary, e.g. 'But he answered me that, wherever he might find himself, there he   5
would find other children', the answer Herodotus[33] records of the Egyptian
mutineers. Slip in anything else that the judges will enjoy.

The defendant will make less of the narration. He has to maintain that the
thing has not happened, or did no harm, or was not unjust, or not so bad as is
alleged. He must therefore not waste time about what is admitted fact, unless this   10
bears on his own contention; e.g. that the thing was done, but was not wrong.
Further, we must speak of events as past and gone, except where they excite pity or
indignation by being represented as present. The story told to Alcinous is an
example of a brief chronicle, when it is repeated to Penelope in sixty lines. Another
instance is the epic cycle as treated by Phayllus, and the prologue to the   15
Oeneus.

The narration should depict character; to which end you must know what
makes it do so. One such thing is the indication of choice; the quality of purpose
indicated determines the quality of character depicted and is itself determined by
the end pursued. Thus it is that mathematical discourses depict no character; they
have nothing to do with choice, for they represent nobody as pursuing any end. On   20
the other hand, the Socratic dialogues do depict character. This end will also be
gained by describing the manifestations of various types of character, e.g. 'he kept
walking along as he talked', which shows the man's recklessness and rough
manners. Do not let your words seem inspired so much by intelligence, in the
manner now current, as by choice: e.g. 'I willed this; aye, it was my choice; true, I   25
gained nothing by it, still it is better thus'. For the other way shows good sense, but
this shows good character; good sense making us go after what is useful, and good
character after what is noble. Where any detail may appear incredible, then add the
cause of it; of this Sophocles provides an example in the *Antigone,* where Antigone
says she had cared more for her brother than for husband or children, since if the   30
latter perished they might be replaced,

> But since my father and mother in their graves
> Lie dead, no brother can be born to me.[34]

If you have no such cause to suggest, just say that you are aware that no one will
believe your words, but the fact remains that such is your nature, however hard the   35
world may find it to believe that a man deliberately does anything except what pays
him.

Again, you must make use of the emotions. Relate the familiar manifestations
of them, and those that distinguish yourself and your opponent; for instance, 'he

[33]II 30.   [34]Sophocles, *Antigone* 911–2.

1417ᵇ1 went away scowling at me'. So Aeschines described Cratylus as 'hissing with fury and shaking his fists'. These details carry conviction: the audience take the truth of what they know as so much evidence for the truth of what they do not. Plenty of such details may be found in Homer:

5   Thus did she say: but the old woman buried her face in her hands:[35]

a true touch—people beginning to cry do put their hands over their eyes.

Bring yourself on the stage from the first in the right character, that people may regard you in that light; and the same with your adversary; but do not let them see what you are about. How easily such impressions may be conveyed we can see 10 from the way in which we get some inkling of things we know nothing of by the mere look of the messenger bringing news of them. Have some narrative in many different parts of your speech; and sometimes let there be none at the beginning of it.

In political oratory there is very little opening for narration; nobody can 'narrate' what has not yet happened. If there is narration at all, it will be of past events, the recollection of which is to help the hearers to make better plans for the 15 future. [[Or it may be employed to attack someone's character, or to eulogize him.]][36] Only then you will not be doing what the political speaker, as such, has to do.

If any statement you make is hard to believe, you must guarantee its truth, and at once offer an explanation, and then furnish it with such particulars as will be expected. Thus Carcinus' Jocasta, in his *Oedipus,* keeps guaranteeing the truth of her answers to the inquiries of the man who is seeking her son; and so with Haemon 20 in Sophocles.

17 . The duty of the arguments is to attempt demonstrative proofs. These proofs must bear directly upon the question in dispute, which must fall under one of our heads. If you maintain that the act was not committed, your main task in court 25 is to prove this. If you maintain that the act did no harm, prove this. If you maintain that the act was less than is alleged, or justified, prove these facts in the same way. If the dispute is about whether the act took place, do not forget that in this sort of dispute alone is it true that one of the two parties is necessarily a rogue. Here ignorance cannot be pleaded, as it might if the dispute were whether the act was 30 justified or not. This argument must therefore be used in this case only, not in the others.

In epideictic speeches you will develop your case mainly by arguing that what has been done is, e.g., noble and useful. The facts themselves are to be taken on trust; proof of them is only submitted on those rare occasions when they are not easily credible or when they have been set down to some one else.

35   In political speeches you may maintain that a proposal is impracticable; or that, though practicable, it is unjust, or will do no good, or is not so important as its

[35]*Odyssey* XIX 361.   [36]Marked by Kassel as a later addition by Aristotle himself.

proposer thinks. Note any falsehoods about irrelevant matters—they will look like proof that his other statements also are false. Argument by example is highly suitable for political oratory, argument by enthymeme better suits forensic. 1418ᵃ1 Political oratory deals with future events, of which it can do no more than quote past events as examples. Forensic oratory deals with what is or is not *now* true, which can better be demonstrated, because not contingent—there is no contingency in what has now already happened. Do not use a continuous succession of enthymemes: 5 intersperse them with other matter, or they will spoil one another's effect. There are limits to their number—

Friend, you have spoken as much as a sensible man would have spoken[37]—

'as much' says Homer, not 'as well'. Nor should you try to make enthymemes on every point; if you do, you will be acting just like some students of philosophy, whose 10 conclusions are more familiar and believable than the premises from which they draw them. And avoid the enthymeme form when you are trying to rouse feeling; for it will either kill the feeling or will itself fall flat: all simultaneous motions tend to cancel each other either completely or partially. Nor should you go after the 15 enthymeme form in a passage where you are depicting character—the process of demonstration can express neither character nor choice. Maxims should be employed in the arguments—and in the narration too—since these do express character: 'I have given him this, though I am quite aware that one should "Trust no man"'. Or if you are appealing to the emotions: 'I do not regret it, though I have been wronged; if he has the profit on his side, I have justice on mine'. 20

Political oratory is a more difficult task than forensic; and naturally so, since it deals with the future, whereas the pleader deals with the past, which, as Epimenides of Crete said, even the diviners already know. (Epimenides did not practise divination about the future; only about the obscurities of the past.) Besides, in 25 forensic oratory you have a basis in the law; and once you have a starting-point, you can prove anything with comparative ease. Then again, political oratory affords few chances for those leisurely digressions in which you may attack your adversary, talk about yourself, or work on your hearers' emotions; fewer chances, indeed, than any other affords, unless your set purpose is to divert your hearer's attention. Accordingly, if you find yourself in difficulties, follow the lead of the Athenian speakers, and that of Isocrates, who makes regular attacks upon people in the 30 course of a political speech, e.g. upon the Lacedaemonians in the *Panegyricus,* and upon Chares in the speech about the allies. In epideictic oratory, intersperse your speech with bits of episodic eulogy, like Isocrates, who is always bringing someone forward for this purpose. And this is what Gorgias meant by saying that he always found something to talk about. For if he speaks of Achilles, he praises Peleus, then 35 Aeacus, then Zeus; and in like manner the virtue of valour, describing its good results, and saying what it is like.

Now if you have proofs to bring forward, bring them forward, and also talk

[37]*Odyssey* IV 204.

about character; if you have no enthymemes, then fall back on character: after all, it
is more fitting for a good man to display himself as an honest fellow than as a subtle
reasoner. Refutative enthymemes are more popular than demonstrative ones: their
logical cogency is more striking: the facts about two opposites always stand out
clearly when the two are put side by side.

5   The reply to the opponent is not a separate division of the speech but part of the
arguments. Both in political speaking and when pleading in court, if you are the
first speaker you should put your own arguments forward first, and then meet the
arguments on the other side by refuting them and pulling them to pieces
beforehand. If, however, the case for the other side contains a great variety of
10 arguments, begin with these, like Callistratus in the Messenian assembly, when he
demolished the arguments likely to be used against him before giving his own. If
you speak later, you must first, by means of refutation and counter-deduction,
attempt some answer to your opponent's speech, especially if his arguments have
been well received. For just as our minds refuse a favourable reception to a *person*
15 against whom they are prejudiced, so they refuse it to a speech when they have been
favourably impressed by the speech on the other side. You should, therefore, make
room in the minds of the audience for your coming speech; and this will be done by
getting your opponent's speech out of the way. So attack that first—either the
whole of it, or the most important, successful, or vulnerable points in it, and thus
20 inspire confidence in what you have to say yourself—

> First, champion will I be of Goddesses. . .
> Never, I ween, would Hera. . .[38]

where the speaker has attacked the silliest argument first. So much for the
arguments.

    With regard to the element of character: there are assertions which, if made
25 about yourself, may excite dislike, appear tedious, or expose you to the risk of
contradiction; and other things which you cannot say about your opponent without
seeming abusive or ill-bred. Put such remarks, therefore, into the mouth of some
third person. This is what Isocrates does in the *Philippus* and in the *Antidosis,* and
Archilochus in his satires. The latter represents the father himself as attacking his
daughter in the lampoon

> Think nought impossible at all,
30 > Nor swear that it shall not befall. . .[39]

and puts into the mouth of Charon the carpenter the lampoon which begins

> Not for the wealth of Gyges. . . .[40]

So too Sophocles makes Haemon appeal to his father on behalf of Antigone as if it
were others who were speaking.

[38]Euripides, *Troades* 969–71.   [39]Frag. 122 West.   [40]Frag. 19 West.

Again, sometimes you should restate your enthymemes in the form of maxims; e.g. 'Wise men will come to terms in the hour of success; for they will gain most if they do'. Expressed as an enthymeme, this would run, 'If we ought to come to terms when doing so will enable us to gain the greatest advantage, then we ought to come to terms in the hour of success'.

18 · Next as to interrogation. The best moment to employ this is when your opponent has so answered one question that the putting of just one more lands him in absurdity. Thus Pericles questioned Lampon about the way of celebrating the rites of the Saviour Goddess. Lampon declared that no uninitiated person could be told of them. Pericles then asked, 'Do you know them yourself?' 'Yes', answered Lampon. 'Why,' said Pericles, 'how can that be, when you are uninitiated?'

Another good moment is when one premiss of an argument is obviously true, and you can see that your opponent must say 'yes' if you ask him whether the other is true. Having first got this answer about the other, do not go on to ask him about the obviously true one, but just state the conclusion yourself. Thus, when Meletus denied that Socrates believed in the existence of gods, Socrates proceeded to ask whether supernatural beings were not either children of the gods or in some way divine? 'Yes', said Meletus, 'Then', replied Socrates, 'is there any one who believes in the existence of children of the gods and yet not in the existence of the gods themselves?'[41] Another good occasion is when you expect to show that your opponent is contradicting either his own words or what everyone believes. A fourth is when it is impossible for him to meet your question except by an evasive answer. If he answers 'True, and yet not true', or 'Partly true and partly not true', or 'True in one sense but not in another', the audience thinks he is in difficulties, and applauds his discomfiture. In other cases do not attempt interrogation; for if your opponent gets in an objection, you are felt to have been worsted. You cannot ask a series of questions owing to the incapacity of the audience to follow them; and for this reason you should also make your enthymemes as compact as possible.

In replying, you must meet ambiguous questions by drawing reasonable distinctions, not by a curt answer. In meeting questions that seem to involve you in a contradiction, offer the explanation at the outset of your answer, before your opponent asks the next question or draws his conclusion. For it is not difficult to see the drift of his argument in advance. This point, however, as well as the various means of refutation, may be regarded as known to us from the *Topics*.

When your opponent in drawing his conclusion puts it in the form of a question, you must justify your answer. Thus when Sophocles was asked by Peisander whether he had, like the other members of the Board of Safety, voted for setting up the Four Hundred, he said 'Yes'. 'Why, did you not think it wicked?'— 'Yes'.—'So *you* committed this wickedness?'—'Yes', said Sophocles, 'for there was nothing better to do'. Again, the Lacedaemonian, when he was being examined on his conduct as ephor, was asked whether he thought that the other

---

[41]Plato, *Apology* 27C.

ephors had been justly put to death. 'Yes', he said. 'Well then', asked his opponent, 'did not *you* propose the same measures as they?'—'Yes'.—'Well then, would not
35 *you* too be justly put to death?'—'Not at all', said he; '*they* were bribed to do it, and I did it from conviction'. Hence you should not ask any further questions after drawing the conclusion, nor put the conclusion itself in the form of a further
1419ᵇ1 question, unless there is a large balance of truth on your side.

As to jests. These are supposed to be of some service in controversy. Gorgias said that you should kill your opponents' earnestness with jesting and their jesting
5 with earnestness; in which he was right. Jests have been classified in the *Poetics*. Some are becoming to a gentleman, others are not; see that you choose such as become you. Irony better befits a gentleman than buffoonery; the ironical man jokes to amuse himself, the buffoon to amuse other people.

10 **19** · The epilogue has four parts. You must make the audience well-disposed towards yourself and ill-disposed towards your opponent, magnify or minimize the leading facts, excite the required state of emotion in your hearers, and refresh their memories.

15 Having shown your own truthfulness and the untruthfulness of your opponent, the natural thing is to commend yourself, censure him, and hammer home your points. You must aim at one of two objects—you must make yourself out a good man and him a bad one either in yourselves or in relation to your hearers. The commonplaces by which this should be established have been stated.

20 The facts having been proved, the natural thing to do next is to magnify or minimize their importance. The facts must be admitted before you can discuss how important they are; just as the body cannot grow except from something already present. The proper commonplaces to be used for this purpose of amplification and depreciation have already been set forth.

25 Next, when the facts and their importance are clearly understood, you must excite your hearers' emotions. These emotions are pity, indignation, anger, hatred, envy, emulation, pugnacity. The commonplaces to be used for these purposes also have been previously mentioned.

Finally you have to review what you have already said. Here you may properly do what some wrongly recommend doing in the introduction—repeat your points
30 frequently so as to make them easily understood. What you *should* do in your introduction is to state your subject, in order that the point to be judged may be quite plain; in the epilogue you should summarize the arguments by which your case has been proved. The first step in this reviewing process is to observe that you have done what you undertook to do. You must, then, state what you have said and why you have said it. Your method may be a comparison of your own case with that
35 of your opponent; and you may compare the ways you have both handled the same point or make your comparison direct: 'My opponent said so-and-so on this point; I
1420ᵃ1 said so-and-so, and this is why I said it'. Or with modest irony, e.g. 'He certainly said so-and-so, but I said so-and-so'. Or 'How vain he would have been if he had proved all this instead of that!' Or put it in the form of a question, 'What has not

been proved by me?' or 'What has my opponent proved?' You may proceed, then, either in this way by setting point against point, or by following the natural order of the arguments as spoken, first giving your own, and then separately, if you wish those of your opponent. $1420^{b}1$

For the conclusion, the disconnected style of language is appropriate, and will mark the difference between the oration and the peroration. 'I have done. You have heard me. The facts are before you. I ask for your judgement'.

RHETORIC
TO ALEXANDER**

E. S. Forster

1420ª5   ¹[Aristotle to Alexander. Salutation.

You write that you have often sent persons to me to urge upon me the project of noting down for you the principles of public speaking. It is not through indifference that I have put off doing so all this time, but because I was seeking how to write on
10   this subject with more exactitude than any one else who has concerned himself therewith. It was only natural that I should have such an intention; for just as you are desirous to have more splendid raiment than other men, so you ought to strive to attain to a more glorious skill in speech than other men possess. For it is far more
15   honourable and kingly to have the mind well ordered than to see the bodily form well arrayed. For it is absurd that one who in deeds excels all men should in words manifestly fall short of ordinary mortals, especially when he knows full well that, whereas among those whose political constitution is democracy the final appeal on
20   all matters is to the law, among those who are under kingly rule the appeal is to reason. Just as their public law always directs self-governing communities along the best path, so might reason, as embodied in you, guide along the path of their
25   advantage those who are subject to your rule. For law can be simply described as reason defined by the common consent of the community, regulating action of every kind. Furthermore, I think that you are well aware that we praise as good men and true those who employ reason and prefer always to act under its guidance, while we
1420ᵇ5   abhor as savage and brutish those who act in any matter without reason. It is for this reason too that we punish wicked men when they show their wickedness and admire the good when they display their excellence. Thus we have discovered a means of preventing possible wickedness, while we enjoy the benefits of existing goodness. In
10   this way we escape annoyances which threaten us and secure advantages which we did not previously possess. Just as a life free from pain is an object of desire, so is wise reason an object of contentment.

Again, you must realize that the model set before most men is either the law or

---

TEXT: M. Fuhrmann, *Anaximenis Ars Rhetorica*, Teubner, Leipzig, 1966
¹Fuhrmann brackets the introduction as a later addition.

else your life and your reason. In order therefore that you may excel all Greeks and 15
barbarians, you must exert yourself to the utmost, so that those who spend their
lives in these pursuits, using the elements of excellence in them to produce a
beauteous copy of the model thus set before them, may not direct themselves
towards ignoble ends but make it their desire to partake in the same excellence.

Moreover, deliberation is the most divine of human activities. Therefore you 20
must not waste your energies on subordinate and worthless pursuits, but desire to
drink at the very fountain-head of good counsel. For what man of sense could doubt
that, while it is a sign of foolishness to act without deliberation, it is the mark of true 25
culture to accomplish under the guidance of reason anything that reason
commands? It is plain to see that all the greatest politicians of Greece resort to
reason first and then to deeds, and further that those who have won the highest
repute among the barbarians have employed reason before action, knowing full well
that the consideration of expediency by the light of reason is a very citadel of 1421ᵃ1
salvation. It is reason which we must regard as an impregnable citadel, and not look
on any fortress built by man as a sure safeguard.

But I hesitate to say another word, lest I should seem to be writing for effect, 5
bringing forward proofs of facts which are fully known as though they were not
generally admitted. I will therefore say no more, after mentioning only one topic, in
enlarging on which one might spend one's whole life, namely, that reason is the
thing wherein we are superior to all other animals; and we who have received the
highest honour which heaven can bestow will have this above other men. For all 10
animals display the appetites and desire and the like, but none save man possesses
reason. Now it would be most strange if, when it is by virtue of reason alone that we
live happier lives than all other animals, we should through indifference despise and 15
renounce that which is the cause of our well-being. Though you have long been
exhorted thereto, I urge you to embrace with the utmost zeal the study of reasoned
speech. For just as health preserves the body, so is education the recognized
preserver of the mind. Under its guidance you will never take a false step in
anything that you do, but you will keep safe practically all the advantages which 20
you already possess. Moreover, if physical sight is a pleasure, to see clearly with the
eyes of the soul is a thing to be admired. Again, as the general is the saviour of his
army, so is reason, allied with education, the guide of life. These, then, and like 25
sentiments I think I may well dismiss at the present moment.

In your letter you urge me not to let this book fall into other hands than yours,
and this knowing full well that, just as parents love their own offspring more than
supposititious children, so those who have invented something have more affection 30
for it than those to whom the discovery is merely imparted. For men have died in
defence of their words, as they have died for their offspring. For the so-called Parian
sophists, because what they teach is not of their own production, in their gross
indifference feel no affection and barter it away for money. For this reason I exhort 35
you to watch over these precepts, that while they are yet young they may be
corrupted by no moneys, and, sharing in your well-ordered life, when they come to
man's estate, may win unsullied glory.

Following the lesson taught by Nicanor, we have adopted from other authors anything on the same subjects which was particularly well expressed in their

1421ᵇ1   treatises. You will find two such books, one of which is my own, viz. the Oratorical Art which I wrote for Theodectes, while the other is the treatise of Corax. The other points connected with public and forensic exhortations have all been dealt with

5   specially in these treatises. So in these commentaries written expressly for you you will find material for amplifying these two treatises. Farewell.]

1 · Public speeches fall into three classes, deliberative, epideictic, and

10   forensic. They are of seven kinds, being employed in persuasion, dissuasion, eulogy, vituperation, accusation, defence, and inquiry either by itself or in relation to something else. Such are the different kinds of discourses and their number. We shall employ them in public harangues, in lawsuits about contracts, and in private

15   conversation. We shall treat of them most conveniently if we take them each separately and enumerate their qualities, their uses, and their actions. And first let us discuss persuasion and dissuasion, since they are used most of all in private

20   conversations and in public harangues. To speak generally, persuasion is an exhortation to some choice or speech or action, while dissuasion is the prevention of some choice or speech or action. Such being the definition of these things, he who

25   persuades must show that those things to which he exhorts are just, lawful, expedient, honourable, pleasant, and easy of accomplishment. Failing that, when he is exhorting to that which is difficult, he must show that it is practicable and that its execution is necessary. He who dissuades, by pursuing the opposite course, must exert a hindering influence, showing that the proposed action is neither just nor

30   lawful nor expedient nor honourable nor pleasant nor practicable; if he cannot do that, he must urge that it is toilsome and unnecessary. All actions can have both these sets of attributes applied to them, so that no-one who can urge one of these two sets of fundamental qualities is at a loss for anything to say. It is for these qualities therefore that those who seek to persuade or dissuade must look. I will now attempt

35   to define them one by one and show whence we shall supply them for our discourses.

That which is just is the unwritten custom of all or the majority of men which draws a distinction between what is honourable and what is base. We may take as examples the honouring of parents, doing good to one's friends, and returning good to one's benefactors. These and similar duties are not enjoined upon mankind by

1422ᵃ1   written laws, but they are observed by unwritten custom and universal practice. So much for just actions.

Law is a common agreement made by the community, which ordains in writing how the citizens ought to act under every kind of circumstance.

5   Expediency is the safeguarding of existing advantages, or the acquisition of those not already possessed, or the riddance of existing disadvantages, or the prevention of harm which threatens to occur. For individuals you can divide up expediency according as it applies to the body or the soul or external possessions.

10   For the body, strength, beauty, and health are expedient; for the soul, courage,

wisdom, and justice. External possessions are friends, wealth, and property. The contraries of these are inexpedient. For a community such things as concord, strength for war, wealth, a plentiful supply of revenue, and excellence and abundance of allies are expedient. In a word we look upon anything of this kind as expedient and the contrary as inexpedient. Honourable things are those from which good repute and creditable distinction will accrue to the doers. Pleasant things are those which cause joy. Easy things are those which are accomplished with the least expenditure of time, trouble, and money. Practicable things are all those which admit of performance. Necessary things are those the execution of which does not depend upon us but takes place as it were by some necessity divine or human. Such, then, is the nature of things just, lawful, expedient, honourable, easy, practicable, and necessary.

It will be easy to speak about such subjects by the use of the considerations mentioned above and by ones analogous to them and by ones opposed to them and by employing judgements pronounced by the gods or by men or by judges of repute or by our opponents.

We have already described the nature of that which is just. The following are cases where there is an analogy to that which is just: 'As we consider it just to obey parents, on the same principle it behoves sons to imitate the actions of their fathers'; or again, 'As it is just to do good in return to those who do good to us, so it is just to abstain from harming those who have done us no ill'. It is by this method that we must get analogies to justice. Then we ought to make it plain from contraries in the following way: 'As it is just to punish those who do us a wrong, so it behoves us to do good in return to our benefactors'. You will discover what is just in the judgement of men of repute by a consideration such as the following: 'Not only do we hate and do harm to our enemies, but the Athenians also and the Lacedaemonians judge that it is just to punish their enemies'. By following this system you will often discover what is just.

We have already defined the nature of that which is lawful. When it serves our purpose we must introduce the law itself, and any case of analogy to the written law. For example, 'As the lawgiver punishes thieves with very serious penalties, so we ought to inflict heavy chastisement on those who deceive, for they steal away the understanding'; or again, 'Just as the lawgiver has made the nearest relatives the heirs of those who die childless, so I ought in the present case to have authority over the possessions of a freedman; for since those who set him free are dead and I am the nearest relative of the deceased persons, I am justified in assuming control over their freedmen'. This is an example of the way in which an analogy to that which is ordained by law is obtained. The following is an illustration of what is contrary to that which is lawful: 'If the law prohibits the distribution of public property, it was clearly the judgement of the lawgiver that all who divide up such property are doing wrong; for if the laws ordain that those who govern the state well and justly should be honoured, they clearly regard those who make away with public property as deserving of punishment'. The nature of the lawful is thus clearly shown by taking cases of the contrary. It can be demonstrated from previous judgements by a

15

20

25

30

35

40

1422ᵇ1

5

10

15

20

consideration such as this: 'Not only do I hold that the lawgiver made this law to cover such cases as these, but on a former occasion, when Lysithidas gave an explanation similar to that which I am now putting forward, the jury voted in favour
25 of this interpretation of the law'. By this method we shall often be able to demonstrate what is lawful.

The nature of the expedient itself has already been defined. We must, as in the cases already mentioned, introduce the expedient, wherever it is available, into our arguments and often bring it to light, pursuing the same method which we
30 employed for the lawful and the just. The following would be instances of analogies to the expedient: 'As in war it is expedient to station the bravest men in the front rank, so in the state it is advantageous that the wisest and justest men should be the leaders of the people'; or again, 'As it is expedient for the healthy to be on their
35 guard against disease, so too in communities which live in harmony it is expedient to provide against possibilities of faction'. By following this method you will be able to make many analogies to the expedient. The expedient will also be clear if you take
40 contrary cases such as the following: 'If it is advantageous to honour good citizens, it would be expedient also to punish the wicked'; or again, 'If you think it inexpedient that we should make war unaided on the Thebans, it would be expedient to make
1423ᵃ1 the Lacedaemonians our allies and then make war on the Thebans'. This is the method by which you will demonstrate the expedient by arguing from the contrary. You can discover what has been judged to be expedient by judges of repute by
5 considerations such as the following: 'The Lacedaemonians, when they had conquered the Athenians, thought it expedient not to enslave their city, and on another occasion the Athenians and Thebans, when it was within their power to depopulate Sparta, thought it expedient to allow the Lacedaemonians to survive'.
10 By pursuing this method you will have plenty to say about the just, the lawful, and the expedient. You must employ the same methods in the case of the honourable, the easy, the pleasant, the practicable, and the necessary. We shall thus have abundant material on these topics also.

2 · Next let us determine the number and character of the subjects which we
15 discuss in the council-chamber and in the popular assembly. If we have a clear knowledge of these, the actual circumstances will provide us with something appropriate to say on each occasion when we are giving advice. If we have long been familiar with the characteristics common to each class of subject, we shall always be able to apply them readily in practice. We must therefore distinguish the various
20 subjects about which all men hold public deliberation.

To sum the matter up, there are seven subjects on which we shall speak in public. For whether we are addressing the council or the people, we must necessarily deliberate and speak about either sacred rites or laws or the political constitution or
25 alliances and contracts with other states or war or peace or the provision of resources. These, then, are the subjects about which we shall deliberate and address the people. Let us take each of them separately and see how they can be treated in a speech.

There are three ways in which we must deal with the subject of sacred rites; for we shall urge either that they ought to be retained in their existing form, or that they ought to be changed so as to be more magnificent or else less sumptuous. When we are maintaining that the existing form should be retained, we should derive material from the argument of justice, urging that it is regarded by all men as unjust to transgress the customs of our forefathers, and that all the oracles command men to make their sacrifices according to the usages of their forefathers, and that it is of the utmost importance that the religious observances should be continued which were prescribed by those who originally founded cities and set up temples to the gods. On the ground of expediency we shall urge that, if the sacrifices are offered according to ancestral usage, it will be expedient either for individuals or the community at large in view of the payments of money which will be involved, and that it will benefit the citizens by creating a feeling of self-confidence; for if heavy-armed troops, horsemen, and light-armed soldiers join in a religious procession, the citizens, priding themselves on such things, would feel greater confidence in themselves. It can be urged on the ground of what is honourable, if it results in the spectacle of splendid festivals[2]; on the ground of pleasure, because a variety in the sacrifices to the gods is introduced into the spectacle; and on the ground of practicability, if neither defect nor excess has characterized the celebration. Thus when we are speaking in support of the existing state of affairs, we must pursue our inquiry by the above or similar methods and treat the question under discussion as the nature of the subject permits.

When we are advising a change to greater magnificence in the celebration of sacred rites, we shall have a plausible pretext for altering ancestral usages, if we urge that an addition to existing rites involves not their destruction but their extension; again, that it is reasonable to suppose that the gods too are more favourably disposed to those who honour them more; again, that even our fathers used not to perform their sacrifices always in the same way, but regulated their service to the gods, both as a community and as private individuals, according to the occasion and their own prosperity; again, that this is a principle which we follow in all other matters in the government of our cities and our private establishments. You must also mention any advantage in brilliance or enjoyment which is likely to result to the city from the alteration, following the methods which we have described above.

When we are urging a reduction of the scale of our sacred rites, we must in the first place direct our remarks to the circumstances of the moment and show in what respect the citizens are less prosperous now than formerly. Next we must show that it is reasonable to suppose that the gods rejoice, not in the costliness of the sacrifices, but in the piety of those who offer them; again, that both gods and men deem those who do anything beyond their means to be guilty of great folly; next, that public expenditure is not merely a personal question but depends on prosperity and adversity. These and others of the same kind are the arguments which we shall offer on the subject of sacrifices.

---

[2]The text of this sentence is uncertain.

But in order that we may know how to give some indications and offer rules as
to the conditions of the ideal sacrifice, let us define it thus: the best sacrifice of all is
one which is pious towards the gods, moderate in costliness, splendid from a
spectacular point of view, and likely to bring advantage in war. It will be pious
towards the gods, if ancestral usage is not violated; it will be moderate in costliness,
if the accompaniments of the ceremony are not all wasted; it will be splendid from a
spectacular point of view, if gold and such things as are not actually consumed are
used lavishly; and it will be advantageous for war, if horsemen and infantry in full
panoply accompany the procession. By following these rules we shall best provide
for the service of the gods. From what has been said above we shall know how to
speak in public about the performance of sacred rites of every kind.

Let us next deal similarly with laws and the political constitution. Laws may be
briefly described as common agreements made by the community which define and
ordain in writing how the citizens should act under various circumstances.

In democratic states legislation ought to provide for appointment by lot to the
less important and the majority of the offices (for thus faction will be avoided),
while the most important magistrates should be elected by the votes of the
multitude. In this way the people, having the power to bestow honours on
whomsoever they like, will not be jealous of those who obtain them, while the more
prominent men will be encouraged to practice virtue, knowing that it will be to their
advantage to have a good repute among their fellow-citizens. Such are the laws
which ought to be laid down regarding elections in a democratic state. It would be a
lengthy task to go into detail about the rest of the administration. But, to put the
matter briefly, care must be taken that the laws may prevent the multitude from
entertaining designs against the possessors of property and may instil into the
wealthy citizens an eagerness to spend money in undertaking public burdens. The
laws will ensure this if certain distinctions are set aside by law for the owners of
property in return for their expenditure in the service of the state, and if the laws
show more consideration for the tillers of the soil and the sailors among the poorer
classes than for the poor; so that the rich may willingly serve the state, and the
people may prefer work to dishonest means of gain. In addition stringent laws must
be laid down forbidding the distribution of lands and the confiscation of the
property of those who have served the state, and heavy penalties must be imposed on
those who commit these transgressions. Also public land in a good position in front
of the city must be set apart for the burial of those who are killed in war, and their
children must be supported at the public expense until they grow up. Such must be
the character of legislation in a democratic state.

In oligarchical states the laws ought to distribute the magistracies impartially
to all who possess the rights of citizenship; most of them should be bestowed by lot,
but the most important should be assigned by secret vote under oath and with the
strictest precautions. Under an oligarchy the penalties inflicted on those who offer
affronts to any of the citizens ought to be very heavy, for the people are not so much
annoyed at being debarred from holding office as they are angered at being
affronted. Differences between citizens ought to be settled as quickly as possible

and not be allowed to continue. Nor ought the lower classes to be allowed to collect from the country into the city; for the result of such assemblages is that the populace unites and overthrows the oligarchy. Speaking generally, in democratic states the laws ought to hinder the populace from entertaining designs on the property of the rich; in oligarchical states they ought to check the possessors of political rights from insulting those who are weaker than themselves and from imposing upon the citizens. From what I have said you will not fail to perceive what aims the laws and political constitution ought to keep in view.

Anyone who wishes to speak in favour of a law must show that it affects all equally, that it harmonizes with the rest of the laws, and that it is beneficial to the city, particularly in promoting concord; failing this, he must show that it will conduce to virtue among the citizens or that it will benefit the public revenue or the good repute of the city as a whole, or that it will strengthen the power of the state, or that it will confer some similar advantage. If you are speaking against a law, you must consider whether it does not apply to all the citizens; and next, whether, so far from agreeing with the other laws, it is actually opposed to them; and further, whether it will conduce to none of the benefits which we have mentioned, being on the contrary harmful. These considerations will provide us with abundant arguments for making proposals and speaking about laws and the political constitution.

We will now proceed to deal with alliances and contracts with other states. Contracts and arrangements must necessarily be regulated by public agreements. Alliances must be formed on occasions when one party is too weak by itself, or when a war is expected to break out or because they think they will thus prevent certain people from making war. These and a number of similar circumstances are the reasons which induce states to make allies.

When you wish to support the formation of an alliance, you must make it clear that the occasion for doing so exists, and show if possible that the proposed allies are just men, and that they have previously conferred some benefit upon the state, and that they are possessed of considerable power, and that they are situated near at hand. If all these advantages are not present, you must collect in your speech any of them which do exist. When you are trying to prevent an alliance, it is open to you to show in the first place that it is unnecessary at the moment; or again, that the proposed allies are not just men, or that they have wronged us on a previous occasion. . . .[3] Failing that, you can object to them on the ground that they live too far away and are not in a position to help us at the proper moment. With these and similar arguments we shall have abundant material for speaking against and in support of the formation of alliances.

Again, on the subject of peace and war let us use a similar method to obtain our chief kinds of argument. The pretexts for making war on another state are as follows: when we have been the victims of aggression, we must take vengeance on those who have wronged us, now that a suitable opportunity has presented itself; or else, when we are actually being wronged, we must go to war on our own behalf or

10

15

20

25

30

35

1425ª1

5

10

---

[3] Fuhrmann marks a lacuna here.

15 on behalf of our kindred or benefactors; or else we must help our allies when they
are wronged; or else we must go to war to gain some advantage for the city, in
respect either of glory, or of resources, or of strength, or of something similar.

When we are exhorting anyone to go to war we must collect as many of these
20 pretexts as possible, and afterwards show that those whom we are exhorting possess
most of the advantages which bring success in warfare. Now men are always
successful either by the favour of the gods, which we call good fortune, or through
the number and strength of their troops, or through the abundance of their
resources or the wisdom of their general or the excellence of their allies, or through
25 their superiority of position. From these, then, and similar advantages we shall
select and demonstrate those which are most applicable to the circumstances, when
our advice is in favour of war, belittling the points of superiority possessed by the
enemy and exaggerating those which we ourselves enjoy. If we are trying to prevent
a war which is likely to take place, we must first of all show either that the pretexts
30 do not exist at all or else that the grievances are small and insignificant; next we
must show that it is not expedient to go to war, dwelling on the disasters that befall
men in warfare; and further, that the advantages which conduce to victory (which
35 have just been enumerated) are possessed by the enemy rather than by us. These are
the means which we must employ to avert a war which is likely to occur. When we
are trying to stop a war which has actually started, if those to whom our advice is
offered are stronger than their foes, the first point on which we must insist is that
sensible men ought not to wait until they have a fall, but should make peace while
they are strong; also, that it is characteristic of war to ruin many even of those who
1425ᵇ1 are successful in it, but of peace to save the vanquished and to allow the victorious to
enjoy the possessions which they have gained in warfare.[4] We must also dwell upon
the numerous and incalculable vicissitudes of warfare. Such are the methods by
5 which we must exhort to peace those who are victorious in war. Those who have
already met with failure we must urge to make peace on the ground of actual events,
and because they ought to learn from their misfortunes and not be exasperated by
those who have already injured them, and because of the dangers which have
already resulted from not making peace, and because it is better to sacrifice a part
10 of their possessions to an enemy stronger than themselves than to be conquered and
lose their lives as well as their property. And, to put the matter briefly, we must
realize that it is the universal custom of mankind to abandon mutual warfare, either
when they think that the demands of the enemy are just, or when they are at
15 variance with their allies, or weary of war, or afraid of their enemy, or suffering
from internal strife. If, therefore, you collect from amongst all these and similar
arguments those which are most applicable to the circumstances, you will have no
lack of material for speaking about peace and war.

20 Lastly, it remains for us to treat of the provision of resources. First, then, we
must inquire whether any property belonging to the city is neglected, neither
bringing in any revenue nor being dedicated to the gods: I mean, for example, any

---

[4] Reading ἐᾶν ὧν.

public lands which are neglected and might bring in revenue to the city if they were sold or leased to private persons; for this is a very common source of income. If this expedient is lacking, we must impose taxes on rateable property, or order the poor to give their personal service in time of danger, the rich to pay money, and the craftsmen to provide arms. In a word, when we are treating of ways and means, we must say that they affect all the citizens equally and are permanent and ample, while the exact opposite is true of our adversaries' proposals.

From what has now been said we are acquainted with the subjects on which we shall speak in public, when we are seeking to persuade or dissuade, and with their component parts, which will supply us with the material of our orations. Next in order let us set forth and treat of the eulogistic and the vituperative kinds of oratory.

3 . To speak generally, the eulogistic kind is the amplification of creditable choices, deeds, and words, and the attribution of qualities which do not exist; while the vituperative kind is the opposite of this and consists in the minimizing of creditable qualities and the amplification of those which are discreditable. Things worthy of praise are those which are just, lawful, expedient, honourable, pleasant, and easy of execution. The nature of these qualities and the sources from which we can obtain abundant material about them have already been stated. He who is eulogizing must show in his speech that one of these praiseworthy qualities is connected with a certain person because it has either been brought about by his personal exertions, or has been produced through his agency, or has resulted from a certain action of his, or has been done for some object, or could not have come to pass except under certain circumstances which are due to him. Similarly he who is censuring must show that the contrary of this is true of the person whom he is censuring. . . .[5] The following are examples of the results of action; bodily health is the result of a fondness for gymnastics; a man falls into ill-health as the result of not caring for exercise, or becomes wiser as the result of studying philosophy, or lacks the necessities of life as the result of his own carelessness. The following are actions done with an object: men endure many toils and dangers with the object of being crowned by their fellow-citizens, or neglect everything else with the object of pleasing those whom they love. Instances of things which can only take place under certain circumstances are the following: victories at sea can only take place when there are sailors to win them, and drunkenness can only occur as the result of drinking. By pursuing this method on the lines already laid down you will have abundant material for eulogy and vituperation.

Generally speaking you will be able to amplify and minimize under all such circumstances by the following method: first, by showing, as I explained just now, that many good or bad results have been caused by a certain person's actions. This is one kind of amplification. A second method is to introduce something judged to be great—a great good, if you are eulogizing, and an evil if you are censuring—and

----

[5]Fuhrmann marks a lacuna here.

25 then set side by side with it what you have to say and compare the two together, making as much as possible of your own case and as little as possible of the other; the result will be that your own case is magnified. A third plan is to compare that about which you are speaking with the least thing which falls under the same

30 category; for the former will then appear magnified, just as persons of moderate height appear taller than they really are when they stand side by side with persons of unusually small stature. The following is another safe method of amplification: if a certain thing has been considered a great good, then its contrary, if you mention it, will appear to be a great evil, and similarly, if a thing is considered to be a great evil,

35 its contrary, if you mention it, will appear to be a great good. You can also magnify good and bad actions by showing that the doer of them acted intentionally, proving that he had long premeditated doing them, that he purposed to do them often, that he did them over a long period, that no one else ever tried to do them, that he acted in company with others with whom no one else ever acted, or following those whom

1426ᵇ1 no one else ever followed, or that he acted voluntarily or designedly, and that we should be fortunate, or unfortunate, if we all did as he did. You must also prove your point by drawing parallels and amplifying as follows, building them as it were one

5 on the top of another: 'If a man cares for his friends, it is natural to suppose that he honours his parents, and he who honours his parents will also desire to benefit his fatherland'. Generally speaking: if you can prove that a man is the cause of *many* good or bad things, these things will appear to be important. You must also examine the topic on which you are speaking and see whether it appears to have more weight

10 when divided into parts or when treated as a whole, and you must treat it in the manner in which it appears to have more weight. By pursuing these methods you will be able to make the most frequent and effective amplifications.

You will minimize good and bad things in your speeches by following the

15 opposite method to that which we have prescribed for amplification. The best thing is to show that a man's action has produced no result at all, or, if that is impossible, only the smallest and most insignificant results. From these instructions we know how to amplify or minimize any point which we are bringing forward, when we are eulogizing or censuring. These materials for amplification are useful in other kinds

20 of oratory, but they are most effective in eulogy and vituperation. We shall thus be provided with ample material on these topics.

4 · Let us next similarly define the kinds of oratory employed in accusation

25 and defence and the elements of which they are composed and the uses to which they are to be put. The oratory of accusation is, to put the matter briefly, the exposition of errors and crimes; defensive oratory is the disproving of errors and crimes of which a man is accused or suspected. Both styles, then, having these

30 qualities, he who is accusing, when he charges his opponents with wickedness, must declare that their acts are unjust and illegal and detrimental to the interests of the mass of citizens; when he is accusing an adversary of folly, he must declare his acts to be both inexpedient for the actual doer of them and disgraceful and odious and

35 impracticable. These and similar arguments are those which should be directed

against the wicked and foolish. Accusers should also observe against what kinds of offences the punishments ordained by the laws are directed and for what offences juries impose penalties. Where the law has laid down a definite punishment, the accuser must make it his sole object to prove that the offence has been committed. When the jury has to assess the penalty, . . .[6] then the errors committed by one's opponents must be amplified, and, if possible, it must be shown that the offence was committed voluntarily, and not with ordinary intent but after every possible preparation. If you cannot do this, and think that your opponent intends to show that he has somehow made a mistake or that he intended to act honourably in the matter but met with misfortune you must deprive him of any claim to pardon by telling your hearers that evil-doers, instead of declaring that they have made a mistake after they have acted, ought to be careful before they act; and further that, even if he has made mistakes or met with misfortune, he is more deserving of punishment for his misfortunes and mistakes than one who has done neither of these things. Moreover the legislator has not let those who make mistakes go free, but has made them liable to punishment, in order to prevent them from making mistakes again. You must also point out that if they listen to one who makes this kind of defence, they will have many persons doing wrong by choice; for if they are successful, they will simply do what they like, while, if they are unsuccessful, they will declare that they have met with ill-fortune, and they then will be excused from punishment. By such arguments must accusers deprive their adversaries of any claim to pardon, and by means of the amplifications already described their acts must be shown to have caused many evils. These are the component parts of which the oratory of accusation is made up.

Defensive oratory consists of three methods. A man who is defending himself must either prove that he committed none of the acts of which he is accused; or if he is forced to admit them, he must try to show that what he has done is lawful and just and honourable and expedient for the state; if he cannot prove this, he must attribute his acts to an error or to misfortune and show that the harm which has resulted from them is small, and so try to gain pardon. You can define a crime, an error, and a misfortune thus: you must regard as a crime a wicked deed done deliberately, and you must urge that the heaviest penalty be exacted for such deeds; a harmful act done because of ignorance must be called an error; while the failure to accomplish some good intention, not through one's own fault but owing to some one else or to luck, is to be accounted a misfortune. The commission of crime you must declare to be confined to wicked men, while error and misfortune in action are not peculiar to oneself but are common to all men, including those who are sitting in judgement upon you. You must ask for pardon if you are forced to admit that you have committed faults of this kind, pointing out that your hearers are as liable to error and misfortune as you are. A man who is making his defence must observe all the offences for which the laws have laid down punishment and juries assess penalties. When the law fixes a definite punishment, he must show that he has not committed the offence at all, or that he has acted legally and justly. But when the

[right margin line references:]
1427ª1

5

10

15

20

25

30

35

40

1427ᵇ1

5

---

[6]Fuhrmann marks a lacuna here.

jury is empowered to assess the penalty, he must not follow the same course and deny that he has committed the offence, but rather he must try to prove that his action has caused little harm to his adversary and that it was done involuntarily. If we follow these and similar methods, we shall have abundant material in cases of accusation and defence. It remains for us still to deal with the style of oratory employed in an inquiry.

5 · Inquiry may be summarily described as the elucidation of choices, acts, and words which are contradictory to one another or to the rest of a man's mode of life. He who is making an inquiry must try to discover whether either the statement which he is examining or the acts or choices of the subject of his inquiry are in any respect contradictory to one another. The method to be pursued is as follows: he must consider whether in the past the person in question, after having been originally the friend of another man, next became his enemy and then again the friend of the same person, or whether he has acted, or is likely in the future, if opportunities should occur, to act in a manner which contradicts his former acts. Similarly, you must observe whether †in making some statement now, he is speaking in contradiction of his former words or whether he might speak in contradiction of what he is saying or has said before†,[7] and likewise whether he has formed any choice which contradicts his former choices, or would do so if opportunities should arise. By a similar process you must deal with the contradictions which occur in the mode of life of the person whom you are examining in respect of his other and highly esteemed habits of life. If you thus pursue this branch of oratory, there is no method of examination which you will leave untried.

All the various branches of oratory having now been distinguished, we must employ them, when it is fitting, either each separately or in common with one another by mingling their different qualities. For there are very great differences between them, but in actual practice they have much in common. In this respect they resemble the various classes of human beings, who are partly similar and partly dissimilar in their appearance and in their looks. Having thus distinguished the various kinds of oratory, let us next enumerate the requisites which are common to all kinds and explain how they must be used.

6 · First, then, the just, the lawful, the expedient, the honourable, the pleasant, and similar topics are, as I stated at the beginning, common to all the various kinds of oratory, but are chiefly used in persuasive and dissuasive oratory. Secondly amplification and minimization are necessarily useful in all kinds of oratory, but most use is made of them in eulogy and vituperation. Thirdly, there are the proofs, which must necessarily be employed in every department of oratory, but are particularly useful in accusation and defence, since these need most refutation.[8] Further we must deal with anticipations of arguments, postulates, reiterations, elegancies, prolixity of speech, and moderate length of speech, brevity, and method

---

[7] The text of the obelized passage is uncertain.
[8] Fuhrmann obelizes the 'since' clause.

of statement. For these and similar expedients are useful in all the various branches   10
of oratory.

7 . The just, the lawful, and the like I have already defined and explained
their application; I have also dealt with amplification and minimization. I will now   15
explain the other terms, beginning with the proofs.

Proofs are of two kinds; some are derived directly from actual words, acts, and
persons, others are supplementary to words and actions. Probabilities, examples,
evidences, enthymemes, maxims, signs, and refutations are proofs derived from   20
actual words, persons, and actions. The speaker's opinions, testimonies, evidence
given under torture, and oaths are supplementary proofs. We must understand the
nature of each of these kinds of proof, and whence we are to derive material for   25
them, and how they differ from one another.

It is a probability when one's hearers have examples in their own minds of what
is being said. For instance, if any one were to say that he desires the glorification of
his country, the prosperity of his friends, and the misfortunes of his foes, and the
like, his statements taken together will seem to be probabilities; for each one of his
hearers is himself conscious that he entertains such wishes on these and similar   30
subjects. We must, therefore, always carefully notice, when we are speaking,
whether we are likely to find our audience in sympathy with us on the subject on
which we are speaking; for in that case they are most likely to believe what we say.
Such, then, is the nature of a probability.   35

We can divide probabilities into three kinds. One kind consists in the inclusion
in one's speech of the feelings which are naturally found in mankind—if, for
example, certain persons happen to despise or fear a certain other person, or,
further, if they feel pleasure or pain or desire, or have ceased from desire, or if they   1428ᵇ1
have experienced in mind or body or one of the senses any of the feelings whereby
we are all affected. These and similar feelings, being common to all human nature,   5
are well known to our hearers. Such, then, are the natural feelings which are wont to
affect mankind, and for these we say that a place ought to be found in our speeches.
Another division of probabilities falls under the heading of habit (which is what we
do from custom), a third under that of love of gain. For we often for the sake of gain
choose to act in a way which does violence to our nature and character.   10

With these definitions before us, when we are seeking to persuade or dissuade,
we must show in regard to the subject in question that the action to which we are
exhorting our hearers, or which we are opposing, has the effect which we declare
that it has. Failing that, we must show that actions similar to that of which we are   15
speaking either generally or invariably turn out as we say they do. Such must be our
application of probabilities in relation to actions. As regards persons you must show,
if you can, when you are accusing any one, that he has often committed the act in
question on previous occasions; or, if that is impossible, that he has done   20
similar acts. You must also try to prove that it was to his advantage to commit these
acts; for most men, themselves preferring what is to their advantage, think that
others too always act from this motive. If, therefore, you can derive an argument of

25 probability directly from your adversaries, this is the method by which you must infer it. Failing that, you must take similar persons and adduce their customary procedure; for example, when the man whom you are accusing is young, argue that he has committed acts such as persons of that age are in the habit of committing; for your accusations against him will be believed on the ground of this resemblance.

30 Similarly you will gain credence if you can show that his companions have the character which you declare him to have; for owing to his association with them it will appear likely that he has the same pursuits as his friends. Such must be the employment of the argument from probabilities by those who are accusing.

Those who are speaking in their own defence must make it their chief object to show that none of the acts of which they are accused has ever been committed either

35 by themselves or by any of their friends or by any person who resembles them, and that it would have been of no advantage to them to commit such acts. But if you have manifestly done the same deed on a previous occasion, the fault must be attributed to your youth, or some other excuse must be introduced to provide a reasonable pretext for your having done wrong on that occasion. You must declare also that it was of no benefit to you to have acted thus at the time and that it would not have been of any advantage to you now. If no act of the kind alleged has ever

1429ª1 been committed by you, but some of your friends happen to have done such deeds, you must plead that it is not just that you should be slandered because of them, and you must show that others of your associates are honest men; you will thus throw doubt on the crime of which you are accused. If they point out that other persons,

5 who resemble you, have committed the same crimes as they allege against you, you must declare that it is absurd if the fact that other people can be shown to have done wrong is to be regarded as a proof that you have committed any of the deeds of which you are accused. If, then, you deny that you have done the deed with which you are charged, you must thus make your defence by arguing from probabilities;

10 for you will then make the charge appear implausible. If, however, you are obliged to admit the charge, you must point out the resemblance of your acts to the usual practice of mankind, by stating as emphatically as possible that the majority of men, or all men, act under these and similar circumstances exactly as you have

15 done. If you cannot do this, you must take refuge in pleas of misfortune or error, and try to obtain pardon by citing the passions which are common to all mankind and make us lose our reason—love, anger, drunkenness, ambition, and the like. Such is the method by which we shall make the most skilful use of the argument from

20 probability.

8 · Examples are actions which have taken place in the past and are similar to, or the contrary of, those about which we are speaking. They must be used when your statement is not credible and you wish to establish its truth when it does not

25 gain credence from the argument of probability; the object being that your hearers, learning that another action similar to that of which you are speaking has been carried out in the way in which you declare it to have been done, may be more ready to believe what you say.

Examples are of two kinds; for some things turn out according to our expectations, others contrary to them. The former cause credit the latter discredit. For instance, if some one declares that the rich are juster than the poor and instances certain just actions on the part of rich men, such examples are in accordance with our expectation, for one can see that most men think that rich people are juster than poor people. If, on the other hand, some one shows that certain rich individuals have acted unjustly in order to get money, thus employing an example which is contrary to expectation, he would cause the rich to be distrusted. Similarly, if any one brings forward an example of what seems to be in accordance with our expectation—for instance, that on some occasion the Lacedaemonians or Athenians employing a large number of allies utterly defeated their enemies—he then disposes his hearers to take to themselves many allies. For every one is of opinion that large numbers are of no small importance for winning a victory. If, on the other hand, a speaker wishes to prove that numbers do not bring victory, he must give as examples occasions when the unexpected has happened, pointing out, for instance, that the Athenian exiles first seized Phyle with fifty men and then fought a battle against the far more numerous party in the city, who had the Lacedaemonians as their allies, and were thus restored to their own city; or again, that the Thebans, when the Lacedaemonians and practically all the Peloponnesians invaded Boeotia, confronted them alone at Leuctra and conquered the might of the Lacedaemonians; or again, that Dio the Syracusan sailed to Syracuse with three thousand hoplites and defeated Dionysius, whose forces were many times as great; and likewise the Corinthians, when they went to the assistance of the Syracusans with nine triremes, defeated the Carthaginians, although they were blockading the harbours of Syracuse with a hundred and fifty ships and held all the city except the acropolis. To sum the matter up, these and similar instances of unexpected successes often serve to discredit counsels which are based on ordinary probability. Such, then, is the nature of examples.

Examples of both kinds must be employed, when we are urging what may be reasonably expected to happen, in order to show that the suggested course of action for the most part turns out in a particular way; and, when we are predicting some unexpected result, in order to give instances in which satisfactory results have accrued where they seemed to be least expected. If your adversaries use this device, you must show that their instances were the results of good luck, and declare that such things happen rarely, whereas your examples are of common occurrence. This, then, is the method of employing examples. If, on the other hand, we wish to cite instances where the unexpected has happened, we must collect as many of them as possible and show by enumeration that the unexpected happens quite as often as the expected. We must use not only examples derived in this way but also those based on contraries. For instance, you can show that a certain state has acted selfishly towards its allies and that their friendship has thus been dissolved, and then say, 'We on the other hand, if we behave fairly and impartially towards our allies, shall keep their alliance for a long time'; or again, you can show that certain others have gone to war without due preparation and have consequently been defeated, and then

5 say, 'If we were to go to war properly prepared, we should have better hopes of success'. You will be able to derive a number of examples from past and from present events; for actions are generally partly like and partly unlike one another.

10 For this reason therefore we shall have no lack of examples and no difficulty in contradicting those brought forward by the other side. We now know the different kinds of examples and how we are to employ them and whence we are to derive them in abundance.

9 · Evidences exist where the direct contrary of that with which the speech is
15 concerned has occurred,[9] and where the speech is self-contradictory. For most listeners conclude from the contraries which occur in connexion with a speech or action that there is nothing sound in what is being said or done. You will often discover evidences by considering whether your adversary's speech is self-
20 contradictory or whether his action itself contradicts his words. Such is the nature of evidences and the method by which you will obtain the greatest number of them.

10 · Enthymemes arise where contraries occur not only of the speech and
25 action in question but of anything else as well. You will often discover them by pursuing the method prescribed for the oratory of inquiry and by considering whether the speech or the actions are contrary to justice or law or expediency or to what is honourable, practicable, easy, or probable, or to the character of the speaker
30 or the nature of the circumstances. Such are the enthymemes which must be chosen for use against our adversaries. The contraries of these must be employed on our own behalf, and we must prove that our actions and words are the contrary of those
35 which are unjust, unlawful, inexpedient, and of the habits of wicked men—in a word, of those things which are considered evil. We must speak in support of each of these pleas as briefly as possible and express ourselves in the fewest possible words. This then is the way in which we shall obtain a large number of enthymemes and the best method of employing them.

11 · A maxim is, briefly, the expression of an individual opinion on general
1430[b]1 matters. There are two kinds of maxims, those which are reputable and those which are paradoxical. When you are using the former, there is no need to bring forward any reasons for your statement for what you say is well known and does not excite incredulity. But when you are uttering a paradox, you must state your reasons
5 briefly, so as to avoid prolixity and not arouse incredulity. The maxims which you quote must be applicable to the circumstances, in order that your words may not seem inept and far-fetched. We shall form a large number of maxims either from
10 the peculiar nature of the circumstances or by means of hyperbole or by drawing parallels. The following are examples of maxims derived from the peculiar circumstances of a case: 'I do not regard it as possible for a man to become a clever general if he is without experience in affairs'; or again, 'It is characteristic of

[9]Fuhrmann obelizes this clause.

sensible men to profit by the examples of their predecessors and so try to avoid the errors of evil counsel'. Such then are the maxims which we shall form from the peculiar circumstances of a case. Maxims such as the following are formed by hyperbole: 'Thieves are in my opinion worse than plunderers; for the former carry off property secretly, the latter openly'. By this method we shall form a number of maxims by hyperbole. The following are maxims based on parallels: 'Those who appropriate money seem to me to act very like those who betray cities; for both are trusted and wrong those who have trusted them'; or again, 'My opponents seem to me to act very like tyrants; for tyrants claim not to be punished for the wrongs which they have themselves inflicted, while they demand the fullest punishment for the wrongs of which they accuse others; and my adversaries, if they have themselves something which belongs to me, do not restore it, while, if I have received something which belongs to them, they think that they ought to have it restored to them and the interest on it as well'. By following this method then we shall form a number of maxims.

12 · One thing is a sign of another thing, but one thing taken at random is not a sign of something else taken at random, nor is everything a sign of everything else; but the sign of a thing is that which usually occurs before, or simultaneously with, or after it. That which has happened is a sign not only of what has happened but also of what has not happened; and similarly what has not happened is a sign not only of what does not exist but also of what does exist. One sign causes belief, another knowledge; the latter is the best kind of sign, while that which produces the most plausible opinion is second best. To put the matter briefly, we shall obtain an abundance of signs from anything which has been done or is said or seen, taking each separately and also from the greatness or smallness of the resultant disadvantages or advantages. We shall also derive them from testimonies and evidence and from our own supporters or those of our enemies, or from our enemies themselves; also from the challenges issued by the parties and from times and seasons and from many other things. From these sources then we shall have an abundance of signs.

13 · A refutation is that which cannot be otherwise than as . . .[10] as urged by us, and on what is impossible by nature or impossible as urged by our adversaries. An example of something which is naturally necessary is the statement that living creatures require food, and the like. What is necessary as urged by us is such a statement as that those who are scourged confess what their tormentors tell them to confess. Again, an instance of what is naturally impossible is the statement that a small child stole a sum of money, which he could not possibly carry, and went off with it. It will be an impossibility as urged by an adversary, if for example, he declares that on a certain date we made a contract at Athens, whereas we can prove to our hearers that at that time we were absent in some other city. From these and similar materials we shall form an ample supply of refutations.

---

[10]Fuhrmann marks a lacuna.

We have now briefly described all the proofs which are derived from actual words and from acts and from persons. Let us now consider how they differ from one another.

25   14 · A probability differs from an example in this, that the hearers have themselves some notion of the probability, while examples . . .[11] can be derived from contraries and from similars, while evidences can only be constructed from contrarieties of word and deed. Again, an enthymeme always has this distinction

30   from an evidence, that an evidence is a contrariety which is concerned with a word or an action, while an enthymeme selects also contrarieties connected with other kinds of things; in other words, it is impossible for us to obtain an evidence unless there is some contrariety in respect of actions or words, whereas speakers can

35   provide themselves with enthymemes from a variety of sources. Maxims differ from enthymemes in that enthymemes can be constructed only from contrarieties, whereas maxims can be enunciated both in connexion with contrarieties and also by themselves. Signs differ from maxims and all the other proofs already mentioned,

40   because, while all the others engender an opinion in the minds of those who hear them, certain of the signs cause those who judge to have a clear knowledge; also

1431ᵇ1   because it is impossible for us ourselves to provide most of the other proofs, while it is easy to obtain a large number of signs. Further, a refutation differs from a sign, because some signs cause those who hear them merely to entertain an opinion, whereas every refutation teaches the truth to the judges. Thus from what has been

5   said we know the nature of the proofs which are derived from actual words and actions and men, and the sources from which we are to derive them, and how they differ from one another.

Let us next deal with each of the supplementary proofs. The opinion of a

10   speaker is the declaration of his own belief about things. You ought to show yourself to be experienced in the matters about which you are speaking, and point out that it is to your advantage to tell the truth concerning them. One who is contradicting ought first and foremost to show that his adversary has no experience of the matters

15   on which he is talking: if however that is impossible, he ought to show that even persons of experience often make mistakes; and if this is inadmissible, he must say that it is contrary to the advantage of his opponents to tell the truth about these matters. Such is the use which we shall make of opinions expressed by speakers, both when we are ourselves expressing them and when we are contradicting others.

20   15 · Testimony is a confession made voluntarily by one who knows. That which is testified must be either plausible or implausible or of doubtful credit; similarly the witness must be trustworthy or untrustworthy or of doubtful good faith. When therefore the evidence is plausible and the witness truthful, the

25   testimony needs no further support, unless you wish briefly to introduce a maxim or enthymeme for adornment's sake. But when the witness is under suspicion, you

[11]Fuhrmann marks a lacuna.

must prove that such a person would not give false evidence to show gratitude or from motives of revenge or gain. You must also make it clear that it is not to his advantage to bear false witness; for the benefits which he gains are small, while detection is a serious matter, and, if he is found out, the laws punish him not only by fining him but also by damaging his reputation and destroying his credit. By these methods then we shall cause witnesses to be believed.

When we are contradicting evidence, we must cast prejudice on the character of the witness, if he is a bad man, or inquire into the evidence, if it is implausible, or else contradict both the witness and the evidence by bringing together all that is most discreditable to our adversaries. We must also consider whether the witness is a friend to him for whom he is giving evidence, or whether he can in any way be associated with his deed, or whether he is an enemy of the man against whom he is bearing witness, or whether he is poor. For such men are under suspicion of bearing false witness either to show favour or from motives of revenge or for gain. We shall also say that the legislator laid down the law about false testimony to apply to persons of this kind, so that it is absurd that, whereas the legislator did not trust witnesses, those should believe them who are sitting in judgement after having sworn to judge according to the laws. By these methods then we shall cause witnesses to be discredited.

It is possible also to disguise evidence by a proceeding such as the following: 'Bear witness', you say, 'in my favour, Callicles'—'By the gods, I will not', he replies, 'for the accused committed these crimes, though I tried to prevent him'. In this way, though he has given false evidence in his refusal, he will not be liable to punishment as a false witness. This then is the way in which we shall treat evidence, when it is to our advantage to disguise it. If our opponents try to do anything of this kind, we shall expose their wickedness and order them to give their evidence in writing. With these instructions then before us we know how to deal with witnesses and evidence.

16 · Evidence given under torture is a confession on the part of one who knows but is unwilling to state what he knows. When therefore it is to our interest to strengthen such evidence, we must say that individuals take their proofs from evidence under torture in their most serious affairs, and cities in their most important business, and that evidence under torture is more trustworthy than ordinary testimony. For it is often to the interest of witnesses to lie; but those who are under torture gain by telling the truth, for doing so will bring them the speediest relief from their sufferings.

When you wish to discredit evidence given under torture, you must say in the first place that those who are being tortured become hostile to those who have delivered them up to be tortured and for this reason tell many lies against their masters. Secondly, you must say that they often make confessions to their torturers which are not the truth, in order to end their torments as quickly as possible. You must also point out that even free men have often before now lied against themselves under torture to escape the suffering of the moment; it is therefore much

30   more likely that slaves should wish to avoid punishment by lying against their masters, rather than, when they are enduring great bodily and mental pain, retain from falsehood in order to save other people from suffering. By these and similar arguments we shall cause evidence given under torture to be plausible or implausible.

35   17 · An oath is an affirmation without proof accompanied by an invocation of the gods. When we wish to amplify the power of an oath we must say that no one would desire to commit perjury, because he would fear punishment from heaven and disgrace in the eyes of men; we must also point out that, while it is possible to escape the notice of men, it is impossible to elude the gods. When our opponents take refuge in an oath and we wish to belittle it, we must point out that those who do

1432^{b}1   evil deeds are the very men who do not scruple to commit perjury; for a man who thinks that the gods take no notice of him when he does wrong, also thinks that he will not be punished even if he forswears himself. By pursuing a method such as the above in the matter of oaths we shall have no lack of material.

5   We have now briefly carried out our purpose of dealing with all the various kinds of proof and have shown not only the force of each of them, but also how they differ from one another and how they ought to be employed. We will now proceed to explain the other expedients which belong to all seven kinds of oratory and are

10   useful in speeches of every kind.

18 · Anticipation is the method by which we shall counteract the ill-feeling which is felt against us by anticipating the adverse criticisms of our audience and the arguments of those who are going to speak against us. We shall anticipate the

15   criticisms of our audience by such a statement as, 'Perhaps some of you are astonished that, young as I am, I attempt thus to speak in public on important matters'; or again, 'Let no one oppose me through resentment, because I am going to offer you advice on subjects about which certain other people hesitate to speak

20   openly before you'. In matters then which are likely to annoy your hearers you must by anticipations of this kind bring forward reasons, which will show that you are justified in offering advice, pointing out the dearth of public speakers or the greatness of the dangers or the public expediency, or giving some other such reason

25   whereby you will remove the ill-feeling which threatens you. If your audience still cries out just as much against you, you must address them briefly in the form of a maxim or enthymeme, saying, for example, that it is absolutely absurd that they should have come together to take the best counsel about the situation and then think that they can take good counsel without deigning to hear what the speakers

30   have to say; or again, you may say that it is only fair that they should either themselves get up and offer some advice, or else listen to those who have advice to offer, and then vote in favour of any course that recommends itself to them. Such must be the method of employing anticipation in public speaking, and this is how outcries must be faced.

35   In forensic speeches we shall use similar methods of anticipation to the above. If an outcry is raised against us at an early stage of the proceedings, we shall meet it

in this manner: 'Is it not absurd that, while the legislator ordained that each party should be allowed to speak twice, you who are sitting in judgement upon us should have sworn to pass sentence according to the law, and then refuse even to listen to a single speech? And that, while he took such measures to secure that you should give 1433ª1 your vote in accordance with your oath after hearing all that was to be said, you should be so indifferent to his injunctions that, without even listening to the beginnings of the speeches, you already think that you know all the facts perfectly?' Or you can put the matter differently and say, 'How absurd it is that the lawgiver 5 should have ordained that, if the votes are equal, the defendant should win the case, whereas you hold so strongly to the contrary opinion that you do not even listen to the defence offered by those who have been slandered; and that, whereas he granted this advantage in the voting to defendants because they run greater risks, you, while you show no hostility towards the accusers who run no risks, alarm by these outcries 10 those who in terror and danger are defending themselves from the charges brought against them'. Such must be your method of meeting those who raise an outcry against you at the beginning of your speech. If they interrupt you when your speech is well advanced, then, if those who do so are few in number, you must rebuke them 15 and tell them that it is only just that they should listen to you at the moment, in order that they may not prevent the rest from forming a correct judgement, and that, when they have heard you, then they can do what they please. If the majority raises an outcry against you, you should blame yourself and not your judges; for, if you find fault with them, you only make them angry, whereas, if you blame yourself 20 and say that you have made a mistake in your manner of speaking, you will gain their pardon. You must also beg your judges to give a favourable ear to your speech and not at this early stage to show what view they take about the facts on which they are to give their secret vote. In general, we shall meet interruptions in a summary 25 manner with maxims and enthymemes, pointing out that our interrupters are setting themselves in opposition to justice or the laws or the interests of the city or what is honourable; for such methods as these are best calculated to make one's hearers stop interrupting. We now know from what has been said above how to employ anticipations in dealing with an audience and how to meet interruptions. 30

I will next show you how to anticipate what is likely to be said by one's opponents. You can say: 'Perhaps he will bewail his poverty, which is not my fault but has been caused by his own way of life'; or again, 'I hear that he intends to say 35 such and such a thing'. If we are speaking first, we must thus anticipate what our opponents are likely to say and so destroy and invalidate their pleas. For even though the arguments which you forestall are quite forcible, they will appear much less weighty to those who have already heard them.

If we are speaking after our opponents and they have anticipated what we 1433ᵇ1 intend to say, it is necessary to counteract their anticipations and destroy them by speaking as follows, 'My opponent has not only told you many lies to my discredit, but further, well knowing that I shall refute his charges, he has anticipated my plea and discredited it beforehand, in order that you may not give it the attention which 5 you otherwise would, or else that I may not employ it at all, because it has already been torn to pieces by him. I hold, however, that you ought to hear my arguments

from my own lips, not from his, even if[12] he has tried to tear my arguments to pieces
10   by saying things which I declare to be a strong sign that he has no sound plea to
offer'. Euripides has made a clever use of this device in the following lines of his
Philoctetes:

> E'en though he thinks to have destroyed my pleas
> Escaping charge of wrong, yet will I speak;
> From mine own lips mine arguments shall come,
> Let his words show what kind of man he is.[13]

15   We know then from the above how to make use of anticipations in relation both to
our judges and to our opponents.

19 · Postulates in oratory are the demands which speakers make from their
hearers. Some of them are just, others unjust. It is just to ask that they should listen
20   to what you are saying and lead a favourable ear. It is also a just demand that they
should give one the assistance which the laws allow and never vote against the laws
and that they should make allowances for misfortunes. Any demand which is
contrary to the law is unjust, otherwise it is just.[14] Such are the postulates. We have
25   distinguished their different kinds in order that, knowing the just from the unjust,
we may use them on the right occasion, and that it may not escape our notice if our
adversaries make any unjust demand from the judges. From what has been said we
shall have an adequate knowledge on this subject.

20 · Iteration is a means of briefly reminding one's hearers. It must be
30   employed both at the conclusion of a division of a speech and at the final conclusion.
In recapitulating we use iteration when arguing or narrating or recommending or
questioning using irony. I will show you of what nature each of these is. The
35   following is an example of its use in arguing: 'I cannot say what these men would
have done, if they had not manifestly deserted us long ago and were not convicted of
having served against our city and of having never fulfilled any of their promises'.
Such is the use of iteration in an argument. It can be used as follows in narrating: 'I
have shown that they were the first to break the treaty of alliance and the first to
1434ª1   attack us when we were at war with the Lacedaemonians, and that they displayed
the utmost eagerness to enslave our city'. Such is the use of iteration in narrative.
The following is an example of its use in reminding your audience under the form of
recommending a certain course of action: 'You must remember that ever since we
5   entered into friendship with these men we have never suffered any reverse at the
hands of our enemies. For they have often helped us and prevented the Lacedaemonians from devastating our territory, and they have continued to this day to
contribute large sums of money'. Thus shall we remind our hearers by recommend-
10   ing a certain course of action. The following is an instance of iteration in the form of
a question: 'I should like to hear from them, why it is that they do not pay us the
tribute which they owe. For they cannot have the face to say that they are in need of

---

[12]The text of this clause is uncertain.   [13]Frag. 794 Nauck.   [14]Fuhrmann obelizes this sentence.

money, when they can be shown to be receiving such large sums of money annually
from their land, nor yet can they say that they spend much on the administration of   15
their city; for they clearly spend less than all the other islanders'. Such will be our
use of iteration in the form of a question.

21 · Irony is to say something and pretend that you are not saying it, or else
to call things by the names of their contraries. It may take the following form in a
brief reminder of what has already been said: 'I think that I need hardly say that   20
these men, who pretend that they have done the state many services, are shown to
have done it much harm, whereas we, whom they declare to be ungrateful, are
shown to have often helped them and never to have done any one any injury'. Such is
the way briefly to remind your hearers of something under the pretence of omitting   25
it. Secondly, the following is an instance of calling things by contrary names: 'These
noble citizens have clearly done great harm to their allies, while we worthless
mortals have obviously been the cause of many benefits to them'. In this way we   30
shall briefly remind our hearers and employ iteration at the end of the divisions of
our speeches and at their final conclusion.

22 · We will next explain how one can speak elegantly and prolong a speech
to the length which one desires.
     We can speak elegantly in the following manner, by introducing, for example,   35
half enthymemes in such a way that our audience can guess the other half; we must
also include maxims. To some of these we must give a place in every division of the
speech[15] but the actual words must be varied and a similar phrase must never be
applied repeatedly in the same connexion. In this way your speech will be elegant.
     When you wish to lengthen your speech, you must divide up your subject and   1434ᵇ1
in each division explain the nature of its contents and their particular and general
application and state the grounds of your pleas. If we wish to make our discourse
still longer, we must employ a number of words in dealing with each topic. In each   5
division of the speech you must iterate and make your iteration brief; while at the
conclusion of your speech you ought to recapitulate as a whole all that you have
dealt with in detail, and treat the subject generally. In this way your speech will be   10
of a sufficient length.
     If you wish to speak briefly, you should include your whole subject in a single
word and that word the shortest which is applicable to the subject. You must also
employ few conjunctive particles and connect as many things as possible together.
Such must be your choice of words; you must make your language serve a double   15
purpose, and you must do away with the brief iterations in the separate divisions of
the speech and only employ iteration in your final conclusion. This is the way in
which we shall make our speeches brief.
     If you wish to speak at moderate length, you must pick out the most important
divisions of your speech and make them your subject. You must also use the words
of medium length and not the longest or the shortest, and not employ a large   20

---

[15]Fuhrmann obelizes this clause.

number on a single topic but observe moderation. You must neither on the one hand do away entirely with conclusions in the intermediate parts of your speech, nor on the other hand introduce them in every division; but you must make special
25 iterations at the end of those parts to which you wish your audience to pay particular attention. On these principles, then, we shall regulate the length of our speeches, whenever we wish to do so.

If you wish to compose a speech which will be elegant, you must take care as far as possible to adapt the character of your speech to that of your audience. You
30 will achieve this, if you observe their character, whether noble or petty or ordinary.

On these points, then, you will have adequate knowledge from what has been said above. We will now treat of the putting together of words; for this too is essential.

23 · In the first place, then, words are of three kinds, simple, composite, and metaphorical.
35 Similarly there are three ways in which words can be put together: firstly, you can end one syllable with a vowel and begin the next with a vowel; secondly, you can begin a word with a consonant and end the previous word with a consonant; thirdly, you can put consonants and vowels in juxtaposition.

There are four orders in which words can be arranged. First, you can either put similar words side by side or else disperse them; or again, you can use the same
1435ª1 words or else change them into others; thirdly, you can describe a thing in one or many words; fourthly, you can name in their proper order the subjects of which you have undertaken to treat, or else transpose them.

I will next show what is the best method of statement which you can employ.

24 · First of all, you must make your statement by means of a twofold
5 division, and, secondly, you must discourse lucidly. The following are the various forms of this two-fold division. First, one can say that one can oneself do one thing and another; secondly, that this man cannot do a certain thing, but that man can; thirdly, that this man can do a certain thing and something else; fourthly, that neither can one do a certain thing oneself nor can any one else do it; fifthly, that one
10 cannot do a certain thing oneself, but that some one else can; sixthly, that one can do something oneself, but the other person cannot do something else. You can see each of these cases in the following examples. An illustration of the case where one can oneself do one thing and another is: 'I have not only achieved this for you, but also,
15 when Timotheus intended to make an expedition against you, I prevented him'. The following is an example of the case where one man cannot do a thing but another man can: 'This man then is unable to go himself on an embassy for you, but here is a man who is a friend of the Spartan state and would be better able than any one else to carry out the negotiations which you wish carried out'. The case where a man can do a certain thing and something else as well can be thus illustrated: 'Not only has
20 he proved himself a strong man in war, but he can also give as good advice as any

other citizen'. The following is a case where one cannot oneself do a thing and nobody else can: 'Having but a small force I cannot myself conquer our adversaries, nor could any other citizen do so'. The following is an instance in which another man can do a thing, but one cannot do it oneself: 'Yes, he is physically strong, but I am weak'. The following is an illustration of the case where one can oneself do one thing, but some other person cannot do something else: 'I can steer, but this man cannot even pull an oar'. This then is how you will employ forms of twofold statement, following the same course in every subject. We must next consider how you are to treat your subject lucidly.

25 · First, then, call anything of which you speak by its proper name, avoiding ambiguity. Take care not to put vowels next to one another. Be careful to put the so-called 'articles' in the proper place. Consider how you put words together, so that there may be neither confusion nor transposition; for if your discourse has these qualities it is obscure. When you use an introductory particle, employ the corresponding particle afterwards. The following is an example of the use of corresponding particle: 'I *indeed* (μέν) came to the place to which I said I would come, *but* (δέ) you, though you promised to come, did not do so'; or again, when the same particle follows: 'You were *both* (καί) the cause of that *and* (καί) the cause of this'. So much for the particles; from these examples you must infer the use of others.

Words must be put together so as to avoid confusion or transposition. The following is an example of such confusion: 'It is a terrible thing that this man should strike this man'. Here it is not clear which man struck the other; but you will make it clear if you say; 'It is a terrible thing that this man should be struck by this man'.[16] This is an example where there is a confusion in the arrangement of words. . . .[17] The following is an instance of care taken to put the article in the right place: 'This man is wronging this man'. In this case the insertion of the articles makes the diction clear, while their omission will make it obscure; the reverse is sometimes true. So much then for the articles.

Never put vowels in juxtaposition, unless it is impossible to make your meaning clear otherwise, or unless a pause or some other division occurs.

The following is a case where ambiguity must be avoided: the same words are sometimes used in several senses, for example we speak of a threshold (ὀδός) of a door and of a way (ὀδός) along which people walk; in such cases we must always add that which gives the word its distinctive meaning.

If we follow these rules we shall be clear in our use of words, and we shall make statements by means of the twofold method of division already described.

26 · Let us now deal with the antitheses, parisoses, and similarities; for we shall need these also.

An antithesis occurs when both the wording and the sense, or one or other of them, are opposed in a contrast. The following would be an antithesis both of

---

[16]The examples make sense in Greek, where τοῦτον τύπτειν τοῦτον is ambiguous.
[17]Fuhrmann marks a lacuna.

30   wording and sense: 'It is not fair that my opponent should become rich by possessing what belongs to me, while I sacrifice my property and become a mere beggar'. In the following sentence we have a merely verbal antithesis: 'Let the rich and prosperous give to the poor and needy'; and an antithesis of sense only in the following: 'I tended him when he was sick, but he has been the cause of very great

35   misfortunes to me'. Here there is no verbal antithesis, but the two actions are contrasted. The double antithesis (that is, both of sense and of wording) would be the best to use: but the other two kinds are also true antitheses.

27 · Parisosis occurs when a sentence has two equal 'members'. The equality

1436ᵃl   can be that of many small to few great things, and an equality of magnitude can be united with an equality of number. Parisosis takes a form such as the following, 'either through lack of resources or through the magnitude of the war'. These things are neither like nor opposed to one another, but merely equal to one another.

5   28 · Paromoeosis goes further than parisosis; for it makes the 'members' not only equal but also similar, being composed of similar words, in the following, for example: 'If you must imitate the wording, you should simulate the feeling'.[18] Above all you should make the last words similar; for this gives the closest

10   similarity. Words are similar which have similar syllables, in which most of the letters are the same; for example, 'in numbers deficient, in might sufficient'.

        Enough then of these topics. For we are acquainted with the nature of the just,

15   the lawful, the honourable, the expedient and the other qualities, and the sources from which we can derive them in abundance. Similarly we know the nature of

20   amplifications and minimizations, and how we can provide them for our discourses. In like manner we are acquainted with proofs, anticipations, the postulates which we demand from our hearers, iterations, elegances, the means of regulating the length of our speeches, and all the ways of putting words together for purposes of statement. And so knowing from what has been said the qualities which are common to every kind of oratory and their uses, if we accustom and practise

25   ourselves according to the prescribed preparatory exercises, we shall attain to great facility both in writing and speaking.

        It is by taking the component parts separately that you can most accurately distinguish the methods of speaking. I will next treat of the manner in which the words must be organically arranged in the various kinds of oratory, and which parts

30   must be put first and how they must be treated.

        I deal therefore first with proems; for the proem is common to all seven kinds of oratory and it can be fittingly applied to all subjects.

        29 · The proem can be described in a general way as a preparation of one's

35   audience and a declaration of the subject in a summary manner for the benefit of the ignorant, in order that they may know with what the speech is concerned and

---

[18]The text of this example is uncertain.

may follow the argument. It also exhorts them to pay attention and tries, as far as is possible in a speech, to influence their minds in our favour. Such is the preparation at which the proem must aim.

I will first show how the proem must be employed in public speaking and persuasive oratory. The following are examples of the way in which to lay your subject before your hearers and make it clear to them: 'I stand before you to advise that we should go to war on behalf of the Syracusans', or, 'I stand before you to demonstrate the inadvisability of our helping the Syracusans'. This, then, is the way to summarize your subject.

We shall know how to exhort our hearers to pay attention, if we ourselves call to mind to what arguments and facts we pay most attention when deliberating. Do we not pay the closest attention when the subjects of deliberation are important or alarming or else nearly concern us; or when those who address us claim that they will show us that the measures which they are urging us to adopt are just and honourable and expedient and easy and honest; or when they beg us to listen with attention? Just as, therefore, we ourselves attend to others, so if we take those of the points above mentioned which are most applicable to the subjects of which we are treating and lay them before our hearers, we shall make them attend to what we are saying. These, then, are the ways in which we exhort our hearers to pay attention.

We shall secure their goodwill if we first consider what is in fact their attitude towards us, whether they are well or ill disposed or whether they are indifferent. If they are actually well disposed towards us, it is superfluous to talk about goodwill; if, however, we wish to talk about it at all, we must do so briefly, using irony in the following way: 'That I am well disposed towards the state, and that you have often acted expediently by following my advice, and that I observe a just attitude towards public affairs, preferring a personal sacrifice to reaping any advantage at the expense of the state,—these are, I think, statements which it is unnecessary for me to make to you who know well the truth of them. My efforts shall be directed rather to showing you that you will be well advised, if on this occasion too you follow my counsels'. This then is the method by which in a public speech you must remind those who are well disposed towards you of their goodwill.

When your hearers are neither prejudiced against you nor well disposed, you must say that it is right and expedient that they should give a favourable ear to those citizens who have not yet given a proof of their quality as speakers. You must then flatter your audience by praising them, urging them to judge the speeches which they hear with fairness and discrimination as is their custom. Further, you must employ minimization and say, 'I stand before you not through any confidence in my own cleverness, but because I think that the advice which I am about to offer is beneficial to the state'. By such methods you must secure the goodwill of those who are neither well nor ill disposed towards you.

If you are the object of misrepresentation, the misrepresentation must be connected with yourself or the subject on which you are speaking or your actual words. Misrepresentations of this kind can date either from the present or from the past. If then one is under suspicion of wrongdoing in the past, one must employy

1436^{b}1

5

10

15

20

25

30

35

1437^{a}1

anticipation in addressing one's audience and say: 'I am well aware that a prejudice
5   exists against me, but I will prove that it is groundless'. You must then make a brief
defence in your proem, if you have anything to say on your own behalf, or raise
objections to the judgements which have been passed upon you. For whether you
have been publicly or privately misrepresented, judgement must either have been
passed upon you or be impending in the immediate future, or else those who have
10 laid the charge against you are unwilling to submit the matter to judgement; and
you must say that the judgement passed upon you was unfair[19] and that you have
been the victim of party plots. If this is impossible, you must say that your previous
misfortunes were sufficient, and that it is only fair, now that the matter has been
judged and done with, that no further prejudice should be raised against you on the
15 same grounds. If you are expecting to have judgement passed upon you, you must
say that you are ready to submit the misrepresentations now to the judgement of
your present audience; adding that, if you are proved to have wronged the state, you
consider yourself worthy of death. If your accusers do not press their charges
against you, you must use this very fact as a sign that their misrepresentations of
20 you are groundless; for it will seem hardly likely that those who are bringing true
accusations against you can be unwilling to submit the matter to judgement. You
must always denounce misrepresentation and declare it to be outrageous and
universal and the cause of endless evil. You must also point out that many have
before now been ruined through unjust misrepresentation. You must show more-
25 over that it is foolish that men, when they are consulting about matters of
public interest, should allow themselves to be disturbed by the misrepresentations of
individuals instead of listening to the advice of all and then considering what true
policy requires. You must also promise to prove that the advice which you have
undertaken to give is just and expedient. Such then is the method which those who
30 have been misrepresented in the past must adopt in public speaking in order to
refute misrepresentation.

In reference to the present time the first thing which creates a prejudice
against speakers is their age. If a man who is quite young or quite old is speaking in
public, his hearers feel annoyance; for they think that the former ought not yet to
35 have begun to speak, while the latter ought before now to have ceased speaking.
Secondly, a prejudice is created against a man, if he is a frequent speaker, for it
looks as if he were a busybody; or again, against a man who has never spoken before,
for it looks as if he had some motive of private gain in thus speaking in public
contrary to his usual custom. Such, then, are the ways in which prejudices in
reference to the present are likely to be created against a public speaker.

Excuses must be made by a young man by urging the dearth of advisers and
1437b1 the special suitability of the speaker; for instance, if the question concerns the
superintendence of the torch-races or the gymnasium or arms or horses or war—in
such matters a young man has no small interest. He must also urge that, if he has
not yet the wisdom of years, he has at any rate that wisdom which comes from
5   natural endowments and diligent application. He should also point out that,

---

[19]Fuhrmann obelizes this clause.

whereas unsuccessful advice reflects only upon its unhappy proposer, the benefit conferred when the policy succeeds is shared by the whole community. Such then are the excuses which must be urged by a young man. Excuses must be made when an old man is speaking by pointing out the dearth of advisers and his experience of the subject. Furthermore he may urge the magnitude and unusual character of the crisis and the like. When a man is in the habit of speaking too frequently, he may point to his wide experience and urge that it would be wrong that one who was formerly in the constant habit of speaking should not express his opinion on this occasion. One who is not in the habit of speaking must urge the magnitude of the crisis and that it is essential that every one who has a stake in the community should express his opinion on the present situation. Such then are the means by which we shall attempt to break down the prejudices raised against the persons of public speakers.

Prejudice is created against the subject matter of a speech when the speaker advises the rupture of peaceful relations with[20] those from whom we have received no injury or who are stronger than we, or when he advises a discreditable peace or urges a reduction of the expenditure on sacrifices or makes some other such proposal. On such subjects, first, one should employ anticipation in addressing one's hearers; secondly, one ought to lay the blame upon necessity and fortune and the times and expediency, and say that it is not those who are giving advice but the circumstances which are to be blamed for such proposals. Such are the methods by which we shall free advisers from prejudices which are due to their subject matter.

The actual speech in a public harangue creates a prejudice when it is too lengthy or old-fashioned, or lacks credibility. If it be long, this must be attributed to the abundance of material; if it be old-fashioned, it must be pointed out that such a style is opportune at the moment; if it is implausible, you must promise that you will prove it to be true in the course of your oration. These then are the considerations which will have a place in our public speeches.

Next, what arrangement shall we employ? If there be no prejudice against either ourselves personally or our speech or our subject, we shall lay down our proposition at the very beginning, and we shall afterwards exhort our hearers to pay attention and give our words a favourable hearing. If any prejudice has been created against us in previous speeches, we shall anticipate the judgement of our audience and, after briefly defending and excusing ourselves from the prejudices thus caused, shall then state our proposition and exhort our hearers to give us their attention. This, then, is the way in which public speeches should be constituted.

30 · Next we must either narrate events which have happened in the past or recall them to the minds of our hearers, or explain events which are occurring at the moment or else predict what is likely to occur in the future. When therefore we are reporting the details of an embassy, we must make a lucid statement of everything that was said, in order that our speech may carry weight (for it will be a report and nothing else, and no other style will find its way in); next, if we have been

[20]Reading συμβουλεύῃ λύειν.

10 unsuccessful, our object will be to make our hearers think that the failure of the negotiations was due to some other cause and not to our negligence; whereas, if we have met with success, they must be made to suppose that the result has been due not to chance but to our zealous efforts. This they are ready to believe, if, not having
15 been present at the negotiations, they observe the zeal displayed in our speech in omitting nothing but accurately reporting every detail. So, when we are describing the results of an embassy, we must for the reasons which I have stated report everything just as it happened.

20 When we are ourselves describing in a public speech some past event or explaining the events of the moment or predicting what will happen in the future, we must do each of these things briefly, clearly, and convincingly. We must be clear, in order that our hearers may grasp the events which we are describing, and concise, in order that they may remember what we have said; and we must speak convincingly, in order that they may not reject our statements before we have
25 supported them with proofs and justifications.

The clearness of our explanations will be due to the facts or to the words which we use; to the facts if we do not present them in an inverted order, but mention first
30 those which have occurred or are occurring or are going to occur first, and arrange the subsequent events in their proper order, and do not desert the subject about which we have undertaken to speak, and deal with some other subject. Thus, then, we shall speak clearly as far as our facts are concerned. Our actual words will be
35 clear, if we describe actions as far as possible in words which are appropriate to them, and if we employ usual words and do not put them in an inverted order but always arrange together those which naturally follow one another. If we observe these rules, our narrative will be clear.

We shall be concise if we omit all facts and words the mention of which is not
1438ᵇ1 essential, keeping only those the omission of which will render our speech obscure. Our narrative will then be concise.

We shall speak convincingly if, in support of facts which are implausible, we bring forward reasons which will make the events which we describe seem likely to have taken place. We must omit anything the occurrence of which seems too
5 unconvincing. If you are obliged to mention such things, you must make it clear that you have definite knowledge of them, and you must pass lightly over them, weaving them into your speech by the figure of 'pretended omission', and promise to show their truth as your speech progresses, making the excuse that you wish first to demonstrate the truth or justice (or the like) of your previous statements. This is the
10 way in which we shall remedy incredulity in our hearers.

In a word, by employing all the above-mentioned devices we shall make our reports, expositions, and predictions clear, brief, and convincing.

31 · There are three different methods in which we shall arrange them. If
15 the actions about which we are speaking are few in number and well known to our audience, we shall include the narration of them in our proem, in order that this part of our speech may not in itself be too short. If the actions which we are recounting

are too numerous and not familiar to our audience, we shall present them in every case in a connected form and show that they are just, expedient, and honourable, in order that we may not only make our tale plain and unembellished by simply relating facts but may also win the attention of our hearers. If the facts which we are recounting are unimportant and unfamiliar, we ought to insert the report or exposition or prediction of them bodily in the proem .This we shall do by recounting them from beginning to end and including nothing extraneous but merely relating the bare facts. We shall thus know how to arrange narratives in our proem.

32 · Next comes confirmation, whereby we confirm that the facts which we have already mentioned are of the nature of which we have undertaken to prove them to be, by adducing proofs and by considerations of justice and expediency. When therefore . . .[21] you must make sure they are connected. The proofs which are best suited to public orations are those based on the customary course of events and examples and supplementary enthymemes and the opinion of the orator; but any other proofs which present themselves may also be employed. They must be arranged in the following way: first, the opinion of the orator must be mentioned, or, if that is not done, the customary course of events must be indicated, showing that what we are asserting, or something similar, is what usually occurs. Following on this we must cite examples, and any point of similarity must be introduced to support what we are saying. The examples which we take must be closely akin to our subject and the nearest in time or place to our hearers. In the absence of such examples we must employ the most striking and best known that we can find. Next we must cite maxims. Also, in the parts where we introduce probabilities and examples we must end with enthymemes and maxims. This is the manner then in which we must introduce proofs where facts are concerned.

If our statements of facts are believed as soon as they are made, we must omit all proofs and confirm the facts which we have already stated by appeals to justice and lawfulness and expediency and considerations of what is honourable, pleasant, easy, possible, or necessary. Where an appeal to justice is possible, it must be given the first place, and we must explain our statements in relation to justice or a resemblance to justice or its contrary or what has been judged to be just. You must also cite examples similar to the cases of justice which you are instancing. You will also be able to produce numerous examples of what is regarded as just under special circumstances and in the actual city in which your speech is made, and in other states. When, following this method, we have said what we have to say, adding at the end maxims and brief enthymemes of different kinds, if this division of our speech is long and we wish it to be remembered by our hearers, we shall give a concise iteration; if, however, it is short and still fresh in their memory, we shall bring the division itself to a close and begin another one. The following is an example of what I mean: 'In what I have already said I think that the justice of our helping the Syracusans has been sufficiently demonstrated; I will now attempt to

[20]

[25]

[30]

[35]

1439ª1

5

10

15

20

25

---

[21]Fuhrmann marks a lacuna.

show the expediency of our doing so'. You will next treat the question of expediency by a similar method to that which we employed above in the case of justice, and at the end of that division add an iteration or definite conclusion, and then bring
30   forward some other considerations with which you have to deal. This is the way in which you must connect one division with another and keep up the thread of your speech. When you have employed every possible means to confirm your advice, you must in addition to all this show in a summary manner with the help of enthymemes
35   and maxims that it is unjust and inexpedient and dishonourable and unpleasant not to adopt your suggestion, and in a summary way you must contrast with this the justice, expediency, honourableness, and pleasure of doing what you are recommending. When you have made a sufficient use of maxims, you must end your exhortations with a definite conclusion. This then is the way in which we shall
1439ᵇ1   confirm the proposals which we make. The next division of our treatise will be concerned with the anticipation of contrary arguments.

33 · Anticipation is the method by which you anticipate and demolish the
5   objections which can be brought against your speech. You must minimize the arguments of your opponents and amplify your own, as you have already learnt to do from the instructions about amplification. You must set a single argument against another when yours is the stronger, and several against several and one against many and many against one, using every possible kind of contrast to
10   magnify your own arguments and weaken and minimize those of your adversaries. This is the manner in which we shall employ anticipations. Having done this we shall conclude with an iteration using the forms of argument or narration or recommendation or questioning or irony which we have already mentioned.

34 · If we are urging that help should be given to someone, whether to
15   private individuals or to states, it will be fitting briefly to mention any friendship or cause for gratitude or pity which already exists between them and the assembly which you are addressing. For they are most willing to help those who stand in such relations to them. All men feel an affection for those from whom, or from whose
20   friends, they think they themselves, or those for whom they care, have received or are receiving or are going to receive some deserved kindness. They feel gratitude towards those from whom, or from whose friends, they think they themselves or those for whom they care have received, are receiving, or will receive some undeserved benefit. If any feelings of this kind are present in their minds, we must
25   briefly dwell upon them and so move our hearers to pity. We shall have no difficulty in arousing as much pity as we wish, if we realize that all men pity those whom they suppose to be closely connected with themselves or think to be unworthy to suffer misfortune. You must prove that this is the condition of those for whom you wish to
30   excite pity, and show that they either have been or are in an evil plight, or will be so unless your hearers assist them. If this is not possible, you must show that those on whose behalf you are speaking have been or are being or will be deprived of advantages which all or most other people enjoy, or else have been or are without

some advantage, or never will obtain it unless those whom you are addressing take 35
pity on them now. These are the ways in which we shall incline our audience to
pity.

In dissuasion we shall employ the contrary method, using the same kind of
proem and narrating the facts and giving the proofs and showing our hearers that
what they are attempting to do is unlawful, unjust, inexpedient, disgraceful, 1440ª1
unpleasant, impracticable, burdensome, and unnecessary. The arrangement of our
speech will be similar to that used in persuasion. Such, then, is the way in which
those who are employing dissuasion on their own account must arrange their
speech.

Those who are opposing the advice given by others must in the first place state 5
in their proem the views which they intend to oppose and then add one by one the
other parts of the proem. After the proem the speaker must first bring forward
separately each of the points in the previous speech and show that the recommendations of his adversary are not just or lawful or expedient or the like. This you will do
by proving that what he says is unjust or inexpedient or bears a resemblance to 10
injustice or inexpediency, or is the opposite of the just or expedient or what has been
judged to be so. You must treat the other points in a similar manner. This, then, is
the most effective method of dissuasion. If this course is impossible, you must try to 15
dissuade your audience by using the technique of omission: for example, if your
opponent has shown that a certain course is just, you must attempt to prove that it is
discreditable or inexpedient or toilsome or impracticable or whatever else you can;
or if he has expediency on his side, you must show that his suggestion is unjust and 20
whatever else you can as well. You must amplify your own contentions and
minimize those of your adversary, employing the method already prescribed for
persuasive oratory. You must also introduce maxims and enthymemes, as in
persuasion, and refute anticipations, and in conclusion employ iteration. 25

In addition to this† we must show, when we are seeking to persuade our
hearers, that friendship exists between them and those whom we are urging them to
help, or that they owe a debt of gratitude to those who are asking for their
assistance; but when we are trying to prevent help from being given, we must show
that they are worthy objects of anger or envy or hostility.†[22] We shall implant a
sentiment of hostility in those whom we are seeking to dissuade by showing that 30
either they themselves, or those for whom they care, have received undeserved
ill-treatment at the hands of the other party or their friends. We shall arouse anger,
if we show that they, or those for whom they themselves care, have been wrongfully
treated with contempt or injustice by the other party or their friends. We shall
create a feeling of envy, to put the matter briefly, against those whom we show to 35
have enjoyed unmerited prosperity, or to be now doing so, or to be likely to do so in
the future; or not to have been deprived of some advantage, or not to be being
deprived or not likely to be so; or never to have suffered some misfortune in the past,
or not to be doing so now, or to be never likely to do so in future. This, then, is the

[22]Obelized by Fuhrmann.

method by which we shall implant envy or hostility or anger; while we shall create
1440ᵇ1 feelings of friendship, gratitude, and pity by the methods which we indicated in
treating of persuasion. We shall give these sentiments their place and arrangement
according to the various methods already mentioned. We now know the nature of
persuasive oratory and its component parts and how it must be employed.

5   35 · Let us next set before ourselves the consideration of eulogistic and
vituperative oratory.† Here too we must first of all state our propositions†[23] in the
proem, and refute misrepresentation by the same method as in persuasive oratory.
We must also exhort our hearers to give us their attention by the methods already
10 described under public speeches and in particular by saying things which will cause
astonishment and attract remark, and showing that the subjects of our speech and
those who usually incur praise or blame have acted in the same manner.[24] Speeches
of this kind are usually made not in order to fight a case but for display.

15   First, we shall arrange the proem on the same principle as in persuasive and
dissuasive speeches. After the proem, we must distinguish those good qualities of
our subject which are outside the sphere of excellence and those which fall within it,
as follows[25]: those which fall outside the sphere of excellence we shall divide into
good birth, physical strength, personal beauty, and wealth, while we shall divide
20 excellence into wisdom, justice, courage and reputable habits of life. The qualities
which pertain to excellence are proper subjects of eulogy; those which fall outside it
must be disguised, for we ought to congratulate rather than praise those who are
strong and handsome and well-born and wealthy. Having made these distinctions
we shall give the genealogy of the subject of our speech the first place after the
25 proem; for this is the first thing which brings repute or disrepute upon men and also
upon animals. [We shall therefore be justified in giving the genealogy of a man or
any other animal; and when we are praising any one's feeling or action or speech or
possession, we shall be justified in beginning our eulogy by mentioning the
reputable qualities which he possesses.][26]

30   The following is the way to treat a man's genealogy: if his ancestors were good
men and true, you ought to mention them all from the earliest times down to the
subject of your eulogy and give a brief account of some glorious achievement
performed by each of his forefathers. If it is only his earliest ancestors that were
good men while the rest failed to do anything remarkable, you must mention the
35 former in the manner already described and omit the undistinguished members of
the family, excusing yourself by saying that, his ancestors being so numerous, you
do not wish to weary your audience by speaking of them, and that every one knows
that men who are born of a good stock usually resemble their forefathers. If his
early ancestors were undistinguished but those who come nearer his own time were
men of repute, you must dwell upon his descent from the latter and say that it would

---

[23]Obelized by Fuhrmann.
[24]Reading καὶ αὐτοὺς κατ' ἴσον for καὶ αὐτὸν ἴσον.
[25]The text is uncertain.
[26]Excised by Fuhrmann.

be tedious to speak at length about his early forefathers, and you must show that the 1441ᵃ1
immediate ancestors of those whom you are eulogizing were good men; adding that
it is quite clear that *their* ancestors must have been good men and true, for it is
hardly likely that such excellent and worthy persons can have been born of bad 5
parents. If there is nothing reputable in the ancestry of the subject of your eulogy,
you must insist on his personal nobility and suggest that all those who have a natural
predisposition for excellence are well born, and you must censure those other orators
who dwell upon ancestral glories, pointing out that many men of reputable ancestry
have proved themselves unworthy of their forefathers. You must also insist that
your task on the present occasion is to praise the man himself, not his ancestors. A 10
similar use must be made of genealogies to discredit one whose ancestors were men
of evil repute. Such then is the place which genealogy must occupy in eulogy and
vituperation.

If the subject of your eulogy owes some distinction to good luck, . . .²⁷ observing 15
this one principle that you say what befits his various ages, and do not speak at too
great length. For example, in children it is generally considered that orderliness and
self control are due not to themselves but to those who have charge of them, and so
they must be dealt with briefly. When you have thus described his early years, after
concluding with an enthymeme or maxim at the end of this division of your speech, 20
you will, when you come to the early manhood of the subject of your eulogy, state
your subject, viz. his achievements or character or habits, and you must amplify
them on the principle which we laid down at the beginning in treating of eulogistic
oratory, explaining that it was at this age that such and such a glorious deed was 25
done by him whom you are eulogizing, or through his agency or that he inspired it or
supplied the motive or was essential to it. You must also compare the notable
achievements of other young men and show that his actions far surpass theirs,
relating the least important of their deeds and the most important of the 30
achievements of the subject of your eulogy. You must set deeds of others which are
notable but less important side by side with those which you are relating, and so
exaggerate the importance of the latter. You must also amplify his achievements by
conjectures of the following kind: 'Yet one who at this early age became so great a
philosopher, if he had been older would have advanced yet further'; or again, 'A 35
man who so stoutly endures the toils of the gymnasium, will gladly welcome the love
of toil which philosophy demands'. By conjectures of this kind we shall amplify his
good qualities.

When we have dealt with the events of his early manhood, we shall put maxims
and enthymemes at the end of this section too; and, after either briefly iterating what 1441ᵇ1
we have said, or bringing it to a final conclusion, we shall next treat of the
achievements of the subject of our eulogy after reaching full manhood, and after
setting forth his justice first and amplifying this topic by the method already 5
described we shall proceed to deal with his wisdom, if he possesses this quality;
having similarly dealt with this we shall set forth his courage, if he possesses any,
and after going through the process of amplifying this also, when we have reached

---

²⁷Fuhrmann marks a lacuna.

the end of this section and described all his various qualities, we shall repeat and
10   summarize what we have said and bring the whole speech to a conclusion with a
maxim or an enthymeme. It will be suitable in eulogies to treat the various points at
considerable length and to employ a dignified diction.

15   We shall use the same method to compose our accusations when we are dealing
with wicked men. But we must not scoff at the man with whom we are finding fault,
but we must describe his life; for statements have more effect than scoffs, bringing
conviction to our hearers and causing annoyance to those with whom we are finding
fault; for scoffing is directed against outward appearance and circumstance, while
20   statements about a man are the picture, as it were, of his habits and character. Be
on your guard against calling disgraceful actions by disgraceful names, so as not to
violate conventional feeling, but express such things by indirect hints and explain
the facts in words which are really applicable to different actions. In finding fault
25   you must employ irony and laugh at the points on which your adversary prides
himself; in private, and in the presence of a few listeners, you should seek to
discredit him, but before the multitude you should abuse him by levelling only
ordinary accusations against him. You must employ the same methods of amplification and minimization in finding fault as in eulogy. From what has been said we
shall know how to practise these kinds of oratory.

30   **36** · It remains for us to deal with the oratory of accusation and defence and
inquiry. Let us next discuss how we shall compose and arrange these in the forensic
type of oratory. We shall first set forth in the proem, as in the other kinds, the action
which is to be the subject of our accusation or defence. We shall exhort our hearers
35   to attention by the same means as we employed in the persuasive and dissuasive
styles.

†Again, as regards the goodwill of the audience, when they are well-disposed
towards the subject of our speech in connexion with either the past or in the present
and he is not the object of prejudice because they are irritated against him or his
1442ª1   action or his speech, we must secure their goodwill by the method described in
dealing with the other kinds of oratory. When they are neither well nor ill-disposed
towards him in connexion with either the past or the present, or when his personality
or his action or his words are the object of prejudice, we must bring forward reasons
5   for goodwill towards him, sometimes blending them together and sometimes taking
them separately.†28 Such, then, is the method by which we must conciliate
goodwill.

Those who are the objects neither of goodwill nor of illwill must briefly
eulogize themselves and dispraise their adversaries. They must praise themselves in
10   connexion with the qualities which most nearly concern their hearers, calling
themselves, for example, patriotic, true to their friends, grateful, compassionate;
while they will dispraise an adversary by applying to him epithets which will arouse
the anger of their audience, such as unpatriotic, untrue to his friends, thankless,
15   pitiless, and the like. They must also conciliate the jury by praising their justice and

---

28The text of this paragraph, which Fuhrmann obelizes, is uncertain.

the intelligence which they bring to their task. They must also mention any point in which they are at a disadvantage compared with their opponents, whether in word or deed or anything else which concerns the suit; and they must further introduce the considerations of justice, legality, expediency, and the like. It is by these means 20 that we must win goodwill in the minds of the jury for one who is the object of neither kindly nor unkindly feeling.

When a man is an object of prejudice, if the prejudice dates from the past and is concerned with his person or with what he has said, we know from what has already been remarked how to remove it. If it dates from the present time, it must necessarily be concerned with the man's personality[29] if he is represented as unfit to 25 bring the case in question, or his character as contradicting the charges he brings or consistent with the accusation brought against him. It would be a case of unsuitability if too young or too old a man pleaded on behalf of another; of contradiction, if a strong man accused a weak man of assault, or if a violent man brought a charge of violence against a self-controlled man, or if a very poor man 30 went to law against a very rich man charging him with embezzlement. These are cases where there is a contradiction between the accusations and those who bring them. There will be consistency with the charge where a strong man is prosecuted for assault by a weak man or one who has the reputation of being a thief is put on his trial for theft. In a word, there will seem to be consistency with the charge in the 35 case of persons who cause an opinion to be formed about them which corresponds with their character. Such, then, will be the misrepresentations which arise at the moment against a man's personality. Prejudice will be raised against a man's action if he goes to law with his own friends or guests or relatives, or on petty or 1442ᵇ1 discreditable pleas; for these things bring disrepute upon the parties in a suit.

I will now show how we are to get rid of the above mentioned prejudices. I maintain that there are two principles which hold good in all cases. First, when you think your opponents are likely to impress the jury, anticipate them and make the 5 impression yourself. Secondly, when it is a question of acts, you should, if possible, turn the blame upon your adversaries, or failing that, upon some one else, urging as an excuse that you have been dragged into the suit against your will and under compulsion from your opponents. Against each particular prejudice you must urge such excuses as these: a young man, for example, should allege a lack of older 10 friends to fight the case on his behalf, or the enormity or number of his opponent's misdeeds, or the short limit of time allowed, or some other such excuse. If you are speaking on some one else's behalf, you must say that you are pleading his cause from motives of friendship for him or hatred of his opponent, or because you were present at the events in question, or for the public good, or because your client 15 stands in need of friends and is a victim of injustice. If his character agrees with the charge brought against him or is in contradiction to the accusation which he brings, you must make use of anticipation and say that it is not just or lawful or expedient to judge from an opinion or suspicion before listening to the facts. Such, then, is the 20 way in which we shall get rid of prejudices against a man's personality; those which

[29]Deleting the comma after ἄνθρωπον.

concern his action we shall repudiate by transferring the blame to his adversary, or by accusing the latter of libel or injustice or greed or contentiousness or anger,
25 alleging as an excuse that our client could not possibly obtain justice in any other way. This is how we shall get rid of personal prejudices in the law courts; those which concern a man's public life we shall refute by the various methods prescribed for the kinds of oratory already dealt with.

We shall arrange the proems of forensic speeches in the same manner as those
30 of public orations, and on the same principle we shall include the narration of facts in the proem or show them to be trustworthy and just in detail or else insert them bodily by themselves.

Next will follow confirmation, by means of proofs if the facts are disputed by
35 our opponents, or, if they are admitted, by considerations of justice, expediency, and the like. Of proofs we must put testimony first and admissions made under torture, if there are any. Next we must confirm our statements, if they are plausible, by maxims and enthymemes, but, if they are not entirely plausible, by considerations
1443ᵃ1 of probability, and afterwards by examples, evidences, signs, and refutations, and lastly by enthymemes and maxims. If the facts are admitted, we must leave proofs
5 alone and make use of justification as already described. Such, then, is the method of confirmation which we shall employ.

After such confirmation we shall next state the arguments which we can urge against our opponents, and anticipate what they are likely to say. If they deny the facts, we must amplify the proofs which we have already stated and criticize and
10 minimize those which they are likely to bring forward. If they admit the actions but intend[30] to show that they are legal and just according to written laws, we must attempt to show that the laws which we bring forward, and laws similar to them, are just and right and to the common advantage of the state, and that this is the opinion
15 generally held about them, while the contrary is true of the laws which our opponents are bringing forward. If it is impossible to say this, you must remind the jury that they have to give their verdict not on a point of law but on a point of fact, and that they have sworn to vote according to the established law, and you must tell them that they must not pass laws now but upon the proper days fixed for that
20 purpose. If it so happens that what has been done contravenes laws which appear to be bad,[31] we must say that here we have not law but the negation of law; for law is laid down for the public benefit, but this law is harmful to the state. We must say
25 that they will not be acting illegally if they vote in contravention of this law, but will be legislating to prevent the use of bad and illegal ordinances. You can also point out that no law forbids the conferring of a public benefit and that it is a benefaction to the state to annul bad laws. Regarding laws, then, of which the meaning is clear,
30 we shall easily be able, by such methods of anticipation, to speak against any of them with which we are concerned. When there is ambiguity, if the jury understand a law in a sense which favours you, you must give it that interpretation; but if they give it the construction which your opponent puts upon it, you must tell them that

---

[30]Reading μέλλωσιν for ὦσιν.
[31]Reading μοχθηροὺς δοκοῦντας εἶναι νόμους.

this is not what the lawgiver meant but that he interpreted it as you do, and that it is to the advantage of the jury to put the construction which you do upon it. If you cannot twist the law round, point out that it cannot mean anything but what you say it means. If you follow this method you will have no difficulty as to the way in which to deal with laws.

Generally speaking, if they admit the facts and intend to base their defence on pleas of justice and legality, you must employ these methods to anticipate what they are likely to say. But if they admit the facts but claim to be pardoned, you must deprive your opponents of such arguments in the following manner. First, you must say that their conduct is all the more reprehensible and that it is only when they have been found out that they admit their mistake in so acting, adding, 'If, therefore, you pardon the defendant, you will absolve every one else from punishment'. You can say, 'If you acquit those who admit their mistakes, how will you be able to condemn those who do not do so'? You must urge that 'even if he has made a mistake, there is no reason why I should suffer through his mistake'. Furthermore, you must say that the lawgiver does not pardon those who make mistakes, and so the jury in giving their verdict according to the laws should not do so either. Such then, as we have stated at the beginning, are the means by which we shall refute their appeals for pardon, and, speaking generally, we shall anticipate by the method already mentioned anything which our opponents intend to say with a view either to proof or justification or pardon.

Next we must iterate the whole story of the case in summary form, and, if possible, in a few words instil into the minds of the jury a feeling of hostility or anger or envy towards our opponents and of goodwill or gratitude or pity for ourselves. How this is done we have already stated in dealing with public speaking and persuasion and dissuasion, and we shall again allude to it finally in treating of the defensive style of oratory. This, then, is the way in which we shall compose and arrange our speech when we are the first to speak and are the accusers in a forensic case.

When we are defending a case, we shall frame our proem in the same way as when accusing, and we shall make no mention of the accusations, of which our opponent has informed our hearers, but after the proem we shall set forth and refute the opinions which he has put into their minds and throw discredit on his witnesses and the testimony given under torture and the oaths, in the manner already described to you. If the facts are credible, we must put our defense against them . . .[32] changing to the technique of omission, and if the witnesses or those who have been examined under torture are trustworthy, we must have recourse to argument or statement of fact or any other strong point which we can bring against them. If your adversary accuses you by bringing a charge which accords with your advantage or habitual practice, you must defend yourself, if you can, by showing that the crime with which you are charged does not accord with your advantage; or, failing that, you must urge that it has not been the custom either of yourself or of persons like you to do such things, or to do them in such a manner. This is how you

[32]Fuhrmann marks a lacuna.

will refute the argument of probability. When he employs an example, you must first show, if you can, that it does not resemble the crime with which you are charged, or, failing that, yourself bring forward another example to the contrary which has occurred against probability. If he employs an evidence, you must refute it by giving reasons why it implies the exact opposite, while you must show that his maxims and enthymemes are either paradoxical or ambiguous. His signs you must prove to be signs of a number of other things and not only of the charge which he is bringing against you. This, then, is the way in which we shall cause our adversary's contentions to be discredited by either interpreting them in a contrary sense or reducing them to ambiguity.

If, on the other hand, we admit that we have done the acts with which we are charged, we shall base our plea on justice and legality and try to prove that our acts are juster and more legal. If this is impossible, we must resort to pleas of error or misfortune, and try to win pardon by showing that the harm which has resulted is small, pointing out that error is common to all men, while wrongdoing is peculiar to the wicked. You must urge that it is right and just and expedient to pardon errors; for no man knows whether it may not fall to his lot to commit such an error. You must also point out that your opponent claimed pardon when he committed an error.

Next will come the anticipations which your adversaries have made in their speeches. Anticipations of other kinds we shall easily be able to refute by an appeal to the facts; but if they misrepresent us by saying that we read our speeches or practise them beforehand, or that we are pleading for the sake of some reward, we must meet such accusations with irony and say with regard to the writing of speeches that the law does not forbid a man to read out a written speech any more than it forbids his opponent to speak without notes; for, while it prohibits the doing of certain actions, it allows a man to make a speech in any way he likes. You must also say: 'My opponent considers that the wrongs which he has committed are so serious that he does not think I am doing justice to the accusation which I am bringing against him, unless I write out and take a long time to think over my speech'. Such then is the way in which we must meet the misrepresentation of having written out our speech. If our opponents declare that we learn and rehearse our speeches, we shall admit it and say: 'We who, according to you, learn what we are going to say, are not litigious, whereas you, who declare that you do not know how to speak, have been convicted of bringing vexatious suits in the past and are doing so now against us'; and we shall draw the conclusion that it would apparently therefore be better for the citizens, if our opponent also learned to be an orator, for then he would not be such a scoundrel and pettifogger. We shall meet the accusation that we are paid to plead in court by a similar argument—admitting it and speaking ironically and pointing out that our accuser and every one else does so. You must distinguish between the different kinds of pay and say that some men plead in court for money, others as a favour, others for vengeance, others for honours. You must show that you are yourself pleading as a favour, and say that your opponent pleads for no small payment; for he is going to law that he may make money unjustly, not in order to avoid having to pay it. We must follow the same method if any one accuses us of teaching others how to plead and of composing speeches to be delivered in court. You must point out that every one else, as far as lies within his power, helps his friends by instruction and advice. Thus you will have an answer in such cases in accordance with the rules of rhetoric.

You must not be slow in any questions and answers which occur in cases of this kind; but you must make a clear distinction in your answers between admissions and denials. The following are examples of admissions: 'Did you kill my son'?—'Yes, I did kill him, when he, unprovoked, raised a sword against me'; or again, 'Did you thrash my son'?—'Yes, but he first assaulted me'; or again, 'Did you break my head'?—'Yes, when you were forcing your way into my house at night'. Such admissions are made in reliance on the legality of your action. Denials, on the other hand, aim at diverting the course of law, for example: 'Did you kill my son'?—'No, it was not I, but the law that killed him'. This is the kind of answer which you must always make when one law enjoins, while another forbids, a certain course of action. Out of all these various methods you will gather the means to meet your adversaries.

Next will follow an iteration by way of brief reminder of what you have said. It is useful on all occasions and should therefore be employed in every part and in every kind of speech. It is very suitable in accusation and defence and also in persuasion and dissuasion. In my opinion we ought here not only to remind our audience, as in eulogistic and vituperative speeches, of what has been said, but we ought also to dispose our judges to be favourable towards ourselves and unfavourable to our opponents; we shall make this the last part of our speech. It is possible to refresh your hearer's memory in a summary manner either by arguing or by narrating the points which you have mentioned, or by picking out the best of your own points and the worst of your opponent's, or, if you like, you can use the form of a question. The nature of these methods we know from what has already been said.

We shall win a favourable hearing for ourselves and an unfavourable one for our opponents if, as in persuasion and dissuasion, we show briefly how we ourselves (or our friends) have benefited or are benefiting or will benefit those who are now seeking to wrong us (or those for whom they care); and point out to them that now is the opportunity to show us gratitude for our good services; and also, when it is possible, induce them to pity us. This we shall do by showing that a close tie binds us to our hearers and that we are suffering undeserved misfortune, having been unfairly treated in the past, or being so now, or being likely to be so in the future, unless they help us now. If such arguments are inapplicable, we must describe the advantages of which we have been, or are being, or are likely to be deprived, if our prayers are rejected by our judges; or show that we never have been, or are not now, or are never likely to be in enjoyment of some benefit, unless they help us. For it is by these means that we shall win pity and gain the goodwill of our audience.

We shall cause a prejudice and feelings of envy against our opponents by employing the opposite method and pointing out that our hearers, or those for whom they care, have received undeserved ill-treatment, or are receiving it, or are likely to receive it at the hands of our opponents or their friends; for by such arguments they

will be induced to entertain feelings of hatred and anger against them. Where this is impossible, we shall collect together all the arguments by which we can create in our hearers a feeling of envy against our opponents; for envy is very near to hatred. They
20 will be objects of envy, to put the matter briefly, if we can show that they have met with undeserved prosperity and that no close ties bind them to our hearers, and point out that they have unjustly received, or are receiving, or are about to receive many benefits; or that they have never in the past been without some advantage, or are not without it now, or likely to be so in the future; or that they have never met
25 with some misfortune, or are not now meeting with it, or likely to do so, unless the judges punish them now. By these means then we shall in the peroration of our speech win favour for ourselves and disfavour for our opponents, and by following all the instructions given above we shall be able to arrange speeches for accusation and defence according to the rules of rhetoric.

30 37 · The inquisitive kind of oratory generally occurs, not separately, but in connexion with the other styles; it is especially useful in dealing with contradictions. However, in order that we may know the arrangement of this kind of speech also, when we have to inquire into the words or manner of life or deeds of men or the
35 administration of a city, I will describe it also in a summary manner. When conducting an inquiry of this kind we must begin in the same way as when refuting a prejudice; and so, after first adducing plausible pretexts so as to make our action appear reasonable, we shall then proceed to conduct our inquiry. The following are suitable pretexts: in political assemblies, that we are adopting such a course not
1445ᵇ1 from party-spirit but in order that it may not escape the attention of our hearers, or again, that our adversaries molested us first. In private suits our excuse will be a feeling of hatred or the bad character of the subjects of our inquiry or our friendship towards them in order to make them realize what they are doing and not do it again.
5 In public trials our pretexts will be legality, justice, and the general interest. After first treating of these and similar subjects we shall next in order set forth and inquire into each utterance or deed or intention of our opponents, showing that these
10 are opposed to justice and legality and private and public expediency, and examining them all to see whether in any respect they contradict one another or the practice of good citizens or probability. But, not to be tedious by going into details, the more we can prove to our hearers that the conduct of the subjects of our inquiry
15 is opposed to reputable pursuits, acts, words or habits, the greater will be the disrepute which attaches to them. We ought to conduct our inquiry not in a bitter but in a gentle spirit; for words if thus spoken will appear more persuasive to our hearers, and those who utter them will be less likely to bring prejudice upon
20 themselves. When you have carefully inquired into everything and amplified the results, you must conclude with a brief iteration and remind your hearers of what you have said. By arranging them thus we shall be able to employ all the various kinds of oratory according to the rules of rhetoric.

25 38 · Both in speaking and writing we must try as far as possible to make our

words accord with the principles laid down above, and accustom ourselves to practise each principle readily, and we shall have many technical expedients to enable us to make speeches according to the rules of art in private and public suits and in conversation with others; but an orator ought to be careful not only about his words but also about his personal behaviour, regulating it according to the principles already laid down; for the manner of a man's life contributes to the persuasive influence which he exercises and to the establishment of a good reputation.

In the first place you must divide up your subject-matter according to the general system of division in which you have been instructed, and decide what you must treat of first, secondly, thirdly, and fourthly. Next you must prepare your hearers to receive you, as I have described in dealing with the attitude to be taken towards your audience in proems. You will dispose them well towards you, if you are true to your promises and if you keep the same friends all your life and show yourself unchanging in your other habits and always following the same course. They will listen attentively to you, if you treat of great and noble deeds and such as promote the public good.

Their goodwill having been won, when you come to practical suggestions they will accept as expedient to themselves those which procure the avoidance of evils and the provision of benefits, and reject those which involve the contrary results.

In order that your exposition may be quick and lucid and may command credit, you ought to make your practical suggestions as follows. You will perform your task quickly, if you do not try to do everything at once, but take the first point first and then the next. You will speak lucidly, if you do not suddenly leave your subject and go on to other points before you have finished it. You will command credit, if you do not act contrary to your usual character, and further if you do not pretend that the same persons are your enemies and your friends.

As regards proof, where we have sure knowledge, we shall prefer to follow its guidance in prescribing plans of action, but, where we lack knowledge, we shall take what holds for the most part as our guide; for it is safest in such cases to act with a view to what usually happens.

When we have adversaries to contend with, if it is a question of words, we shall obtain confirmation in support of our case from the actual words uttered; in suits about contracts we shall do so by dealing with them in accordance with unwritten and written laws with the support of the best possible testimony and within definite limits of time.

As regards our peroration we shall remind our hearers of what has been said by a summary repetition of the facts; while we shall remind them of our past deeds by reference to our present deeds, when we are undertaking actions identical with, or similar to, former actions.

Our hearers will be well disposed to us, if we follow a course of action which will result in their thinking themselves well treated in the past, present, or future. We shall add weight to our actions, if we deal with transactions which are likely to produce great credit.

Such then is the manner in which an orator must regulate his personal

35   behaviour; while he must practice the art of oratory according to the principles already laid down.

[33][Sacrifices must be conducted, as we have already indicated, so as to be reverent towards the gods, moderate in costliness, splendid from a spectacular point of view, and likely to bring advantage to the citizens. They will be reverent towards the gods, if we sacrifice according to ancestral custom; they will be moderate in
1446[b]1   costliness, if the accompaniments of the ceremony are not used up as well as the money actually expended; they will be splendid from a spectacular point of view, if they are magnificently appointed; they will be beneficial to the citizens, if horsemen
5   and infantry in full panoply accompany the procession. Our dealings with the gods will be reverently performed if carried out thus.

We shall establish friendly relations with those who are of like character to our own and have the same interests, and with whom we are obliged to co-operate in matters of great importance; for such friendship is most likely to be permanent. We
10   must make those men our allies, who are most righteous and are possessed of considerable power and live near at hand; those who are the contrary must be our enemies. We must undertake war against those who are trying to injure the state or her friends or her allies. The protection of the state must be secured either by
15   personal service or by the help of allies or by mercenaries; the first method is preferable to the second, and the second to the third.

As regards the supply of resources, we must provide them first and foremost from our own revenues and possessions, secondly by taxes on rateable property, and thirdly by personal service on the part of the poor, and the provision of arms by the
20   craftsmen, and of money by the wealthy.

As for political constitution, the best form of democracy is that under which the laws bestow the posts of dignity on the best citizens, and the people are not deprived of the rights of electing and voting; the worst form is that under which the
25   laws deliver up the wealthy to the insolence of the mob. Oligarchies are of two kinds, being based either on political partisanship or on a property qualification.

Alliances must be formed when the citizens are unable by themselves to protect their own territory and strongholds or hold the enemy in check. An alliance
30   must be dispensed with when it is unnecessary or when the proposed allies are too far distant and unable to arrive at the opportune moment.

A good citizen is one who provides the state with useful friends and few and feeble foes, and who procures for her the greatest revenue without confiscating the
35   property of a single private citizen, and who, while conducting himself righteously, exposes those who attempt any injury to the state.

Men always bestow presents either in the hope of benefiting themselves or in grateful return for previous services. Service is always given either for gain or
1447[a]1   honour or pleasure or fear. All dealings are carried out either by choice or unwillingly; for all facts are done either under compulsion or through persuasion or fraud or on some pretext.

In war one side gains the upper hand either through luck, or superiority of

---

[33]Excised by Fuhrmann.

numbers or strength or resources, or advantage of position, or excellence of allies, or 5 skill on the part of a general. It is generally held that men should abandon their allies either because it is expedient to do so or because they have brought the war to a close.

1447^{b}1

To act justly is to follow the common customs of the state, to obey the laws, and to abide by one's personal promises.

Physical advantages are good condition, beauty, strength, and health; mental 5 advantages are wisdom, prudence, courage, self-control, and justice. Wealth and friends are advantages alike to mind and body. The opposites of these are disadvantageous. To a state a multitude of good citizens is an advantage.]

POETICS

I. Bywater

1447ª10 1 · I propose to speak not only of poetry in general but also of its species and their respective capacities; of the structure of plot required for a good poem; of the number and nature of the constituent parts of a poem; and likewise of any other matters in the same line of inquiry. Let us follow the natural order and begin with first principles.

Epic poetry and tragedy, as also comedy, dithyrambic poetry, and most
15 flute-playing and lyre-playing, are all, viewed as a whole, modes of imitation. But they differ from one another in three ways, either in their means, or in their objects, or in the manner of their imitations.

Just as colour and form are used as means by some, who (whether by art or
20 constant practice) imitate and portray many things by their aid, and the voice is used by others; so also in the above-mentioned group of arts, the means with them as a whole are rhythm, language, and harmony—used, however, either singly or in certain combinations. A combination of harmony and rhythm alone is the means in
25 flute-playing and lyre-playing, and any other arts there may be of the same description, e.g. imitative piping. Rhythm alone, without harmony, is the means in the dancer's imitations; for even he, by the rhythms of his attitudes, may represent men's characters, as well as what they do and suffer. There is further an art which imitates by language alone, and one which imitates by metres, either one or a plurality of metres. These forms of imitation are still nameless today. We have no
1447ᵇ10 common name for a mime of Sophron or Xenarchus and a Socratic Conversation; and we should still be without one even if the imitation in the two instances were in trimeters or elegiacs or some other kind of verse—though it is the way with people to tack on 'poet' to the name of a metre, and talk of elegiac poets and epic poets,
15 thinking that they call them poets not by reason of the imitative nature of their work, but generally by reason of the metre they write in. Even if a theory of medicine or physical philosophy be put forth in a metrical form, it is usual to describe the writer in this way; Homer and Empedocles, however, have really nothing in common apart from their metre; so that, if the one is to be called a poet, the other should be termed a physicist rather than a poet. We should be in the same
20 position also, if the imitation in these instances were in all the metres, like the *Centaur* (a rhapsody in a medley of all metres) of Chaeremon; and Chaeremon one

TEXT: R. Kassel, OCT, Oxford, 1965

has to recognize as a poet. So much, then, as to these arts. There are, lastly, certain other arts, which combine all the means enumerated, rhythm, melody, and verse, e.g. dithyrambic and nomic poetry, tragedy and comedy; with this difference, however, that the three kinds of means are in some of them all employed together, and in others brought in separately, one after the other. These elements of difference in the above arts I term the means of their imitation.

2 · The objects the imitator represents are actions, with agents who are necessarily either good men or bad—the diversities of human character being nearly always derivative from this primary distinction, since it is by badness and excellence men differ in character. It follows, therefore, that the agents represented must be either above our own level of goodness, or beneath it, or just such as we are; in the same way as, with the painters, the personages of Polygnotus are better than we are, those of Pauson worse, and those of Dionysius just like ourselves. It is clear that each of the above-mentioned arts will admit of these differences, and that it will become a separate art by representing objects with this point of difference. Even in dancing, flute-playing, and lyre-playing such diversities are possible; and they are also possible in the nameless art that uses language, prose or verse without harmony, as its means; Homer's personages, for instance, are better than we are; Cleophon's are on our own level; and those of Hegemon of Thasos, the first writer of parodies, and Nicochares, the author of the *Diliad,* are beneath it. The same is true of the dithyramb and the nome: the personages may be presented in them with the difference exemplified . . .[1] in the Cyclopes of Timotheus and Philoxenus. This difference it is that distinguishes Tragedy and Comedy also; the one would make its personages worse, and the other better, than the men of the present day.

3 · A third difference in these arts is in the manner in which each kind of object is represented. Given both the same means and the same kind of object for imitation, one may either speak at one moment in narrative and at another in an assumed character, as Homer does; or one may remain the same throughout, without any such change; or the imitators may represent the whole story dramatically, as though they were actually doing the things described.[2]

As we said at the beginning, therefore, the differences in the imitation of these arts come under three heads, their means, their objects, and their manner.

So that as an imitator Sophocles will be on one side akin to Homer, both portraying good men; and on another to Aristophanes, since both present their personages as acting and doing. This in fact, according to some, is the reason for plays being termed dramas, because in a play the personages act the story. Hence too both tragedy and comedy are claimed by the Dorians as their discoveries; Comedy by the Megarians—by those in Greece as having arisen when Megara became a democracy, and by the Sicilian Megarians on the ground that the poet Epicharmus was of their country, and a good deal earlier than Chionides and

---

[1]The text is corrupt here.
[2]The text of the last clause is uncertain.

35 Magnes; and Tragedy is claimed by certain of the Peloponnesian Dorians. In
support of this claim they point to the words 'comedy' and 'drama'. Their word for
the outlying hamlets, they say, is *comae,* whereas Athenians call them *demes*—thus
assuming that comedians got the name not from their *comoe* or revels, but from
their strolling from hamlet to hamlet, lack of appreciation keeping them out of the
1448ᵇ1 city. Their word also for 'to act', they say, is *dran,* whereas Athenians use *prattein.*
So much, then, as to the number and nature of the points of difference in the
imitation of these arts.

5   **4** · It is clear that the general origin of poetry was due to two causes, each of
them part of human nature. Imitation is natural to man from childhood, one of his
advantages over the lower animals being this, that he is the most imitative creature
in the world, and learns at first by imitation. And it is also natural for all to delight
in works of imitation. The truth of this second point is shown by experience: though
10 the objects themselves may be painful to see, we delight to view the most realistic
representations of them in art, the forms for example of the lowest animals and of
dead bodies. The explanation is to be found in a further fact: to be learning
something is the greatest of pleasures not only to the philosopher but also to the rest
15 of mankind, however small their capacity for it; the reason of the delight in seeing
the picture is that one is at the same time learning—gathering the meaning of
things, e.g. that the man there is so-and-so; for if one has not seen the thing before,
one's pleasure will not be in the picture as an imitation of it, but will be due to the
20 execution or colouring or some similar cause. Imitation, then, being natural to
us—as also the sense of harmony and rhythm, the metres being obviously species of
rhythms—it was through their original aptitude, and by a series of improvements
for the most part gradual on their first efforts, that they created poetry out of their
improvisations.
Poetry, however, soon broke up into two kinds according to the differences of
25 character in the individual poets; for the graver among them would represent noble
actions, and those of noble personages; and the meaner sort the actions of the
ignoble. The latter class produced invectives at first, just as others did hymns and
panegyrics. We know of no such poem by any of the pre-Homeric poets, though
there were probably many such writers among them; instances, however, may be
30 found from Homer downwards, e.g. his *Margites,* and the similar poems of others.
In this poetry of invective its natural fitness brought an iambic metre into use; hence
our present term 'iambic', because it was the metre of their 'iambs' or invectives
against one another. The result was that the old poets became some of them writers
of heroic and others of iambic verse. Homer, just as he was in the serious style the
35 poet of poets, standing alone not only through the excellence, but also through the
dramatic character of his imitations, so also was he the first to outline for us the
general forms of comedy by producing not a dramatic invective, but a dramatic
picture of the ridiculous; his *Margites* in fact stands in the same relation to our
1449ª1 comedies as the *Iliad* and *Odyssey* to our tragedies. As soon, however, as tragedy
and comedy appeared in the field, those naturally drawn to the one line of poetry
became writers of comedies instead of iambs, and those naturally drawn to the

other, writers of tragedies instead of epics, because these new modes of art were   5
grander and of more esteem than the old.

If it be asked whether tragedy is now all that it need be in its formative
elements, to consider that, and decide it theoretically and in relation to the theatres,
is a matter for another inquiry.

It certainly began in improvisations—as did also comedy; the one originating   10
with the authors of the dithyramb, the other with those of the phallic songs, which
still survive as institutions in many of our cities. And its advance after that was little
by little, through their improving on whatever they had before them at each stage.
It was in fact only after a long series of changes that the movement of tragedy
stopped on its attaining to its natural form. The number of actors was first increased   15
to two by Aeschylus, who curtailed the business of the Chorus, and made the
dialogue take the leading part in the play. A third actor and scenery were due to
Sophocles. Tragedy acquired also its magnitude. Discarding short stories and a
ludicrous diction, through its passing out of its satyric stage, it assumed, though   20
only at a late point in its progress, a tone of dignity; and its metre changed then from
trochaic to iambic. The reason for their original use of the trochaic tetrameter was
that their poetry was satyric and more connected with dancing than it now is. As
soon, however, as a spoken part came in, the very nature of the thing found the
appropriate metre. The iambic, we know, is the most speakable of metres, as is   25
shown by the fact that we very often fall into it in conversation, whereas we rarely
talk hexameters, and only when we depart from the speaking tone of voice. Another
change was a plurality of episodes. As for the remaining matters, the embellish-
ments and the account of their introduction, these must be taken as said, as it would   30
probably be a long piece of work to go through the details.

5 · As for comedy, it is (as has been observed) an imitation of men worse
than the average; worse, however, not as regards any and every sort of fault, but
only as regards one particular kind, the ridiculous, which is a species of the ugly.
The ridiculous may be defined as a mistake or deformity not productive of pain or   35
harm to others; the mask, for instance, that excites laughter, is something ugly and
distorted without causing pain.

Though the successive changes in tragedy and their authors are not unknown,
we cannot say the same of comedy; its early stages passed unnoticed, because it was
not as yet taken up in a serious way. It was only at a late point in its progress that a
chorus of comedians was officially granted by the archon; they used to be mere   1449ᵇ1
volunteers. It had also already certain definite forms at the time when the record of
those termed comic poets begins. Who it was who supplied it with masks, or
prologues, or a plurality of actors and the like, has remained unknown. The making   5
of plots, however, originated in Sicily; of Athenian poets Crates was the first to drop
the comedy of invective and frame stories and plots of a general nature.

Epic poetry, then, has been seen to resemble tragedy to this extent, that of
being an imitation of serious subjects in metre. It differs from it, however, in that it   10
is in one kind of verse and in narrative form; and also by its length—which is due to

its action having no fixed limit of time, whereas tragedy endeavours to keep as far as possible within a single circuit of the sun, or something near that. This, I say, is another point of difference between them, though at first the practice in this respect
15 was just the same in tragedies as in epic poems. They differ also in their constituents, some being common to both and others peculiar to tragedy—hence a judge of good and bad in tragedy is a judge of that in epic poetry also. All the parts of an epic are included in tragedy; but those of tragedy are not all of them to be
20 found in the epic.

      6 · Reserving hexameter poetry and comedy for consideration hereafter, let us proceed now to the discussion of tragedy; before doing so, however, we must gather up the definition resulting from what has been said. A tragedy, then, is the
25 imitation of an action that is serious and also, as having magnitude, complete in itself; in language with pleasurable accessories, each kind brought in separately in the parts of the work; in a dramatic, not in a narrative form; with incidents arousing pity and fear, wherewith to accomplish its catharsis of such emotions. Here by 'language with pleasurable accessories' I mean that with rhythm and harmony; and
30 by 'the kinds separately' I mean that some portions are worked out with verse only, and others in turn with song.
      As they act the stories, it follows that in the first place the spectacle must be some part of the whole; and in the second melody and diction, these two being the means of their imitation. Here by diction I mean merely this, the composition of the
35 verses; and by melody, what is too completely understood to require explanation. But further: the subject represented also is an action; and the action involves agents, who must necessarily have their distinctive qualities both of character and thought,
1450ª1 since it is from these that we ascribe certain qualities to their actions, and in virtue of these that they all succeed or fail. Now the action is represented in the play by the plot. The plot, in our present sense of the term, is simply this, the combination of the
5 incidents, or things done in the story; whereas character is what makes us ascribe certain qualities to the agents; and thought is shown in all they say when proving a particular point or, it may be, enunciating a general truth. There are six parts consequently of every tragedy, that make it the sort of tragedy it is, viz. a plot,
10 characters, diction, thought, spectacle, and melody; two of them arising from the means, one from the manner, and three from the objects of the dramatic imitation; and there is nothing else besides these six. Of these, its formative elements, then, not a few of the dramatists have made due use, as every play, one may say, admits of spectacle, character, plot, diction, melody, and thought.[3]
15   The most important of the six is the combination of the incidents of the story. Tragedy is essentially an imitation not of persons but of action and life. [All human happiness or misery takes the form of action; the end for which we live is a certain kind of activity, not a quality. Character gives us qualities, but it is in our actions
20 that we are happy or the reverse.][4] In a play accordingly they do not act in order to portray the characters; they include the characters for the sake of the action. So

----

[3]The text of this sentence is uncertain.
[4]Excised by Kassel.

that it is the action in it, i.e. its plot, that is the end and purpose of the tragedy; and the end is everywhere the chief thing. Besides this, a tragedy is impossible without action, but there might be one without Character. The tragedies of most of the moderns are characterless—a characteristic common among poets of all kinds, and with its counterpart in painting in Zeuxis as compared with Polygnotus; for whereas the latter is strong in character, the work of Zeuxis is devoid of it. And again: one may string together a series of characteristic speeches of the utmost finish as regards diction and thought, and yet fail to produce the true tragic effect; but one will have much better success with a tragedy which, however inferior in these respects, has a plot, a combination of incidents, in it. And again: the most powerful elements of attraction in Tragedy, the peripeties and discoveries, are parts of the plot. A further proof is in the fact that beginners succeed earlier with the diction and characters than with the construction of a story; and the same may be said of nearly all the early dramatists. We maintain, therefore, that the first essential, the life and soul, so to speak, of tragedy is the plot; and that the characters come second—compare the parallel in painting, where the most beautiful colours laid on without order will not give one the same pleasure as a simple black-and-white sketch of a portrait. We maintain that tragedy is primarily an imitation of action, and that it is mainly for the sake of the action that it imitates the personal agents. Third comes the element of thought, i.e. the power of saying whatever can be said, or what is appropriate to the occasion. This is what, in the speeches in tragedy, falls under the arts of politics and rhetoric; for the older poets make their personages discourse like statesmen, and the moderns like orators. One must not confuse it with character. Character in a play is that which reveals the choice of the agents—hence there is no room for character in a speech on a purely indifferent subject. Thought, on the other hand, is shown in all they say when proving or disproving some particular point, or enunciating some universal proposition. Fourth among the literary elements[5] is the diction of the personages, i.e., as before explained, the expression of their thoughts in words, which is practically the same thing with verse as with prose. As for the two remaining parts, the Melody is the greatest of the pleasurable accessories of Tragedy. The spectacle, though an attraction, is the least artistic of all the parts, and has least to do with the art of poetry. The tragic effect is quite possible without a public performance and actors; and besides, the getting-up of the spectacle is more a matter for the designer than the poet.

7 · Having thus distinguished the parts, let us now consider the proper construction of the plot, as that is at once the first and the most important thing in tragedy. We have laid it down that a tragedy is an imitation of an action that is complete in itself, as a whole of some magnitude; for a whole may be of no magnitude to speak of. Now a whole is that which has beginning, middle, and end. A beginning is that which is not itself necessarily after anything else, and which has naturally something else after it; an end is that which is naturally after something itself, either as its necessary or usual consequent, and with nothing else after it; and a middle, that which is by nature after one thing and has also another after it. A

_____
[5]Text uncertain.

well-constructed plot, therefore, cannot either begin or end at any point one likes;
beginning and end in it must be of the forms just described. Again: to be beautiful, a
35   living creature, and every whole made up of parts, must not only present a certain
order in its arrangement of parts, but also be of a certain definite magnitude.
Beauty is a matter of size and order, and therefore impossible either in a very
minute creature, since our perception becomes indistinct as it approaches instanta-
neity; or in a creature of vast size—one, say, 1,000 miles long—as in that case,
1451ᵃ1   instead of the object being seen all at once, the unity and wholeness of it is lost to the
beholder. Just in the same way, then, as a beautiful whole made up of parts, or a
beautiful living creature, must be of some size, but a size to be taken in by the eye,
5   so a story or plot must be of some length, but of a length to be taken in by the
memory. As for the limit of its length, so far as that is relative to public
performances and spectators, it does not fall within the theory of poetry. If they had
to perform a hundred tragedies, they would be timed by water-clocks, as they are
said to have been at one period.[6] The limit, however, set by the actual nature of the
10   thing is this: the longer the story, consistently with its being comprehensible as a
whole, the finer it is by reason of its magnitude. As a rough general formula, a
length which allows of the hero passing by a series of probable or necessary stages
from bad fortune to good, or from good to bad, may suffice as a limit for the
15   magnitude of the story.

8 · The unity of a plot does not consist, as some suppose, in its having one
man as its subject. An infinity of things befall that one man, some of which it is
impossible to reduce to unity; and in like manner there are many actions of one man
which cannot be made to form one action. One sees, therefore, the mistake of all the
20   poets who have written a *Heracleid,* a *Theseid,* or similar poems; they suppose that,
because Heracles was one man, the story also of Heracles must be one story.
Homer, however, evidently understood this point quite well, whether by art or
instinct, just in the same way as he excels the rest in every other respect. In writing
25   an *Odyssey,* he did not make the poem cover all that ever befell his hero—it befell
him, for instance, to get wounded on Parnassus and also to feign madness at the
time of the call to arms, but the two incidents had no necessary or probable
connexion with one another—instead of doing that, he took as the subject of the
Odyssey, as also of the *Iliad,* an action with a unity of the kind we are describing.
30   The truth is that, just as in the other imitative arts one imitation is always of one
thing, so in poetry the story, as an imitation of action, must represent one action, a
complete whole, with its several incidents so closely connected that the transposition
or withdrawal of any one of them will disjoin and dislocate the whole. For that
35   which makes no perceptible difference by its presence or absence is no real part of
the whole.

9 · From what we have said it will be seen that the poet's function is to
describe, not the thing that has happened, but a kind of thing that might happen, i.e.

[6]Text uncertain.

what is possible as being probable or necessary. The distinction between historian and poet is not in the one writing prose and the other verse—you might put the work 1451[b]1 of Herodotus into verse, and it would still be a species of history; it consists really in this, that the one describes the thing that has been, and the other a kind of thing that might be. Hence poetry is something more philosophic and of graver import than 5 history, since its statements are of the nature rather of universals, whereas those of history are singulars. By a universal statement I mean one as to what such or such a kind of man will probably or necessarily say or do—which is the aim of poetry, though it affixes proper names to the characters; by a singular statement, one as to 10 what, say, Alcibiades did or had done to him. In comedy this has become clear by this time; it is only when their plot is already made up of probable incidents that they give it a basis of proper names, choosing for the purpose any names that may occur to them, instead of writing like the old iambic poets about particular persons. In Tragedy, however, they still adhere to the historic names; and for this reason: 15 what convinces is the possible; now whereas we are not yet sure as to the possibility of that which has not happened, that which has happened is manifestly possible, otherwise it would not have happened. Nevertheless even in tragedy there are some plays with but one or two known names in them, the rest being inventions; and there 20 are some without a single known name, e.g. Agathon's *Antheus,* in which both incidents and names are of the poet's invention; and it is no less delightful on that account. So that one must not aim at a rigid adherence to the traditional stories on which tragedies are based. It would be absurd, in fact, to do so, as even the known 25 stories are only known to a few, though they are a delight none the less to all.

It is evident from the above that the poet must be more the poet of his plots than of his verses, inasmuch as he is a poet by virtue of the imitative element in his work, and it is actions that he imitates. And if he should come to take a subject from actual history, he is none the less a poet for that; since some historic occurrences 30 may very well be in the probable order of things; and it is in that aspect of them that he is their poet.

Of simple plots and actions the episodic are the worst. I call a plot episodic when there is neither probability nor necessity in the sequence of its episodes. 35 Actions of this sort bad poets construct through their own fault, and good ones on account of the players. His work being for public performance, a good poet often stretches out a plot beyond its capabilities, and is thus obliged to twist the sequence 1452[a]1 of incident.

Tragedy, however, is an imitation not only of a complete action, but also of incidents arousing pity and fear. Such incidents have the very greatest effect on the mind when they occur unexpectedly and at the same time in consequence of one another; there is more of the marvellous in them than if they happened of 5 themselves or by mere chance. Even matters of chance seem most marvellous if there is an appearance of design as it were in them; as for instance the statue of Mitys at Argos killed the author of Mitys' death by falling down on him when he was looking at it; for incidents like that we think to be not without a meaning. A plot, therefore, of this sort is necessarily finer than others. 10

10 · Plots are either simple or complex, since the actions they represent are naturally of this twofold description. The action, proceeding in the way defined, as one continuous whole, I call simple, when the change in the hero's fortunes takes place without reversal or discovery; and complex, when it involves one or the other, or both. These should each of them arise out of the structure of the plot itself, so as to be the consequence, necessary or probable, of the antecedents. There is a great difference between a thing happening *propter hoc* and *post hoc.*

11 · A reversal of fortune is the change of the kind described from one state of things within the play to its opposite, and that too as we say, in the probable or necessary sequence of events; as it is for instance in *Oedipus:* here the opposite state of things is produced by the Messenger, who, coming to gladden Oedipus and to remove his fears as to his mother, reveals the secret of his birth. And in *Lynceus:* just as he is being led off for execution, with Danaus at his side to put him to death, the incidents preceding this bring it about that he is saved and Danaus put to death. A discovery is, as the very word implies, a change from ignorance to knowledge, and thus to either love or hate, in the personages marked for good or evil fortune. The finest form of discovery is one attended by reversal, like that which goes with the discovery in *Oedipus*. There are no doubt other forms of it; what we have said may happen in a way[7] in reference to inanimate things, even things of a very casual kind; and it is also possible to discover whether some one has done or not done something. But the form most directly connected with the plot and the action of the piece is the first-mentioned. This, with a reversal, will arouse either pity or fear—actions of that nature being what tragedy is assumed to represent; and it will also serve to bring about the happy or unhappy ending. The discovery, then, being of persons, it may be that of one party only to the other, the latter being already known; or both the parties may have to discover each other. Iphigenia, for instance, was discovered to Orestes by sending the letter; and another discovery was required to reveal him to Iphigenia.

Two parts of the plot, then, reversal and discovery, are on matters of this sort. A third part is suffering; which we may define as an action of a destructive or painful nature, such as murders on the stage, tortures, woundings, and the like. The other two have been already explained.

12 · The parts of tragedy to be treated as formative elements in the whole were mentioned in a previous chapter. From the point of view, however, of its quantity, i.e. the separate sections into which it is divided, a tragedy has the following parts: prologue, episode, exode, and a choral portion, distinguished into parode and stasimon; these two are common to all tragedies, whereas songs from the stage and *Commoe* are only found in some. The prologue is all that precedes the parode of the chorus; an episode all that comes in between two whole choral songs; the exode all that follows after the last choral song. In the choral portion the parode is the whole first statement of the chorus; a stasimon, a song of the chorus without

---

[7]Text uncertain.

anapaests or trochees; a *Commos,* a lamentation sung by chorus and actor in concert. The parts of tragedy to be used as formative elements in the whole we have   25 already mentioned; the above are its parts from the point of view of its quantity, or the separate sections into which it is divided.

13 · The next points after what we have said above will be these: what is the poet to aim at, and what is he to avoid, in constructing his plots? and what are the conditions on which the tragic effect depends?   30

We assume that, for the finest form of tragedy, the plot must be not simple but complex; and further, that it must imitate actions arousing fear and pity, since that is the distinctive function of this kind of imitation. It follows, therefore, that there are three forms of plot to be avoided. A good man must not be seen passing from good fortune to bad, or a bad man from bad fortune to good. The first situation is   35 not fear-inspiring or piteous, but simply odious to us. The second is the most untragic that can be; it has no one of the requisites of tragedy; it does not appeal either to the human feeling in us, or to our pity, or to our fears. Nor, on the other   1453ᵃ1 hand, should an extremely bad man be seen falling from good fortune into bad. Such a story may arouse the human feeling in us, but it will not move us to either pity or fear; pity is occasioned by undeserved misfortune, and fear by that of one like ourselves; so that there will be nothing either piteous or fear-inspiring in the   5 situation. There remains, then, the intermediate kind of personage, a man not preeminently virtuous and just, whose misfortune, however, is brought upon him not by vice and depravity but by some fault, of the number of those in the enjoyment   10 of great reputation and prosperity; e.g. Oedipus, Thyestes, and the men of note of similar families. The perfect plot, accordingly, must have a single, and not (as some tell us) a double issue; the change in the subject's fortunes must be not from bad fortune to good, but on the contrary from good to bad; and the cause of it must lie   15 not in any depravity, but in some great fault on his part; the man himself being either such as we have described, or better, not worse, than that. Fact also confirms our theory. Though the poets began by accepting any tragic story that came to hand, in these days the finest tragedies are always on the story of some few houses, on that of Alcmeon, Oedipus, Orestes, Meleager, Thyestes, Telephus, or any others   20 that may have been involved, as either agents or sufferers, in some deed of horror. The theoretically best tragedy, then, has a plot of this description. The critics, therefore, are wrong who blame Euripides for taking this line in his tragedies, and giving many of them an unhappy ending. It is, as we have said, the right line to take.   25 The best proof is this: on the stage, and in the public performances, such plays, properly worked out, are seen to be the most truly tragic; and Euripides, even if his execution be faulty in every other point, is seen to be nevertheless the most tragic certainly of the dramatists. After this comes the construction of plot which some   30 rank first, one with a double story (like the *Odyssey*) and an opposite issue for the good and the bad personages. It is ranked as first only through the weakness of the audiences; the poets merely follow their public, writing as its wishes dictate. But the   35 pleasure here is not that of tragedy. It belongs rather to comedy, where the bitterest enemies in the piece (e.g. Orestes and Aegisthus) walk off good friends at the end, with no slaying of any one by any one.

1453ᵇ1   14 · The tragic fear and pity may be aroused by the spectacle; but they may also be aroused by the very structure and incidents of the play—which is the better way and shows the better poet. The plot in fact should be so framed that, even without seeing the things take place, he who simply hears the account of them shall
5   be filled with horror and pity at the incidents; which is just the effect that the mere recital of the story in *Oedipus* would have on one. To produce this same effect by means of the spectacle is less artistic, and requires extraneous aid. Those, however, who make use of the spectacle to put before us that which is merely monstrous and
10   not productive of fear, are wholly out of touch with tragedy; not every kind of pleasure should be required of a tragedy, but only its own proper pleasure.

The tragic pleasure is that of pity and fear, and the poet has to produce it by a work of imitation; it is clear, therefore, that the causes should be included in the incidents of his story. Let us see, then, what kinds of incident strike one as horrible,
15   or rather as piteous. In a deed of this description the parties must necessarily be either friends, or enemies, or indifferent to one another. Now when enemy does it on enemy, there is nothing to move us to pity either in his doing or in his meditating the deed, except so far as the actual pain of the sufferer is concerned; and the same is true when the parties are indifferent to one another. Whenever the tragic deed, however, is done among friends—when murder or the like is done or meditated by
20   brother on brother, by son on father, by mother on son, or son on mother—these are the situations the poet should seek after. The traditional stories, accordingly, must be kept as they are, e.g. the murder of Clytaemnestra by Orestes and of Eriphyle by
25   Alcmeon. At the same time even with these there is something left to the poet himself; it is for him to devise the right way of treating them. Let us explain more clearly what we mean by 'the right way'. The deed of horror may be done by the doer knowingly and consciously, as in the old poets, and in Medea's murder of her
30   children in Euripides. Or he may do it, but in ignorance of his relationship, and discover that afterwards, as does the Oedipus in Sophocles. Here the deed is outside the play; but it may be within it, like the act of the Alcmeon in Astydamas, or that of the Telegonus in *Ulysses Wounded*. A third possibility is for one meditating some
35   deadly injury to another, in ignorance of his relationship, to make the discovery in time to draw back. These exhaust the possibilities, since the deed must necessarily be either done or not done, and either knowingly or unknowingly.

The worst situation is when the personage is with full knowledge on the point of doing the deed, and leaves it undone. It is odious and also (through the absence of suffering) untragic; hence it is that no one is made to act thus except in some few
1454ᵃ1   instances, e.g. Haemon and Creon in *Antigone*. Next after this comes the actual perpetration of the deed meditated. A better situation than that, however, is for the deed to be done in ignorance, and the relationship discovered afterwards, since there is nothing odious in it, and the discovery will serve to astound us. But the best of all
5   is the last; what we have in *Cresphontes*, for example, where Merope, on the point of slaying her son, recognizes him in time; in *Iphigenia*, where sister and brother are in

a like position; and in *Helle,* where the son recognizes his mother, when on the point of giving her up to her enemy.

This will explain why our tragedies are restricted (as we said just now) to such a small number of families. It was accident rather than art that led the poets in quest of subjects to embody this kind of incident in their plots. They are still obliged, accordingly, to have recourse to the families in which such honours have occurred.

On the construction of the plot, and the kind of plot required for tragedy, enough has now been said.

15 · In the characters there are four points to aim at. First and foremost, that they shall be good. There will be an element of character in the play, if (as has been observed) what a personage says or does reveals a certain choice; and a good element of character, if the purpose so revealed is good. Such goodness is possible in every type of personage, even in a woman or a slave, though the one is perhaps an inferior, and the other a wholly worthless being. The second point is to make them appropriate. The character before us may be, say, manly; but it is not appropriate in a female character to be manly, or clever. The third is to make them like the reality, which is not the same as their being good and appropriate, in our sense of the term. The fourth is to make them consistent and the same throughout; even if inconsistency be part of the man before one for imitation as presenting that form of character, he should still be consistently inconsistent. We have an instance of baseness of character, not required for the story, in the Menelaus in *Orestes;* of the incongruous and unbefitting in the lamentation of Ulysses in *Scylla,* and in the speech of Melanippe; and of inconsistency in *Iphigenia at Aulis,* where Iphigenia the suppliant is utterly unlike the later Iphigenia. The right thing, however, is in the characters just as in the incidents of the play to seek after the necessary or the probable; so that whenever such-and-such a personage says or does such-and-such a thing, it shall be the necessary or probable outcome of his character; and whenever this incident follows on that, it shall be either the necessary or the probable consequence of it. From this one sees that the dénouement also should arise out of the plot itself, and not depend on a stage-artifice, as in *Medea* or in the story of the departure of the Greeks in the *Iliad.* The artifice must be reserved for matters outside the play—for past events beyond human knowledge, or events yet to come, which require to be foretold or announced; since it is the privilege of the gods to know everything. There should be nothing improbable among the actual incidents. If it be unavoidable, however, it should be outside the tragedy, like the improbability in the *Oedipus* of Sophocles. As tragedy is an imitation of personages better than the ordinary man, we should follow the example of good portrait-painters, who reproduce the distinctive features of a man, and at the same time, without losing the likeness, make him handsomer than he is. The poet in like manner, in portraying men quick or slow to anger, or with similar infirmities of character, must know how to represent them as such, and at the same time as good men . . .[8]

All these rules one must keep in mind throughout, and, further, those also for

[8]The text is corrupt here.

such points of stage-effect as directly depend on the art of the poet, since in these too one may often make mistakes. Enough, however, has been said on the subject in one of our published writings.

16 · Discovery in general has been explained already. As for the species of
20   discovery, the first to be noted is the least artistic form of it, of which the poets make most use through mere lack of invention, discovery by signs. Of these signs some are congenital, like the 'lance-head which the Earth-born have on them' or 'stars', such as Carcinus brings in his *Thyestes;* others acquired after birth—these latter being either marks on the body, e.g. scars, or external tokens, like necklaces, or the boat in
25   the discovery in *Tyro.* Even these, however, admit of two uses, a better and a worse; the scar of Ulysses is an instance; the discovery of him through it is made in one way by the nurse and in another by the swineherds. A discovery using signs as a means of assurance is less artistic, as indeed are all such as imply reflection;
30   whereas one bringing them in all of a sudden, as in the *Bath-story,* is of a better order. Next after these are discoveries made directly by the poet; which are inartistic for that very reason; e.g. Orestes' discovery of himself in *Iphigenia:* whereas his sister reveals who she is by the letter, Orestes is made to say himself what the poet rather than the story demands. This, therefore, is not far removed
35   from the first-mentioned fault, since he might have presented certain tokens as well. Another instance is the voice of the shuttle in the *Tereus* of Sophocles. A third species is discovery through memory, from a man's consciousness being awakened
1455ᵃ1   by something seen. Thus in *The Cyprioe* of Dicaeogenes, the sight of the picture makes the man burst into tears; and in the *Tale of Alcinous,* hearing the harper Ulysses is reminded of the past and weeps; the discovery of them being the result. A fourth kind of discovery through reasoning; e.g. in *The Choephoroe;* 'One like me is
5   here; there is no one like me but Orestes; he, therefore, must be here'. Or that which Polyidus the Sophist suggested for *Iphigenia;* since it was natural for Orestes to reflect: 'My sister was sacrificed and I am to be sacrificed like her'. Or that in the *Tydeus* of Theodectes: 'I came to find a son, and am to die myself'. Or that in *The*
10   *Phinidae:* on seeing the place the women inferred their fate, that they were to die there, since they had also been exposed there. There is, too, a composite discovery arising from bad reasoning on the part of the audience. An instance of it is in *Ulysses the False Messenger:* that he stretched the bow and no one else did was invented by the poet and part of the argument, and so too that he said he would
15   recognize the bow which he had not seen; but to suppose from that that he would know it again was bad reasoning. The best of all discoveries, however, is that arising from the incidents themselves, when the great surprise comes about through a probable incident, like that in the *Oedipus* of Sophocles; and also in *Iphigenia;* for it was probable that she should wish to have a letter taken home. These last are the
20   only discoveries independent of the artifice of signs and necklaces. Next after them come discoveries through reasoning.

17 · At the time when he is constructing his plots, and engaged on the diction in which they are worked out, the poet should remember to put the actual

scenes as far as possible before his eyes. In this way, seeing everything with the vividness of an eye-witness as it were, he will devise what is appropriate, and be least likely to overlook incongruities. This is shown by what was censured in Carcinus, the return of Amphiaraus from the sanctuary; it would have passed unnoticed, if it had not been actually seen; but on the stage his play failed, the incongruity of the incident offending the spectators. As far, as may be, too, the poet should even act his story with the very gestures of his personages. Given the same natural qualifications, he who feels the emotions to be described will be the most convincing; distress and anger, for instance, are portrayed most truthfully by one who is feeling them at the moment. Hence it is that poetry demands a man with a special gift for it, or else one with a touch of madness in him; the former can easily assume the required mood, and the latter may be actually beside himself with emotion. His story, again, whether already made or of his own making, he should first simplify and reduce to a universal form, before proceeding to lengthen it out by the insertion of episodes. The following will show how the universal element in *Iphigenia,* for instance, may be viewed: a certain maiden having been offered in sacrifice, and spirited away from her sacrificers into another land, where the custom was to sacrifice all strangers to the Goddess, she was made there the priestess of this rite. Long after that the brother of the priestess happened to come; the fact, however, of the oracle having bidden him go there, and his object in going, are outside the plot of the play. On his coming he was arrested, and about to be sacrificed, when he revealed who he was—either as Euripides puts it, or (as suggested by Polyidus) by the not improbable exclamation, 'So I too am doomed to be sacrificed, as my sister was'; and the disclosure led to his salvation. This done, the next thing, after the proper names have been fixed as a basis for the story, is to turn it into episodes. One must ensure, however, that the episodes are appropriate, like the fit of madness in Orestes, which led to his arrest, and the purifying, which brought about his salvation. In plays, then, the episodes are short; in epic poetry they serve to lengthen out the poem. The argument of the *Odyssey* is not a long one. A certain man has been abroad many years; Poseidon is ever on the watch for him, and he is all alone. Matters at home too have come to this, that his substance is being wasted and his son's death plotted by suitors to his wife. Then he arrives there himself after his grievous sufferings; reveals himself, and falls on his enemies; and the end is his salvation and their death. This being all that is proper to the *Odyssey,* everything else in it is episode.

18 · Every tragedy is in part complication and in part dénouement; the incidents before the opening scene, and often certain also of those within the play, forming the complication; and the rest the dénouement. By complication I mean all from the beginning of the story to the point just before the change in the subject's fortunes; by dénouement, all from the beginning of the change to the end. In the *Lynceus* of Theodectes, for instance, the complication includes, together with the presupposed incidents, the seizure of the child and that in turn of the parents . . . ;[9]

---

[9]Kassel marks a lacuna.

and the dénouement all from the indictment for the murder to the end. There are four distinct species of Tragedy—that being the number of the constituents also that have been mentioned: first, the complex tragedy, which is all reversal and discovery; second, the tragedy of suffering, e.g. the Ajaxes and *Ixions;* third, the tragedy of character, e.g. *The Phthiotides* and *Peleus.* The fourth constituent is that of . . .[10] exemplified in *The Phorcides,* in *Prometheus,* and in all plays with the scene laid in the nether world. Now it is right, when one speaks of a tragedy as the same or not the same as another, to do so on the ground before all else of their plot, i.e. as having the same or not the same complication and dénouement. Yet there are many dramatists who, after a good complication, fail in the dénouement. But it is necessary for both points of construction to be always duly mastered. The poet's aim, then, should be to combine every element of interest, if possible, or else the more important and the major part of them. This is now especially necessary owing to the unfair criticism to which the poet is subjected in these days. Just because there have been poets before him strong in the several species of tragedy, the critics now expect the one man to surpass that which was the strong point of each one of his predecessors. One should also remember what has been said more than once, and not write a tragedy on an epic body of incident (i.e. one with a plurality of stories in it), by attempting to dramatize, for instance, the entire story of the *Iliad.* In the epic owing to its scale every part is treated at proper length; with a drama, however, on the same story the result is very disappointing. This is shown by the fact that all who have dramatized the fall of Ilium in its entirety, and not part by part, like Euripides, or the whole of the Niobe story, instead of a portion, like Aeschylus, either fail utterly or have little success on the stage; for that and that alone was enough to ruin even a play by Agathon. Yet in their reversals of fortune, as also in their simple plots, the poets I mean show wonderful skill in aiming at the kind of effect they desire—a tragic situation that arouses the human feeling in one, like the clever villain (e.g. Sisyphus) deceived, or the brave wrongdoer worsted. This is probable, however, only in Agathon's sense, when he speaks of the probability of even improbabilities coming to pass. The Chorus too should be regarded as one of the actors; it should be an integral part of the whole, and take a share in the action—that which it has in Sophocles, rather than in Euripides. With the later poets, however, the songs in a play of theirs have no more to do with the plot of that than of any other tragedy. Hence it is that they are now singing inserted pieces, a practice first introduced by Agathon. And yet what real difference is there between singing such inserted pieces, and attempting to fit in a speech, or even a whole act, from one play into another?

19 · The plot and characters having been discussed, it remains to consider the diction and thought. As for the thought, we may assume what is said of it in our Art of Rhetoric, as it belongs more properly to that department of inquiry. The thought of the personages is shown in everything to be effected by their language— in every effort to prove or disprove, to arouse emotion (pity, fear, anger, and the

[10]The text is corrupt; most editors read ὄψις, 'spectacle'.

like), or to maximize or minimize things. It is clear, also, that their mental procedure must be on the same lines in their actions likewise, whenever they wish them to arouse pity or horror, or to have a look of importance or probability. The only difference is that with the act the impression has to be made without 5 explanation; whereas with the spoken word it has to be produced by the speaker, and result from his language. What, indeed, would be the good of the speaker, if things appeared in the required light even apart from anything he said?

As regards the diction, one subject for inquiry under this head is the turns given to the language when spoken; e.g. the difference between command and prayer, simple statement and threat, question and answer, and so forth. The theory of such matters, however, belongs to acting and the professors of that art. Whether 10 the poet knows these things or not, his art as a poet is never seriously criticized on that account. What fault can one see in Homer's 'Sing of the wrath, Goddess'?— which Protagoras has criticized as being a command where a prayer was meant, 15 since to bid one do or not do, he tells us, is a command. Let us pass over this, then, as appertaining to another art, and not to that of poetry.

20 · The diction viewed as a whole is made up of the following parts: the 20 letter, the syllable, the conjunction, the article, the noun, the verb, the case, and the speech. The letter is an indivisible sound of a particular kind, one that may become a factor in a compound sound. Indivisible sounds are uttered by the brutes also, but no one of these is a letter in our sense of the term. These elementary sounds are either vowels, semivowels, or mutes. A vowel is a letter having an audible sound 25 without the addition of another letter. A semivowel, one having an audible sound by the addition of another letter; e.g. S and R. A mute, one having no sound at all by itself, but becoming audible by an addition, that of one of the letters which have a sound of some sort of their own; e.g. G and D. The letters differ in various ways: as 30 produced by different conformations or in different regions of the mouth; as aspirated or not aspirated; as long, short, or of variable quantity; and further as having an acute, grave, or intermediate accent. The details of these matters we must leave to the students of metre. A syllable is a non-significant composite sound, made 35 up of a mute and a letter having a sound; for GR, without an A, is just as much a syllable as GRA, with an A.[11] The various forms of the syllable also belong to the theory of metre. A conjunction is a non-significant sound which, when one significant sound is formable out of several, neither hinders nor aids the union, and 1457ª1 which naturally stands both at the end and in the middle but must not be inserted at the beginning; e.g. μέν, or δέ. Or a non-significant sound which naturally makes one significant sound out of several significant sounds. An article is a non-significant 5 sound marking the beginning, end, or dividing-point of a sentence, its natural place being either at the extremities or in the middle. E.g. ἀμφί, περί etc. Or a non-significant sound which neither prevents nor makes a single significant sound out of several, and which is naturally placed both at the end and in the middle.[12] A 10

---

[11]The text of this sentence is uncertain.
[12]The text from 1456ᵇ38–1457ª10 is highly uncertain.

noun or name is a composite significant sound not involving the idea of time, with parts which have no significance by themselves in it. It is to be remembered that in a compound we do not think of the parts as having a significance also by themselves; in the name 'Theodorus', for instance, the δῶρος means nothing. A verb is a

15 composite significant sound involving the idea of time, with parts which (just as in the noun) have no significance by themselves in it. Whereas the word 'man' or 'white' does not signify a time 'he walks' and 'he has walked' involve in addition to the idea of walking that of time present or time past. A case of a noun or verb is

20 when the word means 'of' or 'to' a thing, and so forth, or for one or many (e.g. 'man' and 'men'); or it may consist merely in the mode of utterance, e.g. in question, command, etc. 'Did he walk'? and 'Walk'! are cases of the verb 'to walk' of this last kind. A sentence is a composite significant sound, some of the parts of which have a certain significance by themselves. It may be observed that a sentence is not always

25 made up of noun and verb; it may be without a verb, like the definition of man; but it will always have some part with a certain significance by itself. In the sentence 'Cleon walks', 'Cleon' is an instance of such a part. A sentence is said to be one in two ways, either as signifying one thing, or as a union of several speeches made into one by conjunction. Thus the *Iliad* is one speech by conjunction of several; and the

30 definition of man is one through its signifying one thing.

21 · Nouns are of two kinds, either simple, i.e. made up of non-significant parts, like the word earth, or double; in the latter case the word may be made up either of a significant and a non-significant part (a distinction which disappears in the compound), or of two significant parts. It is possible also to have triple, quadruple, or higher compounds, like many of the names of people from Massalia: e.g. 'Hermocaïcoxanthus' and the like.

1457ᵇ1 Whatever its structure, a noun must always be either the ordinary word for the thing, or a strange word, or a metaphor, or an ornamental word, or a coined word, or a word lengthened out, or curtailed, or altered in form. By the ordinary word I mean that in general use in a country; and by a strange word, one in use elsewhere. So that

5 the same word may obviously be at once strange and ordinary, though not in reference to the same people; σίγυνον, for instance, is an ordinary word in Cyprus, and a strange word with us. Metaphor consists in giving the thing a name that belongs to something else; the transference being either from genus to species, or from species to genus, or from species to species, or on grounds of analogy. That

10 from genus to species is exemplified in 'Here stands my ship'; for lying at anchor is a sort of standing. That from species to genus in 'Truly ten thousand good deeds has Ulysses wrought', where 'ten thousand', which is a particular large number, is put in place of the generic 'a large number'. That from species to species in 'Drawing the life with the bronze,' and in 'Severing with the enduring bronze'; where the poet

15 uses 'draw' in the sense of 'sever' and 'sever' in that of 'draw', both words meaning to 'take away' something. That from analogy is possible whenever there are four terms so related that the second is to the first, as the fourth to the third; for one may then put the fourth in place of the second, and the second in place of the fourth. Now and then, too, they qualify the metaphor by adding on to it that to which the

word it supplants is relative. Thus a cup is in relation to Dionysus what a shield is to 20
Ares. The cup accordingly will be described as the 'shield of Dionysus' and the shield as the 'cup of Ares'. Or to take another instance: As old age is to life, so is evening to day. One will accordingly describe evening as the 'old age of the day'—or by the Empedoclean equivalent; and old age as the 'evening' or 'sunset of life'. It may be that some of the terms thus related have no special name of their own, but 25 for all that they will be described in just the same way. Thus to cast forth seed-corn is called 'sowing'; but to cast forth its flame, as said of the sun, has no special name. This nameless act, however, stands in just the same relation to its object, sunlight, as sowing to the seed-corn. Hence the expression in the poet, 'sowing around a god-created flame'. There is also another form of qualified metaphor. Having given 30 the thing the alien name, one may by a negative addition deny of it one of the attributes naturally associated with its new name. An instance of this would be to call the shield not the 'cup of Ares', as in the former case, but a 'cup that holds no wine' . . . .[13] A coined word is a name which, being quite unknown among a people, is given by the poet himself; e.g. (for there are some words that seem to be of this origin) ἔρνυγες for horns, and ἀρητήρ for priest. A word is said to be lengthened out, 1458ª1 when it has a short vowel made long, or an extra syllable inserted; e.g. πόληος for πόλεως, Πηληιάδεω for Πηλείδου. It is said to be curtailed, when it has lost a part; e.g. κρῖ, δῶ, and ὄψ in μία γίνεται ἀμφοτέρων ὄψ. It is an altered word, when part is left as 5 it was and part is of the poet's making; e.g. δεξιτερόν for δεξιόν, in δεξιτερὸν κατὰ μαζόν.

The nouns themselves are either masculines, feminines, or intermediates. All ending in N, P, Σ, or in the two compounds of this last, Ψ and Ξ, are masculines. All 10 ending in the invariably long vowels, H and Ω, and in A among the vowels that may be long, are feminines. So that there is an equal number of masculine and feminine terminations, as Ψ and Ξ are the same as Σ. There is no noun, however, ending in a mute or in a short vowel. Only three (μέλι, κόμμι, πέπερι) end in I, and five in Υ. . . .[14] 15 The intermediates end in the variable vowels or in N, P, Σ.

22 · The excellence of diction is for it to be at once clear and not mean. The clearest indeed is that made up of the ordinary words for things, but it is mean, as is shown by the poetry of Cleophon and Sthenelus. On the other hand the diction 20 becomes distinguished and non-prosaic by the use of unfamiliar terms, i.e. strange words, metaphors, lengthened forms, and everything that deviates from the ordinary modes of speech. But a whole statement in such terms will be either a riddle or a barbarism, a riddle, if made up of metaphors, a barbarism, if made up of 25 strange words. The very nature indeed of a riddle is this, to describe a fact in an impossible combination of words (which cannot be done with a combination of other names, but can be done with a combination of metaphors); e.g. 'I saw a man glue brass on another with fire', and the like. The corresponding use of strange words 30 results in a barbarism. A certain admixture, accordingly, of unfamiliar terms is necessary. These, the strange word, the metaphor, the ornamental equivalent, etc.,

[13]Kassel marks a lacuna.
[14]Kassel marks a lacuna.

will save the language from seeming mean and prosaic, while the ordinary words in it will secure the requisite clearness. What helps most, however, to render the diction at once clear and non-prosaic is the use of the lengthened, curtailed, and altered forms of words. Their deviation from the ordinary words will, by making the language unlike that in general use, give it a non-prosaic appearance; and their having much in common with the words in general use will give it the quality of clearness. It is not right, then, to condemn these modes of speech, and ridicule the poet for using them, as some have done; e.g. the elder Euclid, who said it was easy to make poetry if one were to be allowed to lengthen words as much as one likes—a procedure he caricatured by reading Ἐπιχάρην εἶδον Μαραθῶνάδε βαδίζοντα, and οὐκ †ἂν γεράμενος† τὸν ἐκείνου ἐλλέβορον as verses. A too apparent use of these licences has certainly a ludicrous effect, but they are not alone in that; the rule of moderation applies to all the constituents of the poetic vocabulary; even with metaphors, strange words, and the rest, the effect will be the same, if one uses them improperly and with a view of provoking laughter. The proper use of them is a very different thing. To realize the difference one should take an epic verse and see how it reads when the normal words are introduced. The same should be done too with the strange word, the metaphor, and the rest; for one has only to put the ordinary words in their place to see the truth of what we are saying. The same iambic, for instance, is found in Aeschylus and Euripides, and as it stands in the former it is a poor line; whereas Euripides, by the change of a single word, the substitution of a strange for what is by usage the ordinary word, has made it seem a fine one. Aeschylus having said in his *Philoctetes:*

φαγέδαιναν ἥ μου σάρκας ἐσθίει ποδός,

Euripides has merely altered the ἐσθίει here into θοινᾶται. Or suppose

νῦν δέ μ᾽ ἐὼν ὀλίγος τε καὶ οὐτιδανὸς καὶ ἀεικής

to be altered, by the substitution of the ordinary words, into

νῦν δέ μ᾽ ἐὼν μικρός τε καὶ ἀσθενικὸς καὶ ἀειδής.

Or the line

δίφρον ἀεικέλιον καταθεὶς ὀλίγην τε τράπεζαν

into

δίφρον μοχθηρὸν καταθεὶς μικράν τε τράπεζαν.

Or ἠιόνες βοόωσιν into ἠιόνες κράζουσιν. Add to this that Ariphrades used to ridicule the tragedians for introducing expressions unknown in the language of common life, δωμάτων ἄπο (for ἀπὸ δωμάτων), σέθεν, ἐγὼ δέ νιν, Ἀχιλλέως πέρι (for περὶ Ἀχιλλέως), and the like. The mere fact of their not being in ordinary speech gives the diction a non-prosaic character; but Ariphrades was unaware of that. It is a great thing, indeed, to make a proper use of these poetical forms, as also of compounds and strange words. But the greatest thing by far is to be a master of metaphor. It is the one thing that cannot be learnt from others; and it is also a sign of genius, since a good metaphor implies an intuitive perception of the similarity in dissimilars.

Of the kinds of words we have enumerated it may be observed that compounds are most in place in the dithyramb, strange words in heroic, and metaphors in 10 iambic poetry. Heroic poetry, indeed, may avail itself of them all. But in iambic verse, which models itself as far as possible on the spoken language, only those kinds of words are in place which are allowable also in a prose speech, i.e. the ordinary word, the metaphor, and the ornamental equivalent.

Let this, then, suffice as an account of tragedy, the art imitating by means of 15 action on the stage.

23 · As for the poetry which narrates, or imitates by means of versified language, the construction of its plots should clearly be like that in a tragedy; they should be based on a single action, one that is a complete whole in itself, with a beginning, middle, and end, so as to enable the work to produce its own proper 20 pleasure with all the organic unity of a living creature. Nor should one suppose that there is anything like them in our usual histories. A history has to deal not with one action, but with one period and all that happened in that to one or more persons, however disconnected the several events may have been. Just as two events may take place at the same time, e.g. the sea-fight off Salamis and the battle with the 25 Carthaginians in Sicily, without converging to the same end, so too of two consecutive events one may sometimes come after the other with no one end as their common issue. Nevertheless most of our poets, one may say, ignore the distinction.

Herein, then, to repeat what we have said before, we have a further proof of 30 Homer's marvellous superiority to the rest. He did not attempt to deal even with the Trojan war in its entirety, though it was a whole with a definite beginning and end—through a feeling apparently that it was too long a story to be taken in in one view, or if not that, too complicated from the variety of incident in it. As it is, he has singled out one section of the whole; many of the other incidents, however, he brings 35 in as episodes, using the Catalogue of the Ships, for instance, and other episodes to relieve the uniformity of his narrative. As for the other poets, they treat of one man, or one period; or else of an action which, although one, has a multiplicity of parts in 1459ᵇ1 it. This last is what the authors of the *Cypria* and *Little Iliad* have done. And the result is that, whereas the *Iliad* or *Odyssey* supplies materials for only one, or at most two tragedies, the *Cypria* does that for several and so does the *Little Iliad* [for 5 more than eight: for an *Adjudgment of Arms*, a *Philoctetes*, a *Neoptolemus*, a *Eurypylus*, a *Ulysses as Beggar*, a *Laconian Women*, a *Fall of Ilium*, and a *Departure of the Fleet*; as also a *Sinon*, and a *Woman of Troy*].[15]

24 · Besides this, epic poetry must divide into the same species as tragedy; it must be either simple or complex, a story of character or one of suffering. Its parts, too, with the exception of song and spectacle, must be the same, as it requires 10

[15]Excised by Kassel.

reversals, discoveries, and scenes of suffering just like tragedy. Lastly, the thought and diction in it must be good in their way. All these elements appear in Homer first; and he has made due use of them. His two poems are each examples of
15 construction, the *Iliad* simple and a story of suffering, the *Odyssey* complex (there is discovery throughout it) and a story of character. And they are more than this, since in diction and thought too they surpass all other poems.

There is, however, a difference in the epic as compared with tragedy, in its length, and in its metre. As to its length, the limit already suggested will suffice: it must be possible for the beginning and end of the work to be taken in in one view—a
20 condition which will be fulfilled if the poem be shorter than the old epics, and about as long as the series of tragedies offered for one hearing. For the extension of its length epic poetry has a special advantage, of which it makes large use. In a play
25 one cannot represent an action with a number of parts going on simultaneously; one is limited to the part on the stage and connected with the actors. Whereas in epic poetry the narrative form makes it possible for one to describe a number of simultaneous incidents; and these, if germane to the subject, increase the body of the poem. This then is a gain to the epic, tending to give it grandeur, and also variety
30 of interest and room for episodes of diverse kinds. Uniformity of incident by the satiety it soon creates is apt to ruin tragedies on the stage. As for its metre, the heroic has been assigned it from experience; were any one to attempt a narrative poem in some one, or in several, of the other metres, the incongruity of the thing would be apparent. The heroic in fact is the gravest and weightiest of metres—
35 which is what makes it more tolerant than the rest of strange words and metaphors, that also being a point in which the narrative form of poetry goes beyond all others. The iambic and trochaic, on the other hand, are metres of movement, the one
1460ᵃ1 representing that of life and action, the other that of the dance. Still more unnatural would it appear, if one were to write an epic in a medley of metres, as Chaeremon did. Hence it is that no one has ever written a long story in any but heroic verse; the very nature of the thing, as we have said, teaches us to select the metre appropriate to such a story.

5 Homer, admirable as he is in every other respect, is especially so in this, that he alone among epic poets is not unaware of the part to be played by the poet himself in the poem. The poet should say very little in his own character, as he is no imitator when doing that. Whereas the other poets are perpetually coming forward in person, and say but little, and that only here and there, as imitators, Homer after a
10 brief preface brings in forthwith a man, a woman, or some other character—no one of them characterless, but each with distinctive characteristics.

The marvellous is certainly required in tragedy. The epic, however, affords more opening for the improbable, the chief factor in the marvellous, because in it
15 the agents are not visibly before one. The scene of the pursuit of Hector would be ridiculous on the stage—the Greeks halting instead of pursuing him, and Achilles shaking his head to stop them; but in the poem the absurdity is overlooked. The marvellous, however, is a cause of pleasure, as is shown by the fact that we all tell a story with additions, in the belief that we are giving pleasure to our hearers.

Homer more than any other has taught the others the art of framing lies in the

right way. I mean the use of paralogism. Whenever, if one thing is or happens, 20
another is or happens, men's notion is that, if the latter is, so is the former—but that
is a false conclusion. Accordingly, if the first thing is untrue, but there is something
else that on the assumption of its truth follows as its consequent, the right thing then
is to add on the latter. Just because we know the truth of the consequent, we are in
our own minds led on to the erroneous inference of the truth of the antecedent. 25
There is an instance of this in the *Bath-story* in the *Odyssey*.

A likely impossibility is always preferable to an unconvincing possibility. The
story should never be made up of improbable incidents; there should be nothing of
that sort in it. If, however, such incidents are unavoidable, they should be outside
the piece, like Oedipus' ignorance in *Oedipus* of the circumstances of Laius' death; 30
not within it, like the report of the Pythian games in *Electra,* or the man's having
come to Mysia from Tegea without uttering a word on the way, in *The Mysians.* So
that it is ridiculous to say that one's plot would have been spoilt without them, since
it is fundamentally wrong to make up such plots. If the poet has taken such a plot,
however, and one sees that he might have put it in a more probable form, he is guilty
of absurdity as well as a fault of art.[16] Even in the *Odyssey* the improbabilities in the
setting-ashore of Ulysses would be clearly intolerable in the hands of an inferior
poet. As it is, the poet conceals them, his other excellences veiling their absurdity. 1460[b]1
Elaborate diction, however, is required only in places where there is no action, and
no character or thought to be revealed. Where there is character or thought, on the
other hand, an over-ornate diction tends to obscure them. 5

25 · As regards problems and their solutions, one may see the number and
nature of the assumptions on which they proceed by viewing the matter in the
following way. The poet being an imitator just like the painter or other maker of
likenesses, he must necessarily in all instances represent things in one or other of
three aspects, either as they were or are, or as they are said or thought to be or to 10
have been, or as they ought to be. All this he does in language, with an admixture, it
may be, of strange words and metaphors, as also of the various modified forms of
words, since the use of these is conceded in poetry. It is to be remembered, too, that
there is not the same kind of correctness in poetry as in politics, or indeed any other
art. There is, however, within the limits of poetry itself a possibility of two kinds of 15
error, the one directly, the other only accidentally connected with the art. If the poet
meant to describe the thing . . .[17] lack of power of expression, his art itself is at fault.
But if it was through his having meant to describe it in some incorrect way (e.g. to
make the horse in movement have both right legs thrown forward) that the
technical error (one in a matter of, say, medicine or some other special science), 20
have got into his description, his error in that case is not in the essentials of the
poetic art. These, therefore, must be the premises of the solutions in answer to the
criticisms involved in the problems.

As to the criticisms relating to the poet's art itself. Any impossibilities there
may be in his descriptions of things are faults. But from another point of view they

---

[16]The text of this sentence is uncertain.
[17]Kassel marks a lacuna.

are justifiable, if they serve the end of poetry itself—if (to assume what we have
25 said of that end) they make the effect of either that very portion of the work or some
other portion more astounding. The Pursuit of Hector is an instance in point. If,
however, the poetic end might have been as well or better or no worse attained
without sacrifice of technical correctness in such matters, the impossibility is not to
be justified, since the description should be, if it can, entirely free from error. One
30 may ask, too, whether the error is in a matter directly or only accidentally
connected with the poetic art; since it is a lesser error in an artist not to know, for
instance, that the hind has no horns, than to produce an unrecognizable picture of
one.

　　If the poet's description be criticized as not true to fact, one may urge perhaps
that the object ought to be as described—an answer like that of Sophocles, who said
that he drew men as they ought to be, and Euripides as they were. If the description,
35 however, be neither true nor of the thing as it ought to be, the answer must be then,
that it is in accordance with opinion. The tales about Gods, for instance, may be as
1461ª1 wrong as Xenophanes thinks, neither true nor the better thing to say; but they are
certainly in accordance with opinion. Of other statements in poetry one may
perhaps say, not that they are better than the truth, but that the fact was so at the
time; e.g. the description of the arms: 'their spears stood upright, butt-end upon the
ground'; for that was the usual way of fixing them then, as it is still with the
5 Illyrians. As for the question whether something said or done in a poem is right or
not, in dealing with that one should consider not only the intrinsic quality of the
actual word or deed, but also the person who says or does it, the person to whom he
says or does it, the time, the means, and the motive of the agent—whether he does it
to attain a greater good, or to avoid a greater evil.

　　Other criticisms one must meet by considering the language of the poet: by the
10 assumption of a strange word in a passage like οὐρῆας μὲν πρῶτον, where by οὐρῆας
Homer may perhaps mean not mules but sentinels. And in saying of Dolon, ὅς ῥ' ἦ
τοι εἶδος μὲν ἔην κακός, his meaning may perhaps be, not that Dolon's body was
deformed, but that his face was ugly, as εὐειδής is the Cretan word for handsome-
15 faced. So, too, ζωρότερον δὲ κέραιε may mean not 'mix the wine stronger', as though
for topers, but 'mix it quicker'. Other expressions in Homer may be explained as
metaphorical; e.g. in πάντες μέν ῥα θεοί τε καὶ ἀνέρες εὗδον παννύχιοι, as compared
with what he tells us at the same time, ἦ τοι ὅτ' ἐς πεδίον τὸ Τρωικὸν ἀθρήσειεν, αὐλῶν
συρίγγων τε ὅμαδόν, the word πάντες, 'all', is metaphorically put for 'many', since
20 'all' is a species of 'many'. So also his οἴη δ' ἄμμορος is metaphorical, the best known
standing 'alone'. A change, as Hippias of Thasos suggested, in the mode of reading
a word will solve the difficulty in δίδομεν δέ οἱ εὖχος ἀρέσθαι, and in τὸ μὲν οὗ
καταπύθεται ὄμβρῳ. Other difficulties may be solved by another punctuation; e.g. in
Empedocles, αἶψα δὲ θνήτ' ἐφύοντο, τὰ πρὶν μάθον ἀθάνατ' εἶναι ζωρά τε πρὶν κέκρητο.
25 Or by the assumption of an equivocal term, as in παρῴχηκεν δὲ πλέω νύξ where πλέω
is equivocal. Or by an appeal to the custom of language. Wine-and-water we call
'wine'; and it is on the same principle that Homer speaks of a κνημὶς νεοτεύκτου
κασσιτέροιο, a 'greave of new-wrought tin'. A worker in iron we call a 'brazier'; and
30 it is on the same principle that Ganymede is described as the 'wine-server' of Zeus,

though the Gods do not drink wine. This latter, however, may be an instance of metaphor. But whenever also a word seems to imply some contradiction, it is necessary to reflect how many ways there may be of understanding it in the passage in question; e.g. in Homer's τῇ ῥ᾽ ἔσχετο χάλκεον ἔγχος one should consider the possible senses of 'was stopped there'—whether by taking it in this sense or in that one will best avoid the fault of which Glaucon speaks: 'They start with some improbable presumption; and having so decreed it themselves, proceed to draw inferences, and censure the poet as though he had actually said whatever they happen to believe, if his statement conflicts with their own notion of things'. This is how Homer's silence about Icarius has been treated. Starting with the notion of his having been a Lacedaemonian, the critics think it strange for Telemachus not to have met him when he went to Lacedaemon. Whereas the fact may have been as the Cephallenians say, that the wife of Ulysses was of a Cephallenian family, and that her father's name was Icadius, not Icarius. So that it is probably a mistake of the critics that has given rise to the problem.[18]

Speaking generally, one has to justify the impossible by reference to the requirements of poetry, or to the better, or to opinion. For the purposes of poetry a convincing impossibility is preferable to an unconvincing possibility; and if men such as Zeuxis depicted . . .[19] the answer is that it is better they should be like that, as the artist ought to improve on his model. The improbable one has to justify either by showing it to be in accordance with opinion, or by urging that at times it is not improbable; for there is a probability of things happening also against probability. The contradictions found in the poet's language one should first test as one does an opponent's confutation in a dialectical argument, so as to see whether he means the same thing, in the same relation, and in the same sense, before admitting that he has contradicted either something he has said himself or what a man of sound sense assumes as true. But there is no possible apology for improbability or depravity, when they are not necessary and no use is made of them, like the Euripides' Aegeus and the baseness of Menelaus in *Orestes*.

The objections, then, of critics start with faults of five kinds: the allegation is always that something is either impossible, improbable, corrupting, contradictory, or against technical correctness. The answers to these objections must be sought under one or other of the above-mentioned heads, which are twelve in number.

26 · The question may be raised whether the epic or the tragic is the higher form of imitation. It may be argued that, if the less vulgar is the higher, and the less vulgar is always that which addresses the better public, an art addressing any and every one is of a very vulgar order. It is a belief that their public cannot see the meaning, unless they add something themselves, that causes the perpetual movements of the performers—bad flute-players, for instance, rolling about, if quoit-throwing is to be represented, and pulling at the conductor, if Scylla is the subject of the piece. Tragedy, then, is said to be an art of this order—to be in fact just what the later actors were in the eyes of their predecessors; for Mynniscus used to call

---

[18]The text of this sentence is uncertain.
[19]Kassel marks a lacuna.

Callippides 'the ape', because he thought he so overacted his parts; and a similar
view was taken of Pindarus also. All tragedy, however, is said to stand to the Epic as
the newer to the older school of actors. The one, accordingly, is said to address a
cultivated audience, which does not need the accompaniment of gesture; the other,
an uncultivated one. If, therefore, tragedy is a vulgar art, it must clearly be lower
than the epic.

In the first place, one may urge that the censure does not touch the art of the
dramatic poet, but only that of the actor; for it is quite possible to overdo the
gesturing even in an epic recital, as did Sosistratus, and in a singing contest, as did
Mnasitheus of Opus. Again, one should not condemn all movement, unless one
means to condemn even the dance, but only that of ignoble people—which is the
point of the criticism passed on Callippides and in the present day on others, that
their women are not like gentlewomen. Again, tragedy may produce its effect even
without movement or action in just the same way as epic poetry; for from the mere
reading of a play its quality may be seen. So that, if it be superior in all other
respects, this element of inferiority is no necessary part of it.

In the second place, one must remember that tragedy has everything that the
epic has (even the epic metre being admissible), together with a not inconsiderable
addition in the shape of the music which very clearly gives pleasure. Next, the
reality of presentation is felt in the play as read, as well as in the play as acted.
Again, tragic imitation requires less space for the attainment of its end; which is a
great advantage, since the more concentrated effect is more pleasurable than one
with a large admixture of time to dilute it—consider the *Oedipus* of Sophocles, for
instance, and the effect of expanding it into the number of lines of the *Iliad*. There is
less unity in the imitation of the epic poets, as is proved by the fact that any one
work of theirs supplies matter for several tragedies; the result being that, if they
take what is really a single story, it seems curt when briefly told, and thin when on
the scale of length usual with their verse. In saying that there is less unity in an epic,
I mean an epic made up of a plurality of actions, in the same way as the *Iliad* and
Odyssey have many such parts, each one of them in itself of some magnitude; yet
the structure of the two Homeric poems is as perfect as can be, and the action in
them is as nearly as possible one action. If, then, tragedy is superior in these
respects, and also, besides these, in its poetic effect (since the two forms of poetry
should give us, not any or every pleasure, but the very special kind we have
mentioned), it is clear that, since it attains the poetic effect better than the epic, it
will be the higher form of art.

So much for tragedy and epic poetry—for these two arts in general and their
species; the number and nature of their constituent parts; the causes of success and
failure in them; the objections of the critics, and the solutions in answer to them.

CONSTITUTION OF ATHENS

F. G. Kenyon

1 · ... [They[1] were tried] by a court empanelled from among the noble families, and sworn upon the sacrifices. The part of accuser was taken by Myron. They were found guilty of the sacrilege, and their bodies were cast out of their graves and their race banished for evermore. In view of this expiation, Epimenides the Cretan performed a purification of the city.

2 · After this event there was contention for a long time between the upper classes and the populace. Not only was the constitution at this time oligarchical in every respect, but the poorer classes, men, women, and children, were the serfs of the rich. They were known as Pelatae and also as Hectemori, because they cultivated the lands of the rich at the rent thus indicated. The whole country was in the hands of a few persons, and if the tenants failed to pay their rent they were liable to be haled into slavery, and their children with them. All loans were secured upon the debtor's person up to the time of Solon, who was the first to appear as the champion of the people. But the hardest and bitterest part of the constitution in the eyes of the masses was their state of serfdom. Not but what they were also discontented with every other feature of their lot; for, to speak generally, they had no share in anything.

3 · Now the ancient constitution, as it existed before the time of Draco, was organized as follows. The magistrates were elected according to qualifications of birth and wealth. At first they governed for life, but subsequently for terms of ten years. The first magistrates, both in date and in importance, were the King, the Polemarch, and the Archon. The earliest of these offices was that of the King, which existed from ancestral antiquity. To this was added, secondly, the office of Polemarch, on account of some of the kings proving feeble in war; for it was on this account that Ion was invited to accept the post on an occasion of pressing need. The last of the three offices was that of the Archon, which most authorities state to have come into existence in the time of Medon. Others assign it to the time of Acastus,

TEXT: F. G. Kenyon, OCT, Oxford, 1920
[1]Sc. the Alcmeonidae. The papyrus begins in the middle of a sentence.

and adduce as proof the fact that the nine Archons swear to execute their oaths 'as in the days of Acastus', which seems to suggest that it was in his time that the descendants of Codrus retired from the kingship in return for the prerogatives conferred upon the Archon. Whichever way it be, the difference in date is small; but that it was the last of these magistracies to be created is also shown by the fact that the Archon has no part in the ancestral sacrifices, as the King and the Polemarch have, but exclusively in those of later origin. So it is only at a comparatively late date that the office of Archon has become of great importance, through the dignity conferred by these later additions. The Thesmothetae were appointed many years afterwards, when these offices had already become annual, with the object that they might publicly record all legal decisions, and act as guardians of them with a view to determining the issues between litigants. Accordingly their office, alone of those which have been mentioned, was never of more than annual duration.

Such, then, is the relative chronological precedence of these offices. At that time the nine Archons did not all live together. The King occupied the building now known as the Bucolium, near the Prytaneum, as may be seen from the fact that even to the present day the marriage of the King's wife to Dionysus and its consummation take place there. The Archon lived in the Prytaneum, the Polemarch in the Epilyceum. The latter building was formerly called the Polemarcheum, but after Epilycus, during his term of office as Polemarch, had rebuilt it and fitted it up, it was called the Epilyceum. The Thesmothetae occupied the Thesmotheteum. In the time of Solon, however, they all came together into the Thesmotheteum. They had power to decide cases finally on their own authority, not, as now, merely to hold a preliminary hearing. Such then was the arrangement of the magistracies. The Council of Areopagus had as its duty the protection of the laws; but in point of fact it administered the greater and most important part of the government of the state, and inflicted punishments and fines summarily upon all who misbehaved themselves. For the Archons were elected under qualifications of birth and wealth, and the Areopagus was composed of those who had served as Archons; for which reason the membership of the Areopagus is the only office which has continued to be a life-magistracy to the present day.

4 · Such was, in outline, the first constitution; but not very long after the events above recorded, in the archonship of Aristaechmus, Draco enacted his ordinances. Now his constitution had the following form. The franchise was given to all who could furnish themselves with a military equipment. The nine Archons and the Treasurers were elected by this body from persons possessing an unencumbered property of not less than ten minas, the less important officials from those who could furnish themselves with a military equipment, and the generals and commanders of the cavalry from those who could show an unencumbered property of not less than a hundred minas, and had children born in lawful wedlock over ten years of age. These officers were required to hold to bail the Prytanes, the generals, and the cavalry commanders of the preceding year until their accounts had been audited, taking four securities of the same class as that to which the generals and the cavalry commanders belonged. There was also to be a Council, consisting of four hundred

and one members, chosen by lot from among those who possessed the franchise. Both for this and for the other magistracies the lot was cast among those who were over thirty years of age; and no one might hold office twice until every one else had had his turn, after which they were to cast the lot afresh. If any member of the Council failed to attend when there was a sitting of the Council or of the Assembly, he paid a fine, to the amount of three drachmas if he was a Pentacosiomedimnus, two if he was a Knight, and one if he was a Zeugites. The Council of Areopagus was guardian of the laws, and kept watch over the magistrates to see that they executed their offices in accordance with the laws. Any person who felt himself wronged might lay an information before the Council of Areopagus, on declaring what law was broken by the wrong done to him. But, as has been said before, loans were secured upon the persons of the debtors, and the land was in the hands of a few.

5 · Since such, then, was the organization of the constitution, and the many were in slavery to the few, the people rose against the upper class. The strife was keen, and for a long time the two parties were ranged in hostile camps against one another, until, by common consent, they appointed Solon to be mediator and Archon, and committed the whole constitution to his hands—he had written the poem, which begins with the words:

> I behold, and within my heart deep sadness has claimed its place,
> As I mark the oldest home of the ancient Ionian race
> Slain by the sword.

In this poem he fights and disputes on behalf of each party in turn against the other, and finally he advises them to come to terms and put an end to the quarrel existing between them. By birth and reputation Solon was one of the foremost men of the day, but in wealth and position he was of the middle class, as is generally agreed on other grounds, and is, indeed, established by his own evidence in these poems, where he exhorts the wealthy not to be grasping.

> But ye who have store of good, who are sated and overflow,
> Restrain your swelling soul, and still it and keep it low:
> Let the heart that is great within you be trained a lowlier way;
> Ye shall not have all at your will, and we will not for ever obey.

Indeed, he constantly fastens the blame for the conflict on the rich; and accordingly at the beginning of the poem he says that he fears 'the love of wealth and an overweening mind', evidently meaning that it was through these that the quarrel arose.

6 · As soon as he was at the head of affairs, Solon liberated the people once and for all, by prohibiting all loans on the security of the debtor's person; and in addition he made laws and cancelled all debts, public and private. This measure is commonly called the Seisachtheia[2] since thereby the people had their loads removed

---

[2] 'Removal of burdens'.

from them. In connexion with it some persons try to traduce the character of Solon. It so happened that, when he was about to enact the Seisachtheia, he communicated his intention to some members of the upper class, whereupon, as the partisans of the popular party say, his friends stole a march on him; while those who wish to attack his character maintain that he too had a share in the fraud himself. For these persons borrowed money and bought up a large amount of land, and so when, a short time afterwards, all debts were cancelled, they became wealthy; and this, they say, was the origin of the families which were afterwards looked on as having been wealthy from primeval times. However, the story of the popular party is more plausible. A man who was so moderate and public-spirited in all his other actions, that when it was within his power to put his fellow-citizens beneath his feet and establish himself as tyrant, he preferred instead to incur the hostility of both parties by placing his honour and the general welfare above his personal aggrandisement, is not likely to have consented to defile his hands by such a petty and palpable fraud. That he had this absolute power is indicated by the desperate condition of the country; moreover, he mentions it himself repeatedly in his poems, and it is universally admitted. We are therefore bound to consider this accusation to be false.

7 · Next Solon drew up a constitution and enacted new laws; and the ordinances of Draco ceased to be used, with the exception of those relating to murder. The laws were inscribed on the wooden stands, and set up in the King's Porch, and all swore to obey them; and the nine Archons made oath upon the stone, declaring that they would dedicate a golden statue if they should transgress any of them. This is the origin of the oath to that effect which they take to the present day. Solon ratified his laws for a hundred years; and the following was the fashion in which he organized the constitution. He divided the population according to property into four classes, just as it had been divided before, namely, Pentacosiomedimni, Knights, Zeugitae, and Thetes. The various magistracies, namely, the nine Archons, the Treasurers, the Commissioners for Public Contracts [Poletae], the Eleven, and the Exchequer Clerks [Colacretae], he assigned to the Pentacosiomedimni, the Knights, and the Zeugitae, giving offices to each class in proportion to the value of their property. To those who ranked among the Thetes he gave nothing but a place in the Assembly and in the juries. A man had to rank as a Pentacosiomedimnus if he made, from his own land, five hundred measures, whether liquid or solid. Those ranked as Knights who made three hundred measures, or, as some say, those who were able to maintain a horse. In support of the latter definition they adduce the name of the class, which may be supposed to be derived from this fact, and also some votive offerings of early times; for in the Acropolis there is a votive offering, a statue of Diphilus, bearing this inscription:

> The son of Diphilus, Anthemion hight,
> Raised from the Thetes and become a Knight,
> Did to the gods this sculptured charger bring,
> For his promotion a thank-offering.

And a horse stands in evidence beside the man, implying that this was what was meant by belonging to the rank of Knight. At the same time it seems more reasonable to suppose that this class, like the Pentacosiomedimni, was defined by the possession of an income of a certain number of measures. Those ranked as Zeugitae who made two hundred measures, liquid or solid; and the rest ranked as Thetes, and were not eligible for any office. Hence it is that even at the present day, when a candidate for any office is asked to what class he belongs, no one would think of saying that he belonged to the Thetes.

8 · The elections to the various offices Solon enacted should be by lot, out of candidates selected by each of the tribes. Each tribe selected ten candidates for the nine archonships, and among these the lot was cast. Hence it is still the custom for each tribe to choose ten candidates by lot, and then the lot is again cast among these. A sign that Solon regulated the elections to office according to the property classes may be found in the law still in force with regard to the Treasurers, which enacts that they shall be chosen from the Pentacosiomedimni. Such was Solon's legislation with respect to the nine Archons; whereas in early times the Council of Areopagus summoned suitable persons according to its own judgement and appointed them for the year to the several offices. There were four tribes, as before, and four tribe-kings. Each tribe was divided into three Trittyes, with twelve Naucraries in each; and the Naucraries had officers of their own, called Naucrari, whose duty it was to superintend the current receipts and expenditure. Hence, among the laws of Solon now obsolete, it is repeatedly written that the Naucrari are to receive and to spend out of the Naucraric fund. Solon also appointed a Council of four hundred, a hundred from each tribe; but he assigned to the Council of the Areopagus the duty of superintending the laws, acting as before as the guardian of the constitution in general. It kept watch over the affairs of the state in most of the more important matters, and corrected offenders, with full powers to inflict either fines or punishment. The money received in fines it brought up into the Acropolis, without assigning the reason for the mulct. It also tried those who conspired for the overthrow of the state, Solon having enacted a process of impeachment to deal with such offenders. Further, since he saw the state often engaged in internal disputes, while many of the citizens from sheer indifference accepted whatever might turn up, he made a law with express reference to such persons, enacting that any one who, in a time of civil factions, did not take up arms with either party, should lose his rights as a citizen and cease to have any part in the state.

9 · Such, then, was his legislation concerning the magistracies. There are three points in the constitution of Solon which appear to be its most democratic features: first and most important, the prohibition of loans on the security of the debtor's person; secondly, the right of every person who so willed to claim redress on behalf of any one to whom wrong was being done; thirdly, the institution of the appeal to the jury-courts; and it is to this last, they say, that the masses have owed their strength most of all, since, when the people are master of the voting-power, it is

master of the constitution. Moreover, since the laws were not drawn up in simple and explicit terms (but like the one concerning inheritances and wards of state), disputes inevitably occurred, and the courts had to decide in every matter, whether public or private. Some persons in fact believe that Solon deliberately made the laws indefinite, in order that the final decision might be in the hands of the people. This, however, is not probable, and the reason no doubt was that it is impossible to attain ideal perfection when framing a law in general terms; for we must judge of his intentions, not from the actual results in the present day, but from the rest of his legislation.

10 · These seem to be the democratic features of his laws; but in addition, before the period of his legislation, he carried through his abolition of debts, and after it his increase in the standards of weights and measures, and of the currency. During his administration the measures were made larger than those of Pheidon, and the mina, which previously had a standard of seventy drachmas, was raised to the full hundred. The standard coin in earlier times was the two-drachma piece. He also made weights corresponding with the coinage, sixty-three minas going to the talent; and the odd three minas were distributed among the staters and the other values.

11 · When he had completed his organization of the constitution in the manner that has been described, he found himself beset by people coming to him and harassing him concerning his laws, criticizing here and questioning there, till, as he wished neither to alter what he had decided on nor yet to be an object of ill will by remaining in Athens, he set off on a journey to Egypt, with the combined objects of trade and travel, giving out that he should not return for ten years. He considered that it was not right for him to expound the laws personally, but that every one should obey them just as they were written. Moreover, many members of the upper class had been estranged from him on account of his abolition of debts, and both parties were alienated through their disappointment at the condition of things which he had created. The mass of the people had expected him to make a complete redistribution of all property, and the upper class hoped he would restore everything to its former position, or, at any rate, make but a small change. Solon, however, had resisted both classes. He might have made himself a despot by attaching himself to whichever party he chose, but he preferred to incur the enmity of both, by being the saviour of his country and the ideal lawgiver.

12 · The truth of this view of Solon's policy is established alike by common consent and by the mention he has himself made of the matter in his poems. Thus:

I gave to the mass of the people such rank as befitted their need,
I took not away their honour, and I granted naught to their greed;
While those who were rich in power, who in wealth were glorious
    and great,

I bethought me that naught should befall them unworthy their splendour
and state;
So I stood with my shield outstretched, and both were safe in its sight,
And I would not that either should triumph, when the triumph was not
with right.

Again he declares how the mass of the people ought to be treated:

But thus will the people best the voice of their leaders obey,
When neither too slack is the rein, nor violence holdeth the sway;
For indulgence breedeth a child, the presumption that spurns control,
When riches too great are poured upon men of unbalanced soul.

And again elsewhere he speaks about the persons who wished to redistribute the
land:

So they came in search of plunder, and their cravings knew no bound,
Every one among them deeming endless wealth would here be found,
And that I with glozing smoothness hid a cruel mind within.
Fondly then and vainly dreamt they; now they raise an angry din,
And they glare askance in anger, and the light within their eyes
Burns with hostile flames upon me. Yet therein no justice lies.
All I promised, fully wrought I with the gods at hand to cheer,
Naught beyond in folly ventured. Never to my soul was dear
With a tyrant's force to govern, nor to see the good and base
Side by side in equal portion share the rich home of our race.

Once more he speaks of the abolition of debts and of those who before were in
servitude, but were released owing to the Seisachtheia:

Of all the aims for which I summoned forth
The people, was there one I compassed not?
Thou, when slow time brings justice in its train,
O mighty mother of the Olympian gods,
Dark Earth, thou best canst witness, from whose breast
I swept the pillars broadcast planted there,
And made thee free, who hadst been slave of yore.
And many a man whom fraud or law had sold
Far from his god-built land, an outcast slave,
I brought again to Athens; yea, and some,
Exiles from home through debt's oppressive load,
Speaking no more the dear Athenian tongue,
But wandering far and wide, I brought again;
And those that here in vilest slavery
Crouched 'neath a master's frown, I set them free.
Thus might and right were yoked in harmony,

> Since by the force of law I won my ends
> And kept my promise. Equal laws I gave
> To evil and to good, with even hand
> Drawing straight justice for the lot of each.
> But had another held the goad as I,
> One in whose heart was guile and greediness,
> He had not kept the people back from strife.
> For had I granted, now what pleased the one,
> Then what their foes devised in counterpoise,
> Of many a man this state had been bereft.
> Therefore I showed my might on every side,
> Turning at bay like wolf among the hounds.

And again he reviles both parties for their grumblings in the times that followed:

> Nay, if one must lay blame where blame is due,
> Were't not for me, the people ne'er had set
> Their eyes upon these blessings e'en in dreams—
> While greater men, the men of wealthier life,
> Should praise me and should court me as their friend.

For had any other man, he says, received this exalted post,

> He had not kept the people back, nor ceased
> Till he had robbed the richness of the milk.
> But I stood forth a landmark in the midst.
> And barred the foes from battle.

13 · Such, then, were Solon's reasons for his departure from the country. After his retirement the city was still torn by divisions. For four years, indeed, they lived in peace; but in the fifth year after Solon's government they were unable to elect an Archon on account of their dissensions, and again four years later they elected no Archon for the same reason. Subsequently, after a similar period had elapsed, Damasias was elected Archon; and he governed for two years and two months, until he was forcibly expelled from his office. After this it was agreed, as a compromise, to elect ten Archons, five from the Eupatridae, three from the Agroeci, and two from the Demiurgi; and they ruled for the year following Damasias. It is clear from this that the Archon was at the time the magistrate who possessed the greatest power, since it is always in connexion with this office that conflicts are seen to arise. But altogether they were in a continual state of internal disorder. Some found the cause and justification of their discontent in the abolition of debts, because thereby they had been reduced to poverty; others were dissatisfied with the political constitution, because it had undergone a revolutionary change; while with others the motive was found in personal rivalries among themselves. The parties at this time were three in number. First there was the party of the Shore, led by

Megacles the son of Alcmeon, which was considered to aim at a moderate form of government; then there were the men of the Plain, who desired an oligarchy and were led by Lycurgus; and thirdly there were the men of the Highlands, at the head of whom was Pisistratus, who was looked on as an extreme democrat. This party was reinforced by those who had been deprived of the debts due to them, from motives of poverty, and by those who were not of pure descent, from motives of personal apprehension. A proof of this is seen in the fact that after the tyranny was overthrown a revision was made of the citizen-roll, on the ground that many persons were partaking in the franchise without having a right to it. The names given to the respective parties were derived from the districts in which they held their lands.

14 · Pisistratus, who had the reputation of being an extreme democrat, and had also distinguished himself greatly in the war with Megara, wounded himself, and by representing that his injuries had been inflicted on him by his political rivals, he persuaded the people, through a motion proposed by Aristion, to grant him a bodyguard. After he had got these 'club-bearers', as they were called, he made an attack with them on the people and seized the Acropolis. This happened in the archonship of Comeas, thirty-one years after the legislation of Solon. It is related that, when Pisistratus asked for his bodyguard, Solon opposed the request, and declared that in so doing he proved himself wiser than half the people and braver than the rest—wiser than those who did not see that Pisistratus designed to make himself tyrant, and braver than those who saw it and kept silence. But when all his words availed nothing he carried forth his armour and set it up in front of his house, saying that he had helped his country so far as lay in his power (he was already a very old man), and that he called on all others to do the same. Solon's exhortations, however, proved fruitless, and Pisistratus assumed the sovereignty. His administration was more like a constitutional government than the rule of a tyrant; but before his power was firmly established, the adherents of Megacles and Lycurgus made a coalition and drove him out. This took place in the archonship of Hegesias, five years after the first establishment of his rule. Eleven years later Megacles, being in difficulties in a party struggle, again opened negotiations with Pisistratus, proposing that the latter should marry his daughter; and on these terms he brought him back to Athens, by a very primitive and simple-minded device. He first spread abroad a rumour that Athena was bringing back Pisistratus, and then, having found a woman of great stature and beauty, named Phyë (according to Herodotus, of the deme of Paeania, but as others say a Thracian flower-seller of the deme of Collytus), he dressed her in a garb resembling that of the goddess and brought her into the city with Pisistratus. The latter drove in on a chariot with the woman beside him, and the inhabitants of the city, struck with awe, received him with adoration.

15 · In this manner did his first return take place. But later, about six years after his return, he was again expelled. For he did not hold power for long: he refused to treat the daughter of Megacles as his wife, and being afraid in

consequence of a combination of the two opposing parties, he retired from the country. First he led a colony to a place Called Rhaicelus, in the region of the Thermaic gulf; and thence he passed to the country in the neighbourhood of Mt. Pangaeus. Here he acquired wealth and hired mercenaries; and not till ten years had elapsed did he return to Eretria and make an attempt to recover the government by force. In this he had the assistance of many allies, notably the Thebans and Lygdámis of Naxos, and also the Knights who held the supreme power in the constitution of Eretria. After his victory in the battle at Pallene he captured Athens, and when he had disarmed the people he at last had his tyranny securely established, and was able to take Naxos and set up Lygdamis as ruler there. He effected the disarmament of the people in the following manner. He ordered a parade in full armour in the Theseum, and began to make a speech to the people. He spoke for a short time, until the people called out that they could not hear him, whereupon he bade them come up to the entrance of the Acropolis, in order that his voice might be better heard. Then, while he continued to speak to them at great length, men whom he had appointed for the purpose collected the arms and locked them up in the chambers of the Theseum hard by, and came and made a signal to him that it was done. Pisistratus accordingly, when he had finished the rest of what he had to say, told the people also what had happened to their arms; adding that they were not to be surprised or alarmed, but go home and attend to their private affairs, while he would himself for the future manage all the business of the state.

16 · Such was the origin and such the vicissitudes of the tyranny of Pisistratus. His administration was temperate, as has been said before, and more like constitutional government than a tyranny. Not only was he in every respect humane and mild and ready to forgive those who offended, but, in addition, he advanced money to the poorer people to help them in their labours, so that they might make their living by agriculture. In this he had two objects, first that they might not spend their time in the city but might be scattered over all the country, and secondly that, being moderately well off and occupied with their own business, they might have neither the wish nor the time to attend to public affairs. At the same time his revenues were increased by the thorough cultivation of the country, since he imposed a tax of one tenth on all the produce. For the same reasons he instituted the local justices, and often made expeditions in person into the country to inspect it and to settle disputes between individuals, that they might not come into the city and neglect their farms. It was in one of the progresses that, as the story goes, Pisistratus had his adventure with the man of Hymettus, who was cultivating the spot afterwards known as 'Tax-free Farm'. He saw a man digging and working at a very stony piece of ground, and being surprised he sent his attendant to ask what he got out of this plot of land. 'Aches and pains', said the man; 'and that's what Pisistratus ought to have his tenth of'. The man spoke without knowing who his questioner was; but Pisistratus was so pleased with his frank speech and his industry that he granted him exemption from all taxes. And so in matters in general he burdened the people as little as possible with his government, but always cultivated

peace and kept them in all quietness. Hence the tyranny of Pisistratus was often spoken of proverbially as 'the age of gold'; for when his sons succeeded him the government became much harsher. But most important of all in this respect was his popular and kindly disposition. In all things he was accustomed to observe the laws, without giving himself any exceptional privileges. Once he was summoned on a charge of homicide before the Areopagus, and he appeared in person to make his defence; but the prosecutor was afraid to present himself and abandoned the case. For these reasons he held power long, and whenever he was expelled he regained his position easily. The majority alike of the upper class and of the people were in his favour; the former he won by his social intercourse with them, the latter by the assistance which he gave to their private purses, and his nature fitted him to win the hearts of both. Moreover, the laws in reference to tyrants at that time in force at Athens were very mild, especially the one which applies more particularly to the establishment of a tyranny. The law ran as follows: 'These are the ancestral statutes of the Athenians; if any persons shall make an attempt to establish a tyranny, or if any person shall join in setting up a tyranny, he shall lose his civic rights, both himself and his whole house'.

17 · Thus did Pisistratus grow old in the possession of power, and he died of illness in the archonship of Philoneus, thirty-three years from the time at which he first established himself as tyrant, during nineteen of which he was in possession of power; the rest he spent in exile. It is evident from this that the story is mere gossip which states that Pisistratus was the youthful favourite of Solon and commanded in the war against Megara for the recovery of Salamis. It will not harmonize with their respective ages, as any one may see who will reckon up the years of the life of each of them, and the dates at which they died. After the death of Pisistratus his sons took up the government, and conducted it on the same system. He had two sons by his legitimate wife, Hippias and Hipparchus, and two by his Argive consort, Iophon and Hegesistratus, who was surnamed Thessalus. For Pisistratus took a wife from Argos, Timonassa, the daughter of a man of Argos, named Gorgilus; she had previously been the wife of Archius of Ambracia; one of the descendants of Cypselus. This was the origin of his friendship with the Argives, on account of which a thousand of them were brought over by Hegesistratus and fought on his side in the battle at Pallene. Some authorities say that this marriage took place after his first expulsion from Athens, others while he was in possession of the government.

18 · Hippias and Hipparchus assumed the control of affairs on grounds alike of standing and of age; but Hippias, as being the elder and also naturally of a statesmanlike and shrewd disposition, was really the head of the government. Hipparchus was youthful in disposition, amorous, and fond of literature (it was he who invited to Athens Anacreon, Simonides, and the other poets), while Thessalus was much junior in age, and was violent and headstrong in his behaviour. It was

from his character that all the evils arose which befell the house. He became enamoured of Harmodius, and, since he failed to win his affection, he lost all restraint upon his passion, and in addition to other exhibitions of rage he finally prevented the sister of Harmodius from taking the part of a basketbearer in the Panathenaic procession, slanderously alleging that Harmodius was a person of loose life. Thereupon, in a frenzy of wrath, Harmodius and Aristogeiton did their celebrated deed, in conjunction with a number of confederates. But while they were lying in wait for Hippias in the Acropolis at the time of the Panathenaea (Hippias, at this moment, was awaiting the arrival of the procession, while Hipparchus was organizing its dispatch) they saw one of the persons privy to the plot talking familiarly with him. Thinking that he was betraying them, and desiring to do something before they were arrested, they rushed down and made their attempt without waiting for the rest of their confederates. They succeeded in killing Hipparchus near the Leocoreum while he was engaged in arranging the procession, but ruined the design as a whole; of the two leaders, Harmodius was killed on the spot by the guards, while Aristogeiton was arrested, and perished later after suffering long tortures. While under the torture he accused many persons who belonged by birth to the most distinguished families and were also personal friends of the tyrants. At first the government could find no clue to the conspiracy; for the current story, that Hippias made all who were taking part in the procession leave their arms, and then detected those who were carrying secret daggers, cannot be true, since at that time they did not bear arms in the processions, this being a custom instituted at a later period by the democracy. According to the story of the popular party, Aristogeiton accused the friends of the tyrants with the deliberate intention that the latter might commit an impious act, and at the same time weaken themselves, by putting to death innocent men who were their own friends; others say that he told no falsehood, but was betraying the actual accomplices. At last, when for all his efforts he could not obtain release by death, he promised to give further information against a number of other persons; and, having induced Hippias to give him his hand to confirm his word, as soon as he had hold of it he reviled him for giving his hand to the murderer of his brother, till Hippias, in a frenzy of rage, lost control of himself and snatched out his dagger and dispatched him.

19 · After this event the tyranny became much harsher. In consequence of his vengeance for his brother, and of the execution and banishment of a large number of persons, Hippias became a distrusted and an embittered man. About three years after the death of Hipparchus, finding his position in the city insecure, he set about fortifying Munichia, with the intention of establishing himself there. While he was still engaged on this work, however, he was expelled by Cleomenes, king of Lacedaemon, in consequence of the Spartans being continually incited by oracles to overthrow the tyranny. These oracles were obtained in the following way. The Athenian exiles, headed by the Alcmeonidae, could not by their own power effect their return, but failed continually in their attempts. Among their other failures, they fortified a post in Attica, Lipsydrium, above Mt. Parnes, and were

there joined by some partisans from the city; but they were besieged by the tyrants and reduced to surrender. After this disaster the following became a popular drinking song:

> Ah! Lipsydrium, faithless friend!
> Lo, what heroes to death didst send,
> Nobly born and great in deed!
> Well did they prove themselves at need
> Of noble sires a noble seed.

Having failed, then, in every other method, they took the contract for rebuilding the temple at Delphi, thereby obtaining ample funds, which they employed to secure the help of the Lacedaemonians. All this time the Pythia kept continually enjoining on the Lacedaemonians who came to consult the oracle, that they must free Athens; till finally she succeeded in impelling the Spartans to that step, although the house of Pisistratus was connected with them by ties of hospitality. The resolution of the Lacedaemonians was, however, at least equally due to the friendship which had been formed between the house of Pisistratus and Argos. Accordingly they first sent Anchimolus by sea at the head of an army; but he was defeated and killed, through the arrival of Cineas of Thessaly in support with a force of a thousand horsemen. Then, being roused to anger by this disaster, they sent their king, Cleomenes, by land at the head of a larger force; and he, after defeating the Thessalian cavalry when they attempted to intercept his march into Attica, shut up Hippias within what was known as the Pelargic wall and blockaded him there with the assistance of the Athenians. While he was sitting down before the place, it so happened that the sons of the Pisistratidae were captured in an attempt to slip out; upon which the tyrants capitulated on condition of the safety of their children, and surrendered the Acropolis to the Athenians, five days being first allowed them to remove their effects. This took place in the archonship of Harpactides, after they had held the tyranny for about seventeen years since their father's death, or in all, including the period of their father's rule, for forty-nine years.

20 · After the overthrow of the tyranny, the rival leaders in the state were Isagoras son of Tisander, a partisan of the tyrants, and Cleisthenes, who belonged to the family of the Alcmeonidae. Cleisthenes, being beaten in the political clubs, called in the people by offering the franchise to the masses. Thereupon Isagoras, finding himself left inferior in power, invited Cleomenes, who was united to him by ties of hospitality, to return to Athens, and persuaded him to 'drive out the pollution', a plea derived from the fact that the Alcmeonidae were supposed to be under the curse of pollution. On this Cleisthenes retired from the country, and Cleomenes, entering Attica with a small force, expelled, as polluted, seven hundred Athenian families. Having effected this, he next attempted to dissolve the Council, and to set up Isagoras and three hundred of his partisans as the supreme power in the state. The Council, however, resisted, the populace flocked together, and Cleomenes and Isagoras, with their adherents, took refuge on the Acropolis. Here

the people sat down and besieged them for two days; and on the third they agreed to let Cleomenes and all his followers depart, while they summoned Cleisthenes and the other exiles back to Athens. When the people had thus obtained the command of affairs, Cleisthenes was their chief and popular leader. For the Alcmeonidae were perhaps the chief cause of the expulsion of the tyrants, and for the greater part of their rule were at perpetual war with them. But even earlier than the attempts of the Alcmeonidae, Cedon made an attack on the tyrants; whence there came another popular drinking song, addressed to him:

> Pour a health yet again, boy, to Cedon; forget not this duty to do,
> If a health is an honour befitting the name of a good man and true.

21 · The people, therefore, had good reason to place confidence in Cleisthenes. Accordingly, now that he was the popular leader, three years after the expulsion of the tyrants, in the archonship of Isagoras, his first step was to distribute the whole population into ten tribes in place of the existing four, with the object of intermixing the members of the different tribes, and so securing that more persons might have a share in the franchise. From this arose the saying 'Do not look at the tribes', addressed to those who wished to scrutinize the lists of the old families. Next he made the Council to consist of five hundred members instead of four hundred, each tribe now contributing fifty, whereas formerly each had sent a hundred. The reason why he did not organize the people into twelve tribes was that he might not have to use the existing division into trittyes; for the four tribes had twelve trittyes, so that he would not have achieved his object of redistributing the population in fresh combinations. Further, he divided the country into thirty groups of demes, ten from the districts about the city, ten from the coast, and ten from the interior. These he called trittyes; and he assigned three of them by lot to each tribe, in such a way that each should have one portion in each of these three localities. All who lived in any given deme he declared fellow-demesmen, to the end that the new citizens might not be exposed by the habitual use of family names, but that men might be officially described by the names of their demes; and accordingly it is by the names of their demes that the Athenians speak of one another. He also instituted Demarchs, who had the same duties as the previously existing Naucrari—the demes being made to take the place of the naucraries. He gave names to the demes, some from the localities to which they belonged, some from the persons who founded them, since some of the areas no longer corresponded to localities possessing names. On the other hand he allowed every one to retain his family and clan and religious rites according to ancestral custom. The names given to the tribes were the ten which the Pythia appointed out of the hundred selected national heroes.

22 · By these reforms the constitution became much more democratic than that of Solon. The laws of Solon had been obliterated by disuse during the period of the tyranny, while Cleisthenes substituted new ones with the object of securing the

goodwill of the masses. Among these was the law concerning ostracism. Four years after the establishment of this system, in the archonship of Hermocreon, they first imposed upon the Council of Five Hundred the oath which they take to the present day. Next they began to elect the generals by tribes, one from each tribe, while the Polemarch was the commander of the whole army. Then, eleven years later, in the archonship of Phaenippus they won the battle of Marathon; and two years after this victory, when the people had now gained self-confidence, they for the first time made use of the law of ostracism. This had originally been passed as a precaution against men in high office, because Pisistratus took advantage of his position as a popular leader and general to make himself tyrant; and the first person ostracized was one of his relatives, Hipparchus son of Charmus, of the deme of Collytus, the very person on whose account especially Cleisthenes had enacted the law, as he wished to get rid of him. (The Athenians, with the usual leniency of the democracy, allowed all the partisans of the tyrants, who had not joined in their evil deeds in the time of the troubles, to remain in the city; and the chief and leader of these was Hipparchus.) Then in the very next year, in the archonship of Telesinus, they for the first time since the tyranny elected, tribe by tribe, the nine Archons by lot out of the five hundred candidates selected by the demes, all the earlier ones having been elected by vote; and in the same year Megacles son of Hippocrates, of the deme of Alopece, was ostracized. Thus for three years they continued to ostracize the friends of the tyrants, on whose account the law had been passed; but in the following year they began to remove others as well who seemed to be more powerful than was expedient. The first person unconnected with the tyrants who was ostracized was Xanthippus son of Ariphron. Two years later, in the archonship of Nicodemus, the mines of Maroneia were discovered, and the state made a profit of a hundred talents from the working of them. Some persons advised the people to make a distribution of the money among themselves, but this was prevented by Themistocles. He refused to say on what he proposed to spend the money, but he bade them lend it to the hundred richest men in Athens, one talent to each, and then, if the manner in which it was employed pleased the people, the expenditure should be charged to the state, but otherwise the state should receive the sum back from those to whom it was lent. On these terms he received the money and with it he had a hundred triremes built, each of the hundred individuals building one; and it was with these ships that they fought the battle of Salamis against the barbarians. About this time Aristides the son of Lysimachus was ostracized. Three years later, however, in the archonship of Hypsichides, all the ostracized persons were recalled, on account of the advance of the army of Xerxes; and it was laid down for the future that persons under sentence of ostracism must not live between Geraestus and Scyllaeum, on pain of losing their civic rights irrevocably.

23 · So far, then, had the city progressed by this time, growing gradually with the growth of the democracy; but after the Persian wars the Council of Areopagus once more developed strength and assumed the control of the state. It did not acquire this supremacy by virtue of any formal decree, but because it had

been the cause of the battle of Salamis being fought. When the generals were utterly at a loss how to meet the crisis and made proclamation that every one should see to his own safety, the Areopagus provided eight drachmas to each member of the ships' crews, and so prevailed on them to go on board. On these grounds people bowed to its prestige; and during this period Athens was well administered. At this time they devoted themselves to the prosecution of war and were in high repute among the Greeks, so that the command by sea was conferred upon them in spite of the opposition of the Lacedaemonians. The leaders of the people during this period were Aristides, son of Lysimachus, and Themistocles, son of Neocles, of whom the latter appeared to devote himself to the conduct of war, while the former had the reputation of being a clever statesman and the most upright man of his time. Accordingly the one was usually employed as general, the other as political adviser. The rebuilding of the fortifications they conducted in combination, although they were political opponents; but it was Aristides who, seizing the opportunity afforded by the discredit brought upon the Lacedaemonians by Pausanias, guided the public policy in the matter of the defection of the Ionian states from the alliance with Sparta. It follows that it was he who made the first assessment of tribute from the various allied states, two years after the battle of Salamis, in the archonship of Timosthenes; and it was he who took the oath of offensive and defensive alliance with the Ionians, on which occasion they cast the masses of iron into the sea.

24 · After this, seeing the state growing in confidence and much wealth accumulated, he advised the people to lay hold of the leadership of the league, and to quit the country districts and settle in the city. He pointed out to them that all would be able to gain a living there, some by service in the army, others in the garrisons, others by taking a part in public affairs; and in this way they would secure the leadership. This advice was taken; and when the people had assumed the supreme control they proceeded to treat their allies in a more imperious fashion, with the exception of the Chians, Lesbians, and Samians. These they maintained to protect their empire, leaving their constitutions untouched, and allowing them to retain whatever dominion they then possessed. They also secured an ample maintenance for the mass of the population in the way which Aristides had pointed out to them. Out of the proceeds of the tributes and the taxes and the contributions of the allies more than twenty thousand persons were maintained. There were 6,000 jurymen, 1,600 bowmen, 1,200 Knights, 500 members of the Council, 500 guards of the dockyards, besides fifty guards in the Acropolis. There were some 700 magistrates at home, and some 700 abroad. Further, when they subsequently went to war, there were in addition 2,500 heavy-armed troops, twenty guard-ships, and other ships which collected the tributes, with crews amounting to 2,000 men, selected by lot; and besides these there were the persons maintained by the Prytaneum, and orphans, and gaolers, since all these were supported by the state.

25 · Such was the way in which the people earned their livelihood. The supremacy of the Areopagus lasted for about seventeen years after the Persian

wars, although gradually declining. But as the strength of the masses increased, Ephialtes, son of Sophonides, a man with a reputation for incorruptibility and public virtue, who had become the leader of the people, made an attack upon that Council. First of all he ruined many of its members by bringing actions against them with reference to their administration. Then, in the archonship of Conon, he stripped the Council of all the acquired prerogatives from which it derived its guardianship of the constitution, and assigned some of them to the Council of Five Hundred, and others to the Assembly and the law-courts. In this revolution he was assisted by Themistocles, who was himself a member of the Areopagus, but was expecting to be tried before it on a charge of treasonable dealings with Persia. This made him anxious that it should be overthrown, and accordingly he warned Ephialtes that the Council intended to arrest him, while at the same time he informed the Areopagites that he would reveal to them certain persons who were conspiring to subvert the constitution. He then conducted the representatives delegated by the Council to the residence of Ephialtes, promising to show them the conspirators who assembled there, and proceeded to converse with them in an earnest manner. Ephialtes, seeing this, was seized with alarm and took refuge in suppliant guise at the altar. Every one was astounded at the occurrence, and presently, when the Council of Five Hundred met, Ephialtes and Themistocles together proceeded to denounce the Areopagus to them. This they repeated in similar fashion in the Assembly, until they succeeded in depriving it of its power. Not long afterwards, however, Ephialtes was assassinated by Aristodicus of Tanagra. In this way was the Council of Areopagus deprived of its guardianship of the state.

26 · After this the administration of the state became more and more lax, in consequence of the eager rivalry of candidates for popular favour. During this period the moderate party, as it happened, had no real chief, their leader being Cimon son of Miltiades, who was a comparatively young man, and had been late in entering public life; and at the same time the general populace suffered great losses by war. The soldiers for active service were selected at that time from the roll of citizens, and as the generals were men of no military experience, who owned their position solely to their family standing, it continually happened that some two or three thousand of the troops perished on an expedition; and in this way the best men alike of the lower and the upper classes were exhausted. Consequently in most matters of administration less heed was paid to the laws than had formerly been the case. No alteration, however, was made in the method of election of the nine Archons, except that five years after the death of Ephialtes it was decided that the candidates to be submitted to the lot for that office might be selected from the Zeugitae as well. The first Archon from that class was Mnesitheides. Up to this time all the Archons had been taken from the Pentacosiomedimni and Knights, while the Zeugitae were confined to the ordinary magistracies, save where an evasion of the law was overlooked. Four years later, in the archonship of Lysicrates, the thirty 'local justices', as they were called, were re-established; and two years afterwards, in the archonship of Antidotus, in consequence of the great increase in

the number of citizens, it was resolved, on the motion of Pericles, that no one should be admitted to the franchise who was not of citizen birth by both parents.

27 · After this Pericles came forward as popular leader, having first distinguished himself while still a young man by prosecuting Cimon on the audit of his official accounts as general. Under his auspices the constitution became still more democratic. He took away some of the privileges of the Areopagus, and, above all, he turned the policy of the state in the direction of sea power, which caused the masses to acquire confidence in themselves and consequently to take the constitution more and more into their own hands. Moreover, forty-eight years after the battle of Salamis, in the archonship of Pythodorus, the Peloponnesian war broke out, during which the populace was shut up in the city and became accustomed to gain its livelihood by military service, and so, partly voluntarily and partly involuntarily, determined to assume the administration of the state itself. Pericles was also the first to institute pay for service in the law-courts, as a bid for popular favour to counterbalance the wealth of Cimon. The latter, having private possessions on a regal scale, not only performed the regular public services magnificently, but also maintained a large number of his fellow-demesmen. Any member of the deme of Laciadae could go every day to Cimon's house and there receive a reasonable provision; while his estate was guarded by no fences, so that any one who liked might help himself to the fruit from it. Pericles' private property was quite unequal to this magnificence and accordingly he took the advice of Damonides of Oea (who was commonly supposed to be the person who prompted Pericles in most of his measures, and was therefore subsequently ostracized), which was that, as he was beaten in the matter of private possessions, he should make gifts to the people from their own property; and accordingly he instituted pay for the members of the juries. Some critics accuse him of thereby causing a deterioration in the character of the juries, since it was always the common people who put themselves forward for selection as jurors, rather than the men of better position. Moreover, bribery came into existence after this, the first person to introduce it being Anytus, after his command at Pylos. He was prosecuted by certain individuals on account of his loss of Pylos, but escaped by bribing the jury.

28 · So long as Pericles was leader of the people, things went tolerably well with the state; but when he was dead there was a great change for the worse. Then for the first time did the people choose a leader who was of no reputation among men of good standing, whereas up to this time such men had always been found as leaders of the democracy. The first leader of the people, in the very beginning of things, was Solon, and the second was Pisistratus, both of them men of birth and position. After the overthrow of the tyrants there was Cleisthenes, a member of the house of the Alcmeonidae; and he had no rival opposed to him after the expulsion of the party of Isagoras. After this Xanthippus was the leader of the people, and Militades of the upper class. Then came Themistocles and Aristides, and after them Ephialtes as leader of the people, and Cimon son of Miltiades of the wealthier class. Pericles followed as leader of the people, and Thucydides, who was connected by

marriage with Cimon, of the opposition. After the death of Pericles, Nicias, who subsequently fell in Sicily, appeared as leader of the aristocracy, and Cleon son of Cleaenetus of the people. The latter seems, more than any one else, to have been the cause of the corruption of the democracy by his wild undertakings; and he was the first to use unseemly shouting and coarse abuse on the Bema, and to harangue the people with his cloak girt up short about him, whereas all his predecessors had spoken decently and in order. These were succeeded by Theramenes son of Hagnon as leader of the one party, and the lyre-maker Cleophon of the people. It was Cleophon who first granted the two-obol donation and for some time it continued to be given; but then Callicrates of Paeania ousted him by promising to add a third obol to the sum. Both of these persons were subsequently condemned to death; for the people, even if they are deceived for a time, in the end generally come to detest those who have beguiled them into any unworthy action. After Cleophon the popular leadership was occupied successively by the men who chose to talk the biggest and pander the most to the tastes of the majority, with their eyes fixed only on the interests of the moment. The best statesmen at Athens, after those of early times, seem to have been Nicias, Thucydides, and Theramenes. As to Nicias and Thucydides, nearly every one agrees that they were not merely men of birth and character, but also statesmen, and that they ruled the state with paternal care. On the merits of Theramenes opinion is divided, because it so happened that in his time public affairs were in a very stormy state. But those who give their opinion deliberately find him, not, as his critics falsely assert, overthrowing every kind of constitution, but supporting every kind so long as it did not transgress the laws; thus showing that he was able, as every good citizen should be, to live under any form of constitution, while he refused to countenance illegality and was its constant enemy.

29 · So long as the fortune of the war continued even, the Athenians preserved the democracy; but after the disaster in Sicily, when the Lacedaemonians had gained the upper hand through their alliance with the king of Persia, they were compelled to abolish the democracy and establish in its place the constitution of the Four Hundred. The speech recommending this course before the vote was made by Melobius, and the motion was proposed by Pythodorus of Anaphlystus; but the real argument which persuaded the majority was the belief that the king of Persia was more likely to form an alliance with them if the constitution were on an oligarchical basis. The motion of Pythodorus was to the following effect. The popular Assembly was to elect twenty persons from among those over forty years of age, who, in conjunction with the existing ten members of the Committee of Public Safety, after taking an oath that they would frame such measures as they thought best for the state, should then prepare proposals for the public safety. In addition, any other person might make proposals, so that of all the schemes before them the people might choose the best. Cleitophon concurred with the motion of Pythodorus, but moved that the committee should also investigate the ancient laws enacted by Cleisthenes when he created the democracy, in order that they might have these too before them and so be in a position to decide wisely; his suggestion being that the

constitution of Cleisthenes was not really democratic, but closely akin to that of Solon. When the committee was elected, their first proposal was that the Prytanes should be completed to put to the vote any motion that was offered on behalf of the public safety. Next they abolished all indictments for illegal proposals, all impeachments and public prosecutions, in order that every Athenian should be free to give his counsel on the situation, if he chose; and they decreed that if any person imposed a fine on any other for his acts in this respect, or prosecuted him or summoned him before the courts, he should, on an information being laid against him, be brought before the generals, who should deliver him to the Eleven to be put to death. After these preliminary measures, they drew up the constitution in the following manner. The revenues of the state were not to be spent on any purpose except the war. All magistrates should serve without remuneration for the period of the war, except the nine Archons and the Prytanes for the time being, who should each receive three obols a day. The whole of the rest of the administration was to be committed, for the period of the war, to those Athenians who were most capable of serving the state personally or pecuniarily, to the number of not less than five thousand. This body was to have full powers, to the extent even of making treaties with whomsoever they willed; and ten representatives, over forty years of age, were to be elected from each tribe to draw up the list of the Five Thousand, after taking an oath on a full and perfect sacrifice.

30 · These were the recommendations of the committee; and when they had been ratified the Five Thousand elected from their own number a hundred commissioners to draw up the constitution. They, on their appointment, drew up and produced the following recommendations. There should be a Council, holding office for a year, consisting of men over thirty years of age, serving without pay. To this body should belong the Generals, the nine Archons, the Amphictyonic Registrar [Hieromnemon], the Taxiarchs, the Hipparchs, the Phylarchs, the commanders of garrisons, the Treasurers of Athena and the other gods, ten in number, the Hellenic Treasurers [Hellenotamiae], the Treasurers of the other non-sacred moneys, to the number of twenty, the ten Commissioners of Sacrifices [Hieropoei], and the ten Superintendents of the mysteries. All these were to be appointed by the Council from a larger number of selected candidates, chosen from its members for the time being. The other offices were all to be filled by lot, and not from the members of the Council. The Hellenic Treasurers who actually administered the funds should not sit with the Council. As regards the future, four Councils were to be created, of men of the age already mentioned, and one of these was to be chosen by lot to take office at once, while the others were to receive it in turn, in the order decided by the lot. For this purpose the hundred commissioners were to distribute themselves and all the rest as equally as possible into four parts, and cast lots for precedence, and the selected body should hold office for a year. They were to administer that office as seemed to them best, both with reference to the safe custody and due expenditure of the finances, and generally with regard to all other matters to the best of their ability. If they desired to take a larger number of persons into counsel, each member might call in one assistant of his own choice, subject to

the same qualification of age. The Council was to sit once every five days, unless there was any special need for more frequent sittings. The casting of the lot for the Council was to be held by the nine Archons; votes on divisions were to be counted by five tellers chosen by lot from the members of the Council, and of these one was to be selected by lot every day to act as president. These five persons were to cast lots for precedence between the parties wishing to appear before the Council, giving the first place to sacred matters, the second to heralds, the third to embassies, and the fourth to all other subjects; but matters concerning the war might be dealt with, on the motion of the generals, whenever there was need, without balloting. Any member of the Council who did not enter the Council-house at the time named should be fined a drachma for each day, unless he was away on leave of absence from the Council.

31 · Such was the constitution which they drew up for the time to come, but for the immediate present they devised the following scheme. There should be a Council of Four Hundred, as in the ancient constitution, forty from each tribe, chosen out of candidates of more than thirty years of age, selected by the members of the tribes. This Council should appoint the magistrates and draw up the form of oath which they were to take; and in all that concerned the laws, in the examination of official accounts, and in other matters generally, they might act according to their discretion. They must, however, observe the laws that might be enacted with reference to the constitution of the state, and had no power to alter them nor to pass others. The generals should be provisionally elected from the whole body of the Five Thousand, but so soon as the Council came into existence it was to hold an examination of military equipments, and thereon elect ten persons, together with a secretary, and the persons thus elected should hold office during the coming year with full powers, and should have the right, whenever they desired it, of joining in the deliberations of the Council. They were also to elect a single Hipparch and ten Phylarchs; but for the future the Council was to elect these officers according to the regulations above laid down. No office, except those of member of the Council and of general, might be held more than once, either by the first occupants or by their successors. With reference to the future distribution of the Four Hundred into the four successive sections, the hundred commissioners must divide them whenever the time came for the citizens to join in the Council along with the rest.

32 · The hundred commissioners appointed by the Five Thousand drew up the constitution as just stated; and after it had been ratified by the people, under the presidency of Aristomachus, the existing Council, that of the year of Callias, was dissolved before it had completed its term of office. It was dissolved on the fourteenth day of the month Thargelion, and the Four Hundred entered into office on the twenty-first; whereas the regular Council, elected by lot, ought to have entered into office on the fourteenth of Scirophorion. Thus was the oligarchy established, in the archonship of Callias, just about a hundred years after the expulsion of the tyrants. The chief promoters of the revolution were Pisander, Antiphon, and Theramenes, all of them men of good birth and with high reputations

for ability and judgement. When, however, this constitution had been established, the Five Thousand were only nominally selected, and the Four Hundred, together with the ten officers on whom full powers had been conferred, occupied the Council-house and really administered the government. They began by sending ambassadors to the Lacedaemonians proposing a cessation of the war on the basis of the existing position; but as the Lacedaemonians refused to listen to them unless they would also abandon the command of the sea, they broke off the negotiations.

33 · For about four months the constitution of the Four Hundred lasted, and Mnasilochus held office as Archon of their nomination for two months of the year of Theopompus, who was Archon for the remaining ten. On the loss of the naval battle of Eretria, however, and the revolt of the whole of Euboea except Oreum, the indignation of the people was greater than at any of the earlier disasters, since they drew far more supplies at this time from Euboea than from Attica itself. Accordingly they deposed the Four Hundred and committed the management of affairs to the Five Thousand, consisting of persons possessing a military equipment. At the same time they voted that pay should not be given for any public office. The persons chiefly responsible for the revolution were Aristocrates and Theramenes, who disapproved of the action of the Four Hundred in retaining the direction of affairs entirely in their own hands, and referring nothing to the Five Thousand. During this period the constitution of the state seems to have been admirable, since it was a time of war and the franchise was in the hands of those who possessed military equipment.

34 · The people, however, in a very short time deprived the Five Thousand of their monopoly of the government. Then, six years after the overthrow of the Four Hundred, in the archonship of Callias of Angele, the battle of Arginusae took place, of which the results were, first, that the ten generals who had gained the victory were all condemned by a single decision, owing to the people being led astray by persons who aroused their indignation; though, as a matter of fact, some of the generals had actually taken no part in the battle, and others were themselves picked up by other vessels. Secondly, when the Lacedaemonians proposed to evacuate Decelea and make peace on the basis of the existing position, although some of the Athenians supported this proposal, the majority refused to listen to them. In this they were led astray by Cleophon, who appeared in the Assembly drunk and wearing his breastplate, and prevented peace being made, declaring that he would never accept peace unless the Lacedaemonians abandoned their claims on all the cities allied with them. They mismanaged their opportunity then, and in a very short time they learnt their mistake. The next year, in the archonship of Alexias, they suffered the disaster of Aegospotami, the consequence of which was that Lysander became master of the city, and set up the Thirty in the following manner. One of the terms of peace stipulated that the state should be governed according to 'the ancient constitution'. Accordingly the popular party tried to preserve the democracy, while that part of the upper class which belonged to the political clubs,

together with the exiles who had returned since the peace, aimed at an oligarchy, and those who were not members of any club, though in other respects they considered themselves as good as any other citizens, were anxious to restore the ancient constitution. The latter class included Archinus, Anytus, Cleitophon, Phormisius, and many others, but their most prominent leader was Theramenes. Lysander, however, threw his influence on the side of the oligarchical party, and the popular Assembly was compelled by sheer intimidation to pass a vote establishing the oligarchy. The motion to this effect was proposed by Dracontides of Aphidna.

35 · In this way were the Thirty established in power, in the archonship of Pythodorus. As soon, however, as they were masters of the city, they ignored all the resolutions which had been passed relating to the organization of the constitution, but after appointing a Council of Five Hundred and the other magistrates out of a thousand selected candidates, and associating with themselves ten Archons in Piraeus, eleven superintendents of the prison, and three hundred 'lash-bearers' as attendants, they kept the city under their own control. At first, indeed, they behaved with moderation towards the citizens and pretended to administer the state according to the ancient constitution. They took down from the hill of Areopagus the laws of Ephialtes and Archestratus relating to the Areopagite Council; they also repealed such of the statutes of Solon as were obscure, and abolished the supreme power of the law-courts. In this they claimed to be restoring the constitution and freeing it from obscurities; as, for instance, by making the testator free once and for all to leave his property as he pleased, and abolishing the existing limitations in cases of insanity, old age, and undue female influence, in order that no opening might be left for professional accusers. In other matters also their conduct was similar. At first, then, they acted on these lines, and they destroyed the professional accusers and those mischievous and evil-minded persons who, to the great detriment of the democracy, had attached themselves to it in order to curry favour with it. With all of this the city was much pleased, and thought that the Thirty were doing it with the best of motives. But so soon as they had got a firmer hold on the city, they spared no class of citizens, but put to death any persons who were eminent for wealth or birth or character. Herein they aimed at removing all whom they had reason to fear, while they also wished to lay hands on their possessions; and in a short time they put to death not less than fifteen hundred persons.

36 · Theramenes, however, seeing the city thus falling into ruin, was displeased with their proceedings, and counselled them to cease such unprincipled conduct and let the better classes have a share in the government. At first they resisted his advice, but when his proposals came to be known abroad, and the masses began to associate themselves with him, they were seized with alarm lest he should make himself the leader of the people and destroy their despotic power. Accordingly they drew up a list of three thousand citizens, to whom they announced that they would give a share in the constitution. Theramenes, however, criticized this scheme also, first on the ground that, while proposing to give all respectable citizens a share

in the constitution, they were actually giving it only to three thousand persons, as though all merit were confined within that number; and secondly because they were doing two inconsistent things, since they made the government rest on the basis of force, and yet made the governors inferior in strength to the governed. However, they took no notice of his criticisms, and for a long time put off the publication of the list of the Three Thousand and kept to themselves the names of those who had been placed upon it; and every time they did decide to publish it they proceeded to strike out some of those who had been included in it, and insert others who had been omitted.

37 · Now when winter had set in, Thrasybulus and the exiles occupied Phyle, and the force which the Thirty led out to attack them met with a reverse. Thereupon the Thirty decided to disarm the bulk of the population and to get rid of Theramenes; which they did in the following way. They introduced two laws into the Council, which they commanded it to pass; the first of them gave the Thirty absolute power to put to death any citizen who was not included in the list of the Three Thousand, while the second disqualified all persons from participation in the franchise who should have assisted in the demolition of the fort of Eëtioneia, or have acted in any way against the Four Hundred who had organized the previous oligarchy. Theramenes had done both, and accordingly, when these laws were ratified, he became excluded from the franchise and the Thirty had full power to put him to death. Theramenes having been thus removed, they disarmed all the people except the Three Thousand, and in every respect showed a great advance in cruelty and crime. They also sent ambassadors to Lacedaemon to blacken the character of Theramenes and to ask for help; and the Lacedaemonians, in answer to their appeal, sent Callibius as military governor with about seven hundred troops, who came and occupied the Acropolis.

38 · These events were followed by the occupation of Munichia by the exiles from Phyle, and their victory over the Thirty and their partisans. After the fight the party of the city retreated, and next day they held a meeting in the marketplace and deposed the Thirty, and elected ten citizens with full powers to bring the war to a termination. When, however, the Ten had taken over the government they did nothing toward the object for which they were elected, but sent envoys to Lacedaemon to ask for help and to borrow money. Further, finding that the citizens who possessed the franchise were displeased at their proceedings, they were afraid lest they should be deposed, and consequently, in order to strike terror into them (in which design they succeeded), they arrested Demaretus, one of the most eminent citizens, and put him to death. This gave them a firm hold on the government, and they also had the support of Callibius and his Peloponnesians, together with several of the Knights; for some of the members of this class were the most zealous among the citizens to prevent the return of the exiles from Phyle. When, however, the party in Piraeus and Munichia began to gain the upper hand in the war, through the defection of the whole populace to them, the party in the city deposed the original

Ten, and elected another Ten, consisting of men of the highest repute. Under their administration, and with their active and zealous co-operation, the treaty of reconciliation was made and the populace returned to the city. The most prominent members of this board were Rhinon of Paeania and Phayllus of Acherdus, who, even before the arrival of Pausanias, opened negotiations with the party in Piraeus, and after his arrival seconded his efforts to bring about the return of the exiles. For it was Pausanias, the king of the Lacedaemonians, who brought the peace and reconciliation to a fulfilment, in conjunction with the ten commissioners of arbitration who arrived later from Lacedaemon, at his own earnest request. Rhinon and his colleagues received a vote of thanks for the goodwill shown by them to the people, and though they received their charge under an oligarchy and handed in their accounts under a democracy, no one, either of the party that had stayed in the city or of the exiles that had returned from the Piraeus, brought any complaint against them. On the contrary, Rhinon was immediately elected general on account of his conduct in this office.

39 · This reconciliation was effected in the archonship of Eucleides, on the following terms. All persons who, having remained in the city during the troubles, were now anxious to leave it, were to be free to settle at Eleusis, retaining their civil rights and possessing full and independent powers of self-government, and with the free enjoyment of their own personal property. The temple at Eleusis should be common ground for both parties, and should be under the superintendence of the Ceryces and the Eumolpidae, according to ancient custom. The settlers at Eleusis should not be allowed to enter Athens, nor the people of Athens to enter Eleusis, except at the season of the mysteries. The secessionists should pay their share to the fund for the common defence out of their revenues, just like all the other Athenians. If any of the seceding party wished to take a house in Eleusis, the people would help them to obtain the consent of the owner; but if they could not come to terms, they should appoint three valuers on either side, and the owner should receive whatever price they should appoint. Of the inhabitants of Eleusis, those whom the secessionists wished to remain should be allowed to do so. The list of those who desired to secede should be made up within ten days after the taking of the oaths in the case of persons already in the country, and their actual departure should take place within twenty days; persons at present out of the country should have the same terms allowed to them after their return. No one who settled at Eleusis should be capable of holding any office in Athens until he should again register himself on the roll as a resident in the city. Trials for homicide, in which one party had either killed or wounded another, should be conducted according to ancestral practice. There should be a general amnesty concerning past events towards all persons except the Thirty, the Ten, the Eleven, and the magistrates in Piraeus; and these too should be included if they should submit their accounts in the usual way. Such accounts should be given by the magistrates in Piraeus before a court of citizens in Piraeus, and by the magistrates in the city before a court of those rated.[3] On these terms

---

[3]The text is uncertain.

those who wished to do so might secede. Each party was to repay separately the money which it had borrowed for the war.

40 · When the reconciliation had taken place on these terms, those who had fought on the side of the Thirty felt considerable apprehensions, and a large number intended to secede. But as they put off entering their names till the last moment, as people will do, Archinus, observing their numbers, and being anxious to retain them as citizens, cut off the remaining days during which the list should have remained open; and in this way many persons were compelled to remain, though they did so very unwillingly until they recovered confidence. This is one point in which Archinus appears to have acted in a most statesmanlike manner, and another was his subsequent prosecution of Thrasybulus on the charge of illegality, for a motion by which he proposed to confer the franchise on all who had taken part in the return from Piraeus, although some of them were notoriously slaves. And yet a third such action was when one of the returned exiles began to violate the amnesty, whereupon Archinus haled him to the Council and persuaded them to execute him without trial, telling them that now they would have to show whether they wished to preserve the democracy and abide by the oaths they had taken; for if they let this man escape they would encourage others to imitate him, while if they executed him they would make an example for all to learn by. And this was exactly what happened; for after this man had been put to death no one ever again broke the amnesty. On the contrary, the Athenians seem, both in public and in private, to have behaved in the most unprecedentedly admirable and public-spirited way with reference to the preceding troubles. Not only did they blot out all memory of former offences, but they even repaid to the Lacedaemonians out of the public purse the money which the Thirty had borrowed for the war, although the treaty required each party, the party of the city and the party of Piraeus, to pay its own debts separately. This they did because they thought it was a necessary first step in the direction of restoring harmony; but in other states, so far from the democratic parties making advances from their own possessions, they are rather in the habit of making a general redistribution of the land. A reconciliation was made with the secessionists at Eleusis two years after the secession, in the archonship of Xenaenetus.

41 · This, however, took place at a later date; at the time of which we are speaking the people, having secured the control of the state, established the constitution which exists at the present day. Pythodorus was Archon at the time, but the democracy seems to have assumed the supreme power with perfect justice, since it had effected its own return by its own exertions.[4] This was the eleventh change which had taken place in the constitution of Athens. The first modification of the primaeval condition of things was when Ion and his companions brought the people together into a community, for then the people were first divided into the four tribes, and the tribe-kings were created. Next, and first after this, having now

---

[4]Kenyon obelizes this sentence.

some semblance of a constitution, was that which took place in the reign of Theseus, consisting in a slight deviation from absolute monarchy. After this came the constitution formed under Draco, when the first code of laws was drawn up. The third was that which followed the civil war, in the time of Solon; from this the democracy took its rise. The fourth was the tyranny of Pisistratus; the fifth the constitution of Cleisthenes, after the overthrow of the tyrants, of a more democratic character than that of Solon. The sixth was that which followed on the Persian wars, when the Council of Areopagus had the direction of the state. The seventh, succeeding this, was the constitution which Aristides sketched out, and which Ephialtes brought to completion by overthrowing the Areopagite Council; under this the nation, misled by the demagogues, made the most serious mistakes in the interest of its maritime empire. The eighth was the establishment of the Four Hundred, followed by the ninth, the restored democracy. The tenth was the tyranny of the Thirty and the Ten. The eleventh was that which followed the return from Phyle and Piraeus; and this has continued from that day to this, with continual accretions of power to the masses. The democracy has made itself master of everything and administers everything by its votes in the Assembly and by the law-courts, in which it holds the supreme power. Even the jurisdiction of the Council has passed into the hands of the people at large; and this appears to be a judicious change, since small bodies are more open to corruption, whether by actual money or influence, than large ones. At first they refused to allow payment for attendance at the Assembly; but the result was that people did not attend. Consequently, after the Prytanes had tried many devices in order to induce the populace to come and ratify the votes, Agyrrhius, in the first instance, made a provision of one obol a day, which Heracleides of Clazomenae, nicknamed 'the king', increased to two obols, and Agyrrhius again to three.

42 · The present state of the constitution is as follows. The franchise is open to all who are of citizen birth by both parents. They are enrolled among the demesmen at the age of eighteen. On the occasion of their enrolment the demesmen give their votes on oath, first whether the candidates appear to be of the age prescribed by the law (if not, they are dismissed back into the ranks of the boys), and secondly whether the candidate is free born and of such parentage as the laws require. Then if they decide that he is not a free man, he appeals to the law-courts, and the demesmen appoint five of their own number to act as accusers; if the court decides that he has no right to be enrolled, he is sold by the state as a slave, but if he wins his case he has a right to be enrolled among the demesmen without further question. After this the Council examines those who have been enrolled, and if it comes to the conclusion that any of them is less than eighteen years of age, it fines the demesmen who enrolled him. When the youths [Ephebi] have passed this examination, their fathers meet by their tribes, and appoint on oath three of their fellow tribesmen, over forty years of age, who, in their opinion, are the best and most suitable persons to have charge of the youths; and of these the Assembly elects one from each tribe as guardian, together with a director, chosen from the general body of Athenians, to control them all. Under the charge of these persons the youths

first of all make the circuit of the temples; then they proceed to Piraeus, and some of them garrison Munichia and some the south shore. The Assembly also elects two trainers, with subordinate instructors, who teach them to fight in heavy armour, to use the bow and javelin, and to discharge a catapult. The guardians receive from the state a drachma apiece for their keep, and the youths four obols apiece. Each guardian receives the allowance for all the members of his tribe and buys the necessary provisions for the common stock (they mess together by tribes), and generally superintends everything. In this way they spend the first year. The next year, after giving a public display of their military evolutions, on the occasion when the Assembly meets in the theatre, they receive a shield and spear from the state; after which they patrol the country and spend their time in the forts. For these two years they are on garrison duty, and wear the military cloak, and during this time they are exempt from all taxes. They also can neither bring an action at law, nor have one brought against them, in order that they may have no excuse for requiring leave of absence; though exception is made in cases of actions concerning inheritances and wards of state, or of any sacrificial ceremony connected with the family. When the two years have elapsed they thereupon take their position among the other citizens. Such is the manner of the enrolment of the citizens and the training of the youths.

43 · All the magistrates that are concerned with the ordinary routine of administration are elected by lot, except the Military Treasurer, the Commissioners of the Theoric fund, and the Superintendent of Springs. These are elected by vote, and hold office from one Panathenaic festival to the next. All military officers are also elected by vote.

The Council of Five Hundred is elected by lot, fifty from each tribe. Each tribe holds the office of Prytanes in turn, the order being determined by lot; the first four serve for thirty-six days each, the last six for thirty-five, since the reckoning is by lunar years. The Prytanes for the time being, in the first place, mess together in the Tholus and receive a sum of money from the state for their maintenance; and, secondly, they convene the meetings of the Council and the Assembly. The Council they convene every day, unless it is a holiday, the Assembly four times in each prytany. It is also their duty to draw up the programme of the business of the Council and to decide what subjects are to be dealt with on each particular day, and where the sitting is to be held. They also draw up the programme for the meetings of the Assembly. One of these in each prytany is called the 'sovereign' Assembly; in this the people have to ratify the continuance of the magistrates in office, if they are performing their duties properly, and to consider the supply of corn and the defence of the country. On this day, too, impeachments are introduced by those who wish to do so, the lists of property confiscated by the state are read, and also applications for inheritances and wards of state, so that nothing may pass unclaimed without the cognizance of any person concerned. In the sixth prytany, in addition to the business already stated, the question is put to the vote whether it is desirable to hold a vote of ostracism or not; and complaints against professional accusers, whether Athenian or aliens domiciled in Athens, are received, to the number of not more than three of either class, together with cases in which an individual has made some promise to the people and has not performed it. Another Assembly in each prytany is assigned to the hearing of petitions, and at this meeting any one is free, on depositing the petitioner's olive-branch, to speak to the people concerning any matter, public or private. The two remaining meetings are devoted to all other subjects, and the laws require them to deal with three questions connected with religion, three connected with heralds and embassies, and three on secular subjects. Sometimes questions are brought forward without a preliminary vote.

Heralds and envoys appear first before the Prytanes, and the bearers of dispatches also deliver them to the same officials.

44 · There is a single President of the Prytanes, elected by lot, who presides for a night and a day; he may not hold the office for more than that time, nor may the same individual hold it twice. He keeps the keys of the sanctuaries in which the treasures and public records of the state are preserved, and also the public seal; and he is bound to remain in the Tholus, together with one-third of the Prytanes, named by himself. Whenever the Prytanes convene a meeting of the Council or Assembly, he appoints by lot nine Proedri, one from each tribe except that which holds the office of Prytanes for the time being; and out of these nine he similarly appoints one as President, and hands over the programme for the meeting to them. They take it and see to the preservation of order, put forward the various subjects which are to be considered, decide the results of the votings, and direct the proceedings generally. They also have power to dismiss the meeting. No one may act as President more than once in the year, but he may be a Proedrus once in each prytany.

Elections to the offices of General and Hipparch and all other military commands are held in the Assembly, in such manner as the people decide; they are held after the sixth prytany by the first board of Prytanes in whose term of office the omens are favourable. There has, however, to be a preliminary consideration by the Council in this case also.

45 · In former times the Council had full powers to inflict fines and imprisonment and death. When it had consigned Lysimachus to the executioner, and he was sitting in the immediate expectation of death, Eumelides of Alopece rescued him from its hands, maintaining that no citizen ought to be put to death except on the decision of a court of law. Accordingly a trial was held in a law-court, and Lysimachus was acquitted, receiving henceforth the nickname of 'the man from the drum-head'; and the people deprived the Council thenceforward of the power to inflict death or imprisonment or fine, passing a law that if the Council condemn any person for an offence or inflict a fine, the Thesmothetae shall bring the sentence or fine before the law-court, and the decision of the jurors shall be the final judgement in the matter.

The Council passes judgement on nearly all magistrates, especially those who have the control of money; its judgement, however, is not final, but is subject to an appeal to the law-courts. Private individuals, also, may lay an information against any magistrate they please for not obeying the laws, but here too there is an appeal to the law-courts if the Council declare the charge proved. The Council also examines those who are to be its members for the ensuing year, and likewise the nine Archons. Formerly the Council had full power to reject candidates for office as unsuitable, but now they have an appeal to the law-courts. In all these matters, therefore, the Council has no final jurisdiction. It takes, however, preliminary cognizance of all matters brought before the Assembly, and the Assembly cannot vote on any question unless it has first been considered by the Council and placed on the programme by the Prytanes; since a person who carries a motion in the Assembly is liable to an action for illegal proposal on these grounds.

46 · The Council also superintends the triremes that are already in existence, with their tackle and sheds, and builds new triremes or quadriremes, whichever the Assembly votes, with tackle and sheds to match. The Assembly appoints master-builders for the ships by vote; and if they do not hand them over completed to the next Council, they cannot receive the donation—that being normally given during the term of the following Council. For the building of the triremes it appoints ten commissioners, chosen from its own members. The Council also inspects all public buildings, and if it is of opinion that the state is being defrauded, it reports the culprit to the Assembly, and on condemnation hands him over to the law-courts.

47 · The Council also co-operates with the other magistrates in most of their duties. First there are the treasurers of Athena, ten in number, elected by lot, one from each tribe. According to the law of Solon—which is still in force—they must be Pentacosiomedimni, but in point of fact the person on whom the lot falls holds the office even though he be quite a poor man. These officers take over charge of the statue of Athena, the figures of Victory, and all the other ornaments of the temple, together with the money, in the presence of the Council. Then there are the Commissioners for Public Contracts [Poletae], ten in number, one chosen by lot from each tribe, who farm out all the public contracts. They lease the mines and taxes in conjunction with the Military Treasurer and the Commissioners of the Theoric fund, in the presence of the Council, and grant, to the persons indicated by the vote of the Council, the mines which are let out by the state, including both the workable ones, which are let for three years, and those which are let under special agreements for ten years. They also sell, in the presence of the Council, the property of those who have gone into exile from the court of the Areopagus, and of others whose goods have been confiscated, and the nine Archons ratify the contracts. They also hand over to the Council lists of the taxes which are farmed out for the year, entering on whitened tablets the name of the lessee and the amount paid. They make separate lists, first of those who have to pay their instalments in each prytany, on ten several tablets, next of those who pay thrice in the year, with a separate tablet for each instalment, and finally of those who pay in the ninth prytany. They also draw up a list of farms and dwellings which have been confiscated and sold by order of the courts; for these too come within their province. In the case of dwellings the value must be paid up in five years, and in that of farms, in ten. The

instalments are paid in the ninth prytany. Further, the King-archon brings before the Council the leases of the sacred enclosures written on whitened tablets. These too are leased for ten years, and the instalments are paid in the ninth prytany; consequently it is in this prytany that the greatest amount of money is collected. The tablets containing the lists of the instalments are carried into the Council, and the public clerk takes charge of them. Whenever a payment of instalments is to be made he takes from the pigeon-holes the precise list of the sums which are to be paid and struck off on that day, and delivers it to the Receivers-General. The rest are kept apart, in order that no sum may be struck off before it is paid.

48 · There are ten Receivers-General [Apodectae], elected by lot, one from each tribe. These officers receive the tablets, and strike off the instalments as they are paid, in the presence of the Council in the Council-chamber, and give the tablets back to the public clerk. If any one fails to pay his instalment, a note is made of it on the tablet; and he is bound to pay double the amount of the deficiency, or, in default, to be imprisoned. The Council has full power by the laws to exact these payments and to inflict this imprisonment. They receive all the instalments, therefore, on one day, and portion the money out among the magistrates; and on the next day they bring up the report of the apportionment, written on a wooden notice-board, and read it out in the Council-chamber, after which they ask publicly in the Council whether any one knows of any malpractice in reference to the apportionment, on the part of either a magistrate or a private individual, and if any one is charged with malpractice they take a vote on it.

The Council also elects ten Auditors [Logistae] by lot from its own members, to audit the accounts of the magistrates for each prytany. They also elect one Examiner of Accounts [Euthunus] by lot from each tribe, with two assessors [Paredri] for each examiner, whose duty it is to sit at the ordinary market hours, each opposite the statue of the eponymous hero of his tribe; and if any one wishes to prefer a charge, on either public or private grounds, against any magistrate who has passed his audit before the law-courts, within three days of his having so passed, he enters on a whitened tablet his own name and that of the magistrate prosecuted, together with the malpractice that is alleged against him. He also appends his claim for a penalty of such amount as seems to him fitting, and gives in the record to the Examiner. The latter takes it, and if after reading it he considers it proved he hands it over, if a private case, to the local justices who introduce cases for the tribe concerned, while if it is a public case he enters it on the register of the Thesmothetae. Then, if the Thesmothetae accept it, they bring the accounts of this magistrate once more before the law-court, and the decision of the jury stands as the final judgement.

49 · The Council also inspects the horses belonging to the state. If a man who has a good horse is found to keep it in bad condition, he is mulcted in his allowance of corn; while those which cannot keep up or which shy and will not stand steady, it brands with a wheel on the jaw, and the horse so marked is disqualified for

service. It also inspects those who appear to be fit for service as scouts, and any one whom it rejects is deprived of his horse. It also examines the infantry who serve among the cavalry, and any one whom it rejects ceases to receive his pay. The roll of the cavalry is drawn up by the Commissioners of Enrolment [Catalogeis], ten in number, elected by the Assembly by open vote. They hand over to the Hipparchs and Phylarchs the list of those whom they have enrolled, and these officers take it and bring it up before the Council, and there open the tablet containing the names of the cavalry. If any of those who have been on the roll previously make affidavit that they are physically incapable of cavalry service, they strike them out; then they call up the persons enrolled, and if any one makes affidavit that he is either physically or pecuniarily incapable of cavalry service they dismiss him, but if no such affidavit is made the Council vote whether the individual in question is suitable for the purpose or not. If they vote in the affirmative his name is entered on the tablet; if not, he is dismissed with the others.

Formerly the Council used to decide on the plans for public buildings and the contract for making the robe of Athena; but now this is done by a jury in the law-courts appointed by lot, since the Council was considered to have shown favouritism in its decisions. The Council also shares with the Military Treasurer the superintendence of the manufacture of the images of Victory and the prizes at the Panathenaic festival.

The Council also examines infirm paupers; for there is a law which provides that persons possessing less than three minas, who are so crippled as to be unable to do any work, are, after examination by the Council, to receive two obols a day from the state for their support. A treasurer is appointed by lot to attend to them.

The Council also, speaking broadly, co-operates in most of the duties of all the other magistrates; and this ends the list of the functions of that body.

50 · There are ten Commissioners for Repairs of Temples elected by lot, who receive a sum of thirty minas from the Receivers-General, and therewith carry out the most necessary repairs in the temples.

There are also ten City Commissioners [Astynomi], of whom five hold office in Piraeus and five in the city. Their duty is to see that female flute- and harp- and lute-players are not hired at more than two drachmas, and if more than one person is anxious to hire the same girl, they cast lots and hire her out to the person to whom the lot falls. They also provide that no collector of sewage shall deposit any of his sewage within ten stadia of the walls; they prevent people from blocking up the streets by building, or stretching barriers across them, or making raised drain-pipes with a discharge into the street, or having doors which open outwards; they also remove the corpses of those who die in the streets for which purpose they have a body of state slaves assigned to them.

51 · Market Commissioners [Agoranomi] are elected by lot, five for Piraeus, five for the city. Their statutory duty is to see that all articles offered for sale in the market are pure and unadulterated.

Commissioners of Weights and Measures [Metronomi] are elected by lot, five for the city, and five for Piraeus. They see that sellers use fair weights and measures.

Formerly there were ten Corn Commissioners [Sitophylaces], elected by lot, five for Piraeus, and five for the city; but now there are twenty for the city and fifteen for Piraeus. Their duties are, first, to see that the unprepared corn in the market is offered for sale at reasonable prices, and secondly, to see that the millers sell barley meal at a price proportionate to that of barley, and that the bakers sell their loaves at a price proportionate to that of wheat, and of such weight as the Commissioners may appoint; for the law requires them to fix the standard weight.

There are ten Superintendents of the Mart, elected by lot, whose duty is to superintend the Mart, and to compel merchants to bring up into the city two-thirds of the corn which is brought by sea to the Corn Mart.

52 · The Eleven also are appointed by lot to take care of the prisoners in the state gaol. Thieves, kidnappers, and pickpockets are brought to them, and if they plead guilty they are executed, but if they deny the charge the Eleven bring the case before the law-courts; if the prisoners are acquitted, they release them, but if not, they then execute them. They also bring up before the law-courts the list of farms and houses claimed as state-property; and if it is decided that they are so, they deliver them to the Commissioners for Public Contracts. The Eleven also bring up informations laid against magistrates alleged to be disqualified; this function comes within their province, but some such cases are brought up by the Thesmothetae.

There are also five Introducers of Cases [Eisagogeis], elected by lot, one for each pair of tribes, who bring up the one-month cases to the law-courts. The one-month cases are these: refusal to pay up a dowry where a party is bound to do so, refusal to pay interest on money borrowed at 12 per cent., or where a man desirous of setting up business in the market has borrowed from another man capital to start with; also cases of slander, cases arising out of friendly loans or partnerships, and cases concerned with slaves, cattle, and the office of trierarch, or with banks. These are brought up as one-month cases and are introduced by these officers; but the Receivers-General perform the same function in cases for or against the farmers of taxes. Those in which the sum concerned is not more than ten drachmas they can decide summarily, but all above that amount they bring into the law-courts as one-month cases.

53 · The Forty are also elected by lot, four from each tribe, before whom suitors bring all other cases. Formerly they were thirty in number, and they went on circuit through the demes to hear causes; but after the oligarchy of the Thirty they were increased to forty. They have full powers to decide cases in which the amount at issue does not exceed ten drachmas, but anything beyond that value they hand over to the Arbitrators. The Arbitrators take up the case, and, if they cannot bring the parties to an agreement, they give a decision. If their decision satisfies both parties, and they abide by it, the case is at an end; but if either of the parties appeals to the law-courts, the Arbitrators enclose the evidence, the pleadings, and the laws

quoted in the case in two urns, those of the plaintiff in the one, and those of the defendant in the other. These they seal up and, having attached to them the decision of the arbitrator, written out on a tablet, place them in the custody of the four justices whose function it is to introduce cases on behalf of the tribe of the defendant. These officers take them and bring up the case before the law-court, to a jury of two hundred and one members in cases up to the value of a thousand drachmas, or to one of four hundred and one in cases above that value. No laws or pleadings or evidence may be used except those which were adduced before the Arbitrator, and have been enclosed in the urns.

The Arbitrators are persons in the sixtieth year of their age; this appears from the schedule of the Archons and the Eponymi. There are two classes of Eponymi, the ten who give their names to the tribes, and the forty-two of the years of service. The youths, on being enrolled among the citizens, were formerly registered upon whitened tablets, and the names were appended by the Archon in whose year they were enrolled, and by the Eponymus who had been in course in the preceding year; at the present day they are written on a bronze pillar, which stands in front of the Council-chamber, near the Eponymi of the tribes. Then the Forty take the last of the Eponymi of the years of service, and assign the arbitrations to the persons belonging to that year, casting lots to determine which arbitrations each shall undertake; and every one is compelled to carry through the arbitrations which the lot assigns to him. The law enacts that any one who does not serve as Arbitrator when he has arrived at the necessary age shall lose his civil rights, unless he happens to be holding some other office during that year, or to be out of the country. These are the only persons who escape the duty. Any one who suffers injustice at the hands of the Arbitrator may appeal to the whole board of Arbitrators, and if they find the magistrate guilty the law enacts that he shall lose his civil rights. The persons thus condemned have, however, in their turn an appeal. The Eponymi are also used in reference to military expeditions; when the men of military age are despatched on service, a notice is put up stating that the men from such-and-such an Archon and Eponymus to such-and-such another Archon and Eponymus are to go on the expedition.

54 · The following magistrates also are elected by lot: Five Commissioners of Roads [Hodopoei], who, with an assigned body of public slaves, are required to keep the roads in order; and ten Auditors, with ten assistants, to whom all persons who have held any office must give in their accounts. These are the only officers who audit the accounts of those who are subject to examination, and who bring them up for examination before the law-courts. If they detect any magistrate in embezzlement, the jury condemn him for theft, and he is obliged to repay tenfold the sum he is declared to have misappropriated. If they charge a magistrate with accepting bribes and the jury convict him, they fine him for corruption, and this sum too is repaid tenfold. Or if they convict him of unfair dealing, he is fined on that charge, and the sum assessed is paid without increase, if payment is made before the ninth prytany, but otherwise it is doubled. A tenfold fine is not doubled.

The Clerk of the Prytany, as he is called, is also elected by lot. He has the charge of all public documents, and keeps the resolutions which are passed by the Assembly, and checks the transcripts of all other official papers and attends at the sessions of the Council. Formerly he was elected by vote, and the most distinguished and trustworthy persons were elected to the post, as is known from the fact that the name of this officer is appended on the pillars recording treaties of alliance and grants of consulship and citizenship. Now, however, he is elected by lot. There is, in addition, a Clerk of the Laws, elected by lot, who attends at the sessions of the Council; and he too checks all the transcripts. The Assembly also elects by open vote a clerk to read documents to it and to the Council; but he has no other duty except that of reading aloud.

The Assembly also elects by lot the Commissioners of Public Worship [Hieropoei], known as the Commissioners for Sacrifices, who offer the sacrifices appointed by oracle, and, in conjunction with the seers, take the auspices whenever there is occasion. It also elects by lot ten others, known as Annual Commissioners, who offer certain sacrifices and administer all the quadrennial festivals except the Panathenaea. There are the following quadrennial festivals: first that of Delos (where there is also a sexennial festival), secondly the Brauronia, thirdly the Heracleia, fourthly the Eleusinia, and fifthly the Panathenaea; and no two of these are celebrated in the same place. To these the Hephaestia has now been added, in the archonship of Cephisophon.

An Archon is also elected by lot for Salamis, and a Demarch for Piraeus. These officers celebrate the Dionysia in these two places, and appoint Choregi. In Salamis, moreover, the name of the Archon is publicly recorded.

55 · All the foregoing magistrates are elected by lot, and their powers are those which have been stated. To pass on to the nine Archons, as they are called, the manner of their first establishment has been described already. At the present day six Thesmothetae are elected by lot, together with their clerk, and in addition to these an Archon, a King, and a Polemarch. One is elected from each tribe. They are examined first of all by the Council of Five Hundred, with the exception of the clerk. The latter is examined only in the law-court, like other magistrates (for all magistrates, whether elected by lot or by open vote, are examined before entering on their offices); but the nine Archons are examined both in the Council and again in the law-court. Formerly no one could hold the office if the Council rejected him, but now there is an appeal to the law-court, which is the final authority in the matter of the examination. When they are examined, they are asked, first, 'Who is your father, and of what deme? who is your father's father? who is your mother? who is your mother's father, and of what deme?' Then the candidate is asked whether he possesses an ancestral Apollo and a household Zeus, and where their sanctuaries are; next if he possesses a family tomb, and where; then if he treats his parents well, and pays his taxes, and has served on the required military expeditions. When the examiner has put these questions, he proceeds, 'Call the witnesses to these facts'; and when the candidate has produced his witnesses, he next asks, 'Does any one wish to make any accusation against this man?' If an accuser appears, he gives the parties an opportunity of making their accusation and defence, and then puts it to

the Council to pass the candidate or not, and to the law-court to give the final vote. If no one wishes to make an accusation, he proceeds at once to the vote. Formerly a single individual gave the vote, but now all the members are obliged to vote on the candidates, so that if any unprincipled candidate has managed to get rid of his accusers, it may still be possible for him to be disqualified before the law-court. When the examination has been thus completed, they proceed to the stone on which are the pieces of the victims, and on which the Arbitrators take oath before declaring their decisions, and witnesses swear to their testimony. On this stone the Archons stand, and swear to execute their office uprightly and according to the laws, and not to receive presents in respect of the performance of their duties, or, if they do, to dedicate a golden statue. When they have taken this oath they proceed to the Acropolis, and there they repeat it; after this they enter upon their office.

56 · The Archon, the King, and the Polemarch have each two assessors, nominated by themselves. These officers are examined in the law-court before they begin to act, and give in accounts on each occasion of their acting.

As soon as the Archon enters office, he begins by issuing a proclamation that whatever any one possessed before he entered into office, that he shall possess and hold until the end of his term. Next he assigns Choregi to the tragic poets, choosing three of the richest persons out of the whole body of Athenians. Formerly he used also to assign five Choregi to the comic poets, but now the tribes provide the Choregi for them. Then he receives the Choregi who have been appointed by the tribes for the men's and boy's choruses and the comic poets at the Dionysia, and for the men's and boy's choruses at the Thargelia (at the Dionysia there is a chorus for each tribe, but at the Thargelia one between two tribes, each tribe taking its turn in providing it); he transacts the exchanges of properties for them, and reports any excuses that are tendered, if any one says that he has already performed this service, or that he is exempt because he has performed some other service and the period of his exemption has not yet expired, or that he is not of the required age; for the Choregus of a boys' chorus must be over forty years of age. He also appoints Choregi for the festival at Delos, and a chief of the mission for the thirty-oar boat which conveys the youths thither. He also superintends sacred processions, both that in honour of Asclepius, when the initiated keep house, and that of the great Dionysia—the latter in conjunction with the Superintendents of that festival. These officers, ten in number, were formerly elected by open vote in the Assembly, and used to provide for the expenses of the procession out of their private means; but now one is elected by lot from each tribe, and the state contributes a hundred minas for the expenses. The Archon also superintends the procession at the Thargelia, and that in honour of Zeus the Saviour. He also manages the contests at the Dionysia and the Thargelia.

These, then, are the festivals which he superintends. The suits and indictments which come before him, and which he, after a preliminary inquiry, brings up before the law-courts, are as follows. Injury to parents (for bringing these actions the prosecutor cannot suffer any penalty); injury to orphans (these actions lie against their guardians); injury to a ward of state (these lie against their guardians or their husbands); injury to an orphan's estate (these too lie against the guardians); mental derangement, where a party charges another with destroying his own property through unsoundness of mind; for appointment of liquidators, where a party refuses to divide property in which others have a share; for constituting a wardship; for determining between rival claims to a wardship; for granting inspection of property to which another party lays claim; for appointing oneself as guardian; and for determining disputes as to inheritances and wards of state. The Archon also has the care of orphans and wards of state, and of women who, on the death of their husbands, declare themselves to be with child; and he has power to inflict a fine on those who offend against the persons under his charge, or to bring the case before the law-courts. He also leases the houses of orphans and wards of state until they reach the age of fourteen, and takes mortgages on them; and if the guardians fail to provide the necessary food for the children under their charge, he exacts it from them. Such are the duties of the Archon.

57 · The King in the first place superintends the mysteries, in conjunction with the Superintendents of Mysteries. The latter are elected in the Assembly by open vote, two from the general body of Athenians, one from the Eumolpidae, and one from the Ceryces. Next, he superintends the Lenaean Dionysia, which consists of a procession and a contest. The procession is ordered by the King and the Superintendents in conjunction; but the contest is managed by the King alone. He also manages all the contests of the torch-race; and to speak broadly, he administers all the ancestral sacrifices. Indictments for impiety come before him, or any disputes between parties concerning priestly rites; and he also determines all controversies concerning sacred rites for the ancient families and the priests. All actions for homicide come before him, and it is he that makes the proclamation requiring polluted persons to keep away from sacred ceremonies. Actions for homicide and wounding are heard, if the homicide or wounding is willful, in the Areopagus; so also in cases of killing by poison, and of arson. These are the only cases heard by that Council. Cases of unintentional homicide, or of intent to kill, or of killing a slave or a resident alien or a foreigner, are heard by the court of Palladium. When the homicide is acknowledged, but legal justification is pleaded, as when a man takes an adulterer in the act, or kills another by mistake in battle or in an athletic contest, the prisoner is tried in the court of Delphinium. If a man who is in banishment for a homicide which admits of reconciliation incurs a further charge of killing or wounding, he is tried in Phreatto, and he makes his defence from a boat moored near the shore. All these cases, except those which are heard in the Areopagus, are tried by the Ephetae on whom the lot falls. The King introduces them, and the hearing is held within sacred precincts and in the open air. Whenever the King hears a case he takes off his crown. The person who is charged with homicide is at all other times excluded from the temples, nor is it even lawful for him to enter the market-place; but on the occasion of his trial he enters the temple and makes his defence. If the actual offender is unknown, the writ runs against 'the doer of the deed'. The King and the tribe-kings also hear the cases in which the guilt rests on inanimate objects and animals.

58 · The Polemarch performs the sacrifices to Artemis the huntress and to Enyalius, and arranges the contest at the funeral of those who have fallen in war, and makes offerings to the memory of Harmodius and Aristogeiton. Only private actions come before him, namely those in which resident aliens, both ordinary and privileged, and agents of foreign states are concerned. It is his duty to receive these cases and divide them into ten groups, and assign to each tribe the group which comes to it by lot; after which the magistrates who introduce cases for the tribe hand them over to the Arbitrators. The Polemarch, however, brings up in person cases in which an alien is charged with deserting his patron or neglecting to provide himself with one, and also of inheritances and wards of state where aliens are concerned; and in fact, generally, whatever the Archon does for citizens, the Polemarch does for aliens.

59 · The Thesmothetae in the first place have the power of prescribing on what days the law-courts are to sit, and next of assigning them to the several magistrates; for the latter must follow the arrangement which the Thesmothetae assign. Moreover they introduce impeachments before the Assembly, and bring up all votes for removal from office, challenges of a magistrate's conduct before the Assembly, indictments for illegal proposals or for proposing a law which is contrary to the interests of the state, complaints against Proedri or their president for their conduct in office, and the accounts presented by the generals. All indictments also come before them in which a deposit has to be made by the prosecutor, namely, indictments for concealment of foreign origin, for corrupt evasion of foreign origin (when a man escapes the disqualification by bribery), for blackmailing accusations, bribery, false entry of another as a state debtor, false testimony to the service of a summons, conspiracy to enter a man as a state debtor, corrupt removal from the list of debtors; and adultery. They also bring up the examinations of all magistrates, and the rejections by the demes and the condemnations by the Council. Moreover they bring up certain private suits in cases of merchandise and mines, or where a slave has slandered a free man. It is they also who cast lots to assign the courts to the various magistrates, whether for private or public cases. They ratify commercial treaties, and bring up the cases which arise out of such treaties; and they also bring up cases of perjury from the Areopagus. The casting of lots for the jurors is conducted by all the nine Archons, with the clerk to the Thesmothetae as the tenth, each performing the duty for his own tribe. Such are the duties of the nine Archons.

60 · There are also ten Commissioners of Games [Athlothetae], elected by lot, one from each tribe. These officers, after passing an examination, serve for four years; and they manage the Panathenaic procession, the contest in music and that in gymnastic, and the horse-race; they also provide the robe of Athena and, in conjunction with the Council, the vases, and they present the oil to the athletes. This oil is collected from the sacred olives. The Archon requisitions it from the owners of the farms on which the sacred olives grow, at the rate of three-quarters of a pint from each plant. Formerly the state used to sell the fruit itself, and if any one dug up

or broke down one of the sacred olives, he was tried by the Council of Areopagus, and if he was condemned, the penalty was death. Since, however, the oil has been paid by the owner of the farm, the procedure has lapsed, though the law remains; and the oil is a state charge upon the property instead of being taken from the individual plants. When then, the Archon has collected the oil for his year of office, he hands it over to the Treasurers to preserve in the Acropolis, and he may not take his seat in the Areopagus until he has paid over to the Treasurers the full amount. The Treasurers keep it in the Acropolis until the Panathenaea, when they measure it out to the Commissioners of Games, and they again to the victorious competitors. The prizes for the victors in the musical contest consist of silver and gold, for the victors in manly vigour, of shields, and for the victors in the gymnastic contest and the horse-race, of oil.

61 · All officers connected with military service are elected by open vote. In the first place, ten Generals [Strategi], who were formerly elected one from each tribe, but now are chosen from the whole mass of citizens. Their duties are assigned to them by open vote; one is appointed to command the heavy infantry, and leads them if they go out to war; one to the defence of the country, who remains on the defensive, and fights if there is war within the borders of the country; two to Piraeus, one of whom is assigned to Munichia, and one to the south shore, and these have charge of the defence of the Piraeus; and one to superintend the symmories, who nominates the trierarchs and arranges exchanges of properties for them, and brings up actions to decide on rival claims in connexion with them. The rest are dispatched to whatever business may be on hand at the moment. The appointment of these officers is submitted for confirmation in each prytany, when the question is put whether they are considered to be doing their duty. If any officer is rejected on this vote, he is tried in the law-court, and if he is found guilty the people decide what punishment or fine shall be inflicted on him; but if he is acquitted he resumes his office. The Generals have full power, when on active service, to arrest any one for insubordination, or to cashier him publicly, or to inflict a fine; the latter is, however, unusual.

There are also ten Taxiarchs, one from each tribe, elected by open vote; and each commands his own tribesmen and appoints captains of companies [Lochagi]. There are also two Hipparchs, elected by open vote from the whole mass of the citizens, who command the cavalry, each taking five tribes. They have the same powers as the Generals have in respect of the infantry, and their appointments are also subject to confirmation. There are also ten Phylarchs, elected by open vote, one from each tribe, to command the cavalry, as the Taxiarchs do the infantry. There is also a Hipparch for Lemnos, elected by open vote, who has charge of the cavalry in Lemnos. There is also a treasurer of the Paralus, and another of the Ammonias, similarly elected.

62 · Of the magistrates elected by lot, in former times some, including the nine Archons, were elected out of the tribe as a whole, while others, namely those who are now elected in the Theseum, were apportioned among the demes; but since

the demes used to sell the elections, these magistrates too are now elected from the whole tribe, except the members of the Council and the guards, who are still left to the demes.

Pay is received for the following services. First the members of the Assembly receive a drachma for the ordinary meetings, and nine obols for the 'sovereign' meeting. Then the jurors at the law-courts receive three obols; and the members of the Council five obols. The Prytanes receive an allowance of an obol for their maintenance. The nine Archons receive four obols apiece for maintenance, and also keep a herald and a flute-player; and the Archon for Salamis receives a drachma a day. The Commissioners for Games dine in the Prytaneum during the month of Hecatombaeon in which the Panathenaic festival takes place, from the fourteenth day onwards. The Amphictyonic deputies to Delos receive a drachma a day from the exchequer of Delos. Also all magistrates sent to Samos, Scyros, Lemnos, or Imbros receive an allowance for their maintenance. The military offices may be held any number of times, but none of the others more than once, except the membership of the Council, which may be held twice.

63 · The juries for the law-courts are chosen by lot by the nine Archons, each for their own tribe, and by the clerk to the Thesmothetae for the tenth. There are ten entrances into the courts, one for each tribe; twenty rooms in which the lots are drawn, two for each tribe; a hundred chests, ten for each tribe; other chests, in which are placed the tickets of the jurors on whom the lot falls; and two vases. Further, staves, equal in number to the jurors required, are placed by the side of each entrance; and counters are put into one vase, equal in number to the staves. These are inscribed with letters of the alphabet beginning with the eleventh (lambda), equal in number to the courts which require to be filled. All persons above thirty years of age are qualified to serve as jurors, provided they are not debtors to the state and have not lost their civil rights. If any unqualified person serves as juror, an information is laid against him, and he is brought before the court: if he is convicted, the jurors assess the punishment or fine which they consider him to deserve. If he is condemned to a money fine, he must be imprisoned until he has paid up both the original debt, on account of which the information was laid against him, and also the fine which the court has imposed upon him. Each juror has his ticket of box-wood, on which is inscribed his name, with the name of his father and his deme, and one of the letters of the alphabet up to *kappa;* for the jurors in their several tribes are divided into ten sections, with approximately an equal number in each letter. When the Thesmothetes has decided by lot which letters are required to attend at the courts, the servant puts up above each court the letter which has been assigned to it by the lot.

64 · The ten chests are placed in front of the entrance used by each tribe, and are inscribed with the letters of the alphabet from *alpha* to *kappa*. The jurors cast in their tickets, each into the chest on which is inscribed the letter which is on his ticket; then the servant shakes them all up, and the Thesmothetes draws one ticket from each chest. The individual so selected is called the Ticket-hanger

[Empectes], and his function is to hang up the tickets out of his chest on the bar which bears the same letter as that on the chest. He is chosen by lot, lest, if the Ticket-hanger were always the same person, he might tamper with the results. There are five of these bars in each of the rooms assigned for the lot-drawing. Then the Archon casts in the dice and thereby chooses the jurors from each tribe, room by room. The dice are made of bronze, coloured black or white; and according to the number of jurors required, so many white dice are put in, one for each five tickets, while the remainder are black, in the same proportion. As the Archon draws out the dice, the crier calls out the names of the individuals chosen. The Ticket-hanger is included among those selected. Each juror, as he is chosen and answers to his name, draws a counter from the vase, and holding it out with the letter uppermost shows it first to the presiding archon; and he, when he has seen it, throws the ticket of the juror into the chest on which is inscribed the letter which is on the counter, so that the juror must go into the court assigned to him by lot, and not into one chosen by himself, and that it may be impossible for any one to collect the jurors of his choice into any particular court. For this purpose chests are placed near the Archon, as many in number as there are courts to be filled that day, bearing the letters of the courts on which the lot has fallen.

65 · The juror thereupon, after showing his counter again to the attendant, passes through the barrier into the court. The attendant gives him a staff of the same colour as the court bearing the letter which is on his counter, so as to ensure his going into the court assigned to him by lot; since, if he were to go into any other, he would be betrayed by the colour of his staff. Each court has a certain colour painted on the lintel of the entrance. Accordingly the juror, bearing his staff, enters the court which has the same colour as his staff, and the same letter as his counter. As he enters, he receives a voucher from the official to whom this duty has been assigned by lot. So with their counters and their staves the selected jurors take their seats in the court, having thus completed the process of admission. The unsuccessful candidates receive back their tickets from the Ticket-hangers. The public servants carry the chests from each tribe, one to each court, containing the names of the members of the tribe who are in that court, and hand them over to the officials, five in number,[5] assigned to the duty of giving back their tickets to the jurors in each court, so that these officials may call them up by name and pay them their fee.

66 · When all the courts are full, two ballot boxes are placed in the first court, and a number of bronze dice, bearing the colours of the several courts, and other dice inscribed with the names of the presiding magistrates. Then two of the Thesmothetae, selected by lot, severally throw the dice with the colours into one box, and those with the magistrates' names into the other. The magistrate whose name is first drawn is thereupon proclaimed by the crier as assigned for duty in the court which is first drawn, and the second in the second, and similarly with the rest.

---

⁵Reading ἀριθμῷ πέντε.

The object of this procedure is that no one may know which court he will have, but that each may take the court assigned to him by lot.

When the jurors have come in, and have been assigned to their respective courts, the presiding magistrate in each court draws one ticket out of each chest (making ten in all, one out of each tribe), and throws them into another empty chest. He then draws out five of them, and assigns one to the superintendence of the water-clock, and the other four to the telling of the votes. This is to prevent any tampering beforehand with either the superintendent of the clock or the tellers of the votes, and to secure that there is no malpractice in these respects. The five who have not been selected for these duties receive from them a statement of the order in which the jurors shall receive their fees, and of the places where the several tribes shall respectively gather in the court for this purpose when their duties are completed; the object being that the jurors may be broken up into small groups for the reception of their pay, and not all crowd together and impede one another.

67 · These preliminaries being concluded, the cases are called on. If it is a day for private cases, the private litigants are called. Four cases are taken in each of the categories defined in the law, and the litigants swear to confine their speeches to the point at issue. If it is a day for public causes, the public litigants are called, and only one case is tried. Water-clocks are provided, having small supply-tubes, into which the water is poured by which the length of the pleadings is regulated. Ten gallons are allowed for a case in which an amount of more than five thousand drachmas is involved, and three for the second speech on each side. When the amount is between one and five thousand drachmas, seven gallons are allowed for the first speech and two for the second; when it is less than one thousand, five and two. Six gallons are allowed for arbitrations between rival claimants, in which there is no second speech. The official chosen by lot to superintend the water-clock places his hand on the supply-tube whenever the clerk is about to read a resolution or law or affidavit or treaty. When, however, a case is conducted according to a set measurement of the day, he does not stop the supply, but each party receives an equal allowance of water. The standard of measurement is the length of the days in the month Poseideon[6]. . . . The measured day is employed in cases when imprisonment, death, exile, loss of civil rights, or confiscation of goods is assigned as the penalty.

68 · Most of the courts consist of 500 members . . . ;[7] and when it is necessary to bring public cases before a jury of 1,000 members, two courts combine for the purpose, . . .[8] The ballot balls are made of bronze with stems running through the centre, half of them having the stem pierced and the other half solid. When the speeches are concluded, the officials assigned to the taking of the votes give each juror two ballot balls, one pierced and one solid. This is done in full view of the rival litigants, to secure that no one shall receive two pierced or two solid balls.

---

[6]The next ten lines in the papyrus are mutilated.
[7]The papyrus is mutilated at this point.
[8]The papyrus is mutilated here.

Then the official designated for the purpose takes away the jurors' staves, in return for which each one as he records his vote receives a brass voucher marked with the numeral 3 (because he gets three obols when he gives it up). This is to ensure that all shall vote; for no one can get a voucher unless he votes. Two urns, one of bronze and the other of wood, stand in the court, in distinct spots so that no one may surreptitiously insert ballot balls; in these the jurors record their votes. The bronze urn is for effective votes, the wooden for unused votes; and the bronze urn has a lid pierced so as to take only one ballot ball, in order that no one may put in two at a time.

When the jurors are about to vote, the crier demands first whether the litigants enter a protest against any of the evidence; for no protest can be received after the voting has begun. Then he proclaims again, 'The pierced ballot for the plaintiff, the solid for the defendant'; and the juror, taking his two ballot balls from the stand, with his hand closed over the stem so as not to show either the pierced or the solid ballot to the litigants, casts the one which is to count into the bronze urn, and the other into the wooden urn.

69 · When all the jurors have voted, the attendants take the urn containing the effective votes and discharge them on to a reckoning board having as many cavities as there are ballot balls, so that the effective votes, whether pierced or solid, may be plainly displayed and easily counted. Then the officials assigned to the taking of the votes tell them off on the board, the solid in one place and the pierced in another, and the crier announces the numbers of the votes, the pierced ballots being for the prosecutor and the solid for the defendant. Whichever has the majority is victorious; but if the votes are equal the verdict is for the defendant. Then, if damages have to be awarded, they vote again in the same way, first returning their pay-vouchers and receiving back their staves. Half a gallon of water is allowed to each party for the discussion of the damages. Finally, when all has been completed in accordance with the law, the jurors receive their pay in the order assigned by the lot.

FRAGMENTS

Selected and translated by
Jonathan Barnes and Gavin Lawrence

CONTENTS

PREFACE

In the twelfth volume of the Oxford Translation, Sir David Ross published a selection of fragments from Aristotle's lost works. Ross limited his attention to passages bearing upon Aristotle's dialogues and upon his logical and philosophical writings. He presented those passages at generous length, including large amounts of context and often transcribing several variants of the same report.

Like Ross, we have attempted to give a fairly full collection of the fragments of Aristotle's *juvenilia,* which have occupied much scholarly attention in the past five decades, and also of the texts relating to the more philosophically interesting of his lost works. But we have been less generous than Ross in matters of context, repetitious variants, and dubiously valuable reports.

Unlike Ross, we have paid some attention to the fragments of Aristotle's other lost works—fragments which account for some two thirds of our total information about the lost writings. Here we have, for want of space, been highly selective: our aim has been to give a fair sample of the range of Aristotle's intellectual concerns, as it is exhibited in the fragments, and at the same time to illustrate those parts of his work which are less well represented in the surviving treatises.

We have prefaced the selection with a translation of the Catalogue of Aristotle's works; and we have closed it with versions of his letters and of his poems.

All the translations have been done afresh from the originals; but we have based ourselves on Ross's versions where those are available, and for the fragments of the *Protrepticus* we have leaned heavily on Düring's translation. As for the Greek texts, we have generally taken the latest, or the standard, editions of the various authors concerned. For much of the *Protrepticus* we have again made use of Düring's work; for *On Ideas* we have followed Harlfinger's edition of the text of Alexander.

We present the passages in the order in which they occur in Rose's third edition of the *Fragmenta* (Teubner, Leipzig, 1886). "*F 1 R³*" thus refers to fragment one in this edition. The few passages not occurring there have been interpolated at the most appropriate points. We have retained Rose's division of the fragments into ten categories. Rose's arrangement is not ideal; but we felt that, on balance, any fresh arrangement would have caused more inconvenience than it produced enlightenment.

Finally, a few words of caution. Most of the passages we print are not, in the strict sense, fragments of Aristotle's lost works: most of the passages do not purport to quote Aristotle's actual words. Rather, they offer paraphrases or summaries of his opinions and arguments; and in many cases they are little more than casual allusions to his views. Some of the passages we quote refer to works which were in all probability not written by Aristotle at all; several of the passages may plausibly be construed as relaxed allusions to the extant treatises rather than as close paraphrases of lost works; and in some cases—and those not the least celebrated— we ourselves are not convinced that any genuinely Aristotelian matter is conserved.

J.B.

G.L.

CATALOGUE OF ARISTOTLE'S WRITINGS

(Diogenes Laertius, V 22–27)

He wrote a vast number of books, which I have thought it appropriate to list because of the man's excellence in all fields of enquiry:—

On Justice, 4 books
On Poets, 3 books
On Philosophy, 3 books
On the Statesman, 2 books
On Rhetoric, or Grylus, 1 book
Nerinthus, 1 book
Sophist, 1 book
Menexenus, 1 book
Eroticus, 1 book
Symposium, 1 book
On Wealth, 1 book
Protrepticus, 1 book
On the Soul, 1 book
On Prayer, 1 book
On Good Birth, 1 book
On Pleasure, 1 book
Alexander, or On behalf of Colonies, 1 book
On Kingship, 1 book
On Education, 1 book
On the Good, 3 books
Excerpts from Plato's Laws, 3 books
Excerpts from Plato's Republic, 2 books
Economics, 1 book
On Friendship, 1 book
On being affected or having been affected, 1 book
On the Sciences, 2 books
On Eristics, 2 books
Eristical Solutions, 4 books
Sophistical Divisions, 4 books
On Contraries, 1 book
On Genera and Species, 1 book
On Properties, 1 book

Notes on Arguments, 3 books
Propositions on Excellence, 3 books
Objections, 1 book
On things spoken of in many ways or by addition, 1 book
On Feelings or On Anger, 1 book
Ethics, 5 books
On Elements, 3 books
On Knowledge, 1 book
On Principles, 1 book
Divisions, 16 books
Division, 1 book
On Question and Answer, 2 books
On Motion, 2 books
Propositions, 1 book
Eristical Propositions, 4 books
Deductions, 1 book
Prior Analytics, 9 books
Great Posterior Analytics, 2 books
On Problems, 1 book
Methodics, 8 books
On what is better, 1 book
On the Idea, 1 book
Definitions prior to the Topics, 1 book
Topics, 7 books
Deductions, 2 books
Deduction and Definitions, 1 book
On the desirable and on accidents, 1 book
Pre-topics, 1 book
Topics aimed at definitions, 2 books
Feelings, 1 book
Division, 1 book
Mathematics, 1 book
Definitions, 13 books

Arguments, 2 books
On Pleasure, 1 book
Propositions, 1 book
On the Voluntary, 1 book
On the Noble, 1 book
Argumentative theses, 25 books
Theses on love, 4 books
Theses on friendship, 2 books
Theses on the soul, 1 book
Politics, 2 books
Lectures on Politics (like those of Theophrastus), 8 books
On Just Acts, 2 books
Collection of Arts, 2 books
Art of Rhetoric, 2 books
Art, 1 book
Art (another work), 2 books
Methodics, 1 book
Collection of the Art of Theodectes, 1 book
Treatise on the Art of Poetry, 2 books
Rhetorical Enthymemes, 1 book
On Magnitude, 1 book
Divisions of Enthymemes, 1 book
On Diction, 2 books
On Advice, 1 book
Collection, 2 books
On Nature, 3 books
Nature, 1 book
On the Philosophy of Archytas, 3 books
On the Philosophy of Speusippus and Xenocrates, 1 book
Excerpts from the Timaeus and from the works of Archytas, 1 book
Against Melissus, 1 book
Against Alcmaeon, 1 book
Against the Pythagoreans, 1 book
Against Gorgias, 1 book
Against Xenophanes, 1 book
Against Zeno, 1 book
On the Pythagoreans, 1 book
On Animals, 9 books
Dissections, 8 books

Selection of Dissections, 1 book
On Composite Animals, 1 book
On Mythological Animals, 1 book
On Sterility, 1 book
On Plants, 2 books
Physiognomonics, 1 book
Medicine, 2 books
On Units, 1 book
Storm Signs, 1 book
Astronomy, 1 book
Optics, 1 book
On Motion, 1 book
On Music, 1 book
Memory, 1 book
Homeric Problems, 6 books
Poetics, 1 book
Physics (alphabetically ordered), 38 books
Additional Problems,[1] 2 books
Standard Problems, 2 books
Mechanics, 1 book
Problems from Democritus, 2 books
On the Magnet, 1 book
Conjunctions of Stars, 1 book
Miscellaneous, 12 books
Explanations[2] (arranged by subject), 14 books
Claims, 1 book
Olympic Victors, 1 book
Pythian Victors in Music,[3] 1 book
On Pytho, 1 book
Lists of Pythian Victors, 1 book
Victories at the Dionysia, 1 book
On Tragedies, 1 book
Didascaliae, 1 book
Proverbs, 1 book
Rules for Messing, 1 book
Laws, 4 books
Categories, 1 book
On Interpretation, 1 book
Constitutions of 158 States (arranged by type: democratic, oligarchical, tyrannical, aristocratic)

---

[1] Reading ἐπιτεθειμένων.   [2] Text uncertain.   [3] Reading Πυθιονῖκαι μουσικῆς ά.

Letters to Philip
Letters about the Selymbrians[4]
Letters to Alexander (4), to Antipater (9), to Mentor (1), to Ariston (1), to Olympias (1), to Hephaestion (1), to Themistagoras (1), to Philoxenus (1), to Democritus (1)

Poems, beginning: "Holy one, most honoured of the gods, far-shooting . . . "
Elegies, beginning: "Daughter of a mother of fair children . . . "

Appendix:

(A) Titles found in the *Vita Menagiana* but not in Diogenes:

Peplos
Hesiodic Problems,[5] 1 book
Metaphysics, 10 books
Cycle on Poets, 3 books
Sophistical Refutations or On Eristics
Prior Analytics, 2 books
Messing Problems, 3 books
On Blessedness, or Why did Homer invent the cattle of the sun?
Problems from Archilochus, Euripides, Choerilus, 3 books
Poetical Problems, 1 book
Poetical Explanations
Lectures on Physics, 16 books
On Generation and Destruction, 2 books
Meteorologica, 4 books
On the Soul, 3 books
History of Animals, 10 books
Movement of Animals, 3 books

Parts of Animals, 3 books
Generation of Animals, 3 books
On the Rising of the Nile
On Substance in Mathematics
On Reputation
On Voice
On the Common Life of Husband and Wife
Laws for Man and Wife
On Time
On Vision, 2 books
Nicomachean Ethics
Art of Eulogy
On Marvellous Things heard
Eulogies or Hymns
On Differentia
On the Nature of Man
On the Generation of the World
Customs of the Romans
Collection of Foreign Customs

(B) Titles in the *Life* of Ptolemy but neither in Diogenes nor in the *Vita Menagiana:*

On Indivisible Lines, 3 books
On Spirit, 3 books
On Hibernation, 1 book
Magna Moralia, 2 books
On the Heavens and the Universe, 4 books
On Sense and Sensibilia, 1 book
On Memory and Sleep, 1 book
On Length and Shortness of Life, 1 book

Problems of Matter, 1 book
Platonic Divisions, 6 books
Divisions of Hypotheses, 6 books
Precepts, 4 books
On Regimen, 1 book
Farming, 15 books
On the Moist, 1 book
On the Dry, 1 book
On Relatives, 1 book

[4]Reading περὶ Σηλυμβριανῶν.   [5]Reading Ἡσιοδείων for θείων.

I · DIALOGUES

F 1-111 R³

(Cicero, ad Atticum *IV xvi 2):*
... since I am having a preface in each book, as Aristotle does in the books he calls exoteric ...

(Cicero, ad Atticum *XIII xix 4):*
In what I have written recently, I have followed the Aristotelian custom, according to which the conversation of the others is so arranged that the writer himself has the chief part.

(Plutarch, adversus Colotem *1115BC):*
As for the Ideas, over which he upbraids Plato, Aristotle attacks them everywhere and introduces all the puzzles about them—in his ethical works, in his metaphysics, in his physics, in his exoteric dialogues: to some he seemed more ambitious than philosophical ... [1] these doctrines, as though proposing to subvert Plato's philosophy; so far was he from following Plato.

(Numenius, apud *Eusebius,* Praeparatio Evangelica *XIV vi 9–10):*
Cephisodorus, when he saw his master Isocrates being attacked by Aristotle, was ignorant of and unversed in Aristotle himself; but, seeing the repute which Plato's views enjoyed, he thought that Aristotle was following Plato. So he waged war on Aristotle, but was really attacking Plato. His criticism began with the Ideas and finished with the other doctrines—things which he himself did not know; he was only guessing at the meaning of the opinions held about them. This Cephisodorus was not attacking the person he was at war with, but was attacking the person he did not wish to make war upon.

(Asclepius, Commentarius in Metaphysica *112. 16–19):*
About these first principles, he [sc. Aristotle] says, we have already spoken in the *Physics;* and he promises to speak about these in Book α [sc. of the *Metaphysics*], and to raise and solve the puzzles about them in the work *On Philosophy.*

F 1 R³ (Plutarch, adversus Colotem *1118C):*
Of the inscriptions at Delphi that which was thought to be the most divine was "Know Thyself"; it was this, as Aristotle has said in his Platonic works, that started Socrates off puzzling and inquiring.

---

[1]Pohlenz marks a lacuna.

F 2 R³ (Diogenes Laertius, II 23):
Aristotle says that he [sc. Socrates] went to Delphi.

F 3 R³ (Porphyry apud Stobaeus, Anthologium III xxi 26):
What and whose was the sacred injunction at Delphi, which bids him who is to seek anything from the god to know himself? . . . or was it even before the time of Chilon already inscribed in the temple that was founded after the one of feathers and bronze, as Aristotle has said in his work *On Philosophy*?

F 4 R³ (Clement, Stromateis I xiv 61.2):
Aristotle and his followers think that it [sc. "Give a pledge and you're ruined"] comes from Chilon.

F 5 R³ (Etymologicon Magnum *s.v. σοφιστής):*
Aristotle calls the Seven Sages sophists.

F 6 R³ (Diogenes Laertius, I 8):
Aristotle in the first book of *On Philosophy* says that they [sc. the Magi] are more ancient than the Egyptians, and that according to them there are two first principles, a good spirit and an evil spirit, one called Zeus and Oromasdes, the other Hades and Arimanius.

F 7 R³ (Philoponus, Commentarius in de Anima 186. 24–26):
Aristotle says "so-called . . . " because the poems are thought not to be the work of Orpheus, as he himself says in the books *On Philosophy*: the opinions are those of Orpheus, but they say that Onomacritus set them to verse.

F 7 R³ (Cicero, de natura deorum I xxxviii 107):
Aristotle says the poet Orpheus never existed; the Pythagoreans ascribe this Orphic poem to a certain Cercon.

(Sextus Empiricus, adversus mathematicos X 46):
Its existence [i.e. the existence of motion] is denied by Parmenides and Melissus, whom Aristotle has called immobilists[1] and unnaturalists—immobilists because they maintain the immobility of things, unnaturalists because nature is a source of motion and in saying that nothing moves they abolished nature.

F 8 R³ (Proclus, apud Philoponus, de aeternitate mundi II 2):
. . . and in his dialogues, where he [sc. Aristotle] announces most clearly that he cannot agree with this doctrine [sc. the Theory of Ideas], even if he should be thought to be opposing it from ambition.

[1]Omitting τῆς φύσεως.

F 9 R³ (Syrianus, Commentarius in Metaphysica *159.35–160.3):*

This is shown by what he [sc. Aristotle] says in the second book of the work *On Philosophy:* "Thus if the Ideas are a different sort of number, not mathematical number, we can have no understanding of it; for of the majority of us, at all events, who understands any other number?"

(Alexander, Commentarius in Metaphysica *117.23–118.1):*

Aristotle sets out their view, which he has also stated in the work *On Philosophy.* Wishing to refer the things that exist (he always calls the things that exist substances) to the first principles which they assumed (for them the first principles of existing things were the great and the small, which they called the indefinite dyad)—wishing to refer everything to this, they said that the first principles of length were the short and the long (on the grounds that length takes its origin from a long and short, i.e. a great and small, or that every line falls under one or other of these), and that the first principles of the plane were the narrow and wide, which are themselves also great and small.

(Simplicius, Commentarius in de Anima *28.7–9):*

Aristotle now [sc. in the *de Anima*] applies the name *On Philosophy* to his work *On the Good* (taken down from Plato's seminar), in which he relates both the Pythagorean and the Platonic opinions about what exists.

([Alexander], Commentarius in Metaphysica *777.16–21):*

The principle of the One, he [sc. Aristotle] says, they did not all introduce in the same way. Some said that the numbers themselves introduced the Forms into magnitudes, e.g. the number 2 doing so for line, the number 3 for plane, the number 4 for solid (Aristotle relates this about Plato in the work *On Philosophy,* and that is why he here [sc. in the *Metaphysics*] expounds their theory only briefly and concisely); while others explained the form of the magnitudes by participation in the One.

F 10 R³ (Sextus Empiricus, adversus mathematicos *IX 20–23):*

Aristotle used to say that men's concept of god sprang from two sources—the experiences of the soul and the phenomena of the heavens. From the experiences of the soul, because of its inspiration and prophetic power in dreams. For, he says, when the soul gets by itself in sleep, it then assumes its nature and foresees and foretells the future. The soul is also in such a condition when it is severed from the body at death. At all events, he accepts even Homer as having observed this; for he has represented Patroclus, in the moment of his death, as foretelling the death of Hector, and Hector as foretelling the end of Achilles. It was from such events, he says, that men came to suspect the existence of something divine, of something in itself akin to the soul and of all things most knowledgeable. And from the heavenly bodies too: seeing by day the revolution of the sun and by night the well-ordered movement of the other stars, they came to think that there was a god who is the cause of such movement and order.

F 12 R³ (Cicero, de natura deorum *II xxxvii 95):*

Thus Aristotle brilliantly remarks: 'Suppose there were men who had always lived underground, in good and well-lighted dwellings, adorned with statues and pictures, and furnished with everything in which those who are thought happy abound. Suppose, however, that they had never gone above ground, but had learned by report and hearsay that there was a divine spirit and power. Suppose that then, at some time, the jaws of the earth opened, and they were able to escape and make their way from those hidden dwellings into these regions which we inhabit. When they suddenly saw earth and seas and skies, when they learned the grandeur of clouds and the power of winds, when they saw the sun and realized not only its grandeur and beauty but also its power, by which it fills the sky with light and makes the day; when, again, night darkened the lands and they saw the whole sky picked out and adorned with stars, and the varying light of the moon as it waxes and wanes, and the risings and settings of all these bodies, and their courses settled and immutable to all eternity; when they saw those things, most certainly would they have judged both that there are gods and that these great works are the works of gods'. Thus far Aristotle.

F 14 R³ (Seneca, quaestiones naturales *VII xxx 1):*

Aristotle excellently says that we should nowhere be more modest than in discussions about the gods. If we compose ourselves before we enter temples, . . . how much more should we do so when we discuss the constellations, the stars, and the nature of the gods, lest from temerity or impudence we should make ignorant assertions or knowingly tell lies.

F 15 R³ (Synesius, Dio *48A):*

. . . as Aristotle claims that those who are being initiated are not to learn anything but to experience something and be put into a certain condition . . .

F 16 R³ (Alexander, apud *Simplicius,* Commentarius in de Caelo *289.1–15):*

He [sc. Aristotle] speaks of this in his *On Philosophy.* In general, where there is a better there is also a best. Since, then, among existing things one is better than another, there is also something that is best, which will be the divine. Now that which changes is changed either by something else or by itself, and if by something else, either by something better or by something worse, and if by itself, either to something worse or through desire for something nobler. But the divine has nothing better than itself by which it will be changed (for that other thing would then have been more divine), nor is it right for the better to be affected by the worse; besides, if it were changed by something worse, it would have admitted something bad into itself—and nothing in it is bad. Nor yet does it change itself through desire for something nobler, since it lacks none of its own nobilities; nor yet does it change itself for the worse, since not even a man willingly makes himself worse, nor does it possess anything bad such as it would have acquired from a change to the worse. This proof too Aristotle took over from the second book of Plato's *Republic.*

F 17 R³ (Scholia in Proverbia Salomonis, cod. Paris gr. 174, fol. 46a):

Aristotle: 'There is either one first principle or many. If there is one, we have what we are looking for; if there are many, they are either ordered or disordered. Now if they are disordered, their products are more so, and the world is not a world but a chaos; and that which is contrary to nature exists while that which is in accordance with nature does not exist. If on the other hand they are ordered, they were ordered either by themselves or by some outside cause. But if they were ordered by themselves, they have something common that joins them, and that is the first principle'.

F 18 R³ (Philo, de aeternitate mundi III 10–11):

Aristotle was surely speaking piously and devoutly when he objected that the world is ungenerated and imperishable, and convicted of grave ungodliness those who maintained the opposite and thought that the great visible god, which contains in truth sun and moon and the remaining pantheon of planets and fixed stars is no different from an artefact; he used to say in mockery (we are told) that in the past he had been afraid for his house lest it be destroyed by violent winds or by fierce storms or by time or by lack of proper maintenance, but that now a greater fear hung over him, from those who by an argument were destroying the whole world.

F 19 R³ (Philo, de aeternitate mundi V 20–24):

The arguments which prove the world to be ungenerated and imperishable should, out of respect for the visible god, be given their proper precedence and placed earlier in the discussion. All things that admit of being destroyed are subject to two causes of destruction, one inward, the other outward. Iron, bronze and such-like substances you will find being destroyed from themselves, when rust invades and devours them like a creeping disease, and from without when a house or city is set on fire and they catch fire from it and are destroyed by the fierce rush of flame; and similarly death comes to living beings from themselves when they fall sick, and from outside when they have their throats cut or are stoned or burned to death or suffer the unclean death by hanging. Thus if the world, too, is destroyed, it must be either by something outside or by one of the powers in itself. Now each of these is impossible. For there is nothing outside the world, since all things have contributed to its completeness. For so will it be one, whole, and ageless: one, because if some things had been left out another world like the present world would come into being; whole, because all substance has been expended on it; ageless and diseaseless, because bodies caught by disease and old age are destroyed by the violent assault from without of heat and cold and the other contrary forces, none of which powers can escape and circle round and attack the world, since all without exception are entirely enclosed within it. If then there *is* anything outside, it must be a complete void or an impassive nature which cannot suffer or do anything. Nor again will the world be destroyed by anything within it—first, because the part would then be both greater and more powerful than the whole, which is most absurd; for the world, wielding unsurpassable power, directs all its parts and is directed by none; secondly, because, there being two causes of destruction, one within and one without, things that can suffer the one are susceptible also to the other. Oxen and horses and men and such-like animals, because they can be destroyed by iron, will also perish by disease. For it is hard, or rather impossible, to find anything that is naturally subject to the external cause of destruction and entirely insusceptible to the internal. Since, then, it was shown that the world will not be destroyed by anything without, because absolutely nothing has been left outside, neither will it be destroyed by anything within, because of the preceding demonstration to the effect that that which is susceptible to the one cause is also by nature susceptible to the other.

F 20 R³ (Philo, de aeternitate mundi *VI 28-VII 34):*

This may be put in another way. Of composite bodies all that are destroyed are dissolved into their components; dissolution is then nothing but return to the natural state of each thing, so that conversely composition has forced into an unnatural state the parts that have come together. And indeed it seems to be so beyond a doubt. For we men were put together by borrowing little parts of the four elements, which belong in their entirety to the whole universe—earth, water, air and fire. Now these parts when mixed are robbed of their natural position, the upward-travelling heat being forced down, the earthy and heavy substance being made light and seizing in turn the upper region, which is occupied by the earthiest of our parts, the head. The worst of bonds is that which is fastened by violence; this is brief and shortlived, for it is broken sooner by the things bound, because they shake it off through longing for their natural movement, to which they hasten to return. For, as the tragic poet says, "Things born of earth return to earth, things born of an ethereal seed return to the pole of heaven again; nothing that comes into being dies; one departs in one direction, one in another, and each shows its own form."[1] For all things that perish, then, this is the law and this is the rule prescribed—when the parts that have come together in the mixture have settled down they must in place of their natural order have accepted disorder, and must move to the opposite places, so that they seem to be in a sense exiles; but when they are separated they turn back to their natural lot. Now the world has no part in the disorder which is found in the things we have spoken of. For let us consider: if the world is perishing, its parts must now each have been arranged in a region unnatural to it. But this it is not right to suppose; for to all the parts of the world have fallen perfect position and harmonious arrangement, so that each, as though fond of its own country, seeks no change to a better. For this reason, then, earth was assigned the midmost position, to which all

[1] Euripides, frag. 836 Nauck.

earthy things, even if you throw them up, descend. This is an indication of their natural place; for that region in which a thing brought thither stays and rests, when under no compulsion, is its allotted home. Water is spread over the earth, and air and fire have moved from the middle to the upper region, to air falling the region between water and fire, and to fire the highest region of all. And so, even if you light a torch and throw it to the ground, the flame will none the less strive against you and lighten itself and return to the natural motion of fire. If, then, the cause of destruction of other creatures is their unnatural situation, but in the world each of its parts is arranged according to nature and has its proper place assigned to it, the world may justly be called imperishable.

F 21 R³ (Philo, de aeternitate mundi *VIII 39–43):*

The most demonstrative argument is that on which I know countless people to pride themselves, as on something most precise and quite irrefutable. They ask why god should destroy the world. Either to save himself from continuing in world-making, or in order to make another world. The former of these purposes is alien to god; for what befits him is to turn disorder into order, not order into disorder; and further, he would be admitting a change of mind, and hence an affection and disease of the soul. For he should either not have made a world at all, or else, if he judged the work becoming to him, should have rejoiced in the product. The second alternative deserves full examination. For if in place of the present world he is to make another, the world he makes is bound to be either worse or like or better, and each of these possibilities is open to objection. If it is worse, its artificer too will be worse; but the works of god are blameless, free from criticism and incapable of improvement, fashioned as they are by the most perfect art and knowledge. For, as the saying goes, 'not even a woman is so lacking in good judgement as to prefer the worse when the better is available'; and it is fitting for god to give shape to the shapeless and to deck the ugliest things with marvellous beauties. If the new world is like the old, its artificer will have laboured in vain, differing in nothing from silly children, who often when playing on the beach make great piles of sand and then undermine them with their hands and pull them down again. Much better than making a similar world would be neither to take away nor to add anything, nor change anything for better or for worse, but to leave the original world in its place. If he is to make a better world, the artificer himself must become better, so that when he made the former world he must have been more imperfect both in art and in wisdom—which it is not right even to suspect. For god is equal and like to himself, admitting neither slackening towards the worse nor tautening towards the better.

F 22 R³ (Cicero, Academica *II xxxviii 119):*

When your Stoic sage has said all these things to you syllable by syllable, Aristotle will come, pouring out his golden flow, to say that the Stoic is talking nonsense; he will say that the world was never generated, because there was never a beginning based on a new plan for such a brilliant work, and that it is so well designed in every part that no force can effect such great movements and so great a change, and no old age can come upon the world by lapse of time, so that this splendid world should ever fall to pieces and perish.

F 23 R³ (Cicero, de natura deorum II xv 42):

Since some living things have their origin in earth, others in water, others in air, Aristotle thinks that it is absurd to suppose that in that part which is fittest to generate living things no animal should be born. Now the stars occupy the ethereal region; and since that region is the most rare and is always in movement and activity, any animal born in it must have the keenest perception and the swiftest movement. Thus since it is in ether that the stars are born, it is proper that in these there should be perception and intelligence. From which it follows that the stars should be reckoned among the gods.

F 24 R³ (Cicero, de natura deorum II xvi 44):

Aristotle is to be praised, too, for judging that all things that move do so either by nature or by force or voluntarily, and that the sun and moon and all the stars are in movement, and that things that move by nature are carried either downwards by their weight or upwards by their lightness, neither of which happens to the stars, because their movement is in an orbit or circle. Nor again can it be said that some greater force makes the stars move contrary to nature; for what force can be greater? What remains, then, is that the movement of the stars is voluntary.

F 25 R³ (Censorinus, de die natali XVIII 11):

There is, further, the year which Aristotle calls greatest (rather than great), which the spheres of the sun, the moon and the five wandering stars complete when they return together to the same point where once they were all together; the winter of such a year is a great cataclysm or flood, the summer an ecpyrosis or conflagration of the world; for at these alternate periods the world seems now to be consumed in fire, now to be covered in water.

F 26 R³ (Cicero, de natura deorum I xiii 33):

Aristotle, in the third book of his *On Philosophy,* creates much confusion by dissenting from his master Plato. For now he ascribes all divinity to mind, now he says that the world itself is a god, now he sets another god over the world and ascribes to him the part of ruling and preserving the movement of the world by a sort of backward rotation. Then he says that the heat of the heavens is a god, not realising that the heavens are a part of the world, which he has himself elsewhere called a god.

(Cicero, Academica I vii 26):

The fifth kind, from which are made stars and minds, Aristotle thought to be something distinct, and unlike the four I have mentioned above.

(Cicero, Tusculanae disputationes *I x 22):*

Aristotle, who far exceeded all others—Plato I always except—both in intellect and in industry, after taking account of the four well-known kinds of first principles from which all things were derived, considers that there is a fifth kind of thing, from which comes mind; for thought, foresight, learning, teaching, discovery, remembering many things, love and hate, desire and fear, distress and joy, these and their like he thinks cannot be included in any of those four kinds; he adds a fifth kind, which lacks a name, and so he calls the mind itself by a new name, ἐνδελέχεια, as being a sort of continuous and endless movement.

(Aristoxenus, Elementa harmonica *II 30–31):*

This, as Aristotle was always saying, was the experience of most of those who heard Plato's lecture *On the Good.* Each of them attended on the assumption that he would hear about one of the recognised human goods—such as wealth, health, strength, and in general some marvellous happiness. When Plato's lectures turned out to be about mathematics—numbers, geometry, astronomy—and to crown all about the thesis that the good[1] is one, it seemed to them, I fancy, something quite paradoxical; and so some people despised the whole thing, while others criticised it.

(Philoponus, Commentarius in de Anima *75.34–76.1):*

By the books *On Philosophy* Aristotle means the work entitled *On the Good;* in this Aristotle reports Plato's unwritten seminars; the work is genuine. He relates there the view of Plato and the Pythagoreans about what exists and about first principles.

*F 27 R³ (*Vita Aristotelis Latina *33):*

In the work *On the Good* he says: 'Not only he who is in luck but also he who offers a proof should remember he is a man'.

F 28 R³ (Alexander, Commentarius in Metaphysica *55.20–56.35):*

Both Plato and the Pythagoreans assumed numbers to be the first principles of existing things, because they thought that that which is primary and incomposite is a first principle, and that planes are prior to bodies (for that which is simpler and not destroyed along with something else is primary by nature), and on the same principle lines are prior to planes, and points (which the mathematicians call *sêmeia* but they called units) to lines, being completely incomposite and having nothing prior to them; but units are numbers; therefore numbers are the first of existing things. And since Forms or Ideas are prior to the things which according to him have their being in relation to them and derive their being from them (the existence of these he tried in several ways to establish), he said that the Forms are numbers.

---

[1]Reading τἀγαθόν.

For if that which is one in kind is prior to the things that exist in relation to it, and nothing is prior to number, the Forms are numbers. This is why he also said that the first principles of number are first principles of the Forms, and the One is the first principle of all things.

Again, the Forms are the first principles of all other things, and the first principles of number are first principles of Ideas since they are numbers; and he used to say that the first principles of number are the unit and the dyad. For, since there are in numbers both the One and that which is other than the One (i.e. the many and the few), he assumed that the first thing there is in number, apart from the One, is the first principle both of the many and of the few. Now the dyad is the first thing apart from the One, having in itself both manyness and fewness; for the double is many and the half is few, and these are in the dyad; and the dyad is contrary to the One, since the latter is indivisible and the former is divided.

Again, thinking to prove that the equal and the unequal are first principles of all things, both of things that exist in their own right and of opposites (for he tried to refer all things to these as their simplest elements), he assigned equality to the monad, and inequality to excess and defect; for inequality involves two things, a great and a small, which are excessive and defective. This is why he called it an indefinite dyad—because neither the excessive nor the exceeded is, as such, definite; they are indefinite and unlimited. But when limited by the One the indefinite dyad, he says, becomes the numerical dyad; for this kind of dyad is one in form.

Again, the dyad is the first number; its first principles are the excessive and the exceeded, since it is in the dyad that the double and the half are first found; for while the double and the half are excessive and exceeded, the excessive and the exceeded are not thereby double and half; so that these are elements of the double. And since the excessive and the exceeded when they have been limited become double and half (for these are no longer indefinite, nor is the treble and third, or the quadruple and quarter, or anything else that already has its excess limited), and this is effected by the nature of the One (for each thing is one in so far as it is a 'this' and is limited), the One and the great and the small must be elements in the numerical dyad. But the dyad is the first number. These then are the elements in the dyad. It is for some such reasons that Plato used to treat the One and the dyad as the first principles both of numbers and of all existing things, as Aristotle says in his work *On the Good*.

F 28 R³ (Simplicius, Commentarius in Physica *151.6–11):*

Alexander says that according to Plato the first principles of all things, and of the Ideas themselves, are the One and the indefinite dyad, which he used to call great and small, as Aristotle relates in his work *On the Good*. One might gather this also from Speusippus and Xenocrates and the others who were present at Plato's lecture on the Good; for they all wrote down and preserved his doctrine, and they say he used these as first principles.

F 28 R³ (Simplicius, Commentarius in Physica *453.25–30):*

They say that Plato maintained that the One and the indefinite dyad were the first principles of sensible things as well. He placed the indefinite dyad also among the objects of thought and said it was unlimited, and he made the great and the small first principles and said they were unlimited, in his lectures on the Good; Aristotle, Heraclides, Hestiaeus, and other associates of Plato attended these and wrote them down in the enigmatic style in which they were delivered.

F 29 R³ (Sextus Empiricus, adversus mathematicos *III 57–58):*

But Aristotle says . . . that the length without breadth of which they [sc. the geometers] speak is not inconceivable, but that we can without any difficulty arrive at the thought of it. He rests his argument on a rather clear and illuminating example: we grasp the length of a wall, he says, without considering also its breadth, so that it must be possible to conceive of the length without any particular breadth of which the geometers speak—for the phenomena are our way of seeing what is non-evident.

F 30 R³ (Alexander, Commentarius in Metaphysica *59.28–60.2):*

One might ask how it is that, though Plato mentions both an efficient cause . . . and also that for the sake of which and the end . . . , Aristotle mentions neither of these causes in his account of Plato's doctrines. Is it because he mentioned neither of them in what he said about causes (as he has shown in *On the Good*), or because he does not treat these as causes of things that come into being and perish, and did not even work out any theory about them?

F 31 R³ (Alexander, Commentarius in Metaphysica *250.17–20):*

For the proof that practically all contraries are referred to the One and plurality as their first principle, Aristotle sends us to the *Selection of Contraries,* where he has treated expressly of the subject. He has also spoken about this selection in the second book *On the Good.*

F 34 R³ (Pliny, naturalis historia *XXX ii 3):*

Eudoxus related that this Zoroaster lived six thousand years before the death of Plato; Aristotle agrees.

F 37 R³ (Cicero, de divinatione *I xxv 53):*

What, is the singular, the almost divine, intellect of Aristotle in error, or does he wish others to fall into error, when he writes that his friend Eudemus of Cyprus while on a journey to Macedonia came to Pherae, a Thessalian town of considerable note at that time, but held in cruel subjection by the tyrant Alexander? Now in that town, he says, Eudemus fell so ill that all the doctors feared for his life. He dreamed

that a handsome young man told him that he would soon recover, that in a few days
the tyrant Alexander would die, and that five years later Eudemus himself would
return home. And indeed, Aristotle writes, the first two predictions were fulfilled
forthwith: Eudemus recovered and the tyrant was killed by his wife's brothers. But
towards the end of the fifth year, when the dream had led him to hope that he would
return from Sicily to Cyprus, he died in battle at Syracuse. And so the dream was
interpreted as meaning that when Eudemus' soul had left his body it had returned to
its home.

(al-Kindi, cod. Taimuriyye Falsafa 55):

Aristotle tells of the Greek king whose soul was caught up in ecstasy, and who
for many days remained neither alive nor dead. When he came to himself, he told
the bystanders of various things in the invisible world, and related what he had
seen—souls, forms, and angels; he gave the proofs of this by foretelling to all his
acquaintances how long each of them would live. All he had said was put to the
proof, and no-one exceeded the span of life that he had assigned. He prophesied too
that after a year a chasm would open in the country of Elis, and after two years a
flood would occur in another place; and everything happened as he had said.
Aristotle asserts that the reason for this was that his soul had acquired this
knowledge just because it had been near to leaving his body and had been in a
certain way separated from it, and so had seen what it had seen. How much greater
marvels of the upper world of the kingdom would it have seen, then, if it had really
left his body.

F 38 R³ (Themistius, Commentarius in de Anima *106.29–107.4):*

Almost all the weightiest arguments that he [sc. Plato] used about the
immortality of the soul make reference to the intellect. . . . as is also the case with
the more convincing of those worked out by Aristotle himself in the *Eudemus.*

F 39 R³ (Elias, Commentarius in Categorias *114.25–115.3):*

Aristotle establishes the immortality of the soul in his acroamatic works as
well, and there he establishes it by compelling arguments; but in the dialogues he
naturally uses plausible arguments. . . . In his dialogues he says that the soul is
immortal because all we men instinctively make libations to the departed and swear
by them, but no-one ever makes a libation to or swears by that which is completely
non-existent . . . [115.11–12]. It is chiefly in his dialogues that Aristotle seems to
announce the immortality of the soul.

F 40 R³ (Proclus, Commentarius in Timaeum *323.31–324.4):*

Aristotle in emulation of him [sc. Plato] treats scientifically of the soul in the
de Anima, saying nothing either about its descent or about its fortunes; but in his
dialogues he dealt separately with those matters and set down the preliminary
discussion.

F 41 R³ (Proclus, Commentarius in Rem Publicam *II 349.13–26):*

The excellent Aristotle also gives the reason why the soul on coming hither from there forgets the sights it saw there, but on going hence remembers there its experiences here. We must accept the argument; for he himself says that on their journey from health to disease some people forget even the letters they have learned, but that no-one ever has this experience when passing from disease to health; and that life without the body, being natural to souls, is like health, and life in the body, as being unnatural, is like disease. For there they live according to nature, but here contrary to nature; so that it not unreasonably results that souls that pass thence forget the things there, while souls that pass hence thither continue to remember the things here.

F 42 R³ (Damascius, Commentarius in Phaedonem *530):*

That there must actually be a whole race of men which is nourished in this way is shown by the case of the man who was nourished by the sun's rays alone, as recorded by Aristotle from his own observation.

F 43 R³ (Plutarch, quaestiones convivales *733C):*

Aristotle has related how in Cilicia Timon's grandmother used to hibernate for two months each year, showing no sign of life apart from breathing.

F 44 R³ ([Plutarch], Consolatio ad Apollonium *115BE):*

Many wise men, as Crantor says, not of today but of long ago, have wept for the human lot, thinking life to be a punishment and birth the beginning of the greatest disaster for a man. Aristotle says that Silenus stated this opinion to Midas after he had been captured—but let me set down the philosopher's actual words; he says this in the work entitled *Eudemus* or *On the Soul:*

'For that reason, best and most blessed of all men, in addition to thinking that the dead are blessed and happy, we hold it impious to speak any falsehood about them or to slander them, since they have now become better and greater. And these customs are so ancient and long-established among us that no one at all knows when they began or who first established them, but they have been continuously acknowledged for an indefinite age. In addition to that, you observe the saying which has been on men's lips for many years'.

'What is that?', he said.

He said in reply: 'That not to be born is best of all, and to be dead better than to be alive. Heaven has given this testimony to many men. They say that when Midas had caught Silenus he interrogated him after the hunt and asked him what was the best thing for men and what the most desirable of all. Silenus at first would not say anything but maintained an unbroken silence; but when, after using every device, Midas with difficulty induced him to address him, he said under compulsion: "Shortlived seed of a toiling spirit and a harsh fortune, why do you force me to say what is better for you not to know? For a life lived in ignorance of its own ills is most painless. It is quite impossible for the best thing of all to befall men, nor can they share in the nature of what is better. For it is best, for all men and women, not to be born; and second after that—the first of things open to men—is, once born, to die as quickly as possible." It is clear that he meant that time spent dead is better than time spent alive'.

F 45 R³ (Philoponus, Commentarius in de Anima *141.33–142.6, 144.21–145.7):*

Some . . . thought that the soul was an attunement of the body, and that the different kinds of soul answered to the different attunements of the body. This opinion Aristotle states and refutes. In the present work [i.e. the *de Anima*] he first merely records the opinion itself, but a little later on he also sets out the arguments that led them to it. He had already opposed this opinion elsewhere—I mean, in the dialogue *Eudemus*—and before him Plato in the *Phaedo* had used five arguments against the view. . . .

These are Plato's five arguments. Aristotle himself, as I have said, has used the two following arguments in the dialogue *Eudemus.* One goes thus: 'Attunement', he says, 'has a contrary, lack of attunement; but the soul has no contrary. Therefore the soul is not an attunement'. . . . Secondly: 'The contrary of the attunement of the body is the lack of attunement of the body; and the lack of attunement of the living body is disease, weakness, and ugliness—of these, disease is lack of attunement of the elements, weakness lack of attunement of the uniform parts, ugliness lack of attunement of the instrumental parts. Now if lack of attunement is disease, weakness, and ugliness, then attunement is health, strength and beauty; but soul is none of these—I mean, neither health nor strength nor beauty; for even Thersites, the ugliest of men, had a soul. Therefore the soul is not an attunement'.

F 45 R³ (Damascius, Commentarius in Phaedonem *383):*

Aristotle in the *Eudemus* argues as follows: 'Lack of attunement is contrary to attunement; but soul has no contrary—for it is a substance. And the conclusion is obvious. Again, if the lack of attunement of the elements of an animal is disease, their attunement must be health, not soul'.

F 46 R³ (Simplicius, Commentarius in de Anima *221.28–30):*

And because of this he [sc. Aristotle] says in the *Eudemus,* his dialogue on the soul, that the soul is a sort of form. . .

F 47 R³ ([Plutarch], de musica *1139B):*

On the theme that harmony is something noble, divine and grand, Aristotle, the pupil of Plato, says: 'Harmony is heavenly, by nature divine, beautiful and inspired; having by nature four parts potentially, it has two means, the arithmetical and the harmonic, and the parts of it, their extents, and their excesses one over another, have numerical and proportionate relations; for tunes are arranged in two tetrachords.'

F 48 R³ (Olympiodorus, Commentarius in Phaedonem *9):*

Proclus would have heavenly bodies possess only sight and hearing, as Aristotle also would; for of the senses they have only those which contribute to well-being, not those that contribute to being, which is what the other senses do. The poet testifies to this, saying, "Sun, who seest and hearest all things"—which implies that the heavenly bodies have only sight and hearing. Also because these senses, most of all, have knowledge by way of activity rather than of passivity, and are fitter for the unchanging heavenly bodies.

F 49 R³ (Simplicius, Commentarius in de Caelo *485.19–22):*

That Aristotle has the notion of something above mind and substance is shown by his saying clearly at the end of his book *On Prayer* that god is either mind or something even beyond mind.

F 50 R³ (Stobaeus, Anthologium *IV xxxii 21):*

Zeno said that Crates, while sitting in a cobbler's workshop, read [B1][1] Aristotle's *Protrepticus* which he wrote to Themison, king of Cyprus, saying that no-one had more goods than he for devoting himself to philosophy; for he had great wealth, so that he could spend money on this, and a good reputation as well.

F 57 R³ (Oxyrrhynchus Papyrus 666; cf. Stobaeus, Anthologium *III iii 25):*

[B2] . . . prevents them from choosing and doing what they should; hence, contemplating the misfortune of these men, we ought to avoid it and believe that happiness consists not in the acquisition of much property but rather in the manner of the disposition of the soul. For one would not say that it is a body adorned with splendid clothing that is blessed, but one which is healthy and has a good disposition, even if it has none of the things just mentioned; in the same way, if the soul is educated, such a soul and such a man must be called happy, not the man splendidly adorned with external goods but himself worthless. It is not the horse that has a golden curb-chain and costly harness but whose nature is bad that we think worth anything; rather we praise the one that has a good disposition. [B 3] Besides, when worthless men get abundant possessions, they come to value these even more than the goods of the soul; and this is the basest of all conditions. For just as a man would be a laughing-stock if he were inferior to his own servants, so too those for whom possessions are more important than their own nature must be considered miserable. [B 4] This is indeed so: surfeit, as the proverb says, breeds insolence; lack of education combined with power breeds folly. For those who are ill-disposed in soul neither wealth nor strength nor beauty is good; the more lavishly one is endowed with these conditions, the more grievously and the more often they hurt him who possesses them but lacks understanding.[2] The saying 'No knife for a

---

[1]These signs refer to the fragments in Düring's edition.
[2]'Understanding' and its cognates here, and throughout the *Protrepticus* fragments, translate φρόνησις and its cognates.

child' means 'Do not give bad men power'. [B 5] But all men would agree that understanding comes from learning and from seeking the things that philosophy enables us to seek; surely, then, we should pursue philosophy unhesitatingly and. . .

F 51 R³ (Alexander, Commentarius in Topica *149.11–15):*

E.g. if someone were to say that one should not philosophize, then, since [B 6] to philosophize is both to inquire into the very question whether one should philosophize or not, as he [sc. Aristotle] himself said in the *Protrepticus,* and also to pursue philosophical contemplation, by showing that each of them is proper for a man we shall wholly refute the view stated.

(Iamblichus, Protrepticus *37.13–22 Pistelli):*

[B 9] Again, some kinds of knowledge produce the good things in life, others use the first kind; some are ancillary, others prescriptive; and in these last, as being more authoritative, rests the true good. If, then, only that kind of knowledge which involves correctness of judgment and uses reason and contemplates the good as a whole—that is to say, philosophy—can use all other kinds of knowledge and prescribe to them according to nature, we ought in every way to philosophize, since philosophy alone comprises right judgment and an infallible prescriptive understanding.

(Iamblichus, Protrepticus *49.3–51.6 Pistelli):*

[B 11] Of things that come into being some come from some kind of thought or art, e.g. a house or a ship (for the cause of both of these is a certain art and process of thought), while others come into being through no art but by nature; for nature is the cause of animals and plants, and all such things come into being according to nature. But some things also come into being as a result of chance; for of most of the things that come into being neither by art nor by nature nor of necessity, we say that they come into being by chance. [B 12] Now of the things that come into being by chance none comes into being for the sake of anything, nor have they an end; but in the case of things that come into being by art there is an end and that for the sake of which (for he who possesses the art will always tell you the reason why he wrote, and for the sake of what he did so), and this is better than that which comes into being because of it. I mean the things of which art is the cause by its own nature and not by accident; for we should properly describe medicine rather as the art of health than as that of disease, and architecture as the art of building houses, not of pulling them down. Everything, therefore, that is according to art comes into being for the sake of something, and this is its best end; but that which comes into being by chance does not come into being for the sake of anything: something good might come into being by chance, yet in respect of chance and insofar as it results from chance it is not good—for that which comes into being by chance is always indeterminate.

[B 13] But that which comes into being according to nature does so for the sake of something and is always constituted for the sake of something better than the product of art; for nature does not imitate art, but art nature, and art exists to aid nature and to fill up what nature leaves undone. For some things nature seems able to complete by itself without aid, but others it does with difficulty or cannot do at all; an example close to hand is what happens when something comes into being: some seeds obviously generate without protection, whatever ground they fall into, others need the art of farming as well; similarly, some animals too attain their full nature by themselves, but man needs many arts for his preservation, both at birth and in the matter of nutrition later. [B 14] If, then, art imitates nature, it is from nature that the arts have derived the characteristic that all their products come into being for the sake of something. For we should assume that everything that comes into being rightly comes into being for the sake of something. Now that which comes into being well, comes into being rightly; and everything that comes or has come into being according to nature, comes into being well, since that which is contrary to nature is bad and the opposite of that which is according to nature; natural coming into being, therefore, is for the sake of something. [B 15] This one can see from any one of our parts; if, for example you consider the eyelid, you would see that it has come into being not in vain but to aid the eyes, in order to give them rest and to ward off things that fall on to them. Thus that for which something has come into being is the same as that for which it should have come into being; e.g. if a ship ought to have been built to provide transport by sea, it is for the sake of that that it has come into being.

[B 16] Now either absolutely all animals belong to the class of things that have come into being by nature and according to nature, or the best and most honourable of them do; for it makes no difference if someone thinks most animals have come into being contrary to nature because of some destruction and evil. The most honourable of the animals in the world is man; so that clearly he has come into being by nature and according to nature.

(Iamblichus, Protrepticus 51.16–52.5 Pistelli):

[B 17] If, then, the end of each thing is always better than the thing (for everything that comes into being does so for the sake of its end, and that for the sake of which is better and the best of all things), and if a natural end is that which is completed last in order of generation when this proceeds continuously; now the bodily parts of man are completed first, the parts concerned with the soul later, and the completion of the better is somehow always later than its generation; now soul is later than body, and understanding is what emerges last in soul (for we see that it is by nature the last thing to come into being for men, and this indeed is why old age lays claim to this alone of good things): therefore, some form of understanding is by nature our end and the exercise of it the final activity for the sake of which we have come into being. Now if we have come into being, clearly we also exist to understand and to learn.

(Iamblichus, Protrepticus 51.6–15 Pistelli):

[B 18] Then what is it among existing things for the sake of which nature and god have brought us into being? Pythagoras, when asked about this, answered, 'To observe the heavens', and used to say that he was an observer of nature and had come into life for the sake of this. [B 19] And when somebody asked Anaxagoras for what end one would choose to come into being and to live, he is said to have answered the question by saying, 'To observe the heavens and the stars, moon and sun in them', everything else being worth nothing.

(Iamblichus, Protrepticus 52.6–16 Pistelli):

[B 20] According to this argument, then, Pythagoras was right in saying that every man has been made by god in order to acquire knowledge and contemplate. But whether the object of this knowledge is the universe or some other nature we must consider later; what we have said suffices as a first conclusion; for if understanding is our natural end, to understand must be the best of all things. [B 21] Therefore the other things we do we ought to do for the sake of the goods that are in man himself, and of these those in the body for the sake of those in the soul, and excellence for the sake of understanding; for this is the supreme end.

(Iamblichus, Protrepticus 34.5–35.18 Pistelli):

[B 23] As possessing reason, nature of every kind does nothing at random but everything for an end, and banishing chance cares for the end in a higher degree than the arts—for they are, as we know, imitations of nature. Since man is by nature composed of soul and body, and soul is better than body, and that which is inferior is always servant to that which is superior, then the body must exist for the sake of the soul. Recalling that the soul has a rational and an irrational part, we conclude that the irrational part exists for the sake of the rational part. Mind belongs to the rational part: the demonstration thus compels us to state that everything exists for the sake of mind. [B 24] The activities of mind are thoughts, and thinking is the seeing of objects of thought, just as the activity of the faculty of sight is seeing the objects of sight. It is, then, for the sake of mind and thinking that everything is desirable for man; for other things are desirable for the sake of the soul, mind is the best part of the soul, and the other things exist for the sake of the best. [B 25] Again, of thoughts, those are free which are pursued for their own sake, but those which bring about[1] knowledge for the sake of something else are like slaves; a thing pursued for itself is always superior to one pursued for something else, so that[2] that which is free is superior to that which is not. [B 26] Now if in our actions we use our intellect, even though we take into account our own advantage and consider things from that point of view, yet we follow the guidance of our intellect; we also need our body as a servant and are exposed to chance too. . . .[3] [B 27] Of acts of thought, then, those which are done just because of pure

---

[1]Text uncertain.
[2]Reading ὥστε for ὅτι.
[3]Text corrupt.

contemplation itself are more honourable and better than those useful for some other ends. Contemplative thinking is in itself honourable and wisdom of the mind is in this kind of thinking desirable; but thinking which involves understanding is honourable because of the actions it produces. The good and the honourable, then, is found in contemplation involving wisdom, but certainly not in every kind of contemplation. . . . [B 28] Man deprived of perception and mind is reduced to the condition of a plant; deprived of mind alone he is turned into a brute; deprived of irrationality but retaining mind, he becomes like god.

(Iamblichus, Protrepticus *36.7–13 Pistelli):*

[B 29] For what distinguishes us from the other animals shines through in this sort of life alone, a life in which there is nothing ordinary or of little value. For animals too have some small sparks of reason and understanding, but are entirely deprived of contemplative wisdom . . . ;[1] as to sense-perception and impulses, man has less exactness and strength than many animals.

F 52 R³ (Iamblichus, Protrepticus *37.22–40.1 Pistelli):*

[B 31] Moreover, since everyone chooses what is possible and expedient, we must admit that these two characteristics are found in philosophy, and also that the difficulty of acquiring it is more than outweighed by its usefulness; for we all do with greater pleasure that which is easy. [B 32] It is easy to show that we are capable of acquiring the sciences that deal with the just and the expedient and also those that deal with nature and the rest of reality. [B 33] The prior is always more knowable than the posterior, and that which is better by nature than that which is worse. For knowledge is more concerned with things that are defined and ordered than with their contraries, and more with causes than with effects. Now good things are more defined and ordered than bad things, just as a good man is more defined and ordered than a bad man: there must be the same difference. Besides, things that are prior are causes rather than things that are posterior; for if the former are removed, the things that have their substance from them are removed—lines if numbers are removed, planes if lines are removed, solids if planes are removed, the so-called syllables if letters are removed. [B 34] Therefore, if soul is better than body (being by nature more able to command), and there are arts and forms of understanding concerned with the body, namely medicine and gymnastics (for we reckon these as sciences and say that some people possess them), clearly with regard to the soul too and its excellences there is a care and an art, and we can acquire it, since we can do this even with regard to things of which our ignorance is greater and knowledge is harder to come by.

[B 35] So too with regard to nature; for it is far more necessary to have understanding of the causes and elements than of things posterior to them; for the latter are not among the highest realities, and the first principles do not arise from them, but from and through the first principles all other things manifestly proceed

---

[1]Text corrupt.

and are constituted. [B 36] For whether it is fire or air or number or any other natures that are the causes and principles of other things, if we are ignorant of them we cannot know any of the other things; for how could one recognise speech if one did not know the syllables, or know these if one knew none of the letters? [B 37] So much, then, on the theme that there is a science of truth and of the excellence of the soul, and that we can acquire these.

[B 38] That it [sc. understanding] is the greatest of goods and the most useful of all will be clear from what follows: we all agree that the best man and he who is by nature strongest ought to rule, and that the law alone is ruler and has authority; and the law is a sort of understanding and a formula based on understanding. [B 39] Again, what accurate standard or what boundary-marker of what is good do we have apart from the man of understanding? For the things that such a man will choose if his choice follows his knowledge are good and their contraries bad. [B 40] Now since all men choose what accords with their own dispositions (the just man choosing to live justly, the brave man to live bravely, the temperate man to live temperately), similarly it is clear that the man of understanding will choose above all things to understand; for that is the task of this capacity. It is clear, then, that according to the most authoritative opinion understanding is the greatest of goods.

(Iamblichus, Protrepticus *41.6–11 Pistelli):*

[B 41] One would see the same point more clearly from the following argument. To understand and to come to know is in itself desirable for men (for it is not possible to live a human life without these activities), and useful too for life; for no good comes to us unless it is accomplished after we have calculated and acted in accordance with understanding.

F 58 R³ (Iamblichus, Protrepticus *52.16–54.5 Pistelli):*

[B 42] To seek from all knowledge a result other than itself and to demand that it must be useful is the act of one completely ignorant of the distance that from the start separates good things from necessary things; for they differ completely. For the things that are loved for the sake of something else and without which life is impossible must be called necessities and joint-causes; but those that are loved for themselves, even if nothing else follows from them, must be called goods in the strict sense; for this is not desirable for the sake of that, and that for the sake of something else, and so *ad infinitum*—there is a stop somewhere. It is really ridiculous, then, to demand from everything some benefit besides the thing itself, and to ask 'What is the gain to us'? and 'What is the use'? For in truth, as we maintain, such a man is in no way like one who knows the noble and the good or who distinguishes causes from joint-causes. [B 43] One would see the absolute truth of what we are saying if someone as it were carried us in thought to the Isles of the Blest. For there there would be need of nothing and no profit from anything; and there remain only thought and contemplation, which even now we describe as the free life. If this is true, would not any of us be rightly ashamed if when the chance was given us to settle in the Isles of the Blest, he were by his own fault unable to do so? The reward that knowledge brings men is, then, not to be despised, nor is the good that comes from it slight. For as, according to the wise among the poets, we receive the gifts of justice in Hades, so, it seems, we gain those of understanding in the Isles of the Blest.

[B 44] It is not at all strange, then, if it [sc. understanding] does not show itself useful or advantageous; for we call it not advantageous but good, and it should be chosen not for the sake of something else but for itself. For as we travel to Olympia for the sake of the spectacle itself, even if nothing more were to follow from it (for the spectacle itself is worth more than much money), and as we view the Dionysia not in order to gain anything from the actors (indeed, we spend money on them), and as there are many other spectacles we should prefer to much money, so too the contemplation of the universe is to be honoured above all things that are thought useful. For surely we should not take great pains to go to see men imitating women and slaves, or fighting and running, and yet not think it right to view without payment the nature and reality of things.

(Iamblichus, Protrepticus *54.10–56.12 Pistelli):*

[B 46] But that contemplative understanding is also of the greatest usefulness to us for our practical life can easily be seen from the arts. For as clever doctors and most experts in physical training pretty well agree that those who are to be good doctors or trainers must have a general knowledge of nature, so good lawmakers too must have a general knowledge of nature—and indeed much more than the former. For the former only produce excellence in the body, while the latter, being concerned with the excellences of the soul and claiming to teach about the happiness and misery of the state, need philosophy still more. [B 47] For just as in the ordinary crafts the best tools were discovered from nature, as for instance in the builder's art the plumbline, the ruler and the compasses—for some come from water, others from light and the rays of the sun—, and it is by reference to these that we determine what is to the senses sufficiently straight and smooth, in the same way the statesman must have certain boundary-markers taken from nature itself and from truth by reference to which he will determine what is just, what is good, and what is expedient. For just as there these tools excel all others, so too the best law is that which has the greatest possible conformity to nature.

[B 48] Nobody, however, who has not practised philosophy and learned truth is able to do this. Furthermore, in the other arts and crafts men do not take their tools and their most accurate reasonings from first principles and so attain something approaching knowledge: they take them from what is second or third hand or at a distant remove, and base their reasonings on experience. The philosopher alone imitates that which is exact; for he looks at the exact things themselves, not at imitations. [B 49] Consequently, as a man is not a good builder if he does not use the ruler or any other such instrument but takes his measure from other buildings, so presumably if a man either lays down laws for cities or performs actions by looking at and imitating other human actions or constitutions, whether of Sparta or Crete or of any other state, he is not a good or serious lawgiver; for an imitation of what is not good cannot be good, nor can an imitation of what is not divine and stable in its nature be immortal and stable. But it is clear that to the philosopher alone among craftsmen belong laws that are stable and actions that are right and noble. [B 50] For he alone lives by looking at nature and the divine. Like a good helmsman he moors his life to that which is eternal and unchanging, drops his anchor there, and lives his own master.

[B 51] This knowledge is indeed contemplative, but it enables us to frame all our practice in accordance with it. For just as sight makes and shapes nothing (since its only work is to judge and to show us everything than can be seen), yet enables us to act as it directs and gives us the greatest assistance towards action (for we should be almost entirely motionless if deprived of it), so it is clear that, though knowledge is contemplative, yet we do innumerable things in accordance with it, choose some things and avoid others, and in general gain as a result of it everything that is good.

F 52 R³ (Iamblichus, de communi mathematica scientia 79.15-80.1 Festa):

[B 52] Now he who is to consider these matters must not forget that all things good and useful for human life reside in use and action, not in mere knowledge; for we become healthy not by knowing the things that produce health but by applying them to our bodies; we become wealthy not by knowing wealth but by possessing much property; most important of all, we live well not by knowing something of that which exists, but by doing well; for this is true happiness. It follows that philosophy too, if it is useful, must be either a doing of good things or useful as a means to such acts.

(Iamblichus, Protrepticus 40.1–41.5 Pistelli):

[B 53] Now we ought not to flee philosophy if it is, as we think, the acquisition and exercise of wisdom, and wisdom is among the greatest goods; and if in pursuit of gain we run many risks by sailing to the pillars of Hercules, we should not shrink from labour or expense in the pursuit of understanding. It is slave-like to desire to live rather than to live well, to follow the opinions of the many instead of expecting the many to follow one's own, to seek money but show no concern at all for what is noble.

[B 54] As to the value and the greatness of the thing, I think we have sufficiently proved our case; that the acquisition of wisdom is much easier than that of other goods, one might be convinced by the following arguments. [B 55] The fact that those who pursue philosophy get no reward from men to spur them to the considerable efforts they make, and[1] that having spent much on acquiring other skills, nevertheless in a short time their progress in exact knowledge is rapid, seems to me a sign of the easiness of philosophy. [B 56] So too that all men feel at home in philosophy and wish to spend their lives in the pursuit of it, leaving all other cares, is no small evidence that it is pleasant to sit down to it; for no-one is willing to

---

[1]Reading πολύ τε.

work hard for a long time. Besides, the exercise of philosophy differs very much from all other labours: those who practise it need no tools or places for their work; wherever in the whole world one sets one's thought to work, one is everywhere equally able to grasp the truth as if it were actually present. [B 57] Thus it has been proved that philosophy is possible, that it is the greatest of goods, and that it is easy to acquire; so that on all counts it is fitting that we should eagerly lay hold of it.

(Iamblichus, Protrepticus *41.15–42.29 Pistelli):*

[B 59] Further, part of us is soul, part body; the one rules, the other is ruled; the one uses, the other is present as its instrument. Again, the use of that which is ruled, i.e. the instrument, is always arranged to fit that which rules and uses. [B 60] Of the soul one part is reason (which by nature rules and judges in matters concerning ourselves), the other part follows and is of a nature such as to be ruled; everything is well arranged in accordance with its appropriate excellence—for to attain this is good. [B 61] And indeed, when the most authoritative and most honourable parts attain their excellence, then it is well arranged; now the natural excellence of that which is naturally better is the better, and that which is by nature more fit to rule and more authoritative is better, as man is in relation to the other animals; consequently soul is better than body (for it is fitter to rule), and of soul, that part which has reason and thought (for such is that which commands and forbids and says that we ought or ought not to act). [B 62] Whatever excellence, then, is the excellence of this part must be, for all beings in general and for us, the most desirable of all things; for one would, I think, maintain that we are this part, either alone or especially.

[B 63] Further, when a thing best produces that which is—not by accident but in itself—its product, then that thing must be said to be good too, and that excellence in virtue of which each thing can achieve precisely this result must be termed its supreme excellence. [B 64] Now that which is composite and divisible into parts has several different activities; but that which is by nature simple and whose substance does not consist in a relation to something else must have only one proper excellence of its own. [B 65] If, then, man is a simple animal and his substance is ordered according to reason and mind, he has no other product than the most exact truth and a true account of the things that exist; but if he is composed of several faculties, it is clear that when someone can produce several things, the best of them is always his product, e.g. health is of the doctor and safety of the helmsman. Now we can name no better product of thought and the thinking part of the soul than truth. Truth therefore is the supreme product of this part of the soul.

[B 66] Now this it does, generally speaking, by knowledge, and more so by knowledge of a more perfect kind; and the supreme end of this is contemplation. For when of two things one is desirable for the sake of the other, the latter is better and more desirable for the same reason as the other is desirable; e.g. pleasure than pleasant things, health than healthy things; for these are said to be productive of those. [B 67] Now nothing is more worthy of choice, when one state is compared with another, than understanding, which we maintain to be the faculty of the supreme element in us; for the cognitive part, whether taken alone or in combination with the other parts, is better than all the rest of the soul; and its excellence is knowledge.

[B 68] Therefore none of what are called the particular excellences is its product; for it is better than all of them and the end produced is always better than the knowledge that produces it. Nor is every excellence of the soul in this way its product; nor is happiness. For if it is to be productive, it will produce results different from itself; as the art of building produces a house but is not part of a house. But understanding is part of excellence and of happiness; for we say that happiness either comes from it or is it. [B 69] According to this argument too, then, it cannot be a productive knowledge; for the end must be better than that which is coming to be and nothing is better than understanding, unless it is one of the things we have named—and none of these is a product distinct from it. Therefore we must say that this form of knowledge is contemplative, since it is impossible that its end should be production.

[B 70] Hence understanding and contemplation are the product of the soul, and this is of all things the most desirable for men, comparable, I think, to eyesight. For one would choose to have sight even if nothing other than sight itself were to result from it. [B 71] Again, if we love one thing because something else necessarily results from it, clearly we shall wish more for that which possesses this quality more fully; e.g. if a man chooses walking because it is healthy but finds that running is more healthy and that he can get it, he will prefer running and, if he knows, would choose to run. If, therefore, true opinion is similar to understanding, and if true opinion is desirable precisely according to the manner and extent to which it is like understanding by reason of being true, then if this is found more in understanding, understanding is more desirable than believing truly.

(Iamblichus, Protrepticus *43.25–27 Pistelli):*
[B 72] Again, if we love sight for its own sake, that is sufficient evidence that all men love understanding and knowing most of all.

(Iamblichus, Protrepticus *44.26–45.3 Pistelli):*
[B 73] For in loving life they love understanding and knowing; they value life for no other reason than for the sake of perception, and above all for the sake of sight; they evidently love this faculty in the highest degree because it is, in comparison with the other senses, simply a kind of knowledge.

(Iamblichus, Protrepticus *44.9–26 Pistelli):*
[B 74] Indeed, living is distinguished from not living by perception, and life is determined by its presence and power: if this is taken away life is not worth living; it is as though life itself were removed by the loss of perception. [B 75] Now of perceptions the power of sight is distinguished by being the clearest, and it is for this reason that we prefer it to the other senses; but every sense is a cognitive power

which works through the body, as hearing perceives sound through the ears. [B 76] Therefore, if life is desirable for the sake of perception and perception is a kind of knowing, and if it is because the soul can come to know by means of it that we desire to live; [B 77] further, if, as we said just now, of two things, the one which possesses the desirable quality more fully is always more desirable, then of the senses sight must be the most desirable and honourable; and understanding is more desirable than it and than all the other senses, and than life itself, since it has a stronger grasp of truth; hence all men aim at understanding, most of all things.

(Iamblichus, Protrepticus 56.13–59.17 Pistelli):

[B 78] That those who have chosen to live according to mind also enjoy life most will be clear from the following argument. [B 79] Things are said to be alive in two senses, in virtue of a potentiality and in virtue of an actuality; for we describe as seeing both those animals which have sight and are naturally capable of seeing, even if they happen to have their eyes shut, and those which are using this faculty and are looking at something. Similarly with knowing and cognition: we sometimes mean by it the use of the faculty and contemplation, sometimes the possession of the faculty and having knowledge. [B 80] If, then, we distinguish life from non-life by the possession of perception, and perceiving has two senses—properly of using one's senses, in another way of being able to use them (it is for this reason, it seems, that we say even of a sleeping man that he perceives)—it is clear that living will correspondingly be taken in two senses: a waking man must be said to live in the true and proper sense; as for a sleeping man, because he is capable of passing into the activity in virtue of which we say that a man is waking and perceiving something, it is for this reason and with reference to this that we describe him as living. [B 81] When, therefore, each of two things is called by the same term, the one by being active the other by being passive, we shall say that the former possesses the property to a greater degree; e.g. we shall say that a man who uses knowledge knows to a greater degree than a man who possesses knowledge, and that a man who is looking at something sees to a greater degree than one who can do so. [B 82] For we use 'to a greater degree' not only in virtue of an excess (in the case of things which share a single account) but also in virtue of priority and posteriority; e.g. we say that health is good to a greater degree than healthy things, and that what is by its own nature desirable is so to a greater degree than what is productive of this; yet we see that there is not a single account[1] predicated of both when we say both of useful things and of excellence that each is good. [B 83] Thus we say that a waking man lives to a greater degree than a sleeping man, and that a man who is exercising his soul lives to a greater degree than a man who possesses it; for it is because of the former that we say that the latter lives, because he is such as to be active or passive in this manner. [B 84] The use of anything, then, is this: if the capacity is for a single thing, then it is doing just that thing; if it is for several things, then it is doing whichever is the best of these. E.g. a flute: a man uses a flute only or especially when

---

[1]Reading οὐχ εἷς for οὐχ ᾗ.

he plays it—for the other cases presumably also fit here. Thus we must say that he who uses a thing aright uses it to a greater degree; for he who uses something well and accurately uses it for the natural end and in the natural way.

[B 85] Now thinking and reasoning are, either alone or above everything else, the products of the soul. It is now simple and easy for anyone to infer that the man who thinks aright lives to a greater degree, and that he who reaches truth in the highest degree lives in the highest degree, and that this is the man who understands and contemplates according to the most precise knowledge; and it is then and to these men that perfect life must be ascribed—to those who understand and are men of understanding. [B 86] Now if for every animal to live is the same as to exist, it is clear that the man of understanding will exist to the highest degree and in the most proper sense, and most of all when he is exercising this faculty and contemplating what is most knowable of all things.

[B 87] Again, perfect and unimpeded activity contains in itself delight; so that the activity of contemplation must be the most pleasant of all. [B 88] Further, there is a difference between enjoying oneself while drinking and enjoying drinking; for there is nothing to prevent a man who is not thirsty, or is not getting the drink he enjoys, from enjoying himself while drinking—not because he is drinking but because he happens at the same time to be looking at something or to be looked at as he sits. So we shall say that such a man enjoys himself, and enjoys himself while drinking, but not that he does so because he is drinking, nor that he is enjoying drinking. In the same way we shall say that walking, sitting down, learning, any activity, is pleasant or painful, not if we happen to feel pain or pleasure in the presence of these activities, but if we are all pained or pleased by their presence. [B 89] Similarly, we shall call that life pleasant whose presence is pleasant to those who have it; and we shall say that not all who have pleasure while living enjoy living, but only those to whom living is itself pleasant and who rejoice in the pleasure that comes from life.

[B 90] So we assign life to the man who is awake rather than to him who is asleep, to him who understands rather than to him who is foolish, and we say the pleasure of living is the pleasure we get from the exercise of the soul—for that is true life. [B 91] If, then, there is more than one exercise of the soul, still the chief of all is that of understanding as well as possible. It is clear, then, that necessarily the pleasure arising from understanding and contemplation is, alone or most of all, the pleasure of living. Pleasant life and true enjoyment, therefore, belong only to philosophers, or to them most of all. For the activity of our truest thoughts, nourished by the most real of things and preserving steadfastly for ever the perfection it receives, is of all activities the most productive of joy.

(Iamblichus, Protrepticus *59.19–60.10 Pistelli):*

[B 93] If we should not only infer this from the parts of happiness but also go deeper and establish it on the basis of happiness as a whole, let us state explicitly that as philosophizing is related to happiness so it is related to our character as good or bad men. For it is as leading to or following from well-being that all things are worthy of choice, and of the sources of happiness some are necessary others pleasant. [B 94] Thus we lay it down that happiness is either understanding and a form of wisdom, or excellence, or genuine pleasure, or all of these. [B 95] Now if it is understanding, clearly philosophers alone will enjoy a happy life; if it is excellence of the soul or enjoyment, then too it will belong to them alone or most of all—for excellence is that which governs our life, and understanding is, if one thing is compared with another, the most pleasant of all things. Similarly, if one says that all these things together are identical with happiness, it must be defined by understanding. [B 96] Therefore all who can should practise philosophy; for this is either the perfect life or of all single things most truly the cause of it for souls.

F 55 R³, F 59 R³, F 60 R³, F 61 R³ (Iamblichus, Protrepticus 45.4–48.21 Pistelli):

[B 97] It is no bad thing to throw light on the subject by adducing what appears clearly to everyone. [B 98] To everyone this much is quite plain, that no-one would choose to live in possession of the greatest[1] possible wealth and power but deprived of understanding and mad, not even if he were to be pursuing with delight the most violent pleasures, as some madmen do. All men, then, it seems, shun folly above all things. Now the contrary of folly is understanding; and of two contraries one is to be avoided, the other to be chosen. [B 99] Thus as illness is to be avoided, so health is to be chosen. Hence according to this argument too, in the light of common conceptions, it seems that understanding is most desirable of all things, and not for the sake of anything that follows from it. For even if a man had everything but were destroyed and diseased in his understanding, his life would not be desirable, since even the other good things could not profit him. [B 100] Therefore all men, insofar as they can come within reach of understanding and taste its savour, reckon other things as nothing, and for this reason not one of us would endure being drunk or a child throughout his life.

[B 101] For this reason too, though sleep is a very pleasant thing, it is not desirable, even if we suppose the sleeper to have all possible pleasures, because the images of sleep are false while those of waking men are true. For sleep and waking differ in nothing else but the fact that the soul when awake often knows the truth but in sleep is always deceived; for the whole nature of dreams is an image and a falsity. [B 102] Further, the fact that most men shrink from death shows the soul's love of learning. For it shrinks from what it does not know, from darkness and obscurity, and naturally seeks what is manifest and knowable. This is, above all, the reason why we say we ought to honour exceedingly those who have caused us to see the sun and the light, and to revere our fathers and mothers as causes of the greatest of goods—they are, it seems, the causes of our understanding and seeing. It is for the same reason that we delight in things and men that are familiar, and call dear those whom we know. These things, then, show plainly that what is knowable and manifest and clear is a thing to be loved; and if what is knowable and clear, then also knowing and understanding.

---

[1]Retaining μεγίστην.

[B 103] Besides this, just as in the case of property it is not the same possession that conduces to life and to a happy life for men, so it is in the case of understanding too: we do not, I think, need the same understanding with a view to mere life and with a view to the good life. The majority of men may well be pardoned for doing this: they certainly pray for happiness, but they are content if they can merely live. But unless one thinks one ought to endure living on any terms whatever, it is ridiculous not to suffer every toil and bestow every care to gain that kind of understanding which will know the truth. [B 104] One might recognise this from the following facts too, if one viewed human life in a clear light. For one will find that all the things men think great are mere scene-painting; hence it is rightly said that man is nothing and that nothing human is stable. Strength, size, beauty are a laugh and of no worth; . . .² only because we see nothing accurately. [B 105] For if one could see as clearly as they say Lynceus did, who saw through walls and trees, would one ever have thought a man endurable to look at if one saw of what poor materials he is made? Honours and reputation, things so envied, are more than other things full of indescribable folly; for to him who catches a glimpse of things eternal it seems foolish to crave for these things. What is there among human things that is long-lived or lasting? It is owing to our weakness, I think, and the shortness of our life that even this appears great. [B 106] Which of us, looking to these facts, would think himself happy and blessed? For all of us are from the very beginning (as they say in the initiation rites) shaped by nature as though for punishment. For it is an inspired saying of the ancients that the soul pays penalties and that we live for the punishment of great sins. [B 107] For indeed the conjunction of the soul with the body looks very much like this. For as the Etruscans are said often to torture captives by chaining dead bodies face to face with the living, fitting part to part, so the soul seems to be extended throughout and affixed to all the sensitive members of the body.

[B 108] Mankind possesses nothing divine or blessed that is of any account except what there is in us of mind and understanding: this alone of our possessions seems to be immortal, this alone divine. [B 109] By virtue of being able to share in this faculty, life, however wretched and difficult by nature, is yet so cleverly arranged that man seems a god in comparison with all other creatures. [B 110] For mind is the god in us—whether it was Hermotimus or Anaxagoras who said so—and mortal life contains a portion of some god. We ought, therefore, either to philosophize or to say farewell to life and depart hence, since all other things seem to be great nonsense and folly.

F 51 R³ (Elias, Prolegomena Philosophiae *3.17–23):*
. . . or like Aristotle in his work entitled *Protrepticus;* for he puts it like this: If you ought to philosophize you ought to philosophize; and if you ought not to philosophize you ought to philosophize: therefore, in any case you ought to philosophize. For if philosophy exists, we certainly ought to philosophize, since it exists; and if it does not exist, in that case too we ought to inquire why philosophy

²Text corrupt.

does not exist—and by inquiring we philosophize; for inquiry is the cause of philosophy.

F 53 R³ (Cicero, Tusculanae disputationes *III xxviii 69):*
Thus Aristotle, accusing the old philosophers who taught that philosophy had been perfected by their own talents, says that they were either very stupid or very conceited; but that he sees that, since in a few years a great advance has been made, philosophy will in a short time be brought to completion.

F 54 R³ (Calcidius, Commentarius in Timaeum *225.21–226.2 Waszink):*
. . . Aristotle agrees, saying that at first children, before they are weaned, think that all men are their fathers and all women their mothers, and that as they grow older they make the distinction but they are not always successful in distinguishing and often are taken in by false images and stretch out their hands towards the image.

F 54 R³ (Calcidius, Commentarius in Timaeum *226.8–15 Waszink):*
It is the height of madness not merely to be ignorant but not to realize that you are ignorant and therefore to assent to false images and to suppose that true images are false—as when men think that wickedness is advantageous and virtue an impediment that brings destruction; and such an opinion accompanies to their last years many men who believe that doing injury is very expedient and acting rightly disadvantageous, and who are therefore reviled. Aristotle calls such people aged children, because their minds hardly differ from those of children.

F 56 R³ (Plutarch, Pelopidas *279B):*
For of the majority of people, as Aristotle says, some do not use it [sc. wealth] through meanness, and others misuse it through extravagance—and the latter spend their lives as slaves to every passing pleasure, the former as slaves to their business.

F 61 R³ (Cicero, de finibus *II xiii 40):*
. . . man, as Aristotle says, was born for two things, understanding and action, as though he were a mortal god.

F 62 R³ (Plutarch, quaestiones convivales *734D):*
Coming into contact with Aristotle's *Scientific Problems,* which had been brought to Thermopylae, Florus himself came to teem with many puzzles—as is normal and proper to philosophical natures—and passed them on to his companions; he thus bore witness to Aristotle's remark that much learning is the beginning of many puzzles.[1]

[1]The text of the last clause is disputed.

F 63 R³ (Diogenes Laertius, IX 53):

He [sc. Protagoras] was the first to discover the so-called 'knot' on which they carry their burdens, as Aristotle says in his *On Education;* for he was a porter, as Epicurus too says somewhere.

F 64 R³ (Themistius, orationes 295CD):

This man, after some slight association with my studies or amusements, had almost the same experience as the philosopher Axiothea, Zeno of Citium, and the Corinthian farmer.... The Corinthian farmer, after coming into contact with Gorgias—not Gorgias himself, but the dialogue Plato wrote in criticism of the sophist—at once gave up his farm and his vines, mortgaged his soul to Plato, and sowed and planted Plato's views there. This is the man whom Aristotle honours in his Corinthian[1] dialogue.

F 65 R³ (Diogenes Laertius, VIII 57):

Aristotle in the *Sophist* says that Empedocles was the first to discover rhetoric, Zeno dialectic.

F 66 R³ (Diogenes Laertius, VIII 63):

Aristotle says that he [sc. Empedocles] was a free spirit and averse to all authority, if (as Xanthus says in his account of him) he refused the kingship which was offered to him, plainly setting more value on simplicity.

F 67 R³ (Diogenes Laertius, IX 54):

Pythodorus, son of Polyzelus, one of the Four Hundred, accused him [sc. Protagoras]; but Aristotle says that Euathlus did.

F 68 R³ (Diogenes Laertius, II 55):

Aristotle says that a vast number of people wrote eulogies and memorials to Grylos, partly in the wish to please his father.

F 69 R³ (Quintilian, II xvii 14):

Aristotle, as is his custom, has in the *Grylos* produced for the sake of inquiry certain arguments of his usual subtlety [to show that rhetoric is not an art] . . .

F 70 R³ (Diogenes Laertius, VIII 57–58):

In his *On Poets* he [sc. Aristotle] says that Empedocles was both Homeric and skilled in his diction, using metaphor and the other devices of poetry; and that although he wrote other poems too—the Crossing of Xerxes, and a Prelude to

---

[1]Perhaps read Νηρίνθῳ.

Apollo—a sister of his (or, as Hieronymus says, a daughter) later burned them, the Prelude by accident, the Persian verses deliberately because they were unfinished. And he says in general that he also wrote tragedies and works on politics.

F 71 R³ (Diogenes Laertius, VIII 51–52):
Eratosthenes, in his *Olympic Victors*, says that Meton's father[1] won his victory in the seventy-first Olympiad: his authority is Aristotle. . . . Aristotle, and also Heraclides, say that he [sc. Empedocles] died at the age of sixty.

F 72 R³ (Athenaeus, 505C):
Aristotle in his work *On Poets* writes thus: 'Are we then to deny that the so-called mimes of Sophron, which are not even in verse,[1] or those of Alexamenus of Teos, which were written before[2] the Socratic dialogues, are dialogues[3] and imitations?' Thus Aristotle, the most learned of men, says outright that Alexamenus wrote dialogues before Plato.

F 73 R³ (Diogenes Laertius, III 37):
Aristotle says that the form of his [sc. Plato's] writings was in between poetry and prose.

F 74 R³ (Macrobius, V xviii 19–20):
I will quote Aristotle's own words in the second book of his *On Poets*, where he says this about Euripides: 'Euripides says that the sons of Thestius went with their left foot unshod—at all events, he writes that:

In their left step they were unshod of foot, while the other had sandals, so that they should have one knee light.

Now the custom of the Aetolians is just the opposite: their left foot is shod, the right unshod—I suppose because the leading foot should be light, but not the one which remains fixed'.

F 75 R³ (Diogenes Laertius, II 46):
He [sc. Socrates] had as rivals, according to Aristotle in the third book of his *On Poetry*, a certain Antilochus of Lemnos and Antiphon the soothsayer—just as Pythagoras had Cylon of Croton; Homer when alive Syagrus and when dead Xenophanes of Colophon; Hesiod when alive Cercops and when dead the aforesaid Xenophanes; Pindar, Amphimenes of Cos; Thales, Pherecydes; Bias, Salaros of

---

[1]Meton was Empedocles' father.
[1]Reading ἐμμέτρους ὄντας τούς.   [2]Reading πρότερον for πρῶτον.
[3]Reading διαλόγους for λόγους.

Priene; Pittakos, Antimenidas and Alcaeus; Anaxagoras, Sosibius; and Simonides, Timocreon.

F 76 R³ ([Plutarch], Vita Homeri *3):*

Aristotle in the third book of his *On Poetry* says that in the island of Ios, at the time when Neleus the son of Codrus was leading the Ionian settlement, a certain girl who was a native of the island became pregnant by a spirit which was one of the companions of the Muses in the dance. Being ashamed of what had happened because of the size of her belly, she went to a place called Aegina. Pirates raided the place, enslaved the girl, and took her to Smyrna which was then under the Lydians; they did this as a favour to Maeon, who was the king of Lydia and their friend. He fell in love with the girl for her beauty and married her. While she was living near the Meles the birth-pangs came upon her and she gave birth to Homer on the bank of the river. Maeon adopted him and brought him up as his own child, Critheis having died immediately after her delivery. Not long after, Maeon himself died. When the Lydians were being oppressed by the Aeolians and had decided to leave Smyrna, and their leaders had called on any who wished to follow them to leave the town, Homer, who was still an infant, said he too wished to follow (ὁμηρεῖν); for which reason he was called Homer instead of Melesigenes.

F 78 R³ (Cicero, ad Quintum fratrem *III v 1):*

. . . Aristotle says in his own name what he has to say about the state and the outstanding man.

F 79 R³ (Syrianus, Commentarius in Metaphysica *168.33–35):*

In the second book of the *Politicus* he [sc. Aristotle] says the same as his predecessors about this subject—his words are: 'The good is the most accurate measure of all things'.

F 80 R³ (Seneca, de ira *I ix 2):*

Anger, Aristotle says, is necessary, nor can any battle be won without it—unless it fills the mind and kindles the spirit. But we must treat it not as a commander but as a soldier.

(Philodemus, Volumina Rhetorica *II.175, frag. XV):*

A hare that makes its appearance among hounds cannot escape, Aristotle says, nor can that which is deemed despicable and shameless survive among men.

F 82 R³ (Demetrius, de elocutione *28):*

At all events, in Aristotle's work *On Justice*, if the speaker who is bewailing the fate of Athens were to say 'The enemy city they captured, their own they forsook,' he would have used the language of emotion and lament; but if he makes it assonant—'The enemy city they took, their own they forsook'—by heaven he will not rouse any emotion or pity but only tears of laughter.

F 83 R³ (Athenaeus, 6D):

Others call Philoxenus a fish-lover, but Aristotle calls him simply a dinner-lover. He writes, I think, as follows: 'When they are making speeches to crowded audiences they spend the whole day in relating marvels, and that to men who have just sailed in from the Phasis or the Borysthenes, when they have read nothing themselves but the *Dinner* of Philoxenus—and not the whole of that.'

F 84 R³ (Suetonius, de blasphemiis 84 Taillardat):

Aristotle in the first book of his *On Justice* says that he [sc. Eurybatos] was a thief who, when he was caught and put in chains, was encouraged by the warders to show how he got over walls and into houses: on being set free, he fastened the spikes to his feet and took the sponges—then he easily climbed up, broke through the roof, and got away.

F 86 R³ (Plutarch, de Stoicorum repugnantiis 1040E):

... he [sc. Chrysippus] says in criticism of Aristotle on the subject of justice that he is not right in saying that if pleasure is the end justice is destroyed, and with justice each of the other excellences.

F 87 R³ (Boethius, Commentarius in de Interpretatione, ed. 2, I i 27):

In his work *On Justice* he [sc. Aristotle] makes it clear that nouns and verbs are not sounds that signify objects of perception; he says: 'the objects of thought and the objects of perception are from the start distinct in their natures'.

F 89 R³ (Cicero, de officiis II xvi 56–57):

How much more serious and true is Aristotle's criticism of us for not being astonished at these vast sums of money spent on captivating the populace. For he says[1] that if men besieged by an enemy should be compelled to pay a mina for a pint of water, that seems at first incredible to us and everyone is astonished; but when they think about it, they pardon it as due to necessity. Yet in the case of this enormous outlay and endless expenditure, we are not greatly astonished at all—even though necessity is not being relieved or respect increased, and the pleasure of the populace itself lasts only a very short time and moreover derives from the most trivial of objects where at the moment of gratification even the memory of the pleasure dies. He rightly infers that these things gratify children,

---

[1]Reading *ait enim* for *at ii.*

womenfolk, slaves, and slavelike free men; but they can in no way be approved of by a serious man who weighs events with a sure judgment.

(Philodemus, de oeconomia *XXI 28–35):*
    ... which happened to Aristotle in respect of the argument in the work *On Wealth*[1] to show that the good man is also a good money-maker and the bad man a bad money-maker (as Metrodorus proved).

F 91 R³ (Stobaeus, Anthologium *IV xxix A 24):*
    From Aristotle *On Good Birth*. 'In short, with regard to good birth, I for my part am at a loss to say whom one should call well-born.'
    'Your difficulty', I said, 'is quite reasonable; for among the many and even more among the wise there is division of opinion and obscurity of statement, particularly about its value. What I mean is this: is it a valuable and good thing, or, as Lycophron the sophist wrote, something altogether empty? For, comparing it with other goods, he says the nobility of good birth is obscure, and its dignity a matter of words—the preference for it is a matter of opinion, and in truth there is no difference between the low-born and the well-born.'

F 92 R³ (Stobaeus, Anthologium *IV xxix A 25):*
    In the same book. 'Just as it is disputed what height is good, so it is disputed who those are who ought to be called well-born. Some think it is those born of good ancestors, which was the view of Socrates; he said that because Aristides was good his daughter was nobly born. They say that Simonides, when asked who it is that are well-born, said "those whose family has long been rich"; but at that rate Theognis' reprimand is wrong, and so is that of the poet who wrote "Mortals honour good birth, but marry rather with the rich". Good heavens, is not a man who is rich himself preferable to one who had a rich great-grandfather or some other rich ancestor, but is himself poor?'
    'Surely', he said.
    'And one ought to marry with the rich rather than with the well-born; for it is people who were once rich who are well-born, but people who are now rich who are more powerful. Is it not much the same, then, if one supposes that it is not those born into a once rich family but those born into a once good family who are well-born? One would suppose that recent goodness is better than ancient, that a man has more in common with his father than with his great-grandfather, and that it is more desirable to be good oneself than to have a great-grandfather or some other ancestor who was good.'
    'You are right', he said.
    'Well, then, since we see that good birth does not consist in either of these things, should we not look elsewhere to see what it consists in?'[2]

---

[1]Text uncertain.
[2]Reading τίνι τοῦτο ἔνι ποτέ.

'We should', he said.

' "Good (τὸ εὖ)" means, I suppose, something praiseworthy and excellent; e.g. having a good face or good eyes means, on this showing, something good or fine.'

'Certainly', he said.

'Well then, having a good face is having the excellence proper to a face, and having good eyes is having the excellence proper to eyes, is it not?'

'Yes', he said.

'But one family (γένος) is good, another bad and not good.'

'Certainly', he said.

'And we say each thing is good in virtue of the excellence proper to it, so that a family is good in the same way.'

'Yes', he said.

'Clearly, then', I said, 'good birth (εὐγένεια) is excellence of family.'

F 93 R³ (Diogenes Laertius, II 26):

Aristotle says that he [sc. Socrates] had two wives, first Xanthippe from whom he had Lamprocles, and secondly Myrto, the daughter of Aristides the Just, whom he took without a dowry and from whom he had Sophroniscus and Menexenus.

F 93 R³ (Plutarch, Aristides 335CD):

Demetrius of Phaleron, Hieronymus of Rhodes, Aristoxenus the writer on music, and Aristotle (if the work *On Good Birth* is to be reckoned among his genuine works) relate that Myrto, grand-daughter of Aristides, lived with the sage Socrates, who was married to another woman but took Myrto under his protection when she was widowed because she was poor and lacking in the necessities of life.

F 94 R³ (Stobaeus, Anthologium IV xxix C 52):

From Aristotle's work *On Good Birth:* 'It is evident, then', I said, 'on the subject which has for so long puzzled us, why those born into once rich or once good families are thought to be better born than those whose possession of these advantages is recent. For a man's own goodness is nearer to him than that of a grandfather, and on that basis it would be the good man who is well born. And some have said this, claiming by this deduction to argue against good birth: Euripides, for example, says that good birth belongs not to those whose ancestors have long been good, but to a man who is himself good, simply. That is not so; those are right who give preference to ancient excellence. Let us state the reasons for this. Good birth is excellence of family, and excellence is good; and a good family is one in which there have been many good men. Now this happens when the family has had a good origin; for an origin has the power of producing many products like itself: this is the function of an origin—to produce many results like itself. When, then, there has been one man of this kind in the family, a man so good that many generations inherit his goodness, the family is bound to be good. There will be many good men if the family is human, many good horses if it is equine, and so too with the other animals. Thus it is reasonable that not rich men nor good men but those born into once rich or once good families should be well born. The argument has its eye on the truth: the origin counts more than anything else. Yet not even those born of good ancestors are in every case well born, but only those who have among their ancestors originators who are good.[1] When a man is good himself but has not the natural power to beget many like him, the origin has not in such a case the power we have ascribed to it. . . .[2] People are well born if they come of such a family—not if their father is well born but if the originator of the family is so. For it is not by himself that a father begets a good man, but because he came of such a family.'

F 96 R³ (Athenaeus, 564B):
Aristotle said that lovers look to no other part of the bodies of their beloved than their eyes, in which modesty dwells.

F 97 R³ (Plutarch, Pelopidas 287D):
It is said also that Iolaus, who was the beloved of Hercules, shares in the contests of the Thebans and fights alongside them. Aristotle says that even in his day lovers and their beloved still pledged their troth on the tomb of Iolaus.

F 98 R³ (Plutarch, Amatorius 761A):
Aristotle says that Cleomachus died in a different way, after defeating the Eretrians in battle, and that the man embraced by his lover was one of the Chalcidians from Thrace who had been sent to help the Chalcidians in Euboea—hence the Chalcidian song, 'O children . . . '.

(al-Dailami, cod. Tübingen Weisweiler 81):
It is said in a certain book of the ancients that the pupils of Aristotle assembled before him one day. And Aristotle said to them: 'While I was standing on a hill I saw a youth who stood on a terrace roof and recited a poem, the meaning of which was this: whoever dies of passionate love, let him die in this manner—there is no good in love without death'. Then said his pupil Issos: 'O philosopher, inform us concerning the essence of love'. And Aristotle replied: 'Love is an impulse which is generated in the heart; when it is once generated, it moves and grows; afterwards it becomes mature. When it has become mature it is joined by affections of appetite whenever the lover in the depth of his heart increases in his excitement, his perseverance, his desire, his concentrations, and his wishes. And that brings him to cupidity and urges him to demands, until it brings him to disquieting grief, continuous sleeplessness, and hopeless passion and sadness and destruction of mind'.

---

[1]Reading ὄντες ἀγαθοί.
[2]There is a lacuna in the text.

F 101 R³ (Athenaeus, 674F):

Aristotle in the *Symposium* says that we offer nothing mutilated to the gods, but only what is perfect and whole; and what is full is perfect; and garlanding signifies a certain sort of filling.

F 103 R³ (Apollonius, Historiae mirabiles *25):*

Aristotle in his *On Drunkenness* says that Andron of Argos, though he ate many salty and dry foods, remained all through his life without thirst and without drink. Besides, he twice travelled to Ammon through the desert, eating dry barley-groats but taking no liquid.

F 104 R³ (Athenaeus, 641DE):

Aristotle, in his *On Drunkenness*, talks of second courses in the same way as we do, thus: 'We must consider that a sweetmeat differs entirely from a foodstuff, as much as what is eaten differs from what is nibbled ('nibbles' was the old Greek word for things served as sweetmeats); so that the first person to speak of 'second courses' seems to have been justified—for the eating of sweets is a sort of extra dinner, and the sweetmeats form a second meal'.

F 105 R³ ([Julian], Letters *391BC):*

The fig . . . is so useful to mankind that Aristotle actually says that it is an antidote to every poison, and that for precisely that reason it is served at meals both as an hors d'oeuvre and as a dessert—as though it were being wrapped round the iniquities of the food in preference to any other sacred antidote.

F 106 R³ (Athenaeus, 447AB):

Aristotle in his work *On Drunkenness* says . . . : 'Something peculiar happens in the case of the barley-liquor which they call *pinon*. Those who are drunk on other intoxicants fall in all directions—to left, to right, face down, face up: those who are drunk on *pinon* only[1] fall backwards and face up'.

F 107 R³ (Athenaeus, 429CD):

Aristotle in his work *On Drunkenness* says: 'If wine is boiled down slightly, it is less intoxicating when drunk; for when it is boiled down its potency becomes weaker. Older men', he says, 'get drunk very quickly because of the scarcity and weakness of the natural heat in them; and very young men get drunk fairly quickly because of the abundance of heat in them—for they are easily overcome by the added heat from the wine. And of the lower animals, pigs get drunk when they are fed on masses of pressed grapes, ravens and dogs when they have eaten the so-called wine-plant, monkeys and elephants when they drink wine. That is why men hunt for monkeys and ravens after getting them drunk on wine or on the wine-plant'.

---

[1]Reading μόνον for μόνοι.

F 108 R³ (Plutarch, quaestiones convivales *650A):*

Florus was surprised that Aristotle, having written in his work *On Drunkenness* that old men are most susceptible to drunkenness and women least so, did not work out the cause, although he does not normally omit such inquiries.

F 109 R³ (Athenaeus, 429F):

Aristotle says that a pint and a half of watered Samagorian wine, as they call it, will make more than forty men drunk.

F 110 R³, F 111 R³ (Athenaeus, 464CD):

Aristotle in his work *On Drunkenness* says: 'The cups they call Rhodian are introduced at drinking-parties both because of their taste and because when heated they make the wine less intoxicating. For they put myrrh, rushes, and other such stuffs into water and bring it to the boil; when this is added to the wine it is less intoxicating'. In another part of the work he says: 'Rhodian cups are made by boiling together myrrh, rushes, dill, saffron, balsam, cardamom, and cinnamon. The liquor resulting from this is added to the wine and inhibits intoxication to such an extent that, by working on the spirits, it even dispels sexual desire'.

II · LOGIC

F 112-124 R³

F 112 R³ (Alexander, Commentarius in Topica *63.11–13):*

But problems put forward in this way are physical problems, as he [sc. Aristotle] has said in his *On Problems;* for physical phenomena whose causes are unknown constitute physical problems.

F 114 R³ (Diogenes Laertius, III 80):

Plato, Aristotle says, used to divide things in this way: of goods, some are in the soul, some in the body, some external. For example, justice, wisdom, courage, temperance, and the like are in the soul; beauty, good condition, health, and strength in the body; friends, the happiness of one's country, and wealth fall among external goods.

F 114 R³ (Diogenes Laertius, III 109):

Thus of existing things, some exist in their own right, others are relative. And according to Aristotle, he [Plato] used to divide the primary things too in this way.

F 116 R³ (Simplicius, Commentarius in Categorias *65.2–10):*

But in which [sc. category] are negations, privations, and the various inflexions of the verb to be placed? This question Aristotle himself answered in his *Notes.* For in his *Methodics,* in his *Divisions,* and in another set of *Notes* entitled *On Language* (which, even if it is thought by some not to be a genuine work of Aristotle, is at all events the work of some member of the school)—in all of these, after putting forward the categories, he adds 'I mean these with their cases' (i.e. inflexions), and he connects his exposition of them with negations, privations, and indefinite terms.

F 117 R³ (Ammonius, Commentarius in Categorias *13.20–25):*

It should be known that in the old libraries forty books of *Analytics* have been found and two of *Categories.* One began: 'Of existing things, some are called homonymous, others synonymous'. The other is the one now before us. . . . This version has been preferred as being superior in order and in matter, and as everywhere proclaiming Aristotle as its begetter.

F 118 R³ (Simplicius, Commentarius in Categorias *387.17-388.1):*

But now that the language of Aristotle has been clarified, let us see what the more famous interpreters make of the passage. For since the Stoics pride themselves on their working out of logical problems, they are anxious in the matter of contraries—as well as in all other matters—to show that Aristotle furnished the starting point for everything in one book which he called *On Opposites,* in which there is an immense number of problems set forth. Of these the Stoics have set out a small portion: the rest it would not be reasonable to include in an introduction, but those which the Stoics set out in agreement with Aristotle must be mentioned. There has been laid down an ancient definition of contraries, which we have mentioned previously, viz. that they are the things which differ most from one another within a genus: in his work *On Opposites* Aristotle subjected this definition to all kinds of tests, and amended it. He asked whether things that differ are contraries, and whether difference can be contrariety, and whether complete divergence is maximum difference, and whether the things that are furthest apart are identical with those that differ most, and what distance is, and how we are to understand maximum distance. Since all this proves to lead to absurdity, something must be added to the genus, so that the definition comes to be 'the things that are furthest apart in the same genus'. He pointed out the absurdities consequent upon this; he asked whether contrariety is otherness,[1] and whether the things that are most different are contraries, and added many other criticisms. . . . [388.13–14] This is only a small part of the difficulties raised by Aristotle in his work *On Opposites.*

F 119 R³ (Simplicius, Commentarius in Categorias *389.5–10):*
    He [sc. Aristotle] in his book *On Opposites* says that justice is contrary to injustice, but that the just man is not said to be contrary, but to be contrarily disposed, to the unjust man. If these too are contraries, he says, 'contrary' will be used in two ways: things will be called contraries either in themselves, like excellence and badness, movement and rest, or by virtue of sharing in contraries, e.g. that which moves and that which rests, or the good and the bad.

F 120 R³ (Simplicius, Commentarius in Categorias *389.28-390.5):*
    This distinction was first drawn by Aristotle, who held that a simple term is not contrary to the definition of its contrary, e.g. that wisdom is not contrary to ignorance of things good, bad and neutral; but that, if there is contrariety here at all, definition is to be opposed to definition, and the definitions should be said to be contrary by being definitions of contrary things. He elaborates further on this by saying that a definition is contrary to a definition if their subjects are contrary in genus or in differentiae or in both; e.g. let the definition of beauty be mutual symmetry of parts; mutual asymmetry of parts is contrary to this, and the contrariety is in respect of the genus; but in other cases it is by virtue of differentiae: e.g. white is colour that pierces the sight, black is colour that compresses it—in these the genus is the same, but there is contrariety in respect of the differentiae.

[1]Reading ἑτερότης.

F 121 R³ (Simplicius, Commentarius in Categorias *390.19–25):*

Aristotle himself in his book *On Opposites* considered whether if someone who has lost one of two things does not of necessity gain the other, there must be something between the two; or whether this is not in all cases so. For a man who has lost a true opinion does not necessarily acquire a false one, nor does he who has lost a false one necessarily acquire a true—sometimes you pass from one opinion to a complete absence of opinion or else to knowledge. But there is nothing between true and false opinion, if ignorance and knowledge are not.

F 122 R³ (Simplicius, Commentarius in Categorias *402.30-403.1):*

Aristotle took his distinction between state and privation not from the realm of custom but from that of nature, where the antithesis of state and privation is properly applied. . . . In his book *On Opposites* he himself says that some privations are privations of natural states, others of customary states, others of possessions, others of certain other things—blindness a privation of a natural state, nakedness a privation of a customary state, loss of money a privation of something acquired in practice. There are several other types of privation, and some it is impossible some possible to lose.

F 124 R³ (Simplicius, Commentarius in Categorias *409.30-410.2):*

In the book *On Opposites* he added to these types of contrariety also that of things neither good nor bad to things neither good nor bad, saying that it is in this way that white is contrary to black, sweet to bitter, high to low, rest to movement.

III · RHETORIC AND POETICS

F 125–179 R³

F 136 R³ (Cicero, de inventione II ii 6–7):

Aristotle brought together in a single compilation the ancient writers on the art of rhetoric, going right back to their founder and inventor, Tisias; with great care he sought out the main tenets of each author name by name, wrote them down clearly, and meticulously expounded the difficult passages. And with the charm and brevity of his diction he so excelled the inventors themselves that no-one looks to learn their precepts from the original books, but everyone who wants to understand what they were resorts to Aristotle as a far more convenient expositor. Thus Aristotle published his own views and also those of his predecessors, so that from this work we become acquainted both with his own views and with the others.

F 137 R³ (Cicero, Brutus XII 46–48):

Eloquence is the companion of peace, the ally of leisure, and, so to say, the offspring of a well-ordered state. And for this reason, Aristotle says, it was when the tyrants in Sicily had been removed and restitution in private matters was after a long interval being sought in the courts, that for the first time—since that people was sharp and born to controversy—the Sicilians Corax and Tisias wrote *Arts* and *Precepts* of rhetoric; for before that no-one was accustomed to speak with the methodical application of technique, although there were several who spoke carefully and precisely. Some discussions of important topics—what are now called commonplaces—were written and prepared by Protagoras; Gorgias too did the same thing, writing speeches in praise and condemnation of particular topics, because he thought that the ability to inflate a topic with praise and again to belittle it with disparagement was the most essential part of being an orator; Antiphon of Rhamnous produced some similar works (and Thucydides, a reliable source, who actually heard him, says that no-one ever offered a better defence against a capital charge than he did when defending himself). Lysias indeed began by claiming to be versed in the art of rhetoric; but later, seeing that Theodorus was more sophisticated in matter of theory though weaker in his speeches, he took to writing speeches for others and abandoned theory; in a similar fashion, Isocrates began by denying that there was any art of rhetoric, during which period he wrote speeches for others to use in the law-courts; but when he found himself repeatedly in court on a charge of breaking the law against circumvention by judicial procedure, he gave up writing speeches for others and devoted himself entirely to composing *Arts*.

F 140 R³ (Dionysius of Halicarnassus, Isocrates XVIII 576–77):

Let no-one suppose that I do not know either that Aphareus (who was an ancestor of mine and was adopted by Isocrates) claimed in his speech against Megacleides on the Antidosis that his father wrote no speeches for the law-courts, or that Aristotle says that a large number of volumes of Isocrates' forensic speeches were published by the book-sellers. I am indeed aware of these men's statements, and I neither believe Aristotle (because he wanted to discredit the man) nor fall in with Aphareus (who was putting together a fine-seeming speech on his behalf). I think that Cephisodorus the Athenian is a sufficient judge of the truth here: he lived with Isocrates, was a most faithful pupil, and made a splendid speech for the defence in the counter-pleas against Aristotle. And so I believe that Isocrates did write some speeches for the law-courts—but not many.

F 144 R³ (Athenaeus, 556DF):
One might be surprised, Aristotle says, that nowhere in the *Iliad* did Homer portray a concubine sleeping with Menelaus, yet presented everyone else with women. Indeed, even the old men—Nestor and Phoenix—sleep with women according to him. For they had not exhausted their bodies in their youth through drunkenness or sex or even through the dyspeptic effects of gluttony, and so not unnaturally they are enjoying a vigorous old age. Thus the Spartan seems to respect his wife Helen, on whose behalf he had actually collected the army; and this is why he avoids sleeping with any other women. Agamemnon is disparaged by Thersites as a womaniser. . . . But it is hardly likely, Aristotle says, that this number of women was for use—it was rather a mark of status; after all, it was not for getting drunk that he had a large supply of wine.

F 149 R³ (Porphyry, apud Scholiast to Homer, Iliad III 277):
Why, having said the sun looks over all things and hears all things, did Homer portray him as needing a messenger in the case of his oxen?. . .
Aristotle resolves this by saying that it is either because the sun indeed sees all things but not at one and the same time; or because Lampetia was messenger to the sun in the way sight is to man; or because, he says, it was appropriate to speak in this way both for Agamemnon when swearing the oath in the Single Combat—'and sun, you who look over all things and hear all things'—and for Odysseus when addressing his companions; for he does not also see what goes on in Hades.

F160 R³ (Porphyry, apud Scholiast to Homer, Iliad X 153):
The placing of the spears on their spikes is thought to be poor; especially since a single one of them, by falling over, had already created panic everywhere at night. Aristotle resolves this by saying that Homer always portrays things as they were at that time. And the ancient practice was the same as present practice among the barbarians; and this is the custom of many of the barbarians.

F 161 R³ (Porphyry, apud Scholiast to Homer, Iliad X 252):
For example, it is agreed that the following is one of the old puzzles: 'and now the star had advanced, and more than two parts of the night had passed, and a third part still remained'. For how is it that if two parts and more have gone, yet the third

part is left and not a fraction of the third?. . . . Aristotle thinks to resolve it as follows, where he says: 'Division into two may in this case be division into equal parts. Now since[1] what is more than half is indeterminate, when it is increased to such an extent that a third of the whole is left, a stickler for accuracy would determine this and indicate how much remains in order to make clear by how much the half of the whole has been increased. For example, 3 is half of 6. If 6 were divided into two equal parts, they will be 3. If one part is increased, it is unclear whether this is by a fraction or by a whole unit. Now if it becomes larger by a whole unit[2], the part still remaining will be a third of the whole; and if you say "one of the two parts became more and left a third part," you indicate that the increase has been by a unit—since the three have become four and there remain two, which is a third of the original six. Now since the twelve parts of night can be divided into two equal divisions—into sixes—and one of these parts was increased and became larger, and it was unclear by how many hours it had been increased (for the increase could have been by one, two, three, or more hours), the poet determines the size of this indeterminate "more" and, because it was increased by two hours, he adds that a third was left—since eight hours have gone by and four remain, which is a third of the whole. Thus too, if something had 18 parts (dividing into two nines) and you were to say that more than one part of the two-part division has gone and the third part remains, you would make clear, by saying that the third (i. e. 6) remains, that you mean that 12 have been taken. Suppose we ask the same question of the hours of a full day, and suppose someone to say that more than one part of the two-part division of the hours has passed—still without determining how much—and to add that the third part of the whole remains: it is clear that, since the two-part division is into 12 and 12 and a third of the whole (i.e. 8) remains, the "more" of the one part amounts to 4, so that 16 hours have passed in all and 8 remain. Thus when there is a division into two and into three equal parts, anyone who adds to one part of the two-part division and leaves a third of the three-part division, determines in how much more the increase consists. Thus the poet cleverly indicates how large the indeterminate part[3] of the increase of the half was—that it consisted of two hours and that the eighth hour has passed[4]—by saying "and a third part still remained." For, if you know that the night contains 12 hours in all, and that division into two parts gives 6 and 6, and division into three 4 and 4 and 4,[5] and if you hear that more than one part of the two-part division has passed and then learn that a third of the three-part division, i.e. 4 hours, remains, you know at once that two hours have gone by since midnight'.

F 166 R³ (Porphyry, apud Scholiast to Homer, Iliad XXIV 15):
    Why did Achilles go on dragging Hector around the tomb of Patroclus, treating the corpse contrary to established custom? There is a solution, Aristotle

---

[1] Reading ἐπεὶ δή, and placing a comma before ὅταν.
[2] Comma after γένηται, no comma after ἀπολειπόμενον.
[3] Omitting τρίτον.   [4] Text uncertain.
[5] Adding καὶ δ'.

says, referring to the customs of the time—they were like that, since even today in Thessaly men drag [corpses] around the tombs.

F 170 R³ (Scholiast to Homer, Odyssey V 93):
    'And she mixed red nectar':
    If the gods drink nothing but nectar, why does Calypso give it to Hermes after mixing it? For if it has been mixed with water, they drink not only nectar but water also. And yet, he says, she served him plain ambrosia 'and mixed red nectar'. Now Aristotle in resolving this says that 'she mixed' means either to combine one liquid with another one or to pour out; for 'to mix' means both. So here 'and she mixed red nectar' means not to combine but simply to pour out.

F 171 R³ (Scholiast to Homer, Odyssey V 334):
    Aristotle asks why he speaks of Calypso and Circe and Ino alone as 'having speech (αὐδήεσσα)'; for all the others had voices. He did not want to solve this, but emends the text, in some places to αὐλήεσσα—by which he says is meant that they were solitary—and in the case of Ino to οὐδήεσσα—for this characteristic belonged to all and only these people since they all resided on earth.

F 172 R³ (Scholiast to Homer, Odyssey IX 106):
    Aristotle asks how Polyphemus the Cyclops was a Cyclops himself when neither his father (who was Poseidon) nor his mother was a Cyclops. He himself solves it by reference to another myth; for horses were sired by Boreas, and the horse Pegasus had Poseidon and Medusa as parents.

F 175 R³ (Eustathius, 1717, on Homer, Odyssey XII 130):
    It should be recognized that they say that Aristotle gives an allegorical account of these herds, and especially of the herds of oxen, associating them with the days of the twelve lunar months, which number three hundred and fifty; for that is also the number of the seven herds which each contain fifty beasts. That is why Homer says that they neither are born nor die; for those days never vary in amount.

IV · ETHICS

F 182 R³ (David, Prolegomena Philosophiae *74. 17–25):*

He [sc. Aristotle] also wrote on economy, where he discusses household management (he says there that four things must come together in a household: the relation of man to wife, love of father for children, fear of slaves for masters, and that expenditure be commensurate with income—for each lack of measure is ignoble: if income is found to be large, expenditure small, there is something ignoble—such a man is found to be miserly; if income is small, expenditure large, there is something ignoble—such a man is found to be extravagant).

F 183 R³ (Clement, Paedagogus *III xii 84):*

I would advise even married men not to kiss their wives at home in front of the servants; for Aristotle does not even allow us to laugh in front of our slaves, still less to let our wives be seen to be embraced in their presence.

F 185 R³ (Syrianus, Commentarius in Metaphysica *120.33–121.4):*

That he [sc. Aristotle] has nothing more than this to say against the theory of Forms is shown both by the first book of this treatise [i.e. the *Metaphysics*] and by the two books he wrote *On the Forms;* for it is by taking everywhere practically these same arguments, and sometimes cutting them up and subdividing them, sometimes putting them forward more concisely, that he tries to correct his predecessors in philosophy.

F 186 R³ (Scholiast to Dionysius Thrax, 116.13–16 Hilgard):

And one must realize that it is of universals and things eternal that there are definitions, as Aristotle too has said in *On Ideas,* which he wrote against Plato's Ideas. For while particular things all change and never remain in the same condition, universals are unchangeable and eternal.

(Alexander, Commentarius in Metaphysica *79.3–88.2):*

They [sc. the Platonists] made further use of the sciences in establishing the Ideas, and in more ways than one, as he [sc. Aristotle] says in the first book of *On Ideas;* and the arguments he seems to have in mind at the present moment [i.e. 5 in the *Metaphysics*] are the following sort. If every science performs its task by referring to some one and the same thing and not to any of the particulars, then there will be with respect to each science something different apart from perceptible individuals, eternal and a pattern for the things produced in each science; and such a thing is the Idea. Again, the things of which there are sciences exist; the sciences are of certain different things apart from particulars (for the latter are infinite and indeterminate, while the sciences are of determinate things); so there are certain 10 things apart from particulars, and these are the Ideas. Again, if medicine is not a science of this particular health but of health simply, there will be a certain health-itself; and if geometry is not a science of this particular equal and this particular commensurate, but of equal simply and the commensurate simply, there will be a certain equal-itself and a commensurate-itself; and these are the Ideas. 15

Now such arguments do not prove the thesis at issue, which was that there are Ideas; but they do prove that there are certain things apart from particulars and perceptibles. But it does not follow that if there are certain things which are apart from particulars, these are Ideas; for the common objects, which we say are also the objects of the sciences, are apart from the particulars. Again, these arguments show that there are also Ideas of the things that fall under the arts. For every art too 20 refers what is produced by it to some one thing, and things of which there are arts exist, and the arts are of certain different things apart from particulars. And the last argument, besides equally failing to prove that there are Ideas, will also be thought to establish Ideas of things for which they do not wish there to be Ideas. For if, because medicine is not a science of this particular health but of health simply, there is some thing health-itself, then such will be the case also in each of the arts. For an art is not of the particular nor of *this*, but of that simply which is its concern, e.g. carpentry is of chair simply but not of this particular one, and of bed simply but not of this particular one; and sculpture, painting, building, and each of the other arts are similarly related to the things that fall under them. So there will be an Idea of each of the things that fall under the arts—which they do not want.

They also use the following argument to establish the Ideas. If each of the many men is a man, and each of the animals is an animal, and similarly in the other cases; and if in the case of each of these it is not that something is predicated of itself but that some one thing is being predicated of all of them while not being the same as any one of them, then there will be something which is apart from the particulars which exist, separated from them and eternal; for it is predicated always alike of all the changing particulars. And that which is one over many, both separated from them and eternal, is an Idea; so there are Ideas.

This argument, he [sc. Aristotle] says, establishes Ideas even of negations and of things that do not exist. For one and the same negation is predicated of many things and of things which do not exist, and is not the same as any one of the things which it is truly predicated of. For 'not-man' is predicated of horse and of dog and of everything apart from man, and for this reason is one thing over many and is not the same as any one of the things of which it is predicated. Again, it always remains alike true of like things; for 'not-musical' is true of many things (of everything non-musical), and similarly 'not-man' of non-men; consequently, there are Ideas also of negations. But that is absurd; for how could there be an Idea of non-being? For if one were to accept that, there would be a single Idea for things that are of *different* kinds and that differ in every respect—of, as it might be, line and man; for all these are non-horses. Again, there will be a single Idea both of things that are indeterminate and of things that are infinite. But also of what is primary and what is secondary; for both man and animal are non-wood, of which the one is primary, the other secondary—and they did not want there to be either genera or Ideas of such things. Clearly, this argument too fails to show that there are Ideas; but it too tends to show that what is commonly predicated is other than the particulars of which it is predicated. Again, the very people who wish to prove that what is commonly predicated of several things is some single thing and in fact an Idea, try to establish it from negations. For if someone in denying something of several things will do so by referring to some single thing (for someone who says of a man that he is not white and of a horse that it is not white is not in each case denying something peculiar to it but is making reference to some single thing and denying the same white of each), then someone in affirming the same thing of several things will not be affirming something different in each case but there will be some single thing which he is affirming, e.g. man, with reference to some one and the same thing; for as with negation so with affirmation. So there is something that is different apart from what is in the perceptibles, which is the cause of the affirmation that is both true of several things and common, and this is the Idea. Now this argument, he says, produces Ideas not only of things that are affirmed but also of things that are denied; for in both cases there is a similar reference to something single.

The argument that tries to establish that there are Ideas from thinking is as follows. If whenever we think of man or footed or animal, we are thinking of something that is both among the things that exist yet is not one of the particulars (for when the latter have perished the same thought remains), clearly there is something apart from particulars and perceptibles, which we think of whether the latter exist or not; for we are certainly not then thinking of something non-existent. And this is a Form and an Idea. Now he says that this argument also establishes Ideas of things that are perishing and have perished, and in general of things that are both particulars and perishable—e.g. of Socrates, of Plato; for we think of these men and keep some image of them even when they no longer exist. And indeed we also think of things that do not exist at all, like a Hippocentaur, a Chimaera: consequently neither does this argument show that there are Ideas.

The argument that tries to establish Ideas from relatives is as follows. In those cases where some same thing is predicated of several things not homonymously but as revealing some single nature, it is true of them either by their strictly being what is indicated by what is predicated, as when we say Socrates is a man and Plato is; or by their being likenesses of the genuine things, as when we predicate man of painted men (for in the case of these latter we reveal the likenesses of men by indicating the same particular nature in all of them); or on the grounds of one of them being the pattern, while the rest are likenesses, as if we were to call both Socrates and likenesses of him men. And we predicate the equal itself of things here, although it is predicated of them only homonymously; for neither does the same account fit all of them, nor do we indicate things that are truly equal; for among perceptibles quantity changes and shifts continuously and is not determinate. Nor moreover do any of the things here accurately receive the account of the equal. And no more indeed on the grounds of one of them being pattern, the other likeness; for one is no more pattern or likeness than the other. And even if someone were to accept that the likeness is not homonymous with its pattern, it still follows that these equal things are equal as likenesses of that which is strictly and truly equal. And if this is the case, there is some equal itself quite strictly, relative to which things here, as likenesses, are both produced and called equal, and this is an Idea, a pattern for those things which are produced relative to it.

This argument, Aristotle says, establishes Ideas even of relative terms. At any rate the present proof has been advanced in the case of the equal, which is a relative; but they used to say that there were no Ideas of relatives because while Ideas, being for them kinds of substances, existed in their own right, relatives had their being in their relationship to one another. And again, if the equal is equal to an equal, there will be more than one Idea of the equal; for the equal-itself is equal to an equal-itself; for if it were not equal to something, it would not be equal at all. Again,

by the same argument there will have to be Ideas of unequals too; for opposites are
30   in a similar case—there will or will not be Ideas of both; and the unequal is admitted
by them too to involve more things than one.

The argument which introduces the third man is as follows. They say that what
are commonly predicated of substances both are strictly such things and are Ideas.
84.1   And again, things that are like each other are like each other by sharing in the same
certain thing, which is strictly the thing in question; and this is the Idea. But if this is
the case, and what is commonly predicated of certain things, if it is not the same as
any one of those things of which it is predicated, is some other thing apart from it
(for that is why man-himself is a genus—because while being predicated of the
5   particulars it is not the same man as any of them), then there will be some third man
apart both from the particular, e.g. Socrates and Plato, and from the Idea; and this
too will be itself one in number.

And there was an argument presented by the sophists introducing the third
man as follows. If when we say 'a man is walking' we are saying neither that man as
10   an Idea is walking (for the Idea is not capable of motion) nor that some particular
individual is (how could we when we do not know who it is? For while we know that
a man is walking we do not know which particular man it is of whom we are saying
it), we are saying that some other third man apart from these is walking: so there
15   will be a third man of whom we predicated the walking. Now this argument, which
is sophistical, is given encouragement by those who separate what is common from
the particulars, as those who posit the Ideas do. And Phanias says, in *Against
Diodorus,* that the sophist Polyxenus introduced the third man by saying "If it is
both by participation and sharing in the Idea, i.e. in man-himself, that man exists,
then there must be some man who will have his existence relative to the Idea. But
20   neither man-himself, i.e. the Idea, exists by participation in the Idea, nor does any
particular man. It remains then that there is some third man who has his existence
relative to the Idea."

The third man is proved also in the following way. If what is predicated truly
of several items is also something other apart from the things of which it is
predicated, separated from them (for it is this that those who posit the Ideas think to
25   prove; for in their opinion man-himself is something because man is predicated
truly of particular men, who are more than one in number, and is different from
these particular men)—but if this is so, there will be some third man. For if the man
that is predicated is different from those of whom he is predicated, and exists on his
own, and man is predicated both of the particular men and of the Idea, then there
85.1   will be some third man apart both from the particular and from the Idea. On this
basis there will be also a fourth man, predicated of the third man, of the Idea, and of
the particulars; and similarly also a fifth, and so on *ad infinitum.*

This argument is the same as the first; this comes about for them because they
5   supposed that like things were like by sharing in the same thing; for both men and
the Ideas are like. Now he refuted both these arguments though they were thought
to be rather refined, the one on the grounds that it established Ideas even of relative
terms, and the other because it introduces a third man and then multiplies men to

infinity. And a similar multiplication will be suffered by any of the other things of which they say there are Ideas. While others have used the first exposition of the third man—there is a specially clear use by Eudemus in his *On Diction*—the last was used by Aristotle himself both in the first book of *On Ideas* and a little later on in the present work [i.e. the *Metaphysics*].

Now they are more—in fact most—concerned to establish that there are first principles; for first principles are for them first principles of the Ideas themselves. And the one and indefinite dyad are first principles, as he has said a little earlier and has himself explained in his *On the Good;* but in their view these are the first principles of number too. Now he says that these arguments for establishing the Ideas destroy these first principles.

And if these are destroyed, the things after the first principles will also be destroyed, given that they come from the first principles; so consequently the Ideas too will be. For if in the case of all things which have a common predicate it is both separated and an Idea, and if the dyad is predicated of the indefinite dyad too, there will be something primary and an Idea of this latter; and consequently the indefinite dyad will no longer be a first principle. But nor will the dyad in its turn be both primary and a first principle; for number is predicated of it in its turn since it is an Idea; for the Ideas are assumed by them to be numbers: consequently number, being a kind of Idea, will be primary for them. And if this is so, number will be prior to the indefinite dyad, which is for them a first principle, but not the dyad to number; and if this is so, the dyad would no longer be a first principle, if it is what it is by sharing in something. Again, while it is assumed to be a first principle of number, yet according to the argument just stated number becomes prior to it; but if number is relative (for every number is a number of something), and number is first of the things that exist, given that it is prior even to the dyad which they assumed as a first principle, then on their view what is relative will be prior to what exists in its own right. And that is absurd; for everything relative is secondary. For a relative indicates the condition of a pre-existing nature, which is prior to that condition which happens to belong to it. . . . But even if someone were to say that number is a quantity and not a relative, it would have as a consequence that quantity was prior to substance.

Again, they are committed to saying that what is relative is both a first principle of and prior to what exists in its own right, in so far as the Idea is in their view a first principle of substances, and what it is for an Idea to be an Idea lies in its being a pattern, and a pattern is relative; for a pattern is a pattern of something. Again, if being for Ideas lies in their being patterns, then things that come into being in relation to them and of which they are Ideas will be likenesses of them; and so someone might say that according to them all naturally constituted things become relative; for all things are likenesses and patterns. Again, if being for Ideas lies in their being patterns, and a pattern exists for the sake of what comes into being relative to it, and what exists on account of something else is less worthy than that thing, then the Ideas will be less worthy than what comes into being relative to them.

The following are some of the arguments which, in addition to those already stated, through the positing of Ideas destroy their first principles. If what is
87.5 commonly predicated of certain things is both the first principle and Idea of those things, and if first principle is commonly predicated of the first principles and element of the elements, there will be something prior to and a first principle of the first principles and of the elements; and in this way there will be neither first principles nor elements. Again Idea is not prior to Idea; for all Ideas similarly are first principles. And the one-itself and the dyad-itself are alike Ideas—as is
10 man-itself and horse-itself and each of the other Ideas; so there will not be any of these that is prior to any other—so that none will be a first principle either; so it is not the case that the one and the indefinite dyad are first principles. Again, it is absurd that an Idea should be given form by an Idea; for all are Forms; but if the one and the indefinite dyad are first principles, there will be Ideas given form by Ideas; for the dyad-itself will be given form by the one-itself; for it is in this way that they say that these are first principles—in the sense that one is form, the dyad
15 matter; so these are not first principles. And if they say that the indefinite dyad is not an Idea, then first there will be something prior to it although it is a first principle; for there is the dyad-itself, by sharing in which even this is a dyad, since this is not the dyad-itself; for it is by virtue of sharing that dyad will be predicated of it, since the same goes for particular dyads. Again, if the Ideas are simple, they will not come from different first principles, but the one and the indefinite dyad are
20 different. Again, the number of dyads will be amazing if one is the dyad-itself, another the indefinite dyad, another the mathematical dyad, which we use in counting and which is not the same as either of the former, and again besides these another in numerable and perceptible things. This is absurd; so that clearly by
88.1 following the very assumptions made by them it is possible to destroy the first principles, which are for them more important than the Ideas.

(Alexander, Commentarius in Metaphysica *97.27–98.24):*
That it is not, as Eudoxus and some others thought, by mixture with the Ideas that other things exist: Aristotle says it is easy to infer many impossibilities as consequences of this opinion. If the Ideas are mixed with the other things, in the
98.1 first place, they will be bodies; for it is of bodies that there is mixture. Again, they will be contrary to each other; for mixture occurs with respect to contrariety. Again, mixture will occur in such a way that either a whole Idea will be in each of the things with which it is mixed or else part of one. But if a whole, then what is one in number will be in several things; for an Idea is one in number. While if in parts, a
5 man will be what participates in a part of man-himself, not what participates in man-himself as a whole. Again, Ideas will be divisible and partible, although they are impassive. Then they will be uniform if all things which have some part from it are like each other. But how can the Forms be uniform? For part of man cannot be a
10 man, as a part of gold is gold. Again, as Aristotle himself says a little later [sc. in the *Metaphysics*], in each thing there will not be one Idea mixed but many; for if there is one Idea of animal and another of man, and a man is both an animal and a man,

he will participate in both Ideas. And man-himself, the Idea, insofar as it is also an animal, will also itself participate in animal; and consequently the Ideas will no longer be simple but composed from many, and some of them primary, others 15 secondary. But if it is not an animal, surely it is absurd to say that man is not an animal? And again, if they are mixed with things that are relative to them, how can they still be patterns, as they say they are? For it is not in this way, as the result of a mixture, that patterns are causes of the similarity that their likenesses have to them. And again, they will be destroyed along with the destruction of the things they are in. Nor yet will they be in themselves separable, but will be in the things that 20 participate in them. In addition to these points, they will no longer be unchange-able—and all the other absurdities which Aristotle in his examination of this opinion in the second book of his *On Ideas* showed it to have. For it was for this reason that he said 'for it is easy to infer many impossibilities against this view'—for they were inferred there.

F 191 R³ (Apollonius, historiae mirabiles *6):*

Again in Caulonia, according to Aristotle ...[1] in addition to much other information about him, he says that in Tyrrhenia he killed a deadly biting snake by biting it himself. He also says that Pythagoras foretold to the Pythagoreans the coming political strife; that is why he departed to Metapontum unobserved by anyone, and while he was crossing the Cosas he, with others, heard the river say "Good morning, Pythagoras"—and those present were terrified. He once appeared both at Croton and at Metapontum on the same day and at the same hour. Once, while sitting in the theatre, he stood up—so Aristotle tells—and showed those sitting there his own thigh, which was golden.

F 191 R³ (Aelian, varia historia *II 26):*

Aristotle says that Pythagoras was called by the people of Croton the Hyperborean Apollo. The son of Nicomachus adds that Pythagoras was once seen by many people, on the same day and at the same hour, both at Metapontum and at Croton; and at Olympia, during the games, he got up and showed that one of his thighs was golden.[2] The same writer says that while crossing the river Cosas he was hailed by the river, and that many people heard him so hailed.

F 192 R³ (Iamblichus, vita pythagorica *VI 31):*

Aristotle relates in his books *On the Pythagorean Philosophy* that the following division was preserved by the Pythagoreans as one of their greatest secrets: of rational living creatures, some are gods, some men, and some beings like Pythagoras.

---

[1]There is a lacuna here.
[2]Text uncertain.

F 193 R³ (Apuleius, de deo Socratis XX 166–7):

But I suppose Aristotle is a sufficient witness to the fact that the Pythagoreans marvelled greatly at anyone who said he had never seen a divine being.

F 194 R³ (Aulus Gellius, IV xi 12):

Since the fact is unexpected, I add Plutarch's own words: 'Aristotle says the Pythagoreans abstain from eating womb and heart, the sea anemone, and certain other such things, but use all other kinds'.

F 194 R³ (Diogenes Laertius, VIII 19):

Aristotle says that at times they [sc. the Pythagoreans] abstain from womb and red mullet.

F 195 R³ (Diogenes Laertius, VIII 34):

Aristotle says in his work *On the Pythagoreans* that he [sc. Pythagoras] enjoyed abstention from beans either because they are like the genitals or because they are like the gates of Hades . . .[1] (for they alone have no joints), or because they are destructive, or because they are like the nature of the universe, or because they are oligarchical (being used in the choice of rulers by lot).

F 196 R³ (Porphyry, Vita Pythagorae 41):

Pythagoras used to say certain things in a mystical and symbolic way, and Aristotle has recorded many of these; e.g. that he called the sea the tears of Cronos, the Bears the hands of Rhea, the Pleiades the lyre of the Muses, the planets the dogs of Persephone; the ringing sound of bronze when struck was, he said, the voice of a divine being imprisoned in the bronze.

F 197 R³ (Porphyry, Vita Pythagorae 42):

There was also another kind of symbol, of the following sort: 'Do not step over a balance', i.e. do not be covetous: 'Do not poke the fire with a sword', i.e. do not vex with sharp words a man swollen with anger; 'Do not pluck the crown', i.e. do not offend against the laws which are the crowns of cities. Or again, 'Do not eat heart', i.e. do not vex yourself with grief: 'Do not sit on the corn ration', i.e. do not live in idleness; 'When on a journey do not turn back', i.e. when you are dying, do not cling to this life; 'Do not walk the highway', i.e. do not follow the opinions of the many but pursue those of the few and educated; 'Do not receive swallows in your house', i.e. do not take into your house talkative men who cannot control their tongues; 'Add to the burdens of the burdened, do not lighten them', i.e. contribute to no man's sloth, but to his excellence; 'Do not carry images of the gods in your rings', i.e. do not make your thought and speech about the gods manifest and obvious, nor show it to many; 'Make your libations to the gods at the ear of the cup', i.e. celebrate and honour the gods with music, for this goes through the ears.

---

[1]There is a lacuna in the text.

F 198 R³ (Martianus Capella, VII 731):

(Philosophy speaks). 'Although Aristotle, one of my followers, reasoning from the fact that it [sc. the unit] itself is one alone and wishes always to be sought after, asserts that it is called Desire because it desires itself, since it has nothing beyond itself and, never carried beyond itself or linked with other things, turns its own ardours on itself'.

F 199 R³ (Theo of Smyrna, p. 22. 5–9 Hiller):

But Aristotle in his *Pythagoreans* says that the One partakes of the nature of both; for added to an even number it makes an odd, and added to an odd an even, which it could not do if it did not share in both natures; and that for this reason the One was called even-odd.

F 200 R³ (Simplicius, Commentarius in de Caelo, 386.20–23):

Right, above and before they called good, and left, below and behind evil, as Aristotle himself related in his collection of Pythagorean doctrines.

F 201 R³ (Stobaeus, Eclogae I xviii 1c):

In the first book of his work *On the Philosophy of Pythagoras* Aristotle writes that the heaven is one, and that time and breath and the void, which divides for ever the regions of different things, are drawn in from the infinite.

F 202 R³ (Alexander, Commentarius in Metaphysica 75.15–17):

Of the arrangement in the heavens which the Pythagoreans assigned to the numbers, Aristotle informs us in the second book of his work *On the Belief of the Pythagoreans.*

F 203 R³ (Alexander, Commentarius in Metaphysica 38.8–41.2):

He [sc. Aristotle] has shown what likenesses the Pythagoreans said there were between numbers and the things that exist and come into being; for assuming that reciprocity and equality were properties of justice and finding them to exist in numbers, they said, for this reason, that the first square number was justice, for in every case the first of a number of things that admit of the same definition is most truly that which it is said to be. Now this number some declared to be the number 4, because, being the first square number, it is divided into equals and is itself equal (being twice 2), while others declared it to be the number 9, which is the first square number produced by multiplying an odd number (3) by itself. Again, they said the number 7 was season; for natural things seem to have their perfect seasons of birth and completion in terms of sevens, as in the case of man. Men are born after seven months, they begin to grow their teeth in seven months, they reach puberty about the end of the second set of seven years, and grow beards about the end of the third. The sun, too, since it is itself thought to be (as he says) the cause of seasons, they maintain to be established where the number 7 resides, which they identify with season; for the sun holds the seventh place among the ten bodies that move round

39.1 the centre and hearth of the universe; it moves after the sphere of the fixed stars and the five spheres of the planets; after it come the moon, eighth, and the earth, ninth, and after the earth the counter-earth. Since the number 7 neither generates nor is generated by any of the numbers in the decad, for this reason they also said that it

5 was Athene. For the number 2 generates 4, 3 generates 9 and 6, 4 generates 8, and 5 generates 10, and 4, 6, 8, 9 and 10 are generated, but 7 neither generates any number nor is generated from any; and so too Athene was motherless and ever virgin. Marriage, they said, was the number 5, because it is the union of male and female, and according to them the odd is male and the even female, and 5 is the first

10 number generated from the first even number, 2, and the first odd number, 3; for the odd is for them (as I said) male, and the even female. Mind (which was the name they[1] gave to soul) and substance they identified with the One. Because it was unchanging, alike everywhere, and a ruling principle they called mind both a unit

15 and one; but they also applied these names to substance, because it is primary. Opinion they identified with the number 2 because it can move in both directions; they also called it movement and addition. Picking out such likenesses between things and numbers, they assumed numbers to be the first principles of things, saying that all things are composed of numbers.

20 But they also saw the harmonies to be constituted according to particular numbers, and said that numbers were the first principles of these also; the octave depends on the ratio 2:1, the fifth on the ratio 3:2, the fourth on the ratio 4:3. They said, too, that the whole universe is constructed in accordance with a certain harmony . . . because it consists of numbers and is constructed in accordance with

25 number and harmony. For the bodies that move round the centre have their distances in a certain ratio, and some move faster and others slower, and in their movement the slower strike a deep note and the faster a high one, and these notes,

40.1 being proportionate to the distances, make the resultant sound harmonious; and since they said that number was the first principle of this harmony, they naturally made number the first principle of the heavens and of the universe. For they thought the sun to be, say, twice as far from the earth as the moon, Venus to be

5 three times as far, Mercury four times, and each of the others to be in a certain ratio, and the movement of the heavens to be harmonious, and the bodies that move the greatest distance to move the fastest, those that move the least distance the slowest, and the intermediate bodies to move in proportion to the size of their orbit.

10 On the basis of these likenesses between things and numbers, they supposed existing things both to be composed of numbers and to be particular numbers.

Thinking numbers to be prior to nature as a whole as to natural things (for nothing could either exist or be known at all without number, while numbers could be known even apart from other things), they laid it down that the elements and

15 first principles of numbers are the first principles of all things. These elements were, as has been said, the even and the odd, of which they thought the odd to be limited and the even unlimited; of numbers they thought the unit was the first principle, composed of both the even and the odd; for the unit was at the same time even-odd,

---

[1]Reading εἶπον.

which he used to prove from its power of generating both odd and even number: added to an even it generates an odd, added to an odd it generates an even.   20

As regards the agreements which they found between numbers and harmonious combinations on the one hand, and the attributes and parts of the heavens on the other, they took these for granted straight off, as being obvious, and showed that the heavens are composed of numbers and arranged in harmony. If any of the celestial phenomena seemed to fail to conform with the numerical principles, they made the   25 necessary additions themselves and tried to fill the gap so as to make their whole treatment of the matter consistent. At least, treating the decad straight off as the perfect number, and seeing that in the visible world the moving spheres are nine in number—seven spheres of the planets, the eighth that of the fixed stars, the ninth the earth (for this, too, they thought, moves in a circle about the resting hearth of   30 the universe, which according to them is fire)—they added, in their system, a counter-earth, which they supposed to move in an opposite direction to the earth, and to be for that reason invisible to those on earth.

Aristotle speaks of these matters both in the *De Caelo* and, with greater   41.1 precision, in his *Beliefs of the Pythagoreans.*

F 204 R³ (Simplicius, Commentarius in de Caelo *511.26–31):*

The Pythagoreans . . . do not say that the earth is about the centre, but that the centre of the universe is a fire, and that about the centre the counter-earth moves, being itself an earth but called a counter-earth because it is on the opposite side to our earth. 'After the counter-earth came our earth, itself also moving about the centre, and after the earth the moon': so he himself [sc. Aristotle] relates in his work *On the Pythagorean Doctrines.*

F 204 R³ (Simplicius, Commentarius in de Caelo *512.12–13):*

For this reason, some call it [sc. fire] the tower of Zeus, as Aristotle himself related in his work *On the Pythagorean Doctrines* . . .

F 205 R³ (Simplicius, Commentarius in de Caelo *392.16–32):*

How can he [sc. Aristotle] say that the Pythagoreans place us in the upper part and on the right side of the universe, and those opposite to us in the lower part and on the left side if, as he himself relates in the second book of his collection of Pythagorean doctrines, they say that one part of the whole universe is up and the other down, and that the lower part is right and the upper left, and that we are in the lower part? Is it that he has used the words 'upper' and 'on the right' here [sc. in the *de Caelo*] in accordance not with his own view but with that of the Pythagoreans? They coupled up and before with right, down and behind with left. But Alexander thinks that the statement in Aristotle's collection of Pythagorean doctrines has been altered by someone and should run thus—'the upper part of the universe is on the right, the lower part on the left, and we are in the upper part,' not in the lower as the text now runs. In this way it will agree with what he says here, that we, who say we live in the lower part and therefore on the left side (since the lower part is coupled with the left side) are in opposition to the Pythagorean statement that we live in the upper part and on the right side. That the text has been altered is perhaps likely, since Aristotle knows that the Pythagoreans coupled the higher position with the right side and the lower with the left.

F 206 R³ (Simplicius, Commentarius in de Caelo 296.16–18):

In his epitome of Plato's Timaeus he [sc. Aristotle] writes: 'He says it [sc. the universe] is generated; for it is perceptible, and he is assuming that what is perceptible is generated and that what is intelligible is not generated.'

F 207 R³ (Damascius, dubitationes et solutiones 306):

Aristotle in his work on Archytas relates that Pythagoras too called matter 'other', as being in flux and always becoming other.

F 208 R³ (Simplicius, Commentaria in de Caelo 294.33–295.22):

A few words quoted from Aristotle's On Democritus will reveal the line of thought of those men [sc. the Atomists]:—Democritus thinks the nature of the eternal entities consists of small substances infinite in number; he supposes a place for them, different from them and infinite in extent, and to this he applies the names 'void', 'nothing', and 'the infinite', while to each of the substances he applies the names 'thing', 'solid', and 'existent'. He thinks the substances are so small as to escape our senses, but have all sorts of shapes and figures, and differences of size. From these, then,[1] as from elements, are generated and compounded visible and perceptible masses. The substances are at variance and move in the void because of their dissimilarity as well as the other aforesaid differences, and as they move they collide with each other and interlock in such a way that, while they touch and get close to each other, yet a single substance is never in reality produced from them; for it would be very simple-minded to suppose that two or more things could ever become one. The cause of these substances remaining with one another for some time he ascribes to the bodies fitting into one another and catching hold of one another; for some of them are scalene, others hook-shaped, others concave, others convex, and others have countless other differences. He thinks that they cling to one another and remain together until some stronger necessity arriving from the environment scatters them apart and separates them. He ascribes the genesis and the separation opposed to it not only to animals but also to plants, and to worlds, and generally to all perceptible bodies.

---

[1]Reading ἤδη for ἤδει.

VI · PHYSICS

F 209–278 R³

F 209 R³ (Aulus Gellius, XX iv 3–4):

. . .I sent him words excerpted from a book of Aristotle's entitled *Standard Problems:* 'Why are the Dionysian artists for the most part bad? Because they have hardly any share in reason and philosophy, since the great part of their life is involved in necessary skills, and because for a large part of the time they are in a state of incontinence, and sometimes in a state of poverty—and both of these conditions incline to produce badness'.

F 211 R³ (Simplicius, Commentarius in de Caelo 505.23–25):

Aristotle too makes this clear in his *Scientific Problems,* where he raises puzzles for the assumptions of the astronomers from the fact that the sizes of the planets do not appear equal.

F 214 R³ (Aulus Gellius, XIX v 9):

I have extracted from the book a few of Aristotle's own words and written them down: 'Why is water from snow and ice bad? Because whenever water is frozen the finest and lightest part turns to vapour. A sign of this is that when it freezes and then thaws it becomes less than before; therefore, once the healthiest part has gone, of necessity in every case what is left behind is worse'.

F 215 R³ (Plutarch, quaestiones naturales 912A):

Why are trees and seeds naturally nourished more by rain water than by running water? . . . Or is what Aristotle says true?—that it is because rain water is recent and fresh while pool water is stale and old.

F 225 R³ (Galen, de simplicium medicamentorum temperamentis XII 164 K):

Now astringent things once they have been burnt lose much of their heat, while things that are not of that sort gain in heat. But nothing which has been burnt is completely cold. For there is left behind in it as it were a kind of ember (that is how Aristotle names it); and this is what is cleaned away in washing. It is the lightest part of the substance of burnt things, and when it departs along with the water, what is left of the burnt thing is an earthy substance; for the burning exhausts all the moisture, and what is left behind is earthy together with what Aristotle calls the ember.

F 232 R³ (Apollonius, historiae mirabiles *51):*

Aristotle talks of something worthy of note in his *Scientific Problems:* he says that a man who has fed and drunk weighs the same as when he is fasting; and he also attempts to give an account of the cause of this.

F 234 R³ (Apollonius, historiae mirabiles *9):*

Aristotle in his *Scientific Problems* says: 'Those who eat only one meal a day are likely to have more irritable characters than those who eat two'.

F 235 R³ (Athenaeus, 692BC):

Aristotle, the most learned of men, asks in his *Scientific Problems:* 'Why is it that those who use hair-oil are greyer? Is it because the oil is a drying agent because of the herbs in it (hence those who use hair-oil are dry), and dryness makes men greyer? For either greyness is a drying up of the hair or it is a lack of heat—and dryness puts out fire. That is why felt caps also make men go grey more quickly; for the natural moisture of the hair is drawn out'.

F 237 R³ (Apollonius, historiae mirabiles *28):*

Aristotle in *Pertaining to Animals:* 'Wax in the ears, being bitter, becomes sweet in long illnesses'. And this, he says, has been observed to occur in many cases. And in the *Scientific Problems* he also gives the cause of this occurrence.

F 242 R³ (Plutarch, quaestiones convivales *734DF):*

. . . what they say about dreams—that they are particularly uncertain and false during the months when the leaves fall—somehow came up after dinner. . . . Your friends—my sons—thought that Aristotle had solved the puzzle, and they believed that there was no need to argue or search any further, except to say as he does that the harvest is the cause. For fruit, when it is fresh and juicy, generates a quantity of disorderly wind in the body; for it is not likely that wine alone boils and protests or that oil alone when newly pressed causes the lamps to sputter as the heat makes the wind rise in waves—rather, we see that new grain and all fruits stretch and swell until they exhale gaseous and unconcocted matter. To show that some foods bring bad dreams and disturb our sleeping visions, they adduce beans and the head of the octopus, from which those who resort to divination through dreams are ordered to abstain.

F 243 R³ (Aulus Gellius, XIX vi 1):

In the *Problems* of the philosopher Aristotle, this is written: 'Why is it that those who are ashamed turn red and those who are afraid turn pale, although those emotions are very similar? Because the blood of those who are ashamed runs from the heart to all the parts of the body and thus rises to the surface, while the blood of those who are afraid rushes together to the heart and thus leaves the other parts'.

F 244 R³ (Aulus Gellius, I xi 17–19):

However, Aristotle in the books of *Problems,* wrote that the custom of marching into battle to the tunes of flute-players was begun by the Spartans in order that the confidence and keenness of the soldiers might become more evident and more certain. For, he says, marching in this manner is least compatible with lack of confidence and fear, and men depressed and fearful are incapable of such an intrepid and seemly mode of advance. I have added a few words of Aristotle's on the matter: 'Why is it that whenever men are about to run into danger, they advance to the flute? In order that they may recognise the cowards by their failure to keep time. . . .'[1]

F 246 R³ (Photius, Bibliotheca *249, 441b6–15):*

Aristotle dealt with this topic [sc. the flooding of the Nile]. For he himself actually thought the matter out on the basis of nature, determining to send Alexander of Macedonia to those parts and to discover by inspection the causes of the Nile's increase. That is why he says that this is no longer a problem; for it has been plainly observed that it increases from the rains, and—what is paradoxical—that in the driest parts of Ethiopia where there is neither winter nor water there occur rainstorms in the summer.

F 252 R³ (Scholiast to Aratus, 1095, p. 547 Maass):

Aristotle says: 'Whenever the air is cold and wet, then at that time the islands, being moistened, produce vegetation and supply food for the birds there; but whenever the air is arid and dry, then since the islands produce no vegetation at all, the island birds flee to the mainland where they can find at least a little nourishment. And when the jackdaws fly from the islands it is a sign to farmers of drought and poor harvests; but if they migrate in season they indicate a good harvest'.

F 267 R³ (Athenaeus, 652A):

Aristotle in *On Plants:* 'Of seedless dates, which some call "eunuchs" and others "stoneless". . . .'

---

[1]There is a lacuna in the text.

VII · BIOLOGY

F 279–380 R³

F 284 R³ (Strabo, XV xxii 695):

Aristotle relates that there have been cases of septuplets [sc. in Egypt], and himself calls the Nile very fertile and nourishing, because of the moderate concoction from the periods of the sun which leave behind the nourishing factor while evaporating the superfluous.

F 286 R³ (Pliny, naturalis historia XI cliv 273):

I am surprised that Aristotle not only believed but actually stated that there are certain signs of longevity in the body itself. And although I think that his view is baseless and should not be published without hesitation (lest everyone anxiously hunts for such signs in himself), nevertheless I shall touch on it because so learned a man did not despise it. Thus he lays down that signs of a short life are few teeth, long fingers, leaden complexion, and a large number of broken lines on the palm; on the other hand, long life is given to those who have sloping shoulders, one or two long lines on their palms, more than thirty two teeth, and big ears.

F 288 R³ (Apollonius, historiae mirabiles 27):

Aristotle in *Pertaining to Animals* (for there are two works by him, *On Animals* and *Pertaining to Animals*) says: 'Lice on the head do not perish during long illnesses; but when the patient is on the point of death the lice are found on the pillows, having abandoned the head'.

F 294 R³ (Athenaeus, 305D):

Aristotle in *On Animals:* 'Others are toothless and smooth, like the needlefish; some are stoneheaded, like the cremys; some are very hard and rough-skinned, like the boar-fish; some have two stripes, like the seserinus; some have many stripes and red lines, like the saupe'.

F 297 R³ (Athenaeus, 286F):

Aristotle, in the work entitled *Pertaining to Animals* or *On Fish*, says: 'Those with dorsal markings are called bogues, those with oblique markings mackerel'.

F 298 R³ (Athenaeus, 313D):

Aristotle in his *Pertaining to Animals* writes thus: 'Fish with speckled tails include the blacktail and the sarg—they have many black markings'.

F 299 R³ (Athenaeus, 305C):

Aristotle in his *Pertaining to Animals:* 'Some have black speckles, like the blackbird; others variegated speckles, like the thrush'.

F 308 R³ (Athenaeus, 277E):

Now when some bonito had been served, someone said: 'Aristotle records that these have covered gills, that they are saw-toothed, belong to the gregarious and carnivorous groups, and have a gall-bladder and a spleen as long as their gut. And it is said that when they are caught they jump up and bite off the hook, thus escaping'.

F 311 R³ (Athenaeus, 298B):

Aristotle says that eels like very clean water. So eel-breeders pour clean water on them—for they are stifled in turbid water. That is why those who hunt them stir up the water in order to stifle them. For they have small gills and the ducts are immediately blocked by the mud. Thus during storms too, when the water is disturbed by the winds, they stifle. They copulate by twining together, and they then release a glue-like substance from themselves which, left in the mud, becomes a living creature. Eel-breeders say that they feed at night and lie still in the mud during the day; and they live, for the most part, for eight years.

F 346 R³ (Athenaeus, 389AB):

Aristotle says this about the creature: 'The partridge is a land animal, with divided feet; it lives for fifteen years, though the female lives for even longer (for among birds the female are longer-lived than the males). It broods over its eggs and hatches them like a domestic hen. When it realizes that it is being hunted, it runs out in front of its nest and limps along by the hunter's legs, giving him the hope of catching it; and it deceives him until the nestlings have flown away—whereupon it flies away itself. The creature is bad-natured and mischievous; it is also salacious. That is why it breaks the female's eggs—so that it may tread her again. Thus the female, recognising this, runs away to lay'.

F 363 R³ (Aelian, de natura animalium XVI 33):

Aristotle says that the horns and ears of the cattle among the Neuri grow out of the same spot and are knitted together. The same author says that a certain place in Libya has goats with their udders suspended from their breasts. The following too is from the son of Nicomachus: he says that among the Boudini who live by the Cariscus white sheep are not to be found—they are all black.

F 366 R³ (Aelian, de natura animalium V 8):

Aristotle says that the land of the Astypalaeans is hostile to snakes, just as—so the same author tells us—Rhenea is to weasels.

F 368 R³ (Aelian, de natura animalium *IV 57):*

Aristotle says that a man who has been bitten by a water-snake immediately gives off a very heavy smell, so that no-one is able to approach him. According to the same author, anyone who has been bitten is overcome by drowsiness—and in fact a great mist comes over his eyes, and madness and very violent trembling ensue, and he dies two days later.

F 373 R³ (Galen, Commentarius in Hippocratis de natura hominis *XV 25–26 K):*

And if you want to investigate the opinions of the old doctors, you can read the volumes of the medical collection which are ascribed to Aristotle but are agreed to have been written by his pupil Menon—which is why some call them the *Menonia.* It is clear that Menon carefully sought out those books of the old doctors which were still extant in his time, and thence collected their opinions.

*F 380 R³ (*Vita Aristotelis Marciana *170–5 Gigon):*

And in mathematics he showed that the cone of the lines of sight is acute-angled because the line of sight extends further than the magnitude which it sees. And for this reason none of the things seen is seen as a whole at one and the same time, and hence the axis is larger than the base and the cone is acute-angled.

VIII · HISTORICAL WORKS

F 381–644 R³

F 472 R³ (Athenaeus, 272D):
In the *Constitution of the Aeginetans* Aristotle says that they had 470,000 slaves.

F 473 R³ (Strabo, VII vii 2):
Aristotle's *Constitutions* show that from of old they [sc. the Leleges] were nomads, both in association with them [sc. the Carians] and by themselves. For in the *Constitution of the Acarnanians* he says that while the Curetes held part of it [sc. of Acarnania], the Leleges, and then the Teleboae, held the western part. And in that of the Aetolians he calls Leleges those who are now Locrians, and he says that they also held Boeotia. Similarly in those of the Opuntians and of the Megarians. In that of the Leucadians he also names an autochthonous Lelex, his grandson Teleboa, and the latter's twenty-two children, the Teleboae, some of whom settled in Leucas.

F 476 R³, F 510 R³ (Pollux, IV 174):
Aristotle, in the *Constitution of the Acragantines,* having said that they used to levy a fine of fifty litres, adds that 'the litre is worth an Aeginetan obol.' And in the *Constitution of the Himerans* he says that the Siceliots call two bronze pieces a dizas, one an ounce, three a trias, six a half-litre, an obol a litre, a Corinthian stater a decalitre (which is worth ten obols).

F 486 R³ (Scholiast to Pindar, Pythian I 89):
Aristotle says in the *Constitution of the Geloans* that Hieron's brother died of dropsy, and, in the *Constitution of the Syracusans,* that Hieron himself suffered from cystitis.

F 491 R³ (Strabo, VIII vi 15):
Epidaurus used to be called Epicarus. For Aristotle says that the Carians held it, as they also held Hermione; but that when the Heraclidae returned, Ionians from the Attic Tetrapolis followed them to Argos and settled with the Carians.

F 492 R³ (Harpocration, s.v. Ἑλλανοδίκαι):
… Aristotle in the *Constitution of the Eleans* says that to begin with the Eleans appointed one Hellanodikes, but after a time two, and finally eight.

F 496 R³ (Eustathius, 1747, on Odyssey XIII 408):
The same author [sc. Pausanias] says that Aristotle relates that when a plague struck them [sc. the Boeotians] and a large flock of crows appeared, the men hunted

down the crows, purified them with incantations, and let them go free; and they said to the plague: 'Go to the crows'.

F 497 R³ (Harpocration, s.v. τετραρχία):
Aristotle in the *Constitution of the Thessalians* says that in the time of Aleuas the Red Thessaly was divided into four portions.

F 498 R³ (Scholiast to Euripides, Rhesus 311):
Aristotle in the *Constitution of the Thessalians* writes as follows: 'Dividing up the government . . .'[1] Aleuas ordered that each group according to lot should provide fifty cavalrymen and eighty peltasts. A *peltê* is a shield without a rim, not bronze-covered but made of stretched sheep- or goat-skin (not of cow-hide). And they all carried three javelins and a short spear called a *schedion*'.

F 501 R³ (Scholiast to Dionysius Thrax, p. 183.1–5 Hilgard):
Others, including Ephorus in his second book, say that Cadmus was the inventor of the alphabet. But some say that he conveyed to us the invention of the Phoenicians—as Herodotus says in his *Histories* and as Aristotle relates. For they say that while the Phoenicians invented the alphabet, Cadmus introduced it to Greece.

F 501 R³ (Scholiast to Dionysius Thrax, p. 190.19–21 Hilgard):
Cadmus is the inventor of the alphabet, as Ephorus and Aristotle say; but others say that it was the invention of the Phoenicians and that Cadmus imported it to Greece.

F 501 R³ (Pliny, naturalis historia VII lvi 192):
Aristotle holds that 18 [sc. of the letters of the Greek alphabet] are original, and that two—psi and zeta—were added by Epicharmus rather than by Palamedes.

F 504 R³ (Etymologicon Magnum, s.v. Ἀρκείσιος):
Aristotle, in the *Constitution of the Ithacans,* says that Cephalus, while living in the Cephallenian islands which got their name from him, had been childless for a long time, and on inquiring of the god was ordered to copulate with anything female he should happen to meet. Now arriving back in his own country he fell in with a she-bear, and in obedience to the oracle copulated away: the bear, becoming pregnant, turned into a woman and gave birth to a child, Arceisios (from ἄρκτος ['bear']).

F 512 R³ (Scholiast to Apollonius Rhodius, IV 982–92):
The island is Corcyra. This previously used to be called Scheria. Aristotle gives the reason in his *Constitution of the Corcyreans.* For he says that Demeter was

---

[1] There is a lacuna in the text here.

afraid that the rivers flowing from the mainland would make it part of the mainland, and so she begged Poseidon to divert the courses of the rivers. Thus, since the rivers had been held back, it was called Scheria instead of Drepane.

F 515 R³ (Athenaeus, 618EF):

Aristotle at any rate says in the *Constitution of the Colophonians:* 'And Theodorus himself also died later by a violent death. And he is said to have become rather soft-living, as is clear from his poetry; for even today the women sing his songs at the time of the festivals'.

F 519 R³ (Scholiast to Pindar, Pythian *II 127):*

Aristotle says that Achilles was the first to have used the war-dance (πυρρίχη) at the pyre (πυρά) of Patroclus (this is the dance, he says, that is called the *prulis* among the Cyprians); so he takes the word πυρρίχη to derive from pyre.

F 532 R³ (Scholiast to Pindar, Isthmian *VII 18):*

The Aegeidae are a phratry of the Thebans, from whose number some came to help the Spartans in their war against the Amycleans; their leader was Timomachus, who was the first man to instruct the Spartans in all military matters, and who received great honours from them. And his bronze breastplate is put on display at the Hyacinthia—the Thebans used to call this a 'weapon'. Aristotle relates this in the *Constitution of the Spartans.* . . . Aristotle says that when the Spartans were engaged in their war with the Amycleans, having ascertained from the god that they should take the Aegeidae as allies, they set out for Athens. But while lodging in Thebes they were invited to the banquet of the Aegeidae phratry. On hearing the priest praying after dinner that the gods would give good things to the Aegeidae, they interpreted the oracle and concluded their alliance in Thebes.

F 533 R³ (Plutarch, Lycurgus *39E):*

Least of all is there agreement about the date at which he [sc. Lycurgus] lived. Some say that he flourished at the same time as Iphitus and joined with him in establishing the Olympic truce—among them, Aristotle the philosopher, who cites as evidence the discus at Olympia on which is preserved an inscription of Lycurgus' name.

F 540 R³ (Harpocration, s.v. μόρων):

Aristotle has discussed this in the *Constitution of the Spartans.* He says that there are six named *morae* and that all the Spartans are divided among the *morae.*

F 544 R³ (Scholiast to Euripides, Andromache *445):*

In the next lines he [sc. Euripides] berates them [sc. the Spartans] in particular for their love of money. Aristotle too relates this in his *Constitution of the Spartans,* and he adds the verse pronounced by the god: 'Love of money, nothing else, will ruin Sparta'.

F 547 R³ (Polybius, XII v 4–5):

Nevertheless, I have no compunction in saying and writing that the account we have received from Aristotle about the colonisation [of Locri] is truer than that given by Timaeus. For I am aware that the Locrians agree that the tradition about the colonisation handed down to them from their fathers is the one Aristotle, not the one Timaeus, told. And they would offer the following proofs of it . . .

F 549 R³ (Athenaeus, 576AB):

Aristotle too relates that something similar happened when he writes in the *Constitution of the Massaliots* as follows: 'Phocaean merchants from Ionia founded Massilia. Euxenus the Phocaean was the guest of Nanos the king (that was his name). Now this Nanos was celebrating the marriage of his daughter and he invited Euxenus, who happened to be there, to the feast. The marriage took place in the following way: the girl had to come in after dinner with a cup of mixed wine and give it to any of the suitors present she wished—the man she gave it to would be the bridegroom. Now the girl came in and, either by chance or for some other reason, gave it to Euxenus. (The girl's name was Petta.) When this occurred, and her father asked him to take her since the gift was sanctioned by the gods, Euxenus took her for his wife and lived with her, changing her name to Aristoxene. And there is a family in Massilia that traces its origins back to her and is still called the Protiadae—for Protis was the son of Euxenus and Aristoxene'.

F 551 R³ (Athenaeus, 235E):

Aristotle in the *Constitution of the Methonians* says: 'There were two parasites for each magistrate, and one for each military official; and they received fixed contributions from various sources and, in particular, fish from the fishermen'.

F 554 R³ (Photius, Lexicon s.v. τὸ Μηλιακὸν πλοῖον):

Aristotle says that when Hippotes was setting out to found a colony he laid a curse on those who were unwilling to sail with him. For those who stayed behind excused themselves by saying that their wives were sickly or that their ships were leaky; so he laid a curse that their ships might never be watertight and that they might always be ruled by their wives.

F 558 R³ (Athenaeus, 348AC):

Aristotle in the *Constitution of the Naxians* writes about this proverb as follows: 'Most of the rich men in Naxos lived in the town, while the rest were scattered among the villages. Now in one of the villages, called Leistadae, there lived Telesagoras, a very rich man with a good reputation who was honoured by the people in various ways including the daily sending of gifts. And when they came down from the town and haggled over anything being sold, the sellers used to say that they would rather give it to Telesagoras than sell it at such a price. Now some young men were buying a large fish, and when the fisherman made the usual remark they were annoyed at hearing it so often; so, being tipsy, they roistered round to his house. Telesagoras received them civilly; but the young men assaulted him and his two daughters, who were of marriageable age. The Naxians were enraged at that, took up arms, and attacked the young men. And there was then serious unrest, the Naxians being led by Lygdamis who from this generalship became tyrant of his country'.

F 562 R³ (Harpocration, s.v. ˝Αμφισσα):
Aristotle in the *Constitution of the Opuntians* says this: 'Andraimon was the founder, and he called it Amphissa because the place was surrounded by mountains'.

F 577 R³ (Plutarch, Pericles 166D):
Aristotle says that Pericles himself was earlier defeated in a sea-battle by Melissus.

F 583 R³ (Athenaeus, 520CD):
So far gone in luxury were they [sc. the Sybarites] that they actually trained their horses to dance to the pipe at their feasts. Now the Crotoniates knew this, and when they made war against them, as Aristotle says in his account of their constitution, they struck up the dance music for the horses—for they had pipers among their soldiery. And when the horses heard the pipers they not only danced but actually deserted, carrying their riders, to the Crotoniates.

F 588 R³ (Athenaeus, 435DE):
Aristotle in his *Constitution of the Syracusans* says that he [sc. Dionysius the younger] was sometimes drunk for ninety days on end, and that that is why his sight became somewhat dim.

F 593 R³ (Stephanus of Byzantium, s.v. Τένεδος):
[On the proverb, 'an axe of Tenedos.'] Or rather, as Aristotle says in the *Constitution of the Tenedians*, because a certain king in Tenedos laid down a law that anyone who caught an adulterous pair should kill both with an axe. Now it happened that his son was caught committing adultery, and he confirmed that the law should be observed even in the case of his own son; after his son had been killed, the matter gave rise to a proverb for cruel treatment.

F 609 R³ (Dionysius of Halicarnassus, Antiquitates Romanae I lxxii 3–4):
Aristotle the philosopher relates that certain of the Achaeans who were returning from Troy sailed round Cape Malea and were caught in a violent storm; for a time they were carried by the winds and wandered all over the sea, but at last

they came to that part of Opice which is called Latinium and lies on the Tyrrhenian Sea. Overjoyed at the sight of land, they beached their ships there and spent the winter months preparing to sail at the beginning of spring. But their ships burned one night, and having no way to leave they were compelled willy-nilly to settle in the spot where they had landed. This happened because of certain female prisoners whom they had brought from Troy: they burned the ships because they feared that if the Achaeans sailed home they would be made into slaves.

F 614 R³ (Ammonius, de adfinium vocabulorum differentia *334):*

Aristotle, in his *Claims of the Cities,* records the following: 'At the same time, Alexander the Molossian, when the Tarentines summoned him to make war against the barbarians, sailed with fifty ships and numerous vessels for horse- and troop-transport'.

F 615 R³ (Plutarch, Solon *83F):*

For the Amphictyons were persuaded by him [sc. Solon] to go to war, as several authors testify, including Aristotle who, in his *List of Pythian Victors,* ascribes the decision to Solon.

F 637 R³ (Scholiast to Aristides, Panathenaicus *189.4):*

The order of the festivals according to Aristotle is this: first, the Eleusinia, because of the harvest of Demeter; second, the Panathenaea, for Aster the giant who was killed by Athena;[1] third, the festival founded in Argos by Danaus because of the marriage of his daughters; fourth, the one founded in Arcadia by Lycaon and called the Lycaea; fifth, the one at Iolcus, begun by Acastus[2] for his father Pelias; sixth, the one at the Isthmus, introduced by Sisyphus for Melicertes; seventh, the Olympic festival, introduced by Hercules for Pelops; eighth, the one at Nemea, which the Seven against Thebes founded for Archemorus;[3] ninth, the one at Troy which Achilles instituted for Patroclus; tenth, the Pythian festival which the Amphictyons founded for the death of Pytho. This is the order of the old and ancient festivals set out by Aristotle who composed the *Peploi.*

[1] Reading ὑπὸ Ἀθηνᾶς ἀναιρεθέντι.
[2] Reading Ἀκάστου.
[3] Reading Ἀρχεμόρῳ.

IX · LETTERS

F 645–670 R³

F 645 R³ (Athenaeus, 697 A):

And Aristotle himself, in his defence against the charge of impiety (if the speech is not a forgery) says: 'If I had decided to sacrifice to Hermeias as an immortal I would not have prepared a memorial to him as a mortal, and if I had wished to immortalise his nature I would not have adorned his body with burial honours'.

*F 646 R³ (*Vita Aristotelis Marciana *94–96 Gigon):*

In order to confer a benefit on all mankind, he [sc. Aristotle] wrote a book to Alexander on kingship, instructing him on how to rule.

F 647 R³ (Themistius, orationes 107CD):

We should do honour to Aristotle, who slightly altered Plato's words and made his thesis truer. He said that it was not merely unnecessary for a king to be a philosopher, but actually a disadvantage; rather, a king should be attentive and obedient to true philosophers, since then he would fill his reign with good deeds not with words.

F 651 R³ (Harpocration, s.v. ὅτι ξένους):

. . . Aristotle, in one of his letters to Philip, says that he [sc. Philip] released the daughters of Apollophanes to Satyrus the actor.

*F 652 R³ (*Vita Aristotelis Marciana *34–40 Gigon):*

When he [sc. Aristotle] was seventeen, he received an oracle from the Pythian god to become a philosopher in Athens. There he attended on Socrates, and stayed with him for the short time that remained before the latter's death; after him, he attended on Plato and stayed with him too until death, a period of some twenty years as he himself says in a letter to Philip.

*F 654 R³ (*Vita Aristotelis Marciana *121–27 Gigon):*

. . . and he can be seen in his letters expressing his admiration for Plato and recommending to the kings those connected to Plato by birth.

*F 655 R³ (*Vita Aristotelis Marciana *73–80 Gigon):*

He [sc. Aristotle] was so valued by Philip and Olympias that they set up a statue of him with themselves; and the philosopher, being such a considerable part of the kingdom,[1] through his philosophy used his power as an instrument for benefaction, doing good both to individuals and to entire cities and to all men at one and the same time. For the benefits he bestowed on individuals are revealed in the letters which he wrote on various subjects to the royal couple. . . .

F 656 R³ (Demetrius, de elocutione 233):

Aristotle, however, actually uses demonstrations in his letters; for example, wishing to get it across that one should benefit large and small states alike, he says: 'For the gods in both are equal; hence, since the Graces are goddesses, equal grace will accrue to you from both'.

F 657 R³ (Dio Chrysostom, XLVII 9–11):

I used sometimes to congratulate Aristotle, who, coming from Stagira (a small town in Olynthia), after the fall of Olynthus managed through his intimacy with Alexander and Philip to secure the refounding of the site; and I used to say that he was the only man to have had the good fortune to be the founder of his own country. Now the other day I chanced on a letter in which Aristotle is repenting and lamenting and saying that some of the people in question were trying to destroy the king and the governors he had sent, so that no good had come of it nor had the city been established at all. But if it pained some men that, having been stateless fugitives, they should acquire a country and live in freedom according to the laws, and if they preferred to live in villages like barbarians rather than have the form and name of a state, why should we be amazed if anything else pains men? Aristotle writes in his letter that he has given up the business—for he says that he is putting his hands up.

F 658 R³ (Plutarch, de Alexandri fortuna 329B):

He [sc. Alexander] did not do as Aristotle advised—act towards Greeks as their leader, towards foreigners as their master, treating the former as friends and kinsmen and the latter as animals or plants—and so fill his reign with many wars and banishments and festering factions.

F 659 R³ (Aelian, Varia Historia xii 54):

Aristotle, wishing to pacify Alexander's rage and to put a stop to his anger with so many people, wrote to him as follows: 'Anger and rage are directed not against lesser men but against greater; and you have no equal'.

F 660 R³ (Stobaeus, Anthologium III xx 55):

Just as smoke stings our eyes and prevents us from seeing what is under our feet, so anger, once aroused, clouds our reason and does not allow our mind to anticipate the absurdity which will result from it.

---

[1]Reading βασιλείας for φιλοσοφίας.

F 661 R³ (Stobaeus, Anthologium *III xx 46):*

Or do you not see that when anything is done in rage our reason goes abroad, fleeing anger as a harsh tyrant?

F 663 R³ (Aristocles, frag. 2 Heiland = Eusebius, Praeparatio Evangelica *XV ii 14):*

... as for his [sc. Aristotle's] marriage to Pythias, he himself has given a full enough defence in his letters to Antipater. For he married her on Hermeias' death because of his regard for Hermeias: she was a modest and good woman, and in unfortunate circumstances because of the disasters that had overtaken her brother.

F 664 R³ (Plutarch, de tranquillitate animi *472E):*

Aristotle in writing to Antipater said: 'It is not just Alexander who has good reason to be proud because he has power over many men: pride is no less appropriate on the part of those who possess correct beliefs about the gods'.

F 665 R³ (Demetrius, de elocutione *225):*

Who would speak to a friend as Aristotle does to Antipater in a letter on behalf of some exile who was an old man? He says: 'If this man has journeyed as an exile in every land without ever returning home, clearly no reproach attaches to men who wish to return home to Hades'.

F 666 R³ (Aelian, Varia Historia *xiv 1):*

Aristotle ... wrote to Antipater when someone deprived him of the honours voted him at Delphi, commenting thus: 'As to what was voted me at Delphi and of which I have been deprived, my present attitude is neither one of great concern nor yet one of complete indifference'.

*F 667 R³ (*Vita Aristotelis Marciana *184-91 Gigon):*

When the Athenians rose against him, he withdrew to Chalcis, hinting at his reasons: 'I will not allow the Athenians to wrong philosophy twice.' And, since citizens and foreigners did not have the same duties to the state of Athens, he writes in a letter to Antipater: 'Life at Athens is difficult—for pear grows old on pear and fig on fig,' punning on the succession of informers.[1]

F 668 R³ (Demetrius, de elocutione *144):*

Elegance comes both from colloquial words, as when Aristotle says 'For the more I am a loner the more fond of stories have I become,' and also from coined words, as for example the same author in the same passage: 'For the more I am a

---

[1]Fig = σῦκος, informer = συκοφάντης.

selfer and a loner, the more fond of stories have I become' (the word 'loner' is of somewhat colloquial usage, while 'selfer' is coined from 'self').

F 669 R³ (Demetrius, de elocutione 29):

However, they [sc. homoeoteleuta] are sometimes useful, as when Aristotle says: 'I came to Athens from Stagira because of the great king, from Stagira to Athens because of the great winter'.

F 670 R³ (Demetrius, de elocutione 230):

Aristotle, who has a high reputation as a letter-writer, says: 'I am not writing to you on this matter; for it is not suitable for a letter'.

(Ptolemy, Life of Aristotle p. 214 Düring):

Thereupon, one of the priests which are called hierophants, by name Eurymedon, came forward with the purpose of denouncing him. He indicted him for impiety, claiming that Aristotle did not hold the gods in honour. He was prompted by a grudge which he bore to him in his heart, and Aristotle speaks of this in a letter to Antipater.

(Ptolemy, Life of Aristotle p. 215 Düring):

With what zest he practised goodness and strove to do good services to his fellow men is apparent from his open letters and his books and from what the reader can gather in these writings concerning the numerous interviews he had with contemporary kings and individuals, by which negotiations he promoted their affairs and proved useful to them.

X · POEMS

F 671–675 R[3]

F 650 R[3], F 673 R[3] (Olympiodorus, Commentarius in Gorgiam 41.9):
 That Aristotle actually honours him [sc. Plato] as his teacher is clear from the fact that he wrote a whole speech in praise of him; for he narrates his biography and lavishes praise upon him. And it is not just in the encomium that he praises him: in the elegy addressed to Eudemus he praises Plato himself in the following lines:

> Coming to the fair land of Cecropia
> he piously founded an altar of holy friendship
> for a man whom the wicked may not properly even praise;
> he, alone or the first of mortals, showed clearly
> by his own life and by the courses of his arguments
> that a man becomes good and happy at the same time:
> but now none can grasp this any more.[1]

F 675 R[3] (Diogenes Laertius, V 7; Athenaeus, 696BE; Didymus, in Demosthenem col. 6):

> Excellence, greatly striven for by mankind,
> noblest quarry in life,
> for your form, maiden,
> to die is an enviable fate in Greece
> and to endure violent untiring labours.
> Such is the fruit you cast into the mind,
> immortal, better than gold
> and parents and the soft rays of sleep.
> For your sake Hercules, son of Zeus, and the children of Leda
>   underwent much, with their deeds
> hunting your power.
> From desire for you Achilles and Ajax went
>   to the house of Hades.
> For the sake of your dear form the nursling of
>   Atarneus forsook the rays of the sun.
> Therefore, celebrated for his deeds and immortal,
>   the Muses will magnify him,
> daughters of Memory, magnifying the honour of Zeus,
>   god of guests, and the reward of steadfast friendship.[1]

---

[1]Text uncertain.
[1]Text often uncertain.

ARISTOTLE'S WILL

(Diogenes Laertius, V 11–16):

It will be well; but if anything should happen, Aristotle has made the following provisions:

Antipater is to be executor in all matters and in perpetuity; but until Nicanor arrives, Aristomenes, Timarchus, Hipparchus, Dioteles, and Theophrastus (if he is willing and able) are to take care of the children and of Herpyllis and of the estate.

And when my daughter comes of age, they are to marry her to Nicanor; and should anything happen to her—may it not, nor will it—before her marriage or after she has married but before there are children, Nicanor is to be responsible for administering the affairs of my son and the others in a fashion worthy both of himself and of us. Let Nicanor take care of both my daughter and my son Nicomachus in whatever way he judges appropriate to their affairs, as though he were both father and brother to them.

If anything should previously happen to Nicanor—may it not—either before he has taken my daughter or after he has taken her but before there are children, then if he has made arrangements let these take effect. If Theophrastus wishes to live with my daughter, let the same provisions stand as with Nicanor; if he does not, the executors, after consultation with Antipater, are to administer the affairs both of my daughter and of my son in whatever way they think best.

The executors and Nicanor are to remember me in taking care also of Herpyllis (for she was good to me) in all respects, and in particular, if she wants to take a husband, they are to see to it that she is given away in a fashion not unworthy of us. And in addition to what she has previously been given, they are to give her also a talent of silver from the estate and three woman servants, if she wishes, and the maidservant which she has, and the slave from Pyrrha. And if she wants to live in Chalcis, she is to have the guest-house by the garden, if in Stagira the family house; and whichever of these she wants, the executors are to furnish with whatever seems both proper to them and satisfactory to Herpyllis.

Nicanor is also to take care of the slave Murmex, so that he is conveyed in a fashion worthy of us to his own people, together with those of his belongings which we received. They are to free Ambracis and to give her on the marriage of my daughter five hundred drachmae and the maidservant which she has. They are also to give to Thale, in addition to the maidservant which she has (the one who was purchased), a thousand drachmae and a maidservant. As for Simo, apart from the money which has earlier been given him for another slave, they are either to buy him a slave or to give him money. Tacho is to be freed on the marriage of my daughter, as are Philo and Olympius and his child. Do not sell any of the slaves who served me, but employ them; and when they come of age, send them away free men as they deserve.

They are to take care too that the statues which I commissioned from Gryllio are completed and set up—both the one of Nicanor and the one of Proxenus (which I intended to commission), and the one of Nicanor's mother; as for the one of Arimnestus which is already completed, set it up as a memorial to him since he died childless. They are to dedicate the statue of my mother to Demeter in Nemea or wherever seems best. Wherever they make my grave they are to take and deposit there Pythias' bones too, just as she instructed. And Nicanor, if he is preserved (which is a prayer I have offered on his behalf) is to set up statues in stone four cubits in height to Zeus Saviour and Athena Saviouress at Stagira.

INDEXES

REFERENCES give Bekker page-, column-, and approximate line-numbers: these numbers are to be found in the margins of the present translation. References of the form "*CA n*" give section-numbers in the *Constitution of Athens*. References to the fragments are all of the form "p. *n*" and give page-numbers of the present translation.

The Index of Names is largely confined to writers or thinkers mentioned by Aristotle. It does not include historical figures who occur mainly in the *Politics*. A few historical figures—and also a few geographical locations—are given in the General Index.

For reasons of space, the General Index is highly selective, both in its headings and (for all but the major items) in the passages it cites. Entries are not analytical. The reader who requires more detailed information must consult Bonitz's *Index Aristotelicus* (Greek) or Organ's *Index to Aristotle* (English)—or else turn to the indexes in the several volumes of the original Oxford translation.

INDEX OF NAMES

GENERAL INDEX

Essence (*cont.*)
  1007a20, 1025b29, 1029b12-1032a11, 1034b20-
  1038a35, 1182b19, 1343a13. *See* Accident, Definition
Evaporation [*anathumiasis:* exhalation], 340b26,
  341b7, 344a10, 359a19, 369a26, 378a18,
  384b33, 394a9-b19, 438a4, 440a15, 443b2,
  464a6, 469b31
Example [*paradeigma*], 68b38-69a16, 71a10,
  916b25, 1356b1-25, 1357a14-21, 1357b25,
  1393a25-1394a18, 1402b14, 1403a5, 1429a21-
  1430a13, 1431a24
Excellence [*aretē:* virtue], 8b34, 13a26, 113b31,
  116b1, 118a27, 121b38, 124b20, 128b39, 131b1,
  142b14, 144a9-19, 153b8, 1098a17, 1100a4,
  1103a4-b26, 1104b4-1108b18, 1113b6-1115a6,
  1126a8-31, 1129b26, 1144b1-1145a11, 1156b6-
  1157a24, 1177a13, 1178a16, 1185a36, 1186a19-
  27, 1197b36-1198a9, 1220a13-1234b13,
  1259b21-1260a9, 1276b17-1277a13, 1288a32-
  b2, 1309a33-b14, 1323a27, 1324a5-1325b32,
  1332a8-b11, 1337a33-b23, 1366a23-1368a39
Exchange, 1132b13, 1133a2-b26, 1256b40-
  1257b23, 1258a32-40
Excluded middle, law of, 18a28-19b4, 77a30,
  88a39, 1011b24-1012a28
Experience [*empeiria*], 46a18, 100a6, 703a9,
  981a2, 981a13-b9, 1143b13, 1250a35
Extremes, 1108b11-1109a19, 1222a23-b4,
  1234b6-14, 1234a34-b5, 1296a22-1297a13,
  1320a2-17. *See* Mean
Eye, 437a24-438b20, 454a28, 491b18-492a13,
  743b32-744b12, 779a28-781a14, 811b14-29,
  957a36-960a33
Eyelid, 421b29, 657a25-658a10, 744a36-b9

Faction, 1172b11-22, 1196a22-36, 1302a8,
  1306a6
Fallacy, 108a26-36, 162b3-15, 168a17-169a22,
  172a9-28, 175a1-183a26, 1401a23-1402a27
False cause, fallacy of, 65a38-66a15, 166b26,
  167b21-36, 168b22, 169b13, 181a31, 1401b30
Falsity, 88a25, 281b3-25, 980a10, 1011b26,
  1024b17-1025a13, 1027b17 1028a5, 1051a34-
  1052a12. *See* Truth
Familiar [*gnōrimos:* intelligible, knowable],
  71b33-72a5, 129b3-130b10, 131a2-26, 141a26-
  142b19, 184a16. *See* Prior
Family, 1252a26-b27, 1259a37-b17, 1260b13,
  1303b1-14
Fat, 388a7, 520a6-b9, 651a20-b19, 672a1-b8,
  725b30-726a6
Fatalism, 18a28-19b4, 337a34-338b5, 401b9-24,
  463b27. *See* Necessity
Fear, 660b25-30, 667a20, 947b12-949a20,
  1105b22, 1107a33, 1110a4, 1115a7, 1128b11,
  1179b11, 1191a30-36, 1220b12, 1382a19-
  1383b11; and tragedy, 1449b27, 1452a2,
  1452b32-1453a6, 1456a38
Feet, 494a12, 499b7, 690a4-b11, 706a33, 734b29

Female, 608a22-b25, 648a12, 737a28, 738b20-27,
  766a22-b26, 1058a29-b26, 1254b14, 1259a39,
  1343b30. *See* Male, Woman
Final cause [*telos, hou heneka:* end, goal, that for
  the sake of which], 94b8-37, 194a27-35, 194b32,
  195a24, 198a24, 198b10-199b33, 200a22,
  200a33, 324b14-18, 335b5, 415b2-20, 416b24,
  420b19, 432b21, 433a14, 434b24, 435b20,
  455b17, 471b25, 639b12-641a17, 642a1,
  663b14-23, 778a16-b19, 778a35, 994b9,
  1013a33, 1013b26, 1023a34, 1044b1, 1050a7,
  1051a15, 1072b2, 1094a4, 1097a25, 1111b27,
  1112b12, 1214b6, 1252b32, 1257b25, 1331b29,
  1339b32, p. 2405
Fire, 103a29, 130a10, 134b29-32, 137b37, 146a15,
  214b14, 217a1, 293a20-b15, 303b9-304b23,
  330b3, 330b33-331a6, 335a5-20, 336a1-12,
  339a16, 340b22, 341b14, 379a16, 392a33-b5,
  416a9-18, 469b21-470a19, 646a10, 699b25,
  761b20, 809b7-17. *See* ELement
Fissile, 385a16, 386b25-387a11
Flavour, *see* Taste
Flesh, 388a16, 390b5, 432b26, 426b15, 484a16,
  485b20, 519b26-520a5, 653b19-654a31
Flexion of limbs, 494b3, 4498a2-b4, 499a20,
  503b32, 687b25, 692a15, 708b22-79b33, 711a8-
  713b21
Food, *See* Nutrition
Form [*eidos*], 79a7, 187a20, 192a14-24, 193a30,
  194a22-27, 194b15, 198b3, 199a31, 207b1,
  209a2-210a13, 277b26-278b9, 310b15, 312a12,
  318b16, 321b16-322a4, 322a28, 324b4-22,
  403b2, 412a8, 414a12-18, 424a18, 429a15,
  432a2, 640a17, 645a32-37, 701b20, 999b17,
  1015a16, 1016b9, 1017b35, 1029a5, 1032b1,
  1033a24-1034a8, 1035a21, 1036a26-1037b6,
  1042a30, 1043a19, 1044b12, 1069b35, 1070a15,
  1084b10; Platonic, 77a5, 83a33, 85b19, 113a27,
  137b3-13, 143b23, 147a3, 148a13, 1541a19,
  193b35, 203a8, 278a16, 335b9-24, 404b20,
  987b5-22, 988a10, 988b1-16, 990a33-993a10,
  1002b11-32, 1028b19-27, 1031b14, 1033b5-
  1034a8, 1036b14-30, 1039a24-b19, 1040a8-b4,
  1040b28-1041a5, 1042a18, 1045a16, 1050b35,
  1059a10, 1069a35, 1070a18, 1071b21, 1073a18,
  1075b18, 1076a17-33, 1078b6-1080a11,
  1081a1-1083a20, 1086a18-1090a1, 1095a27,
  1096a13-1097a13, 1182b9-13, 1183a28-b7
  1217b1-1218b26, p. 2389, p. 2390, p. 2391, p.
  2397, p. 2435, p. 2438
Form of expression, fallacy of, 166b10-19, 169a29-
  b2, 178a4-179a10, 179a20
Freedom, *see* Liberty
Friendship, 116b38, 118a1-5, 126a12, 1126b20,
  1155a3, 1172a15, 1208b3-1212b23, 1234b18-
  1246a25, 1262b3-24, 1287b33, 1295b24,
  1313a41, 1360b20, 1361b36, 1380b34-1382a18,
  1386a10, 1388b5, 1439b15, 1440a26, 1446b7-
  16
'From', 724a20-35, 991a20, 994a19-b6, 1023a26-
  b11, 1044a24, 1092a33

Frost, 347a16-b33, 349a10, 378a31, 388b12, 784b15, 888b30, 938a34, 939b36, 940b8

Function [ergon], 436a4, 454a26, 645b15, 687a10, 1094a5, 1097b25-32, 1098a7, 1152b19, 1153a23, 1168a9, 1219a1-27

Generals, 1277b10, 1305a7-28, 1312a11, 1321a16, CA 4, 22, 26, 30, 31, 44, 61

Generation [genesis: becoming, coming into being], 15a13, 186a14, 191b13, 193b27, 201a14, 223b21, 225a13-226a16, 230a31, 249b20, 258b17, 270a15, 279b4, 280b1-20, 288a34, 298b15, 301b2, 302a10, 304624, 305a34, 314a6, 315a26, 317a17-22, 317a32-320a2, 331a23-b4, 337a1-7, 338a4-b11, 415a27, 416b15, 509a1-511a34, 729a34-730b32, 737b26-739b35, 771a18-772b12, 981a17, 994a22-b6, 1010a21, 1032a20, 1033a24-1034a7, 1034b7, 1042a30, 1044b21-28, 1049b28, 1070a15, 1077a27, 1088a33. See Alteration, Change, Growth

Genus, 1b16, 11a20, 15a4, 96b21-25, 101b17, 102a31, 107a18, 107b19-26, 111a20-29, 120b12-128b70, 133a35, 134b1, 139b3, 143a12, 189a14, 201b19, 209a4, 210a18, 448b25, 449b15, 465a4, 486a23, 490b7-491a26, 505b26, 816a13, 995b29, 998b13-999a23, 1014b10, 1016a24, 1022a27, 1024a29-b16, 1037b19, 1038b1-1039a22, 1042a22, 1053b22, 1057a26. See Differentia, Species

Geometry, 75a39, 75b12-19, 76b9, 76b39, 77a40-b27, 87a33, 194a10, 279b35, 450a2, 452a3, 709a1, 709a15-30, 956a15, 983a20, 992a21, 997b27, 998a2, 1005a11, 1051a21, 1078a25, 1089a21, 1098a29, 1142a12, 1143a3, 1175a32, 1187a36, 1189b9, 1216b8, 1247a17

Gestation, 727b27, 746a32, 777a32-778a12, 891b25

Gnat, 490a21, 551b27-552a8, 601a3

Goat, 573b17-574a15, 610b25-611a6

God, 105a5, 109b33, 116b12, 122b12, 126a34, 136b6, 268a15, 270b7, 271a33, 284a12, 286a9, 336b27-34, 397b9-401b24, 462b20, 463b16, 464a21, 700b35, 983a8, 986b24, 997b10, 1026a18, 1074b1-14, 1096a24, 1101b20, 1122b20, 1123a10, 1134b28, 1137a28, 1145a23, 1158b35, 1160a24, 1162a5, 1164b5, 1166a22, 1178b8-26, 1179a25, 1207a6-12, 1208b27, 1212b33-1213a8, 1243b12, 1244b8, 1245b13-19, 1247a27, 1248a26, 1249b13-21, 1252b24, 1259b12, 1323b21, 1325b28, 1326a32, p. 2391, p. 2392, p. 2395, p. 2396, p. 2403, p. 2410

Good, 113a1-14, 114a39-115a2, 116b1, 123b8-12, 142a23, 147b18, 700b20, 701a1, 807b33-808a2, 983a31, 1013a22, 1075a12-24, 1091a29-1092a21, 1094a2, 1095a14, 1097a12, 1098b12, 1105a9, 1113a16, 1114a32, 1129b4, 1152b32-1153a7, 1166a20, 1182a34-b5, 1183a8-23, 1252a2, 1261b9, 1332a27, 1363b5-1365b27; senses of, 106a5, 107a5-11, 1096a23, 1096b13, 1152b27, 1182b6-10, 1217b25, 1218b3, 1128b18; absolute)(relative, 49b10, 115b15-35,

116b8, 142b12, 700b35, 1129b4, 1152b26, 1155b21, 1156b14, 1182b2, 1235b30, 1237a13; form of, 996a28, 1095a27, 1096a11-1097a13, 1182b10, 1183a28-68, 1217b1-1218a38; classification of goods, 1098b13, 1123b20, 1154a15, 1169b10, 1183b19-1184a14, 1217a30, 1218b37, 1235b30, 1323a21-38, p. 2408

Good birth, 1136b22, 1207b19-1208a4, 1248b8-1249a16, 1283a33-68, 1360b31, 1390b16, p. 2422

Good fortune, 1098b26, 1099b8, 1124a14, 1129b3, 1153b22, 1155a8, 1169b14, 1171a21-b28, 1179b23, 1183b34, 1206b34, 1207a1-19, 1213a28, 1214a25, 1246b37-1248b7, 1361b39, 1369a32, 1389a1, 1390b13-1391b7. See Chance

Good temper, 125b21-7, 1103a8, 1108a6, 1109b17, 1125b26-1126b10, 1129b22, 1191b23-38, 1220b38, 1222a42, 1231b5-26, 1250a40, 1380a5-b33

Good will, 1155b33-1156a5, 1158a7, 1166b6-1167a20, 1211b40-1212a13, 1241a1-14, 1436b17, 1441b37-1442a27, 1444b35-1445a10

Government, 1252a14, 1275a39, 1279a18-b10, 1288a34-1290a29, See Constitution

Grammar, 102a19, 104a17, 111a37, 142b31-5, 146b6, 1003b20, 1205a19, 1226a37, 1246b28

Great year, 352a20, p. 2396

Growth [auxēsis: increase], 111b5, 111b25, 270a23, 284b28, 288b15, 310a27, 310b20, 314b13, 319b30, 320a8-322a33, 325b3, 327a22, 406a13, 411a30, 413a27, 415b29, 434a24, 441b30, 442a5, 450b7, 100a27, 744b30-745b9, 916a12-17, 1042a35, 1088a32

Habit [hexis: condition, state], 8b27-9a12, 11a22, 928b23-929a5, 1022b4-14, 1148b18-34, 1220b18, 1222b5-14

Hail, 347b14-349a11, 369b32, 388b12, 940a13

Hair, 90b5, 386b14, 388a16, 517b2-519a29, 658a16-b11, 745a11, 781b30, 785b16, 797a34-799b20

Haloes, 344b2, 346a5, 371b18-373a31, 373b34, 374a10, 377b34, 912b34

Hand, 432a1, 493b27, 687a5-b21

Happiness [eudaimonia], 1095a18-1102a17, 1152b6, 1153b15, 1169b28, 1176a30-1181b32, 1184a10-1185a26, 1204a28, 1206b30, 1207b16, 1208a31, 1214a1-1215b14, 1217a20-40, 1219a28-b25, 1255b9, 1264b11, 1323b20-1326b7, 1329a23, 1332a25, 1337b33-1338a13, 1339b11-42, 1360b8-1362a14, p. 2403, p. 2414

Hard, 314b17-26, 326a8, 329b19, 330a8, 654a1, 783a34

Hare, 542b31, 579b30-580a5, 667a20, 774a35

Harmonics, 75b16, 76a10, 76a24, 76b38, 79a1, 997b21, 1077a5, 1078a14, 1093b22

Harmony, 123a33, 139b33, 396b8-397a5, 1448b21, of the spheres, 290b12-291a29, 986a2, 1093b4; and soul, 407b27-408a28

'Have', 15b17-33, 1023a7-25, 1184b10. See Habit

Induction, 28b21, 42a3, 67a23, 68b8-37, 69a16, 71a6, 72b30, 77b35, 78a35, 81a38-69, 90b14, 91b35, 92a37, 100b4, 105a13-18, 108b7, 111b38-112a5, 113b17, 115a5, 112a17, 155b34-156a7, 156b14, 157a7, 160a37, 164a12, 185a14, 210b8, 224b30, 229b3, 252a24, 992b33, 1048a36, 1078b28, 1098b3, 1139b27, 1182b32, 1356b1-25, 1393a26, 1394a13, 1398a32-b18

Infinity, 187b8, 200b17, 202b30-208a23, 233a22-b15, 237b23-238b22, 239b4-240b8, 271b1-276a17, 303a5, 304b28, 318a20, 337b25, 440a23, 445b3, 742b20, 987a16, 994a1-b30, 999a27, 1000b28, 1022b9, 1030b35, 1048b9, 1066a35, 1083b37-1085a2

Inflexion, see Case

Inherence, 1a20-b5, 116b17, 125a33, 127b1-4, 132b19-34, 145a33-b11, 150a26, 151a32-b2

Injustice, see Justice

Insects, 475a1-b4, 531b19-532b18, 542a1-17, 550b2-557b31, 682a2-683b3, 710a2-22, 758b7-37

Intuition, see Thought

Involuntary, see Voluntary

'Is', see Being

Judges, 1132a7-30, 1268b8, 1270b38, 1291a22, 1300b38-1301a10, 1321b40-1322a18, 1354a34-b22

Justice, 106a4-8, 106b30, 107a5-8, 108a1, 109a21-b1, 116a24, 118a3, 120a30, 121b26-30, 125b22-27, 143a15, 145b35-146a2, 150a3-21, 173a11, 180a21-39, 950a21-953a7, 1103b1, 1105a18-b10, 1108b7, 1120a20, 1127a34, 1129a3-1138b14, 1144b5, 1155a22-28, 1159b25-1160a8, 1161a11-b10, 1173a18, 1177a29, 1178a10, 1193a39-1196b3, 1216b4, 1218a10, 1234a31, 1242a30, 1246a36, 1248b21, 1253a15, 1255a7, 1259b21-1260a20, 1276b16-30, 1280a7-34, 1281a25-36, 1318a11-28, 1324a35-1325a15, 1358b25, 1362b12, 1366b1, 1375b6, 1421b36, p. 2427

Kidneys, 506b24-31, 671a27-672a8

King, 1113a8, 1150b14, 1160b3-11, 1161a11-19, 1180a20, 1252a13, 1271a21, 1277a17, 1284b22-34, 1286b27-40, 1288a15-30, 1310b9, 1366a2. See Monarchy

Kingfisher, 542b4-25, 593b10, 615b29, 616a14-34

Knowledge, 67b4, 71a1-b12, 74b26-39, 76a4, 88b30-89b6, 103a8, 111a23, 121a1, 130a19-22, 131a23-26, 134a36, 139b32, 145a36, 155b32, 163a3, 247b10, 441b23, 465a23, 639a1, 806a15, 980a21, 983a5, 995a20, 1003b10, 1008b28, 1028a32, 1039b33, 1087a15, 1094a27, 1112b7, 1139b16-36, 1145b36, 1146a24, 1276b11, 1220b28, 1246a26-35, p. 2404; types of, 71a11-b8, 145a16, 157a10, 982a1, 993b27, 1025b19-27, 1026b5, 1046b3, 1103b27, 1139a27, 1216b11; objects of, 71b15, 73a21, 114a21-3, 121a21-25, 124b23, 125a29, 143a11, 982b1,

983a25, 987a34, 994b21, 1003a14, 1025a6, 1026b3, 1027a20, 1031b6, 1035a8, 1036a6, 1057a8, 1077635, 1086b3, 1087a15, 1139b23, 1140b34, 1180b15; and perception, 87b28-88a17, 99b15-100b17, 105a28, 108a4, 114a21, 125a28, 156b11, 441b23, 980a28, 999b3, 1142a27, 1147b15. See Contemplation, Science, Thought

Language, 535a30, 898b30, 1403b7-1404a12, 1404b27, 1405b34-1406b19, 1407a18-b10, 1408a10-b21, 1447a21, 1448a11, 1449b25, 1456a37. See Speech, Voice

Laughter, 673a4-10, 1371b35, 1415a36, 1419b3, 1448b37, 1449a34, 1458b14

Law, 140a7, 141a20, 173a7-30, 1129a32-1130b15, 1133a32, 1137b73-1138a11, 1164b13, 1180a24, 1195a1-8, 1268b26-1269a27, 1282b10, 1284a11, 1286a7-1287b36, 1289a13-20, 1292a32, 1326a29, 1354a32-b22, 1368b8, 1373b2-17, 1374a19-b22, 1375a22-b25, 1424a9-67, p. 2408

Law-courts, 1300b73-1301a15, 1320a27, CA 41, 52-55, 63-69. See Judges

Legs, 687b25-688a12, 708a22-b19, 711a8-713b22

Legislators, 1102a11, 1103b3, 1113b23, 1128a30, 1137b18-23, 1155a23, 1160a13, 1180a25, 1180b24, 1265a17, 1267a19-37, 1273b21, 1283b40, 1289a7, 1296a18, 1332a28, 1332b25, 1334b29, 1337a11-21

Leisure, 1177b4, 1269a34, 1273a32-b7, 1328b33, 1333a33-1334a10, 1337b23-1338b8

Lever, 255a22, 709b25, 847b10, 850a30, 853a9-854a15. See Mechanics

Liberality, 1099a19, 1103a6, 1107b9, 1108b22, 1115a20, 1119b22-1122a17, 1125b3, 1151b7, 1158a21, 1191b39-1192a20, 1221a5, 1231b27-1232a17, 1250a13, 1250b25, 1263b11, 1265a33, 1326b31

Liberty, 1280a5, 1291b30-38, 1294a11, 1301a28, 1308a11, 1310a25-36, 1370b1-17, 1318a5, 1319b30, 1330a32

Lice, 556b28-557a28, p. 2450

Life, 123a25, 134a32, 148a27-38, 223b24, 404a10, 412a15, 413a24, 415a25, 467b12, 1215b15-1216a25, 1244b21-25, 1245a11-27, 1335b34; types of, 1095b18, 1215a32, 1216a27, 1324a25-1325b32, p. 2412

Light, 146a15, 342b6, 345a26, 367b22, 374a27, 418b9, 419a11, 430a15, 437b16, 438a29, 439a18, 446b27, 791b7-17, 904b15, 905a35-b23, 939a10

Light/heavy, 106a18, 201a8, 205b27, 212a25, 217b18, 255b11, 260b9, 703a25. See Heavy

Lightning, 364b30, 369a10-370a33, 371b14

Like, 105a25, 108b7, 114b25-36, 117b10-27, 124a15-30, 136b33-137a7, 152a1, 156b10-17, 741b15, 769a15, 1018a15, 1021a11, 1054b3-12

Line, 5a9, 141b15, 143b11-20, 193b32, 215b19, 231a24, 241a3, 709a7, 997a27, 1001b18, 1001b26-1002b12, 1016b26, 1017b7, 1028b17,

Middle classes, 1295a25-1297a13, 1297b26, 1302a15, 1308b30

Middle term, 26b36, 41a3, 47a38-b14, 53a15-b3, 72b24, 75b10, 80b18, 89b36-90a34, 93b6, 94b19, 99a31, 702b15

Milk, 521b17-523a12, 587b19-588a2, 653b9-18, 676a11-16, 776a15-777a31

Milky Way, 338b22, 339a34, 342b25, 345a9-346b15

Mind [*nous:* intuition, thought], 203a31, 250b26, 265b22, 404a31, 404b22, 405a15, 407a4, 408b18, 410b14, 413b25, 415a12, 415b16, 429a10-431b19, 432b26, 433a15, 445b16, 472a22, 984b14, 989b15, 993b11, 1025b32, 1070a26, 1075a7, 1270b40, p. 2416. *See* Soul, Thought

Minor term, 26a22, 26b38, 28a14

Mirrors, 342b12, 372a33, 373b8-22, 793b31, 915b30. *See* Reflection

Mixture [*mixis:* combination], 315b4, 322b8, 324b35, 327a30-328b24, 334b8-20, 440a31, 442a12, 989b2, 1042b29, 1082a21, 1092a24

Mnemonics, 163b29, 427b19, 453a5. *See* Memory

Modality, 27a34-23a26, 25a1, 29b29-40b16, 45b28-35. *See* Necessity, Possibility

Molluscs [*malakia:* cephalopods], 523b21-525a29, 534b13-535a25, 536b34-537b4, 549b30-550b21, 621b28-622a34, 678b25-679a32, 684b13-685b26, 720b17-721a2

Monarchy, 1160a32-b10, 1160b24, 1255b19, 1279a33, 1284b35-1288b5, 1310a39-1313a17, 1366a2, 1420a22. *See* Constitution, Kings

Money, 1109a27, 1119b32-1123a32, 1133a18-b28, 1137a4, 1164a1, 1178b15, 1250b25, 1257a34, 1258b39-1259a33, 1346a33-1353b27, *CA* 10

Monopoly, 1259a5-33

Monsters, 767b10, 769b11-771a17, 772b13-773a30, 878a20, 898a9-19

Moon, 290a26, 291b19, 297b30, 341a22, 396a26, 399a7, 582b1, 699b19, 738a18, 761b21, 778a4, 911b35-912a33

Motion [*kinēsis:* movement], 120b24, 123a15, 125b17, 200b12-202b29, 214a22, 222b30-223a15, 227b3, 229a7-b22, 234b21-235b5, 243a12, 248a10-253a21, 260a20-261a27, 261b37-265a12, 268b15, 279a16, 288a14-289a10, 300a20, 336a18, 337a20-33, 338a14-b5, 698a10, 858a17-22, 989a32, 1004b29, 1010a36, 1012b23, 1025b21, 1036b29, 1048b18, 1049b35, 1053a9, 1071b11, 1072a21, 1073a29, 1078a13; types of 15a13-33, 192b14, 201a8, 225b7-226b9, 243a6, 260a26, 261a9, 310a23, 336a18, 406a13, 700a27-b3, 1068a15; of animals 284b32, 285a29, 398b30, 404b8, 405b31-407b11, 408a34-b33, 415b22, 432a15-434a21, 446a20, 459a29, 666b15, 671b30, 700b4-704a3, 1020b20, 1022a7, 1023a18. *See* Change, Flexion, Locomotion, Movers, Zeno

Mouse, 488a21, 580b10-581a1

Mouth, 502a5, 662a16-b23, 746a20, 963b18-964b19

Movers, 202a12-b29, 241b24-245b1, 254b8-258b9, 318a3-8, 323a12-33, 324a24-b13, 699a5, 1012b31, 1071b34. *See* Prime Mover

Mule, 577b5-578a5, 747a24-749a5, 1033b33

Murex, 546a18-547b11, 603a13-19, 795b11-21

Music, 111a37, 128a31, 917b19-923a3, 1180b2, 1254a33, 1281b7, 1337b28-1338b8, 1339a11-1342b34, 1447a24. *See* Harmonics

Nails, 517a6-34, 687b22-24

Nature, 184a15, 187b7, 192b8-193b22, 194a12-28, 199a30, 200a30-b9, 208b8, 230b4, 268b16, 301b17, 639b12-641a17, 724b20, 770b11, 981b4, 1005a34, 1014b18, 1024a4, 1032a12, 1033a24-1034a7, 1042a7, 1070a11, 1103a19-26, 1114b14, 1134b25, 1143b9, 1148b31, 1152a30, 1153a2, 1223a11, 1247a31, 1254a36, 1255b3, 1329a13, 1342b22, 1369a35, 1370a4, p. 2405

'Nature does nothing in vain', 198b10-199b33, 268a20, 271a33, 288a3, 290a30, 291a25, 293a2, 336b27, 379b25, 415b16, 432b21, 434a30, 455b17, 471b26, 476a13, 477b19, 485a3-27, 485b5-8, 639b12-641a17, 652a12, 655a27, 658b30, 661b30, 663a18, 665b20, 683a1, 691b4, 695b19, 704b15, 708a10, 711a7, 717a16, 730b35, 738b1, 744b17, 760a31, 781b23, 788b22, 125261, 1253a9, 1256b20, 1263a41. *See* Final cause.

Necessity, 18b5-36, 19a22-b4, 21b26, 24b19, 29b29-40b16, 946b37, 112b1, 121a10, 152b32, 196b13, 199b34, 337b10-338a17, 451b12, 455b26, 639b25-640a12, 642a32, 699b15, 778b5, 789b15, 1006b31, 1015a25-b15, 1025a15, 1026b28, 1112a32, 1224a14, 1357a23-b20

Neck, 664a18-665a25, 686a19-24

Negation, 13a37-b35, 17a9, 51b5-52b34, 72a14, 978a32, 990b13, 1004a12, 1012a9, 1056a17, 1079a9

Nests, 552b27-556b5, 562b2-564b13, 599a1-14, 612b18-620b8, 622b9-629b2

Nile, River, 98a31, 350b15, 351b33, 353a16, 356a28, 393b31, 597a5, p. 2449

Noble, *see* Good birth

Nose, 492b5-24, 656b33, 781b2-12, 961b9-963a16

Noun, 16a19, 16a23, 16b1-5, 1404b27, 1407b7, 1456b21, 1457a10, 1457a32-1458a7

Now, 218a6-27, 219b12-220a21, 233b34-234a24, 237a6-25, 251b20, 262a30, 971a16. *See* Time

Number, 4b23-31, 120b4, 142b9, 150a24, 219b6, 220a27, 223a24, 286b34, 300a15, 425a19, 969a12-15, 978b35, 985b26, 986a9, 987a19, 991b9-20, 1001a25, 1036b12, 1039a12, 1043b34, 1053a30, 1073a18, 1076a20, 1080a12-1086a18, 1087a28-1093b29, 1316a2-17, p. 2391, p. 2443. *See* Mathematics, One